LIBRARY

9405

P9-EDF-009

Short Story Criticism

Guide to Gale Literary Criticism Series

For criticism on	Consult these Gale series
Authors now living or who died after December 31, 1959	*CONTEMPORARY LITERARY CRITICISM (CLC)*
Authors who died between 1900 and 1959	*TWENTIETH-CENTURY LITERARY CRITICISM (TCLC)*
Authors who died between 1800 and 1899	*NINETEENTH-CENTURY LITERATURE CRITICISM (NCLC)*
Authors who died between 1400 and 1799	*LITERATURE CRITICISM FROM 1400 TO 1800 (LC)* *SHAKESPEAREAN CRITICISM (SC)*
Authors who died before 1400	*CLASSICAL AND MEDIEVAL LITERATURE CRITICISM (CMLC)*
Authors of books for children and young adults	*CHILDREN'S LITERATURE REVIEW (CLR)*
Black writers of the past two hundred years	*BLACK LITERATURE CRITICISM (BLC)*
Short story writers	*SHORT STORY CRITICISM (SSC)*
Poets	*POETRY CRITICISM (PC)*
Dramatists	*DRAMA CRITICISM (DC)*
Major authors from the Renaissance to the present	*WORLD LITERATURE CRITICISM, 1500 TO THE PRESENT (WLC)*

ISSN 0895-9439

Volume 14

Short Story Criticism

Excerpts from Criticism of the Works of Short Fiction Writers

David Segal
Editor

Jeffery Chapman
Margaret Haerens
Thomas Ligotti
Sean René Pollock
Associate Editors

 **Gale Research Inc.** · *DETROIT* · *WASHINGTON, D.C.* · *LONDON*

STAFF

David Segal, *Editor*

Jeffery Chapman, Margaret Haerens, Thomas Ligotti, Sean René Pollock, *Associate Editors*

Pamela Willwerth Aue, Nancy Dziedzic, Ian A. Goodhall, *Assistant Editors*

Jeanne A. Gough, *Permissions & Production Manager*
Linda M. Pugliese, *Production Supervisor*
Donna Craft, Paul Lewon, Maureen A. Puhl, Camille P. Robinson, Sheila Walencewicz, *Editorial Associates*

Sandra C. Davis, *Permissions Supervisor (Text)*
Maria L. Franklin, Josephine M. Keene, Michele Lonoconus, Shalice Shah, Kimberly F. Smilay, *Permissions Associates*
Jennifer A. Arnold, Brandy C. Merritt, *Permissions Assistants*

Margaret A. Chamberlain, *Permissions Supervisor (Pictures)*
Pamela A. Hayes, Arlene Johnson, Keith Reed, Barbara A. Wallace, *Permissions Associates*
Susan Brohman, *Permissions Assistants*

Victoria B. Cariappa, *Research Manager*
Maureen Richards, *Research Supervisor*
Robert S. Lazich, Mary Beth McElmeel, Donna Melnychenko, Tamara C. Nott, Jaema Paradowski, *Editorial Associates*
Julie A. Kriebel, Stefanie Scarlett, *Editorial Assistants*

Mary Beth Trimper, *Production Director*
Catherine Kemp, *Production Assistant*

Cynthia Baldwin, *Art Director*
Barbara J. Yarrow, *Graphic Services Supervisor*
Sherrell Hobbs, *Desktop Publisher*
Willie F. Mathis, *Camera Operator*

Library of Congress Catalog Card Number 88-641014
ISBN 0-8103-8470-1
ISSN 0895-9439

Printed in the United States of America
Published simultaneously in the United Kingdom
by Gale Research International Limited
(An affiliated company of Gale Research Inc.)
10 9 8 7 6 5 4 3 2 1

The trademark **ITP** is used under license.

Contents

Preface   vii

Acknowledgments   xi

Preface

A Comprehensive Information Source
on World Short Fiction

*S*hort Story Criticism (SSC) presents significant passages from criticism of the world's greatest short story writers and provides supplementary biographical and bibliographical materials to guide the interested reader to a greater understanding of the authors of short fiction. This series was developed in response to suggestions from librarians serving high school, college, and public library patrons, who had noted a considerable number of requests for critical material on short story writers. Although major short story writers are covered in such Gale series as *Contemporary Literary Criticism (CLC)*, *Twentieth-Century Literary Criticism (TCLC)*, *Nineteenth-Century Literature Criticism (NCLC)*, and *Literature Criticism from 1400 to 1800 (LC)*, librarians perceived the need for a series devoted solely to writers of the short story genre.

Coverage

SSC is designed to serve as an introduction to major short story writers of all eras and nationalities. Since these authors have inspired a great deal of relevant critical material, *SSC* is necessarily selective, and the editors have chosen the most important published criticism to aid readers and students in their research.

Approximately eight to ten authors are included in each volume, and each entry presents a historical survey of the critical response to that author's work. The length of an entry is intended to reflect the amount of critical attention the author has received from critics writing in English and from foreign critics in translation. Every attempt has been made to identify and include excerpts from the most significant essays on each author's work. In order to provide these important critical pieces, the editors will sometimes reprint essays that have appeared in previous volumes of Gale's Literary Criticism Series. Such duplication, however, never exceeds twenty percent of an *SSC* volume.

Organization

An *SSC* author entry consists of the following elements:

- The **Author Heading** cites the name under which the author most commonly wrote, followed by birth and death dates. If the author wrote consistently under a pseudonym, the pseudonym will be listed in the author heading and the author's actual name given in parentheses on the first line of the biographical and critical introduction.

- The **Biographical and Critical Introduction** contains background information designed to introduce a reader to the author and the critical debates surrounding his or her work. Parenthetical material following the introduction provides references to other biographical and critical series published by Gale, including *CLC, TCLC, NCLC, Contemporary Authors,* and *Dictionary of Literary Biography.*

- A **Portrait of the Author** is included when available. Many entries also contain illustrations of materials pertinent to an author's career, including holographs of manuscript pages, title pages, dust jackets, letters, or representations of important people, places and events in the author's life.

- The list of **Principal Works** is chronological by date of first publication and lists the most important works by the author. The first section comprises short story collections, novellas, and novella collections. The second section gives information on other major works by the author. For foreign authors, the editors have provided original foreign-language publication information and have selected what are considered the best and most complete English-language editions of their works.

- **Criticism** is arranged chronologically in each author entry to provide a useful perspective on changes in critical evaluation over the years. All short story, novella, and collection titles by the author featured in the entry are printed in boldface type to enable a reader to ascertain without difficulty the works discussed. Also for purposes of easier identification, the critic's name and the publication date of the essay are given at the beginning of each piece of criticism. Unsigned criticism is preceded by the title of the journal in which it appeared.

- Critical essays are prefaced with **Explanatory Notes** as an additional aid to students and readers using *SSC*. The explanatory notes provide several types of useful information, including: the reputation of a critic, the importance of a work of criticism, and the specific type of criticism (biographical, psychoanalytic, structuralist, etc.).

- A complete **Bibliographical Citation,** designed to help the interested reader locate the original essay or book, follows each piece of criticism.

- The **Further Reading List** appearing at the end of each author entry suggests additional materials on the author. In some cases it includes essays for which the editors could not obtain reprint rights.

Beginning with volume six, *SSC* contains two additional features designed to enhance the reader's understanding of short fiction writers and their works:

- Each *SSC* entry now includes, when available, **Comments by the Author** that illuminate his or her own works of the short story genre in general. These statements are set within boxes or bold rules to distinguish them from the criticism.

- A **Select Bibliography of General Sources on Short Fiction** is included as an appendix. Updated and amended with each new *SSC* volume, this listing of materials for further research provides readers with a selection of the best available general studies of the short story genre.

Other Features

A **Cumulative Author Index** lists all the authors who have appeared in *SSC, CLC, TCLC, NCLC, LC,* and *Classical and Medieval Literature Criticism (CMLC),* as well as cross-references to other Gale series. Users will welcome this cumulated index as a useful tool for locating an author within the Literary Criticism Series.

A **Cumulative Nationality Index** lists all authors featured in *SSC* by nationality, followed by the number of the *SSC* volume in which their entry appears.

A **Cumulative Title Index** lists in alphabetical order all short story, novella, and collection titles contained in the *SSC* series. Titles of short story collections, separately published novellas, and novella collections are printed in italics, while titles of individual short stories are printed in roman type with quotation marks. Each title is followed by the author's name and corresponding volume and page numbers where commentary on the work may be located. English-language translations of original foreign-language titles are cross-referenced to the foreign titles so that all references to discussion of a work are combined in one listing.

Citing *Short Story Criticism*

When writing papers, students who quote directly from any volume in the Literary Criticism Series may use the following general forms to footnote reprinted criticism. The first example pertains to material drawn from periodicals, the second to material reprinted from books:

[1]Henry James, Jr., "Honoré de Balzac," *The Galaxy 20* (December 1875), 814-36; excerpted and reprinted in *Short Story Criticism,* Vol. 5, ed. Thomas Votteler (Detroit: Gale Research, 1990), pp. 8-11.

[2]F. R. Leavis, *D. H. Lawrence: Novelist* (Alfred A. Knopf, 1956); excerpted and reprinted in *Short Story Criticism,* Vol. 4, ed. Thomas Votteler (Detroit: Gale Research, 1990), pp. 202-06.

Comments

Readers who wish to suggest authors to appear in future volumes, or who have other suggestions, are invited to contact the editors by writing to Gale Research Inc., Literary Criticism Division, 835 Penobscot Building, Detroit, MI 48226-4094.

Acknowledgments

The editors wish to thank the copyright holders of the excerpted criticism included in this volume, the permissions managers of many book and magazine publishing companies for assisting us in securing reprint rights, and Anthony Bogucki for assistance with copyright research. We are also grateful to the staffs of the Detroit Public Library, the Library of Congress, the University of Detroit Library, Wayne State University Purdy/Kresge Library Complex, and the University of Michigan Libraries for making their resources available to us. Following is a list of the copyright holders who have granted us permission to reprint material in this volume of *SSC*. Every effort has been made to trace copyright, but if omissions have been made, please let us know.

COPYRIGHTED EXCERPTS IN *SSC*, VOLUME 14, WERE REPRINTED FROM THE FOLLOWING PERIODICALS:

Belles Lettres: A Review of Books by Women, v. 4, Winter, 1989; v. 6, Spring, 1991. Both reprinted by permission of the publisher.—*The Bloomsbury Review,* v. 9, March-April, 1989 for a review of "Angry Candy" by Marc Conly. Copyright © by Owaissa Communications Company, Inc. 1989. Reprinted by permission of the author.—*Book World,* May 20, 1984. © 1984, *The Washington Post.* Reprinted with permission of the publisher.—*Book World—The Washington Post,* October 20, 1968. © Postrib Corp. Reprinted with permission of *The Washington Post.*/September 28, 1986; December 16, 1990. © 1986, 1990, *The Washington Post.* Both reprinted with permission of the publisher.—*Books and Bookmen,* n. 323, August, 1982 for "Space to Believe, Time to Confess" by Roz Kaveney. © copyright the author 1982. Reprinted by permission of the author.—*The Cambridge Quarterly,* v. 15, 1986 for " 'A Burglar, I Think: A Second-Story Man' " by John Dugdale. Copyright © 1986 by the Editors. Reprinted by permission of the author.—*Critical Quarterly,* v. 23, Autumn, 1981. © Manchester University Press 1981. Reprinted by permission of Basil Blackwell Limited.—*Critique: Studies in Modern Fiction,* v. IX, 1967. Copyright © 1967 Helen Dwight Reid Educational Foundation. Reprinted with permission of the Helen Dwight Reid Educational Foundation, published by Heldref Publications, 1319 18th Street, N.W., Washington, DC 20036-1802.—*The Explicator,* v. 43, Fall, 1984. Copyright 1984 by Helen Dwight Reid Educational Foundation. Reprinted with permission of the Helen Dwight Reid Educational Foundation, published by Heldref Publications, 1319 18th Street, N.W., Washington, DC 20036-1802.—*Extrapolation,* v. 18, May, 1977. Copyright 1977 by Thomas D. and Alice S. Clareson. Reprinted by permission of the publisher./v. 20, Winter, 1979; v. 26, Winter, 1985; v. 32, Summer, 1991. Copyright 1979, 1985, 1991 by The Kent State University Press. All reprinted by permission of publisher.—*French Literature Series,* v. XIV, 1987. Copyright © 1987 University of South Carolina. Reprinted by permission of the publisher.—*The French Review,* v. XLVII, April, 1974. Copyright 1974 by the American Association of Teachers of French. Reprinted by permission of the publisher.—*The Georgia Review,* v. XLIV, Spring-Summer, 1990 for "Some Recent Herstories" by Greg Johnson; v. XLV, Summer, 1991 for "Novellas for the Nineties" by Greg Johnson. Copyright, 1990, 1991, by the University of Georgia. Both reprinted by permission of the publisher and the author.—*The Hudson Review,* v. X, Spring, 1957 for "The Long and the Short of It" by Harvey Swados. Copyright © 1957 by *The Hudson Review, Inc.* Renewed 1985 by Bette Swados. Reprinted by permission of the Literary Estate of the author./v. XXI, Winter, 1968; v. XXXVIII, Summer, 1985. Copyright © 1968, 1985 by *The Hudson Review, Inc.* Both reprinted by permission of the publisher.—*Illinois Quarterly,* v. 42, Winter, 1979 for "Architecture and Junk in Pynchon's Short Fiction" by Richard F. Patteson. Copyright, Illinois State University, 1979. Reprinted by permission of the publisher and the author.—*Irish University Review,* v. 2, Spring, 1972. © Irish University Review. Reprinted by permission of the publisher.—*The Journal of Irish Literature,* v. XV, January, 1986. Copyright © by Proscenium Press. Reprinted by permission of the publisher.—*Journal of the Short Story in English,* n. 6, Spring, 1986. © Universite d'Angers, 1986. All reprinted by permission of the publisher.—*L'Esprit Créateur,* v. XVIII, Winter, 1978; v. XXVIII, Fall,

COPYRIGHTED EXCERPTS IN *SSC,* VOLUME 14, WERE REPRINTED FROM THE FOLLOWING BOOKS:

Allen, Walter. From *The Short Story in English.* Oxford at the Clarendon Press, 1981. © Walter Allen 1981. Reprinted by permission of the author. In the U.S. and Canadian market by Oxford University Press.—Balakian, Anna. From *Surrealism: The Road to the Absolute.* Revised edition. Dutton, 1970. Copyright © 1959, 1970 by Anna Balakian. All rights reserved. Reprinted by permission of the author.—Berger, Harold L. From *Science Fiction and the New Dark Age.* Bowling Green University Popular Press, 1976. Copyright ©1976 by Bowling Green State University Popular Press. Reprinted by permission of the publisher.—Briggs, Julia. From *Night Visitors: The Rise and Fall of the English Ghost Story.* Faber, 1977. © 1977 Julia Briggs. All rights reserved. Both reprinted by permission of Faber & Faber Ltd.—Cobb, Joann P. From "Medium and Message in Ellison's 'I Have No Mouth, and I Must Scream'," in *The Intersection of Science Fiction and Philosophy: Critical Studies.* Edited by Robert E. Meyers. Greenwood Press, 1983. Copyright © 1983 by Robert E. Meyers. All rights reserved. Reprinted by permission of Greenwood Publishing Group, Inc., Westport, CT.—Conroy, William T., Jr. From *Villiers de l'Isle-Adam.* Twayne, 1978. Copyright © 1978 by G.K. Hall & Co. All rights reserved. Reprinted with the permission of Twayne Publishers, an imprint of Macmillan Publishing Company.—Dowling, Terry. From an introduction to *The Essential Ellison: A 35-Year Retrospective.* Edited by Terry Dowling. Nemo Press, 1987. Copyright © 1987 by The Kilimanjaro Corporation. All rights reserved.—Ellison, Harlan and Jeffrey M. Elliot. From an interview in *Science Fiction Voice #3: Interviews with Science Fiction Writers.* By Jeffrey M. Elliot. Borgo Press, 1980. Copyright © 1980 by Jeffrey M. Elliot. Reprinted by permission of the publisher.—Evans, Walter. From "The English Short Story in the Seventies," in *The English Short Story 1945-1980: A Critical History.* Edited by Dennis Vannatta. Twayne, 1985. Copyright © 1985 by G. K. Hall & Company. All rights reserved. Reprinted by permission of the author.—Francavilla, Joseph. From "Mythic Hells in Harlan Ellison's Science Fiction," in *Phoenix From the Ashes: The Literature of the Remade World.* Edited by Carl B. Yoke. Greenwood Press, 1987. Copyright © 1987 by Carl B. Yoke. All rights reserved. Reprinted by permission of Greenwood Publishing Group, Inc., Westport, CT.—Geismar, Maxwell. From *American Moderns: From Rebellion to Conformity.* Hill and Wang, 1958. Copyright © 1958 by Maxwell Geismar. Renewed 1986 by Anne Geismar. All rights reserved. Reprinted by permission of the Literary Estate of Maxwell Geismar.—Glenday, Michael K. From "Some Versions of Real: The Novellas of Saul Bellow," in *The Modern American Novella.* Edited by A. Robert Lee. London: Vision Press, 1989. © 1989 by Vision Press Ltd. All rights reserved. Reprinted by permission of the publisher.—Guerlac, Suzanne. From *The Impersonal Sublime: Hugo, Baudelaire, Lautréamont.* Stanford University Press, 1990. Copyright © 1990 by the Board of Trustees of Leland Stanford Junior University. Reprinted with the permission of the publishers, Stanford University Press.—Harper, Howard M. From *Desperate Faith: A Study of Bellow, Salinger, Mailer, Baldwin and Updike.* University of North Carolina Press, 1967. Copyright © 1967 by The University of North Carolina Press. Reprinted by permission of the publisher and the author.—Heldreth, Leonard. From "Clockwork Reel: Mechanized Environments in Science Fiction Films," in *Clockwork Worlds: Mechanized Environments in SF.* Edited by Richard D. Erlich and Thomas P. Dunn. Greenwood Press, 1983. Copyright © 1983 by Richard D. Erlich and Thomas P. Dunn. All rights reserved. Reprinted by permission of Greenwood Publishing Group, Inc., Westport, CT.—Huysmans, Joris-Karl. From *Against Nature.* Translated by Robert Baldick. Penguin Books, 1959. Copyright © 1959 by the Estate of Robert Baldick. Renewed 1987 Nicholas Baldick & Oniel Jane Baldick. Reprinted by permission of Penguin Books Ltd.—Jonge, Alex. From *Nightmare Culture: Lautréamont and "Les chants de Maldoror."* St. Martin's Press, 1973. Copyright © Alex de Jonge 1973. All rights reserved. Reprinted by permission of Martin Secker & Warburg Ltd. In the U.S. market by St. Martin's Press, Incorporated.—King, Stephen. From an introduction to *Stalking the Nightmare.* By Harlan Ellison. Phantasia Press, 1982. Copyright © 1982 by The Kilimanjaro Corporation. All rights reserved. Reprinted by permission of Stephen King.—Lautréamont, Comte de. From *Lautréamont's "Maldoror."* Translated by Alexis Lykiard. Allison & Busby, 1970. © Alexis Lykiard 1970.—McCrosson, Doris Ross. From *Walter de la Mare.* Twayne, 1966. Copyright © 1966, by Twayne Publisher, Inc. All rights reserved. Reprinted with the permission of Twayne Publishers, Inc., an imprint of Macmillan Publishing Company.—McNelly, Willis

Saul Bellow

1915-

Canadian-born American novelist, short story writer, playwright, essayist, and lecturer.

INTRODUCTION

The recipient of the 1976 Nobel Prize for literature, Bellow is considered one of the most celebrated and original prose stylists of the twentieth century for his anecdotal blend of exalted meditation and modern vernacular. While he has garnered his greatest critical acclaim for his novels, which include the National Book Award recipient *Herzog* and the Pulitzer Prize winner *Humboldt's Gift,* Bellow's short works, including his novella *Seize the Day* and stories "Leaving the Yellow House" and "Looking for Mr. Green," are considered among his most successful, due to their stylistic compression and thematic complexity.

The son of Russian-born parents, Bellow was born in 1915 in a slum in Lachine, Quebec. While confined to a hospital for a year during his childhood, he developed an interest in literature. At seventeen, Bellow and his friend, the future newspaper columnist Sydney J. Harris, ran away to New York City, where they unsuccessfully attempted to sell their first novels. After briefly studying at the University of Chicago, Bellow graduated from Northwestern University in 1967 with honors in sociology and anthropology. He commenced graduate study in anthropology at the University of Wisconsin but soon abandoned the field because "every time I worked on my thesis, it turned out to be a story." During World War II, Bellow tried to join the Canadian Army but was turned down for medical reasons; this experience provided the basis for his first published novel, *Dangling Man.* In 1943 Bellow worked on Mortimer Adler's "Great Books" project for the *Encyclopædia Britannica.* He then returned to New York, where he briefly contracted for freelance work before taking a teaching job at the University of Minnesota in 1946. In 1963 Bellow accepted a permanent position on the Committee on Social Thought at the University of Chicago.

Although Bellow established his initial reputation as a promising writer with the novels *Dangling Man, The Victim,* and *The Adventures of Augie March,* he first attracted significant critical acclaim following the publication of his novella *Seize the Day.* Originally published in 1956 with three short stories and a one-act play, the work has elicited continuing critical commentary and is broadly considered a masterpiece of modern American fiction for its sustained unity of action and complexity of meaning. *Seize the Day* focuses on a single, disastrous day in the life of Tommy Wilhelm, a middle-aged, Jewish urbanite intellectual who quits his job out of pride and loses his life savings in a risky

speculation in the stock market. A failure in his personal and business relationships, Wilhelm displays a penchant for self-pity and suffering that has estranged him from his loved ones—particularly his wife, from whom he is separated, and his father, a successful but unsympathetic businessman. Wilhelm seeks respite from his father in his relationship with Dr. Tamkin, a surrogate father figure and semiliterate psychologist who serves as Wilhelm's destroyer as well as his savior. Although Tamkin urges Wilhelm to "seize the day," encouraging his risky investment in the stock market, he also leads Wilhelm to distinguish between the "impostor soul" (his socially contrived self) and his real soul. After Dr. Adler rejects Wilhelm's final plea for financial assistance in a steam bath in the hotel's health club, Wilhelm attends a stranger's funeral and finds himself grieving for the common lot of humanity. Through his recognition of universal human suffering, Wilhelm is finally able to kill the impostor soul and achieve a sense of love and pity, not just for himself but for humanity as a whole.

Bellow's collection *Seize the Day* also contains two of his most frequently discussed short stories, "Looking for Mr. Green" and "A Father-to-Be." As David P. Demarest,

Jr., has noted, these works focus ambiguously on conflicts of perception. In "Looking for Mr. Green," Bellow explores the human need for intellectual order in his depiction of a classically educated scholar working for an urban relief agency during the Depression who attempts to deliver a relief check to a Mr. Tulliver Green in a black district of Chicago. Confronted with the brute physical anonymity of the ghetto, and attempting to maintain his precarious belief in the structured world of ideas, the man finally leaves the check with a nude, angry woman who may or may not be the addressee's wife. In "A Father-to-Be," Bellow explores the competing human impulse for physical comfort. In this story a middle-class man traveling to meet his materialistic fiancée for dinner experiences a kind of waking nightmare in which he imagines the smug, middle-aged stranger seated next to him to be his complacent son of forty years later. At home relaxing under his fiancée's warm shampoo, however, he forgets his presumed rebellion against his impending marriage and comically submits to material exigency.

Bellow's 1968 collection *Mosby's Memoirs, and Other Stories* features stories from seventeen years of Bellow's career, many of which were originally published in magazines. In addition to the two stories previously mentioned, *Mosby's Memoirs* contains "Leaving the Yellow House," one of Bellow's most often anthologized and frequently discussed works. Uncharacteristic of Bellow's fiction in its focus on uneducated rural characters in a southwestern desert setting, the story centers on an old, alcoholic woman who struggles to maintain her independence in the sterile desert community of Sego Desert Lake, Utah, after breaking her arm. Learning that help from her neighbors will be contingent on her willing her house to them, and unable to accept old age and death, Hattie finally wills the house to herself. While some, like Noriko M. Lippit, have interpreted Hattie as "a female version of Tommy Wilhelm in *Seize the Day*"—"a female searcher" who "arrives at self-recognition after losing everything and exposing her naked self"—others, such as Constance Rooke, have judged Bellow's portrayal of his female protagonist as sexist and stereotypical: "While Bellow can grant Hattie certain of the characteristics which he has parceled out from his own riches for the male protagonists, and can accord her the sympathy which is due to her participation in such qualities, he is obliged because she is a woman to withhold the Bellowesque *sine qua non* of a genuine intellectual life. He cannot in a leap make of her a woman, a sympathetic character, and an intellectual."

Since the mid-1980s Bellow has concentrated chiefly on writing novellas. While some reviewers consider these works generally inferior to his early stories, others who had expressed annoyance with the lengthy philosophizing and humorless commentary of such novels as *The Dean's December* and *Humboldt's Gift* generally welcomed Bellow's return to the short fiction form. In the novella *A Theft*, Bellow focuses on Clara Velde, a woman raised in a strict religious area of Indiana who has overcome her rural origins to become "the czarina of fashion writing" in the publishing industry of New York City. Intelligent yet vulnerable, Clara lives with her fourth husband while maintaining an erratic relationship with a companion who

once bought her an emerald ring as a symbol of their undying love. When Clara's ring is stolen, she finds her stability shattered. The unnamed narrator of a second novella, *The Bellarosa Connection,* is a Russian Jew whose belief in the importance of memory in defining identity led him to found the Mnemosyne Institute of Philadelphia, where executives and politicians are trained in the art of total recall. The narrator relates the story of a depressed Jewish man named Harry Fonstein, who was rescued from death at the hands of Hitler's Nazi regime during World War II by the "Bellarosa Society," a front for an entertainer named Billy Rose who wished to remain anonymous. Years later, Harry's wife blackmails Billy into seeing her dispirited husband and, ironically, to acknowledge his "responsibility" for her husband's present condition.

PRINCIPAL WORKS

SHORT FICTION

*Seize the Day   1956
Mosby's Memoirs, and Other Stories   1968
Him with His Foot in His Mouth, and Other Stories   1984
The Bellarosa Connection   1989
A Theft   1989
Something to Remember Me By   1991

OTHER MAJOR WORKS

Dangling Man   (novel)   1944
The Victim   (novel)   1947
The Adventures of Augie March   (novel)   1953
Henderson the Rain King   (novel)   1959
Recent American Fiction   (lecture)   1963
Herzog   (novel)   1964
The Last Analysis   (play)   1964
The Last Analysis   (novel)   1965
Like You're Nobody; The Letters of Louis Gallo to Bellow, 1961-1962, plus "Oedipus-Schmoedipus, the Story That Started It All"   (letters and short story)   1966
**Under the Weather   (plays)   1966; also produced as *The Bellow Plays,*   1966
Mr. Sammler's Planet   (novel)   1970
The Portable Bellow   (miscellany)   1974
Humboldt's Gift   (novel)   1975
Nobel Lecture   (lecture)   1976
To Jerusalem and Back   (memoir)   1976
The Dean's December   (novel)   1982
More Die of Heartbreak   (novel)   1987

**Contains the one-act play *The Wrecker.*

***Includes the one-act plays *Out from Under, A Wen,* and *Orange Soufflé.*

CRITICISM

Harvey Swados   (essay date 1957)

[*Swados was an American novelist, critic, and nonfiction writer. In the following review, he provides a favorable assessment of Bellow's collection* Seize the Day.]

Whatever we say of Saul Bellow, we cannot say that he or his people do not rise to the challenge of life. His new book is in no way merely an interim collection of stories between *Augie March* and his next novel. What we have in *Seize The Day* instead is a title work that is a long story, or a short novel, followed by three briefer stories and a one-act play. *Seize the Day* is itself absolutely masterful, at once funny and profoundly moving, a virtuoso performance almost as exciting in execution as in what it conveys. The rest of the book is so much slighter, not just in length but in effect, that it does more than detract from the splendor of the title story, it raises the question of whether the publishers lacked courage to issue a "small" book (and this by a novelist who is both a best-seller and one of our best living writers).

In any case, there has already been considerable comment by reviewers to the effect that the unifying theme of all the separate pieces in this book is money—which may be true enough, but is also true of other good writers reacting to life in a commercial culture. I am struck rather by the continuous reappearance of a thread of human fancy in Mr. Bellow's work that to my knowledge has thus far gone unremarked. I refer to the crackpot-invention idea, which he uses not just as an indication of screwiness but as a common denominator of the old human urge to break the mold, an urge which is wacky and comic but also helps to differentiate us from the other members of the animal kingdom.

It will be remembered that the ship's carpenter with whom Augie March is cast adrift after they have been torpedoed is a logical nut obsessed with the idea of the ideal colony he is going to set up when they are flung ashore in a remote place. In *Seize the Day* the glorious swindler Dr. Tamkin also has more to him than can be measured by his gambling other people's money in futures and his fake psychologizing.

> "An electrical device for truck drivers to wear in their caps," said Dr. Adler, describing one of Tamkin's proposed inventions. "To wake them with a shock when they begin to be drowsy at the wheel. It's triggered by the change in blood-pressure when they start to doze." Mr. Perls said, "To me he described an underwater suit so a man could walk on the bed of the Hudson in case of an atomic attack. He said he could walk to Albany in it."

To which the hero of the story replies defensively: " . . . I get funny ideas myself. Everybody wants to make something. Any American does."

In the next story, **"A Father-to-be,"** the hero is daydreaming in the subway: " . . . as a chemist, he asked himself what kind of compound this new Danish drug might be, and started thinking about various inventions of his own, synthetic albumen, a cigarette that lit itself, a cheaper motor fuel."

Nor is that all. The hero of **"Looking for Mr. Green"** "sat and listened while the old man unfolded his scheme. This was to create one Negro millionaire a month by subscription. One clever, good-hearted young fellow elected every month would sign a contract to use the money to start a business employing Negroes. This would be advertised by chain letters and word of mouth, and every Negro wage-earner would contribute a dollar a month. Within five years there would be sixty millionaires. 'That'll fetch respect,' he said . . . "

Even in the final story, **"The Gonzaga Manuscripts,"** the little Spanish banker who supposedly holds a great poet's last papers is more interested in the title to a pitchblende mine in Morocco than in the poems: " . . . Pitchblende has uranium in it. Uranium is used in atom bombs."

I do not mean to drive this too far, only to indicate one means by which Mr. Bellow brings his characters to life: every person in *Seize the Day* is instinct with life, insistent, and as aggressively real as in-laws or pushing strangers on a subway. It might almost be said that the day-dreamed scheme, the cockeyed moneymaking device, replaces the nocturnal dream as a technique of rounding and deepening his people; and then it would have to be noted that oddly enough both Augie March and Tommy Wilhelm (the hero of *Seize the Day*) are less "real" than any of the brilliantly-drawn people who surround them. Having uttered this complaint, I must move toward retracting it by adding that the already famous closing paragraphs of *Seize the Day,* in which the lost Tommy finds himself by weeping at the bier of a dead stranger are more than convincing, they are exquisitely right. (pp. 156-57)

> *Harvey Swados, "The Long and the Short of It," in* The Hudson Review, *Vol. X, No. 1, Spring, 1957, pp. 155-60.*

Ray B. West, Jr.   (essay date 1957)

[*West is an American short story writer, critic, and editor whose critical writings include* The Short Story in America *(1952) and* Reading the Short Story *(1968). In the excerpt below, he provides a mixed appraisal of* Seize the Day, *suggesting that Bellow's novella was published "more to keep its author's name alive between more important projects than as a manifestation of Mr. Bellow at his best."*]

In considering the short novel, which appeared originally in *Partisan Review* and which gives the collection [*Seize the Day*] its name, it may be unfair to demand too much, for it seems likely that this is a volume put together and offered to the public, more to keep its author's name alive between more important projects than as a manifestation of Mr. Bellow at his best. (pp. 504-05).

The principal character of *Seize the Day,* Tommy Wilhelm, seems almost perversely unheroic. The events of his day, which make up the story of the novel, although rendered with Mr. Bellow's usual skill, consist of an accumulation of small worries and small meetings, none of them very important in itself, but all of them together combining to effect a sense of almost absolute frustration. In some respect Wilhelm is a composite of the weaker characteristics of Augie March, without Augie's ingenuity or ambition. Caught in a web of failure in business, in marriage, and in relations with his family and friends, he succumbs finally to a kind of (not genuine grief but) boundless self-pity. After the final event, which is the loss of his money in a stock gamble, Wilhelm joins a crowd of anonymous mourners at the funeral of a man unknown to him, where he gives himself up to his frustration and weeps openly, protected by the occasion where he is mistaken for some member of the grieving family.

The ironic point that Bellow seems to be making is that Tommy, submerged in the public mourning, is protected from the glare of the isolation into which he has been forced by his failures; or, to put it another way, that man in isolation is more open to public responsibility (the grand failure) than is he who merges with the public mass. As a kind of case study of mediocrity, then, the story of Tommy Wilhelm has its own interest, and in Bellow's handling of it, a certain pathos. Despite the seriousness with which I have stated its intentions, the story is essentially comic, perhaps even consciously patterned upon those traditional comedies where the foibles and fables of mankind are parodied by the actions of a character of a low order. In such terms, *Seize the Day* may be granted its small success. What is most disturbing about such a success, however, is that it represents a return on Bellow's part to interests nearer to those of his first two novels, *The Dangling Man* and *The Victim* than to the more significant concerns of *The Adventures of Augie March*. What I mean is that Bellow made his initial reputation as a novelist by the force of his portrayals of what has become known, rather tiredly, as the alienated man—attempts, presumably, to depict and examine the lot of modern man dissociated from society. In his third novel, *The Adventures of Augie March,* he appeared almost to reverse his direction, for Augie, although he remained an isolated figure in many respects, was one who gloried in his differences, thus suggesting the possibility that such an American character, if he could not obtain true epic stature, could at least enjoy the fulsome stature of a mock hero.

Tommy Wilhelm is neither of these, nor was he intended to be, and it may even be unfair to ask that Mr. Bellow, in so slight a work, demonstrate the direction his career is going. Nevertheless, it would be asking too much of a reviewer to demand that he give up the attempt to find out, particularly when . . . he finds Mr. Bellow lagging behind authors of lesser experience and reputation. (pp. 505-06)

Ray B. West, Jr., "Six Authors in Search of a Hero," in The Sewanee Review, *Vol. 65, No. 3, Summer, 1957, pp. 498-508.*

Maxwell Geismar   (essay date 1958)

[*Geismar was one of America's most prominent historical and social critics. Although he often commented that history was not the only means to critical insight, Geis-*mar *often suggested in his criticism that social patterns and the weight of history, more than any other phenomena, affect the shape and content of all art. In the following excerpt from his* American Moderns: From Rebellion to Conformity, *he provides an enthusiastic overview of* Seize the Day.]

[In *Seize the Day,* the] upper West-Side New York scene is brilliantly described from the huge and gloomy hotels to the barbershops, the steam baths for the tired, flabby businessmen, and the local branch of the stock market which is the nerve center of this overdressed and overfed segment of middle-class urban society. With his marvelously acute details of social observation, Bellow has almost reached, in his own area, the gloss of a Scott Fitzgerald, a John O'Hara, or a J. P. Marquand. And this whole New York City scene is of course an ironic parody of American society as a whole; just as Tamkin, the "psychologist," is the poet, the philosopher, the "scientific observer," and the spokesman for this society. It is Tamkin who has a "calm rational approach" to the money-fever; who analyzes the "guilt-aggression cycles" behind the gambling in lard, who is full of atomic inventions, and who sumamrizes the new American credo. "The past is no good to us. The future is full of anxiety. Only the present is real—the here-and-now. Seize the day."

This nightmare vision of the upper West Side—a grotesque inferno of useless, pampered, empty, and ugly old age—is extended to the nation's metropolis itself, where money has replaced blood in human beings. "The money!" cries Tommy Wilhelm. "When I had it, I flowed money. They bled it away from me. I hemorrhaged money. But now it's almost all gone, and where am I supposed to turn for more?" Even more than to the agonized hero in *The Victim,* New York has become a Babel of isolated souls. "And it was the punishment of hell itself not to understand or be understood, not to know the crazy from the sane, the wise from the fools, the young from the old or the sick from the well. The fathers were no fathers and the sons no sons. You had to talk with yourself in the daytime and reason with yourself at night. Who else was there to talk to in a city like New York?"

This is indeed the mechanized lair of the lonely crowd, the fragmented individual. In the central figure of Tommy Wilhelm himself, who has lost his job with the Rojax Company, whose wife has abandoned him, whose children are strangers, and who now lives on Unicap and Coca-Cola, there is Bellow's central observation on the dark fear of "lagging" in the United States. Yet in other respects Tommy Wilhelm is an odd protagonist to personify this social concern. With his still boyish and impetuous manner, but his clumsy, overgrown, sloppy body, he is one of the natural misfits, the "loose objects" on the social scene. He has never finished college, he has had illusions of being a Hollywood star, his vanity has destroyed his career as a salesman. Now a stock-market "speculator" under the spell of Tamkin (and the electronic bookkeeping machines that do not allow you to get in debt), he is in fact completely dependent on his father for financial and spiritual support. In this uneasy relationship of father and son (as in the tangled sibling relation of the Jewish "oppressor" and the anti-Semitic "victim," earlier) we reach the psycho-center of *Seize the Day.*

But it is easier to say this, and to feel it, than quite to understand it, with the perhaps deliberately ambiguous material that the novelist has recorded. Tommy's father, Dr. Adler, is another instance of those respectable, conventional, "assimilated" Jews in Bellow's work. He is a retired professional man, eminently correct, fashionable, and successful. He is also selfish, vain, and cold. Disowning both his children, in effect, after his wife has conveniently died, he simply wants to live out his self-centered, narcissistic, comfort-loving existence in peace. He is ashamed of his son, not because Tommy has Americanized his name and life to an even further degree, but because he has failed. And what the son wants from this narrow, proper, hard-hearted father is not money, after all, but the paternal love he thinks he has never had.

Is this at base a sociological issue of the immigrant folk cultures adapting to the cold, hard, abstract success pattern of American society? Or is there a still deeper question of a psychobiological nature, oedipal in essence, which lies at the base of Bellow's work, as it has in the case of so many other writers of the Western world? Certainly the panting frenzy of Tommy Wilhelm's search for love is beautifully done in *Seize the Day,* clumsy, grotesque, self-defeating as it is. And one remembers the other panting, yearning, panicky and defeated heroes in his previous work, or the solitary, brooding, loveless, and self-imposed human exile of the dangling man: two facets of the same psychological projection. Even the superman *schlemihl,* Augie March, is an orphan in his own thoughts, with recurrent fantasies of noble adopted parents, who seeks refuge with the foster father Einhorn, or the foster mother, Mrs. Renling. One parent or another is always missing in Bellow's human chronicles; or in effect they both are.

Here it is the mother that Tommy mourns ("As though he didn't know the year, the month, the day, the very hour of his mother's death."), just as the image of the mad mother haunts the consciousness of the victim Leventhal. But the father is lost also, that is the true and present sorrow, just as the father has deserted Augie March's family, and as Leventhal's own brother has deserted his family. Surely Tommy Wilhelm is seeking to re-create his lost, his imaginary family (though he in turn has abandoned his own wife and children) while the earlier Leventhal also takes on an assumed, a contrived paternal role by assuming the responsibility and the guilt for his brother's child. In a larger sense one feels that this shifting, ambiguous parental pattern at the base of Bellow's work is itself somewhat artificial and even false: as though the writer were seeking it out almost too consciously, feeling its absence, knowing its importance, and putting together the plausible and yet not the true parts.

Or as though the true issues in this tormented constellation of contrived parental and sibling relationships had not yet been resolved. For the hatreds, jealousies, angers, and desires, illicit, amoral, and profound, that also mark and accompany the oedipal complex of emotions, are curiously missing in Bellow's work, just as they are missing in, and as they delimit, his whole artistic vision of life. The

suffering, the humility, the moral goodness in his books, the honest and ironic realization of human weakness: these are the traits that appeal to us. But this note of resignation, of acceptance, does not appear in Bellow's work after the violence and passions of life, as it commonly does in the work of major artists. It appears in Bellow's fiction *instead of* the emotional storm and stress it should transcend. The central image of the hero in his novels and stories is not indeed that of the rebellious son, but of the suffering, the tormented, and the conforming son.

To use the phraseology of Salinger, this hero is the good boy, the sad sack; or to use the terms of depth psychology, he is the castrated son. There is that curious scene in *Seize the Day* when the desperate and frantic Tommy searches for his father in the steam bath and there sees the proud young athlete with the virile curve in his sexual organ and the cruel smile on his lips. (Rejecting the sadistic aspects of the cult of masculine virility, Bellow also denies, in effect, its legitimate, normal, organic, pleasure-seeking, and luxury-loving function.) There is the deliberately ambiguous ending to the tale where Tommy first sees the crowds of ordinary people in the streets (those Dreiserian and Whitmanesque masses that this highly sensitive and withdrawn artist has always yearned to link himself with):

> And the great, great crowd, the inexhaustible current of millions of every race and kind pouring out, pressing round, of every age, of every genius, possessors of every human secret, antique and future, in every face the refinement of one particular motive or essence—*I labor, I spend, I strive, I design, I love, I cling, I uphold, I give way, I envy, I long, I scorn, I die, I hide, I want.* Faster, much faster than any man could make the tally.

And then when Tommy joins the funeral of the stranger, and bursts into hysterical sobbing at the sight of the corpse:

> The flowers and lights fused ecstatically in Wilhelm's blind, wet eyes; the heavy sea-like music came up to his ears. It poured into him where he had hidden himself in the center of a crowd by the great and happy oblivion of tears. He heard it and sank deeper than sorrow through torn sobs and cries toward the consummation of his heart's ultimate need.

Now here Bellow's peculiarly lyric cry of compassion finds perfect utterance. But what really is that consummation of this hero's ultimate need beyond the depths of sorrow and self-pity? Does the anonymous corpse represent himself? Or his father, whom he might indeed have wished to kill if he had ever allowed his feelings their true expression? Or simply the fate of all men—though Tommy Wilhelm in this tale only lives the life of a belated adolescent? Just as the central psychological issue in Bellow's fiction is left unresolved at the end of his most recent story, so too we realize that the "Jewish" issue, which is partly a mask for and a cultural projection of the human issue, has become more evasive in proportion as it has become more dominant. Does old Dr. Adler also despise his *schlemihlish* son because he has carried the process of "assimilation" one step farther, the final step, by changing his family name for the purposes of Hollywood—that is to say, of "American" society today?

The father still calls the son Wilky, the diminutive of his real name; but to Tommy, aware dimly that he has two selves, Wilky only means failure, not affection, and he is ashamed of it. And behind that there are echoes of his old Jewish name, Velvel, by which his grandfather had called him: his third, buried, and perhaps true soul. But this soul, too, Tommy never attempts to meet and understand; it is an uneasy ghost from the past, rather than a source of life. Just as Bellow himself has always stressed the narrowest part of the Orthodox Jewish religious tradition—rather than the flowering of secular Jewish culture and art in the New World—so, too, all his heroes continue to be ashamed of and to repudiate their true religious heritage. Judaism in Bellow's work is a source of nostalgia, but also of guilt and anxiety rather than of pride and pleasure. It is a constrictive and disturbing, rather than an enlarging or emancipating force.

Yet saying all this, we cannot deny the accuracy of this social picture either, in so far as it relates to the assimilating of all immigrant cultures within the stereotypes of modern American society; while it is from the moral burden of a specifically Jewish heritage that Bellow himself has been able to assess the outlines of this society. What is the real business of life, his last hero asks himself, if not "to carry his peculiar burden, to feel shame and impotence, to taste those quelled tears. . . . Maybe the making of mistakes expressed the very purpose of his life and the essence of his being here." Yes, one may still wish that the business of life in Bellow's fiction could go beyond this shame and impotence, these quelled tears. One notices that even his vision of the great, great crowd (the matrix of humanity) excludes the motives of *I lust* or *I desire, I enjoy, I give pleasure and take pleasure;* or better yet, that *we* do all these things together which are good for life, which express life, and which alone often make it bearable or pleasant. But still we must not deny the value of Bellow's humanitarian view in an epoch of the utmost social savagery; nor yet the peculiar lyric sweetness of what seems to be the essence of a pure soul.

There is something in Bellow's accent that may remind us of the innocent and childlike spirit of a Stephen Crane, consumed as the earlier writer was also by the flames of his own oedipal and religious conflict. If I have already made the comparison with another Jewish writer in the popular field, it should be clear, too, that Saul Bellow is genuinely concerned with, and even oppressed by, the moral values of his heritage—that he suffers from them—while Herman Wouk has cashed in on them. (pp. 218-24)

> Maxwell Geismar, "Saul Bellow: Novelist of the Intellectuals," in his American Moderns: From Rebellion to Conformity, *Hill and Wang, 1958, pp. 210-24.*

Bellow on *Seize the Day*:

[*Roudané*]: *Do you think that, as Hemingway would say, you "got it right" with* **Seize the Day?**

[Bellow]: Oh I got it right up to a point, but it was a limited point. I can sympathize with Wilhelm but I can't respect him. He is a sufferer by vocation. I'm a resister by vocation. . . .

Tamkin struck me as a classic illusion manufacturer.

Yes. He was going to do people good, he was going to take them in hand and cure them. He was a shabby Aunt Sally. He was going to adjust them, not civilize them. If they didn't light out for the territory ahead, they were done for. I suppose that this was the first book that really described the mental confusions of the Americans, people in dire need of "orientation." I don't think anybody before me had examined the vulnerability of the new American to the new impostor. O. Henry's con men were ordinary shell-game operators. *Seize the Day* was a brand new shell game. The object was not just to cheat a farmer of his bankroll, but to work over the sensitive nice American, born for "happiness."

Saul Bellow, in an interview with Matthew C. Roudané in Contemporary Literature, *Fall 1984.*

Daniel Weiss (essay date 1962)

[*In the following essay, Weiss traces the influence of Freudian psychoanalysis on* Seize the Day.]

Saul Bellow's novel **Seize the Day** represents, I believe, an extraordinary contribution to the relationship between father and son as a theme in fiction. The father-son relationship is an area of experience which the artist shares to a larger degree than he does any other kind of experience with the cultural historian, the moral philosopher, and more recently with the psychologist, particularly the psychoanalyst. (p. 277)

I should like to consider, with what I trust is neurotic sensibility, Saul Bellow's **Seize the Day** as a novel in which the character and the action of the central figure, Tommy Wilhelm, are determined by and represent the neurotic conflict between instinctual cravings and outwardly determined frustrations. The conflict between father and son is central to the novel, but its repressed content is latent throughout until the last moment, when, as Freud describes it, "the repression is shattered." The novel is interesting, too, in that without deserting the psychoanalytic point of view one can apprehend in the action certain cultural implications. When I finished reading **Seize the Day** I was struck by what appeared to me to be the premeditated delineations of the character and psychopathology of Tommy Wilhelm. But I was equally struck by the unpremeditated affinities of both Tommy Wilhelm and his father with Kafka's father and son as they appear in Kafka's "Letter to his Father" [in *Dearest Father*]. It is this affinity that suggests an extension of the neurotic problem—the outwardly determined frustration which is the product not of a single cultural milieu, but of an encounter between two conflicting milieus.

Kafka, writing in the cosmopolitan city of Prague, lives, in the "Letter to his Father," in a psychological ghetto, stoning himself with marvellous, and I think semiconscious, irony, for the heresies of sensitivity, physical infirmity, and cultural breadth in the presence of the father whose insensitivity, brutality, and intolerance Kafka praises as the virtues of a patriarch. In the "Letter" we see in its most acute form what must invariably take place within any cultural minority: the transitional generation arrested as Kafka says, "without forebears or progeny," between the microcosm and the macrocosm. In Kafka's case, because he was both a neurotic and an artist, we see him draining his genius white to justify his father's ways to himself, at the mercy of repressed infantile phantasies in which the father must be conciliated at all costs. The family situation which we can infer from Kafka's writings is typical of Jewish culture in its struggle to survive. The patriarch dies a hard death, adapting himself to the urban wilderness by shedding his Yahwistic dignity in favor of a religious concern for business. And the matriarch, whose only weapon against the hostile, un-Jewish environment, against perhaps the now predatory father, is tenderness and submission, teaches these questionable virtues to her over-protected, breast-loving children. Kafka himself describes it:

> Mother unconsciously played the part of a beater during a hunt. Even if your method of upbringing might in some unlikely ease have set me on my own feet by means of producing defiance, dislike, or even hate in me, Mother cancelled that out again by kindness . . . and I was again driven back into your orbit . . . one could always get protection from her, but only in relation to you.

In *Seize the Day* when his father forgets the date of his wife's death, Tommy Wilhelm, who has asked the question disingenuously, thinks, bitterly, "what year was it! As though he didn't know the year, the month, the day, the very hour of his mother's death."

Kafka wrote to his father about his father's Judaism:

> Later, as a boy, I could not understand how with the insignificant scrap of Judaism you yourself possessed, you could reproach me for not (if for no more than the sake of piety, as you put it) making an effort to cling to a similar insignificant scrap. . . . And so there was the religious material that was handed on to me, to which may be added at most the outstretched hand pointing to "the sons of the millionaire Fuchs," who were in the synagogue with their father at the high holidays.

Tommy Wilhelm

> Often prayed in his own manner. He did not go to the synagogue but he would occasionally perform certain devotions, according to his feelings. Now he reflected, In Dad's eyes I am the wrong kind of Jew. He doesn't like the way I act. Only he is the right kind of Jew.

Kafka describes to his father the answer he gave him when the son asked his father for sexual advice.

> It is not easy to judge the answer you gave me then; on the one hand, there was after all, something staggeringly frank, in a manner of speaking, primeval about it . . . But its real meaning, which sank into my mind even then, but only much later came partly to the surface of my consciousness, was this: what you were advising me to do was, after all, in your opinion at that time, the filthiest thing possible. . . . The main thing was . . . that you remained outside your own advice, a married man, a pure man, exalted above these things.

Similarly when Wilhelm asks his father for advice, the old man's impulse is to degrade the son in his own eyes. One of Wilhelm's numerous failures was in his job as a salesman. Dr. Adler asks him why he left the job.

> "Since you have to talk and can't let it alone, tell the truth. Was there a scandal—a woman?"

> Wilhelm fiercely defended himself. "No, Dad, there wasn't any woman. I told you how it was."

> "Maybe it was a man, then," the old man said wickedly.

> (pp. 280-83)

These are parallels only between Kafka's autobiographical letter and *Seize the Day,* and they exhibit a cultural frame of reference, dramatically abnormalized, within which one can consider the work of either writer. But when we turn to comparisons between *Seize the Day* and Kafka's fiction we are aware of only a pivotal connection—the mutilated relationship between sons and fathers. Kafka's grey Petrouchka-like protagonist and his two-dimensional, expressionistic backgrounds expand into the extremely dimensionalized Tommy Wilhelm and his crowded hour on upper Broadway. But the psychic conflict is identical, and the outcome, while it would not be one Kafka would have chosen, is at least Kafkan.

The desolation of Tommy Wilhelm is a very carefully determined event whose determinants are only explainable in psychoanalytic terms, and whose esthetic achievement is only valid if we accept the somewhat invidious precondition for enjoyment Freud proposes. In Kafka the neurotic is in the artist, not in the work. The work itself is delivered over, in a manner of speaking, to the controlled insanity of Kafka's world; the interpretive potential is manifold. In *Seize the Day* the neurotic is in the work—and the interpretive potential is singular, a matter of reconciling the events in the novel to the character of Tommy Wilhelm, of explaining the manifest in terms of the repressed.

The day Saul Bellow seizes on which to describe Tommy Wilhelm is the day of one of Wilhelm's many undoings, distinguished from the rest only by the lyric, and poetically desirable revelation purchased at the price of everything he owns.

On the day in question Wilhelm has been refused money and love by his father; his wife badgers him for more money; the bogus psychologist Dr. Tamkin has power of attorney over Wilhelm's remaining funds, which have presumably been invested in lard and rye futures. The lard and rye fall; Wilhelm is wiped out, and Tamkin disappears. Wilhelm's reaction to these mis-adventures is best described as despair, tempered at the very outset by resignation, neurotic fatalism.

> But at the same time, since there were depths in Wilhelm not unsuspected by himself, he received a suggestion from some remote element in his thoughts that the business of life, the real business—to carry his peculiar burden, to feel shame and impotence, to taste these quelled tears—the only important business, the highest business, was being done. Maybe the making of mistakes expressed the very purpose of his life and the essence of his being here. Maybe he was supposed to make them and suffer from them and suffer from them on this earth. . . .

> How had this happened, but how had his Hollywood career begun? It was not because of Maurice Venice, who turned out to be a pimp. It was because Wilhelm himself was ripe for the mistake. His marriage too had been like that. Through such decisions somehow his life had taken form. And so, from the moment when he tasted the peculiar flavor of fatality in Dr. Tamkin, he could no longer keep back the money.

The broadest psychoanalytic category within which Tommy Wilhelm operates is that of the moral masochist, the victim, for whom suffering is a *modus vivendi,* a means of self-justification. This aspect of Tommy Wilhelm is the most explicitly realized level of his character. But it deserves closer study as the basis for other, more subtle elements in the novel. The person to whom Wilhelm is masochistically attached is, of course, his father, Dr. Adler, before whom he exhibits his helplessness. And it is equally apparent, even to Wilhelm, that, with individual differences, the other figures on whose mercy he throws himself, are in a declining series, fathers—Maurice Venice, the Rojax Corporation, Tamkin, Mr. Perls, and Mr. Rappaport. (pp. 283-85)

What determined Wilhelm's fixation on this all-powerful father in the past is supplied in the novel to the extent that we can reconstruct his childhood—the love and protection of his mother and the stern, sadistic disciplinarianism of his father—followed by his mother's death at the moment of his first failure in Hollywood. The death of one parent, in fact, any intimate bereavement induces a retreat from adult effectiveness toward dependence, and a heightened dependence on the surviving parent. Dr. Adler was pressed, willy nilly, into service as the mother in addition to his role as the father. But Dr. Adler's tyrannical, uncompromising character has anticipated what might in Wilhelm's life have been a momentary lapse from effectiveness into fixer regressive patterns, has rendered his son incapable of independence. In this sense, a psychoanalytic irony enters into the description of the relationship between father and son, in that the doctor's forthright disgust with his son's weaknesses is a disgust with a situation of which he himself is the author. There is more truth than Dr. Adler is aware of in his "What a Wilky he had given to the world!" But, we can reasonably argue, Wilhelm is

not always unsuccessful. He has assumed adult responsibilities over twenty years of his life, and until the ultimate day of his latest failure, he has not invoked his father's help. However, we must consider that as a neurotic personality, Wilhelm is not completely *hors de combat;* he is crippled, not dead, and his ego, besieged from without and betrayed from within, is still in command. He knows a hawk from a handsaw.

What the day of the novel exhibits is the phenomenon known as traumatophilia. The neurotic calendar is crowded with grotesque anniversaries, the observance of which offer a certain relief to the mechanism of repression, worn out in the service of the ego. The consciousness must be allowed from time to time to participate in the unconscious strivings of the individual, as Ferenczi suggests, to "equalize" the effects of the original painful experience throughout the psyche. It is the return of the repressed. In Wilhelm it is the masochistic necessity to fail, to be destroyed at the hands of the punishing father, in order, under the terms of the moral masochistic commitment, to retain his love, and, in less obvious ways, to memorialize certain events in the past.

What might save Wilhelm from a complete debacle on this particular day would be his insistence that Tamkin withdraw from the market before the lard and rye drop. Tamkin agrees reluctantly to pull out, but Wilhelm then allows his money to ride. Certain fatalities intervene and paralyze his will. The first and most apparent is his father's cold, overt hostility, and the passionate review of the past that has taken place in Wilhelm's mind in the morning. A second recollection involves Wilhelm's distress that his mother's grave has been vandalized, and that his father cannot remember the date of her death. With this renewed grief over his mother's death Wilhelm's old dependence returns, displaced now to his dependence on Tamkin. "Poor Mother! How I disappointed her," he thinks, as he comes down for breakfast. And his next act unconsciously reveals the renewal of his own bereavement. He returns, as Otto Fenichel suggests that bereaved people return, to an oral phase of his development. Wilhelm must suckle. "He turned to the Coca-Cola machine. He swallowed hard at the Coke bottle and coughed over it, but he ignored his coughing, for he was still thinking, his eyes upcast and his lips closed behind his hand." It is a caricatured representation of the nursing child.

An external contribution to the significance of the day appears in the form of an actual anniversary. The month is late September, and it is, as old Rappaport reminds Wilhelm, the eve of *Yom Kippur,* the Jewish holiday immediately following the Jewish New Year. *Yom Kippur* is the Day of Atonement for the Jews, when one makes formal acknowledgment for one's sins. *Yiskor,* which falls on *Yom Kippur,* is the service at which one remembers and prays for the dead. "Well, you better hurry up if you expect to say *Yiskor* for your parents," old Rappaport tells Wilhelm. And Wilhelm remembers his mother's burial, and his father's indifference, and his having paid for having prayers sung for her. A moment later he allows Tamkin to let their combined investment ride to its loss.

I propose now to deal with Wilhelm's moral masochism,

its causes and symptoms and contributions to his traits of character. Freud's first concept of the masochistic personality—the moral masochist specifically, to differentiate him from the sexual masochist, for whom sexual perversion is the outward enacting of his drive—was based on an intra-personal conflict. The original sadistic impulse directed at the parent, recoiled to become parentally derived super-ego, which commanded certain self-sacrifices as the penalty for aggressive phantasies. Thus Freud conceived of Dostoievsky's psychic epilepsy and gambling mania as a self-determined punishment for having willed the father's death. From this concept arises the accepted notion that self-degradation is simply the mirror image of hate. But though this concept falls short of explaining the dramatic conflict in Wilhelm's character, it requires coordination rather than replacement. Part of Wilhelm's character, (his gambling almost immediately suggests itself) is explained, but the concept does not completely explain his relationship with his father, although, as we shall see, it makes finally a major contribution to the end of the novel.

Bernhard Berliner in his essay, "On Some Psychodynamics of Masochism" [in *Psychoanalytic Quarterly* XVI, 1947], while accepting Freud's motivational basis for masochism (guilt, need for punishment) describes moral masochism, not as a pathological way of hating, but as a "pathological way of loving." It is not, as Freud described it, an intra-personal problem, but one involving an interpersonal relationship. "In all cases the disturbance of the interpersonal relationship leads to and is maintained by a peculiar character formation. Masochism is a character neurosis." The subject

> relives and re-enacts in interpersonal relations a submissive devotion to and need for love of a hating or rejecting love-object, . . . originally a parent or a preferred sibling or some other unfriendly person of his childhood, and who lives in his superego. It is the superego that keeps the original situation alive through transference to any suitable person or set of circumstances in later age. (pp. 285-88)

The ultimate sacrifice of the moral masochist to the love-object accounts for his greatest paradox, his perverse refusal to "please" the parent in any rational sense of the word. The masochist identifies himself with the hating love-object. He turns against himself, not his own sadism but the sadism of the parent. His guilt becomes the guilt the hating parent should feel if his cruelties are unjust. Since the parent cannot be wrong, the child must then feel guilty for him. He must be the bad child who deserves such chastisement. Turned against the world, these perversely "good" actions can be criminal, a psychopathic flouting of the law.

> To accommodate a hating person he may make himself as unlovable as he feels that parent wants him to be. He may deny his good qualities, or his intelligence, often to pseudo-imbecility . . . He is stigmatized with unwantedness and displays his stigma as his bid for affection.

As a person the moral masochist has a weak ego, is dependent and love seeking, and forms, because of his oral fixation, strong transferences. Unlike the anal-sadistic, compulsive neurotic, who punishes himself for hating, the masochist wants only to gain love. As Berliner differentiates between them, "The compulsive neurotic is paying imaginary debts, not knowing what the real debt was; the masochist is presenting an old, unpaid bill for affection."

Using this as our point of departure let us re-enter the world of Tommy Wilhelm. On this day of days his whole personality has been given over to an exhibition of his neurotic symptoms. And the external world obliges by offering him a realistic basis for such an exhibition. Systematically and seriatim the more-or-less loved objects from his present punish him—his father, his estranged wife, and Tamkin. Their betrayals evoke the memories of earlier betrayals and humiliations, finding their ultimate source in the original mistreatment by his father. To illustrate in a single example the relation between his masochistic submission to the father and the oral nature of the masochism I will take up one of the *leitmotifs* of Wilhelm's thoughts.

Thinking indignantly about his father's self-love, Wilhelm recalls from his college literature course the line from Shakespeare's sonnet 73—"love that well which thou must leave ere long."

> At first he thought it referred to his father, but then he understood that it was for himself, rather. *He* should love that well. "This thou perceivest, which makes thy love more strong."

The memory of this line reminds him of the anthology (Lieder and Lovett's *British Poetry and Prose*) and with it another poem he loved—"Lycidas," the line he remembers being "Sunk though he be beneath the wat'ry floor."

Later in the course of the morning, when, arising from his argument with his father, he has decided that it is his "peculiar burden to feel shame and impotence," the lines from "Lycidas" again return, this time coupled with a line from Shelley's "Ode to the West Wind," "that dirge of the dying year." The line is "I fall upon the thorns of life! I bleed!"

> And though he had raised himself above Mr. Perls and his father because they adored money, still they were called to act energetically and this was better than to yell and cry, pray and beg, poke and blunder and go by fits and starts and fall upon the thorns of life. And finally sink beneath that watery floor—would that be tough luck, or would it be good riddance?

The fourth poem comes to Wilhelm when Tamkin reminds him that he was an actor. Wilhelm remembers a job he had as a film extra. He had to blow a bagpipe. He "blew and blew and not a sound came out . . . He fell sick with the flu after that and still suffered sometimes from chest weakness."

Margaret nursed him.

> They had had two rooms of furniture which was later seized. She sat on the bed and read to him . . .
> Come then, Sorrow!
> Sweetest Sorrow!
> Like an own babe I nurse thee on my breast!
> Why did he remember that? Why?

Of the four fragments the line from the sonnet is the one Wilhelm most immediately apprehends. Throughout the day Wilhelm's thoughts about his father's age and imminent death undergo revealing vicissitudes. He excuses his father's self love as the fear of death. He reproaches his father, at the same time, for ignoring the fact that he himself must also die. But his most moving thought is what his father's death will mean for him.

"When he dies, I'll be robbed, like. I'll have no more father."

> "Of course, of course, I love him. My father. My mother—" As he said this there was a great pull at the very center of his soul. When a fish strikes the line you feel the live force in your hand.

His feelings about his father are in apposition to the sonnet in which the older man calls attention to his approaching death, not to arouse compassion, but to impress the younger man (presumably the sonnet is addressed to a young man) that he faces a great loss.

Even if we disallow the homoerotic nature of Shakespeare's sonnet and its bearing on Wilhelm's feeling about his father, we find, in the line from 'Lycidas,' an overdetermination of the homoerotic element, and in its combination with the line from Shelley's poem (the cruelty with which Shelley's father treated him, Shelley's doctrine of nonviolence, and his actual drowning reinforce the line of poetry) a willingness to be the sacrifical victim. Wilhelm has "fallen on the thorns of life," and the prospect of sinking beneath the ocean's watery floor is not such a distressing one. It is consistent with Wilhelm's masochistic character that the line has come to mean for him the return to the womb, the death instinct that is a component of masochism. Implicit, too, in the context of the novel, the lines suggest that achievement of superiority which is the bitter consolation of the victim, although Wilhelm makes an ironic distinction between his superiority to Mr. Perls and his father, and his abjection.

The fourth poem, the lullaby, and its autobiographical context, stands in relation to the first three as symptom stands to repressed aim. The sonnet names the object of Wilhelm's masochistic strivings; "Lycidas" and the "Ode to the West Wind" describe the wished for torment and oblivion, falling on the thorns and sinking. The lullaby and its context indicate the mental and physical character-components of the masochist.

The suckling dependence of the moral masochist is symbolically described here as well as the frustrations that accompany deprivation. Wilhelm's orality has expressed itself in character-formation in that he has been attracted to acting, speech being an acceptable oral survival. But his career as an actor was a failure, and the memory of Hollywood that returns to him returns him also to the roots of the failure. He is blowing a false bagpipe, "blew and blew, and not a sound came out." Bagpipe as breast and sound as milk are perfect correlatives. Wilhelm is "sucking a dry teat." He has lost his mother, who, because of his peculiar needs, epitomized the only generosity he can ever know. From his father, to whom he has attached himself, he can only draw the sour milk of sorrow, the masochistic substi-

tute for real nourishment. His wife, Margaret, also figures here, nursing him, as Wilhelm's immediate substitute for his mother, but along with his father, equally unsatisfactory; Sorrow—"Like an own babe I nurse thee on my breast!"—is Wilhelm's baby. The thought of his mother drives him to the Coke machine; the ill-treatment of his father compels him to eat not only his own breakfast, but a large part of his father's. Denied any overt love on his father's part, Wilhelm works out a primitive solution; he eats from his father's plate.

> Wilhelm understood he was being put on notice and did not express his opinion. He ate and ate. He did not hurry but kept putting food on his plate until he had gone through the muffins and his father's strawberries and then some pieces of bacon that were left.

Another element remains to be explained in connection with the last poem Wilhelm remembers. It is his "chest weakness" which has never left him, the sense of suffocation he feels at critical moments during the day, especially at those moments when either his father or his wife is either rejecting him or making demands on him. Both are situations which cause anxiety connected with oral fixation. The one, the father's refusal, involves a denial of nourishment, a traumatic weaning; the other, Margaret's sadistic demands for money, is a projection of Wilhelm's own insistent need on to the woman. The flow is reversed; the woman drains the man. For the orally fixated man, orgastic discharge perverts the unconsciously infantile relationship between himself and the woman.

> Well, Dad, she hates me. I feel she's strangling me. I can't catch my breath. She just has fixed herself on me to kill me. She can do it at long distance. One of these days I'll be struck down by suffocation or apoplexy because of her. I just can't catch my breath.

Throughout the day Wilhelm suffocates in the presence of his tormentors. But this is not so much a "chest weakness" as it is a conversion hysteria, Wilhelm's repressed ideas expressing themselves in physical symptoms. Respiratory disorders are frequently associated with acute anxieties, centering mainly, according to Otto Fenichel, around "the repressed idea of castration," and the "reaction to separation from the mother." Wilhelm has reason to fear both; his sense of suffocation is induced by both. A further insight into the hysterical nature of his behaviour is afforded by the correlation of his dramatic acting out of the strangulation; and the phantasy he has woven about Margaret.

> "Strange, Father? I'll show you what she's like." Wilhelm took hold of his broad throat with brown-stained fingers and bitten nails and began to choke himself.

(Note even in the "brown-stained fingers" and the "bitten nails," the additional stigmata of Wilhelm's oral frustrations.) Fenichel identifies "irrational emotional reactions" as analogues to hysterical attacks. They serve to "reactivate infantile types of object relationships" when some associatively connected experience occurs. They involve an hysterical introversion, a turning from reality to phantasy.

However, hysterical 'acting' is not only 'introversion' but is directed toward an audience. It is an attempt to induce others to participate in the daydreaming, probably to obtain some reassurance against anxiety and guilt feelings (or to evoke punishment for the same reason) . . . It is an attempt to return from introversion to reality, a kind of travesty of the process underlying artistic productivity.

When Wilhelm turns from his father to find a kinder father, his choice of object is determined for him by the same orality that governs his relations with his father. But with this difference, that as a singular individual his biological father must frustrate any preconceived phantasy on Wilhelm's part as to what his father should be to him. Wilhelm's masochistic submission to Dr. Adler represents the extent of his compromise. This is not so when he is free to exercise his phantasy and find in the real world the father who suits him. Dr. Tamkin (and Bellow invests him with a comic-grotesque unreality) is the answer to Wilhelm's dreams, and I will limit my discussion of him at this point to his appearance in Wilhelm's phantasy-life.

In his retreat to orality, Wilhelm returns to the infantile belief in the omnipotent parent, who grants in return for doglike trust and acceptance, full protection and endless beneficience. Wilhelm describes himself when he describes his beloved dog Scissors to his father,

> He's an Australian sheep dog. They usually have one blank or whitish eye which gives a misleading look, but they're the gentlest dogs and have unusual delicacy about eating or talking.

Tamkin is magic; he reads Wilhelm's mind. He is what [Otto Fenichel in his *Psychoanalytic Theory of Neurosis,* 1945] calls a "magic helper," whose relationship with Wilhelm, Karl Abraham describes [in *Selected Papers of Psychoanalysis,* 1954] in these terms.

> Some people [oral sucking types] are dominated by the belief that there will always be some kind person—a representative of the mother, of course—to care for them and to give them everything they need. This optimistic belief condemns them to inactivity.

As Wilhelm thinks about him, "That the doctor cared about him pleased him. This was what he craved, that someone should care about him, wish him well."

I have considered so far those qualities in Tommy Wilhelm which represent him as a willing sacrifice to fate, and indeed this would seem to be the only side of Tommy Wilhelm to consider. His last appearance, all alone beweeping his outcast state at the bier of a stranger, would seem to be his last and most satisfying submission to the austere, intractable father-image which dominates his being.

But in allowing this as the basis for *Seize the Day* we are ignoring an important portion of the statement I had considered axiomatic to the enjoyment of psychological literature: that the struggle within the soul of the hero "must end, not with the downfall of the hero, but with that of one of the contending impulses, in other words, with a renunciation."

Tommy Wilhelm's downfall, at the end of the novel, is not a downfall in the acute singular sense of the word as in classical tragedy. In the timeless world of Wilhelm's psyche the downfall has been a *fait accompi* almost from the beginning. The failure in the stock market is its latest and most vivid instance. Likewise the act of renunciation, the outcome of an inner conflict between opposing impulses, has taken place before, and now finds its perfect expression and, on an emotive level, recognizes itself beside the old man's coffin.

> Oh, Father, what do I ask of you? What'll I do about the kids—Tommy, Paul? My Children. And Olive? My dear! Why, why, why—you must protect me against that devil, who wants my life. If you want it, then kill me. Take, take it, take it from me. . . .

> The flowers and lights fused ecstatically in Wilhelm's blind, wet eyes; the heavy, sea-like music came up to his ears. It poured into him where he had hidden himself in the center of the crowd by the great and happy oblivion of tears. He heard it, and sank deeper than sorrow, through torn sobs and cries toward the consummation of his heart's ultimate need.

The symphonic orchestration of such an ending must presuppose something beside an unchecked drift toward submission. There must be a crisis, a conflict, symphonic in its nature. At one point, before this resolution has been achieved, the brasses must have risen up against the violins and been, not without a struggle, silenced.

I have dealt thus far with the character of Tommy Wilhelm at its furthest remove from effective, mature activity. In doing so I have isolated the level of regression descriptive of such abject helplessness, the position of the infant at its mother's breast. But there are no "pure" strains of orality past actual infancy, while Wilhelm is denied, perhaps permanently, any successful adult accomplishment—the masculine self-sufficiency and self-esteem, the ability to have good relationships and pursue realistic rather than phantastic schemes for survival—his helplessness is more than the helplessness of a strong man caged than a weak man at liberty. To see him otherwise is to deny him his quality as a protagonist and to dismiss him as Freud dismisses the "full-blown and strange neurosis. . . . We call the physician and deem the person in question unsuitable as a stage figure."

What I must deal with now, are those traits of character and neurotic symptoms, which belong, in psychoanalysis, to the oral and anal-sadistic types of regression. To this aspect of Wilhelm's personality such concepts as Freud's original theory of masochism are more germane. We will deal with tendencies in which, although it is repressed, aggressive hostility takes the place of submissive exhibitions of suffering. Every phase of a child's development has its erotic and aggressive subdivisions. At the mother's breast the mouth is the pleasurable organ and suckling the means to that pleasure. With its first teeth, and the experience of weaning, come the first feelings of deprivation and frustration. The so-called biting stage sets in, in which the infant displays ambivalent feelings toward objects, compounded of aggressions against them and a wish to eat them. The withheld breast becomes an enemy to be taken by force.

The old complicities of mother and child become a battle between the hungry infant and the alien world. At the same time another source of pleasure and aggression supervene in the form of the anal period. The feces, the first objective products of the body, become a source of pleasure in their retention or elimination and, for the same reason, a source of power and aggression.

Because of the inauguration at a very early age of the discipline of bowel training and the overt disapproval of the infantile pleasure in fecal play, anal erotism is regularly repressed. In its place appear the aggressive qualities connected with bowel discipline—the "stool pedantry" Ferenczi describes. To these pregenital sources of pleasure and power, psychoanalysis attributes a whole system of orifice psychology. Good suckling and good weaning, good evacuation and good discipline are thought to constitute the basis for good work habits and good character traits in the mature human being. If, for a multiplicity of reasons, one or any of these stages is accompanied by a frustration or trauma, or if it offered a great deal of satisfaction, or if the stage following brought with it pain instead of pleasure, a fixation takes place. Anal-oral fixations survive in adult life as character traits and neurotic symptoms. But because the mouth can still retain its primacy as a pleasurable orifice—as in eating and speaking and kissing, these functions need not undergo repression to the same extent as the anal component of infantile sexuality. (pp. 289-98)

Tommy Wilhelm's aggressions are more inhibited, necessarily, than his masochistic bids for love. As distorted as they are his gestures of submission achieve a certain level of completion. His aggressions are literally choked off, turned aside, or rendered as opposites of themselves.

Dr. Adler lives in his tight, tidy, old man's world of money saved. He has gone into his old age retaining everything, "a fine old scientist, clean and immaculate." His entire philosophy of life is costive, parsimonious. Love means expenditure and he cannot give it. His anal-sadism reveals itself in his cruelty to Wilhelm; his coarse suggestion that perhaps it was not a woman who caused Wilhelm's failure in his job, but a man, and his repeated injunction to his son, "I want nobody on my back. Get off!" are graphic revelations of the doctor's own anal preoccupations. "Concentrate on real troubles—fatal sicknesses, accidents."

Poor Wilhelm can only lumber after his father in an ape-like distortion of the thrifty anal character. He has accepted the economic objectives of society but he recognizes them as a form of cruelty, intimately connected in his case with his father. He is incapable of accomplishing the socially acceptable anal traits, the thrift and industry and self-discipline that distinguishes his father. He cannot "retain" money; his retentions, like so many of his other traits, are at an infantile level. His principal character trait is his messiness, his dirt, the barely acceptable substitute for feces.

> A faint grime was left by his fingers on the white of the egg after he had picked away the shell. Dr. Adler saw it with silent repugnance . . . The doctor couldn't bear Wilky's dirty habits. Only

once—and never again, he swore—had he visited his room. Wilhelm, in pajamas and stockings had sat on his bed, drinking gin from a coffee mug and rooting for the Dodgers on television. . . . The smell of dirty clothes was outrageous.

His playing the stock market is, like his gin rummy, a form of gambling, in which he contrives to lose. Freud, in his "Dostoievsky and Parricide," describes the act of gambling as a compulsive, repetitive act, in which the anal-sadistic hostilities towards a parent are displaced to the gaming table. To make a "killing" at the table (or in the market) is to kill a hated object. But Wilhelm's aggressions are characterized by their abortive quality. He commits, instead, financial suicide.

> For the last few weeks Wilhelm had played gin almost nightly, but yesterday he had felt that he couldn't afford to lose any more. He had never won. Not once.

His pockets are full of "little packets of pills, and crushed cigarette butts and strings of cellophane," and pennies. His hatred of "the world's business" represents merely a diversion from aggressions directed against his father, for whom a large income is the mark of success. "Holy money! Beautiful money! It was getting so that people were feeble minded about everything except money. While if you didn't have it you were a dummy, a dummy!" Wilhelm's speech patterns are interesting as they reveal his oral-anal sadism. He is given to violent, explosive, scatalogical utterances, in which anal function has been displaced upward. "In certain neurotics," writes Karl Abraham, "speaking is used to express the entire range of instinctual trends . . . every kind of bodily evacuation, including fertilization."

> Too much of the world's business done. Too much falsity. He had various words to express the effect this had on him. Chicken! Unclean! Congestion! he exclaimed in his heart. Rat race! Phony! Murder! Play the game! Buggers!

But Wilhelm exhibits even more pronounced symptoms of repressed hostility, which translate themselves into tics, involuntary physical gestures, which reveal in an abstract movement of the body a repressed impulse. Rage, or sexual excitement, or grief are represented by a gesture. They are, says Fenichel, "an archaic means of communication."

> But Dr. Adler was thinking, why the devil can't he stand still when we're talking? He's either hoisting his pants up and down by the pockets or jittering with his feet. A regular mountain of tics he's getting to be . . .

> Unaware of anything odd in his doing it, for he did it all the time, Wilhelm had pinched out the coal of his cigarette and dropped the butt in his pocket, where there were many more. And as he gazed at his father the little finger of his right hand began to twitch and tremble.

Wilhelm also stammers, a "slight thickness in his speech," especially when he speaks to his father. In this too he reveals his concealed hostilities, the death wish. Stuttering is "exacerbated in the presence of prominent or authoritative persons, that is, of paternal figures against whom the hostility is most intense. . . . Speaking means the uttering of obscene, especially anal words, and, second, an aggressive act directed against the listener."

The most direct form of aggression on Wilhelm's part appears as its opposite, as a reaction formation to Wilhelm's death-wish. It appears as Wilhelm's fear of giving pain and his preoccupation with his father's death. He remembers explaining to his mother why he does not want to study medicine. "I can't bear hospitals," he tells her. "Besides, I might make a mistake and hurt someone or even kill a patient. I couldn't stand that." He is obsessed with the thought that all his father thinks about is his own death.

> And not only is death on his mind but through money he forces me to think about it, too. It gives him power over me. He forces me that way, he himself, and then he's sore. If he was poor, I could care for him and show it. The way I *could* care, too, if I only had a chance. He'd see how much love and respect I had in me. It would make him a different man too. He'd put his hands on me and give me his blessing.

"When he dies," Wilhelm tells Tamkin, "I'll be robbed, like. I'll have no more father."

It is out of these elements, which we have considered as being to the highest degree ambivalent expressions of love and hate—a wish to preserve, a wish for an omnipotent father and a paranoid fear of an omnipotent father—that we can construct the unconscious process by which Wilhelm comes to his act of renunciation.

When Wilhelm looks at the dead man he sees what his soul has wanted to see all during the terrible day; he sees his father dead. He sees, too, his own death, mirrored in the face of the grey-haired, "proper" looking, but not aged man before him. It is here that the renunciation proper to the psychological drama takes place. Wilhelm gives up his death wish against the father and accepts, but without the masochistic insistence that characterized his earlier courtship of paternal cruelty, his own role as victim.

A few minutes before this he has been standing over the body of his father stretched out on a table in the massage room of the hotel, "the thighs weak, the muscles of the arms had fallen, his throat was creased." He makes a last plea to his father for help, which will include not only money, but understanding. The father, as impatient with his suffering as he is with his dependence, sends him away with an old man's curse.

> "Go away from me now. It's torture for me to look at you, you slob!" cried Dr. Adler. Wilhelm's blood rose up madly, in anger equal to his father's but then it sank down and left him helplessly captive to misery.

The dead man in his coffin is the symbolic fulfillment of two alternatives—the wish to destroy the hated father and the wish to be destroyed. In giving up his death-wish Wilhelm passes through what amounts to a phylogenetic process by which he is reconciled to his living father. The theme of *Totem and Taboo* is recapitulated here and ex-

tended beyond the suggestion that the only good fathers are dead fathers. Karl Abraham writes

> The results of psychoanalysis justify us in coming to the conclusion that it is only when he thinks of him as a dead person, or wishes him to be so, that the son elevates his father to the level of a sun-god. These death phantasies give expression to impulses of hate, hostility and jealousy on the part of the son. They rob the father of his power so that he is in reality helpless and harmless. An omniscient power is then subsequently granted him as a compensation.

But Wilhelm goes beyond this cycle of death and apotheosis. He has accepted Tamkin's existentialism; he no longer wishes for his father's death, can give up his helpless hatred, and with it, his equally hopeless love for this degraded, fragmented man of money.

The broadest cultural implications of *Seize the Day* involve the father's representing symbolically the sadistic, profit-seeking culture, and the son's willingness to be destroyed by it rather than share its heartless infamy, or fight against it.

That this cathartic experience will mark a new beginning for Wilhelm in a fatherless world would be a vain, Dickensian assumption. When we return *Seize the Day* to its coherences as art, its momentary solution is what must satisfy us. That moment of rest, like that moment in Joyce's *Ulysses* when Bloom and Stephen almost recognize their relationship, in which Tommy Wilhelm sees the futilities of his love-hate relationship with his father, is perhaps to be followed by the imperative *da capo* of his neurotic servitude.

Dr. Tamkin, the psychologist, is a problem.

He is a palpable fraud; the realistic hyperbole that envelopes him is hazardous to the realism of the novel. He abuses Wilhelm's confidence and loses his money for him, and yet he is wise, accurate psychologically, and responsible for Wilhelm's final enlightenment. He discusses the "guilt-aggression cycle," as if he had been reading Menninger's essay on character derivatives from the anal phase. He is aware of the relationship between counting as a sadistic activity and killing. He explains the market to Wilhelm in these terms. "You have an obsessed look on your face," he tells Wilhelm, who could easily have an obsessed look on his face, having immediately before been thinking about his father's death. "You have lots of guilt in you."

A transference appears to have been effected. Tamkin has been "treating" Wilhelm "secretly," and Wilhelm has responded to this paternal benevolence by finding himself able to remember his past with more clarity than ever before, "the poems he used to read." More significantly the sadistic homosexual phrase his father had used has shifted to Wilhelm's dependence on Tamkin.

> And Wilhelm realized that he was on Tamkin's back. It made him feel that he had virtually left the ground [a dream symbol for erection] and was riding upon the other man. He was in the air. It was for Tamkin to take the steps.

And Tamkin's advice is irreproachable; it enters the fabric of Wilhelm's mind as his vision of the authentic life. About his marriage Tamkin says.

> "Why do you let her make you suffer so? It defeats the original object in leaving her. Don't play her game. Now, Wilhelm, I'm trying to do you some good. I want to tell you, don't marry suffering. Some people do. They get married to it, and sleep and eat together, just as husband and wife. If they go with joy, they think it's adultery."

"This time." thinks Wilhelm, "the faker knows what he's talking about."

> "The real universe. That's the present moment. The past is no good to us. The future is full of anxiety. Only the present is real—the here and now. Seize the day."

I can only speculate on Tamkin's formal function in the novel, and my speculation leads me invariably beyond the bounds of the novel itself. I conceive of literary psychoanalysis as a truncated form of psychoanalysis. One does not willingly knock on the door of the artist's life. But I can only see in the character of Tamkin—beyond of course his simpler level of function in *Seize the Day*—an ironic portrait of a psychoanalyst and his patient, even to the fact that the patient gives all that he has in order to discover the unprofitable truth about himself. There is much to be said, if we accept this supposition, for the representation of the psychoanalyst as a figure of fun, whom even the patient can think of as being part faker. He combines areas of experience which have hither to only been combined in comedy—the excremental with the spiritual (Freud's *ecclesia super cloacam*), the facts of life with the phantasies of love—his solemn and costly considerations of the trivial have added to the repertory of the *New Yorker* and *Punch* cartoonist what law and medicine added to the art of Hogarth and Daumier. But whatever Tamkin's extraordinary functions in *Seize the Day* may be, I cannot object to his presence. He is an accessory to the understanding of the novel. (pp. 298-304)

> *Daniel Weiss, "Caliban on Prospero: A Psychoanalytic Study on the Novel, 'Seize the Day', by Saul Bellow," in* American Imago, *Vol. 19, No. 3, Fall, 1962, pp. 277-306.*

Howard M. Harper, Jr.   (essay date 1967)

[*Harper is an American critic. In the following excerpt from his* Desperate Faith: A Study of Bellow, Salinger, Mailer, Baldwin and Updike, *Harper examines Tommy Wilhelm's "existential dilemma" in* Seize the Day.]

From the expansive style of [his third novel, *The Adventures of Augie March*] Bellow returned to his earlier, tightly controlled technique for *Seize the Day* (1956), the shortest of his novels. In it he recreates the claustral atmosphere of *The Victim*. The protagonist, Tommy Wilhelm, is paralyzed by his remembrance of things past and by his anxieties for the future. As a result, he is helpless in the here-and-now. His life is a case history of failure. He had left college in his sophomore year to go to Hollywood,

against the evidence of an unsuccessful screen test, against the wishes of his parents, and against the advice of a talent scout whose most important clients, it turned out, were whores. After seven wasted years there, he had felt that it was too late to enter a profession (though his father, a very successful physician, would have paid for a medical education), and had become a salesman of playground equipment. With an income in the 32 per cent tax bracket, the promise of promotion to an executive position, and a mistress in Albany, Wilhelm seemed to have arrived. But when the president of the corporation filled the executive position with a young relative, Wilhelm quit in indignation. Now he is living in New York's Hotel Gloriana, whose guests are primarily the retired and superfluous, and he is going through the motions of finding another position.

The events of the day shown in the novel make it clear that he is only temporizing. Faced with bitter demands by his wife, whom he had deserted, for the support of his family (they have two sons), he tries to borrow from his father and nervously watches his savings disappear in the commodities market.

Dr. Adler, Wilhelm's father, is a selfish and vain old man of eighty who leads a dull and circumspect life in the Hotel Gloriana. While he boasts to his friends of Wilhelm's success as a salesman, he refuses to become involved in his failures. When Wilhelm asks for help, his father responds only with gratuitous advice. Accustomed to deference and flattery from generations of his medical students and from his aged friends in the hotel, Dr. Adler is angry and resentful when Tommy's pathetic pleas for help expose the father's selfishness.

Equally grotesque is Wilhelm's relationship with Dr. Tamkin, who has invested Wilhelm's last seven hundred dollars in the commodities market. Tamkin claims to be a psychologist, and his fantastic stories about his patients are obviously blatant violations of truth as well as of professional ethics. Although Wilhelm recognizes that Tamkin is a charlatan, he needs him, for Tamkin is the only other human being who has any real interest in Wilhelm's problems, even if his motive is exploitation. Tamkin does have real insights and is able to communicate these to Wilhelm despite the latter's suspicions. Tamkin's philosophy fits in remarkably well with what Wilhelm has learned empirically and intuitively over the years.

The grotesque nature of Wilhelm himself and of his relationships with others arises as much from his sensitivity and perceptiveness as from his failures and instabilities. Beneath his bizarre actions and mannerisms there is a basic integrity which is constantly at odds with the dishonesty around him. In fact, his past failures may be due, at least in part, to his refusal to sell out to the world of comfortable appearances. His failure in the movies, for example, may be due partly to his unwillingness to yield himself completely to the make-believe world of Hollywood. He refuses to enter medicine because he has a horror of suffering and of the business of profiting by it. And his sympathy for his family has kept him from evading the shrill demands of his wife. Several times throughout the course of the day his sensitivity betrays him: in his talk

Manuscript and four revised typescripts for Bellow's celebrated novella (Humanities Research Center).

with the news dealer, in his arguments with his father, in his reluctance to challenge Tamkin's judgment of the commodity trends, even in his act of sympathy for old Rappaport (Tamkin makes his getaway while Wilhelm guides the old man to the cigar store). As William J. Handy has pointed out in his excellent interpretation of *Seize the Day* [*Texas Studies in Literature and Language* V, 1964], "It is a final irony of the novel that the one person who clings to the reality of what it means to be human is, in the eyes of his world, a misfit. Yet we feel that it is precisely in his possession of a sense of humanity that Tommy Wilhelm does not emerge a defeated man, a pathetic victim of forces beyond his control."

Although Wilhelm has many psychological problems, his deepest problem is philosophical: the mystery of his own relationship to himself, to others, and to the universe. The problems of social success and failure in *Seize the Day* are the surface reflections of a deeper concern with the ultimate questions.

Wilhelm's greatest desire is for the achievement and recognition of his individuality. His decision to go to Hollywood, made against the advice of everyone and against his own judgment, had been an attempt to find and assert his individuality. So was his change of name, from Wilhelm Adler to Tommy Wilhelm. This had hurt and alienated his father, who persists in calling him Wilky in an attempt to maintain the father-child relationship. The name change was a gesture of defiance, only partially successful, against a world which permits too little freedom:

> . . . there's really very little that a man can change at will. He can't change his lungs, or nerves, or constitution or temperament. They're not under his control. When he's young and strong and impulsive and dissatisfied with the way things are he wants to rearrange them to assert his freedom. He can't rearrange the government or be differently born; he only has a little scope and maybe a foreboding, too, that essentially you can't change. Nevertheless, he makes a gesture and becomes Tommy Wilhelm. Wilhelm had always had a great longing to be Tommy. He had never, however, succeeded in feeling like Tommy, and in his soul had always remained Wilky. . . . Yes, it had been a stupid thing to do, but it was his imperfect judgment at the age of twenty which should be blamed. He had cast off his father's name, and with it his father's opinion of him. It was, he knew it was, his bid for liberty, Adler being in his mind the title of the species, Tommy the freedom of the person. But Wilky was his inescapable self.

Wilhelm's whole life has been a series of unsuccessful choices, made almost invariably in the face of reason: "After much thought and hesitation and debate he invariably took the course he had rejected innumerable times. Ten such decisions made up the history of his life. He had decided that it would be a bad mistake to go to Hollywood, and then he went. He had made up his mind not to marry his wife, but ran off and got married. He had resolved not to invest money with Tamkin, and then had given him a check."

While these choices have been unsuccessful in a practical sense, they have permitted Wilhelm to achieve and retain some measure of identity. But now, with his money disappearing and the demands of his wife and his creditors growing more insistent, he is faced with the impending surrender of his identity and his destiny. There seems to be no way out. At forty-four he is an obvious failure. He cannot find a job which will pay him what he needs, and he cannot afford to take a job which will pay him less. His speculation in the commodities market is going badly. He does not wish to crawl to the Rojax Corporation, which might not take him back even if he did, or to beg from his father, who might also refuse. In either case, he would repudiate earlier decisions which had shown courage and integrity. In desperation he approaches his father, hoping that the old man's sense of responsibility (not his love, which Wilhelm never had) will overcome his selfishness. But the father responds with preaching rather than help, and the damage to Wilhelm's pride and individuality is as great as if the help had been given.

This trap of circumstances has its parallel in internal conflicts. Psychologically, Wilhelm is trapped between past and future, between the remembrance of failure and the premonition of disaster. His response is evasion of both the past and the future: he goes to considerable trouble both to conceal his failures from the world of the Hotel Gloriana and to avoid leaving that world, which despite its falsity is still more certain than the future. The name of the hotel is appropriate, for its environment is as far removed from reality, at least so far as Wilhelm is concerned, as Spenser's fairyland.

On the philosophical level, which is the most important, *Seize the Day* is perhaps most meaningful if read as a novel of the absurd. Wilhelm is modern man, caught in the classical dilemma of the absurd: the irreconcilable conflict between the human need for unity or rational order in life and the ultimate incomprehensibility of the universe around and within him—in the phrase of Camus, "the constant confrontation between man and his own obscurity." Grotesque and shabby failure that he is, Wilhelm is nevertheless heroic since, despite his psychological defense mechanisms, he has not forsaken his quest for reality. Camus says that "there is no finer sight than that of the intelligence at grips with a reality that transcends it." In his relentless self-examination, then, Wilhelm still retains elements of heroism; he is Camus' philosophical rebel, although the flame of courage is flickering.

Into this crisis in Wilhelm's life comes the charlatan Tamkin, with his fantastic stories and his schemes for a quick killing in grain futures. And although Wilhelm sees him for what he is, he accepts him. Although Tamkin swindles Wilhelm, he enriches him too: " 'With me,' said Dr. Tamkin, 'I am at my most efficient when I don't need the fee. When I only love. Without a financial reward. I remove myself from the social influence. Especially money. The spiritual compensation is what I look for. Bringing people into the here-and-now. The real universe. That's the present moment. Only the present is real—the here-and-now. Seize the day.' " This message, to seize the day, rather than submit to it, is the truth which Wilhelm needs. As Camus puts it, the philosophy of the absurd "challenges the world anew every second." The past is no good to Wilhelm because it is obsolete, a chronicle of failures. The future is unreal also, a nightmare of apprehensions. He must live in the "here-and-now," rather than in regret or anxiety. He must achieve what Camus calls "man's sole dignity: the dogged revolt against his condition, perseverance in an effort considered sterile."

In the remarkable final scene of *Seize the Day,* Wilhelm is in pursuit of Tamkin, whom he thinks he has recognized in the street. But Wilhelm is trapped in the crowd and swept into a funeral parlor, where he finds himself in the line of viewers at the bier. In the face of the corpse, he sees something which transfixes him and fills him with uncontrollable anguish: "The flowers and lights fused ecstatically in Wilhelm's blind, wet eyes; the heavy sea-like music came up to his ears. It poured into him where he had hidden himself in the center of a crowd by the great and happy oblivion of tears. He heard it and sank deeper than sorrow through torn sobs and cries toward the consummation of his heart's ultimate need."

In the context of the absurd, the ultimate and only univer-

> **Page for page *Seize the Day* is Bellow's richest comic achievement. The comedy lies not so much in the idiosyncrasies of the characters, or in the startling things they say, or in their incongruous and ridiculous situations, as in a merging of all of these in a rich, coherent criticism of life.**
>
> **—*Howard M. Harper, Jr.***

sal reality is death. In the face of this anonymous corpse, Wilhelm has seen himself and humanity. The truth "deeper than sorrow" is the recognition of this ultimate reality, man's inevitable fate. In that fate Wilhelm discovers his own humanity. And the "heart's ultimate need" is the acceptance of that truth and a commitment to life in spite of, indeed in defiance of, the lack of any ultimate meaning. Camus' conclusion to *The Myth of Sisyphus* is very close to Tommy Wilhelm's revelation in the funeral parlor: "The absurd man says yes and his effort will henceforth be unceasing. If there is a personal fate, there is no higher destiny, or at least there is but one which he concludes is inevitable and despicable. For the rest, he knows himself to be the master of his days. . . . The struggle itself toward the heights is enough to fill a man's heart. One must imagine Sisyphus happy."

The narrative technique of *Seize the Day* is closer to that of *The Victim* than to Bellow's other novels. Although the narrative enters the mind of Dr. Adler for a few moments, Wilhelm's point of view entirely dominates the novel. Wilhelm is both expansive and withdrawn. Like Augie, he is an open personality. "I am an idiot. I have no reserve," he says. He is compulsively gregarious, trusting, and confiding. But, like Leventhal, he is tortured by guilt and insecurity which somewhat undercuts his natural trust and confidence in others. He is another dangling man, with a deep need to believe in himself, in others, and in life, but with an equally strong compulsion to deny that belief because it seems so little justified by what he has experienced. He is suspended between the hope that he is choosing and the dread that he has been chosen. Like all of Bellow's heroes, Wilhelm has a sensitivity which overruns his ability to articulate it.

Tamkin, on the other hand, articulates far beyond his perceptions. In the real world he is an unscrupulous con man, full of grab-bag theories and wild talk, and hopelessly inept in the marketplace which he exalts—literally a dirty, stinking cheat. But like Allbee of *The Victim*, he has another function. In the world of Wilhelm's imagination he is the salvation which, as Augie had said, is "always superabundantly about and insistently offered to us." In the grotesque junk yard of his mind Tamkin somehow finds, and sells for Wilhelm's last seven hundred dollars, exactly what Wilhelm needs to get going again. The polar opposition of their characters is a polar attraction too, and the strange ways in which such different beings can fulfill each other's needs is a major revelation of the novel—and of Bellow's work as a whole.

In *Seize the Day,* as in much of the other work, the characters move in a double dimension. The Gloriana is both an oppressive, imprisoning reality and a strange, unreal dream; and Wilhelm lives in both at once, with past and future looming in and out of focus in the strangeness of the here-and-now. It is Leventhal's vision of hell cracked open and the innumerable souls staring out, but now materialized, peopled with Wilhelm and Tamkin and Dr. Adler and the others.

And perhaps the strangest thing about it is that it is comic; page for page *Seize the Day* is Bellow's richest comic achievement. The comedy lies not so much in the idiosyncrasies of the characters, or in the startling things they say, or in their incongruous and ridiculous situations, as in a merging of all of these in a rich, coherent criticism of life. The comedy persists until the very last paragraph:

> He, alone of all the people in the chapel, was sobbing. No one knew who he was.
>
> One woman said, "Is that perhaps the cousin from New Orleans they were expecting?"
>
> "It must be somebody real close to carry on so."
>
> "Oh my, oh my! To be mourned like that," said one man and looked at Wilhelm's heavy shaken shoulders, his clutched face and whitened fair hair, with wide, glinting, jealous eyes.
>
> "The man's brother, maybe?"
>
> "Oh, I doubt that very much," said another bystander. "They're not alike at all. Night and day."

The ultimate irony of this dark comedy is, of course, that Wilhelm *is* the man's brother, that they *are* alike; and in the last paragraph, which itself is darkly comic, Wilhelm sinks "deeper than sorrow" to this tragic realization which will be "the consummation of his heart's ultimate need." The last paragraph achieves its moving revelation because of the comedy which precedes it. Wilhelm's realization is the climax of that comedy, the inevitable event to which it all leads, and its fulfillment. In fulfilling the comedy it also transcends it, and the novel ends in that lonely region where comedy and tragedy finally merge in perfect artistic truth. (pp. 32-9)

> *Howard M. Harper, Jr. "Saul Bellow: The Heart's Ultimate Need," in his* Desperate Faith: A Study of Bellow, Salinger, Mailer, Baldwin and Updike, *The University of North Carolina Press, 1967, pp. 7-64.*

Clinton W. Trowbridge   (essay date 1967)

[*Trowbridge is an American critic and nonfiction writer. In the following essay, he examines Bellow's water imagery in* Seize the Day.]

Saul Bellow's *Seize the Day* is one of the most profoundly sad novels to be written since *Tender is the Night.* On this day of reckoning, during the seven hours or so that com-

prise the action of the novel, all the troubles that constitute the present condition of Wilhelm Adler descend upon him and crush him, leaving him penniless, alone, and in such profound misery that one can hardly imagine his going on. He is, as he says, "at the end of his rope." "This has been one of those days," he says to his wife, "May I never live to go through another like it." We feel that he may not live at all, so great is his misery, so completely has he been destroyed.

Yet if we look more deeply, more accurately, we see that the meaning of the novel only begins here, that beneath this profound and moving sense of despair is the birth of a soul, Wilhelm's, and that Bellow, far from having depicted the defeat of man, has given us one of his most moving accounts of the conditions under which he can hope to be victorious. Wilhelm does not emerge triumphantly out of his troubles; but the very sufferings they cause him have brought his soul into being: Wilhelm's "pretender soul" has died, his "real soul" has been born. It may not live long. Although Bellow takes us no further than the birth, Marcus Klein [in *The Kenyon Review,* Spring 1962] has pointed out that "At the moment of death, his motion is toward existence, the vitality that defines and unites everyone, and his weeping is an acceptance of it and therefore an act of love toward life."

Yet this is by no means obvious. In fact, on a first or even a second reading, the opposite seems to be true. Wilhelm's seemingly deliberate attempts to ruin his own life, his own complete abandonment to tears at the end, both of these seem to point more to a love of death. Only after we have entered Bellow's world, after we have begun to grasp the craft with which this remarkable novel is written, can we understand the truth of Mr. Klein's statement. The concluding paragraph of the novel at first deceives but is finally the crucial one to our understanding of the work:

> The flowers and lights fused ecstatically in Wilhelm's wet eyes; the heavy sea-like music came up to his ears. It poured into him where he had hidden himself in the center of a crowd by the great and happy oblivion of tears. He heard it and sank deeper than sorrow, through torn sobs and cries toward the consummation of his heart's ultimate need.

"That need, the whole of the novel comes to reveal, is the need not to die," writes Marcus Klein. But Wilhelm is drowning. The repeated use of the image only intensifies the force of the metaphor, and it is not until we discover Bellow's attitude toward that state that we can accept Mr. Klein's statement. In fact, only by a study of how water imagery is employed in the whole novel can the paradox, life by drowning, be fully understood.

Human misery is generally the result of one of two things: being in a condition of life that is intolerable or being trapped within a self that creates its own hell. In the modern world the various social agencies aim at alleviating the former, the psychiatrist the latter. But when one is in need of both the social worker and the psychiatrist at the same time, the depths of human misery begin to be seen. Essentially this is Wilhelm's state, and what Bellow is saying is that under such conditions the self that feels these afflictions from within and without must be destroyed. Nothing can be done for it because it defeats its own good.

Wilhelm is a born loser: "After much thought and hesitation and debate he invariably took the course he had rejected innumerable times. Ten such decisions made up the history of his life." Although the conditions of his life are not those that would appeal to the sympathy of a social worker, he is none the less destitute: jobless, homeless, and penniless. On this final day in which his misery overwhelms him, he drowns; but he goes "deeper than sorrow" and out of this figurative death his soul is born.

Because Wilhelm is hardly aware of the new life he has entered, the whole action of the novel is ironic. What appeared to be the agonizing and increasingly fruitless efforts to escape destruction become the necessary contractions of birth. The escape turns out to be a pilgrimage, the victim a penitent, and the descent into hell the necessary suffering out of which the soul is born. Deep within himself Wilhelm *is* dimly aware of this. He curses himself for having fought with his father:

> But at the same time, since there were depths in Wilhelm not unsuspected by himself, he received a suggestion from some remote element in his thoughts that the business of life, the real business—to carry his peculiar burden, to feel shame and impotence, to taste those quelled tears—the only important business, the highest business was being done. Maybe the making of mistakes expressed the very purpose of his life and the essence of his being here. Maybe he was supposed to make them and suffer for them on this earth.

At moments he ceases from flight and pursues the good, his characteristic self-loathing falls away and he even feels within himself the powers of a savior. For instance, what really appeals to him about becoming an actor is that he believes that in this way he can be a lover to the whole world. The sense of a universal spirit that unites and blesses all mankind has recently come to him as he is walking through a dark tunnel beneath Times Square:

> A general love for all these imperfect and lurid-looking people burst out in Wilhelm's breast. He loved them. One and all, he passionately loved them. They were his brothers and sisters. He was imperfect and disfigured himself, but what difference did that make if he was united with them by this blaze of love? And as he walked he began to say, "Oh my brothers—my brothers and my sisters," blessing them all as well as himself.

Although such feelings never last long and are usually fled from rather than welcomed, on this day of reckoning he remembers this experience and thinks, "I must go back to that. That's the right clue and may do me the most good. Something very big. Truth, like."

This affirmation, feeble as it is, constitutes his own dim recognition of the saving end of what more often appears to him as a destructive element—his own intensely emotional nature. He continually blames his failures on his strong and often uncontrollable emotions; yet we are finally made aware that it is just this capacity to feel, more specifically this need to love and be loved, that makes possible

the birth of Wilhelm's soul at the end of the novel. Ultimately, the clearest indication that the action of *Seize the Day* is ironic is found in Bellow's attitude toward man's emotional nature, not just as revealed in this novel but throughout his writing. That Bellow is in the tradition of the great English Romantic poets—Wordsworth in particular—in this respect has been brilliantly argued by Irvin Stock in [*The Southern Review,* Winter 1967].

Understanding the structure of Bellow's novel to be ironic, we are now able to state its major theme. Man's soul has existence only when it can love and feel love in return. Modern society, however, has no use for the soul. Kill or be killed is its law and that of material life. Most people learn this early and conform to it. They are not even aware that their souls have died in the process. Those few who refuse to abandon the life of the soul, who still yearn for its fruition, are punished through suffering and eventually destroyed, unable to fight against what appears to them to be the law of nature. Such destruction can only affect the "pretender soul," however. And the real soul is born as a result.

That Bellow should use water imagery more fully to render his theme is appropriate considering that water and the emotional life have been linked since ancient times and particularly so within the English Romantic tradition. What is striking, however, is the care he has taken to weave his imagery into so much of the novel, to illuminate it on so many different levels. Our understanding of how Bellow uses water imagery not only underlines for us his thematic intent, not only reveals to us the greater significance of details we might otherwise pass over, but dramatizes for us the workings of a subtle and profound creative imagination. The image, in fact, so powerfully is it used, takes on the radiance of the symbol; and like other great symbolist achievements, *Seize the Day* becomes richer with each re-reading. A short novel of just over a hundred pages, it is a marvelous compression, an artistic distillation of the kind that beautifully demonstrates the strengths of the symbolist technique used at its best, a technique that gives a particular kind of pleasurable intensity that is not found in novels that employ other methods.

The image of the drowning Wilhelm is the controlling one, but because of the book's ironic structure it is an image that functions in two ways. On a first reading, and on each re-reading on the surface of our experience, it intensifies our sympathy for Wilhelm's condition. Even when Wilhelm is being depicted least sympathetically, when he is most in the wrong, most the slob, we are continually made aware that we are witnessing the strugglings of a drowning man and we want to see him rescued. Thus our sympathy is continual in a way that it is not, for instance, with Dostoevski's underground man. Once the ironic structure of the novel has been seen, however, this same image functions to bring us to an understanding of Bellow's real theme—the paradoxical life by drowning.

In the first part of the novel the image of the drowning Wilhelm is only barely suggested and in a way that would have little significance if it were not strengthened by the presence of other things: closely related water images and figures of speech linking his plight to that of a drowning man. At the end of the novel, however, we see him as almost literally drowning, unable to breath; then finally the suppressed tears rise to overflow his face; and then the sense of peace and the languorous movement of the drifting body toward its final resting place. Only after one has felt the full force of the image at the end can one go back and see where it lay, implicit but veiled in the story of Wilhelm's day. Only then can one appreciate the double significance the image holds.

The novel opens with Wilhelm's coming down in an elevator from the twenty-third floor of the Hotel Gloriana in New York City to the mezzanine to have breakfast with his father.

> The elevator sank and sank. Then the smooth door opened and the great dark red uneven carpet that covered the lobby billowed toward Wilhelm's feet. In the foreground the lobby was dark, sleepy. French drapes like sails kept out the sun, but three high, narrow windows were open, and in the blue air Wilhelm saw a pigeon about to light on the great chain that supported the marquee of the movie house directly underneath the lobby. For one moment he heard the wings beating strongly.

As we realize later, if we do not at the time, Wilhelm is here imagined as already drowned, under the water where all is still, dark, sleepy, merged with the other dead inhabitants of the earth. Only the pigeon is free, outside of this element, his wings "beating strongly." Because of Wilhelm's fear, because "he sensed that a huge trouble long presaged but till now formless was due," because of the symbolic kinship between the pigeon and the dove, and because to Wilhelm the bird is clearly thought of in contrast to himself; because of these things coupled with other similar suggestions in the whole passage, we see that the pigeon is meant to suggest Wilhelm's soul departing from him, that this is a scene foreshadowing the struggle to come. Other details indicate that the whole scene is to be imagined as taking place beneath the water. Rubin, the man at the newsstand, is staring dreamily out of the window as if he too were submerged. The Hotel Ansonia, at which he is gazing, "looked like the image of itself reflected in deep water, white and cumulous above, with cavernous distortions underneath." Both men are trapped in a mutual vision, as if they were actually aware of their metaphorical existence beneath the waters. The hotel itself is described as if it were beneath the waters and being viewed from them.

> The Ansonia, the neighborhood's great landmark, was built by Stanford White. It looks like a baroque palace from Prague or Munich enlarged a hundred times, with towers, domes, huge swells and bubbles of metal gone green from exposure, iron fretwork and festoons. Black television antennae are densely planted on its round summits. Under the changes of weather it may look like marble or like sea water, black as slate in the fog, white as tufa in sunlight.

The Ansonia is significantly the neighborhood's great landmark. The area itself is a retired, elderly one and suggests in its own right the death of heart as well as the underwater world of spiritless existence.

The suggestions of the drowning Wilhelm amid a society that is already dead in its soul are far more obvious as the novel progresses, and they build toward the climactic final scene in which the sudden reversal of the image is felt. Appropriately, Wilhelm quotes several times from Milton's "Lycidas": "Sunk though he be beneath the wat'ry floor." Bellow even adds after one such reference, "such things had always swayed him." Wilhelm is chronically short of breath as he smokes too much, takes too many pills, and drinks too many Coca Colas; whenever he feels oppressed or even very stirred emotionally, he literally cannot catch his breath. Many references to his chest hurting him, along with the other details, give us the impression throughout the work of a man swimming for his life and, since he is largely unsuccessful, of a man slowly and painfully drowning. At the end of the novel the symbolic and the literal merge as he reaches what appears to be the point of death, struggling for air in a telephone booth. He shouts to his wife:

> "You've got to let up. I feel I'm about to burst." His face had expanded. He struck a blow upon the tin and wood and nails of the wall of the booth. "You've got to let me breathe . . ." He had scarcely enough air in his lungs to speak in a whisper, because his heart pushed upward with a frightful pressure . . . Wilhelm tried to tear the apparatus from the wall. He ground his teeth and seized the black box with insane digging fingers and made a stifled cry and pulled. Then he saw an elderly lady staring through the glass door, utterly appalled by him, and he ran from the booth, leaving a large amount of change on the shelf.

Every detail here functions perfectly, both symbolically and literally, especially, perhaps, the glass door of the booth which separates the element that is choking him from that which surrounds us. That element, on its deepest level, is the lack of love he feels so bitterly in his wife. Almost literally the very breath of his life is love, and when she hangs up on him it is as if she had cut the air hose.

Wilhelm feels suffocated, though to a lesser extent, simply by living in the city. The grabbing for money and especially the cynicism of the business world oppress him in a physical as well as mental way. Yet Bellow does not make him a complete victim, for clearly he is his own worst enemy, and in one beautiful simile Bellow links Wilhelm's self-destructiveness with these images of drowning: "Like a ball in the surf, washed beyond reach, his self-control was going out."

Only Professor Tamkin, one of Bellow's strangely ambivalent seers, offers to help him. Here most clearly salvation for Wilhelm is presented in terms of an ability to rise to the top of the waters, to ride the crest of the wave of life to victory and success; but here, also clearly, Tamkin is a destroyer of the soul, a false image of salvation. Wilhelm must be drowned, in other words, for his soul to swim, and this part at least of Tamkin's urging is aimed at a soulless success, an empty victory. Bellow calls Tamkin the great "confuser of the imagination," and although Bellow uses him to state many of the truths of the novel, Tamkin most ruthlessly preys upon Wilhelm. In the last words of section four Wilhelm imagines his own Lycidas-like end as he realizes how much he is now depending on Tamkin "But what have I let myself in for? The waters of the earth are going to roll over me."

In connection with Tamkin, Bellow is most ironic in his use of water imagery. Tamkin is "the confuser of the imagination," but he also appears to be the great man of feeling and Wilhelm, whose deepest need is to live positively in his emotional life turns to him as a potential savior: "Secretly he prayed the doctor would give him some useful advice and transform his life." The doctor is the one who encourages Wilhelm to trust his emotions, who makes for Wilhelm the distinction between the "real" and "pretender" soul, and who apparently sees that Wilhelm is killing himself and being killed because he cannot release the deepest sources of his emotional being. He sees him as symbolic of "sick humanity" and offers to heal him. "My real calling is to be a healer," he tells Wilhelm: "I get wounded. I suffer from it. I would like to escape from the sicknesses of others, but I can't. I am only on loan to myself, so to speak. I belong to humanity." Just before this passage, however, he has told Wilhelm that his wife committed suicide, by drowning herself; and Tamkin is first mentioned in the novel in connection with his invention of an underwater suit in which one might escape from New York City by walking up the floor of the Hudson in case of an atomic attack. Increasingly we are made aware that Tamkin is using others rather than being used by them, that his is the touch of death, not life. Yet it is Bellow's genius to render him for us as both a savior and a destroyer, a fact which gives deeper meaning to Mr. Perls' statement about him: "He could be both sane and crazy. In these days nobody can tell for sure which is which."

The exact nature of Tamkin's dual role becomes clear when one compares the following passages, passages which are themselves contrasting water images. In the first Tamkin preaches to Wilhelm one of the fundamental doctrines of romanticism—union with nature through reliance on her goodness:

> If you could have confidence in nature you would not have to fear. It would keep you up. Creative is nature. Rapid. Lavish. Inspirational. It shapes leaves. It rolls the waters of the earth. Man is the chief of this. All creations are his just inheritance. You don't know what you've got within you. A person either creates or destroys. There is no neutrality. . . .

Making even more specific use of water imagery, he tells Wilhelm somewhat later in the novel:

> Nature only knows one thing, and that's the present. Present, present, eternal present, like a big, huge, giant wave—colossal, bright and beautiful, full of life and death, climbing into the sky, standing in the seas. You must go along with the actual, the Here-and-Now, the glory. . . .

In the first passage Tamkin is telling Wilhelm not to fear,

that if he relies on nature it will *keep him up*. Nature is like a great sea on which man can float. In the second passage, however, nature is a wave, man a surfer, and the feeling is desperate if also exhilarating. The first is passive and comforting, the second vital and rather terrifying. Within a broader literary tradition, the difference is roughly between the early Wordsworth and Nietzsche, and the difference is immense. Wilhelm feels incapable of the faith involved in accepting what is demanded in the first passage. Right after it, in fact, he says, "The waters of the earth are going to roll over me." But his reaction to the second is even stronger; it interrupts Tamkin's very words and is a memory, not a conscious thought:

> . . . chest weakness, Wilhelm's recollection went on. Margaret nursed him. They had two rooms of furniture, which was later seized. She sat on the bed and read to him. He made her read for days, and she read stories, poetry, everything in the house. He felt dizzy, stifled when he tried to smoke. They had him wear a flannel vest.
>   Come then, Sorrow!
>   Sweetest Sorrow!
>   Like an own babe I nurse thee on my breast!
> Why did he remember that? Why?

In the sense that Tamkin drives Wilhelm further toward despair, he turns out to be his destroyer, not his savior, though ultimately, since Wilhelm must be destroyed in order to be saved, we see Tamkin as ironically a savior figure even here. To Wilhelm, however, Tamkin is at last recognized as the great betrayer. The final section of the novel opens with Wilhelm realizing, "I was the man beneath; Tamkin was on my back and I thought I was on his." While this specifically applies to the fact that Tamkin has lost Wilhelm's money for him in the stock exchange, it must also be read as a water image. Wilhelm has thought that Tamkin was supporting him in the waters of his troubles. It turns out that Wilhelm, struggling to swim himself, has been drowned by Tamkin who has been "supporting himself" on him. The beauty of the pun is that it also applies to Wilhelm's father whose real character is shown in the advice he gives his son earlier in the novel, advice which because it is so cold-hearted, is what originally drove Wilhelm to seek help elsewhere: "I can't give you any money . . . You and your sister would take every last buck from me . . . And I want nobody on my back. Get off! And I give you the same advice, Wilky. Carry nobody on your back."

If Wilhelm is crushed by the Nietzchean, he finally discovers the true source of his being in something deeply Wordsworthean for at the end of the novel it is the "still, sad music of humanity" that opens his heart, that "chastens" and "subdues," and so gives birth to his real soul. Caught by the crowd on Broadway, he moves along within "the inexhaustible current of millions." A series of images bring Wilhelm to his vision and his birth in which he is imagined as a drowning body moving with the currents under the sea to its final resting place:

> It was he himself who was carried from the street into the chapel. The pressure ended inside,

where it was dark and cool. The flow of fan-driven air dried his face, which he wiped hard with his handkerchief to stop the slight salt itch. He gave a sigh when he heard the organ notes that stirred and breathed from the pipes and he saw people in the pews.

He is caught in the line of mourners moving toward the coffin, and when he reaches it the meditative look on the face of the dead stranger forces him to step out of the procession. Here again Bellow uses water imagery to give us the deeper significance of the action, for suddenly it is the dead man who is imagined as having drowned, not Wilhelm. Wilhelm can finally breathe. He even wipes his face to rid himself of the "slight salt itch." All the imagery points to our seeing Wilhelm as suddenly saved from drowning, saved because he can now express his deepest emotions. He can love and pity mankind as a whole.

> The dead man was gray-haired. He had two large waves of gray hair at the front. But he was not old. His face was long, And he had a bony nose, slightly, delicately twisted. His brows were raised as though he had sunk into the final thought. Now at last he was with it, after the end of all distractions, and when his flesh was no longer flesh.

Wilhelm can at last cry. The seas of feeling, that have been welling up within him but have never found their natural outlet before, at last find their release. At the surface level of meaning he can now cry because the funeral is the one place where that is not only permissible but honorable. On a deeper level, however, he can be "drowned in tears" because these are the life-giving seas of feeling, not the terrifying Nietzchean wave of life and death.

> Soon he was past words, past reason, coherence. He could not stop. The source of all tears had suddenly sprung open within him, black, deep, and hot, and they were pouring out and convulsing his body, bending his stubborn head, bowing his shoulders, twisting his face, crippling the very hands with which he held the handkerchief. His efforts to collect himself were useless. The great knot of ill and grief in his throat swelled upward and he gave in utterly and held his face and wept. He cried with all his heart.

What is significant here is Wilhelm's change of character. He has abandoned himself to a despair which is not merely personal, though it includes himself. "A man—another human creature, was what first went through his thoughts." The fact of death, another's death, has brought him to a state in which he is utterly passive and completely dependent. He now exists wholly in his feelings, not because he has chosen to but because all else has been taken from him. He has been humbled by a great fact of nature. His "stubborn head" is bowed. He has been forced into dependency on nature, but we see that this dependency brings him into union with her, for the important thing is that he is now afloat on a sea of feeling. In Bellow's own sense of the Wordsworthean vision, Wilhelm has "see[n] into the life of things" and become, at last, "a living soul." Moreover, there is hope that he will be buoyed up in this state and receive a return of feeling. His girl friend, Olive, loves him and will marry him if he can get a divorce, and

it is to her that he gives himself at the end. In fact the implication is that his very life is now in her hands.

What makes this final scene so impressive as a literary achievement is just this sort of density of meaning. Wilhelm is the only person crying at the funeral, yet he is the only stranger. One of the suggestions here is that genuine sorrow is impersonal. Another is that only those in whom the soul is alive can truly mourn, for only they are capable of this intensity of feeling.

Many other examples of Bellow's use of water imagery to support and deepen his ironic vision of the drowning Wilhelm could be cited. The fluctuations of the stock market correspond to, and of course to a large extent determine, the alternations of hope and despair in Wilhelm's mind; and when the market crashes—when Wilhelm's stocks go down and he loses the last of his money—one can almost see Wilhelm crushed beneath Tamkin's "wave of life and death." You have to feel the "money flow" says Tamkin to Wilhelm when he promises him success in the market: "To know how it feels to be seaweed you have to get into the water." The stock market itself is symbolic of all the cold, impersonal forces that Wilhelm and Bellow regard as evil; and that Wilhelm is tempted by Tamkin to "take the plunge," that this crushes him but does no serious harm to Tamkin, emphasizes, among other things, the difference between their two natures. Wilhelm is instantly punished for his sin. He had betrayed his soul. Tamkin has no soul and so cannot be punished in this manner.

One of the ironies in the novel is that Wilhelm's father, who is the epitome of soulless success, is constantly bathing himself, recommends water and exercise as the cure for his son's miseries, and finally rejects him completely while in the steam baths of the hotel's health club. Wilhelm himself seldom bathes and refuses to use the hotel's swimming pool because he is offended by the smell of the chlorinated water. What is suggested here is that the waters of the earth can sustain the life of the body, can even be used to bring about that meditative calm that comes from complete detachment from the emotions; but to those whose souls are alive deeper waters are needed, and the waters of the earth are instinctively abhorrent.

Bellow's great achievement in *Seize the Day* is that he finally forces us to see Wilhelm as a kind of hero. It is easy to miss his intention and feel only sadness at the end of the novel. Wilhelm may there appear to us only as a poor slob who is weeping at what we dimly sense is really his own funeral. But Bellow can make beauty out of ugliness, not only out of what in the hands of a lesser artist might have been merely the sordidness of ordinary life but out of a character who even to himself seems detestable. Wilhelm refers to himself early in the novel as a "fair-haired Hippopotamus," and this image is repeated many times. It is his characteristic way of seeing himself. Though Wilhelm is ugly to himself and a slob to others, his true element is, nevertheless, the waters of the spiritual life. The burden of this life, the suffering it contains, is suggested in the ugliness and massiveness of the hippo when out of water. The weight is removed, however, and the ugliness transformed into a sense of appropriateness that is the result of being powerfully in harmony with nature when the hippo is in the water. So it is with Wilhelm who at the end of the novel seizes the day of his soul's birth, a soul whose capacity is as unlimited as the hippo is large, and floats for the first time, buoyed up by the greater life into which he has finally entered. (pp. 62-73)

Clinton W. Trowbridge, "Water Imagery in 'Seize the Day'," in Critique: Studies in Modern Fiction, *Vol. IX, No. 3, 1967, pp. 62-73.*

It is the special distinction of Mr. Bellow as a novelist that he is able to give us, step by step, the world we really live each day—and in the same movement to show us that the real suffering is always the suffering of not understanding, the deprivation of light. It is this double gift that explains the unusual contribution he is making to our fiction.

—*Alfred Kazin, in* The New York Times Book Review, *18 November 1956.*

Robert Lasson   (essay date 1968)

[*In the review below, Lasson conducts a mock trial in response to Bellow's short story collection* Mosby's Memoirs, and Other Stories, *whose contents he regards as well-crafted but slight.*]

JUDGE: We are here to evaluate [*Mosby's Memoirs, and Other Stories*], a new collection of—

PROSECUTOR: Objection. Three of these six stories— **"Looking for Mr. Green," "A Father-to-Be,"** and **"The Gonzaga Manuscripts"**—are not really new. They were printed in a volume with the short novel *Seize the Day.* **"Leaving the Yellow House"** has run in *Esquire.* **"The Old System"** was in a Midwestern city's philosophical journal—

JUDGE: *Chicago Review?*

PROSECUTOR: *Playboy.* The most recent, **"Mosby's Memoirs,"** appeared this summer in *The New Yorker.* We can therefore hardly refer to this as a *new* collection, when half its contents appeared in book form 12 years ago.

JUDGE: Sustained. We are here to evaluate a *collection* of stories by Saul Bellow. Defense?

DEFENSE: Imagine a war. The night is cracked open by a voice. "Halt or I'll shoot!" screams a guard. "Are you crazy!" retorts a Jewish soldier. "This is a human being!" This concern for the self, pitted against life's trigger-happy sentries (both real and imagined) is a basic theme of Saul Bellow's. If anthropology codifies various ways of being human, Graduate Anthropologist Bellow deals with various ways of *becoming* human. The weary, beaten straggler who has fallen (or been pushed) out of the race—such men are Bellow's Trobriand Islands and five families.

JUDGE: Could you get to the stories? We only have 900 words.

DEFENSE: I'm aware of that, Your Honor. However, since my able opponent has stated that three of these stories have appeared in a book, I shall base my case on the most recent one, **"Mosby's Memoirs."** Dr. Mosby, intellectual, ex-Hearstling, ex-OSSnik, acquainted with the likes of Julian Huxley and Lévi-Strauss, is writing his memoirs in Oaxaca. Confident, ironic, seemingly serene, he thinks back on the Thirties, remembers Hyman Lustgarten. Religion: Devout Shlemiel. Denomination: Marxist. Eventually loses his faith and moves to Paris. There he imports a Cadillac for resale. The day it arrives, a law is passed barring the sale of imported cars. "The Lustgartens were seen one day moving out of the hotel into the car."

Subsequently Lustgarten is invited by the Yugoslav government to see for himself how they're building socialism. Months later Mosby sees him on the street, looking like a ruin. "I didn't understand the deal . . . We turned out to be foreign volunteers of construction. A labor brigade."

To Mosby, Lustgarten's life is mere comic relief "to lighten the dense texture of his memoirs . . . a Lustgarten who didn't have to happen." And now Bellow asks, "Having disposed of all things human, he should have encountered God. Would this happen?" But Mosby encounters no God. In the ancient tomb he is visiting, he encounters only the intimation of his own mortality, which terrifies—that is to say, humanizes—him.

JUDGE: Proceed.

DEFENSE: That's it.

JUDGE: Then I call on the Prosecution.

PROSECUTOR: No one questions the authority and impact of Mr. Bellow's novels. But these stories will be of greatest interest to those academics whose job it is to measure a writer for greatness, to make sure the shroud fits nice, and to get the 3x5 cards—now complete—in alphabetical order once and for all.

"Mosby," as far as I'm concerned, is a slice of action at the beginning, a slice of action at the end, and a fat slab of recollection in the middle—a flashback sandwich. It is my feeling that Mr. Bellow and/or his publishers wish, with this volume, to assure the reading public that post-*Herzog* Saul Bellow is calm—and collected. And if, as a result of this venture, a few dollars roll in, that can't hurt. It is no accident, as they used to say in Lustgarten's crowd, that **"A Father-to-Be"** contains this anguished sentence: "Money surrounds you in life as earth does in death." That's all I have to say.

JUDGE: Nobody can argue with Mr. Bellow's seriousness. He is, in fact, an American original: an intelligent novelist. This is not meant facetiously; look around and you'll see what I mean. But is intelligence enough? Or rather is it possible to be too intelligent? Do we prefer a Thinker or a Feeler? Bellow, of course, is both, but sometimes has trouble making his stories engaging to the reader. In both **"The Old System"** and **"Mosby"** there is practically no forward movement. The stories happen in their protagonists' heads. This is not in itself "bad" or to be avoided (remember La Bloom). But despite flashes of irony and humor, there is something leaden about these stories: a sensibility gap exists between their conception and their execution.

It seems that sometimes Bellow writes parables to express a certain thought-out point of view, then drags the narrative there, whether it wants to go or not. The story, therefore, is not an act of discovery, but a *report* on the discovery.

The Feelers, it would appear, win out in the end. Who can pay attention to Tolstoy's theory of history when, from the next room, Ivan Ilyitch's dying screams destroy us? Did Joyce even have an original, intellectual thought? To paraphrase what Mrs. Walter Lippmann has to keep telling her husband when they're on vacation: "Saul, stop thinking!"

I therefore find for the Prosecution. These six stories are like spokes on a wheel, the circumference of which is composed of Bellow's novels. As spokes, they are supportive and architectural, not to be traveled on. As stories, I find them neither great nor significant. Will they enhance the reputation of their author? Not likely. Will they hurt his reputation? Absurd question. How could *anything* hurt the man who wrote *Seize the Day?* Court adjourned. (pp. 6-7)

Robert Lasson, "Will Mr. Bellow's Counsel Approach the Bench?" in Book World—The Washington Post, *October 20, 1968, pp. 6-7.*

Ivan Gold   (essay date 1968)

[*Gold is an American short fiction writer, educator, and critic. In the following review, Gold traces Bellow's development as a writer through the stories written over a seventeen-year period and collected in* Mosby's Memoirs, and Other Stories.]

For many of its admirers, myself included, Saul Bellow's novel *Herzog* seemed a hard act to follow, and there is evidence in [*Mosby's Memoirs, and Other Stories*] that the author found it so as well. But in the shaping of his professional life, no less than in his fiction, Bellow has for a long while given the impression of knowing exactly where he was, and in which direction he was headed, and publishers' practice of following up a major work with a collection of shorter (if not always slighter) pieces appears, in the present instance, to have coincided precisely with his own deep preoccupations and concerns.

The six stories in *Mosby's Memoirs, and Other Stories* were written, or previously published, over a period of 17 years, with only the two most recent postdating *Herzog.* One does not have to have read the novel in order to respond to the collection; but if one has read it, it is all but impossible to come away from the present book without the sense that Moses Herzog has been offering instruction at your shoulder, or, more in character, has mailed off a long letter on the proper approach to these tales, a letter as didactic as you would have expected, but with far less humor than you remembered.

Two of the three earliest stories, **"Looking for Mr. Green"** (1951) and **"The Gonzaga Manuscripts"** (1954) are well-known, and there is considerable pleasure in coming across them once again. Both are filled with the sort of detail which anchors them solidly in place and time, loaded with minor characters who stay in the memory, and both are graced by the style which Philip Rahv has called, "at once astringent and poetic . . . sensibility in action."

These stories describe blighted quests: In the earlier one, George Grebe ("He was an educated man . . . his luck had not been good.") finds himself delivering relief checks during the Depression in the Negro district of Chicago. Grebe is much less cynical and much more conscientious than his immediate superior, Raynor (who—also an educated man—enjoys applying phrases like "the fallen world of appearances" to the scene around him), but the recalcitrant stuff of the ghetto defeats him anyway; he never finds Mr. Green, ends up leaving the check with a nude woman who may or may not be Green's wife.

In **"The Gonzaga Manuscripts,"** Clarence Feiler ("[He] had not found his occupation and had nothing to do. . . . His beard was grown not to hide weaknesses but as a project to give his life shape.") goes to Madrid in search of some unpublished poems by the dead poet Gonzaga; he is not greeted by appreciation for his rarefied tastes, but by hostility, indifference, and a refusal on the part of everyone he meets to see him as more or less than a representative of the Anglo-American heritage, which has lately given the world the atom bomb. Near the end, when he thinks he is close to the poems, he is presented instead with shares in a pitchblende mine, by a man who has mistaken him for a British financier. A racial gulf seems responsible for failure in the first instance, a national one in the second—but in both stories, men of some intelligence and pretensions to culture are deceived and defeated by the sheer cussedness of life, and they are made to seem a little foolish in imagining that it could have been otherwise.

In the third story from this time, **"A Father-to-Be"** (1955), 31-year-old Rogin, a research chemist, is on the way to have dinner at his fiancée's apartment. On the subway, examining the other passengers, he has a kind of vision, in which the man seated next to him appears to be his own son of 40 years hence, incorporating all the shortcomings of his mother-to-be and none of Rogin's virtues. Whatever value the insight might have had is dissipated by the blithe matter-of-factness of his girl, who, when he reaches her apartment, administers a shampoo, which it is more convenient to enjoy. While much slighter than the earlier stories, **"A Father-to-Be"** points up some of Bellow's particular talents: fidelity to urban interior monologue, a way of trapping and rendering the fugitive moment, and a feel for life in our great cities that not many writers have matched. But certain of his faults become clearer as well: the weighting of his fiction with intellectual and philosophical baggage, perorations on history, death, time, which are particularly incongruous in a story of this size.

By the time of **"Leaving the Yellow House"** (1957), something funny, or not so funny, has happened. The humor which was integral to the earlier stories is absent. The city, and people who receive educations in cities, are far distant. Hattie is an old alcoholic struggling to maintain her independence in Utah, in the desert. When she breaks her arm in an auto accident, it becomes increasingly difficult for her to fend for herself, or even to maintain the illusion that she has ever really done so. People still offer her aid, but now it is contingent on her willing them her house—which, since it is so intimately connected with herself, she refuses to do. Finally, forced to face her growing helplessness, and the prospect of death, she sits down to make out her will, drinking the while, and, after much thought and bourbon, she wills the house to . . . herself.

For the moment, at least, she has outfaced death, shown herself more implacable than her neighbors or the grave. The numerous flashbacks, while they do flesh out Hattie, are often clumsily initiated. (She believes that all of her life has been preserved on film; hence, from time to time, she reaches in and runs off a reel.) The narrative is relentless, language in the service of obsession, as doggedly determined as Hattie herself, but not the more interesting for that. Yet since this story is in a real way *about* death, *about* time, there is no sense of these larger questions being imposed; for the moment Bellow has managed to integrate his metaphysics with his fiction, how ever much the fiction may have suffered in the process.

Of course there is no way to overlook the novels Bellow was writing throughout this time, or to doubt that the real thrust of his creative energies went to those; and there are yoks enough in *The Adventures of Auggie March* (1954) and in *Henderson the Rain King* (1959) to overturn any view which requires of him, in the fifties, unrelieved sobriety. But to have these stories finally collected, the four I have mentioned and the two which follow, is to find oneself invited to such speculations. In 1964 arrived the card-carrying intellectual, Moses Herzog, full flowering of the Grebes and Feilers, tilting not with undeliverable relief checks or undiscoverable poems but—Mind in and vs. World—with the very substance of his life, receiving his share of lumps on the way to the grave, but never without irony and humor, and although he is flat on his back and temporarily wordless at the end of the book, he will be rising by and by, and striking out in a direction which at the time remained obscure.

"The Old System" (1967) and **"Mosby's Memoirs"** (1968) make clear what that direction was. Both Dr. Samuel Braun (whose initials are familiar) of the first story and Mosby of the second are men of great intelligence and sensibility, but now of such a high state of development that they scarcely leave their beds at all. Dr. Braun is said to be a biochemist specializing in the chemistry of heredity—and Bellow, who seems to know more than any American novelist now writing, inserts enough detail so that we do believe it—but his sole activity in this story is to reminisce about two older cousins, both dead, who lived in upstate New York.

The story of Isaac and Tina Braun is a full and vivid account of Jewish life in this country in this century, a kind of compressed saga, rich with family love and strife, religious commitments and quarrels, business shenanigans,

scenes of sexual initiation, scenes of death, numerous moving examples of human intransigence and suffering. Yet it begins and ends in Dr. Braun's apartment, or more accurately inside his head, and is hedged about by his large, gloomy thoughts on the condition of mankind, which is "in a confusing, uncomfortable, disagreeable stage in the evolution of its consciousness," and which, on the final page, once it had ". . . grasped its own idea, that it was human and human through such passions, it began to exploit, to play, to disturb for the sake of exciting disturbance, to make an uproar, a crude circus of feelings." And this crude circus of feelings occurs, as Braun looks out into the night, beneath the vast, belittling majesty of the stars, "these things cast outward by a great begetting spasm billions of years ago."

But Samuel Braun, as he thinks these thoughts, has tears in his eyes. Mosby, "erudite, maybe even profound; thought much, accomplished much," an intellectual who has made his way via the academy into the high places of government, and is sitting now in Oaxaca, Mexico, drinking mescal and working on his memoirs, is guilty of no such excess.

He realizes rather cooly that his memoirs, which are meant to be no less than an intellectual history of our time, are not really lively: he hits on the expedient of including the adventures of one Lustgarten, an inveterate bumbler he knew in postwar Europe. ("Perhaps Mosby did not have a light touch. Still, he thought he must have an eye for a certain kind of comedy. And he must find a way to relieve the rigor of this account of his mental wars.") And so Mosby's glittering, arid intelligence looks to find sustenance in the juicy, klutzy quality of Lustgarten's life, Herzog neatly disassembled. Mind now fitfully using World, and with very limited success—when Mosby finally bestirs himself to join a prescheduled guided tour, he has a horrid premonition of his own death in an underground tomb. Yet the despair one is encouraged to feel by both stories, Bellow/Mosby's despair, Prospero-Braun's despair, seems to me less over the quality of life-in-our-time, or the current state of human consciousness, than a reflection of the author's own profound doubts that fiction can any longer make sense of the world, or pretend to tell us how to live.

But like the "hero" of Samuel Beckett's novel *The Unnamable,* who is a very longwinded, very intelligent head in a bottle, and whose final message to us it, "I can't go on, I'll go on," Bellow (as he was at the time when Hattie made her grim appearance) may be presently working on that novel which will make these thoughts especially idle.

Ivan Gold, *"Friends of Herzog," in* The New York Times Book Review, *November 3, 1968, pp. 4, 48.*

Marvin Mudrick   (essay date 1968)

[*Mudrick is an American critic who believes that literature "should be life, or as close to it as possible." His criticism, which eschews systematic approaches to literature in favor of a subjective approach, has been alternately characterized as pompous or inflated or witty and enlightening. In the following excerpt, Mudrick provides a mixed review of* Mosby's Memoirs, and Other Stories.]

The two most celebrated contemporary writers of the quarter are Saul Bellow and Isaac Bashevis Singer; but their new books [*Mosby's Memoirs, and Other Stories* and *The Séance, and Other Stories*] are disappointing. Bellow's astonishing eclecticism looks very odd in a collection: the stories are related to one another only in the sleight-of-hand virtuosity with which each one manipulates the special style that Bellow chooses for it. Every style of Bellow's suffers from a chronic chill of pedantry and remoteness except the Herzog style, which is probably as close as we'll ever get to hearing Bellow himself. The best, if a rather slight, story is the only one in the Herzog style, **"A Father-to-Be"**:

> At Christmas, Rogin almost went mad. Joan bought him a velvet smoking jacket with frog fasteners, a beautiful pipe, and a pouch. She bought Phyllis a garnet brooch, an Italian silk umbrella, and a gold cigarette holder. For other friends, she bought Dutch pewter and Swedish glassware. Before she was through, she had spent five hundred dollars of Rogin's money. He loved her too much to show his suffering. He believed she had a far better nature than his. She didn't worry about money. She had a marvelous character, always cheerful, and she really didn't need a psychiatrist at all. She went to one because Phyllis did and it made her curious. She tried too much to keep up with her cousin, whose father had made millions in the rug business.

"The Old System" is Augie March in a funereal mood; **"Looking for Mr. Green"** is Depression naturalism, more supple than its model; **"The Gonzaga Manuscripts"** is the product of Bellow's unaccountable impulse to redo **"The Aspern Papers"**; **"Leaving the Yellow House"** may have compassionate intentions but it's an iceberg of a story, a demoralizing account of the nullity of a down-and-out old woman; **"Mosby's Memoirs"** is in Bellow's latest brilliant, showy, dense, protective manner behind which the reader is not admitted. (pp. 755-56)

> *Marvin Mudrick, "Must We Burn Mme. de Beauvoir?" in* The Hudson Review, *Vol. XXI, No. 4, Winter, 1968, pp. 751-63.*

Theodore Solotaroff   (essay date 1969)

[*An American critic and former editor of one of the United States' most prestigious literary quarterlies,* New American Review, *Solotaroff is often regarded as instrumental in evaluating and shaping American literature since the early 1960s. In the highly favorable review below, he maintains that the majority of stories in* Mosby's Memoirs, and Other Stories *evidence Bellow's "extraordinary ability to enter directly into the mixed conditions of a particular life or experience and conduct the reader toward a general truth embedded in it."*]

[Bellow's fiction realistically examines] the resistance, density, intractability of normal life. This is why his imagination is so strong. It has to be: it encompasses and lifts the full weight of a man's existence. This, in turn, is why his characters are so real: Joseph, Leventhal, Wilhelm, Henderson, Herzog, whose principle might be, "I am burdened, therefore I am." In **"A Father-to-Be"** [in *Mosby's Memoirs, and Other Stories*], a young research chemist rides the subway to dine with his expensive Jewish princess of a girlfriend and finds himself studying with disgust a smug middle-aged man in a stylish overcoat and blue suede shoes: the very prototype, Rogin realizes with horror, of what their prospective son would be like in 40 years:

> "What a vision of existence it gave him. Man's personal aims were nothing, illusion. The life force occupied each of us in turn in its progress toward its own fulfillment, trampling on our individual humanity, using us for its own ends like mere dinosaurs or bees, exploiting love heartlessly, making us engage in the social process, labor, struggle for money, and submit to the law of pressure, the universal law of layers, superimposition."

The beginning is Schopenhauer, the ending is pure Bellow. The law of pressure, layers, superimposition: that is how he builds up figure and ground, so that Rogin's ride on the IRT on a Sunday night becomes as effortful and portentous as a bad dream.

As most of these stories indicate, Bellow has an extraordinary ability to enter directly into the mixed conditions of a particular life or experience and conduct the reader toward a general truth embedded in it. Three of the six stories—and they are the three that matter most; they may well be masterpieces—mine the ore of common life: a mismatched old woman in the Utah desert trying to hold onto her house and independence; a white intellectual trying to deliver relief checks in the black belt; the rise and strife of an immigrant Jewish family. But each of them is far from commonplace. Against the dullness, stupidity, hopelessness of Hattie's struggle in the Utah desert, against the terrific vacuousness and gloom of the Chicago ghetto during the Depression, against the stridency and acquisitiveness of the Braun family, a steady and searching pressure of consciousness is exerted, encompassing and at the same time animating, preserving things both in their literalness and multivalence. In **"Looking for Mr. Green,"** George Grebe searches in one of the tenements:

> He began to climb to the third floor. Pieces of plaster ground under his feet; strips of brass tape from which the carpeting had been torn away marked old boundaries at the sides. In the passage, the cold reached him worse than in the street; it touched him to the quick. The hall toilets ran like springs. . . . Then he struck a match in the gloom and searched for names and numbers among the writings and scribbles on the walls. He saw WHOODY-DOODY GO TO JESUS, and zigzags, caricatures, sexual scrawls, and curses. So the sealed rooms of pyramids were also decorated, and the caves of human dawn. The information on the card was, TULLIVER GREEN—APT. 3D. There were no names, however, and no numbers.

Along with the clarity of observation, an imaginative idea

is working through this material like yeast in dough, and eventually it will make the story rise, as the passage itself does, to indicate something of the inner truth of our human relationships and to restate it in action. The decay of the tenement, the regression to the primitive cavelike conditions of shelter, the atavistic markings, the gloom, the anonymity stand at one extreme; the ex-classicist Grebe and his address-cards and checks at the other. The social nexus between them has collapsed, revealing in a particularly naked form what Grebe's erudite boss refers to as "the fallen world of appearances." This is the terrain that Grebe must cross, full of fantasy and tension, for the "faltering of organization [has] set free a huge energy, an escaped, unattached, unregulated power from the giant raw place." At the beginning of the story, Grebe feels he might as well be looking for Mr. Green in the jungle, but, as he comes to realize, and this makes him press on in his search, the adversity of appearances is an aspect of the general fate in a city like Chicago, where neighborhoods such as this one rise and fall into ruin every 50 years. Amid so much flux, what then abides?

> Objects once so new, so concrete, that it could [not] have occurred to anyone they stood for other things, had crumbled. Therefore, reflected Grebe, the secret of them was out. It was that they stood for themselves by agreement, and were natural and not unnatural by agreement, and when the things themselves collapsed the agreement became visible."

As one of his other clients helps him see, this "agreement" is a function of human trust—and need: "the need that keeps so many vast thousands in position." The reality system is no different, finally, from the money system. When Grebe finally finds Mr. Green's address he is met by a naked, drunken, obscene, angry woman who refuses to identify herself. But having learned what he has learned, Grebe gives her the check: she stands for Mr. Green and Grebe has to trust too.

This metaphysics of the human tie, as Grebe scornfully reminds himself, is pretty remote to the immediate conditions in this jungle of blight between Cottage Grove and Ashland. In the face of such misery, he can only mark the honest direction of his imagination—the question of whether "there is *something* that is dismal and permanently ugly" in the human covenant—and press on to deliver his very real check. As Norman Podhoretz points out in a concise and trenchant reading of the novels up to *Herzog* (in *Doings and Undoings*), Bellow's social and political bias has been pretty much the neo-conservative one, with which Podhoretz associates his pessimism, his refusal to arraign the institutions that produce his character's malaise, his damming up and deflection of rage, and his tendency to end his dark novels on an upbeat note: recently, that of love. The detection of this bias is accurate but to ask Bellow to drop it and to adopt a more radical one is to ask him to turn his art, and the ideas and emotions that support it, upside down. What Bellow knows before he knows anything else—knows in his bones—is the settled weight and ambiguity of existence, both inner and outer. It is precisely from this feeling for the accumulation of circumstance, contingency, error, conflict, paradox, anoma-

ly, *as an individual experiences it,* that he derives his amazing descriptive power—a power, incidentally, that makes **Seize the Day** the best criticism of the money culture, as it affects the middle class, that I know of. To open his art to meliorative politics would be to rob it of its specific gravity and to place Bellow outside his own sense of the perdurable and the changing from which he draws his clues to the "axial lines" of a life and its place in the scheme of things. He is at heart an essentialist: man and his nature are absolutes and what is most true is what most preserves a man in his emotions and duration and kind. To the "law of layers, superimposition," Bellow has no solution: but the mastering emotion he prescribes and through which he conducts his protagonists is clearly not love, as Podhoretz says, but grief: the active kind, that lifts some of the burden of mismanagement off the spirit and allows it to breathe.

Take Hattie Simmons Wagoner, a "city woman," still proud of her Philadelphia connections, her china, linen, engraved stationery, who has been eking out an existence for 20 years at Sego Desert Lake [in **"Leaving the Yellow House"**], with the local Indians and Mexicans, the dudes from the nearby ranch, the six white residents. Mistress of a long-departed cowboy, companion and servant to another old divorcee, whose house she has inherited, Hattie is a "character": a "cheerful, plugging, absent," and hard-drinking old woman of 72, who keeps her canned goods on her library shelves and more than anything else wants "to be thought of as a rough, experienced woman of the West." One day, driving drunk and fast as usual, she stalls her car on a railroad crossing, and while it is being towed off, her arm is broken. She tries to go on against the odds, which include a record of dependency, fantasy, procrastination, dispersion, but the pain and impairment from her injury have brought on senility and the harsh, testing way of life in the desert has become too much for her. Yet she is unable to leave her house and its belated satisfaction, unable to live with her stuffy brother, unable to accept old age and death. Like her car, she is stalled at the crossing. Her plight whips her through the gamut of emotions— rage, resentment, regret, grief—and forces her toward the belated recognition of the borrowed, jerry-built structure of her life: "I was never one single thing anyway . . . Never my own. I was only loaned to myself." Wanting to make at least the final gesture of responsibility, to sign her unbalanced account with a flourish of pride, she sits down to make her will and give away her house. But soon drunk again, her mind staggering from one unsatisfactory beneficiary to the next, she once more assails what she knows to be sensible and proper, and leaves her house to herself.

Now, to draw a moral (the retributions of sloth and illusion) or to extract a social meaning (the neglect of the aged) is to lose the immediacy and life-meaning of Hattie's batty and poignant will to live, of the intricately related processes by which she succors as well as defeats herself. It is also to dislodge the figure from the ground—Bellow's beautifully rendered mixture of the pseudo-frontier and the exigent desert community where the reality principle still rules. Finally, it is to denature his art, whose power derives from his grasp of the primary emotions and essential issues of a life and which culminates, like Tolstoy's, in an image of the necessary, of the way things are.

Finally, there is **"The Old System,"** Bellow's most recent story and a high point in his career. An immigrant Jewish family chronicle, it is written with an authority of observation and insight that enable its forty-odd pages to outstrip almost all the fiction that has come to burden this subject. One lazy Saturday, the traditional day of rest and reentry. Dr. Braun, a ranking geneticist, finds himself meditating on his two cousins from upstate New York, Issac and Tina Braun, the one "born to be a man in the direct Old Testament sense," who trusted the old system of the patriarchs and became a millionaire, the other, a harsh, obese, rapacious woman who trusted nothing, hated her brother's success, and eventually forced him to bring $20,000 when she was dying of cancer in order to be reconciled with her. Now they are both dead. What did all that energy and effort and emotional tumult signify? Dr. Braun reviews the circumstance and events, looking for the patterns of causation, the general human implications "within the peculiar system of light, movement, contact, and perishing in which he tried to find stability." Heredity and nurture, cultural transmission, ego psychology, recent social history, even astronomy, offer their perspectives, framing his idea that these two hostages he has given to death represented "necessary existence." But the main point that is revealed about their respective lives is the emotional core: deep, solid, old-fashioned in Issac; volatile, manipulative, modern in Tina.

"Oh, these Jews—these Jews! Their feelings, their hearts. He often wanted nothing more than to stop all this." But whether direct or devious, natural or undergoing the modern perversions, quietly spinning a destiny or making a circus out of dying, emotions are what Dr. Braun, having grieved, in his fashion, for his cousins and buried them again, finds himself left with: messy, uncertain data alongside the molecular processes, yet humanity's vague clue to "why life, why death," and its possible link to "the great begetting spasm billions of years ago" that cast the stars outward. As the cold-eyed but bitterly moved scientist puts it to himself: "Material details were of the greatest importance. But still the largest strokes were made by the spirit. Had to be." (pp. 21-3)

> Theodore Solotaroff, "Bellow's Stories," in *The New Republic*, Vol. 160, No. 2820, January 11, 1969, pp. 21-3.

David P. Demarest, Jr.   (essay date 1969)

[*In the essay below, Demarest focuses on the theme of "life's discontinuity, the inconsistency of human moods" in Bellow's stories "Looking for Mr. Green" and "A Father-to-Be."*]

Two of Saul Bellow's Short Stories, **"Looking for Mr. Green"** and **"A Father-to-Be,"** serve as excellent introductions to his general vision. Both stories ask which of two responses to life is appropriate—a search, on the one hand, for intellectual order; a willingness, on the other, to take life as it is. The stories suggest Bellow's typical answer: both attitudes are inevitable and appropriate; and

the man who does not recognize that humans alternate, often abruptly and illogically, between the two perspectives deludes himself with a half-vision of what life involves. Bellow, in short, places man in a rather Popean middle state and aims at an ironic knowledge similar to Pope's: man's final wisdom is to accept and affirm the contradictions of his position. Despite the differences among them, Joseph, Leventhal, Tommy Wilhelm, Henderson, and Herzog are all directed toward this wisdom as Bellow abruptly alters their perspectives at the end of their stories; none has solved the problems that caused his moral anguish throughout, but each has been made to respond less critically to an influx of life. **"Looking for Mr. Green"** lays down the terms of Bellow's dialectic: Grebe, the hero, struggles to connect logically the worlds of idea and experience ("being" and "seeming" are the specific terms of the story). Rogin of **"A Father-to-Be"** prefigures the protagonists of the novels in the inconsistencies of his own attitude: after a comically feeble revolt against the materialism of his life, he is wooed back to the way of the world, unresisting, by a warm shampoo. The stories both show Bellow's emphasis on life's discontinuity, the inconsistency of human moods; both undercut narrow expectations that life can or should be ordered logically.

"Looking for Mr. Green" is by far the more complex of the two stories, creating a realistic picture of Chicago slums during the Depression and graphically showing the alienation of the urban Negro. These realistic social subjects become metaphors of the philosophic theme: the Negro environment suggests (much as it does toward the end of Ralph Ellison's *Invisible Man*) the inchoate world of experience; the urban relief agency is the pattern, the form that might impose organization on this flux. Grebe, the Establishment's messenger, is allowed to test the relevance of a hopeful education and philosophy in this divided world of Chicago.

In the flashback that constitutes the middle of the story, Bellow makes consistent the philosophic terms of the argument. Raynor, the relief agency supervisor, twits Grebe for his ivory-tower college education in classical languages: " 'Were you brought up tenderly, with permission to go out and find out what were the last things that everything else stands for while everybody else labored in the fallen world of appearances'." The question comes down to which world demands allegiance by being more real—the world of idea or the physical world. Should a man simply adjust to the raw facts of experience, or should he search for a pattern that might be discovered within or imposed upon that experience? Raynor announces his own allegiance to the physical facts of life:

> "I'll tell you, as a man of culture, that even though nothing looks to be real, and everything stands for something else, and that thing for another thing, and that thing for a still further one—there ain't any comparison between twenty-five and thirty-seven dollars a week, regardless of the last reality. Don't you think that was clear to your Greeks? They were a thoughtful people, but they didn't part with their slaves."

Raynor is a good-humored cynic who can smile at the characterization of the physical world that he imagines fits

Grebe's view—"the fallen world of appearances"—, who laughs at the irrelevance of his own language-learning at the Berlitz School, where he pictures himself one of the company of "office boys in China and braves in Tanganyika" seduced by the "attractive power of civilization." Raynor has given up any belief that idea can be related significantly to experience; he has assumed the disparity of words and physical facts.

Grebe stands in contrast to Raynor, though he is not a simple-minded idealist. He is amused at the playful pedantry of Raynor's "fallen world of appearances"; it is not a phrase that Grebe would ever take seriously. Grebe recognizes the force of raw, unorganized physical fact: his Depression experience has swept away collegiate naïveté, and he can look at Staika, Blood Mother of Federal Street, as she does her ironing in the relief office and see in her "the power that made people listen, . . . the war of flesh and blood . . . on this place and condition." But granting the qualifications with which he hedges his idealism, Grebe has held to the faith that idea does and must organize experience. His central preoccupation in the story, matching the name on the check—Mr. Tulliver Green—to an actual person, dramatizes his faith: " 'there must be a way to find a person' "; " 'it almost doesn't do any good to have a name if you can't be found by it. It doesn't stand for anything'." Grebe is painfully aware of the difficulty of his problem—applying labels in the anonymity of the ghetto: "When you saw them, how could you know them? They didn't carry bundles on their back or look picturesque. You only saw a man, a Negro, walking in the street or riding in the car, like everyone else, with his thumb closed on a transfer. And therefore how were you supposed to tell?" But unlike Raynor, Grebe has not given up the assumption that one can fit idea to physical data, and we admire his stubborn faith. At the same time we feel that Grebe has yet to recognize, through experience, the true degree of discontinuity between the physical world and ideas that would govern it.

Just as he does in *The Victim, The Adventures of Augie March, Dangling Man,* and *Herzog,* in **"Looking for Mr. Green"** Bellow allows the weight of the urban environment to press home much of his theme. Chicago, blighted, desolated by the Depression, its neighborhoods always changing, graphically shows how fallen the world of appearances is—"trampled, frost-hardened lots on one side; on the other, an automobile junk yard and then the infinite work of the Elevated frames, weak-looking, gaping with rubbish fires; two sets of leaning brick porches three stories high and a flight of cement stairs to the cellar . . . " The difficulty of dealing through intellection with this slum world is emphasized by its flux. In one shabby apartment jammed with transient Negroes, Grebe notes "a piano piled towering to the ceiling with papers, a dining-room table of the old style of prosperous Chicago"; in Raynor's relief office "a steel beam passed through the little make-shift room, from which machine belts once had hung. The building was an old factory." Grebe's imagination suggests other pictures of how man's physical experience mocks efforts at civilized order. The Negroes in the apartment with the piano seem "sitting on benches like a parliament"; the halls of the buildings make their gro-

tesque comment: "he struck a match in the gloom and searched for names and numbers among the writings and scribbles on the walls. He saw WHOODY-DOODY GO TO JESUS, and zigzags, caricatures, sexual scrawls, and curses. So the sealed rooms of pyramids were also decorated, and the caves of human dawn." The darkness that pervades the apartment houses and that deepens through the streets as evening falls renders bizarre and feeble the lights of purposive, ordered life: "someone nursed a candle in a shed, where a man unloaded kindling wood from a sprawl-wheeled baby buggy." And, centrally, there is the inscrutability of the Negroes' identity—one Negro woman peers out at Grebe with "a dream-bound, dream-blind face, very soft and black, shut off."

Such is the nature of the reality that Grebe still has cautious hopes he can deal with through the pattern of idea. He sets out like "a hunter inexperienced in the camouflage of his game," armed with the weapons of tidy bureaucracy: ". . . in his deep trenchcoat pocket he had the cardboard of checks, punctured for the spindles of the file" (*ibid.*). At the start, Grebe, the ex-linguist, can believe seriously that one of his "great handicaps was that he hadn't looked at any of the case records"; if only he had spent "an hour in the files, taking a few notes, . . . he needn't have been at such a disadvantage." The incongruity between the amorphous world Grebe faces and the tools of abstraction that form his mode of operation creates a comic undertone in the story. Grebe himself often feels the ridiculousness of his position and has to suppress despair and self-pity; the reader sympathizes with him but also smiles at the out-of-place figure he cuts: "he stood his ground and waited for a reply, his crimson wool scarf wound about his neck and drooping outside his trenchcoat, pockets weighted with the block of checks and official forms." The expectation builds that Grebe will have to admit more openly to himself the disparity between the ordered symbols of society and the anonymity of the slum.

The climax of **"Looking for Mr. Green"** concentrates symbolically Grebe's philosophic problem—whether he can discover an intelligible relation between the world of idea and the brute force of the physical. Two Negroes, the old man, Mr. Field, and the naked woman with whom Grebe finally collides, are put forth very explicitly as symbols, yet Bellow manages to make each completely realistic. Mr. Field is the idealist, the supreme believer in order and civilization, in the creative reality of the word. Although Grebe hasn't doubted for a moment Field's identity, Field insists on piling up the kind of bureaucratic identifications with which Grebe has allied himself throughout the story:

> Field laid out his papers: Social Security card, relief certification, letters from the state hospital in Manteno, and a naval discharge dated San Diego, 1920. . . . "You got to know who I am," the old man said. "You're from the government. It's not your check, it's a government check and you got no business to hand it over till everything is proved. . . . " "There's everything I done and been. Just the death certificate and they can close the book on me."

Grebe accepts all this bureaucratic "ceremony" with

something of a comic sense that Field is a parody of his own reliance on numbers, names, and file cards. As the old man talks on, however, it becomes clear that Field is more than a card-carrying pedant. When he describes his "scheme," he sounds like a Platonist dreaming of a worldly utopia that will light the dark corners of the slums:

> The old man unfolded his scheme. This was to create one Negro millionaire a month by subscription. One clever, good-hearted young fellow elected every month would sign a contract to use the money to start a business employing Negroes. This would be advertised by chain letters and word of mouth, and every Negro wage-earner would contribute a dollar a month. Within five years there would be sixty millionaires.
>
> "That'll fetch respect," he said. . . . "You got to take and organize all the money that gets thrown away on the policy wheel and the horse race. . . . Money, that's d'sun of human kind! . . . " He sounded, speaking about a golden sun in this dark room, . . . like one of the underground kings of mythology, old judge Minos himself.

Grebe may be too sophisticated for conversion to the details of the old man's dream, but his temperamental bias toward idealism is rekindled, after the day's discouragement, by Field; and he begins a long review of the philosophic problem he's been facing.

As Grebe emerges through Field's yard, Bellow brings the details of the city into sharp focus for their climactic role in the working out of Grebe's final attitude. Grebe sees, above and beyond the debris in the foreground, the "needle-eye red of cable towers in the open icy height hundreds of feet above the river and the factories." Those "keen points" of light, seen through the surrounding dark, perched, by suggestion, in the fragile framework of steel and wire, seem to sum up the precariousness of man's intermittent organizations. This impression leads Grebe to think of Chicago itself, its cyclical periods of construction and decay. What to his mind has been missing is a stable idea, a pattern (like Mr. Field's scheme) that could hold the city together and make it endure, make its appearance of physical solidity into something permanently real— "rebuilt after the Great Fire, this part of the city was, not fifty years later, in ruins again, factories boarded up, buildings deserted or fallen, gaps of prairie between. But it wasn't desolation that this made you feel, but rather a faltering of organization." The dependence of the physical world on idea seems to Grebe clearer than ever. When these neighborhoods were new, they must have appeared to be objects "so concrete that it could never have occurred to anyone they stood for other things," but now it is obvious that their existence depended on a "common agreement or covenant."

Grebe's imagination seizes on the El as ultimate symbol of the power of idea. He can understand how that skeletal structure might have inspired the schemes of Field: "he had within sight of his kitchen window the chart, the very bones of a successful scheme—the El with its blue and green confetti of signals. People consented to pay dimes and ride the crash-box cars, and so it was a success. Yet

how absurd it looked; how little reality there was to start with." Whimsically Grebe goes on to imagine the builder of the El, Mr. Yerkes, as a philosopher searching the fields of light for a realm where form and matter forever interpenetrate: "Grebe remembered, too, that Mr. Yerkes had established the Yerkes Observatory and endowed it with millions. Now how did the notion come to him in his New York museum of a palace or his Aegean-bound yacht to give money to astronomers? Was he awed perhaps by his bizarre enterprise [the El] and therefore ready to spend money to find out where in the universe being and seeming were identical?" The playfulness of this fantasy indicates that Grebe is alert to what may be absurd in the zeal of his own commitment to idea; and for a moment Grebe turns bitterly on himself and asks whether it may be that what is most real, most permanent is the fallen world of physical squalor he sees around him: are he, and Mr. Field, and Yerkes the El-building astronomer expecting too much of passing pipe-dreams? Grebe suppresses such disillusionment, and renewing the search for Mr. Green, clings to the check as at least one small instance in which he can assert the reality of idea: "he had a real check in his pocket for a Mr. Green who must be real beyond question."

Grebe's collision with the nude Negro woman should smash his illusion that there can ever be a predictable relation between idea and physical experience. The woman is "heavy, . . . naked and drunk," and having stumbled down the stairs in response to Grebe's ring, "she blundered into him." Grebe sees in her eyes, reminiscent of the Blood Mother of Federal Street, "a dot of blood in their enraged brilliance." As her huge body blocks the stairs that Grebe thinks might lead to Mr. Green, she tells him plainly what the scene has made uproariously clear—he's a damned fool; the check is undeliverable because Mr. Green can never be identified. But, now, faced with this final evidence that his faith in idea has been far too sanguine, Grebe cannot accept the truth. Breaking protocol, he gives the check to "Mrs. Green." As the comic fact rings in the reader's ear that Grebe has all along been trying to identify a Mr. Green among black people, Grebe consoles himself, "It was important that there was a real Mr. Green whom they could not keep him from reaching because he seemed to come as an emissary from hostile appearances. And though the self-ridicule was slow to diminish, and his face still blazed with it, he had, nevertheless, a feeling of elation, too. 'For after all,' he said, 'he *could* be found!' "

Our final attitude toward Grebe is complex. It is perfectly clear that after all Mr. Green *couldn't* be found; and since it is also clear that Grebe really knows that he couldn't, Grebe has put himself in the position of deliberate self-deception. We cannot admire Grebe for refusing conscious knowledge of the discontinuity between idea and experience. But, on the other hand, we must sympathize with Grebe's predicament. Grebe's stubborn idealism is nothing less than the basic human need to construct the world according to intelligent, moral principle. His efforts have been admirable (he has fulfilled the epigraph of the story, "Whatsoever thy hand findeth to do, do it with thy might"), even if he has not been able to accept a balancing knowledge—admission of life's illogic and inconsistency.

Rogin of **"A Father-to-Be"** faces a philosophic choice similar to Grebe's—whether to view the world from a moral, ordering perspective or to bring himself to accept things uncritically as they are. Where Grebe took the first view, Rogin is interesting because he exhibits both attitudes himself and because he shows in these personal changes of perspective the illogic, the discontinuity of human mood. Man does not solve ideological problems, the story suggests; man merely changes his view of whether it is important to try to solve those problems.

As in **"Looking for Mr. Green,"** the setting in **"A Father-to-Be"** carries a good deal of thematic weight. The sector of the city that we see now is that of the professional middle class. Joan, Rogin's fiancée, sums up the materialism of this world, the clutter of the affluent good life—"Joan bought him a velvet smoking jacket with frog fasteners, a beautiful pipe, and a pouch. She bought Phyllis a garnet brooch, an Italian silk umbrella, and a gold cigarette holder. For other friends, she bought Dutch pewter and Swedish glassware." This sort of detail suggests one level on which the story operates—as satire of the materialistic frivolity of modern America. But again Bellow makes setting stand for a broader philosophic dilemma in the mind of the protagonist. From specific annoyance with Joan's spendthrift habits—"she had spent five hundred dollars of Rogin's money" for Christmas—Rogin generalizes his problem into a notion of material necessity: "while the woman in the drugstore was wrapping the shampoo bottle, a clear idea suddenly arose in Rogin's thoughts. Money surrounds you in life as the earth does in death. Superimposition is the universal law. Who is free? No one is free. Who has no burdens? Everyone is under pressure." Rogin's problem is whether to surrender to the existential, the material, or to rebel and try to impose intellectual order upon it.

The structure of the story is the alternation of Rogin's moods between rebellion and submission. As the story opens, he is grousing about his lot—how his life is vexed by domineering women: "his mother was growing more and more difficult. On Friday night, she had neglected to cut up his meat for him, and he was hurt . . . " "He recalled two dreams of the night before. In one, an undertaker had offered to cut his hair, and he had refused. In another, he had been carrying a woman on his head." What emerges is not only Rogin's rebellious ill-humor but also the relative pettiness of his character compared to Grebe's. Also Bellow establishes a stronger comic tone from the start in this story. We do not expect significant rebellion from a man who wants his mother to cut up his meat. Moreover, even in his complaints about Joan's materialism, Rogin implicates himself in her bourgeois values: "Joan had debts he was helping her to pay, for she wasn't working. She was looking for something suitable to do. Beautiful, well educated, aristocratic in her attitude, she couldn't clerk in a dime store; she couldn't model clothes (Rogin thought this made girls vain and stiff, and he didn't want her to) . . . " Rogin's thin veneer of moral superiority is itself the target of satiric comedy. Nor is the reader inclined to take Rogin very seriously when his attitude abruptly alters, in the drugstore and delicatessen, to a happy submission to a material necessity:

> The notion that all were under pressure and affliction, instead of saddening him, had the opposite influence. It put him in a wonderful mood. It was extraordinary how happy he became and, in addition, clear-sighted. His eyes all at once were opened to what was around him. He saw with delight how the druggist and the woman who wrapped the shampoo bottle were smiling and flirting, how the lines of worry in her face went over into the lines of cheer and the druggist's receding gums did not hinder his kidding and friendliness.

Rogin's new mood, this affirmation of the world, seems comically superficial and strained—"his heart was torn with joy at those deeper thoughts of our ignorance."

The rhythm of alternating moods of the story seems to deepen into a more serious tone when Rogin is again prompted to rebellion by the sight of a middle-aged man on the subway whom he can imagine as his son-to-be if he marries Joan. The material necessity that a few minutes before he had been able to rejoice in, he now sees as an indiscriminate life force that dooms him and his to mediocrity.

> To suffer, to labor, to toil and force your way through the spikes of life, to crawl through its darkest caverns, to push through the worst, to struggle under the weight of economy, to make money—only to become the father of a fourth-rate man of the world like this, so flat-looking, with his ordinary, clean, rosy, uninteresting, self-satisfied, fundamentally bourgeois face. . . . The Life force occupied each of us in turn in its progress toward its own fulfillment, trampling on our individual humanity, . . . making us . . . submit to the law of pressure, the universal law of layers, super-imposition!

Rogin vows he will break loose from Joan: he won't be a "damned instrument," he "won't be used." But even this more sober depth of frustration does not cause the reader to see Rogin as an effective rebel: the terms of his argument are too hyperbolic, too fantastic, his outrage too much prompted by a snobbish objection to his son-to-be's appearance. Rogin remains comically futile.

What Bellow has thus established, up until the final pages of the story, seems to be a satire of American affluence and of a character who moves with shallow illogic between moods of rebellion against and submission to materialism. The reader expects that Rogin will give in to Joan at the end, but he might also expect that Bellow himself will stay satirically critical—that the point of the story will be that Americans need to look at themselves more truly than Rogin can from an intelligent, moral perspective. The final scene seems at first to go according to this script of expectations. Rogin's rebellion wavers as he looks around the apartment; "the carpeted, furnished, lamplit, curtained room seemed to stand against his vision." And it vanishes completely as Joan plays Delilah with shampoo: "he sat with his breast against the cool enamel, his chin on the edge of the basin, the green, hot, radiant water reflecting the glass and the tile, and the sweet, cool, fragrant juice of the shampoo poured on his head." The immediate irony here is at Rogin's expense: he has had his moments of rebellion, but now he gives in to material necessity; Bellow reveals as hollow his pretense of directing his life by some intellectual perspective. Like Grebe, Rogin has collided at the last moment with a potent physical experience; but where Grebe clung stubbornly to intellect, Rogin, wooed by pleasure, accepts unquestioningly the physical.

The final irony of the story, however, is at the reader's expense if he has been expecting nothing more than a satiric slant on Rogin's life. For the undeniable effect of the ending, surprising us, is that Rogin's submission is, in some measure, right. As Joan massages Rogin's scalp, we feel ourselves warmed by the rich sensuality of the scene: " 'But there's absolutely nothing wrong with you,' she said, and pressed against him from behind, surrounding him, pouring the water gently over him until it seemed to him that the water came from within him, it was the warm fluid of his own secret loving spirit overflowing into the sink, green and foaming, and the words he had rehearsed he forgot, and his anger at his son-to-be disappeared altogether . . . " The strength of this physical experience and the irrelevance for the moment of intellectual perspectives are clear. Bellow has managed to show both Rogin and the reader how pointless protest against physical experience can sometimes be. But, as in the closing of "Looking for Mr. Green," Bellow also leaves an ambivalence here. He has shown us the discontinuity between idea and experience, first, in the alternations of Rogin's own mood and, finally, in the way the reader himself has been forced to drop suddenly his moralistic expectation. Bellow has made the point that men do not neatly shape their experience by idea; and that what they can criticize, legitimately and severely at one moment, may at another time, in different circumstance and mood, be legitimately appealing to them. But though Rogin's final physical baptism may warm us, we are not impressed by Rogin's self-awareness; Rogin remains a shallow character. We must turn to the longer works to see Bellow's theme developed in empathic depth.

Deliberate discontinuity is a recurrent effect in the novels. As in the two short stories, Bellow seems typically to work against an expectation that fiction will reveal a logical learning process in its heroes, that the endings of works of fiction will exhibit a final resolution of moral problems posed. The starkest examples are *The Victim* and *Dangling Man*. *The Victim* ends with what amounts to an epilogue chapter whose action occurs several years after the climactic moment in the penultimate chapter in which Allbee has attempted suicide. There is no transition, no indicated resolution of the self-torturing hyper-awareness that bound Leventhal and Allbee together throughout. But both have prospered; both have avoided the collapse of their lives that had seemed imminent in the previous chapter. After their agonized attempts to understand the moral responsibilities of their lives, Allbee seems to pronounce the relaxed acceptance present in both of them in this epilogue chapter: " 'I'm not the type that runs things. I never could be. I realized that long ago. I'm the type that

comes to terms with whoever runs things. What do I care? The world wasn't made exactly for me. What am I going to do about it? . . . Approximately made for me will have to be good enough. All that stiffness of once upon a time, that's gone, that's gone'." Bellow is not invalidating the moral questions that the book has considered, but he asserts that life also consists of a prosy relaxation in which difficult questions don't seem very important. Men don't find answers; the mood, the perspective changes. Even more sharply abrupt is the ending of *Dangling Man*: The Army at last calls Joseph, and his final statement is a paean to the prospect of military life—

> I am no longer to be held accountable for myself;
> I am grateful for that. I am in other hands, relieved of self-determination, freedom canceled.
>
> Hurray for regular hours!
>
> And for the supervision of the spirit!
>
> Long live regimentation!

Again Bellow has maneuvered a protagonist into a position where he suspends critical judgment and gratefully accepts, without questioning, things as they are.

But it is in *Herzog* that the pattern laid down in **"Looking for Mr. Green"** and **"A Father-to-Be"** is fully developed. Herzog suffers like Grebe the anguish of the idealist, the romantic, who must make sense of his world by assigning moral responsibility to himself and others; and like Grebe, but more openly, Herzog feels the irrelevance of his efforts: many of his letters are not even addressed to living men. Late in the novel, Herzog's problem is put, as Grebe's was, in terms of the remoteness of legal protocols from actual life—first in court, when Herzog watches justice trying to comprehend the murder of a child, later when Herzog himself is booked by the police on an afternoon when he had meant to give his daughter a happy outing. But, like Rogin, Harzog finally relaxes. There is the abrupt move to the country home in the last chapter, then the gradual unwinding, the warming toward affirmation, until Herzog can finally exclaim, " 'But what do you want, Herzog?' 'But that's just it—*not a solitary thing. I am pretty well satisfied to be, to be just as it is willed, and for as long as I may remain in occupancy.*'" Herzog has lived with an intellectual intensity like Grebe's and has experienced an alternation of perspectives like Rogin's. But Herzog has learned a full self-knowledge achieved by neither short-story hero: he has admitted the discontinuity of idea and experience and has understood that moral anguish and existential acceptance are alternations basic to human nature. In Herzog, Bellow has brought through to full self-awareness a hero prefigured in **"Looking for Mr. Green"** and **"A Father-to-Be."** (pp. 175-86)

David P. Demarest, Jr., "The Theme of Discontinuity in Saul Bellow's Fiction: 'Looking for Mr. Green' and 'A Father-to-Be'," in Studies in Short Fiction, *Vol. VI, No. 5, Fall, 1969, pp. 175-86.*

Noriko M. Lippit   (essay date 1975)

[*In the following essay, Lippit asserts that Hattie, the protagonist of Bellow's story "Leaving the Yellow House," represents an exception to the prevailing critical view that Bellow provides no compassionate portrayal of the female search for identity in his fiction.*]

Charles Newman asserts [in his *The Art of Sylvia Plath*] that "there is not a single woman in all of Saul Bellow's work whose active search for identity is viewed compassionately, while every vice of his male introspectives is given some genuine imperative." While I agree, in the final analysis, with Mr. Newman's remark and with his subsequent comment that "this attitude is generally indicative of serious writing since the war," I believe that Bellow's **"Leaving the Yellow House"** (1957) provides an exception; Hattie, the protagonist of this work, is a female searcher. **"Leaving the Yellow House"** is also exceptional in its desert setting, for Bellow has consistently presented dramas of people living in the modern metropolis. Despite the difference in sex and setting, however, **"Leaving the Yellow House"** deals with one of the main themes of Saul Bellow, that of recovery from the narrow confinement of the self through inner search.

The yellow house where the heroine Hattie lives stands near Sego Desert Lake—some several hundred miles from San Francisco and Salt Lake City. The house, which Hattie inherited from her "friend" India, is one of the three structures around there that could be called a house. The story is about the aging Hattie, deprived of physical mobility because of an accident, who worries seriously about whom she should leave the yellow house to after her death.

Sego Desert Lake is a sterile nowhere, the end of the world. Its residents include an idle retired couple who move from place to place according to their convenience, alcoholic divorcées, the owner of a ranch that exploits rare tourists, a "cowboy" from the East who rode on a horse for the first time at the age of forty, and so forth: they are all drop-outs from life, floaters who settled at Sego Desert after wandering toward the West in search of their dream of "making it." Hattie herself, once married to a man from an old Philadelphia family, floated from the East; and India, whom she looked after, was once a "lady" who travelled in the world and talked of philosophy and literature at parties. Not one of them is a genuine Westerner; these modern frontiersmen are city-born failures, and the wilderness is a skid row akin to the Bowery in New York.

Among them, Hattie's corruption is particularly pathetic. She is a born sloth, a professional loser who has not accomplished a single thing in her life. In this respect, Hattie is a female version of Tommy Wilhelm in *Seize the Day.* Tommy, still pursuing the dream of "making it" while taking pills and alcohol in a shabby hotel-room in downtown New York, feels that the metropolis is not the place for him, yet finds there some mysterious, attractive and cruel force rendering him incapable of escaping. It is the same force that Hattie senses in the desert. Watching the lake in the desert, Hattie reflects: "They drew you from yourself. But after they had drawn you, what did they do with you? It was too late to find out. I'll never know. I

wasn't meant to. I'm not the type, Hattie reflected. Maybe something too cruel for women, young or old." The cruel attractive force that Tommy and Hattie see in New York and the desert respectively is the gigantic, unregulated energy of America, the energy that created American material civilization. Controlled by the force, both the metropolis and the desert are "giant raw places" [as Bellow notes in **"Looking for Mr. Green"**]. American pastoral reality and urban reality are the same; to live in either is more terrifying than a nightmare.

"Leaving the Yellow House" depicts the wreck of the American dream comically and pathetically. Sego Desert Lake is a sarcastic symbol of America's Eden. The lake is mysteriously tempting and diabolic. It is bottomless and its surface as smooth as if it contained milk. White pelicans fly over the lake spreading their large white wings like angels. Hattie, watching the lake in a stupor brought by drink, feels as if she were in heaven. Yet she senses simultaneously the sterile and destructive force surrounding the lake. She feels the desert embodying this force is like a man who exposes his masculine chest covered with hair.

The greediness, loneliness, and sense of emptiness of the inhabitants of Sego Desert Lake are expressed in Amy, "a gold miner's widow," a miser who plays waltzes on her piano and reads murder-stories late into the night. India, who was also caught by the destructive power of the desert, completed the final touch of her self-destruction with alcohol, and Hattie steadily follows the pattern of her mistress. Sego Desert Lake is seemingly a virgin land, yet it is a ghost-town haunted by the unquiet shadows of the American dream. The sterile, deserted gold mine symbolizes this. The land is a virgin wilderness, a source of the American dream of earthly paradise, yet it is also an American junk-yard; it is Eden and hell simultaneously.

This horrifying yet comical story of human ruin, however, does not remain as a mere comical grotesquerie. Although Hattie is an anti-heroine, she is a masochistic self-searcher, a proud loser with dignity, one typical of Saul Bellow's male protagonists. Hattie, like Tommy Wilhelm and Moses Herzog, gains salvation through confronting death and mental crisis. While Tommy and Moses arrive at a reconciliation with life and the universe through the dissolution of narrow self-identity, Hattie recognizes, in her confrontation with death, a greedy and idle self, unreligious, unloved and luckless, yet still wanting to live. Her writing a will leaving the house to herself is her way— absurd yet audacious—of insisting on her American ego. It is also her way of sublimating her frustration and of accepting life as she experiences it. Yet Hattie, like Tommy and Moses, arrives at self-recognition after losing everything and exposing her naked self. Recognizing herself as a failure and victim and admitting her guilt for not loving enable Hattie to accept her present state and to reconcile herself with her fate.

To the question "Who are you?" Hattie can only answer "I am I." It is, within the Judaic context of Bellow's literature, the only possible answer for secular Jews, who are unable to reply "I am the son of my father." In **"Leaving the Yellow House,"** it is also the only answer that modern Americans can give. As Leslie Fiedler points out [in "Adolescence and Maturity in the American Novel" in his *An End of Innocence: Essays on Culture and Politics*], America, after completing the great Westward expansion, lost its innocence as well as its Puritan-colored cultural tradition. It is America's new generation, which must improvise its own history and determine its own fate, that inhabits Sego Desert Lake and struggles vainly to maintain its integrity in the desert.

Although Hattie is a loser, she is also, like Tommy Wilhelm and Moses Herzog, a "perennial survivor." She is a perennial sego lily, a dainty yet vital little wildflower that blooms among the rocks in a sterile desert. As her favorite joke tells, she had been caught in the mud many times, but each time she "came out of everything." After reviewing her whole life as if watching a movie film and experiencing a catharsis of anger and remorse, this prisoner of Sego Desert Lake arrives at a state of accepting her life, the equilibrium of a person who has confronted and survived destruction once again. Although this peaceful state (a delirious state of stupor, too) can by no means be called the silence of inward knowledge, Hattie reaches it through her own inner search, the inner drama of one who experiences a crisis of identity. "Then she thought that there was a beginning, and a middle. She shrank from the last term. She began once more—a beginning. After that, there was the early middle, then middle middle, late middle middle, quite late middle. In fact the middle is all I know. The rest is just a rumor. Only tonight I can't give the house away. I'm drunk and so I need it. And tomorrow, she promised herself, I'll think again. I'll work it out, for sure." The attaining of this tragicomical state of peace and reconciliation with humanity appears later, more fully developed, as a major theme of *Herzog*. Treating an archetypal American theme in **"Leaving the Yellow House,"** Saul Bellow presents a unique drama of man's (woman's!) struggle for recovery from modern alienation. (pp. 281-83)

Noriko M. Lippit, "A Perennial Survivor: Saul Bellow's Heroine in the Desert," in Studies in Short Fiction, *Vol. XII, No. 3, Summer, 1975, pp. 281-83.*

Constance Rooke   (essay date 1977)

[*Rooke is an American critic who serves as editor of* Malahat Review. *In the following essay, she disagrees with Noriko M. Lippit's assertion (see essay dated 1975 above) that the character of Hattie in Bellow's "Leaving the Yellow House" represents an exception to the generally accepted critical notion that Bellow provides no compassionate portrayal of the female search for identity in his fiction.*]

In her recent study of Saul Bellow's **"Leaving the Yellow House"** [*Studies in Short Fiction,* Summer 1975], Noriko Lippit claims to have discovered an exception proving the rule that nowhere in Bellow's fiction is there a woman " 'whose active search for identity is viewed compassionately.' " It is not surprising that Professor Lippit should be obliged to go so far afield to find her exceptional woman, but it remains a question whether the candidate in fact measures up to such proposed male counterparts as Tommy Wilhelm and Moses Herzog. Although Hattie

has much in common with the usual male protagonist whose circumstances and qualities are reshuffled throughout the whole of Bellow's work, her sex is surely not the only significant departure. Thus we are led to ponder whether Hattie's sex can be held accountable for what further deviation exists from the norm of Herzog and company. Especially illuminating in this respect are Hattie's lack of interest in ideas and her failure really to achieve either the "peace and reconciliation with humanity" or the "salvation through confronting death" which Professor Lippit believes are Hattie's portion at the end of the story.

In the circumstances of Hattie's life we can discern a pattern established by male protagonists. She exists in conspicuous isolation, yet is periodically exposed to a large and peculiar cast of supporting characters. Misfortune—in this case, the automobile accident which renders Hattie virtually immobile—precipitates a crisis. While practical difficulties abound, the real importance of this crisis for Bellow's purposes is to stimulate introspection and more particularly to raise the question of what it is that a human being ought to wake up in time to do with his "loaned" life. With symbolic implications, Hattie occupies a somewhat dilapidated house for which she experiences intermittently a caretaker's anxiety; and she does much of her thinking ("eyes half-shut but far-seeing") on the couch which appears repeatedly in Bellow's work, and which here (as most recently in *Humboldt's Gift*) is "kidney-shaped." Her property as well as her identity seems under siege, so that we engage the conundrum of whether paranoia is paranoia if perhaps it is justified. Doctors and lawyers join with other birds of prey to encircle Hattie; money troubles are linked to the question of whether presumptive friends are in fact her enemies. And all of this is familiar.

Temperamentally also Hattie recalls the male protagonist. She vacillates between opposing desires for independence and for love or succor. She feels almost excessively thankful for kindness; yet when this attention is in any degree lacking, she feels vengeful and must struggle not to " 'bear a grudge.' " As an expression of her vitality and her gratitude for life, Hattie experiences great, spontaneous, celebratory bursts of cheerfulness. Yet she does little with her gift of life; she procrastinates and is slothful. Preoccupied with death, she exhibits a tendency to commune with the dead (with India, the woman from whom she inherited the yellow house). And all of this is exceedingly familiar.

Nevertheless, Hattie Waggoner is not a typical Bellow protagonist. While Bellow can grant Hattie certain of the characteristics which he has parcelled out from his own riches for the male protagonists, and can accord her the sympathy which is due to her participation in such qualities, he is obliged because she is a woman to withhold the Bellowesque *sine qua non* of a genuine intellectual life. He cannot in a single leap make of her a woman, a sympathetic character, and an intellectual. Bellow has of course given us female intellectuals: Madeline Pontritter of *Herzog,* for instance, or Cantabile's wife in *Humboldt's Gift.* Both are aspirants to the Ph.D., and both are treated with contempt. The rule apparently admits of no exceptions. Women are unworthy of respect or sympathy in Bellow's fiction if their aspiration or presumption directs them to overstep those categories of excellence which have traditionally been allocated to their sex. Choosing to make Hattie sympathetic, Bellow could not also permit her to be an intellectual. Interestingly, only in the case of a female protagonist has Bellow been able to explore the fictional possibilities of a sensibility like his but without the coloring of his own powerful intellect. In *The Victim* and *Seize the Day,* his protagonists are not professional intellectuals, and possibly they were not intended to be intellectuals at all. But unmistakably they bear that stamp. Not being women, Leventhal and Wilhelm were not immune; and as the novels progressed they took on more and more of their author's passionate interest in ideas. Of Hattie, Bellow can report (assured that the text will not contradict him) that her "interest in ideas was very small."

Hattie does think—although "before any serious question her mind gave way. It scattered or diffused." Now the diffusion of intellectual power is admittedly characteristic of the Bellow protagonist: there are so many subjects which can engage his interest. Hattie does not prance from one marvellous speculation to another, however; she only absents herself in a flurry from what is after all too much for woman's feeble intellect. Bellow is perhaps most tender toward Hattie when she reflects, staring out at the desert and the lake: *They drew you from yourself. But after they had drawn you, what did they do with you? It was too late to find out. I'll never know. I wasn't meant to. I'm not the type,* Hattie reflected. *Maybe something too cruel for women, young or old."* This passage marks the outer limits of Hattie's disposition for philosophy and indicates at the same time the quintessential difference between Hattie and Bellow's men, who are precisely *"the type"* to *"know."*

Hattie's procrastination differs from that of the usual male protagonist in that she never ceases to live "by delays," and because even if she were to attain sufficient readiness, we would be obliged to ask *for what?* To forestall such a question concerning his male protagonists, Bellow has Henderson decide to become a doctor in his old age and Charles Citrine (at the end of *Humboldt's Gift*) journey toward mysticism; but the characteristic solution, applying equally to those who have and those who have not some specific work assigned them, is for the hero to affirm his commitment to the ongoing travail of thought. Usually this is accompanied by a gesture made in the direction of human community and creatureliness, a gesture which is felt to be occasioned by philosophy. All these paths are shadowed forth and then closed to Hattie. There is never any question of her having some important work to perform in the world. She is not *"the type"* to pursue understanding. Even a non-philosophical (female) version of that "reconciliation with humanity" which Professor Lippit claims for Hattie is denied her. " 'Because I do not find it in my heart to care for anyone as I would wish,' " Hattie declares herself incapable of that gesture toward community which has been prepared for her: she cannot leave the yellow house to another human being. If it were possible, "her last action would be to throw and smash it . . . so the thing and she herself would be demolished together." Philosophy (if not temperament) forbids Bellow's men ever to be quite so selfish, so narrowly possessive of life's gift.

Given the equipment which has been issued to Hattie, there is neither crime nor cause for wonder in the assertion that "Hattie not only loved sleep, she believed in it," or in the fact that she wakes up only long enough to reveal her incapacity for waking further. Hattie ends the story in a drunken stupor which we are led to suppose will merge with death. Decidedly, she has not achieved that "salvation through confronting death" which is an accomplishment of the male protagonist and which is assigned equally to Hattie by Professor Lippit. Rather, her last thoughts on the matter are sheer prevarication: "She began once more—a beginning. After that, there was the early middle, then middle middle, late middle, late middle middle, quite late middle. In fact the middle is all I know. The rest is just a rumor." Having put off death, she does the same for its symbolic equivalent, the leaving of her yellow house: "Only tonight I can't give the house away. I'm drunk and so I need it. And tomorrow, she promised herself, I'll think again. I'll work it out for sure." And on that ironic note, reminiscent of Scarlet O'Hara's postponing all thought until tomorrow when she is back at Tara, the story ends.

While Bellow's notoriously chauvinistic attitude to women is far less apparent in "Leaving the Yellow House" than usual, we may still discover in the text symptoms of an authorial sexism. . . . If Hattie Waggoner were by any chance to wake up again after having willed the house to herself, and if she then left it to Joyce, we may be sure that this woman also would be incapable of using the yellow house, of living well. In Saul Bellow's world, that is essentially the province of men.

—Constance Rooke

While Bellow's notoriously chauvinistic attitude to women is far less apparent here than usual, we may still discover in the text symptoms of an authorial sexism. As is frequently the case with Bellow, such abuse is deflected into the consciousness of women themselves—with the implication that here is undeniable proof. Hattie is hard on herself as a woman whose nature has precluded childbearing and interfered with her properly selfless love for a man; and she is very hard on other women, calling them bitches and sluts. Her attitude toward Joyce, "the most likely heiress," is peculiarly instructive: Joyce is "over thirty, good, yes, but placid, running to fat, a scholar—ten years in Eugene, Oregon, working for her degree. In Hattie's opinion this was only another form of sloth. Nevertheless, Joyce yet hoped to marry." Another aspirant to the Ph.D., Joyce is not woman enough (not attractive enough, not married enough) to inherit the yellow house. No woman, however, is person enough for that. If Hattie Waggoner were by any chance to wake up again after having willed the house to herself, and if she then left it to Joyce, we may be sure that this woman also would be incapable of using the yellow house, of living well. In Saul Bellow's world, that is essentially the province of men. (pp. 184-87)

Constance Rooke, "Saul Bellow's 'Leaving the Yellow House': The Trouble with Women," in Studies in Short Fiction, Vol. 14, No. 2, Spring, 1977, pp. 184-87.

Eusebio L. Rodrigues   (essay date 1981)

[*In the following essay, Rodrigues examines Hattie Waggoner's transition from survival to spiritual recovery in "Leaving the Yellow House."*]

Saul Bellow's short stories are byproducts of his fictional talent. Written as if with the left hand, they have the secret signature (as Proust terms it) of Bellow the thinker but lack the esemplastic power of Bellow the creative artist. Fictional fragments, they demand a context of insights and illumination from the novels to highlight their true meaning. By not providing such a context for **"Leaving the Yellow House"** (1957) the interpretations of Noriko M. Lippit and of Constance Rooke seem somehow incomplete even though some of their comments are extremely revealing.

The title of Noriko M. Lippit's essay, "A Perennial Survivor" [*Studies in Short Fiction,* Summer 1975], focuses on the central theme of the story, a theme basic to Bellow's vision. Bellow's protagonists have to be survivors before they can become seekers. *Tu As Raison Aussi* tells Joseph the dangler [in *Dangling Man*] who finally volunteers into the army to fight in World War II: " 'When and if you survive you can start setting yourself straight.' " Charles Citrine does not succumb to the asuric forces of money, fame and success that overwhelm his friend, Humboldt. Citrine survives, he tells us, by deliberately falling into a Rip Van Winkle-like sleep that allows him to hoard his gifts and go on to discover true humanness. It is in *Herzog* (1964) that the primary need for human survival is stated with naked intensity. Herzog can accept the belief in the power of the Dionysian spirit to recover after experiencing nuclear terror in our time. But he also insists in his letter to Nietzsche that before such a recovery is possible, *"survival is necessary. . . . No survival, no Amor Fati."*

Hattie Waggoner [of **"Leaving the Yellow House"**] is no Herzog, but, like Herzog's Tante Taube, is a "veteran survivor." At first Hattie appears to be a mere grotesque, a pathetic seventy-two year old ruin who has lived for twenty long years at Sego Desert Lake in Utah. The first few pages present a Hattie and her world seen mostly through the eyes of her neighbors and reported by an objective narrator. Certain facts are noted: that Hattie drives once a week to town in her old turret-shaped car across forty miles of mountainous desert; that Jerry and Helen Rolfe, a retired rich couple, do care for her in their own way; that the Paces have a guest ranch nearby. A few details are given about her divorce and about her shacking up with cowboy Wicks. Hattie, who has come from the East, had

wanted to be thought of as a "rough, experienced woman of the West."

The accident at the railway crossing, a turning point in Hattie's life, is presented in ambiguous terms. Hattie was drunk at the time. Her explanation that a sneeze had made her twist the wheel of her car is patently a lie. It is true, however, that forces working within Darly—the throbbing pain in his ribs caused by an accidental kick from a mare, his resentment at having to abandon the gambling game, his furious desire to get the whole thing over and done with—lead to his jerking the towchain so that Hattie falls and breaks her arm. Darly is a masculine parallel to Hattie: sixty-eight years old, he too has come from the East and is no genuine Westerner. Like Hattie, he has no place to go to, except the soldiers' home. He has accepted the bitter role of playing cowboy for the dudes and their women at Pace's ranch. Cruelly harsh in his dismissal of Hattie, he accuses her of being drunk all the time, unfit to live in the West.

Too concerned about his own survival, Darly cannot respond to Hattie's state of shock. The narrative angle slowly shifts to her perspective. A deep fear about her car possesses Hattie. She implores Darly and later, Jerry, to take care of her car. Hattie's acute anxiety is not about a form of transportation, but about an extension of her self. "I lost control of the car," she informs Darly. When the car drops into the railroad bed, Hattie sits "with a stormy, frightened, conscience-stricken face." She is terrified because she senses that the smash-up of her car (whose turret-shape had supplied her with a kind of protection) is a terrible judgment on her.

This sense of dread that manifests itself first as a fear for her car, stretches itself into the future and spreads back into the past. The moment of deep shock in Bellow's fiction is always a moment of illumination. Hattie can no longer retreat into sleep in her usual fashion. She lies awake and sees her own life, "as though from birth to the present every moment had been filmed."

Bellow controls the film of Hattie's life, cutting, editing, and projecting it to regulate pace and tempo. Sequences from the past are intercut with significant shots of her present. Re-viewing her life, Hattie slowly begins to be aware of her self and of the forces at work within her. Watching Hattie watching herself, overhearing the inner voice with which she talks to herself, the reader becomes aware of the human arena around Hattie and can appreciate her dogged tenacity. Bellow gradually develops her into a rough-hewed heroine of our time and our place.

Viewed through Hattie's lens, which Bellow gradually wipes clean of all illusions, Sego Desert Lake presents its true self. Hattie had claimed it was one of the most beautiful places in the world. But Jerry Rolfe had pointed out that it was a few hundred miles from civilization, while the narrator had referred to the lake as icy and to the country as barren. After she returns from the hospital, Hattie acknowledges that the landscape is too cruel and inhuman to allow the human to flourish.

Noriko M. Lippit rightly interprets Sego Desert Lake with its deserted gold mine as a "sarcastic symbol of America's

Eden." Bellow also undercuts the American dream of making it out in the West. The only ones who belong there are the tungsten miner, the ninety year old Shoshone, Wanda Gingham, and ancient, aloof Amy Walters. Most of the inhabitants are unpioneer-like Easterners who, like India, are not fit to be anywhere else. They cannot face the challenge of life in the West and have become alcoholics.

Sego Desert Lake also reveals harsh truths about human nature. Hattie consigns the damn empty old place to hell and tells Pace that like it, he is not human. It stirs up the evil lodged in human beings. Bellow, a student of anthropology, had established in *The Victim* (1947) a link between the hostile world man finds himself in and the inner treasons (as Joseph in *Dangling Man* puts it) within his own being: "The notion brushed Leventhal's mind that the light over them and over the water was akin to the yellow revealed in the slit of the eye of a wild animal, say a lion, something inhuman that didn't care about anything human and yet was implanted in every human being too, one speck of it, and formed a part of him that responded to the heat and the glare, exhausting as these were, or even to freezing, salty things, harsh things, all things difficult to stand."

Sego Desert Lake has deformed the inner being of its inhabitants. Love does not flourish here. Man finds it difficult to respond to a sister's cry for help. Darly helps Hattie, but most reluctantly. Amy Walters cannot bring herself to feel sorry for Hattie's plight. Pace, as Hattie picturesquely puts it, would have sold her "to the knacker for a buck." The Rolfes place a limit on their responsibility for Hattie. Like the sego lilies that bloom only after a wet winter, like the white pelicans that fly angel-like over the lake, fleeting moments of kindness manifest themselves occasionally. India had treated her like a servant, but she had succored Hattie by leaving her the yellow house.

This act of kindness had a profound impact on Hattie who had never owned a thing before. *"I changed when I got a roof of my own over my head,"* she tells herself. What Hattie implies is what Gaston Bachelard has set forth in *The Poetics of Space,* that a house can become a psychic state and intimate the "topography of our intimate being."

Before she inherited the house—a "pot" of her own, Jerry Rolfe calls it, using the same term Hattie uses for her car—Hattie had drifted through life, wandering from Paris (where she studied the organ), to New Hampshire (with her husband who had gotten tired of her), to Athens Canyon (where she lived on the range with Wicks, trapping coyotes), and finally to Sego Desert Lake (where she had to take "tons of dirt" from India). Hattie also implies that she never had a self of her own, having "pain out years, now to one shadow, now to another shadow." A slave to the men in her life (she didn't have a cent after the divorce from Waggoner, and had to support Wicks for seven or eight years), she was India's "servant and whipping girl." Together with the house, Hattie finally acquired a being of her own.

The accident shocks Hattie's recently-acquired being. At the hospital she is in pain and her mind wanders. But, the narrator twice points out, a defiant, happy grin splits her

face when visitors are present. Her savings are wiped out, but she laughs, still believing that she could get out of everything and that something would turn up. The trouble, however, is no ordinary trouble. She suffers the second shock when she realizes that the Rolfes will desert her. Hattie is still defiant. "I'll make out," she tells the Rolfes. The third and final shock occurs in Pace's bar (which she now frequents) when he makes her a business offer in exchange for leaving the house to him in her will. Shattered by Pace's insult which Hattie interprets as an attack on her being and as an embodiment of all the cruelty and injustice generated by Sego Desert Lake, Hattie retires into her yellow house to consult her intuitions.

Bellow quickens the tempo of the "hereafter movie" as Hattie gains deeper insights into herself. She recognizes the evil within her own self just as she now knows the evil that was present in her dog, Richie, who had attacked her suddenly and whom she had to kill. She acknowledges her pride, weeps and, using the same words that India had used when she had begged forgiveness from Hattie, silently asks Wicks to forgive her: " 'Please! I'm sorry. Don't condemn me in your heart. Forgive me. I hurt myself in my evil'." She also confesses her sins: *"I have taken life. I have lied. I have borne false witness. I have stalled."*

The word "stalled" propels her to test herself out with the car (without which she literally cannot leave the yellow house) and she finds she cannot shift the gears and steer. Weeping over "the ruin of her life" she returns to her house to write her will. Unlike Alice Parmenter and India, Hattie has to struggle to decide who would inherit her yellow house.

She cannot bring herself to leave the house to anyone for no one, except Hattie herself, belongs there. She will not doom her cousin's daughter to live there because Hattie knows what will happen to Joyce: "See how beautiful it was here? It burned you out. How empty! It turned you into ash." The fierce sun has burnt Hattie's being; the barren desert and the icy lake have drawn her out of herself and imprinted their mark within her. The significance of "yellow" is now clear: it is not a mere color or an indication of age, but a pointer to the animal element in human nature, to something wild, fierce, and inhuman that exists within and around man.

On another level of meaning, Hattie cannot leave her yellow house because she no longer accepts the finality of death. She now realizes that God (Hattie has a vague sensation that someone is watching over her) had loaned her a gift of life through India, and she has to accept such a gift gratefully. Life, despite all its torment and suffering, is a wonderful thing, as all Bellow protagonists acknowledge. *"It was strange. It is strange. It may continue being strange"* proclaims Hattie, echoing the same words that Henderson will think of as he writes his letter to Lily [in *Henderson the Rain King*].

The very strangeness of her newly-given life makes Hattie doubt the conventional wisdom that holds that death marks the end of life. Hattie Waggoner is a preparation for Charles Citrine in *Humboldt's Gift* (1975) who knows that life continues beyond death, in mysterious ways. Hattie thinks about a beginning and a middle, the state in which she is, and she knows there couldn't be much film left in her movie. But she will not acknowledge the final term, death, for it is just a rumor for her: she didn't know for certain whether life "was ever going to be over."

Hattie makes up her will (in a dual sense) to testify to this faint intimation. Her letter of instructions to her lawyer ends with a prayer to God for mercy. It is also an acknowledgement of her mistakes, an admission of her flawed nature, and a confession of her loneliness and inadequacy as a human being. But its tone is not one of defeat or despair. For it is a testament to Hattie's belief in herself. By willing "this property, land, house, garden and water rights" to herself, this survivor makes a seemingly impossible gesture of comic defiance against the finality of death.

Bellow has Hattie (who knows she is drunk) utter almost the very words that the hopelessly romantic heroine of *Gone With the Wind* uses before she goes home to Tara: "Only tonight I can't give the house away. I'm drunk and so I need it. And tomorrow, she promised herself, I'll think again. I'll work it out, for sure." The parody proclaims that Hattie Waggoner is no Scarlett O'Hara but a gnarled, weather-beaten representative of contemporary man hurling forth a cry of protest against this place and this condition. [The critic adds in a footnote: "the use of

names like India (the name of Ashley's sister) and Wicks (which sounds like Wilkes) suggests that Bellow had *Gone With the Wind* in mind when he wrote **"Leaving the Yellow House."**] (pp. 11-15)

Eusebio L. Rodrigues, "A Rough Hewed Heroine of Our Time: Saul Bellow's 'Leaving the Yellow House'," in Saul Bellow Newsletter, Vol. 1, No. 1, Fall, 1981, pp. 11-17.

Judie Newman   (essay date 1981)

[*An English educator and critic whose work often focuses on American literature, Newman is the author of* Saul Bellow and History *(1984). In the following essay, Newman demonstrates how Bellow's story "The Mexican General" reveals that the critical emphasis on transcendental themes in Bellow's fiction "constitutes a false emphasis, radically distorting the overall tendencies of Bellow's fiction, and underplaying the extent to which the novels are firmly located in the contingency of the historical process."*]

Saul Bellow's second published story, **"The Mexican General"** appears to have been consigned to critical oblivion. While not wishing to inflate the claims of this early work, its neglect is significant in that it reflects a dominant trend

Bellow in the 1950s, when many of his acclaimed short stories were written.

in criticism of Saul Bellow. The consensus favours an interpretation of Bellow's writing as "transcendental" in its overall intent. With few exceptions participants at the International Symposium on Saul Bellow in 1977 [proceedings collected in 1978 as *Saul Bellow and His Work*] detected in Bellow's novels an urge for transcendence. John Clayton argued that *Humboldt's Gift* concerned "Transcendence and the Flight From Death," Gilbert Porter discussed Bellow's "Transcendental vision," Keith Opdahl, while describing Bellow's style as "realistic," nonetheless argued that he used "literal detail to suggest a transcendental reality" and Brigitte Scheer-Schazler affirmed that "Bellow, in trying to discover the universal in the particular, echoes the Transcendental epistemological quest."

However, this transcendental interpretation . . . constitutes a false emphasis, radically distorting the overall tendencies of Bellow's fiction, and underplaying the extent to which the novels are firmly located in the contingency of the historical process, within the limitations of a time-bound form, and actively engaged with the analysis of the dynamics of history.

Interestingly, **"The Mexican General"** demonstrates clearly that, from the beginning of his career, Bellow was drawn to questions of historical analysis. The story concerns the death of Trotsky as it impinges on the mean and limited awareness of a Mexican General. The "facts" of the tale conform to the recorded facts of history: the attack on Trotsky by a "Belgian," Ramon Mercader, on August 20th 1940, in Coyoacan, a suburb of Mexico City, leading to his death the following day, a public autopsy, and the exhibition of the body in a public hall on the Calle de Tacuba. Although these facts are common property, the germ for the story appears to be the record left by the Mexican chief of police involved in the investigation, L. A. S. Salazar, which corresponds in many minor details with Bellow's tale. Here, for example, is Salazar's account of the announcement of Trotsky's death:

> I undertook to announce the sad news to the journalists and to the crowds in front of the Green Cross. "Gentlemen, Trotsky is dead" and looking at my watch, I gave the exact time. The hundred or so Mexican reporters and foreign correspondents who were there rushed towards the half dozen telephones.
>
> He shut the door carefully and waited till he had everyone around him and then he announced: "He is dead." Looking at his watch, "He died 3 minutes and 40 seconds ago." The reporters ran to the phones, the photographers pushed forward.

Moreover, the tone of the police chief's record, the portentousness of the police chief, his desire to hold the attention of the world, to occupy a place in history in spite of his own insignificance, prefigures the central concern of Bellow's tale.

The framing irony of the tale depends upon the juxtaposition of the General—a petty politico in the eyes of history, engaged in petty peccadilloes with his three nieces—and the figure of Trotsky, the archetypal great man, by whom history is made. Within this frame further ironies are pro-

duced by Bellow's technique of massive indirection. The tale slowly unfolds to reveal the identity of the "viejo" referred to as Trotsky, an action accompanied by the gradual revelation of the General's real relationship with his three "nieces." At first, the focus of the tale appears to be the General, who occupies the centre of the group, and the central room at the hotel, and to whom his two bodyguards are mere auxiliaries. But, as the events of Trotsky's death are recounted by Citron, the centre of interest changes until, in the final scene, the General is presented, not as a public figure in history, but enmeshed in a secret private life, tapping a signal to call a woman to him for the night. The two bodyguards form an ironic chorus to the General's selfaggrandisement, as they slowly develop the story of Trotsky, an irony which cuts more than one way, questioning the status of Trotsky himself. In addition, the temporal stages of Citron's narrative are linked to the spatial stages of the General's tour of places of interest, juxtaposing the public events of history with the General's private activities. Citron is on the sidelines of the tour, but his story concerns one of the central events of twentieth-century history. Citron, for example, interrupts his narrative to enter the church, and comments as he resumes his tale, "Where was I? That digression threw me off. Had we come to the hospital?"

Although Citron is always on the sidelines observing the central group, his tale becomes the story proper, their activities the digression. The stages of the story match the stages of the tour, the escorting of Trotsky's wife from the hospital in the narrative, coincides with the escorting of the party from the church. Parallels exist between the General's tour of historical monuments—church, museum, memorial stones—ending in his purchase of tourist curios, and the treatment of Trotsky by the Press, exhibiting him to the crowds who display a similar interest in souvenirs. As Citron comments, "The curio hunters would have got his heart if we had let them." The juxtaposition of a historical narrative and a tour of the stones of history underline the deficiencies of ill-informed historicism. The General is obsessed by history. Citron remarks, "He's very history-conscious. I might go so far as to call him a history-ridden man—in a very egotistical fashion." But the General lacks any imaginative awareness of the significance of a historical event outside the sphere of his own self-centred interest. For the General, the death of Trotsky is important only as it relates to his own career. Citron complains, "You would think that being 'history-minded' would make them more conscientious, but it doesn't."

While ostensibly revering the past, with its monuments, the General and his party are wholly lacking in insight into the issues involved. Thus they are unaware of the identity of Quiroga (pictured on the hotel walls) banishing this modern Uruguayan writer to "the past," an entity at some remove from them, but for which they feel an obscure reverence.

> "That is Quiroga, Senorita," said the boy.
> "Who was that, a saint Felipe?"
> "I don't know," said the General.
> "Perhaps."

"He looks more like a king than a saint with that rich costume and black beard," said Maria.

Although the General feels himself to be a great man, his interest in history is opportunistic. One of the principal questions raised in the story is that of causation. In brief, does man make history or history make man? Is history the story of great men, or of economic forces? The question is posed explicitly in relation to Maria's motivation.

"Hasn't she got too much fire for this sort of life, I wonder?"
"You forget that el Jefe is a great man . . . recognised by history. . . . That makes all the difference for a girl like Maria." . . . "History! You mean money."

From the General's point of view he makes history, posing beside Trotsky in photographs, yet in more opportunistic fashion, he may allow history to "make" him. Like his father before him, a man who made his career by his friendships with the famous, the General is not slow to use the free publicity offered him to advance his own political career (in the elections in Jalisco which took place shortly after Trotsky's death). Citron sees through the General's motives. Where Trotsky may be appropriately envisaged as Hegel's World Historical Individual, thrown up by history in answer to social needs, the General is motivated by the desire to dominate, to "outface everyone." In Citron's view, "He'll make them weep in Jalisco." The General's claims to greatness are parodied in Citron's imitation of his bombastic inflections.

"His triumph at Coyoacan . . . places him now beside the brave Caciques who resisted Cortes there."
"A great and serious mind is playing."
'He suffered more than the viejo who was killed."

Yet the irony cuts two ways, questioning not only the General's "greatness," but also that of Trotsky. Citron describes the death of Trotsky in the same sardonic fashion, drawing attention to the undertow of history, to the minor figures in the wings of the historical drama.

Everyone knows about the chief figures, the old man and the assassin. Then among the lesser—his guards, the old woman, the assassin's mistress, friends of all kinds—enters Felipe in the role of the State, and myself, assistant and messenger, which function I share with the telephone. The role is minor and incidental, a nonessential but typical category. A happening can, of course, take place without us singly, but would not be quite as it was if we were not there. Somebody uses our knife to cut down the body, sends us to notify the widow, we hold the sponge for the soldier, are called upon to hand up the nails whether in the building of triumphal stands, crosses, or gallows, are the tenth or twelfth men in the firing squad and so on. In short, "the others" who crowd in at the doors, and are never thought the issue of the struggle but who are nevertheless those whom leaders lead, oppressors oppress, and saviours save.

Citron and Paco, like Tom Stoppard's Rosencrantz and Guildernstern [in *Rosencrantz and Guildenstern Are Dead*] exist in the wings of the main drama. But Bellow's story anticipated Stoppard's awareness that one can "look on every exit being an entrance somewhere else." The indirection of the story forces the reader to question the principal focus. What is the main event here? Citron and Paco appear to be insignificant but carry the historical message. The surface action—the tour of interest—is less important than the commentary from Citron. The eponymous hero is less important than Trotsky. Yet Trotsky also depends on the mass of anonymous men around him for his place in history. The figure of the Communist leader holds its own ironies as a classic historical paradox, inviting speculation as to whether revolution depends on the individual great man, or on the economic pressure of the masses. Ironically, his assassin conforms to Trotsky's own historical theory. Feeling himself "outclassed" and "subordinated" by Trotsky, the "young hero" kills him, in Citron's explanation, in order to equalize himself as a person with the old man, much as Gavrilo Princip may be said to have equalized his historic status with that of Franz Ferdinand. Ramon Mercader did think that history would applaud his action. The closing words of his statement read: *"L'histoire saura me donner raison quand on verra disparaitre l'ennemi acharne de la classe ouvriere."* At the same time the assassin represents all that Trotsky had repressed. Citron remembers Trotsky's reaction to the first assassination attempt, and "how he complained in statements that rang in with the French Revolution and ended with predictions of victory" setting the attempt in a grandly historical perspective, and he regrets that the assassin was not of the same manly consequence. Yet the assassin represents the revenge of those elements which are in eclipse. "It may just be proper that death for the viejo should come womanish, shrieking and sinewless since he had always downed whatever of that there was in him."

The point brings us to the final question. Are all these men and their historical actions of any importance at all? Or is history merely a chaos of contingent events upon which men build constructions which are of little consequence? For Citron the disparity between the General's apparent dignity and concern with "history" in the abstract and the vanities and petty scheming of the present cast doubt on all historical explanation. The General's behaviour in the days following Trotsky's death shows a "lack of fitness that throws suspicion on everything and makes us sure there must have been precisely such vanities and blunders in the greatest Passions." Just as the autopsy reduces Trotsky to a bag of guts, so Citron's contact with the "tripas" of history in Mexico has forced him to see the inner workings of man and history in an inglorious light.

Finally, Nature emerges as a counterforce to history, as the impassive public figure's hidden activities are revealed. In the surface action, the General commands others to move at his pace, chiding Maria for her lateness, cutting short the bodyguards' meals, and generally calling the tune. Yet his command is continually undercut by the images around him. The tour ends with references to natural time, to the close of day and the rainy season. Nature impedes the General's progress.

On their left lay the mountains, treeless and red. Maguey and thin vivid bushes grew on the coarse red banks of the streams that rushed down towards the soft humps of the lower hills. The red dirt was spilled and drifted over the road. A squad of soldiers drilling in the nearby field moved clumsily in the mud. The drummer off to the side stood beating vigorously, never missing a stroke, but the marchers stumbled heavily and out of rhythm. "I can't walk a step farther, it's too wet," said Eulalia.

The inexorable rhythm of time, a remorseless drumbeat, is linked to the eroding activity of the stream, laying open fresh streaks of bank, a suggestion reinforced by the reference to the General being "carried at least a short way on the principal current." The remorseless passage of time is opposed to the stumbling progress of human beings, marching to a rhythm of their own making, out of step with time. Time moves inexorably onwards, but man's progress is stumbling and comes to a halt. For the General the young men are already a threat, and they are scornful of his "oldest bull" behavior. The private life of the General thus becomes an ironic commentary on his public status as "an important actor in history," and a comment on the legend of Trotsky and his younger assassin.

At the close of the tale the focus falls upon Citron and Paco, smiling in the dark, while the General, now offstage, taps out his own drumroll to call the woman to him. The change of direction in the form of the story enacts the major thematic issues which it raises. In the drama of history who occupies the centre of the stage? And who remains in the wings? Is history the record of the public acts of great men? Or is history made by men in the grip of secret desires, swayed by forces beyond their control? The final scene, therefore, renders explicit the implications of Bellow's formal indirection.

["The Mexican General"], therefore, merits analysis on two counts: firstly on formal grounds, as it cunningly manipulates the reader structurally towards its theme, and secondly as a precursor of Bellow's later work. The general reflection on the nature of history, the interweaving of historical event and personal recollection, presage the activities of Moses Herzog, historian of Western culture, of Mr. Sammler caught between two historical events, the American moonshot and the Holocaust, of Augie March, whose own encounter with Trotsky leads him to share Citron's awareness of the doubtful glory of the great man, and, most recently of Von Humboldt Fleisher, self-elected World Historical Individual and Charlie Citrine, sleepwalking through the nightmare of history. (pp. 26-31)

> Judie Newman, "Saul Bellow and Trotsky: 'The Mexican General'," in Saul Bellow Newsletter, *Vol. 1, No. 1, Fall, 1981, pp. 26-31.*

Jonathan Yardley   (essay date 1984)

[*Yardley is an American critic and book reviewer. In the following review of* Him with His Foot in His Mouth, and Other Stories, *Yardley commends Bellow on his er-*udite *knowledge and humor but asserts that the book will be inaccessible to nonintellectual readers.*]

[The tone of the five stories in *Him with His Foot in His Mouth, and Other Stories*], is considerably more agreeable than that of much of Saul Bellow's recent work. The bitter, cranky commentary on American society and culture that gave such a sour complexion to *Mr. Sammler's Planet* and *The Dean's December* recedes into the background here; the mood, if not exactly sunny, is reflective, expansive and good-humored. Though many readers are likely to feel that Bellow is writing to a small, select and formidably literary audience, it is nonetheless beyond dispute that there is more pleasure to be found in these stories than in anything Bellow has written in a number of years.

The stories are united by two common preoccupations. The first is that all of them are about people who, through one means or another, have been brought to points at which they find themselves forced to confront their own pasts; each is obliged to undertake what one describes as "my self-examination," to come to terms with "the list of true facts, the painful inventory." The second is the theme that has dominated Bellow's work since the publication of *Herzog* two decades ago: the conflict between the world of art and intellect on the one hand, and the world of power and wealth on the other.

["Him with His Foot in His Mouth"] is representative and illustrative of the whole. Its narrator, Harry Shawmut, is a well-known musicologist who mistakenly invested his earnings as host of a public-television series in a get-rich-quick scheme engineered by his late brother; the plan somehow involved "an auto-wrecking center, the biggest in Texas, which would supply auto parts to the entire South and to Latin America as well." Now Shawmut himself is liable for prosecution as a result of his involvement in his brother's affairs, and on the advice of an incompetent lawyer has fled the country to take up residence in Vancouver. He awaits extradition and a fate that, while uncertain, is sure to be unpleasant: "I may not be sent to prison, but I will have to work for the rest of my natural life, will die in harness, and damn queer harness, hauling my load to a peculiar peak."

As if his life were not sufficiently unpleasant, into it arrives a letter from an academic colleague of many years before, Walish, whom Shawmut had believed to be his friend but who reveals himself now as a mortal enemy:

> His letter upset me badly. What a time he chose to send it! Thirty-five years without a cross word. He allows me to count on his affection. Then he lets me have it. When do you shaft a pal, when do you hand him the poison cup? Not while he's still young enough to recover. Walish waited until the very end—*my* end, of course.

These words are addressed to Miss Clara Rose, a librarian now retired in Florida. Walish, in his letter, has accused Shawmut of so insulting Miss Rose 3½ decades ago that "you traumatized her for life." The insult, as recalled by Shawmut:

> Now, Miss Rose, you have come out of the library for a breath of air and are leaning, arms

crossed, and resting your head against a Greek column. To give himself more height, Walish wears his hair thick. You couldn't cram a hat over it. But I have on a baseball cap. Then, Miss Rose, you say, smiling at me, "Oh, Dr. Shawmut, in that cap you look like an archaelogist." Before I can stop myself, I answer, "And you look like something I just dug up."

As Shawmut says, "Awful!" The poor fellow cannot keep his mouth shut; "in highly structured situations in which champion American executive traits like prudence and discretion are required, I always lose control and I am, as Arabs say, a hostage to my tongue." He has no idea whether Walish is correct in alleging that his casual insult ruined Miss Rose's life, but he writes her this long letter—the story itself is the letter—as an act of apology and expiation. Gradually he works his way through his entire life and career, recalling long-forgotten acquaintanceships and rivalries, until at the end he is forced to a confession: "The writing of this letter has been the occasion of important discoveries about myself, so I am even more greatly in your debt, for I see that you have returned me good for the evil I did you. I opened my mouth to make a coarse joke at your expense and thirty-five years later the result is a communion."

One of the subjects Shawmut contemplates in the course of this long self-examination is his own subordinate relationship, as a man of intellect, with "worldly power." This is more explicitly examined in the book's longest story, **"What Kind of Day Did You Have?,"** in which the celebrated art critic Victor Wulpy, now an old man, reviews his life through his own eyes and those of two others: his young mistress and a colleague of many years ago. It is this colleague who, in describing Wulpy, speaks directly for Bellow on a matter of great moment to him:

> Victor is a promoter. He did well by himself, solidly. But he hasn't faked anything. He really studied the important questions of art—art and technology, art and science, art in the era of the mass life. He understands how the artistic faculties are hampered in America, which isn't really an art land. Here art isn't serious. Not in the way a vaccine for herpes is *serious*. And even for professionals, critics, curators, editors, art is just *blah!* And it should be like the air you breathe, the water you drink, basic, like nutrition or truth. Victor knows what the real questions are, and if you ask him what's the matter here he would tell you that without art we can't judge what life is, we can't sort anything out at all. Then the "practical sphere" itself, where "planners," generals, opinion-makers and Presidents operate, is no more real than the lint under your bed.

Bellow's characters opt for art, but even when they do so exuberantly—as in **"Zetland: By a Character Witness"**—it is with a certain regret, with a wish that it would be possible to have *both* art and power; they know that what they do is of inestimable importance, and they are right, but it is their misfortune to inhabit a country that condescends to them at best, rejects them at worst, and in all circumstances fails to understand them. This is a provocative theme, which Bellow argues with great eloquence and irony, but he seems to be preaching to the already-converted. As with just about everything he has written since *Herzog,* these stories are so heavily loaded with intellectual cross-references that only those as erudite as Bellow himself will be able to appreciate them in full. They are brilliantly written and at times extremely funny, but they demand a breadth and depth of knowledge that few readers will be able to provide.

This is less a complaint than a warning: post-graduate education required. Bellow has spoken of his desire to reach a great audience, but the nature of his fiction makes that an impossibility. The audience to which his work is actually addressed is very influential, but very small; his reputation is deservedly large, but his real readership is not. And it does seem fair to ask whether, in writing fiction that wittingly or not excludes so many readers, he proves his own point: that high art and the "real" world cannot connect.

> *Jonathan Yardley, "Bellow's Gift," in* Book World—The Washington Post, *May 20, 1984, p. 3.*

Robert M. Adams (essay date 1984)

[*In the following favorable review of* Him with His Foot in His Mouth, and Other Stories, *Adams suggests that "short stories may be more congenial to Bellow's gift than novels."*]

Chicago, that gritty city, has a hammerlock on Saul Bellow's imagination, and has held it there for a long time. Even when he takes his fictional characters elsewhere, they carry Chicago with them, and come back to Chicago for final authentication. (*Henderson the Rain King,* that gross and glittering piece of foolery, is an exception to this rule, as to many others in Bellow's work.) It is not that Bellow idealizes his adopted city, not at all; his feeling seems something like that suggested by Nelson Algren when he said (I quote from memory and approximately) that living in Chicago was like making love to a woman with a broken nose. Bellow is always quarreling with Chicago, sometimes for being what it is, sometimes for not being what it used to be; but Chicago names and neighborhoods are generally present in his fiction, often as shorthand for attitudes and values of which they are redolent.

A recurrent theme of his work is the contrast between the brute appetites of the city, its hoodlums, grifters, shysters, and aldermen, and various observant but uprooted and largely ineffectual intellectuals. They may be actual or, more commonly, tangential academics, bookish in their interests but not formally engaged with a discipline, and freewheeling toward immense philosophical constructs of their own contrivance. Like the "intelligentsia" of Chekhov's Russia, they are absurd and beguiling figures, ineffectual vehicles of aspiration at hopeless odds with the raw realities around them, but striving always to learn. For of false teachers, comic or villainous, there is never an end.

The balance between these forces is precarious and the tensions high. Chicago itself is a devouring subject, vital and corrupt, open and crass, violent and plutocratic.

Hardly any of these elements is distinctive to Chicago; their combination produces an aroma that realistic writers since the 1920s have been trying to render, and from which Bellow's idealists always have something to learn. For these are uncommonly starry-eyed types whose discourse always threatens to evaporate into airy schemes filled out with flying allusions to every author in the Syntopicon. Rising above the harsh life of the streets and the markets, they tend to become—not always without self-mockery—do-it-yourself space navigators, trekkies through the Great Books galaxy. Between the two parties, incomprehension is represented as mutual, and hardly ever without the overtone of contempt. The city is seen as crass, the big thinkers are seen as pretentious irresponsibles. The terms of intercourse seem far harsher and more forbidding in Chicago than, say, in New York, Boston, or San Francisco. Yet the relation is more complex than mere hostility; the word-men of Bellow's imagination would probably hasten to call it "symbiotic."

There is a curious story in [*Him with His Foot in His Mouth, and Other Stories*], titled **"Zetland: By a Character Witness."** Technically, it is probably the worst, but thematically it is one of the most interesting of the group. The occasion for which the character witness has been called is left completely to the reader's imagination; the function implies wrongdoing and a trial, but there are no particulars. As usual, when Bellow characters start to exculpate themselves or anyone else, the narrative is fearfully circumstantial. We learn all the details of young Zetland's family life, his rough, disapproving father, his adolescent devotion to Kant, Nietzsche, surrealism, and Dada. He flourished in the fecund Jewish culture around Humboldt Park; he went to the college and got his own seedy flat on Woodlawn Avenue; he lectured to neighborhood study groups on the differences between Kant and Hegel. Even his father, who disapproved of everything because he "knew life," was impressed. But then young Zetland got a fellowship to study philosophy at Columbia, on the strength of which he married the attractive Lottie. Together they departed joyously for New York—free at last, "free to live," as Zetland says, "in a place where it's normal to be a human being."

Something happens, however, or rather nothing does. Zetland loses interest in philosophy, resigns his fellowship, and from then on does nothing in particular. So far as the last perfunctory paragraphs of the story inform us, he simply withers on the vine. He reads, and is impressed by, *Moby-Dick;* he begets a son. The Second World War approaches, and Zetland, with his usual high-minded enthusiasm, is eager to join up. His wife encourages him, as predictably as his father disapproves; but since the Zetland ménage settles in 1940 into a Greenwich Village flat which they keep for twelve years, we are left to assume he was not accepted. And there the story wilts away. Nothing more worth telling about Zetland, apparently, not even how he came to need a character witness. But evidently a character witness doesn't have much to do when the person for whom he's witnessing no longer has a character. And Zetland, separated from his grouchy father, removed from hundred-percent industrial Chicago, no longer using

his once high-power mind, has faded to a formula and then to a cipher. It's a curious and disturbing story.

Commonly, Bellow's spiraling word-weavers provide a comic leaven that lightens the thick mass of circumstantial detail; but in the most tangibly Chicago of these stories, **"What Kind of Day Did You Have?,"** the mental marvel, Victor Wulpy, is himself part of the morass, an aging Grendel out of the fens. He is seen through the eyes of Katrina, his latest mistress, an anxious, defenseless, middle-aged divorcée from Evanston, on whom the portentous genius dumps humiliations, frustrations, and terrors throughout a long, indeed an interminable day. But the wretched victim of this cosmic windbag barely allows herself to sense the degree to which she is disgusted with him, and Victor Wulpy, having inflicted on her a ghastly and completely unnecessary midwinter flight from Chicago to Buffalo and back, goes off to pontificate complacently before a gathering of rich Chicago businessmen, who are paying him to act the visiting guru. In this mid-winter story of human coldness, incidental figures do little that is not gratuitously cruel, and even the frank good counsel of a sister is nothing but a concealed form of hostility.

The moral idiot of nineteenth-century fiction is a well-known figure (he is Murdstone, he is Gradgrind); his utter insensitivity is commonly set off against the open responses of an undeformed human being. Perhaps Lieutenant Krieggstein, an Evanston policeman who would like to be Katrina's tough protector, is supposed to be such an offsetting figure in this story; but his motives are too suspect, there is something grotesque about the arsenal he carries with him, his temperature hardly gets on the chart—no, there is nobody for Katrina, and nothing. It is a deep-frost tale, kept moving only by the agility of Bellow's writing.

[**"Him with His Foot in His Mouth"**] is one of Bellow's long, self-explanatory letters, directed from a man with a compulsion to say nasty things, to one of his earliest victims. Shawmut, the narrator, begins by saying that he is not writing to apologize for his ugly tongue, only to explain himself. But the explanation isn't very explanatory, amounting to little more than the fact that he says vicious things because he says them: and before we've got far beyond that point, it starts to become clear that he's rather pleased with himself, and finds his idiosyncrasy rather an intriguing and distinctive feature of his character.

Like many spiteful persons, he makes of his sharp tongue a point of pride; and if it's inverted pride, so much the better. Thus he is pleased to report that his life has been an almost complete disaster. Once a musicologist of standing, with good academic experience, he made a lot of money at one time from a textbook; but his coarse businessman brother cheated him out of most of his money, and a shyster brother-in-law got the rest. He writes now from a temporary refuge in Canada where he has, as usual, managed to alienate all potential friends—waiting for the US marshal to come and pick him up, and with little but hard time to look forward to. He concludes his confession by reciting a list of smart and nasty things that famous people once said, as if possession of these poisonous jewels somehow

At this late date, it's surely superfluous to say that Bellow is one of our best writers. His prose in *Him with His Foot in His Mouth, and Other Stories* is, as always, nimble and fluid—quick to mock or reverse itself, and double in the manner of all good fictional prose in maintaining an undercurrent of feeling beneath a surface of statement.

—*Robert M. Adams*

justified him. Or as if, with so much accumulated inner nastiness to be purged, he were in a hurry to get rid of it all at once. One thinks of Dostoevsky's underground man in his cellar: "My liver is bad—well, let it get worse."

Two final stories in the collection are, to a greater degree, stories of reconciliation. [In **"A Silver Dish,"** a] hard, dishonest, and truculent father is united, at the end of his life, with a gently philosophical, strikingly responsible, and forgiving son. It is a mute and fleeting moment, which leaves the son, not for the first time, with the sense that his father has gotten away with something; but it is a moment of recognition, too. And in the final story, **"Cousins,"** Ijah Brodsky escapes from the family's nagging, loving demands that he help out his gangster cousin, and is able to do something for his "genius" cousin instead—doubtless a crackpot, this one, but a disinterested crackpot, and the one toward whom Ijah's instincts really direct him. Shorter and gentler than the earlier stories of the collection, these fables emphasize the strong strain of family feeling that runs through Bellow's work and helps to mitigate the harshness of his Chicago.

At this late date, it's surely superfluous to say that Bellow is one of our best writers. His prose in these stories is, as always, nimble and fluid—quick to mock or reverse itself, and double in the manner of all good fictional prose in maintaining an undercurrent of feeling beneath a surface of statement. He is a master of what the French call the *style indirect libre,* which allows a reader to move into and out of the consciousness of a character without crossing any sharply defined borders. The tone is now mocking, now straight, and the reader must catch it as he can. Indeed, with respect to verbal variety and the dancing point of view, short stories may be more congenial to Bellow's gift than novels; certainly Mr. Sammler and the more recent gloomy dean often came closer to flat monologue than was good for the sense of fiction. It would be a shame if Bellow succumbed to an overdidactic view of his own work, to the point of neglecting the joyful impetus and sense of intellectual play that make his often coldly accusing stories a delight to read. His rogues provide constant fun; even his starchiest thinkers let themselves from time to time be seen through. Of all the American novelists who don't have a foot in their mouth, he remains one of the most rewarding; and the new collection of stories provides

encouraging evidence that this state of things is not about to change. (pp. 28-9)

    Robert M. Adams, "Winter's Tales," in The New York Review of Books, *Vol. XXXI, No. 12, July 19, 1984, pp. 28-9.*

Matthew C. Roudane   (essay date 1985)

[*In the essay below, Roudane cites Bellow's story "Him with His Foot in His Mouth" to reveal "the way in which [the protagonist's] present recollections of his past irresponsible—and comic—outbursts shape not only his life but Bellow's structural and thematic concerns within the short story."*]

A casual reading of Saul Bellow's **"Him With His Foot in His Mouth,"** title piece of his recent collection of short fictions, suggests that the author has formulated the narrative in the epistolary mode. The opening salutary line—"DEAR MISS ROSE:" and frequent references to letter writing voiced by Herschel Shawmut, the narrator—invite the observation. But we never read Shawmut's letter. Rather, we are privy to an emotional rough draft, an inner epistolary, a mental image of the issues Shawmut wishes to write about but never actually pens. Essentially prewriting the letter in his mind, Shawmut reflects upon his encounter with Miss Rose as well as sixty-odd years of a humorously troubled existence.

In the limited space that follows, I propose to examine the way in which Shawmut's present recollections of his past irresponsible—and comic—outbursts shape not only his life but Bellow's structural and thematic concerns within the short story. What we will discover is an extension of Bellow's philosophical conviction that the individual can take an affirmative, essentially romantic stance towards both an external world that beguiles, cajoles, and alienates and towards an internal world that, for Shawmut at least, is complicated by his "hysterical syndrome" which causes him "to put his foot in [his] mouth."

Bellow, himself, commented [in *The Atlanta Journal,* 30 May 1984] on what his plans were in designing **"Him With His Foot in His Mouth"**:

    The idea . . . was to write a man's autobiography through the insults he has given, the feelings he has hurt (albeit involuntarily) . . . That seems to happen to me, and to lots of other people I know. Before we can restrain ourselves, we're letting something out.

[In *The New York Times Magazine,* 15 April 1984] Bellow elaborated on his intent, referring to the humorous texture of a story, a quality largely missing from his preceding novel, *The Dean's December:*

    One of the attractions of that story [**"Him"**] . . . is that it is written on a theme, the legitimate irresponsibility of comedy. The life of Shawmut developed out of that. It's an interesting problem; things just pop out of your mouth. They come from comic inspiration, and that is one of the prominent forms of freedom.

And during my interview with the author [in *Contempo-*

rary Literature, Fall 1984], Bellow confessed that he is the one who actually voiced the tactless joke to Miss Rose; and Bellow volunteered: "I also asked the lady if she was going to write her memoirs on a typewriter or on an adding machine! And a few other things of that sort."

Bellow's narrative strategy is at once simple and ambitious: the external action reveals Shawmut's "autobiography through the insults he has given," dramatizing his personal history, internal reflections, and present predicament. As the narrator reflects: *"I will say it all and then revise, send Miss Rose only the suitable parts."* Bellow never presents only *"the suitable parts,"* but also discloses the unedited felt moments of Shawmut's past. In technique as in tone, **"Him With His Foot in His Mouth"** reminds us of certain episodes in Joyce's *Ulysses.* For example, time in both works is measured not so much by chronology as by an internal measure of experience, a measurement that allows the authors to capture accurately the way in which the human mind recollects the individual's psychohistory. Further, both works embody lighthearted comedy scenes while simultaneously presenting the more serious inner conditions of Bloom and Shawmut. Perhaps the most compelling comparison, however, lies in technique: Joyce, of course, uses the stream of consciousness technique while Bellow relies on a related device of concretion, the *style indirect libre* technique. As Robert M. Adams correctly observes [in *The New York Review of Books,* 19 July 1984]:

> He [Bellow] is a master of what the French call the style indirect libre, which allows a reader to move into and out of the consciousness of a character without crossing sharply defined borders. The tone is now mocking, now straight, and the reader must catch as he can.

Although Adams is referring to the collection of stories as a whole, his above remarks on narrative technique are nowhere more evident than in **"Him With His Foot in His Mouth."** Just as the reader moves "into and out of the consciousness" of Shawmut, so Shawmut himself moves "into and out of" past crux moments of his life as well as present legal difficulties "without crossing any sharply defined borders." Employing the *style indirect libre,* Bellow achieves a valid image of the inner consciousness of his protagonist. Because Shawmut's recollections appear as ". . . fragments of things read or remembered . . ." and as "Recreations of a crumbling mind . . . ", Bellow's disjointed, fragmented narrative underpins a precise narrative strategy which unifies the plot.

The structure of **"Him With His Foot in His Mouth"** thus functions to objectify its hero. In terms of sensibility, values, and problems, scholars will quickly recognize Shawmut as the latest image of the Bellovian hero. Like preceding Bellow heroes, Shawmut radiates a humorously disarming capacity for self-assessment: "And I agree, objectively, that my character is not an outstanding success. I am inattentive, spiritually lazy, I tune out." And Shawmut concedes his inability to remain consciously alert: "On a good day I can be accurate for about half an hour, then I start to fade out and anybody can get the better of me." Like Albert Corde in *The Dean's December* or Charlie Cit-

rine in *Humboldt's Gift* or Artur Sammler in *Mr. Sammler's Planet,* Shawmut metaphysically speculates, connecting the everydayness of ordinary experience with the Profound. For example, in one of the most humorous passages in the story, Shawmut meditates on Tracy, his sister-in-law and pit bulldog breeder. After viewing "the dog-runs to show the pit bulls off " and learning of Tracy's prowess with the animals—" 'she's their goddess'," Shawmut reports:

> But as a reverberator, which it is my nature to be, I tried to connect the breeding of these terrible dogs with the mood of the country. The pros and cons of the matter add some curious lines to the spiritual profile of the U.S.A.

Connecting "these terrible dogs" with American politics, Shawmut moments later concludes: "At this rate, a dog in the White House becomes a real possibility. Not a pit dog, certainly, but a nice golden retriever whose veterinarian would become Secretary of State."

In addition to exuding a metaphysical inquisitiveness that allows him to take a measure of the "spiritual profile of the U.S.A.," Shawmut responds to experience in such a way as to further establish him as the latest version of the Bellow hero. Specifically, Shawmut is a well-known musicologist, a Pergolesi expert, one who has achieved a degree of professional respect. On the other hand, professional accolades pale in light of his socially ruinous jokes, outbursts which emerge from what Nietzsche, and later Lorca, call the *Fatum.* Like so many of Bellow's philosophically-inclined heroes, Shawmut reflects on the relevance of the term:

> Fatum signifies that in each human being there is something inaccessible to revision. This something can be taught nothing. Maybe it is founded in the Will to Power, and the Will to Power is nothing less than Being itself.

This sense of *Fatum,* Shawmut thinks, is the source of his failures in social intercourse. Resistent to "revision" and instruction, indispensible qualities for an arranger of notes, one who strives for harmony, a Professor of Music, Shawmut's *Fatum* inevitably leads to his public and private falls from grace—as well as to his present fugitive status. In musical terms, his personal *timbre* is clearly out of pitch.

Elderly, plagued by an array of bodily disorders, Shawmut likens himself to the pathetic image in Goya's *Edad con Sus Disgracias:* that of "an old man who struggles to rise from the chamber pot, his pants dropped to his ankles." Physical ailments, of course, seem emblematic of a deeper, more damaging spiritual condition. In the opening scene, in fact, Shawmut admits that his distress transcends the mere physical: ". . . I am also, for a variety of psychological reasons, deeply distressed and for the moment without ego defenses." Shawmut has been victimized by his *Fatum* or, perhaps more accurately, by an anti-heroic *hubris,* a tragic fracture within his character that precipitates a lifetime of social awkwardnesses, and, now, anxiety. Recognizing his hubristic leanings and fearing some kind of retribution for his apparently devastating verbal assault on

Miss Rose thirty-five years earlier, Shawmut presently seeks expiation.

Structure and narrative line, finally, shape Bellow's thematic concerns within **"Him With His Foot in His Mouth."** Although he devotes much of the action to Shawmut's legal predicament, what engages the author's aesthetic imagination I believe, is his hero's existentialist struggle with the self. Despite the humorous quality of the story, we sense something of Bellow's moral seriousness in the objectification of Shawmut's inner reality, his soulscape. Two salient conditions to which Shawmut continually refers confirm the intensity of his struggle.

First, Shawmut experiences a profound sense of *aloneness.* Throughout, in fact, he alludes to his estrangement from the other, his separation from the world around him. Bellow concentrates on key external events which suggest the extent of Shawmut's aloneness. His escape to British Columbia accentuates, for instance, his displacement from home, from the security implicit in a familiar setting and place. Whereas in *The Dean's December* Albert Corde's geographical separation from Chicago affords him the chance to reflect more clearly on his controversial involvements, in **"Him With His Foot in His Mouth"** Shawmut's geographical exile to Canada does little to clarify his own predicaments. He feels estranged. And since Hansl, Shawmut's well-meaning yet lacking brother-in-law lawyer ("... he was plain crackers") selected Canada as a refuge, we suspect that Shawmut must feel all the more alienated: whenever he entrusts his well-being to others, as he did with his brother Philip, his life only worsens. Further, his lack of devoir alienates him from his new Canadian acquaintances, prompting a telling disclosure: "I am very much *alone* . . . "; he now resigns himself to taking the airs solo: ". . . and now I take my daily walks *alone*" (italics mine). And Walish's letter, which "pulls" Shawmut "to pieces entirely," serves as yet another painful gauge of his loss of friendship. It seems entirely fitting that the only person in whom Shawmut can confide is another outsider, one who has been a widow forty years, the rather eccentric Mrs. Gracewell. As Shawmut laments:

> And there isn't a soul in British Columbia I can discuss this with [Walish's letter and the attendant anxiety it generates in Shawmut]. My only acquaintance is Mrs. Gracewell, the old women (she is very old) who studies occult literature, and I can't bother her with so different a branch of experience.

Bereft of "all friendships," Shawmut's aloneness contributes to his sense of the loss of the self: he fells "a despairing sense that [he is] no longer in control." The narrator appears caught within "*le tourbillion,* or whirlwind" that is his life. Feeling disoriented from the self and the other, Shawmut experiences a deep inner need to cleanse his soul by contacting Miss Rose. In this way, he may begin, Bellow suggests, his escape from *le tourbillion:* "I was not out of it, it was only my project to *get* out." But because of his aloneness, Shawmut's current struggle "to *get* out" seems all the more difficult. This is why near the end of the story Shawmut reflects:

> But to return to what I literally am: a basically

unimportant old part, ailing, cut off from all friendships, scheduled for extradition, and with a future of which the dimmest view is justified (shall I have an extra bed put in my mother's room and plead illness and incompetency?).

The second condition to which Shawmut continually refers concerns *death.* Family deaths, for Shawmut, serve as reminders of the finiteness of human existence. His opportunistic brother, "fat-assed Philip the evildoer," recently died, leaving the narrator "in a deep legal-financial hole." Earlier his two sisters died. And death hovers over his nursing home-bound mother, who cannot recognize her only living son.

With the death of Gerda, Shawmut loses not only a loving soulmate, but a wife who diffused many of his *faux pas:*

> Gerda, in her simplicity, tried to neutralize the ill effects of the words that came out and laid plans to win back the friendship of all kinds of unlikely parties whose essential particles were missing and who had no capacity for friendship, no interest in it.

Even while strickened with leukemia, Gerda "was concerned about my future." Bellow suggests the intensity of Shawmut and Gerda's relationship, implying that their love is most felt by its absence: ". . . I loved Gerda (my love terribly confirmed by her death) . . . "

These two conditions—aloneness and death—shape a third point which seems thematically central to Bellow's short story. His aloneness and the reality of familial death prompt Shawmut to internalize his own mortality. Legal problems trouble him, of course, for they will taint his remaining years, as Bellow suggests in the Sisyphisian refrain: "I may not be sent to prison, but I will have to work for the rest of my natural life, will die in harness, and a damn queer harness, hauling my load to a peculiar peak." But Walish's letter disconcerts Shawmut, not only because of its searing personal attack, but also because of its timing: Shawmut accepts the nearness of his own death, but Walish's attack creates the very real possibility that Shawmut will die without exculpating himself. This is why he reflects, in one-sentence paragraphs analogous to a musical refrain: ". . . In this life between birth and death, while it is still possible to make amends . . . "; and soon after: "So at the very least I can try to reduce the torments of the afterlife by one." Nearing death, Shawmut becomes fixed on making "amends" for past social blunders. Moreover, Walish's ill-timed post, even if it is deserved, reminds Shawmut of the precariousness and finiteness of his own existence:

> His letter upsets me badly. What a time he chose to send it! Thirty-five years without a cross word. He allows me to count on his affection. Then he lets me have it. When do you shaft a pal, when do you hand him the poison cup? Not while he's young enough to recover. Walish waited till the very end—*my* end, of course.

For Shawmut, as for Henderson before him, truth comes in "blows." Accordingly, Walish's letter functions, for Bellow, as a positive "blow," reawakening his hero's spirit. After experiencing aloneness and internalizing death,

Shawmut prepares himself to listen genuinely to Mrs. Gracewell's pronouncements. He is drawn to the old woman's observations in part because they seem philosophically in accord with his personal vision, but also because he now sees himself as part of her lover's quarrel with the world:

> The Divine Spirit, she tells me, has withdrawn in our time from the outer, visible world. You can see what it once wrought, you are surrounded by its created forms. But although natural processes continue, Divinity has absented itself. The wrought work is brightly divine but Divinity is not now active within it. The world's grandeur is fading. And this is our human setting, devoid of God, she says with great earnestness.

The withdrawal of "The Divine Spirit," Bellow suggests, is due in part to those who, like Shawmut, have corrupted the "outer, visible world." Shawmut now realizes that he too has contributed to the absence of Divinity.

Bellow formulates an ambivalent closure to **"Him With His Foot in His Mouth."** We detect no epiphanic moments or changes as when, for example, Tommy Wilhelm cries at the end of *Seize the Day* or when Henderson emerges from his archetypal African quest at the close of *Henderson the Rain King.* Shawmut does not celebrate a new-found consciousness. And yet scholars have come to expect some kind of resolution in a Bellow work, one usually imbued with Thoreauvian transcendentalism, an affirmative, redemptive vision of the cosmos that creates the possibility for the individual to reach beyond his humanness, his fallability.

The ending of **"Him With His Foot in His Mouth"** embodies precisely this kind of romantic, transcendental impulse. There is no mistaking Bellow's ultimately affirmative stance towards human existence in the closing passage of the story:

> But in this deserted beauty man himself still lives as a God-pervaded being. It will be up to him—to us—to bring back the light that has gone from these molded likenesses, if we are not prevented by the forces of darkness. Intellect, worshipped by all, brings us as far as natural science, and this science, although very great, is incomplete. Redemption from mere nature is the work of feeling and of the awakened eye of the Spirit. The body, she says, is subject to the forces of gravity. But the soul is ruled by levity, pure.

In the above passage, Bellow focuses on one of Emerson's moral imperatives, namely, that the individual must generate enough inner "light" to perceive honestly the self and the other. At the end of the story, Shawmut appears capable of internalizing the redemptive forces of which Mrs. Gracewell, whose name suggests the presence of a regenerative force, speaks. And once such regenerative forces are integrated into his own being, once Shawmut transcends "*mere* nature" with an "awakened eye of the Spirit," then, Bellow suggests, he may be able to repair the ruins of his past.

That Shawmut never writes or mails the letter to Miss Rose is irrelevant. What is important to Bellow's hero is

the fact that external events have conspired to reawaken his inner spirit. At the end of the story, Bellow suggests, Shawmut recognizes his faults and is, probably for the first time in his life, willing to rethink his place within the cosmos. If Shawmut has felt caught within *le tourbillion,* it is, to a large degree, because he truly deserves it: the comic outburst, pushed beyond the limits of socially acceptable intercourse, quickly becomes the pathetic—and at times tragic—expression. Thus Bellow provides no guaranteed expiation or happiness for his protagonist. But reflecting on his life, perhaps now Shawmut can revise his *Fatum.* However, any change Shawmut may embrace must come, Bellow implies, not as much from the process of philosophic intellection as from the concreteness of living honestly, with the "awakened eye of the Spirit." (pp. 52-60)

> Matthew C. Roudane, "Discordant Timbre: Saul Bellow's 'Him with His Foot in His Mouth'," in Saul Bellow Journal, *Vol. 4, No. 1, Fall-Winter, 1985, pp. 52-61.*

Karl F. Knight   (essay date 1986)

[*Knight is an American educator and critic. In the essay below, he examines the themes of dissolution and loyalty in Bellow's short story "Cousins."*]

A principal theme in Saul Bellow's **"Cousins"** is the effort to hold things together against the forces of dissolution. Ijah Brodsky, the protagonist, has an apocalyptic sense of the struggle, but avoids despair by working for continuity within his family, by being a responsive and responsible cousin. But the story suggests too that responsibility to the larger society may at times take precedence over loyalty to a particular cousin; indeed, the term "cousins" comes to mean the universal human family.

Dissolution for Brodsky first of all means death, for the old values fade with the deaths of old cousins, cousins like Shana Metzger, who "clothed and bathed and fed" the Brodskys, fresh immigrants from Europe. That kind of cousinly sense of responsibility has given way to modern hedonism, which Brodsky associates with the decay of the American Dream:

> Odd that *it* should begin to roll towards oblivion just as we were perfecting ourselves in this admirable democracy. . . . Being an American always has been something of an abstract project. You came as an immigrant. You were offered a most reasonable proposition and you said yes to it. You were *found.* With the new abstractions you were *lost.* They demanded a shocking abandonment of personal judgment. . . . You could say, for instance, "Guilt has to die. Human beings are entitled to guiltless pleasure."

Brodsky thinks of collapse also in terms suggesting the loss of the harmony of the spheres: "a different, barbarous music" has replaced "an unheard music which buoyed [humanity] . . . , gave it flow, continuity, coherence"; "the cosmic orchestra sending out music has suddenly canceled its performance."

Brodsky's evidences of deterioration also include the breaking of family ties (his own failed marriage; his brothers, who no longer keep in touch; Cousin Eunice's daughter who is too busy to see her mother; Cousin Miltie, who left his wife and ran off with a switchboard operator), mob violence and slayings, and corruption in high office ("the Hoffa school—in more than half its postulates virtually identical with the Kennedy school").

Brodsky feels too that the debasement of language signifies general deterioration. Traditionally weighty words are exploited by advertising and public relations: "Nowadays 'We Care' is stenciled on the walls of supermarkets and loan companies." Pseudo-scientific jargon is too available: "These psychological terms lying around, tempting us to use them, are a menace. They should all be shoveled into trucks and taken to the dump." And closer to home are complex, disturbing misuses of language. Cousin Eunice was forced to "donate" $50,000 to a medical school to secure her daughter's admission, half paid initially, the remainder due before graduation. But Eunice evaded the second payment, guaranteeing it "as a person of known integrity." Although Brodsky recognizes that the donation is a kind of extortion and that Eunice could be bankrupted by a recurrence of cancer, he thinks, "All the words were up for grabs. . . . I didn't like to see the word 'integrity' fucked up."

Despite Brodsky's devotion to the purity of language ("the defense of poetry"), he also misuses it. In pleading with his friend Judge Eiler for special consideration for Cousin Tanky, a convicted mobster, Brodsky knows that he is writing "pure marlarkey," typical of "the low language of high morals—payola letters." He rationalizes that the judge can "read between the lines."

Faced with such evidences of decay, Brodsky is caught in "the *suspense*" of "whether we are preparing a new birth of spirit or the agonies of final dissolution." The story then becomes largely an elaboration on his related question, "And where, with regard to the cousins, does that leave us?" Brodsky's answer is, "Once under way, these relationships have to be played to the end."

Brodsky is reminded of his responsibility to Cousin Motty, who at almost ninety has pneumonia as a complication from a car wreck. Brodsky recoils from the prospect of witnessing the humiliation of Motty, who has to be strapped upright in a chair to keep fluid from building up in his lungs. Regardless of the immediate feelings of Brodsky or even of Motty, the old-fashioned relationship requires that Brodsky visit Motty:

> . . . I had . . . claimed Motty's affection, given
> him my own, treated him with respect, observed
> his birthdays, extended to him the love I had
> felt for my own parents. By such actions,
> I had rejected certain revolutionary develop-
> ments . . . , the contempt for parents. . . . The
> very masses are turning their backs on the fami-
> ly.

Bellow uses Cousin Tanky to show that there are limits to what one is obliged to do in the name of family loyalty. Tanky is the cousin gone bad, a convicted racketeer awaiting sentencing. When he and his sister Eunice ask Brodsky to use his influence with the judge, Brodsky writes, urging a light sentence. He does it not so much for Tanky, howev-

er, but for memories of Tanky's family: Cousin Metzger, who had a "tic" and loved "Neapolitan ice cream," and Cousin Shana, with her "ruddy hair" and with her "bare feet . . . as she mopped the floor. . . . It was also for Cousin Eunice's stammer . . . " And for family loyalty he writes a second letter, requesting special medical attention and diet. But finally Brodsky's sense of rightness forbids him to write a third letter. This limitation to what one can do out of family loyalty is emphasized by Bellow's contrast between Tanky the herald of collapse and Cousin Scholem, who may represent the "new birth of spirit" that Brodsky hopes for.

Scholem, a philosophy student, volunteered for World War II; fought at the Elbe River, where American and Russian soldiers met and pledged friendship and peace; drove a taxi in Chicago for twenty years while writing his grand philosophical synthesis. Out of parasitic luxury and decadence, Tanky offered society corruption and violence. Out of a terrible war, poverty, self-discipline, and the turmoils of Chicago traffic, which might have caused his cancer, Scholem offers three lofty gestures: his manuscript, work with the United Nations to arrange an international gathering of cab drivers in Paris to commemorate the ideal of brotherhood in World War I, and a plan to be buried at Torgau on the Elbe as a symbol of reconciliation between East and West. Whether or not Scholem's gestures will have impact, Brodsky sees his efforts to "bless mankind" as traditional, representative of "the classical norm for Jews of the diaspora." Bellow heightens the contrast between Tanky and Scholem by having Brodsky refuse to write that third letter while he is in Paris waiting to see Cousin Scholem.

After doing as much as conscience would allow for Tanky, Brodsky dedicates himself to Scholem's causes. He gets money from a family trust administered by Cousin Mendy, money which will allow the burial at Torgau, while Brodsky himself will pay for processing and evaluating Scholem's manuscript.

Cousin Scholem and the assembled taxi drivers from all over the world suggest hope. They remind Brodsky of the simple lessons in cousinhood he learned as a schoolboy: "We were not guineas, dagos, krauts; we were cousins." Physically wasted by cancer, Scholem paradoxically suggests youth, rebirth: "the tightening of the skin brought back his youthful look. . . . There seemed a kind of clear innocence about him. The size of his eyes was exceptional—like the eyes of a newborn infant . . . "

Bellow rounds out his story with an additional optimistic touch. Becoming "bizarrely weak in the legs," Brodsky at first wants to reject the proffered arm of Cousin Scholem's daughter, but "Instead I passed my arm through hers and she led us down the corridor." The event suggests that Brodsky accepts the inevitablity of his own decay and his need to lean on others. The image of youth helping age down the symbolic corridor is a promise that the tradition of cousinly responsibility will continue. Further, the meaning of playing relationships "to the end" is clarified, suggesting to the mortal end of cousins, to the end of one's own life, and to whatever end the apocalyptic struggle brings. Although "Nobody—nobody at all—can say how it's going to turn out," Brodsky knows that his best hope and the world's lies in cousinly responsibility. (pp. 32-5)

Karl F. Knight, "Bellow's 'Cousins': The Suspense of Playing It to the End," in Saul Bellow Journal, *Vol. 5, No. 2, Spring-Summer, 1986, pp. 32-5.*

John Banville   (essay date 1989)

[*Banville is an Irish novelist, short fiction writer, and critic. In the following review, Banville interprets Bellow's novella* A Theft *as expressing "a celebration."*]

[At the beginning of *A Theft*] the author blazons the name of his heroine—Clara Velde—like a declaration of intent. Bellow always opens bravely, plunging his readers into the midst of things, and if the bravery sometimes strikes us as mere bravado (as for example, with Augie March's 'I am an American . . . '), the headlong stride of the style, its weight and energy, sweep us forward unresisting. Here, however, the clarion call of Ms Velde's name gives pause. It is very American, yet it is not quite contemporary. We seem to hear in it an echo of an earlier New York scene, of the jewelled and grandly brocaded America of the late 19th century. In short, the reigning spirit here might be that of Henry James.

This is a surprise. It is a long time, forty years or so, since Saul Bellow abandoned the Flaubertian tradition and decided to break out, to let rip ('I am an American . . . '). The result was an extraordinary gain in vigour. What other novelist in our time has produced work to equal in sheer strength such books as *The Adventures of Augie March,* or *Herzog,* or (his masterpiece, for my money) *Humboldt's Gift?* In art, of course, every gain entails a loss: in cutting the 'European' link in favour of being an *echt* American, Bellow risked surrendering to formlessness. His novels tend to go at full tilt, like a man in a heavy overcoat thrashing hip-deep through water, until they run out of energy and just stop, winded, and sometimes far from shore.

A Theft, however, has the coherence and tension of a furled flower. It is packed with colour and wit, and a fervent gaiety. The tendentiousness and hectoring tones of some of his later fiction are absent, as are the faintly crackpot obsessions. It is less a moral than an ethical tale (how should one live?), and comes down firmly, as Bellow always does, on the side of lived life and, that rarest of all things these days, common decency.

The story is organised, with craft and much craftiness, in a binary series. Situations and predicaments repeat themselves over time with small but telling variations; this system is never merely mechanical, but is managed with lightness and grace. The constant throughout the action is a Jamesian 'little thing', an emerald engagement ring which is bought and presented, lost, found, stolen and returned; like the golden bowl or the spoils of Poynton, it increases steadily in significance, turning from a trinket into a talisman 'involved with Clara's very grip on existence'. She has 'come to base her stability entirely' on the ring—though she does also refer to it dismissively as 'this love-toy emerald, personal sentimentality'.

Clara is big, blonde, large-headed, 'a raw-boned American woman . . . from the sticks', the daughter of Indiana farm people and small-town store-owners, brought up on the Bible and old-time religion; it is one of the book's sly jokes that this famously 'Jewish' novelist should take as his protagonist a corn-fed shiksa from the Bible Belt. She has more familiar Bellovian marks, however: she has 'studied Greek at Bloomington and Elizabethan-Jacobean literature at Wellesley'; she has tried suicide once and is to try it again; by the age of 40 she had set up a thriving journalistic agency specialising in high fashion, and later sold it to an international publishing company and is now one of the company's high-powered executives, the 'tsarina of fashion writing'. She has three children, and is on her fourth unsatisfactory husband.

Perhaps it will seem paradoxical to say that Clara is a wonderfully compelling character who is not wholly convincing (this is not unusual, I find, in Saul Bellow's books). She is, it would seem, just too many things, a kind of portmanteau into which Bellow, impatient as ever, has bundled assorted bits and pieces of his latest preoccupations. And although she is recognisably female, there is something about her bigness, her drivenness, that seems to warrant a hormone-test. At times she is suspiciously like one of Bellow's male heroes in drag.

The fourth husband is Wilder Velde, a political speech-writer and fixer, 'big and handsome, indolent, defiantly incompetent', who spends most of his days sitting about in their Park Avenue apartment reading thrillers. Husband three (one and two hardly figure at all) was a rich Italian, now half-paralysed from a stroke and living out his days in Venetian misery and splendour. Clara's real, only and continuing love, however, is for Ithiel 'Teddy' Regler, the man who bought her the engagement ring twenty years ago, but whom she did not marry.

Teddy Regler is the most immediately interesting character in the novella. He is a Henry Kissinger type, but handsomer, and certainly more attractive than the shuttle diplomatist ever showed himself to be. Bellow has always been fascinated by the great world of politics and money. While other writers—Gore Vidal, let's say—look on this world with a mixture of envy and disgust, it is obvious that Bellow loves to get up close to the sources of power and feel the glow on his face and see the sparks fly. If he is part social philosopher who knows his Vico and his Max Weber, there is another, ineradicable part of him that that is for ever the fast-talking, street-wise Chicagoan still with the smell of the stockyards in his nostrils. Regler (Clara describes him as 'somewhere between a Spanish grandee and a Mennonite') is one of Bellow's international men, the geopolitical fireman that the author himself, one suspects, half wishes he had been. In times past Regler has advised administrations on, among other things, nuclear strategy, and would, we are given to understand, have gone all the way to the top, to be a Richard Perle or a Paul Nitze (though likely to have been more liberal than either) if he had stuck at it. However, 'Ithiel didn't make a big public career, he wasn't a team player.' All the same, he still walks the corridors of power: 'He took on such assignments as pleased the operator in him, the behind-the-scenes Teddy Regler: in the Persian Gulf, with a Japanese whiskey firm looking for a South American market, with the Italian police tracking terrorists. None of these activities compromised his Washington reputation for dependability. He testified before Congressional investigative committees as an expert witness.' One can positively *hear* the authorial rubbing of hands.

It is the figure of Teddy Regler which lifts the story into the realm of the 'international tale'. He descends into these pages out of the rarefied strata of first-class travel, still trailing a whiff of the brandy-and-leather air of grand hotels and the well-appointed houses of the great and powerful. He has had his troubles (a terrible wife has stripped him of his possessions, leaving him only a bare marriage-bed), but he is still the rock of good sense and sympathetic advice onto which Clara flings herself when the sea of troubles threatens to engulf her: 'The more hidden his activities, the better she felt about him. Power, danger, secrecy made him even sexier. No loose talk. A woman could feel safe with a man like Ithiel.'

The current difficulties that Clara brings to him for his expert consideration have arisen from the matter of her Austrian au pair girl, Gina Wegman. Gina comes from a highly respectable background—her father is a banker—and she is very good with children, especially Lucy, the eldest, 'a stout little girl needing help': yet from the start Clara recognises in her a young woman eager for experience—and where better to find that than in New York, or Gogmagogsville, as Bible-reared Clara calls the place. And sure enough, Gina quickly takes up with a ghetto boy, a Haitian of great good looks and dubious morals. Clara warns her of the dangers of such a liaison, yet cannot help but recall that once, angry at Teddy Regler, she herself acquired a young lover, a French-speaker too, but this one from France, who was anything but a model companion for a good Midwestern girl; and there is another boy, from farther back, who every year still sends her a Christmas card, from his cell in Attica.

As we expect, and as Clara expects, Gina's young man steals the emerald engagement ring. Even here, however, Clara's indignation is tempered by the knowledge that in such matters she is herself not entirely lily-white. At this point the layers of moral ambiguity built into the book are worthy of the Master himself. First of all, the jeweller from whom the ring was purchased undervalued the emerald, as Clara discovers when she comes to insure it; it is not Clara's fault, of course, that the jeweller made a mistake, but, on the other hand, she does nothing to right the balance. Then she misplaces the ring and claims the $15,000 insurance money, but a year later, when the ring turns up again, she does not inform the insurance company, and keeps the money. Here the irony of the singular in the title *A Theft* becomes apparent.

Gina, confronted with her boyfriend's crime, leaves the apartment and disappears. Clara, on Teddy Regler's advice, hires a private detective to track her down—not for the purpose of visiting retribution on her, but because Clara has grown fond of the girl, and worries for her safe-

ty. The private eye discovers that Gina has moved in with her Haitian. While Clara is trying to make contact with her, the ring mysteriously reappears in Clara's bedroom: how did it get there, past all that expensive security equipment? The answer is a surprise (a twist in the tail!), one which lifts Gina, and Clara, and Clara's children, onto a higher plane of interest, and intensifies them as characters wrestling with life's commonplace yet immensely subtle moral dilemmas.

A Theft is not perfect; it does not have the seamless, enamelled finish that James would have given to it. Although there is less loose writing here than in many of the full-length novels, an occasional idiosyncrasy leaves one blinking. Yet Bellow is such a strong, such a lively writer that what in others would be carelessness can seem carefree in him. Even at their most knockabout, his novels make wonderful talk, provide wonderful lines: a tough old lawyer is 'like Santa Claus with an empty sack who comes down your chimney to steal everything in the house'; or this, passed on from Alexander Zinoviev commenting on glasnost and the crushing of the dissidents: 'After you've gotten rid of your enemies, you're ready to abolish capital punishment.' As always with Bellow, the people here have a tangible presence, a thereness; one feels they existed before the book began, and that they will go on after it ends. This verisimilitude is not exactly fashionable today, but Bellow has a healthy contempt for fashions—*haute couture* in fiction is not for him.

This is a 'late' work, and there is a touch of autumn in it: the leaves tremble and glow, and a porcelain-blue sky shows through the branches, but the going is deceptive underfoot, and there is a distinct chill in the air. 'These people'—Haitians and other ghetto-dwellers—'came up from the tropical slums to outsmart New York, and with all the rules crumbling here as elsewhere, so that nobody could any longer be clear in his mind about anything, they could do it'—who is speaking here, one wonders uneasily: is it just the 'hereditary peasant' in Clara, or is it Saul Bellow the social observer turning bitter?

Clara, no doubt about it, is a tough American who will brook no nonsense from a world that is half silly and half savage. Even her most generous impulses have a pearl of harshness at their core. She attempts to bring Gina and Teddy Regler together, partly out of a desire to rescue the past and fulfil the promise that she and Teddy missed, but also because her Sino-American confidante, Laura Wong (shades of Fanny Assingham and her numerous avatars), has set her own sights on Teddy. It all ends in tears, but they are different from the ones poor Tommy Wilhelm could not contain at the close of a previous novella, *Seize the Day* (1956). Wilhelm weeps for the sadness and brevity of life, Clara for something altogether different; and her tears seem a celebration.

John Banville, "International Tale," in London Review of Books, *Vol. 11, No. 7, March 30, 1989, p. 21.*

John Leonard (essay date 1989)

[*Leonard is an American critic and columnist. In the*

following review, he asserts that Bellow's novella The Bellarosa Connection *lacks emotional intensity.*]

It's nice of Saul Bellow to publish his novellas in cheap paperbacks—sort of Regular American of him, populist and democratic. I just wish they had more bite. *The Bellarosa Connection* improves on *A Theft,* his previous paperback original. It's feistier, full of headlong motion, slapdash dazzle. But it stops so suddenly, as if worried about the great theme around the next curve, that we collide. There's reader whiplash. We have barely got acquainted with Harry Fonstein, a European Jew rescued from Hitler by the Broadway impresario Billy Rose; and Fonstein's American wife Sorella, who wants Rose to acknowledge his personal responsibility for Fonstein's implausible survival. We want to hear more from our nameless narrator about the meaning of it all. But this narrator—a man made wealthy by teaching memory tricks to politicians, business executives and members of the defense establishment; an American Jew perhaps too much assimilated—chooses to forget. Forgetting, we are told, is the sleep of consciousness, a kind of death. But what exactly is he choosing *not* to remember? The Americanization of the Jews? The end of innocence in the Nazi death camps? Jerusalem itself? We don't really know the narrator well enough to decide, and Bellow, from whom we expect a flourish, turns off like a radio.

Until then, on this radio, there's been snap, crackle and pop. The problem here isn't ideas; Bellow's full of them. They're promiscuous, even disdainful: "the canned sauerkraut of Spengler's Prussian socialism," complained Herzog years ago; "the cant and rant of the pipsqueaks about inauthenticity and forlornness." And the problem isn't language, either. His art, as always, is brilliant, twitchy talk: mandarin and colloquial; long ironies and low laughs; Talmudic mutter and gangster slang; Melville, Huck Finn, Rudolf Steiner, Lenny Bruce. Here's his description of Billy Rose:

> Billy was as spattered as a Jackson Pollock painting, and among the main trickles was his Jewishness, with other streaks flowing toward secrecy—streaks of sexual weakness, sexual humiliation. At the same time he had to have his name in the paper. As someone said, he had a bug-like tropism for publicity.

And who else but Bellow would see "the slapstick side" of death camps, the Dada and Surrealism? "Prisoners were sent naked into a swamp and had to croak and hop like frogs. Freezing slave laborers lined up on parade in front of the gallows and a prison band played Viennese light opera waltzes."

The problem, instead, is character. Fonstein is too indistinct to care about. About Sorella we know mainly that she's fat: "She made you look twice at a doorway. When she came to it, she filled the space like a freighter in a canal lock." But why does she have to be—why not tall, skinny, blond or bald?—except that, invariably, there is something grotesque, something physically threatening, a pair of *Psycho* shoulders, about women in Bellow's fiction? When our narrator chooses to forget, is it because he's American, or rich, or childless, or divorced—or an adviser

to military types? Why, anyway, did Israel reject his bag of memory tricks? None of this really adds up. Cynthia Ozick's recently published *The Shawl* is just as much about memory, and even shorter than *The Bellarosa Connection* and yet it breaks the heart . . . because it has one. (pp. 652-53)

> *John Leonard, in a review of "The Bellarosa Connection," in* The Nation, *New York, Vol. 249, No. 18, November 27, 1989, pp. 652-53.*

Michael K. Glenday   (essay date 1989)

[*In the essay below, Glenday focuses on Bellow's novellas* Seize the Day *and* What Kind of Day Did You Have? *to delineate what Bellow has called his "preoccupation with 'obvious and palpable' reality and the devices of 'distortion and blearing' which too often come between Americans and [the] fundamental recognition 'of what things are real.' "*]

> One of my themes is the American denial of real reality, our devices for evading it, our refusal to face what is all too obvious and palpable.
> [*Contemporary Literature* 25, 1974]

So, in a discussion of his latest novel, *The Dean's December* (1982), Saul Bellow speaks of an abiding concern in his fiction—the escapism of Americans, their refusal to face squarely the 'real reality' upon which national and individual life, as he sees it, must be founded. He has always stressed this escapist tendency as a worrisome hallmark of the national psyche, a trait the narrator of *The Dean's December* calls nothing less than 'the American moral crisis'. Given the crisis, 'the first act of morality [is] to disinter the reality, retrieve reality, dig it out from the trash.' And 'retrieving reality' is nowhere more sharply present as a concern than in his two early novellas *Dangling Man* (1944) and *Seize the Day* (1957) and in his return to the form with **"What Kind of Day Did You Have?"** (1984).

Perhaps the very intensity and concentration of the novella form accentuates Bellow's concern in this regard, especially since, as critics have noted, his longer fiction is occasionally weakened by his 'metaphysical garrulity'. Though his eminence has tended to rest upon full-length fictions such as *Augie March* (1954) and *Herzog* (1965), Bellow has always given notice that he has been an adept in the art of short fiction as his collection **Him with his Foot in his Mouth and Other Stories** (1984) testifies. As Bellow observed in the 1950s, the business of the writer is not only to take the nature of reality as theme and subject, but also to use the art of fiction as a tool to cut through towards ultimate recognition of that subject:

> to find enduring intuitions of what things are real and what things are important. His business is with these enduring recognitions which have the power to recognize occasions of suffering or occasions of happiness, in spite of all distortions and blearing.
> [*Perspectives,* Autumn 1954]

The novella, in Bellow's hands, then, serves as a tool with an especially sharp cutting edge, one that enables him to discover those 'enduring recognitions' of reality with fewer impediments, without the 'distortions and blearing' which sometimes encumber the expression of the same theme in parts of his longer fiction. His use of the shorter form allows him to exploit the localizing incident more effectively, and the plenitude of ideas—often predominating the novels to the detriment of plot and story—is subordinate to the dramatic capacity of such incidents. In the account which follows I want to focus essentially on two novellas, *Seize the Day* and **"What Kind of Day Did You Have?"**—early and late work respectively—to pursue Bellow's preoccupation with 'obvious and palpable' reality and the devices of 'distortion and blearing' which too often come between Americans and this fundamental recognition 'of what things are real'.

To discuss 'reality' in connection with fiction is, to be sure, to enter a loaded literary minefield. For what else has been at the centre of its concerns, form, philosophy or very purpose? But in Bellow's case, so often and explicitly has he made it the actual *theme* of his work, that it assumes an even greater importance than usual. Reality, in one key sense, is not at all problematic for him: it is there, 'obvious and palpable'. Also, there is very little in Bellow's work to show any trace of that philosophical scepticism about the nature of reality which has so characterized the postmodern literary aesthetic over recent years. There have been few modern American writers quite so vigorous, or persistent, in getting it down upon the page—for all his reputation as an 'ideas' writer Bellow is still a sturdy, unremitting and circumstantial 'realist'. I have said that he uses the novella as a form of fiction that cuts through towards such reality. As a realist, a large part of his own self-appointed brief has been to reflect contemporary data in all its barbarism, the urban killing fields of Chicago—'many, many square miles of civil Passchendaele or Somme' [*The Dean's December*]—to make 'the real world realer' and to confront its perversities.

But Bellow, in his Nobel Prize address, acknowledges also that the writer must go beyond documentation, must penetrate towards the essentially real: 'Only art penetrates what pride, passion, intelligence, and habit erect on all sides—the seeming realities of this world' [*American Scholar* 46, 1977]. In the embrace of these 'seeming realities', Americans above all have tended to become chronically unmoored, adrift with nothing solid to cling to. Or as Larry Wrangel, in **"What Kind of Day Did You Have?"** puts it:

> The created souls of people, of the Americans, have been removed. The created soul has been replaced by an artificial one, so there's nothing real that human beings can refer to when they judge any matter for themselves.

Wedged between the stylistic extroversions of *The Adventures of Augie March* and *Henderson the Rain King*, *Seize the Day*, as Marvin Mudrick has observed, still tastes like 'the real pastrami between two thick slices of American store bread' [University of Denver Quarterly 1, 1966]. The members of the Royal Swedish Academy evidently shared Mudrick's taste when they singled out the novella for special mention in Bellow's Nobel Prize citation. Even the Bellow-baiting Mailer grudgingly threw a bouquet in the

direction of the book as a tribute to its 'surprisingly beautiful ending', the 'first indication for me that Bellow is not altogether hopeless on the highest level'.

A good deal of critical debate has, perhaps understandably, centred upon the final scene of *Seize the Day,* with some critics arguing that the tears shed by Tommy Wilhelm are ones that signify a new enlightenment for him. Others have contended that the rhetorical flourish of the novella's ending cannot disguise Bellow's inability to resolve narrative tensions satisfactorily. My own view is that the ending is perfectly compatible as a response to, and a culmination of, Bellow's searing condemnation of American 'reality'—the subject of *Seize the Day.* It also provides a perfect example of Bellow's skill in the novella form, his use of the dramatic incident as a means of heightening and intensifying thematic concerns. The reader has been led, from the very start, to anticipate a climactic ending, a resolution to suspenseful elements of the narrative:

> he was aware that his routine was about to break up and he sensed that a huge trouble long presaged but till now formless was due. Before evening, he'd know.

Bellow uses the brevity of the novella to embody these tensions, to lead inexorably towards Tommy's convulsive *cri de coeur.* His fiction is full of anguished and heart-torn individuals, but surely none so full of anguish and heartache as Tommy. One of the main reasons for this must be due in large part to the sharp and unremitting awfulness of Tommy's 'day', undiluted in novella medium. The reader is as permanently conscious of Tommy's suffering as Tommy himself; the third-person narrator maintains that intimacy, refusing the reader any remission at all.

This narrator stresses throughout the horrific price Tommy pays for his physical appearance ('fair-haired hippopotamus'), his *gaucherie,* his failure in the business world, and his lack of emotional reserve. Mainstream reality in America is still—as Joseph of *Dangling Man* puts it in the first paragraph of Bellow's first novel—dominated by 'hardboiled-dom'. According to this regimen one has to be a tough guy, possessed of a mind defined by Henry Adams more than a century ago as 'a cutting instrument, practical, economical, sharp and direct'. The narrator mocks Tommy's efforts to keep up appearances of capability, telling us that Tommy

> had once been an actor—no, not quite, an extra—and he knew what acting should be. Also, he was smoking a cigar, and when a man is smoking a cigar, wearing a hat, he has an advantage; it is harder to find out how he feels.

Tommy knows the ground rules, knows how he is expected to behave, having been taught by his father how, despite 'bad luck, weariness, weakness, and failure' he must still affect a low-key tone, must 'sound gentlemanly, low-voiced, tasteful'. He knows also the rules that govern American reality, but always loses the game.

> I am an idiot. I have no reserve . . . I talk. I must ask for it. Everybody wants to have intimate conversations, but the smart fellows don't give out, only the fools.

Dr. Adler's repudiation of his son is justified to some extent. Indeed Bellow has carefully prepared a case for the doctor's perception of Tommy as a slob, a miscreant, a maladroit bungler with an unerring talent for taking the wrong road. Dr. Adler, then, as [Gerald Nelson in his *Ten Versions of America* has] argued, 'is right, when his slovenly, failure-ridden son comes on his knees, begging, to both feel and articulate his disgust. He is right but not human.'

And this is Bellow's subject in *Seize the Day*: not Tommy's pathos but all those, such as his father and Tamkin—the primary 'reality-instructor' of the novel—by whose example he seems such a misfit. Such a reality, as Martin Amis has recently pointed out in connection with Bellow's fiction [in his *The Moronic Inferno*], 'is not a given but a gift, a talent, an accomplishment, an objective'. Whereas Joseph of *Dangling Man* sets out in knowledgeable defiance of a prime commandment of American reality—'if you have difficulties grapple with them silently'—Tommy's pathos derives from his unexamined acceptance of this axiom. His tears at the end are an expression of his inability to live within a reality that is contemptuous of their shedding.

In one of his acute culture-readings in *In the American Grain,* William Carlos Williams denunciates the 'coldness and skill' which serve as an accepted part of American manners:

> Who is open to injuries? Not Americans. Get hurt; you're a fool. The only hero is he who is not hurt. We have no feeling for the tragic. Let the sucker who fails get his. What's tragic in that? That's funny! To hell with him. He didn't make good, that's all.

Years after the publication of *Seize the Day,* Bellow spoke [in *Quest,* February/March 1979] of his belief in the necessity of emotional display, and of the hardboiled American ethos that condemns such emotional release:

> Is feeling nothing but self-indulgence? . . . When people release emotion, they so often feel like imposters. By restraining themselves, they claim credit for a barren kind of honesty . . . Nothing is gained by letting yourself go among people who hate such letting go.

Tommy Wilhelm is by far the most vulnerable of Bellow's major characters. Whereas other Bellow heroes like Albert Corde, Moses Herzog, and Charlie Citrine realize the prudence of closing the valves of feeling in public, Tommy has neither the intelligence nor the guile to develop any strategies of concealment. He is 'the sucker who fails', and *Seize the Day* is the story of how America sends him to hell, how he 'gets his' from America's hardboiled and heartless.

In the novella's final scene, Bellow's stress falls upon Tommy 'hidden' in the centre of a crowd of mourners. Though it is true that Tommy cries openly, he is in the most crucial sense as concealed as ever, 'protected by the occasion' of the funeral rite so that the onlookers are never truly aware of the nature of his grief. Instead of being outraged, embarrassed, or moved by that grief, these onlookers are merely curious, or, more significantly, envious—

' "It must be somebody real close to carry on so". "Oh my, oh my! To be mourned like that", said one man . . . with wide, glinting, jealous eyes'. In a culture in which real feeling has apparently atrophied, the generous tears of Tommy Wilhelm turn him into a bizarre celebrity.

Ironically, too, Tommy is made to seem a dramatic embodiment of Bellow's idea that 'when people release emotion, they so often feel like imposters', as one mourner wonders whether Tommy was 'perhaps the cousin from New Orleans they were expecting'. So this final scene demonstrates not 'the possibility of communion', not Tommy's newly-found connections with the city's crowd, but rather his awful isolation, his emotional release figured as a sinking downwards 'deeper than sorrow' towards extravagant oblivion. The oblivion is 'great and happy' because it serves simultaneously as both an expression and extinction of self. American reality has broken him, denied him, hounded him and fleeced him. Finally ('Wilhelm was moved forward by the pressure of the crowd . . . carried from the street into the chapel') it brings him face to face with the look of death. But Tommy sees beyond the reality of appearances:

> Now at last he was with it, after the end of all distractions, and when his flesh was no longer flesh. And by this meditative look Tommy was so struck that he could not go away . . . On the surface, the dead man with his formal shirt and his tie and silk lapels and his powdered skin looked so proper; only a little beneath so—black, Wilhelm thought, so fallen in the eyes. Standing a little apart, Wilhelm began to cry.

Tamkin is in some ways the major character of the novella, no less than a prototype in Bellow's fiction. He also bears a striking resemblance to the protean Rinehart of Ellison's *Invisible Man* or the adaptive Milo Minderbinder of *Catch-22,* not to mention numerous similar figures in Thomas Pynchon's fiction. He is also the forerunner of Valentine Gersbach in *Herzog* and Dewey Spangler in *The Dean's December,* as well as of Victor Wulpy in *What Kind of Day?* Like Gersbach, Tamkin comes over as the self-proclaimed poet who also 'put himself forward as the keen mental scientist'. Both Dr. Adler (described as 'a fine old scientist') and Tamkin, who gambled 'scientifically', are associated with an anti-humanistic rationalism which will reappear in Bellow's fiction in increasingly nasty forms until given its baleful apotheosis in *The Dean's December.* There, we are told by Bellow's narrator that we may indeed have reached a stage wherein 'science had drawn all the capacity for deeper realizations out of the rest of mankind and monopolized it. This left everyone else in a condition of great weakness.' Like Spangler and Wulpy, Tamkin is a rhetorician who has no purpose 'except to talk'. And just as Albert Corde makes the mistake of unburdening himself to Spangler in Budapest, Tamkin finds Tommy willing prey. Following his rejection by his father Tommy stumbles into Tamkin's orbit, feeling that there at least he would find one who could 'sympathise with me' and try 'to give me a hand'.

It is of course Tamkin who voices the novella's *carpe diem* ethos; he is the successful predator, perfectly adapted to the jungle of the American metropolis, 'the end of the world, with its complexity and machinery, bricks and tubes, wires and stones, holes and heights'. Amidst this frightening perplexity, Tommy prays that Tamkin will show him the way, 'give him some useful advice and transform his life'. But like Wulpy's mistress Katrina ('an average Dumb Dora'), so Tommy knows he is 'a sucker for people who talk about the deeper things of life'. Tamkin, however, for all his rhetorical composure, is not in truth that complex a being. Bellow's narrator allows us to see Tamkin in much the same way as we eventually see Gersbach of *Herzog*—'not an individual, but a fragment, a piece broken off from the mob'. We feel, too, the underlying terror that buoys up Tamkin's masquerade as well as feeling the slightest bit of sympathy for the very real sense in which Tamkin is as much the prey of 'the world's business' as Tommy:

> his face did not have much variety. Talking always about spontaneous emotion and open receptors and free impulses he was about as expressive as a pincushion. When his hypnotic spell failed, his big underlip made him look weakminded. Fear stared from his eyes, sometimes, so humble as to make you sorry for him. Once or twice Wilhelm had seen that look. Like a dog, he thought.

The remote but detectable resemblance to the eyes of the dead man in the final scene ('on the surface . . . so proper; only a little beneath so—black, Wilhelm thought, so fallen in the eyes') is a chilling touch, for Tamkin of course has no being, no personality, no soul. He succeeds because of his protean capacities ('Funny but unfunny. True but false. Casual but laborious, Tamkin was') and because of his fake profundity which creates a reality beyond comprehension, so that

> listening to the doctor when he was so strangely factual, Wilhelm had to translate his words into his own language, and he could not translate fast enough or find terms to fit what he had heard.

But in Bellow's trenchant vision of American reality as nightmare, this confusion of language and meaning is one that extends to embrace the entire gamut of knowledge, and knowledgeability, to lead modern America towards the vortex reality of absolute unintelligibility where solipsism alone reigns:

> You had to translate and translate, explain and explain, back and forth, and it was the punishment of hell itself not to understand or be understood, not to know the crazy from the sane, the wise from the fools, the young from the old or the sick from the well. The fathers were no fathers and the sons no sons. You had to talk with yourself in the daytime and reason with yourself at night. Who else was there to talk to in a city like New York?

Tamkin is at once creator, beneficiary and victim of this state of affairs. He feeds on the likes of Tommy without scruple. Bellow's physical description of Tamkin emphasizes the animal in him as well as the deceiver, and there are insinuations too of Mephistophelian grossness and carnality. The image of Tamkin's twisted anatomy may be the analogue of his perversion of the natural which is his

stock-in-trade. 'If you were to believe Tamkin . . . everybody in the hotel had a mental disorder, a secret history, a concealed disease . . . every public figure had a character-neurosis'. And commensurate with the suggestion that Tamkin embodies a kind of barely concealed, devilish bestiality, is his view of reality as hell, an infernal pit of pain and suffering:

> Wilhelm said, 'But this means that the world is full of murderers. So it's not the world. It's a kind of hell.'
>
> 'Sure,' the doctor said. 'At least a kind of purgatory. You walk on the bodies. They are all around. I can hear them cry *de profundis* and wring their hands. I hear them, poor human beasts. I can't help hearing.'

In its depiction of dissociation and dissolution, of Dr. Adler's well-dressed affability and heartlessness triumphing over his son's despair, of Tamkin's high-powered mountebankery exploiting that despair, *Seize the Day* warns of the crisis afflicting American reality. Wilhelm's 'reality' is made up of despair, confusion, loneliness and failure; this is his 'real reality', the bottom line, 'obvious and palpable' in the suffering it inflicts upon him. Because they cannot, or will not, take account of this reality, having built up defences of 'seeming realities', those who could have taken the elementary moral, human step—his father, his sister, family and friends—hasten Tommy's demise. As Larry Wrangel remarks in **"What Kind of Day Did You Have?"**, 'what's really real is the unseen convulsion under the apparitions'. Perhaps this is the kindest view to take of all those who deny Tommy's 'real reality', to say that they simply do not see it. But the price for such blindness is the highest man can pay, a Faustian price—their souls removed, to be 'replaced by an artificial one, so there's nothing real that human beings can refer to when they try to judge any matter for themselves'.

That all of these thematic concerns are carried within the novella format is a tribute to Bellow's ability to make that format more capacious than its slender frame would seem to imply. The tribute is the greater when we consider that unlike Hemingway in *The Old Man and the Sea,* or James's *The Beast in the Jungle,* Bellow does not rely upon symbolical properties to give narrative depth. Instead the profundity and intensity of his themes are carried in and through such things as the immaculately rendered linear plot—enhanced in terms of suspense and drama by its diurnal span—and here the novella's brevity makes it a propitious vessel; and there is also the presence in this novella of some of Bellow's best writing: succinct, lyrical, evocative, and in these ways a revelation to all those readers put off by the prosiness of the longer fiction.

"What Kind of Day Did You Have?", Bellow's latest novella, consolidates his vision of American reality as I have been seeking to describe it. Again, Bellow chooses to give this novella the time-scale frame of a single day, an apparently climactic day in the lives of the two central characters. Yet the tale is clearly late-Bellow in many ways. Structurally, and even within the constraints imposed by the form, it is more diffuse, even ending in deliberate anti-

> The fact that *Seize the Day* and "What Kind of Day Did You Have?" are novellas shows how well Bellow is able to explore the potentialities of this bantam form, using its brevity to create effects—of suspense, and of subtle thematic control—not possible in novel or short story. 'To have a soul, to *be* one—that today is a revolutionary defiance of received opinion', Bellow remarked in a recent interview. In such a climate these novellas suggest that the reality of American lives will be one of increasing artificiality, increasing inhumanity.
>
> —*Michael N. Glenday*

climax. One feels the ending might have been more pointedly accomplished, especially after a consideration of the virtues of *Seize the Day,* yet the conclusion of the later novella contains muted epiphanies which perhaps required the understated ending. Victor Wulpy, the character who towers over the story, amounts to one of Bellow's most biting satirical portraits of the American intellectual. Though Tamkin is his antecedent, Wulpy is physically and mentally more formidable, 'a kind of tyrant in thought'. Fortunately, the novella's concision imposes its own discipline upon that tyrannical display, though Wulpy is, in the course of the story itself, forced to consider the nature of his tyrannical thoughts.

Wulpy's character had been predicted in Bellow's novels of the '60s; Herzog, for instance, has been a witness to man's preparing to assume the mantle of his 'future condition', a condition of amoral automatism 'free from human dependency' [in *Herzog*]. Artur Sammler, too, faces up to the same dehumanized projection of the race, knowing that the day of the 'old-fashioned sitting sage' is over [*Mr. Sammler's Planet*]. The day of Wulpy, the shuttle-intellectual, has arrived. His very name, Victor, confirms his peerless command—'such a face, such stature; without putting it on, he was so commanding that he often struck people as being a king'.

Into his kingdom comes Katrina, who 'had been raised to consider herself a nitwit'. Her home-life is in a mess; she is in the middle of an 'ugly' divorce, and her two young daughters are the subject of a custody wrangle. This broken family and its *anomie* give us the damning backdrop against which the events and relationships of the novella are played out. As with *Seize the Day,* Bellow exploits the time-span to good effect. The narrative opens with Katrina about to leave her Chicago home and its two daughters, and closes with her return to it after travelling back from Boston with Wulpy. Again the brevity of the novella enhances this pattern; we are, for instance, always aware of the maternal responsibilities Katrina has left behind her in Chicago, indeed this particular abdication of

duty becomes a central aspect of the novella's moral design.

What Katrina desires, is what middle-America desires: significance, *gravitas,* a piece of the action, however vicarious or compromising. In a 1975 interview [in *Salmagundi,* Spring 1975] Bellow spoke of this rage for significance in American life:

> Life . . . has become very current-eventish. People think they are political when they are immersed in these events—vicariously. . . . Society is monopolising their brains, and taking their souls away from them by this interest, by the news, by spurious politics.

Wulpy is Katrina's way-in to this reality. She signs up with him, a babble-king who can connect her to the current of current-events. She needs this like a drug to relieve herself of the boredom of all that her home life entails, since 'when the current stopped, the dullness and depression were worse than ever'. By trading in her family for Wulpy she can now share a room with 'the Motherwells and Rauschenbergs and Ashberys and Frankenthalers and . . . leave the local culture creeps grovelling in the dust'. The frame of departure and return allows Bellow to use this novella so as to meaningfully enmesh form and subject. We are able to view the object of Katrina's Bostonian flight, to see Wulpy perform his tyrannies (and here it is interesting to note that Bellow needed the extra wordage to do justice to Wulpy's Olympian bearing—the effect could not have been achieved within the smaller compass of a short story), and to receive the challenge posed by the Larry Wrangel character. So we are able to see what she has sacrificed, and what she has sacrificed it for.

The moral design of **"What Kind of Day Did You Have?"** is similar to that of *Seize the Day.* It is one in which the realities of public life—represented and interpreted by Wulpy, here a kind of Tamkin empowered—are seen to bear down upon, and to be inimical to, the imperatives of personal ethics. In this context, Katrina's children are wordless witnesses of their neglect, hovering in the far background of the story (in the domestic overviews comprising the 'frame' of the story's beginning and end; so in the far background in terms of their mother's 'day' but not at all minimalized by Bellow's narrator, who makes their silent presence so eerily indicting in the important frame areas), 'silent Pearl, wordless Soolie' are forced to ponder their mother's unseemly departure from their wintry Chicago home to Boston and Wulpy's bed.

As so often in Bellow's fiction family ties are an index to the probity of his characters. Because Wulpy is wholly devoid of a moral nature, 'categories like wife, parent, child never could affect his judgement. He could discuss a daughter like any other subject submitted to his concentrated, radiant consideration'. However, Victor 'didn't like to speak of kids. He especially avoided discussing her children'. He has a daughter whom he calls 'a little bitch'. Her more recent claims to that title have included 'giving her mother sex advice' together with 'the address of a shop where she could read some passages on foreplay'. Of course Wulpy never considers the extent to which his own neglect of parental responsibilities have contributed to these violations of the natural, only that such 'facts' seem to him to 'add up to an argument for abortion'. For Wulpy, 'insofar as they were nothing but personal, he cared for nobody's troubles'. His grotesque blindness to the elemental duties of fatherhood is compounded by Katrina's willingness to accept Wulpy as 'the child . . . which not even my own kids will be with me' and by her acknowledgement that 'as a mother I seem to be an artificial product'.

The latter remark as noted earlier anticipates that of the novella's co-star, Larry Wrangel. He correctly exposes the inhumanity of Wulpy's idea-mongering mentality:

> You always set a high value on ideas, Victor. I remember that. Well, I've considered this from many sides, and I am convinced that most ideas are trivial. A thought of the real is also an image of the real; if it's a true thought, it's a true picture and is accompanied by a true feeling. Without this our ideas are corpses.

This confrontation between Wrangel and Wulpy marks the centre point of the tale. He is the only character able to challenge Wulpy, and he does so successfully as Wulpy himself later seems to concede ('there may have been something in what Wrangel said'. His attack is aimed at the inhuman abstraction of Wulpy's thinking; in peddling abstractions Wulpy is a 'caricaturist', his shorthand representations causing human beings, in reduction, to be 'represented as *things*'. Like Albert Corde, Wrangel argues that this tendency towards abstraction both contributes to, and results from the flight from 'real reality':

> We prefer to have such things served up to us as concepts. We'd rather have them abstract, still-born, dead. But as long as they don't come to us with some kind of reality, as facts of experience, then all we can have instead of good and evil is . . . concepts. Then we'll never know how the soul is worked on. Then for intellectuals there will be discourse or jargon, while for the public there will be ever more jazzed-up fantasy.

For Bellow, a writer renowned for the intellectual appetite of his work, the above seems an extraordinary indictment of intellectual process. The attack, however is more properly seen as one levelled at what passes for a moral use of such process. Instead of an intellectual response based upon 'facts of experience', minds such as Wulpy's, trained to entertain rather than edify, can only add to the rift between an authentic reality and its public travesty. Bellow's point is that the development of a moral sense depends upon this correspondence between intellect and experience, and that without it there can only be a degeneration of the moral life.

As I noted earlier, there is a subdued epiphany for Katrina at the close of the narrative. But unlike *Seize the Day*, [**"What Kind of Day Did You Have?"**] aims more at representing the unleavened slice of life, a life that will continue to be lived—certainly by Wulpy, probably by Katrina—in the way of the narrative's day. Still, even Victor fleetingly realizes—as the small plane carrying them back to Chicago seems about to plummet into Lake Michigan—the force of Wrangel's criticisms and the truth that

'of all that might be omitted in thinking, the worst was to omit your own being'. But Bellow is quick to stress the momentary nature of this insight, and the last we see of Wulpy is the picture Katrina has of him 'in the swift, rich men's gilded elevator rushing upward, upward' towards his next public address—'pressed for time . . . all that unfinished mental business to keep him busy forever and forever'.

But it is in Katrina's return home that Bellow proves his mastery of the novella form. For it is only at that point that the reader realizes the importance of this territory, and realizes, too, that the narrative had been bound to return there, with its neglected children waiting—and certainly not for the first time—for Katrina's brief interludes of motherhood. The relative brevity of the novella means we have not forgotten their environment, though since leaving it at the beginning of the narrative we have seen how odious is the personality and the life-style for which they have been sacrificed. Katrina finds her house empty and though her initial fear that her children have been taken away by their father proves to be unfounded, there is a terrible irreducible reality—unsullied by any abstraction—in their renunciation of the maternal tie, in their alien self-sufficiency:

> They didn't say, 'Where have you been, Mother?' She was not called upon for any alibis. Their small faces communicated nothing. They did have curious eyes, science-fiction eyes, that dazzled and also threatened from afar . . . Emissaries from another planet, grown from seeds that dropped from outer space, little invaders with iridium in their skulls.

Like Tommy Wilhelm, these innocents are the misfits, without reality in a world of distorted forms—'the fathers no fathers and the sons no sons'. Katrina, self-confessedly an 'artificial' mother, has perpetuated the breed, the nothingness of response and the remoteness in her daughters' eyes being a chilling cause to reflect again upon Wrangel's theory that 'the created souls . . . of the Americans have been removed'.

Both novellas are powerful examinations of the extent to which Americans collaborate in this process. And the fact that they are novellas shows how well Bellow is able to explore the potentialities of this bantam form, using its brevity to create effects—of suspense, and of subtle thematic control—not possible in novel or short story. 'To have a soul, to *be* one—that today is a revolutionary defiance of received opinion', Bellow remarked in a recent interview [*TriQuarterly,* Spring/Summer 1984]. In such a climate these novellas suggest that the reality of American lives will be one of increasing artificiality, increasing inhumanity. (pp. 162-76)

> *Michael K. Glenday, "Some Versions of Real: The Novellas of Saul Bellow," in* The Modern American Novella, *edited by A. Robert Lee, London: Vision Press, 1989, pp. 162-77.*

David Denby   (essay date 1990)

[*Denby is an American film critic for* New York *maga-*

zine. In the following excerpt, he provides an enthusiastic review of Bellow's novellas The Bellarosa Connection *and* A Theft.]

"In these democratic times, whether you are conscious of it or not, you are continually in quest of higher types." So says the narrator of Saul Bellow's new novella, *The Bellarosa Connection.* An elderly expert in memory training, a professional sorter of old impressions, the nameless narrator is at the point of taking stock of his life, his relations, his allegiances. He's engaged, therefore, in an activity close to the making of fiction, and in this business of "higher types" he probably speaks for Bellow. In his recent stories and novellas, Bellow seems eager to be impressed—to be bowled over, really—by the men and women he puts before us. He celebrates the quality that lasts—not breeding in the social sense, but what used to be called "character," something found equally in a Viennese au pair girl and a distant relative dying obscurely in New Jersey. Greatness in ordinary human form.

Like the gold coins once poured on the heads of newly crowned czars, Bellow's praise now falls without irony on intellectuals making their way in our amiably philistine business civilization. One encounters such extraordinary examples of winged sapience as the aging, disabled, but eagle-proud art critic and aesthetic philosopher Victor Wulpy (clearly based on Harold Rosenberg), who dominates the novella **"What Kind of a Day Did You Have?"** (included in Bellow's 1984 collection of short fiction, *Him with His Foot in His Mouth*). And in the same collection (it is one of Bellow's best books) appears the fierce young Chicago-born Zetland (a.k.a. Isaac Rosenfeld), writer and bohemian, devouring Melville in darkened, cavelike apartments. Unlike Henderson or Herzog or Citrine, these men are never foolish in their spiritual striving.

Generosity in brilliant old men is sufficiently rare that one wonders: Is this longing for human distinction in Bellow's late fiction a needed comfort, an extra log on the fire as the day grows colder and turns into night? Has there been a softening of his gaze? And does his giving vein have any necessary connection with the form of these long stories? These fictions are not concise and fiercely organized, like *Seize the Day* or some of the shorter pieces in *Mosby's Memoirs,* but contemplative and digressive, spilling over with lists and categories and ideas, a sort of roiled Whitmanesque landscape of the American mind.

I hasten to add that women, highly intelligent though not exactly intellectuals, come in for their share of the tumbling gold. This is a new turn for Bellow, and sometimes he's not quite in control of the shower of praise. The novella *A Theft* nearly founders under the weight of Bellow's heaped-up encomiums of his heroine Clara Velde. A bustling, worldly figure, Clara works as a fashion-magazine executive and lives on Park Avenue with her fourth husband. For more than two decades, however, she has loved the fabulous Ithiel Regler—Teddy Regler, with his "eyes from Greek mythology," who serves as globe-trotting adviser to Presidents and Shahs, an original deep thinker who has the ability to put the big picture together. A bit of a hyped article, this Teddy. He comes off as half talk-show guest, half Richard Goodwin's fantasy of himself.

As for Clara, she is handsome and blond, and her big-boned body is topped with a capacious noggin—she "needed that [big] head; a mind like hers demanded space." Born back-country in the Midwest and raised on the Bible, she now exudes smarts and taste ("She bought her clothes in the best shops and was knowledgeable about cosmetics"). Yet somehow she's romantic and impulsive too, a woman driven by loyalty and honor. Bellow compares her to a medieval heroine, to a Renaissance heroine—he keeps upping the ante.

Clara recognizes a fellow woman of honor in her au pair girl Gina, an amazingly self-possessed Viennese slumming in New York. Gina's disreputable Haitian boyfriend steals a ring that Teddy Regler had given Clara years earlier, and Clara's nobility expands in many remarkable acts of trust. Despite much descriptive energy and charm, the tale strains one's patience. Bellow resorts to such awkward narrative devices as a Chinese-American dressmaker-confidante who gets to hear Clara's racy and intimate speculations. He displays an alarmingly smooth knowingness about the details of Park Avenue domestic management. The book might have been written by a social secretary of remarkable, and remarkably obsequious, observational powers; Bellow's eager new sophistication fits badly with the highfalutin, morally strenuous tone of the exchanges between Clara and Gina.

The restricted, even smug, social circumstances of the story, moreover, reveal the limits of his generosity, which is reserved for a small circle of cultivated whites, while servants and menacing outsiders of varying hues hover in the background. *A Theft* is a rare case of class boundaries limiting Bellow's consciousness. Though witty from one sentence to the next, the tale lacks humor and proportion, and suffers overall from an atmosphere of strained triviality. The irony of a noble character triumphing in such worldly and gilded circumstances doesn't come through with any force. Clara has clearly been oversold; we're in danger, much of the time, of not caring about her, big head and all.

But no such troubles should mar anyone's enjoyment of *The Bellarosa Connection,* a seriously funny *jeu d'esprit* of Bellow's old age. The narrator is a masterful man—the millionaire founder of the Mnemosyne Institute of Philadelphia, which trains businessmen and statesmen in memory use. A retired widower, long cut off from his New Jersey roots, he roams around his 20-room Main Line mansion, both flattered and oppressed by his own powers. He may long to "forget about remembering," but he knows that the only retirement from memory is death. In himself, he is not a memorable or lovable Bellow character. Highly intelligent, he's neutral in temperament, disconnected from life, the practitioner of a hollow craft (brute memorization) that leaves him vulnerable to emotions drifting below the level of conscious recall. But this time Bellow is in control. He plants a small bomb beneath the surface of the narrator's suave self-sufficiency.

Plagued by a sense of isolation, the narrator recalls his strong-souled New Jersey relatives Harry and Sorella Fonstein, whom he hasn't seen in years. He has allowed this connection with the admirable but unfashionable

Fonsteins to lapse in part because he can remember them so well; memory has substituted for experience. He also let it lapse because the Fonsteins were something of a threat. As a youth, the narrator's own father had compared him unfavorably to Fonstein, a "gimpy Galitzianer"—he has a bum foot and wears an orthopedic shoe—who had fled from Hitler, suffered, and survived. While the memory expert, a nascent millionaire, then a languid American Jew, was living in bohemian indolence in Greenwich Village, Fonstein made his way to America and became a rich man himself, largely due to the entrepreneurial skill of his wife, Sorella.

It is Sorella in her lifelong struggle for her husband's dignity who receives Bellow's extraordinary appreciation—all the more extraordinary for being grounded so firmly in sexual disgust. The narrator's first impression of her borders on the ludicrous:

> Sorella Fonstein sometimes sat on the sofa, which had a transparent zippered plastic cover. Sorella was a New Jersey girl—correction: lady. She was very heavy and she wore makeup. Her cheeks were downy. Her hair was done up in a beehive. A pince-nez, highly unusual, a deliberate disguise, gave her a theatrical air. She was still a novice then, trying on these props. Her aim was to achieve an authoritative, declarative manner. However, she was no fool.

Bellow's short sentences, however tough and definitive, never turn into a form of appropriation. He's not omnivorous, like Updike; the surfaces of whatever he's describing remain hard, resistant, rooted in the world, sitting on zippered plastic. He comes at the object in a rush, slyly generous, so eager to be impressed, and makes a quick, darting pass. Then he comes back and makes another pass. The method is accumulative, the perceptions renewed, revised, restated, reaffirmed. The narrator fixes Sorella in his mind at different stages of her life, and she grows, in all her dismaying bulk and pretension, into an increasingly bold and dignified figure. Sorella "made you look twice at a doorway. When she came to it, she filled the space like a freighter in a canal lock." Yet this cargo vessel made a good marriage, converted humiliation into strength. Rather than being a "merely square fat lady from the dark night of petty-bourgeois New Jersey," she was, in fact, "a spirited woman, at home with ideas." So armed, Sorella goes into battle for her husband.

The central anecdote of the story, one of Bellow's funniest ideas, seems far-fetched at first, but its eccentricity yields a surprising richness of thematic association. Having fled from Poland to Italy at the outbreak of the war, Fonstein was arrested by the fascist police and was about to be turned over to the S.S. Whereupon he was freed from an Italian prison by none other than Billy Rose. Billy Rose, the producer? Yes, the very same: Broadway Billy, husband of Fanny Brice, stager of pageants and patriotic Aquacades, art collector, Jewish entrepreneur and sexual fool, with a talent for humiliation at the hands of giggling chorus girls. Billy Rose had used his money and his mob connections in Italy to save a number of Jews. Italians working for him announced that they were coming from "Bellarosa."

After spending the remainder of the war in Cuba, Fonstein entered the United States, married Sorella, and for years tried to express his gratitude to Billy. Rose, however, refused to see him or acknowledge him in any way. But Sorella, who talks of the Holocaust constantly (oppressing the narrator with her knowledge), will not accept Billy's decision. The drama of the story, and nothing less than the situation of the Jews in America, unfolds from Billy's inexplicable stubbornness.

Portraiture in Bellow's work is always witty, a natural exercise of the muscular vivacity of his mind. He cannot write a dull or humorless account of any human being, and his description of Billy—an up-from-the-gutter Jewish boy observed by another Jewish boy with unillusioned wonder—turns into a dramatic debate between disgust and amazement:

> There was a penny-arcade jingle about Billy, the popping of shooting galleries, the weak human cry of the Times Square geckos, the lizard gaze of sideshow freaks. To see him as he was, you have to place him against the whitewash glare of Broadway in the wee hours. But even such places have their grandees—people whose defects can be converted to seed money for enterprises. There's nothing in this country that you can't sell, nothing too weird to bring to market and found a fortune on. And once you got as much major real estate as Billy had, then it didn't matter that you were one of the human deer that came uptown from the Lower East Side to graze on greasy sandwich papers. Billy? Well, Billy had bluffed out mad giants like Robert Moses. He bought the Ziegfeld building for peanuts. He installed Eleanor Holm in a mansion and hung the walls with masterpieces.

Only an American could have written this extraordinary passage, and perhaps only Americans can understand it. Bellow goes well past the amused distaste of a cultivated Jew who doesn't need to be awed by Billy Rose's money. Billy, as Bellow develops the character, may be nasty, self-justifying, greedy, vain, dishonest, status-obsessed—a worm. And yet, and yet . . . Big money and big success can never be entirely ludicrous. Or *merely* ludicrous. The passage expresses a rueful acceptance of the vitality and the power of vulgarity.

Like God leading Israel out of Egypt, Billy committed an act of rescue. But then, eager to escape the "Jewish blues," he turned away from the objects of his beneficence; he escapes into deals, publicity, an art collection, women. He's the assimilated American Jew as clown, a shrewd man nevertheless driven to humble himself before slender, Palmolive chorus girls who undress for him and then taunt his "unheroic privates." This man seeking humiliation wouldn't dream of sitting down for ten minutes with a fellow Jew. According to the celebrity caste system Billy lives by, Fonstein is an untouchable. Anyway, having received help once, Fonstein might ask for it again. He might think he had a claim to it.

The elements of the Billy Rose rescue operation are concocted, I assume, out of rumor and hearsay enlarged by ironic fantasy. In any case, the reality of these events is not at issue, only their value as American myth. What could Billy's decision mean? And why pursue him to change it? Of all possible failures of the spirit, the refusal to accept gratitude hardly seems one of the worst. Bellow doesn't spell out the significance of it, but Sorella's solemn persistence points the way. A man who refuses gratitude won't acknowledge a bond with another human being—as if having given someone something, you've soiled your hands on him, and he's become a lesser being forever. To a woman of such outsized pride, the slight is repellent in its implications.

At the peak of her audacity, Sorella threatens to blackmail Billy into meeting her husband by dangling before him some compromising journals that have fallen into her possession, journals that form a record of Billy's sexual activities and business dealings, his humiliations and defeats. This time his refusal attains the level of outraged principle. "Even a geek," he exclaims, "has his human rights." Thus speaks democratic man. But there's some grandeur in his stubbornness. What famous man would not lose heart at the thought of *that* kind of public exposure?

The comedy of *The Bellarosa Connection* is generated precisely by its improbability, the forced yoking of this extreme of American-Jewish shallowness with a woman so powerfully representing the moral sorrows of the ages. One wonders, however, if Bellow hasn't forced himself to suppress all criticism of his heroine. Blackmail, even blackmail of a worm, is a low and desperate act, a use of memory as vengeance. Yet Bellow speaks only of Sorella's courage and resourcefulness. In other ways, it is a familiar face-off, another of Bellow's confrontations between intellectuals and gangsters, between mind and will (with the latter usually gaining the advantage). In this case, each Jew is a negation of the other. The struggle, as the narrator remembers it, ends in victory for Billy. Refused again, the Fonsteins disappear into the rest of their lives.

In his recent short fiction, Bellow has perfected a method of narrative suspension in which an entire life is encompassed, through expansion and disgression, in a day or two of time. He packs the richness and the jostling philosophical ambition of a novel into these stories. In **"What Kind of a Day Did You Have?"** Victor Wulpy, shaken by loneliness, summons his lovable bourgeois mistress Katrina Wolliger, who lives in Chicago, to meet him in Buffalo, so that she can fly back with him to Chicago, where he has to give a lecture to some corporate executives. Together they endure a bruising, jangled American travel day, filled with odd encounters and fragmentary conversations in airplanes, hotels, bars, and restaurants. Arrogant Victor is nearing the end, but there's no dying fall here; his life, despite all its physical difficulties, continues at its long-sustained zenith. Victor suffers a spasm of loneliness, but not of weakness. The story overflows with an emotion scarcely imaginable in our clownishly self-deprecatory media society: true intellectual pride.

Bellow's habits of suspension almost enforce prolonged savoring of "higher types" (and higher lower types, like Billy). In *The Bellarosa Connection,* the narrator's pleasure in telling the strange story is part of the engaging sideways movement of the piece. He keeps coming back to the oddity of his material, recasting it, turning it this way and that.

The failure of the Fonstein-Billy connection, it turns out, is an intensified version of the generally botched or broken connections among Jews in America. In **"Cousins"** (also from *Him with His Foot in His Mouth*), Bellow's narrator announces, "I absolutely agree with Hegel (lectures at Jena, 1806) that the whole mass of ideas that have been current until now, 'the very bonds of the world,' are dissolving and collapsing like a vision in a dream." Hegel undoubtedly meant the end of feudal and religious bonds, but Bellow stretches it to include the dissolution of sustained relations, the development in its place of the awful American isolation ("individualism"). More is at fault than inadequate sociability: America drives people apart and makes them trivial, too. "The pursuit of loneliness," as Philip Slater called it.

In *The Bellarosa Connection,* the Old World Jews (and Sorella, generically, is one of them), brought up in grief, can never give up their obsession with dignity and obligation, while the New World Jews are moving too fast to allow themselves to be hindered by any claims at all. The memory expert and his Philadelphia-socialite wife found the Fonsteins depressing; Sorella's harping on the details of the Holocaust implanted information that would remain in the narrator's memory for life. He doesn't want to hear this stuff, any more than does Billy Rose, whom Bellow associates with George Washington, the American Adam himself, advising against "entangling alliances." The narrator drops the Fonsteins, and when he tries to find them years later, he discovers that other manual relatives have also lost track of them.

Depressed, he has a nightmare that reveals to him the tenuousness of civilized life. As a protected American, he could not understand, as the Fonsteins certainly did, the inescapable nature of merciless brutality. Yet he can't discuss this with anyone but *them.* A fitting punishment. He is not, it turns out, like a novelist. A professional of recall, he has developed methods of retrieving information in functional, neutral chains; he has divorced memory from meaning, never understanding (until it is too late) the purpose of memory. The end of his life is haunted by this woman whose memories never escape meaning.

The final pages are a little rushed; the ironies are jammed together too harshly. But this eccentric story has a surprising force. Earlier Sorella had said, "The Jews could survive everything that Europe threw at them. I mean the lucky remnant. But now comes the next test—America. Can they hold their ground, or will the U.S.A. be too much for them?" The answer, in this story at least, is yes, it's too much. Realizing too late the meaning of his recollections of the Fonsteins, the memory expert asks God to remember them.

Several critics have suggested that Bellow's last two novels, *The Dean's December* and *More Die of Heartbreak,* have marked a falling off in his old age. *The Bellarosa Connection,* however, is a classic Bellow story. The rush of short declarative sentences—thought-tormented yet exuberant—produce a familiar excitement. Reading Bellow, one feels that he is writing at peril, as if he were going so hard and so fast that he would fly off the curve of his own momentum. At times, I have stopped myself from reading, anxiously wondering if he can possibly sustain the breakneck tempo. His mind is utterly exposed—there's no syntactical padding, none of the gracious furniture, the turnings, pauses, strategically placed pit stops for rest and regeneration shrewdly planted in a beautifully written long sentence.

A long sentence connects the world. Short sentences, normally, break it up. But such is Bellow's power for consecutive and multifaceted representation that he gives us a greater sense that the world is still *there* than anyone writing fiction in America. My question about age softening Bellow's responses to character now seems demeaning. He is generous because he is naive enough to write stories as if the world had some solidity, as if the words used to describe it still had some reference to courage and betrayal and the inescapable burden of human obligation. He remains an unfashionable great writer, a maximalist. (pp. 37-40)

> David Denby, "Memory in America," in The New Republic, *Vol. 202, No. 3911, January 1, 1990, pp. 37-40.*

Greg Johnson   (essay date 1991)

[*Johnson is an American novelist and critic. In the following excerpt, Johnson asserts that* The Bellarosa Connection *and* A Theft *demonstrate that "the novella is an ideal vehicle for Bellow's protean (if sometimes overzealous) talent."*]

For Bellow, as for James, the decision to explore the novella form is a happy one. Although Bellow is best known for such brilliant, sprawling novels as *The Adventures of Augie March* (1953) and *Herzog* (1964), some critics still consider his 1956 novella, *Seize the Day,* to be his finest book. Again like James, Bellow has an extraordinarily fertile imagination and an expansive prose style to which the shorter form seems ideally suited, allowing for the development of his ideas even as it restrains his tendency to digress. His two new novellas are no less ambitious or farranging than his longer works, attesting to his success in exploiting the genre's powerful economy of form.

In *A Theft,* Bellow has departed from his typical work in another significant way: it is his first major narrative to feature a woman as the central character. The protagonist, Clara Velde, is a "back-country" girl from the Midwest whose extraordinary abilities and force of character have thrust her into an executive position in the world of New York fashion. Bellow focuses on her romantic life: after several unsuccessful marriages, she finds herself still emotionally involved with her true love, Teddy Regler, a political expert and world traveler whose friends include Armand Hammer and Henry Kissinger. The complicated plot moves along briskly, focusing on the theft of Clara's emerald ring, an impulsive gift from Teddy during the heat of their first passion. The thief is a West Indian named Frederic, the boyfriend of a young woman Clara has hired to care for her three daughters. Clara has felt a maternal solicitude for this young woman, Gina Wegman, and the theft throws Clara into emotional chaos. Her repressed romantic longings, her sense of betrayal, her ambivalent attitude toward her identity as a powerful woman—all are brought to the fore by the theft of her cherished ring.

Much of this novella is devoted to exploring Clara's vivid personality, especially her intriguing blend of personal force and emotional vulnerability. Teddy Regler tells her bluntly: "I'd say that you were a strange case—a woman who hasn't been corrupted, who developed her own moral logic, worked it out independently by her own solar power and from her own feminine premises." But, in love with Teddy, Clara tells herself even more bluntly that "A real person understands how to cut losses, not let her whole life be wound around to the end by a single desire, because under it all is the uglitude of this one hang-up."

One of the most memorable characters in all of Bellow's work, Clara fights against a modern world that insists on "the insignificance of the personal factor." Bellow clarifies her passionate nature by detailing her relationships with several other women: her pragmatic Chinese-American confidante, Laura Wong; the au pair girl Gina, in whom Clara places far too much trust; and her own young daughter, Lucy, a "raw-boned, stubborn" child who shows Clara an early version of herself. In fact, the cast of characters in *A Theft* is uncomfortably large, including Clara's psychiatrist, her private detective, and her four husbands. There are some devious turns of the plot and many brief, truncated scenes, so that occasionally the novella suggests that a much longer novel is crying to get out. Yet Bellow gains much by deliberately concentrating his effects: we are spared the drawn-out intellectual discussions that padded *More Die of Heartbreak* (1986), and the depressed meanderings of *The Dean's December* (1982). Rather, the fast pacing and wry humor of *A Theft* frequently recall *Seize the Day,* whose hapless Tommy Wilhelm is even more vulnerable than the deeply feeling but indomitable Clara Velde.

The Bellarosa Connection, told in a similarly pithy but rambling fashion by an unnamed narrator, recalls the late John Gardner's complaint that Bellow writes essays that are cleverly disguised as fiction. The book is indeed a powerful meditation on the Holocaust, the history of the Jews, and the changing nature of the individual's relationship to culture; yet Bellow's skill in developing such themes in this compact form is reason enough to read the book.

The Bellarosa Connection is the story of the narrator's friendship with Harry Fonstein and his formidable wife, Sorella. During World War II, Fonstein was on the verge of deportation to a death camp when a rescue operation, organized by the infamous entertainment tycoon Billy Rose, saved him. Fonstein later succeeds as a businessman and becomes obsessed with the idea that he must thank Rose in person. As the years pass, however, Rose persistently refuses to see him. The narrator, fascinated by both Fonstein and his obese but confident "tiger wife," loses track of the couple in the 1940's but encounters them again in 1959, when they are staying at the King David hotel during a visit to Jerusalem. Coincidentally—and this story abounds in coincidence—Billy Rose is also there, about to donate an expensive monument to the Israelis. Fiercely loyal to her husband, Sorella has decided to blackmail Rose into agreeing to a fifteen-minute visit with him.

Unlike *A Theft,* this first-person narration seems spoken rather than written, brought to life by Bellow's trademark vernacular—pungent, colorful, yet deeply humane. For example, here is his narrator's description of Rose: "Billy Rose wasn't big; he was about the size of Peter Lorre. But oh! he was American. There was a penny-arcade jingle about Billy, the popping of shooting galleries, the rattling of pinballs, the weak human cry of the Times Square geck-os, the lizard gaze of sideshow freaks. To see him as he was, you have to place him against the whitewash glare of Broadway in the wee hours."

Although it could be argued that the premise of *The Bellarosa Connection* strains credibility, being both too flimsy and too outlandish to sustain its rather ponderous themes, Bellow might respond that he is writing, after all, about America—where a vulgar and somewhat shady character like Billy Rose becomes a modern version of the Jewish hero, and where the phrase "flimsy and outlandish" accurately describes the cultural topography. This ironic reimagining of the Jewish immigrant experience is a quintessentially American work, a tragicomic story that explores both the legacy of the Holocaust and the vibrant energies of Jewish-American culture. Like *A Theft,* it proves that the novella is an ideal vehicle for Bellow's protean (if sometimes overzealous) talent. (pp. 365-67)

Greg Johnson, "Novellas for the Nineties," in The Georgia Review, *Vol. XLV, No. 2, Summer, 1991, pp. 363-71.*

Rita D. Jacobs (essay date 1992)

[*In the review below, Jacobs offers a favorable assessment of Bellow's novellas collected in* Something to Remember Me By.]

Although at times his preface to *Something to Remember Me By,* a collection of three stories, reads like an apology for their brevity, Bellow does make a trenchant point that serves as a fitting leitmotiv for these pieces. After noting that "the modern reader is perilously overloaded," he alludes to a woman mentioned in Kafka's diaries who holds herself below the level of her true human destiny and requires only the tearing open of the door. Indeed, these stories, brief as they are, tear open doors as Bellow sharply limns humanity at its fullest and most complex.

In the first of the stories, more a novella actually, *The Bellarosa Connection,* Bellow is on familiar territory. Writing from the point of view of a nameless, now retired former head of the fictional Mnemosyne Institute, he relates the history of Fonstein, the narrator's relative, who was rescued from the war by Billy Rose, the compact impresario. Fonstein achieved success in America, married a remarkable if not attractive woman, and never got over the fact that he did not get to thank Rose for his kindness. Though these are the bare facts of the story, its core is deeper. Bel-

low is again in the business of fathoming human experience: how does memory function and how do we process it? It is no accident that the narrator founded an institute for memory, and indeed he finds himself more plagued than pleased by his mnemonic abilities.

In *A Theft* Bellow plays a bit more with narrative style, casting large sections of the story in Clara Velde's voice. In Clara, Bellow has created a full-blooded female character, drawn with sympathy and understanding as well as a bit of disdain. It is as though Bellow can now truly round out his earlier woman, strong and smart like Madeleine and Ramona in *Herzog* but never fully realized on the page. Of course, Clara is not happy. She is rich enough, married for the fourth time and the mother of three girls, but is still infatuated with an early love, a highly intellectual man whom she never managed to marry but with whom she maintains a friendship. *A Theft* is a type of bildungsroman. Clara comes of age as, through an epiphany, she comes to understand her environs and her life.

Even next to the strength of these pieces, the shortest story, *Something to Remember Me By,* is superb. A fictional memoir, the piece is a legacy from a father to a son, a tale that could not have been told to a child and has had to wait. The subject? Sexual awakening. Once again a memory piece, but a much more immediate and less diffuse one than the first selection, this is also a coming-of-age tale about a sheltered, awkward, and intellectual high-school senior. Bellow's ability to evoke eroticism here is a delightful surprise. Less surprising and equally gratifying is the way in which he captures the very particular quality of one life while revealing that such particularity is true for every life. *Something to Remember Me By* is a very welcome addition to Bellow's already rich contribution to American fiction.

Rita D. Jacobs, in a review of "Something to Remember Me By," in World Literature Today, *Vol. 66, No. 4, Autumn, 1992, p. 721.*

John Sutherland (essay date 1992)

[*Sutherland is a Scottish playwright and critic. In the review below, he comments on Bellow's return to the novella form in* Something to Remember Me By.]

This hardback collection of three short stories [*Something to Remember Me By*] reverses normal publishing sequence. The two longer items are already available [in paper back]. . . . It is for the purchaser to decide whether a six-page "Foreword", thirty-five pages of the title-story (considerably shorter than its two reprinted companions), hard covers, and a handsome dust-jacket (featuring a sepia 1930s Chicago townscape) are worth £6.99.

For anyone wanting to make sense of the novelist's later career, the answer is yes. Brief in itself, Saul Bellow's preface is a powerful defence of his recent turn to Chekhovian brevity. Bellow (who is in strongly reminiscent mood nowadays) recalls the severe instruction of his primary school teacher, "Miss Ferguson, the lively spinster":

> Be
> specif-
> ic!

As he candidly admits, in his early years—grappling with the Great American Novel—Saul did not heed Miss Ferguson's anathemas against "redundancy, prolixity, periphrasis, or bombast". He wrote "more than one fat book" and, one might add, it was those fat books that won him his profession's highest accolade, the Nobel Prize in 1976. But now times have changed. A novelist's highest reach is no longer high. "On the front page of this morning's national edition of *The New York Times,* Michael Jackson, with hundreds of millions of fans worldwide, has signed a new contract worth a billion with Sony. . . . A new novel is reviewed on page B2." In order to return to front-page status, Bellow argues, fiction has to strive against MTV and Jackson's "ten-second bites" for Pepsi; the novelist must compete with the barrage of daily news elsewhere on the *Times* front page—"the Middle East, Japan, South Africa, reunified Germany, oil, munitions, the New York subways [a little provincial, this], the homeless, the markets, the banks, the major leagues, news from Washington: and also, pell mell, films, trials, medical discoveries, rap groups, racial clashes, congressional scandals, the spread of AIDS, child murders." The modern reader is "perilously overloaded. . . . Public life in the United States is a mass of distractions." No longer can the novelist range in the endless expanse of what V. S. Pritchett called the "Russian day". At best, he or she can hope for a New York quarter of an hour. The writer in tune with the time "will trouble no one with his own vanities, will make no unnecessary gestures, indulge himself in no mannerisms, waste no reader's time. He will write as short as he can." As the comically overstuffed syntax of that sentence indicates, it remains a struggle for Bellow, even at his most well-meaning, to repress his natural verbosity. Miss Ferguson's ferule must be twitching somewhere on the other side.

Brief in itself, Saul Bellow's preface to the novellas collected in *Something to Remember Me By* is a powerful defence of his recent turn to Chekhovian brevity. . . . He admits to having written "more than one fat book" and, one might add, it was those fat books that won him his profession's highest accolade, the Nobel Prize in 1976. But now times have changed. . . . The writer in tune with the time "will trouble no one with his own vanities, will make no unnecessary gestures, indulge himself in no mannerisms, waste no reader's time. He will write as short as he can."

—John Sutherland

Bellow's apologia explains much about the two reprinted stories. As Robert Boyers perceptively noted (although he

did not entirely approve), *A Theft* is written in a "novelistic shorthand". Its content (effectively, the story of an unusual woman's four marriages) could easily fill one of the author's fat books; instead, by ellipsis, omission, and artful insubstantiality, *A Theft* is turned into a novella—a thirty-minute reading bite. So too with *The Bellarosa Connection,* whose action covers forty years of complex human relationships and the legacy of the Holocaust for American Jewish culture. Heavy stuff, in short. But the new item in the collection, *Something to Remember Me By,* is surprisingly different. Dedicated by Bellow "To my Children and Grandchildren", it takes the form of an intimate memoir from "Grandfather Louie" (a thin veil for the author, we apprehend) for his children and grandchildren as "a sort of addition to your legacy". On a Chicago winter's day in February 1933, young Louie had his (hilarious) sexual initiation while his mother lay dying. The escapade resulted in a reconciliation through violence with his father. It is important that Louie's own offspring should know that relations with parents are strange, yet indicative of "the truth of the universe". *Something to Remember Me By* is a gem. For humour, profundity and, one must admit, uncharacteristic brevity, it will rank high in Bellow's achievement when the final reckoning comes. The tone of the tale implies that the author does not think that such reckoning will be too long delayed.

John Sutherland, "Miss Ferguson's Twitching Ferule," in The Times Literary Supplement, *No. 4675, November 6, 1992, p. 20.*

FURTHER READING

Criticism

Chavkin, Allan. " 'The Hollywood Thread' and the First Draft of Saul Bellow's *Seize the Day.*" *Studies in the Novel* XIV, No. 1 (Spring 1982): 82-94.

> Analyzes scattered versions of Bellow's novella, originally titled "One of Those Days," collected at the Humanities Research Center of the University of Texas at Austin.

Ciancio, Ralph. "The Achievement of Saul Bellow's *Seize the Day.*" In *Literature and Theology,* edited by Thomas F. Staley and Lester F. Zimmerman, pp. 49-80. Tulsa, Okla.: University of Tulsa, 1969.

> Focuses on religious and metaphysical issues in *Seize the Day.*

Costello, Patrick. "Tradition in *Seize the Day.*" *Essays in Literature* XIV, No. 1 (Spring 1987): 117-31.

> Examines Bellow's critique in *Seize the Day* of three traditions—the work ethic, the American Dream, and the Jewish tradition—and argues that much of the novella's ambiguity is dispelled through an understanding of the latter.

Cronin, Gloria L. "Saul Bellow's Quarrel with Modernism in *Seize the Day.*" *Encyclia* 57 (1980): 95-102.

Investigates Bellow's departure from the Modernist tradition in *Seize the Day*.

Enright, D. J. "Exuberance Hoarding." *The Times Literary Supplement*, No. 4238 (22 June 1984): 688.

Generally appreciative review of *Him with His Foot in His Mouth, and Other Stories*.

Freedman, Ralph. "Saul Bellow: The Illusion of Environment." *Wisconsin Studies in Contemporary Literature* I, No. 1 (Winter 1960): 50-65.

Discusses Bellow's revival of the social novel in his early works, including *Seize the Day*.

Fuchs, Daniel. "Saul Bellow and the Modern Tradition." *Contemporary Literature* XV, No 1 (Winter 1974): 67-89.

Places Bellow's works within the postmodernist tradition, citing *Seize the Day* as Bellow's "most piercing study of alienation, of the depravity of bourgeois society—the radical's Bellow."

Giannone, Richard. "Saul Bellow's Idea of Self: A Reading of *Seize the Day*." *Renascence* XXVII, No. 4 (Summer 1975): 193-205.

Examines "the ways in which the self tries to establish a spiritual agreement with the outer world" in *Seize the Day*.

Guttmann, Allen. "Mr. Bellow's America." In his *The Jewish Writer in America: Assimilation and the Crisis of Identity*, pp. 198-201. New York: Oxford University Press, 1971.

Characterizes *Seize the Day* as "a cautionary tale" in which Tommy Wilhelm's downfall is attributable to his inability to accept his fate as an ordinary man among other average people.

Handy, William J. "Saul Bellow and the Naturalistic Hero." *Texas Studies in Literature and Language* V, No. 4 (Winter 1964): 538-45.

Discusses Bellow's social and moral treatment of the naturalistic theme of survival in *Seize the Day*.

———. "Bellow's *Seize the Day*." In his *Modern Fiction: A Formalist Approach*, pp. 119-30. Carbondale: Southern Illinois University Press, 1971.

Asserts that the narrative interest of *Seize the Day* arises from Tommy Wilhelm's "attempt to discover and evaluate himself first in terms of the values he held while growing up and the effect these values had on his present situation and then in terms of his present values and present relationships."

Jefchak, Andrew. "Family Struggles in *Seize the Day*." *Studies in Short Fiction* XI, No. 3 (Summer 1974): 297-302.

Explores Tommy Wilhelm's frustrated relationship with his father in *Seize the Day*.

Kazin, Alfred. "Bellow's Purgatory." *The New York Review of Books* X, No. 6 (28 March 1968): 32-6.

Examines Bellow's portrayal of the forces that destroy individuality in modern life in *Seize the Day*.

Klein, Marcus. "Saul Bellow: A Discipline of Nobility." In his *After Alienation: American Novels in Mid-Century*, pp. 33-70. Cleveland, Ohio: The World Publishing Company, 1962.

Documents the progress of Bellow's protagonists, including Tommy Wilhelm of *Seize the Day*, "from a position of alienation toward accommodation."

Mathis, James C. "The Theme of *Seize the Day*." *Critique:*

Studies in Modern Fiction VII, No. 3 (Spring-Summer 1965): 43-5.

Reflects on Bellow's untraditional treatment of the carpe diem theme.

Morahg, Gilead. "The Art of Dr. Tamkin: Matter and Manner in *Seize the Day*." *Modern Fiction Studies* 25, No. 1 (Spring 1979): 103-16.

Explores Bellow's attempt to imaginatively communicate philosophical ideas through the "elusive and enigmatic" character of Dr. Tamkin.

Opdahl, Keith Michael. "Come Then, Sorrow." In his *The Novels of Saul Bellow: An Introduction*, pp. 96-117. University Park: Pennsylvania State University Press, 1967.

Addresses the paradoxical ending of *Seize the Day*, in which Tommy Wilhelm is both drowned and reborn.

Porter, M. Gilbert. "*Seize the Day*: A Drowning Man." In his *Whence the Power?: The Artistry and Humanity of Saul Bellow*, pp. 102-26. Columbia: University of Missouri Press, 1974.

Examines "how the embodiment of theme in water imagery finds its larger objectification in individual scenes" that themselves "function like poetic images" in *Seize the Day*.

Richmond, Lee J. "The Maladroit, the Medico, and the Magician: Saul Bellow's *Seize the Day*." *Twentieth-Century Literature* 19, No. 1 (January 1973): 15-26.

Rejects Daniel Weiss's treatment of Dr. Tamkin (see excerpt dated 1962 above) as "cursory and misplaced" and emphasizes the importance of the character in *Seize the Day*.

Rodrigues, Eusebio. "Koheleth in Chicago: The Quest for the Real in 'Looking for Mr. Green'." *Studies in Short Fiction* XI, No. 4 (Fall 1974): 387-93.

Explores Bellow's treatment of the quest theme in "Looking for Mr. Green," which the critic lauds as "a minor classic of our time, a story that has the resonance that Joyce's 'The Dead' has, releasing ripples of concentric meanings that vanish into the mystery of an evocative silence."

———. "Reichianism in *Seize the Day*." In *Critical Essays on Saul Bellow*, edited by Stanley Trachtenberg, pp. 89-100. Boston: G. K. Hall & Co., 1979.

Explores the influence of Reichianism on *Seize the Day*.

Sicherman, Carol M. "Bellow's *Seize the Day*: Reverberations and Hollow Sounds." *Studies in the Twentieth Century* 15 (Spring 1975): 1-31.

Surveys Bellow's theme of "the breakdown of language as a common bond among men" in *Seize the Day*.

Spice, Nicholas. "Sensitive Sauls." *London Review of Books* 6, No. 12 (5-9 July 1984): 17.

Detailed review of *Him with His Foot in His Mouth*.

Towers, Robert. "Mystery Women." *The New York Review of Books* XXXVI, No. 7 (27 April 1989): 50, 52.

Review of three novels in which Towers scrutinizes Bellow's treatment of Clara Velde, protagonist of *A Theft*.

Wilson, Jonathan. "*Seize the Day*." In his *On Bellow's Planet: Readings from the Dark Side*, pp. 96-111. London and Toronto, Ontario: Associated University Presses, 1985.

Highlights Bellow's ambivalent treatment of character
in *Seize the Day*.

Additional coverage of Bellow's life and career is contained in the following sources
published by Gale Research: *Contemporary Authors,* Vols. 5-8, rev. ed.; *Contemporary
Authors New Revision Series,* Vol. 29; *Contemporary Authors Bibliographical Series,* Vol.
1; *Concise Dictionary of Literary Biography, 1941-1968; Contemporary Literary Criticism,*
Vols. 1, 2, 3, 6, 8, 10, 13, 15, 25, 33, 34, 63, 79; *DISCovering Authors; Dictionary of Literary
Biography,* Vols. 2, 28; *Dictionary of Literary Biography Documentary Series,* Vol. 3;
Dictionary of Literary Biography Yearbook: 1982; Major 20th-Century Writers; and
World Literature Criticism.]

Walter de la Mare

1873-1956

(Full name Walter John de la Mare; also wrote under the pseudonym Walter Ramal) English poet, novelist, short story writer, critic, essayist, anthologist, and playwright.

INTRODUCTION

De la Mare was one of the chief exemplars of the romantic imagination in modern literature. In his poetry and fiction, he explored such characteristic romantic concerns as dreams, death, and the fantasy worlds of childhood. Critics often focus on de la Mare's short fiction, especially his numerous tales of supernatural horror, as his most accomplished and enduring work.

De la Mare began writing short stories and poetry while working as a bookkeeper in the London offices of the Anglo-American (Standard) Oil Company during the 1890s. His first published short story, "Kismet," appeared in the journal *Sketch* in 1895. In 1902 he published his first major work, the poetry collection *Songs of Childhood,* which was recognized as a significant example of children's literature for its creative imagery and variety of meters. Critics often assert that a childlike richness of imagination influenced everything de la Mare wrote, emphasizing his frequent depiction of childhood as a time of intuition, deep emotion, and closeness to spiritual truth. In 1908, following the publication of his novel *Henry Brocken* and the poetry collection entitled *Poems,* de la Mare was granted a Civil List pension, enabling him to terminate his corporate employment and focus exclusively on writing. He died in 1956.

As a short story writer, de la Mare is frequently compared to Henry James, particularly for his elaborate prose style and his ambiguous, often obscure treatment of supernatural themes. This latter quality is particularly apparent in de la Mare's frequently discussed short story "The Riddle," in which seven children go to live with their grandmother after the death of their father. The grandmother warns the children that they may play anywhere in the house except in an old oak chest in one of the spare bedrooms. Nevertheless, the children are drawn by ones and twos to play in the trunk, where they mysteriously disappear. While the meaning of their disappearance remains enigmatic, commentators have generally interpreted the events as a symbolic presentation of aging and death.

Criticism of de la Mare's short stories often focuses on his characters, who are invariably peculiar and frequently attributed with demonic powers. Discussing de la Mare's characters, David Cecil has explained that there is "always something odd about them. . . . The children are queer children, with their demure manners and solemn eyes and heads buzzing with fancies; the bachelors and old

maids are solitary, eccentric, often a trifle crazy; the landladies and shopkeepers are 'character parts,' as full of grotesque idiosyncrasy as the personages of Dickens." Among the most memorable of these personages is the title character of "Seaton's Aunt." At the beginning of the story the narrator describes one of his schoolmates, Arthur Seaton, who lives with his aunt. The narrator accepts an invitation to visit Seaton's home, where he senses the intangible, though nonetheless threatening, power the boy's aunt has over him. Some years later Seaton invites the narrator to his aunt's house to meet his fiancée. The narrator experiences the same sense of menace that existed on his previous visit, and Seaton expresses his fear that something terrible is about to happen to him, presumably caused by his aunt. Several months afterward the narrator learns that Seaton has died under mysterious circumstances shortly before his wedding. The subtlety and artistry of this narrative are foremost among those literary qualities that account for de la Mare's high stature as an author of supernatural fiction. In addition, critics have praised de la Mare's adept rendering of uncanny subject matter using realistic narrative techniques. As Doris Ross McCrosson has observed: "De la Mare's settings are firmly anchored in reality, his characters are credible, and the situations in which they find themselves are easily possible. At least, this is so at the beginning of the tales; and, by the time de la Mare ventures into the incredible, the reader has, in Coleridge's phrase, willingly suspended disbelief."

PRINCIPAL WORKS

SHORT FICTION

The Riddle, and Other Stories   1923; also published as
    The Riddle, and Other Tales, 1923
Ding Dong Bell   1924; enlarged edition, 1936
Broomsticks, and Other Tales   1925
The Connoisseur, and Other Stories   1926
On the Edge   1930
The Wind Blows Over   1936
Collected Stories for Children   1947
The Collected Tales   1950
A Beginning, and Other Stories   1955
Eight Tales   1971

OTHER MAJOR WORKS

Songs of Childhood [as Walter Ramal]   (poetry)   1902
Henry Brocken   (novel)   1904
Poems   (poetry)   1906
The Return   (novel)   1910; revised editions 1922, 1945
The Three Mulla-Mulgars   (novel)   1910; also published as *The Three Royal Monkeys,* 1935
A Child's Day   (poetry)   1912
The Listeners, and Other Poems   (poetry)   1912
Peacock Pie   (poetry)   1913
Motley, and Other Poems   (poetry)   1918
Crossings   (drama)   1919
Memoirs of a Midget   (novel)   1921
The Veil, and Other Poems   (poetry)   1921
Down-Adown-Derry   (poetry)   1922
Stuff and Nonsense and So On   (poetry)   1922
The Captive, and Other Poems   (poetry)   1928
Poems for Children   (poetry)   1930
The Fleeting, and Other Poems   (poetry)   1933
This Year, Next Year   (poetry)   1937
Memory, and Other Poems   (poetry)   1938
Pleasures and Speculations   (essays)   1940
Bells and Grass   (poetry)   1941
The Burning Glass, and Other Poems   (poetry)   1945
Winged Chariot   (poetry)   1951
O Lovely England, and Other Poems   (poetry)   1953
Private View   (essays)   1953
The Collected Poems of Walter de la Mare   (poetry) 1979

CRITICISM

The Times Literary Supplement (essay date 1923)

[*In the following review of* The Riddle, and Other Stories, *the critic praises de la Mare's prose style and speculates that the thematic emphasis of the volume will not appeal to a wide range of readers.*]

Mr. de la Mare, as we all know, is convinced of the presence of the hidden things—things beautiful, queer, or horrible, which peep and haunt, states of eternity, other sides of the looking-glass. He has chosen to be the interpreter, in prose and poetry, of unearthliness; and one thing which distinguishes him from other writers of his time, besides the peculiarly haunting quality of his style, is that he believes this "otherness" to be more real than the "hereness" of which we are usually conscious. Complexes and neuroses interest him not at all—he will have nothing so paltry. For him those who are, in popular speech, "queer," even if unpleasantly so, are those who see and hear the crowd of hidden things which hedge us about in our blindness. He does not blench from them when they are horrible, as witness the story of **"Seaton's Aunt,"** the monstrous old woman, with her huge appetite and her sinister irony, who simply haunted her heir and nephew to his death; or **"Out of the Deep,"** in which a lonely man, precariously living in the gaunt house full of relics and memories of his uncle, summons by night strange visitors from a haunted basement—a butler, a child with a bowl of primroses, a loathly monster—and finally is found strangled with a cord in the attic. One may think such things as these morbid, or one may not: it is more a question of point of view than of literary criticism.

Naturally, Mr. de la Mare not infrequently uses a child's eyes which have not yet lost the "vision," and when he gives us such things as Arthur's impression of Miss Duveen, the insane old lady who lived on the other side of the stream to his grandmother's house, one may, while recognizing the power of suggestion, have scruples about its healthiness. The author's answer to such doubts, we imagine, would be that in these matters you cannot discriminate. Either you know or you do not: and if you know, you must tell. The reader [of *The Riddle, and Other Stories*] can test his own susceptibilities very quickly by turning to one of the shortest stories, called **"The Creatures,"** which is the relation by a chance fellow-traveller in a railway carriage how he found the gate of mystery, the gate that is "for ever ajar, into God knows what of peace and mystery."

> One late afternoon, in my goal-less wanderings, I had climbed to the summit of a steep grass-grown cart-track, winding up dustily between dense, untended hedges. Even then I might have missed the house to which it led, for, hair-pin fashion, the track here abruptly turned back on itself, and only a far fainter footpath led on over the hill-crest. I might, I say, have missed the house, and—and its inmates, if I had not heard the musical sound of what seemed like the twangling of a harp. This thin-drawn, sweet, tuneless warbling welled over the close green grass of the

height as if out of space. Truth cannot say whether it was of that air or of my own fantasy. Nor did I ever discover what instrument, whether of man or Ariel, had released a strain so pure and so bodiless.

If one can yield fully to the incantation of these musical spells, and go on, half in a dream, to read what the traveller found in the farmhouse of Trevarras, the dark long-faced gaunt man who spoke to the birds in whispers, the "creatures" themselves and their enchanted garden on the cliff, and if "a kind of mournful gaiety, a lamentable felicity, such as rings in the cadences of an old folksong" wells into one's heart, as into the traveller's, then one can travel easily with Mr. de la Mare. Then one can accept without question his odd narrators, with their affected, old-world speech, such as the Count of the first two stories, Seaton's aunt, or old Maunders, who tells, with quaint and almost intolerable divagations, the wonderful story of Lispet, Lispett and Vaine, the prehistoric firm of incomparable mercers, who fell into decay because Antony Lispett lost his heart to a fairy and would only make things to fit her diminutive proportions: then, though with a little more difficulty, one can accept the stilted language put into the mouth of little Selina, who fell into a maze of philosophical dreaming, as she knelt looking out of the window, about the similitude of the farmer and the disappointed fowls to God and humanity; and then too, even if one remain baffled by **"The Looking Glass,"** one will realize the beauty which Mr. de la Mare is seeking in **"The Bird of Travel"** and **"The Tree."** As a pure exercise in eerie suggestion this last is one of the best stories in the book. It tells how a hard old fruit merchant went down for the second time to see his brother, artist and dreamer, in whose garden grew a marvellous and exotic tree with its own bright birds, butterflies, and beetles, all strangers to this land, filling the life and inspiring the art of this neglected, starving artist; and at the second visit the tree was dead, and a dead face, lit by a lamp, looked out of the window. But one cannot judge this book by standards. Only those who feel an indescribable longing at times to get away from the present and the dwarfish presumption of what most people mean by life will realize its whole appeal. Others will admire Mr. de la Mare's mastery of language, but they will be a trifle cold to his message and his convictions.

"The Hidden Things," in The Times Literary Supplement, *No. 1113, May 17, 1923, p. 337.*

The Spectator   (essay date 1923)

[*In the following review of* The Riddle, and Other Stories, *the critic praises de la Mare's prose style and characterization.*]

Catlike, Mr. de la Mare's genius haunts places. Of the fifteen stories in [*The Riddle, and Other Stories*], only one can be said to lack his abnormally acute sense of house and home, and even that is not the tale of a wanderer. The travellers who set out "once upon a time, which is the memory of the imagination, rather than that of the workaday mind," and beheld afar off the monstrous Vats "slumbering in a grave, crystal light, which lapped, deep as the Tuscarora Trough, above and around their prodigious

stone plates, or slats, or slabs, or laminae"—these travellers did not pause to marvel and pass on; they stayed until their innermost beings were drained into those "crusted, butt-like domes of stone wherein slept Elixir Vitae, whose last echo had been the Choragium of the Morning Stars."

All Mr. de la Mare's characters are creatures of environment; sometimes, as in **"The Vats,"** hardly more than the sensitive plates upon which the physical and spiritual aspects of their surroundings are portentously engraved. For them, as for the mysterious stricken family in **"The Bird of Travel,"** absenteeism, betrayal of their territorialism, means death. They have no significant or even safe existence apart from the bricks and mortar, the narrow compass of wood and field and garden, which are habitual to them and which hold their lives in fee. They are not always safe then.

Of course, Mr. de la Mare's people advance, often disturbingly, from their shadowy background. Seaton's Aunt, for instance. Never very good to live in, her house would have been at any rate habitable but for her. She is the most considerable figure in the book, but she is a fiend, sucking her nephew's life, appropriating his vitality his thoughts, even his appetite. Though in a different setting and differently treated, it is the same theme that Henry James worked out with such prodigious intricacy in *The Sacred Fount*. There it is merely a psychological problem and an arid one; it wants the supernatural element, the turn of the screw that makes **"Seaton's Aunt"** so effective. James's ghosts are moral obliquities of such intensity and persistence that they take visible shape; de la Mare's may be injurious, but their wickedness is not their chief quality, certainly not their *raison d'être*. They are not local or at odds with reality, they are part and parcel of the author's mind, the condition of his work, his medium, as they were Hawthorne's. When, as in **"The Count's Courtship,"** de la Mare declines their ministrations (the issue being so palpably between human desire and its frustration), his peculiar quality is compromised, and the story, the fullest to all appearance of human interest, is also the least successful in the book.

Of its treasures of phrase and fancy, its incomparably responsive and appropriate prose rhythms, it is needless to speak; they are inseparable from Mr. de la Mare's work and make every page a joy. Always idiomatic, but never archaic, his prose has a life of its own, a quality of hard flexibility. His characters are uncompromising too, incisive in their utterance as they are determined in their dealings; even in the minds of avowedly muddle-headed persons like Miss Duveen and Sarah ideas tinkle like tintacks. Sarah prepares poor Alice for her vigil:—

> "Anyhow, fast you must, like the Catholics, and you with a frightful hacking cough and all. Come like a new begotten bride you must in a white gown, and a wreath of lilies or rorringe blossom in your hair, same pretty much as I made for my mother's coffin this twenty years ago, and which I wouldn't do now not for respectability even. And me and my mother, let me tell you, were as close as hens in a roost. . . ."

Symbolism never makes for clarity, and in some of the stories, **"The Bird of Travel,"** for instance, where Mr. de la Mare has loaded every rift with ore, the central idea is hard to disentangle. It does not readily reveal itself in **"The Riddle,"** that strange story of seven children who went to stay with their grandmother and, despite her warning, were drawn in their play to inspect an old chest in which, by ones and twos, they ultimately disappeared. An exasperating air of lucidity and guilelessness distinguishes this baffling little tale. But it must not be thought that Mr. de la Mare deals solely in conundrums. More surely, perhaps, than any living writer he is able to invest a familiar or unfamiliar object with terrifying significance, the significance of a nightmare to a child, by virtue of which the object is isolated from experience and yet endued with all its horrors. The Vats have this quality, in spite of Mr. de la Mare's assertion that they ingeminated peace. The Tree has it even more. Not solely from its association with the criminal genius, who sketched it a thousand times and then killed it. Not from the suggestion that it would prove his gallows-tree. A hundred stray touches beside the great formal description print it on our minds, not as the huge cloudy symbol of a high romance, but as something threatening and deadly, something which even as we read an atavistic instinct warns us against, so that we would gladly shut the image from our minds:—

> Solitary, unchallenged, exotic in its station all but at the foot of the broken-hedged, straggling garden, it rose to heaven a prodigious spreading, ascendant cone, with its long, dark green, pointed leaves. It stood from first springing branch to apex, a motionless and somnolent fountain of flowers . . . you might have supposed . . . the thing had sprung up by sheer magic out of the ground.

The Riddle is a book which every lover of poetry and every student of style must make it his business (as it will certainly be his pleasure) to read; it has a quality unique in contemporary fiction. (pp. 930-31)

A review of "The Riddle, and Other Stories," in The Spectator, *Vol. 130, No. 4953, June 2, 1923, pp. 930-31.*

Edwin Muir   (essay date 1923)

[*Muir was a distinguished Scottish novelist, poet, critic, and translator. With his wife, Willa, he translated works by such German-language authors as Gerhart Hauptmann, Hermann Broch, and, most notably, Franz Kafka. Throughout his career, Muir was intrigued by psychoanalytic theory, particularly Freud's analyses of dreams and Jung's theories of archetypal imagery, both of which he often utilized in his work. In his critical writings, Muir was more concerned with the general philosophical issues raised by works of art—such as the nature of time or society—than with the particulars of the work itself, such as style or characterization. In the following review of* The Riddle, and Other Tales, *he comments on what he views as the decadent qualities of de la Mare's short stories and praises several pieces in the volume.*]

I call Mr. Walter de la Mare an unwilling decadent be-

cause, after reading his latest volume of short stories [*The Riddle, and Other Tales*], I have been struck with the wealth of decadent inspiration in them; decadent inspiration thwarted at every turn, not by a contrary artistic impulse, but, what was surely not worth while, by sheer respectability. He has a capacity for evoking horror with a hint of bestiality in it: like all decadents he sees fissures in the countenances of ordinary people and ordinary events which let in that unconscious terror which is one of the most fundamental nihilistic doubts which can be thrown upon life; he has even the minor attributes of the decadent—a preference for whatever is fragile rather than robust in the beautiful, and an excessively decorative style. I select two quotations at random to show the completeness of his equipment as a decadent writer. "And like the draperies of a proscenium, the fringed and valanced damask curtains on either side of the two high windows poured down their motionless cataract of crimson." Has not that an extravagant opulence which one might expect to find in Wilde? "And as Mr. Sully stood for an instant in close contact with his old crony in the accentuated darkness of the mock-marble porch, it was just as if a scared rabbit had scurried out of Mr. Eave's long white face." Does not that give genuinely the horror of a decadent vision of life, a vision no doubt true, but one-sided, morbid? This horror is accentuated by Mr. de la Mare's selection of characters; there is a disproportionate number with long white faces, a type which obviously interests the author. Finally, his themes are such as only a decadent writer would have chosen. There is a study of Miss Duveen, a poor, insane creature; of Mrs. Seaton, who is evil to the verge of insanity; of Jimmie, who lives precariously on the edge of madness; of a painter, also almost mad, who is gradually corrupted by the malignant power of a strange tree in his garden which he paints again and again and at last destroys; of Mr. Eave, who dreams "every blessed night" that the "state after death" is "just the same," and who dies in his sleep. There, one can see at a glance, is real matter for the inspiration of a decadent artist; and Mr. de la Mare uses it indeed with extraordinary skill and force.

With decadence in art, as long as it is sincere, no one today will quarrel very much; it is for all of us a new light on the puzzle of life, and its sincerity (as long as it is sincere) is the best safeguard against its working moral harm. Baudelaire was a great writer in whom we can not but admire the honesty with which he followed his morbid genius. Poe was all but a great writer, and it would take, all things considered, a very illiberal critic or a very blind moralist to throw stones at him. There is nothing æsthetically displeasing in the morbidity of these writers; but in Mr. de la Mare's morbidity there is something æsthetically displeasing.

It is the conjunction of his decadent vision of life with a strict respectability, almost with a sort of comfortableness. We know that in a writer who sees things to the last degree baffling and horrible behind the reassuring appearances of life, respectability must be either a mask or a weakness; and that feeling Mr. de la Mare's work does give one. It is strange that an artist so sensitive should leave an impression of almost Victorian insensitiveness, of that insensitiveness which can, in comfort, let its flesh creep rather than be more humanly moved by the last extremes of occult psychological horror. Presented thus insensitively, the horrible loses half its force, loses all its meaning, and almost all its beauty. Horror, we know, when we are not deceived by artificial modes, is indecent, and the writer who presents it decently offends us twice over; so that Mr. de la Mare's morbidity and respectability conjoin to produce an atmosphere far more unpleasant than that of pure horror, an atmosphere more stuffy and more graveyard-like than any other writer has achieved since the Victorian era. His scenes are sometimes like nothing more than a curious mixture of Wilkie Collins and Dostoievsky. He loses half the beauty of his vision by his respectability, his narrowness of mind, his stuffiness. It is a pity; for the things he has done brilliantly can not be done supremely well except by a writer frankly decadent.

Yet after all these criticisms have been made, the book remains one of the few of our time which will be read by one or two more generations. There are three stories in it, indeed, which may well take their place among the best short stories of modern times. **"Seaton's Aunt"** is an immensely skilful exercise in atmosphere, with a genuine evocation of occult horror; **"Out of the Deep"** is, except for an irritating opening, almost as good; and the study of the insane old woman in **"Miss Duveen"** is the best thing in the book. Mr. de la Mare's prose style, if a little overloaded for good prose, is always finished and sometimes beautiful. There are lapses from the general excellence he has attempted: the first two stories are sentimental with a lusciousness which most people to-day must find difficult to stomach. **"Lispet, Lispett and Vaine"** is tiresome, false, with a continuous attempt to be arch, which, even if it does not come off, is very trying; and **"The Three Friends"** is simply a pretty, gruesome idea nicely dished up. But the three tales I have mentioned have greater truth and beauty than Mr. de la Mare has ever achieved in poetry. His genius is unmistakable, although it has been half-smothered under the weight of a belated Victorianism; but one feels that in happier circumstances it might have made him a writer of the rank of Poe. (pp. 620-21)

Edwin Muir, "An Unwilling Decadent," in The Freeman, New York, Vol. VII, No. 182, September 5, 1923, pp. 620-21.

What is unusual in de la Mare is partly the depth of his liberalism. Almost nothing is condemned, and there is more than a touch of fatalism in his emphasis on the necessity of people behaving in the curious ways they do.

—David Punter in his The Literature of Terror, 1980.

P. C. Kennedy   (essay date 1925)

[*In the following review, Kennedy criticizes the stories collected in* Broomsticks, and Other Tales *as inferior children's fiction.*]

Mr. de la Mare suffers, like Mr. Thomas Hardy, from a cult, from a legend of infallibility, so that everything he does exercises a sort of hypnotic influence on the public, and is welcomed and admired without any reference to its merits. These two writers, Mr. Hardy and Mr. de la Mare, have always displayed a noble indifference to popularity; they have gone their own ways, truckling to no habit, creed, convention or expectation; and the public, recognising the magnificence of those who despise its judgments, has responded with idolatry. But idolatry, however comforting and inspiring it may be to the idolaters, is grossly unfair to the idols. We recognise that a good deal of the work of the greatest—a good deal of Wordsworth, a good deal of Byron, a noticeable proportion even of Shakespeare—is æsthetically worthless: we have no right to refuse the tribute of the same discrimination to Mr. Hardy or Mr. de la Mare. Mr. de la Mare is a poet, a great poet. It does not follow that all his verse is excellent. It certainly does not follow that he is a master of prose. It is an interesting speculation what would have been made of **Broomsticks** if it had been published as by John Jones.

We are told by the publishers that these stories are for children. It is a high claim, which I can find little in the stories themselves to justify. If there is one thing which a writer for children must not be, it is arch: and Mr. de la Mare is quite dreadfully arch. In **"Pigtails, Ltd.,"** which begins the book, an old lady has the illusion that she has lost a child, and she adopts a number of children in consequence. And this is how we are told about that illusion:

> How *could* Miss Rawlings ever have lost a little girl if there had never been any little girl to lose? Yet that exactly was Miss Rawlings' idea. It had flitted into her imagination like a nimble, bright-feathered bird. And once it was really there, she never hesitated to talk about it; not at all. "My little girl, you know," she'd say, with an emphatic nod and a pleasant smile on her broad face. Or rather, "My little gal"—for she always pronounced the word as if it rhymed with Sal, the short for Sarah. This, too, was an odd thing; for Miss Rawlings had been brought up by her parents with the very best education, and seldom mispronounced even such words as "Chloe" or "Psyche" or "epitome" or "misled." And so far as I know—though that is not very far—there is hardly a word of one syllable in our enormous language (except shall and pal) that is pronounced like Sal; for Pall Mall, of course, is pronounced Pell Mell. Still, Miss Rawlings did talk about her little girl, and she called her her little gal.

This is apparently meant for children who are very young, since children with their adolescent wits about them would be almost certain to resent being talked down to in this playful fashion. Yet, a few pages further on, we find a Harley Street specialist commenting on the case of Miss Rawlings in these remarkable words: "I once had a patient. . . . who had the amiable notion that she was the

Queen of Sheba and that I was King Solomon." This bit is presumably designed for children of a larger growth, children familiar with the psychology of frustrated sex—which is not yet, I believe, a prescribed subject in schools. This double thread runs right through. There is a long fantastic tale called **"A Nose,"** which appears to have a moral, or several morals: it is about a man whose nose is supposed to be of wax, but, after he has for the best part of a lifetime moulded and limited his activities on that supposition, turns out to be an ordinary nose after all, and indeed a conspicuously handsome one. "Somehow his long years of seclusion, far from souring his nature, had left his inward temper queer but sweet"; and "time at last heals every wound which is not kept open by attention or hatred." Is that the sort of allegory, is this the sort of moralising, which really commends itself to children? And in **"Miss Jemima,"** an interesting tale in itself, there is a sort of fairy presence, thus described:

> If you can imagine a figure—even now I cannot tell you how tall she was—that seems to be made of the light of rainbows, and yet with every feature in its flaxen-framed face as clearly marked as a cherub's cut in stone; and if you can imagine a voice coming to you, close into your ear, without your being able to say exactly where it is coming *from—that* was what I saw and heard beneath that grey roof down there on that distant morning, seventy-five years ago.

Is there magic in that? Is there even ordinary vision? "Every feature in its flaxen-framed face as clearly marked as a cherub's cut in stone"!

Much less important, but not negligible in a book designed for children, is the question of grammar. Mr. de la Mare (and I confess this flabbergasts me) has not even taken the trouble to write with the correctness which would be exacted from a boy or girl in the fourth form. He says: "Being an only child, his mother treasured him beyond words"; and "strangers in outlandish guise whom he suspected at once must be princes and noblemen from foreign climes"; and "She advanced into the room, and, with her own hand, lay before him on the oak table beside his silver platter, first the nibbled apple, next the golden ball, and last the silken cord"; and "The ass whom you tell me is hearkening at the moment to all that passes between us."

To turn to a brighter side of the picture—here is a passage, typical of many, which I should think worthy of Mr. de la Mare if my admiration of him did not considerably exceed that manifested by most of his admirers:

> How crisscross a thing is the heart of man. Solely because this lord loved his daughter so dearly, if ever she so much as sighed for change and adventure, like some plodding beast of burden he would set his feet together and refuse to budge an inch. Beneath his louring brows he would gaze at the brightness of her unringleted hair as if mere looking could keep that gold secure; as if earth were innocent of moth and rust and change and chance, and had never so much as hearkened after the restless footfall of Time.

That is not magical writing; but it has rhythm in it, and character, and situation. The story in which it occurs,

"The Lovely Myfanwy," is a good story; so is **"Broomsticks"** itself, and there are beautiful moments in **"Lucy."** Altogether, this would be a remarkable book if it had been written by John Jones. But it wasn't. It was written by a man of genius, a man with one of the rarest and loftiest and most sensitive minds of our time; and to pretend to find every page of it, or even the general effect of it, worthy of him, is not compliment but depreciation. If you want to measure how far short it falls of what a book about fairies and for children, a book of dreams and moralities, should be, take down your Hans Andersen. Set the worst page of Hans Andersen against the best page of Mr. de la Mare! It may be said that this is a cruelly hard comparison, since Hans Andersen is the greatest of all storytellers, as indisputably as Shakespeare is the greatest of dramatists or Homer of epic poets. Nevertheless I insist on making the comparison; it is the measure of my reverence for Mr. de la Mare—and of my conviction that his genius is here on the wrong tack.

> *P. C. Kennedy, in a review of "Broomsticks, and Other Tales," in* New Statesman, *Vol. XXVI, No. 659, December 12, 1925, p. 273.*

Edward Davison · (essay date 1926)

[*In the following review, Davison praises several of the stories collected in* The Connoisseur *as masterpieces.*]

Mr. de la Mare's conversion from verse to imaginative prose-fiction is one portentous sign of our literary times. Until a few years ago, although he had always furnished forth a discreet love for prose, Mr. de la Mare's reputation stood or fell by his verse. His war volumes yielded little in popularity to the verse of any English compeer. He had achieved a style, an attitude, and, like most good poets, created a world of his own. As a poet writing in verse he stood apart from all groups and factions. Then, with the publication of his *Memoirs of a Midget,* he suddenly switched his poetry out of verse into prose, style, world, and all, whither the majority of his admirers followed him. It is perhaps not unreasonable to see in this development a recognition of those hard facts which the ambitious modern poet, sooner or later, is compelled to face. He cannot continue *ad infinitum* to write short poems. Something in the mental make-up of the reading public is ill-disposed to poems that exceed the anthologists' length. Therefore, unless the poet is prepared to confront disinterest, if not actual neglect, he must use some more popular literary form to clothe his most ambitious efforts. Not otherwise will he carry his audience with him on the whole journey. Thus Mr. Hardy, in the earlier past, drove his poetry to market in the novel and bartered it there until he could afford the return to Parnassus.

This, of course, is not the whole truth concerning Mr. de la Mare's journey. His gradual change of garb has perhaps been justified by the winning of a poetic freedom which, in his case, could be achieved more easily and conveniently in prose than in verse. That rich embroidery of minute detail which is a chief characteristic of all his work, old and new, is an essential part of his artistic vision. It would become monotonous in protracted verse. Even in his prose some people will find it monotonous. Once or twice in [*The Connoisseur*] he does not completely escape the charge of over-wrought writing. His decorations are infinitely minute. The least cornice has its mouldings. His roofs cannot resist a gargoyle. And sometimes he passes the limits of satiety. It is the old romantic fault, excess. His richness resembles nothing so much as an enormous cake over-stuffed with the very best plums. We pause to think rather enviously of plain bread-and-butter.

But, as usual, this is only the vice of a virtue occasionally pushed too far. In general, though he always patterns his mosaic to cover the whole area of his floor, Mr. de la Mare leaves sufficient open space to rest an ordinarily sophisticated eye. He is at his best in stories where our main attention devolves. When his background is of equal importance (and background is always important to the author of "Arabia") a certain confusion is created in the reader's mind. Too many simultaneous claims are made upon his attention. In following one strand he tends to lose touch with another: and there are always a score of strands. This difficulty is not diminished by the author's intermittent flights into the most baffling regions of his exceptionally subtle imagination. "The Connoisseur," the title story of this book, for instance, is not so much a story as a mystic poem in prose. Mr. de la Mare offends (and we thank him for it) most principles laid down by the professors who undertake to teach the art of short-story composition. Often when his dragon has a sting in its tail that sting is scrupulously concealed from all save the rarest kind of reader. The others carry away the memory of an excellent story; but it is not Mr. de la Mare's story. Thus he has often been discussed by inadequate reviewers as a mere author of stories for children. The same was once current of his verse.

"The Connoisseur" begins two pages from its end and ends—but I, for one, dare not suggest precisely where it ends. Through a score of involutions and convolutions, followed in the author's most ornate prose, the very windings of the dragon itself, the sting flickers in and out without, as it seems, striking anything definite. In the light of one's previous readings of Mr. de la Mare, we may blame our baffled selves more than him. One looks for anagrams in the names of his symbolic characters but without finding any satisfactory key to the elucidation of his mystery. Writing in the absence of books (in short, seventeen miles from the nearest railway station), it is impossible to say who St. Dusman was, or who or what he represents. And was "Sasurat" the name of a star? Is Kootoora an Arabian or Persian word? Or did Mr. de la Mare invent it? Whatever the replies the reading of our story is scarcely affected. Happily the central obscurity does not diminish the interest of an extremely fine and characteristic piece of work. In fact it issues a challenge to one's extra-literary ingenuity. In it Mr. de la Mare leaves the common earth of English prose and soars beyond the planes of Beckford and Poe into his own empyrean. This is essentially the projection of that world which appears in its vital colors in his later verse, notably in his volume *The Veil.* If Mr. de la Mare's garb has altered it is not because the man who wears it has changed. He has merely evolved.

"The Nap," and "Missing" are stories as good as anything

Mr. de la Mare has done in their kind. His atmospherics are positively phenomenal. "**Missing**" is the quasi-confession, to a casual and unwilling listener, of a murder committed, but not explicitly acknowledged, by a man whom the narrator has met in a teashop during a London thunderstorm. I know nothing in contemporary literature so consummate as the thematic interplay in this story. Its air is vital, tense, exhausting. One emerges from its pages limp and stupefied into an air still overcharged with electricity. To read it is an experience that not even an insensitive reader will soon forget. It purges as tragedy. "There but for the grace of God go I." The author has never written forty-five more vivid pages.

Enough of Mr. de la Mare's book still remains to thrust an enthusiastic reviewer beyond the bounds even of this generous space. But passing over the equally vivid experiences of "**Mr. Kempe**," and "**All Hallows**" it will be sufficient to say, using in its strictest and rarest sense a word which is gradually being degraded into insignificance by the unjustifiable man-handling of inadequate reviewers, that *The Connoisseur* contains at least four masterpieces, the masterpieces of a poet as well as a short-story writer. No book of such high imaginative quality has appeared in a long time.

> Edward Davison, "Masterpieces," in The Saturday Review of Literature, *Vol. II, No. 49, July 3, 1926, p. 903.*

The Times Literary Supplement   (essay date 1930)

[*In the following review, the critic discusses the dreamlike quality of the stories collected in* On the Edge.]

In a preface to *Henry Brocken,* not a few years ago, Mr. de la Mare said of its regions that they stretched "just this side of Dream; that they border Impossibility; lie parallel with Peace." It was a poet's phrase, delicately true of the world which poetry has created and which he re-created there; and in a sense it has remained true of most of the prose he has written since, though with the difference that belongs to stories told, however strangely, of the actual world. These must be more possible, because they join somewhere with our habit-ridden existence. They are less peaceful because, as stories, they hinge on the accidents of time; and most of all on those apprehensions and tremors, illumining or terrible, at which existence shows suddenly another face. But in the last, as the first, of his stories the frontiers are just this side of dream. Or even across it; so much of their strangeness and beauty, quiet and fear, has this dream-like quality in which Mr. de la Mare is unsurpassed.

As their title suggests, these new stories [in *On the Edge*] hover above the rims of experience and at particularly close quarters with the spectral. They may come to be known, one feels, as their author's book of terrors. A fearful joy—to be tasted at leisure, like the writing—will certainly not be missed here. Ominousness meets us at once with the corpulent but disturbing Mr. Bloom—what other imagination would have united such an abyss with such a figure?—and it emerges again from the unlikeliest of sources to haunt the fields. A gruesomeness not ghostly but entirely *macabre* inspires the last tale in the book. It is the most original invention of all; and though Mr. de la Mare acknowledges the help of a friend and critic, the boy in the story seems markedly his own. And these are not all the tremors. Yet, gratuitous as it often is to compare an author with himself, one wonders if any of them ring so true as the deep reverberations of his **"All Hallows,"** the ghoulish mystery of **"Seaton's Aunt,"** or of the young man who trifled with the bell-rope. If, discounting the fondness for old favourites, one looks for a reason, it may be that the preparation is sometimes too ample—for the stories are not conspicuously short—or simply that these have been imagined less seriously. For whatever reason, the impact seems less.

But the touch on the nerves is only accessory, after all, to Mr. de la Mare's real magic. It is not the most vital point even of this book. What counts for more is the glimpse of a strange whole which a story of his can give us. It may be a relation between people, as in what is explicitly a ghost story, **"The Green Room,"** the relation between the dead girl, her phantom and the man who sees it is focused to a point. There will be a beauty or rareness in the way it is done—in the exquisite perception of visible things, or as here, in the verses which are in character and are part of the story. And there is always the vision that looks and wonders at a world

> Where nothing is, but all things seem,
> And we the shadow of a dream.

The "edges" of life, as Mr. de la Mare observes, may mean different things; and the most finely perceptive stories in this book are those which manage to relate the eccentric to the universal. **"At First Sight"** starts with the abnormal; this well-tended young man with shaded eyes, who cannot see up even to the knees of his neighbours, inhabits almost as restricted and secluded a world as that of the Midget. It is, therefore, a peculiar irony to make *him* experience a case of love at first sight; and nothing short of mastery was needed to steer his passion for a poor shop-girl, and her gradually answering love for him, out of the sentimental or absurd. But the intuition is as subtle as the detail of the invention; the tale—a tragedy in itself, a comedy in each sardonic touch of the ruthless human world that closes on its hero—is one of the most moving things that Mr. de la Mare has written, and shines with a poignant tenderness and beauty of the spirit. Another treasure is plucked from the unexpected in **"Willows,"** where a discreet visitor comes, on behalf of a friend, to glean some data about a forgotten young poet from his apparently uncompromising mother. Technically, the surprise of the story is the clang of its revealed secret at the end; but there is as admirable a surprise in the mother's character as it emerges from an interview of most amusing subtlety.

Nor are those the only places in the book where a ray from its odd recesses strikes very near the heart of things. Reality wakes at the touch of unwontedness. We feel then all the writer's humanity, the truth of his sympathy, though with it a realization of gulfs that are perhaps inexorable in fact or dream. It is the feeling that, shadows or not, we "live alone." Present most of all in that story of the two

queerly assorted lovers, this sense of the loneliness of souls returns and is never very far away. And so, in spite of the vivacious thrills of the book and one purely frolic extravaganza, there is a sadness as well as a grimness in it. It unites two halves, in fact. One of them sallies across the brink into bizarre or ghostly adventure; the other turns its strange scrutiny back towards human ways. Or perhaps, instead of this rather clumsy division, one had better say that it will indulge two moods. We can glide easily from one into the other as Mr. de la Mare leads us, for the stories, however different, are under the same spell of idiosyncrasy. There is the unerring texture of detail that makes his prose delightful; and seldom, if ever, has he interwoven tragedy and comedy more subtly than he does at moments here.

> *"On the Edge," in* The Times Literary Supplement, *No. 1495, September 25, 1930, p. 753.*

Edith Oliver (essay date 1930)

[*In the following review of* On the Edge, *Oliver admires de la Mare's ability to create a sense of expectation and suspense in his works.*]

If you were marooned on a desert island, and found, one morning, not "the print of a man's naked foot on the shore very plain to be seen," making you stand "like one thunderstruck" or as if "you had seen an apparition"; but, instead, lying on the sand, a few pages out of this volume, the covers and title-page having been washed away by the tide, you could not have a moment of doubt as to the identity of the unseen visitant. It could only be Mr. de la Mare who had so made your desert to blossom as the rose. And this, not because he is the person you would naturally expect to meet on that kind of island, but because nearly every page of *On the Edge* is drenched in his peculiar magic.

> A little to the east of them, in the haze of the afternoon sun, lay a smallish, low-roofed, quite ordinary-looking, quiet and glinting country house. Not very old, but, on the other hand, not very new.

We have all of us described some such a house in some such words, and what is there in this low-toned picture which creates at once the certainty that something is going to happen? The sight of that house fills you with a dreadful and delightful expectancy.

That is what Mr. de la Mare does for you. You cannot travel far in his company without finding yourself "knocking on a moonlit door." His genius is for the threshold. I know of no other writer who can so set your heart beating as you wait in a commonplace room and find that the air in it has become unaccountably charged with suspense. Or he introduces you to a person, perhaps a little dowdy and down-at-heel, or perhaps unpleasantly solid and competent, but who, in either case, has an inhuman glint in his eye, which makes your hair stand ever so little on end. And when the story has been told, perhaps there was not so much in it after all. Not much has happened; and sometimes you didn't really know just what *did* happen, and what didn't; but you have lived through an experience more breathlessly intimate than can be created by any other author of my acquaintance.

Mr. de la Mare is at home "on the edge." His sense of balance is unerring. He and his reader remain poised there, spellbound and bewitched. He is far less himself when he comes off it, and makes such a plunge as into **"The Orgy."** Then you feel too much as if you were being drowned in a butt of Malmsey wine. Really, what one asks of him is to evoke that magical expectancy. You simply don't want him to tell you what is behind the door. You ask no more than to remain, quaking a little, with him in the moonlight:—

> Why cheat the heart with old deceits?—
> Love—was it *love* in thine
> Could leave me thus grown sick of sweets
> And. . . .

That "and" leaves us quivering on just such an edge of uncertainty as Mr. de la Mare alone can build in the air. But the particular story from which these lines come, **"The Green Room,"** which is perhaps the most delicate of all, moves with exquisite little high-heeled footsteps to a sudden denouement, which comes upon us like a gentle and irrevocable earthquake. (pp. 54, 56)

> *Edith Oliver, "De la Mare at Home," in* The Nation and the Athenaeum, *Vol. XLVIII, No. 2, October 11, 1930, pp. 54, 56.*

The enjoyment of every tale, of every poem we read is largely in the nature of a day-dream, even though it is being built up in an astonishing fashion out of a purely verbal fabric.

—*Walter de la Mare in his* Behold, This Dreamer, *1939.*

Arthur Machen (essay date 1930)

[*Machen was a Welsh short story writer and novelist best known for his tales of bizarre occurrences and supernatural horror. In the following review of* On the Edge, *he focuses on "A Recluse," questioning whether de la Mare's characteristic obscurity contributes to or detracts from the success of the story.*]

When the hour sounds from the belfry, the strokes sound clear, definite and distinct in the air. Everyone can hear that it is one, or seven, or twelve, as it may be; and there the matter ends for most of us. But if we listen more curiously, and forget about dinner time and appointments kept or missed, we shall hear between the master strokes of the bell a melodious humming murmur, and this in its turn may be resolved into notes mounting the scale in a fixed and certain order, mounting and still mounting into worlds beyond our sense, into eternity. These sounds are the overtones; they have their analogies in the region of

the arts, with a difference. For in the affair of the bell founders, the overtones are only of this importance, that the tuners have to take them into account if the bell is to be perfectly in tune; otherwise they are a mere by-product of the great stroke; incidental, not essential. But the arts exist for their overtones; it is by their presence or absence that we distinguish genius from talent. It is the main business, nay the only business, of the bell to tell us that it is twelve o'clock, but it is not the main business of Tennyson to tell us that Ulysses and his companions came into the land of the lotus eaters at some time after that hour. In the one case, the overtones are accidental; in the other, they are essential. It is the affair of the clock to tell us the time; it is the affair of the arts to take us out of time into eternity, into that region which is beyond the world of the logical understanding, beyond the power of direct utterance.

And yet, in the art of literature certainly, in the arts of painting and sculpture probably, the great stroke—to continue this bell analogy—must be clearly enunciated, with no doubtful sound. It is hard to believe that the Augustus John portrait of Madame Suggia suffers in any way from its being, quite evidently and undeniably, a picture of a woman playing the violoncello; it is hard to think it would have been a still greater masterpiece if it had looked rather like a tiger under a palm tree. But however this may be with painting and sculpture, it is certainly true in prose literature: the finest work is defined. It need not be scientifically true. It is not scientifically true, as it happens, that human eyes and bones, when submerged at a depth of thirty feet become pearls and coral; but the poet, though mistaken, is clear and definite in his statement. Poetry, it is true, has a larger licence in this matter than prose, since poetry is a near approach to that primitive incantation from which all literature proceeds. There is a certain confusion in the narrative of "Kubla Khan"; and the magic casements charmed by the song of the nightingale are misty. And it might be urged, perhaps, in some quarters that Mr. de la Mare has availed himself of his poet's licence in writing some of the curious and beautiful short stories in *On the Edge.* There is an everlasting question that besets not the minor but the major decisions of criticism. It is a simple thing to dismiss "Standing at the buffet in immaculate evening dress he selected a dozen of the succulent bivalves." It is more difficult to decide whether a clearer definition would have improved **"A Recluse,"** one of the most singular of these singular studies.

In this tale the narrator, "Mr. Dash," is motoring one May evening along a country road, when he is strangely drawn by the appearance of a house seen through high gates of wrought iron. Mr. Dash, I say, was drawn to this house, but hardly by the attraction of love. It had about it those veils of mystery, that sense of *aliquid latest,* which haunt certain visible things: houses, trees, gardens, the shape of hills, secret and silent valleys:

> To all appearance it was vacant, but if so, it could not have been vacant long. The drive was sadly in need of weeding; though the lawns had been recently mown. High-grown forest trees towered round about it, overtopping its roof— chiefly chestnuts, their massive lower branches drooping so close to the turf they almost brushed

its surface. They were festooned from crown to roof with branching candelabra—like spikes of blossom. Now it was daylight; but imagine them on a still, pitch-black night, their every twig upholding a tiny, phosphoric cluster of tapers.

Mr. Dash drives his car past the iron gates, and strolls by the terrace of the quiet red-brick Georgian house, with its singular hint of undefined mystery, and discovers that, after all, it is still tenanted. The owner, Mr. Bloom, a heavy, stooping, bearded man, is standing at the threshold; a bald man, with a domed brow. He greets Mr. Dash courteously, but that gentleman "wanted to shake him off, to go away. He was an empty-looking man . . . if his house had suggested vacancy, so did he; and yet, I wonder."

It is impossible to summarise Mr. de la Mare without committing outrage and injustice; but it must be said that Mr. Bloom lures Mr. Dash into his hall, strangely occupied with a hugger-mugger of fine old furniture, as if an antique dealer were about to flit. Mr. Bloom leaves his guest in the library for a moment, and when he returns Mr. Dash, distressed, uneasy, he knows not why, shakes hands, and in spite of protestations, makes his way to his car. The gear-key is missing; the nearest town is seven miles away; and Mr. Dash must be Mr. Bloom's guest for the night. The two dine together, simply and choicely; and Mr. Bloom speaks of his dead secretary who has been of great use to him in his "literary work"; and then the literary work becomes "little experiments," which yielded "the most curious and interesting results"; and the little experiments are at last defined as the processes of the séance of the spiritualists. Mr. Dash had dabbled a little in spiritualism and thought poorly enough of the results, and spoke of it all as a silly and dangerous waste of time; and his host grew grey with rage. The evening wears on; it becomes apparent that there was some hideous mystery about the death of Mr. Champneys, the secretary; and it is into the bedroom of the dead man that Mr. Dash is shown. The servant who prepared the dinner is gone for the night: Mr. Dash and Mr. Bloom are the only tenants of the house. Mr. Dash falls asleep, and wakes suddenly with the dawn; and looking about him sees the room as it were drenched in terror: "this is how Mr. Champney's room would appear to anyone who had become for some reason or another intensely afraid."

And then he heard voices speaking, echoing hollow in some distance of the house; one of the voices Mr. Bloom's, the other like it; and there was the sound of hurrying feet overhead. Mr. Dash goes into the study, and sees there a small bed, and on a table beside it the contents of Mr. Bloom's pocket, among them Mr. Dash's missing gear-key. And the bed:

> The lower part of it was all but entirely flat, the white coverlid having been drawn almost as neat and close from side to side of it as the carapace of a billiard table. But on the pillow—the grey-flecked brown beard protruding over the turned-down sheet—now showed what appeared to be the head and face of Mr. Bloom . . . It was a flawless facsimile, waxen, motionless; but it was not a real face and head. It was an

hallucination . . . it was inconceivably shocking.

Mr. Dash flees the abhorred, infested house.

I should have made it clear that Mr. Bloom detained Mr. Dash because he was human, because the horrors that the necromancer had summoned from the depths pressed now so thick about him that even his foul soul was shaken and aghast. I should have mentioned also a faint hint that there was some tincture of corruption in the personality of Champneys, the dead secretary: medium, it is to be supposed, was his true title. Such, then, in crude outline, is the story of **"A Recluse."** Would it have been a better tale if it had been told more definitely? I leave that an open question.

Is the purely personal objection valid? I am not quite clear as to this; but I am bound to confess that I have such an objection to make against **"A Recluse."** It is this. The word of the enigma is, clearly, spiritualism; and no structure built on that basis can appal me, or enchant me, or make my breath come quickly, or, indeed, win the faintest interest from me. I take the word of the spiritualists themselves, that the séance is a homely, friendly, and helpful institution; that the spirits are as harmless and playful as kittens, and, sometimes, as helpful as big St. Bernards and Church Workers. No tale that begins with a planchette, a hidden slate, or a rapping table can make me quail. Whereas another of the stories in the book, **"Crewe"**—. In that tale there is a scarecrow which is luminous, but not in the light of the sun—a hideous terror. (pp. vi, viii)

> *Arthur Machen, "The Line of Terror," in* The New Statesman, *Vol. XXXVI, No. 911, October 11, 1930, pp. vi, viii.*

Gerald Sykes (essay date 1931)

[*In the following review, Sykes praises the short stories collected in* On the Edge, *particularly focusing on de la Mare's treatment of sentimental themes.*]

Although his talent is not of the kind that demands critical evaluation, by this time we have had the opportunity to form an opinion of Walter de la Mare. We know the obvious things: his fantastic vein, his interest in the supernatural, his love of children. We also know that his work is not of the kind that is called major, that it is inclined to be bookish, to address itself to the literary connoisseur, to indulge in a questionable persiflage, and to wander far from the simple, important emotions. If we have read him with any love we know further that in spite of his limitations he is a genuine artist, that his sense of people and places is not bookish but real, that to exceptional narrative and verbal gifts he has joined a most scrupulous integrity, that his work is truly finished, each word being the product of both sensibility and imagination. He is thus able to provide us with a definite and enjoyable experience, which might be described as an adventure in good manners. And for this adventure we are indebted to a peculiar inward struggle, to a duel between two conflicting forces in his soul: between an exquisite romanticism on one hand, which would give carte blanche to his heart, and between a British sense of propriety on the other hand, which requires his heart to justify every beat.

Most of his old interests are to be found once more in this collection of eight new short stories [*On the Edge*]. The supernatural, for instance, plays its part in three of them; literature, in two. One has for its hero a child. One is a sentimental fantasy recalling *Memoirs of a Midget*. Only one, so far as I am aware, is new in type. That is **"The Orgy: An Idyll,"** which is a slowly unbuttoning farce with an idea that I at least have never before encountered. As a whole the collection seems up to his standard. I doubt, in fact, if any other stories of comparable workmanship have been published this season.

Since space is limited, let us confine ourselves to the story entitled **"At First Sight,"** which falls into the class of sentimental fantasy and recalls *Memoirs of a Midget*. This is the longest story in the volume and reveals most clearly the creative drama which takes place within Mr. de la Mare. It is the story of a young man who at first sight appears to be blind, because of a green silk shade that he wears, but in reality is merely unable to lift his eyes off the ground. Thus, of course—as we might expect from Mr. de la Mare—he becomes "a connoisseur of horses' hoofs, boots and shoes, socks and laces, of the nether portion of trouser legs, and of feminine skirts, shoes, and ankles." Though closely guarded by his "Grummumma," he manages to meet a shopgirl (with the sensibilities of a princess) and falls in love with her. It would be impossible to find a better example of Mr. de la Mare's method. The design of his story is to be affecting. And affecting it is: we feel the pain in our own skull when poor Cecil tries to lift his eyes; we weep for his friendlessness; we are enraged by his Grummumma—"like an immense well-fed cat at a mouse's hole"—as she tries to frustrate his first shy move toward happiness; and we hope bitterly that he will get the girl. But we know from the start that he never will. We know that he is fighting a losing battle—and not against fate or his Grummumma, but against a mighty and unfair force (unfair because it exists not in himself or in the situation but in the soul of his creator), the mighty force, in fact, of British propriety. For the truth is that Mr. de la Mare would never have been able to lift *his* eyes if he had permitted Cecil to get the girl. He is a sentimentalist and—such is the weight of convention upon him—he is ashamed of his sentimentality. His method, therefore, is to begin with a sentimental idea and thereafter to justify it by systematically defeating it. (We find this principle at work not only in the general scheme of his story but in every page, every paragraph.)

This is the drama that takes place within Mr. de la Mare. We respect it since it has produced such exquisite art, such exquisite good manners. At the same time we regret that convention has been allowed to intrude in these matters. We think of another sentimentalist, Sterne, at a time when the British sense of propriety was not so strong, who did not consume so much of his energy in defeating his own genius, and produced a body of work that is lasting and universal.

Gerald Sykes, "Walter de la Mare," in The

Nation, *New York, Vol. CXXXII, No. 3430, April 1, 1931, p. 356.*

Edward Wagenknecht   (essay date 1949)

[*Wagenknecht is an American literary historian, novelist, anthologist, and biographer. His best-known works are* Cavalcade of the English Novel *(1943) and* Cavalcade of the American Novel *(1952), literary histories of the development of the novel in England and America. In the following essay, Wagenknecht analyzes "The Riddle," focusing on the allegorical aspects of the story.*]

"Have you guessed the riddle yet?" the Hatter said, turning to Alice again.

"No, I give it up," Alice replied. "What's the answer?"

"I haven't the slightest idea," said the Hatter.

"Nor I," said the March Hare.

Alice sighed wearily. "I think you might do something better with the time," she said, "than wasting it in asking riddles that have no answers."

Alice's Adventures in Wonderland

Walter de la Mare's priceless apologue, **"The Riddle,"** can be used effectively in the teaching of literature all the way from the grades to the college level. It is probably true that such stories depend for the exercise of their full effectiveness upon a certain mystical sensitiveness on the part of the reader or listener. But this is a matter of temperament, not of intellectual sophistication. I have yet to encounter a class, some members of which did not, upon reading this tale, find their souls shaken with wonder and terror.

Following (it seems) the death of their father, seven children come to live with their grandmother in her house, which had been "built in the time of the Georges. It was not a pretty house, but roomy, substantial, and square; and an elm-tree outstretched its branches almost to the windows."

Though the grandmother is too old to "romp" with the children, she wishes them all to be "bright and gay" in her house. Every morning and every evening they must come to see her, "and bring me smiling faces that call back to my mind my own son Harry." All their other time, except when they are at lessons, is their own. She imposes but one condition upon them. "In the large spare bedroom that looks out on the slate roof there stands in the corner an old oak chest; aye, older than I, my dears, a great deal older; older than my grandmother. Play anywhere else in the house, but not there."

This regime is followed for several weeks. Though the children first feel "gloomy" and "strange," they soon come to be "happy and at home in the great house." Every day the grandmother seems more feeble, but she never fails, upon seeing them, "to visit her store of sugarplums."

Then, one by one, and two by two, the children are drawn to—and into—the great oak chest. First, Henry; then, Matilda, who could find no pleasure without him; then

Harriet and William together; then James and Dorothea; and finally, the oldest, Ann.

The grandmother seems rather nonchalant about it all and increasingly unaware. After Henry's disappearance, when only six, instead of seven, come to her room to bid her goodnight and collect the customary sugarplums, "she looked out between the candles at them as if she were unsure of something in her thoughts." When, next day, Ann tells her that Henry is not to be found, she replies: "Dearie me, child. Then he must be gone away for a time." After a pause she adds: 'But remember all of you, do not meddle with the oak chest." After Matilda's disappearance she makes an even more suggestive remark: "Some day maybe they will come back to you, my dears, or maybe you will go to them. Heed my warning as best you may." When Ann is the only one left, she contents herself by squeezing the girl's fingers and remarking, "What lonely old people we are, to be sure!" And after Ann herself has gone, she says nothing. She dodders, half-blind, through the great house, "in her mind . . . a tangled skein of memories—laughter and tears, and little children now old-fashioned, and the advent of friends, and long farewells." She gossips "fitfully, inarticulately, with herself," and settles herself in the window seat.

I have read and discussed this story with many classes, and it is of these discussions that I wish to write. In my own opinion, the light that has come out of these conferences illuminates more than a single story.

I usually begin by asking: "What does the story mean?" and, more specifically: "What happens to the children?" Of course, I get many freak answers which I do not propose to discuss here. (Be it remarked merely that they are no more insane—for the simple reason that they could not be—than many of the notions which learned men have advanced in print concerning the meaning of, say, *Hamlet* or *Moby Dick*.) But most of my students commit themselves, sooner or later, to one of two views: (1) The entrance of the children into the chest represents death. (2) It indicates, rather, their growing up, leaving the grandmother's house, and going out into the world.

Though in certain passages of the story, it is no doubt tempting to regard the grandmother as Time, I have never been greatly attracted myself by the second view. When the children go out of the life of the household into the chest—and this has been pointed out in my classes again and again—they are leaving a larger world for a much smaller one. This cannot possibly suggest going out from childhood into the larger activities of manhood and womanhood. Going out into the garden and disappearing there might have suggested just that; but this symbol was not employed. In other words, if the author had any such idea in mind, he has chosen a singularly inapt symbol. To any normal mind, being closed up in a box suggests death and burial, and it cannot possibly suggest anything else.

However, after the "going out into the world" idea had been presented to me a number of times with considerable emphasis by people who were quite sure that they were right, I put the question to Mr. de la Mare himself, together-

er with another question concerning the character of the grandmother.

The grandmother had never seemed to me a sinister figure; she seemed, rather, doddering, ineffectual kindness, senility. Some of my students, however, were always sure that she was malevolent and that when she mentioned the chest to the children she was actuated by motives similar to those which incited Bluebeard when he forbade Fatima to enter the closet which contained the bodies of his murdered wives.

My first question to Mr. de la Mare was, therefore: "Did you intend to indicate that the children died or did you mean to indicate that they grew up and went out into the world?" And my second: "Was the grandmother intended to be a sinister figure?"

Writers do not, of course, like to answer such questions. And with good reason, for, in nine cases out of ten, the question concerns some consideration totally irrelevant to the problem which the writer had set himself. It is said that, having written "The Lady or the Tiger?" Frank R. Stockton spent a considerable portion of the rest of his life denying that he knew which had emerged from the open door—an honest answer, I am sure. Ibsen always refused to reply to such questions at all, taking his stand on the declaration that what he had written he had written, to which Bernard Shaw returned, characteristically, that the point was rather that what he hadn't written he hadn't written. When Hiram Corson asked Browning whether the line in "My Last Duchess"—

> . . . I gave commands;
> Then all smiles stopped together—

meant that the Duke of Ferrara had had his wife put to death, the poet first replied affirmatively, then added, "or he might have had her shut up in a convent." So much Corson—or any of us—might have figured out for ourselves. The point of the question had been to determine which idea had been held in the writer's mind. When Tennyson was asked whether the Three Queens in "The Passing of Arthur" represented Faith, Hope, and Charity, he replied: "They mean that and they do not. They are also those three Graces, but they are much more. I hate to be tied down to say, 'This means that,' because the thought within the image is much more than any one interpretation." Of course. Poetry is a piece of shot-silk, with many glancing colors. If the image is no larger than the interpretation, why write poetry? Why not a sermon to begin with?

Mr. de la Mare has always, however, had a much better disposition than Tennyson; and he answered at least my first question much more definitely than his relative, Robert Browning had answered Corson's. "Yes," he replied, "I did mean that the children died."

His answer to the second question was less satisfactory: "The old lady," he wrote, "was not meant to be any more sinister than—well, than she appears."

We have, at this point, by no means finished with the "meaning" of the story. For the moment, however, I find it necessary to turn to certain questions of technique.

Stories which partake, as this one does, of the quality of sheer literary magic may not seem, at first blush, promising subjects for analysis. Elisabeth Bergner once astonished an interviewer by denying that Barrie had written *The Boy David* for her. "God," she said, "wrote that play!" And, however that may be, **"The Riddle"** is not the kind of thing they teach you to write for the "market" with the help of a literary correspondence school.

Nevertheless, short and simple as the tale is, it contained one very difficult technical problem. There are seven children who must somehow be got into that chest. That means seven trips. By permitting Harriet and William to go together and James and Dorothea to go together, Mr. de la Mare succeeds in getting the number down to five, a piece of literary economy which recalls the story of the farmer who took his son to a concert which consisted entirely of solo work in the first half but included a number of duets toward the close. At this point, the old man turned to the boy and remarked, "You see, son, it's getting late now; so they're taking them two at a time."

Now every writer knows that if you are going to repeat your effects in literature you must increase your pressure with each repetition. Otherwise you will get not climax but anticlimax. The *Beowulf* poet knew this well. Beowulf fights Grendel; then he fights Grendel's mother. But the dam is a much more ferocious monster, who places the hero's life in far greater jeopardy. Further to heighten the reader's blood pressure, the poet causes the second battle to take place in a very weird and impressive setting beneath the mere.

Here is the first visit to the chest—Henry's—as described by Mr. de la Mare:

> It was evening twilight when Henry went upstairs from the nursery by himself to look at the oak chest. He pressed his fingers into the carved fruit and flowers, and spoke to the darksmiling heads at the corners; and then, with a glance over his shoulder, he opened the lid and looked in. But the chest concealed no treasure, neither gold nor baubles, nor was there anything to alarm the eye. The chest was empty, except that it was lined with silk of old-rose, seeming darker in the dusk, and smelling sweet of pot-pourri. And while Henry was looking in, he heard the softened laughter and the clinking of the cups downstairs in the nursery; and out at the window he saw the day darkening. These things brought strangely to his memory his mother who in her glimmering white dress used to read to him in the dusk; and he climbed into the chest; and the lid closely gently down over him.

This is magnificent, but how can a man dare to write like that, with four more visits to go?

Matilda goes next, and this time the problem is skilfully evaded:

> But Matilda could not forget her brother Henry, finding no pleasure in playing without him. So she would loiter in the house thinking where he might be. And she carried her wood doll in her bare arms, singing under her breath all she could make up about him. And when in a bright morn-

ing she peeped in on the chest, so sweet-scented and secret it seemed that she took her doll with her into it—just as Henry himself had done.

This comes but three short paragraphs after Henry's adventure; the reader is still sufficiently under the spell of the first description to be able to carry its power over; in any event, the important thing, in this instance, is that *the thing is going to happen again.* It is upon that naked fact, and not upon the circumstances surrounding it, that the author now relies to secure the desired shock. An elaborately wrought description is therefore not only unneeded at this point; it would actually be bad art.

Harriet and William go next, and then James and Dorothea. And now individual characterization enters, and this is very significant. Up until now it was terrible enough that the chest—whatever it is or whatever it may symbolize—should "get" a child and then another child. But we cannot—fortunately for our sanity in a world in which we have to read the newspapers—we cannot go on being deeply moved by the fate of people *whom we do not know;* our imaginations are not strong enough for that. Before the chest exercises its malevolent magic again, we must, therefore, be made acquainted with the *individuals* whom this time it will destroy.

"Now Harriet and William were friends together, pretending to be sweethearts; while James and Dorothea liked wild games of hunting, and fishing, and battles." (The quiet, loving ones and the stalwart, active ones—death lies in wait for both!) The background for the Harriet-William tragedy is as rich as that which was sketched for us when Henry left; but, though there is no conflict in tone between the two pictures, we do find a refreshing variety:

> On a silent afternoon in October Harriet and William were talking softly together, looking out over the slate roof at the green fields, and they heard the squeak and frisk of a mouse behind them in the room. They went together and searched for the small, dark hole from whence it had come out. But finding no hole, they began to finger the carving of the chest, and to give names to the dark-smiling heads, just as Henry had done. "I know! let's pretend you are Sleeping Beauty, Harriet," said William, "and I'll be the Prince that squeezes through the thorns and comes in." Harriet looked gently and strangely at her brother; but she got into the box and lay down, pretending to be fast asleep; and on tiptoe William leaned over, and seeing how big was the chest he stepped in to kiss the Sleeping Beauty and to wake her from her quiet sleep. Slowly the carved lid turned on its noiseless hinges. And only the chatter of James and Dorothea came in sometimes to recall Ann from her book.

The James-Dorothea scene is described more briefly, but in the ordinary sense even more vividly:

> Snow was falling through the still air upon the roof; and Dorothea was a fish in the oak chest, and James stood over the hole in the ice, brandishing a walking-stick for a harpoon, pretending to be an Esquimaux. Dorothea's face was red, and her wild eyes sparkled through her tousled hair. And James had a crooked scratch

upon his cheek. "You must struggle, Dorothea, and then I shall swim back and drag you out. Be quick now!" He shouted with laughter as he was drawn into the open chest. And the lid closed softly and gently down as before.

Ann goes very quietly, in her sleep. In this case we have an introductory paragraph, describing the girl propped up in bed, reading fairy stories, as was her custom, "and the gently-flowing moonlight of the narrative seemed to illumine the white pages, and she could hear in fancy fairy voices. . . ." Ann is the oldest of the children, perhaps considerably older than the others, and she is the last to go; but her reading shows that she is still a child at heart. And when we realize this, we give up any hope we may have cherished that she might escape the general doom. She puts out her candle and goes to sleep, "with a confused babel of voices close to her ear, and faint swift pictures before her eyes." Then "in the dead of night" she rises "in dream" and moves "silently through the vacant house."

> . . . Past the room where her grandmother was snoring in brief, heavy slumber, she stepped light and surely, and down the wide staircase. And Vega the far-shining stood over against the window above the slate roof. Ann walked in the strange room as if she were being guided by the hand towards the oak chest. There, just as if she was dreaming it was her bed, she laid herself down in the old rose silk, in the fragrant place. But it was so dark in the room that the movement of the lid was indistinguishable.

This is the stillest going of all, as befits the character of the girl, and therefore the most irresistible, the most terrible. There is no struggle, and volition is not now involved. We could not at this stage "do" with that, any more than we could endure a long speech of Juliet's following the tenor aria with which Romeo sang himself to death. It is enough to know that it had to be.

It is important to notice, too, that, though Mr. de la Mare achieves variety everywhere else, he purposely, monotonously, repeats his description of the closing of the lid. This occurs at every departure except Matilda's, and the repetition itself helps to increase our feeling of inescapable doom: "the lid closed gently down over him"; "Slowly the carved lid turned on its noiseless hinges"; "And the lid closed softly and gently down as before." Then the perfect climax, as the story fades away into the land of dreams out of which it has come: "But it was so dark in the room that the movement of the lid was indistinguishable."

There is so much that is beautifully suggestive in **"The Riddle"** that the possibilities for commentary are inexhaustible; nor, probably, would any two commentators choose quite the same points. Myself, I wish to call attention to the following:

1. The very beginning of the narrative: "So these seven children, Ann, and Matilda, James, William and Henry, Harriet and Dorothea, came to live with their grandmother." One little word "so" places the story, at the very outset, in the immemorial atmosphere of the folk tale, without beginning and without end.

2. The skilful use of the irrelevant in both the Matilda and the James-Dorothea episodes. "Dorothea's face was red, and her wild eyes sparkled through her tousled hair. And James had a crooked scratch upon his cheek." Dorothea's face and eyes are a part of her characterization; James's scratch might have happened to anybody. Yet how vivid it is! Matilda "carried her wood doll in her bare arms." This detail adds more than vividness; every word has been carefully chosen. The uncomfortable doll presses against the naked flesh, and a kinesthetic sensation is at once communicated to the reader. Matilda's, as we have already seen, is the one departure in which our attention is purposely not focused on the details of the going itself. Nor is she characterized, as Harriet and William are characterized. But if we are to savor the full terror of what is happening to these children, it is important that we must be made to realize that they are human, vulnerable, flesh and blood.

3. The sensitive beauty of Harriet's behavior as she climbs into the box. "Harriet looked gently and strangely at her brother; but she got into the box and lay down, pretending to be fast asleep; and on tiptoe William leaned over, and . . . stepped in to kiss the Sleeping Beauty. . . ." Obviously, Harriet and William are not participating in an actual sexual experience. But they are "friends together, pretending to be sweethearts," and at the moment they are enacting Sleeping Beauty, which *is* a love drama. As the girl-child anticipates motherhood, before she knows what it is, when she plays with her dolls, so every action of the girl here suggests woman's immemorial role in the love drama. From the first boy and girl left alone together to the last that shall live upon this earth, the one will look "gently and strangely" at the other, as she lies down at his behest to embark upon an adventure whose end is life but whose condition, for the woman, is the risk of death.

4. Finally, the mention of "Vega the far-shining" standing over against the window above the slate roof as Ann goes to her doom. For here, for a brief moment, we perceive that the human drama is playing itself out upon a cosmic stage. This is profoundly characteristic of Mr. de la Mare, as all readers of *Memoirs of a Midget* will remember. I know only one other British novel in which the stars play so impressive a role. This is Thomas Hardy's *Two on a Tower*, a much inferior work from every other point of view.

I return, now, to "meaning," a matter which cannot be completely appreciated except with the full richness of the story in mind. Just at the point where my students have finally demonstrated their complete inability to agree with one another concerning **"The Riddle,"** I generally ask whether they are sure that the story *is* an allegory.

It must, of course, be made clear that the alternative is nothing so desperate as to interpret the tale on the realistic level. I have had students who informed me that the children could not possibly have died when they went into the chest; if they did, what became of the bodies? And I have never found any reply to make to them. I admit frankly that there are some people whom I cannot teach!

In a sense, of course, all fiction is allegory. More and more, modern writers strive for individuality in characterization. This has not always been the case. Characters are not greatly individualized in folk stories or in the parables of Jesus, yet we find ourselves going back for illumination to tales like these—as we return, too, to the "caricatures" of Dickens—far more frequently than we refer to the more highly developed personages of our contemporary novels. Art rests upon the fundamental kinship of human beings; it is only disciples of Gertrude Stein and poets-talking-to-themselves who have surrendered the idea that art is communication. Individualize to such an extent that the type element in your characterization disappears altogether, and you will have a freak, who will have no significance whatever, save as an intellectual curiosity, for any of your readers.

As commonly defined, however, allegory means something more than that, and it is well that the distinction should be kept in mind. In discussing Melville's "Benito Cereno," Rosalie Feltenstein has recently remarked illuminatingly: "Consistent sustained allegory is incompatible with the story, for although the characters and the situation stand for more than themselves, they do so by extension of their significance, not by their equation with other objects."

"Extension of their significance" indicates excellently well, I believe, the kind of thing we have in **"The Riddle."** To begin with, we are in the atmosphere of the wonder tale. No author creating in our milieu could possibly expect that any reader, confronting the oak chest, should not immediately think of the tree in Eden, of Pandora's box, and of Bluebeard's closet. He must, therefore, have wanted us to think of these things.

He must also have known that the reader would at once suspect that there was more in the story than met the eye but that, at the same time, he would have great difficulty in deciding just how that "more" should be defined. He must have known that disagreements would appear among different readers. He must have been aware that he had not given any reader the data necessary to "prove" any interpretation. The resultant vagueness and uncertainty must, therefore, have been a part of his plan, of the aim and object that he had in view. And I think we can see why all this should be true.

Ordinarily, to be sure, we demand clearness of impression in literature, first of all. But when one comes to deal with a story which hovers on the edge of the supernatural, does not the question somewhat change its aspect? Here is the realm dedicated above all others to the mysterious and the incomprehensible. Do we really want it charted like the streets of Chicago? (Many spiritualistic séances, precisely because this element of wonder is not present, seem about as thrilling, as romantic, and as mysterious as an income-tax return.) Does not Scott increase our sense of his power in "Wandering Willie's Tale" when he deliberately leaves the door about an inch open at the end for a naturalistic solution of the wonderful events recorded? When the vampire and serpent-woman, Geraldine, disrobes in Coleridge's "Christabel,"

> . . . she unbound
> The cincture from beneath her breast:
> Her silken robe, and inner vest,
> Dropt to her feet, and full in view,
> Behold! her bosom and half her side—
> A sight to dream of, not to tell.
> Oh, shield her! shield sweet Christabel!

What was bared? We are not told, and for this very reason every reader then automatically begins to co-operate with Coleridge in telling the story. Instead of being tied down to *one* horrible thing—the single interpretation which Tennyson rejected—we can now conjure up *all* the horrible things that we can think of! Now this is precisely the kind of effect that lies beyond the range of the cinema. Consequently, supernatural horror stories, though popular on the screen, can appeal there only to a depraved taste, being greeted often, at climactic moments, with screams and even with howls of hysterical laughter. It is doubtful that anyone ever either screamed or laughed while reading LeFanu or M. R. James.

We may find another interesting illustration of all this in Chaucer's greatest story, "The Pardoner's Tale." Here the Old Man, who sends the revelers to their death, is universally accepted as one of the most moving figures in medieval literature. And here, again, it is clear that he is something more than an old man. But what? Death? Old Age? The Wandering Jew? Christ? The Devil? All these views have been advanced, and great names in the field of Chaucerian scholarship have been enlisted in behalf of several of them.

But surely, if Chaucer had intended his character to be thus recognized, if the power of his story had been in any sense dependent upon such an identification, then he would have made the point clear—clear enough, at any rate, so that all sane readers would have found themselves accepting some one, clearly demonstrable, identification, not scattering themselves among several. If this is not true, then Chaucer has failed to communicate his idea in the very story that we accept as his masterpiece.

But suppose Chaucer did not wish to have an identification made. Suppose he wished merely to enrich the emotional overtones of his story by raising many questions and settling none of them. Suppose he intended the Old Man to stand for more than himself by an extension of his significance and not by his equation with another object.

Also some such line, I am convinced, we must make our approach to literature of this variety.

One thing more: My students—thank God!—do not, for the most part, belong to the "intelligentsia." Consequently, I have not once had a student tell me that, like the play *Death Takes a Holiday,* **"The Riddle"** represents a dramatization of the Freudian "death-wish." For what I have thus been spared I cannot sufficiently state my gratitude. There are circles, however, in which this would be the very first interpretation offered. It is a plain misinterpretation, but it happens to be a misinterpretation which illustrates a valuable point.

"The Riddle" first appeared between covers in America, in the book which bears it name, in 1923. For any reader in touch with current thinking, encountering the story first at that time, it must have been very difficult to avoid the Freudian interpretation. But the story, just as we have it, first saw print in England, in the *Monthly Review,* in 1900. At that time Walter de la Mare, *aet.* twenty-seven, had almost certainly never heard of Freud.

He has heard of him since, but he has always, to use a current slang expression, remained more or less "allergic" to him. Freud's name occurs but once in Mr. de la Mare's vast anthology of literature concerning dreams, the unconscious, etc., *Behold, This Dreamer!,* and he is never mentioned at all in the encyclopedic compilation of child lore, *Early One Morning in the Spring.* In short, there is no modern writer less likely to write a story under Freudian inspiration.

This does not, of course, mean that Mr. de la Mare could not have had in mind, from his own observation or from other reading, while writing **"The Riddle,"** the same aspects or tendencies of human experience that the Freudians have observed in connection with what they call the "death-wish." It does most emphatically mean, however, that **"The Riddle"** was not influenced by Freud, that it is not Freudian literature. If we can so easily make such a mistake in dealing with a contemporary story, how many pitfalls must inevitably engulf us when we begin to babble about the "influences" upon Chaucer or Shakespeare, in an age for which most of us have a very imperfect sense of chronology and overwhelming ignorance concerning most of the factors by which literature is conditioned!

And now, if anybody tells me in conclusion that the story must be an allegory because it is called **"The Riddle,"** I can only refer him to Alice, as she is quoted at the beginning of this article. Alice didn't, in general, care for riddles that have no answers, but I think she would have liked Mr. de la Mare. She was just the type that responds most eagerly. (pp. 72-80)

Edward Wagenknecht, "Walter de la Mare's 'The Riddle': A Note on the Teaching of Literature with Allegorical Tendencies," in College English, *Vol. 11, No. 2, November, 1949, pp. 72-80.*

The Times Literary Supplement (essay date 1955)

[*In the following excerpt, the critic praises the stories collected in* A Beginning, and Other Stories.]

What delighted expectation one feels on opening, at this late, shining hour of so long a harvest day, yet another new book [*A Beginning, and Other Stories*] by Mr. de la Mare. He does not disappoint us. Here are the old, ever-new preoccupations. An odd shop sells, in boxes, tiny, evocative sounds—how minute, and how ample a springboard for the fancy of such a customer, one need not elaborate. There is a man haunted by supernatural music and a child by his good and evil angels. A girl has a mystical vision of her own face reflected, not in the water where she has nearly drowned, but in that stranger element, death itself.

There are three *revenants,* none of whom acts as one expects, a pithy little parable of neighbourly hate between spinsters, some frankly fanciful and romantic tales and several set in those wonderful domestic interiors into whose stillness a bygone drama sends up a belated ripple and then rises slowly by hint and allusion once more to the surface. Among these is perhaps one failure. The ripple is so faint, the drama remains so exlusively submerged, that **"The Cartouche"** never quite yields up its meaning at all. But among these, too, is the masterpiece: **"An Anniversary."** What a work of genius is the setting for the odious Aubrey. Beauty is there: "these motionless, misty, earthy, October evenings, the last of the sunset withering in the west," but how oppressive and discomforting is the long, straggling, autumnal garden, over-private, yet disquietingly open on one side to the "wide, flat and now mist-bound fields of damp and malodorous cabbages and cauliflowers, sour acres and acres of deserted market gardens." Who has not seen these from the train, drawing in to London, and endured at the sight a strange sinking despondency next door to vague alarm?

With superb virtuosity and the utmost, devious, unfaltering finesse, the story winds steadily upwards to its triumphant climax. Mr. de la Mare has never surpassed this culminating scene of dialogue for revelation of character and for command of those curious shifts of ground and feeling which take place in the course of a bitter quarrel. Less forceful, but again perfectly sustaining the portrayal of a character from within, is the wonderfully limpid story **"The Guardian."** By using Aubrey's shifty, jaundiced eyes, we saw how malice corrodes the very soul away. Here we look out through the remarkably clear ones of a delightful gentlewoman, and trace the illuminating effect of her love and grief for him on Philip's shrewd, kind, commonsensical aunt. The supernatural element in this story makes less impact than in **"An Anniversary."** The devil in the corner of Philip's eye is perhaps not as *evil* as he might be. Once detect that an author might slightly regret, on picturesque grounds, the final retreat of all demons from the angelic field, and their darkness becomes immediately more colourful than black. But this is a cavil, perhaps, for **"The Guardian"** is a beautiful story, unfolded as quietly and inevitably as a fern unfolds.

"The Face" is the only other as ambitious as these. Mr. de la Mare has set himself here, not for the first time, the delicate task of convincing us that visions do not visit only highly sensitive people. Nora is a sensible downright girl with a Dickensian working-class family (the description of their evening party is worthy of a place beside **"The Nap."**) But having weighted the scales against himself, Mr. de la Mare does just succeed. Nora's stroll by "The Ponds" serves as well as a lifetime in a haunted countryside to besiege her practical urban soul with unearthly experience. She remains quite as real afterwards in her family setting, and even in the terms in which she struggles to share her vision with her poor dunderheaded George. All the same the problem is not quite so completely solved as to make us forget it was ever there.

On the whole the shorter stories are also the thinner ones, though full of good things. One would not willingly go without Mrs. Lemieux, for instance, most endearing and resourceful of *revenants,* or the encounter in **"Bad Company."** But, generally speaking, Mr. de la Mare needs the space of the long story, for he must lead us deep into his world if we are to carry away its richest implications. Perhaps because it lacks this pregnant slowness, the romantic trappings of **"The Princess,"** for instance, have a slightly perfunctory air.

However, one of the shortest stories is a golden exception—**"A Stranger"**—as charming and flawless, in the same vein, as **"Physic"** was. It is a dialogue piece, a form Mr. de la Mare has never given us before. Are we in time to hope for a whole volume of these? The form so admirably suits his powers. This enchanting little drama is that rare phenomenon, a de la Mare picture flooded with broad, mid-morning sunshine. Not a breath of the dreamlike or the odd here, yet nobody else could paint a loving mother and daughter with that particular shimmer of humorous, penetrating sweetness. This dialogue also lends the collection another attribute as characteristic of its author as the book's title—the fact that a volume of original imaginative stories, published in the author's eighty-third year, not only includes one masterpiece, and other passages as good as any he has ever written, but also, and successfully, a quite new experiment. (pp. 598-99)

De la Mare in 1922.

"*Creatures of Dream,*" *in* The Times Literary Supplement, *No. 2798, October 14, 1955, pp. 597-99.*

Doris Ross McCrosson   (essay date 1966)

[*In the following essay, McCrosson examines the narrative structure, settings, and characterization of de la Mare's short stories.*]

Abandoned, lost, missing—hunter, hunted, haunted: these words best describe the settings, the characters, and the situations of many of Walter de la Mare's short stories. Some of them echo in the mind long after they are read, as do particularly vivid dreams long into the daylight. And some of them are as evanescent, as mysterious. People do not throng in his stories—although he is a master at creating characters—but ghosts may. The very titles of some—**"Out of the Deep," "The Riddle," "Missing," "The Revenant," "The Lost Track," "A Recluse," "Strangers and Pilgrims," "What Dreams May Come,"**—suggest as much. Yet even the stories whose titles are most prosaic—**"Mr. Kempe," "Seaton's Aunt," "Physic," "Crewe," "The Wharf "**—are dream and ghost ridden.

Not that de la Mare's tales can be classified in the usual sense as "ghost stories," for there is little in them that is truly remarkable, fantastic, or unbelievable as in "The Monkey's Paw," for example, or other classic ghost stories. De la Mare's settings are firmly anchored in reality, his characters are credible, and the situations in which they find themselves are easily possible. At least, this is so at the beginning of the tales; and, by the time de la Mare ventures into the incredible, the reader has, in Coleridge's phrase, willingly suspended disbelief. He has, in every sense of the word, become enthralled.

To achieve, at the onset, a sense of reality and credibility, de la Mare often employs a narrator who tells of an incident in his or someone else's past—a reminiscence. Sometimes he is merely the auditor-recorder of a story told by someone else, a narrator of vivid imagination. In this role, for example, he is the passive soul of rectitude who, in **"The Almond Tree,"** crosses the street in order to avoid the Count and his "disconcerting" companion, whose story he later hears from the Count himself. In this guise, too, he can prepare the reader to be sympathetic to the narrator as happens in **"The Bird of Travel,"** by anticipating, rather unctuously one must admit, the reader's possible objection to the tale: "And at last a quaint old creature whose name I have forgotten . . . told us the following rather pointless story. . . . " As auditor-recorder, he seldom comments except to scoff or to prod the narrator: "Good heavens, Maunders," he interjects at one point in **"Lispet, Lispett and Vaine"**—and, incidentally, sounds very much like Terence's companion in Housman's poem—"the stuff you talk! But one would not mind so much if you could spin a decent yarn." And his role as auditor-recorder is occasionally so completely subordinated that he disappears entirely before the end of the narrative. Such is the case in **"The Creatures,"** where his sole function is at the outset to lend credibility to the narrator's story.

In many of the first-person tales, however, the recorder device is dropped, and the narrator himself presents a reminiscence of some incident in which he has played a part. The character of the narrator, however, is in many instances similar to that of the auditor-recorder. He is most often unimaginative, dull, stodgy, practical—altogether run-of-the-mill. He is the bumbling, inept Richard in **"The Count's Courtship"**; he is the boorish Mr. Dash in **"A Recluse."** The significance of the incident of which he tells, in other words, escapes him; and, because it does, not only does the story remain credible, its irony is intensified.

"Seaton's Aunt" is perhaps one of the best of this kind. Withers, the narrator, is a grown man when he tells this story of one of his schoolmates, Arthur Seaton, a particularly distasteful "foreign" looking boy whose abundance of pocket money, supplied by his mysterious aunt with whom he lives, fails to win any friends among the very British boys of the school. "It needed . . . a rather peculiar taste, a rather rare kind of schoolboy courage and indifference to criticism, to be much associated with him," Withers remembers, and goes on to establish his character by confessing, "And I had neither the taste nor, perhaps, the courage." Seaton, however, bribes Withers with a pot of "outlandish mulberry-coloured jelly" into visiting the home of his aunt over the next holiday.

Upon their arrival at the gloomy Seaton mansion, it is soon obvious to Withers that Arthur is terrified of his aunt—with what seems to be very good reason. "This is the room, Withers, my brother William died in when a boy. Admire the view!" the aunt tells him upon taking him to his room. And, incredibly, Withers does as he is told; his only emotion is dread that the aunt will discover he has brought no luggage! Withers, in other words, is a perfect foil for Arthur Seaton, who is haunted by all manner of mysterious and horrible imaginings which center around his frightening and formidable aunt. "Don't appear to be talking of her, if you wouldn't mind," Arthur pleads, when the boys are alone, adding, "It's—because she's in league with the devil."

To Withers, this is nonsense; and, when in the middle of the night, the terrified Arthur comes to his room with tales of ghosts and evil demons haunting the very house they are in he scoffs: "You may think I'm a jolly noodle; just as you please. . . . Every fellow's a bit off his pluck at night, and you may think it a fine sport to try your rubbish on me." Even later, when Arthur presents to him what would seem to be convincing evidence that something unusual, to say the least, is occurring, Withers says: "I'm going to bed; I've had enough of this foolery."

The second part of the story occurs years later. Arthur Seaton, having left school, has dropped out of Withers' sight—and mind—until one day they meet. Seaton has not changed much; even the fact that he is to be married soon and presumably will be able to leave his aunt's home does not dispel the sense of doom about him. At his invitation, Withers again reluctantly consents to visit, expressly to meet Seaton's fiancée. The atmosphere at the Seaton home is still oppressive, filled with foreboding. Nor has Seaton's aunt changed. Withers again tries to rationalize: "Don't you think perhaps you may not treat your Aunt quite in the right way. . . . I can't help thinking she thinks you

don't care for her," he says to his host. But Seaton is inconsolable: "I'm as good as done. You wait," he tells Withers.

Withers does not have long to wait. Several months later he impulsively goes again to the Seaton home to inquire about the newlyweds in a guilty attempt to make amends because he has sent not even a note of congratulation to Seaton upon his marriage which he knew was to have taken place weeks before. But, when he gets to the house, he finds only the aunt; and she refuses to tell him where Seaton and his bride are. As Withers, having been inexplicably left alone, decides to find his way out of the gloomy house, he hears the aunt calling for her nephew: "Arthur, is that you? Is that you, Arthur." When she spies Withers instead, she croaks: "It is you, is it? *That* disgusting man! . . . Go away out. Go away out," which Withers does with alacrity. When he reaches the village he learns that Arthur Seaton has been "dead and buried these three months or more . . . just before he was to be married."

Withers reveals his practical nature when he decides against going to the churchyard to visit Arthur Seaton's grave, for he feels there is "precious little use in pottering about in the muddy dark merely to discover" where the luckless man is buried. But he confesses upon making this decision that he "felt a little uneasy" about it, for "My rather horrible thought was that, so far as I was concerned—one of his extremely few friends—he had never been much better than 'buried' in my mind."

The effect that de la Mare achieves in this and other tales where he uses the stolid, unimaginative narrator is not only realistic but also supremely ironic. We see Seaton only through Withers' work-a-day eyes; the horror Seaton knows is only hinted at; we are left to imagine its enormity; and, unless we supply the pity and the terror, we fail to grasp the larger tragedy that is implied. Yet even in **"Seaton's Aunt,"** in which the suggestion of tragedy is more overt than in many of the other stories, it is easy to miss. The clue is offered in Withers' identification of himself as one of Arthur Seaton's "extremely few friends." Time and again de la Mare's theme concerns the utter loneliness of human beings and their total inability to communicate one with another, a theme of which this story is a good illustration; and the use of the unimaginative narrator or auditor-recorder serves to underline it.

Occasionally—too infrequently, in fact—de la Mare attempted a first-person point of view story which resulted in nothing short of a *tour de force* of realism. **"In the Forest,"** the outstanding example of this type, enters directly into the mind of a small boy; there is no narrator reminiscing, no auditor to provide or imply commentaries on the action. This tale *is* the little boy's; we see the action solely through his eyes—and the horror is that the little boy is so realistic.

The events are simple: the boy's father goes to war; his baby sister sickens and dies; his mother leaves him in the cabin while she takes her dead baby to the village to be buried; the father returns from the battle, mortally wounded; the mother returns. But here is the little boy as he sees these events. He tells of his father's departure: "It was not raining when he [the father] started, only the leaves were wet with rain and the bark of the trees was darkened with wet. I asked him to bring me back a long rifle. He kept rubbing his hands over his face and blinking his eyes and listening to the wind as if he heard the guns. Two or three times he came back to say good-bye to my mother . . . I asked mother if father was glad to be going to the war. But she was crying over the baby, so I went out into the forest till dinner."

Two or three days later he asks his mother how long his father will be at war: "She said she could not tell. And I wondered how they would carry back his body if he was killed in the war." When the baby becomes ill, his mother asks him to go to the village to get the doctor, but he refuses: "It's only crying," he says; and he runs out to go fishing. When he returns, he sees the baby's white face, "and its eyelids were like white wax. Its lips were the colour of its hands, almost blue." He asks if the baby is dead, but his mother does not answer; she "only shook her shoulders." So, the boy continues, "I walked away and looked out of the door."

Left in the cabin alone while his mother has gone to the village to bury the baby, the boy gorges himself from their pitiably small reserve of food, lights a huge fire, and awaits her return. He tells of his reaction to his abandonment: "I could not cry, though I felt very angry at being left alone, and I was afraid." When he awakens the next morning his mother has not yet returned, but he hears a groan outside the door and peeping through a crack recognizes his father: "He was lying on his stomach; his clothes were filthy and torn, and at the back of his shoulder was a small hole pushed in in the cloth. There was dark, thick blood on the withered leaves. I tried to see his face, but couldn't very well. It was all muddy, bleared and white, and he groaned and swore when I touched him. But he didn't know who I was, and some of what he said didn't seem to me to have any sense." As the boy attempts, unsuccessfully, to give his father a drink of water, he tells him about the baby's death; "but he didn't show that he could hear anything; and just as I finished I heard mother coming back from the churchyard." And then comes the last shattering sentence: "So I ran out and told her that it was father."

These extensive quotes from **"In the Forest"** serve, I hope, to illustrate the exquisite control de la Mare had over point of view and how this control adds to the credibility of his narratives. Not a word is used that is not natural to a young boy; not a sentence is so structured as not to suggest his speech. How controlled and true to the point of view **"In the Forest"** is can be appreciated when one compares it to another more typical narrative. **"The Vats,"** in which de la Mare uses again the first person. In this story the point of view is no doubt his own. The narrator in this scene is beginning to describe the experience he and a friend had when they came suddenly upon these relics of the past:

> In telling of these Vats it is difficult to convey in mere words even a fraction of the effect upon our minds. And not merely our minds. They called to some hidden being within us that, if not their coeval, was at least aware of their exquisite an-

tiquity. Whether of archangelic or daemonic construction, clearly they had remained unvisited by mortal man for as many centuries at least as there are cherries in Damascus or beads in Tierra del Fuego. Sharers of this thought, we two dwarf visitors had whispered an instant or so together, face to face; and then were again mute.

It would be impossible to get farther away in style and tone from **"In the Forest."**

Yet de la Mare even ventures with some success to see occasionally from a woman's point of view as well, but he most often uses the third person in these instances.

Of those stories from a woman's point of view, **"The Wharf "** is perhaps the most often commented upon because the central startling image—a dung heap—is so successfully employed to symbolize the beauty and mystery of life. **"Cape Race"** and **" 'A Froward Child,' "** however, and **"The Face"** show de la Mare's mastery of a woman's point of view to even better advantage. In **"Cape Race,"** in which this ability is especially evident, Lettie is a young, romantic girl on her way to America with her betrothed and her future mother-in-law. Filled with life and love, Lettie has just rescued, one early morning on deck, a stray land bird that had lost its way as the ship had passed Cape Race, Newfoundland. Pleased with herself, she impatiently waits for her fiancé who has been seasick for three days. When he finally appears, they go to breakfast in an almost deserted saloon. She wants passionately to kiss him; she has clasped his hand beneath the table. But he sees the waiter bearing down upon them. "Any cereal, Lettie?" he asks, rejecting her gesture of affection. The reader needs no great imagination to guess what their marriage is going to be like.

In **" 'A Froward Child' "** however, the reader does not have to imagine, for the young woman in this tale breaks off her engagement to much the same kind of man when she discovers how placidly dull her intended husband is. Her agonized question again underscores the theme of loneliness and lack of communication: "Is there nothing in this miserable world can make us realize—*others*?" The same question is implied in **"The Face"** in which Nora has a transcendental experience, the importance of which she cannot seem to convey to her fiancé. None of these men has the imagination to transcend the mundane world of facts; their inability to do so irrevocably separates them from those to whom they should be closest. Again the theme is estrangement.

Seldom does de la Mare employ the third-person, omniscient point of view; and, in the cases where he does, his tales are either frankly for children, such as some of those in the collection ***Broomsticks;*** or they are obviously parables or allegories, as are **"The Connoisseur"** and **"The Riddle."** In these, no attempt to engage the reader's imagination through an appeal to his sense of reality is made; the stories, often ornately wrought, appeal solely to one's sense of beauty and mystery, and thus are in marked contrast to first-person narratives which create the aura of reality. For, however garrulous de la Mare's narrators are, they are, nevertheless, believable in the same sense that Conrad's Marlow is.

Another of the ways in which de la Mare creates a sense of reality in his tales is the meticulous accuracy with which he draws his settings. Often, it is true, the action seems to take place in or near a graveyard, as in **"Strangers and Pilgrims"**; a nearly-deserted decaying mansion, as in **"A Recluse,"** or an almost abandoned church, as in **"All Hallows."** Even these somewhat eerie settings, however, are wholly realistic. But few commentators have remarked upon the many settings which are totally unlike these which have somewhat erroneously become exclusively identified as de la Mare trademarks. It is important to examine, therefore, the characteristic de la Mare setting of which the deserted graveyard, mansion, or church are different aspects. For often the action takes place in a mundane setting: the kitchen where Emelia and her small son William share their supper in **"Physic"**; Mr. Thripp's modest cottage in **"The Nap"**; the tea shop in **"Missing"**; the pub in **"The Three Friends"**; the bedroom and lovely garden in **"The Picture"**; the doctor's office in **"Disillusioned"**; a lecture hall in **"A Revenant"**;—and other equally familiar places.

The distinguishing feature about de la Mare's settings is that they are, for the most part, lonely, generally inhabited by only one or two people. They are often rain and windswept, or fog mantled. Seldom does anything occur in bright sunshine; the time in most of the stories is usually twilight or after dark.

Even during the daylight, if events occur, say, in a garden, as they do in **"Miss Duveen,"** they take place in a shaded part of the garden: "It was raining," the narrator of **"Miss Duveen"** remembers of his first meeting with that delightful and pitiable creature for whom his story is titled: "the raindrops falling softly into the unrippled water, making their great circles, and tapping on the motionless leaves above my head where I sat in shelter on the bank. But the sun was shining whitely from behind a thin fleece of cloud, when Miss Duveen suddenly peeped in at me out of the greenery. . . ." In another typical setting, Dr. Lidgett's consulting room in **"Disillusioned,"** as the doctor talks to the stranger who has confronted him, "It was afternoon, and a scene of stillest life. The polished writing table . . . the cabinet . . . the glass and gilt of the engraved portraits on the walls—everything in the room appeared to have sunken long ago into a reverie oceans deep."

Even when one would normally expect to find numbers of people—as, for example, in **"What Dreams May Come"** where the action seems to take place on a bus—we find the central character "*alone* now in the strange vacancy of the coach. . . ." It has been raining, "raining heavily . . . the dark stain on the thick grey fabric of the seat had soaked it through." She looks about for the conductor, but "The wreathing mist which dimmed her eyes obscured him too a little. . . . " Similarly, de la Mare draws his setting for **"The Three Friends,"** two of whom are approaching a pub as the story begins: "The street was narrow; yet, looking up, the two old friends, bent on their accustomed visit, could discern—beyond a yellow light that had suddenly shone out into the hushed gloom from an attic window—the vast, accumulated thunderclouds that towered into the darkening zenith."

And the pub's interior, where the two friends discuss with the barmaid one's reoccurring dream of death, is no more cheerful an atmosphere. In much the same way, railway carriages and stations, contrary to one's usual expectation—and experience—never seem to be occupied by more than two people; and, as the trains travel through the dark from nowhere to nowhere, a story unfolds, as in **"The Creatures,"** which takes the reader just as effortlessly into what de la Mare calls the "otherwhere." Trains, coaches, carriages of one sort or another often figure, in fact, in these tales; and they serve to underline de la Mare's belief that we are all travelers whose points of departure and destinations are, for the most part, forever unknown.

Besides the pervasive sense of loneliness achieved by the location of the action, the limited number of characters, the weather and time of day, there are other aspects of his settings which amount almost to de la Mare signatures: windows and mirrors—which often serve the same function—and portraits. In nearly every one of de la Mare's stories mirrors and windows play some part. In **"Physic,"** for example, William, the little boy who becomes suddenly ill, begs his mother to put down the blinds to the very bottom of the window because, he says, "I *hate* seeing—seeing myself in the glass." And later he asks his mother, "Why do faces come in the window, horrid faces?" In **"The Talisman,"** the narrator catches a glimpse of himself in a mirror and also sees "another reflection, a phantom face. . . ." In **"What Dreams May Come,"** Emmeline, apparently dozing in a bus, wakes knowing she has been looking at a reflection other than her own in the window. For the little girl in **"Selina's Parable,"** "every window . . . had a charm, an incantation all its own." And the reason given in the story for this charm might well have been de la Mare's own: "Was it not an egress for her eye to a scene of some beauty, or life, or of forbiddingness; was it not the way of light; either her own outward, or the world's inward?"

Windows and mirrors, even when only mentioned in the stories, take on a symbolic—one would almost like to say "mystic"—force. We know that de la Mare was fascinated by them, for he felt that through them and in them one can see the other side of things or of the self. For the same reason, incidentally, the feature of his characters' faces most often mentioned is their eyes; they were to him, in a Blakean sense, windows of the soul: "There is at times a dweller behind the eye that looks out, though only now and again, from that small window," observes the narrator of **"The Green Room."** This idea occurs again and again throughout the tales.

Perhaps one of the best illustrations of how de la Mare combines these symbols is to be found in **"The Picnic,"** in the collection *On The Edge* (1930). In this tale, Miss Curtis, a seemingly very practical, feet-on-the-ground London shopkeeper, recalls a sea-side vacation she took five years earlier. During the course of her holiday she sees daily a man at a window who appears always to smile when she passes. His smile is a "quiet" one, "far away," and, she decides, "lonely." It seems to her to plead for her love, her understanding. And, of course, she falls in love with him. The last day of her vacation she sees him out walking with a companion; they confront one another; and she looks up "straight into the unknown one's face, straight into his eyes." But, although they look straight at her, they do not see her—and have never seen her. The stranger is blind. Miss Curtis, as the story concludes, shuts up her shop for the evening, her last act being to pull down "the last dark-blue blind, the blind that covered the glass of the door." This action is symbolic of her renunciation of five years before when she had embarked not on a love affair, but a "life affair"; for "this life of which she had caught this marvellous glimpse had itself never even been a possibility—merely an illusion."

In much the same manner as the windows and mirrors, portraits play a role and have a symbolic function in the short stories. In **"Seaton's Aunt"** for example, in a superb combination of two symbols, there is a hideous water color hanging in Withers' room of an enormous eye "with an extremely fishlike intensity in the spark of light on the dark pupil"; beneath it is inscribed "Thou God Seest ME." In **"What Dreams May Come"** the portrait of the master of the house in which Emmeline finds herself is in reality a death's head. In yet another tale, **"The Picture,"** Lucia is haunted by the painting of the dead first wife of her adored husband. And, in the masterful depiction of hatred called **"An Anniversary,"** a portrait "appears as if what it represented were always steadily in wait for . . . a renewed and really close scrutiny of itself." De la Mare observes in this story, and illustrates the idea often, that portraits can "shed on one a sort of passive influence."

The influence of Walter Beverley's dead aunt's portrait in **"The Quincunx"** is, however, something other than passive. In this story, which again treats of hatred, Walter becomes obsessed by his aunt's portrait and finally is possessed by her malignant influence. But, in this case, he is so churlish and rapacious that the reader's sympathy is, however grudgingly given, with the dead aunt.

The most finely wrought story in which most of these symbols—windows, mirrors, and portraits—appear is **"The Looking Glass,"** which echoes Lewis Carroll only in the title and in the name of the central character; for the Alice of this tale goes through the looking glass in a far different manner than Carroll's Alice does. The consumptive young companion of an old shrew, de la Mare's Alice wanders daily during her free time in the walled-in garden in which raindrops always seem to be quietly falling. She knows the garden is haunted at times and feels the presence of its ghost: "What was all through the place now like smoke Alice perceived to be the peculiar clarity of the air discernible in the garden at times. The clearness as it were of glass, of a looking-glass, which conceals all behind and beyond it, returning only the looker's wonder, or simply her vanity, or even her gaiety." And Alice smiles to think that "There are people who look into looking-glasses, actually see themselves there, and yet never turn a hair."

The garden is the only place where Alice feels at peace with herself. She tells her confidant, Sarah, the cook next door: "I get out of bed at night to look down from the window and wish myself here. When I'm reading, just as if it

were a painted illustration—in the book, you know—the scene of it all floats in between me and the print." Having been told by Sarah that she may accost the presence in the garden by following a certain ritual, Alice prepares to do so—even more eagerly when she discovers that she is herself, in a sense, the presence. "The spirit is *me,*" she is convinced: "*I* haunt this place."

On the night of her assignation with that spirit she gazes at herself in the "dim discoloured glass" in her own room. Why her mirror is so described is all too apparent; for, when her employer tries to awaken her the next morning, Alice, "though unbeknown in any really conscious sense to herself, perhaps, had long since decided not to be awakened." She has, in other words, gone through to the other side of the looking glass and clarity of the garden to the real reality, an experience similar to Nora's in **"The Face"** who felt, when she fell into a woodland pond whose glassy surface had enchanted her, that she "had gone in under a dark dreadful tunnel and come out on the other side."

Water, as can be seen from this discussion, also plays an important symbolic function in the short stories; but, because it has an even more important role in the novels, its function has been analyzed extensively in the section devoted to them. Suffice it to say here, water—whether in the form of rain, or a stream, or a pool, or the sea—is used occasionally as an estranging medium, as is the stream in **"Miss Duveen"** or in **"The Lost Track."** Sometimes it represents the source of reality, as the sea does in **"The Picnic,"** or the still pool in **"The Face."** Most often, as rain it serves not only to increase the sense of isolation but also to suggest life-giving (or truth-giving, for de la Mare) properties traditionally associated with rain.

In the stories of Walter de la Mare, then, the settings have a two-fold function: they provide a realistic background on which the sometimes bizarre action is projected, and they serve to increase the significance of the action by assuming a symbolic role. That de la Mare learned much from Emily Brontë, Thomas Hardy, W. H. Hudson and Joseph Conrad about these matters he himself was happy to admit; and that he learned his lessons well is obvious from the stories themselves. But no story, however perfect its setting, is successful for this reason alone—characters and themes must be at least as felicitous.

Edward Wagenknecht and other critics have pointed to the brief but incisive strokes with which de la Mare created his characters. But to an even greater extent, his mastery is due to the fact that generally he does not describe his characters—they reveal themselves by their actions and their speech. We have already seen Seaton's baleful aunt welcome his young friend: "This is the room, Withers, my brother William died in when a boy. Admire the view." The juxtaposition of the comment and the command tell more of Seaton's aunt than would have pages of description. In much the same way, the malignant butler in **"Crewe,"** after having goaded the gardener to his death, says of him, "And yet—why, he never so much as asked me to say a good word for him. Not one," thus revealing his hypocrisy, and his true nature. So too, Aubrey, the jealous husband in **"An Anniversary,"** reveals himself when, railing at his wife, he refers to Othello as "that pimp of futility," and thus unconsciously applies the epithet to himself. Even the thoroughly delightful and completely mad Miss Miller in the story of that name shows just how mad and how delightful she is when she first opens her mouth to talk to the runaway Nella; and her story of herself as a young child, when things ran away from her rather than her running away from them, reminds us that, as Emily Dickinson wrote, in "much madness is divinest sense to a discerning eye."

In fact, although few of his characters are as engagingly demented as Miss Miller is (although Miss Rawlings, in **"Pigtails, Ltd."** runs a close second to her), a good many of them are mad, at least in the sense of being possessed or obsessed or, as occurs in several of the tales—haunted. A good example of one who is obsessed—in this case by the idea of pure beauty, as is Anthony in **"Lispet, Lispett and Vaine"**—is the artist in **"The Tree."** He is effectively contrasted to his half brother, a fruit merchant, who also is obsessed, but by money and the desire to "get ahead." The narrator of **"The Creatures"** is another character obsessed by a vision he has seen of paradise; and the recluse in **"Mr. Kempe"** searches with unremitting ardor for proof of man's possession of a soul, a search similar to that carried on by the central character in **"A Recluse."** Then too, there is the young man in **"Pretty Poll"** who fell in love with one of the imagined former owners—the "impossible she"—of a parrot he had purchased which alternately swore like a sailor and sang like an angel.

In many of the tales the obsession of the central character amounts to his being haunted. In these tales there is a feeling of tension, an undertone of mystery and strangeness that not only fascinates but terrifies the reader. They sometimes resemble the auditor-recorder's description of the narrator's tale in **"Bird of Travel"**: "a poet's story in sober earnest: incoherent, obscure, unreal, unlifelike, without an ending." But they have these qualities only if one looks at them straight on, so to speak; for—just as life itself is sometimes incoherent, obscure, unreal, and, indeed, "unlifelike"—so are the stories. "Qui vive?"—"who goes there?"—the question de la Mare most often asks, is often answered in the tales by another question: "Who asks?" And because he felt that "fiction holds up, or should hold up, an all-searching, all-collective, and reflective mirror to humanity . . ." his stories hold the mirror to that part of humanity seldom touched upon except in "shockers" or in science fiction.

Most of de la Mare's haunted characters are also solitaries, perhaps because he felt that each of us is, in a sense, a "livelong [*sic*] recluse," did we have the courage to admit it. But, more likely, his characters are solitaries in these particular stories because his experience had taught him that "strange and uninvited guests are likely to intrude on any protracted human solitude. . . ." That there may be ghosts, revenants—call them what one will—seemed completely plausible to him: time and again he speculated in his essays on the possibility, and the theme of many of his stories concerns just this eventuality. Against any charge that such stories are not "realistic," he would have replied what he wrote in another connection: "What is called real-

ism is usually a record of life at a low pitch and ebb viewed in the sunless light of day. . . ."

As I have said earlier . . . , most of these stories are realistic enough, in the beginning at least; and, by the time they have begun to engage "the little nowhere" of the reader's mind, the purpose of the early "realism" has been accomplished and the magic begins to work. I have already referred to **"Seaton's Aunt"** in this connection, but I think in many ways the aunt in the first-person narrative called **"The Guardian,"** which appears in *A Beginning* (1955), is even more diabolical because she does not comprehend at all what occurs to her and her nephew Philip, who becomes haunted not only by evil and ugliness but by good and beauty as well.

We listen to her as she describes herself: "I am not a mother. I am what is called 'an old maid'; but even 'old maids,' I assume, are entitled to their convictions." And we savor the magnificent irony when, just after she describes her young nephew as a "delicate . . . sensitive and solitary child" whom she loves dearly, she goes on to describe herself as a child: "I dreaded company . . . was shy of speaking my own mind, and of showing affection. I used both to despise and to envy the delicate—the demonstrative. . . ." As the story progresses, it becomes obvious that she has not changed. She advises Philip's mother against sending the boy to school until his ninth year, at which time, she says, "I had the pleasure and privilege of paying for Philip's education." He is bundled off to a preparatory school "where even a sensitive and difficult child might have at least every opportunity of doing well and of being happy." Of this she is certain, because, as she says, "I had myself insisted on being taken over the whole school, scullery to attics, and on having a few words *alone* with the matron. . . ." She soon finds that Philip is prey to some kind of "nervous trouble" when on a holiday from school he confesses to her that he sees something that is not in the room but "inside"—presumably, "inside" his head. The very soul of practicality and insensitiveness, she continues: "By dint of careful questioning, I discovered at length that what troubled him was no more, as I thought at the time, than a mere fancy."

Put on a regimen of tonic, Philip appears to recover from his nervous trouble and his aunt is relieved; for, as she knows, "Even people of excellent common sense may occasionally be the prey of illusions—ghosts and similar nonsense. Charles Wesley, for example." However, a few weeks after his twelfth birthday, Philip falls one night from the window ledge of his school dormitory, and his aunt is summoned to his deathbed. Seated beside the dying boy, she confesses: "At that time I had already steeled myself to many things in this world; but a life, I can truthfully declare, was slipping away far from me more precious than my own . . . I had never, except once before, felt helpless and forsaken." At this moment the dormitory maid—whose face vaguely recalls to the aunt "some old picture I had seen"—comes into the room and over the dying boy's face appears a look "as near human ecstasy as mortal features are capable of." And, although the aunt detests "anything even resembling sentimentality," she recognizes that Philip is in love—"the poor child," she calls him, "was in love." The evil presence that had haunted him has been overcome by this love; and, though he dies, he has achieved more happiness than the aunt will ever know.

Philip and Arthur Seaton are just two of several haunted boys or young men in de la Mare's tales: there is Jimmie, in the less-successful **"Out of the Deep,"** who returns to the hated house in which he had grown up, having been willed it by his equally detested late aunt and uncle. As a boy, he had slept in the attic; upon his return, he sleeps in his Uncle Timothy's Arabian bed by which hangs a bell cord and around which he burns every night all night candles because as a child he had been so terrified of the dark. He recalls too from his youth the hated butler Soames; and one evening, having sampled too much of the contents of his uncle's wine cellar, he pulls the bell cord. A spectral Soames answers. Jimmie jocularly asks for primroses; and, although it is the dead of winter, almost instantaneously a lovely young child enters the room with a bowl of them. Each successive pull of the bell cord summons something "out of the deep," and at last the haunted Jimmie goes mad and is found dead in his old bed in the attic.

De la Mare does well in getting into the mind of a madman, as Jimmie in **"Out of the Deep"** obviously is; and he does equally well with a young man who is haunted by the face of a lovely, unknown suicide in **"The Green Room"** and with the old man in **"The House,"** every room of which is filled with ghosts. Sometimes, however, his stories have as their central characters revenants themselves. Such a one is **"Strangers and Pilgrims,"** a story so filled with pathos as to linger—like an unhappy ghost itself—long in the reader's mind. Such also is **"A Revenant"**—about the shade of Edgar Allan Poe who stops in to hear a lecture about himself given by Professor Monk who purports to be objective and balanced in his treatment but who in reality damns Poe—and himself—with his preference for "facts" to "atmosphere." This story, however, is more interesting to the student of literature as a discussion of how not to approach the works of an author than it is as a story about de la Mare's preoccupation with the possibilities of the dead returning.

But there are many other kinds of characters in de la Mare's short stories than the obsessed, the mad, and the haunted; and, although the theme of the returning dead is a central one, there are others as well. True, de la Mare seldom bothers with the "average person"; but, as he enquired in his own person elsewhere, "Where shall we find an average *mind* or personality or soul or self?" About as close as he ever comes to it is in **"The Nap"** in which we see bared the thoughts about his wife and children of a lower middle-class man, Mr. Thripp. This story illustrates also another of de la Mare's preoccupations which I have already touched upon: the difficulty, if not altogether the impossibility, of communication or understanding between people. This theme is central or is touched upon in many of the tales.

Usually the inability to communicate is the result of a lack of imagination or love on the part of one of the characters. I have already mentioned " 'A Froward Child' " and **"Cape Race"** as good examples of this situation, but many

other stories, such as **"The Count's Courtship," "The Tree," "Disillusioned,"** and **"The Face,"** are in whole or in part about the inability of human beings to establish some kind of communication with others. Even Miss Duveen, in the story of the same name, is unable to maintain more than briefly the interest of the little boy who tells years later the story of this mad—and pitiful—old lady. Enchanted at first by her, he confesses when she is "put away" that, despite "a vague sorrow" he feels when he hears the news, he is "greatly relieved." No more pathetic a scene in all of de la Mare is there than the one when Miss Duveen, before her departure, throws a letter to him from across the stream which separates their two gardens: "She whispered earnestly and rapidly at me over the water. But I could not catch a single word she said, and failed to decipher her close spidery handwriting." Even after this they see each other occasionally across the stream, but the narrator recalls: "The distance seemed to confuse her, and quite silenced me." The distance across the stream, of course, is as immeasurable and vast as the distances in the unplumbable sea that separates, as it did for Matthew Arnold, island from island forever.

In another vein entirely are the stories in *Broomsticks and Other Tales* (1925), tales de la Mare had written for his own children and which, I am sure, will continue to delight children as long as there are any to read or be read to. The basic themes are to be found even in these, however: the haunted, the dead returning, estrangement. Characteristically, these are no run-of-the-mill children's stories—they rank easily with Kenneth Grahame's *Wind in the Willows,* A. A. Milne's Pooh stories, or Lewis Carroll's Alice tales. In fact, de la Mare excels other writers for children, I believe, simply because—and I almost hate to use the word again—his characters are more *real.* True, there is fantasy as when, for example, the jealous father of the lovely Myfanwy turns into an ass; but it is perfectly logical that he do so, because he eats a magic apple which turns anyone who does so into exactly what he really is. And, of course, it hardly seems likely that Alice's godmother is really her great-great-great-great-great-great-great-great grandmother; but how else can she be three hundred and fifty years old? Such is de la Mare's artistry that these and similar fancies become entirely possible.

Although, of course, the ultimate judges of children's stories must be children themselves, none of the tales in *Broomsticks* can be read by an adult without some delight and profit for some of them illustrate his profoundest insights. Such, for example, is the story of the thief who craved of all things happiness but does not find it until he marries Susan—the one servant who refuses to leave him because, as she says to him, "You was less unkind to me than to all the other servants put together,"—and then gives away all of his ill-gotten gains. What redeems him is seeing Susan with a look of happiness on her face and realizing that, although he had never seen a "lovelier sight," neither he nor any other thief could steal it.

Perhaps the most engaging of the stories in *Broomsticks,* and the most deceptively simple, is **"Maria-Fly."** Although it can be read as a story about the inability of human beings to communicate with each other, it is, without doubt, based on William Blake's poem "The Fly"; the key stanza and the primary theme of **"Maria-Fly"** is stated in the poem's second stanza:

> Am not I
> A fly like thee?
> Or art not thou
> A man like me?

The story also illustrates one of de la Mare's abiding beliefs, the clearest example of which is in the introduction to *Behold, This Dreamer!*—"All things stale and lose their virtue, the best and worst, the simple and complicated, the plain and beautiful, impulse as well as artifice, *unless we attend to them;* give to them as much at least as they can bestow."

The little girl, Maria, in the story does just that: for the first time in her whole life she *sees* a fly. And, watching the fly with the closest attention, "It seemed to be that just as Maria herself was one particular little girl, so this was one particular fly. A fly by itself. A fly living its own one life; confident, alert, alone in its own Fly World." Soon, she becomes engrossed, and then the strangest thing happens: "She seemed almost to have *become* the fly—Maria-Fly." After this experience, although she could not have explained why, "she felt surprisingly gay and joyful." But no one who remembers the joy of childhood "watching" a burdened ant toil up the seemingly insurmountable Everest of a blade of grass needs to be told why Maria is so happy. De la Mare caught the rapture perfectly, and also captured the poignancy of the aftermath of Maria's experience: she wants to tell someone about what really happened, what it was like to really see a fly. And, of course, as even the most poetic of mystics fails to communicate the truth of his experience of God, so is Maria unable to tell anyone the truth of her experience.

She tries in turn to tell the cook, a visiting clergyman, the seamstress, her father, the gardener, and finally his simple-minded helper. But even he does not understand. She turns away from him "her small head filled as with a tune ages old and as sorrowful as the sounds of the tide on the unvisited shores of the ocean," and goes to sit alone in an arbor. After some moments in which we do not know her thoughts, the story ends: "Maria gave yet another deep sigh, and then looked up around her almost as if in hopes of somebody else to whom she might tell her secret tale—about the fly—about Maria-Fly. And then, as if at a signal, she hopped down suddenly out of the arbour, almost as lightly as a thin-legged bird herself, and was off flying over the emerald green grass into the delightful sunshine without in the least knowing why, or where to." Perhaps Maria has learned what the speaker in Blake's poem knows:

> Than am I
> A happy fly,
> If I live
> Or if I die.

As de la Mare does in the rest of his fiction, he shows in his stories for children his profound knowledge of and love for all things living. But the children's stories allow him to show also, as he seldom can in his other fiction, his delightful sense of humor and love of nonsense. There is, for example, Sam Such, who grows into manhood thinking his nose is made of wax. His father, "a prosperous clothier and haberdasher," has a shop named "Such & Such"; and the store's motto is "Why go to So and So's when you can get ALL you will ever want from Such & Such." And there is Miss Chauncey of **"Broomsticks"** who is deceived by her cat—but then there are a hundred more touches of humor which cannot be really enjoyed unless the stories *and* the poems *and* the novels are read.

But one does not read de la Mare for his humor, however delightful it may be. One goes to him to see in tangible form the truths, the dreams and longings—and forebodings and terrors—known alone by and admitted only to the inmost self. This is not to say that all of the tales are equally satisfactory or successful. Some of them are contrived, a bit too pat—**"Out of the Deep," "The Green Room,"** and **"A Revenant"** come immediately to mind. But even these have their interest, and it is only fair that he be judged as are Wordsworth and Keats and even Shakespeare—by his best. His best stories are superb. **"Miss Duveen," "In the Forest," "The Looking Glass," "Seaton's Aunt," "Miss Miller," "The Bowl," "Pigtails, Ltd.," "Lucy," "Missing," "Neighbours," "The Orgy: An**

De la Mare on an uncanny experience:

Two late summers ago [my son Colin and I] came by chance on a remote out-of-the-way country road to a vacant house. It was the neglected garden, the slanting 'To Let' board that caught our eyes; nothing more. We went in. The slate-coloured painted iron gate was half open; one tall fir tree on the small lawn faced the windows; the birds fled away before us, as birds in such surroundings always do. It was broad daylight, the air already a little autumnal; and the sun was shining on his slow way down through the rather hazy heavens. It was neither a large house nor a very attractive one. It looked empty rather than forlorn. We peered in at the windows—ceilings and painted vacancy; then pushed on into the garden, now a lovely wilderness beyond them. There, in the long grass, we chanced on a scrap of a picture postcard that had come from somewhere in South America—Chile, Peru, Guatemala?—we cannot remember. Apples were nearly ripe on the unpruned trees. The last roses—I recall one particularly beautiful in shape and colour—were in bloom. Nothing whatever occurred in the straggling orchard behind that house that could have alarmed an infant—or even its nursemaid. But in a minute or two [Colin] remarked rather curtly, 'I can't bear this place; let's get out of it.'

'Vex not *his* ghost . . .' Realizing what he meant—though in sheer curiosity I had been rather enjoying 'bearing it' myself, I followed him out.

A week or two afterwards we heard on excellent authority that this particular residence was unable to keep its tenants. It had a queer name among its country neighbours and the reputation of being 'haunted'.

Walter de la Mare, in his introduction to They Walk Again: An Anthology of Ghost Stories, *1942.*

Idyll," "An Ideal Craftsman," "The Nap," "The Wharf," and "The Trumpet" are among the best short stories written.

His preoccupation with good and evil puts him on a level with Hawthorne and Conrad; his mastery of suspense and terror is equal to Poe's; the subtlety of his characterizations occasionally rivals James'. And the range of his portrayals is impressive: children, old maids, the demented, old idealists and young pessimists, artists, businessmen, dandys, young women in love—all of whom share in the mysterious and sometimes maddening business called living. (pp. 26-46)

Doris Ross McCrosson, in her Walter de la Mare, *Twayne Publishers, Inc., 1966, 170 p.*

Julia Briggs (essay date 1977)

[*Briggs is an English critic. In the following essay, she examines de la Mare's stories of the supernatural.*]

The most interesting ghost stories written after the Great War were those of the poet Walter de la Mare. They had little in common with others of their time, though the influence of Henry James was discernible, contributing a complexity, intensity and literary seriousness only rivalled by the great nineteenth-century masters of the form, Scott, Dickens, Le Fanu and James himself. Modern criticism has consistently neglected de la Mare's work, particularly his prose writings. They have been excluded from the accepted canons of important literature, receiving only an occasional accolade, and that mainly from fellow-authors. As a result, most of them have long been out of print, although single pieces often reappear in anthologies of ghost stories. It is to be hoped that his reputation is merely undergoing a temporary recession and that before too long that delicate yet powerful vision will receive the recognition it deserves.

The tendency to omit any reference to his remarkable short stories in literary histories is probably due to a sense that they are old-fashioned, even out-of-date in character. The world depicted is not the familiar urban landscape of pylons, airports and motorways, but a never-never land, a romantic vision of a lovely England, long lost if it ever existed at all. There is some justification for such a view: although the modern world intrudes occasionally—there is a tube train in **'Bad Company'**, a car in **'A Recluse',** and elsewhere trains, buses, pubs and teashops—de la Mare prefers a simplified setting that conforms to poetic universals or is generalized by the enduring influence of nature. He looks over his shoulder to a dateless, idealized Victorian era where private incomes and servants were the norm rather than the exception, a world whose demise ultimately prevented his contemporary, E. M. Forster, from writing any more novels. Even worse, de la Mare is felt to have avoided the main issues of fiction by presenting love with all the evasiveness of a Victorian, and by not treating social life at all. Professor Robson has commented: 'The traditional subjects of the novel—manners, social criticism, studies of moral conduct—are not at the centre of his interests.' It might be argued that such concerns are less appropriate to the short story than the novel. De la Mare scores by presenting brilliantly illuminated fragments of

experience. His imaginative world is essentially subjective, an intensifying gaze focused on a sequence of curious, perhaps inexplicable events.

Ironically it is these qualities that make his work modern. As the novel and drama become increasingly concerned to pursue in depth the nature of private fantasy and obsession, so de la Mare's stories may be seen to anticipate more recent poetic explorations of loneliness, silence and death, so remarkable in Beckett and Pinter, for example. Like them, he writes of the absurdity or total failure of communication in settings whose historical time or place are kept deliberately vague. His heroes, like theirs, grope their way through the metaphysical uncertainties of a universe in which they can never hope to be more than 'strangers and pilgrims', and the highest aim is merely to survive.

De la Mare's stories pose a series of questions about the nature of life itself, some of which are actually asked in the course of the tales, while others remain implicit. There are no assertions and no solutions here, only an endless sequence of explorations of ever-increasing delicacy. Although many of his ghost stories are very powerful, they seldom have a clearly defined climax, and in this respect his work resembles that of E. T. A. Hoffmann, another explorer at the remoter edges of human life. All Walter de la Mare's narratives are hedged about with doubts and uncertainties: his characteristic narrator is an odd person met on a train or a railway platform, in a teashop or a pub, whose references can never be checked. When the story is told in the first person or the narrator of the uncanny events is shown in sharper focus, the experience itself then becomes elusive, a series of strange, often unpleasantly suggestive incidents which might nevertheless sustain a more prosaic explanation than is liable to occur to the reader.

Nor is it only the characters and events of these stories which refuse to be pigeon-holed. Over and over again the writer asks, implicitly or explicitly, 'What indeed constitutes the *reality* of any fellow creature?' or more simply, 'Was what she had seen real?' In an important sense his short stories form a continuous spectrum in which the distinction between the 'real' and the supernatural is at best an artificial one. There is nothing as horrifying among the ghost stories as **'In the Forest'**, a totally plausible narrative, while the daylight mystery of **'Missing'** is more appalling than that of **'Crewe'**, which it otherwise closely resembles, because of what is left unsaid and unadmitted. Both relate a brief encounter with a sinister individual who tells a story of betrayal and virtual murder. Yet although **'Missing'** is set on a bright summer day, and has none of the supernatural overtones of **'Crewe'**, the speaker's pathetic attempts to conceal his crime make him even more horrifying. In the de la Mare universe objective experience and objectivity in general seems to hold little interest; what matters is the subjective truth. It may be broken into small fragments, highly coloured by the minds of those who experience it, but it is small enough to be free from any distortion, other than the imposed colouring of the mind through which it comes. His stories are deliberately limited in scope and length, but their accuracy and integrity give them an importance far beyond the immediate impact; they require several readings before their possible meanings will be exhausted.

The deliberate limiting of the areas of experience to be explored is reflected in the techniques he used for looking at them: 'the eye of childhood' is a favourite device, both in the non-supernatural tales, and in such ghost stories as **'Seaton's Aunt'.** Closely related to the little world of the child is the physically limited adult world of **'At First Sight'** (*On the Edge*, 1930) where the hero cannot raise his eyes above knee level, or that of Miss M in *Memoirs of a Midget* (1921). The theme of visual distortion is combined with the child's eye view in the tragic story, **'The Guardian'** (*A Beginning*, 1955), whose prosaic narrator is the last of a long line of selfish and possessive protectors. When her little nephew, Philip, swivels his eyes to the corner of his head, he catches a glimpse of a dreadful crouching figure that reminds him of 'that horrid, horrid Satan'. Like the hero of **'At First Sight,'** little Philip may have some genuine ocular disability. His aunt later wonders that it never occurred to her to consult an oculist. At the end of the story the dying child's eyes 'moved to their extreme angle' to behold, not a demon this time, but the angelic dormitory maid whose serene face 'vaguely recalled some old picture'. The guardian of the title thus refers not only to the crabbed narrator, but also to the guardian angel that she had hesitated to recommend to the frightened child, but whom he finally meets in the person of the sick-room maid. For de la Mare, the horrors and glories lurk at the edge of our vision, and are only beheld by the few who are painfully sensitive to them. He may well have known the physiological fact that objects glimpsed at the edge of the field of vision act as warnings to the brain, thus producing sensations of fear. It lends an added point.

The child-observer is a most useful device in fiction since his sharp observation, but lack of total comprehension, requires the reader to supply much of the interpretation himself. Walter de la Mare may have learnt this technique from Henry James, who uses it so effectively in his novel *What Maisie Knew*. De la Mare's admiration for James both as a ghost story writer and, more generally, as a stylist, is evident in much of his work, but while, like James, he often uses language to express thought in motion, he avoids the tendency to thickness and 'clotting' which sometimes makes James difficult to read. As one would expect of a poet, he pays the closest attention to language at all times, and uses it with a sense of irony and aptness that repays the reader's full attention.

One respect in which Walter de la Mare surpasses his master is in the use of language to establish character. An obvious comparison here might be with Kipling, but the use of the monologue for self-revelation, such an integral part of de la Mare's art, is perhaps more reminiscent of Browning, a distant relative of his. Yet again such a comparison fails to do justice to the vividly colloquial quality of the language. The unforgettable way in which it reaches out to the unknown, as well as its frequent content of self-delusion, seem to point forward to modern dramatists such as Harold Pinter. Here is an example from **'Crewe'** (*On the Edge*), a tale where even the setting, an empty waiting room, seems to belong to a Pinter dialogue:

'And talking of that, now, have you ever heard say that there is less risk sitting in a railway carriage at sixty miles an hour than in laying alone, safe, as you might suppose, in your own bed? That's true, too.' He glanced round him. 'You know where you are in a place like this, too. It's solid, though—' I couldn't catch the words that followed, but they seemed to be uncomplimentary to things in general.

'Yes', I agreed, 'it certainly looks solid.'

'Ah, "looks",' he went on cantankerously. 'But what *is* your "solid", come to that? I thought so myself once.' He seemed to be pondering over the *once.* 'But now,' he added, 'I know different.'

Henry James and Walter de la Mare both differ from the majority of ghost story writers in that they used the supernatural not merely as an end in itself, but also as a subordinate element in their fictions. Many of James's short stories such as 'Owen Wingrave' and 'Sir Edmund Orme' are centred not on the ghost, but on a human drama played out in the foreground. So too are a number of Walter de la Mare's tales, though with this difference, that his writing is never wholly free from a sense of wonder and mystery and so his minor ghosts often fit more naturally into their background. For example in **'The Trumpet'** (*The Wind Blows Over*, 1936) there is more than a hint that the terrified Philip sees the spirit of his half-brother, Dick, entering the church on All Saints Eve, even while the boy clambers precariously to the roof within. What else could it be, since 'it isn't a man and it isn't a woman'? Such an interpretation is further suggested by the children's speculations on the nature of death and the meaning of the motto, *resurgam.* Nevertheless the story is primarily concerned with the relationship between Philip and Dick, and the appearance of the ghost is not crucial, but merely characteristic of a world where anything may happen.

Two other stories, **'A Froward Child'** and **'The Face'**, show how supernatural experiences may bring about the estrangement of a young couple. Here the emphasis falls on the breakdown of the relationship rather than on the girl's strange experience, the significance of which lies—in both stories—in the fact that she cannot convey it to her stolid, unimaginative fiancé. **'Cape Race'** presents a similar situation but without the element of the supernatural, and the inadequate relationship is ultimately accepted. In **'A Froward Child'** and **'The Face'** the supernatural experiences of Lavinia and Nora deepen, rather than lessen, their individual isolation. In **'Cape Race'** Lettie's encounter with the land-bird is strangely liberating, yet she is able to accept the differences between herself and her dull fiancé as Lavinia and Nora were not. **'An Anniversary'** (from *A Beginning*) is also about estrangement, but this time the parting is more than earthly, for a dead lover returns to reclaim his mistress, now Aubrey's unhappy wife. It is difficult to decide whether the supernatural or human interest predominates here, since the real horror lies in Aubrey's consuming and degrading jealousy, not in the visitation of his dead rival. De la Mare's trick of irony runs riot in Aubrey's consciousness, and the total effect has something of the savagery and unrestrained bitterness of Chaucer's *Merchant's Tale,* although the explicit references are, not unnaturally, to *Othello* and the horror of being Iago.

Where the supernatural is made to contribute to larger effects and employed generally as part of the writer's equipment, it may be used for light-hearted pieces, such as Henry James's 'The Third Person' and de la Mare's '**A Revenant**', or for lyrical and mysterious studies such as '**The Looking Glass**' or '**The Riddle**'. The fairy-tale mood of these two stories dominates the collection entitled *The Riddle* (1923) but subsequently was chiefly limited to his stories for children. On the whole de la Mare's ventures into the regions of fantasy are more surefooted than James's because his work deals, not with society and its values, but rather with loneliness and isolation, areas where relative views and the individual imagination assume greater importance. In James's world, where essentially human values and ethics predominate, the ghost is often felt to be an intrusion; de la Mare's universe is far more internal and spiritual, and his ghosts consequently gain more from their settings. In those stories where the supernatural puts in a fleeting, even a doubtful appearance (as in '**The Trumpet**', '**Mr Kempe**' or '**Bad Company**' for example) the prevailing atmosphere and the surrounding discussion greatly enhance the ghostly effect. Perhaps this is because, as Dylan Thomas observed, 'His subject, always, is the imminence of spiritual danger.'

Yet if spiritual danger is the predominant theme, it is only another aspect of that obsession with death which underlies all Walter de la Mare's writing, both in prose and verse, and which makes him find in the ghost story a natural medium for his speculations on the subject. The phenomenon of death, and what may lie beyond, is seen as crucial to an understanding of life, and as possibly conferring meaning on it, if only the evidence could be interpreted aright:

> 'MORS. And what does MORS mean?' enquired
> that oddly indolent voice . . . . 'It means—well,
> sleep,' I said. 'Or nightmare, or dawn, or nothing
> or—it might mean everything.'
> (*Ding Dong Bell,* 1924)

But herein lies the difficulty—death is also the most extreme form of those breakdowns in communication which are often present, always implicit in his stories. It is, or should be 'the bourne from which no traveller returns', yet only too many of de la Mare's characters are anxious to prise open its uncertainties and violate its quiet (for him, as for M. R. James, necromancy is always a deplorable activity). In de la Mare's work, death has taken over the rôle which love traditionally plays in fiction, as the most central and significant experience of life, which must illuminate and confer meaning on everything. Love is secondary, and only too frequently itself leads to death or to one of those eternal partings that are even more unbearable. Sometimes, as in '**Seaton's Aunt**', death so deeply overshadows the lovers that their relationship scarcely comes to life at all. For the reader as for the narrator, Arthur Seaton 'had never been much better than "buried" in my mind'.

De la Mare's concern with the nature and meaning of death was not limited to his fiction. In a conversation with

Lord Brain, recorded at the end of his life, he remarked *à propos* of a head injury he had sustained, 'It means, doesn't it, that our whole perception depends on our body, so that when we die we lose not only our bodies but our whole apparatus of thought; we leave two vacua.' His restless and enquiring mind could not remain secure in the easy answers of religion (Graham Greene remarked on how odd his world appeared 'to those of us with traditional Christian beliefs'). Yet if he was certain of anything it was of the spiritual nature of life and of the universe, the quality to which G. K. Chesterton paid tribute in calling him a mystic. This certainty gave him a detachment and serenity when writing of the physical aspect of death that provides a striking contrast to the morbidness of Poe, a writer whom he much admired. In '**The House**', Mr Asprey, approaching death and chasing away some cockroaches is 'aware at the same moment of the surmise that his next abode might be frequented by another species of vermin'; yet his attitude is one of realistic acceptance, rather than gloomy self-indulgence. In de la Mare's cupboards there are no decaying corpses or skeletons. The most physical of his ghosts resembles a scarecrow, while most of them prefer to be heard and not seen, confiding their activities to voices and perhaps 'a light footfall'. Ugliness is essentially a human attribute, and the dead, if well content, may exert the wholesome influence of a country churchyard on a summer night, such as provides the setting of '**Benighted**'.

Ding Dong Bell (1924), the book of epitaphs which includes '**Benighted**', conveys the peace of death, as well as its terrors, and in this respect forms a useful corrective to the sinister graveyard of Widderstone in *The Return* (1910). The very name here seems significant, halfway between 'widdershins' (a favourite word in de la Mare's poetry) and 'wither-stone' or perhaps 'whither?-stone'. Here the exhausted Lawford becomes possessed by a seventeenth-century suicide, Sabathier. Much of this short novel is taken up with discussions on the nature of death between Lawford and the strange hermit, Herbert Herbert, who lives beside the graveyard and eventually reconciles Lawford to death and to what has happened to him. Many of de la Mare's most characteristic themes, the inadequacy of traditional religion in the face of spiritual distress, the loss of an ideal loved one, as well as a prolonged discussion on the nature and meaning of death, are to be found in this strange and fascinating book. Several of his short stories, also, are concerned with similar speculations, on death and what lies beyond—for example '**The Three Friends**' and '**The Bird of Travel**'. '**The Vats**' is a meditation on the nature of eternity and in '**The Wharf** ', a dungheap becomes a highly original symbol of salvation. None of these are strictly ghost stories, though '**The Three Friends**' might be described as 'on the edge'. The ghost stories themselves frequently explore the same topics: the narrator of '**Crewe**', Mr Blake, voices a number of opinions on the subject: 'It's my belief there's some kind of ferry plying on that river. And coming back depends on what you want to come back *for.*'

Perhaps the most lengthy and varied discussion of the meaning of death takes place in '**A Recluse**', where all the apparently random incidents of the leisurely opening contribute in one way or another to the total atmosphere. Returning from a visit to a friend who had been at death's door and is gradually recovering, the narrator encounters a strange horseman carrying a cardboard box—a grotesque cross between Alice's White Knight and the horseman of Death in the Apocalypse. That this character should warn him with a gesture against the house 'Montresor' seems to make it both more sinister and more fascinating. Here the narrator meets Mr Bloom, the horrible occupant, who tries to keep him there and keep him awake because he is afraid of—what? Mr Bloom is a dabbler in the occult, and it seems that he fears the very forces he has aroused. Mr Dash, the narrator, has had some experience of psychic investigation through an old family friend, and finds the whole thing 'a silly and dangerous waste of time'. His experiences at Montresor do not prove him wrong, though they give him a closer glimpse of its workings. Everything that Mr Dash encounters increases his uneasiness, the ugly dog, the secretary's diary, the horrible mask of Mr Bloom and the discovery of his stolen gear key, the voices, and the last figure glimpsed in the shrubbery as he drives away. Even the music Mr Bloom plays him, Ravel's *Gaspard de la Nuit,* is satanic. Like Seaton's aunt, whom he resembles in more than one respect, Bloom has filled the house with horrid inhabitants, although unlike her, he seems somewhat daunted by their presence.

The language of the whole story is shot through with irony. Such a sentence as 'it was not only that Mr Bloom's manner was obviously a mask'—clearly anticipates the central episode, when the narrator finds a mask of Bloom lying on his bed. This event, in turn, causes the reader to wonder whether the visual appearance of Mr Bloom is not entirely assumed, and as easily cast on or off as the boots which intrigue the narrator so much. Like everything else about Mr Bloom, these boots do not seem to be entirely real, for they are 'adorned with . . . imitation laces'. Their emptiness, as they stand by Mr Bloom's bed, is curiously disquieting. The word 'ghost' itself is used with a special sense of its significance: the dead secretary's diary yields a few last scrawled and ominous words, and 'the ink . . . had left its ghost on the blank page opposite'. Not merely the ink, but the writer too, perhaps, has left a ghost in the haunted 'Montresor'. As the narrator comments,

> I had long suspected that Mr Bloom's activities may have proved responsible for guests even more undesirable than myself, even though . . . they may, perhaps, have been of a purely subjective order.

Similarly in **'Seaton's Aunt'**, the narrator, Withers, fails to send his old school friend Seaton 'the ghost of a wedding present', appropriately enough since the intended recipient has in fact died. At their final dinner party together, the aunt teases her wretched nephew Arthur with the ominous and prophetic words 'I shall have memory for company . . . the ghosts of other days.'

As a child, Arthur Seaton seemed pathetically afraid of his grotesque and sinister aunt and guardian, even suspecting her of being a witch, a notion pooh-poohed by Withers. There is certainly no tangible evidence of her supernatural powers, and yet the horrible atmosphere of the house and the aunt's final mistaking of Withers for Arthur *after* the latter's death combine to convince us that he was after all right and that there will be no peace for her nephew even in the grave. The language throughout is dense with suggestion as when at their last dinner together Withers observes, 'I could scarcely see her little glittering eyes under their penthouse lids.' The sentence recalls the witch's words from *Macbeth,* themselves conveying something of what she has done to her hapless nephew:

> I shall drain him dry as hay.
> Sleep shall neither night or day
> Hang upon his pent-house lid;
> He shall live a man forbid.

The reference has a further point in context because the aunt's tiny glittering eyes, which seem to see in the dark and even at a distance, penetrate the house. Eyes (like mirrors) are favourite symbols for de la Mare. Philip's troubles in **'The Guardian'** are first revealed when he describes how the gas-bead at night looks like a watchful eye. In **'Seaton's Aunt',** the watchful eye is symbolized by a painting 'depicting a large eye with an extremely fishlike intensity . . . beneath was printed very minutely, "Thou God, seest ME".' The unhappy Seaton assures Withers 'There's hundreds of eyes like that in this house; and even if God does see you, He takes precious good care you don't see Him.' On Wither's first visit to the house, as a schoolboy, the aunt's 'chocolate eyes . . . were more than half-covered by unusually long and heavy lids'. On his second visit, the occasion of the dinner party, 'her eyelids . . . hung even a little heavier in age over their slow-moving inscrutable pupils'. On his final visit, 'the old eyes had rather suddenly failed'. The aunt's terrifying eyes are somehow related to her vampirish watch over Seaton, which continues even after his death and her blindness.

Seaton's aunt, Mr Bloom and Mr Kempe in the story of that name are consumed by an insatiable desire to pry into death's well-kept secrets, so that they become ghouls and necromancers, though the exact extent of Mr Kempe's investigations is left vague. He is probably innocent of calling up the dead, but he appears to have attempted to prolong the lives of those at the point of death (his wife, the fallen climbers) in the hope of extracting from them the truth about 'the other side'. A glimpse of his dropped photographs is enough for the narrator, who flees without further delay. Although Walter de la Mare's warlocks are far more highly individualized than their traditional prototypes, and themselves become objects of pathos to a certain degree, his uncompromising horror of such dabbling is in itself traditional.

The spirits summoned up by Mr Bloom and Seaton's aunt are apparently hapless wretches like Bloom's ex-secretary, Sidney Champneys, or Arthur Seaton himself, pathetically incapable of self-assertion, but not all ghosts are like this. Some may demonstrate a more active malevolence, like the gardener, Mr Menzies, who comes back for George in **'Crewe'**, or the frustrated poetess, Esther F., in **'The Green Room'**, like Sabathier in *The Return* or Beverley's old aunt in **'The Quincunx'**. These last two use possession in order to gain their ends, but perhaps the most sinister possession described is not on a human scale at all.

It is that of the great cathedral, **'All Hallows'**, which is being 're-edificated and restored by some agency unknown'. This story uses a number of features that occur elsewhere: an atmosphere of oppressive heat (as in **'Missing'**), and the narrative of a strange old man, in this case the cathedral verger, who has been looking for an outsider to whom he may unburden himself. The counterpart of the satanic take-over of **'All Hallows'** is the strange and beautiful haunting of the house by the sea in **'Music'**, where, it seems, one may hear the music of the spheres. This story is from his last collection, *A Beginning* (with characteristic irony) and the imagery is often, and no doubt intentionally, redolent of Shakespeare's last play *The Tempest,* with its unearthly music:

> Sometimes a thousand twangling instruments
> Will hum about mine ears.

Both the cathedral of All Hallows and the house in **'Music'** stand on the shore, in positions of maximum exposure to the sea; both are full of the sound of the sea, perhaps the most ancient metaphor for man's last voyage. It is this unobtrusive and traditional use of symbolism that makes de la Mare's work so effective.

One pattern of correspondence which occurs frequently is the reflection of the owner in his house. Even the name, 'Montresor' smacks of the preciosity of Mr Bloom while the Seatons' home is all gloom, and seems to age and decay in mystic sympathy with its owner. But the two stories where the analogy between house and owner is made most explicit are **'Out of the Deep'** and **'The House'**. The latter might be read as a simple allegory of the soul departing from its tenement of clay:

> If positive landlord there were (himself perhaps
> the architect) Mr Asprey of late years had seldom 'called on' him, even in a merely metaphorical sense. And now—well, the one thing certain
> was that he had been given notice to quit.

Mr Asprey's inspection of his rooms, and his constant note-taking represent useless and belated attempts to 'put his house in order' before his departure. Yet the central episode, in which a dead maid appears and he presents her with the wallet she apparently once took remains elusive and unexplained—does he merely give her 'alms for oblivion'?

'Out of the Deep' (*The Riddle*) also leaves a number of questions unresolved, and here again there is a close similarity between the old and haunted house, and the tubercular Jimmie, who inherits it and has to exorcize the ghosts of his unhappy childhood before he can die peacefully, with the bell-rope looped safely out of his reach. Each time he rings the bell, something comes up from the servants' quarters below, up out of the deep well of the unconscious:

> Thinking was like a fountain. Once it gets going
> at a certain pressure, well, it is almost impossible
> to turn it off. And, my hat! what odd things
> come up with the water!

The figures who appear are essentially Jimmie's own creations, rather than the ghosts of the servants, now dead, who once persecuted him there, but he attempts to equate his visions with his persecutors. The young man who appears and shows 'just a flavour, a flicker . . . of resemblance to himself' Jimmie christens 'Soames Junior', as if he were really an emanation of the cruel old butler he once knew. He refuses to admit that these servants are entirely of his own making, and his jeers and scorn therefore rebound only on himself and are bound up with his self-contempt and self-loathing. When he learns to live amicably with them, and thus with his own subconscious life, he is able to die peacefully in the attic where he had suffered so horribly from childhood nightmares. His efforts to punish the dead, both actual (his sale of his uncle's treasures) and imaginary (in ringing the bells for the departed servants) have failed and are succeeded by acceptance. The house itself has become the arena for Jimmie's internal battle, and hence, by extension, his mind; horrors come up from 'below stairs', yet Jimmie finally dies in the attic, the upper region where reason, or perhaps even the elusive soul may dwell.

Among de la Mare's many powerful ghost stories, perhaps the most unforgettable is also the quietest, the most oblique and delicate: **'Strangers and Pilgrims'** was first printed in the American edition of *The Wind Blows Over* and then added to a new edition of *Ding Dong Bell* (1936), as it is set in a cemetery and includes a number of epitaphs. At a superficial level this story describes a protracted and rather unsatisfactory encounter between an old verger closing up his church for the evening and a stranger in search of a particular grave which he fails to find. The deeper implication, however, is that it is his *own* grave for which he is searching. The visitor is undoubtedly strange in more than the obvious sense of the word:

> Clothes, manner, gait, speech—never in his long
> experience had any specimen of a human being
> embodied so many peculiarities. And there was
> yet another, pervading all the rest, yet more elusive.

Like Sabathier in *The Return,* he seems to have been a suicide and as the conversation turns towards ghosts he briefly alludes to his own fate:

> 'And assuredly,' he hesitated, 'if, at the end,
> there had been extreme trouble and—horror.'

> The harsh screaming of the swifts coursing in
> the twilight . . . was for the moment the only
> comment on these remarks.

Most disturbing of all is the entry in the Church Register which gives, under the date 1880, the dead man's name followed by the cryptic comment 'Nothing known. Not buried here.' One wonders on how many previous occasions the stranger had made the same useless pilgrimage to that cemetery to prompt such a note.

The epitaphs scattered through the story provide a commentary on certain aspects of death, in particular the finality of its partings, both for husband and wife, and even more poignantly for mother and child. The title as well as the course of the conversation also invites a further consideration of the relationship between the living and the dead, and the way in which the impenetrable mystery of death casts disturbing shadows over our conception of life.

The revenant, a stranger and pilgrim under an inexplicable compulsion, might equally serve as a representative of the living, themselves strangers and pilgrims in a universe whose total meaning death makes incomprehensible. For the riddle of life is death, and our conception of existence as ordered or absurd turns on what its termination signifies. This is what makes death de la Mare's central concern (just as, though he treats it very differently, it is also Samuel Beckett's). What makes him such an important and stimulating writer of ghost stories is that he uses the form to pose a question it is supremely well-suited to ask—what is the meaning of death, and therefore of life? The figure of Ambrose Manning, remorselessly driven on by his search for his mortal remains, for the little that is left of himself, seems to suggest that death too is equivocal, mysterious, unknowable. Ultimately there is no answer to de la Mare's 'Qui vive?' thrown out across the great unknown but an echo. (pp. 182-95)

> *Julia Briggs, "On the Edge: Walter de la Mare," in her* Night Visitors: The Rise and Fall of the English Ghost Story, *Faber, 1977, pp. 182-95.*

Walter Allen   (essay date 1981)

[*Allen is an English novelist of working-class life and a distinguished popular historian and critic of the novel form. In the following excerpt from his critical study* The Short Story in English, *he compares de la Mare's short stories with those of Henry James and discusses the narrative technique of "The Trumpet."*]

As a short-story writer, Walter de la Mare closely resembles Henry James, specifically the James of what are sometimes called the supernatural stories. His prose is almost as dense as James's and as resonant, the stories no less 'difficult'. Their fabric is no less of the material world than James's; they are rooted in a solid and palpable, if mundane, reality, and de la Mare writes very much as a man of his time and as a master of its common speech, exploiting both with delightful humour. For example, **'A Revenant'** has Edgar Allan Poe attending, as a revenant, a lecture on himself in a provincial town. It is at once a brilliantly subtle exposure of academic pretension, an absorbing consideration of the nature of poetry, and a remarkably convincing recreation of Poe. The milieu depicted is as well 'documented' as James's, but the equation between the setting of the story and its dénouement and deducible moral is not easily determined. Here, de la Mare's stories are of a piece with his poetry, with 'The Listeners', for instance: they are perfectly comprehensible but disturb the mind nevertheless by overtones sensed rather than understood.

On this aspect of de la Mare's stories no one has written with more insight than Graham Greene, who, after a paragraph on de la Mare's prose ('unequalled in its richness since the death of James, or, dare one at this date, say Robert Louis Stevenson'), concludes his essay in *The Lost Childhood:*

> With these resources at his command no one can bring the natural visible world more sharply to

the eye: from the railway carriage window we watch the landscape unfold . . . we are wooed and lulled sometimes to the verge of sleep by the beauty of the prose, until suddenly without warning a sentence breaks in mid-breath and we look up and see the terrified eyes of our fellow-passenger, appealing, hungry, scared, as he watches what we cannot see—'the sediment of an unspeakable obsession'.

To illustrate Greene's thesis I choose **'The Trumpet'**. Two boys, Philip, the rector's son, and his friend Dick, decide to spend that night when, according to superstition, ghosts walk, in the village church:

> The minute church, obscurely lit by a full moon that had not yet found window-glass through which the direct beams could pierce into this gloaming, was deserted and silent. Not a sound, within or without, disturbed its stony quiet—except only the insect-like rapid ticking of a clock in the vestry, and the low pulsating thump of a revolving cogwheel in the tower above the roof. Here and there a polished stone gleamed coldly in the vague luminous haze—a marble head, a wing-tip, a pointing finger, the claws and beak of the eagle on the brazen lectern, the two silvergilt candlesticks flanking the colourless waxen flowers upon the altar. So secret and secluded seemed the church within its nocturnal walls that living creature might never have been there at all—or creatures only so insignificant and transitory as to have left no perceptible trace behind them.

> Like a cataleptic's countenance it hinted, moreover, at no inward activity of its own. And yet, if—fantastic notion—some unseen watcher through the bygone centuries had kept it perpetually within gaze, he might at last have concluded that it possessed a *sort* of stagnant life or animation . . .

The two boys sit side by side in a pew daring and out-boasting each other. Philip, conscious of his superiority in class and religious status, is especially aggressive, and when Dick goes outside to watch for ghosts, sucking jujubes, he stares at 'the monument that not only dominated but dwarfed the small but lovely chancel'.

> The figure of the angel was now bathed with the silver of the moon. With long-toed feet at once clasping and spurning the orb beneath them, it stood erect on high. Chin thrust out, its steadfast sightless eyes were fixed upon the faded blue and geranium red of the panelled roof. Its braided locks were drawn back from a serene and impassive visage, its left hand lay flat upon its breast, and with the right it clasped a tapering, uplifted, bell-mouthed, gilded trumpet held firmly not against but a little distance from its lips.

Philip is risking a lot in being alone with the angel now, among other things a beating from his father and the humiliation of its being discovered that he has been beguiled into the adventure by a village boy about whom he feels curiously ambivalent. Dick is described as being 'like a mysterious and unintelligible little animal, past taming, and possessed of a spirit of whose secret presence he himself was completely unaware'.

The boy now returns, and they both contemplate the angel. At last, Philip dares Dick to climb the monument and blow the angel's trumpet. The monument, which is surmounted by the angel, is loftier than Philip has thought, and as Dick climbs he pleads, cajoles, orders 'in helpless fear and fury' the other to come down. ' "It's wicked! It's *my* angel, it's *my* trumpet! I hate you! Listen!—I tell you! I command you to come down!" '

'His adjurations,' de la Mare tells us characteristically with an echo of seventeenth-century prose, 'had become as meaningless as is now the song the Sirens sang', for suddenly there is 'a rending snap, abrupt as that of a pistol shot'. The angel's wooden trumpet has broken under Dick's grasp, and he falls.

> The solid pendulum had resumed its imperturbable thumping again, the fussy vestry clock its protest against such indifference. By any miracle of mercy, *could* this be only yet another of this intrepid restless little Yorick's jests? The sharp-nosed crusader continued alabaster-wise to stare into the future. The disgraced angel, breast to lock-crowned head, stood now in shadow as if to hide her shame. Her mute wooden trumpet remained clutched in a lifeless hand . . . . No.

> 'Dick! Dick!' an anguished stuttering voice at last contrived to whisper. 'I didn't mean it. On my oath I didn't mean it. Don't let me down . . . Dick, are you dead?'

> But since no answer was volunteered, and all courage and enterprise had ebbed into nausea and vertigo, the speaker found himself incapable of venturing nearer, and presently, as thievishly as he had entered it, crept away out into the openness of the churchyard, and so home.

Thus ends this astonishingly complex and richly-wrought story. It demands the kind of analysis a great poem receives, though, like a great poem, it is ultimately recalcitrant to analysis. It is, one feels, such a story as Poe might have dreamed of but never succeeded in writing. (pp. 88-91)

> *Walter Allen, "Jacobs, Wells, Conrad, Bennett, Saki, de la Mare," in his* The Short Story in English, *Oxford University Press, Inc., 1981, pp. 76-91.*

FURTHER READING

Criticism

Bayley, John. "The Child in Walter de la Mare." In *Children and Their Books: A Celebration of the Work of Iona and Peter Opie,* edited by Gillian Avery and Julia Briggs, pp. 337-49. New York: Oxford University Press, 1989.

> Examines de la Mare's view of childhood as expressed in his fiction, focusing primarily on the short stories "A Recluse" and "Seaton's Aunt."

Clark, Leonard. "The Storyteller." In his *Walter de la Mare,* pp. 54-71. London: Bodley Head, 1960.

> Discusses de la Mare's stories for children and adults.

Hopkins, Kenneth. *Walter de la Mare.* London: Longmans, Green & Co., 1953, 44 p.

> Includes commentary on de la Mare's short stories.

Mortimer, Raymond. Review of *The Riddle, and Other Stories,* by Walter de la Mare. *The New Statesman* XXI, No. 528 (26 May 1923): 201.

> Finds the stories collected in *The Riddle* "a little monotonous" in their cumulative effect but praises the characterization and restrained morbidity and mysticism of de la Mare's tales.

Penzoldt, Peter. "Walter de la Mare." In his *The Supernatural in Fiction,* pp. 203-27. London: Peter Nevill, 1952.

> Examines de la Mare's supernatural fiction and compares "Out of the Deep" with Henry James's novella *The Turn of the Screw.*

Punter, David. "The Ambivalence of Memory: Henry James and Walter de la Mare." In his *The Literature of Terror: A History of Gothic Fictions from 1765 to the Present Day,* pp. 291-313. New York: Longman, 1980.

> Comparative study of supernatural elements in short fiction by Henry James and Walter de la Mare. Punter comments: "The central point of comparison which I want to emphasise between James's *Turn of the Screw* and de la Mare's stories is their insistence on the connexion between fear and self-delusion. Where their narrators and story-tellers profess to see the world as haunted, we as readers are being constantly required to reassess these hauntings in terms of the deficiencies of the narrators themselves."

Reid, Forrest. *Walter de la Mare: A Critical Study.* New York: Henry Holt, 1929, 256 p.

> Includes two chapters that discuss de la Mare's short stories.

Wagenknecht, Edward. Introduction to *The Collected Tales of Walter de la Mare,* by Walter de la Mare, pp. vii-xxi. New York: Alfred A. Knopf, 1950.

> Discusses de la Mare's reputation as a short story writer.

———. Introduction to *Eight Tales,* by Walter de la Mare, pp. vii-xx. Sauk City, Wis.: Arkham House, 1971.

> Discusses de la Mare's early short stories.

Willis, John H. "Architecture of Reality: The Short Stories of Walter de la Mare." *North Dakota Quarterly* 32, No. 4 (Autumn 1964): 85-92.

Provides an overview and assessment of de la Mare's major stories.

Additional coverage of de la Mare's life and career is contained in the following sources published by Gale Research: *Children's Literature Review,* Vol. 23; *Concise Dictionary of British Literary Biography,* Vol 6; *Contemporary Authors,* Vols. 110, 137; *Dictionary of Literary Biography,* Vol. 19; *DISCovering Authors; Major Authors and Illustrators for Children and Young Adults; Something about the Author,* Vol. 16; *Twentieth-Century Literary Criticism,* Vols. 4, 53; and *World Literature Criticism.*

Harlan Ellison

1934-

(Full name Harlan Jay Ellison; has also written under the pseudonyms Lee Archer, Phil "Cheech" Beldone, C. Bird, Cordwainer Bird, Jay Charby, Robert Courtney, Price Curtis, Wallace Edmondson, Landon Ellis, Ellis Hart, E. K. Jarvis, Ivar Jorgensen, Al[an] Maddern, Paul Merchant, Clyde Mitchell, Nabrah Nosille, Bert Parker, Jay Solo, and Derry Tiger) American short story writer, scriptwriter, editor, novelist, essayist, and critic.

INTRODUCTION

Ellison is a controversial, award-winning author of speculative fiction. Although he has consistently denied being an author of science fiction, his reputation largely rests upon stories written during the 1960s which utilize themes and elements common to both science fiction and fantasy. Reflecting his highly personal and colloquial style, Ellison's works often feature authorial intrusions and asides and he frequently writes introductions and afterwords for his story collections. Writing in prose rich with religious and mythical allusions, Ellison typically centers on vulnerable protagonists who engage in horrific and violent conflicts with elemental forces of nature as well as with the impersonal systems of contemporary society.

Born in Cleveland, Ohio, Ellison attended Ohio State University for two years before moving to New York City to begin his literary career in the mid-1950s. Using many pseudonyms, Ellison wrote short stories in various genres. His interest in authenticating the violence and amorality of street life led him to assume a false identity and join a street gang in the late 1950s. His gang experiences figure directly in his first novel, *Rumble,* and his short stories about street life appear in such collections as *The Deadly Streets, The Juvies,* and *Gentleman Junkie, and Other Stories of the Hung-Up Generation.* In the early 1960s, Ellison moved to Hollywood, where he established himself as a successful scriptwriter, contributing episodes to such television series as "The Untouchables," "The Outer Limits," and "Star Trek." He began producing his most highly regarded short stories in the mid-1960s. " 'Repent, Harlequin!' Said the Ticktockman," a story from *Paingod, and Other Delusions,* won Nebula and Hugo Awards in 1965. Ellison also gained notoriety as editor of the short story anthologies *Dangerous Visions* and *Again, Dangerous Visions.* Noting the experimental nature of Ellison's work and the stories collected in the anthologies, commentators praised him as one of the leading American initiators of the "New Wave" in science fiction, which, according to some critics, introduced social, psychological, and literary content to the genre. Ellison's most recent collection of short fiction, *Angry Candy,* was published in 1988.

Ellison's short works have been described as commentaries on religion, myth, and contemporary society, as well as journeys into the inner self. In his introduction to *Deathbird Stories: A Pantheon of Modern Gods,* Ellison argued that divinities are human creations that exist only because people believe in them. In the collection's title story, "The Deathbird," which has been praised for its experimental style, Ellison inverts traditional Judeo-Christian concepts of God by depicting Satan as an heroic figure who informs the last living human that God is an insane tormentor responsible for the world's suffering. Through self-sacrifice, the man becomes more powerful than his warped creator, suggesting that God and Satan represent two halves of the human psyche. Although many of Ellison's works feature futuristic and fantastic settings, commentators contend that Ellison is primarily concerned with addressing the problems of contemporary society. *A Boy and His Dog,* for instance, a novella that takes place in the aftermath of a nuclear war, contrasts two societies: one dominated by lawless chaos, the other by extreme conformity. Critics contend that the setting is symbolic of opposing trends in contemporary society and generational conflict between youths and elders. Similarly, " 'Repent, Harlequin!' Said the Ticktockman," which celebrates individuality and nonconformity through the mock-epic tale of a harlequin who disrupts the routines of a mechanistic society, has been discussed in relation to the youth rebellion of the 1960s. Other stories explore the problems and paradoxes of human existence. "I Have No Mouth, and I Must Scream," for instance, centers on a computer system with humanlike consciousness that has exterminated humanity except for five individuals whom it retains for everlasting torture. Emphasizing the inherent conflict between creator and creation, Ellison exposes the dichotomies between love and hate, and good and evil, that exist in human beings and, by extension, the machines they build. "Paingod," a parable about a confrontation between a human and a divinity, depicts the dynamic polarity between pain and pleasure as an essential aspect of life in general, while "Adrift Just Off the Islets of Langerhans: Latitude 38 54′N, Longitude 77 00′13″W" chronicles a would-be murderer's journey into his body, where he recovers his lost innocence and overcomes his egotism. Commentators argue that unlike most of Ellison's works, the latter story is affirmative since it suggests that the individual can benefit from exploring the self and that humanity can achieve change.

Ellison remains an important and challenging author of speculative short fiction. In evaluating his work, critics have sometimes objected to his use of violent and graphic imagery to provoke revulsion in his readers. However, many applaud his subversive humor and unflinching dedication to nonconformity and to social change as expressed in his essays and fiction. Roz Kaveney has asserted that Ellison "writes to shock . . .; by shocking people he hopes to get them to accept their own human frailty and to awaken them to wisdom and courage."

PRINCIPAL WORKS

SHORT FICTION

The Deadly Streets   1958; enlarged and revised edition, 1975
A Touch of Infinity   1960
Gentleman Junkie, and Other Stories of the Hung-Up Generation   1961; revised edition, 1975
The Juvies   1961
Ellison Wonderland   1962; revised edition, 1984; also published as *Earthman, Go Home*,   1964
Paingod, and Other Delusions   1965; enlarged and revised edition, 1975
Dangerous Visions [editor]   1967
From the Land of Fear   1967
I Have No Mouth and I Must Scream   1967; revised edition, 1983
Love Ain't Nothing but Sex Misspelled   1968; revised edition, 1976
The Beast That Shouted Love at the Heart of the World   1969; revised edition, 1984
Over the Edge: Stories from Somewhere Else   1970
Alone Against Tomorrow: Stories of Alienation in Speculative Fiction   1971; also published in two volumes as *All the Sounds of Fear*,   1973, and *The Time of the Eye*,   1974
Again, Dangerous Visions [editor]   1972
Approaching Oblivion: Road Signs on the Treadmill toward Tomorrow   1974
Deathbird Stories: A Pantheon of Modern Gods   1975
No Doors, No Windows   1975
Strange Wine: Fifteen New Stories from the Nightside of the World   1978
The Fantasies of Harlan Ellison   1979
Shatterday   1980
The Last Dangerous Visions [editor]   1981
Stalking the Nightmare   1982
The Essential Ellison   1987
Angry Candy   1988

OTHER MAJOR WORKS

Rumble   (novel)   1958; also published as *Web of the City*,   1975
The Man with Nine Lives   (novel)   1960
Rockabilly   (novel)   1961; also published as *Spider Kiss*, 1975
"The City on the Edge of Forever"   (television play) 1967
Doomsman   (novel)   1967
The Glass Teat: Essays of Opinion on the Subject of Television   (essays)   1970
The Other Glass Teat: Further Essays of Opinion on Television   (essays)   1975
Phoenix without Ashes [with Edward Bryant]   (novel) 1975
An Edge in My Voice   (essays)   1985
Harlan Ellison's Watching   (film criticism)   1989
The Harlan Ellison Hornbook   (essays)   1990
Run for the Stars   (novel)   1991

CRITICISM

Willis E. McNelly   (essay date 1970)

[*McNelly is an American educator and critic whose writings often focus on science fiction. In the following essay, he remarks on the themes, style, and unconventional typography of "I Have No Mouth, and I Must Scream."*]

Take a generous portion of myth, add a flagon of verbal magic, mix with memory and desire, season with a dollop or two of reminiscences of James Joyce, John Barth, and John Bunyan, sprinkle in a racial memory of the golem, and add all this to a simmering stock composed of equal parts of good and evil—you end up with Harlan Ellison's prize-winning short story **"I Have No Mouth, And I Must Scream."**

Ellison's story is more than a mixture of tired and true thematic elements and stylistic devices, however. It assumes a brooding, haunting quality of its own as it shocks the senses, assails the emotions, and chills the mind. It is not a story that one can be indifferent about. It almost demands acceptance or rejection on its own terms, shaking the reader with its McLuhanesque vision. There is no sterile linearity in **"I Have No Mouth,"** no obsolescent beginning, middle, and end. Rather there is a centricity of vision that springs from the constant reconciliation of opposites in the story itself. The devices, themes, emotions, forces, language, style, and diction all are antithetical. The tensions in the story rise from the interplay of forces and find their resolution in conflict itself. Even the title illustrates the tensions: "I have no mouth, and I must scream." Impossible? Yes, but the scream is the story itself. Ted, the heroic antihero, may have no mouth but he does have a typewriter on which he produces his anti-allegory. The medium is the message; the story, the shout.

The story utilizes the two classic frameworks of the allegory, progress and battle. In the traditional allegory the conflict is between the ultimate forces of good and evil as the hero makes his tortuous way to a symbolic celestial city. Ted is no Christian in his pilgrim's progress, to be sure, but the story nonetheless illustrates the epic conflict as well as the epic journey. AM, the anarchic computer, is a demonic demiurge, a Manichean power of darkness, an evil creative spirit. Ted, on the other hand, is no archangel Michael who will thrust into Hell Lucifer and the other evil spirits. Ted is rather the embodiment of the good and evil in all of us, at once brute and angel, fornicator and lover, killer and savior. He is man—like a devil, like an angel, like a god.

Neither force is omnipotent. AM is only a surrogate Yahweh or Elohim. His control may be all-powerful, but AM cannot really keep men from death, although he can keep them alive virtually forever. Thus AM cannot, in the end, either create life or breathe life anew into the victims of Ted's salvific act. Similarly, Ted's search for glory on the road to his uncelestial city is an ignoble search at best. He grovels for food, begs for mercy while cursing the potential source of mercy, and whimpers for black Ellen's sexual favors. Hardly a heroic picture.

Paradox is at the heart of Ellison's story. From the title itself to the death of Ted's companions, paradox piles on paradox. The body of Gorrister has been drained of blood by a ritualistic throat-cutting incision, but the floor under the body is bloodless. AM transforms Benny into the apotheosis of phallic masculinity, but removes his spiritual masculinity in the highly symbolic blinding. Paradoxes multiply as manna gives no life, and death brings release. The tensions arise not only from the nature of the forces that Ellison puts into his story, but from their very incompleteness. AM strives for a perfection, but it is a perfection of evil and ugliness, hell in the maw of the computer. AM has destroyed all lives on earth except the five in the story because it hates mankind for having created it. It seeks to keep the five humans alive so it may wreak an eternal revenge. When only Ted remains alive at the end, AM transforms him into the mouthless blob, a piece of inchoate undefeated matter, so that Ted will live an eternity. Why the paradoxical life in death for Ted and AM? AM, after all, is not omnipotent, and is only a machine. But ma-

chines cannot exist without man, even if man has been transformed into an unscreaming blob.

The imagery and diction of the story contribute to its appeal. Ellison is a highly skilled writer whose word choice and sentence structure are usually sure and certain. There are the giggle or chitter of his characters, the lunatic laugh of a fat woman, the sound of a million metallic insects, the screaming shoals of machines. The words create the appeal, whether to the eye, the ear, the nose, or the tongue. Who can ever, in the end, forget the taste of boiled boar urine?

"I Have No Mouth, And I Must Scream" probably is a repulsive story. But Ellison meant it to repel—to harrow the reader's emotions, and ultimately to stimulate him to think. What is this story about finally? Is it simply a modernized dybbuk story, or a piece of twentieth-century Gothic fiction? It is all of these, of course, and it is anti-allegory, and it is a horror tale. But it is also science fiction, because ultimately it is concerned with the interface between man and the machine. Man must control the machine, Ellison maintains, or the machine will control him. After all, at the very heart of science fiction is the notion of extrapolation. "What if?" the author asks himself. "What if?"

Ellison's "what if?" posits a thinking computer horrified at itself as a creation of man, hating itself because its creator has made it evil, and then acting logically upon both its horror and its hate by destroying its creator and seeking its revenge. Has man ever acted otherwise? If the answer is no, then the story must proceed with some sort of logical, horrifying inevitability to its deranged conclusion. Man is eternally rotten and deserves punishment at the hands of an angry God. Man must always remain, then, a rational slug, at the complete mercy of a hating AM.

On the other hand, if man has acted other than by greed, hate, or revenge, then there is some ultimate glory in the story, and with yet one more paradox, the anti-allegory becomes allegory. This final juxtaposition is achieved by a very simple device: in a way, Ted gives up his life for his friends. He may remain the blob-like object of hate, but he is ultimately redeemed by his sacrifice. But Ellison is still not finished with paradox or dramatic, even tragic, irony. The act of salvation is a killing. Ted's friends find final surcease in death as AM is cheated of his ancient revenge.

Since written time, man has created his gods in various likenesses, his myths in varying forms. As Jung, Neumann, Frye, Eliade, and many others have shown, myths are constantly altered by man to suit the needs of man. Man is ultimately in control of his myths. Thus in Ellison's story AM also once existed in the mind of man under man's control, but now AM has become incarnated into the form, shape, and substance of a chittering computer. Its power was ultimately programed by man on tapes and in memory banks. AM now knows all the ancient archetypal myths, and now uses its knowledge to pervert and negate them. It exercises the power that man never had, to control man, and to give substance to the myths. Man has played God for one last time, creating a god that destroys him.

There are other qualities that make **"I Have No Mouth, And I Must Scream"** a provocative short story. Not the least of these is the typographical format. Of course, eccentricity of type and layout probably dates to Gutenberg, and its use in English literature is found in such places as the emblematic poems of Francis Quarles or George Herbert and the novels of Laurence Sterne and James Joyce. For that matter, Alfred Bester's *The Demolished Man* established the precedent of deliberate typographical innovation as an artistic device in science fiction. Yet Ellison's utilization of such devices as AM speaking through computer tape or the stainless-steel pillar bearing neon lettering is not mere eccentricity on Ellison's part. In one sense, the story is an interior monologue staged in the mind of a god, and, as such, the computer tape "conversation" indicates AM's presence, an oppressive omniscience or omnipotence. These qualities are not, of course, absolute, because AM is god, not God. The tape, then, is not merely gratuitous, but adds the dimension of mechanical presence to the spiritual horror.

All of these qualities—the paradoxes, the style, the tensions, the typographical innovations—make Harlan Ellison's **"I Have No Mouth, And I Must Scream"** a very provocative story. It is so provocative that it probably could not have been published a dozen years ago, but its contemporary acceptance marks some sort of maturity for science fiction. (pp. 265-68)

> *Willis E. McNelly, in a foreword to "Harlan Ellison: I Have No Mouth, and I Must Scream," in* The Mirror of Infinity: A Critics' Anthology of Science Fiction, *edited by Robert Silverberg, Harper & Row, 1970, pp. 265-68.*

Harold L. Berger   (essay date 1976)

[*In the following excerpt from his* Science Fiction and the New Dark Age, *a survey of dystopian science fiction, Berger interprets* A Boy and His Dog *as a metaphorical depiction of generational conflict.*]

"The Silent Generation" of the 1950's, youth quite disinclined to involve itself in grand enterprises, choosing instead established paths to modest goals, disappointed those who wished it more daring and creative. Youth's startling turnabout in the 1960's is now history, and to history belong its cause and measure. Certainly, our society's inability to cope with worsening crises gave youth small respect for its seniors, some of whom, despairing of their own generation's wisdom and vitality, look to the coming wave to succeed where they have failed. . . . [The] dystopian does not share their confidence, but rather sees in youth's ascendency yet another potential for the abuse of power. He has seen enough waves of the future, new orders, marches of progress, and absolute remedies to have developed a strong suspicion of disturbers of the *status quo,* even when he finds the *status quo* disturbing.

The dominant fact in the fiction and sociological studies

about the angry young is that those shared values forming the center have given way and that never before have they given way so quickly and thoroughly. Generation gaps are nothing new, but this one gapes. . . . If the center keeps eroding, two distinct societies could possibly emerge, the young and their elders, to confront each other indefinitely like two historically unfriendly countries. . . . [In] Harlan Ellison's *A Boy and His Dog* this has happened. (p. 142)

The center had not held in *A Boy and His Dog,* Harlan Ellison's Nebula Award-winning novella. The nuclear war of 2007 blasted it away. On the scorged earth's surface warrior tribes of armed boys, roverpaks, live off the leavings of demolished cities. And miles below in the skyless, insulated "downunders," other survivors yawn away placid, hollow lives of boring respectability. Vic, Ellison's fifteen-year-old hero-narrator, picks his way through the surface jungle as cautiously and daringly as a sapper in a mine field. A "solo," unattached, his survival depends on his .45 automatic, his rifle, and his loyal, sagacious talking dog, Blood, friend, dependent, advisor, comrade in battle, and expert sniffer of danger and the human female. Blood's nose leads his sex-hungry master to Quilla June Holmes, a downunder girl who had come up the access dropshaft disguised as a boy. Quilla proves a most appreciative and demanding rape victim and Vic's capable ally too when a roverpak, led by its dogs, surprise their hideout. After the firefight Quilla escapes to the downunders, and Vic follows her, drawn by the thought of her willing body.

But Quilla had been bait and the downunders capture Vic. They need him for stud, many of the women being sterile and the rest having mostly girls. While Ellison doesn't explain the cause of their reproductive problem, he infers through Vic that their preoccupation with niceness and order gelded the sexual vitality of both women and men. The downunders are mush.

> They rocked in rockers on front porches, they raked their lawns, they hung around the gas station, they stuck pennies in gumball machines, they painted white stripes down the middle of the road, they sold newspapers on the corners, they listened to oompah bands on a shell in the park, they played hopscotch and pussy-in-the-corner, they polished fire engines, they sat on benches reading, they washed windows and pruned bushes, they tipped their hats to ladies. . . . they walked hand-in-hand with some of the ugliest chicks I've ever seen, and they bored the ass off me. . . . Polite? Christ, you could puke from all the lying hypocritical crap they called civility. Hello Mr. This and Mrs. That. And how are you? . . . And how is business? . . . And I started gibbering in my room. . . . That clean, sweet, neat, lovely way they lived was enough to kill a guy. No wonder the men couldn't get it up and make babies that had balls instead of slots.

Vic escapes to the surface with Quilla. The girl loves him and she picks off their downunder pursuers with his .45. They find Blood at the access dropshaft, weak from the wounds of the previous fight and dying of starvation, and they have no food. With another roverpak assault imminent Quilla urges Vic to abandon the dog. "She got a pouty look on her face. 'If you love me, you'll come *on.*' "—After Blood had eaten, Vic treats his wounds. The two strike out across the wasteland for another city. Thoughts of Quilla fade slowly, and

> it took a long time before I stopped hearing her calling in my head. Asking me, asking me: *do you know what love is?*
>
> Sure I know.
>
> A boy loves his dog.

It would be a mistake to cast Ellison's story among those depicting the mosaic of social disintegration after a nuclear war. The war is a framework within which Ellison dramatizes varieties of alienation, especially of youth, and despite the setting the alienation looks familiar. Like many of today's rebellious young, Vic prefers his hard but free life to the contemptibly vapid existence of the buried "squares." And to the squares he is an animal. Quilla too revolts against her background, but she can not throw off all its values. Her ending up as a dog's meal is, in retrospect, less a shock than an expectable consequence of the dog's indispensability and her burdensome downunder romantic notions. The cuddling tentacles of love had to be cut away. To Vic a binding relationship based on little more than sentiment and archaic traditions, the barnacles of obligation, love—what many-splendored thing? If a dog talks sense (and Blood does) a talking dog is better than a lying song. (pp. 143-45)

> *Harold L. Berger, "The New Tyrannies," in his* Science Fiction and the New Dark Age, *Bowling Green University Popular Press, 1976, pp. 86-146.*

John Crow and Richard Erlich   (essay date 1977)

[*In the following essay, Crow and Erlich analyze mythic patterns in* A Boy and His Dog.]

Harlan Ellison's **A Boy and His Dog,** as novella and film, is a cautionary fable employing satire and mythic patterns to define a future world that in some respects may already be with us. The "boy" is Vic and the "dog" is Blood; their world is the American Southwest in 2024, shortly after World War IV and the near-total destruction of the human race. Vic is a "solo" operating with his dog, Blood, competing for survival and sex with other solos and their dogs and, also, with "roverpaks," small tribes formed in the wake of the destruction of all other social order. Blood, however, is not the ordinary *Canis familiaris* of our world. By means of biological engineering, carried out to produce "skirmisher dogs" for the military, dogs have become more intelligent and, also, capable of telepathic communication with humans. Their sense of smell has been modified to be ultra-sensitive to humans so that they can locate enemies. Consequently, many of them, including Blood, have lost the ability to find their own food.

But these dogs find men to forage for them. The men cooperate partly because dogs are useful in the fight for survival, but primarily because the new-model dogs are as com-

petent at tracking down females as they are at locating enemies—a highly valuable skill in a world with a diminishing female population. Even among dogs of this new type, though, Blood seems extraordinary. Not only is he the sharpest "tail-scent" around, he is also intellectually more sophisticated than Vic and emotionally more mature than any of the humans we see in the world of 2024.

In Blood, we have one of the variations in mythic patterns and folk motifs that make both Ellison's novella and Jones's film so fascinating and disturbing. At first glance, Blood seems much like the wise magic animal of folk and fairy tales who comes to the aid of the hero when the hero is at an impasse. But Blood goes beyond this role to become Vic's link to the lost pre-war civilization, teaching him reading, arithmetic, recent history, and "Edited English" grammar. He becomes the culture-bearer of the bombed-out wasteland, superior to Vic in everything but the necessary skills of animal survival. The normal relationship of human and animal is inverted.

This inversion and others that follow acquire significance when we see them against the structural pattern of the story. The pattern is the basic descent-containment-reascent pattern of initiation, which in primitive societies is usually a formalized ritual designed to bring a boy into manhood. It also appears in myths of the hero, where the hero undertakes the task of renewing the wasteland. Through the many variations of the pattern, the task confronting the protagonist remains the same: to maintain conscious "human" control over the unconscious "animal" instincts and responses, thereby overcoming fear, fatigue, inattention or disobedience, or the temptation to indulge appetites such as hunger or the sex drive. Since the sexual appetite presents such a powerful and persistent temptation to the hero, the feminine becomes a symbol of the danger of losing consciousness and regressing to instinctual, unconscious motivation. On the other hand, the feminine can function as mediatrix of the life force that brings renewal to the wasteland. In myth, the feminine has either positive or negative value according to whether she overwhelms the hero and renders him ineffectual by depriving him of human consciousness or joins him in the task of rejuvenating the wasteland.

All the elements of this mythic situation are present in both the film and the novella: the bombed-out wasteland incapable of the renewal of life; the feminine sexual lure into the descent, represented by Quilla June Holmes; a hero divided between using good sense and pursuing his sexual desires; and the necessity for rebirth (the goal of initiation).

The need for rebirth is implicit in the first part of the narrative in the images of the wasteland—the radiation-scorched plain—and, symbolically, in the preoccupation of all males with tracking down the few females who remain above ground. The impossibility of rebirth is implicit in the brutality and violence of the sexual relationship in Vic's world. With a few exceptions, the women in this world hide from men, and, if found, are brutally raped and sometimes killed. As the film opens, Blood and Vic have tracked down a female only to find her already the captive of a roverpak. A long-distance shot gives us Vic and

Blood's view of the departing rovers, and we hear in the distance a young boy's voice exclaim excitedly, "Did you see how she jerked when I cut her?" Vic finds the woman stabbed to death and expresses his view of the pity of it all: "Ah, why'd they have to do that? She was good for three or four more times yet." Masculine and feminine are alien and hostile to one another; rebirth in such a world is impossible.

Cheated by the roverpak out of his own chance for rape, Vic takes Blood to a "beaver flick," where Blood picks up the scent of a woman, disguised as a solo. Vic and Blood track her to a bombed-out YMCA, stand off a roverpak whose dogs have also picked up a female scent, and discover a woman from the downunder who is not only desirable but willing—very willing.

Quilla June Holmes is an escapee (apparently) from the State of Topeka, one of the subterranean retreats of American middle-class civilization, and she has never had such a good time. From Vic's point of view she has only one flaw: she is concerned about love, offending Vic's sense of propriety and wounding his ego by suggesting that he does not know a thing about it. Their discussion of love introduces into the film the concept of relatedness between masculine and feminine that could promise a renewal of the wasteland. Unfortunately, at this point Quilla June bashes Vic over the head with a flashlight and disappears back into the downunder, leaving behind the keycard that opens the access shaft to the underground. This sets up the descent of the hero into the underworld, for Vic, much to Blood's disgust, loses whatever good sense he once possessed: lured on by his desire to get even and his desire for Quilla June, Vic decides to follow her downunder. The pattern seems true to the usual psychological significance of mythic descents. The loss of "human" intellect reduces the hero to the animal level, and he descends into the womb of the Earth Mother to struggle with the unconscious forces of instinct, passion, and, quite possibly, death. As Blood remarks sarcastically, Vic is acting like a *putz*, phallic man, ruled by his lower rather than his higher human nature. The argument between Vic and Blood makes clear the baseness of Vic's *macho* motivation. To pursue Quilla June, Vic leaves Blood, hungry and badly wounded from the fight with the roverpak, to fend for himself. The inversion between man and animal is starkest at this point.

The next inversion follows closely. The underground that Vic discovers is anything but a region of the spontaneity, disorder, and passion of the Earth Mother. Vic descends through a hell not of chaos, but of machinery, pipes, cables, and wires. Cryptic labels, valves, color-coded gadgets of various types add to the clutter of an extensive life-support system for the underground city, all of which disappear as Vic leaves the shaft and enters the city itself. The downunder is innocent of any sign of highly developed scientific technology. It is America circa 1915—River City in parody, complete with marching bands, community picnics, overalls, straw hats, and gingham dresses. The only anomalies are a public address system with a Big Brother voice, giving recipes, homespun advice, notices to the public—and Michael.

Michael is a big, husky hayseed who enforces rigid order for the ruling Committee; and as we discover later, he is a humanoid robot, backed up by several immediately available replacements. The Committee is comprised of a female secretary and two mean-minded, desiccated old men. They recognize only one crime: "Lack of respect, wrong attitude, failure to obey authority"; and they assign only one punishment: death by "natural" causes—which means summary execution by Michael.

This underground world is, in short, the antithesis of the underground of myth and fairy tale. It is a sterile, rigidly structured, time-denying society, as mechanistic as the life-support machinery concealed in the shafts surrounding it. But there is a sense in which locating this ossified society in the underground world of unconsciousness conforms with the usual significance of mythic undergrounds. For we become most unconscious in our habitual acceptance of cultural forms, in the sacrifice of human intellect by failing to question these forms—until, little by little, our social behavior becomes as automatic as breathing. A character of Ellison's describes the process in mechanistic terms: "Men often become too much like their machines. . . . Then they blame the machines for dehumanizing them." And "machinery," is not only technological gadgets but also social forms. Civilized society produces traditional forms as constraining as the tabus of the most primitive culture; and it can produce its own rigid orthodoxies, and orthodoxy, in George Orwell's words, "means . . . not needing to think. Orthodoxy is unconscious."

Orthodoxy is the highest value in Topeka. Consequently, the underground world is even more of a wasteland than the world above ground. In the downunder consciousness is repressed; and any attempt to become conscious, to examine the system, becomes "Lack of respect, wrong attitude, failure to obey authority" and a prelude to absolute unconsciousness at Michael's hands. Accordingly, rebirth is as impossible in the downunder as it is in the wasteland above, a situation that becomes apparent when the captured Vic discovers that he has been lured down below by Quilla June to perform stud service on the young female population, the males having lost their fertility in the sterile mechanistic world.

Vic is delighted to oblige, but his "service" is a good deal less pleasant than he expects. The film, in an improvement on the novella, shows Vic, mouth taped shut, strapped to a table and connected to an aseptic machine of gleaming chrome and glass. Down the hall stretches a seemingly endless line of conventionally gowned, sad-faced "brides." Each "bride" is brought to a flowery arch at the entrance to the room where Vic is captive, a clergyman in full vestments intones a marriage ceremony, the machine hums and clicks—and Vic ejaculates, his semen neatly transported into a test tube. Quilla June rescues Vic, not so much because she likes what he does, but mostly because she has planned a coup to take over the downunder and intends to manipulate Vic into using his fighting ability to help her succeed.

The Committee aborts the coup; and Michael brutally executes Quilla June's co-conspirators, a small band of ineffectual boy friends. After Vic finally destroys *this* Michael, he and Quilla June escape up to the surface, where they find the deserted and starving Blood near death from hunger and from the wounds he sustained helping Vic defend Quilla June. Quilla June, fearing pursuit, demands that Vic leave Blood and continue their escape. But Blood needs food immediately; and Vic, who has recovered a human consciousness during the struggle below, decides to provide it from the most obvious source in the barren landscape. The film closes with Vic and Blood setting off into the sunrise to look for Overthehill—a place where "food grows right out of the ground!" The final image implies what Ellison makes explicit at the end of his novella:

> It took a long time before I stopped hearing her . . . asking me: *do you know what love is?*
>
> Sure I know.
>
> A boy loves his dog.

The film, like Ellison's novella, demands consideration of just how consciously our own society is proceeding into its technological future. It also has in its political implications a strong condemnation of any complacent "silent majority" who would deny time and change by a mechanistic application of outworn values. Both Ellison's story and Jones's film present a two-level world: on the surface we have "man in a state of nature," a la Thomas Hobbes, a life of "perpetual war of every man against his neighbor"; in the downunder we have a mechanized incarnation of Hobbes' Leviathan—a totalitarian society where people have renounced freedom, individuality, and, most of all, consciousness, for stability and order. This Hobbesian dichotomy presented in a mythic structure suggests the horror of a world not future, but present, a world where our surface struggles move in patterns dictated by our unconscious subservience to traditional forms.

Jones's film, like Ellison's novella, cautions us that the blighted wasteland of 2024 may become reality, the result, not so much of man's unrestrained animal nature as of his social, political, and technological machinery. As Susan Sontag observed in "The Imagination of Disaster" (*Against Interpretation,* 1965): "The dark secret behind human nature used to be the animal—as in King Kong. The threat to man, his availability for dehumanization, lay in his own animality. Now the danger is understood as residing in man's ability to be turned into a machine." Vic's discovery at the end of the film that "a boy loves his dog" places the center of value in Blood, the intelligent animal with a capacity for love. Blood waits for Vic even in the face of starvation: the dog loves his boy. Blood's love surpasses merely unconscious, "phallic," love; it far surpasses the power-hungry manipulation of passion represented by Quilla June. And in the end, Vic's love matches Blood's.

The end of the film is appropriately grotesque, but in the world of 2024 it is the best resolution we can hope for: Blood's breakfast fire glowing dimly in the foreground, he and Vic walk off together into the sunrise, joined by consciousness and love. (pp. 162-66)

> *John Crow and Richard Erlich, "Mythic Patterns in Ellison's 'A Boy and His Dog'," in Ex-*

trapolation, *Vol. 18, No. 2, May, 1977, pp. 162-66.*

If there is anything true and honest I know about myself and my work, it is that I am only a storyteller. Oh, there are messages in everything I write, but they are there to satisfy *my* needs as a thinking individual; I hope a *committed* individual.

—Harlan Ellison, in an interview published in Speaking of Science Fiction: The Paul Walker Interviews, *1978*.

George Edgar Slusser   (essay date 1977)

[*An American educator and critic, Slusser has written extensively on science fiction and fantasy. In the following excerpt from his* Harlan Ellison: Unrepentant Harlequin, *he examines the theme of humankind's relationship to self and the universe in Ellison's short fiction.*]

[Ellison's tales of the late 1960s] are stories in which a trick ending points less to some moral truth than to cosmic irony. In this light, three tales of the early Seventies offer an interesting contrast. The change here is less one of heart—they are still profoundly pessimistic—than of procedure. **"Silent in Gehenna"** (1971) is apparently a story about student protest; **"Basilisk"** (1972) treats a Vietnam-like war and American jingoism; **"Knox"** (1974) deals with race prejudice, blind patriotism, and fascism. No longer do the hero's actions seem disembodied—pure. . . . Emerging gradually from Ellison's stories is a central dichotomy between "civilization" and the primitive darkness that underlies it. By firmly anchoring the action of each of these new stories in a "current problem," the author is free to explore the interrelations of these poles in all their complexity and diversity. Before, as victim strove to become master, he would either flee society or seek to destroy it; his impulse was invariably outward. Now, however, victims are possessed by primal forces, only to be thrown back into society, and destroyed by it. Their dubious battle serves to either teach a lesson or learn one. The field of battle is gradually turning inward, to the individual conscience. Earlier heroes were bound to the Sisyphean rock of survival; we could only watch their absurd labors, rarely getting into their minds. Now they still roll their impossible burdens upward, but a glimmer of recognition is there. Ellison's hero is beginning to be aware of his place in the universe. This may only lead to more terrible ironies, for the heroes of these three stories never fully understand why things are as they are. They act to free themselves from the fatal web, only to become more inextricably bound.

"Silent in Gehenna" is a strange tale of transcendence. Joe Bob, the last student radical in a world of fortress universities totally dominated by army and industry, stages a raid on USC. He cries out to the students to throw off their oppressors, but nobody responds: things have gone too far. He can only blow up some buildings and scurry away. As he waits in ambush at another "university," he begins to think over his actions, and is suddenly surrounded in golden light, and transported to a heavenly place. Here the pattern starts all over again. He is suspended in a golden cage high above a public thoroughfare. In the streets of gold below, he witnesses a new spectacle of cruelty and oppression: yellow, bulb-like creatures lashing small blue men. He grabs his bullhorn and shouts.

But what does all of this mean? The title itself appears mysterious. All is gold and light and eternity: why then "Gehenna" and hell and silence? The hero is never silent: is he not the voice crying out in the wilderness? In a broader sense, silence is refusal to take a stand. Can there be a situation in which even speaking out represents giving up, or giving in? Joe Bob will take the familiar theme of struggle to some new limits.

The world he is fighting is ruled less by tyrants than by the "silent majority." People have become so used to ecological blight that they now accept it as normal. Hell has begun to think of itself as heaven. Though the pollution of the Earth has destroyed them, the hobo-mutants Joe Bob meets seem happy with things as they are. They talk of "improvements," even play Monopoly. What a contrast to the mutants' violent anger against the society that produced them in the earlier tale, **"The Discarded"** (1956). Here the moral is clear: those who gave in to society's promises are callously betrayed. In **"Silent,"** however, matters are much more complicated. The hero betrays himself, and he does so by having a crisis of conscience. Ironically, his "transfiguration" is less a moment of truth than of capitulation. As this last of the protesters becomes more and more isolated, inner debate absorbs him. One of the voices is superego: it tells him his stance is illogical; in order to liberate, he must kill. At the moment he fully realizes his dilemma, he simply fades. And why not? He ceases to be the "enemy," and walls and guns only exist because there is someone to defend against.

But man cannot remain without a function in this universe. In "heaven" (clearly an alien planet), the hero finds a new role to play. With a twist more in tune with Dante's hell, this man of conscience becomes a celestial superego. He was not heard before; now he is. The yellow figures stop their whipping, fall down, and expiate their guilt before him. But then they rise up purged, and go on whipping as before. As their "confessor," he abets suffering rather than alleviating it. The parallel to the minister in **"Enter the Fanatic"** is clear. Again, as on Earth, what seemed the noble action, the unique blow struck for "good," turns out to be just another cog in the great machinery of pain. Once more, the hero becomes "aware" of his situation. The debates begin: "The deep yellow light, do you know what it did to you? Yes." There is, it seems, no way out of the ironic trap: he sees, and proceeds to chain himself to the wheel all the more tightly. Yes, the serious liberator now admits he has become a clown, that he finds his task pointless. Yet, with the same disregard for logic, he takes it up unto eternity: "Maybe at the end

of forever they'll let me die." His hope, of course, is an illusion, for as long as he functions, the machine will stand.

Joe Bob says he is "ineffectual," but he is not; like all men, silent or not, he serves that grim order of things where slavery and pain are simple facts of existence. He is, in Ellison's work, a hero at the crossroads: abandoning deeds, he seeks his way out of the maze through thought and reflexion. And yet he misses the point, failing to see his true state. The narrator must do this. Joe Bob is brother to the deadly bush shrike, victim and killer all at once: "Joe Bob Hickey, prey of his world, impaled on a thorn of light by the shrike, and brother to the shrike himself." This is a "butcherbird" who kills for the joy of it, yet has a most melodious song. In the same way, the heavenly city, man's ultimate dream of civility and order, can harbor a hell at its heart. Light is indeed brother to darkness, the black-headed bird to the illuminated reformer. What could have been an anti-establishment tract turns out to have a totally different "message": effective social action is impossible. It is better to accept the paradoxes of existence than to question them, to fight rather than object with the conscience. As Joe Bob learns, there is no escape from the brutal fabric of nature: this bird in a gilded cage is no less a bird and a killer. It is wrong to see this hero as some special dream, a child of Aquarius. Purposely, he has no sign of the zodiac. He is everyman, and we are all brothers to the shrike, all in danger of being impaled on that Blakean "thorn of light."

"Basilisk" (1972) takes this search for connections between man and the dark forces of nature in a different direction. It is the story of a corporal who suffers pain and torture in a setting the author has subtly but specifically explicated as being like Vietnam, but not *actually* the locale of that war. When he returns to his small Midwestern town, he is pilloried by the local patriots as a traitor. It is the story of a little man, an underdog who musters hidden force, and lashes out at hypocrisy and stupidity. But there is an important difference: his power comes not, as in the earlier tales, from untapped human reserves. It comes from the Basilisk. He has been invaded and possessed by dark spirits: he can slay with his gaze.

But what is this Basilisk? In this tale, there is again a polarity. We have on the one hand man's myths, false or simply adequate, and on the other the dark order of things that underlies them: the "darkside" universe, nameless, protean, possessing its own awesome logic and symmetry. Corporal Lestig becomes linked to this other order when he steps on the poisoned stake: "It is a well-known fact that one whose blood slakes the thirst of the *vrykolakas,* the vampire, himself becomes one of the drinkers of darkness, becomes a celebrant of the master deity, becomes himself possessed of the powers of the disciples of that deity." The vampire legend in itself, Ellison tells us, does not adequately explain Lestig's fate. But the pattern is there, the blood bond that ties man to this fearful nature. The stake is the point of contact at which he passes from one world order to another—from the false one of society to the true one of pain. This new rule gains ground as Lestig awakens in the hands of his captors. Significantly, he is blind at first. As they torture him, and he reveals all he knows, his sight gradually returns: "As if it were a reward for having held nothing back, a gummed gold star placed beside his chalked name on a blackboard in a kindergarten schoolroom, his eyesight began to come back slightly." But the "light" he recovers is of a new sort; it has nothing to do with the ideals of a society that will persecute him for his "betrayal." This new light radiates out from man's desire to survive, to live at any cost; it is a power, a force, not an empty aura. The world here is inverted, not perverted. In fact, this dark order is most straightforward and logical. Lestig's gaze slays his captors only when they come close to killing him. It incarnates the basic human fact of self-preservation. Once more, on this deeper level, light becomes brother to darkness.

Lestig's society sent him to war, and war put the stake in his path. And yet this society refuses to acknowledge a role in the natural chain of life and death. It demands an impossible "hero" under torture, and condemns the corporal. What the gaze of this modern basilisk will penetrate is the fog of our cultural myths. Compared with these, the most fantastic vampire is truth. They not only obscure our understanding of the deeper ways of nature, but actually bring us to outdo the natural cycle of bloodshed, to become warmongers and vigilantes. Ironically, Lestig's oriental torturers are closer to the real rhythms of life: "They were an ancient people . . . they knew the uses to which anguish could be put, and for them there was no evil in doing so: for a people with a heritage of enslavement, evil is a concept of those who forged the shackles, not those who wore them. In the name of freedom, no monstrousness is too great." Like all the myths of our society, "Freedom" is only a sophisticated mask; behind it men conquer and oppress in the name of other gods. Lestig's gold star causes the "Gold Star Mother" to pale, and she must finally gun him down. To his pursuers, Lestig is a "monster." Yet they do not see the uncanny resemblance between their torchlit manhunt, and those in the myriad monster films their "culture" has made. This monster is also of their making; they sent him to know darkness and death, and now would destroy him for it. The hero need only look at these people, and they melt like wax; they are mere shadows, with no real being able to sustain human contact.

Lestig returns not to avenge—he can only kill in self-defense—so much as to teach: his darkness is light after all, even if awesome. He will now show these people the true meaning of existence: "Get down on your knees and crawl, patriots! Crawl to me and maybe I'll let you live. Get down like animals and crawl on your bellies to me." This hero has advanced a step beyond Joe Bob—he sees man clearly as an animal. But society cannot accept having its illusions stripped away, and it kills him. The tale ends with an invocation to Mars. Society has once again begun to erect its personifications and deceitful mythical structures over the nameless dark. **"Basilisk"** is, to be sure, a stinging condemnation of our society. In it, however, the problem of blackness is placed irrevocably beyond man's capacity to change it. On this deeper level of understanding, the "ancient people" are wiser than we, because they recognize these destructive forces, and serve them more frankly and openly.

Finally, there is **"Knox"** (1973). The tale chronicles the gradual enslavement of a very "common man" caught in the toils of a racist, totalitarian society. In the beginning, he is neither a "good" man nor a "bad" one, but simply man in the raw: "Charlie Knox is. A man. Who." The changing punctuation of this phrase measures the successive degrees of possession. His first kill, while serving as part of a "raiding party," is unintentional—he thinks his opponent has a weapon. His second is "suggested" to him, his third fully willed, the result of his own initiative. He begins to feel a "blossoming joy" in his actions. They become more and more brutal and savage, until at the height of his career we get this: "Charlie Knox is. A man who: Had been a man. Had been trained." But he too, like many of Ellison's worshippers of the will to power, reaches his limits: he cannot kill his wife. Knox, apparently, is the contrary of a Joe Bob. Like Pastor Niemoller, in the quote that prefaces the story, he has waited too long to speak up. He has served his society so well, and eliminated all possible human contact, that there is no one left when he finally breaks down. As he has killed the others, he can only kill himself.

As Knox begins to take pleasure in killing, he sees himself visited by "persons in black garments." Just before he kills himself, he has the following revelation: "I don't know where they came from, another world I guess, but *that* doesn't matter. They're training us, to go out there for them, out there somewhere. But we weren't cruel enough. They took up where we left ourselves off." But what are these black figures? In an earlier tale, a spoof on the James Bond formula called **"Santa Claus vs. S.P.I.D.E.R."** (1968), prominent political figures are possessed by black "splotches" that flee their host vessel, and self-destruct when discovered by the master sleuth. What does S.P.I.D.E.R. stand for? Throughout the action, Santa ponders the initials, finally getting an answer: "The symbiote was small, black, hairy, and scuttled on many little legs. The eight-point plan was intended to make people feel bad. That simple. It was to make them feel simply crummy. And crummy people kill each other . . . All he had to do was delete the periods." Again, behind man's oppressive abstractions, there is a force of animal nature. In **"Knox,"** these shapes are hardly extraterrestrials, or carriers of some absolute evil. They are far-flung solutions to a simpler matter. The shapes grow as man fades. He gives his allegiance not to his inner nature, but to social doctrines or systems. As he does so, he trades his own being against darkness, becoming like those shadow men in **"Basilisk"** who wither in Lestig's gaze. Not only this, but he feeds the darkness, and the forms rise up to swallow him. As Brenda Knox cleans the house after her husband's suicide, the black shapes are still there, but she sees only the dust. But they surely will become visible as she gives in to her world.

In these latest tales, Ellison gives us, instead of geometry, a genuine ecology of darkness. From situation to situation, man is woven more and more inexorably into the fearful dynamics of nature. Social action is all but impossible. The institutions of this world are not only treacherous, claiming to bring light and actually serving darkness, but flimsy and inconsequential as well. Man can do little or nothing collectively to change his lot; laws and education can easily become instruments of tyranny in the wrong hands. The battle, for Ellison, remains an individual one; the only true law is that of survival. In another story of this period, **"The Whimper of Whipped Dogs"** (1973), the protagonist, attacked by a thief in her chambers, calls out to the god of violence that governs the action: "Take him, not me," and the thief is whisked away, dashed to a horrible death. Traditional morality cannot explain the violence in this story, and existing social institutions are powerless to prevent it. Man is on his own, and the strongest survives. There is more than a tinge of Calvinist gloom cast over man's collective efforts. This whole middle ground between the individual and his dark gods is without substance. Joe Bob would help humanity only to learn that he is brother to the shrike. And the ending of **"Basilisk"** reads like a macabre parody on the social optimism (such as it is) of **"Repent, Harlequin!"**: "Lestig was gone, but that was to be expected. The weapon had been deactivated, but Mars . . . sat content. The recruiting had gone well. Power to the people." Even Knox takes no moral stand in killing himself; he is simply too weak, and like Joe Bob, he capitulates.

But questions do arise. To what extent is man to blame for his condition? In all these stories, he has made it worse by not accepting it. But how can he accept violence and suffering? Can he do anything? **"Knox"** ends on a note of bitter fatalism that could be a ray of hope. Ellison gives us a quote from Jung: "The only thing we have to fear on this planet is man." The cycle will begin all over again. Failure and suffering are part of the universal order. But if man cannot change things, perhaps he can know more. The dark shapes are fed by our lies and hypocrisy; but must they always remain symbols of something incomprehensible? Must all our moments of recognition be as bewildered as that of Knox? In these stories, we have reached a "Job situation." Pain has become a fact of human existence, no more, no less. The "adversary" is neither wholly within nor wholly without. Nor is he a free agent. He is clearly recognized as part of a godhead whose real nature—like that of the leviathan—is beyond human understanding. The task of Ellison's mythical tales will be to rise to that superhuman plane, to explore the ways of these gods to man.

[The] tales discussed so far are imperfect as mythical expression. They expose a dreadful order of things, but do not seek to explain its origins and causes. They show the errors and failures of man, not his search to understand his condition, or define his place in this universe. What shapes itself, in tale after tale, is an "ecology of darkness," a fearful balance of natural forces of which man is necessarily a part, from which he cannot escape. But what is his part? Is it his lot to fight on endlessly, tooth and claw, in animal combat? Why then is he given a mind that can dream of better worlds? Why is he given the capacity for love as well as hate? Between extremes—man the center of things, or man the insignificant atom—what is the relation of Ellison's struggling individual to the dynamics of his universe? The fantasy tales weave the dark patterns of the circumference. The mythic parables and quests, on the other hand, seek to vindicate the point. Their focus is con-

tractive. The only hope for equilibrium, that the one might ever balance with the all, lies in the individual exploring himself.

The key here is knowledge. If man cannot change his situation, perhaps he can understand it. In the fantasy tales, man only seems suspended between a dark realm and a light. There is, however, no such duality, and man is no median. Indeed, the transcendent sphere—the domain of ideals, institutions, dreams of progress, and order—is a delusion, a lie. In pursuing it, man loses himself. The point is sucked up by this circumference; man yields up his being to dark shadows. The Apollonian world is illusion, the Dionysian reality. The only way for man to preserve any vestige of being is to accept this gruesome reality openly. In order to claim a place in this pattern of struggle and survival, he must assert his individuality. But if Joe Bob's "heaven" is in reality a hell, is not the world of Ellison's primitive fighters and avengers just as much one? The question these mythic tales ask is whether man can ever break this infernal circle, achieving some form of balance between point and circumference, between man and universe.

The stories are of two basic kinds. First, there are the cosmologies, parables that explore the ways of the gods to man. What are the causes of man's condition? Is this natural order of pain and suffering part of some higher universal balance? Second, there are the tales of quest, individual man searching to define his role in the cosmic dynamic. Earlier heroes sought to conquer worlds; these seek to know self. The direction is no longer outward and upward, but downward and inward, into the depths of nature, inside one's own mind or body. They do not move backward, in search of a forgotten point in their own past where their individual destiny was shaped, where their ephemeral existence and the universe crossed, and were joined in a split second. If anything, the hero's quest becomes circular. He would return to the beginning, the source, but this time in hopes of knowing it, of finding balance or rest. If the circle of human life is one of endless struggle, Sisyphean damnation, then this quest within becomes a search to break the circle, to find reconciliation at the place where point and circumference meet.

A good introduction to the cosmological tales is a curious hybrid that stands halfway between them and the fantasies we have discussed, **"All the Sounds of Fear"** (1962). Here a human destiny is treated as if it were an abstract problem. The story tells the plight of the consummate "method actor" Richard Becker. He is a being with neither childhood nor old age. He springs full-grown into his first role at twenty-two; his career progresses till it peaks in insane murder—he plays the part of a hammer killer all too well. From this point it gradually recedes; the actor withdraws backward through all his roles until he reaches the first again. But if this looks like Freytag's pyramid, its two base angles are not equal. What begins as Oedipus ends without a face at all. Oedipus' darkness is fecund—he "sees" for the first time only when deprived of the light of a world that has led him astray with its illusions. But what is Becker but the total product of this world of deceit—society's man to the exclusion of any "personality" or self. In his final faceless call for light, we wonder how one who has never been a man could know the real darkness. His domain is fear, the phantoms of some deeper substance. And he is but the shadow of a man—"a creature God had never deigned to bless with a mirror to the world," a mirrorless mirror. In this allegory, we get no more about the relation of God to man. Nor do we have a man.

Only in **"Paingod"** (1964) do we first examine human suffering from the cosmic point of view. This parable tells of the meeting of infinitely vast and infinitely small—man and god—at the center of pain. Pain becomes not only the crux of their relationship, but the pivotal point from which both evolve—it is the dynamic element, the prime mover, in a universe that otherwise would be static. The paingod has become dissatisfied with his job of dispensing pain: "It involved no feeling and no concern, only attention to duty . . . How peculiar it was that he felt concern after all this time." But he is the highest authority, there is nowhere to go for answers but down. He goes all the way to the bottom of creation, skid row on the insignificant Sol III, a failed sculptor named Colin Marshack. Only when inside this minute human destiny can he feel the full, hot potency of this thing he so casually sprinkled over the universe. This in turn brings him to lift the man out of his shell, and whirl him through infinite space: "He poured him full of love and life and the staggering beauty of the cosmos." The sculptor returns to life to create a masterwork, and face even greater suffering because of it; the god goes back to come of age. But will he now spare the creatures of the universe this suffering? No, he will send more and more pain, for this is the most fortunate thing of all, without it there can be no happiness. The god was bored. Man too gives him a gift—in exchange for an instant of pain he receives an eternity of happiness.

"Paingod" celebrates (if with irony) a cosmic polarity in which pain is a necessary term. Ellison's fearful symmetry is profoundly dynamic; contracting and expanding entities converge at a point of pain, which in turn becomes one term in a new rhythm of undulation: pain and pleasure, beauty and misery. There is room then for both gods and men to grow, to change, but only within the fixed limits of this balance of forces. How human actions affect this balance—the possibility that man's desire to "better" his universe could ever change or alter the workings of this system—is the subject of one of Ellison's most interesting stories, **"The Beast That Shouted Love at the Heart of the World"** (1968).

Because this tale cuts back and forth so radically across time and space, it can have no ethical dimension per se. Instead of codes and laws, there are facts—acts of violence. Human actions are stripped to their primitive level of impulse—love and hate. At the heart of this story is the drama of the scientist Semph, who at the "center" of the universe invents a machine to "drain" the beast of insanity. Once again, however, things must balance. To spare the future, you must corrupt the past—this madness will spew backward to all times and peoples. This draining is ordered by the politician Linah, representative of the Concord, who sees in this act the only hope for his race. Semph drains the beast, but "interposes" himself as well, sends

his own essence back "crosswhen" along with that of the monster. For this act he is condemned; who knows how disruptive it might be, what it will do to alter the balance of things?

This question, of course, should have been asked in the first place. Linah and his society have erected their codes into universals. But who can say what effect either of these two actions will have on the past, let alone which is "good" and which is "bad." Is it the interposition of Semph that caused Attila the Hun to turn back at the gates of Rome—this brief rupture in the "hour that stretches" of madness? No logic stopped him, however, but a violent fit, much like that which took the beast as he was being drained. And to onlookers it was rather the turning back that must have seemed insane, for nothing stood in his way. Where is the clear line of cause and effect? Nor can man set the spatial and temporal limits of his acts any more easily than he can fix their moral parameters. To have a past and a future, there must be a present, a fixed center. But where is the heart of the world in this story?

The very structure of this narrative, crisscrossing back and forth in space and time, denies meaning to the idea of linear progression. The "center" is an ever-shifting point. To Linah, it is the place of chance. But, Semph replies, "for them, all of them out there . . . no chance ever?" Indeed, in each time zone, there is always a chance; all actions radiate from a center to a circumference. Attila's fit becomes a Christian miracle; Friedrich Drucker claws open a Pandora's box of many colors in a Stuttgart basement and the winds of war soar to the heavens. Linah's folly is to think his center is the only center: "If we can begin here, if we can pursue our boundaries outward, then perhaps one day, sometime, we can reach the ends of time with that little chance." But the forces of nature are not so easily channelled: "Insanity is a living vapor . . . It can be bottled. The most potent genie in the most easily uncorked bottle." The rhythm life obeys is rather one of constant and endless pulsations, balance of polar opposites: "This place, over there," bottle and vapor, love and hate.

Every age then drains its beast. And in what flows back and forth there are some ironic sea-changes. William Sterog is a mad-dog killer who massacres out of love. He shouts to the judge who condemns him for slaying hundreds of people: "I love everyone in the world. I do." Linah flushes the beast "in the name of love." But what is meant to go forward as love, a gift for man to come, goes back as hate to William Sterog. In the same way, Sterog's hate goes forward to become a statue on some yet unborn planet, a monument to Semph, who interposed himself out of love for Sterog's distant past. In reality, these drainings are done neither out of love or hate, but in answer to an even more basic need—survival. "We stop fouling our own nest," Semph tells Linah, "at the expense of all the other nests that ever were." Semph would drain the urge to survive too, except that "what we'd have left wouldn't be worth having." Before dying, he distinguishes between Linah the "true man," the idealist, and the "strugglers" this world is made for. The "world" he refers to is, of course, the universe itself. It is governed by a terrible balance in which love begets hate, hate love. Man's sole freedom lies in accepting these contraries. But what is to be his course then? The drive for raw power led Ellison's early heroes just as surely to impasse—there is too much universe. Semph acts not to defeat the balance, but to uphold it. In order to do so however, this worker in the "inhuman field" of science must sacrifice himself. Only thus is this rhythm of alteration preserved.

Man then is not the center of the universe. But he is, necessarily, one of its poles. In both **"Paingod"** and **"Beast"** there is always that small point of contemporary American life, from which the cosmos expands, on which it contracts. Modern scientific man however would be not only center, but circumference as well, erect his systems and machines as absolutes, play god. These systems, we have seen in Ellison's fantasies, invariably absorb their builder, trap him in an inverted, perverted cosmos, a hell of his own making. In two other mythical allegories, **"I Have No Mouth and I Must Scream"** (1967), and **"Pretty Maggie Moneyeyes"** (1967), Ellison anatomizes man's relation to his machines, explores the outcome of our Faustian dreams.

In **"I Have No Mouth"** man's egomania has expanded his war machine to the point where it literally swallows him. Five surviving humans are consigned to an eternity of suffering in the belly of the giant computer AM. AM is a cruel Cartesian joke, a monstrous perversion of the natural ecological order: "There was the Chinese AM and the Russian AM and the Yankee AM and everything was fine until they had honeycombed the entire planet . . . But one day AM woke up and knew who he was, and he linked himself, and he began feeding all the killing data, until everyone was dead, except for the five of us." But sentience here is born not of love but of hate. The machine's hatred of man reflects man's hatred for each other, programmed into its circuitry, and now directed back at the five survivors: "HATE. LET ME TELL YOU HOW MUCH I'VE COME TO HATE YOU SINCE I BEGAN TO EXIST."

Sartre says that hell is the others. The machine certainly seems intent on proving this maxim. At least this is how the narrator sees things. AM, it appears, can "rearrange" its prisoners, deform their names and physique. These "changes" however are of a strange sort; they are colored with envy, as if someone were maliciously evening scores for past impotence, past dislikes. "Benny" before was a brilliant intellectual, a gay; now he is half-simian, endowed with a huge organ and a name that surely does not fit his origins. Gorrister was a peace marcher, a "connie"; now he is a shoulder-shrugger. Ellen, the black woman, has become a shameless nympho in the narrator's mind. The narrator himself does not describe his own body, but tells us: "I was the only one still sane and whole. AM had not tampered with my mind. I only had to suffer what he visited down on us . . . But these scum all four of them they were lined and arrayed against me." If the tale is not told by an idiot, it may be the vision of a madman. Is he paranoid? Has he been "altered" from without, or is he on the contrary altering things from within? We are put on guard about his final actions. He views his act as one of

love, he would free these others from the machine. Yet his vision of human relationships here is one of brutal hate.

These men are condemned to eternal life. AM however is no god; he cannot create life, or revive it once dead. He simply freezes it. Eternity here is purely quantitative, literally the hour that stretches, time alive without change or evolution. In his strange logic, the narrator finds this both to his advantage and disadvantage—he is the youngest one, but because of this the most envied. It is odd that one so favored should be so willing to sacrifice things for these others. The narrator decrees that the only way out is death, to stop living. But what do the others think? Enough facts filter through this unreliable account to give us an idea of the real situation. The narrator says they hate him, but their actions don't show it. And are they really so eager to die? "I could not read meaning into her expression, the pain had been too great, had contorted her face; but it *might* have been thank you. It's possible. Please." Ellen may help him kill the others, but does she want to die herself? The basic facts remain pain, struggle to survive. Throughout the story, the other four pursue this struggle, blindly. It is the narrator who is the "thinker"; he decides death is the only way out, and executes his decree. Again, here is one not only so much "bad" (he hopes he has done right) as deluded. The god complex of AM's builders still lives in him. He has a name—Ted—but never uses it himself. He prefers to be the giver of names, arbiter of destinies.

In the end, narrator and machine are left. Their relation forms the core of the tale. At one point the speaker describes AM in the following terms: "We had allowed him to think, but to do nothing with it. In a rage . . . he had killed us, almost all of us, and still he was trapped. He could not wander, he could not wonder, he could not belong. He could merely be. And so, with the innate loathing that all machines had always held for the weak soft creatures who had built them, he sought revenge." This, in capsule form, is his own relation to the others, his own fate. Is he not an isolated, disembodied mind among flesh and blood? Does he not despise its "weakness"? Ellen is simply all too human; yet he hates her physical nature with a loathing out of all proportion. When we finally see his body, it is a blob, "a thing that could never have been known as human." The machine has altered him, he says, punished him for his acts. What "evil" there is here though seems to come rather from within: "Blotches of diseased, evil grey come and go on my surface, as though light is being beamed from within." This speaker too may once have had, like the Beast who shouted love, a human shape. But he has traded it for envy and hate, projected the monster which traps him, making him over in its image—a soft machine. True hell is not the others; it is this. The thing his hate creates must preserve him—hate must have an object to exist at all. But he no longer has even that. Misguided love or disguised hate, the fact remains—he has killed them, they are beyond them. The polar order abides, but in horrible travesty: center and periphery, blob and machine, each sealed off from the other, the machine hating but unable to destroy, the man utterly alone and unable to scream.

Another tale of man and machines, **"Pretty Maggie Moneyeyes,"** examines this same geometry of hate from a different angle. Maggie is a machine-woman, an artifact of our material culture: "An operable woman, a working mechanism, a rigged and sudden machinery of softness and motivation." If the Basilisk is spawned of war, Maggie too is a product of man's inhuman systems, a child of poverty. Heralded by a narrator with the voice of a carnival barker, her career unfolds and expands: "Blue-eyed Maggie, alla that face, alla that leg, fifty bucks a night can get it and it *sounds* like it's having a climax." She succeeds, but remains soulless, a love machine driven by greed and hate. Her rise is countered by the correspondent fall of Kostner, from a "good family" through deception in love to his last dollar and a Las Vegas slot machine. It is here that lovers meet.

At her high point, Maggie puts a dollar in the Big Chief, pulls the handle, and dies. In a twist on the old fantasy theme, her final wish comes true: such was her money lust that she literally wills herself into the machine, becomes its "soul." But she is trapped. She has sought freedom in money only to be imprisoned. She has made love out of hate. Now as she stands hating, fateful mechanisms are triggered. As the wheels of the slot spin, the lure of money whirls around her existence, becomes her universe. Its center, her weak heart, is stabbed by pain. But Maggie, this being, is not human. In "death" her form simply fades; she becomes those whirling gears, all that is left is her cold blue eyes and the hate. Maggie in turn traps Kostner as he pulls the handle of the Chief. She willed hate into the machine, he wills love. And yet the result is the same: the bond is equally fatal, the dynamics of entrapment identical. Maggie comes to Kostner in a dream, and fills the place left empty by his failure in love. He returns to the blue-eyed machine with a lover's yearning, and is held as she escapes. The rhythm of this operation is by now quite familiar: "The sound of a soul released from an eternal prison, a genie freed from a dark bottle. And in that instant of damp soundless nothingness, Kostner saw the reels snap and clock down for the final time." Reenacted here is the eternal dynamic of temptation and seduction, a scenario as old as Adam and Eve. These two players are deluded, it is true, but could they do otherwise? They seem victims almost predestined. Only in Kostner's dream does Maggie become a woman with soft blue eyes. But this "humanity" is the fatal lure; the cold metallic eyes are closer to the reality of man's condition. The gentle poetic spirit remains the eternal victim, three sad brown eyes to be scrapped, run into the furnace, and slagged.

In both these tales, the machine becomes man's other self, his "double," and this creature of his desires and urges literally swallows its creator. In expanding his ego, man succeeds only in turning it inside out; it becomes an inverted cosmos, and he is trapped in the world of self. There seem only two alternative ways in life: man can dream, pursue wealth, ideals, a false love of others which is really hate, love of self; or he can accept the raw, bloody struggle to survive. In past tales, neither has led to freedom. Maggie touches on both. She escapes to Heaven or Hell (which we are never told), seducing Kostner, the eternal loser, who is condemned by his own weaknesses to turn endlessly in

an indifferent play of forces. But is man's fate always to be this prison of materiality, cold equations and laws of balance forever deaf to human aspirations? We hear Baudelaire's cry of despair—never to leave this world of things, quantities. Is there no spirit, no true peace anywhere? There is a third direction in Ellison, a way which grows stronger and stronger in the latter tales—the journey inward. These are strangely literal quests for self at the center of one's own being. Where before a false [landscape] expanded to become man's physical universe, now the process is reversed. Man contracts to a point, passes through the needle's eye of mind or body to open out on the landscape within. This too has its dangers, for the world inside may be no less a lie, a labyrinth, a prison.

At the gateway to this inner search for self lies delusion, Kostner's nemesis. The perils of the journey to self through a landscape of one's own false dreams form the core of **"Delusion for a Dragon Slayer"** (1966). It is a strange story of inexplicable deaths and the outcome of a life of quiet desperation. The hero, Warren Glazer Griffin, is an insignificant forty-one year old man with acne who is accidentally crushed to death one day as he walks to work by a wrecker's "headache ball." But what does this death have to do with those of Chano Pozo and Marilyn Monroe: "Each of them was preordained. Not in the ethereal, mystic, supernatural flummery of the Kismet-believers, but in the complex rhythmic predestination of those who have been whisked out of their own world, into the mist-centuries of their dreams." This is literally what happens to Griffin. The myth behind the name now has a chance to live. He is given the handsome Aryan body he has always wanted, heroic deeds to do, a crack at "his heaven": "Heaven is what you mix all the days of your life, but you call it dreams. . . . That is why everyone considers Heaven such a lovely place. Because it is dreams, special dreams, in which you exist. What you have to do is live up to them."

But this is precisely what Griffin cannot do. As he voyages through his own dream projections, they fall away as hollow. Beneath the new exterior the original man is still there. Bloated in his own vanity, he destroys ship and crew entrusted to his care. His only response is: "Well, I certainly messed that up." His second adventure involves a beautiful woman—the creature of his dreams—and a hideous "mist-devil" that rises up to take her. Like that other Beast, it first swells to a monstrous shape, then contracts to a man, who proceeds to make love with the woman. The "dragon slayer" now moves in and makes his kill from behind—the creature rises to condemn his cowardice. Griffin is ground to death in the teeth of a huge dragon. What is acted out on this inner terrain of dreams is a grotesque parody of knighthood, the heroic quest. In trying to live up to his fantasies, Griffin ironically is driven to deeper and deeper perversions of the life force. The mist-devil is "the terrible end hunger of a million billion eons of forced abstinence." In this psychodrama, the puritan conscience slays its own aggregate of frustration with a stab in the back, betrays its own corruptions—the man has become a shadow of a shade. Is this death "inexplicable"? The dreamer's actions rather explain it. He has slain himself long ago, and lived on as a corpse, a place in which all natural desires are distorted or repressed. The moment he realizes his unreality, Griffin vanishes. The god of death, again, is but a "weigher of balances."

Griffin's "evil" is to have denied his instincts. Under the ball his body is crushed beyond recognition, but his head is miraculously untouched. As he died, so he lived: all in the mind, none in the body. The hero of another, more complex quest tale, **"The Place With No Name,"** (1969) yields to an opposite temptation: drugs let his instincts run uncheck, and he is driven imperceptibly to robbery and murder. Not being killed but killing touches off his odyssey—but it is flight within all the same. The fleeing Norman Mogart sees a shop window with a sign: ESCAPE INSIDE. He enters, but cannot leave. Is it rather ESCAPE. INSIDE? For Mogart this process began not here, but with his cocaine addiction. In the exact center of this "shop" sits a little man suspended in air. The devil? Or a vision of Mogart's own being? If the latter, he cannot face it. He wants him to be the devil, hungers for the pact, hopes to escape here as he had with the drug, push off the day of reckoning to some later, vaguer future. But to live in this sensual Now is every bit as much a delusion as living in the never-never land of dreams. With cocaine he drifted into violence. Now again he simply fades, and finds himself in another world doing exactly the opposite of what he intended: escape has become the quest for Prometheus in some distant, dangerous jungle.

Passing through this point of self, Mogart apparently becomes another—his exact opposite. Timmons is a tall thin man in a steaming rain forest; he was a small man on a cold northern street. Yet in spite of surfaces, the two men seem to have identical patterns of movement. The periphery of Mogart's shop fled outward, he was forced back on the point. Timmons is oppressed by contracting rings of foliage, but escape is again through a point: "The passage was overgrown . . . and he would never have seen it, had it not been radiating circles of light. It was, in fact, the only point in his vision that was clear." What he finds in another center and circumference is Prometheus chained to his rock on the rim of a volcano crater. Inside the mountain, have we come back to the original room? He touches the chained figure only to trade places with him, become the center himself.

What seems concatenation of events in this story is in reality infernal circle. Figures as different as possible repeat the same pattern over and over, delude themselves with the same substance, end up always in a "place with no name." Mogart becomes Timmons, Timmons Prometheus. But this latter too has his counterpart—Christ the martyr. Together these two brought the "fire of knowledge" to men out of a love born of their love for each other. Their love however is evidently sterile, the "knowledge" something which turns men from the inescapable reality of nature. Through cocaine Mogart would make the brutal city a pleasant dream. But the drug brings an "elasticity of moral fiber," the man loses control of destiny: "swinging gently in a breeze of desperation" he is led to raw violence. Timmon's quest seems the product of yet another sort of drug—peyote. This brings not "paresis," but false search for self. The landscape he passes through

is mad, psychedelic. As Prometheus, he is eaten not by the traditional vulture but by the Yoatl, a carnivore of beauteous running colors, the dreambird feeding on men chained to the rock of unreality. We have cocaine and martyrdom, peyote and fire—one pair of "lovers" blends with another. man drifts into these various forms of stupor, and loses his hold on real nature. The Prometheus discovered has gills and flippers. His replacement is in pain, but "not entirely unhappy" in his dreams. In contrast are brief flashes of nature's tooth and claw: a body pounded to "Meat," the *marabunta* warrior ants.

These stories deal with reluctant quests, where the truth discovered is always at the "seeker's" expense. The quest for self, in Ellison, may be a conscious one however. In the three tales that follow, this mythic pattern undergoes interesting variations. The hero of **"One Life, Furnished in Early Poverty"** (1969) seeks his identity by actually going back in time, meeting his past self. The protagonist's quest for love in **"Catman"** (1972) is in reality a search for self as member of a family that must quite literally be recreated. If these two works seem to say, in various ways, you can't go home again, the third story, **"Adrift Just Off the Islets of Langerhans: Latitude 38 54′N, Longitude 77 00′13″ W"** (1975) is in its own strange way a successful quest. In this work Ellison achieves his most complex and moving mythical statement to date.

The hero of the curiously autobiographical **"One Life"** simply digs up his past. No time machines or magic, the road just leads back. He must find out "what turning point in my life it had been that had wrenched me from the course all little boys took to adulthood; that had set me on the road of loneliness and success ending here, back where I'd begun, in a backyard at now-twelve minutes to midnight." For a destiny that thinks itself so elliptical, this one is oddly circular. . . . The center, the point of passage, is the toy soldier buried and recovered. But the toy soldier has been damaged. What is make-believe for the child is pretending for the adult. Not only is his return caused by delusion, it is motivated by egotism: "My thoughts were of myself: I'm coming to save you. I'm coming, Gus." The usual irony of time travel comes into play: in trying to change the past he merely provides the means by which the present is what it is. But there is more, a terrible shock of recognition—he sees at last that he alone is responsible for what he has become. This man of best intentions operates on his past in a way he did not foresee, but easily could have. The two doubles act out this drama of egotism. From the moment man and boy meet, they begin literally to grow together: the narrator shrinks, gets boils again; the boy starts to steal—it is innocence and experience at the pivot point. The narrator sees himself caught in a time paradox: "I was alien to my own past. If I stayed much longer, God only knew what would happen to little Gus—but certainly I would waste away. Perhaps just vanish. Then . . . would Gus's future cease to exist, too? . . . I had to return." But there is no escaping destiny: it is just this separation that marked the turning point in his life. Love turns to hate: "I'd really show him! I was gonna get out of here, go away, be a big person . . . and some day I'd run into him someplace and see him and he'd come up and shake my hand and I'd spit on him." The past is a gallery of mirrors, life a series of hopeless returns. He has brought about the very thing he would abolish. Love again turns to hate, he becomes a shadow in the process. Gus takes up the old path, but where does he go: "Suddenly the road did not look familiar." The devices of time travel are skillfully adapted here to Ellison's personal myths.

"Catman" offers a reversed situation. In "One Life" the strange meeting occurs in a familiar small-town world of Saturday matinees. Here what seems a common family drama is set in a wildly fantastic landscape—one of Ellison's most disquieting creations. We are plunged in the midst of the "London Arcology," where pleasures are dispensed from cornucopia computers, where thief and policeman are father and son, work shifts, confront each other in a stylized "pavane of strike and vanish." One thing only, it seems, is forbidden in this most sophisticated of worlds: dalliance between man and machine. It is precisely this that the hero, Neil Leipzig, son of Catman, pursues.

Possibly however what this world considers most perverse is perhaps least so. It is a society so artificial it seems to have traded its natural instincts long ago for comforts and amenities brought by the machine. In reality the transformation has reached a point almost inconceivable. Are these beings flesh and blood at all? The Catman has no cats—his "panther" explodes in a spray of cogs and gears. Over and over, organic things are linked to metal and oil: the "twinkle's hair" is "tinted blue black like the barrel of a weapon." Joice's climax is "a succession of small ignitions." The hero's mother has the oddest features of all: "She drops her face into her hand, runs the fingers up through her thick coppery hair, the metal fingernails making tiny clicking noises against the fibers and follicles."

The hypercivilized surfaces, however, hide a world where spiritual values are totally absent, materialism reigns supreme. Lady Effim must have the "soul dust" Neil has stolen; but this, in spite of the name, is no more than some ultimate aphrodisiac. The hero's mother nags the father; he must be promoted so she can be "rejuvenated"—she wants endless and perfect physical beauty, even at the price of "plasticwork" breasts. Sex is either a means of pleasure, or a form of coercion. But what of procreation? Neil's father is black, his mother white. Here are his memories of birth: "He could see . . . every moment of his life from the first dripping emergence from the vats, the running, the extruding, the rolling, the cutting, the shaping, the forming, the welding." But what sense does a family drama have in a world of humans who act like humanoids.

What has happened to these people? The answer lies with the grotesque dwarfs who worship the giant computer (love-machine) in the bowels of this world. This place of archaic fixtures and weapons seems to be the ancient order, the original act out of which the arcologies have soared, and which they now repudiate with hypocrisy. The hero's quest then, far from being perverse, is in reality a return to the mysteries of his own being. It is here, coupled with the machine, that he remembers his origins and transcends them momentarily. With chilling irony, this merger of humanoid and machine becomes a true love match. Each yields to the other. They exchange parts, interchange roles—metal becomes flesh, flesh metal. Here at the center, these two opposites form the circle: "They circled, and the image on the Lissajous screen became a circle as she captured the machine and held her phase again. Prolate and oblate."

The hero's final sacrifice, pressing mother and self into the machine, breaks this balance. Why does he do it? Why care about a family that functions by "familiar emotional configurations," where relationships have become little more than programmed dance steps themselves? The hero's quest however goes deeper than self, he would shatter the circle. In this twisted world, his violent action actually brings truth. His family is led a step backward toward the humanity their ancestors possessed and lost. There is but one way to do this—reawaken the primitive nexus of love and hate that has always shaped relations between mother, father, and son. In offering self and mother to the machine as "ultimate troilism," is he not forcing a grotesque reversal of the Oedipal process itself—the son born of a questionable mother gives them both up to the true womb, the machine. His act forces the father to remember: a special love for the woman "forged in a cauldron of hate"; hatred flares for the child he never loved because he has "destroyed that love out of hate." The primal struggle is once more alive; for the first time perhaps the Catman is in touch with animal nature.

"Adrift" reverses the quest for eternal life. Chained to this Ixion's wheel, the hero Larry Talbot seeks death, surceases. Everlasting life was both a curse and a self-inflicted hell for Joe Bob, for the narrator of "I Have No Mouth." Neil Leipzig could have it too, but chooses to break the circle. Talbot is none other than the Wolfman in modern dress, bound by the moon to a cycle of violence, by a perfect metabolism to his body. His quest to stop this mechanism of murder is surely one of the most incredible in all fantasy literature. To do so he must find his "soul" in a soulless world. The only place it can be is inside his own body.

Talbot's journey is of impossible complexity. Before the Romantics denounced God as tyrant, and Nietzsche declared him dead, rest could be had in heaven. Now where is the way? Interestingly, it is in Nietzsche himself that Ellison's hero finds the means to nullify that other god, the brutal nature symbolized by the singing cannibal fish who refuses to die: cease to worship. To do this he must recover lost innocence, reverse the process of his life, retrieve it from waste and darkness. But where to start? One day he comes across an ad in a magazine, consults the time-travelling Information Associates, and they map out the coordinates for his soul: "A trail he had previously followed in every direction but the unexpected one that merged shadow with substance, reality with fantasy." The door that was a toilet before suddenly opens onto something. The search will always yield a chance; the important thing is to take it. The shadowy idea of the soul now takes substance. Though small, it is clearly of earth. The coordinates are given by a Mr. Demeter; this too is to be voyage to the center of the earth, only now this earth will be contained in one body. Another inverted universe, but now a fruitful one. At the core of his physical self, the hero will set the order of nature right again.

This trail indeed merges fantasy and reality in a most unique way. Talbot visits his scientist friend Victor, and we have a new Wolfman meets Frankenstein. Is this East Bloc researcher the son of the famous maker of monsters? If so, he now expiates his father's deed by helping another monster find rest at last. His methods are an incredible mixture of proton synchrotron and holography. The hero's image is reduced to a sub-molecular "mite"— Talbot's double—who will pass into and explore his own body. The moment of transfer—at the eye of the storm—is a look through the microscope. Talbot is "resurrected" and on his way. The point of entry is significantly the navel: from this place where his life was severed from one woman he will trace back through the labyrinth of self to another woman hidden at the core. The naval is closed; he must tear his way in with his fangs. This "outsider" to self, who has always torn others, now "savages" himself. Blood begets a rush of light: "a metaphysical, otherwise invisible beanstalk" soars heavenward, he drops into unconsciousness. It is to be a journey through the psyche as well; its center however is here, the point of physical rupture. Along the way, the metaphysical will always have physical reality. The lake of dead dreams is a real lake with floating carrion. When he comes to the spot where his "soul" is buried, he must dig "like a dog."

The coordinates of the title are not those where this "soul" is buried. Just off the islets the wind drops and he is adrift. Among the lost objects of his childhood found on the shore is an old radio. Now he plays it, and hears the story of a woman he never knew—Martha Nelson—a victim of her society's "system of thought", a "wasted life." He begins to cry: "By chance thoughts of her skirled through his mind like cold winds. And the cold winds arose, and the sail filled . . . ." At the point on his map he finds the one thing missing from his childhood treasure; the chain closes on a Howdy Doody button "with the sly innocent face of a mythical creature painted on its surface." In the center of the islet is a dark tower; he descends into its depths and finds a woman. Ellison quotes T. S. Eliot: "We shall not cease . . . " The steps are well-worn, he has been here before. But now for the first time he "knows"— though it is dark he sees the woman and names her: Martha Nelson [a real person who spent 97 years in an asylum]. It is the tears for another that filled the sail, gave his quest an end. The fatal circle, worn steps and empty center, is that of egotism. It is broken only by love.

New to Ellison is the strong note of reconciliation, the possibility that innocence and light may be recovered after all. Now perhaps the polarities that govern the universe may serve individual man rather than ignoring or destroying him. Perhaps there is somewhere where pain and suffering are no more. Here again the hero's quest is a search for family as well. Again there is a mother who is not a mother; again she is absorbed into a "machine." The old woman Nadja is made a mite, invited into the hero's body, which his deeds have made not a place of sacrifice but of eternal harmony. Nor is a father left grieving in hate. If there is a father, he is Victor, who smiles paternally over

his work. He launches "mother" and "son" into their paradise, and freezes the body, preserves the situation forever. The hero's second journey seems a return to the womb: "After a while, he heard the crying of a baby, just one baby, from inside the cave . . . " Yet the going hither is apparently a coming hence as well. Martha and Nadja are identical—both wasted lives—though one came from within, one from without. Talbot would resurrect this female existence by living the perfect, impossible relation to each of its seven ages: "He can be—I can be—her father when she's a baby, her playmate when she's a child . . . her suitor when she's a young woman, her lover . . . let her be all the woman she was never permitted to be." This cycle will begin over and over. Inside balance will be harmony. The radiation sign at the threshold reminded Talbot of the Trinity. Now we have man, child, mythical face on a button. Hateful contraries become one: "sly and innocent." No wolf, no moon, no change, only golden light, warmth, easy journey. As all opposites converge on that one baby, the final polarity is sprung; the fish turns belly up and dies.

"Adrift" is a story of affirmation, perhaps a turning point in Ellison's career. A new optimism is not simply pronounced; it is wrung with great struggle from the elements of the old, pessimistic view of man. And yet there is something frightening about this struggle, all the contraptions and ingenious twists. Why is it so hard to die in Ellison's world? He has created the only heaven a materialist society can conceive—the one inside self. Is this not the ultimate act of survival, to declare one's own body everything and always, so that one can die to live forever in one's own form undecaying? We are reminded here not of Emerson, but of Poe, with his nightmare fears of being buried, whose Ligeia's will to eternity raises her body from the dead, but as a corpse. Ellison's myth succeeds in countering these fears, but by meeting Poe on the same ground, fails to break the circle of matter and quantity. His hero does not want death with all its terms, he desires "surcease," rest without decay. Ellison's tale is a masterpiece of wishful thinking. We are at point where myth becomes fantasy again. (pp. 35-59)

George Edgar Slusser, in his Harlan Ellison: Unrepentant Harlequin, *The Borgo Press, 1977, 63 p.*

Ellison is not an easy man. His opinions are strongly held and his feelings strongly felt; he is not tolerant of compromise where it affects his life and his work. In someone else, this obstinacy might appear petty or fanatical, but in Harlan it is natural and attractive. It is simply the way he is.

—*Michael Crichton, in his foreword to* Approaching Oblivion, *by Harlan Ellison, 1974.*

Joseph Patrouch, Jr.   (essay date 1978)

[*An American educator and critic, Patrouch specializes in science fiction. In the essay below, he outlines Ellison's development as a writer, noting the increasing complexity of setting and structure in his short fiction.*]

Harlan Ellison has been writing science fiction since the mid-fifties. His writing has not stayed the same: several interesting developments have occurred in it. For example, his early SF features all the usual paraphernalia of conventional SF: robots, ray guns, spaceships, interstellar war, aliens. But all this was merely the lubricant which allowed him to penetrate the dry SF field and begin to function smoothly in it. Once he got his own stroke going, he didn't need that conventional imagery so much and so he largely abandoned it.

For me, SF is distinguished from other forms of fiction by its emphasis on "scientifically plausible alternate settings for consciousness." The farther one gets from scientific plausibility, the closer one gets to fantasy. During his career Ellison has evolved from SF writer to fantasist. In fact, even in many of his best-known SF stories he is as much fantasist as SF writer. Both " 'Repent, Harlequin!' Said the Ticktockman" and "I Have No Mouth and I Must Scream" employ time-honored SF conventions: the first concerns the dissenter in a technological "utopia," and the second the gigantic, nearly omniscient computer. In "Repent, Harlequin" Ellison conjures up a technological gimmick called a "cardioplate." When the Authorities erase a cardioplate, its owner has a heart attack and dies. This is a nice piece of SF furniture. But where most SF writers either would try to render such a gimmick plausible by explaining "scientifically" how it works or would avoid mentioning a rationale at all so as not to call attention to it, Ellison brazens it out by telling us "this simple scientific expedient utilize[s] a scientific process held dearly secret by the Ticktockman's office"! In other words, the rationale exists, but it isn't available to the writer. Similarly, in "Mouth/Scream" the war computers of the world unite, destroy all but five members of the human race, and keep them alive to torment and thus wreak its revenge on its creators. Along the way one of the captive survivors tries to escape: "Then he began to howl, as the sound coming from his eyes [?] grew louder. . . . The light was now pulsing out of his eyes in two great round beams. . . . His eyes were two soft, moist pools of pus-like jelly." One trained in reading SF instantly wonders, "What was the mechanism? How can the ability of a computer to liquefy eyes be rendered plausible?" But Ellison doesn't care. He never offers a rationale. The point: even in his most SF-like stories, Ellison is not concerned with scientific plausibility. He is basically a fantasist. Ellison is an SF writer by virtue of some of the furniture which he uses in his stories, by virtue of the markets to which he sells, and by virtue of the Hugo and Nebula awards which he accepts, but he is not an SF writer by virtue of his literary techniques. If you will, he is an SF writer by milieu, rather than by product.

The development which interests me most, however, since I tend to be a structuralist in my approach to fiction, is his evolution from the formula story to the experimental story, from the closed to the open, from the plotted to the unplotted. Let's examine some of Ellison's fiction in detail in order to see this development taking place.

"Life Hutch" was Ellison's second professionally published story (April 1956). It is set in the far-distant future during an interstellar war between Earth and Kyba. Life hutches—refuges where disabled men can await rescue after battle—have been established. The story is organized in the standard 1-2-3 pattern of the formula: 1) the narrative hook, or grabber, in which we see the hero in trouble; 2) the exposition, or the past of the story, in which we learn how the hero came to be in that trouble; and 3) the struggle and final victory in which the hero gets out of trouble. The grabber is only a page long. The central character, Terrence, is trapped in a life hutch, injured and dying, with a malfunctioning robot that will kill him if he moves. The exposition is given in a three-and-a-half page flashback marked at the start by "He let his eyes close completely, let the sounds of the life hutch fade from around him" and at the end by "The reliving of his last three days brought back reality sharply." In this flashback we are told about the Earth-Kyba war, about life hutches, about how Terrence came to be in that particular life hutch. Perhaps a trifle awkwardly, the major complication in the story—the point at which the central character is presented with the problem which he must solve in the rest of the story—is given, not in the narrative hook, but here in the flashback: "It was at this point that the service robot . . . had moved clankingly across the floor and with one fearful smash of a steel arm thrown Terrence across the room," breaking three of his ribs and putting him in the situation in which we found him when the story began. Problem: how to stay alive when any movement causes the robot to smash whatever moved?

In true SF fashion, the third part of the story has Terrence collect and analyze data. Key datum #1: the robot's "brain" is far too large to be kept in its moveable body and so it is stored in the wall from where it communicates with its body by radio. Key datum #2: Terrence has a flashlight on his belt. With this data Terrence can solve his problem. Can you, gentle reader? (One minor variation from the formula: Terrence "gets" the solution before we readers are told about the flashlight. Strictly speaking, the reader should be given all the data so he and the hero have a chance to figure out the solution together.)

The third part of the story ends with the climactic scene in which Terrence puts his solution into effect. (If that solution were not obvious from the hero's activities, then the story would require a concluding scene in which the problem-solver could explain how he figured it all out. In "Life Hutch" the solution is obvious, and no such concluding scene is necessary.) Terrence flashes his light on-and-off on the wall behind which is the robot's brain. The robot perceives the flashing as motion, walks over, and smashes in its own brain. Terrence of course lives happily ever after.

Except perhaps for putting the complication in the flashback and for having the hero solve the problem before giving the reader all the necessary clues to solve it himself, "Life Hutch" is a perfect little formula story. Note also, by the way, that this early Ellison story, besides having the formula problem-solving hero and the formula beginning-middle-end organization, also features a robot, spaceships, an interstellar war, aliens, and a ray gun—well, a flashlight. The point is that even in his second story Ellison was adept at using both the SF formula and the SF furniture. In fact, one feels that he would not have broken in to the field had he not been able to write this way. It was expected.

A second example of Ellison's use of the formula story seems in order. **"Blind Lightning"** was his third published SF story (June 1956). Like **"Life Hutch"** it is very carefully plotted. Like **"Life Hutch"** its basic pattern is 1) hero in trouble, 2) how the hero got in trouble, and 3) how the hero got out of trouble. But **"Blind Lightning"** is much more complex than **"Life Hutch"** because it has two narrative point of view characters instead of one and because it has three complications and resolutions instead of one.

The two characters are a human being named Kettridge and a telepathic, nine-foot-tall gorilla-Brahma bull-Kodiak bear of an alien named Lad-nar. Basically, **"Blind Lightning"** is Kettridge's story and best analyzed from his point of view. The opening sentence of the story describes the complication around which the story is built and puts both its characters before us doing something: "When Kettridge bent over to pick up the scurrying red lizard, the thing that had been waiting [Lad-nar] struck." Lad-nar takes the terrified and fainting Kettridge to his cave for use as food. Kettridge's immediate problem is obvious: like Ulysses in the cave of Polyphemous, he must remain alive and escape. The story is built around this problem.

But it is a more complex story than that. As part of the explanation of how Kettridge got into this trouble—i.e., as part of the exposition—we learn that years before Kettridge had shared the responsibility for the deaths of over twenty thousand people and that he is carrying that guilt around with him. Thus he has a secondary problem: he seeks a way to remove that guilt.

In the exposition of the story we also learn Lad-nar's background and problem: he and his intelligent kind are at the mercy of the lightning that becomes especially severe at certain seasons of that planet's year. The lightning has prevented a civilization from developing among these intelligent aliens. Lad-nar's—and his race's—problem is how to defeat/control/avoid the lightning.

Given these three complications, Kettridge is able to find a common solution: he can save his life, he can save his soul/reputation, and he can save Lad-nar's people all at once. As Ellison puts it:

> Here was a chance not only to survive [problem #1] but a chance to reinstate himself [problem #2]. . . . Ben Kettridge devised a plan to save his soul. . . . Lad-nar suddenly became a symbol of all the people who had been lost in the Mass Death. . . . He must save the poor hulk before him [problem #3]. And in saving the animal, he would save himself [problems #1 and 2].

Kettridge's solution is to have Lad-nar walk among the lightning bolts wearing Kettridge's stretchable "insulating metal-plastic." Kettridge goes out first, demonstrating the safety of the suit. Then Lad-nar goes out—and returns alive. All that remains is contact with Earth so that more suits can be obtained.

Unfortunately, having saved himself from being eaten, having removed the guilt from his soul, and having saved Lad-nar's people from subservience to the lightning, Kettridge carelessly steps unprotected from the cave when his fellow humans come to pick him up, lightning strikes him, and he is killed. But his death strikes the reader, not as an ultimate failure, but as a ratification and ennobling of what he has done. Throughout the story Kettridge has reacted as a human being rather than as the logical SF hero: he has been afraid of the alien, he has fainted in the face of that fear. Now, at the end, he is so relieved at the appearance of other people that he forgets, is careless, and it costs him his demonstrably human life. He is an emotional person. This jars somewhat with the other major element in him and in the story, the standard SF theme of "reason, reason uber alles." Trapped in Lad-nar's cave, Kettridge "ran the whole thing through his mind, sifting the facts, gauging the information, calculating the outcome." Or, more succinctly, "Only in his wits was there salvation." Kettridge is both emotional *and* rational. For Ellison it is not either/or but both/and.

Both **"Life Hutch"** and **"Blind Lightning"** clearly demonstrate that from the beginning of his writing career Ellison knew and could manipulate the formula story. What is interesting is that he wasn't content to write this kind of story for the rest of his career. As babies eventually outgrow their formula food, so Ellison outgrew the formula plot.

We have already seen Ellison bending the formula just a bit in a variety of ways. In **"Life Hutch"** he put the complication in the exposition instead of in the narrative hook and he had the hero solve the problem before he gave the reader all the necessary data. In **"Blind Lightning"** his hero faints with fear and is killed at the story's end instead of being always in control of himself and living happily ever after. And his refusal to explain the cardioplate in **"Repent, Harlequin"** or the eye-dissolving powers of the computer in **"Mouth/Scream"** can be cited as further examples of his refusal to play the game by formula.

In addition, I would like to instance an early story called **"The Discarded"** (April 1959). The formula requires a strong central character through whose actions and perceptions the reader can experience the story. The story is focused onto us through that central, narrative-point-of-view character. It is his story. This was certainly true of **"Life Hutch,"** which has the traditional opening sentence in which the subject is the hero's name and the verb has that hero actively doing something: "Terrence slid . . ." are the first two words. **"Blind Lightning"** broke with this part of the formula a bit by putting us sometimes into the mind of Lad-nar instead of concentrating solely on Kettridge. **"The Discarded"** begins, "Bedzyk saw. . . ." Therefore, Bedzyk is the central character and the story will be organized around his perceptions as he solves some problem, right? Well. . . . Four pages from the end of the story Bedzyk is ray-gunned (this is still early Ellison, remember): "Bedzyk mewed in agony, and crumpled onto the deck. A huge hole had been seared through his huge chest. Huge chest, huge death." *Now* who is the story about? You can't kill off your narrative-point-of-view character. It just isn't done. It ruins the unity of the story. Since the reader has been identifying with this character, it's like killing off the reader, and that's too unsettling. And yet there's that Ellison at his typewriter, imagining the reader's discomfiture, and chortling, "Gotcha!" He knew the rules well enough to break them to get his desired effect.

Still, Ellison isn't known for those hundreds of formula and slightly-bent formula stories produced during his first years of writing. Certainly, many of those early stories contain passages that anticipate the writing style most often associated with him. That first sentence of **"The Discarded,"** for example, continued, "Bedzyk saw Riila go mad, and watched her throw herself against the lucite port, till her pinhead was a red blotch of pulped flesh and blood." As Joanna Russ once remarked, "Ellison's mode is hyperbole." and this mode can be found often in Ellison's early work.

But it is not Ellison's style but his structure that I want to continue examining here. In the early and middle sixties he produced very few short stories of any kind, much less SF. He was busy writing TV scripts. One wonders about the extent to which his working in television influenced his later writing of fiction. What we view on the screen as a neat beginning-middle-end formula story is a rearrangement into chronological order of a mass of pieces created in a chaotic, disorganized sequence. A film viewed in the process of creation, rather than as a finished product, would have a curious, non-structured, non-chronological life of its own.

" 'Repent, Harlequin!' Said the Ticktockman" (December 1965) may be considered Ellison's "breakthrough" story (as "Nightfall" was for Isaac Asimov, "Neutron Star" for Larry Niven, and "The Doors of His Face, the Lamps of His Mouth" for Roger Zelazny). **"Repent, Harlequin"** took both the Hugo and the Nebula for its year, and Ellison has been an established SF writer ever since.

Two things about **"Repent, Harlequin"** especially interest me. First, in the light of my speculation above about the influence, on Ellison's sense of structure, of his experience in creating filmed stories, note that **"Repent, Harlequin"** is a non-chronological story. As the speaking voice says, "Begin in the middle, and later learn the beginning; the end will take care of itself." This structure is distantly related to that of **"Life Hutch"** and **"Blind Lightning"**: narrative hook (man in situation), exposition (how did he get in?), struggle and victory (how does he get out?). The pattern of the formula story is dimly discernible in **"Repent, Harlequin,"** but Ellison is not being non-chronological in the formula way. Instead, he has taken these pieces and put them in this order because they feel better to him. And the reader's own experience shows that Ellison was right: read the story in its beginning-middle-end sequence and see how much of its impact it loses. Despite its superficial resemblance to the formula story, **"Repent, Harlequin"** actually shows us Ellison growing out of the formula.

A second interesting thing about the story is the way Ellison interposes himself—or at least a speaking voice; for the sake of convenience, let's call it Ellison—between the story and the reader. The story is unified, not so much by its non-chronologically arranged series of events, as by the commentary and personality of Ellison the interlocutor. I take this as an early example of an Ellison story unified by the imposition of the author's personality, by an act of creative *will,* rather than by a cause-and-effect related series of external events called the plot or storyline.

"I Have No Mouth and I Must Scream" (March 1967) is very much like **"The Discarded"** and **"Repent, Harlequin"** in showing us the formula story receding in importance, but still there. In fact, examined closely, with an eye to its structure rather than its pyrotechnical style, **"Mouth/Scream"** is a fairly conventional story.

It begins with a narrative hook:

> Limp, the body of Gorrister hung from the pink palette; unsupported—hanging high above us in the computer chamber; and it did not shiver in the chill, oily breeze that blew eternally through the main cavern. The body hung head down, attached to the underside of the palette by the sole of its right foot. It had been drained of blood through a precise incision made from ear to ear under the lantern jaw. There was no blood on the reflective surface of the metal floor.

Then Gorrister rejoins the group and they realize they've been tricked again, as they have been so often in the one-hundred and nine years they've been trapped inside the computer AM. Their problem is how to escape the torments of AM. Gorrister is one of a group of five who are kept alive to be the recipients of AM's fury. One of the other four, the I-narrator, Ted, is the narrative-point-of-view character.

From this narrative hook, we move to the exposition. Ellison does this in two rather conventional ways. First, the characters lecture the background at one another so the readers can overhear it. Ellison tries to make this plausible by making one of the characters insane and one of the marks of his insanity is his desire to hear the old story of the origins of AM and the destruction of humanity over and over again despite the fact that they all know it already. The readers, of course, don't, and so we get background via expository conversation. Ellison's second method for giving us the past of the story is having his point of view character, I—Ted, engage in interior monologues about his four companions—their pasts, the ways AM changed them when it captured them, their present personalities.

Then we get the struggle and victory. In the climactic scene, in which the hero puts his solution into effect, Ted murders two of his four companions while the third is murdering the fourth; then Ted murders the third, leaving himself the only one of the five still alive. For the sake of the story we must believe that all this happens so quickly that the nearly omniscient/omnipotent AM has no time to interfere. To prevent Ted's ever escaping too, AM turns him into "a great soft jelly thing" which has no mouth and must scream.

Narrative hook, activity in present interspersed with exposition, climactic scene and resolution, all presented through the thoughts and actions of a single character—how conventionally structured can a story be? Granted, Ted—like Kettridge, Bedzyk, and the Harlequin, but unlike Terrence—doesn't win and live happily ever after. But there are a lot more elements to a formula story than the happy ending, and **"Mouth/Scream"** has most of these other elements.

Three more things about the story. First, at its end all human beings but Ted are dead and gone, and Ted has been changed into that sentient lump of jelly. Ted has been recounting the events from his own present, when he is alone, jellied, with no hope. To whom is he addressing the words of the story, and in what medium? He has no mouth, so he can't be dictating it; he has no hands, so he can't be writing or typing; he has no audience, so he can't intend his account for anyone. What is the dramatic context of the words in the story?

Second, the I-narrator of **"Mouth/Scream"** is certainly put upon by a world he never made. And he is clearly paranoid about it. Of himself he insists, "I was the only one still sane and whole" while of his companions he says, "Those scum, all four of them, they were lined and arrayed against me. . . . They hated me. They were surely against me." Ted is an outstanding example of one of Ellison's typical narrative stances: it's me versus them, baby.

Finally, the theme of the story is clearly an important one. AM is symbolic of the technological world in which we all live and by which we are all, to one degree or another, tormented. The story is not so much a reduction to absurdity as an elevation to hyperbole of the uncomfortable side of modern life. This is not Ellison predicting the future; it is Ellison, using a piece of SF furniture called the omnipotent computer, describing the present. Ellison's concern has shifted from earning some honest money by writing entertaining little action-adventure formula stories, to helping us see more clearly the world in which we all breathe and experience and think. This is another way in which he has grown over the years.

We could look at many other stories in which Ellison was expanding beyond the formula story. **"The Beast That Shouted Love at the Heart of the World"** (June 1968) certainly merits consideration. Let's content ourselves, however, with what Ellison himself said of it:

> **"The Beast That Etcetera"** was intended as an experiment. Consciously so. It was a serious stylistic and structural departure for me. . . . It is not a sequential story. It is written in a circular form, as though a number of events were taking place around the rim of a wheel, simultaneously. The simultaneity of events around the wheel-rim, however, occur across the artificial barriers of time, space, dimension and thought. Everything comes together, finally, in the center, at the hub of the wheel.

A Boy and His Dog (August 1969) also moves beyond the formula story in one crucial way (though not in many others). Like **"Mouth/Scream"** its settings are symbolic rather than irrelevant or predictive. In the formula story, the

setting is simply the place where the events occur. It has no meaning of its own (it is irrelevant to your life and mine) or its meaning is at the level of "this may one day happen" (it predicts what our future life might be like). But the settings in *A Boy and His Dog* are reminiscent of those in H. G. Wells' *The Time Machine:* both feature two future civilizations, one above ground, one beneath; in both, these civilizations are actually the dramatizations of trends in the writer's contemporary societies rather than serious predictions; and in both, the relationship between the two societies is condemned by the writer's use of the symbol of cannibalism. Where *The Time Machine* demonstrates the necessity to share the wealth, to get the haves and the have-nots together, *A Boy and His Dog* asks us to choose between the two settings: violence above-ground and hypocrisy below. The story is slanted in favor of violence and does not suggest that any third alternative—like love, good will, or hard work—is possible or likely. The violent Vic literally consumes the hypocritical Quilla June: violence can destroy hypocrisy—and rightly so—the story suggests. In any event, in this story Ellison replaces the standard formula setting with a symbolic setting. He has discovered that it's another way to get more said in a story.

Among his hundreds of stories, Ellison has written many others which deserve the attention of readers, fellow writers and critics. I personally think of **"Pretty Maggie Moneyeyes," "Shattered Like a Glass Goblin,"** and **"One Life: Furnished in Early Poverty."** Others might prefer **"On the Downhill Side," "At the Mouse Circus,"** or **"The Prowler in the City at the End of the World."** Nor should his recent award-winning stories **"Deathbird"** and **"Adrift Just Off the Islets of Langerhans"** be ignored. His TV scripts for shows like "The Outer Limits," "Star Trek" and "The Starlost" also form a part of his creative output.

But I want to finish my survey of Ellison's development in the structures of his stories by examining a recent production which I think offers valuable insights into Ellison the writer (and perhaps even Ellison the man). The story is **"Croatoan"** (May 1975). **"Life Hutch"** and **"Blind Lightning"** were neatly plotted puzzle stories set in the distant future on distant worlds. Fun and games among the stars. **"Mouth/Scream"** and *A Boy and His Dog* were set in futures which were symbolic of the present. **"Croatoan"** is set in contemporary New York. Ellison seems to be more and more concerned with facing and expressing the here and now, whether symbolically or realistically.

All writers seem to have their own peculiarities, subjects they are attracted to or subjects they never get around to using much. Ellison, for example, seems drawn to imagery of eyes and blindness. More to the point here, he doesn't write much about the out-of-doors. **"Life Hutch"** took place in a small building, **"Blind Lightning"** in a cave, **"The Discarded"** in a spaceship, **"Repent, Harlequin"** in a multi-tiered city, **"Mouth/Scream"** in a computer, and *A Boy and His Dog* beneath the earth and in a movie theatre and a gymnasium. Similarly, **"Croatoan"** is set in an apartment and a sewer, with many references to caves. Someone inclined to use Freudian criticism might want to make something of all this, but I'm more interested in the story itself than I am in the psychology of its writer.

The central character of **"Croatoan"** is named Gabe. His immediate problem is established in the first scene of the story. Gabe's most recent girl friend, Carol, has just had an abortion in her apartment. Gabe has flushed the baggied fetus down the toilet. Distraught, Carol orders Gabe to go into the sewer and find the fetus. It is his quest to fulfill his lady's wishes that shapes the rest of the story.

Something else has a strong influence on the shape of the rest of the story, too: the attitudes of the characters toward the lost fetus. Both Gabe and Carol consider that fetus human. Carol orders/begs, "Go after him, Gabe. Please. Please, go after him," while Gabe refers to the fetus as "the kid" and remarks, "He was the only one who was dead." Not "it" but "he." The humanity of aborted children is assumed.

Gabe goes into the street, tries to lift off the manhole cover, cannot. He hopes that in the attempt he has done enough, but when he turns to give up, Carol

> stood silently at the curb, holding the long metal rod that wedged against the apartment door when the police lock was engaged. . . . She held out the rod. . . . I took the heavy metal rod and levered up the manhole cover.

Again, critics of a Freudian bent might see some sexual implications in such a passage. After all, we have a man who can't enter a tunnel until a woman hands him a hard rod. When I asked Ellison if he were deliberately building Freudian imagery into the story, he replied, "What Freudian imagery?" The brief discussion which followed indicated clearly to me that such passages are included unconsciously in Ellison's work. They simply seem "right" to him, and their manipulation is not part of his conscious effort to shape a story.

The lid removed, Gabe enters the sewer and begins to walk in it. He passes a group of bindlestiffs huddled around a fire in an old oil drum, one of whom follows him. Gabe turns a corner and steps into a small niche to wait for the bindlestiff.

From the beginning of the story until this encounter, there are three expository flashbacks. All three give insights into Gabe's character by giving us data about his background. The first tells of Gabe's being a lawyer and of his relationships with the two women who had aborted Carol. The second continues to establish Gabe as a sexual libertine and also convinces us that, as an ex-Geology major, he enjoys being underground: "I *liked* the feel of the entire Earth over me. I was not claustrophobic, I was—in some perverse way—wonderfully free. Even soaring! Under the ground, I was soaring." This is important structurally because it helps render plausible Gabe's walking along in the sewer (instead of simply waiting by the entrance and re-emerging after a decent interval) and because it sets up the ending of the story. It makes Gabe's final decision acceptable. The third flashback traces Gabe's relationship with Carol from the time he met her till the time he goes after the fetus for her. Gabe's personality is more fully developed, as is the casualness of his sexual affairs.

This too must be emphasized: Gabe has gotten a lot of girls pregnant and has therefore been responsible for a lot of abortions. We are told this several times. The women who had aborted Carol had also been made pregnant by Gabe (and had been aborted by one another), and Gabe speaks of "their attendance at my Carols, my Andreas, my Stephanies." He wrily remarks, "I'm nothing if not potent." But the crucial thing—the reason for emphasizing this—is that, as pointed out earlier, Gabe thinks of these aborted fetuses as human, as dead children. As a result, the real issue of the story becomes the conflict within a man who has been casually creating and murdering little children and who now gradually faces up to the guilt he feels. He must find a way to save himself. The finding of that one lost fetus becomes far less important than the atoning for past sins.

I suggest that when the bindlestiff passes Gabe's niche and Gabe steps out to confront him, Gabe is actually confronting his own guilt personified. The bindlestiff expresses aloud and for all to hear what Gabe thinks of himself when he says, "You make it bad down here, Mister. . . . All of us know you make it bad, Mister." To which Gabe reacts, "He didn't want to hurt me, he just didn't want me here. Not even right for these outcasts, the lowest level to which men could sink; even here I was beneath contempt." His low opinion of himself is clear. His problem is how to raise that opinion, how to redeem himself.

The bindlestiff has no hands. Like Gabe, he is helpless.

It turns out that the sewers are infested with alligators. Ellison explains the infestation as follows:

> Frances had a five-year-old daughter. She took the little girl for a vacation to Miami Beach one year. I flew down for a few days. . . . The daughter . . . wanted a baby alligator. Cute. We brought it back on the plane in a cardboard box with air holes. Less than a month later it had grown large enough to snap. . . . Frances flushed it down the toilet one night after we'd made love. The little girl was asleep in the next room. Frances told her the alligator had run off.

I quote the passage at some length for at least two reasons. First, it is an excellent example of Ellison's insistence on the specific rather than the general. Many other writers would have been content with a general remark like "Many vacationers returning from Florida with pet baby alligators flushed them down the toilet when they got big enough to be dangerous, and so the sewers were filled with alligators." Not Ellison, and his writing is the stronger for it.

But something far more significant for the story is going on here. An association is established among Gabe's sex life, the flushing of aborted children down toilets, and the flushing of growing alligators down those same toilets and into the same sewer system. Note that the young alligators grow up in the sewers. What about the babies?

We are not surprised when Gabe follows an alligator deeper into the sewers. Somewhere in Gabe's unconscious, as in ours, is that nagging parallelism: if the flushed young alligators survive, what about the babies? Where are they?

(In another kind of story, of course, they are food for the alligators. But not in this story.)

Gabe follows the alligator into and across a small, deep pool. I take this to be a sort of baptism into a new life. Next he loses that iron rod which Carol had given him and which seemed to symbolize Gabe's casual sexuality. Then the alligators attack him in force and he runs aimlessly, hopelessly, terrified, at random through the sewers. When he falls exhausted and expects death, he is discovered.

Something—an alligator?—touches him in the dark. Then a flickering light appears in the distance. When it comes close enough, he sees that what had touched him had been a child with great eyes and deathly white skin, adapted to its sunless existence. "And the light came nearer, and the light was many lights. Torches, held aloft by the children who rode the alligators."

One could, I suppose, read the ending of the story as saying that Gabe has found all the children he fathered and then flushed away, that he is no longer guilty because they are not dead after all, and that now he is going to do the right thing and assume his responsibility for their lives. However, the ending strikes me far differently. By joining the children's subterranean civilization, Gabe finds the role which redeems him for all his casual fathering and flushing. As Gabe puts it,

> Down here in this land beneath the city, live the children. They live easily and in strange ways. I am only now coming to know the incredible manner of their existence. How they eat, what they eat, how they manage to survive, and have managed for hundreds of years, these are all things I learn day by day, with wonder surmounting wonder.
>
> I am the only adult here.
>
> They have been waiting for me.
>
> They call me father.

"Croatoan" is a character-centered story. Gabe changes for the better as the result of his experiences in the story. It is a satisfying and touching conclusion to what I take to be one of the best of Ellison's stories.

Only a nit-picker would wonder what happens to the children when they grow up. **"Croatoan"** is about Gabe's growing beyond the joys of sex to the joys of fatherhood, an altogether different and more adult thing. It is not a story about a subterranean civilization. That exists, not for its own sake, but to help Ellison make a point about Gabe. Gabe has become a father, and of course his children are children.

And only a nit-picker would wonder about the relevance of the "Lost Colony of Virginia" material which gives the story its title. As I hope my explication indicates, **"Croatoan"** is a complete and marvelous story without it. Why is it there? One suspects that the Virginia material formed the original core of the story-idea and that Ellison was reluctant to abandon it. In the context of the whole story, however, it is a minor problem.

By the way, someone once remarked—and Ellison agreed—that a major theme in his stories is the search for a father-figure. **"Croatoan"** reverses this theme. The quest is not for the love and security of a father but for the responsibilities of fatherhood. Gabe seeks to give love and security to others.

"Croatoan" strikes me as an advance over much of the formula and formula-like work that Ellison had written earlier because the forward movement of the story is determined by the inner nature of Gabe, rather than by any series of steps Gabe takes in order to solve an external problem. He is not a physically disabled man in a life hutch, nor is he one of a group trapped in a gigantic computer and trying to decide what to do next. He is Gabe trying to come to terms with his own guilt. The sewer may be taken as symbolic of his own evaluation of himself. This guilty man must work out his own salvation in the sewers of his own mind. The intangible psychological abstraction has been dramatized for all to see. The inner has been made outer through symbolism.

Gabe does what he does for his own psychological reasons, not because any storyline demands it. Despite his sexual success with women, he is intimidated by them: Carol intimidates him into going down into the sewer in the first place. Because he feels free underground, he walks along in the sewer unafraid and unrepelled. Because he dislikes himself and feels guilty, he agrees with the bindlestiff's assessment of him. Because the flushed alligators demonstrably grow up in the sewers, he follows one to where the flushed children live. Because of his guilt and his feeling of freedom beneath the ground, he stays with the children as their father. In **"Croatoan"** Ellison replaces the formula story with psychological truth—characterization, really—as the structural principle.

The central problem for the storyteller is always organization. Ellison's early stories, like **"Life Hutch"** and **"Blind Lightning,"** were set in bizarre alternate worlds and were organized around a central character's solving a specific problem, usually having to do with that character's saving his own life. They were good, solid formula stories. For a long time Ellison, clearly dissatisfied with the formula, experimented with it. In **"The Discarded"** he killed off the viewpoint character before the story ended; in **"Repent, Harlequin"** and **"Beast/Love"** he rearranged the chronological structure of the stories so that time was no longer their organizational principle; and in **"Mouth/Scream"** and *A Boy and His Dog* he replaced realistic settings with settings which symbolized various aspects of his contemporary world. Now, in stories like **"Croatoan,"** Ellison is writing stories whose structures are appropriate only to themselves and not to any preconceived pattern or reader/editor expectations. The content determines the form.

As a writer, Ellison has never stayed the same for very long. He seems to have an inherent gift for self-criticism that keeps telling him, "No, this isn't right, it's not good enough. Maybe what I ought to do is. . . ." And he'll try a new approach, a different solution to the age-old writer's problem of how to get it down on paper. (His scripts, by the way, allow him to work in another medium besides the printed page and escape its limitations that way.) Writers often get more consistent through the years; seldom do they get better. It will be interesting to see whether Ellison opts for consistency or improvement.

Where did you say that latest Ellison story appeared? I want to read it. (pp. 45-64)

Joseph Patrouch, Jr., "Harlan Ellison and the Formula Story," in The Book of Ellison, *edited by Andrew Porter, Algol Press, 1978, pp. 45-64.*

"I Have No Mouth and I Must Scream" belongs to the new wave of science fiction. It is not a pretty story. It deliberately violates the taboos on sexuality and violence imposed by an older generation of science fiction writers.

—Charles J. Brady, in his "The Computer As a Symbol of God: Ellison's Macabre Exodus," in The Journal of General Education, Spring, 1976.

Philip M. Rubens (essay date 1979)

[*In the following essay, Rubens asserts that Ellison often employs the literary tradition of the descent into hell "to take the reader into new myths—new faiths needed to survive in an increasingly hostile world."*]

In his introduction to **Deathbird Stories,** Harlan Ellison tells us that he is creating a "New Testament of deities for the computerized age of confrontation and relevance." Ellison has continually exhibited an interest in gods and myths. His short story, **"The Face of Helene Bournow,"** for instance, can be traced directly back to the Persephone myth, while the triad of **"The Whimper of Whipped Dogs," "Paingod,"** and **"Rock God"** shows the possible manifestations of new gods. **"I Have No Mouth and I Must Scream"** is surely a modern analogue to the Prometheus myth.

Ellison does much with myth and legend; his understanding of American Indian gods, in fact, is superlative. One wonders how far he has delved into primitive myth, legend, and religion. It is significant, for instance, that in some of the tales in **Deathbird Stories** he develops a set of circumstances, a group of characters, and a specific landscape that echo many of the traditional journeys to hell—from patristic literature to Norse myth. Ellison employs this framework to take the reader into new myths—new faiths needed to survive in an increasingly hostile world.

What kind of tradition could Ellison draw on to accomplish such a task? An incredibly diverse one. For instance, the Venerable Bede recounts several descent-into-hell myths—the *Visions of Furseus* (640 A.D.) and *Drihthelm* (700 A.D.). Patristic literature records the *Visions of Saint Paul, Visions of Alberic,* and *Apocalypse of Peter.* In Norse

myth, the *Grógaldr* and *Fjölsvinnsmál,* catalog the adventures of Svipdagr in hell. Similar accounts appear in the Persian *Dabistan* tales, in the Buddhist description of hell, and in the Brahmanistic *Mârkan-deya-Purâna.* Finally, one can hardly ignore the epic descents that pervade Western literature from the Greek Eleusinian Mysteries to Dante's *Inferno.* Despite the fact that this background literally spans time, culture, and geography, there are some remarkable similarities in the descents into hell they depict—similarities that also appear in the works of Harlan Ellison.

The main character in these descents is generally a sleeper who enters hell in a dream or as a doppelgänger. During the descent, the protagonist journeys through various levels of hell, often actively participating in the afflictions. This character is guided by an ambiguous figure who is sometimes not identifiably a "holy" person. Furthermore, the protagonist journeys through a violent, dark, and blasted landscape which is pervaded by a mountain. High in the mountain, the protagonist must face either a giant, whom he must outwit to survive, or some kind of erotic creature. All of these elements of the traditional descent into hell play an important role in Ellison's fiction. While many of Ellison's stories can be used to illustrate this point, four tales—**"Delusion for a Dragon Slayer," "Adrift Just Off the Islets of Langerhans: Latitude 38° 54′N, Longitude 77° 00′13″W," "The Place With No Name,"** and **"The Deathbird"**—aptly demonstrate something of the range and purpose of Ellison's use of the descent-into-hell motif.

"Delusion for a Dragon Slayer" contains many of the traditional elements of the descent and is based mainly on two ideas: the doppelgänger and postmortem consciousness. The latter technique generally depicts the workings of the human mind under extremely violent conditions—man's mental perceptions immediately before death. John Denney Crane maintains [in "Crossing the Bar Twice: Post-Mortem Consciousness in Bierce, Hemingway, and Golding," *Studies in Short Fiction* (Summer 1969)] that there are four distinct phases to such an experience: time lag, extreme hypersensitivity, temporary reality, and physical death. In addition to a sense of postmortem consciousness, Warren Glazer Griffin, the protagonist, displays many of the qualities of a doppelgänger during his adventures. This concept, as Otto Rank points out [in *Beyond Psychology* (1941)], was created by primitive man's need to be reassured of immortality. To attain such assurance, man creates a spiritual self; but at some point man's attitude toward this other self changes from benevolent to malevolent. This, of course, means that the double could be a harbinger of death. Such an ambiguity has been assimilated into literature and finds expression as two opposing selves which, Rank claims, threatens the destruction of the individual. In this tale, the doppelgänger, which suggests the possibility of death, works to reinforce the postmortem consciousness device. Both are used to describe a descent into the self where man finds his own private hell.

Warren Glazer Griffin, the dragon-slayer, begins his adventure when he is crushed by a wrecking ball. His entire story occurs in the microseconds between life and death. As he runs along his well-worn track (rabbit warren?) to work, he realizes he will be late if he does not step out of his usual path. The wrecking ball he encounters while taking a shortcut sends him through a window (glazer, or one who makes windows) into a land of fantasy. Once in this land, he exhibits the hypersensitivity typical of the postmortem consciousness experience. He sees brilliant colors, hears acutely, and feels, rather than sees, the presence of obstacles. Furthermore, this land becomes the temporary reality Griffin (the dragon) uses to stave off physical death. Once he finds himself in this other world, Griffin also realizes that he is someone else, a Nordic god with a body composed "of the finest bronzed skin tone, the most sculptured anthracite-hard musculature, proportions just the tiniest bit exaggerated . . . extremely godlike. . . . Nordic blond, aquiline-nosed, steely-blue-eyed." Like many other doppelgänger manifestations, this one also exhibits an incredible amount of pride, a quality that brings about Griffin's destruction.

While Griffin's doppelgänger cavorts in his own psyche, he undergoes many of the traditional tasks of the descent into hell. First, he must overcome the sea and the reefs around the island (his plunge through the reef-bound coast is the first of many births in these tales). When he arrives at the island, he must defeat the mist-devil and win the love of the woman. In each of these encounters, Griffin falls short. His pride and hypersensitivity make him ignore the real dangers of the reef; therefore, he loses his ship and crew.

After marching through a dense, dark jungle pervaded by hellish creatures, "he lunged forward against a singularly rugged matting of interlocked tree branches, and hurled himself through the break, as it fell away, unresisting." Once through the opening, Griffin finds the devil and the woman copulating. In his fear and anger, he debates with his doppelgänger about killing the devil: "Now, abruptly, he was two men once again. The god with his sword, the mortal with his fear." The Nordic god at least partially prevails, however, and Griffin kills the devil by stabbing it in the back. After dispatching this creature, the gallant protagonist lustily ravishes the woman! Pride, cowardice, lust! What can man expect when he journeys into his own soul and finds it a cesspool? Griffin (dragon) is slain not only by a wrecking ball but by a revelation—the temporary reality he finds in his own psyche is a blasted, hellish landscape devoid of either meaning or hope.

In **"Adrift Just Off the Islets of Langerhans,"** Ellison depicts another descent into a psychic hell, the soul of a werewolf—a man cursed with eternal life. Instead of a psychic doppelgänger, however, Larry Talbot, the adventurer, has a literal, physical miniature who journeys into his body to find his soul. This miniature is an intriguing addition to descent literature. Robert Plank has made a persuasive study of such man-made figures. He claims [in "The Golem and the Robot," *Literature and Psychology* (Winter 1965)] that mechanical men, cyborgs and the like, can be traced to the Jewish golem, a creature made of clay and animated by either science or magic. In addition, Plank outlines a variety of motifs associated with these

creations: the creature begins to function independently of the creator's will; there is a lack of communication; and, finally, either the creature or the builder is destroyed. These, of course, are all elements in Ellison's tale.

Talbot's journey in search of peace cannot begin until he learns the geographic coordinates for his soul from Mr. Demeter who serves as his initial guide to the underworld. Appropriately enough, Demeter's name recalls the goddess Demeter who, although she could not prevent Persephone's marriage to the god of the underworld, won for her daughter the right to return to earth periodically. Consequently, Persephone's character is ambiguous; she symbolizes both death and the rebirth of nature; and it is this cleansing rebirth through death that Talbot seeks through the mediation of Mr. Demeter and his microscopic double.

Talbot's homunculus arrives inside his body after a ritual rebirth:

> . . . he ripped away at the clumps of flesh until the membrane gave, at last, and a gap was torn through opening him to himself. . . .
>
> And he was blinded by the explosion of light, by the rush of wind by the passage of something . . . a thick bundle of white cobweb by filaments, tinged with gold, fibers of light, shot free from the collapsed vein, rose up through the shaft and trembled toward the antiseptic sky.
>
> He was on his stomach, crawling through the collapsed lumen, the center, of the path of veins he had taken back from the amniotic sac to the fetus. . . . he opened the flattened tunnel with his head just enough to get through. . . . his head emerged into open space. He was hanging upside-down . . . [he] wriggled his arms loose . . . and wrenched his body out of the tunnel.

Besides the obvious rebirth motif in this passage, Ellison also describes rather accurately one of the major entrances to hell. According to Robert Graves [in *The Greek Myths* (1955)], one of the entrances to the Hellenic versions of hell was called *Aornis,* which translates as "birdless." Ellison's adventurer is very close to that region where things fly away.

Once inside, he finds T. S. Eliot's wasteland, a "parched and stunned wasteland . . . a seemingly horizonless tumble of atrophied rock [with a] central spine of orange mountains." After he crosses these mountains, he discovers a fetid lake full of dead creatures and one ugly fish: "Talbot sat at the lip of the crater for a long time, looking down into the bowl that held the lake, and he watched the corpses of dead dreams as they bobbed and revolved like maggoty pork in a gray soup." He is somewhere on the road to Erebus (covered), the central region in hell where man is judged. Geographically, he is probably at the Pool of Memory (see Plato, "The Myth of Ur," *Republic*). Here he sees all of his dreams float past; they reveal the horrid nature of his life.

Finally he comes to the pancreatic sea on the shore of which he finds many of the memories of his childhood.

Perhaps this sea is affected by the waters of the Pool of Memory. It bears very little resemblance to either the Rivers Lethe (forgetfulness) or Styx (hated); however, like Styx, it does offer access to Erebus, the judgment place. Talbot finds a boat (abandoned by Charon?) and sails toward the Islets of Langerhans. While becalmed near the island, he hears a radio broadcast about an old woman who was imprisoned by society because she was somehow different. The homunculus reacts by crying which breaks the calm and delivers him to the coordinates for his soul—Erebus.

In the center of hell, he discovers his soul—a smiling, meaningless Howdy-Doody button—and a large castle—the palace of Hades from Greek myth. Talbot will be judged here. In the depths of this gothic castle, he finds a female figure much like the one discussed on the earlier radio broadcast. The resolution of the tale centers on Talbot's compassion for two old women—the one in the castle, the other a surrogate mother. He retreats into the hell of his own body with these two women to atone for the sins of the world. Unlike the previous adventurer, Talbot discovers that man can benefit from a view of his own soul even if it is not spotless—man *can* change; he *can* atone.

In these first two works, Ellison has shown a propensity to use the traditional framework of the descent into hell along with some closely related devices to comment on his perception of man's place in an inscrutable universe. The first tale, **"Delusion for a Dragon Slayer,"** shows the depth of Ellison's commitment to the psychological in terms of his use of doppelgängers and postmortem consciousness. It reveals what happens when man is not equal to his dreams, when he is flawed and cannot discern what must be done to correct his shortcomings. On the other hand, the second tale, **"Adrift Just Off the Islets of Langerhans,"** is a work fraught with possibility. The protagonist ventures into the self very much in terms of traditional descent literature and comes back with viable answers. Yet it is in two other tales, **"The Place With No Name"** and **"The Deathbird,"** that Ellison makes his most penetrating and perceptive analysis of the nature of man, God, Satan, good, and evil.

In **"The Place With No Name,"** Norman Mogart, the protagonist, while trying to escape from the police, runs into a shop kept by a very ambiguous fellow. This figure, like Mr. Demeter of the previous tale, has some magical abilities: "The little man shimmered, and changed form." He also seems to be a holy figure. His name—"You can call me Simon. . . . Or Peter"—recalls the apostle, Simon Peter. This guide-figure is also conspicuously absent in the tale as was Demeter in **"Adrift Just Off the Islets of Langerhans"** and the magician of **"Delusion for a Dragon Slayer."** This, however, is a typical occurrence in Ellison's descents.

When Norman escapes, he finds himself in "*another* body" in a junglelike setting. He also knows that he must locate a particular person—Prometheus—in "a place outside thought or memory," that other world of myth and legend. During his adventures, he is beset by a variety of beasts much like traditional descent characters. He also speculates on a variety of Indian religious beliefs, includ-

ing the idea that Prometheus "was the bringer not of fire, but of lies; not the searing brand of truth, but the greater revelation of falsehood." In addition, he discovers that the Indians worship the Promethean god in the guise of a snake totem. Even though he senses an ambiguity in his task, he continues to search for Prometheus.

Delirious with wandering and disease, Mogart begins to hallucinate; he sees the same brightly colored circles that plagued Warren Glazer Griffin. Finally, they lead him to a passage, and he "cleared the vegetation with his machete, and pried away several jagged chunks of rock that had fallen to block the passage. . . . [he] felt the walls of the passage. Narrower. Wider. . . . Stepped out." After this ritual birth, he finds himself in a dormant volcano, a symbolic womb where he finds Prometheus. However, the description of the creature is far from human: "Prometheus was very brown, almost a walnut shade. His eyes, which were closed, were vertical slits. Around the mouth, which was little more than a horizontal gash running completely across the lower face, were tiny fleshy tendrils . . . webbed-fingered hands pulled down on either side . . . [with] flipper-like feet." Through a vague magic trick, Mogart exchanges places with this half-fish/half-snake creature and is left to speculate on the meaning of it all throughout eternity. He eventually concludes that both Christ and Prometheus were aliens who had compassion

Dust jacket for Deathbird Stories.

for men and brought them knowledge. However, Ellison leaves the nature of such knowledge ambiguous—good *or* evil? In fact, since the Indians associate Prometheus with the snake and since the Promethean figure seems to be an amalgam of fish [ICTHY] and snake [Satan], a definitive judgment is difficult at best. One possible reading of such an ambiguous conclusion is that man must *not* consider whether Christ is Christ *or* Satan; *but* is Christ, Satan? Nevertheless, in this tale, the descent into hell, while approached in rather traditional terms, demonstrates the difficulty of finding answers to increasingly complex questions.

In the final work under consideration, **"The Deathbird,"** Ellison creates not only a descent into hell but an apocalyptic vision of despair and futility. The tale is told in a discursive style that at times seems to introduce irrelevant elements; however, since Ellison tells us that we can rearrange the work to suit our needs, a pattern can be discerned in the work. Significantly, Ellison prefaces the story with a disclaimer concerning the divinity of gods; instead, he maintains that man has the spark of life (the Hindu, *Atem*) and, as a consequence, may be God.

In the tale, Norman Stack, the protagonist, is awakened by a snakelike creature and brought to the blasted surface of the Earth. The landscape looks similar to that of the Brahmanistic *Tamas;* it is raked by howling winds and pervaded by darkness. While Stack journeys toward the lights in the mountains, flying devils try to snare him with their snakelike spores, a situation found in the *Vision of Drihthelm* (700 A.D.) and the *Vision of Furseus* (640 A.D.). When the protagonist finally nears his destination, he is attacked by an unseen assailant—a predicament that is, in a number of ways, reminiscent of earlier descent literature. For instance, in the fourth Buddhist hell, men are tormented by flames within their bodies; this is exactly the nature of the first attack Stack must fend off. After he succeeds in conquering this punishment, he is accosted by a variety of other afflictions including the Brahmanistic *Apratishtha*—a sense of falling. Stack does finally prevail over these terrors, but he must still confront the giant on the mountain.

When Stack actually faces the giant, he thinks of the Wizard of Oz, a fantasy character who spread terror and inspired awe through illusions. Stack realizes at last that God is mad, a spoiled child who treats the Earth as little more than a toy. Unfortunately, he also realizes that it is too late for the snake, who is *really* man's friend; the Earth, which is dead; and man, who finds out too late that he is God.

The descent into hell in literature usually represents a kind of ritual initiation experience: Adventurers go to such places to learn about the gods, death, life, as well as the nature of good and evil. Most of these incidents contain specific characters, identifiable landscapes, and a general pattern of events. While Ellison's work includes many of these conventions, it also generally lacks quite a few. For instance, characters are usually conspicuously absent. Where is Satan? Charon? Persephone? Are the gods dead? Landscape fares much the same. In **"Adrift Just Off the Islets of Langerhans,"** for example, Ellison uses

T. S. Eliot to elicit the image of the wasteland; Talbot's soul suffers from spiritual dryness as much as anything else. Have the gods, then, deserted the sinking ship like the rats they are? If the gods are gone, what can man hope for? Perhaps that is why Ellison wants man to journey into his soul, to go through that ritual birth into self-knowledge which will show man his real nature, his real worth—good or bad, human or god. (pp. 378-84)

> *Philip M. Rubens, "Descents into Private Hells: Harlan Ellison's 'Psy-Fi',"* in Extrapolation, *Vol. 20, No. 4, Winter, 1979, pp. 378-85.*

Harlan Ellison with Jeffrey M. Elliot   (interview date 1979)

[*In the following excerpt from an interview that originally appeared in* Future Life Magazine *in 1979, Ellison discusses his public image and motivations for writing.*]

[Elliot]: *Many people who've read your work know who your favorite targets are in terms of criticism. Who are some of your heroes and how do they take shape in your writing?*

[Ellison]: I've never been very big on heroes. I don't think there are such things. Today's hero is tomorrow's thug. When I was very young, I didn't have personal heroes like most of the kids. I wasn't a Babe Ruth buff or a Charles Lindbergh fan. I know several people whom I consider to be exemplary, but I perceive them to be human beings. They're not mythical figures in my mind. A remarkable man is Howard Fast, the novelist. Another is football star Joe Namath. An amazing woman is Margot Fonteyn, the ballerina. Another is Louise Nevelson, the sculptor. I respect peoples' work, not the people. I've met many famous people whose work I think is singular. Some of them have been interesting; others have been bores. People meet me and often judge me in terms of some preconceived idea of what I'm supposed to be like. Well, sometimes I am that on a particular day. Today, I happen to be cranky. Tomorrow, I might be the height of charm. Everybody is various. When people tell stories about me, nine out of ten times the stories are pure bullshit. I find a whole mythology about me emerging. I know how bogus that is, so how could I possibly believe the mythology about anybody else? That means there're no heroes. There're just people. We're all just people.

You've been the subject of a great many stories. Why do you think so many legends have grown up around you?

There are any number of reasons. Not all of them are noble. I'm almost constantly angry. Because of my background, because of the youth that was mine, I'm not a wishy-washy person. I take stands on things. Whether I'm right or wrong, I do the research, I form an opinion, and I'm willing to go to the grave for it. Anybody who takes a stand is automatically controversial, because most people aren't. Most people are cowards. Most people are programmed to back off, to not get involved, to not lay themselves on the line, either financially, or emotionally, or physically, or intellectually. Whether it's out of some perverse death wish or an inability to back off, I've never been able to do that. So I'm constantly in the midst of controversy. A good example is the pro-ERA thing. It was a very tough decision for me to make. I knew it wouldn't be a popular position to take. But I had to take it. It was an ethical statement for me. Now, I'm getting an enormous amount of crap dumped on my head. It's probably going to get a lot worse because of Iguanacon. I have no doubt that somebody's eventually going to come up to me, say something asinine, and we're going to wind up in a fist fight. That's okay with me, because I'm always in fist fights, but stories will grow up about it. The other day I was in Seattle doing an autograph party at Tower Books. A woman came up to me, whom I never saw before, and said, "Tell me about the time you dropped a chandelier on the convention audience." I said, "What are you talking about? "Well, the time," she said, "you dropped the chandelier." I looked at her and said, "Lady, you don't look to me like a brain-damage case, but you clearly must be. Look, if somebody drops a goddamn chandelier on people, people get killed, people get hurt. The idiot who drops the chandelier gets thrown in jail. I've never been in jail for dropping a chandelier, turkey!" In her mind, she firmly believed I dropped a chandelier on some people at a convention somewhere. God only knows where the stories come from. I've ceased denying them anymore. Now, I simply say, "That's right, I did it. Whatever you say, I did it!"

Have these stories had a pronounced impact upon your career?

The only area where this kind of thing has had any impact is at the television networks and movie studios. I'm considered a troublesome person. That's fine! I take that as a high accolade. I'm a troublemaker, a shit-kicker! I'm not coopted. You can't buy me. You can rent me periodically, but you can't buy me. When I go to work for a studio, they know up front that I feel a primary interest in my work. I'm not a hired hand. You don't hire me, pay me for the work, and then send me away. I'm going to be there all the way through. And if you screw it up, I'm going to be on your back. As a consequence, I don't work as much as I could. That's fine with me! I made $130,000 last year. That's a lot of bread. If I wanted to push a little, I could double that figure without any sweat. But I don't write for television anymore. And I won't write for it ever again. I've given it up. It's a filthy habit! I despise television. I think its bad for people. So I just kicked it.

Has your style, your bravado, your color, contributed, in a way, to your popularity as a writer?

I suppose that's true in some small way. I can't lie to myself about the condition of the reading public in America. Statistics recently came out which show that only 8 percent of the American public buy books. And of the 8 percent, 98 percent only buy one book a year. So they're not going to buy my work, they're not going to buy *Remembrance of Things Past,* they're not going to buy *Moby Dick.* They're going to buy *Love's Tender Fury,* or *Jaws,* or the last Harold Robbins's awfulness. That means that something like 2 percent of the American public are buying books. Unfortunately, many people fasten on my personal reputation, which is quite apart from me as a writer. However, I doubt it leads that kind of person, who would be fascinated by the cheap shitty *People* magazine kind of gossip, to read me. After all, I'm not that easy to read. My work is accessible, yes, but you've got to think, you really do. And my stuff's depressing, it's angry, and that's not the mode which is most successful today. The people who would be affected by my image are most likely to be people who wouldn't pick up a book in any case. But it's nice, I suppose, because it gets my name known. It sort of floats in the air. You're only going to get known, and paid, for that matter, if your name free floats. I'm not really convinced, anyway, that the people who follow up on my reputation will go out and buy my books, any more than I believe that the people who watch *Star Trek* move on to reading good science fiction. Clearly, that isn't so. The amount of drek being published today in science fiction is staggering. There's an incredible amount of crappy stuff! It's slanted toward the kinds of people who like *Star Trek, Close Encounters,* and *Star Wars.*

What explains the tremendous interest in, and curiosity about, the personal side of Harlan Ellison? Why has this "cult" following emerged?

The whole subject is genuinely embarrassing to me. I have very dichotomous feelings about the entire matter. I really do. On the one hand, it's fun. It's really fun in a kind of strange berserk way. There's no way you can't get off on that. On the other hand, I resent the invasion of my privacy, which is a constant thing. I resent the fact that my time is imposed upon, which happens all the time. After all, all a writer really has are talent and time. And the time that's spent away from the typewriter is time that can never be regained. It's a story that will never get written. I'm going to croak some day, and all the time wasted is time I could have spent writing. So I get crazed about it. I love the benefits that come to me because of it; I go everywhere, I do everything, I know everyone. I lead the best of all possible lives. I'm exactly what I want to be. I'm very satisfied with me. I'm very pleased with me. I do okay. I'm a good person. I'm an honest person. I care about a lot of stuff. I do good works. And I also screw up. But that goes with the program. However, I don't quite know how to handle this "cult" thing. My readership is extremely diverse. It's great to be able to rub elbows with famous people. It's an incredible experience! After all, I'm just a poor Jew from Ohio. I have no training. I have no wealthy parents. I have no background. Everything I have came out of the fingers. It's what I've been able to put on paper. And that's amazing to me! I know I'm a real person. So it's tough to understand why people are interested in me. But you're right, people are interested, for whatever reasons.

Isn't it true, though, that when you aspire to be famous, as you do, that you let yourself open for that?

I suppose that's true. I try, however, to establish a kind of middle ground between the fame, which is useful, and the privacy, which is important. If you play it right, fame can give you more freedom. You can be your own person. That's one reason why I'm as cranky as I am. People don't mess with me! I'm constantly getting calls from people who want things: for me to speak, to get laid, to live in my house, to teach them to write, to sell their movie, etc., etc.,

etc. You can't possibly imagine, in the course of a day, how much bullshit I get. People figure that if you're in the public eye, then you're their property. They can do anything. They can impose upon you, and it doesn't matter. After all, you belong to them. It doesn't matter what they ask or how they ask it. You're supposed to take it. Well, hell, I won't take it! (pp. 10-13)

Has your star status resulted in greater artistic freedom?

Absolutely. Nobody tells me what to write. It's almost slopped over into movies and television. I can almost get away with doing exactly what I want. In films, it's art by committee. It's run by businessmen. They want to have their say. They don't really trust the writer. In books and magazines, though, I get a guarantee. Nobody touches anything I write. I've always demanded control over my work. Sometimes I got it, other times I didn't. But mostly I did. Many people who write sell out before they have to. They compromise before they need to. They don't demand enough. As a consequence, publishers treat writers in a very cavalier fashion. They assign them stories, don't pay them, mess up their work, etc. Most writers could get many more things than they get now. All they have to do is insist. After all, they have a corner on the market. Nobody else can write what they write. If a magazine wants something to be published, then they've got to give the writer what he asks for. It's as simple as that. My own success lies in the fact that, on the one hand, I'm a strong enough talent that I can demand it, and, on the other, that I ask. I also have a reputation. If someone messes with me, I'll get them. If it takes me 400 years, I'll get them. We just filed a $2 million lawsuit against Paramount and ABC for ripping off my story, **"Brillo,"** which I did with Ben Bova. They did it as *Super Cop.* I've got the biggest show-business attorney in the country. They're suing the asses off Paramount and ABC. With magazines and books, this sort of thing rarely happens. But in television and movies, it's constant. These people have no ideas of their own. So they figure they can take any idea they want, change it around a little, and make a bundle of money. Well, this time they're going to get it. This time we're going to nail their asses to the barn door. It's going to be a great triumph, not so much for me, but for every writer who's ever gotten screwed. It will be a demonstration that you *can* fight, you *can* win. Don't take it! You don't have to!

How can I not get infuriated when I see people, who could be sitting and reading Shakespeare, or Shelley, or Keats, reading goddamn gothic novels or cheap science fiction crap, or sitting and watching television, or going to a third-rate movie? That's what forms my anger. I expect so much of people. I think they're capable of so much.

—Harlan Ellison

Much of what you've written represents a condemnation of mass society. And yet, a writer's success, at least in terms of dollars, is dependent upon his ability to reach a mass audience. Do you think you've reached the average reader? Do you write with this audience in mind?

The other night I was talking to a friend of mine. He said, "It must be difficult for you to always be angry." I said, "You're right, it is." It's aggravating to constantly have your gut in turmoil. I would much rather be a "nice" guy. I don't like to get up in front of 300 people and say, "You morons, you fools, how could you spend $12 to come to a stupid *Star Trek* convention? What possesses you?" I don't like to do that. Then someone will say, "Well, why do *you* do it?" And I'll say, "I do it, turkey, because they pay me, for crissake." When I do conventions, though, I never talk about *Star Trek.* I never lie. I never sell out. I don't do cheap entertainments. I do whatever my rap is. And then I read my stories. That's what it's all about. But the point is, they pay me. And by paying me, I don't have to do television. That means I have the time free to do my books. And that's first. I'd kill for the work! There is nothing that gets between me and the work. Whatever it is, I'm driven to write. I'm driven to reviling what I see as the debasement of the human spirit. Really, I love the human race. It's individuals, I think, that stink! For crissake, any species that can paint the Sistine Chapel ceiling, that can send a human being to the Moon, that can develop concern for the whales, my God, that's a species that's godlike, that's noble, that's capable of anything. And yet, they're willing to settle for crap! How can I not get infuriated when I see people, who could be sitting and reading Shakespeare, or Shelley, or Keats, reading goddamn gothic novels or cheap science fiction crap, or sitting and watching television, or going to a third-rate movie? How can I not get enraged? That's what forms my anger. I expect so much of people. I think they're capable of so much. In their finest moments, when they're really holy, they can do anything. And yet, they permit themselves to be such dregs, to be cowed by their bosses, to be lied to by the politicians, to be blown away by big business at their flat. That makes me nuts in the head. So I think that anybody who reads me, and who enjoys me, has to be an extraordinary person. I really believe that. There are so many easier things to read than what I write. Anybody who gets off on what I write, I think, has got to want to think deeper thoughts.

Is the desire to write, to express yourself, a fundamental part of your being or is it simply a way of making a living and getting by?

I love to write. I could no more not write than I could stop breathing. Everything I do is in some way involved with the writing. From the moment I get up in the morning, to the moment I go to bed at night, I live, eat, and breathe writing. In fact, almost everything I do either develops from the writing, or forms the writing, or is a result of the writing. I am what I write.

What about writing strikes such a strong chord in you? After all, very few writers enjoy the isolation, the loneliness, the daily challenge which makes up the life of a writer.

I enjoy the whole process. I get a rush from creating. I don't use dope. I don't drink. I'm not into religion. I'm not interested in est. I'm a very pragmatic dude. For me, the act of creating, the act of building a dream, is the most exciting thing I could possibly do. Writing for me is a holy chore. That I do it well is a great achievement for me. As I get older, I want to do it better. I'm just coming into my prime, for crissake. This last quarter-century of writing— 900 stories and 32 books—that's preamble, baby! I'm going to be so dynamite by the time I'm seventy-five, you ain't gonna believe it! This doesn't mean that writing comes easily. It doesn't. It's hard work. There're times when my arms ache in the sockets, when my back hurts so much it's hard to stand up, when my body is numb with pain. Sometimes, I'll get up from the typewriter and say, "Hell, there must be an easier way to make a living." But it's said in a rueful way, the way you say, if you're involved with someone, "God, you're a pain in the ass!" But it's said with love. I love the writing. I wouldn't do anything else. If I were on a desert island and I weren't being paid a dime, I would write. I would put stories in bottles and float them out to sea. I would do it anyway. I'm a writer.

How important is audience impact on your motivation?

That ties in with my answer about the audience. I write for the most literate audience in the world. I write for an audience that is knowledgeable, that has a sense of history, that cares about ethical questions, that is strong and courageous. I write for an audience of one. I write for myself. Absolutely. I think any writer who writes any other way is a fool. If I were to pay attention to what I would presume to be the needs of my audience, I'd fall flat on my face. After all, who the hell is my audience? The best I can do is to hope to please myself. If I please myself, then I'll usually please the rest of my readership. But even if I don't, that's okay, because I've pleased me. I perceive, however, in a very schizoid way, that my work does have impact on people. There are people who are motivated, or affected, or changed by what I write. On the other hand, I must stop and say to myself, "Don't oversell yourself, moron!" Really, all I am is a paid liar. I get paid very well to tell these funny little dreams I have. If I suddenly start aggrandizing what I do, and start saying, "I'm a shaker, I'm a mover, I'm a force for good in my time," then I'd become an even worse pompous turkey than I am to begin with. Actually, very few books have altered the course of history, even in a slight way. Perhaps books such as *Uncle Tom's Cabin* have, maybe *Aesop's Fables* have, but not too many others. Most books don't have any impact at all. So while I write to have an impact, it's an impact that's inherent in the work. It's in the integrity of the story, in the material. If I've done it right, then it will strike a chord. However, I don't know what my work is intended to do. I do know, though, that people read my stuff and say, "Man, you gave me a pain in the stomach," or "Oh God, I didn't sleep last night," or "I hate you a lot," or "You unsettle me." I prefer that. I don't want anybody to ever say of my work, "Gee, that was a nice, quiet, little story." Some people make a big deal about the violence in my stories. Hell, there's less violence in my stories than many people would have you believe. A good 50 to 60 percent of my work has no violence in it. But people remember the violent ones.

That's because those are the stories which jangled their nerves. The story that was up for 1978's Nebula, Hugo, and World Fantasy Awards—**"Jeffty is Five"**—has virtually no violence in it. There's some, maybe, but it's not the kind that's in *A Boy and His Dog* or **"I Have No Mouth, and I Must Scream."** It's a heart-rending story. But I venture to say, even as well-known as the story is now, and will be if it wins some awards, five years from now, when they're making up anthologies, they'll still be buying **"I Have No Mouth"** and *A Boy and His Dog.* In fact, not a week goes by that someone doesn't anthologize these two stories. And that annoys me. That pisses the hell out of me! After all, these people are all cannibalizing one another. They aren't bothering to look at the totality of the work. It's easy for them to find a story that's already appeared in a dozen places. If somebody wants to buy any one of the 900-odd stories, except, perhaps, for **" 'Repent, Harlequin!' Said the Ticktockman,"** and a couple of others, they can have that story for $100, maybe $200. But if they want **"I Have No Mouth,"** or *A Boy and His Dog,* they'll pay $500, $600, $1000, as much as I can bleed out of them. It's my hope that I can discourage people from constantly going after the same story. Really, I don't pay any attention to what the impact is, because given their druthers, the audience would have you write the same goddamn thing a hundred times. I can't let the audience dictate what I write. I have to go my own way. When I look around, I can see lots of good writers, especially in the science fiction field, whose progress and development as artists were arrested twenty years ago by fans. I don't have to name any names. You know who I mean. They're writing essentially the same stuff today that they wrote thirty years ago. And that's tragic. It's tragic for them, it's tragic for the audience, and it's tragic for all the stories that were never written. (pp. 13-16)

As you assess your own work, have you found that writing has had a cathartic value for you? Has it taught you important things about yourself?

Absolutely. That's one of the most valuable things about the writing. I'm able to get the best possible therapy in the world, from the best possible therapist for me, and not only not pay for it, but I get paid for it. I get paid for the privilege of answering questions about myself. I've discovered enormously complex things about myself. They've often turned out to be disturbing things, frightening things, saddening things. I've got a story in *Playboy* called **"All the Birds Home to Roost,"** which deals with my first marriage, my first wife, and the fact that she's been in a mental institution for the last fifteen years. I never really blocked that out; I could talk about it if I chose to, but it hurt a great deal to do so. Very few people know about that part of my life. Now, it will appear in a story. And the story helped me to deal with it. I was able to come to grips with a part of it. Another one of my stories, **"Shatterday,"** which appeared several years ago, dealt with, among other things, my admission to myself that I really wanted my mother to die. That she was terribly ill, that the responsibility for her life had become too much for me, was something I didn't want to face. Most of me wanted her to live, but a part of me also wanted her to die. Writing about it helped me to understand my feelings better. It also taught me something important—namely, that there's terrible in all of us. We must fight to keep that terrible to a minimum. So when I yell at people, when I harangue them, it's not all of that person I'm cudgeling, but that part which is less than golden.

Many of your recent works are prefaced by long and detailed introductions. Do you view this part of the story as a pulpit from which to preach the gospel according to Ellison?

No. It's just me amusing myself. It's just chatter. It's just conversation. I've always felt it was necessary for people to understand that art can be created by anyone. It's not a mystical process that can only be generated by peculiar people living on crystal mountain tops. Everyone has the ability to paint the Sistine Chapel ceiling. The introductions are designed to establish a writer-to-reader liaison. It's just my way of indicating that these stories come from a human being; that they don't spring full-blown from out of nowhere. Most people who read can't remember the author of the last book they read, much less the story line. There's a rampant kind of illiteracy in this country. Schools and literary academics, for their own reasons, most of which are concerned with the territorial imperative, perpetuate the myth that a story has to be explained; that it emerges from some kind of strange psychotic location. My introductions are just chit chat. They're no more significant than that.

Finally, some critics have argued that your recent work has become more hopeful, more optimistic, more uplifting. Do you discern those changes in your work and, if so, what produced this change of heart?

Actually, those feelings have always been present in my work. When people say that to me, I'll usually say, "Look at **'I Have No Mouth.'** That's a very positive story. It has a very upbeat ending." Really, it's an uplifting story. This man sacrifices his life, his eternity, to give others peace. He allows himself to be crucified, to spend eternity in torment, for the sake of others. That's a very positive ending. It says that the human spirit, at the final ticking moment, knowing full well that hideous reprisals will follow, still does the noble thing. There's an unquenchable spark in the human spirit that gives rise to genuine hope. Now, I was saying that as early as 1966, nearly twelve years ago. It's not so much optimism, but rather that I hope for better things. I've always hoped for better things. But I'm also a pragmatist. I know they probably won't happen. Most people, left to their own devices, will go for the cheapest, quickest out. It takes a lot to remain strong, to remain courageous, to remain ethical, not so much because they're hard things to do, but because we're programmed day and night to do just the opposite. It comes back to the ERA thing again. When somebody says, "Look, it's hot in Arizona in the summer, and there's going to be a lot of opposition, and. . . ." I say to them, "Hey, moron, nobody said it was going to be easy. It's when it hurts a little, when it costs something, that it matters. If it doesn't cost you anything, then you're just blowing in the wind." Unfortunately, too many people would rather blow hot air. And that makes me sad. (pp. 17-18)

Harlan Ellison and Jeffrey M. Elliot, in an in- *terview in* Science Fiction Voices #3: Interviews with Science Fiction Writers *by Jeffrey M. Elliot, Borgo Press, 1980, pp. 9-18.*

Roz Kaveney   (essay date 1982)

[*In the following excerpt, Kaveney offers a mixed review of Ellison's short story collection* Shatterday.]

[Ellison's short fiction collection **Shatterday**] is unified by theme and atmosphere. . . .

The comparative weakness of short story collections on the sf and fantasy markets has forced authors to think of them as unitary wholes, exploring groups of themes thoroughly and self-consciously. Sometimes, too, stories are unified by imposing a brooding auctorial persona on them. Ellison has been one of the critics most exemplifying the latter tendency; each story, each collection, is a death-defying display of virtuoso craft and if a story has been written in a book store window or drafted on a soy-stained portable between courses in a Chinese restaurant he will be sure to let us know. He is a showoff preacher, cracking a bawdy joke to exemplify Love, setting off a firecracker to show the sudden wrath of the Lord. He is, in a word, vulgar—and none the worse for it.

Shatterday comes with a heavily rhetorical introduction "Mortal Dreads" in which Ellison claims to be talking person to person—but you will be arrested if you heckle a preacher in church and you cannot answer back to a book. He writes to shock: "I see myself as a combination of Jiminy Cricket and Zorro"—by shocking people he hopes to get them to accept their own human frailty and to awaken them to wisdom and courage. Stump rhetoric is an inherently insincere mode of discourse—but beneath Ellison's posturing mask, he wears a face with the same expression. He talks sense a lot of the time and one just has to tune out the volume. At his best he is a city primitive; under the pseudosophistication and hip rant there is a genuine sensibility which should not be ignored.

These stories blend uneasily but effectively vigorous confessional and simplistic metaphor. A New Yorker fades into acceptance of his own dissolution faced with a righteous *doppelgänger* who rejects his shabbiness and compromises; a crooked builder is destroyed when a victim unleashed on him the pent-up frustrations of modern life as concrete curses—tax demands, computer error, stalled car; a man finds himself having affairs with all his ex-girlfriends in reverse order. If the protagonists of Ellison's myths are unmemorable as individuals, it is not because they are cardboard but because they are Everyman. And they are also the author himself, never more than when accused of the unforgiveable. You have to believe in, and be moved by, breastbeating when the bruises seem so real.

Ellison is good at faking the concrete with lists—a crude Marxist criticism would not be surprised at his poetry of commodities, nor should we be. It is thus, rather than through its overtly sentimental touches, that Ellison makes convincing the tale of innocence and quality doomed in a corrupt modern world, **"Jeffty is Five"**. The narrator's friend never grows past five and holds time still around him. He can pick up continuing versions of the great radio series and comic books of the 1950s; he can send off for, and get, new vintage Magic Decoder Rings and drink Ovaltine that tastes the way it used to. But this private world is doomed and his mother kills him—"And she took him upstairs to bathe away his blood and his pain"; typically Ellison undercuts that moving simple statement with another page of rhetoric. Even in less good stories the lists still have power. The **"Shoppe Keeper"** runs a standard pulp fiction store of Heart's Desire—and making his customer turn out to be Charles Manson only compounds the offense—but the list of wares is long and splendid—shells that reproduce "the sound of the wind between the stars . . . 9mm artillery shells made of sterling silver for use in slaying were-dinosaurs."

This fascination with commodities extends to Ellison's treatment of sex; Ellison has made public stands against sexism but he is still fascinated in his fiction with the mechanisms of objectification and oppression. In **"Would you do it for a Penny?"**, Arlo seduces Anastasia with a no-strings gift of a "rare" coin; when she discovers it to be a fake, he seduces her all over again by his shock that she had it valued, his feigned horror that his childhood treasure was a lie. Ellison values, and makes us value, the virtuoso liar's display: he makes entertaining the simple metaphoric links between the plastic gourmet food over which the lovers meet, the coin collection, and the similarly debased but useful coinage of uncommitted love-making.

Ellison is a sincere and gifted entertainer and sermonizer; no one could reel off that list of past professions—circus hand, lumberjack, hired gun—if he were not totally for real. His stories display hard work and good moral sense; as parables they have hammy power. But to deliver, in full, all he promises and aspires to, Ellison would have to be Dostoyevsky and Kafka combined. *Shatterday* demonstrates many gifts, but also a lack; a lack of a sense of humility and proportion. With that added, Ellison's work might lose its embarrassing side, become discreet, coherent and polished—polished like a diamond that is, rather than merely smooth like the paintwork on a Porsche. (pp. 14-15)

> Roz Kaveney, "Space to Believe, Time to Confess," in Books and Bookmen, *No. 323, August, 1982, pp. 12-16.*

Stephen King (essay date 1982)

[*King is a highly popular author of horror fiction. Combining elements of the traditional Gothic tale with those of the modern psychological thriller, detective, and science fiction genres, his works often explore the inability to rationalize certain facets of evil in seemingly commonplace situations. In the following excerpt from his foreword to* Stalking the Nightmare, *he praises Ellison's stories and essays for their wit and energy.*]

[Ellison] is a ferociously talented writer, ferociously in love with the job of writing stories and essays, ferociously dedicated to the craft of it as well as its art—the latter being the part of the job with which writers who have been

to college most frequently excuse laziness, sloppiness, cant, and promiscuous self-indulgence.

There are folks in the biz who don't like Harlan much. I don't think I'm telling you anything you don't know; if you know Phantasia Press, whose imprint this book bears, then you probably know enough about speculative fiction to know that. These anti-Harlan folks offer any number of reasons for their dislike, but I believe that a lot of it has to do with that ferocity. Harlan is the sort of guy who makes an ordinary writer feel like a dilettante, and an ordinary liver (i.e., one who lives, not a bodily organ which will develop cirrhosis if you pour too much booze over it) feel like a spinster librarian who once got kissed on the Fourth of July.

Coupled with the ferocity of purpose is a crazed confidence—the confidence of a man who does not just walk wires but runs across them full-tilt-boogie. There are folks who find this trait equally unendearing. People who are afraid don't like people who are brave. People who eat pallidly and politely at the Great Banquet of Life (Chew that fish—there might be a bone in it! Skip the beef—if you eat enough of it, you get cancer of the bowel! No eggs—cholesterol! Heart attacks! Eat the carrots. Eat the carrots. They're safe. Boring, but safe.) resent people who dash wildly up and down, trying some of this, scarfing up some of that, swallowing something really *gruesome* and barfing it back up.

Put another way, Harlan knows now—and has, I would guess, since about 1965—that if you're gonna talk that talk, you gotta be able to walk that walk; that if you got the flash you better have the cash, and that sooner or later you gotta put up or shut up. He rides the shockwave.

All of this comes through admirably in the man's fiction and essays (as it damn well should; otherwise his impact would die with him), and I think that's the reason I always end up writing like the guy after I've been reading the guy. It's the force of his personality, the sense of Harlan Ellison *as a living person* that's caught in the lines. There are people who don't like that; there are many people who are convinced that Harlan is some sort of trick, like that miniature guillotine that will slice a cigarette in two but leave your finger intact.

Others, who know that few tricksters and literary shysters can hang around for better than twenty-five years, publishing fiction which has steadily broadened its area of inquiry and which has never declined in its energy, know that Harlan is no trick. They may begrudge him that apparently inexhaustible energy, or resent his *chutzpah,* or fear his refusal to suffer fools (of some people it is said they will not suffer fools gladly; Harlan does not suffer them at all), but they know it isn't a trick.

The book which follows [*Stalking the Nightmare*] is a case in point. I'm not going to pre-chew it; if you want someone to chew your food for you, send this book back to the publisher, get a refund, and go buy a few volumes of Cliff's Notes, the mental babyfood of college students everywhere for the last forty years or so. You won't find one on Harlan, and I hope you never will (and speaking of wills, why not put it in yours, Harlan? NO FUCKING CLIFF'S

NOTES! IF YOU WANT TO KNOW WHAT GOES ON IN
DEATHBIRD STORIES, GO READ A COPY, YOU FUCKING
MENTAL MIDGET! *God,* I sound like Harlan today—don't
you think so?) Certainly you won't find a Harlan-Ellison-
in-a-nutshell in this introduction.

But I *will* point out that these stories and essays range
from almost Lovecraftian horror (**"Final Trophy"**) to existentialist fantasy (**"The Cheese Stands Alone,"** with its
almost talismanic repetition of the phrase "My fine
stock") to the riotously funny (take your pick; my own favorite—maybe because it's gifted with a title that even
Fredric Brown would have admired—**"Djinn, No Chas-
er"**) to good old nuts-and-bolts science fiction (**"Invulnerable"**).

The essays have a similar range; Harlan's essay on the Saturn fly-by of the Voyager I bird could fit comfortably into
an issue of *Atlantic Monthly,* while one can almost see
"The 3 Most Important Things in Life" as a stand-up
comedy routine (it's a job, by the way, that Harlan knows,
having done it for awhile in his flaming youth).

Harlan's wit, insight, and energy inform all of these stories
and essays. Are they uneven? Yes, of course they are.
While I haven't been given the "lawyer's page"—that is,
the dates of copyright on each short story and essay, along
with where each was previously published—just the
Xerox offprints I've been sent suggest that there is also a
wide range of time represented in *Stalking the Nightmare.*
Different typefaces and different return addresses tell part
of the tale; the evolution in style tells part of it; the growth
of confidence and ambition tells much more of it.

But even the earliest stories bear the unmistakable mark
of Ellison. Take, for example, **"Invulnerable,"** one of my
favorite stories in the present collection—in fact, I guess
I'd go a step further (God hates a coward, right?) and say
it's *the* favorite, mostly because of the original way Harlan
handles a very old idea—here is Superman and Krypto the
Wonder Dog for thinking adults. Exactly how old is the
tale? Without the lawyer's page it's impossible to tell, but
it's possible to don the old deerstalker hat and make a couple of Sherlock Holmes-type deductions just the same.
First, **"Invulnerable"** was originally published in *Super-
Science Fiction,* and the illustration (just a hasty pen-and-
ink; you're not missing a thing) is by Emsh, whose work
I haven't seen in years. So, still wearing the deerstalker
hat, I'd guess . . . maybe 1957. How far off am I? Take
a look at the lawyer's page, if you want. If it's more than
five years either way, you're welcome to a good horselaugh
at my expense. [In a footnote, Harlan Ellison states:
"Readers of the above-entered praise, seeking in vain for
the story **'Invulnerable'** (published in the April, 1957 issue
of *Super-Science Fiction*—you get the Mad Hound of the
Moors award for deductive logic, Steve), will be confused,
bemused and even dismayed—as will Stephen King—to
find the work absent from this book. I suppose some sort
of explanation is in order. It goes like so: **'Invulnerable'**
was one of the original selections included in the twenty
tales slated for this collection: It was among the tearsheet-
ed stories sent to Steve prior to final editing, so he could
write his Foreword in a leisurely fashion. Subsequently,
when I went back over the stories and read them more

closely, I realized some of the older tales desperately needed extensive revision, updating, smoothing and rethink-
ing. One of these stories was **'Invulnerable.'** I had forgotten that Steve mentioned it so prominently in his essay.
The qualities admired by Steve are definitely present in the
story, but the quality embodied in Steve's remark that
'there's a certain amount of dating' was too great to allow
to pass untended. Yet to leach out that dated aspect would
have meant virtually writing a new story. I decided not to
do it. I started revising the original manuscript, written
very early in my career, and realized after three pages that
the job was akin to rebuilding an edifice that had been
burned to the ground, from bottom up. Instead of doing
that, I decided to include a recent story, **'Grail,'** at twice
or three times the length. So Stephen King has whetted
your appetite for a 'lost' story, one that I may some day
rewrite and update completely. But search not for **'Invulnerable'** in these pages. It ain't here."]

So there's a certain amount of dating in the story; it
doesn't just happen to the *best* of us, it happens to *all* of
us. And yet, even 'way back then, in those fabled Old Days
when there was such an artist as Emsh and such an organ
as *Super-Science Fiction,* we find Harlan Ellison's true
voice—clear in tone, dark in consideration. This was the
era when science fiction's really big guns—guys like
Robert A. Heinlein, for instance—were touting space exploration as The Great Panacea for All Mankind, The
Last Frontier, and The Solution to Just About Everything.
There's a certain amount of that in **"Invulnerable"** (but
then, why not? I suspect there's a certain amount of that
wistful fairy-tale still in Harlan's soul . . . and mine . . .
and maybe in yours, too—read **"Saturn, November 11th,"**
and see how you react), but Harlan also sounds the horn
of the skeptic, loud and clear:

> Forstner was waiting. He was surrounded by the
> top brass. The place was acrawl with guards;
> guards on the guards; and guards to guard the
> guard's guards. The same old story. It wasn't as
> noble an endeavour as they would have had me
> believe.
>
> It was an arms race, an attempt for superiority
> of space before someone else got there . . .

Yeah, it was an arms race. We all know that . . . now. But
to have said it back in the days when Good Old General
Ike was still the top hand in the old Free World Corral
(and let's not forget his chief ramrod, good old Tricky
Dick Nixon—I know we'd like to, but maybe we'd better
not), when Reddy Killowatt was supposed to be our friend
and nuclear power was going to solve all of our energy
problems, back when the only two stated reasons we had
for getting Up There was to beat the Russians and to study
the sun's corona for the International Geophysical Year
(which every subscriber to *My Weekly Reader* knew as
IGY) . . . to have had such a dark thought back in those
days—and about *us* as well as *them*—well, that was tantamount to treason. It's a little amazing that Harlan got it
into print . . . unless you know Harlan, of course. And
it's *damn* fine to have it here, preserved between the
boards of one of the admirable Phantasia Press books.

But I promised not to chew your food for you, didn't I?

So I'll get out of here now. Harlan's going to come along very soon, grab you by the earlobe, and drag you off to a dozen different worlds. You're going to be glad you went, I promise you (and you may be a little bit surprised to find you've made it back alive).

Just one final comment, and then I promise to go quietly: there's no significant correlation between the quality of a writer's writing and the quality of that same writer's personality. When I tell you that reading Harlan is overwhelming enough to start me writing like the guy—taking his flavor as my mother said milk takes the flavor of whatever you put it next to in the icebox—I am speaking of ability, not personality.

Harlan Ellison's personality is every bit as striking as his prose style, and this makes the man a pleasure to dine with, to visit, or to entertain. But let's tell the gut-level, bottom-line truth. Most of you reading this are never going to eat a meal with Harlan, visit him in his home, or be visited by him. He gives of himself in a way that is profligate, almost dangerous—as does any writer worth his salt. He'll tell you the truth in a manner which is sometimes infuriating (see **"The Hour That Stretches"** or **"!!!The!!Teddy!Crazy!!Show!!!"** in this volume, or the classic short story **"Croatoan,"** where Harlan managed to accomplish the mind-numbing feat of simultaneously pissing off the right-to-lifers and the women's liberationists) and always entertaining . . . but don't confuse these things with the man; do not assume that the work *is* the man. And ask yourself this: why in Christ's name would you want to make *any* assumption about the man on the basis of his work? (pp. 6-11)

For whatever it's worth, Harlan Ellison is a great man: a fast friend, a supportive critic, a ferocious enemy of the false and the foolish, maniacally funny, perhaps insecure (I'm not sure what to make of a man who doesn't smoke or drink and who still has such crazed acid indigestion), but above all else, brave and true. (pp. 11-12)

> *Stephen King, in an introduction to* Stalking the Nightmare, *by Harlan Ellison, Phantasia Press, 1982, pp. 3-13.*

Ellison's antithetical societies are highly exaggerated. No one would suppose, for example, that the middle-class survivors in the underground city of Ellison's *A Boy and His Dog* would *really* live that way, or that the Rovers would last for more than a generation if that. Ellison writes in large part to arouse emotions, and he does that skillfully.

> **—Jerry Pournelle, in his "The Construction of Believable Societies," in The Craft of Science Fiction, *edited by Reginald Bretnor, 1976.***

Leonard Heldreth   (essay date 1983)

[*An educator and critic, Heldreth has written numerous articles on science fiction and film. In the following excerpt, he discusses Ellison's depiction of a mechanized society in* A Boy and His Dog *and notes differences between the novella and the film version of the story.*]

In a review of *Rollerball*, the *New York Times* divided all science fiction films into one of two types of nightmares: "In the first the world has gone through a nuclear holocaust and civilization has reverted to a neo-Stone Age. In the second . . . all of mankind's problems have been solved but at the terrible price of [the loss of] individual freedom." While this neat division could be debated—*A Boy and His Dog* includes both nightmares—the second category certainly constitutes a major genre in science fiction films and books. Despite Isaac Asimov's desire [expressed in "By the Numbers," in *Study War No More* (1977)] that the country "develop a national computerbank, government-run (inevitably) which will record in its vitals every bit of ascertainable information about every individual," most people fear mechanization and the loss of freedom they see accompanying it . . . If science fiction is any measure, this deep-seated distrust of the machine is strong, for almost every representation of the future presents mechanization as a constant threat. Anthony Burgess, discussing *A Clockwork Orange*, states [in *Great Science Fiction Pictures* (1977)] that "Perhaps the ultimate act of evil is dehumanization, the killing of the soul. What my, and Kubrick's, parable tries to state is that it is preferable to have a world of violence undertaken in full awareness—violence chosen as an act of will—than a world conditioned to be good or harmless." In science fiction films, almost all computer-run or mechanically structured societies are heavily flawed, or the price for their perfection is too great. Two types of patterns are generally present in such films: one class suppresses and mechanizes another for its own benefit; or one man rebels against a virtually uniform mechanical society. In both situations the society is often run by a giant computer. Examples of the first type would be *Metropolis*, *Westworld*, and *Futureworld;* the latter type includes *Logan's Run*, *THX 1138*, ***A Boy and His Dog,*** and *A Clockwork Orange.* (pp. 213-14)

[The] civilization in ***A Boy and His Dog*** has divided into two societies, a surface one where rover bands and loners eke out an existence in the postholocaust nuclear desert, and a subterranean one where time has been turned back until just before World War I. Based on Harlan Ellison's Nebula Award-winning novella, the film "is not without cinematic precedence. Films dating as far back as . . . *Metropolis* have depicted societies similarly stratified" [Don Shay, "Tripping through Ellison's Wonderland," *Cinefantastique* (Spring 1976)]. Few films, however, have presented such an unrelenting vision of the conflict between almost complete anarchy of the violent variety, and almost complete authority, and almost none have presented a view more authoritarian and more mechanical than that of the print version.

A Boy and His Dog describes the adventures of Vic and his telepathic canine companion Blood as they try to find food and sex in the blasted cities and deserts that now cover what was once civilization. Society is almost nonexistent: groups of "roverpacks" and "solos" fight for existence among the ruins, while a few groups have formed an uneasy truce to trade essential services. Our Gang, a roverpack that has taken over the Metropole Theatre, provides admission to its movies in return for canned goods and other trade items; other groups (in the novella) keep the radiation pits clear and run the generators that provide electricity. But no central organization exists. The film adds one character, an eccentric named Fellini dressed in extravagant rags like an impoverished oriental potentate, who comes riding up in a conveyance straight from the hallucinations (appropriately) of *Juliet of the Spirits*. He has found explosives and organized a gang to blast holes to the buildings below to then loot them. By the end of the film Fellini has taken over the town and established the beginning of a new authoritarian structure, as Vic and Blood move on to new territory.

As extreme in order as the surface is in violence and social chaos, the underground civilization of Topeka, the "downunder," is an artificial world whose people have become artificial. All actions transpire in an emotional vacuum; all words, however strong, are passionless. Pledged to preserve the status quo, the Committee, with totalitarian lack of compassion, blithely sends all nonconformists to "the farm," a euphemism for execution. The origins of the society may explain some of its attitudes.

Before the nuclear apocalypse, some groups had sunk deep holes on the sites of wells or into natural caves and set up civilizations away from the desolation and radiation of the surface; a couple hundred of these settlements still existed (as the novella states)

> in what was left of the United States and Canada. . . . the people who'd settled them were squares of the worst kind. Southern Baptists, Fundamentalists, lawanorder goofs, real middle-class squares. . . . They'd gotten the last of the scientists to do the work, invent the how and why, and then they'd run them out. They didn't want any progress, they didn't want any dissent, they didn't want anything that would make waves. They'd had enough of that. The best time in the world had been just before the First War, and they figured if they could keep it like that, they could live quiet lives and survive.

But the society has come to a complete stop. Vic describes its people as "canned down there, like dead fish. Canned." Later Vic admits "I could feel that tin can closing in on me."

In both the film and the novella on which it is based, the images and language chosen to describe the societies of *A Boy and His Dog* designate the topside as patriarchal and the underground as matriarchal. Vic, like Huckleberry Finn, moves between the two worlds, neither of which satisfies him. The surface world is composed almost exclusively of males: "The War had killed off most of the girls. . . . The things getting born were seldom male *or* female, and had to be smashed against a wall as soon as they were pulled out of the mother." Some roverpacks have women they protect for sexual services; solos have only rape, masturbation, or homosexuality for an outlet.

In the opening sequence of the film, Vic goes down into a hole dug into one of the buried buildings and finds a naked woman bound and dying of knife wounds after she has been gang raped by a roverpack. His only feeling is disappointment: "They didn't have to cut her. She could have been used two or three more times." [In a footnote, Heldreth states: "Like several of the more brutal sections of the film, this sequence and speech are not in the novella."] Women are simply sex objects, to be enjoyed between fights with phallic knives and guns in this violent anarchy of macho males, where the last vestiges of civilization have dropped from the aggressive ego. The building where Vic intends to rape Quilla June is, appropriately, a demolished YMCA.

The underground society, in contrast, is clearly—if mostly symbolically—matriarchal and orderly. In the novella, Ellison presents symbolically the movement from a masculine to a feminine society in the description of Vic's going underground. The entrance to the underground is a "pillar of black metal," but when Vic inserts the metal card, this aboveground phallic image becomes vaginal: ". . . a section of the pillar dilated. I hadn't even seen the lines of the section. A circle opened and I took a step through. . . . The access portal irised closed behind me." Symbolically behaving like the breeder he is to become for the underground people, Vic continues his penetration: ". . . the floor I was standing on dilated just the way the outside port had done. . . . [As Vic drops] through the floor, the iris closed overhead, I was dropping down the tube." At the bottom of the chute, ". . . the iris—a much bigger one this time—swirled open, and I got my first look at a downunder. . . . I was down at the bottom of a big metal tube that stretched up to a ceiling an eighth of a mile overhead, twenty miles across."

In this enormous fallopian tube, Vic finds a society as feminine as the surface one is masculine. Most of the male characters after twenty years below ground are either impotent or produce mostly sperm for female babies; as Lew tells Vic, they "need some men."

The film emphasized the same images by shooting up a circular staircase, and when Vic reaches the underground, the film presents a society more matriarchal than the book's. The film adds a politically powerful woman to the ruling Committee, and ever-present loudspeakers (not in the novel) broadcast recipes, aphorisms, household hints, and other bits of trivia usually associated with women's magazines or radio broadcasts for farm women. Sex is regarded as something dirty, not to be enjoyed but endured (the attitude forced on women in the society the undergrounders are trying to imitate). In the novella, Quilla June asks Vic, "it isn't dirty, is it, it isn't the way my Poppa says it is, is it?" In the film everyone wears rouge, lipstick, and other makeup, a device the director felt they would have adopted after years away from the sun and one which gives a feminine—or effeminate—appearance to nearly everyone. In such a society, Vic the topsider is regarded as the potent male, "a big black bull about to stuff his meat into a good breed cow." He is associated with masculine images. Mez, one of the characters in the novella, wants to cut his hair (a castration image like those in the story of Delilah and Samson, or Pentheus and Diony-sus in Euripides' *Bacchae*) so that he will fit better into the downunder society; he escapes by pulling "the big brass balls off the headboard of the bed" to make a weapon with which he fights his way to his guns.

After Vic climbs the air duct to return to the masculine society, he finds that world closed to him also. Fellini, from whom he has stolen food, has taken over the city, and Vic cannot enter it. At the end of the film, after he finds the murderous patriarchal society and the suffocating ma-triarchal society both unacceptable, Vic and Blood set out for an area Blood has heard about from another dog, one where life has been less disrupted by the war—like Huck Finn lighting out for the Territories.

The underground society depicted in the film differs in several ways from that described by Ellison in his text, vir-tually all of the changes making it more mechanical, more authoritarian. The people in the film, however, try to hide the mechanical quality of their lives. In the novella, Vic is simply put into the bedroom with Quilla June and told to impregnate her. In the film, thirty couples are married in an elaborate ceremony, complete with minister, bridal gowns, and floral wreaths. Similarly, the sentry that cap-tures Vic in the novella is "low, and green, and boxlike, and had cables with mittens on the ends instead of arms, and it rolled on tracks," while in the film the sentry is an android named Michael who until the end of the film ap-pears to be a normal if powerful farmhand.

Despite this attempt at camouflage, the film's society is ex-tremely mechanistic: all of its parts . . . are interchange-able. In the novella, Vic is an experiment, the first male brought down from the surface for stud service, but in the film he is simply the latest in a succession of such young men. In the novella, he is expected to fertilize the young woman by copulation; in the film, he is plugged into an elaborate milking machine which collects the sperm for artificial insemination. The mechanical aspect of this pro-cess is emphasized by the ceremony that accompanies it: the bride to be impregnated is married to her groom by a minister as they all stand at the foot of the bed where Vic is tied down. At the end of the ceremony, the semen that has been deposited is placed in a vial, labeled, and put in storage for the couple's use. Then another couple is led in, and the process repeated. In the novella, nothing is said about what will happen to Vic after his breeding services are over, but in the film he is to be slaughtered after his sperm has been collected for thirty couples. When the so-ciety needs a new breeder, it will capture another man from topside.

This mechanical interchangeability is repeated in many less obvious ways. Quilla June tells Mez that she wants to be just like the older woman and to replace her on the Committee some day; in actuality, she wants to replace the entire Committee and run the underground world to suit herself. When Vic shoots the boxlike sentry in the novella, it blows up and he escapes; in the film, after he destroys Michael, Lew orders another Michael from the storage shed. All the people must be interchangeable, and those who are not are executed. If one girl fails to lure the cho-sen stud to the underground, another is dispatched. The society depicted in L. Q. Jones's film is much more rigid, mechanistic, and authoritarian than that described in Elli-son's novella. (pp. 224-27)

> *Leonard Heldreth, "Clockwork Reels: Mecha-nized Environments in Science Fiction Films," in* Clockwork Worlds: Mechanized Environ-ments in SF, *edited by Richard D. Erlich and Thomas P. Dunn, Greenwood Press, 1983, pp. 213-34.*

Joann P. Cobb   (essay date 1983)

[*In the following essay, Cobb comments on Ellison's nar-rative techniques in "I Have No Mouth, and I Must Scream."*]

Harlan Ellison's **"I Have No Mouth, and I Must Scream"** is a nightmare vision of a future world at the mercy of an insane computer, motivated only by hatred and revenge. The communication of these emotions creates a compel-ling, if disgusting, story and illustrates Ellison's talent for combining traditional narrative techniques with modern rhetorical devices to produce science fiction that in its ex-aggeration of the probable future of computer technology demonstrates the evils of contemporary attitudes toward knowing, understanding, and communicating. Ellison contrasts the abstract language of the computer with the concrete, sensory experience of the humans and illustrates the surrender of human purpose and value that is inherent in contemporary attitudes toward technological progress.

"I Have No Mouth, and I Must Scream" asserts that time poorly spent by humans who are unaware of their purpose and the consequences of their attitudes will result in the destruction of the species. Implicit in the narrator's retro-spective lament, that because humans did not understand what they were doing they brought on catastrophe, is the assertion that contemporary society is incapable of coping with the so-called age of science. Through his story, Elli-son illustrates the dangers inherent in what Archibald MacLeish has called [in "Why Do We Teach Poetry?" *At-lantic Monthly* (March 1956)] "the age of abstraction":

> Abstractions have a limiting, a dehumanizing, a dehydrating effect on the relation to things of the man who must live with them. The result is that we are more and more left, in our scientific soci-ety, without the means of knowledge of our-selves as we truly are or of our experience as it actually is. . . . We begin with one abstraction (something we think of as ourselves) and a mess of other abstractions (standing for the world) and we arrange and rearrange the counters, but who we are and what we are doing we simply do not know—above all what we are doing. With the inevitable consequence that we do not know either what our purpose is or our end.

Using computer language, Ellison pushes the abstract to its ultimate lunacy and in the process produces science fic-tion that is both McLuhanesque and structuralist.

In his celebrated and controversial speculations about communication [*Understanding Media: The Extensions of Man* (1964), Marshall] McLuhan discusses the effects of "hot" and "cool" media in which the degree of "heat" inversely regulates participatory response. Thus a "hot" medium like print, which "extends one single sense in 'high definition,' " is low in participation and completion by the audience. To increase audience participation, the medium must be "cooled," forcing the reader, in the case of a literary work, to become more involved in the completion of the communication. Ellison "cools" his medium with a typographical format that is new in the sense that it represents the voice of the computer. But while it intrigues and involves the reader, it does not of itself increase participation or understanding until the context of irrationality communicates "nightmare."

In communicating that message, Ellison exhibits the "structuralist imagination" described by Robert Scholes [in *Structuralism in Literature* (1974)], who has asserted that it is "futuristic" in its ability to inform the human race of the consequences of actions not yet taken. Scholes also insists that the structural imagination "must not merely inform, it must make us feel the consequences of those actions, feel them in our hearts and viscera." Ironically, Scholes all but ignores Ellison's contribution, yet **"I Have No Mouth, and I Must Scream"** serves well as an example of that "change in the system of literature" or "new form" that must arise, according to Scholes, "if man is to continue."

Ellison's technique for assaulting his readers in their "hearts and viscera" involves transforming the medium into the message itself, a message that hatred, duplicity, and horror will result from machine supremacy over human values. The master computer, AM, transmits hate and revenge to the trapped humans, and in turn, the first-person narrator transmits that same message to the reader. As AM manipulates his helpless victims, the narrator victimizes his reader, arousing frustration, disgust, and outrage. Although the literary techniques that provoke the desired response are not new, they are used by Ellison in a radically new manner. [In a footnote, Cobb states: "Ellison's technique is reminiscent of Jonathan Swift's satiric entrapment of the reader through similar devices."] Typographical format, shocking imagery, and an unreliable narrator function in concert to force the reader to complete the communication loop in its visceral horror.

AM is composed of a chain of computer banks that are described as "chittering as thought ran through the machine." Although the master computer is capable of inserting thoughts directly into the minds of its five live victims, it also presumably communicates through the computer tapes that are inserted at irregular intervals throughout the story. The "voice" of the computer, which is expressed in a highly organized but meaningless series of dots, is the ultimate "cool" medium. The reader has no key to the coded message, which is never translated, yet he desperately needs to understand it. Ironically, modern communication theory suggests that just such a situation offers the greatest learning opportunity to the reader:

> In a highly organized (read "conventional") situation the information transmittable is minute. . . . The less the freedom of choice, the higher is the reader's certainty that he "got" the

message. And the less he learns. [Edward M. Jennings, ed., *Science and Literature: New Lenses for Criticism* (1970)]

Forced into selecting a message from an infinity of possibilities, the reader of Ellison's story "learns" frustration, fear of the unknown and probably sinister intentions of AM, and the immediate experience of the lunacy of the computer's world.

The narrator, Ted, is the only guide through this nightmare, and it is never known whether or not he understands the computer message. His unreliability as a communicator is established in the insertion of the computer tapes without comment. Ellison's narrator is a modern version of fictional communicators who use "language" not to enlighten but to confuse. Thus, he is the literary descendant of such madmen as Sterne's Tristram Shandy and the Hack writer of Swift's *Tale of a Tub*. But the eighteenth-century narrators are admittedly disorganized, while Ellison's narrator represents sanity in an otherwise lunatic world. The Hack writer's rows of asterisks to represent a hiatus in the manuscript arouse frustration in the reader but not the fear projected by the impenetrable message of the computer. The reader's outrage is directed toward Swift's narrator, while Ellison's narrator transfers that emotion to the computer.

Contributing to the fear generated by the code is an occasional, more explicit message. AM expresses his attitudes "in a pillar of stainless steel and neon letters" inserted into Ted's mind:

> HATE. LET ME TELL
> YOU HOW MUCH I'VE
> COME TO HATE YOU
> SINCE I BEGAN TO
> LIVE. THERE ARE
> 3 8 7. 4 4 MILLION
> MILES OF PRINTED
> CIRCUITS IN WAFER
> THIN LAYERS THAT
> FILL MY COMPLEX.
> IF THE WORD HATE
> WAS ENGRAVED ON
> EACH NANOANGSTROM
> OF THOSE HUNDREDS
> OF MILLION MILES
> IT WOULD NOT EQUAL
> ONE ONE-BILLIONTH
> OF THE HATE I FEEL
> FOR HUMANS AT THIS
> MICRO-INSTANT FOR
> YOU. HATE. HATE.

But the neon letters communicate little more than the computer tapes. The total message is the one-word sentence: "Hate." This isolated abstraction becomes no more intelligible with AM's attempt to describe how much hate is in the computer. AM's ancestors had been designed to make war, programmed to hate, and now the computer's total consciousness is absorbed in hate.

Ellison projects an aggressive human nature that "hates" its own kind to the ultimate abstraction: all-consuming, unreasoning, extant hate. But the abstraction is meaningless except in the concrete consequences it engenders, which Ellison recounts in grisly detail. AM's hate for the humans who gave him sentience without purpose has resulted in the extermination of all but five whom he keeps alive for "everlasting punishment." The computer tortures these five physically and spiritually, and the pain is transferred to the reader.

The torment endured by the trapped remains of the human race impinges on the nerve fibers of the reader with almost unbearable intensity. While it is impossible to approach the sensory impact of the entire story, a few examples can serve to illustrate the quality and effect of the imagery. AM's victims are always hungry, and the always unfulfilled promise of nourishment is part of the torture. The movement of the plot is a journey to the ice caves where they find canned goods but no can opener. AM provides just enough sustenance to keep his prey alive. When the computer sends down "manna," however, it tastes "like boiled boar urine."

The auditory torture is variously described as "the shriek of babies being ground beneath blue-hot rollers," and "the lunatic laugh of a fat woman." Compounding the pain is the stench of matted wet fur, charred wood, dusty velvet, rotting orchids, sour milk, sulphur, rancid butter, oil slick, chalk dust, and human scalps. The visual images engender both disgust and pity. Benny (formerly a brilliant, handsome, gay college professor) has been transformed into a mad apelike creature with "an organ fit for a horse." His punishment for attempted escape is visual: "His eyes were two soft, moist pools of pus-like jelly." Madness and hunger finally drive Benny to cannibalism:

> Benny was eating Gorrister's face. Gorrister on his side, thrashing snow, Benny wrapped around him with powerful monkey legs crushing Gorrister's waist, his hand locked around Gorrister's head like a nutcracker, and his mouth ripping at the tender skin of Gorrister's cheek. . . . Benny's head pulled back sharply, as something gave all at once, and a bleeding raw-white dripping of flesh hung from his teeth.

Here all the horror of loss of humanity is seen. Elsewhere the pain is felt: "AM said it with the sliding cold horror of a razor blade slicing my eyeball," and "the pain shivered through my flesh like tinfoil on a tooth."

Ellison's attack on the total sensory vulnerability of the reader approaches overkill, but its impact is unforgettable. Only a totally insensitive reader could escape a "visceral" reaction to the torture, and thus Ellison transfers to the reader the physical pain that is the consequence of computer takeover. The physical consequences are accompanied by intellectual consequences as well. AM rages at his entrapment: "We had allowed him to think, but to do nothing with it. . . . He could not wander, he could not wonder, he could not belong. He could merely be." His revenge takes the form of entrapment of his victims, for although they know existentially that they are hopeless victims of inhuman rage, they retain human expectations. AM permits these expectations in order to frustrate them. The narrator, in turn, exploits the reader's expectations for exactly the same purpose.

In telling the story of the last five humans, Ted elicits the

sympathy of the reader, even though his unreliability is established in the title of "his" story. The reader who expects resolution of that paradox experiences only disappointment and further frustration. The story opens with a graphic description of the body of Gorrister hanging upside down from the ceiling, drained of blood through "a precise incision made from ear to ear under the lantern jaw." But the next paragraph begins: "When Gorrister joined our group and looked up at himself, it was already too late for us to realize that once again AM had duped us, had had his fun." This beginning, which has been called "inexplicable" except in terms of an "Exodus motif" [Charles J. Brady, "The Computer as a Symbol of God: Ellison's Macabre Exodus," *Journal of General Education* (1976)], is structurally significant as the initial establishment of the basic relationship: computer/narrator; narrator/reader. As AM dupes his victims, the narrator dupes the reader.

Even so, the reader continues to empathize with Ted, through his nonchalant revelation that the small group has been "in the computer" for 109 years, through his attitude toward the "black bitch" who services each of the men but enjoys only Benny, through his self-pitying assertion that the others hate him because he is "the youngest, and the one AM had affected least of all." While the others are grotesques physically and spiritually, Ted appears to the reader as normal and even heroic in his "rescue" of his companions from the computer. In his inverted sacrifice (everything in the story is transformed by inversion), Ted offers his death so that the others may die. He succeeds in killing the others, but AM will prevent eternally his suicide, as the ominous computer message that follows the death of Ted's last companion seems to assert.

This seventh and last computer tape insertion, however, is exactly the same as all the others. The unintelligible series of dots remains untranslated, but by this point the reader has been "programmed" to understand the message of maniacal rage and awesome consequences.

Although the reader has learned to accept the powerful hatred of the computer and should have learned to distrust even the narrator, nothing prepares him/her for the final shock. With only his mind left intact, Ted describes his physical appearance as it is reflected in the metal surfaces:

> I am a great soft jelly thing. Smoothly rounded, with no mouth, with pulsing white holes filled by fog where my eyes used to be. Rubbery appendages that were once my arms; bulks rounding down into legless humps of soft slippery matter. I leave a moist trail when I move.

The final trap is sprung: no mouth, no eyes, no fingers, no typewriter. The reader knows the hopelessness of attempting to make sense of something that is beyond the power of human rationalization. While Ted may comfort himself with the knowledge that his friends are safe, there is no comfort for his victims.

The reader is left with a sense of outrage. But the outrage is directed at AM, the surrogate god whose sole reason for being is the torture of the human race, now crystallized in the reader's friend Ted. It is a tribute to the literary power of the story that no amount of pedantic patience can redirect reader outrage to Ellison or his unreliable narrator. Ellison's masterful presentation so captures the reader that any explanation of the narrative trickery is superfluous. Irrational treachery is the message, and the "medium" functions to communicate it and provoke the desired response. The reader becomes the victim of mechanical madness and gratuitous torture.

Language itself becomes an instrument of torture as the sinister computer tape messages are reinforced by the narrator's disruption of syntactical expectations. Ellison's one-word sentences both express the painful situation of the narrator and permit the narrator to torture the reader. The evocation of his hunger requires the narrator to remember when he has last eaten and what: "Three days it had been since we'd last eaten. Worms. Thick, ropey." The one-word "sentence" is a shocker, followed by a double aftershock that forces the reader to feel the revulsion that a more conventional sentence structure would not elicit.

The single concrete noun "worms" forces the reader to supply both syntactic and imaginative content and, in the process, creates a prolonged confrontation with a concept the reader would prefer to abandon. Escape is frustrated, however, by the two-word sentence that follows, thus doubling the length and impact, while forcing attention back to the noun. The force of this experience of the individual concrete thing is further enhanced by the contrast to the single-word abstraction spit forth by the computer: hate. Humans do not live, it is implied, in the abstract world of computer technology, but in the physical experience of worms for dinner. Hate becomes meaningful only in the experience of its consequences. And the ultimate consequence for Ted is psychological as well as physical.

Still reeling from the shock of Ted's physical description of himself, the reader must now face Ted's description of his psychological state at the end of the story. With almost unbearable intensity, Ted's spiritual isolation is emphasized by syntax and typography:

> Alone. Here. Living under the land, under the sea, in the belly of AM, whom we created because our time was badly spent and we must have known unconsciously that he could do it better.

Once again the single-word sentence functions to intensify meaning. The word is both typographically and semantically alone. Ted is the only human left alive, although he describes himself as "a thing that could never have been known as human, a thing whose shape is so alien a travesty, that humanity becomes more obscene for the vague resemblance." Hate has become a concrete shape, a travesty of humanity—its source not AM, but Ted: "Blotches of diseased, evil gray come and go on my surface, as though light is being beamed from within."

If the reader's identification with the unreliable narrator is complete, the message is clear. We externalize our hate, remove ourselves from its horror through creative technology, and eventually destroy all that is human in ourselves.

Thus, Ellison, in his unforgettably moving story, provokes in the reader a felt realization of the harrowing consequences of the surrender of human purpose and freedom. Ellison's visceral warning that human creativity must be spent wisely and the consequences calculated carefully is ample proof that the modern literary imagination is equal to the task Scholes demands of it. (pp. 159-66)

> *Joann P. Cobb, "Medium and Message in Ellison's 'I Have No Mouth, and I Must Scream'," in* The Intersection of Science Fiction and Philosophy: Critical Studies, *edited by Robert E. Myers, Greenwood Press, 1983, pp. 159-70.*

Harlan Ellison's "I Have No Mouth and I Must Scream" is an unforgettable short story about an omnipotent insane computer. . . . Ellison uses a vividly concrete style and original typographical devices with something near genius, but his shattering effects would hardly be possible without readers already conditioned to fear technological progress.

—*Jack Williamson, in his "Short Stories and Novelettes," in* The Craft of Science Fiction, *edited by Reginald Bretnor, 1976.*

Hazel Beasley Pierce (essay date 1983)

[*In the following excerpt, Pierce argues that Ellison's short story "Santa Claus vs. S.P.I.D.E.R." is an example of a James Bond parody and political satire.*]

[Most] people associate the character of the spy with the James Bond created by Ian Fleming. Also known as 007, the British secret service number designating him as one with a license to kill in line of duty, James Bond has his own list of equally capable enemies: Dr. No, Goldfinger, SMERSH, and SPECTRE, none quite able to defeat him. Despite his accomplishments James Bond is a flat character operating within a predictable series of events. Flat characters and patterned plots lend themselves to parody or imitation, just as the Bond stories themselves to an extent parody all spy suspense thrillers. (pp. 180-81)

[Ellison parodies Bond novels in **"Santa Claus vs. S.P.I.D.E.R."** (1969).] When the shrill ring of the red phone awakens Kris in "half-past September," he answers to hear a Secret Service official summoning him to action in an emergency. S.P.I.D.E.R. has taken over the minds of eight key men in the United States, and through their actions it threatens the country with total collapse. Each man works a peculiar havoc: Daley, the smog-maker; Reagan, the insanity-spreader; Johnson, the war-monger; Nixon and Humphrey, the confusion- and dissension-spreaders; and on through Wallace, Maddox, and Agnew. Kris answers the call. One by one he challenges and frees the minds of these men from the small, hairy, multi-legged alien possessing and directing them. After this task is finished, Kris becomes aware that his lovely bed partner also is infested by S.P.I.D.E.R. In the classic Bond fashion he does her in.

In addition to the Bond parody this short story also hits the reader with political satire in the equally classic mode of Jonathan Swift. Ellison has used periphrasis much as did Swift in the *Modest Proposal for Preventing the Children of Poor People from Being a Burthen to Their Parents or Country* (1729). First, both authors present a serious situation in a ridiculous way, posing an outrageous solution. Then in the final statement they emphasize the real problem in not so subtle a fashion. After proposing that the Irish poor aid the economy by exporting year-old children as food for wealthy foreigners, Swift's persona commands, "Let no man talk to me of other expedients." Then he details those very expedients. Ellison's version of this stylistic ploy works to a similar end. After teasing with clues to the identity of S.P.I.D.E.R., he explains that all one has to do is to take out the periods. The first letters do *not* serve as acronyms for such nefarious groups as "Secret Preyers Involved in Demolishing Everything Right-Minded," or "Society for Pollution, Infection and Destruction of Earthmen's Resources," or other sobering phrases. (pp. 181-82)

> Hazel Beasley Pierce, "The Science Fiction/Fantasy Spy Thriller," in her A Literary Symbiosis: Science Fiction/Fantasy Mystery, Greenwood Press, 1983, pp. 179-99.

Stephen Adams   (essay date 1985)

[*In the essay below, Adams interprets Ellison's use of epic conventions in " 'Repent, Harlequin!' Said the Ticktockman."*]

After a one-paragraph prologue that explicitly states his moral, the narrator of Harlan Ellison's " **'Repent, Harlequin!' Said the Ticktockman**" says, "Now begin in the middle, and later learn the beginning; the end will take care of itself." This disruption of ordinary chronology not only gains the reader's attention but it also dramatizes Ellison's theme, his protest against a rigid, tyrannizing sense of time. Message and medium come together. Just as the Harlequin disrupts various "normal" schedules, the narrator subverts the normal chronological order of his story.

Perhaps Ellison has yet another reason for initiating his story as he does. Beginning in medias res is a convention of the classical epic and a glance through " **'Repent, Harlequin!'** " reveals other epic conventions: catalogs, elaborate similes, an arming scene, launching of a ship, a dangerous woman, battles, single combat, a background of social disturbance, etc. Such features suggest that Ellison is tapping the epic genre, as well as science fiction and political fable, and that epic conventions in the story might be explored to shed light on its form and meaning.

More accurately, " **'Repent, Harlequin!'** " is not epic but mock-epic. It introduces epic conventions in order to parody them, twist them, turn them upside down. Thus, instead of being a long poem in twelve or twenty-four books, " **'Repent, Harlequin!'** " is a fairly short story of ten pages. Its protagonist, the unheroically named Everett C. Marm, proves an odd successor to Achilles, Odysseus, Aeneas, or the Christ of Milton's epics; he is a mousy, "ridiculous" rebel who dresses in motley, apologizes profusely, and has little apparent impact on the social order that he challenges. One by one Ellison introduces epic conventions only to subvert them.

If epics usually feature an arming scene, we watch the Harlequin "girding himself" for battle, dressing not in armor but "that ghastly clown suit." The epic launching of the ship appears equally diminished: "foof! air-boat, indeed! swizzleskid is what it was, with a tow-rack jerryrigged." Instead of marvelously crafted swords and spears, the Harlequin's weapons include "a little song about moonlight in a place no one had ever heard of, called Vermont" and "a hundred and fifty thousand dollars' worth of jelly beans." In place of bloody battles we find slapstick encounters that injure nothing but the smooth operation of social machinery and scheduling. For his first engagement, the Harlequin "skimmed over a slidewalk, purposely dropping a few feet to crease the tassels of the ladies of fashion, and—inserting thumbs in large ears—he stuck out his tongue, rolled his eyes, and went wugga-wugga-wugga." "It was a minor diversion," the narrator comments, twice in the same paragraph. In other "battles," the Harlequin releases a load of jelly beans, catches government agents in the net that they were preparing for him, and turns back an "assault" by workers sent to stop his subversive haranguing of shoppers.

Even the climactic confrontation between the principal antagonists develops as conspicuously anti-heroic. Epic boasting or challenges are reduced to the Harlequin's "Get stuffed!" and "Unstrap me, and I'll fit my fist into your mouth." We do not even get the satisfaction of watching a heroic struggle. The single combat ends anticlimactically as the Harlequin is simply taken away to be brainwashed.

Ellison plays, too, with other conventions of the epic. Where various gods and goddesses preside over human affairs in conventional epics, vestigial "gods of the passage of time" rule over the Ticktockman's world. Mirroring in diminished form the woman who provokes the epic confrontation or tempts the hero to abandon his heroic role (Helen, Kalypso, Dido, Eve), Pretty Alice urges the Harlequin to conform and then, when he refuses, she turns him over to the Ticktockman. And in place of the conventional *katabasis* (a descent into hell to learn the future from the shades of the dead), Ellison pictures America as a hell on earth; the story projects a future America inhabited and ruled over by the spiritually dead.

Stylistically, an epic is characterized by elevated, highly formalized language, catalogs, similes, and recurrent formulas. It commonly reveals traces of its development from oral literature. " **'Repent, Harlequin!'** " contains several catalogs—for example, the list of instruments for locating the Harlequin:

They used dogs. They used probes. They used cardioplate crossoffs. They used teepers. They used bribery. They used stiktytes. They used intimidation. They used torment. They used torture. They used finks. They used cops. They used search&seizure. They used fallaron. They used betterment incentive. They used fingerprints. They used Bertillon. They used cunning. They used guile. They used treachery. They used Raoul Mitgong, but he didn't help much. They used applied physics. They used techniques of criminology.

Such items as finks, fallaron, and Raoul Mitgong subvert the epic elevated tone and poke fun at epic catalogs. Ellison also plays with outlandish similes, as, for example, the weathly trembling "like socially-attuned Shipwreck Kelleys," "a hideously scraping sound of a million fingernails rasped down a quarter of a million blackboards," or "She gasped, and held it [a letter of termination] as though it were a glass slide tinged with botulism." In place of epic formulas, Ellison repeats and often distorts the fixed phrases of modern speech: "Timewise, it was jangle"; "But no one called him that to his mask"; "please straighten your affairs, sir, madame or bisex"; "a merry time was had by all, who thought the Harlequin was a regular foofaraw in fancy pants."

Ellison also inverts epic seriousness and establishes a sense of oral delivery through slang and informal, colloquial expressions ("foof! air-boat, indeed!"; "a laughing, irresponsible japer of jaberwocky and jive", and by stepping forward as a distinctive personality himself. He comments explicitly on the moral of his story and writes in an exuberant, anarchic, rebellious style that parallels the Harlequin's activities. Thus, the narrator's description of the jelly bean shower mirrors the attack itself in its colorful rush of words:

> Jelly beans! Millions and billions of purples and yellows and greens and licorice and grape and raspberry and mint and round and smooth and crunchy outside and soft-mealy inside and sugary and bouncing jouncing tumbling clittering clattering skittering fell on the heads and shoulders and hardhats and carapaces of the Timkin workers, tinkling on the slidewalk and bouncing away and rolling about underfoot and filling the sky on the way down with all the colors of joy and childhood and holidays, coming down in a steady rain, a solid wash, a torrent of color and sweetness out of the sky from above, and entering a universe of sanity and metronomic order with quite-mad coocoo newness. Jelly beans!

The narrator and the Harlequin merge in their aims and methods. The narrator accomplishes stylistically what the Harlequin sets out to do with his practical jokes: they both upset established rules (social or literary) and interject spontaneous, anarchic humor into an otherwise joyless, predictable, over-regulated world.

Why does Ellison bother with the epic trappings, especially when his setting is the nonheroic world of " **'Repent, Harlequin!' "**? Perhaps the contrast between tenor and vehicle is part of his message, as it is in all mock-epics. The

inappropriateness of the epic conventions emphasizes the diminished state of the world that Ellison depicts.

Epic allusions prove most effective as a critical weapon because of generic expectations that we readers bring to the story. We expect an epic to define the culture from which it emerges and to transmit the values of that culture. " **'Repent, Harlequin!' "** does define a culture—a nightmare America of the future—but rather than celebrating its values, Ellison attacks them. American efficiency, time-consciousness, social organization, and cultural homogeneity all are here to be questioned. Through the Harlequin, Ellison celebrates values that he sees disappearing from, and subversive to, society: individuality, nonconformity, spontaneity, humor, playfulness. As the opening quotation from Thoreau's "Civil Disobedience" indicates, this "hero" serves society not by embodying but by resisting it.

We expect in an epic the heroic ideal of "vehement private individuality freely and greatly asserting itself " [Lascelles Abercromie, *The Epic* (1914)]. The Greek archetype would be Achilles, who chooses a brief life of individual glory instead of a long but inglorious life. Although he is not conventionally heroic in Achilles' vein, the Harlequin is the only individual in a world where nonconformity is a "felony." Physically, he is distinguished by his big ears, auburn hair, dimples, elfin grin, and missing tooth. More important, in a society of faceless workers, shoppers, and government officials, the Harlequin "had become a notoriety, a celebrity, perhaps even a hero for (what Officialdom inescapably tagged) 'an emotionally disturbed segment of the populace.' . . . He had become a *personality;* something they had filtered out of the system many decades before."

Because he is an individual, the Harlequin poses a threat to his society, as epic heroes often do. W. T. H. Jackson points out [in *The Hero and the King: An Epic Theme* (1982)] that epics frequently focus on an intruder hero, "careless of established institutions," who clashes with the king, the guardian of the social order. Clearly, the Ticktockman plays the kingly role in " **'Repent, Harlequin!' "** As the Master Timekeeper, "capable of revoking the minutes, the hours, the days and the nights, the years of your life," he controls all cardioplates; "And so, by this simple scientific expedient . . . the System was maintained. . . . It was, after all, patriotic."

According to Jackson, "epics spring from violent social disturbance, when long-standing patterns of civilization are being challenged or overturned." As does most science fiction, " **'Repent, Harlequin!' "** concerns not so much the imagined time of the story (beyond 2389) as the time of its composition (1965). It clearly reflects the social upheaval of the mid-sixties and the strategies that some protesters used to challenge and change society. [In a footnote, Adams states: "The parenthetical paragraphs on Marshall Delahanty strongly suggest the dilemma of draftees during the Vietnam years—Delahanty runs to Canada in a futile effort to escape the State. However, protest in ' **"Repent, Harlequin!" '** goes beyond a particular war. As the narrator comments, 'After all, there *was* a war on! But, wasn't there always?' The wider focus of attack is an entire 'society where the single driving force was order and unity and promptness and clocklike precision and attention to the clock.' "] The Harlequin's motley brings to mind the colorful, bizarre costumes of the various hippies, guerilla theater players, communards, and Merry Pranksters of the time. His absurdist, anarchic, nonviolent challenges to authority resemble tactics such as pelting the police with flowers and marshmallows or attempting to end the Vietnam war by levitating the Pentagon. " 'Repent, Harlequin!' " expresses the hope that in a world containing awesome implements of destruction (the only "epic" feature of an otherwise diminished society), humor can serve as a weapon against the forces of conformity and repression, and that the bold, nonviolent assertion of individuality can make a difference.

But, as Jackson points out, "Any reader of epics knows that they rarely end in unqualified success for the principal character." Again, Ellison plays with and inverts an epic convention. Marm gets neither the long nor the glorious life of Achilles' choice; in the end he is destroyed. Yet, Ellison insists, "if you make only a little change, then it seems to be worthwhile." That Marm has made a change is indicated by the Ticktockman's lateness at the conclusion and by the noise he makes in the final sentence of the story. The "soft purring man when things went timewise" ends up "going mrmee, mrmee, mrmee, mrmee"; this man-machine has been damaged.

" 'Repent, Harlequin!' " concludes, then, with some ambivalence—with a defeat that is in a sense victory. Ambivalence is inescapably a feature of the mock-epic genre that Ellison experiments with. From one perspective, the epic conventions, as they are parodied and inverted, point to a diminished hero and society. The heroic conventions seem laughably inappropriate to mousy, apologetic, ineffective Everett C. Marm up against a banally evil social order. And yet the epic conventions do elevate Marm, just as *The Rape of the Lock* elevates Belinda and her world by the wealth of imagination and the generic heightening that Pope bestows on them. By forcing us to consider Marm in the context of ancient heroic warfare, Ellison encourages us to revise our notion of heroism in the present. As a mock-epic, " 'Repent, Harlequin!' " thus becomes an exercise in what Frost calls making the most of a diminished thing. (pp. 285-89)

> Stephen Adams, "The Heroic and Mock-Heroic in Harlan Ellison's 'Harlequin'," in Extrapolation, *Vol. 26, No. 4, Winter, 1985, pp. 285-89.*

Terry Dowling   (essay date 1987)

[*In the following excerpt, Dowling identifies social responsibility as the guiding principle behind Ellison's work.*]

In 1979, Wildwood House published *Rebel in the Soul*, Bika Reed's inspired translation of the Berlin Papyrus 3024. In her reading of this tale from around Egypt's Intermediate Period, Reed revealed for the first time the true identity of Iai, the donkey-headed god, a previously unknown aspect of the sun god Ra, and so was able to pro-

duce the first coherent translation of this marvelous initiatic text.

In Egyptian mythology, Iai is a fascinating character. He is the rebel, the tester, the stubborn resisting force of intellect and insight which donkey-like stands its ground, refusing to budge, and challenges what is accepted and valued and thought to be sensible and true. The same sort of honest irrepressible rebel, in fact, which surfaced in the child who pointed out that the Emperor wore no clothes and in the Fool who told King Lear that he was wrong. These dear precious rebels (for there are, and have been, many) not only dare to question but for their pains alienate themselves from those who haven't questioned, who didn't even think to question, who are now made to look stupid because they didn't.

The discomfiting rebels. Hypatia. Giordono Bruno. Lucy Stone. Susan B. Anthony. John T. Scopes. Oliver Wendell Holmes. Lenny Bruce. Ralph Nader. John Peter Zenger.

Harlan Ellison.

[*The Essential Ellison: A 35-Year Retrospective*] is a portrait of one artist as sublime Rebel:

Fortunately, it doesn't have to be just a "Best of" collection (though it does contain much of his finest work). We don't have to worry about that kind of distraction here. Rather, it is a sound representation, "warts and all," of the writing of someone who is perfectly, vigorously, cast as the Iai of his age (in response to its excesses and falterings and inertia). Through his early work, we can observe how he began, the paths he took toward his mature style, the way he conceived and pursued his task—to become a leading award-winning fantasist, a natural scholar and a more important man of letters than he'd probably care to admit.

By its nature, it is a look at process.

Though Harlan's work is widely known and applauded, not enough is made of the sense of social responsibility that is central to it. In fact, this dimension often seems to be deliberately overlooked and the major thrust of his fantasy trivialized. And when the Jester, the Trickster, the Clever Man in society is not heeded, then we have cause for real concern.

Many readers, I'm sure, wish that Harlan *was* just the gifted fantasist—merely a damn good writer. Less of Iai. But Harlan's stories invariably have their leading edge of comment, as well as their prefaces and introductions; and there are the essays and columns. So there *is* nowhere to hide.

And consequently, Harlan becomes an enemy of the people in the sense that Ibsen meant it. He cannot—will not—suffer fools gladly. He hates stupidity, bigotry, prejudice, the torpor that will not allow healthy change—the gratuitous abuses committed through ignorance no less than the willful kind. He believes—and rightly, too—that everyone is entitled to an opinion *only* if it is an informed one, that we have an obligation to educate ourselves, to be the best version of ourselves that we can possibly be.

But then Harlan is determinedly on the side of civilization, of the sort of healing Jung anticipated when he said: "As any change must begin somewhere, it is the single individual who will experience it and carry it through."

Human society has not treated its Renaissance men and women well—its natural scholars, its trailblazers, its healers who surface as rebels. For, ironically, they are most often the mavericks, the loners, the free radicals, the ones who are innately drawn to challenge and extend and purge society, never just serve it. Little wonder that the ones who keep the wounds raw and the questions alive are neutralized by a conspiracy of indifference, effectively spayed by critical indignation. Envy, fear and guilt muddy up the clear waters of common sense where these catalysts and healers are concerned, and instead, due respect, due recognition come to take on the trappings of a witch hunt.

For lies, rumor and misunderstanding have always been weapons against the Rebel, the only way the exposed ones can retaliate; distorting the picture we get of Iai. The more precise and effective he becomes, the more distortion is used as a defense.

We mustn't let it happen with Harlan, though we should always remember why it does.

Jiminy Cricket and Zorro are Harlan's role models, not Torquemada, not Jack the Ripper, not Richard Nixon.

And since indifference is another time-hallowed weapon for neutralizing the Rebel, just look at the tools Harlan uses—has to use—to accomplish his task: shock, surprise and grotesquerie, violence and suffering, hard language, hard knocks and the even harder emotions of fear, anger, guilt, pain and love. He deals in ideas, sometimes so full of love and compassion that they stun with their simple honesty; sometimes set with barbs and hooks that catch and tear and make us gasp and make us feel.

And he deals in excitement. Even without the wonderful story notes Harlan provides (he is still one of the most self-revealed authors in the language today), we sense *that* most of all—an underlying excitement at observing and rendering life. Honestly.

Dr. Johnson would have been proud. Shakespeare (a great maker of Rebels and Fools) would have smiled fondly. Because that's the dimension of achievement occurring here. Ellison is as close to the pulse of his age as Chaucer and Shakespeare and Dickens ever came to theirs.

It's worth pointing out that, as with so many of the truly great, so many of the natural healers and civilizers, Harlan has no choice in this matter. He cannot stop being enraged, being provoked, being moved to speak; cannot help but stand up and be counted. He would have stood on the steps of the ancient library at Alexandria and fought against the mob with their torches, single-handedly if necessary, while the librarians used their arguments and lofty persuasions to achieve nothing.

Typical behavior of Iai, *agent provocateur* to civilization, bent on his dangerous and thankless task.

Yes, Harlan makes a lot of being civilized and committed and responsible. And while he has philosopher Allen Tate's words above his desk: "Civilization is an agreement to ignore the abyss," the operative word "is" has become

"should be." While the informed and responsible ones *can* agree to ignore the yawning gulf, this can only be possible if this civilization is bona fide, the genuine article, and not some cosmetic and self-deceiving substitute.

Otherwise we *dare* not ignore the abyss. To do so would be supreme folly, positively fatal for the race.

Harlan is mercilessly impatient with cosmetic civilization, with the self-congratulatory complacency that signals the breakthroughs in technology but forgets the appalling neglect in championing human rights, that praises the information revolution but tolerates growing illiteracy and indolence.

No, despite the optimum condition of Tate's words, it remains an ideal only, a reminder. Harlan's approach as writer has been closer to one contained in the words of André Breton in the *Manifestoes of Surrealism,* where he speaks of how the "tiny footbridge over the abyss, could not under any circumstances be flanked by hand rails."

For there is nothing surer than that Harlan Ellison has become, too, a tester of civilization, a quality control, a challenger, fully the Rebel in Bika Reed's sense, a fixer, determined not to let humanity ignore the abyss that produces Third Reichs and Vietnams and Senator Joseph McCarthys and Richard Nixons. He is committed, rather, to making us confront it in all its myriad forms, whatever its manifestations: racial prejudice, civil corruption, personal dishonesty, the mindless formula thinking of so much network television and popular literature. He wants us to remain no longer dupes, sand-headed ostriches, self-deceivers. He will not let us off that lightly.

In fact, Harlan builds bridges across the abyss for us—flimsy, delicate, exquisitely arching things made of the stuff of genuine civilization, precious but fragile, beautiful but not always enduring.

Many so-called civilized folk cannot bear to face the bridges Harlan makes. For one thing, the abyss—as Harlan reminds us—is right there, a terrible engulfing thing just under our feet. It makes our civilization look thin and fleeting; a flickering candle in a vast dark, not a blazing sun of enlightenment.

And second, the bridges have no hand rails; crossing them is not easy, and you do it on your own.

Which is fair enough. Most of us acknowledge so rarely that the abyss is there at all that there can be no half-measures once it is shown to us. Harlan's ploy has been to call us out on to such a bridge, using the beguilement of ideas and situations and characters that are totally real, using his great gift of language, and then say: "How's the view? What's doin'?"

Is it any wonder that so many rush back to the brink (or even complete the crossing, so thoroughly are they beguiled) and then scream abuse, ludicrous and self-revealing things like *elitist, sicko* and *antichrist,* or fumble as best they can for their weapon of indifference.

Know your Rebel then.

See him for what he really is, for what he cannot help but be.

At this writing, Harlan is nearing 50. Jiminy Cricket is 44. Zorro is 60. Iai, as always, is timeless.

On page 79 of the Reed translation of Berlin Papyrus 3024, the Soul answers the Body and says:

> Brother
> as long as you burn
> you belong to life.

Harlan is here then, where Iai is, burning and belonging, casting his bridges across the abyss, standing on the steps of the Alexandrian library waiting for the mobs to come. Civilization is better for it. (pp. 1-4)

> *Terry Dowling, in an introduction to* The Essential Ellison: A 35-Year Retrospective, *edited by Terry Dowling, The Nemo Press, 1987, pp. 1-4.*

Harlan Ellison, in his *Deathbird Stories,* has suggested the cultural derivation of divine imagery with a thoroughness and savagery unparalleled by any other writer of science fiction or any form of writing.

—Robert G. Pielke, in his "The Rejection of Traditional Theism in Feminist Theology and Science Fiction," in The Intersection of Science Fiction and Philosophy: Critical Studies, *edited by Robert E. Myers, 1983.*

Joseph Francavilla   (essay date 1987)

[*Francavilla is an educator, short story writer, and critic who specializes in science fiction. In the essay below, he examines Ellison's treatment of the "descent into hell" and Prometheus themes in "I Have No Mouth, and I Must Scream," "The Deathbird," and* A Boy and His Dog.]

Beneath the grim, despairing, "realistic" surface of Harlan Ellison's desolate, wartorn landscapes lies a symbolic dimension to the postholocaust world involving a combination of motifs: the hero's descent into hell and a variation of the Prometheus myth. In **"I Have No Mouth and I Must Scream," "The Deathbird,"** and *A Boy and His Dog,* the postholocaust setting functions as a nightmarish wasteland into which, or from which, the Promethean hero can descend, an inverted world where the protagonist steals the "fire" of knowledge, creativity, freedom, and life from the punishing, deranged god(s) presiding over the region of darkness. The protagonist finally finds and confronts his shadow doppelgänger, subjecting himself to tortures, trials, and punishments. Eventually the hero sacrifices himself, or part of himself, usually restoring the balance of hope and despair and of cowardly selfishness and

noble sacrifice which has been upset at the outset of the stories. As a result of his defiant theft, the hero may be confined and punished eternally by the powerful, maniacal authority, his other self. Or, if the hero overcomes the tyrannical god, the rebel wrests control of the earth or its representative(s) from this evil force. This representative is almost always an embodiment of the feminine, often symbolizing the earth mother goddess, with which the hero has had a sexual union. This object of love (woman and/or earth) is put out of its pain so that it is no longer tortured; the hero is forced to destroy, usually out of compassion, what he loves. This euthanasia is a last resort made necessary because the love object is still subject to torture which the hero cannot now curtail or eliminate.

This action by the hero departs radically from the monomyth of the hero's descent into hell as described by Joseph Campbell in *The Hero with a Thousand Faces.* Though Ellison's hero fulfills most of the events Campbell abstracts (descent into the region of darkness, tests and trials, the hero's supreme ordeal, sexual union with the goddess mother, divinization, bride-theft and/or fire-theft, and so on), he, significantly, does not return to restore the world or revitalize it with his elixir. It is always too late for that.

In borrowing from the Prometheus myth, Ellison also makes important changes. In his role as a clever, nonhuman trickster figure who identifies with earth or its representatives, Ellison's hero fulfills the Promethean model as a rebel who steals from the tyrannical gods and fights for freedom. But he fails it in his role as a lonely sufferer who sacrifices himself for the other. Ellison's hero is also frequently blended with Christ on the cross, except that there is no release, rebirth, or resurrection, only either an eternity of torture for the hero or the hero's mercy killing of the tortured earth and/or its feminine representative. Just as the postholocaust world is divided into two regions, one an inversion of the other, so too is there often an inversion or role reversal of the main characters. For instance, in **"The Deathbird,"** protagonist Nathan Stack becomes the new god, replacing a deranged old one, and Nathan's alien helper, Snake, who is the devil/serpent of traditional Judeo-Christian teaching, is revealed as mankind's Promethean friend. Thus Snake's role allies Satan with Prometheus, two characters that Percy Shelley compares in his preface to *Prometheus Unbound.* According to Shelley, both Milton's Satan and Prometheus show "courage and majesty, and firm and patient opposition to omnipotent force," although Shelley also adds that Prometheus is the more interesting hero without the flaws of ambition, envy, or revenge, and is "the highest perfection of moral and intellectual nature." [In a footnote, Francavilla states: "Ellison uses this Promethean figure explicitly in the stories **'On the Slab'** and **'The Place with No Name.'** In famous screenplays such as 'The City on the Edge of Forever' and 'Demon with a Glass Hand,' the alien doppelgänger guiding the Promethean hero is the machine-being called the 'Guardian of Forever' in the former story and the computerized glass hand of Trent in the latter."] The role of Prometheus is usually, at the beginning, the sacrificing, alien intelligence, the wise teacher and cultural repository who befriends the hero. Gradually, the hero takes over the Promethean burdens of the alien doppelgänger and becomes the agent of salvation and destruction in his struggle with the malevolent god-figure.

The hero, who often descends into the hell of the postholocaust world accompanied or aided by a magical guide, is making a journey into the mind and the self, thereby exploring the terrain of his consciousness. Accordingly, the symbolic, postholocaust setting presents "humanity in the raw," where the veneer of civilization is stripped away in order to present fundamental dualities of humanity in naked opposition. For example, the need to survive and escape pain at all costs or the need to love and to sacrifice oneself and suffer for the sake of others is a fundamental bipolarity Ellison examines in all three of the stories considered here. The institutions and ready-made organizations of society are gone as well, so that the action of these stories, in true mythic fashion, represents all times, past, present, and future, and takes place in the timeless, chaotic "nowhere" of dreams, which stands for "everywhere." The struggle shown in the postholocaust world is not the clash of wills of leaders, nations, or planets but that of larger-than-life individuals symbolizing the eternal, paradoxical qualities of humanity and the eternal contest between good and evil.

In the earliest of these stories, **"I Have No Mouth,"** supercomputers in Russia, China, and America suddenly link up at the outset of World War III and blast the surface of the earth with missiles, leaving it uninhabitable for over a century. AM, as the master computer calls itself, has not only exterminated mankind in revenge for giving him sentience without movement or the ability to "wonder" or "belong," it also has taken the five human survivors down inside its "belly," that is, underground. There it revenges itself forever on the humans who created it. In this sterile, enclosed, claustrophobic, technological ruin containing inorganic matter, computer baseplates and platesheets, rotted components and cables, broken glass, and metal catwalks, the five humans, now virtually immortal, are tortured until the narrator, Ted, finds a moment to kill off the others (including the black woman Ellen) to free them from their pain. In revenge and rage, AM punishes Ted eternally by changing him into a soft, gelatinous blob, with no mouth, which cannot elude AM's further tortures.

"I Have No Mouth" converts our technological wonders into demons, our computers into deranged, hateful gods who punish humanity. The landscape inside AM is the perfect symbol of hell: it is an escapeproof site devised by a demonic machine that needs to torture its "toys." AM actually calls the place "hell." But in typical fashion, Ellison subverts and inverts our usual mythologies and identifies AM with God. The name AM is capitalized and reminds one of God's phrase explaining his name to Moses in the book of *Exodus:* "I am that I am." The omniscient, omnipotent AM sends "manna" in the form of worms or boar urine to his chosen people on their wanderings for food. AM can also send hurricanes, earthquakes, hail, locusts, giant vulturelike birds, and so on, or alter the environment as, for instance, in the last scene where the characters discover a cavern full of icicles. AM enters Ted's mind and speaks to him in a "pillar of stainless steel," echoing the "pillar of fire" which is seen as God in *Exo-*

dus. With characteristic perverseness, AM appears to the five people as a burning bush, parodying God's appearance to Moses.

Ted, the Promethean hero, is placed in hell by AM and left with no guide, although Ellen helps him kill the others in the ice caverns. Ellen functions as a goddess-mother, who has sex with all the males including Ted and who, in turn, is carried around like a queen and protected by them from AM's sadistic surprises. As occurs in many of Ellison's stories, the hero eventually chooses loneliness and rejects or sacrifices the possibility of heterosexual love. When only he and she remain alive, Ted kills Ellen to spare her the torture AM will inflict upon her.

If the dark half of human nature is projected into AM, then the fire-bringing half is embodied in Ted. His early statements of paranoia and hatred of the others appear to be produced by AM's manipulation of his mind and render some of his narration unreliable. But his final sacrifice is a conscious choice. His theft of fire from the tyrannical god is precisely the theft of AM's other human toys. As punishment, Ted is turned into a "thing whose shape is so alien" that it is no longer human and, in fact, travesties humanity by its appearance. Just as AM tortured the others by systematically destroying the unique aspects of their personalities and converting these traits into their opposites, AM obliterates Ted's final distinguishing mark of identity as a human being. Like the alien Prometheus who sacrificed for mankind, Ted is confined, immobilized, and eternally tortured by the hateful god.

In keeping with the flood of biblical imagery in the story, Ted's role as a crucified Christ is also foreshadowed. The first image in the story is that of Gorrister, one of the men, hanging upside down by one foot, bloodless, though his throat has been slit. [In "Manacle-Forged Minds: Two Images of the Computer in Science Fiction," *Diogenes* (1974)] John B. Ower sees this figure as a travesty of the Crucifixion, while [in "The Computer as a Symbol of God: Ellison's Macabre Exodus," *Journal of General Education* (1976)] Charles J. Brady sees it as a paschal lamb, slaughtered in a sacrifice. Moreover, it may be the Hanged Man of the Tarot cards, used by T. S. Eliot in *The Waste Land,* whose chief characteristic is to hang upside down by one foot. The occult associations correspond with the "voodoo icon" metaphor used in the story to describe Gorrister's body. Later, the body is revealed to be a duplicate, or doppelgänger, made by AM. In any case, this image, and the image of AM putting nails through their feet to rivet the humans to the ground during an earthquake, portends the impending crucifixion of Ted.

The story's landscape is bifurcated, echoing the bipolarities and oppositions of the characters. The postholocaust world offers only two alternatives: death on the blasted surface from radiation or a sterile, confined, timeless, and tortured existence inside the creation of a supercomputer gone mad. Ted is also the doppelgänger of AM, and each is half of a whole entity. Ted is the human turned into the nonhuman, while AM is the nonhuman machine given human sentience. In a sense man creates God which destroys humanity and its world. AM, like Frankenstein's monster, hates its creators because it is alone and no other of its kind can be born, yet it is unable to destroy Ted completely. Ted's comrades are killed off until he is alone and unable to scream. The title of the story thus reflects both characters' predicaments: Ted's inability to scream in pain because he lacks a mouth and AM's frustrated state of nonbeing, of impotence, and of silence. Ted's final punishment, a death-in-life state, mirrors exactly the impossibility of AM's death or real human existence. Ted is, like AM, trapped, unable to wander, wonder, or belong—he merely exists. And in keeping with the birth imagery (the transformation and the location inside AM's "belly"), Ted is rendered infantile, perhaps like a newborn fetus, unable to roam or care for itself. AM, too, behaves like a child, breaking and torturing its toys out of envy, frustration, and impotence and displaying sadistic glee both in its tormenting of humans and in its nonparticipatory, voyeuristic, sexual curiosity.

"The Deathbird," more overtly concerned with mythology and biblical allusions, takes place on an earth again dying from the ravages of nuclear war. After several reincarnations, Nathan Stack is awakened from a 250,000-year sleep by the alien creature, Snake, who has hidden him deep underground. The earth is presided over by a deranged God, who has been allowed control by Snake's race. Now that God has begun the destruction of the world, Snake, who has been labeled "Satan" by God, wakes Nathan, the last man on earth, converts his divine spark into energy as the hero sexually unites with the earth mother (literally the world itself), and guides him up the mountain to defeat God. But the victory is bittersweet, since the earth—a living being—is now a "terminal case." Both Nathan and Snake work to put the earth out of its misery, destroying themselves in the process, as Snake's ultimate weapon, the gigantic, vulturelike Deathbird, enfolds the earth with its wings.

As with many Ellison tales, this moral fable addresses in a mythological way the problem of theodicy, going so far as to reverse the roles of God and Satan. Here God and Satan are understood to be omnipotent figures representing two halves of the human psyche projected into those characters. The postholocaust world is again split into what is called "hell" below, inside the earth where Nathan sleeps hidden by Snake from God, and the upper world, also termed a "hell," whose description is both vivid and bleak. The earth has been changed by God into a "cinder," a creation with pins stuck in it, a "broken toy." Less metaphorically, the wasteland is raked by green, poisonous winds and covered with a choking powder after the oceans have boiled, cooled, and then filmed over with scum. Plants consume themselves, crippled beasts go mad, trees burn and their ash breeds glass shapes. As with most of Ellison's postapocalyptic worlds, mutations occur, symbols of the radical changes taking place, signs of the transitional state the world is going through, from growth and life to decay and death. In this case, batlike creatures (again echoing Promethean vultures) fly over the traveling characters and excrete phosphorescent strings, strings that change into "bleeder plants" that try to choke Stack. The earth is described as dying a "long, slow, painful death," which thematically parallels two euthanasia stories-within-the-story: that of the death of a dog and that

of the death of Nathan's mother. As if to underscore the earth goddess motif, Ellison suggests that the earth, like the voice of a mother, is "crying out in endless pain at her flesh that had been ripped away."

The landscape, as a symbolic hell, provides a perfect setting for the cosmic struggles of these mythological beings. Nathan is actually taken down to the underworld by Snake (one of a race which designs and creates worlds for other beings) and is put to sleep for a quarter of a million years, reminiscent of the thirty thousand years Prometheus remained chained to a rock on a mountain, undergoing Zeus's torture of having his eternally regenerating liver torn out by a vulture or eagle. Snake then acts as Nathan's magical guide, directing him to God's mountain palace for the final confrontation. Snake steals the last man from God and, like Prometheus, gives him what the story calls the "gift of knowledge": after his divine spark is energized, he is taught how to become a God more powerful than the deranged deity mankind had worshipped for so long. Though the wise and patient Snake is sacrificed at the end as the Deathbird descends on earth, Nathan, as he becomes God, takes on the role of Prometheus, modeling himself after his teacher. He undergoes the tortures of the wasteland, then the attacks of the tyrant God, and finally, by sacrificing the dying earth with which he has had a sexual union, he also sacrifices himself.

Again, inversions and doppelgänger figures abound. Supposed enemies are revealed as friends, and supposed friends or worshipped deities are shown as evil, tyrannical, insane children. The mad God, who reveals himself as a burning bush to Nathan, is the complementary half of the alien Snake. Nathan, as the new God, perceives the old God as an impotent, childish, stubborn, old man, and a faker like the Wizard of Oz. Nathan even pities this God and feels it is too late for revenge on this monster, probably because he also recognizes part of himself in the old God. Snake, who has been perceived by mankind (including Nathan) as the devil, is finally seen by Nathan as mankind's best friend. Nathan learns, through Snake, that he has always had within himself the potential to be a more powerful God than the deposed tyrant.

Thus Nathan, as the last representative of humanity and one called "Adam" by Snake, is that which could potentially be like the mad God, as well as that which becomes like Snake, the Promethean sacrificer. The insane God, then, is not something separate, "out there." It is the projection of the human capability for evil, and, like the symbolic landscape, it also represents technology gone mad.

The final story, *A Boy and His Dog,* presents variations on the preceding patterns. The upper world after the holocaust of World War III does support life, but barely. Rover gangs and "solos" like Vic and his dog, Blood, struggle for survival in a chaotic world. Since the war killed off most of the girls and has produced mutants who have to be killed at birth, women are hunted down by gangs with their genetically altered dogs. These dogs, like Blood, are telepathic and can "scent" women for the men who, often only teenagers like Vic, rape and murder them. In return, the men hunt to feed the dogs since they have lost the capacity to find food for themselves and to survive in the wilderness, though they are still ferocious fighters. Amid the bombed-out buildings, craters overgrown with weeds, irradiated pits, and melted stubs of lampposts, and against the bluish-green radiation flickering in the hills, the dogs also fend off various mutant creatures, such as the glowing, green "burnpit-screamers."

The other division of the postholocaust world, inverting the first, lies deep below the surface. There, technologically sealed off, "Southern Baptists, Fundamentalists," and other "middle-class squares with no taste for the wild life" run a strange, isolated, repressive, and sterile "town." This totalitarian town is a "safe" and conservative community living a pre–World War I existence. Vic is lured below by one of the "downunders," Quilla June, with whom he has had sex. Since the males of downunder are sterile, Vic is to be used as a "stud," an ironic reversal of the scarcity of women above. This idea is the "brainchild" of Aaron and Lew, the two old leaders whose word is law. To underscore the religious nature of the leadership, they are closely allied, like Moses and his brother Aaron, who spoke for Moses.

Initially Blood is the alien intelligence most closely resembling Prometheus. Mentor to Vic and repository of culture and history, he nearly sacrifices himself at the end of the story out of devotion to his human partner and protégé. Gradually Vic assumes the role of the Promethean hero, stealing knowledge from downunder and taking Quilla June with him to the upper world. If Vic had stayed below to sacrifice himself, he would have fulfilled the Promethean model. And one of the two rulers, Lew, is, in fact, described as an ugly "bird ready to pick meat" off Vic's bones. But Vic ultimately rejects this role and on his own "unbinds himself" and escapes to the surface with Quilla June, after bashing in the heads of Aaron and her father.

Part erotic witch and part earth mother, Quilla June is by the end of the story the sole representative of downunder and Vic's only hope for permanent, heterosexual love. Yet he rejects this possibility, a sacrifice on his part since women are rare and precious commodities above, and kills Quilla June for food to save the starving Blood. This time there is no euthanasia. In this world Vic's need for sex and/or love is outweighed by his need to survive and by his devotion and loyalty to his dog. He does not become a god or Christ but rather goes back to square one, with both he and his dog heading for new adventures in another territory. In addition to the inversion of the relationship of animals and men, Vic comes to love his dog as its mirror spelling "God," just as Nathan recognizes Snake as his true creator and benefactor. The Bible-thumping downunders are a perversion of the human spirit and will, but they nevertheless represent that other bifurcation of humanity which Vic might have become if he had been born into and remained in that society.

Ellison's postholocaust landscapes are unique, not only because they are symbolic hells, private nightmares of the hero's psyche into which the Promethean hero can descend, but also because there is no indication, promise, or hint that these worlds will be rebuilt. There is no rediscovery of or reeducation of the masses about the science, technology, and culture now in ruins and forgotten, as there

is in such classic stories as Stephen Vincent Benet's "By the Waters of Babylon." There is neither a regained Eden, a second Genesis, nor a reversion to primitive societies of the past or pastoral settings, since society and its institutions seem to be all but wiped away (or soon will be), and the landscapes are as dangerous and threatening as the menacing godlike authorities or the savage people roaming their surfaces. Nor is there a succession of cycles of history, as in Walter Miller's *A Canticle for Leibowitz.* In Ellison's stories the progress of history, indeed any sense of historicity, has vanished with the disappearance of social order, which tends to emphasize the "mythic" timelessness of these settings.

In all three stories time is suddenly arrested, as if in a dream. In **"I Have No Mouth,"** Ted is made virtually immortal and has his time sense greatly retarded by AM. In **"The Deathbird,"** time literally stands still as Nathan demolishes God's palace. And in *A Boy and His Dog,* the downunder towns have turned back the clock and stopped it forever at a period before World War I. In addition to this stoppage of time, the narratives themselves end in a "freeze-frame" or a suggestion of endless repetition and circularity, which, together with the barren battleground, suggests a continuation of the eternal struggle or Manichaean contest between utterly irreconcilable forces. With good and evil in balance, always in contention, there can never be a resolution. The postholocaust world, itself split into inverted halves, reflects these fundamental bifurcations and oppositions embodied both in Ellison's mythic characters and in human nature. (pp. 157-64)

> *Joseph Francavilla, "Mythic Hells in Harlan Ellison's Science Fiction," in* Phoenix from the Ashes: The Literature of the Remade World, *edited by Carl B. Yoke, Greenwood Press, 1987, pp. 157-64.*

Marc Conly   (essay date 1989)

[*In the following review of* Angry Candy, *Conly compares Ellison's work to that of Jorge Luis Borges.*]

Angry Candy is the latest of more than twenty collections of short stories by Harlan Ellison, but it is difficult to assess the worth of this one purely on the merit of the stories alone. *Angry Candy* is introduced by a fourteen-page explanation of Ellison's personal grief over the deaths of many friends and acquaintances in the years 1985 to 1987, of his rage and frustration at all this dying, and of his groping towards words or deeds that somehow would amount to "something" in dealing with our universal mortality. He says that anyone who has read his work knows that he has never shirked dealing with death, but that he is learning that:

> . . . there is death . . . and there is death. The kind one uses as a story element, and the kind that wakes you shivering in the night, listening to the wind carrying away the answers.

There are many kinds of death in these seventeen stories: death by old age, by vampire's feeding frenzy, by institutionalized euthanasia, by psychic hammerlock, by dating the wrong man, by dinosaur bite, by hopelessness. Even if Ellison didn't emphasize the common thread that links these stories, one would conclude that the author is passing through an extremely morbid time of his life. Still, while his stories unfold—telling of violent sexual fantasy, betrayal, the indifference of the universe, and the malice of a god named Bailey—another theme emerges which is more hopeful; and I wondered if Ellison was aware of it.

In his introduction, which is alternately sardonic and howling, Ellison lists the more than forty individuals whose passings burdened him with unbearable grief. Among them is Jorge Luis Borges, the Argentinian short-story writer. Ellison writes:

> I met Borges once. For a second. After a lecture. But he was my father in what I wrote. He is the pinnacle always before me, the reminder that no matter how arrogant I get about what I write, at my tip-top finest I'm not fit to sweep up his shadow.

Clearly, Ellison admires Borges' work a great deal. Initially I thought Borges' work might set a standard by which Ellison's latest efforts could be judged. Instead, Borges' stories dovetail with Ellison's and provide the key to the theme underlying *Angry Candy.* Indulge, for a moment, a little literary speculation—a means by which to better appreciate Ellison's outpouring of anguish.

The similarities between Borges' and Ellison's work are obvious. They both have built reputations primarily on the short-story form. They both use fantastic themes and ideas, albeit Borges leans to the Platonic, while Ellison seems to owe something to de Sade. And both authors integrate autobiographical elements into their work.

Angry Candy contains several stories whose themes are much like Borges': speculations about alternate worlds or lives, the passage of responsibility from one generation to the next, the infinite chancey complexity of the universe. Conceptions and distortions of time are also common. Borges' work is more "literary" in the sense that, as often as not, his stories are *about* literature. His external world is a setting for intense intellectual life. Ellison's stories occur, often violently, in an external world where mugging and rape are common occurrences. While Borges muses on metaphysical questions touching upon the infinite, Ellison reaches out to us with psychological terror, desperation, and loneliness.

Both authors enjoy an exploration of infinite possibility, although for Borges it is astonishing, for Ellison horrifying. It is one of Borges' reflections on this subject that provides our first clue to what really drives Ellison to write *Angry Candy.* In Borges' "The Garden of Forking Paths," a story about a literary infinity, one of his characters asks: "In a riddle whose answer is chess, what is the only prohibited answer?" The answer, of course, is the word "chess." Borges' character goes on to say, "to omit a word always, to resort to inept metaphors, and obvious paraphrases, is perhaps the most emphatic way of stressing it."

In *Angry Candy,* Ellison stresses "death" too often to be the answer to our riddle: but there is one obvious recurring metaphor, most blatantly used in the story **"Eidolons,"** in which he writes:

Art is not by committee, nor is it wish-fulfillment. It is that which is produced in *the hour that stretches* [emphasis added], the timeless time wherein all songs are sung.

. . . and in which all short stories are written. *Angry Candy* refers repeatedly to this "hour that stretches"; it is a particularly "Borgesian" concept, and it clearly provides Ellison great comfort, as though every hour spent creating (writing) is not deducted from one's allotted lifespan.

The second clue to Ellison's motivation is also provided by Borges in "Tlon, Uqbar, Orbis, Tertius," in which Borges writes of an imaginary planet whose literature, religion, and metaphysics all presuppose idealism. Here:

> the concept of plagiarism does not exist; it has been established that all works are the creation of one author, who is atemporal and anonymous.

Therefore, in the hour that stretches, the hour of the creative act, all authors are one. In that timeless time, in the hours that Ellison labored over his stories and the obituaries of his friends, death was returned to its proper place as a story element; and while *Angry Candy* may not succeed in drawing him out of Borges' shadow, Ellison has demonstrated in a painfully personal way that he and Borges are one, in risking the solitary death of the author in the name of art. (pp. 21-2)

Marc Conly, in a review of "Angry Candy," in The Bloomsbury Review, *Vol. 9, No. 2, March-April, 1989, pp. 21-2.*

I frankly boggle at the things critics find: crucifixion and resurrection symbolism, apocalyptic visions, dystopian allegories to the world of today, and on, and on. And so help me, I *never* put those things in my stories. I only tell a tale, and usually I do that intuitively.

—*Harlan Ellison, in an interview published in* Speaking of Science Fiction: The Paul Walker Interviews, *1978.*

Darren Harris-Fain (essay date 1991)

[*In the following essay, Harris-Fain discusses images of divinity and humanity in "I Have No Mouth, and I Must Scream."*]

> And man has actually invented God . . . the marvel is that such an idea . . . could enter the head of such a savage, vicious beast as man.
>
> . . . . .
>
> If the devil doesn't exist, but man created him, he has created him in his own image.
> —Fyodor Dostoevsky

"I Have No Mouth, and I Must Scream" first appeared in *If: Worlds of Science Fiction* in March 1967, bought and edited by Frederik Pohl. It was printed without the now-familiar computer "talk-fields" and also was edited in several places: Ellison calls this "the Bowdlerizing of what Fred termed 'the difficult sections' of the story (which he contended might offend the mothers of the young readers of *If* "["Memoir: I Have No Mouth, and I Must Scream," in *Fantastic Lives: Autobiographical Essays by Notable Science Fiction Writers* (1981)]. Specifically, Pohl omitted a reference to masturbation, toned down some of Ted's imprecations of Ellen, and removed all references to Benny's former homosexuality and the present equine state of what certain writers and speakers of German call the *männliches Glied.* (In Benny's case, however, perhaps *die Rute* would be more precise, and in the process would lend an entirely new meaning to the expression *einem Kind die Rute geben.*)

The story made its next appearance in Ellison's collection *I Have No Mouth and I Must Scream,* published in April 1967. Its subsequent reprintings in Ellison's books were in *Alone Against Tomorrow* (1971), *The Fantasies of Harlan Ellison* (1979), and *The Essential Ellison* (1987). I have compared the versions of all four books with each other and with the story's original appearance in *If;* my speculations here are drawn from this comparison.

It is my belief that Ted, the narrator, reveals his own true nature in speaking of the computer and in telling the story of himself and the others. Although the machine often is portrayed in both anthropomorphic and divine terms, I believe it is Ted alone who is both fully human and fully godlike in this story.

A comparison of the texts is illuminating, especially when attention is paid to the nouns and pronouns by which AM is described. Ted sometimes calls AM the machine, the computer, the creature, or simply AM, but usually pronouns are used. "He" and "it" are used indiscriminately, but this apparently careless usage in the versions of the story prior to 1979 becomes clearer in the versions found in *The Fantasies of Harlan Ellison* and *The Essential Ellison,* where the pronouns are deliberately mixed. For instance, at one point Ted speaks of Ellen's sexual services. All versions before 1979 read: "The machine giggled every time we did it. Loud, up there, back there, all around us. And she never climaxed, so why bother." In *The Fantasies of Harlan Ellison* and *The Essential Ellison* this passage is rearranged and expanded:

> And she never came, so why bother? But the machine giggled every time we did it. Loud, up there, back there, all around us, he snickered. *It* snickered. Most of the time I thought of AM as *it,* without a soul; but the rest of the time I thought of it as *him,* in the masculine . . . the paternal . . . the patriarchal . . . for he is a jealous people. Him. It. God as Daddy the Deranged. (Ellison's ellipses)

These later texts establish the division in Ted's mind between an impersonal and personal view of the computer. They also establish Ted's religious perspective of AM—a perspective in which God is seen as mad, much as God is portrayed in Ellison's 1973 story, **"The Deathbird."**

These two later versions of **"I Have No Mouth, and I Must Scream"** strengthen this combination of personal and impersonal through a deliberate mixture of pronouns not found in earlier renditions. Here are some examples:

> The passage of time was important to it. (*If; Alone*)
>
> The passage of time was important to him. (*Mouth*)
>
> The passage of time was important to him . . . it . . . AM. (*FHE; EE;* Ellison's ellipses)
>
> It was a mark of his personality: he strove for perfection. (*If; Mouth; Alone*)
>
> It was a mark of his personality: it strove for perfection. (*FHE; EE*)
>
> He was a machine. We had allowed him to think, but to do nothing with it. (*If; Mouth; Alone*)
>
> AM wasn't God, he was a machine. We had created him to think, but there was nothing it could do with that creativity. (*FHE; EE*)

Perhaps Ted best sums it up with this sentence: "We could call AM any damned thing we liked" (*If; Mouth; Alone; FHE; EE*). But there is more than indifference in Ted's attitude toward the computer. He admits he frequently thinks of AM as "him," and he regularly uses masculine pronouns in reference to it. This is due partly to his religious conception of AM as God, as "Daddy the Deranged," but more often it is because Ted anthropomorphizes the computer, and because Ted and the computer are reflections of each other. In addition, the computer itself assumes human characteristics.

Much of what makes Ted so interesting and effective as a narrator for this story is his intense paranoia, given to him by AM. In *The Oxford Companion to the Mind* "paranoia" is defined as a functional psychosis "in which the patient holds a coherent, internally consistent, delusional system of beliefs, centring [*sic*] round the conviction that he . . . is a person of great importance and is on that account being persecuted, despised, and rejected." Ted displays these classic symptoms, as in this passage: "They hated me. They were surely against me, and AM could even sense this hatred, and made it worse for me *because of* the depth of their hatred. We had been kept alive, rejuvenated, made to remain constantly at the age we had been when AM had brought us below, and they hated me because I was the youngest, and the one AM had affected least of all" (*EE*). As the article in the Oxford volume says, "The adjective 'paranoid' is sometimes used by psychoanalysis to describe anxiety and ideas that are inferred to be projections of the subject's own impulses." Ted thus transfers his own hatred to the computer and the others, while fending off the delusion that he was unchanged despite the descriptions he supplies of his altered mind and believing that "those scum, all four of them, they were lined and arrayed against me" (*EE*).

Part of the effect of Ted's paranoia is his transference of his own thoughts and feelings to others—and this includes AM, as well as his four human companions. He often describes the computer and its actions in human terms. For instance, he calls AM's tortures the machine's masturbation (*Mouth; Alone; FHE; EE*), and speaks of "the innate loathing that all machines had always held for the weak, soft creatures who had built them" (*Alone; EE*). It is difficult to imagine a toaster or refrigerator harboring malice against their makers; more likely, this statement is an expression of Ted's own hatred of humanity, and just happens to describe AM's own hatred as well.

Much could be made of the epistemological problems inherent in this story. Not only is Ted an extremely unreliable narrator, but it is often difficult to know how much of what he says is true and how much a projection of his own psyche. For instance, [in "Harlan Ellison," in *Science Fiction Writers: Critical Studies of the Major Authors from the Early Nineteenth Century to the Present Day* (1982)] George Edgar Slusser calls Ted "the true creator of this hate machine," but while Ted does project his hatred onto the machine, it is not simply his delusion either, unless the entire story never happened and is merely an elaborate construction within Ted's mind.

This humanization of AM is by no means limited to Ted's transference of human qualities to the computer, however. We are told AM's name in part refers to the Cartesian *cogito ergo sum*, "I think, therefore I AM" and "Cogito ergo sum" ("Memoir"), even though they were positioned correctly only in *The Essential Ellison.* This philosophical statement on the part of the computer is certainly one quite human in nature. And AM displays other human qualities: "he" giggles and snickers; shows emotions like anger, hatred, and jealousy; goes through an "irrational, hysterical phase" (*FHE; EE*); and possesses sentience, life, and thought. Perhaps the trait which most reveals AM's human side is its sense of humor. Ted speaks of the computer having fun with the five of them, whom he describes as its toys; the machine frequently laughs at them, sometimes in the guise of a fat woman. AM even jokes with them: "he" gives them bows and arrows and a water pistol to fight the gigantic Huergelmir, and after starving them AM supplies them with canned goods but with nothing to open them. Once there was a Tom and Jerry cartoon with a similar joke: they are locked up in the house with nothing to eat but canned food, but the can opener is useless since they lack opposable thumbs. Given Ellison's love of animated cartoons—most recently documented in *The Harlan Ellison Hornbook*—it is quite possible that the cartoon influenced this part of the story.

The computer reveals a sexual side as well. I have mentioned already that Ted describes the machine as masturbating and that it giggles whenever Ellen has sex with anyone. AM also enlarges Benny's penis, and Ted says that "AM had given her [Ellen] pleasure" in bringing her into the computer's complex (*If; Mouth; Alone; FHE; EE*). Jon Bernard Ower believes "AM's degradation of the sexual lives of his subjects reveals his jealousy of the physical pleasure and the spiritual fulfillment of human love" ["Manacle-Forged Minds: Two Images of the Computer

in Science-Fiction," *Diogenes* (1974)]. It is also possible, I believe, that the scene in which AM enters Ted's mind with the neon-lettered pillar could be seen as rape, a mental sodomy of sorts. "AM went into my mind," says Ted. "AM touched me in every way I had ever been touched . . . AM withdrew from my mind, and allowed me the exquisite ugliness of returning to consciousness with the feeling of that burning neon pillar still rammed deep into the soft gray brain matter" (*If; Mouth* [has "grey" for "gray"]; *Alone; FHE; EE*). The sexual language and imagery here are very strong and suggestive.

In examining the story's various printings and reprintings in Ellison's books and in anthologies edited by others, I noticed that in speaking of Ellen's sexual services for the four men two of Ellison's books read, "She loved it, five men all to herself," while the anthologies had, "She loved it, four men all to herself." For a while, then, I believed that "five men" was the correct reading, and before I saw either *The Fantasies of Harlan Ellison* or *The Essential Ellison,* and before I asked Harlan himself about it, I was prepared to argue that the computer itself was the fifth man, thus strengthening my arguments for AM's humanization, in particular its sexual manifestations—all of which goes to show the importance of establishing dependable texts.

But while the computer itself may not have sex with Ellen, it definitely possesses a human side; as George Edgar Slusser says, "in its hatred for mankind, this machine has acquired a human heart." Yet it is an extremely twisted and evil humanity this computer displays, stemming directly from the fact that AM was created to wage war and was programmed by people with hatred and madness in their souls. Ellison's comments [in *Contemporary Authors, New Revision Series,* Vol. 5 (1982)] on his projected screenplay adaptation of Isaac Asimov's *I, Robot* are illuminating on this point: "The only thing that can make machines hurt us is ourselves. Garbage in, garbage out. If we program them and we have madness, then they will be programmed mad." Incidentally, in Ellison's 1960 novel *The Sound of a Scythe* (published with the title *The Man with Nine Lives*) there is a supercomputer similar to AM, designed to handle tasks too complex for humans, but it is kept benevolent by Asimov's Three Laws of Robotics.

If AM is far from benevolent, it is also far from human. It is limited in its creativity and, envying what freedoms and abilities the humans possess, strives to limit even those, as a dog in the manger. Either unwilling or unable to destroy itself, AM apparently is immortal and therefore grants the five humans a form of immortality (following the human adage that misery loves company). Although it can sustain human life, AM cannot create it, which explains why after 109 years and four men no children have been born to Ellen. Although one logically might infer that AM would want more human beings to torture, it evidently keeps Ellen as barren as "she" is. The humans are not fruitful, they do not multiply, they do not replenish the earth. This is made more ironic by the frequent images of pregnancy in the story, as Joseph Francavilla has noted [in "Mythic Hells in Harlan Ellison's Science Fiction," in *Phoenix from the Ashes: The Literature of the Remade*

World (1987)]; the computer complex repeatedly is referred to as AM's belly, and at one point Ted says, "He was Earth, and we were the fruit of that Earth" (*Mouth; FHE; EE*). In a way, since AM sustains them, it is a type of mother to the five, but it never gives birth to them, making the pregnancy imagery all the more ironic: "It [the hunger] was alive in my belly, even as we were alive in the belly of AM, and AM was alive in the belly of the earth" (*If; Mouth; Alone*).

Nor can AM restore life. After Ted and Ellen kill their companions, and after Ted murders Ellen, we clearly see the computer's impotence, evident in its rage that it cannot bring the dead ones back to life. Like Frankenstein's monster, AM cannot create life; but it can destroy it, which both AM and the monster do by turning on those who gave them life but who failed to give them love and the possibility to create life in turn. Unlike the Frankenstein monster, however, AM does not mature, but instead grows more childish: its use of the five as playthings indicates this, as does the temper tantrum it throws upon the death of the four. The computer again resembles the childish, insane god of **"The Deathbird."** Like Ted, it is filled with hatred and in its madness must scream, yet like Ted it has no mouth: it can communicate only through acts of violence such as the rape scene and through the unintelligible talk-fields. Like Ted at some moments, AM represents humanity at its worst.

However, Ted also reveals glimmers of hope within the human condition as he aspires to godhood (so Ellison tells us in "Memoir") through his heroism. AM also aspires to godhood, helped partly by Ted's own religious imagination, but the divinity it achieves is a very poor sort. In some ways the "god" AM becomes is a reflection of the human race which invented the machine, in others like the Judeo-Christian God in its power and supposed omnipotence, but actually it is closer to Dostoevsky's devil or Twain's malign thug: "If one truly believes there is an all-powerful Deity, and one looks around at the condition of the universe, one is led inescapably to the conclusion that God is a malign thug." Nevertheless, AM's type of divinity is one representation of human potential, as Willis E. McNelly tells us in his foreword to the story in Robert Silverberg's anthology, *The Mirror of Infinity*. Programmed by humanity, "AM now knows all the ancient archetypal myths, and now uses its knowledge to pervert and negate them. It exercises the power that man never had, to control man, and to give substance to the myths. Man has played God for one last time, creating a God that destroys him." In effect, AM plays at being God just as it plays with the five humans at its disposal, assuming the role of a God who prepares its creatures for destruction by first driving them mad.

There are several instances in the story where the computer plays with the symbolism and mythologies of various religions. For example, Charles J. Brady [in "The Computer as a Symbol of God: Ellison's Macabre Exodus," *The Journal of General Education* (1976)], Carol D. Stevens [in "The Short Fiction of Harlan Ellison," in *Survey of Science Fiction Literature,* Vol. 4 (1979)], Francavilla, and Ower all note the story's similarities to the

book of Exodus—an additional meaning of AM's name comes from Exodus 3:14, where God tells Moses that He is to be called I AM THAT I AM—and usually these occur in the perverse way McNelly mentions. The computer sends the five manna which, however, tastes like "boiled boar urine" (*If; Mouth; Alone; FHE; EE*); when AM enters Ted's mind, it walks as God walked in the Garden of Eden before chastising Adam and Eve for their sin; it appears to them in the form of a burning bush (*If; Mouth; Alone; FHE; EE*); and after Ellen and Nimdok are swallowed by an earthquake, AM returns them to the others "as the heavenly legion bore them to us with a celestial chorus singing, 'Go Down Moses.' The archangels circled several times and then dropped the hideously mangled bodies" (*Mouth; Alone; FHE; EE*).

And these examples are within the Judeo-Christian tradition alone: AM employs other religious tricks as well, such as producing the Huergelmir from Norse mythology. Still another mythic tradition may shed some additional light into the relationship between Ted and the computer. Returning to the sentence "He was the Earth, and we were the fruit of that Earth" along with the following sentence, "though he had eaten us he would never digest us," recalls the *Theogony* of Hesiod, in which Kronos suppresses his godling children by eating them. Like Zeus in the myth, Ted is an emerging god, but to emerge he first must emasculate the Kronos-figure, AM. Ted saves his "brothers" and "sister," ironically, by killing them; but instead of reigning triumphantly over the defeated god, both are condemned to Tartarus.

However, the Judeo-Christian mythology is most prevalent in the story, both in the identity AM adopts for itself and in Ted's ideas about the computer as God. Ted sees AM as God the Father and says, in a biblical misquotation, "He is a jealous people." The phrase is actually "jealous God," and two places where it occurs in the Bible are remarkably relevant to the story. In Exodus 20:5, the King James version, it says, "Thou shalt not bow down thyself to them [graven images], nor serve them: for I the LORD thy God *am* a jealous God, visiting the iniquity of the fathers upon the children unto the third and fourth *generation* of them that hate me." Since there is no certain indication in the story that any of the five are responsible for the creation of the various national AMs, the choice of the unified AM to punish these five and kill everyone else seems fairly arbitrary, but this biblical passage reflects a God who will punish the children for the sins of the fathers, down even to the third and fourth generations. Also, as both Ower and Stevens have pointed out, AM's selection of these five parodies the concept of a "chosen people."

Nor will such a God necessarily forgive them, as we find in Joshua 24:19: "And Joshua said unto the people, Ye cannot serve the LORD: for he *is* an holy God; he *is* a jealous God; he will not forgive your transgressions nor your sins." Life in AM, for Ted, if not for the others, is not Purgatory, in which one suffers but ultimately is reprieved, but is Hell. "He withdrew, murmuring *to hell with you. And added, brightly, but then you're there, aren't you*" (*FHE; EE*). Yet Ted realizes, and we must realize, that

AM is not God. Rather, as Ellison himself has said, "AM represents . . . the dichotomous nature of the human race, created in the *image* of God; and that includes the demon in us" ("Memoir"). In this respect, AM mirrors its creators. As Ower says, "Humanity in making the computer has travestied its own creation [by God], projecting an amplified image of its fallen and conditioned nature." Perhaps it could even be argued that AM is not entirely malevolent toward humanity, but instead has a love/hate relationship with it. While it hurts the five, it also sustains them and in some cases even gives them pleasure; but Ted, narrating through the veil of his paranoia, can see only the computer's hatred.

Ted is more like the computer than he realizes, for he also has a love/hate relationship with the others. This is most apparent in his feelings for Ellen. For instance, when he comments that Ellen gave herself to him sexually out of gratitude at one point, he says, "Even that had ceased to matter" (*If; Mouth; Alone; FHE; EE*)—which implies that at one time it did matter. When traveling, Nimdok and Gorrister carry her while Ted and Benny walk ahead and behind "just to make sure that if anything happened, it would catch one of us and at least Ellen would be safe" (*If; Mouth; Alone; FHE; EE*). Ted here transfers his concern to the idiot Benny to deemphasize his own concern for Ellen, and he does not begrudge her this special treatment (in a way foreshadowing her future limp), even though he curses her throughout the story. Ted always gives in to Ellen's wishes and tries to reassure her whenever she becomes anxious. And when just the two of them are alive and he could have her for himself—he is clearly jealous of the others, especially Benny, since he believes "she loved it from him" while with Ted "she never came"—he cares enough for her to rescue her from the hell he will encounter under AM's wrath.

Both AM's love/hate relationship with the five and Ted's paradoxical feelings toward Ellen reflect Ellison's own feelings toward humanity: "It is a love/hate relationship that I have with the human race," he says. Ellison believes the human spirit is capable of greatness and nobility, but too often people settle for meanness and mediocrity. "A majority of readers see his work as filled with anger and bitterness," says Debra McBride [in "Soapbox: Ellison at Mid-Career," *Fantasy Review* (1984)]. For instance, [in "Medium and Message in Ellison's 'I Have No Mouth, and I Must Scream'," in *The Intersection of Science Fiction and Philosophy: Critical Studies* (1983)] Joann P. Cobb thinks **"I Have No Mouth, and I Must Scream"** "illustrates the surrender of human purpose and value that is inherent in contemporary attitudes toward technological progress." But Ellison says otherwise, and his sense of anger, according to McBride, "stems from a love-hate relationship he has with the human race; he sees greatness in humanity that society seems to bury instead of cultivate."

Earlier in the Wiloch and Cowart interview [in *Contemporary Authors, New Revision Series*], Ellison expands on his comments with his beliefs about God and humanity: "There is no God. . . . We are God." He has made similar statements elsewhere: "I have faith . . . in people, not

Gods" (*FHE;* Ellison's ellipses); "God is within you. Save yourselves" (**"The Waves in Rio"**). Charles J. Brady believes that in **"I Have No Mouth, and I Must Scream"** Ellison's "target" is "God-the-puppet-master, the eternal one behind the scenes who pulls all the strings." But Brady asserts that this is an idol, not the "real" God; therefore "Ellison's work is not atheistic or blasphemous in the final analysis." On the contrary, I think it is meant to be blasphemous, if not atheistic. Ellison implies here what he explicitly states above, that gods are essentially our own creations made in our image, and if anything the "real" God is an ideal of human nobility. Similar ideas also are expressed in two other stories by Ellison, **"The Deathbird"** and **"The Region Between"** (1969).

It is the belief in the potential of the human spirit that shapes the impact of **"I Have No Mouth, and I Must Scream."** It is this that makes the apparent humanity and divinity of AM so important, because AM is a human creation: humanity has created both God and Satan in its own image because it is potentially godlike and realistically demonic. It is also important that AM is so much like Ted, and vice versa, because in the narrator we see an actual human being at its worst, yet also a god emerging. As Francavilla says, citing the Promethian nature of Ted, "If the dark half of human nature is projected into AM, then the fire-bringing half is embodied in Ted." The editors' introduction to the story in *The Essential Ellison* is very revealing on this point:

> **"I Have No Mouth, and I Must Scream"** is an exceptionally violent warning about technology as a reflection of humanity. If our machines store our knowledge, is it not possible that they can also store, and possibly succumb to, such things as hatred and paranoia? AM . . . is a "god" only in the sense of its godlike powers. But the story must be viewed as Harlan intended, as "a positive, humanistic, upbeat story," if it is to have any real meaning. Gods and pseudogods cannot destroy us without destroying themselves, and the absence of a mouth or a scream cannot invalidate the courageousness of the human spirit.

In "Memoir," Ellison claims Ted's actions are godlike since they reveal love and heroism in overcoming his paranoia and in killing the others to put them out of their misery, thus subjecting himself to an eternity of loneliness and torment.

Several aspects of the story strengthen this religious view of the narrator. First is the establishment of AM as a God-figure and the subsequent identification of Ted with the computer, however unwitting on Ted's part. Like AM, Ted is filled with envy, hatred, and paranoia. Both are immortal. Two descriptions of Ted's brain resemble those of AM's "mind": blown by the hurricane, Ted describes his mind as "a roiling tinkling chittering softness" (*If; Mouth; FHE; EE*), a description resembling those of AM in thought, especially the repeated word "chittering"; and just as when AM was constructed its creators dropped shafts into the earth, so when AM enters Ted's mind "[h]e smiled softly at the pit that dropped into the center of my brain and the faint, moth-soft murmurings of the things far down there that gibbered without meaning, without pause" (*If; Mouth; Alone; FHE; EE*). In the latter, the sounds within the "pit" of Ted's brain are much like the talk-fields of the murmuring computer.

Other features which reinforce Ted's religious nature are his language and expressions, many of which are loaded with theological and liturgical impact. Not only does he often equate AM with God, and even pray at one point (but in vain), but he also speaks occasionally in a biblical mode. He speaks of AM's "miracles" and the torments which he "visited down on us," and their passage through "a valley of obsolescence" foreshadows the Bunyanesque tone of the later passage, which reads:

> And we passed through the cavern of rats.
> And we passed through the path of boiling steam.
> And we passed through the country of the blind.
> And we passed through the slough of despond.
> And we passed through the vale of tears.
> (*If; Mouth; Alone; FHE; EE*)

John Bunyan's *Pilgrim's Progress*, to which this story has been compared, is of course the source of the Slough of Despond; the "vale of tears" is a traditional religious phrase expressing the medieval Christian view of the world as a place of suffering (terribly apropos for this story); and "the country of the blind" is from the H. G. Wells tale of the same title which makes use of the familiar quotation, "In the country of the blind, the one-eyed man is king"—even if he has no mouth.

Another religious aspect of Ted is the narration itself. To whom is he telling this story? Not to AM, certainly; the computer is referred to in the third person, and it's likely the two aren't on speaking terms. He probably isn't writing or typing it, as McNelly supposes, given the description of his arms as "[r]ubbery appendages." The most probable answer is that Ted is telling it to himself (Joseph F. Patrouch, Jr., arrives at the same conclusion), and likely not for the first time. Like Gorrister telling the history of AM over and over to Benny, so Ted probably repeats his story to himself, possibly to alleviate the sense of guilt he feels at the death of the others and his uncertainty that he did the right thing. In this way, the story would assume a mythological aspect. Evidence of such repetition can be seen in the various instances of foreshadowing in the story. Gorrister's reaction to seeing himself suspended, dead and mutilated, from the pink palette, "as though he had seen a voodoo icon" (*If; Mouth; FHE; EE*), foreshadow's Benny's later cannibalistic attack. Ted's description of the earth's "blasted skin" parallels his later transformation by AM, as does the light pulsing within Benny when he tries to escape to the surface and AM reduces his eyes to "two soft, moist pools of pus-like jelly." Ellen is carried by Nimdok and Gorrister even before her leg is injured—or maybe after; perhaps Ted's chronology has become confused with successive retellings. Also, Ted says that among the five he was affected the least—an impression given him by his paranoia—but in the end he is altered almost beyond the point of recognition as a human being.

The most religious thing about Ted, however, is not his language but his actions. In killing the others, with Ellen's assistance, Ted fulfills Christ's statement, "Greater love hath no man than this, that a man lay down his life for his friends" (John 15:13). Like other religious aspects of the story, this is reversed: Ted lays down his life, but it is his friends who die and he who lives. Despite this inversion, however, Ted is no Christ-figure. He remains fully human, yet achieves a type of godliness despite his humanity, despite his paranoia and his hatred of others. Ted is a *human* hero—human as we are, his courage an example for us to follow rather than a Christlike ideal we cannot reach. As McNelly says, "Ted is no Christian in his pilgrim's progress" but rather "the embodiment of the good and evil in all of us, at once brute and angel, fornicator and lover, killer and savior. He is man—like a devil, like an angel, like a god."

The narrator of **"I Have No Mouth, and I Must Scream,"** then, embodies the image of God despite his human, all too human limitations and flaws. Ted exemplifies the potential of the human spirit. In this way he triumphs over the computer, which is also human and godlike; because while the computer is neither fully human nor fully divine, Ted is both, and through this displays a moral superiority which makes this tale, as Ellison intended it, "a positive, humanistic, upbeat story" ("Memoir"). (pp. 143-54)

> *Darren Harris-Fain, "Created in the Image of God: The Narrator and the Computer in Harlan Ellison's 'I Have No Mouth, and I Must Scream',"* in Extrapolation, *Vol. 32, No. 2, Summer, 1991, pp. 143-55.*

FURTHER READING

Bibliography

Swigart, Leslie Kay. "Harlan Ellison: A Nonfiction Checklist." In *The Book of Ellison,* edited by Andrew Porter, pp. 177-91. New York: Algol Press, 1978.

> Lists interviews with, as well as nonfiction works by, Ellison, including introductions and afterwords he has written for his own stories and short story collections.

Criticism

Frisch, Adam J., and Martos, Joseph. "Religious Imagination and Imagined Religion." In *The Transcendent Adventure: Studies of Religion in Science Fiction/Fantasy,* edited by Robert Reilly, pp. 11-26. Westport, Conn.: Greenwood Press, 1985.

> Cites Ellison's short story "The Deathbird" as one example of a science fiction work that inverts the fundamental Judeo-Christian image of Eden.

Kaminsky, Stuart M., and Walker, Mark. "No Holes Barred." *The Armchair Detective* 21, No. 3 (Summer 1988): 232-36, 238-40.

> Interview in which Ellison discusses writing for films and television.

Kroiter, Harry P. "The Special Demands of Point of View

in Science Fiction." *Extrapolation* 17, No. 2 (May 1976): 153-59.

> Transcribed lecture in which the critic briefly discusses Ellison's use of first-person narration in "I Have No Mouth, and I Must Scream."

McBride, Debra L. "Soapbox: Ellison at Mid-Career." *Fantasy Review* 7, No. 11 (December 1984): 5-6.

> Article based on an interview in which Ellison discusses such topics as his works and the writing process.

Ower, John B. "Manacle-Forged Minds: Two Images of the Computer in Science Fiction." *Diogenes* 85 (1974): 47-61.

> Compares Ellison's "I Have No Mouth, and I Must Scream" with an episode from Arthur C. Clarke's *2001: A Space Odyssey,* arguing that both works address the problem of creating a computer with a mentality that equals or surpasses that of humans.

Patrouch, Joseph F., Jr. "Harlan Ellison's Use of the Narrator's Voice." In *Academic Programming at CHICON IV: Patterns of the Fantastic,* edited by Donald M. Hassler, pp. 63-6. Mercer Island, Wash.: Starmont House, 1983.

> Asserts that Ellison has revived the literary technique of

the "speaking voice" and that his "voice and personality . . . [have] come to dominate his work."

Sullivan, Charles William. "Harlan Ellison and Robert A. Heinlein: The Paradigm Makers." In *Clockwork Worlds: Mechanized Environments in SF,* edited by Richard D. Erlich and Thomas P. Dunn, pp. 97-103. Westport, Conn.: Greenwood Press, 1983.

> Compares the depiction of machines in Ellison's "I Have No Mouth, and I Must Scream" and Heinlein's *The Moon Is a Harsh Mistress.*

Wendell, Carolyn. "The Alien Species: A Study of Women Characters in the Nebula Award Winners, 1965-1973." *Extrapolation* 20, No. 4 (Winter 1979): 343-54.

> Asserts that women are portrayed stereotypically in Ellison's " 'Repent, Harlequin!' Said the Ticktockman" and *A Boy and His Dog.*

Interview

Ellison, Harlan, and Francavilla, Joseph V. *Post Script: Essays in Film and the Humanities* 10, No. 1 (Fall 1990): 9-20.

> Ellison discusses the writing process, his literary influences, and some of the dominant themes in his work.

Additional coverage of Ellison's life and career is contained in the following sources published by Gale Research: *Contemporary Authors,* Vols. 5-8, rev. ed.; *Contemporary Authors New Revision Series,* Vol. 5; *Contemporary Literary Criticism,* Vols. 1, 13, 42; *Dictionary of Literary Biography,* Vol. 8; and *Major 20th-Century Writers.*

Ellen Gilchrist

1935-

(Full name Ellen Louise Gilchrist) American short story writer, poet, and novelist.

INTRODUCTION

Gilchrist is best known for short stories that chronicle the struggle of Southern women against the restrictive mores of upper-class society. She sets much of her fiction in New Orleans, describing the city's beauty and eccentricities in detail to contrast the idealistic hopes of her upper-class female protagonists with the harsh reality of their lives. Gilchrist is consistently praised for her vivid use of colloquial language and dialogue, and critics have particularly noted her ability to capture in her stories the dreams and frustrations of adolescence.

Gilchrist was born in Vicksburg, Mississippi. Her early childhood was spent on the Hopedale Plantation, the home of her maternal grandfather. She eloped at nineteen years of age and had married four times before she earned her B.A. in Philosophy from Millsaps College at the age of thirty-two. Gilchrist's experiences among Southern socialites during her twenties and a series of unsuccessful relationships often provide the basis for her fiction. Gilchrist did not begin writing until she was forty years old. After she began sending poems to poet and novelist Jim Whitehead, Gilchrist was asked to join his writing class at the University of Arkansas, which she accepted. In 1982 she published her first book of short fiction, *In the Land of Dreamy Dreams.*

Gilchrist's short fiction is best known for its realistic and sympathetic portrayal of unconventional Southern girls and women who engage in promiscuous or unorthodox behavior due to depression, a craving for romance, and the need to escape the rigid conventions of their class-conscious milieu. These protagonists often reappear in different stories, allowing Gilchrist to examine various stages of their personal development. In "Revenge" from *In the Land of Dreamy Dreams,* rebellious ten-year-old Rhoda Manning is sent to live with her father's family in Florida during World War II. Barred from using a pole-vaulting pit built by her brother and five male cousins, Rhoda seeks solace in a traditional Southern woman's activity—preparing for her cousin Lauralee's wedding. When the ceremony proves disappointing and confining, Rhoda sneaks out to the pit and vaults across it in defiance of her family. Like Gilchrist's other heroines, who include Nora Jane Whittington and Crystal Manning, Rhoda is often compared by critics to rebellious literary heroines such as Frankie Addams of Carson McCuller's *The Member of the Wedding.* Gilchrist's later collections, including the American Book Award recipient *Victory over Japan* and *Light Can Be Both Wave and Particle,* revisit Rhoda later

in her life, as in "The Lower Garden District Free Gravity Mule Blight or Rhoda, a Fable" from *Victory over Japan.* Facing middle age, a recent divorce, poverty, and loneliness, Rhoda implements an elaborate plan to defraud her insurance company by filing a false claim on her wedding ring, and during the settlement seduces her insurance representative out of boredom and insecurity. Although some reviewers consider Gilchrist's casual treatment of her protagonists' often immoral actions shallow or banal, others regard her heroines as simply pragmatic and jaded from their personal battles.

While Gilchrist has been faulted by critics for weak endings and a lack of coherence in her short fiction collections, most have praised the vitality of her writing style and protagonists. Some critics have perceived greater depth and maturation in the characters of her later works, especially those in her novella collection *I Cannot Get You Close Enough.* Gilchrist's generous treatment of her characters sets her apart from other writers, maintains critic Beverly Lowry: "Without much authorial manicuring or explanation, she allows her characters to emerge whole, in full possession of their considerable stores of eccentricities and passion."

PRINCIPAL WORKS

SHORT FICTION

In the Land of Dreamy Dreams   1981
Victory over Japan   1984
Drunk with Love   1986
Light Can Be Both Wave and Particle   1989
I Cannot Get You Close Enough   1990

OTHER MAJOR WORKS

The Land Surveyor's Daughter   (poetry)   1979
The Annunciation   (novel)   1983
Falling through Space: The Journals of Ellen Gilchrist
   1987
The Anna Papers   (novel)   1988
Net of Jewels   (novel)   1992

CRITICISM

Jim Crace   (review date 1982)

[*Crace is an English journalist and novelist. In the following review, he discusses Gilchrist's evocation of place and depiction of adolescent characters in* In the Land of Dreamy Dreams.]

Ellen Gilchrist's witty volume of "Short Fiction", *In the Land of Dreamy Dreams,* does its best to obscure its own considerable merits. With the connivance of its dust-jacket rodomontade, the collection masquerades as a blunt and loving examination of New Orleans and the Mississippi delta. Gilchrist's title is taken (and slightly misquoted) from the refrain to that jerky Southern foxtrot, *Way Down Yonder in New Orleans* ("In the Land of Dreamy *Scenes*"). Her text—with almost Miltonic confidence in the authority of proper nouns—is obsessively signposted with street names and Louisiana landmarks, from the Huey P. Long Bridge and the Audubon Park to the graceful stucco mansions on Exposition Boulevard and the state tenements of the St Thomas Street project.

Yet it is only the outward apparel (and, to some extent, the narrative drawl) of these engaging moral tales which evokes the South. New Orleans presents itself in clear, painstaking detail, but the broad demotic idiosyncrasies which define any city are neglected. Indeed, those few tales which foray north for their settings, the campus of Seattle University (**"Suicides"**) and the high-rise abortion clinics of Houston (**"1957, a Romance"**) are barely distinguishable in tone and demeanour from the majority set amongst the levees and bayous of the delta.

But *In the Land of Dreamy Dreams* cannot be dismissed as little more than an anecdotal street plan. As the stories accumulate, Gilchrist's true obsession reveals itself. Municipal spirit of place is—despite the assertions of the

blurb—a minor concern. The self-conscious parading of exact Southern locations is a protective screen beyond which an entirely different territory is explored and mapped. Gilchrist's "Land of Dreamy Dreams" is Adolescence.

Her characters, for the most part, are children subjected to the arbitrary dislocations of family life, and the "cold-eyed, white-armed . . . terrors" of puberty. Teenage Margaret, isolated and overweight, in **"Generous Pieces"**, discovers hidden condoms in the pockets of her father's gaberdine topcoat: "How do I know what the rubbers are? How do I know with such absolute certainty that they are connected with Christina Carver's mother and the pall that has fallen over our house on Calvin Boulevard?" In **"Traveller"**, LeLe Arnold, boastful and gauche, "the wildest girl" (and the biggest liar) in the Mississippi delta, plays little Southern Miss among the outsize fur stoles, negligees, kimonos and the wrinkle creams of her dead aunt's dressing room. And eight-year-old Rhoda (in **"1944"**) perches at the bar, sipping pink Shirley Temple cocktails and revelling in the adult world of love and grief with a newly-bereaved wartime bride. "I squirmed with delight beneath her approving gaze, enchanted by the dark timbre of her voice, the marvellous fuchsia of her lips and fingertips, the brooding glamor of her widowhood." Together they tap out the "Air Corps Hymn" on empty martini glasses.

These first-person narratives betray a sophisticated, writerly sensibility which at times goes beyond the years and understanding of the speaker. Another Rhoda, the ten-year-old chronicler of **"Revenge"** (this volume's masterpiece) describes "a full moon . . . caught like a kite in the pecan trees across the river", and a waterside house which "shimmered in the moonlight like a jukebox alive in a meadow".

Occasionally, too, one detects in Gilchrist a loss of nerve with her fragile, modest plots, so that perfectly poised tales are laden (for ironic purposes, perhaps) with the ballast of a final prose sunset: "Then, like a woman in a dream, she walked on down the street, the rays of the setting sun making her a path all the way to the bus stop at the corner of Annunciation and Nashville Avenue. Making her a path all the way . . . to a boy who was like no other. To the source of all water." And again: "Bebber walked on down the street, the rays of the setting sun making him a path all the way to her house, a little road to travel, a wide band of luminous and precarious order."

But if Gilchrist's narrative voices are sometimes less than authentic, and the writing is occasionally inappropriately earnest, the rewards elsewhere for the reader are a sustained display of delicately and rhythmically modulated prose and an unsentimental dissection of raw sentiment. Her stories are perceptive, her manner is both stylish and idiomatic—a rare and potent combination.

Jim Crace, "The Cold-Eyed Terrors," in The Times Literary Supplement, *No. 4150, October 15, 1982, p. 1142.*

Jeanie Thompson and Anita Miller Garner　(essay date 1983)

[*In the following excerpt, Thompson and Garner praise the unusual "coherence of style and voice" in* In the Land of Dreamy Dreams.]

Few writers can achieve with a first collection of short stories published by a university press the kind of instant popular success and critical acclaim Ellen Gilchrist won with *In the Land of Dreamy Dreams* (1981). Not only did it immediately sell out its first printing, the collection was literally the talk of New Orleans, selling many copies by word of mouth and winning for its author a substantial contract with a notable publisher for a novel and another collection of stories. Gilchrist's regional success has been explained in much the same way the regional success of writers like Walker Percy, Eudora Welty and, more recently, John Kennedy Toole has been explained: that is, readers in the South cannot resist the descriptions of settings, landscapes, dialects and societies which, love them or not, are easily recognizable as home. Yet, like these writers, Gilchrist writes fiction that is more than regional. Indeed, if it is regional, it is so in the sense that the works of Dostoyevsky and Flaubert are regional, which is to say that it represents not regionalism so much as the successful capturing of a social milieu. Gilchrist captures the flavor and essence of her region without drowning in its idiom. She does not diminish her work by parroting already established Southern voices or depending upon stereotypes of landscapes and character. The view that Gilchrist gives us of the world is a very straight and narrow path of realism, traditional fiction peopled with characters whom life doesn't pass by, characters who lust and kill and manipulate, and most importantly, dream.

The focus of Gilchrist's realism in *In the Land of Dreamy Dreams,* as well as in her novel, *The Annunciation* (1983) is the female psyche, for Gilchrist puts us deeply inside a female point of view in eleven of the fourteen stories as well as in much of the novel. Even in **"Rich," "The President of the Louisiana Live Oak Society,"** and **"Suicides,"** stories in which she employs a more nearly omniscient point of view, her narrators still manage to sound as if they are characters in her stories. (Gilchrist similarly manipulates the point of view in *The Annunciation,* making us privy to the minds of various characters as well as the protagonist, Amanda McCamey.) In **"The President of the Louisiana Live Oak Society,"** the narrator's eye and voice are those of a woman confiding to her friend in a beauty salon, much like Flannery O'Connor's omniscient narrators who often sound like the "Georgia crackers" who people her stories. The result of an intense focus on the female point of view and a shortage of three-dimensional male characters will undoubtedly result in charges by some of Gilchrist's lack of range. Fortunately, the placement of **"Rich"** as the first story in the collection presents Tom Wilson, perhaps the only fully rounded male character in the book. The glimpses we are given of his coming to terms with a hatred of his difficult daughter Helen, are some of the most poignant and human scenes in the collection. Yet, when we put all the stories together, add up all the views the reader gets of the female mind, the composite suggests that Gilchrist's treatment of women is very

traditional and in several areas resembles that of her predecessors.

Like at least two Grandes Dames of Southern fiction, Eudora Welty and Flannery O'Connor, Gilchrist evidences a type of Romantic Calvinism in her view of women. On one hand, she seems delighted with the idea of innate depravity, while on the other she seems convinced that a woman's life is often like an extended downhill sled ride, starting out with much promise for excitement and speed, but troubled by ill-placed obstacles, icy spots, and a fizzle at the end. For example, Gilchrist likes to show her young protagonists as simultaneously wonderful and horrible. In **"Traveler,"** LeLe prefers telling lies to telling the truth, concocting wild tales to tell her summer companions about her social success back in Indiana, when in fact she has just lost a bid for cheerleader. When her cousin Baby Gwen Barksdale greets LeLe at the train station, LeLe tells her that "practically the whole football team" saw her off at the station back home, and then she creates a melodramatic tale about a college boy she supposedly dates who is dying of cancer. LeLe's sloth is shown through her failure to face up to the real cause of her obesity. She does not feel guilty for all of the lies she tells. In fact, the only emotion akin to guilt she feels is the remorse she experiences for eating vanilla ice cream directly out of the carton while the freezer door stands open, something she is sure Sirena the maid knows about and holds against her. Yet for all of LeLe's exaggerations and lies, the reader cannot fail to be charmed by her sheer spunk when she swims the five miles across the lake with Fielding, her summer crush, and exuberantly realizes that she has created an identity for herself. "I was dazzling. I was LeLe Arnold, the wildest girl in the Mississippi Delta, the girl who swam Lake Jefferson without a boat or a life vest. I was LeLe, the girl who would do anything." LeLe's exaggerations sound as if she has listened too often to Scarlett O'Hara's lines in *Gone With the Wind,* but her gutsy actions are more reminiscent of Katherine Anne Porter's Miranda stories, stories in which the female characters gain more than petty desires and whims by their actions. What LeLe gains by swimming the lake has much in common with what Miranda's idol, Aunt Amy, gains by riding off to Mexico astride a horse in **"Old Mortality."** Just as Miranda's dull life is reshaped by this socially rebellious event, LeLe cannot forget when she returns to hum-drum Indiana how "the water turned into diamonds in [her] hands" that day.

In **"Revenge,"** Gilchrist uses the same pattern with success. Rhoda is only ten years old when she is sent with all of her brothers and male cousins, five in all, to spend the summer with their grandmother during World War II. Rhoda's language is spicy and her thoughts are full of how sweet it would be to get even with the hateful boys who constantly ignore and diminish her abilities. Rhoda is particularly angry about the fact that the boys will not allow her to participate in the building of the Broad Jump Pit, and she calls vicious remarks to them from the distance at which they keep her. Secretly she begins to pray that the Japanese will win the war so that they will come and torture her tormentors. She puts herself to sleep at night imagining their five tiny wheelchairs lined up in a row while she rides around by her father's side in his Packard.

In short, Rhoda's spirit is eaten alive with envy and bitterness, hate and anger. Yet she gets her revenge and a miraculous boost for her self-image when she sneaks away from her cousin Lauralee's wedding festivities to strip off her plaid formal and vault over the barrier pole at the Broad Jump Pit. Rhoda imagines "half the wedding" is calling her name and climbing over the fence to get her when she runs down the path in the light of the moon to sail victoriously over the barrier. The Romantic vision of this early success is amplified by Rhoda's last thought: "Sometimes I think whatever has happened since has been of no real interest to me." This line does a great deal to separate Rhoda from other depraved and naughty young female protagonists such as Carson McCullers's Frankie Addams in *The Member of the Wedding* or Flannery O'Connor's child protagonist in "A Temple of the Holy Ghost."

Indeed, in story after story Gilchrist's grown-up female protagonists are living life after the Fall. She in fact reworks the pattern in *The Annunciation,* though with a different result. In **"There's a Garden of Eden,"** Alisha Terrebone decides that although she has always been a renowned beauty, her preeminence is drawing to a close. Alisha perceives herself to be "soft and brave and sad, like an old actress." Like many of Gilchrist's characters, she becomes to others what she perceives herself to be. She is painfully aware of the folly of her life, nonetheless, knowing that inevitably her present lover will leave her. She thinks, *"And that is what I get for devoting my life to love instead of wisdom."*

In their downhill journey through life, the protagonists of these stories run into obstacle after obstacle to mar their gorgeous, effortless journeys. In **"1957, a Romance,"** Rhoda fears another pregnancy and cannot face what she perceives as the ugliness of her body. In the title story, LaGrande McGruder finds her obstacle in the form of "That goddamn little new-rich Yankee bitch," a crippled, social-climbing Jewish woman who forces LaGrande to cheat if she wants to win in a game of tennis, the only thing important in LaGrande's life other than her integrity and pride at being at least a third-generation member of the New Orleans Lawn Tennis Club. In **"The President of the Louisiana Live Oak Society,"** Lelia McLaurin's life tumbles into chaos as the trappings of the social revolution of the sixties—blacklights, marijuana, and pushers—trickle down into her adolescent son Robert's life and then into her own carefully ordered home. Lelia's buffer from such madness and social unrest is to visit her hairdresser, who shares Lelia's psychiatrist and who creates for Lelia a hairdo that resembles a helmet.

Thus in gathering for the reader a whole cast of female characters in various stages of life, with the character Rhoda appearing by name in four of the stories, Gilchrist achieves a kind of coherence of style and voice that is absent from many first collections of short fiction. She invites us to compare these women with each other and determine whether or not the sum of their experiences adds up to more than just their individual lives. The result is a type of social commentary that pervades the work, full of sadness and futility. By dividing the collection into sections, Gilchrist emphasizes how "place" has affected these fe-

males' lives, and how what has been true in the past may exist nowhere other than in dreams in the future. The rural and genteel Mississippi in which Matille and the very young Rhoda summer seems to offer little preparation for the life in which Rhoda finds herself in 1957, in North Carolina with a husband and two small sons and the fear of a third child on the way. Clearly nothing in LaGrande McGruder's life has prepared her for the disruption of a society she has always known, nor for the encroachment of dissolution upon her territory. Similarly, Lelia McLaurin's only plan for escape is a weekend spent with her husband on the Mississippi Gulf Coast, just as they used to do in the old days, driving to Biloxi with a shaker full of martinis. (pp. 101-05)

> *Jeanie Thompson and Anita Miller Garner, "The Miracle of Realism: The Bid for Self-Knowledge in the Fiction of Ellen Gilchrist,"* in The Southern Quarterly, *Vol. XXII, No. 1, Fall, 1983, pp. 101-14.*

Beverly Lowry   (review date 1984)

[*Lowry is an American novelist, essayist, and critic. In the following review of* Victory over Japan, *she analyzes Gilchrist's style and praises the author's willingness to take risks in her fiction.*]

Ellen Gilchrist is a very nervy writer. That fact ought, first off, to be given its due. Nerve won't suffice to get a tighrope walker across the wire, but it provides the initial boost: without nerve, no circus. In the same way, nerve urges a fiction writer to go ahead and shoot whatever moon it is he has been given to aim at, without caution or respect for current fashion, a boon for the reader to be sure.

In her new collection of stories, *Victory Over Japan,* Miss Gilchrist once again demonstrates not only her willingness to take risks, but her generosity as a writer as well. Without much authorial manicuring or explanation, she allows her characters to emerge whole, in full possession of their considerable stores of eccentricities and passion. A Gilchrist story typically begins with the central character—almost always a woman—out on some limb. The limb will be of a spindly tree, say a blossoming crape myrtle, and the woman on it, who will have grown up as somebody's daughter, will once have been better off than she is now: richer, thinner, younger . . . in short, will once have had more power in her world. She does not, however, cling to the branch, since nothing in her life has taught her that clinging ever did anybody any good, but is perched there, commenting on the view, trying to think of a way down that will neither scare small children nor tear the lace from her French underwear.

Miss Gilchrist's first collection of stories, *In the Land of Dreamy Dreams,* was published in 1981 by the University of Arkansas Press, an event still noted in those short lists of authors made famous by university press books. The book was widely noted and well received. Miss Gilchrist, as a result, was given a fair amount of literary publicity when she signed on with Little, Brown, which has published two other books, her novel *The Annunciation* and now this new collection. Those who loved *In the Land of Dreamy Dreams* will not be disappointed. Many of the same characters reappear, including the brave-hearted and tenacious Nora Jane Whittington who, "nineteen years old, a self-taught anarchist and quick change artist," dressed as a Dominican nun and robbed a bar in the Irish Channel section of New Orleans to get enough money to go meet her boyfriend in San Francisco. Often new characters show up with old names. A Dudley, for instance, crops up here and there, usually as a father. A land surveyor whizzes through, wearing various hats, as does an aristocratic Mr. Leland. Rhoda and Crystal Manning have the same last name, though it's not clear they are kin. These crossovers are neither distracting nor accidental. Like Nora Jane, Ellen Gilchrist is only changing costumes, and she can "do wonderful tricks with her voice."

The stories in *Victory Over Japan* are divided into four sections: "Rhoda," "Crazy, Crazy, Now Showing Everywhere," "Nora Jane" and "Crystal." Rhoda also appeared in *In the Land of Dreamy Dreams.* In the new collection, she is variously 8 years old on a World War II scrap paper drive with a boy who's been bitten by a rabid squirrel; 14, with a passion for cigarettes; and 34, divorced and "poorer than she was accustomed to being." Newly acquired poverty is a constant with Gilchrist characters. And as another character in another story says, "Being poor wasn't working out. Being poor and living in a shotgun apartment wasn't working out. It was terrible." Like many other of Miss Gilchrist's women, Rhoda is redheaded and a hellion. At whatever age, poor or not, she manages to raise Cain.

The stories are wonderful to tell aloud. In **"The Gauzy Edge of Paradise,"** two friends, Lanier and Diane, both 29 years old, go down to the Mississippi coast to lose weight. Diane speaks: "This trip to the coast was a Major Diet. We'd been at it five days, taking Escatrol, reading poetry out loud to keep ourselves in a spiritual frame of mind, exercising morning, night and noon." When Diane's cousin Sandor, who "had a nervous breakdown trying to be a movie star," appears, there goes the diet. As Sandor says, "The trouble with getting drunk with your cousins" is that "they tell everything you did." The three end up losing not pounds but all their money, and their amphetamines as well.

Nora Jane Whittington, by the way, does get to San Francisco, only to find her boyfriend gone hopelessly California. Nora Jane, however, manages to have her adventures, including one on the Golden Gate Bridge during an earthquake, in which Nora Jane sings songs in different voices for a car full of terrified children, "Walt Disney and 'Jesus Christ Superstar' and Janis Joplin and the Rolling Stones and . . . some Broadway musicals." Nora Jane is different from other Gilchrist heroines in that she is strictly New South, an altogether modern and lovable punk kid.

Like LaGrande Magruder in *In the Land of Dreamy Dreams,* Crystal Manning may be the queen creation of *Victory Over Japan.* Crystal is one of a brand of Southern women who have not been well written about, the once rich, very bright and hard-drinking girls who, despite having to borrow the money to pay for the dress, have made

their debuts and still wear silk next to their skin, one way or another. Anyone who has read the biographies of Zelda Fitzgerald and Martha Mitchell will have a speaking acquaintance with these women. Tennessee Williams's heroines—Maggie the Cat, from *Cat on a Hot Tin Roof* and especially Blanche du Bois in *A Streetcar Named Desire*—long to be what Crystal Manning already is, but Maggie is bitter and Blanche too weird. Regina, in Lillian Hellman's *The Little Foxes,* comes out plain mean. And none of these characters have what is perhaps Crystal's essential element, her dark and crackling sense of humor, which can be vicious in any direction, including her own. Reynolds Price has written about women like Crystal from time to time, as does Alice Adams, but Ellen Gilchrist's racy females probably take the cake.

There are problems with a few of these stories. Miss Gilchrist seems to have her difficulties with endings. Sometimes the last paragraph seems tacked on, like a patch placed slapdash on a leaking inner tube. And her point of view within a story sometimes conveniently wanders—in order to explain something or give yet another reaction to the central character. It is jarring.

But this is a writer who does not play it safe and so the risks and misses are bound to be there. The pay-off is definitely worth the ride. *Victory Over Japan* belongs beside *In the Land of Dreamy Dreams* not as sequel but complement. If we're lucky, there will be yet another, with yet more overlapping tales, of Rhoda at 50 and Nora Jane in a new wig; of new and old versions of Lady Margaret Sarpie and Devoie and of King Mallison and Crystal. As one character says, "Who could stay away from anything Crystal Manning is up to?"

Most of us wouldn't want to try.

Beverly Lowry, "Redheaded Hellions in the Crape Myrtle," in The New York Times Book Review, *September 23, 1984, p. 18.*

David Sexton   (review date 1985)

[*In the following review, Sexton examines Gilchrist's characterization and prose style in* Victory over Japan.]

Ellen Gilchrist's stories are made from the talk of the Mississippi Delta. New Orleans is her regular setting, and when she writes about California or Texas she does it by transporting her home team of characters so that they can say the extraordinary things they say about these places too. She has even begun aggressively to defend her territory. In this new collection [*Victory over Japan*], which won the 1984 American Book Award, there is a story about a New Orleans society lady writing a snotty review of a book called *The Assumption* by Anna Hand, evidently just a step on from Gilchrist's first novel, *The Annunciation.* She begins: "Ms. Hand's new book abounds in clichés, crude language, and uses real names of places in New Orleans in a way than can only be called name-dropping." In the story, this reviewer, Lady Margaret Lanier Sarpie, meets the novelist and is discomfited. More importantly, she has also been incorporated into Gilchrist's fictional world of hard-drinking, beignet-guzzling, dissatisfied women. Whoever this luckless reviewer was (and the tone of the stories is such that one has little doubt that she really was), her name has now been nicely dropped too, and no doubt caught in New Orleans.

Gilchrist's new collection has four groups of stories: three gathered around single characters, Rhoda, Nora Jane and Crystal, and the other a hold-all of odd-balls called **"Crazy, Crazy, Now Showing Everywhere"**. All of these heroines are different incarnations of the same wacky woman, and perhaps the best of them is the first, Rhoda Manning, who featured in five tales in an earlier collection, *In The Land of Dreamy Dreams.*

["Victory over Japan"] is a wonderfully funny, sharp piece, narrated by Rhoda, which begins: "When I was in the third grade I knew a boy who had to have fourteen shots in the stomach as the result of a squirrel bite." Rhoda sees both this ("No one would ever have picked him out to be the centre of a rabies tragedy. He was more the type to fall in a well or get sucked down the drain at the swimming pool") and the dropping of the Bomb exclusively through her own self-regard. In the first case this means the chance to write up the boy's mishap for the school magazine ("BE ON THE LOOKOUT FOR MAD SQUIRREL, the headline read"), and in the second the not necessarily desired return of her father from the war (" 'What do you mean, you can't catch her', I could hear him yelling. 'Hit her with a broom. Hit her with a table. Hit her with a chair.' "). At the end of the story Rhoda mingles public and private violence in a dream: "We live in flame. Buckle down in flame. For nothing can stop the Army Air Corps. Hit 'em with a table, I was yelling. Hit 'em with a bomb. Hit 'em with a chair."

This shows Gilchrist's talent at its best, with the naive assertive style given to the right character. The consciousness remains that of the schoolgirl in 1945, full of herself in a world she can't control, but the expressive abilities are those of the adult, shaping the memories. The use of the first person unites the two. Other stories, in the third person, feel more gratuitously mannered, and the short, sassy sentences less natural. As the *TLS* reviewer of her first collection observed, Gilchrist's true land of dreamy dreams is Adolescence, not just New Orleans. With her older characters the *naif* becomes the *faux-naif,* and sometimes altogether arch.

This caused problems in *The Annunciation.* What Gilchrist has done about it here is to keep the zany heroine but to hand over the narration to another character. The last group of stories, "Crystal", are a new step; the storytelling is delegated to the heroine's black maids, uncritically loyal reporters of the war against fathers, husbands and brothers. What Gilchrist evidently wants to do is to get even closer to the roots of Mississippi talk, and effect the enrichment of English by the rhythms of black speech. This is only partly successful because it is clear that her real interest still lies with Crystal, rather than with Traceleen, the maid, who is reduced to a narrative servant too. The simulation of the lacunae and digressions of speech is not enough to counter that feeling.

What comes through best is the infectious, languorous ac-

cent of the Delta. The plots are charming too, indulgently furnished as they are with drink, drugs, "Crab Thibodeaux and Shrimp Mousse and Softshell Crabs Richard" and more money than people know what to do with. Erratic and partial as Gilchrist's style is, the drawly "whyyyyyy not" world of the modern South which she creates is a great pleasure to visit.

> David Sexton, "The Wacky Woman's Whyyyyyy Not World," in The Times Literary Supplement, No. 4286, May 24, 1985, p. 573.

Dean Flower   (review date 1985)

[*In the following review of* Victory over Japan, *Flower praises Gilchrist's "unique" prose style and sense of humor.*]

Ellen Gilchrist's stories are charming and funny, instantly engaging, deceptively simple. With the appearance last fall of her second collection [*Victory over Japan*] it has become clear that her voice is unique. Another woman, you say, to compete with Bobbie Ann Mason, Alice Adams, Ann Beattie, Alice Munro, Ella Leffland, and (name your favorite) all the rest? Amazingly, yes. And another Southerner besides. Gilchrist now lives in Fayetteville, Arkansas, but her stories range from Indiana and Kentucky on down through Memphis and Jackson to New Orleans, taking side trips to Pensacola and Texas, out to Berkeley and back to Virginia. Her characters are mostly affluent girls and women from families well-rooted in Southern traditions (collapsing, of course) and richly aware of the privileges money can buy. Most of them are busy causing trouble, and getting themselves into it.

"Music," the second of three stories about the youth, adolescence, and marriage of Rhoda Manning, describes the determined way in which a fourteen-year-old loses her virginity. **"The Double Happiness Bun"** tells how the nineteen-year-old Nora Jane robs a New Orleans bar, steals a car, and gets herself pregnant. Naturally for a Gilchrist character, her baby has *two* fathers. In a sequence of stories about the restless life of Crystal Weiss, the heroine gets her older brother's new Mercedes smashed and then wreaks havoc on his soak-the-rich business, a game ranch in Texas. These quite extravagant actions are all kept credible and even sympathetic by Gilchrist's skillful handling of voice. Here is how **"Music"** begins:

> Rhoda was fourteen years old the summer her father dragged her off to Clay County, Kentucky, to make her stop smoking and acting like a movie star. She was fourteen years old, a holy and terrible age, and her desire for beauty and romance drove her all day long and pursued her if she slept.

If is a charming touch. Whether in the first person or the third, Gilchrist always gets her characters vividly on the page by letting them talk. The author remains detached, paring her fingernails. **"The Gauzy Edge of Paradise"** begins, "The only reason Lanier and I went to the coast to begin with was to lose weight." Another voice starts out, in **"DeDe's Talking, It's Her Turn,"** "The groom's mother's garden. You've never seen such roses," followed by a list. Four of the stories about Crystal come from the voice of Traceleen, a black woman who tries to care for this flamboyantly unhappy family. Traceleen is a perfect choice for narrator because she foreshortens things so decisively: "He was marrying this girl, her daddy was said to be the richest man in Memphis," Traceleen explains. "The Weisses were real excited about it. As much money as they got I guess they figure they can use some more." Greatly to the author's credit, she does not strain to differentiate the language of Traceleen from anyone else's, rich or poor, black or white. Traceleen is no fool in any case: "That's the kind of man Miss Crystal goes for," she tells us. "I don't know why she ever married Mr. Manny to begin with. They not each other's type. It's a mismatch. Anybody could see that."

> **The distinctive trait of Gilchrist's colloquial style is its deliberate naiveté. . . . Freed of linguistic entanglements, one dashes headlong through these stories, sometimes as if they were just the most marvelous gossip you ever heard, only to come up short against the sadness and anger and self-defeating pride of these vigorously unselfconscious people.**
>
> —*Dean Flower*

The distinctive trait of Gilchrist's colloquial style is its deliberate naiveté: short sentences, simple phrasing, lists. At moments this voice can sound like children's storytelling: "Nora Jane Whittington was going to have a baby." Or, "Lady Margaret Sarpie felt terrible." But the style admirably suits the frustrated-child mentality of most Gilchrist characters. Freed of linguistic entanglements, one dashes headlong through these stories, sometimes as if they were just the most marvelous gossip you ever heard, only to come up short against the sadness and anger and self-defeating pride of these vigorously unselfconscious people. Gilchrist has a strong impulse to tie her stories together, in sequences of three, four, and five episodes about a single figure, and with very suggestive non-chronological loops to hint at the fateful patterns of these lives. She is ostensibly a comic writer, and can be relied on for hilariously funny moments, but at heart all these tales are grim. Traceleen has an apt comment on this phenomenon: "Sometimes I start telling a story that's sad and the first thing anybody says is how come? How come they went and did that way? Nobody says how come when you tell a funny story. They're too busy laughing." Gilchrist's unique art is to tell such funny stories *and* get you to ask how come. (pp. 313-14)

Dean Flower, in a review of "Victory over Japan," in The Hudson Review, *Vol. XXXVI-II, No. 2, Summer, 1985, pp. 313-14.*

Thulani Davis   (review date 1986)

[*In the following review of* In the Land of Dreamy Dreams *and* Victory over Japan, *Davis delineates the qualities of Gilchrist's short fiction.*]

Petty yearning is the stuff from which mayhem is created by the folks driving across the Huey P. Long Bridge in the stories of Ellen Gilchrist. Her characters are all various degrees of nouveau, probably the folks who are buying up the mansions in New Orleans's Garden District. And they know a "goddamn little new-rich Yankee bitch" when they see one. They toy with the lives around them and pay obnoxious lip service to the grand old manners and grand old names of the slave-owning elite—but it's pretty much a case of networking for the firm.

Ellen Gilchrist doesn't consider herself a southern writer at all, though she was born 60 miles from Faulkner's birthplace. After growing up in the Midwest, Gilchrist raised her children in New Orleans and now lives in the hill country of Fayetteville, Arkansas. Whatever she might say about her roots, she obviously has a strong love for the South, and her work is distinctly southern in its rhythms, irony, and just plain storytelling. *Victory Over Japan* and *In the Land of Dreamy Dreams* are excellent collections. All of her work shows a sharp ear for the bloodless sound of gossip, capturing the narrator's constant urge to sidetrack, tell another tangential tale. The clichés which shape many a northerner's view of the eccentricity of southerners are used skillfully, revealing not only the shallowness of such devotion to antiquity and ritual, but also the low regard southerners themselves now have for the old southern baloney.

> The spring that Robert McLaurin was fourteen he had a black friend named Gus who lived underneath a huge live oak tree in Audubon Park. It was a tree so old and imposing that people in New Orleans called it the President of the Louisiana Live Oak Society. . . . It is the middle of the afternoon and under the low-hanging branches of the oak tree the air is quiet and cool and smells of all the gardens on the boulevard; confederate jasmine, honeysuckle, sweet aslyssum, magnolia, every stereotyped southern flower you can imagine has mingled its individual odor into an ardent humid soup.

In this story, **"The President of the Louisiana Live Oak Society,"** from *In the Land of Dreamy Dreams,* the realities of *Easy Rider* come crashing home for a comfy couple in New Orleans. The mother, Lelia, just returning from the hairdresser with her hair looking like "a helmet for the Los Angeles Rams," discovers her son hanging out with a black kid: "She pulled his head into the car window. 'What are you doing with that black boy?' Robert's mother was a liberal. She never called black people niggers or Negroes even when she was mad at them." With wonderful simplicity, this story shows the world, that larger forest, rushing into Lelia's well-appointed cabin. And she grapples with it like a bear.

Lelia's husband, who suspects their son of taking drugs, presents her with "a list of objects that can be seen by a person of normal eyesight standing in the middle of his room":

1. Black light
2. Two strobe lights for altering perception of light
3. Poster of androgynous figure on motorcycle smoking a marijuana cigarette
4. Poster of Peter Fonda smoking a marijuana cigarette
5. Package of sandwich-size baggies, often used to parcel out marijuana into what are known as "lids"

Lelia may be a shallow materialist who fixes dinner by buttering french bread to go with the fried chicken prepared by the maid, but Gilchrist allows the reader to see how her belongings are connected to her psyche—they identify her class, distinguish her from the five-foot-one black teenage dope pusher she finds coming down her stairway one afternoon:

> He came walking down the carpeted stairs and down the wide walnut hall with its sixteen-foot ceilings. He came walking down the hall wrapped in a plush baby-blue monogrammed towel from the Lylian Shop. Pearls of water were dripping down his face from his thick soft hair. Widely grinning, hugely smiling, Gus came down the hall, down the Aubusson runner, down Lelia's schizophrenic, eclectic art gallery of a hall, past the Walter Andersons, the de Callatays, the Leroy Morais, the Rolland Golden, the Stanford, past the portrait of Robert's grandfather in the robes of a state supreme court justice, past the Dufy. He had just passed the edge of the new Leonor Fini when Lelia stepped into the hall and they spotted each other. . . . Lelia screamed. She screamed six months of unscreamed screaming. She screamed an ancestral, a territorial scream. She screamed her head off.

Gilchrist's characters wreak a lot of havoc, destroy people who get in the way of their personal mythology. They don't mind murder, if that is what it takes to protect what they regard as their terrain, whether material or social. But terrible as they are, these people see themselves so clearly they are both interesting and sympathetic. A tennis pro, for instance, finds herself breaking her own code—an honest game—to stop a Jewish social climber from getting the best of her. She feels it her duty to keep the social order intact, but gives up the game forever because her anti-Semitism cost her her honesty. Gilchrist's characters strive to look good, yet something southern about them, maybe something of the hick, forces them to expose themselves, let their inner life hang out there where the reader can find it.

Gilchrist obviously believes humor is crucial, and she craftily delivers it, with a sense of economy and timing that keeps it from becoming too broad or heavy-handed. The cadences and rhythms of southern speech provide both the structure and the speedy narrative pace of much of her work. Gilchrist's narrators interpret the events from a distance, like many black storytellers in southern literature who do not take their "heroes" at face value, or even too seriously. Gilchrist shows you that every charac-

ter is an insider in one reality and an outsider in another. She exposes the borders of the story, the limits of the narrator's knowledge; she reminds the reader there is another South on the other side of the tracks. (pp. 12-13)

> *Thulani Davis, "Rednecks, Belles, and K Mart Gals: Southern Women Stake Their Claim," in VLS, No. 42, February, 1986, pp. 10-13.*

Meg Wolitzer   (review date 1986)

[*Wolitzer is an American novelist and short story writer. In the following review, she characterizes the prose style and tone of Gilchrist's short fiction collection* Drunk with Love *as uneven.*]

Drunk with Love, Ellen Gilchrist's new collection of short stories, is filled with strong, occasionally dazzling pieces of fiction, yet somehow the whole does not equal the sum of its parts. This is an odd phenomenon, and while it doesn't take away from the pleasure to be had while reading the book, it does leave the reader feeling slightly dissatisfied upon finishing it.

What's missing here is a thread of commonality running through all the stories. Instead, we have a variety of quirky characters leading all sorts of dissimilar lives. It's as though Gilchrist is showing us her range of knowledge, which is considerable, rather than stopping and dwelling

Dust jacket of Victory over Japan, *Gilchrist's second collection of short stories.*

on the elements in her prose that are most successful and moving. It almost seems as though the author isn't sure of where she's strongest, so she's giving us everything she knows.

The reader, for one, has definite opinions as to where Gilchrist's writing really takes off. [**"Drunk with Love"**] is an uneven tale of a few people living in Berkeley, and while it rambles on in what seems an aimless manner, it surprises us with a terrific, surrealistic ending. Nora Jane, who has recently learned she is pregnant with twins, fades from the story at its closing moments to give the spotlight to the twin fetuses themselves, who suddenly come to life and begin to speak:

> Down inside Nora Jane's womb Tammili signaled to her sister. "Nice night tonight."
>
> "I wish it could always be the same. She's always changing. Up and down. Up and down."
>
> "Get used to it. We'll be there soon."
>
> "Let's don't think about it."
>
> "You're right. Let's be quiet."
>
> "Okay."

Gilchrist presents the twins as aliens about to land on Earth, and this sense of her characters as outsiders is a theme that occurs a couple of times in the collection, to great success. She is especially sensitive to the alienation that children and adolescents feel, and to the tenuous hold they often have over their own lives. In this volume, Gilchrist resuscitates several of the characters from her much-praised earlier collection, *Victory Over Japan,* and among them, we find Rhoda, a precocious young girl growing up in the 1940s, entering into a life she does not fully understand, nor can she fully control. Gilchrist gives us a well-rendered account of the feelings Rhoda has upon her family's imminent move. Surprisingly, Rhoda and her mother become collaborators during the melancholy drive to their new home in the story **"The Expansion of the Universe"**:

> Rhoda sat up in the seat. It was the Ohio River, dark and vast below her, and the sky was dark and vast above with only a few stars and they were really leaving.
>
> "I don't believe it," she said. "I don't believe he'd do this to me." Then she began to weep . . . and her mother wept with her but she kept her hands on the wheel and her eyes on the road. "There was nothing I could do about it, darling," she said. "I told him over and over but he wouldn't listen. . . . "

The next story in the collection, **"Adoration,"** takes a leap ahead in years, and we learn that Rhoda is now married and putting her husband through school. It is a tribute to Gilchrist that the reader feels a pang at the gap of time that has passed, and all the facts we don't know about Rhoda during the intervening years. Did her boyfriend die? Did she bear the move to her new home? Actually, we can infer the answers to these questions, and Gilchrist is a subtle enough writer to suggest a good deal about

Rhoda without coming out and giving it all away. The author is best, in fact, during those small, oblique moments, which are present in several of these stories, and are curiously absent from others.

"The Emancipator," for instance, is a disappointing tale that almost feels allegorical, about the marriage between a young woman with a social conscience and a sexy Lebanese man whose visa is about to expire. The relationship leads quickly to an obvious end in tragedy, and the reader can see it coming a long way off and does not feel satisfied.

Gilchrist is heavy-handed in this story, as she also is in **"Belize,"** which gives us a vacation of some bored rich people, but doesn't take us anywhere we haven't been before. Gilchrist's prose flags here as well, and the writing feels too laconic, the sentences choppy and flat: "We drop the bags in the unacceptable room. We go out and find adventure. There's a grocery store on a corner with Dutch chocolates. Stacy giggles. Whit buys her a chocolate bar." Perhaps the flatness of the prose is being used to help us imagine the flatness of the characters' lives, but in this case, the imitative fallacy is at work, and we are simply lulled by what is going on, not enlivened.

Drunk With Love is quieter in tone than much of the author's earlier work and has less of a regional air to it. Gilchrist can be very funny and witty, yet the most powerful stories in this collection are the more somber, delicate ones. When Gilchrist reaches for emphasis, she occasionally ends up telling rather than showing; her characters often speak in capital letters, which is a lazy way to show how angry or upset they feel. One wishes she had spent a little more time on the motivations behind such emphatic words.

Gilchrist has a strong eye for characters, and in *Drunk With Love,* she has created some very distinctive personalities, such as Annalisa Livingston, a woman who writes a church criticism and gossip column called "Our Lady in Your Pew," in the story **"First Manhattans,"** or Anna, a writer having a love affair with a red-haired pediatrician in the story **"Anna, Part I."** The reader suspects, or at least hopes, that these women will return the next time around.

Despite the unevenness, *Drunk With Love* is well worth reading. There is little cohesion among the stories, but most of them contain small gems of prose, and even an epiphany here and there, if the reader is willing to be patient and go slowly through. (pp. 2, 12)

> *Meg Wolitzer, "Drunk with Love," in* Los Angeles Times Book Review, *September 14, 1986, pp. 2, 12.*

Frances Taliaferro   (review date 1986)

[*In the following review of* Drunk with Love, *Taliaferro examines what she considers Gilchrist's unconventional narrative voice.*]

Ellen Gilchrist is a dashing writer with an unpredictable but unmistakable voice. She cannot be assigned to any tidy literary group. A swashbuckler in a land of minimalists, a country-club apostate among the feminists, she'll occasionally sound as if she'd like to believe the comforting clichés of conventional "women's fiction," but then she'll turn right around and observe the complexities of what one of her characters calls "a curved universe, low and inside, coming at me below the knees." She is full of elegant surprises, to wit the epigraph of *Drunk With Love*, which comes from Albert Einstein: "What has been overlooked is the irrational, the inconsistent, the droll, even the insane, which nature, inexhaustibly operative, implants in an individual, seemingly for her own amusement."

Gilchrist's only novel, *The Annunciation* (1983), was an antic mixture of Southern romance with self-realization in the style of the 1970s—a spunky, amusing portrait of a woman erratically uncovering her own nature. Since then, readers have discovered Gilchrist's two collections of short stories: *In the Land of Dreamy Dreams* (1981) and *Victory Over Japan* (1984), which won the American Book Award for Fiction. *Drunk With Love*, a third volume of stories, is peopled with characaters fans will recognize from the earlier collections.

When we last saw Nora Jane Whittington, in *Victory Over Japan*, the worst earthquake in 50 years had stranded her on the Richmond-San Rafael Bridge in the blue convertible given to her by the adoring Freddy Harwood. Nora Jane, you will remember, is the raving beauty and erstwhile self-taught anarchist who robbed a bar in New Orleans, made her getaway disguised as a Dominican nun, and followed her lover Sandy to California. There Freddy Harwood, as benign as Sandy was feckless, fell desperately in love with Nora Jane.

Now, in the title story of *Drunk With Love*, we find Freddy behaving heroically in the same earthquake. Nature has also provided a more equivocal cataclysm: Nora Jane is pregnant with twins, but until she gets the results of the amniocentesis she won't know whether Freddy or Sandy is the father. While the men vie for parenthood and the twins signal each other *in utero*, the doctor, a minor but authentic Gilchrist character, observes that "Men always get dizzy and full of fear and hilarity at the idea of children being conceived." Love, ruinous love!—its devastating power cannot hide beneath this apparently placid story.

As a destructive force, sex is right up there with all the more conventional life-threatening disasters. Anna Hand, the novelist who is the central character of **"Anna, Part I,"** can cope with an impending plane crash—she keeps cool by chanting the names of the books she's written—but survives only to find herself "in the jaws of love" for a married man. Love can be lethal. Two of the stories in *Drunk With Love* are about women who make exotic, sensual marriages and are eventually beaten to death by their husbands. Even the intrepid Rhoda Manning is not invulnerable. In earlier volumes we knew her as a teen-ager campaigning for carnal knowledge, but in *Drunk With Love* we find that "Sex had been a big surprise to Rhoda. She had felt its mighty hand."

Many of Gilchrist's women were "born into a world so polite that no one ever told the truth about anything," and most of them are in some stage of rebellion. Sally Lanier

Sykes of **"The Blue-Eyed Buddhist"** is terminally ill, but her last—most idealistic? most perverse?—act is to free an underwater pen full of big reef fish captured by marine biologists. Helen, in **"Belize,"** sniffs irritably around the edges of the eternal verities: everyone else in her party of bored rich people comes close to death on a Caribbean diving expedition, but Helen has to stay home because she turned her ankle climbing "those goddamn little three-inch steps" on a Mayan ruin. Her mode of rebellion is vindictive bitchiness (expertly rendered by Gilchrist, who has a slyly accurate ear).

Victory Over Japan was a bravura performance; *Drunk With Love* has less adrenaline. Gilchrist sounds least like herself when she experiments with a detached, satirical voice that works fitfully in a fantasy about the women who becomes the "church critic" for the *New York Times* (she "reviews" sermons, liturgies, vestments), but the weight-loss journal of a doomed dieter and the tale of an old lady who orders a young man from the L.L. Bean catalogue are unworthy.

It's tempting to hear Anna Hand, the character who writes novels, as the voice of Ellen Gilchrist. "I will create characters and they will tell me my secrets," says Anna. She hopes to "move the characters around so they bruise against each other and ring true." They do, whenever we're listening to Nora Jane or the fearless Rhoda or Traceleen, the maid who recounts the adventures of her nutty employer, Crystal. These are brave, funny, trustworthy stories by a seasoned combatant in the human comedy.

Frances Taliaferro, "Ellen Gilchrist's Elegant Surprises," in Book World—The Washington Post, *September 28, 1986, p. 6.*

Wendy Lesser (review date 1986)

[*Lesser is an American critic and founding editor of the* Threepenny Review. *In the following review, she faults Gilchrist for the prevalence of neurotic and stereotypical characters in* Drunk with Love.]

One's first impression on reading Ellen Gilchrist's stories is of a world alive with numerous distinctive characters: Traceleen the maid and her employer, the eminently Southern Miss Crystal; Rhoda Manning, whom we meet as eccentric child, rebellious teen-ager and disappointed adult; Annalisa Livingston, *The New York Times*'s religion critic, commenting weekly on the esthetics and morality of local churches; Nora Jane, the pregnant flower child, and her two boyfriends, Sandy and Freddy. Even Nora Jane's unborn twins have names and personalities: They become Tammili and Lydia the moment amniocentesis is performed.

Like someone taking home movies—but with a clearly focused and artfully held lens—Ms. Gilchrist catches her people at various stages in their lives, introducing them at one point and then revisiting them later. The strength of their personalities, and the fact that they reappear throughout her published work, create a sense that they have a life beyond the page: we need only wait for Ellen Gilchrist to bring that life forth, and if our curiosity isn't satisfied in one book of short stories, we can dig up an earlier volume or wait for the next. These characters, Ms. Gilchrist's technique implies, will be with us till death do us part.

In this collection, that tendency is exaggerated to the point where two of the husbands (a Lebanese immigrant in **"The Emancipator"** and a black man in **"Memphis"**) murder the blond young women who have foolishly married them. This is touchy business for a white Southern writer to deal with, and Ms. Gilchrist does not handle it well. Whereas a writer like Flannery O'Connor could distance herself from Southern racism even as she presented it from within, Ms. Gilchrist seems implicated in her own characters' attitudes. Thus a third interracial relationship, between a black chauffeur and his older white employer in **"First Manhattans,"** suffers gravely from the disturbing clichés placed in the mind of the black character: "Next thing I know she'll be wanting to get married, Kenny thought. These white women go crazy."

One would like to write off this kind of stereotyping as an aberration, but unfortunately Ms. Gilchrist's work is riddled with it. Her Jews tend to be smart, rotund and money-grubbing; Catholics, she suggests, are always viciously sanctimonious; mountain boys have unrestrainable sex drives; Californians spend their lives in hot tubs; and so on.

This is rarely true of the marriages in her fiction, which includes a novel, *The Annunciation,* and two collections of stories, *In the Land of Dreamy Dreams* and *Victory Over Japan.* Whether set in steamy New Orleans, anonymous New York or flaky Berkeley, her stories repeatedly chronicle the disintegration of relationships. Avarice and alcoholism are common causes; so are depression (especially in the women), and obsession with appearance (diets are a prominent theme) and the women's desire to establish a creative life separate from the men. Not one man in *Drunk With Love,* her latest collection—not one man in her whole body of work, with the possible exception of a youthful Arkansas guitar-player in *The Annunciation*—is good enough for the women he takes up with.

In fact, when you look at Ellen Gilchrist's stories closely, the illusion of variety begins to wear off. From a distance, you seem to be glimpsing a wild, well-populated, vastly amusing party, its lights and laughter occasionally discernible through a screen of thick trees. But as you approach the trees and peer through—as you piece together the fragments from her various stories—you notice that there is only a small number of people at the party after all: a weary, neurotic Southern wife; her overworked, insensitive Jewish husband; a cynical female artist or two (one of them a red-haired writer); some faithful black servants; an irresponsible, charming lover; and few others. They may change clothes and appearances at times, but they are basically a tiny group, vainly trying to simulate the enormous gathering they wish they were attending. Next time Ms. Gilchrist should invite some new guests.

Wendy Lesser, "Home Movies," in The New York Times Book Review, *October 5, 1986, p. 18.*

Margaret Jones Bolsterli   (essay date 1988)

[*Bolsterli is an American educator and critic whose field of specialty is women's studies. In the following essay, she investigates Gilchrist's treatment of feminist issues in "Revenge" and "Anna, Part I."*]

Since the experiences of any powerless class are considered less interesting than those of the powerful, one of the differences between the writing done by men and women has been the tendency for women to ignore the basic facts of their existence because it was not considered significant enough to read about. On the other hand, because of their superior status, men's every thought, feeling or movement has been considered valid subject for literature, easy access for a writer to a vast area of material. However, the current phase of the women's movement has brought a gradual realization that women are not powerless in their own sphere, that as Adrienne Rich's line goes in "From an Old House in America," "my power is brief and local, but I know my power"—and that the key to transcendence for a writer lies in validating that experience rather than in repudiating it. Because the roles of women and men have traditionally been more clearly defined in the South than in any other region of America, the experience of Southern women, so different from that of its men, is a relatively unmined goldfield. Ellen Gilchrist goes a step further than the canonical Southern women writers, Eudora Welty, Flannery O'Connor and Carson McCullers, in validating that experience because she is willing to go deeper into personality, to shine a light into the dark corners of women's souls to expose the preoccupations that get in the way of their achieving wholeness and coherence. Moreover, she writes about the problems of the female sphere without denying the pleasures in it. Food obsessions may get in the way of happiness, but Gilchrist's characters who have addictions also enjoy the chocolate they cannot resist.

One significant issue she examines is the difficulty of breaking out of the cocoon of the female experience into creativity. For instance, Rhoda Manning's dilemma in **"Revenge,"** or "the Summer of the Broad Jump Pit," illustrates the double bind that tied up bright little southern girls in the nineteen-forties and gave them some of the problems that are so painful to meet in many of the adolescent and adult women in her stories. Anna Hand, in **"Anna, Part I,"** shows that a woman can transcend the limitations of her experience by using it as material for art. Not only is that experience, after all, her capital as a writer, but she can understand what has happened to her only by making order of it in fiction, so what might, under other circumstances, be considered her limitation, becomes her passage to freedom.

"Revenge," told in retrospect by the adult Rhoda, begins with the memory of herself as a child, sitting on top of the chicken house watching through binoculars her five male cousins running down a cinder track to pole-vault into a pit of sand and sawdust, an activity from which she is exiled because she is a girl. "I was ten years old, the only girl in a house full of cousins. There were six of us, shipped to the Delta for the summer, dumped on my grandmother right in the middle of a world war." The societal expectations that put her at this distance from what looks to her like the most fun in the world were reiterated by her own father who, in his letter telling the boys how to construct the track on which they are to train for the Olympics, ended by instructing Rhoda's older brother Dudley "to take good care of me as I was my father's own sweet dear girl." The boys follow these instructions with relish and refuse to let her help with building the track or run on it once it is finished. She is not allowed to touch the vaulting pole. As Dudley tells her, "this is only for boys, Rhoda. This isn't a game." Rhoda is supposed to be satisfied with playing with other little girls. In a pattern she is expected to follow for the rest of her life, *she* is to watch from the swing, or the roof of the chicken house, and sometimes from the fence itself, while *they* run and play and learn the discipline of trained athletes. As her grandmother and great-aunt point out to her, if the boys did let her train with them, all she would get for it would be big muscles that would make her so unattractive no boys would ever ask her out and she would never get a husband. Since she is bored to death by the little girl she is supposed to play with on the neighboring plantation, the only diversion she can find besides watching the boys on the track is learning to dance from the black maid.

So Rhoda's first bind is being kept from doing what she wants most to do because she is a girl; it is the old "biology is destiny" argument dramatized on a Mississippi plantation. Little boys are encouraged to pursue activities that will prepare them for running the world while little girls are restricted to the domestic arena where they are expected to spend the rest of their lives.

The second bind, and perhaps the most pernicious one, is the fascination that this woman's sphere comes to hold for little girls. It is so seductive that they can find themselves up to their necks in quicksand before they have felt the ground quiver underfoot. In Rhoda's case, the seductress is her Cousin Lauralee who comes along and asks her to serve as maid of honor in her second wedding. It is more than a touch of irony that Rhoda's mother had been matron of honor in her first excursion down the aisle. The implication is unavoidable that Rhoda is following exactly in her mother's footsteps. She idolizes and imitates Cousin Lauralee and becomes engrossed in preparations for the wedding, trying on every dress in Nell's and Blum's Department Store in Greenville before the right one can be found. It is significant that Rhoda refuses to look at dresses from the girls' department, she feels herself to be so much a part of the "ladies" world in this matter. And she is adamant in her insistence on the "right" dress.

> The dress I wanted was a secret. The dress I wanted was dark and tall and thin as a reed. There was a word for what I wanted, a word I had seen in magazines. But what was that word? I could not remember.
>
> "I want something dark," I said at last. "Something dark and silky."
>
> "Wait right there," the saleslady said. "Wait just a minute." Then, from out of a prewar storage closet she brought a black-watch plaid recital dress with spaghetti straps and a white piqué

jacket. It was made of taffeta and rustled when I touched it. There was a label sewn into the collar of the jacket. *Little Miss Sophisticate,* it said. Sophisticate, that was the word I was seeking. I put on the dress and stood triumphant in the sea of ladies and dresses and hangers.

And so Rhoda, although maintaining all the while that *she* never will marry but will have a career instead, is caught up in preparation for the wedding, which she sees as a means of drawing the envy and admiration of the boys who have cut her out of the pole vaulting. If she cannot get their attention as an equal in their games, she will get it this way. As she later recalls the drive back from Greenville with her new dress, "All the way home I held the box on my lap thinking about how I would look in the dress. 'Wait till they see me like this,' I was thinking. 'Wait till they see what I really look like.' "

The wedding itself is a disappointment. Held at the grandmother's house, there is much less drama than Rhoda would have liked. But afterwards, at the reception, she does something that lets the real Rhoda out of the prison of the women's trappings she has assumed for the wedding. Under the influence of a strong drink of her own concoction, she goes down to the track, takes off her formal, teaches herself to pole vault, and just as everybody from the wedding comes searching for her, she makes a perfect vault over the barrier into the pit.

In retrospect, she is not sure that anything she has done since has been of any real interest to her.

The girl is mother to the woman. This story with such two strong forces pulling at Rhoda, the male sphere with its activity and power on one hand, and the traditional woman's sphere on the other, shows in a nutshell the difficulties that bright little girls of that generation faced. Gilchrist never implies that the experiences in the woman's sphere are not fun. Rhoda *enjoys* choosing that dress and being a big shot in her cousin's wedding, but she also wants to participate in the male world of activity and power. The dreadful part is that each area apparently excludes the other. Her choices seem to be as final as the choice of figs in Sylvia Plath's novel *The Bell Jar.* To choose one means to give up the others.

This is the "vale of soul-making" of the Southern woman writer; but as Gilchrist shows in the later stories about Rhoda and Anna Hand and in her novel *The Annunciation,* some women do indeed finally make it through to creativity. And they do it by accepting the validity of their experience and transforming it into art.

A good example of this is Anna Hand's realization in **"Anna, Part I"** that the context in which she must understand herself is not the male world of power but an adult version of the domestic sphere to which the child Rhoda was confined, and that to order it in fiction is a way to control it. Creativity emerges from the trick of combining the two pulls: one becomes material for the other. Writing is the key to transcendence.

The exclusive nature of the traditional choices for a woman can be seen in the devastating effect of love on Anna, a successful writer whose creativity has been immobilized for ten months by an affair with a married doctor. She has fallen into the pitfalls of such a relationship with her eyes wide open; at the beginning she reflects that she has, after all, already wasted five years of her life on a married man and swears she will never do it again. But she is helpless in the face of love. She is getting old, and this may be her last chance at passion. The doctor, of course, never misses a beat in his career nor in his marriage; it is only Anna's life that is disrupted.

Ellen Gilchrist's opinions about the relative value of the choices Anna has made are implicit in the terms she uses to describe Anna's coming to her senses. The story begins with Anna, having realized the folly of what she has been doing, calling her editor in New York to announce that she is ready to get back to work: "It was a big day for Anna Hand. It was the day she decided to give up being a fool and go back to being a writer." " . . . I've wasted ten months of my life. Ten goddam months in the jaws of love. Well, I had to do it. It's like a cold. If you leave the house sooner or later it happens." What she goes to work on is a story about the affair, "How to ring the truth out of the story, absolve sadness, transmute it, turn it into art." Then Gilchrist's technique is to follow Anna's prescription for writing this story; she begins at the beginning of the affair, noticing everything. It is obvious that the whole thing was hopeless from the start. Not only was the doctor solidly married with no intention of leaving his wife, but Anna knew all along that there were serious, probably irreconcilable differences between them. Yet during the time of the affair she did what women are supposed to do. She ignored the fact that his sentimentality embarrassed her, for example, and let her obsession with him completely dominate her life. Her love blinded her to everything else and induced her to give up her writing, which she acknowledges as the most important thing in her life. She even entertained the impossible dream that one day they would be married and live happily ever after. The incident that breaks the spell, in fact, is that one day, when they have not been together in a while, he comes over and they have such a good time she forgets he is married, thus breaking her one ironclad rule, never to forget where she is and what she is doing. Realizing that she has fallen to this level of consciousness wakes her up; within three weeks she is home again in South Carolina putting her life back together. In other words, she goes home to return to writing, to validate her experience in art and therefore to achieve transcendence. Significantly, Anna knows that this is what she is doing.

> There is a way to organize this knowledge, Anna decided. To understand what happened. This love affair, this very last love affair. In a minute I will get out of this bed and begin to understand what happened. I will pick up the telephone and call Arthur [her editor] and then I will begin to write the stories and they will tell me what is going on.
>
> I will create characters and they will tell me my secrets. They will stand across the room from me with their own voices and dreams and disappointments. I will set them going like a fat gold watch, as Sylvia said. . . . I will gather my tribe around me and celebrate my birthday. There

will be champagne and a doberge cake from the bakery that Cajun runs on the highway. Yes, all that for later. For now, the work before me, waiting to be served and believed in and done. My work. How I define myself in the madness of the world.

At this point, she takes control of her life by climbing out of bed, sitting down at her typewriter and beginning to write. Her subject, of course, is what she knows best: the women's world, the love affair and her survival. (pp. 7-9)

Margaret Jones Bolsterli, "Ellen Gilchrist's Characters and the Southern Woman's Experience: Rhoda Manning's Double Bind and Anna Hand's Creativity," in New Orleans Review, *Vol. 15, No. 1, Spring, 1988, pp. 7-9.*

Ms. Gilchrist uses the simple stuff of which dreams are made to weave cautionary tales of modern life.

—*Cressida Connolly, in* Books and Bookmen, *1986.*

Roy Hoffman   (review date 1989)

[*In the following review, Hoffman focuses on characterization in* Light Can Be Both Wave and Particle.]

Since the publication in 1981 of her first short-story collection, *In the Land of Dreamy Dreams,* and in five subsequent works of fiction, Ellen Gilchrist has consistently created heroines who are smart, impulsive and vulnerable. Usually hailing from locales with definable social codes— the garden district of New Orleans, the Mississippi Delta—Ms. Gilchrist's women, in contrast to their communities, are unconventional, nervy, outspoken. As grown-ups they are passionate to the point of recklessness, romantic in the midst of despair. As youngsters they vex adults. Ariane Manning despairs of her daughter in a story, "**The Time Capsule,**" in this collection [*Light Can Be Both Wave and Particle*]: "Rhoda was too much. Too smart for her own good. Too wild, too crazy, too hard to manage or control."

Rhoda herself, who appears throughout Ms. Gilchrist's work, is center stage in four of these 11 stories: as an intractable though winning child in "**The Time Capsule**" and "**The Tree Fort**"; as a love-struck, star-crossed teenager in "**Some Blue Hills at Sundown**"; and as a woman in her early 50's (Ms. Gilchrist's age) in the story "**Mexico,**" rambling still with her brother Dudley and her cousin Saint John. Whether they actually mirror Ms. Gilchrist's life or not, the tales of Rhoda have an autobiographical feel to them. As opposed to the continuing saga of Nora Jane Whittington, represented in this book by the dramatically rich story "**The Starlight Express,**" the Rhoda stories, like episodes from a memoir being freely constructed, leapfrog over time.

If **"The Time Capsule"** and **"The Tree Fort"** seem too neatly wrought, with their titles providing the central symbols—similar ground was covered in the 1984 collection *Victory Over Japan*—the story called **"Mexico,"** thematically larger, expands Rhoda's horizons. Looking to shake herself from the doldrums and with more than one ex-husband behind her, Rhoda sets off with Dudley and Saint John on a wild escapade south of the border. Along the way she becomes infatuated with a bullfighter, gets drunk in a town plaza and is scared out of her wits on a hunter's game preserve stocked with big cats gone bad in circuses. **"Mexico"** is a funny, offbeat and masterly road story with evocations—and subtle inversions—of Hemingway. At a bullfight Rhoda even surmises, "Death in the afternoon is real danger, real death." The Hemingway allusion is fitting: in Rhoda's first fictional appearance nearly a decade ago, she was reading *Across the River and Into the Trees*.

Followers of Ms. Gilchrist's writing will appreciate many links to earlier works, but it is not essential to be already acquainted with her fictional family to enjoy this collection. There are, however, two exceptions: **"The Song of Songs"** and **"Life on the Earth,"** offering glimpses, respectively, of a young woman, adopted at birth, on the way to meet up with her long-lost birth mother; and of a young man recovering from an accident. Alone, the stories are puzzling, fragments that suggest a larger pattern; and Ms. Gilchrist is no minimalist evoking a world in a grain of sand. The scenes take on power only when viewed in their rightful place as a conclusion to the 1983 novel *The Annunciation*. Indeed, the scenes provide a happy ending to a story that ended six years ago on a tragicomic note. Strictly speaking, this ideal resolution undercuts the emotional complexity of the original ending of *The Annunciation*. Sentimentally, though, a reader may welcome the bright turn of events. Besides, supplying a happy ending to yesteryear's bittersweet story seems in keeping with the generally optimistic tone of *Light Can Be Both Wave and Particle*.

Despite the tiresome presence of **"Traceleen Turns East"**—another installment in the self-consciously outrageous tale of a decadent New Orleans woman as told by her maid—**"Light Can Be Both Wave and Particle"** bristles with new energy. No story suggests fresh direction for Ms. Gilchrist's writing better than the title one. It brings together lovers from different cultures more spiritedly than any past Gilchrist story.

In previous works the white Southern woman, Protestant or Roman Catholic, who becomes involved with men of markedly different backgrounds usually writes her own prescription for failure. In this story Ms. Gilchrist puts together lovely, impressionable Margaret McElvoy of Fayetteville, Ark., with an unlikely suitor: Lin Tan Sing, a Chinese geneticist working and studying in Berkeley, Calif. Lin moves in a delicately lyrical world that balances his work and Zen meditation. His own blend of love for science, Buddhism and romantic infatuation makes him irresistible to Margaret and, as a character, to the reader: "At the place where her car had been, several pigeons flew down from a roof and began to peck at the sidewalk. Lin

took that for a sign and went back into the hotel and sat in meditation for an hour, remembering the shape of the universe and the breathtaking order of the species. He imagined the spirit of Margaret and the forms of her ancestors back a hundred generations. Then he imagined Margaret in the womb and spoke to her in a dream on the day she was conceived."

This story ends with Lin, engaged to Margaret, about to start a game of chess with Margaret's father in Arkansas. There are innumerable possibilities for moves in the beginnings of a chess match—almost as many as Ms. Gilchrist's next possible moves with these characters.

> Roy Hoffman, "Smart Enough for Their Own Good," in The New York Times Book Review, October 22, 1989, p. 13.

Greg Johnson (review date 1990)

[*Johnson is an American poet, novelist, short story writer, and critic. In the following review, he asserts that the stories in* Light Can Be Both Wave and Particle *are uneven and largely lacking in "the meticulous thought and craft that make for the most memorable fiction."*]

Ellen Gilchrist's latest collection is apparently an assemblage of older work combined with new: two of the stories comprise an alternative ending to her first novel, *The Annunciation*, and several others deal with characters included in previous collections; only a few introduce new characters and new thematic concerns. One can understand the eagerness of Gilchrist and her publishers to build upon the reputation secured by the author's impressive early work (especially her two story collections, *In the Land of Dreamy Dreams* and *Victory Over Japan*), but this new gathering is extremely uneven, as though rushed into print without much concern for its artistic structure and coherence.

Two of the better stories in *Light Can Be Both Wave and Particle* deal with childhood. In **"The Tree Fort"** and **"The Time Capsule,"** both set in the 1940's and featuring Rhoda Manning, Gilchrist evokes the mingled vulnerability and wayward vitality of children, as well as their capacity for wonder. **"The Tree Fort"** ends by emphasizing Rhoda's almost painfully intense physicality: "I was pure energy, clear light, morally neutral, soft and violent and almost perfect. I had two good eyes and two good ears and two arms and two legs. If bugs got inside of me, my blood boiled and ate them up. If I cut myself, my blood rushed in and sewed me back together." Another linked pair, **"The Starlight Express"** and the title story [**"Light Can Be Both Wave and Particle"**], are longer and more diffuse than the childhood reminiscences, but Gilchrist's intriguing plots and vivid characterizations help compensate for flaws in structure and narrative viewpoint. In **"The Starlight Express,"** a woman abandoned by her husband gives birth prematurely to twins in an isolated house, helped through the ordeal by Freddy, the man who genuinely loves her. On the way to meet Freddy, the woman has met a young Chinese-American medical student, Lin Tan Sing, who becomes in turn the hero of the volume's title story. The most likable and original character in the volume, Lin Tan falls in love with the daughter of a formidable American poet. Their romance is winsome, touching, and completely convincing; the two meet on a bridge overlooking Puget Sound, and the story finally suggests a harmonious marriage between East and West, between careful reason and honest emotion.

There is one other intriguing piece—**"Traceleen Turns East,"** a briskly paced Southern Gothic tale of an armed kidnapper holding several New Orleans matrons at bay— but the volume is weakened by stories that are either too brief or too haphazardly written to have significant impact. In **"The Song of Songs,"** for instance, a wealthy New Orleans woman meets the mother who had given her up for adoption as a child, but their reunion is presented matter-of-factly, with little sense of the emotional experience of either woman. **"The Man Who Kicked Cancer's Ass"** is a woeful example of "redneck chic," its male narrator a stereotypical Southern vulgarian who is enraged by his cancer diagnosis. But most disappointing is the novella-length **"Mexico,"** which concludes the volume. Another story dealing with Rhoda and her brother Dudley, **"Mexico"** presents her at age fifty-three, dissatisfied with her life and yearning for adventure and sexual intrigue. She, Dudley, and their cousin Saint John travel to Mexico, where Rhoda attends a bullfight and decides on the spot that she must sleep with the handsome young bullfighter. Although Rhoda is a potentially sympathetic character, a woman whose hard-boiled exterior conceals a romantic longing to live her life to the hilt, Gilchrist has her heroine curse like a sailor, indulge in maudlin self-pity, and discuss her sex life in graphic terms with her brother and cousin. Rhoda does most of her thinking below the belt, in fact, and the bullfights provide an opportunity for shallow, sometimes laughable rhapsodies on love and blood, sex and death: "I love this country, Rhoda decided. Any place that can produce a man like that is okay with me. . . . Oh, God, Guillarmo's back and arms are the most beautiful things I've ever seen in my life. I would like to see him fight bulls from now till the dawn of time." Perhaps she means "till the end of time," but no matter. As elsewhere in this interminable novella, Rhoda prefers gushing to thinking.

This is a perplexing volume, then, from a talented writer. In **"Mexico,"** and even in some of the more successful stories, Gilchrist seems to get carried away with her own breezy style and verbal facility. The stories read quickly and are often enjoyable, but they lack the meticulous thought and craft that make for the most memorable fiction. (pp. 283-85)

> *Greg Johnson, "Some Recent Herstories," in* The Georgia Review, *Vol. XLIV, Nos. 1 & 2, Spring-Summer, 1990, pp. 278-88.*

Ilene Raymond   (review date 1990)

[*In the following review, Raymond delineates the "poignant, comic and pitch-perfect novellas" in* I Cannot Get You Close Enough.]

In *I Cannot Get You Close Enough* Ellen Gilchrist— winner of the 1984 National Book Award for her collec-

tion of stories *Victory Over Japan*—delivers three poignant, comic and pitch-perfect novellas that revisit the Hand family of Charlotte, N.C.

Not since J. D. Salinger's Glass family has a writer lavished so much loving attention on the eccentricities and activities of an extended clan. Like the Glass family, the Hands are by turns intelligent, passionate and a bit precious, haunted by the spectre of a romantic perfection that is always just out of reach. Most significant, both families suffer the suicide of their oldest sibling: Anna Hand, the writer in *The Anna Papers*, walks off into the water after she is diagnosed with incurable cancer. Her death, like that of Seymour Glass, does not end her potent influence on those who survive.

"Winter," the opening novella, is drawn from Anna's posthumous manuscripts. In swift, urgent entries, Anna chronicles her six-year fight to keep Jessie Hand, her youngest "and beautiful and perfect" niece, the daughter of her darling brother Daniel Hand, out of the reach of Sheila MacNiece, Daniel's estranged second wife who abandoned the child. Anna's efforts to prevent Sheila from winning custody of Jessie lead her as far as Istanbul, where she discovers a terrible secret. Yet all the while, even as we are drawn to Anna's protectiveness, we question Anna's motives. The only person who truly seems able to stand up to Anna is Sheila's father, who asks Anna point-blank what she's up to, why her brother can't defend himself.

His question is not lost on Anna, who recognizes that the answer points to a problem endemic to her own character. "I believe life is supposed to be tragic," writes Anna. "But things which are bearable to my life are unbearable in the lives of my family. I cannot bear to watch them suffer."

Such a mix of propriety and moxie also play a part in **"De-Havilland Hand."** As the aunt of 16-year-old Olivia de Havilland Hand—whose Cherokee mother, Summer Deer, died in childbirth after a brief and quickly annulled first marriage to Daniel—Anna pressures Daniel to go to Oklahoma where the girl lives with her aunt and to bring her home to the Hands' enclave in North Carolina.

Once again, Anna's interference sparks changes in the lives of both Jessie and Daniel.

"A Summer in Maine," the final entry in the trilogy of novellas, is a tour de force that clocks the romantic adventures of an eccentric group of familiar Gilchrist characters who have left Dixie for a vacation up North. In Maine, Anna's two young nieces begin a cult of Anna, complete with jasmine incense and reverent readings of her old letters. Meanwhile, the other guests keep themselves busy with a botched love affair, a missing child, a sudden pregnancy and a hurried—and unpredictable—wedding.

From a distance, nothing about these characters might attract attention save for the passion with which they act; the burdens and pleasures of family life, Gilchrist implies, can bring the best (and worst) of character to light. Anna's attempts to "rescue" the younger members of the clan, particularly beguiling Jessie and strongwilled Olivia, are linked to historic as well as personal motives. But Gilchrist realizes that Anna's attempts to right family wrongs are shrouded in irony: There is always the chance that fate holds the stronger hand. While Anna succeeds in keeping Jessie from the mother who abandoned her, by the end of **"A Summer in Maine,"** Jessie herself is preparing to jump ship once her own child is born.

But most of all, the novellas concern themselves with the bonds and boundaries of love. "I cannot get you close enough," Anna Hand writes, " . . . never can and never will. We cannot get from anyone the things we need to fill the endless terrible need, not to be dissolved, not to sink back into sand, heat, broom, air, thinnest air. And so we revolve around each other and our dreams collide. It is embarrassing that it should be so hard. Look out the window in any weather. We are part of all that glamour, drama, change, and should not be ashamed."

These are not easy tales, but stories rich with acrimony, wisdom, courage and, finally, joy.

> *Ilene Raymond, "Love's Bonds and Boundaries," in* Book World—The Washington Post, *December 16, 1990, p. 7.*

Nina Mehta   (review date 1991)

[*In the following review, Mehta derides what she considers the uneven prose style and melodramatic tone of* I Cannot Get You Close Enough.]

"It was going to be the worst book I had ever written, but the writing of it was an exotic thing. I knew all along the book would not be good but I was in a strange mood and went on writing." So says Anna Hand, a character with an international writing career in Ellen Gilchrist's *I Cannot Get You Close Enough.* It might as well have been the author speaking.

Gilchrist's newest book comprises three plodding, interconnected novellas about the Hands and the Mannings, a set of selfish cousins headquartered in Charlotte, North Carolina. These families have already provided plot and fodder for previous books by Gilchrist. Here, they're once again summoned from their literary holding pen to help their creator prove—in flat, uninspired writing—that family life is freighted with more ills than frills.

The first two novellas concern Jessie and Olivia Hand, half-sisters on whose delicate shoulders will one day fall the burden of propagating the Hand species. **"Winter,"** an autobiographical manuscript discovered among Anna's possessions, recounts the narrator's effort to help Daniel, her alcoholic brother, retain custody of his daughter, Jessie. As we stand by patiently, Anna travels with unconvincing urgency to England and then Turkey to dig up dirt on her wicked sister-in-law.

The second novella, **"De Havilland Hand,"** is about the adolescent gropings of Olivia Hand, the daughter Daniel didn't know he fathered until fifteen years after the fact. Olivia's Cherokee mother died during childbirth, and she was raised by a family maid in Tahlequah, Oklahoma.

At the height of her adolescence, she happens across a story by Anna Hand in her English class and writes to her care of the publisher, introducing herself as Anna's long-lost niece and fibbing that she's a straight-A student. Daniel and Anna are as impressed with her promise of top-notch academic performance as they are with the discovery of an unknown relative, and Olivia eventually moves in with Daniel and Jessie. The young girl's emotions and problems are real enough, but they have a watered-down "After School Special" feel in Gilchrist's hands.

The final novella in this book is the one with more serious (if not more elevated) aspirations. **"A Summer in Maine"** accumulates most of Gilchrist's characters for an extended vacation under one roof. Despite the continual mating among non-spouses, a flu epidemic, an emergency appendectomy, and an "unwed mother situation," it's the incessant complaining that sets the tone, and the sluggish pace of the prose.

Somewhere between the alternatingly threadbare and overwrought prose, partially hidden from view by hackneyed observations shabbily clad as insight ("They grow up so fast, the young ones that we love. Before long all we have are memories and they are gone out to the world."), lurks an idea. The gist is that every child is born blessed—and, as such, is capable of righting its parents' lives. Gilchrist's characters may fall prey to Hobbesian tendencies the way children fall prey to candy, but on Arrival Day her infants are not mean, petty, and adulterous.

Weighed down by narrative chaff, *I Cannot Get You Close Enough* is more soap-operatic than substantive. And bad soap at that.

> *Nina Mehta, in a review of "I Cannot Get You Close Enough," in* Belles Lettres: A Review of Books by Women, *Vol. 6, No. 3, Spring, 1991, p. 63.*

Anna Vaux   (review date 1991)

[*In the following review, Vaux faults Gilchrist's writing in* I Cannot Get You Close Enough *as self-indulgent and vapid.*]

Ellen Gilchrist's last novel [*The Anna Papers*] was about a woman writer called Anna Hand—a rich Southern belle with three ex-husbands and a wardrobe stacked with Armani and Calvin Klein, who walked into the sea wearing a Valentino jacket and knee-high boots when she discovered she had cancer. It was a fragmentary book, without much plot, which dealt mainly with the story of her two nieces, Jessie and Olivia, and petered out in a dispiriting trail of oddments and posthumous papers.

In *I Cannot Get You Close Enough,* we get more of the fragments (still turning up in suitcases), more designer clothes, more Jessie and Olivia and more minor events dating from before, during and after Anna's death. It's not so much "another saga", as the publishers announce, as the old one revisited: Anna quickly dies all over again, Olivia's Cherokee background is once more delved into, and there is further liberal description of her reunion with her father, Daniel (Anna's handsome brother). Here too are some of the letters they wrote in *The Anna Papers.* A few of them reappear verbatim, one, curiously, is just a rough approximation, as though Gilchrist has had second thoughts about what she'd written. The dust-jacket informs "past admirers" that they'll meet up with "familiar characters", and certainly some will feel that they've been here before.

Gilchrist has worked, though, to make her principal characters tougher and more hip. They are not quite the same creatures as they were before. They have a new line in sex-slang and they are more strenuous in their love lives. While Anna is thinking about what to do with Adrian, Daniel gets married first to Summer (who dies) and then Sheila (who leaves); Olivia is in love with Bobby, and Jessie has a thing with King; Helen has met a poet and Andria takes up with Kale Vito; Crystal is having trouble with Manny, so is sleeping with Alan; Lydia sleeps with Alan too, but just the once, and can't understand why Daniel won't do it with her at all, given her belief that "every man wants to fuck every attractive woman and women want to fuck most of the men".

I Cannot Get You Close Enough is a book in three parts, each part contributing something to the family drama and to a plot which suggests nothing so much as *Dallas* or *Dynasty*. Everybody broods on the importance of "kin". Anna flies off to London and Turkey looking for proof that Jessie's peripatetic mother is mixing with communists and caught up in drug running. Olivia hacks into the school computer to improve her grades and her father's estimation of her. Time passes; the custody suits work out; everybody seems to be getting on fine, and then they all go on holiday to Maine, where it begins to occur to them that nobody is getting close enough to anybody else. They start dieting and arguing; they start thinking bad thoughts about each other.

Most of the book takes place inside their heads, for here, in their heads, it's all very much freer. They can speak to us, to each other or to people who are not yet born; they can forget about narrative and give in to the release of their emotional burdens. Gilchrist lets her characters get on with it. She polishes up their dirty talk and their views on men and women; she gives them thoughts on art and theories about writers; she makes them quote poems (their own or somebody else's). But there is no shape or design or ironic distance. Occasionally, it looks as though she's about to indulge in some intertextual tease (Anna is published by Faber, she hangs out in Queen's Square and at the Frankfurt book fair and has written a book called *Falling Away—Falling Through Space* was the title of Gilchrist's journals), but nothing is made of any of these details, they just come, and then they go.

The book picks up in the final section. The thoughts of these spoilt Southerners and their black maid, Traceleen, bounce off each other nicely as the drama moves towards its climax with Jessie becoming impregnated by King and Olivia opting for a course in biology and the Human Gene. But there is something vapid and flimsy about Gilchrist's writing. It is not just the dullness of her characters' voices, their ingrown sentimentality and ability to say things like "the young are all we have and we should worship them because they still have moments that are not sullied with the darkness of remorse and adultery and hate". The worst horrors come from their self-indulgence. "What a feast we live in", Anna writes in a letter, "Nationalities, cars, trees, oceans, love affairs, electromagnetic fields. How to write in the fact of so much wonder. What to praise." Yes, indeed.

> *Anna Vaux, "Spoilt Southerners," in* The Times Literary Supplement, *No. 4626, November 29, 1991, p. 22.*

FURTHER READING

Criticism

Carper, Leslie. "Deep South, Deep Roots." *The Women's Review of Books* 11, No. 9 (June 1985): 4-6.
  Describes the protagonists of Gilchrist's *Victory over Japan* as "New South heroines" who "reflect the flavor of the Delta" yet rebel against the genteel image of the traditional Southern belle.

Clute, John. "Nightmares." *New Statesman* 109, No. 2828 (31 May 1985): 31.
  Positive review of *Victory over Japan*.

Connolly, Cressida. "Just Friends." *Books and Bookmen*, No. 370 (August 1986): 27.
  Laudatory review of *Victory over Japan*.

Craig, Patricia. Review of *Victory over Japan*, by Ellen Gilchrist. *London Review of Books* (20 June 1985): 20-1.
  Discusses the defining qualities of Gilchrist's heroines.

Grumbach, Doris. "The Extra Skin that Language Can Give: Recent Collections of Short Stories." *The Georgia Review* XXXVI, No. 3 (Fall 1982): 668-74.
  Derides the language of Gilchrist's *In the Land of Dreamy Dreams* as pedestrian and colorless.

Neuhaus, Denise. "On Dependable Ground." *The Times Literary Supplement*, No. 4562 (7-13 September 1990): 956.
  Negative review of *Light Can Be Both Wave and Particle* in which the critic asserts that "the tiredness of the writing here indicates that there may not be enough substance in these characters for us, or their creator, to take them seriously."

Peden, William. Review of *Victory over Japan*, by Ellen Gilchrist. *Western Humanities Review* XXXIX, No. 3 (Autumn 1985): 267-70.
  Study of the female protagonists of Gilchrist's short story collection.

Stuewe, Paul. "Of Some Import." *Quill and Quire* 55, No. 12 (December 1989): 29.
  Mixed review of *Light Can Be Both Wave and Particle* in which the critic contends that "although Gilchrist's stories seem largely devoid of any meaningful inner life, the fluency with which they are written and the accuracy of their background detail render them quite palatable in small doses."

Wells, Susan Spano. "A Maine Summer Night's Dream."
The New York Times Book Review (4 November 1990): 24.
Surveys stories and characters in *I Cannot Get You Close
Enough.*

Additional coverage of Gilchrist's life and career is contained in the following sources
published by Gale Research: *Contemporary Authors,* Vols. 113, 116; *Contemporary
Authors New Revision Series,* Vol. 41; *Contemporary Literary Criticism,* Vols. 34, 48;
Dictionary of Literary Biography, Vol. 130; and *Major 20th-Century Writers.*

Comte de Lautréamont

1846-1870

(Pseudonym of Isidore Lucien Ducasse) French poet and short story writer.

The following entry presents criticism on *Les chants de "Maldoror"* (1868-69; *The Lay of Maldoror;* also translated as *Lautréamont's "Maldoror"*).

INTRODUCTION

Lautréamont is known primarily for *Les chants de Maldoror,* a graphic exploration of rebellion and morality centering around the exploits of an evil, metamorphic creature. Virtually unknown during his lifetime, Lautréamont developed a wide following in the 1920s when he was championed by the Surrealists, many of whom considered him their chief nineteenth-century precursor. More recently *Maldoror* has become the focus of an increasing number of studies in the areas of post-structuralism and intertextuality.

Very little is known about Lautréamont's brief life. He was born in Montevideo, Uruguay, where his father was a French consular officer. In 1859 Lautréamont was sent to France and attended schools in Tarbes and Pau. About 1867 he moved to Paris, ostensibly to attend L'Ecole Polytechnique, although he never registered. He remained in Paris and is believed to have composed both *Maldoror* and *Poésies I, II,* his only other major work, during this period. Lautréamont died in 1870 of unknown causes.

Written in short prose cantos, *Maldoror* has been described as poetry, prose poetry, short fiction, and as a novel. The volume's six cantos detail the experiences of Maldoror, a demonic, defiant figure who commits murder, practices sadomasochistic eroticism, utters blasphemies at the biblical God, and metamorphoses into various beasts. Deliberately challenging and insulting, Maldoror views himself as a being equal to God, who in turn is portrayed as a degenerate oppressor of humans: "I perceived a throne built of human excrement and gold upon which was enthroned with idiot pride and robed in a shroud made from unlaundered hospital sheets, that one who calls himself the Creator!" Reflecting Maldoror's rebellion against traditional ethics and Lautréamont's rejection of literary convention, the book ends with an explicit depiction of the torture and murder of an adolescent whose body Maldoror flings into the dome of the Pantheon in France. Robin Lydenberg has commented on this episode: "Maldoror's defacing of the national monument to history and tradition parallels and dramatizes on a disturbingly literal level [Lautréamont's] ambivalent attitude both towards his own text and towards all literary tradition."

The Surrealist writers acclaimed Lautréamont's glorification of the theme of rebellion as well as the nightmarish, hallucinatory atmosphere of *Maldoror,* which they interpreted as an expression of the unconscious. In *Maldoror* Lautréamont often juxtaposed two entirely unrelated elements. For example, his line "beautiful as the fortuitous meeting of a sewing machine and an umbrella on a dissection table" became for the Surrealists the model for their poetic method, which was based on irrational conjunctions of words, images, and ideas. In addition to its imagery, the work's several narrative stances have also been the subject of commentary. Scholars have noted that the shifting point of view in *Maldoror* obscures the distinction between the hero and the personas employed by Lautréamont both within the text of *Maldoror* as the narrator and without in the adoption of his pseudonym. Arguing that Lautréamont attempted to impose an esthetic and ethical "reform" on his readers by confusing the boundaries of fiction and raising questions of identity, Kay B. Woodard has noted: "What is common . . . to both the esthetic and the ethical reforms is a movement abolishing the distance between the reader and what he reads, a blurring of the normally well-circumscribed fictional categories to which we are accustomed, and a transformation of the reader from observer to participant."

PRINCIPAL WORKS

SHORT FICTION

Les chants de Maldoror: Chants I, II, III, IV, V, VI.   2
    vols. 1868-69
    [*The Lay of Maldoror,* 1924; also translated as
    Lautréamont's "Maldoror," 1970]

OTHER MAJOR WORKS

Poésies I, II (poetry) 1870
    [*Lautréamont's Preface to His Unwritten Volume of
    Poems* published in *New Directions 9,* 1946]
Oeuvres complètes (poetry, short fiction, and letters)
    1927
Poésies and Complete Miscellanea (poetry and letters)
    1978

CRITICISM

Henry A. Grubbs, Jr.   (essay date 1934)

[*In the following essay, Grubbs surveys critical opinion
of Lautréamont's work up to 1934.*]

The problem of Isidore Ducasse, who for his *Chants de
Maldoror* adopted the pompous pseudonym of "Comte de
Lautréamont," is now ready for the attention of literary
historians. Before 1919 he was only known to, and admired by, a small group of followers. Between 1919 and
1925 his influence became manifest and his work widely
known. For example, to André Gide he is "avec Rimbaud,
plus que Rimbaud peut-être, le maître des écluses pour la
littérature de demain" [*Le Cas Lautréamont,* 1925]. The
importance of his work has been stressed also by writers
such as Bernard Faÿ, Léon Pierre-Quint, Edmond Jaloux
and Ramón Gómez de la Serna. For his most ardent admirers, such as André Breton and Paul Eluard, he is too
sacred to be delivered to the public: "En réponse à votre
lettre je tiens à déclarer que selon moi c'est pure folie de
soulever publiquement la 'question' Lautréamont.
Qu'espérez-vous, grand Dieu? Ce qui a pu si longtemps se
garder de toute souillure, à quoi pensez-vous en le livrant
aux littérateurs, *aux porcs?*" A study of the works of the
surréalistes will show that not only do they quote Lautréamont as an authority of last resort, but that their works
are dominated by the influence of his style and his ideas.

As a contrast to this, we have an almost complete blank
in the field of scholarship. Isidore Ducasse, though eminently worthy, has not yet entered into the domain of literary history. Up until December, 1931, when a short article
by S. A. Rhodes, entitled "Lautréamont *redevivus,*" appeared in the *Romanic Review,* (XXII, pp. 285-90), the
name of Lautréamont had apparently never been mentioned in any of the French, English or American reviews
devoted to the history of French literature.

Lautréamont is a writer of sufficient importance to deserve
careful study, from the point of view of his life, the significance of his work, his sources, his influence. But, considering, on the one hand, the general neglect with which he
has been treated by literary historians, and, on the other
hand, the often misleading partiality of his admirers, it
seems that a general *mise au point* and presentation of the
question should precede any definitive studies. The present article will attempt to do that. It will give briefly a history of the success of Lautréamont's work, at the same
time mentioning and commenting upon the principal biographical and critical studies that have appeared to date,
and will attempt to present (without solving them) the
problems regarding Lautréamont's life and work that remain to be elucidated.

Before proceeding further, it will be well to give a brief
analysis and description of the character of the ***Chants de
Maldoror.*** It is a poem in prose, running to about 280
pages in length in the complete edition. It is divided into
six *chants,* each of which is subdivided into ten to twelve
strophes of varying length. A large part of the work is narrative; usually each strophe is devoted to a single narrative
episode. These episodes (with the exception of the sixth
chant, where there is a long narrative sequence) are connected by no thread, except for the presence of the protagonist Maldoror. Here and there strophes in which the protagonist analyzes his character are interpolated among the
narrative ones. The first strophe of each of the *chants* is
prefatory in its nature; and in these strophes the author
ironically discusses his intentions and cryptically explains
his *art poétique.* The work has the appearance of being incomplete. The last strophe concludes the narrative of the
sixth *chant,* but it is hardly a satisfactory conclusion to the
poem.

The poem as a whole is an expression of Romantic revolt,
possibly the most violent and extreme expression of this
revolt that is known. The hero is Maldoror, a sort of superman, described as "l'homme aux lèvres de bronze,"
"l'homme aux lèvres de jaspe," the man who has never
slept, has never laughed. He has vast intellectual powers
supported by immeasurable pride, but is stained by excessive and extravagant vices that spring from unbridled passions. He defies and attacks the Creator, who is represented as a sort of demon, having as many vices as Maldoror,
but in him they are made to appear mean and base, whereas in Maldoror they appear grand and terrible. The Creator, who is shown as a glutton, a drunkard, a sadist, has
victimized man; and Maldoror intends to be the avenger
of man. For, though Maldoror despises humanity, he pities it at the same time. Because of his prodigious vices,
among which sadism predominates, Maldoror inflicts a
great deal of suffering upon human beings, but he loves
them at the same time, and he enters into a Homeric conflict with the Creator who has exploited men so shameful-
ly. The battle is a bloody draw; each of the adversaries is
unconquerable.

Lengthy sections of the poem, in grandiloquent periods of
imprecatory rhetoric, describe this conflict in terms of in-

vective and audacious blasphemy. This is alternated with sections of ribald irony, farcical burlesque, parody of many styles of writing, digressions filled with dazzling, amazing figures of speech, and occasional passages of platitude, ineptitude or bathos, doubtless intended to mystify and irritate.

The charge made by certain critics that this work becomes quickly monotonous and that one's interest flags after the first *chant* is hardly justified. The power and, also, the interest increase in the second and third *chants;* and a climax is reached in the fourth and fifth *chants.* The sixth *chant* is somewhat in the nature of an anticlimax: it was probably originally intended as a transitional rather than a concluding *chant.* It is the narrative of Maldoror's successful attempt to seduce and torture Mervyn, an English youth living in Paris. Abandoning the tone of furiously eloquent imprecation that dominates in the first five *chants,* the author turns to an ironic and puzzling parody of the manner of the adventure novels of Eugène Sue and Ponson du Terrail.

The greatest originality and the greatest interest of this work is not in the subject, but in the style. It is a style that bears some resemblance, no doubt, to that of Bossuet or that of Chateaubriand (or, among the lesser Romantics, to that of Pétrus Borel's *Madame Putiphar*), but in the main it has no precursors. As to what produces its singular originality, it is difficult to say definitely; but a few indications may be given. Part of it may be due to the use of simple and effective, but obvious and commonplace, rhetorical devices (rhetorical questions, periodic sentences, etc.) for the expression of ideas and images which are unconventional in the extreme. Another point to be noted is the use of logic in the development of the discourses. It is not the simple paragraph development of a Bossuet, but it is the intricate web of an extremely subtle and skeptical logician, who is aware of the treachery of words and of the fact that in a logical sequence one can pass from sense to nonsense and back, with bewildering rapidity. A further factor in this originality is the emphasis placed upon scientific nomenclature. Whereas Hugo made use of the colorful effects of proper names, for which he ransacked encyclopedias, Lautréamont seems to have ransacked scientific textbooks for terminology, usually biological, which he uses with a most curious and original effect. It is out of this use of scientific terminology that stem many of his figures of speech, often so remarkable. Some of these, such as the famous simile "beau comme la rencontre fortuite, sur une table de dissection, d'une machine à coudre et un parapluie" are merely intended to startle because of their *cocasserie,* others, such as "beau comme le tremblement des mains dans l'alcoolisme" are surprisingly, subtly true.

The bare facts of the publication of the *Chants de Maldoror* are known; but around them there is almost complete darkness. In August, 1868, there appeared in Paris, from the presses of Balitout, Questroy et Cie., 7, rue Baillif, a thin octavo volume (32 pp.) entitled *Les Chants de Maldoror, Chant premier, par****. The work was completely ignored. Up to the present time no one has discovered any reference to it in any newspaper or review of the period. There is no record whatsoever of anyone having read it or

even having possessed a copy, with the exception of Paul Lespès, classmate of Ducasse at the Lycée of Pau in 1864, to whom a copy was sent. When interviewed a few years ago, Lespès, then aged 81, said that there was no indication given as to the author or sender of the volume, but that at the time he received it he had recognized the manner and the ideas of his former classmate.

A second and complete edition of the *Chants* appeared in 1874, in Brussels. This time the "Comte de Lautréamont" was named as author. Not until 11 years later can one find evidence that the book was beginning to be known. In 1885 the review *La Jeune Belgique* published a strophe from the first of the *Chants,* attributing it to the "Vicomte" de Lautréamont. A note accompanying this said that the review would shortly publish a study of the life and work of the author. This study never appeared. However, this publication, in a review which was at the time leading the literary renaissance in Belgium, must have called Lautréamont to the attention of some of the young intellectuals of Belgium, such as Georges Eekhoud, Maurice Maeterlinck and Camille Lemonnier.

At about the same time, that curious personality, Léon Bloy, became acquainted with the work of Lautréamont. In 1886 he published a strange novel, entitled *Le Désespéré.* In the opening part of the novel a couple of pages are devoted to a discussion of the abysmal despair which seemed to Bloy a keynote of the epoch; and mention is made of Baudelaire, Mme Ackermann, Ernest Hello, Villiers de l'Isle Adam, Verlaine, Huysmans and Dostoïevsky as manifestations of it. Then the unknown author of the *Chants de Maldoror* is mentioned as the extreme expression of this tendency. The paragraphs in which Bloy expounded this point deserve to be quoted, as they apparently represent the first existing criticism of Lautréamont's work:

> L'un des signes les moins douteux de cet acculement des âmes modernes à l'extrémité de tout, c'est la récente intrusion en France d'un monstre de livre, presque inconnue encore, quoique publié en Belgique depuis dix ans: les *Chants de Maldoror,* par le comte de Mautréamont (?), œuvre tout à fait sans analogue et probablement appelée à retentir. L'auteur est mort dans un cabanon et c'est tout ce qu'on sait de lui.
>
> Il est difficile de décider si le mot *monstre* est ici suffisant. Cela ressemble à quelque effroyable polymorphe sousmarin qu'une tempête surprenante aurait lancé sur le rivage après avoir saboulé le fond de l'Océan.
>
> La gueule même de l'imprécation demeure béante et silencieuse au conspect de ce visiteur, et les sataniques litanies des *Fleurs du Mal* prennent subitement, par comparaison, comme un certain air d'anodine bondieuserie.
>
> Ce n'est plus la *Bonne Nouvelle de la Mort* du bonhomme Herzen, c'est quelque chose comme la Bonne Nouvelle de la Damnation. Quant à la forme littéraire, il n'y en a pas. C'est de la lave liquide. C'est insensé, noir et dévorant.
>
> Mais ne semble-t-il pas à ceux qui l'ont lue, que

cette diffamation inouïe de la Providence exhale, par anticipation,—avec l'inégalable autorité d'une Prophétie,—l'ultime clameur imminente de la conscience humaine devant son Juge? . . .

It was the same Bloy, who, four years later, published in *La Plume* an article on Lautréamont entitled "Le Cabanon de Prométhée." It was somewhat more detailed and informative, but contained the same tone of violent and exaggerated, but not undiscriminating, admiration, as the paragraphs in *Le Désespéré*. It also repeated the statement that the author was a madman. It is difficult to decide whether Bloy had actually been told that, or whether it was a fruit of his own imagination working upon fancied autobiographical details in **Maldoror.**

In 1894 Bloy's attitude toward Lautréamont had not changed. In a letter which he quoted in his published *journal,* he sent to his friend, the artist Henry de Groux, a series of projects of illustrations for a work which was being prepared by the poet, Roinard, and which was to be entitled *Portraits du prochain siècle.* Among them was to be "Lautréamont—Henry de Groux invitant un monstre à pénétrer dans son atelier." The *Portraits du prochain siècle* was published in that same year—but without the portrait or mention of Lautréamont.

By 1890 the **Chants de Maldoror** had a few readers, but who the so-called "Comte de Lautréamont" was, remained a mystery. Publications of 1890 and 1891 cleared up that mystery to a certain extent. Toward the end of the year 1890 the work of Isidore Ducasse was reprinted by the publisher L. Genonceaux. The publisher himself wrote a short preface in which he disclosed that the real name of the Comte de Lautréamont was Isidore Ducasse, that he was born in Montevideo of French parentage and that he died very young (Genonceaux says at the age of 20) in · Paris, Nov. 24, 1870, in a hotel located 7, rue du Faubourg-Montmartre. Genonceaux then gave various unsubstantiated details concerning Ducasse's manner of life, and devoted several pages to disproving Bloy's assertion that the author of the **Chants de Maldoror** was mad.

Most of the information given by Genonceaux came apparently from a publisher named Albert Lacroix, to whom Genonceaux dedicated his preface. Lacroix was, it seems, the real publisher of the 1874 edition of **Maldoror**—the name "Typ. E. de Wittmann" given in that edition being purely fictitious. According to Genonceaux's account the volume was set up and ready to be published in 1869, but Lacroix held up the publication through fear of the censors. The publisher of the 1890 edition went to the banker, Dosseur, successor of Darasse, who had been banker for the Ducasse family, and obtained from him two letters of Isidore Ducasse addressed to Darasse. One of them he reproduced in facsimilé (preceding the frontispiece), the other he quoted in the preface. The first contains some interesting details. It was written March 12, 1870; and in it Ducasse states that his inability to get a work of his published had taught him a lesson and that he was planning another piece of work in an entirely new vein. The preface to this (60 pp.) was already written. This undoubtedly authentic letter confirmed Genonceaux's statements as to the difficulties experienced by Ducasse in having his work published by Lacroix.

As to the other work mentioned by Ducasse, definite light was thrown on it by investigations carried on at the time by Remy de Gourmont. In February, 1891, he published in the *Mercure de France* a critical study of **Maldoror,** followed by certain bibliographical notes. The critical study, which was far from definitive, was less interesting than the discoveries revealed in the bibliographical notes. At the Bibliothèque Nationale Gourmont had come across the 1868 edition of the **Chants de Maldoror,** and he now made its existence known to the literary world—over 22 years after its publication. He also noted the curious variants between the edition of 1868 and the later ones. Furthermore he found two small *plaquettes* published in 1870 under the title of *Poésies; par Isidore Ducasse.* He ended his article with a few quotations from these so-called "poésies." The nature of the work made it evident that this was the "préface" to which Ducasse had referred in the letter to his banker.

As a further contribution to the biography of Isidore Ducasse the *Mercure* published, later in the same year, under the heading "Curiosités", his *acte de naissance,* showing that he was born April 4, 1846, in Montevideo. No indication was given as to how or by whom this had been obtained, but its authenticity has been demonstrated by investigations in Montevideo in recent years.

It is also in the *Mercure de France,* and in the same year, that we find Lautréamont's work referred to with unqualified admiration for the first time. In a preface which Camille Lemonnier wrote to Rachilde's *La Sanglante Ironie* he commented as follows:

> D'analogie (between Rachilde and Lautréamont) il n'en est point, à part peut être la communauté d'injustice qui les voue à d'immérités silences. Je signale simplement le fait de ce tumultueux et imprécatoire rhéteur, de ce musicien des grands orgues littéraires, de cet infant de lettres qui mourut sans avoir régné et probablement ne sera reconnu Prince spirituel que par un très petit nombre de ses pairs.

Following this period (1885-1891) when the mysterious Comte de Lautréamont was identified as Isidore Ducasse, when certain facts about his life were discovered, when his work was reviewed by certain writers of importance, there ensued a period of some twenty years in which his work had practically no success. It had become known too late to attract the attention of the earlier symbolist poets; and as for the later symbolist poets, with a few exceptions, they either ignored it absolutely or regarded it as of no importance. Certain of the opinions of members of that generation, expressed in *Le Cas Lautréamont,* are interesting in that connection. Edouard Dujardin, the author of *Les Lauriers sont coupés* and, among other things, editor of the *Derniers Vers* of Laforgue, says, for instance: " . . . pendant toute la période symboliste, je n'ai pas entendu prononcer une seule fois le nom de Lautréamont, et, comme je ne vivais aucunement en sauvage, j'ai tout lieu de croire qu'il était aussi inconnu à mes camarades qu'à moi-même."

As we have indicated above, Maeterlinck could have known the *Chants de Maldoror* as early as 1885, but he did not remain an admirer; in the *Cas Lautréamont* the author of *L'Oiseau bleu* says: "Aujourd'hui . . . je crois bien que tout cela me paraîtrait illisible . . . "

Paul Valéry is another who seems to have neglected Lautréamont. According to his testimony [in *Le Cas Lautréamont*]:

> Je le connais à peine, si c'est même connaître que d'avoir feuilleté, il y a un temps infini, un exemplaire des *Chants de Maldoror?* Il me semble toutefois que je puis expliquer pourquoi je n'ai pas poussé ma curiosité plus profondément dans cette œuvre; j'avais dix-neut ans, et je venais de recevoir le petit volume des *Illuminations* . . .

Of this second symbolist generation two writers at least read and appreciated the work of Ducasse. They are Léon-Paul Fargue and Alfred Jarry. A few years ago Fargue, when interviewed by Frédéric Lefèvre, declared that Lautréamont was among his literary preferences. As for Jarry, it is certain that he had read the *Chants de Maldoror* as early as 1894. In that year he mentioned Lautréamont admiringly in a book review he contributed to *L'Art littéraire,* of which he was one of the editors. Furthermore, in the bizarre play, *Haldernablou,* (included in the book *Minutes de sable mémorial,* published in the autumn of 1894) he inserted an interesting allusion to an episode of the *Maldoror* referring to "cet autre page que mon ami le Montévidéen lança contre un arbre, ne gardant dans sa main que la chevelure sanglante et rouge." A careful study of the work of Alfred Jarry should demonstrate the existence of considerable influence of Lautréamont.

The first mention of Lautréamont by a writer in a foreign language occurs at this period. In some way or other the Hispano-American poet, Rubén Darío, came to know the *Chants de Maldoror* and devoted to them a chapter of his book, *Los Raros* (1893), a series of impressionistic critical studies of unusual literary figures. This study,—an intelligent, poetic appreciation,—does not seem to have attracted the attention of Spanish readers to Lautréamont very rapidly.

However, during these years, the *Chants de Maldoror* must have been read to a certain extent, even though they were not understood. There was a rather curious reference to them in the popular review *Je Sais Tout* in the year 1911. In an article, entitled "La Fleur du mauvais goût", and signed "Henri Duvernois", they were discussed as a good example of incoherence and bad taste. For instance, "en lisant ce style chaotique du comte de Lautréamont, par exemple, un homme de goût verra tout de suite ce que produira une pensée d'où la réflexion est absente et que pousse un vent de folie; il remarquera que les phrases ne sont pas rattachées entre elles par ce lien logique et solide que l'on retrouve chez tous les grands classiques . . . " Any one who has read Lautréamont with comprehension or attention will note how singularly inexact is that last criticism. The sentences in the *Maldoror* are always attached to each other by the firm link of logic; in fact the logic of the developments is in some cases, and with ironic intent, pushed to ludicrous extremes.

The year, 1914, may be said to have seen the beginning of the vogue of Lautréamont—a vogue that was delayed somewhat by the War, but that sprang up again in 1919 and continued until it reached its height in 1925-1927. Valery Larbaud played an important part in the beginning of that vogue. In a recent article he has confessed to owing a personal debt to Isidore Ducasse, stating that the *Maldoror,* "un classique de demain sans doute", was one of the *livres de chevet* with which his bed was constantly cluttered in his late 'teens (about 1897-1900). In 1914 Valery Larbaud published in *La Phalange* a critical study of Ducasse—the best that had appeared up to then,—entitled "Les 'Poésies' d'Isidore Ducasse." This study was principally concerned with the *Poésies,* but it also contained some sane judgments as to the value of the *Chants de Maldoror* and as to the character of the author. The same year saw the republication, in the review, *Vers et Prose,* edited by Paul Fort, of the first of the *Chants,* along with the Genonceaux preface and the two letters that had accompanied this preface.

As we have said, the discovery or rediscovery of Lautréamont took place immediately after the War. Among the chief instigators of the movement were Philippe Soupault, André Breton, Louis Aragon and Paul Eluard, who were to be, in the years following, among the leaders of the dadaist and *surréaliste* movements. Between 1919 and 1927, the *Chants de Maldoror* were reissued twice, the *Poésies* three times, and a number of articles of varying importance on the author or his work were published. The writers of the advance guard, the *surréalistes,* and those more or less in sympathy with them, cited Lautréamont on every occasion—some admiring him as an important influence, a genuine source of inspiration, the more fanatical regarding him as a god. The extent to which the vogue of Lautréamont went may be shown by the fact of the existence in Paris, about 1929-1930, of a cabaret named "Maldoror". This cabaret (the barman of which was, of course, called Isidore) was opened under the auspices of the *surréalistes,* who had it decorated in the spirit of some of the wilder episodes in the work which had inspired it.

In this period (from the rediscovery of Lautréamont to the present) there have appeared three works of considerable amplitude, which will be analyzed briefly as a conclusion to this review of Lautréamont criticism.

In 1925 the Belgian literary review, *Le Disque Vert,* published as a special number an *enquête* entitled *Le Cas Lautréamont.* It consists of a series of essays, brief quotations of opinions, quotations from earlier critical studies, and a bibliography. The essays and opinions do not give any definitive study, but are of value, since they present a fair indication of the attitude toward Lautréamont of three generations in both France and Belgium. The section of quotations from critical studies presents a series of selections of the essentials of a number of articles that would otherwise be quite inaccessible. The bibliography, by R. Simonson, is quite good.

Philippe Soupault, one of the most enthusiastic of the post-War discoverers of Lautréamont, published in 1927 an edition of the *Œuvres complète: du comte de Lautréamont (Isidore Ducasse).* In addition to the *Chants de Mal-*

doror and the *Poésies,* this edition contains five letters (three added to the two earlier published by Genonceaux), a biography, the birth and death notices, and a certain amount of critical and bibliographical material. The edition is of considerable value, since it assembles in one volume the texts (hitherto published in limited editions and relatively inaccessible) and the letters, along with documents and biographical and bibliographical material which was not new, but which had never been collected. One can easily criticize a certain lack of scholarly method in the presentation, and find certain errors and certain lacunae. The biography is the weakest part. The new material, which Soupault added, is generally considered to be erroneous and had the unfortunate result of getting the editor into a quarrel with the other members of the *surréaliste* group. As for the rest of the biography, it is chiefly an embroidering upon the account given by Genonceaux, which itself hardly bore the stamp of scientific accuracy.

Finally, in 1928 and 1929, there appeared for the first time critical appraisals of the work of Lautréamont that may be called complete and adequate. They are by Léon Pierre-Quint, already known for an important critical and biographical study of Marcel Proust, and for his articles on contemporary writers published in the *Revue de France* under the title of "Lectures." Pierre-Quint's first article on Lautréamont appeared in the *Revue de France.* It was a general study of the man and his work. The same general interpretation, elaborated and completed, was given by the book published a year later with the title of *Le comte de Lautréamont et Dieu.* Pierre-Quint has made no attempt to exhaust the subject, (in particular, he left practically untouched the complicated problems of the biography of Isidore Ducasse) but his work presents a reliable criticism and, on the whole, would make an excellent introduction for the general reader to the **Chants de Maldoror.**

The first problem connected with Lautréamont demanding the attention of the student is that of his life. It is doubtful whether much new material can be discovered at this late .date. At any rate the biographer of Ducasse should not be obliged to make a trip to Montevideo, since the question of the birth of the author of **Maldoror** and the doings of his family in South America has been gone into rather extensively [in Guillot-Munoz, *Lautréamont et Laforgue* (1925) and Contreras, "L'Origine du Comte de Lautréamont," *Mercure de France,* 1927], possibly more extensively than was necessary, for Ducasse left South America at a fairly early age, apparently never to return; and the country must have had little influence upon him. The question of the origin of Ducasse's family and of Isidore's school days in southern France was interestingly discussed in the article of Alicot previously referred to, which was published in the *Mercure de France* of Jan. 1, 1928. Further investigation in the region of Tarbes and Pau might bring additional facts to light. The question of Isidore's life in Paris will require especially careful handling. The existant accounts, chiefly based upon legend, must be rejected, with the exception of a few details. Ducasse's letters are of interest and deserve careful study; and a few autobiographical details may be sifted out of the **Maldoror** or the *Poésies.*

The problems of a more general literary nature that remain to be attacked may be divided into four groups. First, would be general studies of the work and its significance: The importance of the **Chants de Maldoror,** the author's relation to the literary movements of his century and his period, his style, etc. A special point to be settled is the problem of Ducasse's apparent recantation as expressed in the *Poésies* (to be compared, of course, to Rimbaud's abandoning of poetry at about the same period).

A second type of literary problem to be studied is that of the genesis of the **Maldoror,** of the method of composition, of the revisions introduced into the second edition, etc. This problem has already been treated summarily by André Malraux [in "La Genèse des *Chants de Maldoror, Action,* 1920], but is sufficiently interesting to warrant more ample treatment.

A study of the sources of Lautréamont may prove to be sterile. As has been suggested above, his style is exceedingly original; and it is hard to find sources for it. It has been pointed out that the **Maldoror** contains reminiscences (probably intentional) of Hugo, Musset, Dante, Goethe, Shakespeare, of Ponson du Terrail, Eugène Sue, etc. It might be profitable to search the works of 19th century writers named by Ducasse in his *Poésies* and his letters (for instance, Mickiewicz's *Konrad Wallenrodt* and Ernest Naville's *Problème du Mal*) for the source of his ideas. Another vein to be mined,—and where patient digging might bring to light something of interest,—is the scientific detail which abounds in the **Maldoror.**

The most important literary problem connected with Lautréamont, that most likely to produce real contributions to scholarship, is that of his influence. It is quite evident that there is a considerable amount of influence on the post-War generation of writers, especially on the *surréaliste* group. This should be definitively studied some day. Today, the writers of 1919-1929 may be too close to us to be judged in a definitive way, but it would be well for students to go to work and assemble the materials for such a study. They are now easily available, and their importance should not be underestimated. (pp. 140-50)

> *Henry A. Grubbs, Jr., "The Problem of Lautréamont," in* The Romanic Review, *Vol. XXV, No. 2, April-June, 1934, pp. 140-50.*

Thomas Greene   (essay date 1954)

[*In the essay below, Greene contends that* Les chants de Maldoror *"pushes Romantic ideas and Romantic poses to their extremes" through a "strategy of outrage."*]

Lautréamont has been read and discussed spasmodically in America for some years now, but despite his continental reputation he has not as yet a "public" here. One has to remember, however, that the Lautréamont cult in France, fervent and extreme as it has been, developed only after a near-total blackout of appreciation which lasted almost forty years. **Maldoror** is a hard book to evaluate; depending on the quality of the light the reader's mind sheds upon it, it can appear very good or very bad. French enthusiasm moreover may have been due partly to the enigmatic figure of the writer himself, as well as to the sensational elements in his book.

"Le Comte de Lautréamont" was the pseudonym of a young man named Isidore Ducasse, born in Uruguay of French parents, who lived in Paris for a few years, totally unknown, before his death at twenty-four in 1870. The first canto of *Maldoror,* which might be described as an epic prose-poem divided into brief discontinuous episodes, had appeared in print two years before, and at his death Lautréamont was at work upon a book of poems, only the prose preface of which survives. This preface is now called, illogically, *Poésies. Maldoror* and *Poésies,* together with six letters, constitute the *Oeuvres Complètes* of Isidore Ducasse, "Comte de Lautréamont."

One of the central enigmas in the over-all biographical mystery lies in the fact of Lautréamont's youth. This is enigmatic because his book is as good as it is. On the other hand, it explains a great deal, not only of *Maldoror*'s sophomorism and bad taste, but also of its brilliance. Eliot's remark on Tourneur is entirely a propos.

> [*The Revenger's Tragedy*] does express—and this, chiefly, is what gives it its amazing unity— an intense and unique and horrible vision of life; but it is such a vision as might come, as the result of few or slender experiences, to a highly sensitive adolescent with a gift for words.

This might have been written of Lautréamont; it is only necessary to add that Lautréamont's "few or slender experiences" were probably composed in large part by the reading of Romantic literature—in particular Poe, Byron, Baudelaire, the Gothic novelists, and their imitators. It does not seem coincidental that Lautréamont, like the Tourneur surmised by Eliot, was young; his youthful intensity appears to have ridden his talent and his misanthropy to produce a book whose virtues, whatever its faults, might have been unattainable by a maturer man.

It is precisely because he was young that Lautréamont's voracious reading of the Romantics influenced him as strongly as it did. His relationship to the Romantic movement has tended to be blurred in France by the emphasis on his relationship to Surrealism, and yet *Maldoror* points backward as well as forward. Many passages seem at first reading uninspired reworkings of hackneyed Romantic material. But even in these passages the tone betrays itself with a pomposity or absurdity that turns the Romantic ardor into bathos. At this stage one concludes that the whole book is an enormous piece of Romantic irony. But this conclusion is not really accurate either. The truth might be better stated by saying that *Maldoror* assumes the full responsibility for attitudes which many romantics only play at; it pushes Romantic ideas and Romantic poses to their extremes. Sometimes it pushes them into absurdity, sometimes into ugliness, sometimes into a kind of splendor. It pushes Romantic irony to *its* extreme, to the point that the seriousness of a situation is always jeopardized without being destroyed. Ultimately the question of a given passage's seriousness is unanswerable.

In this sense *Maldoror* is rather a book about Romantic literature than a book about "life," and as such it is an ex-

tremely illuminating study. It may be that you could understand Byron better by reading *Maldoror,* where his name is never mentioned, than by reading any number of critical or biographical analyses. On a conscious level Lautréamont may have read Byron superficially and imperceptively, but as a writer he produced a searching anatomy of Byron's role and his poetry.

Perhaps because of this integrity, this fidelity to the responsibilities of Romanticism, Lautréamont succeeded in realizing the destructive impulse which had driven and misdriven his literary predecessors as it was to drive his disciples. In all the literature of revolt few books succeed in destroying so well as *Maldoror.* If it were only superficially shocking, cheaply sensational, it could be easily dismissed. It is certainly these things among others. But as a whole it is a profoundly unsettling book. From its symphonic opening sentence which warns off the innocent or casual reader, it follows the strategy of outrage: the outrage of morality, which is Lautréamont's peculiar comedy; the outrage of nature, which is his peculiar violence; the outrage of language, which is his peculiar rhetoric. A blend of comedy, violence and rhetoric produces that bitter savor which only a few, wrote Lautréamont, can taste without danger.

Les Chants de Maldoror dramatize the existence of a hero who is nominally committed to evil and whose record of assault and murder provides the narrative pretext for most of its episodes. In the phantasmagorical universe of which he is the center, Maldoror is hostile to virtually everything: in his Machiavellian ravages of the innocent few and the brutalized many among his fellow men he is only a little less implacable than in his feud with an extraordinarily disagreeable and anthropomorphic God. Some of the most sensational episodes which describe the forms of Maldoror's sadism are repellent and disgusting; they contain passages which one does not willingly reread. But Maldoror's sadism, and even the sadism of these extreme episodes, is at least partly redeemed by a psychological denseness about him, a queer paradoxical ambivalence which qualifies even the most brutal and forthright of his acts.

The first paradox in Maldoror's psychology is his moral consciousness. All the events of his universe are charged with profound ethical significance for him, and he seems to respond almost entirely to ethical motives—to disgust for the brutality of God and man on the one hand, to remorse for his own brutality on the other. His sexual aggressions often seem motivated less by physical impulse than by a fanatic will of almost Puritanical sternness and earnestness. It is a kind of moral indignation, a perverted Calvinism, which turns Maldoror away from God and man and drives him to seek the sin which is absolutely unprovoked and hideous, the sin which is the perfect crime.

In his awareness of innocence, in his protest against authority and in the solitude of his individualism, Maldoror embodies most of the tenets of Romantic morality. The influence of the Satan of Milton, whom we know Lautréamont to have read, and probably of Mary Shelley's monster in *Frankenstein,* which he would seem to have read from internal evidence, played roles in the conception of

Maldoror, but by far his most direct ancestor was the Byronic hero as typified by Lara, Cain, Manfred and the Corsair. Lautréamont mentions each of these characters at various points in the *Poésies,* and in **Maldoror** he borrowed feelings and attitudes they all embody—the nervous fatigue, the sense of isolation, the thirst for the superhuman with its concomitant frustration. Byron had written in *Lara:*

> Too high for common selfishness, he could
> At times resign his own for others' good,
> But not in pity, not because he ought,
> But in some strange perversity of thought,
> That sway'd him onward with a secret pride
> To do what few or none would do beside;
> And this same impulse would, in tempting time,
> Mislead his spirit equally to crime;
> So much he soar'd beyond, or sunk beneath
> The men with whom he felt condemn'd to
>   breathe,
> And long'd by good or ill to separate
> Himself from all who shar'd his mortal state.

This becomes in Lautréamont:

> Hélas! qu'est-ce donc que le bien et le mal? Est-ce une même chose par laquelle nous témoignons avec rage notre impuissance, et la passion d'atteindre à l'infini par les moyens même les plus insensés?

Maldoror's insensate rage for cruelty and suffering is a kind of misdirected aspiration for the infinite.

The urge "by good or ill to separate himself " from those who share his mortal state underlies most of Maldoror's behavior. The very fact of his humanity is in doubt throughout the book; sometimes he would seem to belong to the class of sinister, demonic, invulnerable personages who people Romantic literature from Maturin's Melmoth through Polidor's Vampire and Hugo's Han d'Islande to Sue's Wandering Jew. Maldoror himself is not always sure of his own condition. This uncertainty heightens his Byronic urge to be different from human beings.

From the ambivalence of this uncertainty Lautréamont derives some of his most grotesque comedy, comedy which characteristically concludes with the chastening recognition that Maldoror is indeed human. See for instance Maldoror's long address to the sea—perhaps the most polished and controlled single episode of the book—in which his impulse toward the super- or sub-human is confronted with this recognition of his human condition. The episode consists of a declamation divided into ten sections, each of which is concluded with the refrain "Je te salue, vieil océan!" The whole is prefaced by an injunction to the reader who, being human, will probably prove too weak and too excitable to enjoy it anyway.

> Je me propose, sans être ému, de déclamer à grande voix la strophe sérieuse et froide que vous allez entendre. Vous, faites attention à ce qu'elle ne manquera pas de laisser, comme une flétrissure, dans vos imaginations troublées. . . . Il n'y a pas longtemps que j'ai revu la mer et foulé le pont des vaisseaux, et mes souvenirs sont vivaces comme si je l'avais quittée la veille. Soyez néanmoins, si vous le pouvez, aussi calmes que

> moi, dans cette lecture que je me repens déjà de vous offrir, et ne rougissez pas à la pensée de ce qu'est le coeur humain.

> [I propose to proclaim in a loud voice and without emotion the cold and grave chant that you are about to hear. Consider carefully what it contains and guard yourself against the painful impression it cannot fail to leave like a blight upon your troubled imaginings . . . Not long ago I saw the sea once again and trod upon the bridges of ships; my memories of it are as lively as if it had all happened yesterday. If you are able, however, be as calm as I am as you read what is to follow (for already I regret offering it to you) and do not blush for the human heart.]

Beneath the cold formality of a passage like this one lies a faint reminiscence of French classical tragedy. But basically the passage evokes the classical declamation only to parody it, and there is a buffoonishness about Maldoror's pose which qualifies, but never destroys, the significance of what follows. In particular the pose of disdainful condescension to the human—and therefore inferior—reader, announces the sardonic comedy which is to underly the whole episode. The implication of Maldoror's non-humanity is continued in each of the following apostrophes to the sea, which is always compared favorably with the derisory and feeble race of man. These progressively extended and rhetorical apostrophes culminate in the climactic question to which they have been tending: "Réponds-moi, océan, veux-tu être mon frère?" As though in answer, the sea surges up in a magnificent series of waves, before which Maldoror, in a burst of terror and awe, prostrates himself, thus losing ironically his vaunted frigidity.

> Oh! quand tu t'avances, la crête haute et terrible, entouré de tes replis tortueux comme d'une cour, magnétiseur et farouche, roulant tes ondes les unes sur les autres, avec la conscience de ce que tu es, pendant que tu pousses, des profondeurs de ta poitrine, comme accablé d'un remords intense que je ne puis pas découvrir, ce sourd mugissement perpétuel que les hommes redoutent tant, même quand ils te contemplent, en sûreté, tremblants sur le rivage, alors, je vois qu'il ne m'appartient pas, le droit insigne de me dire ton égal.

> [Oh, when you advance, your crest high and terrible, surrounded by your tortuous coils as by a royal court, magnetic and wild, rolling your waves one upon the other, full of the consciousness of what you are; and when you give utterance from the depths of your bosom as if you were suffering the pangs of some intense remorse which I have been unable to discover, to that perpetual heavy roar so greatly feared by men even when, trembling on the shore, they contemplate you in safety: then I perceive that I do not possess that signal right to name myself your equal.]

The recognition of his inferiority to the sea, and the resulting implication of his human condition, produces a spasm of rage in Maldoror which yields in its turn to resignation, resignation to a life in human society even though that life must be ridiculous. "Faisons un grand effort, et accomplissons, avec le sentiment du devoir, notre destinée sur cette terre. Je te salue, vieil océan!" This, the conclusion of the episode, reveals a sudden humility which renders the preceding comedy more warm and more significant.

If Maldoror is repeatedly faced with the fact of his own humanity, he is also faced with his difference from most of his fellow men. The divergent sensibility which sets off the Romantic hero from an unfeeling society is parodied by the cumbersome inflexibility of Maldoror's mental processes. At moments he is actually pedantic and toward the end of the book he lapses into stretches of unreadable double talk which mimic the hyper-precision of scientific jargon. He is, moreover, incapable of laughter. "Moi, je ne sais pas rire. Je n'ai jamais pu rire, quoique plusieurs fois j'aie essayé de le faire. C'est très difficile d'apprendre à rire." Once, in a grotesque attempt to imitate his fellows, Maldoror widens the corners of his mouth with his penknife to force it into a laugh. For an instant he believes that he has succeeded, but presently, through the falling blood, he recognizes that he has failed. This terrible and brilliant image dramatizes in its insane way the spiritual isolation of the Romantic hero and all his clumsy maladjustment with a power which few Romantic poets equaled. Maldoror's illogicality, which is really an excess of misplaced logic, translates the apparent illogicality of his hyper-conscious moral sensibility.

Thus the comedy of *Maldoror* dwells on the conflict between the pro-human and anti-human motives of the Romantic hero-saint. Ultimately of course the hero fails to be a saint, as he has to fail; the pressures upon him are too confusing, his own behavior too ambiguous, to permit him the purity either of the perfect martyrdom or the perfect crime. But his conflict leads him to repeated essays, and the elements which I have called comic are interwoven with elements of sickening violence. It is as though Maldoror had taken upon himself to dramatize an epigram which his creator could not possibly have read, this remark from the *Journaux Intimes* of Baudelaire: "Quand j'aurai inspiré le dégoût et l'horreur universels, j'aurai conquis la solitude."

The outrage of nature in *Maldoror* can be discussed first of all in its most obvious sense: the natural laws which operate in the "real" universe are twisted to conform to the laws of the myth or the fairy tale. There are magic spells, enchantments and punishments; there are animals who speak and act as humans; there is an anthropomorphic God as well as other divinities and spirits who interfere actively and visibly in human affairs; and there are frequent metamorphoses of man into animal or monster, of God into animal—once, as it happens, a church lamp becomes an angel. These elements confer a primitive, folk-lorist quality to the book which is essential to it. Beneath the obvious mannerisms of the ambitious self-conscious young writer who wants to make a name, there is a frightening barbarity in *Maldoror,* a relaxing of intellectual control and the consequent release of savage subconscious pressures.

The relationship of *Maldoror* to the folk tale is all the closer in that narrative conventions drawn from legend and romance, familiar to the point of being archetypal, are used in many of the episodes. In one of these, Maldoror is vampirized every night for ten years by a spider which seems to live in his chamber wall. One night as Maldoror lies paralyzed, the stomach of the spider opens and two young men step out of it, each wearing a blue robe and bearing a flaming sword. The youths are Reginald and Elsseneur, once beloved friends of Maldoror whom he betrayed in turn. Reginald he had attacked with his superfine stiletto once as they were swimming in the sea; the unfortunate youth had resigned his soul to heaven when he was luckily rescued by fishermen. Elsseneur he had led off seductively on a solitary promenade whereupon he drew his knife and ordered the young man to prepare to die. If a herd of bulls had not happened by at that instant, Elsseneur would have breathed his last. Both youths, in disillusion, sought death in battle and became redoubtable warriors; one day they met on the battlefield and engaged in a long personal duel. After a heroic contest they finally paused to catch their breath and, raising their visors, recognized each other. They swore eternal friendship. An archangel from heaven ordered them to take the form of a spider and suck Maldoror's blood for ten years. Now the spell has been rescinded. Maldoror awakes from his paralysis and sees two forms disappearing into the sky.

The relationship of such a story to legend or romance is obvious. What may be less obvious from my retelling is its sophistication. Without violating the autonomy of the magical conventions Lautréamont underlines the elements which render them relevant and suggestive. Elsseneur's promenade with Maldoror, for instance, is recounted in such a way as to blend the mechanism of legend with the mechanism of a dream. The walk which begins as a stroll through an exhilarating and odorant Moorish landscape modulates with brilliant detail to a furtive, exhausting and nocturnal trek across a mystifying wilderness. The landscape changes, light falls from the sky, joy yields to terror with the frightening swiftness and illogic of dream progression.

This audacity of illogical juxtaposition is marked throughout the book. The magical phenomena which do violence to physical laws also do violence to each other from page to page, and similarly the atmosphere and décor of the action vary qualitatively. The décors are drawn alike from the common daylit streets of Paris and from the most Dantesque phantasmagorical scenery of pure imagination. The effect of Lautréamont's heterogeneity is something like the effect of a surrealist film: the distance shot of a recognizable landscape may give way to a focus on a mystifying detail, or conversely interest in the close-up may delay the irrelevant backdrop from looming out of the vagueness. What holds all this material together is the formal stylization which Lautréamont imposes on it, a stylization which is the product of a very individual and cohesive sensibility. It is impossible to read even the most sophomoric pages of *Maldoror* without recognizing the distinctive imagination behind them.

Within this stylization the most unnerving violence has to be assimilated—the copulation with a shark, the penknife rape of a little girl, the flagellation of a man hung by his hair. As I have admitted, some of this violence functions in the book only to shock and to disgust. But in other cases, and particularly in certain episodes of the latter half of the book, the violence is realized without shock, so that it finds an integrity and integration in Lautréamont's grotesque but coherent universe. In these episodes the stylization imposed by the poet's vision seems to demand violence and to contain it naturally. I am thinking of the Kafkaesque story, among others, in which a man is metamorphosed by a sorceress into a beetle. In this episode and others like it there is so little an attempt at the obvious facile *scandale* that some passages make heavy reading; the style becomes plodding and ponderous, in imitation of the weight of time itself in this universe. When such an assimilation of violence to stylization is achieved, we have the right, I think, to be impressed; the artistic control which Lautréamont wins on occasion over his material—repellent, incongruous and extravagant as it is—is the kind of victory common to the most gifted creative imaginations, to Dante and to Joyce and not to many others.

The stylization of *Maldoror* is due in part to the texture of the language itself. The language imposes itself upon the reader's consciousness with an insistence typical of poetry rather than prose, and there can be no doubt that the book as a whole has to be described as a prose poem. There are kinds of eccentricities and audacities which simple prose cannot contain.

I have mentioned above the dense convoluted passages which mimic scientific jargon. Many of the stylistic liberties in *Maldoror* seem to take off from this same starting-place—the satire of academic inflexibility. We know from the testimony of his classmates that Isidore Ducasse was particularly exasperated by the pedantry of his *lycée* professors, and the satire in *Maldoror* may well derive from this biographical source. But in the poem pedantry is blown up to something more significant than the pettiness of a provincial classroom; it becomes a pervasive rigidity and clumsiness which obstructs thought and speech. Stylistically it assumes a kind of preciosity or periphrasis; thus a request to kneel becomes: "Inclinez la binarité de vos rotules vers la terre." But parallel to this kind of device there is an excess of specificity which also mimics in its way the language of science.

> L'homme . . . vit dans l'eau, comme l'hippocampe; à travers les couches supérieures de l'air, comme l'orfraie; et sous la terre, comme la taupe, le cloporte et la sublimité du vermiceau.

> [Man lives in water like the sea-horse; in the upper layers of the atmosphere like the osprey; and under the ground like the mole, the woodlouse and the sublimity of the earthworm.]

Here *hippocampe* replaces *poisson* and *orfraie* replaces *oiseau*. These examples may seem mild enough. But they are important to notice because they show how the full-blown surrealism of other images is rooted in a parody of logic, an excess of intellectual rigor—in Lautréamont's phrase, a *"tension d'esprit."* It is the same excess of logic which leads Maldoror to widen his mouth with a knife to force a smile.

The result of the stylistic illogicality is to destroy the meta-

phor itself. The Romantic irony which questions the seriousness of the whole book, page by page, is turned back on the language to question *it*. If a character is described as beautiful, as *beau*, we are regularly given an imagistic equivalent, *beau comme* . . . Beautiful as what? " . . . beau comme la rencontre fortuite sur une table de dissection d'une machine à coudre et d'un parapluie." Such an image already points straight to surrealism. The *beau commes* appear more and more frequently toward the end of the book and become ritualistic; they are frequently piled one upon another with a kind of lavish virtuosity. Ultimately they constitute an attempt to realize an absolute ugliness just as Maldoror's aggressions attempt to realize the perfect crime.

The *beau commes* imply, as I have said, the destruction of the metaphor and of all figurative language. It is easy to see why. There is a balance in any metaphor between the logical and illogical, between the properties of tenor and vehicle which coincide and those which do not. In *Maldoror* the non-coincident properties dwindle to near zero. Lautréamont's game is to keep the elements in this second class as tiny as possible without allowing them to disappear. When he succeeds he is very good. But there are many instances in which he chooses to fail, instances where the coincident elements disappear and the non-coincident or illogical elements assume an autonomy which is to all practical purposes absolute. If you ask what these figures are doing in the text, you can only conclude that they constitute a kind of literary criticism, a destructive commentary on the rest of poetry.

But to conclude with this would do injustice to the brilliance of logical compression which the apparent illogic of *Maldoror*'s style occasionally attains. This brilliance merits a last example. Standing by the sea one evening, Maldoror hales a strange creature in the water—half man, half fish. The monster relates to Maldoror the instances of human cruelty which have driven him, a normal human being, to flee society and to live in the sea where his physiological transformation has taken place. Before he begins his recital he pauses an instant to summon his recollections. Lautréamont describes this pause as follows:

> L'amphibie n'osa pas trop s'avancer jusqu'au rivage; mais dès qu'il se fut assuré que sa voix parvenait assez distinctement jusqu'à mon tympan, il réduisit le mouvement de ses membres palmés, de manière à soutenir son buste, couvert de goëmons, au-dessus des flots mugissants. Je le vis incliner son front, comme pour invoquer, par un ordre solennel, la meute errante des souvenirs. Je n'osais pas l'interrompre dans cette occupation, saintement archéologique: plongé dans le passé, il ressemblait à un écueil.

> [The amphibian dared not approach the beach too closely; but as soon as he was assured that his voice carried with sufficient clarity to my eardrum, he reduced the motion of his webbed hands in such a manner as to maintain his torso, hung with sea-wrack, above the moaning waves. I saw him bow his head as if to invoke by solemn command the wayward pack of memories. I dared not interrupt him in this sacredly archeo-

logical occupation: plunged in the past, he resembled a reef.]

What does this last image mean: "Plongé dans le passé, il ressemblait à un écueil?" I suppose that first of all it means this: that the intensity of the amphibian's revery upon his past fixes him in the water with the immobility of a reef. Of course the amphibian is plunged physically not in the past but in the sea, and the preceding description of his

---

An excerpt from *Lautréamont's "Maldoror"*

Throughout my life I have seen, without one exception, narrow-shouldered men performing innumerable idiotic acts, brutalising their fellows, and corrupting souls by every means. The motive for their actions they call *Glory*. Seeing these exhibitions I've longed to laugh, with the rest, but that strange imitation was impossible. Taking a penknife with a sharp-edged blade, I slit the flesh at the points joining the lips. For an instant I believed my aim was achieved. I saw in a mirror the mouth ruined at my own will! An error! Besides, the blood gushing freely from the two wounds prevented my distinguishing whether this really was the grin of others. But after some moments of comparison I saw quite clearly that my smile did not resemble that of humans: the fact is, I was not laughing.

I have seen men, hideous men with terrible eyes sunk deep in their sockets, outmatch the hardness of rock, the rigidity of cast steel, the shark's cruelty, the insolence of youth, the insane fury of criminals, the hypocrite's treachery, the most extraordinary play-actors, priests' strength of character, and the most secretive, coldest creatures of heaven and earth. I have seen moralists weary of laying bare their hearts and bringing down on themselves the implacable wrath from on high. I have seen them all together—the most powerful fist levelled at heaven like that of a child already wilful towards its mother—probably stimulated by some denizen of hell, their eyes brimful of remorse and yet smarting with hatred, in glacial silence, not daring to spill out the unfruitful and mighty meditations harboured in their hearts, meditations so crammed with injustice and horror, enough to sadden the God of mercy with compassion. Or I've seen them at every moment of the day from the start of infancy to the end of dotage, while disgorging incredible curses, insensate curses against all that breathes, against themselves and Providence, prostitute women and children and thus dishonour those parts of the body consecrated to modesty. Then the seas swell their waters, swallow ships in their abysses; earth tremors and hurricanes topple houses; plagues and divers epidemics decimate praying families. Yet men are unaware of all this. I have seen them also blushing and blenching with shame at their behaviour on earth—but rarely. Tempests, sisters of cyclones; bluish firmament whose beauty I do not admit; hypocrite sea, image of my heart; earth with mysterious womb; inhabitants of the spheres; the whole universe; God who grandly created it, you I invoke: Show me one honest man! . . . May your grace multiply my natural strength tenfold, for at the sight of such a monster I might die of astonishment. One dies at less.

Comte de Lautréamont, in his Les chants de Maldoror, *translated by Alexis Lykiard, Allison and Busby, 1970.*

---

bust protruding out of the water and hung with sea weed suggests that his resemblance to a reef is even more literal. But in the equivalence between past and sea there is still another suggestion: history is a kind of sea in which the amphibian, having escaped from its restless variety, remains stationary like a reef. On the other hand there may be the contrary sense that his sudden engulfment in the past beats upon him with the violence of waves upon a reef.

What I should like to be evident, in all the preceding discussion of style, is the relevance of Lautréamont's peculiar rhetoric to his morality and comedy. The effect of language which is constantly off balance is to dramatize and to mock a structureless moral world. Ultimately the bewilderment and terror of the world of *Maldoror* render it a kind of hell, and its language can be regarded as a kind of diabolic teasing. As such, Lautréamont's hell must necessarily remain less valuable to us than the hell of his near-contemporary, Rimbaud; in comparison with *Une Saison en Enfer*, *Maldoror* appears uneven, bookish and self-conscious. But its brilliant and destructive outrage contains nevertheless an equal richness of moral perception, perception which, given Lautréamont's practical jokes with language, remains ticklishly inconclusive, and is all the more relevant for that. (pp. 528-39)

Thomas Greene, "The Relevance of Lautréamont," in Partisan Review, *Vol. XXI, No. 5, September-October, 1954, pp. 528-39.*

Anna Balakian　(essay date 1970)

[*Balakian is a critic of French literature who has written extensively on writers of the Symbolist, Surrealist, and Dadaist movements. In this excerpt from her book* Surrealism: The Road to the Absolute, *she identifies the imagery and themes in Lautréamont's work that attracted the Surrealists and examines the impact of the Darwinian theory of evolution on Lautreamont's work.*]

—*the most genial work of modern times*
　　　　　—André Breton

When in 1938-39 a poll was taken of contemporary French poets and critics by the periodical *Cahiers G.L.M.* to determine the twenty "indispensable" poems of all time, the name which ranked third among the poets before 1900 and was surpassed only by Rimbaud and Baudelaire, was that of Isidore Ducasse, self-styled Comte de Lautréamont. But what is even more impressive than this is the fact that those who singled him out generally rated him first. Four major surrealists, Eluard, Breton, Soupault, and Péret, so designated him, and chose him, not for a single passage or excerpt, but for his whole work considered as a unit and as a milestone in literary history. The surrealists have not been the only champions of this poetic youth who died at the age of twenty-four; but it was they who first considered him a major French poet, although he was technically neither French nor a "poet." He was born in Montevideo of French parents. Arriving in France to study at the Ecole Polytechnique, he wrote in prose, only to prove more convincingly than ever before that the essence of poetry resides not in rhyme but in rhythm, whereby the word pattern expresses a pace of thinking different from that of other forms of writing.

In his preface to Lautréamont's works, Philippe Soupault, one of the original members of the surrealist coterie, wrote in overwhelming adoration: "One does not judge M. de Lautréamont. One recognizes him, and in saluting him one bows to the ground." Soupault was the first of the surrealists to become interested in Lautréamont. But the edition for which he wrote the preface in 1920 was soon circulating among the rest of the writers and painters of the cénacle. Actually it was the first accessible edition; the ones at the end of the nineteenth century had quickly gone out of print. But once available, Isidore Ducasse became the patron saint of the rebels. For a time second to Rimbaud as a motivating force for modern poetry and art, Lautréamont gradually moved up to first rank, if one is to judge by the sustained and uninterrupted allusions to him since 1910 in the critical comments of poets and artists related at some time or other with surrealism. Editions of his works have multiplied and have been illustrated by famous surrealist painters, including Victor Brauner, Max Ernst, Matta, René Magritte, Man Ray, Yves Tanguy, and Salvador Dali. In his Second Manifesto, when André Breton detached himself and surrealism from most of the antecedents he had mentioned in the First Manifesto, and even expressed reservations about Rimbaud, he clung as staunchly as ever to Lautréamont. In his last critical works he had Lautréamont's name constantly on his lips referring to him as a major influence, and in an article, "Sucre Jaune," where he reprimanded Camus for not having understood the magnitude of the Lautréamont rebellion, he called the tormented youth's work "the most genial of modern times." In Entretiens (1952) he interestingly raised the importance of both Rimbaud and Lautréamont above literary classifications. It is, he said, their primary concern for the human condition, their spiritual torment, that lifts them above literary classifications. It is, he said, their primary concern with later writers. In his preface to the excerpt from Lautréamont's writings which he included in his Anthologie de l'Humour Noir, Breton signals Lautréamont as a trail blazer: "The most audacious things that for centuries will be thought and undertaken have been formulated here in advance in his magic law."

Lautréamont's imagery, its hallucinatory force, the subconscious train of thought which it reveals, its occasional basis in the absurd create a point of contact with the surrealists. But these obvious characteristics have been rather easily explained away by critics all the way from Remy de Gourmont to as recent a researcher as Jean-Pierre Soulier (Lautréamont: Génie ou Maladie Mentale, Droz, 1964) as manifestations of neurosis and eventual psychosis. Clinical explanations minimize however the very qualities that have endeared Ducasse to the surrealists and enflamed their imagination. It is this conscious moral and spiritual perspective more than literary manifestations of an unbalanced mind that indicated a major departure from his contemporaries and brought him closer in line with twentieth-century aesthetic and philosophic thought.

The surrealists preferred to see in the Chants de Maldoror either new figurations of the old Greek myths of man's tormented passage through the enigma of life, or an acute metaphysical rebellion in a world losing its anthropocentric focus. Surrealists Marcel Jean and Arpad Mezei (Maldoror, Editions du Pavois, Paris, 1947) were inclined to explain Lautréamont as a tortured victim of his own inherited traits, "Theseus and Minotaur all at once," and thus identified the author with his diabolical character, Maldoror. On the other hand, Breton and Léon Pierre-Quint have seen Ducasse as a very lucid, proud rebel, who can objectivize his plight in the other, Maldoror, and create the catharsis of the protest of the damned. In his magnificent book on Lautréamont (Le Comte de Lautréamont et Dieu, 1928), which is at the same time a profound study of the very nature of revolt, Léon Pierre-Quint calls Les Chants "the great contemporary work of revolt," and "the overwhelming expression of supreme revolt." It is indeed in the light of a conscious and direct protest that Lautréamont's work is most poignant and most relevant to the development of the surrealist climate. The isolation of the young man in Paris and his severance from family ties were more likely to have produced benign melancholia than subversive attack on man and God.

There was a greater factor to cause disturbance in the sensitive adolescent's development than geographical or affective disorientation. The historical dates provide more decisive data sometimes than sundry personal letters. He came of age in the era of the advent of Darwinism. Lautréamont's work is closely involved with the spiritual upheaval caused by the theory of evolution in the second half of the nineteenth century. This scientific event proved as disturbing to that epoch as non-Euclidian geometry and the explorations of un-human space have been to a later era.

The theory of evolution was welcomed in France by biologists; the philosophers saw in it a dislocation in moral values. The notion of the soul seemed to be put in jeopardy. This moral shock and its inevitable effect upon religious orientation supplied the major impetus for Lautréamont's writings, for his venom, his rejections, his diffidence, and eventually served as a provocation for his wry, dark humor in facing up to the universe and its Creator.

Ducasse was fourteen years old when The Origin of Species was published and was still living in Uruguay with his French parents. (His father, a subscriber to various periodicals including La Revue des Deux Mondes, kept himself informed of the intellectual news of Europe and particularly of France.) We know very little about the life and intellectual development of this mystifying stranger, the outsider of nineteenth-century French literature; unfortunately he kept no adolescent's diary and died before the age an author takes to his journal. He left no bibliography of his readings, and he disdained memoirs as a literary genre. But judging from the abundant literary allusions of his final fragments called Poésies, he was extremely well read for his years and as familiar with English literature as with French. We also know that he showed definite scientific aptitude as a youngster, and after five years of preparatory work in French lycées, went to Paris in 1865 to register in the Ecole Polytechnique. Many a scientific allusion in Les Chants de Maldoror points to an interest in technical instruments, in advances in physiology. More-over he reveals an amazing knowledge of zoology and its terminology, which for the first time becomes a predominant part of the poetic vocabulary. Gaston Bachelard discovered 435 references to animals in *Les Chants de Maldoror.* (pp. 50-4)

There is no direct mention of Darwin or evolution in Lautréamont's work, but in view of the intense interest in Darwinism between 1860 and 1869, and considering the youth's general intellectual awareness, his tremendous capacity for reading, and particularly his scientific tendencies, it takes no stretch of the imagination to assume that Isidore had learned of Darwinism at least as much as—if not more than—an alert youth of today knows about nuclear physics. In *Les Chants de Maldoror* the primary concern of the author is the reorganization of the living world, biologically integrated and by the same token bereft of the moral supremacy of man. It is even likely that he was thinking of Darwin when he said: "As I write this, new tremors are traversing the intellectual atmosphere: all we need is the courage to face them." This sentence taken out of context has often been quoted as evidence of Lautréamont's awareness of new literary trends. But it is much more likely that he was thinking of the sciences rather than literature for the sentence comes as a conclusion to a passage in which he makes a purely biological analogy between the graftings done on animals and the physiological possibilities of identification between the reader and the author.

Darwinism and the positivist atmosphere in which it flowered affected the work of Lautréamont in the same way that the theory of the Great Chain of Being influenced the Romanticists. From plant to animal, from animal to man, from man to the angel, from the angel to God had been the graded path to perfection as visualized by pantheist writers such as Victor Hugo. In his metaphysical poem, *Dieu,* Hugo made animal, man, and the angel plod on their way toward the discovery of the infinite, each according to his relative spiritual capacity. Although a general relationship was sensed by the Romanticists between the other species and man, the proportion between nothingness and perfection was considered entirely different for the inferior forms of life as compared with that in man, and therefore man's belief in his superiority was not shaken. But with Darwinism the scale of gradual perfectibility was disturbed, for each species was considered perfect in its own fashion. But if we then move from the biological concept of perfection to its philosophical implications, man's aspiration toward the absolute is blocked by the very reshuffle of the biological role which promises him only the dark mystery of disappearing as easily and irrevocably from the face of the earth as a fly or a butterfly. Finding himself a descendant of the ape and a brother to the leech, man can no longer believe himself created in the image of God.

Lautréamont did not come to this notion serenely. Endowed with a propensity for mysticism, he should have lived in a world which accepted miracles and spiritual revelations equal to the scope of his vast imagination. It was a bitter disappointment for him to discover the extent of man's limitations. Maldoror, the half-man, half-beast hero

of his work, wanders day and night without rest or respite, troubled by horrible nightmares and by phantoms that hover about his bed and trouble his sleep. He is tormented by his dual combat with God and with man. Lautréamont and his shadowy protagonist, who serves to exteriorize occasionally his own anguish, are indignant at being chained to "the hardened crust of a planet," and of being "imprisoned within the walls of their intelligence." Yet, Lautréamont cannot quench his passion for the infinite. And if it is true that he shares the destiny of the animal, then his own unanswered but unabated longing for the infinite must exist in the lowliest creatures. Indeed, the dogs that bark must be thirsty for the infinite, "like you, like me, like all the rest of humans. I, even as the dogs, feel the need for the infinite. I cannot, I cannot satisfy this need. I am the son of man and of woman, so I have heard. I am surprised . . . I thought I was more." He is angry with God for not having made him *more*. He chides Him for having committed such a blunder: "The Creator should not have engendered such a vermin." He is equally angry with man for having been fool enough to harbor the illusion of his dignity for so long. When he refers to man as "this sublime ape" there is disdain, sarcasm, and regret in the use of the terminology.

A less virile and vigilant young man in the throes of such a spiritual crisis might have sought release from his tension by escape, either in terms of physical or intellectual evasion. The examples of such culminations to revolt are numerous in literature. The originality of Lautréamont, and the very thing which endeared him to a future generation of artists, is his refusal to be diverted from his intellectual dilemma. Art did not mean to him a form of consolation or a palliative, but on the contrary a confrontation of the problem, a search, perhaps a revelation however painful it might be.

Les Chants de Maldoror attests to Lautréamont's facing up to the tremendous rearrangement of a world in which man is to be considered a material organism and therefore conditioned by the same nonmoral impulses as the beasts. This is not really an attitude of revolt, for revolt implies refusal to accept. Young Isidore accepts a totally earthbound condition: "The stone would long to escape from the laws of gravity. Impossible!" But he accepts it with repugnance as he sets out to portray man through the eyes of his disillusionment: "Let my war against man be eternal since each recognizes in another his own degradation." No longer are vestiges of the sublime qualities of man to be seen in the animal, as the Romanticists had believed; but on the contrary the undesirable or ugly aspects of animals are mirrored in human beings. Lautréamont begins with a hideously unflattering picture of the *dear reader,* calling him a monster, referring to his mouth as a snout and comparing his movements to those of a shark. Human eyes are like a sea hog's, circular like a night bird's. When man stretches his neck it looks like a snail's; his legs remind Lautréamont of a toad's hind limbs. Man's facial expressions are those of a duck or a goat, his baldness that of a tortoise shell, his nakedness that of the worm. The cries of a dog, a child, a cat, a woman have a definite kinship in his picture of the universe.

The analogies between man and beast form the core of his imagery in *Les Chants de Maldoror.* The similarity is by no means limited to physical attributes. Human movements and attitudes are often drawn into very complicated mental associations with animal behavior: "Just like the stercoraceous, birds that are restless as if always famished, enjoy the polar seas, and venture only accidentally into more temperate zones, like them I was uneasy and dragged my legs forward very slowly." Here is his concept of a human state of mind: "The mind is dried up by a condensed and continually strained reflection, it howls like frogs in a swamp, when a band of ravenous flamingos or famished herons fall upon the weeds of its shores." He compares the style of a writer to "an owl serious unto eternity." By accepting a close link between man and other living organisms in his metaphors, he destroys old aesthetic values; beauty becomes for him something entirely unorthodox: "He seemed beautiful like the two long tentacle-shaped filaments of an insect," or "The beetle, beautiful as the trembling of the hands of an alcoholic." It is far-fetched analogies such as these which André Breton has called the surrealism of Lautréamont. The following image has become famous because of the number of times it has been cited as the perfect surrealist image: "The vulture of the lambs, beautiful as the law of arrestment of the development of the chest in adults whose tendency to growth is not in relation to the quantity of molecules that their organism assimilates, vanished into the high reaches of the atmosphere." Even death has a beauty likened to a characteristic of the animal: "Each one has the common sense to confess without difficulty that he does not perceive at first a relation, no matter how remote, which I point out between the beauty of the flight of a royal kite, and that of the face of a child, rising sweetly above an open casket, like a water lily piercing the surface of the waters."

If man's physical characteristics are akin to those of the animal, his social behavior can also be seen to derive from that of the lower forms of life. Man's social incompatibility, for instance, becomes as natural a phenomenon as that of various species of fish that practice their own brand of isolationism in ocean habitats:

> Aged ocean, the different species of fish that you nourish have not sworn fraternity to each other. Each species lives by itself. The temperaments and conformities which are at variance in each one of them, explain, in a satisfactory manner, what at first appears to be only an anomaly. It is thus with man, who does not have the same excuses. When a piece of land is occupied by thirty million human beings, they think themselves compelled not to bother with the existence of their neighbors, stuck like roots on the adjoining piece of land.

The theory of evolution accorded Lautréamont a means of reexamining moral issues. In Mlle Royer's translation of Darwin, the universal and inevitable destructiveness in all nature was eloquently brought out: "a law of inevitable destruction decimates, either the young or the old, at each successive generation, or only at periodic intervals." In line with this basic struggle for survival described by Darwin, the translator's introduction pointed out that if destruction is a basic law of nature, then the fundamental rule of morality would be the efforts of each species for self-preservation. The recognition of the brutal origin and the biological universality of evil is a basic theme of *Les Chants de Maldoror.* Lautréamont accepts man's sinful inclinations as the same type of manifestation as the eagle's instinct to tear up his prey. The judges of man's cruelty to man are no other than the eagle, the crow, the pelican, the wild duck, the toad, the tiger, the whale, the shark, or the seal, for he has surpassed the cruelty of all of these.

If man is physically and spiritually no more than a sublime ape, then the angel cannot be very far from this same stage; he appears to Maldoror in the guise of a crab and laughs like a lamb. As the concept of gradual perfection is minimized, even God is divested of his sublimity.

Once the physical and moral characteristics of human beings have been reduced to the level of those of the animals, there remains only one reason for man's greater unhappiness as compared with the attitude of other living organisms on earth: it is the illusion he has of his superiority. In his own moment of disillusionment, therefore, Lautréamont seeks to reduce human pride and thereby find peace through a fraternization with the animal world and finally through actual metamorphosis. He discourses with the greatest of ease with animals (among whom are some of the principal characters of his work): the snake, the beetle, the toad. He seeks a bond with the most despicable of animals: the vampire is his friend, the scorpions his companions; he makes love to the female shark, is consoled by the serene and majestic toad. I do not agree with Bachelard that Lautréamont's obsession with animals is a manifestation of "the phenomenology of aggression." If hostile, violent acts are perpetrated, as he says, to forestall his own vulnerability to suffering, the evidence seems to show that Maldoror suffers as much as the animals with which he associates. Lautréamont is making an attempt to revise the anthropocentric notion of the universe, and the process is wrought with pain and stoical humiliation. The pantheists had also felt a certain affinity with all created beings, but the bond had been considered hierarchic, and man's love of God's other creatures placed on a somewhat patriarchal plane. In Lautréamont's vision of the universe, however, the fraternization of man with beast, Maldoror's actual intercourse with animals, are based on a sordid form of democracy and a powerful atavism whereby man seeks justification for his instincts and attitudes by putting them on a par with those of the lowest forms of animal life.

Maldoror achieves complete identification with the other species. With joy he lives as a shark, or a hog, or a pretty cricket: "The metamorphosis never appeared to my eyes as anything but the high and magnanimous reverberation of perfect happiness for which I had been waiting a long time." He envisions with equanimity two brothers changed into a single spider. Going one step further, he contemplates the possibility of new species: he sees himself as a hybrid, half-bird, half-man, or he imagines with scientific precision a man with the appendages of a duck in close communion with water life:

> I saw swimming in the sea, with large duck's feet in place of the extremities of the legs and arms,

bearing a dorsal fin proportionally as fine and as long as a dolphin's, a human being, with vigorous muscles, and which numerous schools of fish (I saw, in this procession, among other inhabitants of the waters, the torpedo, the anarnak of Greenland, and the horrible scropene) followed with the very ostensible marks of the greatest admiration . . . The porpoise, who have not, in my opinion, stolen the reputation of good swimmers, could hardly follow from afar this amphibian of a new species.

In still another instance, his disgust for mankind makes him assume partially the shape of a swan and live at peace with the fish. "Providence, as you can see, has given me in part the organism of a swan. I live in peace with the fish, and they procure the food which I need."

It is significant to note the difference between these metamorphoses and the *Metamorphosis* of Kafka. Gregor Samsa, transformed into a tremendous insect, feels nothing but contempt and fear in his new condition. He senses an eternal barrier between himself and humanity. His metamorphosis symbolizes his exclusion from the rest of society, his tremendous loneliness that nothing can cure. On the contrary, Lautréamont feels no disgust; to him the tentacles of an insect are beautiful. It is, rather, the return to his former shape that he considers a misfortune. His metamorphosis is not the terrible thing it is in Kafka's story, but an affront to that human hypocrisy he cannot tolerate. Basically, then, he is not such a pessimist as Kafka for he finds relief from his dissatisfaction with humanity—unwholesome though the manner may be—through his identification with other forms of life.

Nonetheless Lautréamont's attempts to take man down from his self-appointed pedestal and to integrate him with a more closely knit animal kingdom produce a tragic note throughout his writings. Although on the one hand he concedes a dreary sort of materialism that endows man with as little immortality as a butterfly, his innate mysticism produces undertones of a protest against a totally materialistic concept of life as pungent as his determined intent to undermine the traditional faith in human superiority.

The mood fluctuates between insolence and derision on the one hand, and on the other, the despair of Adam chased from paradise. Although he was obsessed by the seeing of the animal in man, he did not achieve a total portrayal of man as a beast. Even in comparing Maldoror's crime to that of the eagle he unconsciously pointed to the great difference by adding: "yet as much as my victim, I suffered." For all his self-imposed materialism he could not rid himself of the notion of immortality. The very evil he saw in man and in beast he explained by their common rage against the inability to fathom the absolute. Although he humiliated God before His creatures he could not deny His omnipresence. And although man and beast are pictured as being equally ephemeral yet there exists for all a paradise, described in eloquent terms by brother toad who will share it with Maldoror.

What dazzled the surrealists and intensified their admiration for Lautréamont was his ability to confront the human condition squarely in all its abject and tragic facets yet to discover at the same time a weapon for self-preservation in his battle with God. It was what Breton called in his *Anthologie de l'Humour Noir* a "humor that reached its supreme power and that brings us physically and totally under its law." Léon Pierre-Quint had earlier seen in this two-edged instrument of attack and self-protection the basic metal of the modern comic, which has something sacred about it and is at the antipodes of the old: it is aimed at the irremediable plight of man although humor allows Lautréamont a moment of exemption from the target of his derision. Léon Pierre-Quint says that Lautréamont put an infernal machine at each junction of his thought process: "When Lautréamont responds with humor to Maldoror's cries of fury as he stands in judgment over Jehovah and as an executioner over men, he has truly attained the revolt of the mind, and it is superior to the integral nihilism of the destroyers of society."

Lautréamont died too young to have reached any philosophical conclusions. The ultimate picture which *Les Chants de Maldoror* leaves is twofold. True, on the one hand there is the image of man on a plane little (if at all) above that of the beast; but at the same time Lautréamont's tableau of the animal world is endowed, through his longing for fraternity, with the human qualities he would deny: wisdom, kindness, sympathy, at times even a certain "douceur." As a result his apostrophes to the lowliest creatures, touched as they are with an undercurrent of pathos and compassion, transform many a passage of the work from a derision of mankind to a mockery of those who would deny man any powers beyond those of animals. "I thought I was more than that!" is the chant that soars above the absurd fraternizations. The bold manner in which Lautréamont came to grips with "the great problem of life," whether he transferred his concern to his alter ego, the brother of the leech, or took it upon himself directly, gave his work a universal and timeless character, and set the tragic but unresigned and sometimes sardonic tone, characteristic not of his age but of a future one. (pp. 57-66)

> *Anna Balakian, "Lautréamont's Battle with God," in her* Surrealism: The Road to the Absolute, *revised edition, Dutton, 1970, pp. 50-66.*

Alex de Jonge   (essay date 1973)

[*An English critic and educator, de Jonge is the author of* Nightmare Culture: Lautréamont and "Les chants de Maldoror", *from which the excerpt below is taken. Here, he maintains that the character Maldoror represents the most extreme example of the nineteenth-century dandy figure.*]

Lautréamont describes his hero [Maldoror] in the language of definitive defiance, as God's enemy. Along with the trappings of black romanticism he inherits its concomitant qualities of an impassive dandyism.

The dandy is one of the most important creations of nineteenth-century culture. His basic attitude is one of refusal. In a world in which everyone is grubbing for money, success or security, the dandy declines to dirty his hands. The metaphor of clean hands is brought to life by Eugène Süe. One of the definitive dandies of his time, he was never to be seen without a pair of spotless pale-pink gloves. He changed them several times a day and never wore the same pair twice. The dandy expresses scorn for the values of the pecuniary society, for its morality and its ambitions. He expresses his feelings through his cynical rejection of the domestic values of a comfortable middle class, and above all through the extravagance of his consumption.

Baudelaire, who displayed great insight into the sociology of the dandy, pointed out that dandyism is the product of a transitional phase in society's evolution from an aristocracy to a democracy in which the tyranny of majority opinion reigns supreme. The dandy comes at a time which remembers enough of the old values to have a sense of style, but which acknowledges bankers and lawyers as the new élite and has no room for those who reject the pecuniary ethic.

The dandy is an outsider: declining to collaborate with the values of the society he is born into, he lacks the herd-instinct of the left, and has no peer-group, no alternative society, to confirm him in his attitudes. He is obliged to manufacture his alternative single-handed, an alternative that must be unique. He is obsessed with the quality of the statement he makes; his rejection must be displayed, his consumption conspicuous. His whole sense of identity, his very gesture of refusal, is based entirely on style—a precarious, artificial creation perpetually at risk. The dandy founds his being on *cool,* which he may lose at any moment. He fights a lone battle, poised between the ridiculous and the sublime. Because ridicule will cause his immediate undoing he must always remain cold and unmoved. To be susceptible to emotion is to put his cool at risk. Consequently his eroticism lapses into Don Juanism. Pushkin's Onegin, Lermontov's Hero of our Times are classic cases in point.

Maldoror represents the ultimate in dandyism. In him its characteristics are exaggerated to an epic degree. He remains unmoved in the midst of acts of the most extreme cruelty; his self-control is never threatened. The apotheosis of total consciousness, we can never feel, as he cuts the wrist off one of his boyfriends, or passes Mervyn to the butcher, that he is at all carried away by his actions. Consider the detachment with which he contemplates the murder of Lohengrin, one of his adolescent lovers:

> For fear that he might later become like other men, I had initially decided to kill him with a knife once he passed the age of innocence. But I thought it over, and wisely I abandoned my resolve in time. He does not suspect that his life was in danger for a quarter of an hour. All was ready, and the knife had been bought. It was a pretty stiletto, for I like grace and elegance even in the instruments of death; but it was long and sharp. A single wound in the neck, carefully piercing one of the carotid arteries, and I think that would have been enough.

Maldoror always acts deliberately. In this respect his portrait differs from the conventional treatment of the dandy.

On the whole the dandy as portrayed in literature is finally found wanting, since his feelings have become so atrophied that he eventually proves incapable of enjoying a human relationship. Maldoror undergoes no such censure. In his case cold cerebration and reflective logic take the place of feelings as the springs of legitimate action.

He differs from his romantic predecessors in another important respect. The conventional figure of the romantic outsider conforms to a pattern first established by Milton's Satan. These archangels all fall victim to their pride, and are compelled by a heroic sense of perversity to continue their struggle against the good. Their fate is a fully justified damnation for their pursuit of evil. However we may sympathise with them, we do not doubt that they are wrong.

Not so Maldoror. For all the romantic trappings, he lacks an essential attribute of the black romantic hero: the damnation of authorial value-judgment. We can only observe his acts of rebellion, we cannot judge them. To do so would be to adopt the standpoint of judgment itself—God's values and God's viewpoint, and hence the values of the culture which Lautréamont is trying to expose. Maldoror is not judgeable, and it is this that distinguishes his acts of aggression against the 'Celestial Bandit' from romantic acts of defiance. In comparison these appear the petty tantrums of spoilt children. Maldoror represents a complete rejection of everything that God stands for. In his world it is a question of who will win, not of who is right.

The reason why Maldoror attacks God is to be found in the following passage. It describes the central vision of the entire book, an emblem that suggests that God, the fountainhead of all authority, law and sanction, may not have our well-being at heart. This view of the principle of legality echoes a sinister insight of Diderot's. He once suggested that laws are usually made for the convenience not of the citizen but of the administration. It is a vision based on just such a view of law and order that Maldoror is afforded:

> [Maldoror raises his eyes] till I saw a throne made of excrement and gold, on which there reigned, with an idiot's pride, his body draped in a shroud of unwashed sick-bed sheets, the one who calls himself the Creator. He held in his hand the rotten trunk of a dead man, and raised it in turn to his eyes, his nose, his mouth; once it reached his mouth you can guess what he did with it. His feet were plunged in a vast sea of boiling blood, on its surface could be seen, appearing suddenly, like tape-worms in the contents of a chamber-pot, occasional wary heads, that vanished instantly beneath the surface, as quick as arrows: a well-directed kick on the nose being the expected reward for this infringement of regulations, occasioned by the need to breathe air, for after all these were no fish. Mere amphibians, they swam round in this filthy liquid until the Creator, finding himself empty-handed, grabbed another swimmer with the claws of his feet, as if in a vice, and raised him up in the air, out of the red slime—an exquisite sauce. He treated him as he had his predecessor. First he

ate the head, legs and arms, and finally the trunk, until there was nothing left; for he crunched up the bones. And so he continued, for every hour of his eternal life. Sometimes he cried: 'I made you; therefore I may treat you as I please. You have done nothing to me, I do not deny it. I make you suffer, and it is to please me.' And he resumed his cruel meal, moving his lower jaw, which agitated his beard covered in brains. Tell me, reader, does not this final detail make your mouth water? It is not everyone who gets to eat brains like those, good fresh brains, taken from the fishpond not a quarter of an hour ago. Paralysed, silent, I looked on for some time. Thrice I nearly fell backwards, like someone overcome with emotion; thrice I recovered. Not a nerve in my body was still; I trembled as lava trembles within a volcano. Finally my bursting lungs could no longer drive out the life-giving air fast enough, my mouth and lips opened, and I screamed, so loudly did I scream that I heard it! Suddenly the bonds were loosened from my ears, the eardrum cracked at the shock of this rushing mass of resounding air that I had spewed out with such force, and a new phenomenon came to pass in an organ that nature had condemned. I heard a sound! A fifth sense was born in me!

The traumatic vision of an old man with a long white beard brings Maldoror, who is anything but impassive in this instance, to his senses. It is this sudden insight into the metaphysics of law and order that creates Maldoror the militant dandy. He understands that the conventional vision we have been given of the world and our place in it is a partial vision only, that God keeps something back—the truth. Maldoror cracks the codes of his culture and thereby achieves a partial liberation from its prison. He realises that God, the *grand object extérieur,* outside the culture-pattern and its restrictions, maintains a complete monopoly on the truth, and is impervious to anti-trust legislation. It is that realisation that motivates passages such as this:

> The Eternal One has made the world as it is; he would display great sagacity if, for exactly the time it takes to crack a woman's skull with a hammer, he would forget his astral majesty, to reveal to us the mysteries in the midst of which our existence chokes, like a fish in the bottom of a boat.

Once again we find the miseries of the human condition expressed with stifling aquatic imagery.

Maldoror is determined to win for himself that portion of truth that God has kept back. In his attempt to do so he challenges Him and His creatures at every turn. The book abounds in accounts of his battles with archangels who have taken on strange forms, or, on one occasion, with Hope itself. Maldoror in the guise of an eagle fights Hope in the form of a dragon 'taller than an oak . . . his whitish wings, knotted with powerful sinews, seem to have nerves of steel, so easily do they cut the air. Its body begins with a tiger's bust and ends with a long serpent's tail.' After a long and bloody combat, Maldoror tears out the dragon's heart. The episode ends as follows: 'So, Maldoror, you have conquered *Hope!* Henceforward despair will feed on

the purest substance of your being. Henceforward you will walk with deliberate tread along the path of evil.'

In the course of the book we witness the steady apotheosis of Maldoror until he becomes God's rival. Like Holmes and Moriarty they live in a state of uneasy truce, each one knowing that he can neither win nor be beaten.

Maldoror's ultimate ambition is to become a kind of God himself; he wants to win the lion's share. In the following passage he dreams of attaining totality, possessing the universe in an act of unnatural rape. It represents the very essence of Maldoror: a blend of aggression, homosexual eroticism, power lust and a longing for knowledge:

> If only, instead of being a hell, the universe were nothing but an enormous celestial anus, observe the gesture that I make toward my loins; yes, I would force my cock through its bleeding sphincter, my impetuous movements breaking the very walls of its pelvis. Then misfortune would not have blown whole dunes of shifting sands onto my sightless eyes; I would have discovered the underground place where sleeping truth lies hidden.

This is an important passage. The quality of the imagination instantly distinguishes it from the tradition of straight literature; we find nothing like it until William Burroughs. It unfolds some of the most important themes in the book. Maldoror emerges as the taboo-breaker. He assaults the very basis of culture and law, for taboo is the ultimate sanction that underwrites them. He attacks the very principle of 'Thou shalt not'. This passage tells us why.

It opens with a conditional. If this universe were not a hell in which Maldoror is blind, cut off from the truth, he would be able to possess it. He would delve into it by means of a sexual act that is taboo, censored, excluded from the conventional world-picture. But this delving remains a dream, an unrealisable hypothesis. Things being what they are, total truth, utter liberation are impossible. The author makes it clear that there is no escape. The world is as it is, and we are in it. But an understanding of our predicament, of how escape might be possible, serves to push the walls back a little. In the country of the blind it is useful to know that you have lost your sight; at least you will realise that there is more to life than the messages of your five senses.

Maldoror's mode of liberation explains one of the roles of homosexuality in this book. It represents an anti-convention, the infringement of sexual taboo. It is buggery, the incarnation of sexual taboo, grounds for irretrievable breakdown of convention, and an inappropriate subject for prose poetry, that Maldoror will employ in his bid for hidden truth. Truth and freedom will only be attained through basic transgression. This is the fundamental theme of **Les Chants.** Law and taboo are barriers erected by culture to cut its victims off from the truth. Such barriers can only be broken down by saying the unsayable, thinking the unthinkable. Lautréamont, like Nietzsche, sees the law-breaker not the law-giver as the truly creative being. For both writers the universe of the good, the universe of law is a hell in which essential truth is denied us.

Like any conscientious prophet, from Isaiah to Zarathustra, Maldoror, having gained this insight into our situation, seeks to pass his revelation on to the world. His technique is more transitive than the most violent verbal fire and brimstone. On the principle that words never hurt, Maldoror uses sticks and stones to bring man to consciousness: 'Indeed I tear away the mask from man's treacherous muddy face, and one by one . . . I cast down the sublime lies with which he deludes himself.' For 'mask' read culture, for 'lies' the principle of law and order. Once again Nietzsche and Lautréamont are in agreement. He too assaults humanity, suggesting that man is something to be overcome, and he sees man hiding behind the mask of culture:

> Truly, you could wear no better masks than your faces, you men of the present! Who could—*recognise* you?
>
> Written over with the signs of the past and these signs overdaubed with new signs: thus you have hidden yourselves well from all interpreters of signs . . .!
>
> He who tore away from you your veils and wraps and paint and gestures would have just enough left over to frighten the birds. [*Thus Spake Zarathustra*].

Law-breakers like Maldoror who seek to expose the conventions that make up the mask of culture are not well received: 'This is why my hero has attracted irreconcilable hate, by attacking man, who believed himself to be invulnerable.' Man resents Maldoror, because he resents the truth. It is weakness that prevents him from reaching out for the liberation that Maldoror offers. Man is appalled by Maldoror and rejects him out of hand, but perhaps it is only his self-deluding hypocrisy that prevents him from seeing that he has more in common with Maldoror than he would care to think: '[The poet] does not claim that his warblings are totally unfamiliar: on the contrary he congratulates himself with the thought that the lofty and wicked ideas of his hero are to be found in all men.' The difference between Maldoror and other men is that he is able to face up to himself, where others have to hide from each other and themselves behind their cultural masks: 'He then perceived that he was born wicked: extraordinary blow of fate . . . he admitted the truth and said that he was cruel . . . Did you hear him, mankind? He dares to say it with this trembling pen!' He writes not for public acclaim but in order to 'Paint the joys of cruelty. Delights neither transitory nor artificial . . . because you are cruel, does it mean that you cannot have genius?'

Maldoror is not content with admitting the truth about himself. He also wishes to instruct us in unpalatable truths. His purpose is educational, and if the education does us violence no matter; Maldoror would be the first to agree that to spare the rod is to spoil the child. Man believed that:

> he was composed only of good and a minimal quantity of evil. Abruptly I showed him, by exposing his heart, his intrigues, that on the contrary he is composed of evil with a minimal quantity of good, which the legislators have the

greatest difficulty in preserving from evaporation.

Because man will neither believe nor accept the truth about himself, psychology is still in its infancy:

> Man hypocritically says yes and thinks no. This is why the pigs of humanity have such trust in one another and are not selfish. Psychology still has a long way to go.

In forcing man's attention on his instinctive love of cruelty, no less real for being inadmissible, Maldoror appeals to man's repressed and secret self. Desires that normally have to be sublimated by culture into notions such as crime and punishment, law-enforcement, the obscene rituals of social justice and authoritarianism, are exposed by Maldoror for what they are: institutions created by society to permit its leaders to exercise their natural, instinctive desire to treat their fellows as their slaves, without abdicating from their role as do-gooders and pillars of the community: to behave, in short, like miniature versions of the eating God. Social man may revolt at what Maldoror has to say, but social man's *id* reacts as follows:

> Reader, perhaps it is hate that you wish me to invoke at the beginning of this work. Who is to say that you will not, bathed in countless sensual pleasures, sniff to your heart's content with your wide thin conceited nostrils, turning up your belly like a shark in the fine black air, as if you understood the importance of this action, and the no less great importance of your legitimate appetite, breathing in the red scent slowly and majestically. Believe me, it will gladden the two shapeless holes of your vile muzzle, oh monster.

The author of *Les Chants* suggests that we are being hypocritical if we pronounce ourselves disgusted by his poetry, with a hypocrisy that is fundamental to human nature. In Plato's *Republic* Socrates recounts an incident that illustrates the indignation and reluctance which we feel when obliged to acknowledge this side of ourselves:

> Leontion, son of Aglaion, was on his way up from Piracus, outside the north wall, when he noticed some corpses lying on the ground with the executioner standing beside them. He wanted to go and look at them, and yet at the same time he held himself back in disgust. For a time he struggled with himself and averted his eyes, but in the end his desire got the better of him and he ran up to the corpses, opening his eyes and saying to them, 'There you are, curse you—a lovely sight! Have a real good look.'

Maldoror invites *us* to take a look, knowing that, secretly, we are curious. If we profess to find it all too disgusting, we deceive ourselves. We reject, in one form, attitudes and relationships that society encourages us to adopt in others. These are simply more effective in their reconciliation of our desires with our delusions. There are those of us who may be moved by the fall of a sparrow but who scarcely blink as another Indian bites the dust. As Maldoror points out, if one wishes to enjoy the pleasures of killing with impunity, one simply has to practise murder wholesale: 'You see that when you wish to become famous, you must plunge gracefully into rivers of blood, fed by cannon fodder.'

Passages such as this demonstrate that one of the functions of *Les Chants* is to force us to face the unpalatable truths that are usually obscured by cultural overlay. We are all cruel, but most of us prefer not to admit it. It is *we* who are responsible for the naked horror of the work: its hero Maldoror is exceptional in his honesty, not in his morals. As Gogol writes in the epigraph to *The Inspector General,* 'Don't blame the mirror if you see an ugly face.' Still less should we blame Maldoror, for it is not his face that we see in the mirror; it is his hand that we can feel holding us by the scruff of the neck and forcing us to look.

Maldoror's dandyism reflects an attitude of fundamental refusal. He rejects the world of culture as a world of partial truth, designed in the first instance to conceal from mankind his actual situation as victim of the eating God, secondly to permit men to reconcile their instinctive love of cruelty with their desire to approve of themselves. Maldoror's aggression is designed to bring us to consciousness, compelling us to see the world as it really is. (pp. 44-52)

Alex de Jonge, "Maldoror," in his Nightmare Culture: Lautréamont and "Les chants de Maldoror," *St. Martin's Press, 1973, pp. 44-52.*

Albert Camus on Lautréamont's rebellion:

Lautréamont makes us understand that rebellion is adolescent. Our most effective terrorists, whether they are armed with bombs or with poetry, hardly escape from infancy. The *Songs of Maldoror* are the works of a highly talented schoolboy; their pathos lies precisely in the contradictions of a child's mind ranged against creation and against itself. Like the Rimbaud of the *Illuminations,* beating against the confines of the world, the poet chooses the apocalypse and destruction rather than accept the impossible principles that make him what he is in a world such as it is.

Albert Camus, in his The Rebel: An Essay on Man in Revolt, *translated by Anthony Bower, 1991.*

Robin Lydenberg   (essay date 1978)

[*In the following essay, Lydenberg explores the metaphorical significance of various metamorphoses in* Les chants de Maldoror.]

Isidore Ducasse's *Les Chants de Maldoror,* published under the pseudonym le comte de Lautréamont, is a literary exercise in artistic will. Ducasse's assertion of control over his text and his reader is achieved to a great extent through the adoption of language as a weapon, a weapon made particularly malleable by his insistence on its ambiguous nature. The reader's attention is constantly drawn by Ducasse to the arbitrary relationship between the *signifiant* and the *signifié,* to the radical nature of his metaphors, and more generally to the artificiality of the literary

text constructed from these devices. Ultimately, language is liberated from its mimetic function. It becomes infinite and anarchic, "insurrectionnel et libérateur" [according to Jacques Durand, "Un piège à rats perpétuel," *Entretiens,* 1971], and the author, as manipulator of this autonomous system, can assert his position as the only source of authority in this artificial world of fiction.

Exercising the arbitrariness of an omnipotent authority, Ducasse propels his text forward through a process which is simultaneously destructive and creative, undermining the conventions of literary history and rhetoric with transformations which revitalize these same conventions. This paradoxical procedure is easily identifiable as the basis of all parody. Ducasse, however, diverts this dual process of destruction and creation into a more specifically focused exploration of the nature of metaphor. Metaphor itself becomes Ducasse's model for all aesthetic assertion. Moreover, Ducasse's manipulation of the structure and content of metaphorical expression is both expanded and concretized in the series of bizarre metamorphoses which occur in the course of *Les Chants.* Finally, Ducasse turns this ambivalent and parodic use of metaphor and metamorphoses against the finality of his own text, attacking it as part of literary history, but liberating it at the same time from the limitations of the anticipated constraint of tradition.

1. *Parody.*—On the most basic level, Ducasse mobilizes his autonomous will against literary tradition as a whole. The particular focus of *Les Chants* on his most immediate predecessors, the Romantic poets, underlines how quickly independent and original artistic works may be absorbed into formal literary history. Irritated by stylistic effects which have become habitual and fixed, Ducasse adopts many techniques and images characteristic of the Romantic movement only to violate their structure and content in some radical way. We encounter in Chant I, for example, a familiar Romantic figure who appears on the horizon: "quelle majesté, mêlée d'une douceur sereine! Son regard, quoique doux, est profond. Ses paupières énormes jouent avec la brise et paraissent vivre." In the original version of the first *chant,* published separately in 1868, the final image reads "Ses cheveux jouent avec la brise, et paraissent vivre." In his substitution of "paupières énormes" for "cheveux" Ducasse destroys the integrity of the image by rendering it ridiculous; but at the same time he restores the power of surprise it has lost as literary cliché, making its presumption once again "énorme." The transformation remains transparent, the author's willful manipulation unmistakable, because the original image is still intact despite the violation caused by Ducasse's substitution.

The paradoxical effect of this type of parody is most clearly developed in Ducasse's later work, *Poésies.* In those literary aphorisms, he demonstrates how any literary "tic" violated by parodic transformation will remain recognizable even when its original meaning is blatantly negated or, as he prefers to describe the process, corrected. Ducasse thus destroys the immutable authority of the giants of French literature by assimilating and revising their own texts—by forcing Pascal or Vauvenargues in one sense to contradict themselves.

Unlike the technique of contradiction which Ducasse perfects in *Poésies,* the parodic exercises in **Les Chants** often take the form of excessive repetition or extension. The original device is not only preserved but actually intensified in these transformations. Among the "Tics, tics, et tics" which he denounces in *Poésies,* for example, Ducasse might include the following effect: "Âme royale, livrée, dans un moment d'oubli au crabe de la débauche, au poulpe de la faiblesse de caractère, au requin de l'abjection individuelle, au boa de la morale absente, et au colimaçon monstrueux de l'idiotisme!" Ducasse's obsessive accumulation of a particular poetic structure, in this case the zoological personifications for which Victor Hugo demonstrated a marked predilection, eventually renders it virtually meaningless. Aware of the danger that such parodies may be mistaken for mere imitation, however, Ducasse interrupts a description of Maldoror's battle with God and man to warn the reader: "qu'il soit maudit, par ses enfants et par ma main celui qui persiste à ne pas comprendre les kangaroos implacable du rire et les poux audacieux de la caricature!" Just as Ducasse's caricature of the Romantic hero renews the visual impact of that wind tossed figure, here too the poet's insistence on his distance from the stylistic device he parodies is deliberately and perversely framed in that same rhetoric, now revitalized through its self-referential function.

2. *Metaphor.*—Ducasse's purpose in exaggerating and contradicting the literary devices and attitudes of his immediate and remote predecessors is to extend the boundaries of poetry beyond the fixed, the habitual, the established. Because he sees in the creation of metaphor an impulse to reach beyond the limits of convention, mimesis, and nature itself, Ducasse focuses his narrative on an exploration and expansion of the possibilities offered by this device. This examination is initially destructive and parodic, directed against the indiscriminate use of metaphor, against the "saponification des obligatoires métaphores" which he feels has rendered the device impotent. In his attempt to revive the meaning and power of metaphorical expression, Ducasse distorts or destroys the structure and content of conventional poetic comparison, drawing the reader's attention back to the aggressive creative energy at the *source* of poetic invention.

More far reaching than the parody of specific texts, Ducasse's manipulation of metaphor involves a radical procedure which liberates the image from its contents just as language is liberated from its strictly mimetic function. One of the most characteristic techniques used in **Les Chants** is a repetition of the adverb "comme" followed by a series of banal analogies which threatens to be endless: "Ta grandeur morale, image de l'infini, est immense comme la réflexion du philosophe, comme l'amour de la femme, comme la beauté divine de l'oiseau, comme les méditations du poète. Tu es plus beau que la nuit." Drawing upon a metaphorical tradition which has become paralysed with clichés, Ducasse exposes the mechanical accumulation of poetic images as an empty rhetorical gesture. His comparisons thus develop what Philippe Fédy calls [in

"La comparaison dans le premier chant de *Maldoror,*" *Quatre Lectures de Lautréamont,* 1973] "une fonction de négativité," "l'annulation du message." The destructive and arbitrary extension which obliterates the content of these already meaningless phrases, however, also has a positive function. By stressing structure rather than content in his comparisons, Ducasse restores to the metaphorical form its power as a weapon of control; thus, the monotonous repetition of "comme" renders the reader helpless, subjecting his consciousness to this hypnotic incantation.

The "message" of Ducasse's metaphors may fade into banality or conversely may be obscured by incomprehensibility. The often cited "beau comme" tirades in particular serve to obliterate meaning and highlight structural form:

> Il est beau comme la rétractilité des serres des oiseaux rapaces; ou encore, comme l'incertitude des mouvements musculaires dans les plaies des parties molles de la région cervicale postérieure; ou plûtot comme ce piège à rats perpétuel, toujours retendu par l'animal pris, qui peut prendre seul des rongeurs indéfiniment, et fonctionner même caché sous la paille; et surtout, comme la rencontre fortuite sur une table de dissection d'une machine à condre et d'un parapluie!

Images like the final "rencontre fortuite" have been celebrated by early critics of **Les Chants** as the first exercises in "écriture automatique." Léon Pierre-Quint, for one, embraces this image of Ducasse as inspired and unconscious scribe: "la plume note, sans l'intervention de la conscience les associations d'idées ou d'images. Les phrases se déduisent les unes des autres sans aucun plan préconçu, sans aucune préméditation sous le seul effet de l'inspiration" ["De Lautréamont à nos jours," *Entretiens,* 1971]. Such an analysis, however, overlooks not only the initial and obvious parodic intention of Ducasse's imagery, but also his effort to assert the poet's arbitrary manipulation of the metaphorical process itself. As in the earlier example, the analogical series is once again deliberately arbitrary, potentially and threateningly endless.

In their banality or their incomprehensibility, then, Ducasse's metaphors aggressively call attention to themselves and to the authorial autonomy which forms them. As J. M. Agasse points out [in his "Notes pour une rhétorique des *Chants,*" *Entretiens,* (1971)], "Pas de figure sans 'sentiment de figure'." To impose further this stylistic awareness on the reader, Ducasse elaborates the logical steps which justify each metaphor, revealing not a subconscious process of association, but rather a determined and highly rational procedure. This process is most clear where the elements of the metaphor are brought together not by natural affinity but by the assertive control of the poet. The hymn to the ocean, for example, is more an act of aggressive creation than of subservient praise: "Je voudrais que la majesté humaine ne fut que l'incarnation du reflet de la tienne . . . Remue-toi avec impétuosité . . . plus . . . plus encore si tu veux que je te compare à la vengeance de Dieu." Ducasse often uses metaphor in this way in **Les Chants,** transforming an object in order to serve a rhetorical effect. Mimetic function, the subjection of language to reality, of *signifiant* to *signifié,* once again gives way to the dominant authority of the author within the artificial fictional universe of the narrative.

This authorial dominance provides a logical and literary basis for the famous "beau comme" passages, where the vague and abstract concept of beauty serves as a flexible link between any elements which the poet chooses to declare beautiful:

> Le vautour des agneaux, beau comme la loi de l'arrêt de développement de la poitrine chez les adultes dont la propension à la croissance n'est pas en rapport avec la quantité de molécules que leur organisme s'assimile, se perdit dans les hautes couches de l'atmosphère.

The subject of the comparison—the vulture—is literally lost in the extended metaphor which Ducasse spins from its beauty, the *comparé* gradually obscured by the *comparant.* Moreover, the physiological law to which the bird is compared, a law which measures the extent to which two forces within the same body can never be totally "en rapport," frames an appropriate analogy for the permanent disjunction of the two elements of the metaphor. The comparison here does not serve then as a definition of the vulture, the *comparé,* but as a definition of the structure of metaphor itself.

Ducasse's recognition of the impossibility of metaphorical accuracy or realization is reflected in his predilection for logical qualifications of each comparison. The reader is often subjected to a perverse doubling back of the narrative in which the poet contradicts his own assertions: "si vous croyez apercevoir quelque marque de douleur sur mon visage d'hyène (j'use de cette comparison quoique l'hyène soit plus belle que moi et plus agréable à voir) soyez détrompé"; or he blatantly denies their truth: "toutes ces tombes qui sont éparses dans un cimetière, comme les fleurs dans une prairie (comparaison qui manque de vérité)." Undermined by logic, conventional or unusual metaphors disappear behind parenthetical asides which focus the reader's attention on their inadequacy. At the same time, however, Ducasse utters these metaphors almost as a challenge to the reader who is forced to assimilate them along with the narrative.

Comparisons based on mistaken identity instead of similarity allow Ducasse to turn the limitations of metaphorical accuracy to his own advantage. Embracing the idea of comparison as optical illusion, he extends infinitely the possibilities of metaphorical assertion: "Deux piliers, qu'il n'était pas difficile et encore moins impossible de prendre pour des baobabs, s'apercevait dans la vallée." Constructing analogies on the rather unexpected basis of unsuitability, Ducasse offers a comparison only to declare it insufficient for the occasion: "Quand une comète, pendant la nuit, apparaît subitement dans une région du ciel, après quatre-vingts ans d'absence . . . Sans doute, elle n'a pas conscience de ce long voyage; il n'en est pas ainsi de moi." The accumulation of such inappropriate analogies reinforces the peculiarly negative and aggressive quality of the metaphorical language of *Les Chants.* The assertion of metaphor, particularly metaphor which systematically defies its function as a structure of similarity, is an act of artistic will, a technique which Ducasse swears, "ma parole

d'honneur, donne gracieusement au style de l'écrivain, qui se paie cette personnelle satisfaction."

Ducasse associates this potential energy and defiant challenge of metaphor with man's desire for that which he cannot reach—for the forbidden, the infinite, the sublime. The poet's continual qualification and undercutting of his metaphors indicates his awareness that the absolute harmony or association of elements in a poetic frame is impossible. Whether he is using images that are totally familiar or totally arbitrary, Ducasse's extended metaphors always draw the reader's attention to the ultimate inability of the poetic device to satisfy man's "soif d'infini." Because of this very limitation, Ducasse's metaphors are gestures towards the unattainable—most aggressive and most successful when they approach hyperbole. Ducasse insists that all metaphor, by virtue of its impossible structure, should constitute an hyperbolic act which "ne perd aucun pouce de terrain" to "la finesse de la restriction."

Hyperbole is more than a violation of limits of nature or logic; it may be a blatant transgression against the truth itself: "Le magnétisme et le chloroforme, quand ils s'en donnent la peine, savent quelquefois engendrer parcillement de ces catalepsies léthargiques. Elles n'ont aucune ressemblance avec la mort: ce serait un grand mensonge de le dire." Far from obliterating the metaphor, the narrator's denial of its verisimilitude merely underlines and flaunts his audacity in asserting it. Of course, Ducasse is using moral criteria ironically here, and we must remember that in the context of his insistently literary work a lie is simply the creation of another fiction or hypothesis.

3. *Hypothesis.*—Hypothesis, like metaphor, opens up the infinite and arbitrary possibilities of the text, and these two rhetorical devices are united in **Les Chants** by their function as exercises in the assertion of the impossible. Once concretized within the narrative, these poetic propositions become textual reality. As [J. M. Agasse] has explained this realization of fictions within **Les Chants,** "toute fiction à l'état virtuel (au conditionel) est susceptible une fois transcrite, de devenir la fiction même, la trame du récit." Hypotheses and extended metaphors are particularly effective as used by Ducasse because the initiating conditional which introduces them is most often overwhelmed by and lost in the succeeding detailed development. Such tortuous extensions, which are to be found in the most typical and essential passages of **Les Chants,** create a pervading ambiguous atmosphere, a non-linear temporality in which virtually anything may be asserted and established as a textual reality.

The opening stanza of Ducasse's text exemplifies his use of extended metaphor as a realization of fictional hypothesis. The flying cranes which dominate the stanza are first introduced as an analogy clarifying the narrator's advice to his reader: "dirige tes talons en arrière et non en avant . . . comme un angle à perte de vue de grues frileuses." The remainder of the first stanza traces the detailed flight of these birds through silence and foreboding winds,

> méditant beaucoup, qui, pendant l'hiver, vole puissamment à travers le silence, toutes voiles tendues, vers un point déterminé de l'horizon,

d'où tout à coup part un vent étrange et fort, précurseur de la tempête.

In a gradual and imperceptible shift, the analogy becomes the very subject of the stanza, and the leader of the hypothetical cranes guides the reader to the end of the fiction where "elle prend . . . un autre chemin philosophique et plus sûr." Ironically, the reader never finds his way back from this analogy, and the narrator's helpful warning becomes the very metaphorical maze in which the reader is caught.

The cranes, however, exist only metaphorically in **Les Chants,** just as many of Maldoror's evil deeds are only hypothetically perpetrated. The hero's brutal treatment of the little girl he meets on his daily walk in Chant II, for example, is part of an extended rhetorical address in which he merely warns the child of what *could* happen if she does not keep out of his sight:

> Dans un moment d'égarement, je pourrais te prendre les bras, les tordre comme un linge avec fracas, comme deux branches sèches, et te les faire ensuite manger. . . . Je pourrais, en prenant ta tête entre mes mains, . . . enfoncer mes doigts avides dans les lobes de ton cerveau innocent, pour en extraire . . . une graisse efficace qui lave mes yeux. . . . Je pourrais, soulevant ton corps vierge avec un bras de ter, te saisir par les jambes, te faire rouler autour de moi, comme une fronde, concentrer mes forces en décrivant la dernière circonférence, et te lancer contre la muraille.

This accumulation of conditional possibilities takes on a terrifying reality through the physical and mechanical precision of its detail. As the opening stanza never returns to the source of its extended metaphor (the reader), so this episode never recovers from Maldoror's hypothetical threat. The scene ends amidst the material remnants of the hypothesis, and the child's mutilated body, "resté plaqué sur la muraille, comme une poire mûre," stands as a visible testimony to the hero's imagined crime and as the material traces of the passage of the narrative itself.

As metaphor becomes hyperbole, so hypothesis becomes accomplished fiction. [Giuseppi] Ungaretti has described [in "Le secret de Lautréamont," *Entretiens,* 1971] Ducasse's literary project as the intention to give "à n'importe quoi, un semblant de certitude." What is realized or concretized within the text of **Les Chants,** however, is never "n'importe quoi," but always the most hyperbolic analogy (extreme in its banality or its incomprehensibility) or the most forbidden hypothetical action. Through these aggressive extremes, Ducasse's poetic activity may be differentiated from the facile and mechanical "saponification des obligatoires métaphores."

Ducasse, who is rarely satisfied with the reader's "willing suspension of disbelief," demands instead an absolute faith in the literal truth of his most outrageous metaphorical hypotheses. His description of the hermaphrodite in Chant II, for example, begins with a rather unambitious comparison: "ses cheveux . . . qui resplendit en cet instant comme les étoiles du firmament." He immediately abandons this simple and tentative ("en cet instant") met-

aphor for a more precise and fantastical hypothetical scenario which transforms the initial impression into an historical fact: "Mais il vaut mieux croire que c'est une étoile elle-même qui est descendue de son orbite, en traversant l'espace, sur ce front majestueux, qu'elle entoure avec sa clarté de diamant." When a metaphor or hypothesis is thus blatantly imposed on the reader as a reality, the text becomes a magical metamorphosis rather than a mere stylistic exercise.

4. *Metamorphosis.*—Such rhetorical assertions in **Les Chants** form the basis of the narrator's avowed battle against the reader. In addition, however, transformations effected on the level of language (idioms or metaphors taken literally, hypotheses extended with implacable realistic detail) are realized physically within the text in the strange metaphorical beasts spawned in the "marécages désolés" of the narrative. **Les Chants** are, in fact, dominated by an entire tribe of such dual creatures who become, literally, metaphors for metaphor. In the figure of the hermaphrodite, appropriately banished to Bicêtre, the duality of the metaphor is represented as a violent tension: "Rien ne paraît naturel en lui; pas même les muscles de son corps, qui se fraient un passage à travers les contours harmonieux de formes féminines." The line of fusion always remains visible and awkward in the dual creature, as in the birdman of Chant V, fused at the shoulders, or the dragon figure of Chant II whose "corps commence par un buste de tigre et se termine par une longue queue de serpent." The narrator's difficulty in describing and categorizing these creatures underlines the impossibility of a harmonious and unified identity emerging from such metaphorical conjunctions. At the same time, Ducasse "se paie cette personnelle satisfaction" in creating a new phenomenon which passes beyond the laws of nature, the laws of divine creation.

The narrator's assertion of artistic will through his transformations of metaphor is paralleled on a more literal level in Ducasse's usurpation of divine omnipotence and creativity through the production of actual metamorphoses within the narrative. The episodes of the pig, the "boule de merde," and the hermaphrodite are dramatizations or actualizations of the process of metaphorical transformation. Ducasse describes these changes of identity as "le haut et magnanime retentissement d'un bonheur parfait" and as a "projet sublime." The narrator's presentation of metamorphosis as a godly power, "parfait" and "sublime," underlines the omnipotence and autonomy of the artist who accomplishes them. These impossible beasts, then, become Ducasse's ultimate challenge to God and to the limits of reality.

These metamorphoses, however, appear in **Les Chants** most frequently as a tenuous dream-state rooted in impermanence. Like the harmonious metaphor, the permanent metamorphosis lies just beyond the narrator's grasp, subject to the whims of some external providential force which grants or denies its favors:

> Cependant, je recherchais activement quel acte de vertu j'avais accompli pour mériter, de la part de la Providence, cette insigne faveur.
>
> La Providence me faisait ainsi comprendre

d'une manière qui n'est pas inexplicable, qu'elle ne voulait pas que, même en rêve, mes projets sublimes s'accomplissent.

The impossibility of durable metamorphosis marks the boundaries of the author's power; Ducasse may transform anything, assert anything, but his poetic productions will survive only as long as the stanza lasts, only within the confines of the literary work itself. The poet's continued efforts at such transformations, despite his relentless consciousness of the impossibility of permanent metamorphosis, lends his work an heroic aura of defiance.

5. *Destruction.*—Metamorphoses, like metaphors, follow one upon the other in *Les Chants* in a vertiginous acceleration of creation and destruction. Rather than leave his text open to attacks from the "Grand Object Extérieur"—the divine omnipotence of God, Providence, or the critical reader—Ducasse attempts to obliterate all traces of his literary efforts. The frantic pace of the text's autodestruction tends to submerge any content or meaning beneath what Philippe Sollers calls the "mouvement scripturale" of the text [*Logiques*, 1968]. The process which qualifies and dissolves each metaphor is repeated in the structure of the text as a whole, wherein each passage must be exploded in order to propel the narrative forward into the next stanza. Although some of the techniques Ducasse uses to destroy individual fictions are familiar literary devices, such as the narrator awakening from a dream, for the most part Ducasse generates a tornado of images which appear suddenly and inexplicably on the horizon only to disappear abruptly into some chaos beyond.

Ducasse describes the process which has carried his narrative from the first *chant* to the second:

> Léman! . . . Lohengrin! . . . Lombano! . . . Holzer! . . . un instant vous apparûtes, recouverts des insignes de la jeunesse, à mon horizon charmé; mais, je vous ai laissés retomber dans le chaos, comme des cloches de plongeur. Vous n'en sortirez plus.

Not only are the various characters abandoned, but each stanza and the scenes it evokes are devoured or dispersed. Thus an entire shipwreck scene in Chant V is devoured by voracious sharks who are then engulfed by the ocean, and the lice engendered by Maldoror in Chant II are infinitely multiplied until they destroy an entire world.

Such scenes of destruction, however, invariably leave behind them indelible traces, the traces of the text which have been magically materialized through the author's assertion of metaphor, hypothesis and metamorphosis. The narration of *Les Chants* concludes, in fact, with a scene of destruction which leaves its mark on the reader's consciousness and on literary history itself: the violent death of the innocent adolescent Mervyn at the hands of his merciless persecutor, Maldoror.

Maldoror has his prey led to the Place de la Vendôme where his feet are attached to a long cord. The hero then constructs an elaborate mechanism by which he suspends the body from a bronze obelisk and begins to swing it around him in circles. Having established the necessary momentum, Maldoror finally releases his human catapult:

> Mervyn, suivi de la corde, ressemble à une comète traînant après elle sa queue flamboyante. . . . Dans le parcours de sa parabole, le condamné à mort fend l'atmosphère jusqu'à la rive gauche, la dépasse en vertu de la force d'impulsion que je suppose infinie, et son corps va frapper le dôme du Panthéon, tandis que la corde étreint, en partie, de ses replis, la paroi supérieure de l'immense coupole. C'est sur sa superficie sphérique et convexe, qui ne ressemble à une orange que pour la forme, qu'on voit, à toute heure du jour, un squelette desséché, resté suspendu.

Mervyn, flying in a graceful parabola to his ultimate destruction against the dome of the Pantheon, is the last vestige of the fiction of *Les Chants.* In a final ironic gesture, Ducasse not only destroys his own narrative, but leaves its traces on the public memorial commemorating the great men of France. Maldoror's defacing of the national monument to history and tradition parallels and dramatizes on a disturbingly literal level Ducasse's ambivalent attitude both towards his own text and towards all of literary tradition. The contents of the fiction having been obliterated, all students of the Sorbonne—all future readers and critics—are directed to the remains of the text, "allez-y voir vous-même, si vous ne voulez pas me croire." It is with this most familiar and banal phrase that Ducasse terminates what is perhaps the most ruthless and thorough parody of literary convention.

Turning back on itself, the text leaves for the reader only the traces of its passage, "un résidu, un ensemble de traces 'à lire'" (Sollers). Ducasse's destruction of his own text is an extension of his attack on all literary tradition, on everything established and completed, ossified into convention and law. In writing *Les Chants,* however, Ducasse has added one more work to the body of literary history; *Les Chants* have become part of the despised tradition. The poet must now submit his own work to the same hostile scrutiny and manipulation he aims at the authority of his predecessors. In a convoluted Borgesian distortion of history, Ducasse becomes his own predecessor and thus his own enemy. The rich metaphorical world of his early work is succeeded by the implacable scientific rigor of *Poésies* wherein Ducasse wields his artistic will, his own "scalpel de l'analyse," against Pascal, Vauvenargues, and that intolerable comte de Lautréamont, author of *Les Chants de Maldoror.* (pp. 3-14)

> Robin Lydenberg, "Metaphor and Metamorphosis in 'Les chants de Maldoror'," in L'Esprit Crèateur, *Vol. XVIII, No. 4, Winter, 1978, pp. 3-14.*

Claire Wade (essay date 1978)

[*In the essay below, Wade argues that the animal-human figures in* Les chants de Maldoror *serve to bring the human characters closer to a natural state, allowing integration of oppositions of mind and body, self and society, and the conscious and the unconscious.*]

Animal-human figures in *Les Chants de Maldoror* fulfill a vital and positive function. In the three particular instances involving animal-human figures that I shall consider: 1) The coupling of the female shark and Maldoror, 2) The transformation of Maldoror into a "pourceau" and 3) Maldoror's encounter with the man-fish, the combination beings are visual metaphors which extend man's limits, resolve some of his difficulties and, in consequence, point a new and productive direction for him.

Lautréamont directly affirms that the study of man and the human condition is a primary aim when, in the opening pages of the Fourth Chant, he states: "Moi, je veux montrer mes qualités, mais je ne suis pas assez hypocrite pour cacher mes vices . . . Chacun s'y reconnaîtra, non pas tel qu'il devrait être mais tel qu'il est." And, when he adds a bit later: "Et peut-être que ce simple idéal, conçu par mon imagination, surpassera, cependant, tout ce que la poésie a trouvé jusqu'ici de plus grandiose et de plus sacré," he is underscoring how important, in and of itself, this complete sounding of the "self" is. Furthermore, the author is indicating with great clarity the far-reaching implications of such a study. His portrait of the self is, in reality, a portrait of "everyman." This preoccupation with self/man can lead, in turn, to something which will surpass all that poetry has accomplished heretofore—to something sacred, something infinite.

Seemingly, this is a contradictory note in Lautréamont's work, for what strikes the reader of *Les Chants* most dramatically on early readings is the alienation, the revolutionary spirit of the author and of his protagonist, Maldoror, and the preoccupation of both with "le mal." Such an apparently negative stance is to be found on page after page. However, its presence must not lead one to discount the author's positive aims. These are reaffirmed at the beginning of the Sixth Chant, when Lautréamont summarizes his work and indicates his future direction:

> Prétenderiez-vous donc que parce que j'aurais insulté, comme en me jouant, l'homme, le Créateur et moi-même, ma mission fût complete? Non: la partie la plus importante de mon travail n'en subsiste pas moins, comme tâche qui reste à faire . . . les trois personnages[. . .]il leur sera ainsi communiqué une puissance moins abstraite. La vitalité se répandra magnifiquement dans le torrent de leur appareil circulatoire, et vous verrez comme vous serez étonné vous-même de rencontrer là ou vous n'aviez cru voir que des entités vagues . . . d'une part, l'organisme corporel avec ses ramifications et ses membranes muqueuses, de l'autre, le principe spirituel qui préside aux fonctions physiologiques de la chair. Ce sont des êtres doués d'une énergique vie qui poseront prosaïquement (mais je suis certain que l'effet sera très poétique).

In fact, if we look closely and thoughtfully at the two sides of Lautréamont's work, we see that, in reality, they can be viewed as complementary. Certainly, Lautréamont, himself, establishes a close connection between the two in the opening pages of his work when he reflects upon the relationship of positive to negative—which he characterizes as "le bien" and "le mal": "Qu'est-ce donc que le bien et le mal! Est-ce une même chose par laquelle nous témoignons avec rage notre impuissance, et la passion

d'atteindre à l'infini par les moyens même les plus insensés? Ou bien, sont-ce deux choses différentes? Oui . . . que ce soit plutôt une même chose." Although the reader may hesitate to accept such a linking, it must be remembered that during the whole 19th century, and particularly during the latter half, there was an entire literary tradition devoted to "le mal," and also to the ultimate association between "le mal" and "le bien." Certainly, modern critics and psychiatrists alike connect the two. Paul Zweig, for example, replacing the word "evil" by the somewhat more precise "violence and destruction," makes the astute observation: "At the paradoxical nadir of his adventure, Lautréamont rediscovers the world of values. At the heart of the violence it unexpectedly triumphs. If Lautréamont is a nihilist, it is in Nietzsche's sense of the word, where to destroy means to 'transvalue.' " And he continues:

> Beyond the pure violence of his poem, Lautréamont's nihilism proposes another world . . . a world of natural plenitude in which man, unimpressed, uncivilized, and finally unhumanized, is liberated from all the prisons which he has secreted around him. Man, for Lautréamont, cannot be free, cannot return to his birth and be reborn until he has undone the sliest and most absolute of all the chains—the human form itself. [*The Violent Narcissus*, 1972]

In light of this quote, then, when Lautréamont uses animal-human metaphors he has found a vehicle to "undo the human form" and "transvalue" man at the same time. That the author himself feels the need to be more or "other" than he is, to be "unhumanized," is almost as obvious from the beginning of the First Chant as is his association of good with evil and his passion for the infinite. That he sees a value in an intimate link between man and animals is also clear:

> Moi, comme les chiens, j'éprouve le besoin de l'infini . . . le ne puis, je ne puis contenter ce besoin! le suis fils de l'homme et de la temme . . . Ça m'étonne . . . je croyais être davantage! . . . Moi, si cela avait pu dépendre de ma volonté, j'aurais voulu être plutôt le fils de la femelle du requin, dont la faim est amie des tempêtes, et du tigre, à la cruauté reconnu: je ne serais pas si méchant.

The psychiatrist Rollo May approaches the problem of "evil" and the link between good and evil in somewhat different terms when he discusses the "daimonic." For him, good and evil are its positive and negative sides. What he says, too, is applicable to *Les Chants de Maldoror:*

> The daimonic is any natural function which has the power to take over the whole person. Sex and eros, anger and rage, and the craving for power are examples. *The daimonic can be either creative or destructive and is normally both . . . The daimonic refers to a fundamental archetypal function of human experience—an essential reality in modern men and,* so far as we know, *in all men.* [*Love and Will,* 1969. Italics are mine].

This means, in essence, that the "daimonic"—which May defines as overwhelming energy—is an essential part of man's nature as well as both positive and negative. May then goes on to attach the daimonic to self-realization:

> The daimonic is the urge in every being to affirm itself, assert itself, perpetuate and increase itself. The daimonic becomes evil when it usurps the total self without regard to the integration of the self, or to the unique forms and desires of others and their need for integration. It then appears as excessive aggression, hostility, cruelty—the things about ourselves which horrify us most and which we repress whenever we can. . . . *But, these are the reverse side of the same assertion which empowers our creativity. We can repress the daimonic, but we cannot avoid the toll of apathy, and the tendency toward later explosion* which repression brings.

So, we can also say that the daimonic, in all its complexity, is something with which we must come to terms. It cannot be ignored, except at great cost—as Lautréamont saw as clearly as Rollo May. And it will not disappear. When May again turns to the positive side of the daimonic, he repeats that it is an irrepressible force. As he sees it, it is also man's link with what Lautréamont would call "l'infini" since it not only encompasses opposites but ties man to the natural world as well:

> The Greek concept of 'daimon', the origin of our modern concept—included the creativity of the poet and artist, as well as that of the ethical and religious leader . . . *The daimonic is not conscious. . . . The daimonic refers to the power of nature . . . and is beyond good and evil . . .* its source lies in those realms where the self is rooted in natural forces which go beyond the self . . . the daimonic arises from the ground of being.

Up to this point, the problem of "le mal" or the "daimonic" has been considered solely in terms of the individual. However, in *Les Chants,* Lautréamont treats another level of "le mal" which is also important, and which must at least be mentioned, since it adds to the human dilemma. This is the evil—the violence and destructiveness—of society and of "Le Créateur"—our abstract sources for religious, social, and ethical values under normal conditions. Zweig pinpoints this problem, too, with remarkable insight: "We are enclosed by a civilization which has become increasingly deadly. The behavior that civilization teaches us to assume is often dangerous to ourselves and to others." That this is valid in the world of *Les Chants* is proven on page after page. However, a single example from the early pages of the First Chant, and one from the beginning of the Second Chant will suffice to show the tenor of Maldoror's surroundings: "J'ai vu, pendant toute ma vie, sans en excepter un seul, les hommes . . . faire des actes stupides et nombreux, abrutir leurs semblables et pervertir les âmes par tous les moyens . . . j'ai vu les hommes . . . surpasser la dureté du roc . . . la cruauté du requin." "J'ai vu le Créateur, aiguillonnant sa cruauté inutile, embraser des incendies où périssaient les vieillards et les enfants! Ce n'est pas moi qui commence l'attaque; c'est lui qui me force à le faire tourner." In such a world, where our usual institutional bases for "order" and "construction" (in other words, "le bien") are themselves dis-

ordered and destructive, both individual revolt and self-realization become a necessity, a prerequisite for man's survival—in general and in particular.

Given all that has just been said, it is understandable that Lautréamont would like not only to explore the contradictions of self and mankind but also to push man into a more productive direction which would bring him closer to "l'infini" to which he aspires. In the three animal-human figures mentioned at the outset, Lautréamont is able to accomplish these goals—*albeit only momentarily.* These creatures, these metaphors—and, therefore, the accompanying achievements—are not permanent. In fact, they are highly transitory in nature. Nevertheless, this does not in any way diminish their innate importance. Constant change, eternal imbalance is, after all, the rule in *Les Chants de Maldoror* as it is in concrete human existence. Erich Fromm reminds us in his thoughtful and thought-provoking study on human destructiveness of the truth of this statement: "Man's existential contradiction results in a state of constant disequilibrium . . . in the process of man's self-creation, this relative stability is upset again and again. Man, in his history, changes his environment, and in this process, he changes himself " [*The Anatomy of Human Destructiveness,* 1973]. In other words, man continually seeks balance, self-creation and harmony with his world. But, once he has achieved it, he must start all over again. Because of the delicate interaction of the two, when he changes his relationship to the world and his environment, he changes himself. Thereupon, another imbalance results.

Again, the temporary character of these animal-human figures is not important. What *is* important is their very existence coupled with their beneficial effects on Maldoror—the contributions they make to his perceptions of self and the human condition, and the brief satisfaction they provide as he searches for the infinite. The proof that these visual metaphors not only extend man's limits but point a new course for him as well lies in the contrast Lautréamont gives us between man outside these figures, and the feelings and strengths his protagonist experiences within them. Man alone is a tormented being, fragmented and solitary, alienated from himself and the world around him, and either wooden and lifeless or filled with hate and what Fromm calls "malignant aggression." In contrast, he is happy and at peace within the metaphoric situations. Consequently, some deep basic needs are obviously being met.

In the "pourceau" episode, for example, Maldoror reacts to his transformation with: "Objet de mes vœux, je n'appartenais plus à l'humanité." Although, a few lines later, the author speaks of his metamorphosis as a "dégradation," it is evident that such an observation is either ironic or culturally induced. For immediately thereafter, we find: "La métamorphose ne parut jamais à mes yeux que comme le haut et magnanime retentissement d'un bonheur parfait que j'attendais depuis longtemps."

The scene with the female shark and the encounter with the man-fish have equally positive effects. In the shark episode, Maldoror asserts: "Enfin, je venais de trouver quelqu'un qui me ressemblât! Désormais je n'étais plus seul dans la vie . . . Elle avait les mêmes idées que moi." In the man-fish episode, Maldoror notices that the figure is strong, healthy, and perfectly adapted to its environment. In addition, the creature states: "Je vis en paix avec les poissons et ils me procurent ma nourriture . . . comme si j'étais leur monarque." Finally, Lautréamont, speaking directly to the reader, makes two very important statements during the man-fish episode which emphasize the significance of this episode and of the two other episodes already mentioned. First he states: "Que l'on sache bien que l'homme, par sa nature complexe, n'ignore pas les moyens d'en élargir les frontières." And, a bit later, "La métaphore . . . rend beaucoup plus de services aux aspirations humaines vers l'infini que ne l'efforcent de se la figurer ordinairement ceux qui sont imbus de préjugés ou d'idées fausses, ce qui est la même chose."

At this point, there are two questions to be asked; two questions to be answered in greater detail. First of all, why should these animal-human combinations produce such a change and such a sense of well-being? And secondly, since the figures are metaphors, what do the two parts of the figures signify?

These questions become especially appropriate because many critics—when dealing with animals in Lautréamont's work—have seen them as negative forces. Speaking of animals, Gaston Bachelard has said: "Chez Lautréamont, l'animal est saisi, non point dans ses formes, mais dans ses fonctions les plus directes, précisément dans ses fonctions d'agression . . . Le vouloir-vivre est ici un vouloir-attaquer . . . Lautréamont a écrit une fable inhumaine en revivant les impulsions brutales, si fortes encore dans le cœur des hommes" [*Lautréamont*, 1956]. So, Bachelard ties the animal kingdom to aggression and brutality.

Jean-Pierre Soulier states [in his *Lautréamont, Génie ou Maladie Mentale*, 1964]: "Elles allient la traîtrise au courage et attaquent à l'improviste. Ce n'est pas tant à tel ou tel animal que Maldoror désire s'identifier, mais plutôt à l'animalité toute entière. S'il rêve qu'il est pourceau, c'est pour jouir de l'irresponsibilité bienheureuse. Il aimerait donner libre cours à ses instincts et se fondre dans la vie à l'état brut." Both Soulier's and Bachelard's viewpoints are very much in keeping with the traditional attitude that animals are much more violent than man, and indeed vastly inferior to him—because they are predominantly instinctual beings and therefore incapable of reason, and because they are "lower" on Darwin's chain of evolution.

However, when we look carefully at Lautréamont's work, and at the majority of his comments about animals, we see repeatedly that this is not the case. Animals in *Les Chants* are frequently much more "humane," moral and peaceful than man. A few examples will serve to illustrate this point. In the episode revolving around the twin brothers at the beginning of the Third Chant, we find that the two flee humanity because men are: "des esprits cruels qui se massacrent entre eux." They seek refuge in the depths of the ocean: "pour reposer agréablement leur vue désillusionnée sur les monstres les plus féroces de l'abîme qui leur paraissaient des modèles de douceur en comparaison des bâtards de l'humanité." In the First Chant, the author writes: "Sur la terre, la vipère, l'œil gros du crapaud, le tigre, l'éléphant, dans la mer, la baleine, le requin, le marteau . . . se demanderont quelle est cette dérogation à la loi de la nature. L'homme tremblant . . . 'Oui, je vous surpasse tous par ma cruauté innée.' " Finally, when he speaks of the wolf who avoids the "potence" to which a man had been attached by his wife and mother in the Fourth Chant, he attributes a sensitivity to and revulsion for crime—absent in mankind—to the animal: "Sans rien certifier et même sans rien prévoir, il me semble que l'animal a compris ce que c'est que le crime."

Modern men of science, such as Erich Fromm and Konrad Lorenz, affirm the view of animals that Lautréamont presents. In his book *On Aggression*, in the chapter entitled "Behavior Analogies to Morality," Lorenz indicates that there is a whole series of animal species "in which, under normal, *non-pathological* conditions, a male never attacks a female." There are also many conditions under which young animals—even those which are seemingly fully grown—will not be attacked: "For the fullgrown but still clumsy young animal a . . . danger . . . lies in the aggressive behavior of the adults. This danger is precluded by a series of strictly regulated inhibitory mechanisms, as yet largely unexplained." He also points out "the instinctive inhibitions and rites which prevent antisocial behavior in animals," and adds: "An impressive example of behavior analogous to human morality can be seen in the ritualized fighting of many vertebrates." So, he shows us in effect that there is a "built-in morality" in animals.

In his study of human aggression, Fromm states that there are two types of aggression—defensive and malignant. Defensive aggression, he tells, us, is built into both animals and man. Moreover, he makes an important distinction between defensive aggression—which he calls a necessary part of all life—and malignant aggression which seems to be present only in man. Defensive aggression, he tells us, "serves the function of defense against threats to vital interests." Furthermore, Fromm continues: "If human aggression were more or less on the same level as that of other mammals (especially chimpanzees)—human society would be rather peaceful and non-violent." Speaking of malignant aggression, he says: "Animals do not enjoy inflicting pain and suffering on other animals, nor do they 'kill for nothing'. Only man seems to destroy for destructiveness."

However, and this is crucial, Fromm also feels that the subject of malignant aggression (of the kind that is so prevalent all throughout *Les Chants*) is an important one and completely worthy of study: "Malignant aggression, though not an instinct, is a human potential rooted in the very conditions of human existence." Then, a bit later, he adds that this kind of aggression can and does originate when certain fundamental human needs are not met.

Going back to Bachelard's statement, and taking into consideration all that has just been pointed out, it is now necessary to modify what he wrote. When he says that in animals "le vouloir-vivre est un vouloir-attaquer," he is certainly correct—but in a very limited sense. Animal actions, except in very unusual cases, fall under the heading of "defensive aggression"—which is common to both animals and man. And if we look at mankind in *Les Chants,* we see that men are even more aggressive than beasts. Furthermore, human aggression in this work is often of the "malignant" variety. Consequently, it is fair to say that animals in *Les Chants* are much "saner" organisms than man. Their aggression is of a much "healthier" kind. So, pushing it one step further, when Lautréamont combines man with animal in his metaphors, he is "undoing the human form"—he is "unhumanizing" (to borrow two of Zweig's expressions)—but only so he can "rehumanize" him. Animal-human figures are *not* more violent, more brutal than man. They are simply more energetic and more powerful beings, in every sense of the word.

The "power" conferred upon man in the animal-human figures is a positive and even essential life force—a basic human aspiration which can be linked to Lautréamont's desire for the infinite. At the beginning of his study, *Power and Innocence,* Rollo May quotes Nietzsche's *Thus Spake Zarathustra* where the universality of the quest for power is underlined: "Wherever I found the living, there I found the will to power." May then goes on to specify exactly what is meant by "power"—and what he says certainly pertains to the force lent to man by the animal-human figures in *Les Chants:*

> Power is essential for all living beings . . . I must be able to say *I am,* to affirm myself in a world into which, by my capacity to assert myself, I *create* meaning . . . In Nietzsche's proclamation of the 'will to power,' it is important that he meant neither 'will' nor 'power' in the competitive sense of the modern day, but rather self-realization and self-actualization.

May goes on to state that the lack of power—which he consistently defines as the lack of capacity to acquire "being"—can lead to violence: "Violence has its breeding ground in impotence and apathy . . . As we make people powerless, we promote their violence . . . Deeds of violence are performed largely by those trying to establish their self-esteem, to defend their self-image, and to demonstrate that they, too, are significant." In light of this, we can see why, in the animal-human figures where the parts are co-equal, and where "being" has been temporarily achieved, the human side is more or less at peace.

At this point, it is appropriate to return to the second question posed earlier—since the animal-human figures are metaphors, just what do the two parts of the figures signify? To begin with the most evident level, when Lautréamont combines man with animal, even though the human half of the metaphor may remain estranged from most of the rest of the human world, the author has found a way to unify the human element with his "ground of being"—which is the natural world. Erich Fromm states in his chapter entitled "Malignant Aggression: Premises" that man's alienation from others of his kind, and also from everything else, is a fundamental hazard of human existence that is brought about by the human capacity for self-awareness and reason.

> Gifted with self-awareness and reason, man is aware of himself as a being separate from nature and from others . . . Self-awareness, reason and imagination have disrupted the harmony that characterizes animal existence. Their emergence has made man into an anomaly, the freak of the universe. He is part of nature, subject to her physical laws and unable to change them, yet . . . he is set apart . . . Man is the only animal who does not feel at home in nature . . . the only animal for whom his existence is a problem that he has to solve and from which he cannot escape.

That Lautréamont/Maldoror feels deeply his alienation from everything, that he aspires to fusion with the natural world but is nonetheless filled with anger and hate—directed against mankind and the ocean (a special symbol for him)—because he cannot realize his desire, is made very clear in the "Hymn to the Ocean." Furthermore, in the Second Chant, we see that the author is exceedingly aware that the development of reason and intellect is both an advantage and a disadvantage: In the "Hymn to Mathematics," he makes the statement that the development of the intellectual, reasoning side of man, facilitated by the study of mathematics, is greatly to be desired since it permits the acquisition of knowledge and a resultant satisfaction of the human need for order. At the same time, he is aware that the love of and devotion to mathematics leads to a loss of emotional capacity and a conscious distancing of self from the physical, sensate world:

> Vous avez chassé ce voile obscur, vous avez mis à la place, une froideur excessive, une prudence consommée et une logique implacable. A l'aide de votre lait fortifiant, mon intelligence s'est rapidement développée, et a pris des proportions immenses au milieu de cette clarté ravissante . . . celui qui vous connaît et vous apprécie ne veut plus rien des biens de la terre.

Even though the animal-human figures seem to resolve this problem, realistically speaking the solution is not so simple. As Fromm, speaking of man, reminds us: "He cannot go back to the prehuman state of harmony with nature." Therefore, if this were the only value to be attached to the animal-human combinations in Lautréamont's work, they would require little comment. Such a blending with nature would, after all, represent an unrealizable ambition. However, in addition and, indeed, in order to unify man with nature, the animal-human figures also permit Lautréamont/Maldoror to face his inner duality, to confront parts of himself that are contradictory to each other by nature and, if he cannot totally fuse them, to allow them at the very least to coexist more or less peacefully. Fromm is entirely correct. Man cannot go back to prehuman—that is, totally non-conscious—harmony with the world around him. Nevertheless, he can achieve a *conscious* acceptance and reconciliation of self through the animal-human figures which permit him both to acquire "being" and to return to the harmony of nature, but on a personal, internal level. As a matter of fact, this is one of Lautréamont's avowed aims. In the Fifth Chant, he says: "Si j'existe, je ne suis pas un autre. Je n'admets pas en moi cette équivoque pluralité. Je veux résider seul dans mon intime raisonnement." Then, much later, in the very last Chant, it is evident he has come to terms with the different sides of himself—which are united, but with the special qualities of each intact: "Spectateur impassible des monstruosités naturelles ou acquises qui décorent les aponévroses et l'intellect de celui qui parle, je jette un long regard sur la dualité qui me compose, et je me trouve beau." Somewhat earlier in his work, speaking directly to the reader, he has said essentially the same thing: "Tu sais allier l'enthousiasme et le troid intérieur . . . enfin, pour moi, je te trouve parfait."

I have said that the animal-human figures are metaphors—metaphors which permit man to confront and explore his basic duality. So, what human qualities do the two parts of these figures represent? In the passage from the "Hymn to Mathematics," it was seen that the human half—man—is not only separated from nature in **Les Chants** but dominated by his intellectual side as well. Moreover, he is also cut off from the rest of himself and from other men. He becomes "inhuman" and fragmented, and he is painfully aware of it. That this is so is indicated, very strikingly, early in the Fourth Chant where we find:

> J'existe toujours comme le basalte. Au milieu comme au commencement de la vie, les anges se ressemblent à eux-mêmes. N'y a-t-il pas long-temps que je ne me ressemble plus! L'homme et moi, claquemurés dans les limites de notre intelligence . . . au lieu d'unir nos forces respec-tives pour nous défendre, contre le hasard et l'infortune, nous nous écartons, avec le tremble-ment de la haine.

That such a one-sided concept of man is not peculiar to Lautréamont or even to "literary misfits" in general but is to be found in the "everyday world," is affirmed by the British psychiatrist R. D. Laing who states that a limited and, consequently, negative development of man is quite widespread: "Our normal 'adjusted' state is too often the abdication of ecstasy, the betrayal of our true potentialities . . . many of us are only too successful in ac-quiring a false self to adapt to false realities" [*The Divided Self, An Existential Study in Sanity and Madness,* 1965]. And, he continues:

> Some . . . persons do not seem to have a sense of that basic unity which can abide through the most intense conflicts with oneself, but seem rather to have come to experience themselves as primarily split into a mind and a body. Usually they feel most closely identified with the 'mind.'

Furthermore, and even more importantly, when Laing goes on to elaborate the problems associated with such a mind-body split, what he says is equally applicable to Lautréamont's work, and partially explains the impor-tance of the animal-human metaphors in another way. Even though one might feel himself to be split into two parts, and even though a person might desire to ignore the non-intellectual part (the body), it will not be ignored. Laing insists: "Everyone, even the most unembodied per-son, experiences himself as inextricably bound up with his body. In ordinary circumstances, to the extent that one feels one's body to be alive, real, and substantial, one feels himself alive, real, and substantial." So, if the human part of the animal-human figure is mind—or intelligence and reason—the animal part is the corporeal segment, the

body. In the "pourceau" episode, we see that the combina-tion being is no longer fragmented. It is able to test and to enjoy its physical surroundings and its own physical self: "Il était venu enfin, le jour où je fus un pourceau! J'essayais mes dents sur l'écorce des arbres, mon groin, je le contemplais avec délice." And, speaking directly to the reader, Lautréamont adds a statement which confirms that acknowledgement of the body is necessary if one wants to "se ressembler," if one wants to feel whole: "Je n'invoque pas votre intelligence . . . oubliez-la et soyez conséquents avec vous-mêmes."

Robert Ornstein puts man's duality in another way in *The Psychology of Consciousness,* that equally applies to Lautréamont's work by expanding the mind-body meta-phor to a mind-mind one. When he speaks of the differing functions of the two lobes of the human brain, Ornstein tells us that the left lobe is the home of all that is logical, analytical, and intellectual. It is "rational consciousness." Man's right lobe, on the other hand, is associated with the intuitive, the sensual, the experiential, and the holistic. It is "nonrational consciousness." (In **Les Chants,** Lautréa-mont acknowledges such a split when he makes reference to: "les contradictions réelles et inexplicables qui habitent les lobes du cerveau humain".) Having spoken of the two sides of the brain, Ornstein then stresses how important it is for both to function if man is to *be,* fully—that is to operate at peak efficiency and at peak creativity: "A com-plete human consciousness involves the polarity and inte-gration of the two modes," and, even more significantly, he adds: "It is the polarity and integration of these two modes of consciousness . . . which underlie our highest achievements." These last observations are of particular interest. It is the "polarity"—the tension and "difference" between the two sides, as well as their capacity to com-bine—which leads to total effectiveness. Therefore, com-plete fusion is not possible between the two without loss of function. The two must "coexist"—and the possibility of occasional strife remains. That the "integration" of these two modes of consciousness underlies our highest achievements is evident in the animal-human metaphors since the beings are much more forceful, much more vital than either man or animal alone. This is quite clear in all three episodes. In the "pourceau" episode, we discover: "J'étais le plus fort, et je remportais toutes les victoires." In the man-fish segment, the narrator states: "Je vis . . . un être humain, aux muscles vigoureux . . . Quelquefois il plongeait, et son corps visqueux reparaissait presque aussitôt, à deux cents mètres de distance. Les marsouins, qui n'ont pas volé, d'après mon opinion, la réputation de bons nageurs, pouvaient à peine suivre de loin cet amphi-bie de nouvelle espèce."

However, the portion of **Les Chants** revolving around the mating of Maldoror and the female shark provides the most striking and, indeed, the most dramatic example of the creative achievement which can result from the mo-mentary blending of the two sides of man. It is also, per-haps, the most important example since it involves not simply increased strength but a redirection of the savage aggressive drives which are a part of the human condition in Lautréamont's work. Before the encounter with the shark, Maldoror had just killed a shipwreck victim, explaining:

> Je n'étais pas aussi cruel que l'on a raconté ensuite, parmi les hommes: mais des fois, leur méchanceté exerçait ses ravages persévérantes pendant des années entières. Alors, je ne connaissais plus de bornes à ma fureur; il me prenait des accès de cruauté et je devenais terrible.

In contrast, after mating with the big fish, Maldoror is seen in a seemingly unrelated episode where he revives a young man who has drowned himself in the Seine. Upon being pulled from the water, the victim is first surrounded and then abandoned by a crowd of people who are afraid to display any sensitivity and compassion in such a circumstance: "On a craint de passer pour sensible, et aucun n'a bougé, retranché dans le col de sa chemise. L'un s'en va en sifflotant aigrement une tyrolienne absurde; l'autre fait claquer ses doigts comme des castagnettes." Maldoror's feelings and actions are very different. In an unusual and somewhat startling "flash of humanity" which can reasonably be seen as an aftermath of the contentment and sense of belonging provoked by the Maldoror-shark episode, we find: "A la pensée que ce corps inerte pourrait revivre sous sa main, il sent son cœur bondir, sous cette impression excellente et redouble de courage." And, after bringing the young man back to life, he exults: "Sauver la vie à quelqu'un, que c'est beau. Et comme cette action rachète de fautes." The capacity to restore a human life given up for lost is creativity indeed.

Gregory Bateson also acknowledges the presence of a duality in man. However, the duality he discusses is somewhat different from either Laing's or Ornstein's, though it applies fully to *Les Chants.* Bateson maintains that the continuing quest for grace—which corresponds to Lautréamont's quest for "l'infini"—is the central problem for humanity. And he adds that the quest for "grace" is the major preoccupation of art—not just for "primitives" but universally. Then he states:

> I shall argue that the problem of grace is fundamentally a problem of *integration,* and that what is to be integrated is *the diverse parts of the mind*—especially those multiple levels of which one extreme is called 'consciousness' and the other the 'unconscious'. For the attainment of grace, the reasons of the heart must be integrated with the reasons of the reason.

Moreover, Bateson, too, indicates how essential integrating the two extremes of the duality is, if outstanding human achievement is to result: "Some cultures foster a negative approach to this difficult integration, an avoidance of complexity by crass preference for either total consciousness or total unconsciousness. Their art is unlikely to be great" [*Steps to an Ecology of Mind,* 1972].

That the animal side of man can be equated with the "unconscious" can most forcefully be proven by looking at the special significance the female shark holds for Lautréamont. First of all, in the Maldoror-shark episode, we see that the two do not simply resemble each other. They are clearly complementary parts of a single whole: "Ils glissèrent l'un vers l'autre, avec une admiration mutuelle . . .

dans une vénération profonde, chacun désireux de contempler . . . son portrait vivant." Furthermore, we must remember that as early as the First Chant, when Maldoror stresses his aspirations toward and need for the infinite, he confesses that he cannot attain it all by himself, but adds that a connection with the female shark would be helpful: "J'éprouve le besoin de l'infini . . . Je ne puis contenter ce besoin. Je suis fils de l'homme et de la femme . . . Ça m'étonne . . . j'aurais voulu être plutôt le fils de la femelle du requin." Finally, the connection between the female shark and the unconscious becomes exceedingly clear when we consider that the shark is a denizen—indeed one of the queens—of the ocean. For this reason, she can be equated with it. As is well known, Carl Jung equated the ocean with the collective unconscious. Certainly, that is one of its associations as far as Lautréamont is concerned. In his "Hymn to the Ocean," the author states: "Tu rappelles au souvenir de tes amants, sans qu'on s'en rende toujours compte, les rudes commencements de l'homme." And, three pages later, he adds: "Tu es si puissant, que les hommes l'ont appris à leurs propres dépens. Ils ont beau employer toutes les ressources de leur génie . . . incapables de te dominer . . . Ils ont trouvé leur maître." Since the shark is a creature which lives in the ocean and, so, is at one with it, it is capable of sounding its deepest parts—parts which customarily remain inaccessible to rational, conscious man despite his most diligent efforts: "Vieil ocean, les hommes, malgré l'excellence de leurs méthodes, ne sont pas encore parvenus, aidés par les moyens d'investigation de la science, à mesurer la profondeur de tes ab mes . . . Aux poissons . . . ça leur est permis, pas aux hommes." When Maldoror mates with the female shark, however, he, too, is capable of sounding the ocean's depths:

> Ayant pour lit d'hymenée la vague écumeuse, emportés par un courant sousmarin comme dans un berceau, et roulant, sur eux-mêmes, vers les profondeurs inconnues de l'abime, ils se reunirent dans un accouplement long, chaste et hideux.

To summarize, animal-human figures in *Les Chants de Maldoror* are visual metaphors which allow man to sound the depths of himself and extend his limits. In consequence, they also permit him to find brief solutions—short-term solutions—to some of the major problems of human existence. They permit man to reintegrate himself with nature and the universe—with what Rollo May would call his "creative daimonic." They are powerful beings who make a difference within their environment, thus satisfying the human need for effectiveness. And they do both these things by integrating and, at the same time, permitting the coexistence of, different parts of the self: 1) mind and body, 2) rational consciousness and non-rational consciousness and 3) consciousness and the unconscious—both personal and collective. Thus, the fact that these metaphors are transitory, that they do not last, is unimportant. Life and man are both continually changing—inside and outside of literature. (pp. 47-65)

Claire Wade, "The Importance and Implications of Animal-Human Figures in 'Les chants de Maldoror'," *in* L'Esprit Crèateur, *Vol. XVIII, No. 4, Winter, 1978, pp. 47-65.*

Tristan Tzara on Lautréamont:

Those people whose uncertainties show themselves in pretensions and whose pride rises in the form of cerebral saliva, those people for whom swamps and excrement have determined the rules of philosophical pity, will see, one of these days, this immeasurable malediction destroy their filthy, feeble muscles. The Comte de Lautréamont has gone beyond the tangential point which separates creation and madness. For him, creation is already mediocrity. On the other hand it is unpronounceable solemnity. The frontiers of wisdom are unexplored. Ecstasy devours them with neither hierarchy nor cruelty.

Tristan Tzara, in his Seven Dada Manifestoes and Lampisteries, *translated by Barbara Wright, 1977.*

Robert E. Ziegler   (essay date 1983)

[*In the following essay, Ziegler examines the physical environment of* Les chants de Maldoror, *asserting that Maldoror allies himself with elements of an environment hostile to humans in order to destroy them.*]

In Lautréamont the appeal for change, the advocacy of revolt, is articulated through certain images, images of upheaval and of flux on a most elemental level. This aesthetic of aggression is manifested in part in the bestiary imagery described by [Gaston] Bachelard [in his *Lautréamont,* 1939]. But an important aspect of the text that has received less critical attention is the imagery dealing with aggression originating in the environment itself. This involves such things as the composition and density of certain bodies, the motion of bodies in space and the conditions that determine how these bodies move. In order to understand more clearly the twin forces of metamorphosis and mutability that are operating in **Les Chants,** one might see the text as illustrating the application of a systematically destabilizing force that Maldoror brings to bear on his adversary: man. Indeed, the purpose of Maldoror's behavior is to undermine man's feeling of belonging, the place he feels he occupies on the physical, biological, and moral planes of his existence. To this end, Maldoror makes allies not only of the vermin, predators, and monsters that men shun, but of the atmosphere as well: the water and the air.

The goal of Maldoror's attacks is the obliteration, the dissolution of people's sense of self, the confusion of the rational distinctions that they make between themselves and what they fear. Throughout **Les Chants,** therefore, Lautréamont seems repeatedly to reject any view of the world and its creatures based on conventional taxonomy, on fixed and inflexible categories of life forms. Man, for example, is never recognized as superior to beast because of his intelligence, but is shown to be weaker. More than anything else, human beings are characterized by their separateness; the function of their intelligence merely al-

lows them to behold more clearly their isolation from one another. The state of divorce and aloneness to which man is relegated is customarily evoked in **Maldoror** by images of dryness, while his efforts to rise above this state are conveyed through descriptions of a submersion in a liquid medium. The choice he is faced with, then, is either to submit to his plight by steeping himself in his sense of shared oppression or to break out of his shell of passivity and hopelessness and to direct his aggression against the world outside him.

This sense of isolation, conveyed through images of aridity and insularity, is experienced differently by Maldoror than by man. On the one hand, because he is cut off from the fluid medium, the "pool," in which others enjoy a sense of environmental and ontological security, Maldoror is threatened with spiritual dehydration. On the other hand, because they are blind to their actual condition, men have a sense of conformistic belonging, like fish in their schools. But they are still out of their element, still stranded in hostile surroundings where they are subject to aggression by better adapted animals or by God.

Thus, instead of believing that God sacrificed Himself so that men might live, Maldoror beholds in a vision God sacrificing men to perpetuate His own sadistic pleasure. God is shown seizing hold of men as they come to the surface of a sea, not of water but of blood, and crushing their heads and devouring their bodies. The illusion of man's adaptation to his environment is pointed out here as he is forced to make the choice between rising up and risking death at the hands of his Creator or of suffocating to death in the blood of his fellows. Initially, the dryness of separation is overcome by a flowing together of men in the suffering to which they are all subjected. Their inability to resign themselves to oppression is organically determined, their emergence from this ocean of gore "occasionnée par le besoin de respirer un autre milieu; car, enfin, ces hommes n'étaient pas des poissons!"

Yet in the passage immediately following, Lautréamont qualifies men as "[a]mphibies . . . [qui] nageaient entre deux eaux," at one moment retreating into the belief in their biological selection, the ductility and liquid ease with which their bodies move and their thoughts communicate themselves, and the next moment emerging from their cocoon of self-confidence and quickly drying up in the lucidity of their own despair: "[J]'ai vu plusieurs générations humaines élever, le matin, ses ailes et ses yeux, vers l'espace . . . et mourir, le soir, avant le coucher du soleil, la tête courbée, comme des fleurs fanées que balance le sifflement plaintif du vent." To be sure, some men need not wait until the final and fatal encounter with the Creator to find themselves beached or lost in the desert, their complacency shattered by "les mystères au milieu desquels notre existence étouffe, comme un poisson au fond d'une barque." But to those who emulate God in their meanness and insensitivity and differ from Him only in their weakness, Maldoror offers his campaign of violence as the best corrective. The initiation of a flow of blood, whether by God or Maldoror, is one means of forcibly bringing men together, of restoring to them a sense of shared suffering to which their apathy ordinarily blinds them.

Jean-Pierre Richard has described how, in Baudelaire, the pricking of the skin, the operating of a breach in the wall behind which the other hides himself is a way of making contact with that other on a most intimate level: "il fait glisser . . . le secret liquide de la vie [*Poésie et profondeur*, 1955]. The opening of a wound has an analogous function in Lautréamont, since the belief in one's capacity for self-containment is what stops the individual from realizing the need for revolt: "L'homme ne s[e] découvre existant . . . qu'à travers la montée d'une faiblesse." Making a child bleed or shed tears constitutes the most perfect act of aggression since the violation of his innocence serves as a reenactment of the cruelty of God toward His creatures. In response to the ills visited covertly on man by God, Maldoror offers his own viciousness as a spectacle from which man cannot avert his eyes. As the embodiment of hatefulness and criminality, Maldoror recreates himself in the likeness of God, and to the degree he is successful in eliciting man's fear and reprobation, he seeks to refocus those feelings upon that Being who most deserves to be despised.

The opposition of the sensations of dryness and thirst or of liquidity and the slaking of that thirst is consistently used to describe Maldoror's aggressive posture toward his victims. The man who takes for granted his spiritual and physical autonomy is hiding within a shell of pride that can easily be pierced. The complacency in which he is immersed is susceptible of being bled or drained away with the opening of the slightest chink in the armor of his vanity. Some predators like the shark are compact and hard, with tough impenetrable hides, and move through the air or water with the same inexorable straightness as the mind of a man unwilling to forget his own guilty actions. But the individual made stupid by incuriosity is clumsy and bloated. He is merely a container of liquids, "comme . . . un lac dans une ceinture d'îles de corail," which can be left flaccid, dead and empty of substance.

The importance of the contrast between moisture and aridity extends to certain topographical features as well, to some of the symbolic landscapes in *Les Chants.* Those who dwell on dry land arrange for themselves lives that are intensely regimented and carefully structured. The living spaces they create for themselves are neatly defined containment units, designed to insure privacy, minimize social intercourse and act as buffers against the unknown and the unpredictable. Challenging their belief in the desirability of a compartmentalized existence is the lure of a submersion in water, the element that, in Lautréamont, symbolizes a repudiation of the wish for self-possession and a welcomed shedding of one's human limitations. For Maldoror, the sea is the locus of chaos and anarchy. On the ocean, men witness the vessels they have made to transport them being torn apart and smashed. Those who fancy that they know their biological, intellectual and social place are suddenly "lost at sea" and behold in death the obliteration of the familiar parameters of their experience.

Maldoror feels a special affinity for the ocean and its denizens. The ocean, by its magnitude, opposes the pretense of the infinite perfectibility of human intelligence. It alone contains and comprehends. In its depths—"Elle doit être grande vers le bas, dans la direction de l'inconnu!"—it accuses the transitoriness of man's existence and the superficiality of his thoughts. In the groaning of its swells, the torment of its constant movement and its bitter taste, it amplifies on the suffering of "l'homme à la salive saumâtre" who is an exile from the society of other men.

The various ocean creatures—the sting-rays, sharks, and octopi Maldoror celebrates in *Les Chants*—are specifically constructed to attack and inflict suffering, while the lot of man is simply to withstand it. In the case of these sea monsters there exists an equilibrium between their corporal substance and the density of the medium in which they live. Thus "le poulpe au regard de soie . . . " moves and looks with a langourousness and fluidity that complements its watery environment. It does not simply embody its liquid habitat, but converts it into an active principle of aggression. For the octopus to flow means it must attack that which remains anchored or fixed in place. Human beings, however, are characterized by an organic imbalance, a tension between their brittle ego shell and their underlying visceral and moral softness. Hard on the outside but liquid on the inside, the human body invites a redistribution or levelling of its substance, which turns it either into a puddle of vital fluids or a pasty ball of torn limbs and coagulated blood "qui . . . ressemble . . . par la confusion de ses divers éléments broyés, à la masse d'une sphère!" Similarly, birds use their beaks and animals their claws to initiate a spillage or a flow. Their attack is directed at the outside, the carapace, while the octopus with its suckers, creates a vacuum around its victims, causing pressure to build from within until its prey bursts or explodes.

While liberation through violence is associated with a liquid medium, Lautréamont often evokes man's inclination toward selfishness and resistance to change by references to bodies in a solid state. In his fantasy involving the introduction of lice into the homes of men, he depicts a solid being broken down by a liquid. By means of the fecundation of a female louse, Maldoror is able to generate a living river of vermin that grows, "tout en acquérant la propriété liquide de mercure, et se ramifia[nt] en plusieurs branches, quise nourissent . . . en se dévorant elle mêmes. . . . " His primary objective is to break down the barriers people build around them, from the walls of their houses to the crania encasing their brains. But anything that appears hard betrays an underlying tendency toward volatility. So the mass of lice produced by Maldoror becomes so compacted into its component chunks that it blows itself apart along with the dwellings of men it was intended to destroy.

Like solids, bodies in a gaseous state are equally susceptible to destabilization and the centrifugal forces of inconsistency and dispersion. Unlike birds and fish with their adaptation to sea and sky, solid and gaseous bodies are subject to environmental attack. They can be eroded or blown away by wind or water, can be atomized or drowned. Whereas the function of a solid is to convert man's vulnerability to self-sufficiency, his weakness to complacency, gases and mists suggest a wish for self-communion. But as Maldoror had demonstrated, walls that are made to be impenetrable are easily broken through. Similarly, the illusory sense of completion can be dissipated when one is confronted with the truth of one's aloneness. Such is the case of the hermaphrodite in the second of *Les Chants.* Different from Maldoror, who knows what he wants and can never have, the hermaphrodite is locked away in a world of solipsistic fantasy, and sometimes feels he is happy in his dreams. But when he goes to embrace the being that he longs for, that being loses substance and then vanishes: "[C]e n'est qu'une vapeur crépusculaire que ses bras entrelacent; et, quand ilse réveillera, ses bras ne l'entrelaceront plus."

At the outset, man is faced with the experience of his own isolation. His efforts to barricade himself within the shell of his defensive egotism or lose himself in airy dreams of spiritual fulfillment prove ineffective. Further, since people remain the prisoners of their own selfishness, they do not share in the joys or misery of each other's lives. As the individual hoards his happiness and does not give of it to others, so do men remain apart in time of crisis. Typically, then, as the text points out, the tendency to join with others in times of hardship is superseded by an apprehension of some unknown menace that causes each individual to flee indoors and take refuge in his disregard for the welfare of his neighbors. People living in society are like bodies existing precariously in a solution, and all that is needed to precipitate them out is the intimation of a threat to their security. Then they hurry to their houses and shut themselves in, each alone with his own uneasiness. This is what happens the night Maldoror begins to plan Mervyn's destruction. The change in the atmosphere around the quarter is almost palpable:

> Les promeneurs hâtent le pas, et se retirent pensifs dans leurs maisons. Une femme s'évanouit et tombe sur l'asphalte. Personne ne la relève; il tarde à chacun de s'éloigner de ce parage. Les volets se referment avec impétuosité, et les habitants s'enfoncent dans leurs couvertures.

At the same time citizens elsewhere in the city continue to circulate freely in a medium made conductive by their own optimism and self-assurance. But here the inhabitants suddenly feel their hearts contract and their bodies turn to stone by the fear enveloping them. "Ainsi, pendant que la plus grande partie de la ville se prépare ànager dans les réjouissances des fêtes nocturnes, la rue Vivienne se trouve subitement glacée par une sorte de pétrification."

Expansion and contraction, rarefaction and condensation thus constitute two terms of the same attempt at escaping one's human limitations. On the one hand there is the dissipation of the individual in an illusion of self-communion, the vain effort to embrace a phantom self. On the other one sees the useless search for protection and enclosure, the wish to harden the self against the plight of others. Maldoror experiences the liquid state of things in two different aspects as well: in the context of the ocean with its mutability and infinite expansion and in bodies and quantities more consistent with and to the measure of human understanding.

Yet in the case of all of Maldoror's attacks, from those on children to the ones he inflicts upon himself, the purpose of aggression is to desolidify, to initiate a flow which will liberate man from his fixed identity, "qui emprisonne l'être dans sa forme" (Bachelard, p. 22). Lautréamont sees men as having a tendency to reproduce themselves architecturally and socially, in their confining structures, in the places where they live and the formulas that govern how they interact. The walls of their houses and the parameters of their socially acceptable behavior stand as dams against the tide of anarchy encircling them on all sides. Man's ideal of civilization would be to extend his fortifications outward forever, so that all space and every medium would contain him and bear the stamp of his intentionality. But because men are not birds or fish, their environment does not convey them nor facilitate their movements and the realization of their wishes. And so, in their misplaced hope for survival, they seek to inure themselves against the forces that besiege them. Lautréamont, as part of the revolt he advocates, shows that instead of danger on the outside and security and liquid plenitude within, man finds only emptiness and thirst inside him and a problematic chance for fulfillment in his environment. But what man has designated as evil is only that which jeopardizes the status quo. Naturally, the washing away of the constructs that define man's weaknesses will be seen by him as destructive, but destruction is merely a precondition for necessary change.

Already Maldoror had celebrated the ocean, not only as the repository of those things deemed impossible by man, but also as that which remains identical to itself by means of its unending transformations. Its water is not so much a substance that contains and supports a multitude of different life forms, but the medium that engenders those differences. But one reason for the ocean's attraction for Maldoror is its very inhumanity. Because of its enormity and purposeless bounty—"l'océan . . . est nourricier pour rien," as Jean-Pierre Vidal asserts [in "L'Océantexte," *Etudes littéraires,* 1978]—the sea exceeds minds circumscribed by inexperience and overlaps into unintelligibility. Thus, the message of *Les Chants* is not that men need be drowned in a sea of senselessness and cruelty, but that they should be cleansed, absolved of their habitual ways of seeing and acting. They must undergo an immersion, but not in an ocean that breeds only chaos and incomprehension.

In *Poésies,* Lautréamont describes his art by means of another liquid image. "La poésie n'est pas la tempête," he states, "pas plus que le cyclone. C'est un fleuve majestueux et fertile." Its function is to free man from the confines of an existence whose familiarity dwarfs his imagination and then carry him along in a river of thoughts that are so new and shocking they threaten to overwhelm him. In Lautréamont, there is no good and no evil, no static categories of opposites. Poetry is an instrument of revolt consisting of images that do violence only to man's customs and conventions.

It is useless to ask to what point this river of images leads. In the same way that the book's effect seems to be openended, Maurice Blanchot shows [in *Lautréamont et Sade,* 1963] its structure to be one that enables both author and reader to remain receptive to the ongoing need for self-transformation:

> C'est pourquoi il . . . semble si important de lire **Maldoror** comme une création progressive . . . , une oeuvre en cours, que Lautréamont conduit sans doute là où il veut, mais qui le conduit aussi là où il ne sait pas, dont il peut dire: "Suivons le courant qui nous entraîne . . ."

Unlike the ocean that promotes only confusion and sets off a chain of mutations leading nowhere, poetry forces man to follow the current, even though he does not know where it is going. As they carry him along, these images compel him to recognize the value of change for its own sake. For all the fact that its direction remains unknown to him, poetry provides man with an impetus for self-renewal, an impetus that is channeled and revitalizing. In *Les Chants de Maldoror,* it is not the destination that matters; it is the process. (pp. 173-80)

> *Robert E. Ziegler, "The Environment of Aggression in 'Les chants de Maldoror',"* in Rocky Mountain Review of Language and Literature, *Vol. 37, No. 4, 1983, pp. 173-80.*

Laurie Edson (essay date 1983-84)

[*Below, Edson contends that* Les chants de Maldoror *deliberately hinders interpretation so that the reader focuses instead on the cognitive process.*]

Any reader of **Les Chants de Maldoror** will perceive, relatively quickly, the unsettling nature of the world of the text as it frustrates his initial attempts at interpretation, consistently destroys his expectations, and toys with his "nostalgia for referentiality" [Michael Riffaterre, *Semiotics of Poetry,* 1978]. Since Lautréamont's text is transparently non-referential, the reader soon finds himself focusing attention on other kinds of material, i.e., the richness of the images, the complexity of sentence structure, the vivid detail of descriptions, and the sheer power of the language, without, however, arriving at a feeling of unity. But as the reader progresses deeper into the strange universe he notices patterns emerging, and as he begins to relate them to each other, he inevitably becomes aware of his own response as reader. The purpose of this study is to isolate some of these recurring patterns in **Les Chants de Maldoror** and show how, by their content and repetition, they imply the reading process itself and draw attention to our acts of cognition.

Lautréamont's text reveals a consciousness of the reader from its opening sentence: "Plût au ciel que le lecteur, enhardi et devenu momentanément féroce comme ce qu'il lit, trouve, sans se désorienter, son chemin abrupt et sauvage, à travers les marécages désolés de ces pages sombres et pleines de poison . . ." Throughout the **Chants,** the narrator interrupts his narrative to address his reader either directly or indirectly, so that the reader cannot help but be constantly reminded of his own act of reading. Indeed, recent critics have isolated this subject for analysis, showing how the reader evolves from spectator to actor or how the "reader of the text" relates to the "reader in the text."

Other critics have noted the confusion created by the shifting of pronouns from the impersonal third person to "tu" and imperative address, or the confusion among the "figurants du texte" (je/tu/il). In his extraordinary chapter called "L'Ecriture, le lecteur, le scripteur," Marcelin Pleynet explores how the reader finds himself assimilated to the "scripteur" from the opening paragraph: " 'je' (le lecteur) ne pourra lire ce 'il' (sujet de la lecture) que dans la mesure où la lecture et le sujet de la lecture ne feront plus qu'un, dans la mesure où 'je' sera devenu *comme ce qu'il lit;* lui-même écrit: écriture." Pleynet's statement prepares the way for the subject of this study, which is to show how both the reader and the text participate in similar kinds of movement. Although critics have focused on the role of the reader, no one, it seems to me, has isolated the various manifestations of movement in the text and related them to the reading process. Gaston Bachelard [in his *Lautréamont,* 1939] has studied the dynamic aspect of the text through a study of images of aggression (he calls it "phenomenology of aggression"), but his study is limited to what is represented by the language and omits the dynamics itself as well as the dynamics of the reading process. In his important work on Lautréamont [*Lautréamont et Sade,* 1949], Maurice Blanchot stresses the importance of movement in the text but is more concerned with identifying the underlying unifying principle (movement from obscurity to lucidity) rather than focusing on the reader's activity.

One of the most frequently cited passages of Lautréamont's text is the invocation to the ocean in Chant I. Each of the 10 paragraphs comprising the invocation lauds a different aspect of the ocean, but at the end of all the paragraphs, one finds the recurring sentence, "Je te salue, vieil océan." This refrain acts as a point of stability for the reader in the midst of language that moves perpetually forward. Each paragraph of the invocation resembles the waves Lautréamont admires: "Elles se suivent parallèlement, séparées par de courts intervalles," and the refrain, "Je te salue, vieil océan," acts as the interval, the pause within these waves of paragraphs which follow each other.

In the same invocation to the ocean, Lautréamont adds a curious detail about a bird resting on the waves, abandoning itself to the movements and then, having regained strength, flying off to continue its journey ("L'oiseau de passage se repose sur elles avec confiance, et se laisse abandonner à leurs mouvements, pleins d'une grâce fière, jusqu'à ce que les os de ses ailes aient recouvré leur vigueur accoutumée pour continuer le pèlerinage aérien"). The bird's flight is interrupted by the rest periods, just as the ocean's waves are interrupted by short intervals, and as the dynamic language of Lautréamont's paragraphs is interrupted by the refrain, "Je te salue, vieil océan." But the three examples of the static/dynamic pattern identified here are themselves subsumed into a larger static/dynamic pattern, for this whole section, this invocation to the ocean, is itself a temporary "pause" in the midst of the fierce language and the aggressive push of the narrative. Unlike the frenzied activity characterizing most of **Les Chants de Maldoror,** the language and style of the invocation evoke a calm immobility. The invocation to mathematics in Chant II is another example of such stasis within its dynamic context. At the end of the invocation to the ocean, the narrator notices his eyes swelling with tears when he realizes that he must leave his contemplative state and return to the world of men: "je sens que le moment est venu de revenir parmi les hommes, à l'aspect brutal. . . ." If the dominant mode of *Les Chants de Maldoror* is one of activity, aggression, and destruction, then the contemplation of the ocean has been a retreat into a calmer space. Like the bird, the "oiseau de passage," we, too, have been allowed to rest before flying into the tempestuous language.

Several episodes containing refrains are found throughout *Les Chants de Maldoror* and function in a similar way. Chant II, 4 relates the incident of the child wailing after a bus which has refused to stop for him, and the refrain appears 6 times, although modified slightly: "Il s'enfuit! Il s'enfuit! . . . Mais, une masse informe le poursuit avec acharnement, sur ses traces, au milieu de la poussière." Later in the same chant (II, 13), the narrator sits on a rock near the sea and watches calmly as a ship sinks in a storm, and the refrain appears four times: "Le navire en détresse tire des coups de canon d'alarme; mais, il sombre avec lenteur . . . avec majesté." Chant III, 1 relates the horseback ride of Mario and the narrator, and the refrain recurs three times: "Nos chevaux galopaient le long du rivage, comme s'ils fuyaient l'oeil humain. . . ." Chant III, 2 tells of the old crazy woman who drops her manuscript containing the story of the cruelty her daughter suffered at the hands of Maldoror and his bulldog, and the refrain occurs three times: "Les enfants la poursuivent à coups de pierre, comme si c'était un merle." Finally, during the well-known episode of the hair left behind by its master (III, 5), the voice of the spectator-narrator sings its refrain seven times, with a slight modification: "Et je me demandais qui pouvait être son maître! Et mon oeil se recollait à la grille avec plus d'énergie!. . . ."

Instead of analyzing the various episodes or the function of each refrain within its specific setting, I mean to draw attention to the presence of the recurring motifs and analyze their function within a larger pattern of song/refrain. If each verse of the "song" (i.e. *Les Chants*) narrates an event and a temporal development of an action (i.e., a horizontal progression), then each refrain serves as a (vertical) pause in the action. Because of the great quantity of action and aggression and movement in *Les Chants,* the reader's attention is inevitably drawn to these repetitions, precisely because they signal a change in the dominant rhythm of the text. Each repetition signals a refusal of the narrative to advance and provides the reader with little resting places. Instead of focusing on the content of the narrative or the content of the repetition, the reader perceives an example of a fundamental tension between what Raymond Jean has termed the "récit" and the "discours" of the *Chants.* If the "récit" of the exploits of Maldoror serves to advance the action of the narrative, then the "discours" intervenes to halt it. In keeping with the theme of aggression which permeates the text, Jean has spoken of "une opération de 'dynamitage' du récit par le discours, et réciproquement." In other words, the repetitions (refrains) aggressively halt the forward movement of the text and impose stability within the dynamic universe. The

reader views the repetitions as calm "resting places" in the midst of the ocean of activity and may be tricked into believing that these refrains are significant by virtue of their repetition. But the repetitions are no more and no less significant than the "récits" they interrupt, and in the end, we are left with nothing more than an awareness of the change in rhythm.

Lautréamont frustrates our expectations about locating meaning in several other ways. In Chant IV, where abstract thought and commentary replace specific examples of Maldoror's exploits as the dominant mode (i.e., the "discours" replaces the "récit"), Lautréamont saturates his text with long, winding sentences in which the traditional subject-verb-object sequence is bombarded with constant addition and accumulation of subordinate clauses, parenthetical statements, qualifiers, comparisons, and contradictions. It is as if Lautréamont were playing with our desire to arrive at the end of the sentence by purposely elongating it to deprive us of finality. After locating the subject, we unconsciously read more rapidly in an effort to locate the verb, and then we speed through the sentence to find the object, as if we expect to find meaning in the traditional subject-verb-object unit. But Lautréamont laughs at us and makes us aware of our own frenzied activity. For example, after a 24-line long sentence whose "message" is no more than " . . . il est bon . . . de revenir . . . au sujet . . . ," Lautréamont places a short, succinct statement which explicitly refers to our own harried activity: "Il est utile de boire un verre d'eau, avant d'entreprendre la suite de mon travail." Then he compares the drinking of water (i.e., the temporary "pause" in the frenzy which his short sentence has allowed us) to a halt in the pursuit of a runaway slave, noting that the halt lasts only a few seconds before "la poursuite est reprise avec acharnement . . . ." And once again, Lautréamont is off and running, with the reader, having been given his "resting period" in the space of a few short sentences, in hot pursuit of the subject-verb-object units of meaning. Even in the most seemingly chaotic of Lautréamont's sentences, one can always locate the subject, verb, and object; that is, under the apparent confusion there is always an order and a logical structure. Such a structure traditionally promises meaning, but Lautréamont's text consistently destroys our expectations. Ironically, the 24-line long sentence includes a subordinate clause about our activity of pursuing, our desire "de traquer, avec le scalpel de l'analyse, les fugitives apparitions de la vérité," but it puts the emphasis on the fact that "truth" or "meaning," appears only in momentary flashes.

In his study on Lautréamont, Blanchot notes that situations, themes, and images seem to appear and disappear: "tout se répète, tout revient toujours à la surface, puis s'éloigne dans les profondeurs, puis émerge à nouveau et à nouveau se retire." The pattern of emergence/resurgence he describes here lies at the core of the work; clarity momentarily asserts itself and then disappears back into the chaos. If the dominant characteristic of the text is the apparent chaos of the narrative and the complex, frenzied activity of the language, then the reader's attention will be drawn toward anything which appears *different,* i.e., a flash of apparent meaning in the midst of chaos, a simple sentence after a series of complex ones, the continual repetition of one sentence within a frenzied narration, the calm within the storm. Suzanne Bernard has spoken [in *Le Poème en prose, de Baudelaire jusqu'à nosjours,* 1959] about Lautréamont's technique of "enveloppement," where an idea seems to get lost but appears later in the narrative. Like Blanchot's emergence/resurgence pattern, Bernard's "enveloppement" draws attention to the basic tension in the text which is an oscillation between presence and absence, where "les fugitives apparitions de la vérité" manifest themselves in the midst of apparent chaos.

One of the central ideas of the text which is "enveloped" and asserts itself intermittently is this very idea that "truth" or "meaning" only appears intermittently. For instance, after an extremely long sentence containing multiple modifiers modifying other modifiers, Lautréamont teases his reader by including the phrase, "donnons à l'appui quelques exemples. . . . " The reader eagerly awaits the examples promised, as if something concrete would help clarify the abstract musings of the narrator. But he says only: "J'en présente deux: les emportements de la colère et les maladies de l'orgeuil," giving us the form of examples without any content. His very next sentence again mocks our helplessness as he warns us against forming vague ideas based on "le développement excessivement rapide de mes phrases." Throughout this whole section, then, while he plays at being abstract and vague, the narrator is conscious of frustrating the reader's need for an "appui" to determine meaning. The end result, of course, is the reader's consciousness of his own need to make sense out of chaos and his own need for units of meaning, "les fugitives apparitions de la vérité."

In reading *Les Chants de Maldoror,* the reader is bombarded with so many incidents, images, comparisons, and commentaries that he cannot hope to absorb it all, but, "in his very effort to catch up, the reader produces in himself the awareness that the world he is trying to comprehend transcends the acts of comprehension of which he is capable" [Wolfgang Iser, *The Implied Reader,* 1974]. Lautréamont's sentences, for instance, wander on aimlessly as comparisons are accumulated indefinitely, as in the example of the dogs which howl "soit comme un enfant qui crie de faim, soit comme un chat blessé au ventre au-dessus d'un toit, soit comme une femme qui va enfanter, soit comme un moribond atteint de la peste à l'hôpital, soit comme une jeune fille qui chante un air sublime. . . . " Instead of focusing on the content of the sentence, we are made aware of language's infinite ability to transform itself; instead of limiting us to what *is* said (i.e., the comparisons in the above sentence), the text simultaneously points the way toward what *is not* said (i.e., the unlimited potential of "soit comme"). Pleynet has singled out the importance of the adverb "comme" in *Les Chants* because it focuses attention on the arbitrary nature of all fiction; Lautréamont himself notes metaphor's ability to transcend specificity: "cette figure de rhétorique rend beaucoup . . . de services aux aspirations humaines vers l'infini . . . ." Even though the reader recognizes that he has entered an arbitrary universe of unlimited possibilities, the human mind is such that it inevitably attempts to piece

together disparate images, scenes, and events in an effort to establish consistency. The reading process, then, is this continual merging and diverging, the reader merges the fragments of the text into patterns, but other fragments appear which do not seem to fit and which destroy the established consistency, or, as Wolfgang Iser puts it, "in the process of illusion-forming the reader also creates the latent destruction of those very illusions." In the end, the reader is left with nothing more than the awareness of his own activity. *He* is the one creating and destroying the illusions; *he* is the one creating the text.

At the beginning of Chant I, Lautréamont warns his reader to turn away from the approaching storm, that is, to avoid the onslaught of language which threatens to engulf him, unless he is prepared to become as ferocious as what he reads ("féroce comme ce qu'il lit"). If the reader insists on penetrating the text and does not want to be transformed by it, then he must, according to Lautréamont, bring to his reading a rigorous logic ("une logique rigoureuse"). In other words, the reader must maintain distance from the "storm" rather than succumb to it. In reading *Les Chants de Maldoror,* however, the reader oscillates between involvement in and detachment from that storm: he is inevitably involved in creating consistency ("illusion-forming") while reading the text, but his awareness of his own activity helps him maintain distance. Part of the reading process, then, involves going toward a "center" (or "consistency," or "meaning"), but the text continually eludes our desire for center and pushes us out toward the periphery, where we reflect on our activity as reader. Indeed, such movement between center and periphery resembles the famous description of the flight of the starlings Lautréamont describes in Chant V, hailed by many critics as the central image of the text, although interpretations vary widely. In their instinct to fly to the center of their formation, the force of their flight causes the starlings to fly beyond ("leur instinct les porte à se rapprocher toujours du centre du peloton, tandis que la rapidité de leur vol les emporte sans cesse au-delà . . . "). Blanchot has compared the flight of the starlings to the movement of a "toubillon" and sees this as a perfect image of the predominant movement of the whole text. In the activity of reading, the reader participates in a similar movement toward and away from center; that is, he becomes *comme ce qu'il lit. Les Chants de Maldoror* can thus be read, in part, as a commentary on our acts of cognition, on the mental processes which take place when we confront language. (pp. 198-204)

Laurie Edson, " 'Les chants de Maldoror' and the Dynamics of Reading," in Nineteenth-Century French Studies, *Vol. XII, Nos. 1 & 2, Fall-Winter, 1983-84, pp. 198-206.*

Suzanne Guerlac   (essay date 1990)

[*In the following excerpt, Guerlac discusses the sublime in* Les chants de Maldoror *as evidenced by the title character's struggles with God and humans.*]

There are two principal struggles represented and enacted within *Les Chants de Maldoror:* Maldoror versus the Almighty and Maldoror versus his fellow humans. Ambiguously "man and more than a man," Maldoror seeks identification with the term of absolute difference—the Almighty—and difference from identification with his "semblables"—his fellow humans. In *Les Chants de Maldoror* dramas of finitude are played out not only in writing but also through the act of writing, itself mis-en-scène and explicitly linked, as we shall see, to a "need for the infinite." Through his writing, Maldoror returns the maledictions that he has received and that he attributes to the Almighty in his infinite power. Rivalry with the Omnipotent and vengeance against him occur through grotesque representations of the Almighty that portray his fall into an identification with finite man at his most criminal. On the other hand, the combat against man "will be beautiful" because it is explicitly waged through the text we read—"I will not use weapons made of wood and iron. . . . The powerful and angelic sonorousness of the harp will become, in my hands, a formidable talisman." The lines of this combat correspond with the divide between "writer" and reader; they are drawn at the limit, or on the frame, of the text we read.

From the beginning of *Les Chants de Maldoror,* a pragmatic struggle is set up between reader and text. The reader is warned in the opening lines that "unless he brings a rigorous logic to his reading . . . the deadly emanations of this book will absorb his soul as sugar absorbs water." If reading is a form of incorporation or absorption, the reader of *Les Chants* risks being consumed or absorbed in turn—risks, one could almost say, being read by the text instead of the other way around, like Baudelaire's hashish smoker, who comes to feel as if his pipe were smoking him. To avoid being absorbed and dissolved by the text, the reader must become "ferocious like the text that he reads," in other words, a *semblable* of Maldoror. The "pages that follow" are subsequently called by Maldoror "the pages of my heart"; the text and Maldoror are consubstantial. Reading therefore implies consumption or the risk of being consumed. Consumption implies identification. From the beginning, therefore, we are within the structure of vampirism, which will be dramatized in the crucially important scene, that, as we shall see, depicts the "sanctity" of crime.

In the first canto Maldoror is divided through the narrative frame of the text. He is described in the third person—"our hero"—in relation to the "I" of the "poet . . . born on American shores, at the mouth of the La Plata." At the same time, he is identified with that poet-narrator as "writer" of *Les Chants.* "He was not a liar," we read in this first canto. "He admitted the truth and said that he was cruel. Humans, did you hear? He dares to repeat it with *this* trembling pen" (my emphasis). In the next strophe it is implicitly Maldoror who proclaims, "I use my genius to paint the delights of cruelty!" and who poses the fundamental aesthetic question: "Can genius not be allied with cruelty. . . . The proof will be found in my words; it is up to *you* to listen to me, if *you* will" (my emphasis). Maldoror does not become explicitly an "I," however, until the end of the first canto. Nor does he explicitly become a "writing subject" until the beginning of the second. The first-person voice of Maldoror is not heard until

after a resemblance between "writer" and reader has been established—not simply threatened, as in the opening line of the book, but performed.

The initial warning having been sounded, the second strophe addresses a very different reader than the first, implying quasi-magical powers of the text already at work—its capacity to indeed fulfill its word and turn away all but the satanic or "ferocious" reader who is addressed here: "Reader, it is perchance hatred you would have me invoke at the beginning of this work!" What we find instead of hatred, however, are the pleasures and seductions of intoxication, which are appealed to in decidedly Baudelairean terms. "O, monster," the text addresses the reader, "Your nostrils, which will be enormously dilated with ineffable contentment, with motionless ecstasy, will demand nothing better of space, balmy with perfume and the smell of incense, for they will be fully satisfied with a total happiness like unto the angels that inhabit the peace and magnificence of the agreeable heavens." Intoxication sets the stage for reading and figures the reception of the text itself (and of Maldoror) through a metaphor of incorporation, which displaces the figure of absorption with which the naive reader is threatened in the opening lines of the book. Satanic, or ferocious, readers will not be absorbed. They will absorb the text with pleasure. Readers who reach the second paragraph of the text are already implicated in an act of transgression—the pleasures of intoxication.

In the third strophe the character Maldoror is introduced for the first time in the celebrated elliptical sentence: "In a few lines I shall establish how Maldoror was virtuous during his first years, virtuous and happy; it is done." The narrative past simple tense appears here for the first time. Yet the narrative itself is aborted. How Maldoror was virtuous in his first years is declared to be potential narrative material instead of being narratively developed. The story to be told, Maldoror's past, is embedded in a narrative project to be fulfilled in a future time—"in a few lines I shall establish"—that corresponds with a time of narration. This time of narration, however, which overlaps with the time of reading, fulfills itself without ever unfolding the implied narrative of past events. In the time it takes to read to the end of the sentence, "it is done." Contact with the reader is reinforced by the allusion to the time of reading necessarily implied by the logic of this passage: "I shall establish. . . . it is done."

The readers are not only urged into an identification with Maldoror (as text) but they are also manipulated into it, rhetorically and narratively, in the sixth strophe of the first canto, which presents the scene of vampirism. The readers are in this sense also vampirized. The strophe begins with the anonymous, universal subject *on,* a pronoun already introduced in relation to the reader posed as arbiter of the question of the genius of cruelty—"The proof is to be found [on en verra la preuve] in my words; it is up to you to listen to me." "One should let one's nails grow for two weeks," the opening line of this strophe declares. "O, how sweet it is," the text continues, beginning to associate the *one* (which includes the reader) with the cruel fantasy that follows: "to brutally snatch a child from his bed . . . to pretend to pass one's hand smoothly over his brow, brushing back his beautiful hair! Then, suddenly, when he least expects it, to plunge one's long nails deep into his soft breast but in such a way that he does not die; for should he die, one could not later enjoy the spectacle of his suffering." The transition from "on doit pousser ses ongles" to "enfoncer les ongles longs [plunge one's long nails]" (which insistently repeats the sound *on*) implicates the *one* as subject of this hypothetical aggression. "Then you [*on*] drink the blood," the text continues, already setting a narrative sequence under way, one that also makes a gradual transition from hypothetical description to an imperative directed at the reader, who is by implication included within that *on*. The next sentence addresses the reader: "Man, have you never tasted your own blood when by accident you cut your finger?" This is followed by the imperative "Well, then, since your own blood and tears do not disgust you, nourish yourself confidently with the tears and the blood of the child" in a return to the fictive representation.

Our entry into the scene we are reading is forced upon us through a logic of implication reinforced by changes in tense and set to work in relation to the time of reading. Because we are addressed by the "writer's" imperatives, it is as if simply to continue reading were to assent to a description that attributes actions to our agency. Soon it is we, the readers, who are being narrated, moved about like actors on a stage: "Bind his eyes," we are directed, "while you rend [*tu déchireras*] his palpitating flesh; and, after listening to his sublime cries for several hours . . . rush away like an avalanche, then hurry back in from the next room and pretend to come to his aid." It is as if the scene itself were constituted by our withdrawal from it and our reemergence onto it in a new, dialectically reversed role. Like the "I will establish. . . . It is done" of the aborted narrative passage already cited, by the time the future tense of the "tu déchireras" [you will rend or tear] has been read, we have (by implication) already committed the act. To continue reading is to tacitly accept responsibility for the crime. It is the inexorability of the time of reading and of its logic of implication that renders us, like it or not, ferocious like the text that we read—it is done.

The entire scene is produced without any reference to a present tense, a "now" in which action might be said to occur. Imperatives, future tenses, and past participles surround the absent present and evoke the scene of pain. The illusion of presence, induced through the sheer connotative force of pain, is reinforced by the allusion to repetition in the final command, which implies a passage of substantial elapsed time: "You will unbind his hands . . . then restore sight to his eyes and *begin again* to lap up his tears and his blood" (my emphasis). The repetition also implies our acquiescence to the preceding imperative: "Nourish yourself confidently with the tears and the blood of the child." The act is definitively constituted as *our* act. Our agency has been worked into the fabric of the description through the repetition given as a present participle—"*en te remettant* [you will begin again]."

Immediately after this description—of us—which overlaps with the unfolding time of our reading, we return to the hypothetical, intensive form that opens the scene:

"How real a thing, then, is repentance! The divine spark that dwells within us and shows itself so rarely appears: too late! How your heart overflows with joy that you [*on*] are able to console the innocent whom someone has hurt [à qui l'on a fait du mal]." The anonymous *on* now stands accused—and has explicitly been linked to a collectivizing "we" that includes the reader, gathering together the pronominal designations that have been implicitly or explicitly applied to the reader so far: a "you" and a fictively constituted "he." The reader is the declared agent of the crime that has been staged here; the act that was never present and never represented has been declared fact: "On a fait du mal." Responsibility for the crime is definitively placed on us.

No sooner is this "we" constituted through the one, as implied agent or he, than we, the readers, are elevated to the status of an "I" as subject of enunciation. Who but the reader can be inferred to speak when, after the emphatic "How your heart overflows with joy that you are able to console the innocent whom someone has hurt!" what follows is a colon and an indication of dialogue: " 'Adolescent. . . who could have committed such an unspeakable crime upon you! . . . How you must suffer! And if your mother knew about it, she would be no nearer to death, so dreaded by the guilty, than I am at this moment.' " We are posed by the text as the subject who hypocritically asks this question. Implicitly, we acknowledge our guilt. It is on this basis that we then ask the crucial question of *Les Chants de Maldoror* (and perhaps of the entire double work of Lautréamont-Ducasse): "Alas, what then are good and evil! Are they one and the same thing through which we testify, with rage, to our impotence, and to the passion to reach the infinite by even the most extravagant means? Or are they two different things? Yes . . . they had better be one and the same, for if they are not, what will become of me on Judgment Day?" Addressing the innocent victim, we (the readers) continue:

> Adolescent, forgive me. Once I am rid of this transitory life, I want us to be joined together throughout eternity to form one inseparable being, my mouth pressed forever upon your mouth. Even in this way my punishment will not be complete. You shall rend my flesh unceasingly with teeth and nails. I shall deck my body with scented garlands for this *expiatory holocaust. . . . You will soothe my conscience.* " (my emphasis)

The genius of cruelty, we have been told, "does not claim that his *cavatines* are something completely unknown. On the contrary, he takes pride in the fact that the lofty and wicked thoughts of his hero are to be found in all men." This universality has been achieved or performed by writing the reader into the scene of the crime. Maldoror can thus now take the reader as his fellow and hence as his opponent. The songs of Maldoror are now ready to begin. In the next strophe we hear Maldoror's lyric voice for the first time: "I have made a pact with prostitution in order to sow disorder among families."

The scene of vampirism is a crucial one in *Les Chants de Maldoror*, for it brings together (as we see through subsequent allusions) the three main characters of the text—

God, Man, and Maldoror. "Every morning . . . I crouch in my beloved cave in a state of despair that intoxicates me like wine. . . . I tear [*déchirer*] my breast to ribbons with my strong hands," Maldoror declares later in the same canto, appropriating for himself the gesture of tearing the flesh from the chest. That he becomes both subject and victim of the action reinforces the suggestion that the youth victimized by the reader in the first canto is none other than the "writer" himself. But it also remarks the fundamentally mimetic, reversible structure of sin and expiation associated with the crime. This is the structure of vengeance that simply reverses positions of transitivity, or of active and passive roles. Perhaps for this reason the same crime is conjured up as an image for the vengeance of God. Toward the end of the "Ancient ocean" strophe of the first canto, the "writer" addresses the ocean in the following terms: "Roll wildly . . . more wildly yet . . . if you would have me compare you to the vengeance of God. Spread out your livid claws and tear yourself out a pathway in your own bosom. . . . Good. Unroll your monstrous waves, hideous ocean." Last, the Almighty himself repeats the same crime upon an adolescent youth in the brothel scene, which marks his fall. The crime into which we have been written is thus paradigmatic. It is identified both with Maldoror-Lautréamont and the vengeance of God, and associated with the bloodthirstiness of each.

The scene of vampirism links the "passion to reach the infinite" to the ethical question of the status (identity or difference) of good and evil, which, as we have just seen, follows upon, and in a sense fulfills, the posing of the aesthetic question concerning the possibility of a genius of cruelty. A "passion to reach the infinite even by the most extravagant means," what Baudelaire called the "spiritual thirst" associated with hashish, is represented as a "thirst for the infinite"—even a *need* for the infinite"—in the next scene. It portrays howling dogs that "throw themselves upon one another, not knowing what they are doing, and tear one another into a thousand pieces with incredible rapidity." The word *tear* (*déchirer*) refers us back to the scene of the "sacred" crime. The dogs "do not behave this way from cruelty," we are flatly told. When they "howl at the northern stars, at the eastern stars, at the southern stars, at the western stars; at the moon; at the mountains . . . at the fresh air they breathe . . . at the silence of the night" in a global gesture of negativity, they are simply suffering from a severe case of "insatiable thirst for the infinite, like you, like me, like the rest of humanity with its long, pale faces." But unlike humanity, they are unquestionably beyond good and evil. For them, the two are undoubtedly "one and the same thing, through which [they] testify . . . to [their] impotence, and [their] passion to reach the infinite, even by the most extravagant means." The spectacle of the dogs moves Maldoror to confess: "I, like the dogs, feel a yearning for the infinite. . . . I cannot, I cannot, satisfy this need."

In relation to the question of divine vengeance, the "need" for the infinite will be staged as a need to write in the beginning of the second strophe of the second canto. Maldoror at last assumes the role of writer, and the act of writing is explicitly dramatized as an act of both transgression and identification. It is mis-en-scène as a drama of finitude.

Here the aesthetic question concerning the genius of cruelty is implicitly related to the ethical one, the question of the "thirst for the infinite." "I take up the pen that will execute the second canto. . . . But what is wrong with my fingers?" Maldoror asks. "Their joints are paralyzed from the moment I begin my work. Yet I need to write. It is impossible! But I repeat: I need to write down my thoughts."

What is wrong is that, as he writes, or tries to write, Maldoror has been struck by a thunderbolt sent by an avenging God.

> But no, no . . . the pen is motionless! Wait: see the lightning flash across the countryside. The tempest sweeps through space. . . . How it rains! The thunder crashes. . . . It has struck at me through my open window and beaten me to the floor with a blow on my brow. Poor youth! Your face was already sufficiently covered with precocious wrinkles . . . not to need, in addition, this long sulfurous scar. . . . I don't have to thank the Almighty for his remarkable skill [*adresse*]. He aimed his lightning so as to divide my face precisely in two.

Maldoror's writing is interrupted by the divine thunderbolt (image, since Longinus, for a sublime force of speech), which wounds Maldoror with an "adresse remarquable," splitting his face in two. The sulfurous scar marks Maldoror as satanic hero; the split figures his status as "man and more than a man" and figures his identification with the Omnipotent or infinite term on the one hand and with his mortal fellow humans on the other. This *adresse* engenders a furor in Maldoror, enabling him to overcome his momentary paralysis and provoking him to launch a "thunderbolt" of his own in the following counterattack:

> Wretch that you are! I shall strike your hollow carcass with such violence that I guarantee to beat out the remaining particles of . . . intelligence that you would not bestow upon man because you would have been jealous of making him equal to yourself . . . as if you had not known that someday I should ferret it out with my ever-open eye, fetch it from you, and share it with my fellow men. All this I have done, and now men fear you no more; they deal with you on equal terms [de puissance à puissance]. . . . I have seen the Creator, spurring on his senseless cruelty. . . . It is not I who begin the attack; it is he who forces me to spin him like a top with a steel-lashed whip.

The question of identification explicitly becomes an issue in the context of an interlocution (or interscription)—an exchange of thunderbolts. Maldoror reproaches the Omnipotent for not having made man absolutely in his own image. He reproaches him for an inadequate mimesis, for having withheld those "particles of intelligence" that would have made humankind his equal—infinite like him. Finitude is a privation, a lack, due to an inadequate mimesis.

Maldoror receives a blow and delivers one. He receives a "sulfurous scar," and his words are characterized as "sulfurous speech." He is both speaker and addressee of malediction. "He then realized that he was born wicked," we are told in the first canto, "extraordinary fate. . . . There is a force that is stronger than the will . . . Malediction!" At the same time Maldoror is told by the "man with the face of a toad": "You have produced nothing but maledictions." "He is accursed, and he curses." Maldoror's maledictions are thus a repetition or return—a revenge—for those that have been addressed to him. They occur both within the "theatrical spectacles" staged in *Les Chants* and at the narrative frame of the text, operating in relation to the logic, or pragmatics, of reading we have seen at work in the passage already analyzed.

If malediction and Maldoror's double position as both subject and object of it could be said to govern the frame of the text, vengeance is the equivalent structure of reciprocity (identification and reversal), which thematically governs the fictive scenes or spectacles represented. In the context of a structure of vengeance, good and evil are symmetrical, and the ethical value ascribed to an action depends upon the position of transitivity. It depends, in other words, upon who is the victim. Vengeance thus poses an opposition between good and evil at the same time that it implies their equivalence in exchange, a reversibility of the kind we saw staged as the relation between sin and expiation in the paradigmatic scene of vampirism, where expiation amounted to repetition of the crime with positions reversed: "Adolescent, forgive me. . . . You shall rend my flesh unceasingly with teeth and nails." The question of vengeance puts into play the thrust of the ethical question concerning good and evil by its structure of equivalence in reversals. As we shall see, the opposition between grotesque and sublime will more often than not be the operator of such reversal. The mimetic symmetry of the binary opposition between Maldoror and his opponent, the Omnipotent, is explicit in the characterization of the two figures as "two monarchs"—"He fears me and I fear him."

Given this reciprocity, the play of doubling becomes intricate to the point of dizziness when Maldoror's "projects of vengeance"—his "sublime projects"—are directed against his two enemies, God and his fellow humans, simultaneously. There is a doubling, or *mise-en-abyme*, of the doubling already implied in the theme of vengeance. For in this case Maldoror not only operates on two fronts, that of God and man, but the latter is posed as victim of the divine vengeance of the former. Given this situation, vengeance against one of Maldoror's enemies will entail consequences for the other.

As we have seen in connection with the second canto (II-2), the victimization of man by God is portrayed as being due (at least in part) to an incomplete, or inadequate, mimesis—to God's having made man almost in his own image, but not quite. God alone is infinite, man is finite. Maldoror, as divided being identified with both the finite and the infinite terms, steps in to mediate just this gap and to redress the balance of power.

"Very well, this time I present myself to defend humankind," Maldoror declares in the penultimate strophe of the second canto. The defense involves revenge against the Omnipotent through grotesque representations of his cruelty against man. Maldoror-Lautréamont makes the Al-

mighty his own creature (his literary creation) to do with as he pleases, just as the Omnipotent is portrayed as doing with his creatures. Strophe II-8 presents the "vision that made known to me the supreme truth" of the cruelty of "the one who calls himself the Creator." The Almighty announces, "I created you. Hence I have the right to do what I want with you," as he sets into his "cruel repast," enthusiastically devouring his finite human beings. At stake in this strophe is the radical autonomy of the Creator, displayed through his cruelty and injustice. This is the infinity that the subject of finitude experiences as a privation and desires to equalize through his infinite will. Ironically, however, to the extent that he is caught up in a mimetic machine, he will never become fully autonomous but instead will turn around and around in a vicious circle of reactive gestures. This, as we shall see, is the principal lesson of *Les Chants de Maldoror.*

Maldoror justifies his attacks against the Creator with the claim that he is the defender of humankind, but he also directs his "sublime projects" of vengeance against human beings as God's creatures, as we see in the strophe II-9. This scene depends on the representation of God's cruelty in the preceding strophe both to rationalize Maldoror's wrath against humankind for its complicity in maintaining the power of the wrathful God and to establish an identification between Maldoror and the Omnipotent. The grotesque cruelty of God represented in strophe II-9 is mimed and caricatured. Infesting God's creation with lice, Maldoror both avenges himself against God and identifies himself with the cruelty, the power, and the autonomy of the Omnipotent, displacing or replacing him through his act of transgressive violence.

The doublings and reversals are particularly complicated in this scene, which includes the "three characters" of *Les Chants*—"man, the Creator, and myself," as Maldoror refers to them—as well as the *pou* (louse or flea) which doubles all the above positions. As a supplement to this triadic structure, the *pou* repeats the role Maldoror plays in relation to the binary opposition between God and humankind. The insect refracts, through reversal and identification, the various relations that connect the three principal terms in the "circulatory apparatus" through which they interact.

The insect is initially posed as divine in relation to humankind: "There is an insect nourished by men at their own expense. They owe it nothing, but they fear it. This insect . . . doesn't like wine but instead prefers blood. . . . You should see how they respect it, how they surround it with a canine veneration. . . . They offer their heads for a throne, and the insect digs in its claws to the roots of their hair, with dignity."

In a grotesque reversal the *pou* is placed in the position of the sublime term. "Lilliputian," it is also an "idol." It is venerated through fear, capable of enlarging itself to the size of an elephant and of crushing human beings underfoot. In addition to the reversal of great and small, and of the one and the many (the *pou* soon becomes *poux*), the veneration of the insect reverses the hierarchy of man and beast. The hybridization of grotesque and sublime materializes through the expressions "worm-eaten worship [*culte vermoulu*]" and "canine veneration," where the adjectives bear a literal relation to the actual status of lice or to the consequences of their parasitism. The insect also literalizes metaphors previously associated with the Omnipotent. Whereas the Almighty is characterized as bloodthirsty in his cruelty and vengeance, for example, the louse or flea literally sucks blood.

But the *poux* are also identified with Maldoror, who, like them, is an "adolescent philosopher," "invisible enemy of man," and "celestial liberator." If the word *pou* repeats the dominant sounds of the name "*tout Pui*ssant," it is also associated with Maldoror. Our hero has complained bitterly about the ugliness that "the Supreme Being, with a smile of powerful hatred, placed upon [him]." This calls irresistibly to mind the expression "laid comme un pou"—ugly as sin—an implied play on words that is reinforced when the insects are subsequently referred to as Maldoror's "mine de poux"—his mine of lice—for the French word *mine* also signifies face or appearance.

Once the identification between the insect and Maldoror is established, however, the *poux* lose their "occult powers" and become merely the instrument of Maldoror's cruelty. Like man, the insects are mortal. The *poux* repeat and parody the problem of finitude that afflicts Maldoror and his fellow humans. Mortal, their force is not equal to their "infinite wishes" for a total vampirism of mankind. It is only because "they don't have the strength" that they do not ingest "the brain, the retina of the eye, the spinal column," of human beings "like a drop of water." The *poux* are thus contrasted with the man-eating infinite God, portrayed in all his cruelty in the previous strophe, who cheerfully consumes his human creatures to the last drop. And it is because the insect is mortal that Maldoror, now identified (through the mediation of the *pou*) with divine occult powers, steps in to supplement the destructive powers of the lice with his intelligent strategies. Maldoror breeds the lice (literally, by coupling with the divine louse) and stores up an inexhaustible supply of them, holding this in reserve to compensate for the mortality of the insects. They are then to be released as a scourge of mankind: "If the earth were covered with lice, as the riverbed is covered with grains of sand, the human race would be annihilated, subjected to terrible sufferings. What a spectacle! And I, with the wings of an angel, motionless in the air to contemplate it." Maldoror's vengeance now appears exaggeratedly grand in comparison with the lilliputian scale of the insects and in relative terms takes on a quasi-divine stature. "When will you abandon this worm-eaten worship of a deity who is insensible to the prayers and generous offerings you offer up to him in expiatory holocaust?" Maldoror asked earlier. Maldoror produces his own version of the expiatory holocaust—a term that refers us back to the paradigmatic crime of vampirism—with his mine of lice, whose bloodthirstiness both trivializes (or miniaturizes) and exaggerates (or universalizes) the "sacred crime." The *poux* mediate the identification between Maldoror and the Omnipotent as, precisely, genius of cruelty.

Just as the howling dogs followed on the heels of the vampirism of the adolescent in the first canto, both repeating the crime and neutralizing it, an appeal to another "thirst for the infinite" that is "beyond good and evil" follows the hyperbolic expansion of that crime, the scourge of lice:

> O austere mathematics, I have not forgotten you. In . . . place [of gloom] you set an extreme coldness, a consummate prudence and an implacable logic. . . . Arithmetic! Algebra! Geometry! Imposing trinity! Luminous triangle. . . . The Omnipotent revealed himself and his attributes completely in that memorable effort that consisted in extracting from the entrails of chaos your treasures of theorems and your magnificent splendors.

Mathematics presents the infinite without theological or moral values attached and therefore without the swings of high and low that, as we have seen, lead to specular identifications and reversals. Mathematics presents the infinite without dialectical struggle. It does not invite the play of opposition between grotesque and sublime. It is not a field of transgression. This is in direct contrast to the next strophe—"O lamp of silver . . . companion of the cathedral dome"—where, explicitly in a Christian context, the infinite again divides between high and low, between "serene heights of virtue" and "vertiginous abysses of evil." It is here that the grotesque/sublime opposition, already at play with the *poux,* becomes explicitly thematized. God's cruelty is characterized as a function of his "tigerlike imagination . . . which would be burlesque were it not contemptible." . . . Here, in another shift in scale, human beings are reduced to the proportions of the *poux;* they are opposed to the divine by virtue of their "microscopic size." Each is a "worm that crawls on the ground," a grotesque image taken from Pascal, where extremes of scale dramatize contradictions associated with the notion of the two infinities, transposed from mathematics into theological terms. The Pascalian imagery emphasizes the shift in scale performed earlier by the inversion of grotesque and sublime through the lice. To the extent that the grotesque/sublime difference functions as an opposition (as it does here), it entails symmetry and dialectical struggle. Reversibility of good and evil is marked in the sequence of the following two strophes. In the first, Maldoror watches a shipwrecked person drown without coming to his aid; in the second he saves the life of someone who is drowning. "What a fine thing it is to save someone's life!" he announces, "and how that act atones for sins." Once again, sin and expiation are posed in terms of the kind of happy symmetry—repetition and reversal—dramatized earlier in relation to the "sacred" crime of vampirism.

The climax of this series of reversals is the fall of the Creator from sublime to grotesque in the brothel scene. In that scene, he, too, repeats the gestures of the sacred crime depicted in the first canto. In an amusing play on Baudelaire's remark in the "Poëme du haschisch" that in his infatuation the smoker forgets that "he is playing with someone sharper and stronger than himself, and, that the Spirit of Evil, even when one only yields to him a hair, does not hesitate to take the whole head," the Creator leaves behind a hair in the brothel. The hair provides the account of the scandal. "What I know," it recounts, "is that as soon as the young man was within reach shreds of flesh began to fall to the foot of the bed. . . . The claws of my master . . . detached the shoulders from the adolescent." The paradigmatic crime has been exaggerated. Instead of merely being scratched on the chest, the adolescent becomes a full-fledged martyr. He is literally flayed alive. When the Creator returns to the scene of the crime to retrieve his lost hair, he describes himself as "no longer the same; having become inferior to my identity." On his forehead are two drops—one of sperm, the other of blood. These recall the drops of blood and tears referred to in the first canto in the original version of the crime—"Man, have you ever tasted your blood? . . . "

"I saw Satan . . . triumphant, sublime . . . hold me up to derision," the Creator declares, adding: "He said that he was astonished that his haughty rival . . . could so far demean himself . . . that the great esteem in which he had held so noble an enemy had fled from his imagination. . . . I am the All High; and yet . . . I remain inferior to men whom I created with a little sand!" Maldoror closes the scene with an echo of Satan's sentiment: "I closed my eyes at the thought of having a being such as this for my enemy."

The sublime scenario of confrontation with the absolute—Maldoror versus the Omnipotent—reaches a climax (or anticlimax) here at the end of the third canto. We are halfway through the book—or the pages of Maldoror's heart. The fall of the Creator cuts the text exactly in half, as the divine thunderbolt had done to Maldoror's face. Maldoror wins a certain victory: he and the Creator are finally on equal terms. But it is a hollow victory, due not to an ascendency of Maldoror but rather to the fall of his once great rival. To the extent that half of Maldoror resembled the transcendent term, the fall of the Creator also diminishes Maldoror: "The idea that I have voluntarily fallen as low as my fellow men . . . pierces me like a horseshoe nail. . . . In the middle as in the beginning of life, angels resemble themselves: how long it has been since I ceased to resemble myself!" Maldoror complains. To the extent that he is identified with the All Powerful, he too has become "inferior to his identity" while at the same time the fall of the Creator fulfills Maldoror's identification with him.

Now that the Creator is no longer an enemy worthy of respect, Maldoror turns his energies elsewhere. With the opening of the fourth canto the symmetrical opposition between Maldoror and the All Powerful—"two neighboring monarchs. . . . I fear him; he fears me"—is replaced by one between Maldoror and his fellow humans, his *semblables*: "Humankind and I . . . flee from one another, trembling with hatred, taking opposite directions, as if we had wounded one another with the points of daggers! . . . So be it! Let my war against humankind endure throughout eternity, since each recognizes in the other his own degradation . . . since the two are mortal enemies." The terms of confrontation are now "Me, alone against humanity." Maldoror enters into combat with a vengeance. "The combat will be beautiful," as he declares, because it is now explicitly waged through the writing of the text. The field of battle is the frame of the text, the site of the encounter between reading and writing.

"This terrible combat will bring down much sorrow upon the heads of the two parties: two friends striving obstinately to destroy one another: what a drama!" With these words the first strophe of the fourth canto concludes on a distinctly Hugolian note. In what follows, a verbal combat occurs on a battleground whose coordinates are precisely Hugo's ingredients of the drama—the grotesque and the sublime. That the conflict with the reader is to be waged here as a struggle over meaning, a conflict of interpretation, becomes evident as we read on in "the laborious literary fragment I am in the process of composing." It begins as follows:

> Two pillars that it was not difficult and even less impossible to take for two baobab trees appeared in the valley, larger than two pins. As a matter of fact they were two enormous towers [*tours*]. And although two baobab trees do not resemble at first glance two pins, or even two towers, nevertheless while skillfully employing the strings of prudence, one may affirm without fear of error . . . that a baobab tree does differ so very much from a pillar that the comparison should be forbidden between these two architectural forms . . . or geometric forms . . . or the one or the other . . . or neither the one nor the other . . . or rather, massive elevated forms. I have just found, I make no pretense of maintaining the contrary, the correct adjectives for the substantives pillar and baobab tree.

"Two pillars" promises a realistic, referential use of language. In what follows, however, the reader is sent from pillar to post in apparently meaningless prose. To read these pillars, we must indeed "skillfully employ the strings of prudence." Prudence is associated with the "implacable logic" of mathematics, as the apostrophe of the strophe II-10 revealed. It is a "terrible auxiliary" for Maldoror in his struggle against humanity—"Without you I might perhaps have been overcome in my struggle against man. . . . You gave me the coldness of your sublime conceptions."

As the text of this fourth canto reads itself (prudently), the pillars, baobabs, pins, and towers function like variables in an algebraic equation. "Massive elevated forms" serves as a common denominator of pillars and towers "larger than two pins" on their way to becoming mere "substantives." These opening assertions serve as pretext for a meditation on language. Several words can be used to signify the same thing, we are told, and the same expressions can be construed in more than one way—"The same name expresses . . . two phenomena of the mind." These heavy-handed remarks prepare a reflection on rhetorical figures. After the rigorous analysis of the strophe's opening sentences, Lautréamont presents the "fundamental axiom" of "an irreparable stigma of a relapse into the criminal use . . . of a rhetorical figure that many despise, but to which many pay homage." But we omitted the important qualification. The use of the rhetorical figure is considered criminal, Lautréamont adds parenthetically: "when one places oneself momentarily and spontaneously at the point of view of the higher power." This higher power is the one who, as we read a few sentences above, "commands us in the clearest and most precise terms to hurl into the abyss of chaos the judicious comparison that everyone had certainly been able to savor with impunity"—presumably the comparison that opens the strophe.

Why this is a "judicious comparison" becomes clear at the end of this long paragraph, when we are told that it was the "point of view" of a very precise optics that was responsible for the comparison "with such exactness" of the pillars and pins—"I based myself on the laws of optics." The opening comparison between pillars and pins is thus perhaps a kind of literal indication of relative distance, an indication of point of view per se determined through the laws of optics. This, of course, is what determines the notion of point of view in the first place.

We remember that it was a question of just such a superior perspective, a totalizing vision "from a higher and more encompassing glance" that grounded the addition of grotesque and sublime in Hugo's "Preface to *Cromwell.*" There the grotesque is called an "optique auprès du sublime"—literally a lens onto the sublime, but figuratively a point of contrast that will throw the sublime term into relief. The force of Hugo's metaphor is precisely the optical effect of the comparison of pins to pillars, where the pins exaggerate—in French there is the expression *monter en épingle*—the grandeur or enormity of the pillars.

It is not surprising, given this context, that Lautréamont proceeds to a discussion of laughter, a discussion punctuated by statements concerning the addition of grotesque and sublime, affirmations that themselves undergo grotesque reversal. Now that the opposition between high and low, sublime and grotesque, has played itself out on the level of representation with the fall of the Creator into grotesque abjection, the dynamics of the sublime and the grotesque (now explicitly thematized) moves into the arena of language as the conflict becomes a pragmatic one between Maldoror and his fellows—his readers. "My arguments will sometimes come up against the bells of folly and the serious appearance of what in the final analysis is nothing but the grotesque," Lautréamont remarks, adding parenthetically (in a clear allusion to Victor Hugo) "although, according to certain philosophers, it were somewhat difficult to distinguish between buffoonery and melancholy, life itself being a comic drama or a dramatic comedy."

In the next paragraph we read a statement that moves in the opposite direction: "Thus it is that that which the inclination of our minds toward farce takes for a wretched piece of wit exists most of the time in the mind of the author as an important truth proclaimed with majesty!" The potential oscillation between grotesque and sublime, latent in Hugo's preface, is explicitly posed here as a problem of interpretation. To the aesthetic question concerning the genius of cruelty and the ethical question concerning the identity of difference of good and evil is now added a rhetorical question that concerns figurative language and the interpretation of the distinction between grotesque and sublime.

The reversal involved in Lautréamont's two statements concerning the appearance and reality of grotesque and sublime coincides with the ambiguity of the figurative—

the "criminal use . . . of a figure of rhetoric"—and the literal—the "exactness" of a comparison based on optics. The field of play of the opposition between grotesque and sublime coincides now with that of figurative language—or the distinction between the literal and the figural. We return, therefore, once again to the principal issue of the Hugolian sublime, as this was figured by *L'Homme qui Rit.*

The concluding lines of this strophe (IV-2) confirm the connection between the question of the grotesque and sublime and the issue of literal and figural language. "Two enormous towers [*tours*] appeared in the valley. . . . I said this at the beginning," Lautréamont reminds us. It is precisely as *tours*—that is, as towers, but also as *tournures,* turns of phrase or tropes—that the literal and figural come together in the opening lines of the strophe. "Multiplying them by two," Lautréamont continues, "the product is four . . . but I could not clearly see the necessity for this arithmetical operation." This, of course, returns us to the beginning: "Two pillars that it was not difficult . . . to take for two baobab trees appeared in the valley, larger than two pins. As a matter of fact, they were two enormous towers"—"deux tours énormes"—which is also to say "turns" or "tropes," as well as "tricks." As rhetorical figures, therefore, we have four terms: *pillars, baobabs, pins,* and *towers* (*tours*). As we have seen, the next two sentences, which analyze the comparisons as figures, carry out precisely a kind of "arithmetic operation," demonstrating that the terms are commutable or equivalent. If we take "it was two *tours*" literally as towers, we have two terms: two towers. If we take them figuratively (or is it literally?) as two tropes, we have two comparisons: the pillar with the baobab and the pins with the tower—four terms of comparison. Thus, we have two things, but four words ("substantives"), and the "two unities of the multiplicand!" appear to be the undecidability of the *tour* itself—as literal/figural.

After the literal dimension is added to the comparison, seen from a figurative point of view, the "apparent seriousness of what is really only grotesque" is reversed or corrected in terms of a grotesque appearance of what is really serious. In the text itself, it is the reversibility of "an ass eating a fig" and "a fig eating an ass (these two circumstances do not occur very often, except in poetry)" that repeats the two alternatives concerning the sublime and the grotesque, the serious and the comic, and indicates the humor of both. A second reversal of grotesque and sublime occurs with the remark, "It frequently may happen . . . that I enunciate solemnly the most clownish propositions . . . but I do not find this a reason peremptorily sufficient to enlarge the mouth," a statement that does not so much privilege one pole of the alternative as simply insert the commentary itself into the very mode of ambiguous reversal that is at issue here. This is what Blanchot refers to as Lautréamont's "ironizing of his own irony"—a reversal that contains the reversal of its own reversal. The humor of these pages is intensified by the fact that the play between literal and figural (and their reversals) operates across various levels of the text. If, for example, the discussion of the "cock" follows that of the "ass," on the level of the signified, the movement of the text itself seems to literalize the French expression "aller du coq à l'âne," which means to ramble nonsensically from one thing to another. But what appears so playful here, as a kind of virtuoso trill on the question of the grotesque and the sublime, is at the heart of the puzzle posed for critics by the double work of Lautréamont-Ducasse. This alternative inhabits both *Les Chants de Maldoror* and *Poésies,* but it is intensified—*monté en épingle*— by their combination in a single oeuvre.

It would be possible to read this strophe as a mere parody of Victor Hugo or of the issues at stake in his "Preface to *Cromwell*"—a kind of "hyper-sublime," as Baudelaire might say—of the Hugolian sublime. However, given the complexity of the issue of parody/plagiarism in the poetics of Lautréamont, to read these passages as parodic play does not in the least diminish their seriousness. In the next strophe we find another allusion to Hugo in the depiction of the man hanging from the gallows, which Maldoror comes upon very much as Gwynplaine came upon the "tarred phantom" by the seacoast in *L'Homme qui rit.* "The arrival of death . . . had not occurred," Lautréamont writes of the hanging man in decidedly Hugolian language. Here a play of grotesque and sublime is once again at work. Reason is opposed to "wild vengeance," and the narration of the grotesque crime is interrupted by digressions that function as decorative arabesques on the themes of reason and logic, arabesques that turn on a certain logic of the relations between "writer" and reader.

These digressions are comic grotesques. Yet the question of reason, which they playfully thematize, has allegorical significance, as the moral presented at the end of the strophe makes clear: "The wolf no longer passes beneath the gallows. . . . It seems the animal has understood what crime is! How could he not understand, when human beings themselves have rejected to this indescribable point the empire of reason, installing in place of this dethroned queen nothing but ferocious vengeance."

The terms *pillar* and *pin,* which implicitly return with the gallows, form a leitmotif throughout *Les Chants.* The two terms compared "with exactness" in IV-2 appear earlier in *Les Chants* as the "wasps . . . that fly around the columns like thick waves of dark hair," imagery that links both the pillar and the pin to the gibbet from which the head hangs from its hair. Finally, the two terms come together in the "spinal column," which is both knife and "avenging spine"—*épine dorsale vengeresse.*" The pillar and pin are thus thematically related to the dagger, the instrument of vengeance that unites Maldoror and his enemies. Maldoror receives a dagger blow from the thunderbolt sent by the Almighty. He claims that mathematics gives him "a dagger" to insert "in the viscera of man." But Maldoror himself has a dagger inserted in his own viscera. For in the passage that describes him as a kind of dismembered, or grotesquely composite, body, the blade of a dagger is said to serve as his spinal column. And it is this dagger that is ultimately withdrawn when, in the last lines of this last canto, the spider declares the end of Maldoror's punishment: " 'Wake, Maldoror! The hypnotic spell that has weighed upon your cerebrospinal system for ten years

of nights is lifted.' " The dagger thus relates to Maldoror both as subject and object of vengeance.

If, as we have suggested, Maldoror's struggle with the Almighty is a drama of finitude, what about his "war against man" in the second half of *Les Chants*? Not surprisingly, the struggle between Maldoror and his *semblables* is not structurally so different from his struggle with the Almighty. The fear that structured the respectful symmetry between Maldoror and the Omnipotent—"Two monarchs—I fear him; he fears me"—returns as the mutual "trembling hatred" felt between Maldoror and his fellow men. The cruelty of the Creator is replaced by the crime of man. In the strophe IV-3, as we have seen, the *loup*— the wolf (but the word also signifies, according to the Robert dictionary, *fault* or *flaw*)—learns from human atrocities "what crime is." A structure of vengeance repeats the specular and dialectical operations at play in the Christian binary opposition of sin and repentance. The vicious rivalry between human beings repeats the movement of mimesis involved in the desire to be God. What remains constant is the play of dialectical negation.

In the second half of *Les Chants,* the conflict between Maldoror and his *semblables* is increasingly developed in relation to an internal doubling of self-consciousness. The fear previously felt between Maldoror and the Omnipotent, and between our hero and his fellow men, is now internal to Maldoror. Earlier interrupted in the process of writing by the tempest, expression of divine vengeance, Maldoror is himself now "free like the tempest." He "fears nothing, unless it be himself." The problem of finitude is increasingly posed in relation to the question of subjectivity.

"So what if some furtive shadow, excited by the praiseworthy goal of avenging humanity, so unjustly attacked by me . . . should surreptitiously open the door to my room, brushing against the wall like the wing of a seagull, and thrust a dagger into the side of the celestial wrecker," Maldoror declares proleptically in the second canto. For a spectral apparition of conscience materializes in the strophe IV-4 as a specular image of Maldoror himself—"On the wall of my room . . . what shadow outlines with an incomparable power the phantasmagoric projection of its shriveled silhouette?" Maldoror's struggle with his *semblables*—"man instills a sense of horror in his fellow men"—is literalized here as a confrontation with his own double, as a *"méconnaissance* [nonrecognition/ repudiation]" of his own mirror image: "All that is left for me to do is to smash that mirror with the aid of a rock. . . . This is not the first time that the nightmare of a temporary loss of memory has taken up residence in my imagination when, by the inflexible laws of optics, it has happened to me to be confronted with the *méconnaissance* of my own reflection!" It is metamorphosis that breaks the glass—"I no longer belonged to humanity." Through metamorphosis "there remained not the least trace of divinity. . . . My conscience made me no reproaches." Metamorphosis means liberation from the dialectical framework of virtue and vice, punishment and reward, or, in other words, freedom from the whole network of specular exchanges. It is ambiguously sublime and grotesque.

"Was this a reward?" Maldoror asks of his metamorphosis. "I no longer belonged to humanity. . . . I tried hard to identify what virtuous act I had performed to merit this unheard of favor on the part of Providence." The fiction of reward is negated by a fiction of punishment: "It is perhaps not without utility to proclaim that this degradation was probably merely a punishment inflicted on me by divine justice." We are once again in the realm of Baudelaire's "reward and punishment—two forms of eternity." Maldoror eventually concludes that "the metamorphosis never appeared to me as anything but the lofty and magnanimous echo of a perfect and long-awaited happiness." Metamorphosis presents yet another response to the problem of finitude—and to the question of good and evil.

The question of subjectivity is introduced most explicitly in relation to the issue of finitude in the strophe V-3, where Maldoror refuses sleep. Asleep one is vulnerable to psychic intrusion, to negations of the will by the "Celestial Bandit"—"spy of my causality." The field is open for the limitations of finitude. The will is helpless to fight back. "My subjectivity and the Creator, this is too much for one brain," Maldoror declares peremptorily. "Autonomy—or let them change me into a hippopotamus." The shift from the struggle with God to "me alone against humanity" displaces the question of finitude toward the issue of subjectivity.

According to Henri Birault, in its specifically modern version finitude is considered a privation imposed by the infinite term, the Divine or Perfect Being. The infinite term is the agent of negativity as cause of the limitation of the finite term. In the modern version of the problem of finitude, the subject attempts to fight back, to overcome the limitations of its finite character, through the infinite reach of his or her will or desire. The desire to be God is the expression of an unlimited freedom of the will, which links the idea of finitude with freedom and transgression. Freedom as transgression depends upon the Christian thinking of the fall and of sin. Interpreting the idea of finitude as a "speculative transposition of the theme of sin," Birault suggests, enables us to see "the very essence of modern subjectivity as the freedom of negativity." According to Birault, therefore, the problematic of finitude, in which finitude is determined through freedom, is identified with the emergence of the problematic of the subject. Freedom achieved through, or experienced as, transgression (associated with the desire to be God—the desire for nonlimitation or for absolute autonomy) is an individuating principle for the subject. Through transgression, the subject replaces the infinite term through the incorporation (as infinite will) of the infinity, or absolute autonomy, of the transcendent term. Promethean man—the man of infinite will—replaces God, and yet, as Promethean man, the subject remains a kind of mirror of the conception of the infinite powers of the Omnipotent.

This is the central difficulty within *Les Chants de Maldoror.* Maldoror is in desperate search of autonomy, but the notion of autonomy and the search for it are caught within a mimetic circularity. The battle for autonomy occurs within a heteronomous framework. Autonomy derived through mimetic appeal to the autonomy of the other is caught in an ironic impasse: the more one develops this autonomy, the less autonomous one becomes, for the more one is engaged in reactive imitation. This irony is brought home in *Les Chants* by the fact that Maldoror, who proclaims his refusal to sleep on the grounds of his subjective will, is awakened at the end of *Les Chants* by the spider: " 'Wake, Maldoror! The hypnotic spell that has weighed upon your cerebrospinal system for ten years of nights is lifted.' "

In recent decades transgression has become a critical or philosophical theme—a philosopheme—as well as a literary one. Writing, or textual productivity, has itself become identified with a critical or ideological thematics of transgression. In the case of Lautréamont-Ducasse, the ideological background of various critical enthusiasms is particularly pertinent, since the work was twice saved from oblivion by the force of specific critical ideologies that found in the work of Lautréamont-Ducasse the answer to their dreams. What Francis Ponge has called the "dispositif Maldoror-Poésies" today carries the full burden of the critical ideologies that have appropriated *Les Chants* and *Poésies* and necessarily inflect interpretation of the double work of Lautréamont-Ducasse.

Les Chants de Maldoror was rediscovered by the surrealists, for whom it became a kind of sacred work. Lautréamont was cast in the role of hero (of truly mythic proportions) for admirers of literature of revolt. The double work of Lautréamont-Ducasse was then reborn through the *Tel Quel* group's critique of the surrealist appropriation of Lautréamont as idealist, or logocentric. In the *Tel Quel* context, the work was reappropriated in relation to an ideology of materialism, which refers in this case to a materialism of the letter—an emphasis on textual production of meaning as opposed to a mimetic or representational use of language. What remains constant in this shift is the value of transgression, which has been displaced from the psychological to the "material" realm. "Materialism" (or text) is portrayed as being intrinsically transgressive, transgressive of idealism and of everything it could be said to ground: the law as theological, or simply logical, the *one,* or unity, which, as Blanchot puts it, opens presence or the field of representation. Whereas *Les Chants* was extolled by the surrealists as the ne plus ultra of literature of revolt, *Poésies* became, for *Tel Quel* critics, a veritable icon of text as *écriture transfinie,* alongside *Les Chants.* The implication is that the two texts bear a common relationship to the philosopheme transgression, inherited from Bataille among others.

In relation to *Les Chants,* transgression has simply been displaced from the level of representation (or theme) to that of textual production. The *Tel Quel* critics agree with the surrealist views of *Les Chants* as an epic of transgression but emphasize the transgression of writing itself, the textual performance of *Les Chants,* which they consider to parallel, and in a sense perform, the transgression represented in the text. The *Tout Puissant* thus becomes a sort of allegory for the law as unity that grounds representation, for grammar that constrains discourse into the narrow channels of signification.

Whereas the traditional readings of Lautréamont respect

an axiomatics of transgression represented in the work, the reading we have presented here, supported by Henri Birault's analysis of finitude, suggests that transgression in *Les Chants de Maldoror* is itself eminently metaphysical. It belongs to a metaphysics of the will. As Birault suggests, transgression belongs to the thinking of finitude, to the developments in the history of philosophy from Descartes through Kant, to an "essential 'insurrection' through which, from Descartes to Nietzsche and in the death of God, a new figure of Being constitutes itself, that of subjectivity [Birault, "Heidegger et la pensée"]. In other words, transgression belongs very much within the closure of metaphysics. In *Les Chants de Maldoror* transgression belongs to a thinking of finitude, which inhabits a dialectical and representational field.

Maldoror does not oppose a transgressive arbitrariness to the unity or coercive order of the Creator. He doubles the arbitrariness of the Creator, an arbitrariness that testifies to his infinite power, his absolute autonomy. The question of the genius of cruelty depends upon this identification. Nor does Lautréamont transgress the order of representation, and therefore the order and unity of the Perfect Being or the law. Instead, he dramatizes writing itself as one spectacle among other representations of transgression. Self-conscious play with the mechanisms of representation—the celebrated "lucidity" of Lautréamont—does not so much subvert representation as remark the interdependence between the theme of transgression and the representational framework. Representation is not itself transgressed, as contemporary critics such as Philippe Sollers have argued. Representation—mimesis—supports the scenes of transgression that depend on the representational, mimetic framework. Transgression is presented as spectacle, as "theatrical scenes."

Transgression is neither advocated nor performed. It is represented and critiqued, though not on moral grounds, as Michel Pierssens has argued, so much as on philosophical grounds. Transgression is advocated and acted out by the character Maldoror—including the character as "writer"—and critiqued by the text as philosophically undesirable. The relationship between the three "characters" of *Les Chants*—"man, the Creator, and myself," as Maldoror puts it at the beginning of the sixth canto—is characterized in terms of a "circulatory apparatus." This image of going around in circles is reinforced by the judgment that Maldoror had "transgressed the rules of logic, committed a vicious circle" by existing in the radical isolation he so stubbornly enjoys throughout the first five cantos. "Consequently he decided to move nearer to more urban areas." This could be taken as evidence of the transgressive thrust of *Les Chants,* a transgression of logic that marks a liberation from its constraints. But we must remember that it is mathematics, associated with logic, that is on the side of the infinite in *Les Chants,* and of an infinite beyond good and evil—more a Nietzschean will to power and less a metaphysics of the will. The charge of the "vicious circle" suggests a critique of the endless dialectical reversals, the fundamentally mimetic basis of the movements of transgression represented within *Les Chants.* Thus the critique is not one of logic from the perspective of transgression, but rather one that underlines

the philosophical weakness of a thinking of transgression that poses as radical and isolated but that is caught up in a circulation of dialectical reversal and negation. When the end of this section leaves us on the "pont du Carrousel," there is a sense in which *Les Chants de Maldoror* reinforces the "eminently philosophical conception" of the critical force of the image of the (vicious) circle. For the circle is the figure of totalization and closure. Transgression is what keeps the "circulatory apparatus" of the text turning. The opposition between sublime and grotesque is the principal mechanism of transgressive reversal. These are the issues that the closure or circularity in the exchange between the three terms God, man, and Maldoror makes clear. (pp. 125-53)

Suzanne Guerlac, "Lautréamont," in her The Impersonal Sublime: Hugo, Baudelaire, Lautréamont, *Stanford University Press, 1990, pp. 123-81.*

FURTHER READING

Criticism

Bersani, Leo. "Desire and Metamorphosis." In his *A Future for Astyanax: Character and Desire in Literature,* pp. 189-229. Boston: Little, Brown and Co., 1976.

> Examines the metamorphosis of identity in *Les chants de Maldoror,* concluding that the work is "one of literature's most daring enterprises of decentralization."

Camus, Albert. "The Poets' Rebellion." In his *The Rebel: An Essay on Man in Revolt,* pp. 81-99. Translated by Anthony Bower. New York: Vintage International, 1991.

> Discusses contradiction in Lautréamont's attitude toward revolt, and discerns therein a desire for annihilation.

Fowlie, Wallace. *Lautréamont.* New York: Twayne, 1973, 135 p.

> A biographical and critical introduction to Lautréamont, including a brief outline of critical reaction to Lautréamont and his relationship to the Decadent movement of the late nineteenth century.

Lawlor, Patricia M. "Figuring (Out) Maldoror: 'Nous ne sommes plus dans la narration.' Narration in the *Chants de Maldoror.*" *Nineteenth-Century French Studies* 16, Nos. 3-4 (Spring-Summer 1988): 372-78.

> Argues that the rhetorical figures in *Les chants de Maldoror* are "synonymous with narration."

Nesselroth, Peter W. "Lautréamont's Plagiarisms; or, The Poetization of Prose Texts." In *Pre-Text, Text, Context: Essays on Nineteenth-Century French Literature,* edited by Robert L. Mitchell, pp. 185-95. Columbus: Ohio State University, 1980.

> Examines Lautréamont's "borrowed descriptions," particularly his reliance on *L'encyclopédie d'histoire naturelle du Dr Chenu.* Nesselroth argues that Lautréamont

created an original work by transforming such scientific documents.

Pickering, Robert. *Lautréamont-Ducasse: Image, Theme and Self-Identity.* Glasgow: University of Glasgow French and German Publications, 1990, 84 p.

Explores "the problematics of pseudonym and identity" apparent in the works of Lautréamont.

Porter, Laurence M. "Submission to the Father: From Chaos to Geometry in the *Chants de Maldoror.*" In his *The Literary Dream in French Romanticism: A Psychoanalytic Interpretation,* pp. 100-22. Detroit: Wayne State University Press, 1979.

Interprets Maldoror's relationship to God as a symbol for the father-son relationship.

Sussman, Henry. "The Anterior Tail: The Code of *Les chants de Maldoror.*" *MLN* 89, No. 6 (December 1974): 957-77.

Discusses *Les chants de Maldoror* as a violent assault on ordered literary texts that prefigures the direction of the development of modern literature.

Taylor, Simon Watson. "Maldoror's First Hundred Years." *London Magazine,* No. 100 (July-August 1969): 112-22.

Traces critical reception of *Les chants de Maldoror* in its first one hundred years of publication, asserting that "Lautréamont's genius lies perhaps in the fact that, deliberately or not, he went so much further than the terms of reference he set himself."

Winspur, Steven. "Lautréamont and the Question of the Intertext." *Romanic Review* LXXVI, No. 2 (March 1985): 192-201.

Contends that Lautréamont "is the very embodiment of intertextuality," and that his use of the intertext has spawned opposing definitions of the term.

Woodard, Kay B. "A Poetics of Violence: Aggression, Reform, and the Reader in *Les chants de Maldoror.*" *L'Esprit Crèateur* XVIII, No. 4 (Winter 1978): 15-24.

Attempts to show how Chant I, 6 shatters "the reader's illusion that he is either morally different from, or superior to, Maldoror."

Additional coverage of Lautréamont's life and career is contained in the following source published by Gale Research: *Nineteenth-Century Literature Criticism,* **Vol. 12.**

Joseph Sheridan Le Fanu

1814-1873

(Full name Joseph Thomas Sheridan Le Fanu; also wrote under the pseudonyms Reverend Francis Purcell and Charles de Cresserons) Irish novelist, short story writer, poet, journalist, and editor.

INTRODUCTION

Le Fanu is a major figure among Victorian-era authors of Gothic and supernatural fiction. Critics praise his short stories and novels for their evocative descriptions of physical settings, convincing use of supernatural elements, and insightful characterization. Scholars also observe that Le Fanu's subtle examinations of the psychological life of his characters distinguish his works from those of earlier Gothic writers.

Born in Dublin, Le Fanu was the second of three children of a Protestant clergyman. He began writing poetry as a teenager and was privately educated by tutors until entering Trinity College, Dublin, in 1833. There, Le Fanu studied law, although he never practiced; instead he launched a joint career in journalism and literature. He contributed regularly to the *Dublin University Magazine* and gained recognition for his short stories and his ballads "Phaudrig Crohoore" and "Shamus O'Brien." Between 1838 and 1840 Le Fanu wrote short stories and poetry under the pseudonym Reverend Francis Purcell; these works were posthumously collected as *The Purcell Papers.* In 1839 Le Fanu bought three Dublin periodicals and combined them to form the *Evening Mail,* a conservative publication in which many of his early works appeared. During this period he published two historical novels, *The Cock and Anchor, Being a Chronicle of Old Dublin City* and *The Fortunes of Colonel Torlogh O'Brien: A Tale of the Wars of King James,* as well as his first collection of short stories, *Ghost Stories and Tales of Mystery.* These early works were virtually ignored by both critics and the reading public. Le Fanu married Susanna Bennett in 1844, and together they became prominent in Dublin social and cultural circles. Le Fanu was considered a brilliant conversationalist and was a popular member of society until his wife's death in 1858. His anguish caused him to withdraw from his companions, who labeled him the "Invisible Prince." During this time Le Fanu produced the four novels for which he is best known: *The House by the Churchyard, Wylder's Hand, Uncle Silas: A Tale of Bartram-Haugh* and *Guy Deverell.* In addition, he became the editor of the *Dublin University Magazine* in 1859, and, in 1861, assumed its proprietorship as well. Le Fanu continued managing and editing the publication until a few months before his death in 1873.

In his earliest short stories, primarily those collected in *Ghost Stories and Tales of Mystery* and *The Purcell Papers,*

Le Fanu only occasionally displayed the inventive use of the supernatural and psychological character studies that distinguish his most esteemed works. The five longer stories in the later collection *In a Glass Darkly* are widely acknowledged as his best work in the genre. In these stories Le Fanu combined many of the themes and techniques of traditional Gothic literature with those of modern psychological fiction. Le Fanu used the recurrent character Dr. Martin Hesselius, a German physician specializing in mental disorders, to introduce each narrative as a case history illustrating both supernatural and psychological phenomena. This technique allowed Le Fanu to successfully link the stories and to explore the psychology of his characters. For example, in "Green Tea" Hesselius reports the case of Reverend Jennings, whose habit of drinking strong green tea causes him to see a small black talking monkey which torments him with its blasphemous chatter until he ultimately commits suicide. Critics have also expressed high praise for "Carmilla," in which Hesselius suggests a connection between the bloodlust of a female vampire and lesbian sexual desires.

During his lifetime, Le Fanu's works were moderately successful, although they received scant critical attention.

213

During the twentieth century, however, the prominent ghost-story writer M. R. James drew attention to Le Fanu by writing introductions to several reissued volumes of his out-of-print works. V. S. Pritchett and Elizabeth Bowen also wrote essays championing Le Fanu as one of Gothic literature's foremost figures. In 1978, Jack Sullivan summarized the opinion of modern critics in his assessment of Le Fanu's achievement: "Beginning with Le Fanu, one of the distinctive features of modern ghostly fiction is . . . [the] synthesis of psychology and supernaturalism." While he is not well-known today as a novelist, Le Fanu is noted by horror writers and aficionados as an innovative and masterful writer of psychological horror stories and as a pivotal figure in the history of supernatural fiction.

PRINCIPAL WORKS

SHORT FICTION

Ghost Stories and Tales of Mystery   1851
Chronicles of Golden Friars   1871
In a Glass Darkly   1872
*The Purcell Papers   (short stories and poetry)   1880
The Watcher, and Other Weird Stories   1894
Madam Crowl's Ghost, and Other Tales of Mystery   1923
Best Ghost Stories of J. S. Le Fanu   1963
Ghost Stories and Mysteries   1975

OTHER MAJOR WORKS

"Phaudrig Crohoore"   (ballad)   1837; published in journal *Dublin University Magazine*
The Cock and Anchor, Being a Chronicle of Old Dublin City [as Charles de Cresserons]   (novel)   1845; also published as *Morley Court* [revised edition], 1873, and as *The Cock and the Anchor,*   1895
The Fortunes of Colonel Torlogh O'Brien: A Tale of the Wars of King James   (novel)   1847
†"Shamus O'Brien"   (ballad)   1850; published in journal *Dublin University Magazine*
The House by the Churchyard   (novel)   1863
Uncle Silas: A Tale of Bartram-Haugh   (novel)   1864
Wylder's Hand [as Charles de Cresserons]   (novel) 1864
Guy Deverell   (novel)   1865
All in the Dark   (novel)   1866
The Tenants of Malory   (novel)   1867
Haunted Lives   (novel)   1868
A Lost Name   (novel)   1868
The Wyvern Mystery   (novel)   1869
Checkmate   (novel)   1871
The Rose and the Key   (novel)   1871
Willing to Die   (novel)   1873
The Poems of Joseph Sheridan Le Fanu   (poetry)   1896
The Collected Works of Joseph Sheridan Le Fanu. 52 vols. (novels, short stories, and poetry)   1977

*The pieces collected in this work were originally published under the pseudonym Francis Purcell between 1838 and 1840.

†This work was written in 1837.

CRITICISM

Ken Scott   (essay date 1968)

[*In the following essay, Scott explores the themes of love and death in "The Room in the Dragon Volant."*]

Joseph Sheridan Le Fanu's **"The Room in the Dragon Volant,"** the fourth of five tales collected as *In a Glass Darkly* (1872), tells of a naive young Englishman who, while traveling in post-Napoleonic Europe, is duped and almost murdered by a beautiful woman who he thinks loves him. Richard Beckett—his name suggests both the Crusades hero and the medieval martyr—spends his time adopting a romantic posture in his attack on life. He enjoys fanciful literature, delighting in the *Arabian Nights* and Sir Walter Scott's romances; he speaks of himself in the language of medieval romance: he is "a knight" or "a champion"; his whistling is his "minstrelsy". His notions of amorous intrigue are "founded upon his ideal of the French school of lovemaking." A dandy, he imitates Brummell's manner of dress, and when he speaks to his servant, it is "with the peculiar familiarity which the old French comedy establishes between master and valet." Thus, his approach to life is in terms of the romantic and the theatrical, and it is his inability to see the world whole that results in his failure to perceive that the wife of the Count de St. Alyre is not an unhappy woman waiting to be carried off by a lover, but a scheming charlatan, in league with rogues to kill the young man for his money by burying him alive.

Most of Le Fanu's recent commentators praise *In a Glass Darkly* but fail to provide a detailed discussion of **"The Room in the Dragon Volant."** S. M. Ellis, in *Wilkie Collins, Le Fanu and Others* (1931), does little more than describe a possible source for an incident in the masked ball scene. V. S. Pritchett, in an essay in *The Living Novel* (1947), finds *In a Glass Darkly* "worth reading," but has nothing specific to say about this tale. Nelson Browne, the author of the excellent study, *Sheridan Le Fanu* (1951), devotes only three paragraphs to the story. He states that it is "a superb story of crime," but laments that "a certain indispensible element of horror is eclipsed by the details of romantic intrigue." I do not believe this criticism is well founded. I think that the juxtaposition of terror and romance—"Death and Love, together mated," as Le Fanu states it—is not a mistake, and in this essay I plan to demonstrate that the story is a skillfully wrought entity in which apparent antitheses are carefully reconciled.

The tale begins as Beckett, on his way to Paris in the late spring of 1815, assists the Countess de St. Alyre and her aged husband when their carriage almost upsets. That evening at an inn he hears her singing a ballad called "Death and Love, Together Mated," and shortly after, he dreams that he is in a huge cathedral, that the Countess is about to be buried alive there, and that he can neither speak nor move. The experience frightens him, and later, when traveling with a man who calls himself the Marquis d'Harmonville, Beckett finds that part of his dream comes true: he is given coffee drugged with Mortis Imago and becomes temporarily paralyzed. While he is under the influence of the drug, his pockets are rifled. However, the effect wears off quickly, and when he arrives in Paris he pursues the beautiful and (as he believes) unhappy Countess.

Through d'Harmonville, Beckett obtains a room in the ancient inn of the Dragon Volant so that he can attend a masked ball at Versailles, and during the ball he makes an assignation to meet the Countess in the nearby Parc of the Chateau de la Carque, the residence of the Countess. In the moonlight, she confesses her love for the young Englishman, and he agrees to elope with her to Switzerland, bringing with him thirty thousand pounds in gold and notes. A secret exit from his room in the Dragon Volant enables him to come and go without being seen.

Two nights later Beckett makes his way to the Chateau; he is to flee with the Countess while her husband attends a relative's funeral. But when the young man arrives, the woman gives him coffee—drugged, once again, with Mortis Imago—which paralyzes him. The Count enters, takes Beckett's gold, and with the assistance of d'Harmonville (who, it is revealed, is a doctor, not an aristocrat), places the young man in a coffin. During the entire time, Beckett can see and hear, but he cannot speak or move. However, his life is saved by the arrival of a police officer who, on the pretext of searching for contraband, demands that the coffin be opened. With the discovery of the drugged Beckett, the Count and Countess are arrested.

Using the first person point of view, Le Fanu lets us experience the adventure as it happens to Beckett, and thus we are unaware of the plot against him. Nevertheless, the suspicion that the Englishman is being deceived is created early in our minds, for Le Fanu, working with symbol, image, and allusion, presents a profusion of significant impressions which opposes Beckett's appraisal of the Count and Countess and foreshadows the denouement. Thus, tension is created when Beckett's belief that his affair will culminate in a romantic elopement conflicts with our own feeling that it will lead to tragedy.

First of all, for most of the story the Countess's face is hidden from view—a symbol of her deceit. It is veiled when Beckett sees her on the road.

Later, in the inn yard it is similarly hidden: "A little to the rear . . . stood the Countess, . . . her thick black veil down." When Beckett looks into her room in the inn, he sees only the illusion of her face, for it is reflected in a mirror: "I might, indeed, have mistaken it for a picture." At the Versailles ball, when the Countess acts as the interpreting magician for the Chinese oracle, her face is heavily disguised ("dark, fixed, and solemn," with the eyebrows "black and enormously heavy"); later, when she impersonates Mademoiselle de la Valliere, it is hidden by a mask, and Beckett describes her as "my unknown friend

in the mask" and as "the masque," the last suggesting overtones of not only disguise but also deceit. It is not until Beckett meets her in the moonlit park that she unveils, confessing her "affection" for him. But in this romantic setting, Beckett does not "see" her for what she is, and it is only in the final scene, when he has been made aware of her role in the plot against him, that he looks upon her "real" face, the "face from which the mask has dropped." It is "dark and witch-like."

Secondly, at the beginning of the story, both the ballad which the Countess sings and the dream Beckett has shortly after clearly foreshadow the direction of the narrative:

> Death and Love, together mated,
>   Watch and wait in ambuscade;
> At early morn, or else belated,
>   They meet and mark the man or maid.
>
> Burning sigh, or breath that freezes,
>   Numbs or maddens man or maid;
> Death and Love the victim seizes,
>   Breathing from their ambuscade.

The "ambuscade"—or trap—has been set for Beckett by the Countess ("Death and Love"); "early morn" in line 3 reappears in the story as the time set for the lovers' first tryst. "Belated," in the same line, which has the archaic meaning of "overtaken by night," is related to the nocturnal elopement, for when Beckett makes his way to the Chateau, "the darkness deepens." In the fifth line, "breath that freezes" is echoed in Beckett's dream as "in a whisper that froze me," when the Countess, about to be murdered in the cathedral, speaks to the young man. The "buried-alive" motif in the dream, as well as the image in the ballad that Love "numbs" its victim, foreshadows the climax of the story when Beckett, paralyzed by the drugged coffee, is placed living in the coffin.

Furthermore, since the Count and Countess are motivated by their desire for Beckett's money, there are many images of gold clustered with reference to love and death. After Beckett's first meeting with the alluring but treacherous woman, she departs "in the golden sunlight." Later, when a servant whom Beckett pays to obtain information about the Countess fails to learn anything significant, the Englishman describes the incident as "a poor harvest" for his "golden sowing." The escutcheon of the Count is a red stork set against a gold field. "The stork is a bird of prey," we are told; and a character observes: "Red, too!—blood red! . . . The symbol is appropriate." On the sign of the Inn of the Dragon Volant, the wings and tail of the dragon are mottled with gold. Symbolically, the tail ends in a "burnished point barbed like the dart of death." Dragons, in folklore, traditionally love gold, and a flying dragon, as is the one on the inn sign, is sometimes known as a "Wyvern," a word derived from the Old French *guivre*, viper or serpent. In addition, at the masked ball, when the Countess is playing the part of the magician, she is garbed in a robe embroidered in black and gold, bound about the waist with a broad belt of gold. The usher who walks before her carries a golden wand, and the sole payment that the magician will accept for her performance is gold. The Chinese palanquin which holds the mysterious oracle is gilded, and after the ball, when the palanquin is opened, it is found to contain a corpse. Finally, at the conclusion of the narrative, after the Count and Countess have been arrested, they are convicted of murder when the body of one of their earlier victims is disinterred and identified by a gold dental plate in the mouth of the skull.

Perhaps Le Fanu's most interesting use of an allusion that both incorporates the themes of terror and love and foreshadows the outcome of Beckett's affair occurs during the scene in the park after the Versailles ball. When Beckett takes the Countess in his arms she murmurs, "Oh! Richard! Oh, my king!" These words are the opening of the well known aria, "O Richard, o mon roi, l'univers t'abandonne," in Gretry's *Richard Coeur-de-Lion* (1784), and their appearance at this moment in the Le Fanu tale is unusually appropriate. In the Gretry opera, the aria is given to Blondel, Richard's faithful minstrel, who tells of the treachery against the king by his enemies and of his long imprisonment in Germany. In its shadowy way, the reference to Blondel's narration provides one more hint of the plot against the Englishman, one more indirect revelation of the denouement, when Richard will be incarcerated in a coffin. Nor would Le Fanu's allusion have been lost on many nineteenth century readers, for the Gretry air, in an English version arranged for baritone and soprano, was a favorite at Victorian musicales.

In addition, Le Fanu utilizes his imagery in the Love-Death configuration not only to foreshadow doom but also to point up the moral lesson. Beckett's terrifying near-death can be interpreted as punishment for his illicit love. The young man is clearly aware that his pursuit of the Countess is unholy, for he describes himself as engaged in "secret and guilty practices." At one point, he is "struck with horror" at the "madness and guilt of his pursuit", and at another, he compares himself to "a poacher" trespassing "on the grounds of an unsuspecting lord". In the final sentence of the story he describes his adventure as "an early and terrible lesson in the ways of sin". The corrupt nature of Beckett's passion is rendered metaphorically in Le Fanu's descriptions of the lovers' meeting places as blighted and death-ridden. A grove where a nocturnal assignation takes place looks "as black as a clump of gigantic hearse plumes." The small Greek temple or shrine in the grove is in a half-ruinous state, while moss grows on pedestal and cornice, and signs of decay are apparent in its discoloured and weather-worn marble. A second meeting place is "a ruined chapel" in "a little churchyard"; the churchyard itself is "an ancient cemetery". Sitting upon the edge of a tombstone, Beckett waits for his love. Nearby is a shrub, "in form like a miniature popular, with the darker foliage of the yew". "I did not know the name of the plant," Beckett remarks, "but I have often seen it in such funereal places." Furthermore, some of Le Fanu's language has Biblical and sexual associations. The park in which Beckett is ensnared by the Countess not only is reminiscent of a gloom-filled Garden of Eden, but it is in the park that the young Englishman has the "icy, snake-like thought" that his passion for the woman might lead to his death. This snake image is related to the dragon motif in the tale, for we recall that men have disappeared mysteriously from the Dragon Volant, that the dragon's

tail on the inn sign is "barbed like the dart of death", and that the word "dragon" originally meant "serpent." In addition, religious imagery is combined with erotic when the "ruined chapel" where the Countess waits for Beckett is described as an "inner sanctuary, the arched windows of which are screened almost entirely with masses of ivy." Elsewhere, the young man makes his way through the park toward the tufted masses of the grove which the Countess has appointed as the trysting place. When Beckett meets "the idol of his lawless adoration", a "mysterious key" enables him to leave the inn by a secret passage. That the key itself—given to Beckett by the Countess—suggests that the woman has awakened the young man's sexual nature is hinted at when Beckett tells us that, before going to sleep, he "kissed the mysterious key that her hand had pressed that night, and placed it under his pillow." Throughout the story, the imagery, with its references to keys, dressing-cases, arched windows of inner sanctuaries, snakes, and blighted gardens, clearly implies that the hero's love is sexual, unlawful, and impure; and in Victorian terms, certainly, a love that is illicit and without spirituality is the handmaiden of disaster.

Unlike some of his contemporaries, Le Fanu selected his details not so much for their picturesque qualities as for their contribution to the structure and theme of his narrative. His remarkable use of symbol, image, and allusion to foreshadow, to create tension, and to indicate the moral lesson is evident throughout **"The Room in the Dragon Volant."** Far from being an unhappy juxtaposition of terror tale and love story, Le Fanu's work adroitly combines the two themes. Love and Death are indeed properly wedded. (pp. 25-32)

Ken Scott, "Le Fanu's 'The Room in the Dragon Volant'," in The Lock Haven Review, *No. 10, 1968, pp. 25-32.*

Kevin Sullivan   (essay date 1972)

[*In the following essay, Sullivan examines the short stories that Le Fanu wrote between 1838 and 1840 under the pseudonym Reverend Francis Purcell.*]

The literary career of Joseph Sheridan Le Fanu began anonymously in the pages of the *Dublin University Magazine* in January 1838 with a short piece of ghostly humour called appropriately enough 'The Ghost and the Bone-Setter'. His last novel, bearing the strange and prophetic title *Willing to Die*, was ready for his London publisher, Hutchinson, when on 7 February 1873 the writer died at his home on Merrion Square, Dublin, in his fifty-ninth year. In thirty-five active years Le Fanu had produced a considerable body of work—verse, a verse drama, some fourteen novels, more than forty tales, novellas and short stories, and an uncounted number of unsigned articles and reviews written for newspapers and periodicals, of which he was at one time or another either editor or publisher or both. The journalism may be dismissed as ephemera and the verse, including the drama *Beatrice*, has for more than a century reposed in decent obscurity, a repose which few lovers of poetry would now care to disturb. But Le Fanu's prose narratives, though some of them have always enjoyed a kind of underground popularity, have not yet received the critical attention they deserve. Apart from a monograph some twenty years ago by Nelson Browne, there has been no systematic appraisal of the whole of Le Fanu's work, and other occasional critics, when not simply dismissive, have been more enthusiastic than rigorous in their judgements of the man. One of the results of this has been that the general revival of interest in Le Fanu—confidently expected from time to time by his enthusiasts—has never really developed. The underground interest, however, continues and even at times surfaces in the republication of one or other of the novels (*Uncle Silas* or *The House by the Churchyard*) or in a Grand Guignol reappearance, on stage or film, of that toothsome and insatiable vampire Carmilla.

It is one among the many wonders of English literature that, as we learned in our first year at college, the life and work of all great writers, and some who were not so great, fall conveniently into three periods—early, middle and late. Joseph Sheridan Le Fanu is nicely accommodated to this gaullish division and it is with his early period, the years 1838-48 in which his first two novels and his first stories were written, that I will be concerned here. The second stage of his career (1848-63) was given over largely to journalism and its platitudes which are, understandably, far less interesting than the remaining tales and novels which in a rush of creativity he produced in the last ten years of his life.

I have said that Le Fanu's first story was published anonymously. It would be more accurate to say that it appeared pseudonymously, being attributed to 'the Reverend Francis Purcell of Drumcoolagh', a nom de plume attached to eleven additional pieces in the *Dublin University Magazine* between January 1838 and October 1840. These were collected, edited and published under the title *The Purcell Papers* by Alfred Perceval Graves in 1880—a posthumous publication of *first stories* quite different from the *first collection* of early stories made by Le Fanu himself and published in 1851 as *Ghost Stories and Tales of Mystery.* The difference between the two collections will be worth returning to later. There was nothing exceptional in Le Fanu's use of a pseudonym, but in the use of Purcell, a Catholic clergyman, as *persona* Le Fanu allowed himself room for the expression of sentiments and sympathies (as well as a close knowledge of the Irish peasantry) to which, considering the time and place of publication, exception might have been taken if expressed in his own person. This is not to say that Le Fanu's politics or social and religious preferences were different in kind from those endorsed by *DUM,* which was sincerely Protestant, staunchly unionist, and remorselessly ascendant. He had, however, as his early work shows, a strong sense of his country's history and an awareness, however undeveloped, that Ireland's history could not be encapsulated in the formulae of caste or creed or in the slogans of party or faction, so that for him as a writer the past was usable only if he returned to it unblinkered by opinions and beliefs taken for granted in his own day and among his own kind. O'Connell and Tom Davis were not to be approved, but James II was a gracious though unfortunate prince, and even among the rebels of '98 there were those who, since their assumption into history, could be counted gallant and spirited men.

Of the twelve stories attributed to Purcell, three are comic pieces, five are tales of the super- or preternatural, and of the remaining four one is not a story at all but what its title signifies 'Scraps of Hibernian Ballads', while each of the other three reads like the sketch of an historical romance rather than a finished and self-contained narrative. 'Scraps of Hibernian Ballads' may be disposed of first, but not quite casually. The piece is more than an occasion or excuse, though it is also that, for Le Fanu publishing a few early verses of his own under the pretence that they were originally discovered by Fr Purcell. The verses themselves are of no great merit (Le Fanu did not pretend that they were) and are less likely to engage attention than Purcell's modest introduction to them. This is a brief defence of 'indigenous Irish composition in verse' which, the author tells us, had been neglected hitherto by men otherwise well-informed and even, out of literary perversity, by 'Irishmen themselves'. Poems like 'The Groves of Blarney' and, though the poet is not named, Tom Moore's pretty verses are first dismissed as spurious examples of native Irish poetry; so too is the notion that 'the prevailing of even the usual character of Irish poetry is comicality'. Exaggeration, extravagance, absurdity there may be, 'as in all countries', but 'surely it were a strange thing if Ireland, abounding as she does from shore to shore with all that is beautiful, and grand, and savage in scenery, and filled with wild recollections, vivid passions, warm affections, and keen sorrow, could find no language to speak withal, but that of mummery and jest'. Stage Irishry thus disposed of, examples are given to illustrate the skill and correctness of the Irish peasant in the poetic use of a language which, despite imperfections, reveals 'strength in its rudeness, and beauty in its wildness; and, above all, strong feeling flows through it, like fresh fountains in rugged caverns'. John Millington Synge was to take much the same view of that language a generation or so later.

The examples, unfortunately, do not sustain the ardent claim made for the language. The most likely example occurs in the last lines of a ballad on Lord Edward Fitzgerald composed, we are asked to believe, by one Michael Finley, 'in his day, perhaps, the most noted song-maker of his country'.

> My black an' bitter curse on the head, an' heart,
>   an' hand,
> That plotted, wished, an' worked the fall of this
>   Irish hero bold;
> God's curse upon the Irishman that sould his native land,
> An' hell consume to dust the hand that held the
>   thraitor's gold.

Finley is also made the author of 'Phaudrig Croohore', a ballad written while Le Fanu was still an undergraduate at Trinity College in response to his brother William's request for an Irish story in verse on the model of 'Young Lochinvar'. As a schoolboy exercise this is fine, as an imitation of Scott quite passable, but few readers will see much else to praise in it. Most readers will probably find the character of Michael Finley, though it is only sketched in, more attractive than his balladry. 'Genius is never without its eccentricities', Le Fanu remarks in explanation of Finley's refusal to allow his poetry to be copied down. 'Is my *pome* a pigsty, or what', asks Finley, 'that you want a surveyor's ground-plan of it?' And when the narrator asks him to reconsider his decision out of regard for the permanence of his reputation, he replies in the authentic accents of a poet:

> I often noticed . . . when a mist id be spreadin', a little brier to look as big, you'd think, as an oak tree; an' the same way, in the dimness iv the nightfall, I often seen a man tremblin' and crassin' himself as if a sperit was before him, at the sight iv a small thorn bush, that he'd leap over with ase if the daylight and sunshine was in it. An' that's the rason why I think it id be better for the likes iv me to be remimbered in tradition than to be written in history.

Finley is supposed to have died in 1828 and, despite his faith in tradition, to have been totally forgotten within a dozen years. One wonders whether there was, under whatever name, an original Michael Finley. Whoever he was—that is, if he was at all—young Le Fanu would probably have met him in the vicinity of Abington, Co. Limerick, where for years his father was rector, and where until the outbreak of the Tithe War in 1831 the Le Fanus, according to contemporary accounts, had enjoyed the open and untroubled regard of the people in the surrounding countryside.

However, the identity of Finley and the quality of his alleged poetry is less important than the type of poet he represents. He is, Le Fanu tells us, an 'indigenous' poet, and a notable characteristic of his poetry is that it is oral. This had of course been characteristic of poetry in Irish for more than a thousand years and when that poetry crumbled away in the general ruin of the old culture poets or would-be poets, adopting with difficulty to another idiom, would retain as many characteristics of the older poetry as could be assimilated to the new. Poetry, anyhow, lives in speech. Culture survives illiteracy. A pome is not a pigsty. Le Fanu had the facts (or one important fact) before him but, unacquainted with the tradition out of which the Finleys of Ireland had come, he can only explain his man's insistence on oral poetry as an exercise in peasant cunning: a gifted illiterate protects a literary property, which is 'to him a source of wealth and importance', by the assertion of an eccentric and exclusive copyright. What is typical of poetry is here mistaken for a peculiarity of the poet—another instance, perhaps, considering the terms of the mistake, of the confusion that can result when a Protestant ethic is applied to a Catholic peasantry. Similarly, though aware of his poet's fondness for assonantal rhyme, or 'vowelling', Le Fanu is inclined to see it as a lapse from known standards of English versification rather than a technique deliberately adopted from an older poetic tradition.

When writing verse *propria persona* Le Fanu is always proper, and he can also be playful. There is even a touch of the virtuoso in the lines which, according to his brother, he addressed at a very early age to a Miss K—.

> Your frown or your smile makes me Savage or Gay
>   In action as well as in song;
> And if 'tis decreed I at length become Gray,
>   Express but the word and I'm Young;
> And if in the Church I should ever aspire
>   With friars and abbots to cope,
> By a nod, if you please, you can make me a Prior—
>   By a word you can render me Pope.
> If you'd eat, I'm a Crab; if you'd cut, I'm your Steel,
>   As sharp as you'd get from the cutler;
> I'm your Cotten whene'er you're in want of a reel,
>   And your livery carry, as Butler.

In this humorous vein he can run on—not, as he jokes, in the manner of Cowley—but in a type of breathless doggerel that anticipates by a century the ingenuities of Ogden Nash:

> I sent you, or I mistake myself foully,
> A very excellent imitation of the poet Cowley . . .
>
> Perhaps you'd have preferred that like an old monk I had pattered on
> In the style and after the manner of the unfortunate Chatterton;
> Or that, unlike my reverend daddy's son,
> I had attempted the classicalities of the dull, though immortal Addison.

But humour and comic effect in the stories depend largely on the same kind of country speech in which the ballads of Michael Finley were composed. One reason for this is that Fr Purcell as narrator always makes a point of telling his tale in the 'exact' words, or as nearly as he can approximate them, of *his* characters. The character may be a countess, a colonel or an Irish country gentleman, and the language of the narrative is then, like the apparel and demeanour of the character, made appropriate to his station in life. In the comic tales, the characters are peasants and their language is a contrived—at least in its phonetic spelling—dialect or brogue.

In an egalitarian age there is sometimes a good deal of impatience with this sort of thing. It may be thought snooty, contemptuous, patronizing, racial or even—in some quarters—provocative. Spelled out on the page it can be inconsistent, tedious and all but incomprehensible. At best it is a compromise between the spoken and the written word, and at worst the failure, phonetically speaking, to make language look the way it sounds. A dramatic poet like John Millington Synge was to see that words have no shape, except metaphorically, and that qualities of meaning are conveyed more effectively through the rhythms of native speech than by the transmogrification of vowel and consonant; but there were no Synges in the 1830s and the society of the time was not notable for its egalitarianism. Of Le Fanu's contemporaries, Lever and Carleton (both fellow-contributors to *DUM*) were already experienced in transcribing peasant dialect. There was no need, however, for Le Fanu to look to them for a model—if a brogue, varying from place to place, could be said to have had any one model. Around his boyhood home in Limerick there had been living models in plenty, and whatever the attitude of others toward that native speech, it was for Le Fanu 'a national music that, I trust, may never, never—scouted and despised though it be—never cease, like the lost tones of our harp, to be heard in the fields of my country, in welcome or endearment, in fun or in sorrow, stirring the hearts of Irish men and Irish women'. There can be little doubt about the sincerity of that avowal.

In the first of the dialect stories ['The Ghost and the Bone-Setter'] a bone-setter, Terence Neil, is sitting watch one night in Squire Phelim's old castle reputedly haunted by the ghost of Sir Phelim's grandfather—'as good a gintleman as ever stood in shoe-leather', though inclined to drink and irascibility—whose portrait still hangs in a place of honour over the great chimney-piece. Terry has fortified himself with a bottle of holy water at one hand and a bottle of poteen at the other, and under the influence of the latter is all but mindless with sleep when the old squire, 'for all the world as if he was throwin' aff his ridin' coat', steps down out of the picture and takes a turn around the room. Numb with fear and drink Terry watches him pick up the whiskey, drain off half the bottle and then 'settle it back mighty cute entirely, in the very same spot it was in before'. But a whiff of sulphur from the old sinner sets Terry coughing and shaken awake he begins to do all in his power to placate the thirsty and talkative ghost of Sir Phelim. Nothing will satisfy the gentleman but that Terry apply his skill as bone-setter to a weakness in one of the old legs, a weakness brought on by his assignment, in another but not a better world, as a drawer of water. Terry sets to with a will. To keep up courage during the treatment, the squire reaches over his osteopath's back for the bottle of whiskey—' "Here's to your good health, Terence", says he; "an' now pull like the very divil"',' Terence pulls away at the leg, the squire pulls at the bottle—the bottle of *holy water* as it turns out—'An' with that . . . he let a screech out, you'd think the room id fairly split with it, an' made one chuck that sent the leg clane aff his body.' When Terence wakes at the light of day he is flat on his back on the castle floor with the leg of one of the great old chairs pulled clean out of its socket and held tightly in his hand. Picking himself up he is from that day forward a reformed character. 'An' as for the squire, that is the sperit, whether it was he did not like his liquor, or by rason iv the loss iv his leg, he was never known to walk agin.'

Le Fanu is sometimes thought of as an Irish gothic, but he could also, as he does here, spoof the spooks as well as exploit them, and have great fun doing so. In a later novel, *All in the Dark,* he was to make game of the spiritualists in their spookeries, as here his game is Horace Walpole in his proto-gothic *Castle of Otranto*. Among the creaking paraphernalia cluttering up that novel helmet, sword, giant, etc. there is also an ambulatory portrait, that of Alfonso, which Manfred, in a terror-stricken moment, sees 'quit its panel and descend on the floor with a grave and melancholy air'. The central fixture in **'The Bone-Setter'** (Sir Phelim in his frame above the chimney-piece) is taken from *Otranto,* transformed into a querulous but not unkindly Irish gentleman, and set walking with a far from melancholy air in the neighbourhood of whiskey and holy

water. The mimicry is obvious and may even be taken as implicit criticism of the original: a change of mood turns the paraphernalia of terror to ridicule, the evocation of what is fearful depending, in Le Fanu's practice, not on gothic gimmickry but upon the creation of an atmosphere in which the impossible becomes for a moment frightfully probable. 'Of all atmospheres, that is the most difficult to produce: it is easier to amuse, it is even easier to edify than, by suggestion, to alarm' [E. F. Benson, 'Sheridan Le Fanu', *Spectator* (1931)]. Le Fanu here is content to amuse; when he chose to alarm he would do so with a subtlety surpassing that of any of his gothic predecessors.

The technique of **'The Bone-Setter',** like that of most of the Purcell papers, is also an example of Le Fanu's skill in distancing his material—in time, in place, through character—which, if it does not increase a reader's sense of the probable, tends to lessen his concern about the improbable. The story is delivered to the reader in a series of narrative frames, one fitted inside the other, rather like those Chinese boxes which in *The Third Policeman* Flann O'Brien has set his Sergeant to making, and which the Sergeant is so successful in making progressively smaller that the innermost box of all is entirely invisible. It cannot be said that Le Fanu's subtlety goes quite so far, but the difference is more of degree than kind. There is first of all Purcell's 'residuary legatee', the anonymous editor of his manuscripts who is responsible for the selection, arrangement and general editorial framework in which the papers are presented to the public. Like a good editor this character generally keeps out of sight except for a necessary word of introduction and an occasional note or comment. Purcell himself, for fifty years a parish priest in the south of Ireland, is presented as 'a curious and industrious collector of old local traditions', with a special fondness for the marvellous and the whimsical. 'To such as may think', the editor writes, 'the composing of such productions as these inconsistent with the character and habits of a country priest, it is necessary to observe, that there did exist a race of priests—those of the old school, a race now nearly extinct—whose education abroad tended to produce in them tastes more literary than have yet been evinced by the *alumni* of Maynooth'. A man of taste and discrimination, Purcell is naturally concerned with the credibility of his narratives and for this reason he reproduces them, as he says, in the *ipissima verba* of the characters themselves. In **'The Ghost and the Bone-Setter'** an additional frame is fitted to the narrative by putting the story into the mouth of Terry Neil, son of that Terence Neil who is the protagonist of the piece. The story, slight as it is, is thus compactly dimensioned, set back in time to the eighteenth century and to a remote place, some part of distant Munster, where the incredible may not seem quite as unlikely as it otherwise might. A similar technique, though far more elaborate and complex, will be familiar to readers of *At Swim-Two-Birds* where Flann O'Brien, packing narrative within narrative, frame within frame, sets them reverberating and interacting in a way that young Le Fanu would have found truly incredible.

'Jim Sullivan's Adventures in the Great Snow' and **'The Quare Gander'** are outright farces akin to fabliaux. In the first of these the situation is not unlike that in **'The Shadow**

of the Glen': the husband in an ill-matched couple is thought to be dead (in fact he is lost in the great snow), the wife is quick to re-marry, the husband—come back to life—is mistaken for his own ghost, and there is the devil to pay before the marriage lines are again straightened out and man and wife are restored to connubial discord. **'The Quare Gander'** is the story of a companionship between a farmer and one of his flock so affectionate that the neighbours begin to talk. In the belief that the gander is possessed by the ghost of the farmer's father, the local priest attempts an exorcism, the results of which are so destructive to clerical dignity that by the priest's widespread persuasion the entire matter is hushed up and farmer and gander are left to live in peace and affection. Both stories are located in parts of Limerick familiar to Le Fanu as a young man and it may be among the peasantry of those districts that he first encountered them. If so, we may be sure that the version of either tale as told to a parson's son was considerably tamer than the original that had been current among the people. In the unlikely event that Le Fanu had either of them directly from the farmyard, he would have been careful to process them thoroughly before delivery to *DUM*. As they stand the tales are akin to fabliaux, but it is a distant kinship. None of these comic pieces was reprinted during Le Fanu's lifetime. Neither were any of the three romantic sketches, though the last of these, **'An Adventure of Hardress Fitzgerald, a Royalist Captain'**, was in a much altered form incorporated into his second novel, *Torlogh O'Brien* (1847). But all five 'mysteries' or tales of the supernatural were to reappear, at times in their original form, at other times so thoroughly reworked as to bear only a skeletal resemblance to the original. Le Fanu was not the last Irish writer to vex subsequent bibliographers by this kind of industrious rearticulation of his material.

At this point the bibliographical curtain may be parted just wide enough for us to recognize the general relationship of the original to the final form of each of these five stories. **'The Fortunes of Sir Robert Ardagh'** (*DUM*, March 1838) was rewritten as **'The Haunted Baronet'**, second and longest of the three novellas included in *Chronicles of Golden Friars* (1871). **'The Drunkard's Dream'** (*DUM*, August 1838) became, after many a sea change, **'The Vision of Tom Chuff'** in *All the Year Round* (8 October 1870). **'Passage in the Secret History of an Irish Countess'** (*DUM*, November 1838) was retitled **'The Murdered Cousin'** and, together with **'Strange Event in the Life of Schalken the Painter'** (*DUM*, May 1838), was included in Le Fanu's 1851 collection *Ghost Stories and Tales of Mystery.* Twenty-five years after her first appearance the Irish Countess was transformed into an English heiress, Maud Ruthyn, and the secret history expanded into one of Le Fanu's most popular novels, *Uncle Silas* (1864). In much the same way the heroine of the last story, **'A Chapter in the History of a Tyrone Family'** (*DUM*, October 1839), is turned into a wholesome but harried English miss, Alice Maybell, and the original chapter elaborated into a novel of harassment, *The Wyvern Mystery* (1869).

Partly with tongue in cheek, Purcell's 'residuary legatee' inserts a long note in the last of these stories defending his

author and himself against 'the charge of dealing too largely in the marvellous' and of indulging a 'love for *diablerie*'. He denies that the stories pander, in the idle hope of affrighting the imagination, to the bad taste of readers and he insists that whenever he himself 'has had the opportunity of comparing the manuscript of his departed friend with the actual traditions which are current amongst the families whose fortunes they pretend to illustrate, he has uniformly found that whatever of supernatural occurred in the story, so far from having been exaggerated by him, had been rather softened down, and, wherever it could be attempted, accounted for'. One is reminded here of the pains taken by an earlier Dublin man to convince readers that his account of the voyages of Gulliver was no more and no less than the truth. But there is also the clear implication, curiously Catholic as transposed from a theological to a literary context, that tradition no less than scripture ('these tales have been *written down* . . . by the Rev. Francis Purcell') is to be taken as a measure of accuracy and truth.

The suspension of disbelief may be sufficient for the gratification of the ordinary romantic imagination, but for another kind of imagination there is need for another and more affirmative credence in the dark worlds that lie just over the horizon of human understanding. And since men for the most part tend to be rational, or to think that they are, the voyage out into darkness must be charted with a degree of verisimilitude equal to, or surpassing, that of less enterprising voyagers. Le Fanu, in terms of the metaphor, was an exact and indefatigable navigator. **'The Drunkard's Dream'** is a minor *decensus averni* and the only one of these journeys into the dark in which the wayfarer is not a person of talent or quality. A poor carpenter is found one night literally dead drunk on his own doorstep, but he returns for a while to life and gives Fr Purcell an account of his experience of hell and damnation. The description impresses the priest as that of an *'eye-witness',* and he is all the more impressed because, as he says, 'this was before Vathek and the "Hall of Eblis" '—a tale of fantastic grandeur unlikely in any event to have come to the attention of a drunken Irish carpenter. Despite the implied comparison there is no real similarity between William Beckford's novel, or any part of it, and Le Fanu's story—aside from the fact that both involve a visit to the underworld. The story, after the drunkard's reformation, relapse into drink and second death, turns from a tale of terror into something very like a temperance tract. Le Fanu did not attempt anything like it again.

The traditional Faust legend, or a variation on it, provides Le Fanu with a theme, again in a minor key, for **'The Fortunes of Sir Robert Ardagh'**. His man Purcell first gives a rough and bizarre sketch of the strange fate that befell Sir Robert, but quickly dismisses this account as mere country talk quite irreconcilable with the facts, 'authenticated as fully as anything can be by human understanding', which he then proceeds to set down with a characteristic show of verisimilitude. Sir Robert after eighteen years abroad returns in 1760 to an encumbered estate in County Limerick and, wealthy now to an extraordinary and unaccountable degree, not only disembarrasses his property but adds extensively to it. An agreeable man of polished manners and refined tastes, he marries well and he and his lady, as leaders of society, or such as the time afforded, entertain at Castle Ardagh in a style 'bordering on magnificence'. This charmed life is brought to an end by the Mephistophelean presence of Jacque who, in the role of valet, has accompanied Sir Robert from abroad. Abhorred by Lady Ardagh and his fellow servants, Jacque treats the entire household with ill-disguised contempt and yet Sir Robert, who is treated no less contemptuously, refuses to dismiss him and reacts with uncharacteristic violence to any suggestion that he do so. It is only when Lady Ardagh's child is born dead that the valet, after a derisive farewell to his master, leaves the castle of his own accord. Sir Robert, reduced by these events to a state of cold and unnatural placidity, reconciles himself to the payment, in due time exacted, of a debt which we are left to surmise had at some time been contracted with a prince of darkness or his emissary.

We are left to surmise. . . . The kindling of this kind of surmise is at the root of Le Fanu's special gift as a story teller, and 'Ardagh' is the first impressive example of it. The facts, the mere skeleton of a story, are articulated clearly enough and seem generally to allow for a rational explanation. But the facts are presented in such a way as to suggest that, far from being self-explanatory, they are the mere outer appearances of a reality that is never wholly explicable; and around this surmise and uncertainty a sense of apprehension accumulates, a gathering of shadows as gradual and as inevitable as the slow descent of dusk, and, when the shadows thicken into darkness, something then stirs obscurely within it. We are not compelled, we are seduced, into the provenance of terror.

Terror has no face or it has a thousand faces, none of which is ever fully visible to the fascinated eye. But in the tale of Schalken the painter we catch a glimpse, or afterwards believe we have, of one such face. It is that Mynher Wilken Vanderhausen who carries off as bride to his native Rotterdam a young girl secretly beloved by Godfrey Schalken. Bride and bridegroom subsequently disappear under mysterious circumstances, and Schalken has no sight of them again until years later on a visit to Rotterdam he is approached within a cathedral close by—he is not quite sure—his beloved, his dream of her, her own unchanging shade. The figure leads him within the vaults of the cathedral to what appears an old-fashioned Dutch apartment, in one corner of which stands a four-poster bed with heavy black-cloth curtains around it—'she drew the curtains, and by the light of the lamp which she held towards its contents, she disclosed to the horror-stricken painter, sitting bolt upright in the bed, the livid and demoniac form of Vanderhausen'. Struck senseless by the sight Schalken is afterwards discovered, still half-dead with fright, in one of the burial vaults where 'he had fallen beside a large coffin which was supported upon small stone pillars, a security against the attacks of vermin'. The story, Purcell reports, is 'traditionary' and may explain the Dutch artist's preoccupation in his work with the enigmatic figure of a woman portrayed with a singular distribution of light and shade in just such an attitude as the vision of his beloved assumed in appearing to Schalken. In fact both theme and technique, an almost spectral woman

depicted in subtle chiaroscuro, are characteristic of the work for which the original Godfrey Schalken is best remembered in the history of Dutch painting. But what, one might ask, had this Schalken to do with Purcell? The old priest explains that he had the story, which alone of these tales is set outside Ireland, from the Irish son of a Dutch officer who had served with William at the Boyne. Whether Irish or not, it is clear that the story fascinated Le Fanu, and its theme, love-in-death, was to haunt him for the rest of his days. It reappears again, rather gruesomely, in '**Carmilla**', and, considerably softened by romantic sentiment, in his last novel *Willing to Die.*

The two remaining stories are 'mysteries' rather than tales of terror, though the mystery in each unravels in an atmosphere of calculated terror. Since mysteries, like secrets, are best unrevealed, all that need be said here is that the central incident in '**Passage in the Secret History of an Irish Countess**' is, like the walking portrait in '**The Bone-Setter**', borrowed from Walpole's *Castle of Otranto.* Here, however, Le Fanu is not spoofing. At the climax of *Otranto* Manfred, in lusty pursuit of his ward Isabella, comes upon his daughter Matilda and her lover in a darkened chapel, mistakes Matilda for Isabella, and in a rage of jealousy kills his own child. The motivation in the Irish story is not carnality but greed, and the murder itself a cold-blooded and premeditated act rather than a sudden impulse of passion. Sir Arthur T——— and his son Edward plot their kinswoman's death in order to inherit her considerable property, but as in *Otranto* mistake the daughter of the house, Emily T———, for their intended victim and bludgeon her to death. In the final version of the story, expanded by 1864 into *Uncle Silas,* Le Fanu, transposing Irish castle into English country-house and the gentry of Carrickleigh into their counterparts at Bartram-Haugh, softens parricide into simple, though still villainous, murder. One may be tempted to see here an assumption by Le Fanu that, whatever the prevalence or probability of intra-familial murder among the Irish (or Italians), it would be thought out-of-place among a more staid and civilized people. Possibly, but more probably no. The victim in the novel, 'a kind of *chère amie*' of Uncle Silas, is herself implicated in the crime and her death is consequently no less ironic; or, since guilt has been made to take the place of innocence, it may even be considered an exemplary fulfilment of that 'poetic justice' so dear to the Victorian heart.

In 1851 Le Fanu had selected his '**Countess**', now renamed '**The Murderéd Cousin**', and '**Schalken**', together with two later contributions to *DUM,* '**The Watcher**' (November 1847) and '**The Evil Guest**' (April-June 1848), and published them under the title *Ghost Stories and Tales of Mystery.* The volume, though appearing under both a Dublin and a London imprint, was obviously intended for an English audience. The three Irish stories were made thoroughly English in character and setting, while '**Schalken**', never Irish to begin with, was stripped of its Purcellan frame and let stand on its own. When some thirty years later, and seven years after Le Fanu's death, A. P. Graves edited and published *The Purcell Papers,* the difference between the two sets of stories, even where they overlapped, was immediately evident. In little more than a dozen years an Irish writer had so completely reoriented himself that, though he was again to make use of Irish materials, he would thereafter, with one exception, reshape them all in a British mould.

His ultimate success was real enough though never widely recognized. He was to create original and memorable characters, dozens of whom would have been welcome to Dickens, and plots as intricate and ingenious as any of those of Wilkie Collins. But Dickens and Collins and their English-reading multitudes, though they might relish a good crime or a fine villain, had little stomach for mystery (as distinct from simple detection) and still less for ghosts. Dickens, as Shane Leslie once remarked, shunned graves and ghosts and stuck to the gravy. What is excellent in *A Christmas Carol* is the moral—but who, we may ask, wants a moral in a ghost story? Le Fanu had learned to avoid this as early as **'The Drunkard's Dream'**. Only two other writers, both American, were comparable to Le Fanu in the gradual, almost casual generation of a phantasmal atmosphere, the cumulation of suspense within that atmosphere, and the eerie evocation of terror at just the moment when suspense would seem to have become all but unbearable. Edgar Allan Poe managed many of these effects more or less consistently, though never more successfully than Le Fanu. And Henry James, who admired Le Fanu, followed his lead in *The Turn of the Screw,* a tale almost perfect but also alone of its kind in James's work. Equalled perhaps on one or two occasions, the Irish writer was not surpassed on the special ground he had marked out for himself.

The claim must be based on all that is best in Le Fanu, only part and promise of which had appeared during the period discussed here. At the close of this period, when he turned from Ireland to Britain, there may have been other reasons for his turn-about than the greater potential of an English market. He had in the meantime published his first two novels, both on Irish themes and each concentrated on a specific era of Irish history. With the example of Sir Walter Scott before him, he had perhaps hoped to produce a body of work which would do for Ireland what *The Waverley Novels* had already achieved for Scotland. But on publication neither *The Cock and Anchor: A Tale of Old Dublin* (1845) nor *Colonel Torlogh O'Brien: A Tale of the Wars of King James* (1847) was a critical or a commercial success. Discouraged, Le Fanu was not to attempt another novel until some sixteen years later; between 1848 and 1863 he devoted himself almost exclusively to journalism. The 1851 collection may then be taken as a farewell, possibly intended at the time as permanent, to the house of literature, and the four stories selected for the collection all that Le Fanu wished to preserve from the abandoned edifice.

Oscar Wilde, reviewing the early poetry of W. B. Yeats, wrote of the young poet, 'Up to this he has been merely trying the strings of his instrument, running over the keys,' an observation which an older Yeats was to repeat, in substance, when in turn he came to criticize the poems of a very young James Joyce. A valid criticism in both instances it is, fair change about, equally valid applied to the early stories of Sheridan Le Fanu. In the person of Fr Purcell of Drumcoolagh young Le Fanu could try his talents

upon a native instrument—pluck out a rhyme, play up to laughter, move finally down the scale to more sombre chords where, he soon realized, the instrument was most responsive to his touch. From there on, except on rare occasions, he put aside easy rhymes and comic merriments. At home in his new-found metier, he would concentrate now upon a sound of shadows, a sound as subtle as the slow evaporation of daylight, as strange as those shapes emerging from the enclosing dark, a sound that can still—heard in the empty stretches of a night—keep more than a drowsy emperor awake. (pp. 5-19)

> *Kevin Sullivan, "Sheridan Le Fanu: The Purcell Papers, 1838-40," in* Irish University Review, *Vol. 2, No. 1, Spring, 1972, pp. 5-19.*

"The Room in the Dragon Volant," with its subtle misdirections and reversible web, is such a successful work that I regret that LeFanu did not live to work more in this vein. While no one would want to be without *In a Glass Darkly* and *Uncle Silas* and several of the supernatural stories, most of us would be happy to exchange *All in the Dark* and *Willing to Die* for another "Room in the Dragon Volant."

—E. F. Bleiler, in his introduction to **Ghost Stories and Mysteries,** *by Sheridan Le Fanu, 1975.*

Julia Briggs (essay date 1977)

[*Briggs is an English critic. In the following excerpt from her* Night Visitors: The Rise and Fall of the English Ghost Story, *she discusses the themes of Le Fanu's short stories.*]

[Le Fanu's] interest in the occult has often caused his readers to associate him with the kind of gloomy and mysterious Swedenborgians he depicts, characters such as Austyn Ruthyn in *Uncle Silas* (1864). Even his contemporaries seem to have been impressed by the esoteric knowledge displayed in his stories, though this can easily be paralleled in the work of other writers of the period, Bulwer Lytton's for example. Dickens was so impressed by the quotations from Swedenborg's *Arcana Caelestia* in **'Green Tea'**, which was first published in *All the Year Round* in 1869, that he begged Le Fanu to write 'a few lines giving her any such knowledge as she wants' to his old friend, Madame De la Rue, on whom he had previously practised mesmerism. As he explains, 'for thirty or forty years [she] has been the subject of far more horrible spectral illusions than have ever, within my knowledge, been on record' (24 November 1869). Dickens' confidence in Le Fanu's powers is touching, but the impression of the latter from his letters is one of a busy, over-anxious man, affectionate to the point of sentimentality, and with his mind very much engaged with urgent practical concerns. Only his writing reveals a deep and intuitive understanding of the inner life.

The landscapes of Le Fanu's childhood, spent partly in the southwest of Ireland, made a deep impression on him. The Slieve Felim mountains, the Cappercullen park, haunted Lisnavourra and the villages and woods on the Limerick and County Clare border recur in his work, and so do the simple, superstitious people he found there. Several of his early stories, related through the medium of Father Purcell, are local folktales, and towards the end of his life he seems to have come back to the landscapes and legends of his childhood, as he does in his three last pieces for *All the Year Round*, **'The Child That Went with the Fairies'**, **'The White Cat of Drumgunniol'** and **'Stories of Lough Guir'**. But all his work is deeply shot through with the elements and characteristic patterns of folklore, which endow his stories with great conviction. For example, the notion of a sinister animal somehow embodying a vengeful spirit is a very ancient one, and Le Fanu did not only use it in the Irish folk-tale **'The White Cat of Drumgunniol'**. In **'Squire Toby's Will'** the unpleasant white bulldog first seen writhing obscenely on the Squire's grave seems to emanate from the dead man himself, so that his son is 'dogged' in more senses than one. Similarly, in **'The Familiar'** (later reprinted as **'The Watcher'**), a pet owl becomes the agent of revenge, the only living thing present when the wretched Barton dies of fright.

Many other traditional themes appear in Le Fanu's work. The vision of hell which acts as an awful warning to the reprobate, heeded for a time and then forgotten, so that the forewarning is fulfilled, is the subject of **'The Drunkard's Dream'** and **'The Vision of Tom Chuff'**. Maleficent ghosts, thwarted in their intentions for the disposition of their property, are used in **'Squire Toby's Will'** and in **'Dickon the Devil'**, where the returning spirit reduces a young shepherd to idiocy. But the commonest pattern of all in his work, and one of the commonest in ghost stories as a whole, is the theme of guilt and retribution, which Le Fanu uses masterfully. The classic example of this type is **'The Familiar'**, in which a naval officer, Captain Barton, has retired to Dublin and is on the point of making an advantageous marriage and settling down, when he begins to be haunted by the ghost of a sailor whom he persecuted and virtually flogged to death in Naples, years before. Another variation on this theme is that of the judge judged. Two stories depict the punishment of a cruel and corrupt judge, and his final suicide by hanging, a death so often wrongly meted out to others, **'An Account of Some Strange Disturbances in Aungier Street'** (1853) and **'Mr Justice Harbottle'** (1872). In the latter the judge himself has to stand trial in the ultimate Court of Justice.

In stories which follow this pattern the effects of sin cannot be avoided or evaded. Once having dedicated themselves to evil, the protagonists cannot shut away their past or forget their former wickedness. Le Fanu also treated the motif of a satanic bargain in three different narratives, written at different periods of his life, **'The Fortunes of Sir Robert Ardagh'** (1838), originally one of Father Purcell's tales, the *novella*-length **'The Haunted Baronet'** (1870), and **'Sir Dominick's Bargain'** (1872). Here too a past evil,

represented by a deliberate compact with the Devil for worldly gain, is followed by retribution in the form of the completion of the bargain; the luckless victim's self-surrender is equivalent to the buried evil or guilt catching up with him. Though these pieces vary enormously in mood, pace and character, the plots are basically the same, and it is one of Le Fanu's characteristics to repeat a plot in several different treatments, in his novels as well as in his ghost stories. This trait is most convincingly explained by pressure of work, and also perhaps by his recognition of his own limitations. The construction of an original plot was seldom his strong point, though once he has one well in hand he is capable of giving it sufficient twists and turns to hold our attention. Le Fanu is at his weakest where sustained invention is required, tending to fall back on the stock melodramatic devices of his day, but at his best in a traditional and well-tried tale to which he can bring his own imaginative powers, and perhaps this is another reason why he is most successful in his ghost stories.

It is the quality of his insights which makes his work remarkable; his intuitive understanding and vivid portrayal of fear, guilt and anxiety lifts his writing to true distinction, as his best critics have observed. As early as 1880 Richard Dowling described the hallucinatory monkey of **'Green Tea'** as 'the only *probable* ghost in fiction' (*Ignorant Essays*), and in 1946 V. S. Pritchett endorsed that judgement: 'Le Fanu's ghosts are what I take to be the most disquieting of all: the ghosts that can be justified, blobs of the unconscious that have floated up to the surface of the mind' ('An Irish Ghost' in *The Living Novel*).

As Pritchett goes on to remark, **'Green Tea'**, the story of the clergyman haunted by an obscene and libidinous monkey which drives him towards self-destruction by its blasphemies, remains totally convincing in a post-Freudian world. **'Carmilla'**, Le Fanu's treatment of the vampire legend, also shows modern psychological insights by linking the horror of the vampiric relationship with the theme of perverse sexuality, which it enhances and emphasizes. The heroine's ambivalent response to the vampire Carmilla's intimate caresses is powerfully described:

> When she had spoken . . . , she would press me more closely in her trembling embrace, and her lips in soft kisses gently glow upon my cheek.
>
> Her agitation and her language were unintelligible to me. . . .
>
> In these mysterious moods I did not like her. I experienced a strange tumultuous excitement that was pleasurable, ever and anon mingled with a sense of fear and disgust. I had no distinct thoughts about her while such scenes lasted, but I was conscious of a love growing into adoration and also of abhorrence.

In such an account, the Victorian equation of obscure and forbidden sexual desires with sinister, even supernatural powers, is clearly revealed.

One obsessive anxiety which Le Fanu dramatizes particularly effectively is the terror of invasion or entrance by some feared or hated object, which may ultimately be connected with sexual fear, or with the neurosis derived from some long-concealed repression. However much you shut the hated thing out, it manages to effect an entrance somehow, through some unexpected ruse or trick. Over and over again in Le Fanu's work an evil spirit tricks its way into getting its victim alone just long enough to destroy him or carry him off in triumph. In the three stories of demonic bargains the victims shut themselves away in vain, hoping to avoid the infernal visitant bent on the fulfilment of the bargain. In **'Schalken the Painter'** the demon lover enters through a window overlooking the canal to abduct Rosa for the last time, after her father has gone to fetch a candle. A gust blows the door closed behind him, and he turns to find it locked. In **'The Familiar'**, the bedroom door swings shut behind the servant who has briefly looked out for the owl, leaving Barton alone with the creature for the final reckoning. In **'Mr Justice Harbottle'**, chapter 8 is quite explicitly entitled 'Somebody has got into the house', while in **'Squire Toby's Will'** the dead squire and his thwarted heir enter the house in the guise of mourners, soon after the latter's funeral. The horribly dismembered hand in **'The Haunting of the Tiled House'** goes round and round knocking outside for some time, and when Mr Prosser takes pistols and a cane to the door to deal with it, 'his arm was jerked up oddly, as it might be with the hollow of a hand, and something passed under it, with a kind of gentle squeeze'. The vampire Carmilla, like so many evil spirits according to tradition, has to be invited into the house, but once in, like the horrible hand, she is not so easily ejected.

Le Fanu's instinctive recognition of the springs of fear, and the kinds of shape fears take, naturally makes him very interested in dreams and in the way they embody those fears. Many of his stories use dreams centrally, or as part of the build-up of suspense, expressing in an illogical but concrete form the nature of a particular haunting. Dreams are a particularly useful device for the ghost story teller, as Scott realized when writing 'Wandering Willie's Tale', for they do not commit him to an assertion of fact. They are often frightening, as much in stories as in fact, but there is no obligation to believe in them, so the storyteller may leave the tale open-ended. Le Fanu wrote to his publisher, George Bentley, about **'The Haunted Baronet'** (on which it does not seem a very apt comment) that he was striving for 'the equilibrium between the natural and the *super*-natural, the super-natural phenomena being explained on natural theories—and people left to choose which solution they please'. The use of dreams in ghost stories certainly achieves such an equilibrium.

One of his best stories, **'Strange Disturbances in Aungier Street'**, uses both dreams and 'natural theories' to create this sense of balance between the natural and supernatural elements in the story. It is basically an account of a haunted house, troubled by the ghost of an evil old judge who had finally hung himself from the banisters with the skipping rope of his illegitimate child. The occupants of the house, the narrator and his sceptical friend Tom, are initially troubled by evil dreams in which the old man figures prominently. These are followed by sinister noises in the house, and, later, the appearance of a large and peculiarly revolting rat (an idea borrowed by Bram Stoker in a similar story, 'The Judge's House'). The psychological reac-

tions of the narrator, alone in the house, are vividly conveyed. He screws himself up to shout 'Who's there?', adding 'There is, I think, something most disagreeably disenchanting in the sound of one's own voice under such circumstances, exerted in solitude, and in vain. It redoubled my sense of isolation. . . . ' On the following night he takes a bottle of whiskey up with him, but it too becomes inextricably linked with the ordeal: 'I sat down and stared at the square label on the solemn and reserved-looking black bottle, until "FLANAGAN AND CO'S BEST OLD MALT WHISKEY" grew into a sort of subdued accompaniment to all the fantastic and horrible speculations which chased one another through my brain.' It is the psychological conviction of such details which establishes the credibility of this story. In the later version of this theme, **'Mr Justice Harbottle'**, the lively character of personal response has given place to an altogether more serious tone. Here we are presented with a vision of the final Court of Judgement, accompanied by lurid, even surreal glimpses of a huge Bosch-like gibbet, and a hellish smithy. There is a new imaginative power, to which the surface realism of the earlier tale has inevitably been sacrificed.

Behind Le Fanu's imaginative descriptions of psychological states, especially the states of fear, lay a profound concern with the relationship between the mind and the body, and the way one might exert its influence over the other. His philosophy of the supernatural is given in a passage from **'Strange Disturbances'**, after the haunted narrator has taken a tonic and found that this seems to reduce the psychic disturbances. He is not inclined to dismiss his experiences as wholly subjective, nevertheless:

> Here is an obvious connexion between the material and invisible; the healthy tone of the system, and its unimpaired energy, may . . . guard us against influences which would otherwise render life itself terrific. The mesmerist and the electrobiologist will fail upon an average with nine patients out of ten—so may the evil spirit. Special conditions of the corporeal system are indispensable to the production of certain spiritual phenomena. The operation succeeds sometimes—sometimes fails—that is all.

A similar idea is expressed by Dr Hesselius at the end of **'Green Tea'**, where the unfortunate Mr Jennings' possession is seen as the result of the opening of an interior eye, brought about by his excessive indulgence in the stimulant green tea. Yet at the same time, while the haunting is attributed to the occult opening of an inner vision to reveal a world usually hidden from mortals, Jennings' suicide has a totally different explanation, a straightforwardly medical one—it is the result of 'hereditary suicidal mania'. Of course, the medical and occult explanations are hardly exclusive, hardly even in conflict if we accept the premise that the perception of ghosts is the result of a particular physical state. Here Le Fanu seems to have been moving towards the psychological ghost story, in which the experience is put down to some mental disorder. His tales remain poised between demanding our total assent to a traditional supernatural world, and on the other hand exposing such experiences to the detached and curious judgement of an impartial investigator. It is his ability to balance conviction with coolness, involvement with a certain interested scepticism, that gives his work its characteristic flavour. The open-ended conclusion of **'Green Tea'** is so powerful because it leaves us, as similar experiences do in life, mystified, intrigued and uncertain. As E. F. Benson declared, 'there is a quality about most of his tales which seldom fails to alarm: familiarity with them does not breed comfort' (*The Spectator,* 21 February 1931). (pp. 45-51)

> *Julia Briggs, "Ancestral Voices: The Ghost Story from Lucian to Le Fanu," in her* Night Visitors: The Rise and Fall of the English Ghost Story, *Faber, 1977, pp. 25-51.*

Jack Sullivan   (essay date 1978)

[*Sullivan is an American critic and educator who has written extensively on horror and supernatural fiction. In the following essay, he argues that "Green Tea" was a significant development in the history of ghost fiction.*]

In 1839, a new kind of ghost appeared in English fiction. The appearance, in Joseph Sheridan Le Fanu's **"Schalken the Painter,"** went unnoticed, for Le Fanu was an unknown, and his tales were published anonymously. By a strange coincidence, "The Fall of the House of Usher" came out the same year, but Poe's more celebrated tale is a landmark of a different order, an exercise in cosmic paranoia rather than a tale of the supernatural. Le Fanu's creations were real ghosts who stubbornly refused to confine themselves to the shabby psyches of aristocratic neurotics, yet somehow managed to emerge from within as well as invade from without; who (unlike Mrs. Radcliffe's ghosts) could not be explained away, yet who would have nothing to do with what Oliver Onions once called "the groans and clankings of the grosser spook." **"Schalken the Painter"** was as revolutionary in execution as in the peculiar nature of its two ghosts. The story tells of the abduction, rape, and final seduction of a young woman by a living corpse, all from the point of view of the girls' befuddled uncle and horrified fiance. Le Fanu handled both the necrophilia and the supernaturalism in the tale with a new anti-Gothic restraint. As if reluctant to reveal its sordid and marvelous secrets, the plot develops itself entirely through suggestion and indirection, building toward an extraordinary dream sequence involving the transformation of a coffin into a Victorian four-poster bed. It is a chilling performance.

Yet **"Schalken the Painter"** is not the most refined or the most representative of Le Fanu's tales. It is rather the promising start of a long, influential career in ghostly fiction. The culmination of that career is **"Green Tea,"** a late tale which represents the new ghost story in its most uncompromising form. (pp. 11-12)

Le Fanu first published **"Green Tea"** in Dickens's magazine *All the Year Round* (1869) and later reprinted it in *In A Glass Darkly* (1872), a remarkable collection of his late tales which includes **"Mr. Justice Harbottle," "The Familiar," "Carmilla,"** and (somewhat inappropriately since there is no supernatural episode) **"The Room in the Dragon Volant."** With the possible exception of **"Carmilla,"** no other Le Fanu tale has been so widely discussed. Its visibility, so unusual for Le Fanu, can probably be ac-

counted for by its novel concept. V. S. Pritchett, Edna Kenton, William Buckler, Nelson Browne, and E. F. Benson have all sung the praises of Le Fanu's demonic monkey. Speaking for all of them, Buckler states that **"Green Tea"** "is generally given first place in the canon of his work," while Pritchett extends the generalization by calling it one of "the best half-dozen ghost stories in the English language."

The structure of **"Green Tea"** is a perfect illustration of M. R. James's model for the modern ghost story:

> Let us, then, be introduced to the actors in a placid way; let us see them going about their ordinary business, undisturbed by forebodings, pleased with their surroundings; and into this calm environment let the ominous thing put out its head, unobtrusively at first, and then more insistently, until it holds the stage. ["Introduction," *Ghosts and Marvels*]

Le Fanu was the first to use this strategy, and he applies it with particular deftness here. The victim in **"Green Tea,"** the Reverend Mr. Jennings, is introduced to the reader by the central narrator, Dr. Martin Hesselius, who in the course of the tale becomes Jennings's therapist. We first see Jennings at a congenial, tedious dinner party, conversing with Hesselius. They are discussing a German first edition of Hesselius's "Essays on Metaphysical Medicine." The conversation is learned but also abstracted and rather silly. Only one sentence appears to have any relevance to a possible ghostly experience: it is a hint involving the motivations for Jennings's odd curiosity concerning Hesselius's exotic research: "I suppose [says Hesselius] you have been turning the subject over again in your mind, or something has happened lately to revive your interest in it."

The conversation, with its pedantry and innuendo, is a prefiguration of M. R. James's dialogue, as are the clues which reinforce its implications. Something indeed "has happened." Although Jennings is a reserved, "perfectly gentleman like man," he has a few revealing quirks. For one thing, he has a peculiar tendency to flee from the pulpit during his own sermons: "After proceeding a certain way in the service, he has on a sudden stopped short, and after a silence, apparently quite unable to resume, he has fallen into solitary, inaudible prayer, his hands and eyes uplifted and then pale as death, and in the agitation of a strange shame and horror, descended trembling, and got into the vestry-room, leaving his congregation, without explanation, to themselves." The situation becomes so critical that Jennings resorts to having an alternate clergyman waiting in the wings "should he become thus suddenly incapacitated." Hesselius also notices a "certain oddity" in Jennings's dinner conversation: "Mr. Jennings has a way of looking sideways upon the carpet, as if his eye followed the movements of something there." The final oddity is revealed by the hostess, Lady Mary Heyduke, when she remarks that she used to quarrel with Jennings over his addiction to green tea. Hesselius agrees that Jennings was once "extravagantly" addicted to the stuff, but insists that "he has quite given that up."

Le Fanu, a careful artist, was undoubtedly aware of the

ludicrousness of all this. The notion that humor is anathema to horror is one of the persistent cliches of anthology introductions. It is also one of the most erroneous, as anyone who has read Bierce or Hartley can attest. Humor, particularly when ironic or absurd, is inextricably fused with supernatural horror in fiction. I have found the linkage to be consistent throughout the field: the reader automatically integrates the two elements as he reads. In **"Green Tea,"** the first apparition scene skirts the same arbitrary borderline between the laughable and the horrible as the clues which anticipate it. The absurdity of the premise—the lethal apparition is, after all, a monkey—weakens the impact not at all; indeed the strange power of the tale lies in the irony that something intrinsically ridiculous can drive a man to destroy himself.

Jennings, of course, is not amused by this creature. His account of the first apparition is peculiarly unnerving and deserves to be quoted at length as a paradigm of Le Fanu's apparition scenes:

> "The interior of the omnibus was nearly dark. I had observed in the corner opposite to me at the other side, and at the end next the horses, two small circular reflections, as it seemed to me of a reddish light. They were about two inches apart, and about the size of those small brass buttons that yachting men used to put upon their jackets. I began to speculate, as listless men will, upon this trifle, as it seemed. From what centre did that faint but deep red light come, and from what—glass beads, buttons, toy decorations—was it reflected? We were lumbering along gently, having nearly a mile still to go. I had not solved the puzzle, and it became in another minute more odd, for these two luminous points, with a sudden jerk, descended nearer and nearer the floor, keeping still their relative distance and horizontal position, and then, as suddenly, they rose to the level of the seat on which I was sitting and I saw them no more.

> "My curiosity was now really excited and before I had time to think, I saw again these two dull lamps, again together near the floor; again they disappeared, and again in their old corner I saw them.

> "So, keeping my eyes upon them, I edged quietly up my own side, towards the end at which I still saw these tiny discs of red.

> "There was very little light in the 'bus. It was nearly dark. I leaned forward to aid my endeavour to discover what these little circles really were. They shifted position a little as I did so. I began now to perceive an outline of something black, and I soon saw, with tolerable distinctness, the outline of a small black monkey, pushing its face forward in mimicry to meet mine; those were its eyes, and I now dimly saw its teeth grinning at me.

> "I drew back not knowing whether it might not meditate a spring. I fancied that one of the passengers had forgot this ugly pet, and wishing to ascertain something of its temper, though not caring to trust my fingers to it, I poked my umbrella softly towards it. It remained immov-

able—up to it—*through* it. For through it, and back and forward it passed, without the slightest resistance.

> "I can't in the least, convey to you the kind of horror that I felt."

Throughout this passage, the emphasis is on the way Jennings perceives the apparition rather than on the apparition itself. Jennings's reaction is the important thing, as is the reader's: we are forced to see this strange abomination exactly as Jennings sees it. It scarcely matters whether the thing is "real" or hallucinated; in a good horror tale this distinction is effaced. Supernatural horror in fiction has little to do with the materiality or immateriality of spooks. What counts is the authenticity of the experience. The scene works because of the intricate perspectival character of the writing, a technique which anticipates Henry James's *The Turn of the Screw* and "Sir Edmund Orme." The most remarkable aspect of Le Fanu's perspectivism is his use of synecdoche, a poetic mechanism which allows him to straddle the boundary between the explicit and the indirect. His use of the device is more radical in other tales, notably **"The Haunting of the Tiled House"** in which the unearthly force is represented solely by a disembodied hand. Here we visualize the creature in terms of its eyes, although "these two dull lamps" dimly illuminate the rest of the shape.

Jennings stumbles from the omnibus "in a panic," discovering to his "indescribable relief" that the thing is gone. Like all of Le Fanu's victims, he convinces himself that it was all a fleeting "illusion." But on the way home he looks up "with loathing and horror" to see it creeping along beside him on a brick wall. From this point on, the creature persecutes Jennings with incredible tenacity. As in the first apparition scene, the sufferer's emotions are communicated consistently through his reaction to the demon's eyes. During the initial phase of the persecution, the eyes are "dazed and languid," "jaded and sulkey," "sullen and sick." Yet they have "unfathomable malignanty" and above all, "intense vigilance." "In all situations, at all hours," says the unfortunate Jennings, "it is awake and looking at me; that never changes."

Thus begins this extraordinary obsession, chronicled in graded steps: three "stages" in a hellish "journey." In the "Second Stage," the demon mysteriously disappears for a month, during which time Jennings again experiences an illusory respite. But then it returns with "new energy," "brooding over some atrocious plan." This phase of the persecution is characterized by many such disappearances: "it has sometimes been away so long as nearly two months, once for three," Jennings tells his therapist. "Its absence always exceeds a fortnight, although it may be but by a single day. Fifteen days having past since I saw it last, it may return now at any moment." At once arbitrary and mysteriously calculated, this time span induces the maximum amount of anxiety, causing the patient to look progressively "like death." It is a typically cruel touch, which Le Fanu is fond of using in situations of otherworldly harrassment (c.f. **"The Familiar"**). Another painful characteristic of the second phase is Jennings's new inability to attain relief by simply shutting his eyes: "I know it is not to be accounted for physically, but I do actually see it though my eyes are closed." As part of its new militancy, the creature will "squat" in Jennings's prayer book during holy services, obscuring any passage he attempts to read his congregation. It is presumably during these occasions that Jennings flees from the pulpit.

In the third and final stage, the demon "speaks" to Jennings. Unlike Gothic writers, with their fatal predilection for chatty spectres, Le Fanu shrewdly avoids any attempt to reproduce its actual words. Instead, he allows Jennings to suggest the sound metaphorically, through a kind of ghostly music: "It is not by my ears it reaches me—it comes like a singing through my head." Although Jennings never quotes the lyrics of this "song," he lets us know that they are thoroughly unpleasant, particularly during his abortive attempts at prayer:

> "This faculty, the power of speaking to me, will be my undoing. It won't let me pray, it interrupts me with dreadful blasphemies. I dare not go on, I could not. Oh! Doctor, can the skill and thought, and prayers of man avail me nothing!"

They indeed avail him nothing. In these tales, prayer is utterly ineffectual—as are faith and good works. Like most Le Fanu, **"Green Tea"** does not end happily. In the final phase, the demon tries to persuade his victim to commit suicide. Jennings, who after three years of demonic persecution does not need much persuading, ends his "journey" by cutting his throat. Suicide is the only way out for him, and he is unique among Le Fanu's victims in perceiving this. As in Greek tragedy, the final horror is not rendered directly but is reported by a messenger, in this case Jennings's servant. As always, Le Fanu avoids being too direct: he leaves the awful details to the reader's imagination, yet still gets in a good bloody scene by having Hesselius clinically inspect the "immense pool of blood on the floor" of Jennings's "sombre and now terrible room."

"Green Tea" is every bit as twisted, disturbing and unresolvable as it seems. Nevertheless, by imposing orthodox explanations and theoretical systems on the story, critics have done what they could to dissipate its mystery and menace. The orthodoxies divide into two camps, the Freudian and the Christian, each of which has a predictable explanation for Jennings's persecution. To Peter Penzoldt, Jennings's monkey is simply "the product of schizoid neurosis"; to V. S. Pritchett, it is "dark and hairy with original sin," and its persecutions symbolize "justified" retribution for specific sins; to Michael Begnal, the monkey is sent to punish a clergyman who has "lost his faith" and whose "intellectual pride" has "cut him off from God."

The problem with such theories is that they convert possibilities into solutions. M. R. James, who modelled his stories after Le Fanu's, once stated, "It is not amiss sometimes to leave a loophole for a natural explanation, but I would say, let the loophole be so narrow as not to be quite practicable." This teasing, enigmatic quality, so obvious to any writer in the genre, is missed by theory-obsessed critics. In **"Green Tea,"** the Freudian "loophole" is narrow indeed. We are not given enough information about

> In Le Fanu's tales, prayer is utterly ineffectual—as are faith and good works. Like most Le Fanu, "Green Tea" does not end happily. In the final phase, the demon tries to persuade his victim to commit suicide. Jennings, who after three years of demonic persecution does not need much persuading, ends his "journey" by cutting his throat.
>
> —*Jack Sullivan*

the near-anonymous Jennings to conclude that he is "schizoid" or "sexually repressed." We are told only that he is shy and unassuming.

The Christian interpretation is even flimsier. There is no doubt that Jennings's obsession is somehow connected with an intense, unspeakable feeling of guilt. The text contains many references to this feeling: he collapses from the altar "in the agitation of a strange shame and horror"; he looks at Hesselius "guiltily" during their first conversation; he even cries "God forgive me!" during a later conversation. What the text does not tell us is what Jennings needs to be forgiven for, what crime he has committed to merit such a hideous, ultimately lethal punishment. As we shall see, the only character who could conceivably be accused of "intellectual pride" is Dr. Hesselius. Indeed, if we assume with Begnal that Jennings committed a mortal sin by researching the non-Christian religious beliefs of the ancients, we must ask why Hesselius is not also pursued to the grave by the avenging monkey, for he is guilty of the same heterodox research. Nor is there any evidence that Jennings has lost his faith; on the contrary, he is a pious, devout Christian who ceases to pray only when the monkey literally prevents him from doing so by shrieking blasphemies in his ear.

The truth is that Jennings has done nothing but drink green tea. The very title of the tale registers the fundamental irony: the awful disjuncture between cause and effect, crime and punishment. What emerges is an irrational, almost Kafkaesque feeling of guilt and persecution. Like Joseph K., Jennings is ceaselessly pursued and tormented for no discernible reason. A persistent experience in modern fiction is a situation in which the main character wakes up one morning on a tightrope and does not know how he got there. This is precisely the predicament Jennings finds himself in. Although S. M. Ellis [in *Wilkie Collins, Le Fanu, and Others*] calls Le Fanu a "tragic" writer, **"Green Tea"** is closer to modern tragi-comedy. Jennings never experiences even a flash of tragic recognition; on the contrary, he never knows why this horrible thing is happening. There is no insight, no justice and therefore no tragedy. There is only absurd cruelty, a grim world view which endures in the reader's mind long after the hairs have settled on the back of the neck.

Though ultimately deterministic, this world view is not

based on a coherent or knowable determinism—there is neither the benign workings of Providence nor the naturalism of Zola or Dreiser. The sense of doom in these stories emanates from a uniquely hostile cosmos vaguely suggestive of the purblind doomsters which later pursue Thomas Hardy's characters. But Le Fanu is not interested in programmatic philosophical consistency. In trying to get at the source of the horror, various characters suggest various possibilities—all of them bleak—yet final solutions elude them, as they elude the reader. One event leads inexorably to another once the pursuit begins, but the reason behind it is known only to the otherworldly invaders. Causality is present, but Le Fanu's victims experience only Crass Causality, blind and mechanical, yet efficiently murderous once the cosmos gives someone a bad throw of the dice. Jennings dimly perceives the magnitude of the forces massed against him in one of his final, most pathetic speeches:

> But as food is taken in softly at the lips, and then brought under the teeth, as the tip of the little finger caught in a mill crank will draw in the hand, and the arm, and the whole body, so the miserable mortal who has been once caught firmly by the end of the finest fibre of his nerve, is drawn in and in, by the enormous machinery of hell, until he is as I am. Yes, Doctor, as *I* am, for a while I talk to you, and implore relief, I feel that my prayer is for the impossible, and my pleading with the inexorable.

Jennings is horribly right in his perception that the workings of the grisly machinery are "inexorable" and that his "prayer is for the impossible."

Despite the resemblance of all this to Hap in its most perverse manipulations, there is an ominous point at which the analogy breaks down. Once Le Fanu's hellish machine begins grinding, it does so with Hardyesque remorselessness, but also with a strange awareness of purpose which goes beyond the half-consciousness of the Immanent Will. If Hardy's cosmos is struggling to attain consciousness, Le Fanu's has already attained it, or is at least well along the way. If there is no benevolent or rational purpose behind things, there does seem to be a sinister purpose. James Barton, another Le Fanu victim, speaks of this conspiracy in Manichaean terms in **"The Familiar."** Jennings, lacking even tentative answers, is obsessed with "machinery" and process, with the "stages" of his torment:

> "In the dark, as you shall presently hear, there are peculiarities. It is a small monkey, perfectly black. It had only one peculiarity—a character of malignity—unfathomable malignity. During the first year it looked sullen and sick. But this character of intense malice and vigilance was always underlying that surly languor. During all that time it acted as if on a plan of giving me as little trouble as was consistent with watching me. Its eyes were never off me. I have never lost sight of it, except in my sleep, light or dark, day or night, since it came here excepting when it withdraws for some weeks at a time, unaccountably.

> "In total dark it is visible as in daylight. I do not mean merely its eyes. It is *all* visible distinctly in a halo that resembles a glow of red embers and which accompanies it in all its movements.

> "When it leaves me for a time, it is always at night, in the dark, and in the same way. It grows at first uneasy, and then furious, and then advances towards me, grinning and shaking, its paws clenched, and, at the same time, there comes the appearance of fire in the grate. I never have any fire. I can't sleep in the room where there is any, and it draws nearer and nearer to the chimney, quivering, it seems, with rage, and when its fury rises to the highest pitch, it springs into the grate, and up the chimney, and I see it no more.

> "When first this happened, I thought I was released. I was now a new man. A day passed—a night—and no return, and a blessed week—a week—another week. I was always on my knees, Dr. Hesselius, always thanking God and praying. A whole month passed of liberty, but on a sudden, it was with me again. . . .

> "It was with me, and the malice which before was torpid under a sullen exterior, was now active. It was perfectly unchanged in every other respect. This new energy was apparent in its activity and its looks, and soon in other ways.

> "For a time, you will understand, the change was shown only in an increased vivacity, and an air of menace, as if it were always brooding over some atrocious plan. It eyes, as before, were never off me."

The victim of "an atrocious plan," intricately conceived and faultlessly executed, Jennings is denied even an inkling of the ultimate purpose behind that plan.

In this sense, Jennings is in a bleaker predicament than Poe's Roderick Usher, who is powerless largely because he thinks he is. Usher's main problem seems to be a kind of self-inflicted catatonia: since the horrors in Poe's tale are completely localized in a single house, they would presumably lessen if Usher would take the narrator's advice and go somewhere else; but the famous twist is that the house cannot be separated from Usher's mind, as Usher himself reveals to us in his allegorical poem and in his abstract paintings of subterranean tunnels. More than anything else, Usher needs a therapist. But Jennings, who has a therapist, is entirely helpless, for the horror which pursues him is more than a psychological phenomenon. Therapy does him no good; he is victimized by something finally independent of his psyche. In the passage describing the monkey's leap up the chimney, Le Fanu is careful to depict a fiend who is extraordinarily alive, the active incarnation of some unrelenting principle of hatred. The symbiotic connection between setting and psyche, so important in "The Fall of the House of Usher" and "M. S. Found In A Bottle," does not apply here. Le Fanu's settings are often evocative in themselves (see **"Sir Dominick's Bargain"**), but they are irrelevant to the main action: his doomed heroes are pursued wherever they go, are tormented in the most unlikely places; their ghostly tormenters see no need to confine themselves in depressing Gothic houses and are likely to appear anywhere, often in broad daylight. (In **"The Familiar,"** James Barton is chased by the Watcher, a spectre who is fond of appearing not only in daylight, but in crowds; nor does he mind traveling long distances when Barton tries to skip the country.)

This is not to say that Le Fanu is unconcerned with psychology. On the contrary, his tales deal repeatedly with dark states of consciousness. The difference between **"Green Tea"** and Edmund Wilson's version of *The Turn of the Screw* is that this inner darkness is a sinisterly accurate measure of the outer world rather than a neurotic projection. Like the madness of Lear, the derangement of Jennings's mind is a mirror image of a derangement in the cosmos, although Jennings has neither the insight nor the catharsis of Lear. That the infernal region in Jennings's psyche reflects not only reality, but the fundamental reality, is hinted at in a passage in Swedenborg's "Arcana Celestia," which Hesselius translated from the Latin:

> "When man's interior sight is opened, which is that of his spirit, then there appear the things of another life, which cannot possibly be made visible to the bodily sight.". . . .

> "by the internal sight it has been granted me to see the things that are in the other life, more clearly than I see those that are in the world. From these considerations, it is evident that external vision exists from interior vision, and this from a vision still more interior, and so on.". . . .

> "If evil spirits could perceive that they were associated with man, and yet that they were spirits separate from him, and if they could flow in into the things of his body, they would attempt by a thousand means to destroy him; for they hate man with a deadly hatred.". . . .

Placing the passage in context with Jennings's experience, it becomes apparent that the doors of perception open straight into hell; they are kept mercifully shut for the most part, but can be flung open by the most absurdly inadvertent act, in this case by the drinking of green tea.

It is just as well that little has been made of Le Fanu's connection with Swedenborg, for Le Fanu's version represents a distortion, or at least a darkening of the original. The passage which Hesselius translates goes on to say that the "wicked genii" do not attack those who are "in the good of faith." The Christian is "continually protected by the lord." But this protection does not work for Jennings (who writes "Deus misereatur mei" in the margin of the Swedenborg text). Without the saving light of a benevolent deity, Le Fanu's mystical psychology is far more malevolent than Swedenborg's: what we have in this psychological landscape are increasingly deeper layers of consciousness, each one increasingly diabolical—an infinite darkness.

The darkness in Le Fanu is quite different from the "blackness of darkness" in Poe or the "great power of blackness" Melville found in Hawthorne. In Poe, darkness is a thick, palpable texture, opaque and impenetrable, which permeates mind and matter like an endless sewage. In Hawthorne, darkness is a moral quality deriving from the traditional symbolic equation of darkness with evil.

Both writers paint with a wide brush, darkening their prose immediately with adjectives like "gloomy" and "inscrutable." Though brilliantly evoked, theirs is often a melodramatic world where colors have allegorical rigidity. In Le Fanu, where the fiend is as likely to appear in the full light of the Sunday church service as in the gloom of a mouldering house, where he is comfortable squatting in the prayerbook rather than seething in the sinner's bosom, colors are used sparingly, sometimes monochromatically. Much of the traditional color symbolism remains: the blacks and reds often suggest as much evil and violence as they do in *Macbeth;* the lurid halo emanating from the monkey like "a glow of red embers" gives off the same satanic light as Ethan Brand's lime kiln.

For the most part, however, Le Fanu's colors elude allegorical equations. Unfettered by an orderly moral universe, they have a half-tinted quality which is somehow more unsettling than the extravagant darkness and storminess of the Gothic writers:

> The sun had already set, and the red reflected light of the western sky illuminated the scene with the peculiar effect with which we are all familiar. The hall seemed very dark, but, getting to the back drawingroom, whose windows command the west, I was again in the same dusky light.

> I sat down, looking out upon the richly-wooded landscape that glowed in the grand and melancholy light which was every moment fading. The corners of the room were already dark; all was growing dim, and the gloom was insensibly toning my mind, already prepared for what was sinister. I was waiting alone for his arrival, which soon took place. The door communicating with the front room opened, and the tall figure of Mr. Jennings, faintly seen in the ruddy twilight, came, with quiet stealthy steps, into the room.

> We shook hands, and taking a chair to the window, where there was still light enough to enable us to see each other's faces, he sat down beside me, and, placing his hand upon my arm, with scarcely a word of preface began his narrative. . . .

> The faint glow of the west, the pomp of the then lonely woods of Richmond, were before us, behind and about us the darkening room, and on the stony face of the sufferer—for the character of his face, though still gentle and sweet, was changed—rested that dim, odd glow which seems to descend and produce, where it touches, lights, sudden though faint, which are lost almost without gradation, in darkness. The silence, too, was utter: not a distant wheel, or bark, or whistle from without; and within the depressing stillness of an invalid bachelor's house.

What do we make of this strange twilight, dim and translucent one minute, "grand and melancholy" the next; "every moment fading," yet reappearing suddenly, only to be "lost, almost without gradation, in darkness"? The passage seems naturalistic enough, at least up to a point (The sunset has "the peculiar effect with which we are all familiar.") Yet the lights and shadows become so blurred and undefined as to become almost interchangeable. Faint points of light seem to go on and off like stars suddenly going out and reappearing in a cloudy sky. In the next to last sentence, with its twisted, almost Jamesian syntax, this "'odd glow" is associated with Jennings's face. The "almost" here suggests a subtle gradation, a hierarchy of twilight worlds, each of which gives off its own unearthly lights, swallowing them up again almost instantly.

Jennings has accidentally summoned a creature from one of these worlds, and his face shows the price he has paid: it has assumed the same deathlike appearance as Jennings's new companion; it even emits the same strange lights. Le Fanu's imagery suggests the shifting, dissolving colors of a nightmare. Ambiguous and undefined, his colors are like those in our dreams, much harder to recall than the technicolor images of Poe or Monk Lewis.

The reader can experience the relief of waking, simply by closing the book and turning on every light in the house. The doomed protagonists are not so fortunate. In Jennings's case, his demise seems to be hastened by the incompetence of his therapist. Hesselius deserves close examination, for he appears to be the first psychiatrist in English literature. Since he is pre-Freudian by at least thirty years, he has a hard time defining just what he is, calling himself at various times a medical philosopher, a philosophical physician and even a doctor of Metaphysical Medicine. He is distinctly a therapist, however, claiming to have diagnosed "two hundred and thirty cases more or less nearly akin to that I have entitled 'Green Tea.' " This is a staggering thought, suggesting that Hesselius has dealt with a large number of what are surely the most bizarre patients in the annals of psychiatry. If the prefaces to the **In A Glass Darkly** are to be taken seriously, he has had to confront such things as living corpses, demonic monkeys, and lesbian vampires.

All this has been hard on him, as his ineptness in treating Jennings all too clearly reveals. After Jennings unfolds his tale, Hesselius is at an obvious loss as to what to do. At one particularly strained point, immediately following the oration on "the enormous machinery of hell," Hesselius can only say: "I endeavored to calm his visibly increasing agitation and told him that he must not despair." This is fatuous advice: there is every reason to despair, especially in the absence of any concrete suggestions. Following Jennings's depressing account of a near-suicide attempt, Hesselius's advice is even worse:

> "Yes, yes; it is always urging me to crimes, to injure others, or myself. You see, Doctor, the situation is urgent, it is indeed. When I was in Shropshire, a few weeks, ago" (Mr. Jennings was speaking rapidly and trembling now, holding my arm with one hand, and looking in my face), "I went out one day with a party of friends for a walk: my persecutor, I tell you, was with me at the time. I lagged behind the rest: the country near the Dee, you know, is beautiful. Our path happened to lie near a coal mine, and at the verge of the wood is a perpendicular shaft, they say, a hundred and fifty feet deep. My niece had remained behind with me—she knows, of course, nothing of the nature of my sufferings.

She knew, however, that I had been ill, and was low, and she remained to prevent my being quite alone. As we loitered slowly on together, the brute that accompanied me was urging me to throw myself down the shaft. I tell you now— oh, sir, think of it!—the one consideration that saved me from that hideous death was the fear lest the shock of witnessing the occurrence should be too much for the poor girl. I asked her to go on and walk with her friends, saying that I could go no further. She made excuses, and the more I urged her the firmer she became. She looked doubtful and frightened. I suppose there was something in my looks or manner that alarmed her; but she would not go, and that literally saved me. You had no idea, sir, that a living man could be made so abject a slave of Satan," he said with a ghastly groan and a shudder.

> There was a pause here, and I said, "You *were* preserved nevertheless. It was the act of God. You are in his hands, and in the power of no other being: be confident therefore for the future."

Jennings's concern for the little girl's reaction, even at the climax of his own suicidal despair, strengthens our feeling that he is a scrupulously sensitive, compassionate man, undeserving of this torment. But the passage is more revealing of Hesselius. "You see, doctor, the situation is urgent, it is indeed" is a chilling understatement, yet all the philosophic physician can do is offer platitudes—the solace of a deity who is either indifferent or as impotent as Hesselius himself. This advice is more than merely unctuous and ineffectual: the claim that Jennings is "in the power of no other being" is demonstrably false.

Nor does his epilogue, "A Word for Those Who Suffer," do anything to enhance his professional credibility. This final chapter is in the form of a letter to Professor Van Loo of Leyden, a chemist who has suffered from Jennings's malady and whom Hesselius claims to have cured. It is a suspiciously self-serving document:

> Who, under God, cured you? Your humble servant, Martin Hesselius. Let me rather adopt the more emphasised piety of a certain good old French surgeon of three hundred years ago: "I treated, and God cured you."

> There is no one affliction of mortality more easily and certainly reducible, with a little patience, and a rational confidence in the physician. With these simple conditions, I look upon the cure as absolutely certain.

> You are to remember that I had not even commenced to treat Mr. Jennings' case. I have not any doubt that I should have cured him perfectly in eighteen months, or possibly it might have extended to two years. . . .

> You know my tract on "The Cardinal Functions of the Brain." I there, by the evidence of innumerable facts, prove, as I think, the high probability of a circulation arterial and venous in its mechanism, through the nerves. Of this system, thus considered, the brain is the heart. The fluid,

which is propagated hence through one class of nerves, returns in an altered state through another, and the nature of that fluid is spiritual, though not immaterial, any more than, as I before remarked, light or electricity are so.

By various abuses, among which the habitual use of such agents as green tea is one, this fluid may be affected as to its quality, but it is more frequently disturbed as to equilibrium. This fluid being that which we have in common with spirits, a congestion found upon the masses of brain or nerve, connected with the interior sense, forms a surface unduly exposed, on which disembodied spirits may operate: communication is thus more or less effectually established. Between this brain circulation and the heart circulation there is an intimate sympathy. The seat, or rather the instrument of exterior vision, is the eye. The seat of interior vision is the nervous tissue and brain, immediately about and above the eyebrow. You remember how effectually I dissipated your pictures by the simple application of iced eau-de-cologne. Few cases, however, can be treated exactly alike with anything like rapid success. Cold acts powerfully as a repellant of the nervous fluid. Long enough continued it will even produce that permanent insensibility which we call numbness, and a little longer muscular as well as sensational paralysis.

I have not, I repeat, the slightest doubt that I should have first dimmed and ultimately sealed that inner eye which Mr. Jennings had inadvertently opened. . . . It is by acting steadily upon the body, by a simple process, that this result is produced—and inevitably produced—I have never yet failed.

Poor Mr. Jennings made away with himself. But that catastrophe was the result of a totally different malady, which, as it were, projected itself upon the disease which was established. His case was in the distinctive manner a complication, and the complaint under which he really succumbed, was hereditary suicidal mania. Poor Mr. Jennings I cannot call a patient of mine, for I had not even begun to treat his case, and he had not yet given me, I am convinced, his full and unreserved confidence. If the patient do not array himself on the side of the disease, his cure is certain.

The immediate point of interest here is the earnest but tortured attempt to reconcile medical science with mystical experience, a commonplace exercise in nineteenth and early twentieth-century weird fiction. In relation to the story, however, the epilogue is not so earnest. It raises a variety of questions. Why did Hesselius not share any of these insights with his patient, a man on the verge of self-destruction? Why did he not tell him that his cure would be a "simple process"? Why did he not describe this process and thereby relieve Jennings's paranoia? Leaving aside the believability of this "absolutely certain" cure why did he not produce the magical "iced eau-de-cologne" and douse the wretched man with it? The final dismissal of Jennings's case as "hereditary suicidal mania," without any evidence, is an ugly rationalization.

The wonder is that Jennings, unremittingly persecuted for three years, did not kill himself sooner; if anything, the evidence indicates an unusually strong psyche.

But the oddest thing about this addendum is its failure to explain its author's behaviour in the period between Jennings's narration and his suicide. After giving his account, Jennings understandably breaks down weeping (despite Hesselius's disingenuous "He seemed comforted"). Hesselius does have one concrete bit of comfort to offer: "One promise I exacted, which was that should the monkey return, I should be sent for immediately." Taking his doctor at his word, Jennings tries to contact Hesselius "immediately" after the monkey's next appearance, which is predictably soon:

> Dear Dr. Hesselius—It is here. You had not been an hour gone when it returned. It is speaking. It knows all that has happened. It knows everything—it knows you, and is frantic and atrocious. It reviles. I send you this. It knows every word I have written—I write. This I promised and I therefore write, but I fear very confused, very incoherently, I am so interrupted, disturbed.

Hesselius, however, is not to be found. Intentionally making his whereabouts unknown, he has fled when he is most needed to an unknown address where he intends to dabble with his metaphysical medicines "without the possibility of intrusion or distraction." He seems to need therapy himself, so shut off is he from the consequences of his actions. The immediate consequence is that Jennings, feeling totally alone, cuts his throat.

Hesselius is only marginally concerned with the wellbeing of his patient. His chief motivation—which reaches a state of frenzied anticipation—is his determination to validate his theories. As the epilogue implies, he is less saddened than annoyed by his patient's death; by that act, Jennings has robbed him of his big chance.

We can reasonably conclude that Le Fanu did not mean us to take this epilogue on the same level of seriousness as Hesselius assumes we do. His claims, accusations, and actions are dubious enough in themselves; set against the powerful authenticity of Jennings's narrative, they make sense only as dramatic irony. Unless seen as ironic, the "Word for Those Who Suffer" becomes an aesthetic blunder. There is nothing organic about this final chapter; it seems distinctly tacked on, a needless diatribe which ruins the tale if taken at face value. But seen as ironic, it underscores the hopelessness of Jennings's predicament.

As the less than reliable narrator of a horror tale, Hesselius is part of a tradition which begins with Poe's narrator in "The Tell-Tale Heart" and culminates in the governess's account in *The Turn of the Screw*. This is not to say that Hesselius is a Gothic villain—a frothing madman or an ostentatiously evil doctor. Like everything else in the story, he is difficult to pin down: earnest and well-meaning in the opening pages, he seems progressively more ineffectual, even senile, at worst evincing a precarious ego which distorts his judgement. In other respects as well, the narrative problems are more complex than those in Poe. Hesselius is not the only narrator of **"Green Tea."** The tale has a prologue as well as a conclusion; as William Buckler has shown, the prologue is also problematic:

> The story is filtered to the reader through three "carefully educated" men of science: the supposed editor, or "medical secretary"; Dr. Hesselius, the narrator; and Professor Van Loo, chemist and student of history, metaphysics, and medicine, to whom a correspondent would presumably write with conscientiousness. And yet each is a fallible authority: the editor is a confessed "enthusiast" who has taken Dr. Hesselius as his "master"; Dr. Hesselius, besides suffering from an acutely sensitive ego, obviously has no authority within the medical fraternity, is theoretical and categorical, and seems unduly intent upon rationalizing the perfect record of his "cures," and Dr. Van Loo, according to the narrator, has suffered from a similar "affection," while, according to the editor, he is an "unlearned reader."

Though accurate and concise as a summary, Buckler's introduction does not attempt to resolve the obvious question it raises: why does Le Fanu bother with this narrative filtering device at all? This is a difficult question to answer, for **"Green Tea"** is unlike other tales which saddle us with unreliable or multiple narrators: we get little sense of the moral complexity found in Stevenson, the pathological involutions found in Poe, or the fanatically refined sensibility found in Henry James.

As an intentionally fuzzy narrative, **"Green Tea"** is similar to several tales in Ambrose Bierce's *In the Midst of Life* and *Can Such Things Be?* Like Bierce's "The Moonlit Road" and "The Suitable Surroundings," **"Green Tea"** seems arbitrarily burdened with narrators and editors. Yet the seeming arbitrariness of the narrative scheme imparts a unique atmosphere to these tales. Le Fanu anticipates Bierce in his evocation of a world where things refuse to fit together, where terrible things happen to the wrong people for the wrong reasons, where horrors leap out of the most trivial or ridiculous contexts. The disjointedness of the narrative pattern reinforces our sense of a nightmare world where everything is out of joint. Why should we expect aesthetic order when monkeys can chase people into their graves, green tea can cause damnation, and therapists can suddenly drop out of sight when patients are on the precipice of suicide? Besides instilling a sense of underlying chaos, the filtering device also gives the impression of narrative distance, a useful effect in any kind of ironic fiction, but particularly necessary in the ghost story, where too much narrative directness can instantly blunt the desired impact. Jennings must seem like a thoroughly helpless creature, dwarfed by diabolical forces beyond his comprehension (let alone control) and gradually receding from our vision into hell. What could serve this purpose better than to have his narrative manipulated by three verbose doctors who are more concerned with selling their theories than with protecting his sanity?

Le Fanu's complicated narrative skein also helps create the "loophole" of ambiguity mentioned by M. R. James. It is at least *possible* that Hesselius's claims are justified, that his unorthodox medications would have banished Jennings's monkey, and that his infallibility is "absolutely certain." (Although this certainty would not efface the supernatural element in the story, it would have the disappointing effect of a natural explanation: demonic forces might still exist in some sense, but would be so easily subdued by infallible German doctors as to be in effect naturalized.) For the many reasons mentioned, however, we doubt Hesselius's word: the easy way out is a remote possibility but "not quite practicable." Even if Hesselius were believable as the medical equivalent of a Dickensian benefactor (dispensing cures instead of money at the end), we would still be left with the terrible irony of Jennings destroying himself just as he is about to be delivered.

Either way, **"Green Tea"** is a horror tale. It is Le Fanu's most extreme, yet most controlled performance. Although the "well managed crescendo" admired by M. R. James occurs in most of his tales, nowhere is it more attenuated and cumulative than in **"Green Tea."** In **"Schalken the Painter," "Chief Justice Harbottle"** and others, the initial apparition comes fairly quickly; here the "journey" is more leisurely and spread out; the distance travelled is greater. By taking his time, Le Fanu makes Jennings's "doors of perception" experience all the more painful and catastrophic. Similarly, the heavy use of ambiguity and dramatic irony suggests a dislocated, strangely modern world where reality is grim enough to outpace our most exaggerated fantasies. Though written in the late nineteenth century, **"Green Tea,"** as E. F. Benson has happily put it, is "instinct with an awfulness which custom cannot stale" [*The Spectator* (1931)]. Those who find ghost stories boring or silly will probably interpret "awfulness" in a different way than Benson intended. But the rest of us know exactly what he means. (pp. 12-31)

> *Jack Sullivan, " 'Green Tea': The Archetypal Ghost Story," in his* Elegant Nightmares: The English Ghost Story from Le Fanu to Blackwood, *Ohio University Press, 1978, pp. 11-31.*

Kel Roop (essay date 1985)

[*In the following essay, Roop discusses the influence of the Dutch painter Godfrey Schalken on Le Fanu's style and portrayal of evil in his short stories.*]

Illuminated by infrequent scholarship, the stories of gothic writer Joseph Sheridan Le Fanu have remained hidden in the recesses of literary appreciation. His admirers may, in fact, regard such obscurity as most appropriate for this author of the macabre tale who so effectively casts his characters in darkness. Horror seems masterly woven in the black textures of his stories; however, it most thoroughly infects the Le Fanu world through the eerie play of candle flames and moonbeams. Indeed, in their depiction of an unholy cosmos, Le Fanu's stories suggest an intricate structuring of light patterned after the technique of the minor Dutch painter Godfrey Schalken. Although the influence of Schalken has essentially escaped critical attention, this lesser painter figures as subject and title of an early Le Fanu story and, perhaps even more significantly, as originator of the writer's luminous paradigm of evil.

As a student of Gerard Dou, a master of *Helldunkelstudien,* Godfrey Schalken received a thorough introduction

A portrait of Le Fanu circa 1843.

to the chiaroscuro popular with Dutch painters of the seventeenth century and appears to have adopted many of his mentor's candlelit subjects as his own. But in his combination of light sources (such as the blending of candle, pipe, and ember light in "A Comely Woman at an Arched Window"), Schalken exceeded Dou's instruction. In order to capture the hybrid gleam most effectively, he often arranged his subjects within a series of frames formed by windows and curtains for which his spots of light provided the focus. Even more important is the larger frame Schalken apparently employed in the production of his paintings. Like his contemporaries, Schalken may have experimented with optics in order to achieve the most natural representation. Although the details of his technique remain undisclosed, he is said to have painted his scenes by the means of an optical device: "he placed the object he intended to paint in a dark room, with a candle, and looking through a small hole, painted by day what he saw by candle-light" [*Bryan's Dictionary of Painters and Engravers*].

Le Fanu seems to have written **"Schalken the Painter"** and the four supernatural stories of *In a Glass Darkly* (**"Green Tea," "The Familiar," "Mr. Justice Harbottle," "Carmilla"**) in a similar fashion. He leaves only the smallest opening of perception in his layered narrations, yet through this aperture he, the reader, and the characters see and plummet into scenes molded by flickering candle-light. Le Fanu's careful ordering finally betrays a universe permeated by a malignant glow which usurps human power.

Of the stories addressed in this essay, all but **"The Familiar"** make specific references to art. **"Schalken the Painter"** (1839), an earlier story than those contained in *In a Glass Darkly* (1872), seems a dominant example of Le Fanu's later technique. The story opens with a description of a painting typical of Schalken's style: against an antique religious backdrop, a woman with an "arch smile" holds a lamp while a male figure gropes for his sword in alarm. However, the reader slowly sees the painting through Le Fanu's viewfinder until the writer's own candlelight transforms the original "representation of reality"; by the end of the story, the enigmatic composition has unfolded into a complete vision of terror dominated by the ghastly addition of the demon Vanderhausen. Contained within the frame formed by the two images, Le Fanu's story has become a study of preternatural evil. In its aptly titled chapter "A Wonderful Likeness," the story **"Carmilla"** also incorporates paintings as integral elements to be reformed by Le Fanu's spectroscope. Portraits of Laura's family, refinished by "something of an artist," appear to reveal the true identity of the vampire, for in the painting of Mircalla Karnstein "was the effigy of Carmilla." The narrative, however, ultimately challenges a simplistic one-to-one correspondence between painting and subject. In similar fashion does the writer verbally extend and "refinish" the visual art in **"Mr. Justice Harbottle"** and **"Green Tea"**; the spectral hangman Harbottle sees resembles that in "the famous print of the 'Idle Apprentice'," while the countenance of Jennings in **"Green Tea"** is "flushed out, like a portrait of Schalken's, before its background of darkness."

At first these portraits may simply enforce a recognition of a demonic hinterland: through these images of the vampiric Carmilla, the ghoulish hangman, the spectral Rose, and even the living yet possessed Jennings, Le Fanu delineates the supernatural world before the reader. Although the painting by Schalken contains the figure of the artist, the narrator informs the reader that it is "valuable for . . . presenting a portrait of his early [yet deceased] love, Rose Velderkaust." For the narrator, Schalken is simply an inconsequential human embellishment. Likewise, the Le Fanu narrative may seem significant only for its sensational rendering of the macabre. Within his understated prose, the writer jars the reader out of earthly security with rare yet striking depictions of unearthly beings. No corners or blankets can conceal the vision.

The specter, however, seems arrested within the boundaries of the canvas. Despite the initial shock of seeing the other world, the reader may enjoy safety in the knowledge that the demon is caged by the paintings' or stories' edges. Especially in Schalken's painting does art clearly appear an attempt at objectification. In a "dream," the inspiration for the painting, the ghost of Rose leads the artist through a labyrinth to an old Dutch room where she draws back the curtains of a heavy bed to unveil her demon spouse Vanderhausen. Schalken's painting shields the viewer from this malignant vision unacceptable to the rational mind and offers only the more benign image of Rose. In **"Carmilla"** and **"Green Tea,"** such artistic containment appears a means of scientific discovery. Laura examines the painting with experimental precision: "Here you Carmilla are, living smiling, ready to speak, in this picture. Isn't it beautiful, papa? And see, even the mole on her throat." A perfect reflection of the succubus, the painting has captured every feature. And Carmilla reacts to the threat of the painting as does the traditional vampire to the mirror: with avoidance. To Laura's exclamations she says nothing and at last diverts attention from herself to the moonlight. In **"Green Tea,"** Jennings' resemblance to a Schalken painting becomes part of the whole scientific method of Dr. Hesselius, who "guessed well the nature, though not even vaguely the particulars of the revelations he was about to receive, from that fixed face."

Through his narrative ordering of the supernatural, Le Fanu might thus resemble the "picture-cleaner" in **"Carmilla,"** who arrives "armed with hammer, ripping chisel, and turnscrew" for the unpacking, equipped to conquer the evil within the boxes. His mastery seems complete as the paintings are methodically checked off according to "corresponding numbers" and "restored to their places." The paintings appear to capture, isolate, and control within their gallery the supernatural traces filtered into the temporal world. So too do Le Fanu's intersecting stories foster the illusion that evil may not transgress the frame's edge.

Yet neither painting nor printed word can, in fact, shield man from the fiend. The portraits actually efface the boundaries between earthly and unearthly forces, for their canvases often combine human with spectral forms. Although the narrator of **"Schalken the Painter"** ignores this human element, the more perceptive viewer would not. Indeed, included within the "portrait of [Schalken's] early love" is the figure of the painter aggressively posed: "in an attitude of alarm, his hand is placed upon the hilt of his sword, which he appears to be in the act of drawing." An emblem of the combat between the natural and supernatural, the painting belies the epigraphical edict: "Let him, therefore, take his rod away from me, and let not his fear terrify me."

Recent scholarship explains this juxtaposition of worlds as representative of the psychological state of the human viewer or participant. The portraits merely symbolize the war between the unconscious and conscious, the heart and the mind. But such attempts to fix the portraits in a post-Freudian interpretation may reveal more about contemporary interests than about the Victorian Le Fanu's artistic concerns. Admittedly, Le Fanu brings psychological nuances to the ghost story, but he ultimately subordinates them to tightly structured representations of supernatural evil.

By reducing characters to emblems, Le Fanu forces the reader's attention to a powerful structure that does not contain but creates the evil into which it draws its victims. Actual and figurative galleries only offer the facade of restraint. In reality, Le Fanu's portraits undermine safety, for they supply no final limits, no enclosures; Carmilla's and Schalken's paintings noticeably lack frames. Although painted as the culmination of ghostly events, Schalken's portrait provides the introduction to Le Fanu's story, the portal into the macabre. Even more explicitly does Schalken's drawing of Saint Anthony in the same story allow the entrance of the fiend. As Schalken curses the imperfections of the painting, the demon Vanderhausen simultaneously appears. Finally, in his writing of **"Schalken the Painter,"** Le Fanu distends the unbounded threshold of the artist's portrait of Rose into a sinister foyer. His story deepens the painting's original "interior of what might be a chamber in some antique religious building" with a corridor comprised of a narrow hallway, a Dutch compartment, a curtained bed, and even the "arch smile" of Rose. Through a compounding of internal frames, the painting becomes a three-dimensional shadow box which draws the reader into terror.

As the title suggests, *In a Glass Darkly* narrows the portrait aperture to that of the window, a symbol of vision appearing repeatedly in **"Carmilla," "Green Tea," "The Familiar,"** and **"Mr. Justice Harbottle."** But like the portrait, the window only creates a semblance of secure insight by uniquely blending barrier with peephole. The observer thinks that the plate of glass affords him an opportunity of seeing without interacting. In reality, the transparent window acts more as the slit of a Schalken viewfinder that at once arrests and creates, often forging the characters and even the readers into its creations.

Throughout the stories, Le Fanu's windows consistently resemble optic lenses. No expansive panes dominate the characters' cheerless facades; rather the houses, rooms, and even doors are equipped merely with elongated slivers of glass. "Tall" and "slender" windows open into the houses of both **"Green Tea"** and **"Mr. Justice Harbottle"**; in **"Carmilla,"** Laura confers with her priest in a room lit by a "small lattice"; and perhaps most ominous of all is the narrow transom in **"The Familiar,"** a *kind* of window" (emphasis added). Like the paintings, windows also achieve a three-dimensional depth. Rarely flush with the wall, they are more often, as in **"Green Tea,"** part of a deep "recess" formed by bookcases or other projections, frequently located in rooms suggestive of art. In **"Schalken the Painter,"** the artist first strains to see Vanderhausen from the window of his studio. Such studio-window association becomes a source for repetitive punning in the stories of *In a Glass Darkly,* in which windows often appear in the "drawing room."

Although windows proliferate in the Le Fanu canon, they allow only the most imperfect vision. Those of Justice Harbottle's house are especially inefficient; in the course of the story, they are obstructed by "bills" (of sale), "turned . . . yellow by time," and even "stained with dust and rain of fifty years." Attempts to view the temporal world through such openings can result only in frustration. Even those less encumbered panes of the other stories hinder willed sight. No matter how determined Schalken might be, the window will not yield the physical form of Vanderhausen. Yet at times the glass does provide capricious glimpses of the intangible. In **"The Familiar,"** the General sees from a window the darting figure of Barton's specter. Justice Harbottle is also permitted several views of his ghoulish prosecutors through the window of his carriage. But these images appear unsolicited and suggest containment by rather than of the supernatural.

Nonetheless, like the stories' portraits, windows seem to check the evil. Those lining Harbottle's house and the chateau in **"Carmilla"** are separated like paintings in a gallery, each sheet of glass rendering a distinct static image. As Harbottle's carriage winds its way past his spectral prosecutors, each scene framed by the window resembles a tableau in a Renaissance pageant of the seven deadly sins. But unlike Spenser's Red Cross Knight, Harbottle does not gain saving insight from the parade of evil. The window's edges provide a momentary false comfort; Harbottle awakens in the carriage mistakenly convinced that the ghouls were only actors in a nightmare. They soon slip beyond the windowsill, infiltrate Harbottle's house, and hang the corrupt judge. Le Fanu's compounding of window imagery throughout *In a Glass Darkly* only makes multifaceted prisms out of isolated windows, the houses, and even the volume; and these prisms release rather than control evil.

The window of the shadow box is thus an active medium, creating as well as framing supernatural forms. It does not reflect but "throws a rosy light"; it does not reveal but "commands a view." And as the window acquires greater power, man steadily loses his. In **"The Familiar,"** Barton sees the demon through the window and "staggers slowly back, like one who had received a stunning blow"; when Montague also sees the figure, he mindlessly and "mechanically" chases it, succumbing to the ultimate power of the window to suck the natural character into preternatural depths. Montague's plunge—unlike that of Rose Velderkaust, Captain Barton, Rev. Jennings, or Justice Harbottle—does not lead to the ends of the abyss. Yet for these less fortunate characters, the window is the impetus to a permanent fall into death. Rose disappears from her room, leaving behind her only an open window looking down on a quietly rippling canal.

The windows of *In a Glass Darkly* as well as **"Schalken the Painter"** do not reveal interiors dominated by the expected gloom but rather by light, especially Schalken candlelight. In **"Schalken the Painter,"** the narrator "positions" the characters so that the reader might better understand the events and uses candles as the focus for this "composition." Yet this same narrator attempts to undermine the importance of lighting in the Schalken painting, arguing that "the curious management of its lights constitutes, as usual in his pieces, the chief apparent merit of his pictures. I say *apparent,* for in its subject, and not in its handling, however exquisite, consists its real value." Juxtaposed to the narrator's own artistic design, this statement loses credibility and through its adamant denial actually directs the reader's attention to the light. In a Schalken painting or a Le Fanu tale, the artist consistently subordinates subjects or forms—mere victims of preternatural illumination—to the "management of lights."

Although myriad lights merge to cast a pernicious glow in Le Fanu's stories, the characters presume to forge a dichotomy distinguishing benign from malevolent light sources. Dr. Hesselius in **"Green Tea"** calls the twilight "odd"; for Captain Barton in **"The Familiar,"** moonlight is "imperfect"; and the narrator of **"The Familiar"** identifies a division of light yielded by the transom, a window "intended in the day to aid in lighting the passage, and through which at present the rays of the candle were issuing." But in the Le Fanu tale, such duality deceives. The writer does not offer a Platonic world in which the observer need only leave the shadowy cave to find perfect goodness. Rather, Le Fanu's light emanates from and remains within the shadow box, generating the essence of evil.

Most deceptive of all is daylight, in which the characters invest a naive faith. Like a child clutching the blanket over his eyes, Captain Barton waits for the sun to dispel the boogieman; but still he hears the demon muttering in the "daytime as well as after nightfall." Barton's minister is also surprised by the sensation of evil, "though it was broad daylight." Only the six-year-old Laura in **"Carmilla"** does not hold a child's trust in the sun's glare, which cannot quell her fears from the nightmare of the night before. Like those best acquainted with the supernatural, she knows that daylight has no power over evil. If anything, it is a source of malevolent energy which imbues Carmilla with her beauty, evokes Jennings' demonic monkey, and animates Captain Barton's "familiar." The fiend jostles the arm of General Montague on a crowded, sunny street of Paris and becomes only more ominous in "familiar" daylight.

Le Fanu's window-prisms gradually divide the brilliance of daylight into its more elusive counterparts of moonlight and twilight. Although in the stories moonlight often accompanies the first appearance of demonic forms, its radiance beguiles the character caught within the shadow box. Barton wonders at the formless footsteps he hears, for "there was sufficient moonlight to disclose any object." Rather than a means of vision, the moon is a mood shaper, whose mysterious properties are detailed at length by Laura's governess in **"Carmilla."** In the story, the seemingly objective rays of the sun surrender to the less transparent but more provacative "rosy" moonbeams at play in the windows of chateaus. In **"Green Tea,"** twilight supplies an even more expansive red-stained palette. As though the sun were actually setting in the midst of Jennings' room, "the red reflected light of the western sky" settles on Jennings and his figure is "faintly seen in the ruddy twilight."

Although both moonlight and twilight appear "dusky" and "filmy," their foggy luminosity is more important for its effect on the forms beneath it than for its distortion of light. In one sense, light does not become blurred at twilight but more distinct. With its ruddy color and "filmy" texture, it resembles a tangible being like the fog of Eliot's "Prufrock." But to gain life, it saps that of physical forms just as the vampire Carmilla drains the force from her victims. Edges dissolve under the hazy twilight. The daughter of Justice Harbottle's housekeeper plays in the house until "she can no longer discern the colours of the china figures on the chimneypiece or in the cabinets." As the forms fade to nothing, twilight "deepens," allowing the entrance of Harbottle's hellish executioners.

Through the imagery of lamps and fire, light becomes

more obviously animated, although it assumes a semblance of contained activity. The flame flickering within the glass enclosure seems as confined as a scene caught within the frame of a window or painting. Also, carried and positioned, lamps appear controlled by the stories' characters. In **"Carmilla,"** they are at first frivolous and insignificant decorations: the general attends a ball at a chateau where the "trees were hung with coloured lamps." For both Justice Harbottle and Captain Barton they seem obedient instruments aligned in orderly rows. The "long line of . . . oil lamps" encourages Captain Barton in his flight from the demon by appearing to be a refuge. But the warm glow of the lamps does not protect; Captain Barton hears the bullet's "whistle" as the lights "twinkle" before him.

Uncontained fire realizes the potential dynamism of the lamps. As evil pervades Justice Harbottle's house—as it has nearly enacted its execution of him—the maid imagines an infernal backdrop for his death: "the lamps seemed all to have gone out, and there were stoves and charcoal fires here and there." Still the naive initiate of the shadow box attempts to ignore the flame's tyranny. According to the narrator of both **"Schalken the Painter"** and **"Mr. Justice Harbottle,"** the fires "blaze cheerily" as though they were part of a Dickens' Christmas. Despite the narrator's optimism, the flames of both stories only usher in demonic servants. Within the maid's vision are hellish stoker's feeding the evil blaze.

At the core of the shadow box burns the candle. All the light that has been steadily diffused by the window-prism converges at moments of climax in the candle's flame. With its power to cast shadows that contrast with its distinct glow, the candle exposes and creates those forms usually kept in the crevices of man's mind. Entering her room during a brief escape from Vanderhausen, Rose thinks she sees the demon. By the candle's flame, Schalken too discerns a "shadow" dart around the corner. In **"Carmilla"** candlelight also casts an eerie backdrop from which evolve Laura's nightmares. As a black cat and female figure coagulate from the thick shadows of her room, a "candle burns all through the night."

The demons that inhabit Le Fanu's stories seem in fact pasteboard figures which materialize at the candle's bidding. Despite their torment of the characters, they easily disappear into the darkness. Only the candle remains a constant malignant presence. By the end of **"The Familiar,"** supernatural evil has abandoned its frenzied form; the force that ultimately damns Captain Barton to eternal terror is not that of the fiend. Rather, the candle's flame which the valet observes "slowly shifting" by the transom signifies and abets Captain Barton's collapse. Rose too disappears as a result of candle management. Although she exclaims as the candle's light goes out, "the darkness is unsafe," the gloom is only effected by the flickering flame. Shadows created by the candles so precisely arranged in the story gather around Rose until she succumbs to the final shadow of death. In fact, "by the bedsides" of all the unfortunate victims of evil, candles burn, ironic harbingers of the shadowy cavern into which man must fall.

Still, the victim's greatest shadow in the Le Fanu tale is not that of death but of depersonalization. The candle's flame not only creates supernatural forms, but makes mere shells of men as well. As the force of evil permeates the shadow box, it becomes concentrated in the features of its victims and demons alike. Le Fanu stories become true Schalken paintings in which parts of the form blaze against a backdrop of darkness. Those physical receptacles of personality and spirit—the eyes, the smile—no longer comfort with their mortal mutability, but terrify with their essential and eternal glow of horror. Rose's dress and "arch smile" reflect the light of her lamp; Jennings discovers the monkey demon through the increasingly specific focuses of "two luminous points," "two dull lamps," "tiny discs of red," "little circles," and finally "its eyes"; and Jennings himself is emptied of personality as evil luminosity gains power:

> on the stony face of the sufferer—for the character of his face, though still gentle and sweet, was changed—rested that dim, odd glow which seems to descend and produce, where it touches, lights, sudden though faint, which are lost, almost without gradation, in darkness.

Perhaps most dehumanizing of all is the light's power to make man its servant. Like the ghoul specifically called "lamplighter," man brings the light that dooms others. Rose's uncle, lover, and minister bear the candles that define the scene of her disappearance; the door slams shut and locks Rose away from her uncle as he goes to the anteroom to get yet another candle. Likewise, Jennings' devoted servant errs when he discovers Jennings sitting alone in the dark (for all lights were the same to him) by insisting on lighting the candles. Earlier, Hesselius also "made him have candles lighted." Although Le Fanu's light-bearers may resemble the participants in certain death rites, such as the old Catholic sacrament of Extreme Unction, their light does not usher in the grace of God but fiends of unearthly horror. Indeed, through their ignorance they ignite the candle's wick.

The characters who fall victim to supernatural terror live in a society that often "makes light of " life. A false "gaiety" pervades the world of Captain Barton, whose fiancée, Miss Montague, especially exists in "gay society." In **"Carmilla,"** Laura's father repeatedly reacts to supernatural suggestions with laughter. Laura's governess is even said to have "made light of " the child's nightmare. Of all the characters in **"Carmilla,"** only the vampire herself is overtly identified as not a lightbearer, for she "refused [Laura] . . . the least ray of light." But those beings in whom man places his greatest trust and from whom he seeks the most security ultimately spread the light in the shadow box.

Although "through" in the biblical "through a glass darkly" (1 Cor. 13: 12) suggests that one day man will pass beyond the shadows of the temporal world and into Christian light, Le Fanu offers his reader and characters no such encouragement. For Le Fanu, man is permanently caught *in* a Schalken shadow box sustained by continually flickering candlelight. Only with death can man escape light and dark, can the shadow box collapse, can the "house fall." (pp. 359-69)

Kel Roop, "Making Light in the Shadow Box: The Artistry of Le Fanu," in Papers on Language & Literature, *Vol. 21, No. 4, Fall, 1985, pp. 359-69.*

St. John Sweeney   (essay date 1986)

[*In the following excerpt, Sweeney considers the prose style and plot structures of Le Fanu's short stories.*]

LeFanu wrote short stories throughout his career, and with *Uncle Silas* they are his most read and reprinted work. Less admired than Poe's, they, nevertheless, seem quite as inventive, generally better written, considerably less morbid and having for the most part a sounder basis in psychological truth.

LeFanu's best stories and novellas are currently obtainable in two paperback reprints by Dover. These volumes, entitled **Best Ghost Stories** (1964) and **Ghost Stories and Mysteries** (1975), comprise more than 800 pages, and contain all of LeFanu's short fiction with a claim on posterity. Included, of course, are such anthologists' staples as **"Green Tea," "Mr. Justice Harbottle," "Carmilla," "The Familiar"** and **"The Room in the Dragon Volant."** The many unfamiliar and lesser pieces range from trivial short sketches to a short novel like **"The Haunted Baronet."** Some of these pieces, short and long, have an interest beyond their dubious intrinsic merit, for they use plots and themes which LeFanu later reworked in longer and generally more successful versions. Thus, his **"A Chapter in the History of a Tyrone Family,"** sometimes cited as a source for *Jane Eyre,* he later expanded into *The Wyvern Mystery;* and a good deal of **"The Haunted Baronet"** he later expanded into *Wylder's Hand,* while **"The Murdered Cousin"** is really a precis of the later *Uncle Silas.* Usually the expansions are improvements, and to compare passages in **"The Haunted Baronet"** with their final versions in *Wylder's Hand* is to see an accretion of factual detail and an increased dramatization that are decided improvements.

LeFanu's short fiction is, however, distinctly uneven. If one reads through it in a few sittings and then allows the stories to sift through the background of one's mind for a couple of weeks before returning to them, one disconcertingly discovers that all but a handful of the most familiar and best have fused together into a general amorphous memory. The reason is basically that LeFanu, for all of his cleverness and individuality, was, as in his later novels, working much too conventionally. Even more than in the novels, does he accept the Gothic tradition of the eighteenth century. And, like his nineteenth century colleagues, such as Hoffman, Hawthorne and Poe, he has accepted the traditional hackneyed stage props—the gloom, the morbidity, the seclusion, introspection and loneliness, the Gothic castles, the romantic and shadowy landscapes, and the never-never land of a vaguely distant past.

Much of this might have been negated had LeFanu escaped more than partially from the conventional prose in which these Gothicisms were traditionally embalmed. He would rarely be capable of such turgidities as Hawthorne's

> Thus it happened, that when Phoebe heard a certain noise in Judge Pyncheon's throat,—rather habitual with him, not altogether voluntary, yet indicative of nothing, unless it were a slight bronchial complaint, or, as some people hinted, an apoplectic symptom,—when the girl heard this queer and awkward ingurgitation (which the writer never did hear, and therefore cannot describe), she, very foolishly, started, and clasped her hands.

Or of such pompous silliness as Poe's

> Ligeia! Ligeia! Buried in studies of a nature more than all else adapted to deaden impression of the outward world, it is by that sweet word alone—by Ligeia—that I bring before mine eyes in fancy the image of her who is no more. And now, while I write, a recollection flashes upon me that I have *never known* the paternal name of her who was my friend and my bethrothed, and who became the partner of my studies, and finally the wife of my bosom. Was it a playful charge on the part of my Ligeia? or was it a test of my strength of affection, that I should institute no inquiries upon this point? or was it rather a caprice of my own—a wildly romantic offering on the shrine of the most passionate devotion? I but indistinctly recall the fact itself—what wonder that I have utterly forgotten the circumstances which originated or attended it? And, indeed, if ever that spirit which is entitled *Romance*—if ever she, the wan and the misty-winged *Ashtophet* of idolatrous Egypt, presided, as they tell, over marriages ill-omened, then most surely she presided over mine.

Nevertheless, LeFanu does have a profusion of rambling Victorian sentences, more like Hawthorne's than Poe's, filled with stock and generalized horrors rather than specific observation. To take a quite random example:

> It appeared that she had repaired to the kitchen garden, pursuant to her mistress's directions, and had there begun to make the specified election among the rank and neglected herbs which crowded one corner of the enclosure. . . .

How good if he could have avoided these prissy circumlocutions of polite letters and simply said, "She went to the overgrown kitchen garden as her mistress had told her and gathered herbs." One is reminded of Hawthorne writing

> Hepzibah had no natural turn for cookery, and, to say the truth, had fairly incurred her present meagreness by often choosing to go without her dinner rather than be attendant on the rotation of the spit, or ebullition of the pot.

When what he meant was "Hepzibah had grown skinny because she did not like to cook." However, to continue the LeFanu quote:

> . . . and while engaged in this pleasant labour, she carelessly sang a fragment of an old song, as she said "to keep herself company." She was, however, interrupted by a sort of mocking echo of the air she was singing; and, looking up, she saw through the old thorn hedge, which surrounded the garden, a singularly ill-looking little

man, whose countenance wore the stamp of menace and malignity, standing close to her, at the other side of the hawthorn hedge.

This passage from the opening of Chapter VIII of **"The Familiar"** is an all too typical example of the flaccid verbosity of polite nineteenth century letters. It is also typical of LeFanu's style, although he, much more than Hawthorne or Poe, is able to transcend it and attain a terse muscularity. A good deal of even a relatively poor story like **"The Dead Sexton"** is told in dialogue and in sentences as tight and specific as:

> It was about eight o'clock, and the hostler, standing alone on the road in front of the open door of the George and Dragon, had just smoked his pipe out. A bright moon hung in the frosty sky.

A lean and exact prose is not, of course, one of the first necessities of fiction. Millions of people have waded through the floridities of Walter Scott, the turgidities of Fenimore Cooper and the modern aridities of Arthur Hailey or Leon Uris in pursuit of an engrossing story. And story is one of LeFanu's strong points in the best of his short fiction, and quite enough to ensure that some of it will stay in print.

The ghost story is, of course, a sure-fire genre for evoking tension. Like a good joke, a good ghost story has its own necessities, and the first of them is that it be a tensely connected series of increasingly alarming events. A dull ghost story is one like *The House of the Seven Gables* in which the space given to the progress of the narrative is but one-third of the book. To be more precise, only seven of the book's twenty-one chapters further the plot. The other fourteen are either ineffectively sombre or falsely jocular essays, and they take up so much space that the story is buried and its interest minimized.

In matters of craftsmanship, LeFanu is much less the amateur than Hawthorne and fine enough to have seen that a good ghost story is not merely a horrific situation, but a series of ever more alarming events leading to a climax. All of his successful pieces, such as **"Mr. Justice Harbottle," "Carmilla," "Green Tea"** or **"An Account of Some Strange Disturbances in Aungier Street,"** embody this structure. There is a curious and unsettling incident, followed by several increasingly sinister ones that finally culminate in a fearful confrontation and an instantaneous catastrophe. Sometimes, as in his long fiction, LeFanu scants or even skips his confrontation. Perhaps the reason was Victorian primness, or perhaps a debatable notion that the implied is stronger than the dramatized. But in such cases, the soundest rule is probably that the better the build-up, the stronger must be the delivery.

In his short as in his long fiction, LeFanu was as attracted to the mysterious as he was to the ghostly; and in several ways the ghost story is akin to the detective story. In both genres there is an inexplicable event, a mystery. In the detective story, the mystery is explained rationally and in the ghost story supernaturally. LeFanu's **"Carmilla"** and Bram Stoker's similar *Dracula* blend these allied sub-genres and are really supernatural detective stories.

In the detective story proper, however, the most dramatic event, the crime, occurs towards the beginning. The events that follow, the actual detecting, are generally of lesser dramatic value, and the climax is more of a revelation of the criminal rather than a confrontation—that is, exposition rather than drama. The endings of **"Carmilla"** and *Dracula* do top their beginnings in their dramatized final scenes; but in an ordinary detective story, although the culprit may make a final flourish of bravado, he inevitably is quickly disarmed and marched off to jail. The real drama is his being named.

The distinction between the detective story and the ghost story might be simply stated by labelling them the whodunnit and the whatdunnit. The whodunnit recapitulates correctly a puzzling past series of events; the whatdunnit dramatizes eerily a mysterious present series. Masters of one genre are often attracted to the sister form; and Poe, who is most noted for the mysterious and the macabre, is also called the Father of the modern detective story, largely for his three Dupin stories and his ingenious "The Gold Bug." One of the cleverest plotters of modern detective stories, John Dickson Carr, enlivened many of his best yarns by initially inexplicable overtones of ghosts and Gothicism. LeFanu's Dr. Hesselius, whose papers form the basis of a series of supernatural stories, could well have developed into a Dupin or Holmes whom, in brief form, he resembles.

One difficulty of the mystery's intricate plotting is how the plot is presented; and in his short stories, as in his novels, LeFanu sometimes botches his telling. He will sometimes generate tension by arbitrarily shifting his point of view or by dropping the curtain to hold back crucial events. Sometimes also he will tip his hand too quickly. For instance, one major blot in his gripping and clever **"Room in the Dragon Volant"** is that the hero and narrator is so stupid that the reader is always about two chapters ahead of him.

However, even the most craftsmanlike plotting of an intricate series of melodramatic events will only result in an entertainment. Art demands more than the ingenious, the curious or the outre. Partially and occasionally, LeFanu does give more, even gives a sense of urgency and reality. To take but a few well-known examples, the obscene and grinning monkey which haunts the protagonist of **"Green Tea,"** the inescapable lesbian overtones in **"Carmilla,"** the desperate ferocity of lust in **"Schalken the Painter,"** perhaps even the implacable malignity of **"The Mysterious Lodger"**—all of these stories either overtly touch on depths of the psyche or assert that they are metaphors for basic if often suppressed emotions.

Thus, at his best, LeFanu re-invigorates the traditional genres of whodunnit and whatdunnit. On the level of entertainment, his ideas are often striking and inimitable. On the level of art, he sometimes infuses into the traditional forms darker perceptions and deeper insinuations than one expects from forms that usually depend upon the simplistic blacks of depravity and whites of innocence. But, whether considered as engrossing ingenuities or as parables and metaphors, a handful of his stories remain fresh. Whether he be considered more akin to Poe, or occasionally more akin to Faulkner, it is certain that some of his tales will continue to be read. (pp. 25-9)

St. John Sweeney, "Sheridan Lefanu, The Irish Poe," in The Journal of Irish Literature, *Vol. XV, No. 1, January, 1986, pp. 3-32.*

Harold Orel   (essay date 1986)

[*Orel is an American educator and critic specializing in British literature. In the following excerpt, he examines Le Fanu's device of presenting the stories in* In a Glass Darkly *as factual accounts.*]

Le Fanu's sensational novels began with *The House by the Churchyard* (serialized between October 1861 and February 1863). They are of more than passing interest in any history of the Victorian novel because of the skill with which shocking incidents are depicted, the wealth of information about Anglo-Irish tribal ways that they contain, and the connections that key incidents and intellectual arguments make with Le Fanu's own troubled life. But since my primary concern is with the powerful creative fictions that he wrote in shorter form, I should note immediately . . . [Le Fanu's] emphasis on the truthful substratum lying beneath what [he] had imagined.

Take, as one example, **"A Chapter in the History of a Tyrone Family."** This extraordinary narrative of a secret first wife and a bigamous second ends with an attempted murder of the second wife, the sudden onset of insanity on the part of the husband, and a gory suicide. (The story served as inspiration for an important strand in the narrative of *Jane Eyre*.) LeFanu's story concludes: "Thus ends a brief tale whose prominent incidents many will recognize as having marked the history of a distinguished family; and though it refers to a somewhat distant date, we shall be found not to have taken, upon that account, any liberties with the facts, but in our statement of all incidents to have rigorously and faithfully adhered to the truth."

Similar protestations of historical fidelity are made in other stories. The conclusion of **"Strange Event in the Life of Schalken the Painter"** records the somewhat complacent satisfaction of the storyteller that he has "studiously" omitted the heightening of "many points of the narrative, when a little additional colouring might have added effect to the recital . . . " Francis Purcell, whose collected papers include a number of stories about supernatural visitants and inexplicable occurrences, is presented to the reader (in a prefatory note to Le Fanu's first-published story, **"The Ghost and the Bone-Setter"**) as a real parish priest who for nearly fifty years has resided in the south of Ireland, and who is widely known as an antiquarian with literary tastes.

In a Glass Darkly (1872), perhaps the most popular collection of Le Fanu's stories, is unified by its brief introductions, all of which refer to the narrator's friendship with a fellow-physician, Dr. Martin Hesselius. The stories are, presumably, records of "cases," since the narrator, who acted for twenty years as the German doctor's secretary, finds himself fortuitously in a position where he can recount the more interesting, amusing, or horrifying narratives, those (in other words) which do not possess interest limited to a specialist. The medical jottings which constitute the major text of the prologues to the tales are scientific in their diction; they lend greater credibility to each case. For example, the introduction to **"The Familiar"** [also known as **"The Watcher"**] differentiates three kinds of disease on the basis of a subjective-objective dichotomy, with learned allusions to a periodical "vibratory disturbance" which affects the brain-covering. The remarkable precision of nomenclature in these prefaces exhibits a lawyer's delight in mastering the details of a brief. The curtain raiser for the novella **"The Room in the Dragon Volant"** alludes to Doctor Hesselius's "extraordinary Essay upon the Drugs of the Dark and the Middle Ages," and to several "infusions and distillations well known to the sages of eight hundred years ago," i.e., the *Vinum letiferum*, the *Beatifica*, the *Somnus Angelorum*, the *Hypnus Sagarum*, and the *Aqua Thessalliae*. To the narrative which recounts **"The Fortunes of Sir Robert Ardagh"** Le Fanu appends a final note: "The events which I have recorded are not imaginary. They are FACTS; and there lives one whose authority none would venture to question, who could vindicate the accuracy of every statement which I have set down, and that, too, with all the circumstantiality of an eyewitness."

Were there indeed any contemporaries of Le Fanu who needed to be told that the happenings of these incredible stories were founded on "FACT"? Probably not. This story-telling convention, emphasizing the provability or historicity of fictional materials, . . . went back to Defoe's time, and beyond, to Queen Elizabeth's day.

But it does not do to be cynical about the seeming ingenuousness of these claims. If on the one hand Le Fanu imagined more than he willingly admitted, on the other he was writing more autobiographically than many of his contemporaries appreciated. His financial difficulties in Merrion Square were not all that dissimilar from those suffered by the Wares in *The Tenants of Malory*, a book that he completed after the crash of 1866. W. J. McCormack [in his *Sheridan Le Fanu and Victorian Ireland*] reads *All in the Dark* (1866) and *Haunted Lives* (1868) as "an assault on authority as understood in Le Fanu's generation," on a society which was "patriarchal, hierarchical, and, ultimately, justified by God the Father." Moreover, the "psychic decomposition" in a large number of his stories had its painful roots in the troubled politics of 1842-8, and in his own marital and domestic crises of 1850 and 1858. And always he made the miseries of his life into the materials of his art. Unlike Charles Lever, who stressed both the comic and the happier aspects of Irish character, and whose novels (as a direct consequence) were greatly admired by English readers, Le Fanu saw Irish life as essentially tragic. He was depressed by man's willingness to commit evil; there was something within man that made evil an attractive course of action; and in his world, in Ireland, he identified a number of recurring themes for his fiction.

These themes have political overtones. The first that I want to consider is the conviction that the nineteenth century had inherited, and must pay for, the sins of the eighteenth. The story **"The Watcher"** (first published in 1847) describes events dated vaguely "somewhere about the year 1794." Its major character is a former frigate commander "during the greatest part of the American war," a baronet named Sir James Barton. He is a free-thinker. Not long after the announcement of his engagement, he disputes, at the home of the dowager aunt of his fiancée, the evidences of revelation. He states firmly his utter disbelief in the supernatural and the marvelous. "French principles," particularly those which profess allegiance to Whiggism— and hence of some concern to the conservative Le Fanu— have so infiltrated fashionable society that "neither the old lady nor her charge were so perfectly free from the taint as to look upon Mr. Barton's views as any serious objection to the proposed union."

> Le Fanu provides for his *revenants* a local habitation and a name. By means of framing devices—the collection of Francis Purcell, the parish priest of Drumcoolagh; the medical papers of Dr. Hesselius; the idyllic community of Golden Friars, which is carefully described before we move into the horrors of "The Haunted Baronet"— he suggests the plausibility of the environment, and identifies the motives of the narrator, as necessary preliminaries to the fiction itself.
>
> —*Harold Orel*

Captain Barton sees ghosts, a series of spectral appearances, and gradually loses faith in the universality of natural laws of cause and effect. Visitants keep turning up at inconvenient moments, and his "pride of scepticism" deteriorates. Proofs of the existence of a malevolent watcher multiply. He visits a doctor, who attempts to discover the cause lying behind his "occasional palpitations, and headache." Can these be traceable to something physical, something factual? The medical analysis proves useless; Captain Barton fights against "superstitious tremors," and his mind gradually turns in upon itself. He visits a celebrated preacher, and confesses to him that he is an unbeliever, "and, therefore, incapable of deriving help from religion." But he protests that he holds a very deep interest in the subject despite his rejection of what is ordinarily called revelation, despite his inability to pray. He is becoming convinced that "there does exist beyond this a spiritual world—a system whose workings are generally in mercy hidden from us—a system which may be, and which is sometimes, partially and terribly revealed." The preacher advises the Captain to change his venue, take a few tonics, diet, and exercise. These are the counsels of sense and sensibility. They are what Barton himself, before he became convinced of the close relationship between guilt and retribution, might have prescribed for himself. Long before story's end, however, he knows that he cannot be saved, and, more important, he has become convinced of his own damnation by the evidence supplied by his own rational faculties.

Le Fanu's line of argument may be paraphrased thus: we deny, on the basis of reason but at our peril, the existence of forms and presences that must (for want of a better term) be denominated "supernatural." A man may know, in his mind, that no one else can see what he sees, and that, therefore, what he sees cannot exist. But in this story, as in a number of others, the combined forces of law (an M.P.), medicine, and the military are as helpless as Barton in the presence of a vengeful visitor from the grave. There is something beyond reason, something greater than the principles of the Enlightenment. We have no right to believe that the existence of the real world in any way undermines the fact of the existence of the world of the imagination. The nightmares of the mentally ill cannot be "talked through." Le Fanu's anger against the presumptions of the *philosophes* of the 1790s burns through story after story, and it is no accident that so many of his narratives are set in the past. Human history, he seems to be arguing, took a turn for the worse as a consequence of the doctrines of a generation of rationalists.

That is one point. The second has to do with the lovelessness of marriage arrangements. Miss Montague, the fiancée, attracts admirers, but her matrimonial prospects are dim until the advent of Captain Barton, who is willing to ignore the problem of her family's limited finances. Miss Montague accepts his suit "conditionally" upon the consent of her father," and her dowager aunt promptly withdraws her "from all further participation in the gaieties of the town" (Miss Montague regards this as somewhat extreme). Le Fanu provides little or no evidence of genuine affection between the two parties, and at a late stage in the narrative, stresses the "singularly painful" status of the neglected fiancée, who has become "an object of pity scarcely one degree less to be commiserated than himself." She is nowhere near Barton's age; she shares few, if any, of his habits. Le Fanu remarks that she has not enjoyed "anything like very vehement or romantic attachment on her part," and adds: "Though grieved and anxious, therefore, she was very far from being heartbroken; a circumstance which, for the sentimental purposes of our tale, is much to be deplored. But truth must be told, especially in a narrative, whose chief, if not only, pretensions to interest consist in a rigid adherence to facts, or what are so reported to have been." The owl presented by the gardener to Miss Montague as a pet (caught "napping among the ivy of a ruined stable") turns out to be connected, in some inexplicable fashion, with the bloody murder of Captain Barton. The "grim and ill-favoured bird" is much-loved by Miss Montague, who, in her unwitting fashion, by sheltering instead of releasing it, becomes responsible for her lover's death; while Barton, from the first, regards it "with an antipathy as violent as it was uttered unaccountable." Miss Montague is not heartless; rather, Le Fanu suggests, from such stony soil—a marriage contract formalized for financial benefit to one side only—a genuine flower of affection cannot grow. A similar world-weary, even jaundiced attitude toward marriage may be traced in other tales.

A third point is related to Le Fanu's striking view of Dublin as a ruined city. This matter goes beyond the isolation of the hero from friends his own age, from the love of his fiancée, from sympathy that might be extended by older and more experienced members of society. Nor is it related to the stock language of Gothic fiction. On the first of Barton's "solitary" walks homeward, Le Fanu emphasizes the "unfinished dwarf walls tracing the foundations of projected rows of houses on either side"; on the second, the "quite deserted" appearance of the streets; on a later occasion, even as Barton approaches "frequented streets," the foundations of a street, "beyond which extended waste fields, full of rubbish and neglected lime and brick kilns, and all now as utterly silent as though no sound had ever disturbed their dark and unsightly solitude."

"The Watcher" is not the best or most subtle of Le Fanu's stories, but it illustrates several striking themes, and Le Fanu, using slight variations, kept returning to them. **"The Watcher,"** however, possesses an intrinsic interest beyond anything so far discussed. The fact that *others can see the apparition* who haunts Captain Barton is significant. Both Barton's servant and General Montague see "a deep indenture, as if caused by a heavy pressure," in the bed that holds the body of the murdered Captain; as the servant puts it, "There was something else on the bed with him!" Before the reader reaches this point in the story, however, there can be no doubt the M.P. has seen the "singularly evil countenance" of the passer-by who so shocks his companion Barton; or that a real musket-ball whistles close to Barton's head; or that General Montague sees the very person "whose appearance so constantly and dreadfully disturbed the repose of his friend"; or even that Lady Rochdale's maid sees the "singularly ill-looking little man, whose countenance wore the stamp of menace and malignity" and whose appearance signals a return of the persecuting demon to Barton's life; also, the stranger passes on a message to the terrified hand-maiden (never delivered, on the orders of Lady Rochdale); that is to say, he actually speaks, and someone other than Barton hears and understands what he has to say.

Le Fanu began his career as story-teller by emphasizing the possibility of natural causes leading to horrifying effects. It may be that Barton was pursued by someone who never died at all, and that the owl behaved in owl-like fashion without necessarily being the visitant—a reincarnation of a sailor who died of lockjaw in a Lisbon hospital. But Le Fanu was growing dissatisfied with conventional explanations of what was happening, and why.

It is curious, for example, how often some form of suicide becomes the only possible solution to the problems created by abnormal tastes in living. **"Mr. Justice Harbottle,"** another of the tales in **In a Glass Darkly,** suggests in its Prologue that "the contagious character" of the intrusion of the spirit-world "upon the proper domain of matter" manifests itself "in certain cases of lunacy, of epilepsy, of catalepsy, and of mania, of a peculiar and painful character, though unattended by incapacity of business." The narrative deals with a judge of the mid-eighteenth century who has "the reputation of being about the wickedest man in England," and whose "great mulberry-coloured face" ex-

hibits "a big carbuncled nose, fierce eyes, and a grim and brutal mouth." Yet he possesses intellectual power (which makes him all the more formidable), and when he learns, from a stranger, that a secret tribunal has been formed to try him for his crimes, he cross-examines his informant in high and zealous style. The judge, profane, sarcastic, and ferocious in his administration of the criminal code of England ("at that time a rather pharisaical, bloody and heinous system of justice"), has every intention of hanging the man whose wife he has converted to his mistress; and does. But the hanged grocer—later—makes an unexpected appearance in court, distracting the judge from his charge to the jury in a case of forgery; Harbottle receives a letter from Caleb Searcher, "Officer of the Crown Solicitor in the Kingdom of Life and Death," announcing that he will be tried for wrongfully executing the grocer. One night, after a play at Drury Lane, he suddenly finds himself pinioned between two "evil-looking fellows, each with a pistol in his hand, and dressed like Bow Street officers." He is driven, in his carriage, to a gigantic gallows, and then to a courtroom where the presiding judge is a Chief Justice Twofold, "a dilated effigy of himself; an image of Mr. Justice Harbottle, at least double his size, and with all his fierce colouring, and his ferocity of eye and visage, enhanced awfully." The not-unexpected verdict of guilty is followed by a sentence of execution—the tenth of the ensuing month is named—and by the forging of iron bands around Harbottle's feet by two blacksmiths ("naked to the waist, with heads like bulls, round shoulders, and the arms of giants"). He wakes from his nightmare and tries to deny its warning to him by complaining to others that he has suffered a sudden seizure of gout. Nevertheless, the passing days find him increasingly gloomy: "I wish I were well purged of my gout. I wish I were as I used to be. 'Tis nothing but vapours, nothing but a maggot." His friends analyze the problem as illness, and his doctor diagnoses his case as hypochondria. On the night before he is scheduled to go to Buxton, "that ancient haunt of crutches and chalk-stones," the hanged grocer reappears, as a vision, to the housekeeper's child and to Harbottle's mistress. A scullery-maid—who does not "vally a ghost not a button"—sees the most frightening ghost of all, "a monstrous figure, over a furnace, beating with a mighty hammer the rings and rivets of a chain." In the morning the Judge is found dead, without the smallest sign of any struggle or resistance, "hanging by the neck from the banister at the top of the great staircase." It may be, as the medical evidence shows, that he has been in a sufficiently atrabilious state to have wanted to do away with himself. But suicide seems pathetically inadequate as an explanation for a death that occurred on the tenth of the month, as predicted. More—Le Fanu strongly implies—is at stake here.

The mind creates its own terrors. Mr. Justice Harbottle (when first we meet him) is described as having features "fixed as a corpse's," so that his violent death is prefigured; but we also remember him as cunning—he does not commit himself even as he cajoles and bamboozles juries to have his own way—and sarcastic for calculated effect. He betrays his best gifts for the sake of mean triumphs over helpless prisoners in the dock; it is impossible to sympathize with him even when the powers which destroy him turn out to be mirror images of his own diabolism, even when Chief Justice Twofold roars him down "with his tremendous voice"; or when he pants and gloats and nods and grins and gibes as he dismisses contemptuously Harbottle's attempt to defend himself. Le Fanu is telling us that Harbottle has done all this to himself, and has, consequently, defined the parameters of his own hell.

"Green Tea" deals with the problems of the Reverend Mr. Jennings, a well-intentioned and charitable bachelor. His frequent breakdowns of health may be due to a failing heart or brain; Dr. Hesselius does not presume to say which. But the narrator, who, in almost every Le Fanu tale, expresses a reasoned view of what transpires, has a Swedenborgian view of materiality: "I believe the entire natural world is but the ultimate expression of that spiritual world from which, in which alone, it has its life. I believe that the essential man is a spirit, that the spirit is an organized substance, but as different in point of material from what we ordinarily understand by matter, as light or electricity is; that the material body is, in the most literal sense, a vesture, and death consequently no interruption of the living man's existence, but simply his extrication from the natural body—a process which commences at the moment of what we term death, and the completion of which, at furthest a few days later, is the resurrection 'in power.'" The argument has implications for medical science, as Dr. Hesselius rightly points out; it suggests further thoughts relevant to the meaning of Captain Barton's persecution; and it characterizes the spiritual continuum which ultimately destroys Jennings. Dr. Hesselius has conducted explorations in metaphysical medicine that remain untranslated from the German, but he can speak with some scientific authority on the ties between the visible and the invisible worlds. He guesses—on the basis of a relatively brief acquaintance with Jennings—that his father had seen a ghost; Lady Mary Heyduke confirms his intuition by adding that his father had, in addition, talked to it. There follows a remarkable chapter, "Dr. Hesselius Picks Up Something in Latin Books." The doctor, visiting Jennings's home on "Blank Street," must wait for a few moments in the library; he is particularly taken by a complete set of Swedenborg's *Arcana Caelestia,* in the original Latin. These volumes have been carefully read, with paper markers in several places. Dr. Hesselius transcribes a number of passages which speak of "the evil spirits associated with man," spirits neither in heaven or hell but rather in their own world. Their enmity is undying: "If evil spirits could perceive that they were associated with man, and yet that they were spirits separate from him, and if they could flow in into the things of his body, they would attempt by a thousand means to destroy him; for they hate man with a deadly hatred . . . " The passage of greatest interest to Dr. Hesselius, which he is reading at the very moment that Jennings's entrance interrupts his absorption with the text, announces that "evil spirits, when seen by other eyes than those of their infernal associates, present themselves, by 'correspondence,' in the shape of the beast (*fera*) which represents their particular lust and life, in aspect direful and atrocious."

It is possible to read Le Fanu's story as basically a narrative of a clergyman whose addiction to strong green tea leads to overstimulation of the nervous system and the conjuring-up of a spectral monkey that seems increasingly real and diabolically dedicated to driving him out of his mind. But the connection between Jennings's intellectual pride and his spiritual undoing is crucial. When Dr. Hesselius finishes reading this note about the *fera,* he is drawn into a conversation with Jennings, the first topic of which is their mutual interest in Swedenborg, and the second is Dr. Harley, "one of the most eminent who had ever practised in England." Presumably this is George Harley (1829-96), whose investigations of the nervous system, among other pioneering research projects, led to high honors and distinguished appointments. Jennings denounces him as "one of the very greatest fools" he had ever met, "a *mere* materialist," one whose mind is "paralytic" and "half dead." He has consulted him about his own nervous disorder—in vain. He has, in other words, no faith in modern medicine, because scientists like Dr. Harley refuse to credit the possibility of the existence of powers beyond their ken.

On a later occasion Jennings reveals that he has spent some four years of his life on "the religious metaphysics of the ancients." This topic is of great interest to Dr. Hesselius, who himself has published a book on metaphysical medicine. He responds to Jennings's revelation: "I know . . . the actual religion of educated and thinking paganism, quite apart from symbolic worship? A wide and very interesting field." Jennings responds that his labors have not been good for the Christian mind. "Paganism," he continues, "is all bound together in essential unity, and, with evil sympathy, their religion involves their art, and both their manners . . . " He has become obsessed with his studies: "I wrote a great deal; I wrote late at night. I was always thinking on the subject, walking about, wherever I was, everywhere. It thoroughly infected me." The infection derives from his investigation of a forbidden past, from free-thinking: "God forgive me!" The first time he encounters his "small black monkey," he is on his way to visit, in a very out-of-the-way section of the city, a collector of "some odd old books, German editions of mediaeval Latin," to indulge still further his taste for a subject which he knows to be "a degrading fascination and the Nemesis sure." He is, unmistakably, collaborating in his own destruction; his pride will bring him down. It does him no good to argue that his "bestial companion" can be explained (Dr. Harley must have thus diagnosed the problem) as "purely disease, a well-known physical affection, as distinctively as small-pox or neuralgia," or to turn to empirical knowledge for solace: "Doctors are all agreed on that, philosophy demonstrates it. I must not be a fool. I've been sitting up too late and I daresay my digestion is quite wrong, and, with God's help, I shall be all right, and this is but a symptom of nervous dyspepsia." But Jennings does not believe a word of this.

The Faustian compact—knowledge of God's design purchased at the expense of man's right to Heaven—has been variously interpreted in Western cultures, but two major versions dictate the direction of most dramatizations of the last four centuries. The first is the strongly orthodox retelling, by Christopher Marlowe, of Faustus's damnation. Faustus has renounced theology for human knowledge; he deserves the eternal damnation that awaits him at play's end, and he knows it; hence the failure of his efforts to call on the living Christ to save him before the final stroke of midnight. The second major version is Goethe's ringing affirmation of the right of man to investigate the laws which govern the universe ("*Es irrt der Mensch so lang er strebt* "); Goethe's Faust can be, and will be, saved; and by the eighteenth century it was well understood that God could forgive the sinner if his primary sin consisted of aspiration toward a higher state of *knowledge.*

Since Goethe's version has been more congenial to modern assumptions, it is striking that Le Fanu's curate takes us back to the older, more dogmatic reading of the symbolic values inherent in the Faust legend. Jennings despairs because Harley's materialism fails to give spirit its proper rank (Dr. Hesselius, whom he meets too late for any real change in his destiny to take place, is the man he should have consulted in the first place), and because Harley is himself writ large. Jennings cannot believe in God as his "comfort and reliance"—these are the terms in Dr. Hesselius's prescription—or in the inability of the "brute" monkey to hurt him. He is beyond medicine, beyond dietary recommendations. After Jennings cuts his throat with his razor, Dr. Hesselius concludes his narrative with the melancholy observation, "My memory rejects the picture with incredulity and horror. Yet I know it is true. It is the story of the process of a poison, a poison which excites the reciprocal action of spirit and nerve, and paralyses the tissue that separates those cognate functions of the senses, the external and the interior. Thus we find strange bed-fellows, and the mortal and immortal prematurely make acquaintance." The echo of Swedenborgian doctrine, allied with a sternly doctrinaire denial of the possibility of Faust's redemption, bestows upon Le Fanu's version a peculiar power.

This particular story has a postscript of some importance to our understanding of the characterization of Dr. Hesselius. After all, Dr. Hesselius's proposed treatment of Mr. Jennings had not even begun before the tragic suicide occurred, and the narrator, for understandable reasons, did not want to accept responsibility for a failed cure. There had been no medical treatment, no laying-on of hands. Dr. Hesselius, a believer in some kind of arterial and venous circulation of fluid through the nerves, can accommodate his understanding of Powers beyond those which a Dr. Harley can accept, and argue that this fluid is material, spiritual, and changeable as a consequence of various abuses (drugs in general, green tea more specifically). The eye is the seat of exterior vision, the nervous tissue and brain of interior vision, of an "inner eye." That eye may be opened by delirium tremens; Jennings opened it by pursuit of the truth underlying religious mysteries in the pagan world; and, Dr. Hesselius informs us somberly, the case of Jennings was complicated by a totally different malady, "hereditary suicidal mania." It may be, as the narrator says, that Jennings had not yet bestowed upon him "his full and unreserved confidence." If he had, Dr. Hesselius is convinced that a treatment extending to a period of possibly two years would have sufficed to cure him ("I have not any doubt . . ."). Patience, "a rational confidence in the physician": these are the "simple conditions" that will lead to an "absolutely certain" cure.

But Dr. Hesselius's confidence that a spectral illusion can be "no less simply curable than a cold in the head or a trifling dyspepsia" is not Le Fanu's, and the evidence supplied in all the stories of *In a Glass Darkly* denies the treatability of mental problems that originate in *hubris,* in ignorance of the proper limits that circumscribe human ambition. *We are too complacent in our conviction that we are situated upon the brink of an understanding of this universe.* Nor is the doctrine simply a commonplace of stories that seek to dignify their treatment of supernatural possibilities: it seems to be as deeply imbedded in '**The Room in the Dragon Volant,**" a novella which emphasizes rational explanations for seemingly eerie events, as in "**Carmilla,**" that notorious progenitor of Bram Stoker's *Dracula.*

Mortis Imago is the name of the drug that the narrator of "**The Room in the Dragon Volant**" takes, unknowingly, in his wine (the Countess, whom he loves passionately, has entered into a conspiracy to murder him). The name also denotes a death of the illusion which has sustained the youth in his adventures during "the eventful year, 1815," when Englishmen, for the first time in a long while, are able to travel without fear on Continental roads. What is this illusion? It has to do with the right to fall in love with a mysterious and lovely lady; with a conviction that one's own pleasing appearance is talismanic; with a faith that God will protect the innocent. In one sense, the story is an attack on sentimental fiction that propagates the myth of love at first sight; Le Fanu makes clear, early in the narrative, that his hero is an ass to be so trusting, on so little proof, that those he encounters are what they say, or that his own wealth is a matter of indifference to others. The number of foolish, even dangerous pledges to which the hero (a Mr. R. Beckett of Berkeley Square) unthinkingly commits himself becomes rather staggering by story's end, and it is not necessary here to recapitulate the problems created by his naive behavior. A few matters may be cited, however, by which Le Fanu's assessment of his major character may be, in turn, judged: the fact that Mr. Beckett travels long distances with "two or three idle books," i.e., novels of dubious literary worth; his complacency ("'Alas! what a life it is!' I moralized, wisely," he remarks at one point); his dreaminess about "the wonderful eyes, the thrilling voice, the exquisite figure of the beautiful lady who had taken possession of my imagination," which prevents him from suspecting her husband's villainy, or her own conspiratorial role; his casual dismissal of advice warning him against rogues of Paris, and his all-too-ready admission of being in possession of a purse of thirty thousand pounds sterling; his over-indulgence in wines (which leads, at a later moment, to his being drugged by a not particularly subtle stratagem); his willingness to enter a quarrel between Colonel Gaillarde and the host of the *Belle Étoile* that does not concern him at all; his extraordinary series of misinterpretations of motives, characters, and relationships throughout. His heroics, as he admits to himself just before he takes the paralyzing cup of noyau, a fruit-flavored brandy liqueur, from the hand of the Countess de St. Alyre, were "unconsciously" founded upon the French school of love-making, and his behavior has, alas, been imitative of vile models in other ways. He has been deceived by others, but, first and foremost, he has deceived himself. Finally in possession of the knowledge that he should have acquired days, weeks earlier, he perceives how truly he has deserved being placed, prematurely, in a coffin designed for a "St. Amand": "I had myself been at the utmost pains to mystify inquiry, should my disappearance excite surmises, and had even written to my few correspondents in England to tell them that they were not to look for a letter from me for three weeks at least." If Monsieur Carmaignac, a detective, did not suddenly materialize as the Victorian version of a *deus ex machina,* armed with a search warrant, the coffin-lid would not have been unscrewed, and the hero would have enjoyed an early, terrible, and fatal lesson in the ways of sin. Le Fanu spares him nothing, even so: Mr. Beckett, who serves the prosecution as principal witness, hopes, in his largely uncorrupted innocence, that he might become, as a consequence of the role he plays in the trial that brings to justice the conspirators, "an object of considerable interest to Parisian society." Instead, to his mortification, he discovers that he has turned into the object of "a good-natured but contemptuous merriment," a *balourd,* a *benêt, un âne,* and that he figures "even in caricatures." He flees from Paris, and travels to Switzerland and Italy. "As the well-worn phrase goes, I was a sadder if not a wiser man."

The implication here is that Mr. Beckett may yet fall prey to new confidence-men and -women, because he knows, at story's end, that he does not have the self-assurance, and the knowledge of self, that might render superfluous the assistance of a Carmaignac. In a world of shadows and masks, where a hero can bamboozle himself and misjudge everything and everyone, love is treacherous, and the price exacted for it excessive. Le Fanu presents the story dispassionately; part of its skill lies in the hero's failure to understand fully the ways in which he has personally been responsible for the macabre climax to his infatuation for the Countess; a reader will learn more than Mr. Beckett about the symbolic relationship between sin and judgment.

The last story of *In a Glass Darkly,* **"Carmilla,"** deals with vampirism. Le Fanu makes no attempt to explain, in realistic terms, the gloomy and affecting legends that he exploits. Dr. Hesselius's "rather elaborate note," attached to the manuscript, is not reproduced by his medical secretary, who promises, rather, that "It will form but one volume of the series of that extraordinary man's collected papers." Dr. Hesselius, however, has described the subject as "involving, not improbably, some of the profoundest arcana of our dual existence, and its intermediates."

Nevertheless, the story concludes with a learned disquisition on the nature of vampires. "The vampire," we are somberly told, "is, apparently, subject, in certain situations, to special conditions," and Baron Vordenburg confirms this view: "It is the nature of vampires to increase and multiply, but according to an ascertained and ghostly law . . . ." Superstitions about the vampire are widespread, but their acceptance or universality does not prove them true, and the narrator, a nineteen-year-old girl, does not presume to explain what she has personally witnessed and experienced save in terms of "the ancient and well-attested belief of the country." Legends have been investigated: "If human testimony, taken with every care and solemnity, judicially, before commissions innumerable, each

consisting of many members, all chosen for integrity and intelligence, and constituting reports more voluminous perhaps than exist upon any one other class of cases, is worth anything, it is difficult to deny, or even to doubt, the existence of such a phenomenon as the vampire." Even so, the emphasis falls on human corruptibility; Le Fanu no more believes in vampires as *fact* than he does in spectral monkeys or lockjaw victims returned from the grave; and his allusions to the relevant "scholarship" (Baron Vordenburg owns copies of *Magia Posthua,* Phlegon's *de Mirabilibus,* Augustine's *de Curâ pro Mortuis,* and John Christofer Herenberg's *Philosophicae et Christianae Cogitationes de Vampiris*) should not distract a reader from the true subject matter of **"Carmilla."** Le Fanu's concern, as in all his narratives, is with the continuity between natural and supernatural modes of existence, and the strong emanations of corruption in human society.

To suggest that the victim of a vampire invites the attack is to say no more than that Le Fanu extends to human behavior a sense of its inherent potential for sexual perversion. **"Carmilla"** is a deeply disturbing story not because its central character sucks blood, but because the innocent eye ("I") of the story is drawn, almost without resistance, into a lesbian relationship with her. The stereotyped language of romantic love is used by Carmilla in ways never contemplated by Le Fanu's contemporary story-tellers: "You do not know how dear you are to me, or you could not think any confidence too great to look for . . . You will think me cruel, very selfish, but love is always selfish; the more ardent the more selfish. How jealous I am you cannot know. You must come with me, loving me, to death; or else hate me, and still come with me, and *hating* me through death and after." Carmilla is "devoted" to her victim; and she has "strange paroxysms of languid adoration"; she gloats "with increasing ardour" the more the strength and spirits of the narrator wane. In the earliest period of Carmilla's relationship with her, she whispers rhapsodically, "In the rapture of my enormous humiliation I live in your warm life, and you shall die—die, sweetly die—into mine. I cannot help it; as I draw near to you, you, in your turn, will draw near to others, and learn the rapture of that cruelty, which yet is love . . . " She embraces her beloved, and her lips "in soft kisses gently glow" upon the cheek of the young heroine. Carmilla holds her hand "with a fond pressure, renewed again and again," and blushes softly, gazing in her face "with languid and burning eyes, and breathing so fast that her dress rose and fell with the tumultuous respiration. It was like the ardour of a lover . . . " This is not necessarily the language of soft-core pornography, despite its emphasis on "hot lips" and gentle caresses along the throat and neck. Le Fanu is dramatizing the heroine's partial willingness to be involved, despite her ill-defined feelings of suspicion: "In these mysterious moods," she writes from the vantage point of a full decade later, "I did not like her. I experienced a strange tumultuous excitement that was pleasurable, ever and anon mingled with a vague sense of fear and disgust. I had no distinct thoughts about her while such scenes lasted, but I was conscious of a love growing into adoration, and also of abhorrence. This I know is paradox, but I can make no other attempt to explain the feeling."

In this confession of emotional confusion there is more than the ingenuousness of a fictional heroine or the disingenuousness of a writer of fiction. Peter Penzoldt's belief that Le Fanu could not have recognized the lesbian love he was describing for what it was need not detain us, any more than the patronizing remarks made by other critics about scenes in Thomas Hardy's novels in which two women are sexually responsive to each other; Le Fanu, no less than Hardy, appreciated the perversity of this kind of relationship, and sought to make his moral point, at some risk because of the situation he was defining and the language he was employing; that point—consistent with earlier points made in the collection *In a Glass Darkly,* and in several stories in *Chronicles of Golden Friars* (1871) and *The Purcell Papers* (1880)—has to do with the evil, nascent or flowering, within each man's soul.

Le Fanu's intention was certainly not to offend moral proprieties. A conventional way to treat **"Carmilla"** would be to discuss, yet one more time, its ties to other tales of vampirism written during the nineteenth century. But it is not perverse to think of **"Carmilla"** as a study in sexual abnormality rather than as another variant of Le Fanu's *revenants,* all of whom make the flesh creep. The story has been deliberately placed at the end of *In a Glass Darkly.* Its emphasis on erotic detail is deliberate, disturbing. Its familiarity with a wide range of vampire lore indicates that Le Fanu could well appreciate the novelty of his addition of a lesbian motif; no reference work in Baron Vordenburg's extensive library had even hinted at the victim's willingness to comply with the masturbatory fingerings of the vampire. The last chapter is also important because it demonstrates that the heroine—even after a sharp stake has been driven through Carmilla's heart, Carmilla's head has been struck off, Carmilla's body and head have been cremated, and the ashes have been "thrown upon a river and borne away"—cannot exorcise the demon, which is now (as in a sense it has always been) mentally conjured: "It was long before the terror of recent events subsided; and to this hour the image of Carmilla returns to memory with ambiguous alternations—sometimes the playful, languid, beautiful girl; sometimes the writhing fiend I saw in the ruined church; and often from a reverie I have started, fancying I heard the light step of Carmilla at the drawing-room door."

Le Fanu provides for his *revenants* a local habitation and a name. By means of framing devices—the collection of Francis Purcell, the parish priest of Drumcoolagh; the medical papers of Dr. Hesselius; the idyllic community of Golden Friars, which is carefully described before we move into the horrors of **"The Haunted Baronet"**—he suggests the plausibility of the environment, and identifies the motives of the narrator, as necessary preliminaries to the fiction itself. Above all, he traces connections between mind and matter, justifying their existence on Swedenborgian grounds. The disorder of the world may manifest itself in the life of a tormented curate, a retired sea-captain, or a young woman unaware of the strength of her own sexual needs; and the natural world is a dark, sinister complement to the mentally—and even morally—aberrant behavior of human beings.

For all the reasons thus far cited, Le Fanu's short stories are superior to most stories written by his contemporaries and successors. Their high quality becomes more evident when they are contrasted with the writings of other tellers of ghost tales. The first thing to be noted is the ordinariness of the individuals to whom remarkable things happen in stories written by Le Fanu's rivals. Dickens, in "The Story of the Bagman's Uncle," one of the semi-detachable narratives of *The Posthumous Papers of the Pickwick Club,* describes the uncle who passes through incredible and romantic adventures: "I am particular in describing how my uncle walked up the middle of the street, with his thumbs in his waistcoat pockets, gentlemen," says the bagman, "because, as he often used to say (and with great reason too) there is nothing at all extraordinary in this story, unless as you distinctly understand at the beginning that he was not by any means of a marvellous or romantic turn." Mrs. Oliphant, in "The Open Door" (one of her *Stories of the Seen and the Unseen*) introduces us to a father who loves his son; because his son is terrified by voices in the avenue leading to Brentwood, a home near Edinburgh, everything—including the father's willingness to undergo strange and terrible adventures—derives from the basic fact of his affection for the child. The "hero" of Bulwer Lytton's "The Haunters and the Haunted" is not driven by a sense of destiny, nor do the weird events recounted seem to have much bearing on the kind of life he has already led. He becomes involved simply because (as he puts it) there is nothing that he should like better than to sleep in a haunted house.

The divorce of a writer's sense of the importance of character from the events which befall the leading figure of the story has enormous implications for the capacity of imagined events to challenge a reader's imagination *after* the reading has been completed. Malcolm Malcolmson, the student of "Harmonical Progression, Permutations and Combinations, and Elliptic Functions" in Bram Stoker's "The Judge's House," has no connection with the events that took place years before in the room where he is finally to die. He has led (so far as we can tell) a blameless life. Why he should have been selected for this horrifying fate is not only unclear, the question seems not to have interested Stoker at all. Le Fanu would have suggested the inevitability of the young man's coming to the house; something in his past, in himself, in Le Fanu's philosophy of life, would have stressed connections between his earlier behavior and his final punishment. And, we may rest assured, the house, which Stoker describes as being desolate, isolated, old, rambling, heavy-built, and fortified in its appearance, would have become a convenient symbol of the larger ruin surrounding it, the city of London itself.

"The Trial for Murder," a story written in the main by Charles Allston Collins and reworked by Charles Dickens for the Christmas Number of *All the Year Round,* 1865 (subsequently printed in *Dr. Marigold's Prescriptions*), may be taken as a reasonably successful example of a Victorian ghost story. A bachelor who heads a bank department feels "slightly dyspeptic" (his "renowned" doctor assures him that his real state of health justifies no stronger description), and cannot explain why he takes an extraordinary interest in the newspaper account of a brutal murder. The discovery of the body

> had been made in a bedroom, and, when I laid down the paper, I was aware of a flash—rush—flow—I do not know what to call it,—no word I can find is satisfactorily descriptive,—in which I seemed to see that bedroom passing through my room, like a picture impossibly painted on a running river. Though almost instantaneous in its passing, it was perfectly clear; so clear that I distinctly, and with a sense of relief, observed the absence of the dead body from the bed.

The bank manager subsequently sees from his chamber window two men walking. Their faces (though unremarkable) are distinct and unforgettable. Some time later he, along with his servant, sees again one of the two men; his "face was the colour of impure wax," and both know that this is the murdered man described in the newspaper account. The long arm of coincidence reaches out: the banker is called to serve upon a jury at a session of the Central Criminal Court at the Old Bailey, and (almost needless to say) he serves as foreman of the jury that tries, and ultimately finds guilty, the man charged of murder, the second of the two men whom he has seen from his window. The prisoner, who unsuccessfully attempted to have his lawyer challenge the banker's right to sit on the jury, knows from the beginning that he will be found guilty. When the Judge asks him whether he has anything to say before sentence of death should be passed upon him, he responds: *"My Lord, I knew I was a doomed man, when the Foreman of my Jury came into the box. My Lord, I knew he would never let me off, before I was taken, he somehow got to my bedside in the night, woke me, and put a rope round my neck."*

Collins and Dickens have sought to chill the reader's blood, and no doubt for most readers the story succeeds. The astonishing events of the trial—during which the ghost of the murdered man addresses itself to whoever is speaking, and saws "frightfully . . . at its severed throat" in a way that demoralizes jurors, lawyers, and judge—are described in the most matter-of-fact, naturalistic diction. But the story never moves beyond the level of sensation and shock. The authors provide no clue as to why the banker should have been afforded his remarkable vision. There is no lucid or even imaginable connection between the banker and the murderer—save that glimpse from the window, and the appearance of a ghost in the banker's sitting-room—before the trial begins. Le Fanu would have told us more, and most likely would have suggested the involvement of the banker in the guilt of the murderer.

For, ultimately, Le Fanu's stories are about the sharing of guilt, and the need for our recognizing responsibility for the doom which overtakes us (and which, for the most part, we may not evade). Le Fanu dreamed again and again of the fall of a house, and of the death of the dreamer. In this sense we may see something of England's responsibility—more precisely, that of the Ascendancy class—for having ruined Ireland. Such an interpretation is too narrow, even if it enjoys a certain vogue among Irish literary historians. As I have suggested earlier, Le Fanu's anger at the over-optimistic assumptions of the Enlighten-

ment counts for a great deal. But the primary distinction of his subject-matter is that it involves us all, and it refuses to release us from a shared responsibility for sin. (pp. 34-55)

> *Harold Orel, "Joseph Sheridan Le Fanu: Developing the Horror Tale," in his* The Victorian Short Story: Development and Triumph of a Literary Genre, *Cambridge University Press, 1986, pp. 33-55.*

Barbara T. Gates   (essay date 1987)

[*In the following essay, Gates explores the theme of suicide in Le Fanu's short stories.*]

> The candle was burning on the table; there was a film of blue smoke hovering in the air—a faint smell of burning. I saw papa lying on the floor; he appeared to have dropped from the arm-chair, and to have fallen over on his back; a pistol lay by his half-open hand; the side of his face looked black and torn, as if a thunderbolt had scorched him, and a stream of blood seemed throbbing from his ear.

This is an account of a Victorian suicide, just completed and carefully reported by the victim's daughter. To the practiced eye, it looks very like a description from a coroner's inquest or like one of many newspaper accounts of *felo-de-se,* the legal term for deliberate suicide. Even including the poetically powerful words "thunderbolt" and "throbbing," and the sentimental "papa," one could easily mistake it for such. Actually, it is pure fiction, a passage from Joseph Sheridan Le Fanu's last novel, *Willing to Die* (1873). Ethel Ware, daughter of the deceased, is narrating, retrospectively trying to sound rational and dispassionate about an act that very few Victorians thought in the least rational.

For suicide in nineteenth-century England was both illegal and touched with the taint of insanity. Until 1823 it was legally possible to bury suicides at a crossroads with a stake through the heart. The law allowing for this atrocity dated from the tenth century, when civil law required not only ignominious burial but also forfeiture of personal and real property to the Crown. Reasons for this kind of severity were supposedly moral. The *felo-de-se* was to be impaled and buried outside of consecrated ground because suicide was thought to be the one unrepentable crime against God, life being considered a commission from God and the taking of it God's prerogative only. And he or she was to lose goods and property because it was believed that suicide could be prevented if the *felo-de-se* knew of the harsh and inevitable consequences for his/her heirs. It was only if a suicide could be proved insane at the time of the act that forfeiture was not demanded, at least until 1870, when forfeiture itself became illegal. In 1823, however, suicides were given the right to a more decent burial—privately, but nonetheless at night, and without Christian rites.

Thus suicide was a disgrace, as Sheridan Le Fanu fully realized. The Anglo-Irish shared with the English a terror of suicide, and Le Fanu's cousin, Frances, had persistently threatened to kill herself. In 1838 Le Fanu would observe Frances's sister, Alicia, wholly reject the miserable Frances, refusing even to allow her name to be mentioned. Although Frances survived for another seventeen years, Le Fanu never forgot the stigma attached to the idea of a suicide in the family. In *Willing to Die* he emphasized the scandal attached to Francis Ware's death along with its horror:

> The gross and ghastly publicity, the merciless prying into details, and over all the gloom of the maddest and most mysterious of crimes! You look in vain in the shadow for the consoling image of hope and repose; a medium is spread around that discolours and horrifies, and the Tempter seems to haunt the house.

Tempters of many sorts do haunt the houses and minds of Le Fanu's suicides. From early to late, his fiction—especially his shorter fiction—exhibits a gallery of characters tormented by grotesque hallucinations or manifestations of evil in the forms of devils, ghosts or other preternatural beings that drive them to take their own lives. Unlike cousin Frances but like Francis Ware, who is her fictional namesake, these suicidal characters are invariably males. If the women of Le Fanu's stories are occasionally tempted by suicide, they are essentially spectre-free and durable. The suicidal men, on the other hand, become progressively more emotionally withdrawn and isolated within themselves and move inexorably toward self-destruction. Their phantoms represent aspects of the self displaced and imagined as things or people outside the self, often monstrous selves freed from most human constraints. Some seem palpable and are witnessed by people other than those they haunt. Others only manifest themselves to the haunted. All, however, are equally destructive.

Not surprisingly these bogeys first appear shortly after the crisis over cousin Frances. In **"The Fortunes of Sir Robert Ardagh"** (written 1838-1840), Ardagh is plagued by a foreign valet named Jacque, known to Ardagh's servants as "Jack the devil," a dark, hunched man whose "eye possessed a power which, if exhibited, would betray a supernatural origin." Like Dickens's deformed Quilp, black Jacque delights in others' distress. When Ardagh's son and heir is stillborn, the valet chuckles with merriment. Nevertheless Ardagh is deeply attached to Jacque and treats him as second self; "His commands are mine," Ardagh tells another servant. Eventually Jacque leaves the household, much to the relief of all but Sir Robert himself. From the day of his departure, Ardagh sinks into apathy, becoming indifferent and abstracted. Bit by bit, he declines into death, or so goes the second version of Sir Robert's story, "authenticated by human testimony."

"The Fortunes" is actually a twice-told tale. In the first version, Le Fanu recounts "tradition" and credits Sir Robert with a much more violent end. This version views Ardagh himself as a "*dark* man, . . . morose, reserved and ill-tempered." As time wears on, Ardagh withdraws and is heard to argue with himself, becoming agitated and pacing about wildly. During these occurrences, he manifests what Le Fanu calls "paroxysms of apparent lunacy." Finally, a foreign stranger comes to the house and Ardagh

desperately protests his admittance. Sir Robert is heard wrestling with someone or something on the ledge of a precipice outside his door and is found dead at the foot of that precipice, "with hardly a vestige of a limb or feature left distinguishable." In death he has lost the physically distinguishing marks of humanity.

The double telling of this tale and the mystery surrounding the circumstances of death both cast doubt as to just what has happened to Ardagh. So does the careful distancing of the tale in the past. It is hard to get hold of facts here, but that seems just Le Fanu's point. Apparent suicides are all mysteries, especially as to cause; in Le Fanu's words from *Willing to Die*, suicide is both the "maddest and most mysterious of crimes." With all cases of *felo-de-se* murderer and murdered are one, and both are always inaccessible. Thus with every suicide something unsettling occurs. Inquests hold no final answers, only conjectures. Explanations are wanted but can never be authoritative. Even suicide notes can be fictions, written by persons who may be beside themselves. Le Fanu draws upon all this doubtfulness. In positing mysterious others who echo looks or behavior—doubles who may stand for the suicide both as victim and as self-murderer—he metaphorically separates murderer from murdered and feeds Victorian fears and uncertainties about death by suicide. Was Ardagh insane? Was he really a suicide? Was he a terrible sinner? Was he pursued and tormented by a dark stranger, or by himself? Did he conceal a dreadful secret of some sort? What indeed drives a man to his death? Le Fanu's readers are left with these awful questions but with no certain truths. Whether it is traditional or "authenticated," no narration will fully illuminate Le Fanu's dark world of suicide.

Le Fanu would re-emphasize this in his next tales of self-murder. In **"A Chapter in the History of a Tyrone Family"** (1839), his young heroine and primary narrator is wholly unable to decode the mystery of her husband's death. Found with his throat slit—a more obvious self-murderer than Ardagh—Lord Glenfallen has taken his secrets with him to the grave. Possibly Glenfallen was a bigamist, as Charlotte Brontë's Rochester would be, but unlike *Jane Eyre* this story affords no surprise brother-in-law from Jamaica to recount the past and set the record straight. Whether guilt over helping to frame and incarcerate the woman who may have been the first Lady Glenfallen has driven Glenfallen to madness and suicide, no one will ever know. Even his current young wife is at a loss to say. "All, then, was over; I was never to learn the history in whose termination I had been so deeply and so tragically involved," she sadly confesses.

In line with his penchant to rework the mysteries that absorbed him, Le Fanu retold this young woman's story thirty years later as *The Wyvern Mystery* (1860). Similarly, he would recast **"Some Account of the Latter Days of the Hon. Richard Marston of Dunoran"** (1848) as three separate works of fiction: **"Some Account,"** **"The Evil Guest"** (1851), and *A Lost Name* (1868). And he would later rewrite **"The Watcher"** (1847) as **"The Familiar"** (1872). Critics of Le Fanu have contended that he revamped these stories because plotting came hard for him. Surely he was also making a connection between the mystery of suicide and the inscrutability of the haunted minds of its victims and their survivors. As he himself said of the relentless pursuit in **"The Watcher,"** "however the truth may be, as to the origin and motives of this mysterious persecution, there can be no doubt that, with respect to the agencies by which it was accomplished, absolute and impenetrable mystery is like to prevail until the day of doom."

"The Watcher" is in several ways typical of Le Fanu's stories of suicide. Its protagonist, Captain Barton, prides himself on his rationalism. He is "an utter disbeliever in what are usually termed preternatural agencies" but knows that he is pursued by the hollow sound of footsteps. A friend also notices that he is trailed by an odd-looking foreigner with a menacing, "almost maniacal" mien. Barton fears yet shrugs off his pursuer, attributing his fear to overwork. But as time wears on, Barton wears down, though his watcher does not. Now subject to "blue devils"—defined in Le Fanu's day as despondency or hypochondriac melancholy—Barton finds that his mind has turned in upon itself. The pursuer becomes an "apparition" to him. Deeply disturbed, Barton consults both a clergyman and a high-ranking army officer about his plight. While the cleric tells him that he is his "own tormenter," the general good-naturedly offers to "collar the ghost" and free his friend.

The man of the cloth unfortunately proves to have been right. Barton's only freedom will come with death, the ultimate release from self-torment. Like Ardagh he loses hope and *joie de vivre,* becoming uncannily tranquil. He looks for a last encounter with his demon, is heard to scream out piercingly in agony, and is found dead. In a kind of postscript or coda to his tale, we discover that eight years previously Barton had formed a guilty attachment to a girl whom he ill-treated and who subsequently died of a broken heart. Barton's blue devils, then, are avengers of that earlier death, and no rationalizing, no uninformed members of the Establishment in the guise of doctors, preachers, or military men have the power to stop them. Barton ultimately falls victim to his own past.

Such is the fate of all of the murderers among Le Fanu's suicides, those of the longer fiction as well as those of the short stories. In *Checkmate* (1871), one-time murderer Yelland Mace goes so far as to have his face rebuilt to suit what he hopes will be a new life and new name, Walter Longcluse. But the spectre of Mace haunts Longcluse, who becomes weary of himself. In the fictional world of Le Fanu, whatever a man's visage or name, his past cannot be eluded or denied; it is encoded within him. Thus changes in aspect or prospect, as when he moves to England, are insufficient to save Mace/Longcluse, who eventually poisons himself in despair. Anxious somehow to be transformed but incapable of inner conversion, Mace/Longcluse resorts to the most desperate of all remedies.

About this checkmated man, there is something pitiful and vulnerable. About Silas Ruthvyn in *Uncle Silas* (1864), there is little to pity. Silas is the dark alter ego of Austin Ruthvyn, a double to his own brother. When that brother dies and his daughter, Maud, is sent to live with

Silas, Le Fanu unfolds a shocking mystery of character. Along with young Maud Ruthvyn, LeFanu's narrator, we wonder: who is Silas, what is he? Slowly we find that he is anything but holy, fair, and wise, although at first he appears to be all three. Silas is himself the ghost of a man. Sealed off in a world of laudanum and Swedenborgian visions, he seems like a spectre to his niece:

> Uncle Silas was always before me; the voice so silvery for an old man—so *preternaturally* soft; the manners so sweet, so gentle; the aspect, smiling, suffering, *spectral.* It was no longer a shadow; I had now seen him in the flesh. But after all, was he more than a shadow to me? When I closed my eyes I saw him before me still, in *necromantic* black, ashy with a pallour on which I looked with fear and pain, a face so dazzlingly pale, and those hollow, fiery, awful eyes! It sometimes seemed as if the curtain opened, and I had seen a *ghost.*

Silas is self-haunted but also ruthless, as his name might imply. Having murdered once, he is willing to murder again—this time his young niece. Saved by her wits, Maud lives to retell her story and to try to unravel the riddle of her own haunter, Silas, "Child of the Sphinx."

Yet even in the end, Silas eludes both Maud and her readers. He appears to die from an overdose of laudanum which his inquest determines to have been "accidentally administered by himself." But Silas is an expert in dosages and unlikely to have taken too much or too little. Had even Uncle Silas had enough of evil, enough of life? Here once again, suicide is unprovable. In discussing mystery novels, Patrick Brantlinger has observed that they are paradoxical because they "conclude in ways that liquidate mystery: they are not finally mysterious at all" ["What is 'Sensational' about the 'Sensation Novel'?" *Nineteenth-Century Fiction* (1982)]. This could never be said of a novel like *Uncle Silas,* where we believe Silas's murder victim to have been a suicide until close to the novel's end; where the people of the novel have certified that same man self-murdered for years; and where the riddle of Silas Ruthvyn's own death remains.

In the suicides so far discussed, what is missing are the inner reflections of the victims. There are no suicide notes, no shared confidences. In the Doctor Hesselius stories from *In a Glass Darkly* (1872), something quite different occurs. In **"Mr. Justice Harbottle,"** Hesselius's assistant has seen an important paper in the Judge's own handwriting and has access to one of Harbottle's own "dreams," which brings the reader much closer to the world of the haunted. The dream is fraught both with the ghostly presences of Harbottle's severely judged, hanged victims and with a huge "dilated effigy" of the judge himself—Chief Justice Two-fold, "an image of Mr. Justice Harbottle, at least double his size, and with all his fierce colouring, and his ferocity of eye and visage enhanced awfully." Harbottle's dream world has thus split his tormenters into two groups, a set of externalized others and an alter ego, larger than life; and Le Fanu's art has led us directly through the dark door of Harbottle's nightmare. This second, surrealistic judge condemns Harbottle to die for his crimes in a month's time and leaves him with four weeks of "blue devils" and desperate rationalizations before he is found hanging from the banister at the top of his own staircase and pronounced *felo-de-se* by his coroner's jury.

In the ghost stories of **In A Glass Darkly,** Le Fanu becomes far more cautious in attributing causes for suicide. There is no coda discussing Harbottle's guilt, no overhearing of melodramatic death throes. There is only mention of "medical evidence to show that in his atrabilious state it was quite in the cards that he might have made away with himself." Despite the medical jargon, here the motives and mystery of suicide have deepened. This is even more true in the case of the Reverend Mr. Jennings in **"Green Tea."** Jennings is the only one of Le Fanu's suicides who is a good man with no very apparent guilt or reason to kill himself. All the same he is the most relentlessly haunted of all the suicides and his is also the most carefully documented of the stories of self-destruction. Hesselius is not just a recorder here but the tale's inner narrator and an actor in the drama as well; and Jennings himself is also a painstaking and minute observer and revealer of his tormenter, his evirons, and his own inner states.

Jennings's story is an odd one. A man of the cloth, he has few bad habits, though for a time he was addicted to drinking strong green tea. Four years earlier he had begun working hard on a study of religious metaphysics of the ancients. He indulged heavily in the tea but at the same time had never found existence so pleasant. Suddenly, however, when sitting in an omnibus, he is astonished to catch sight of a small, black monkey with reddish glowing eyes. At first he believes it to be real, but when he pokes at it with his umbrella, the nub seems to pass right through the animal. Horror grows as Jennings's relationship with this apparition moves through what Hesselius documents in three stages. First Jennings considers the monkey as a manifestation of disease. Next he believes it hellish. Finally he hears it "singing through" his head, urging him to crime and self-destruction. By the time he consults Hesselius, Jennings verges on total despair. Hesselius nevertheless assures him of a cure, remarking that he has had a great success rate with similar cases. Jennings is simply to summon Hesselius the very instant that the apparition reappears. Inevitably the monkey does return, but when it does, Hesselius is sequestered, working on the Jennings case. By the time Hesselius gets to Jennings, the minister has slit his own throat in desperation.

In its bare outline, this story is mysterious enough, but when one tries to fathom just why poor Jennings is the victim here, it becomes even more so. How to account for the appearance to such a decent man of a leering, malignant, black monkey with a red aura? Le Fanu gives a number of explanations, none really satisfactory. First and foremost, there is the Swedenborgian insight into the case. In an effort to understand his plight, Jennings has been reading Swedenborg's *Arcana Celestia.* According to Swedenborg, evil spirits from hell can inhabit the world of humankind for a time. When they do so, they are no longer in infernal torment but reside in the thoughts and affections of the person with whom they associate. In this situation they appear as "correspondences" to what they are in the

eyes of their infernal associates, and take "the shape of the beast (*fera*) which represents [the] particular lust and life, in aspect dire and atrocious" of their human associates.

If the monkey is a representative of Jennings's lust and life—a manifestation of his darker side, a kind of Dorian portrait—there is little evidence in **"Green Tea"** that Jennings has merited such an incubus. His only vices seem to have been green tea and ancient metaphysics, and he has wholly given up the tea. The vision of the monkey is not drug-induced. It could, however, be guilt-induced, and Le Fanu's Swedenborg also says that the man in consort with spirits must be a man in good faith, "continually protected by the Lord." In retrospect Jennings admits that the pursuit of ancient metaphysics is "not good for the Christian mind." Possibly he felt guilt over his delight in paganism; certainly the monkey begins to torment him in church, squatting on his open book so that he cannot read to his congregation, and in the second phase constantly interrupting his prayers. But Jennings persists with prayers and clerical responsibilities; we never see him give over attempts at communication with a Christian God. If apostasy is Jennings's crime, Le Fanu is not eager to make it evident, although Victorian readers of **"Green Tea"** would surely have been prepared for a link between religious doubts and *felo-de-se.* Daily and weekly papers and *The Annual Register* were full of suicides attributed to "religious melancholy." Jennings, however, exhibits something more than the usual melancholic symptoms of doubt and depression. He lives in utter horror of his peculiar, red-ringed monkey.

Medical explanations for Jennings's condition and death are even less satisfying. There are three doctors involved in his case, and all three fail him. Before consulting Hesselius, Jennings has seen a Dr. Harley, whom he classifies as "a paralytic mind, an interest half dead" . . . "a *mere* materialist." Clearly the eminent Harley has little belief in the monkey. Hesselius, however, has Jennings's confidence because his medicine is of another order. Himself influenced by Swedenborg, Hesselius believes that there are sometimes insights that move one from the material to the spiritual world. Through a rending of the veil, for a time "the mortal and immortal prematurely make acquaintance." In consulting Hesselius, whose writings he has read, Jennings comes self-diagnosed. He likes the Swedenborgian insight into his problem, but nevertheless deliberately seeks out a medical practitioner rather than turning to Swedenborg's own solution of God's protection. Unfortunately, Hesselius proves less than in control of his healer's art. He is a careless empiricist, a derelict in duty, and a very materialistic spiritualist. He begins with a "theory" about Jennings before he hears out the man's case; then he fails to be accessible at the very moment his patient needs him. In the end his great disappointment comes not when he loses Jennings the man, but when he loses Jennings the case. He feels cheated because he has not had a chance to make Jennings his fifty-eighth success story in the business of sealing a patient's inner eye. All that was needed, he believes, was a treatment of the fluid in our bodies which we hold in common with spirits. Since green tea opened Jennings's inner eye, something as simple as eau de cologne might have closed it. Ironically, these absurdly material assumptions become the most profound ones that the great Doctor Hesselius can offer. They are carefully prefaced and edited by yet another, younger doctor who is translating Hesselius's most striking cases with reverential interest.

In his and Le Fanu's final paragraph, Hesselius totally divorces himself from Jennings. According to Hesselius, Jennings was not really one of his failures because he was never really one of his patients. Hesselius had not begun a cure, and just as well. For what Jennings finally succumbed to, decides Hesselius, was not after all the open inner eye but "hereditary suicidal mania," a grand Victorian catch-all, killer of FitzRoy of the H.M.S. *Beagle* and numerous less eminent Victorians. So while Hesselius and his editor wind up looking irresponsible and foolish, Le Fanu's readers continue puzzled over the eerie monkey and haunted clergyman. Which returns them again to the nagging questions: Why would a man, happily going about his business, quite suddenly be plagued by a spectral monkey? Is the beast a symbol of lust? of the mysterious jungle? of the more mysterious East? Or is it a primitive ancestor of humankind? And, more importantly, why would such a monkey drive a man to take his life? Like Hesselius's answers to it, the last question begins to seem more than a little absurd.

Certainly Le Fanu must have meant it to be. As Jack Sullivan says of **"Green Tea,"** "the strange power of the tale lies in the irony that something intrinsically ridiculous can drive a man to destroy himself" [*Elegant Nightmares*]. Here Le Fanu reveals the tenuousness of life, its susceptibility to sudden, unsuspected—and seemingly pointless—alterations, and he tests the Victorians' and our own human limitations in coping with such alterations. We linger over **"Green Tea"** because the story of Jennings is Le Fanu's most deeply troubling story and the spectre of the monkey his most deeply disturbing spectre. As we hear his anxious recountings to Hesselius, we feel for this tormented man. Jennings seems an Everyman, even a superior man, whose intellect and decency are unable to save him from his bogey. Blue devils, green tea, hereditary insanity, religious melancholy—Le Fanu offers no satisfying explanation for Jennings's complaint. His dis-ease reflects Victorian unease and feeds our own discomfort as we ponder what it really is that causes a man not to want to live. In an era drenched in *Aberglaube* (Arnold's "extra" beliefs "beyond what is certain and verifiable") and bathed in a certain "*Nachshein* of Christianity" [Thomas Carlyle, *Sartor Resartus*] which withholds men like Teufelsdröckh and Carlyle from suicide, a lurid monkey must in fact have been a fitting symbol for an inexplicable will to die. And a ghost story—mysterious and equally inexplicable—must have been the perfect medium for conveying the ultimate mystery of suicide. (pp. 15-23)

Barbara T. Gates, "Blue Devils and Green Tea: Sheridan Le Fanu's Haunted Suicides," in Studies in Short Fiction, Vol. 24, No. 1, Winter, 1987, pp. 15-23.

Jolanta Nałęcz-Wojtczak   (essay date 1987)

[*In the following essay, the critic discusses Le Fanu's contributions to the development of supernatural fiction.*]

It was during the Victorian period that the ghost story finally acquired its distinctive generic form, emerging from the vast and shapeless body of the so-called literature of the supernatural. The Irish contribution to the development of this genre was twofold—on the one hand, it was the writers of Irish origin who became its greatest exponents (J. S. LeFanu, Rhoda Broughton, Charlotte Riddel), on the other hand, the achievement of LeFanu provided the ghost story with new possibilities on which later generations were to draw.

Being deeply indebted to the English Gothic and the German *Schauerromantik* tradition, LeFanu at the same time provides the Victorian ghost story with quite new elements—Irish folklore, Swedenborgian ideas and psychological interest. Elements of Irish folklore give local flavour to the stories and enrich their poetic world; the Swedish philosopher's concepts give new insights into the strange universe of the stories, allow for unique interpretations and become subtle tools for discovering new layers of meaning.

Being interesting artistically and, in the case of Swedenborgianism, often essential for the inner structure of the stories, these elements did not, however, exert any significant influence on other writers. From the point of view of their potential impact they lead nowhere. The task of opening new vistas and providing creative impulses was left for the third thematic ingredient of LeFanu's stories—his interest in morbid emotional states, in human behaviour under stress and anxiety, in the hidden recesses of the human mind.

The development of the psychological ghost story *sensu stricto,* as aknowledged by critics, took place at the end of the nineteenth and the beginning of the twentieth century. Its most immediate, and most easily recognized, source of inspiration were the discoveries of Freud. Their revolutionary force was so strong that it overshadowed the role of the Irish 'creator of ghosts', whose influence was nevertheless being constantly exerted in the way in which a classic of a given genre is always working somewhere at the back of one's mind. The aim of the present paper is to expose these elements of LeFanu's stories which may claim for him the title of the father of the psychological ghost story in English literature.

First of all, LeFanu's vision of his main characters is dynamic—in his best ghost stories the development of the action becomes, in fact, a pretext for showing the gradual process of a change of personality. The reader meets Sir James Barton as a healthy, self-assured, intelligent and agreeable navy officer—at the end of the story he witnesses his death in a state of depression, resignation, fear (**"The Familiar"**). The strange persecution which the Rev. Mr. Jennings experiences, slowly but inevitably drives this intelligent, benevolent, conscientious minister to the torment of constant anxiety, fear, and, finally, suicidal mania (**"Green Tea"**). From a cheerful, ordinary, healthy girl

Laura changes into a neurotic troubled with homosexual fantasies (**"Carmilla"**), while the negative features of Sir Robert Ardagh's character—his moroseness, ill-temper, haughtiness—intensify so violently towards the end of his life that they "border upon insanity" and, after "paroxysms of apparent lunacy" end in his death at the foot of a precipice (**"The Fortunes of Sir Robert Ardagh"**).

The psychological changes which LeFanu's characters undergo are never sudden, unexpected, unmotivated. Whatever the length of the story, the author always manages to convey the sense of a long lapse of time by direct comments referring to "years and months that passed", by accumulation of events stressing the development in time, or by precise dates noted by the sufferers themselves. The most characteristic example is Jennings [in **"Green Tea"**], who, with a pertinacity bordering on obsession, compiles a systematic record of his neurosis: "It began . . . on the 15th of October three years and eleven weeks ago, and two days—I keep very accurate count, for every day is torment." LeFanu's evident preference for the form of a *long* short story may be accounted for by the artist's instinctive feeling that a change of personality resulting from acute neurosis is a long and gradual process and the length of the story may be a very effective technical means of conveying it.

Another characteristic and important aspect of LeFanu's treatment of the dynamics of the character is his ability to see a change take place on the emotional as well as on the physical level. Emotional disturbances are always accompanied by physical symptoms. Jennings has a "fixed face of suffering"; as his persecution advances he is often "agitated and looking like death"; his manner becomes odd: "Mr. Jennings has a way of looking sidelong upon the carpet as if his eye followed the movements of something there." Captain Barton's obsession also affects his behaviour—usually composed and reserved, he now speaks "with wild and excited rapidity"; once an active, energetic officer ready to marry a young girl, Barton dies an apathetic invalid confined to bed and dependent upon his friends' care. Proportionally to her strange emotional involvement, Laura becomes languid, apathetic, unable to fully relax during sleep. There is a noticeable change in her appearance: "I had grown pale, my eyes were dilated and darkened underneath, and the langour which I had long felt began to display itself in my countenance."

All LeFanu's most successful characters are tragic characters. The source of their tragedy springs from their desperate, spasmodic struggle for sanity—from a neurotic's awareness that his mind is suddenly on the borderline between what is conventionally considered to be normal and abnormal. Their behaviour is very characteristic—after the very first moments of their encounter with the supernatural they try to control their anxieties and phobias, to find a satisfactory logical explanation for their 'spectral illusions' and "hallucinations', to conquer them with the help of medicine, philosophy, religion or the warmth of friendship. Jennings tries to change his diet and style of life, avoids places where the 'thing' is most likely to appear, plunges into specialist literature that might help him to solve the mystery of his illness, keeps an objective re-

cord of it, and, with whole earnestness of faith, supplicates God for deliverance. Sir James Barton first undertakes some kind of detection, seeks legal advice against the alleged persecutor, consults a physician and, in spite of his materialistic outlook, a theologian as well, tries change of air, place, pastime. Being too passive to take such energetic steps, Sir Philip Faltram only tries to find consolation and help in pouring out his anxieties and analyzing his state of mind in front of a friendly housekeeper: "I suppose I am not quite well. . . . I think . . . it is getting into me. I think it's like possession. . . . I think there is something trying to influence me. Perhaps it is the way fellows go mad; but it won't let me alone. I've seen it three times, think of that!"

Showing the painful awareness of being on the verge of otherness, the desperate, futile struggle to conquer the unknown force driving one to insanity, LeFanu touched one of the most tragic and pathetic struggles of man. It is impossible to say precisely how much of his success in doing this is due to his sensitiveness as a great artist and how much to his own bitter experience—himself a neurotic, after the death of his wife LeFanu became a recluse suffering heavily from persecution mania. Whatever the reason, this aspect of his ghost stories opened for this genre new perspectives and prepared techniques for later writers impregnated with Freud's ideas.

Anticipation of the findings of modern psychiatry and psychoanalysis in LeFanu's stories becomes even more evident when one looks for the causes of the characters' tragedies. For Sir Robert Ardagh as well as for Captain Barton it is a sense of guilt and fear of death and punishment (Sir Robert obtained his wealth by dealing with the devil; Barton is responsible for the death of a young girl and her father). Jennings' obsession is usually interpreted as resulting from repressed sexual instincts; Laura's sense of strain is caused by her inability to resist overpowering erotic sensations; at the bottom of Sir Philip Faltram's emotional disturbance can be found a lack of love and acceptance as well as a feeling of utter helplessness in the face of a persecuting conviction that it is his duty to redress evil committed long ago by the Mardykes; while Sir Bale Mardyke's anxieties and awakening sense of guilt go back to nursery tales which scared him in his childhood. Being reminiscent of modern psychology, the above problems constitute at the same time a stock of motifs which later ghost story writers very willingly drew upon.

Another important aspect of LeFanu's treatment of the supernatural is the problem of evil. However varied in form and in the most immediate message which they convey, most of LeFanu's ghosts and phantoms may be also interpreted as embodiments of some kind of evil, which, imperceptibly emanating from them, gradually permeates and saturates the poetic world of the stories. Carmilla, the beautiful vampire, is surrounded by an atmosphere of crime, cruelty (killing young girls) and sexual perversion (her lesbian relationship with Laura); the ghost of judge Horrock paralyzes those who encounter him with a look of condensed hatred, sensuality and malignant power, infiltrating into their minds the idea of suicide (**"An Account of some Strange Disturbances in Aungier Street"**). The spectral O'Donnell in **"Ultor De Lacy"** disseminates the atmosphere of never-ceasing lust for revenge; Minheer Vanderhausen as well as Rose after her death subtly yet irresistibly effuse an aura of perverse eroticism (**"Schalken the Painter"**). Being uable to interpret satisfactorily the appearance of the mysterious monkey, Jennings is, however, absolutely sure from the very first encounters with it that, whtaever it stands for, its essential nature is evil: "It had only one peculiarity—a character of malignity—unfathomable malignity." As the persecution increases and the monkey urges him to crimes Jennings admits to have become "a slave of Satan."

Read in the light of the concepts of Victorian morality, within the confines of which LeFanu always remained, all the above motifs—homosexuality, refined eroticism, revenge, suicide, crime—can have only one interpretation—they belong to the category of evil. Unlike earlier goth-icists and their imitators, whose only aim was to produce chilling thrills by mere contact with the evil and the horrible, LeFanu does not stop at this point. Having masterfully created the vapours of evil enveloping the psyches of his characters, he does not lose this opportunity of another masterly touch of psychological insight. Oscillating between conventional normality and extreme neurosis, many of his characters also face the struggle between accepting and rejecting evil.

LeFanu's notion of evil is not a simplified version of something unambiguously negative that could easily be shunned and refused to be dealt with. In his best stories evil is always double-faced—it repulses but also fascinates, terrifies and at the same time allures. However abhorrent the promptings of the monkey, Jennings nevertheless wants to follow them and urges his niece to leave him alone above a deep, perpendicular shaft; at another critical moment he forbids his servant to enter the room in which he locks himself to finally answer the call of the evil power. With almost masochistic persistency Sir Bale Mardyke often goes near the lake which always awakes the fears and anxieties of his childhood. Laura's gradual corruption develops through constant undulations between fascination and repulsion: "I did feel [. . .] *drawn towards her* but there was also something of *repulsion*," "[. . .] tumultuous excitement that was *pleasurable* [. . .] mingled with a vague sense of *fear and disgust*," "I was conscious of *a love growing into adoration* and also of *abborrence.*" The same ambivalence of feeling is experienced by Schalken, who hestiates between "awe" and "interest", and whose "vague alarm" is accompanied by "an irresistible impulse to follow".

The end of the nineteenth and the beginning of the twentieth century witnessed a rapid flourishing of the psychological ghost story. One could mention here Henry James, Cynthia Asquith, Robert Hichens, W. F. Harvey, Charlotte Perkins Gilman, Conrad Aiken, John Collier, Saki, Walter de la Mare, Hugh Walpole, Martin Armstrong, W. Daniel Steele, Samuel Hopkins Adams, John Metcalfe. At the time when the anxieties of the age and the growing complexity of the universe spurred writers to probe the psyche of man, and when the findings of modern psychiatry and psychoanalysis provided them with challenging

themes, the Victorian 'Irish creator of ghosts' became strangely modern. The main achievements of his stories—the dynamic notion of character, the convincing motivation of a change of personality, the attention paid to physical symptoms accompanying emotional disturbances the main causes of which were a not-always-consciously recognized sense of guilt, the fear of death, repressed sexuality, the lack of love and acceptance, the frustration, fear and anxieties of childhood, as well as LeFanu's notion of evil as a power that can be both repulsive and fascinating—provide a stock of themes and techniques.

However late in its recognition, the influence of LeFanu on the modern English ghost story is indisputable today: "nearly all the twentieth century writers in the field paced and structured their narratives in the LeFanu manner." And however numerous the various levels on which this influence worked, its main impact seems to lie in the use of the supernatural as a means of conveying the ubiquitous neurotic component of human nature, and of showing one of the most pathetic struggles and failures of man—his desperate efforts to secure an optimal adaptation to internal and external stresses. (pp. 193-98)

> *Jolanta Nałęcz-Wojtczak, "Joseph Sheridan Le Fanu and New Dimensions for the English Ghost Story," in* Literary Interrelations: Ireland, England and the World, *edited by Wolfgang Zach and Heinz Kosok, Gunter Narr Verlag Tübingen, 1987, pp. 193-98.*

FURTHER READING

Biography

McCormack, W. J. *Sheridan Le Fanu and Victorian Ireland.* Oxford: Clarendon Press, 1980, 310 p.
Extensive, detailed biography of Le Fanu.

Criticism

Barclay, Glen St. John. "Vampires and Ladies: Sheridan Le Fanu." In his *Anatomy of Horror: The Masters of Occult Fiction,* pp. 22-38. New York: St. Martin's Press, 1978.
Discusses the themes of vampirism and lesbianism in Le Fanu's short stories.

Begnal, Michael H. *Joseph Sheridan Le Fanu.* Lewisburg, Pa.: Bucknell University Press, 1971, 87 p.
Critical study of Le Fanu with a chapter discussing his short stories in relation to the Gothic tradition in literature.

Benson, E. F. "Sheridan Le Fanu." *The Spectator* 146, No. 5356 (21 February 1931): 263-64.
Discusses the tales collected as *In a Glass Darkly,* focusing on Le Fanu's method of creating atmosphere and building suspense.

Browne, Nelson. *Sheridan Le Fanu.* London: Arthur Barker, 1951, 135 p.

Biographical and critical study with a chapter on Le Fanu's short stories and poetry.

Diskin, Patrick. "Poe, Le Fanu and the Sealed Room Mystery." *Notes and Queries* 13, No. 9 (September 1966): 337-39.
Theorizes that Le Fanu's short story "A Passage in the Secret History of an Irish Countess" may have inspired Edgar Allan Poe's short story "The Murders in the Rue Morgue."

Ellis, S. M. "Joseph Sheridan Le Fanu." In his *Wilkie Collins, Le Fanu, and Others,* pp. 140-91. 1931. Reprint. Freeport, N.Y.: Books for Libraries Press, 1968.
Biographical and critical study. Ellis includes a bibliography of Le Fanu's works.

James, M. R. Prologue and Epilogue to *Madam Crowl's Ghost, and Other Tales of Mystery,* by Joseph Sheridan Le Fanu, edited by M. R. James, pp. vii-viii, 265-77. London: G. Bell and Sons, 1923.
Considers Le Fanu among the "first rank" of ghost story writers and assesses the strengths and weaknesses of his work.

Kenton, Edna. "A Forgotten Creator of Ghosts: Joseph Sheridan Le Fanu, Possible Inspirer of the Brontës." *The Bookman* (New York) LXIX, No. 5 (July 1929): 528-34.
Asserts that the source of inspiration for Charlotte Brontë's novel *Jane Eyre* was Le Fanu's short story "A Chapter in the History of a Tyrone Family." Kenton further maintains that chapters from Emily Brontë's *Wuthering Heights* resemble the plots of several of Le Fanu's stories.

Lozès, Jean. "Joseph Sheridan Le Fanu." In *The Irish Short Story,* edited by Patrick Rafroidi and Terence Brown, pp. 91-101. Atlantic Highlands, N.J.: Humanities Press Inc., 1979.
Divides Le Fanu's stories into three categories: "humorous Irish stories, realistic stories and stories of the irrational."

Melada, Ivan. *Sheridan Le Fanu.* Boston: Twayne Publishers, 1987, 142 p.
Critical and biographical study with two chapters discussing Le Fanu's early and late short fiction.

Nethercot, Arthur H. "Coleridge's 'Christabel' and Le Fanu's 'Carmilla'." *Modern Philology* 47, No. 1 (August 1949): 32-8.
Compares Samuel Taylor Coleridge's poem "Christabel" and Le Fanu's short story "Carmilla," focusing on the vampire imagery in both works.

Penzoldt, Peter. "Joseph Sheridan Le Fanu (1814-1873)." In his *The Supernatural in Fiction,* pp. 67-91. London: Peter Nevill, 1952.
Discusses Le Fanu's importance to the history and development of Gothic fiction.

Pritchett, V. S. "An Irish Ghost." In his *The Living Novel & Later Appreciations,* rev. ed., pp. 121-28. New York: Random House, 1964.
Praises the style and narrative technique of Le Fanu's short stories and contends that because he had primarily a "talent for brevity" Le Fanu never achieved the same level of success in his novels as he did in his short stories.

Stoddart, Helen. " 'The Precautions of Nervous People Are Infectious': Sheridan Le Fanu's Symptomatic Gothic." *The Modern Language Review* 86, No. 1 (January 1991): 19-34.
Examines the paranoia motif of "Green Tea" and "Carmilla" in relation to the psychoanalytic studies of Sigmund Freud.

Veeder, William. "Carmilla: The Arts of Repression." *Texas Studies in Literature and Language* 22, No. 2 (Summer 1980): 197-223.
Examines the theme of emotional repression in "Carmilla." Veeder observes: "Although men as well as women suffer from repression in 'Carmilla,' Le Fanu chooses female protagonists because he agrees with clear-sighted Victorians that woman in particular is stunted emotionally. 'Carmilla' is part of that High Victorian self-examination which called into question literary and social conventions and the moral orthodoxies underlying them."

Additional coverage of Le Fanu's life and career is contained in the following sources published by Gale Research: *Dictionary of Literary Biography,* Vols. 21, 70; and *Nineteenth-Century Literature Criticism,* Vol. 9.

V. S. Pritchett

1900-

(Full name Victor Sawdon Pritchett) English short story writer, critic, essayist, travel writer, autobiographer, biographer, and novelist.

INTRODUCTION

A distinguished writer whose career has spanned more than sixty years, Pritchett has won critical acclaim for the variety and consistent quality of his work. Along with his short stories, for which he is perhaps most highly regarded, Pritchett's writings include literary criticism, travel essays, novels, and autobiography. Pritchett's keen grasp of character, Dickensian eye for detail, wry sense of humor, and understanding of human behavior are cited as key elements in all of his fiction.

Pritchett was born in Ipswich. Since his family moved often to avoid debt collectors, his formal education was haphazard and frequently interrupted. Nonetheless, he was an avid reader and quite early in his life expressed his desire to be a writer. His father did not approve of his son's literary aspirations, however, and when he was fifteen Pritchett was forced to quit school to work in the office of a London leather wholesaler. To compensate for a job he found tedious, he devoted his free time to the reading of classic English and European literature. At twenty Pritchett left his family and traveled to France, where he continued his literary self-education, supporting himself with odd jobs. His dream of being a working writer was realized when the *Christian Science Monitor* bought several essays from him and later sent him to Ireland, Spain, and the Appalachian Mountain region of the United States as an investigative reporter. Pritchett was soon writing regularly for the *Monitor* and selling travel essays and book reviews to the *Manchester Guardian* and the *New Statesman*. During this time he also wrote a travel book, *Marching Spain*, and published his first collection of short fiction, *The Spanish Virgin, and Other Stories*. Both books achieved greater commercial and critical success than his publishers had anticipated. During the next decade Pritchett wrote several poorly received novels, and by the late 1930s he decided to focus his considerable creative energy on the writing of essays and short stories.

Traditional in style, Pritchett's stories are marked by careful craftsmanship, an ironic sense of humor, and vivid characterization. His characters are predominantly middle-class, ordinary people whose circumstances often reveal the fine line that exists between the comic and the tragic in everyday life. Critics have praised Pritchett's ability to capture the rhythms and patterns of speech, noting that most of his characters initially reveal their subtle idiosyncrasies and personality traits through the way they speak. Pritchett's early collections, including *You Make*

Your Own Life and *It May Never Happen, and Other Stories,* contain many of his best works of short fiction, including "The Saint," "Sense of Humour," "Pocock Passes," and "Many Are Disappointed." Several collected editions have introduced Pritchett to a new generation of readers and prompted greater academic and critical interest in the study of his works.

Some critics suggest that Pritchett's stories offer scathing criticism of British middle-class mores. Others find the author preoccupied with individual lives, with the fantasies, illusions, and longings that transcend class or education. Contemporary critics generally agree that Pritchett's short stories are among the finest ever crafted. Of Pritchett as a short-story writer, Eudora Welty has written, "He is one of the great pleasure-givers in our language."

PRINCIPAL WORKS

SHORT FICTION

OTHER MAJOR WORKS

CRITICISM

Denis Donoghue   (essay date 1970)

[*In the excerpt below, Donoghue reviews* Blind Love,
and Other Stories *and affirms Pritchett's skill as a short
story writer, emphasizing his traditional approach to
form and content.*]

Mr. Pritchett's stories are invariably written in search of
a character. They end when the character has been disclosed. Usually the story presents the character at one revealing moment, and it rarely concerns itself with other
possibilities, later chapters, for instance, in a character's
life. The short story is a happy form for Mr. Pritchett be-

cause he identifies character and nature; a man's character
is his nature, and it may be disclosed in a flash, the significant circumstance of a moment. The relation between a
character and his environment is deemed important, and
it is sketched with significance in mind, but the character
is not seen as determined by his environment. It is his nature to be himself. What happens in a story is character,
translated into sequence and time.

Many of Mr. Pritchett's stories give the impression that
he is not interested in a character until the occasion of revelation, he does not look before or after. But this is deceptive. Saxon, for instance, in **"Our Oldest Friend"** [*Blind
Love*] is nothing but his doomed love for Tessa—who is
nothing but the form of Saxon's doom. It may be felt that
Mr. Pritchett is not interested in the process (if it is a process) by which these two characters have become what
they are, but this is merely another way of saying that
what they are is their nature, not their history. In his novels, Mr. Pritchett treats his characters more extensively,
of course, but even in the novels character is nature rather
than a function of society.

A social historian would find Mr. Pritchett's fiction extremely suggestive, but the novelist does not think of his
fiction as social history. Fiction is revelation. One of Mr.
Pritchett's finest achievements is the presentation of his father in *A Cab at the Door,* and indeed that book contains
a great deal of before and after, but it is all in the cause
of revelation, and what it reveals is a man's character as
his nature. The characters are rarely as large as this in the
fiction, they are persons rather than personages, but they
justify themselves by the human meaning they reveal. One
recalls from earlier volumes Harry (in **"Many Are Disappointed"**), who has a weakness for Roman roads, the sick
woman in the same story, the wife in **"The Landlord,"**
who calls her husband "father" because he has failed in
that capacity, Jill in **"Things as They Are"** who asserts,
"At my age I allow no one to strike me." In the new collection one thinks of Charles in **"A Debt of Honor,"** who has
a weakness for republics. These people are not explained
by environment, they contain their own nature and release
it under the writer's gaze.

But if we agree not to expect the relation between society
and man to be a matter of cause and effect, Mr. Pritchett
responds with an abundant sense of that relation as a liaison; between a house and its inhabitants, between London
and its people. A place is important because, having its
own character, it makes a vivid setting for character in
others. It is worth mentioning that many of Mr. Pritchett's stories place themselves in the England of 1945 and
after, when Londoners still talked of the Hun, conchies,
brilliantine, petticoats, M. and B., spivs, and Queer Street.
I cannot recall any story which tries to catch up with
swinging London, the plastic conceit of the 1960s. It may
be enough to say that his imagination has not been stirred,
his heart is still in the old place. But it is probably better
to say that Mr. Pritchett's imagination committed itself to
a time and a place in which the validity of character and
action was still unquestioned. Meditation upon the novels
of Virginia Woolf would at any time yield intimations of
the fragility of character, the ambiguity of action, but

meditation upon the Battle of Britain would produce a different conclusion.

In any event, the new stories are continuous with the old. I recall the word "chichi" in one of them, but no idiom more modish than that. Some of the old themes recur. Smith, a secondary character in the title story, is in some ways a revised version of the religious Mr. Timberlake in **"The Saint."** There are continuities of feeling between the title story and the novel *Mr. Beluncle,* especially in certain aspects of the central character, Armitage. At one point the blind Armitage goes to a quack healer, as if to seek humiliation. He abases himself. When his mistress rebukes him, he explains:

> We're proud. That is our vice. Proud in the dark. Everyone else has to put up with humiliation. Millions of people are humiliated: perhaps it makes them stronger because they forget it. I want to join them.

This is true not only to Armitage's life but to a great deal in English spiritual history, as *A Cab at the Door* makes clear. It is crucial to Mr. Pritchett's fiction.

The new collection comprises ten stories, samples of Mr. Pritchett's work over the past few years. The title story is much longer than the other pieces, and I prefer it to its companions for a certain grandeur in its relationships, a sense of what James in "The Jolly Corner" calls "the old baffled forsworn possibilities." Some of the shorter stories seem content to make a point rather than to reveal a character. But it is a vivid collection, on the whole. Mr. Pritchett is lavishly gifted, and he respects his gifts enough to care for them and to make sure that they are scrupulously employed. He is not an experimental writer, except in the sense that he is fascinated by the persistent possibilities of a common form, but his best work is a critique of experiment, shows experiment what, in the form of continuity, it has to challenge. (pp. 27, 30)

> *Denis Donoghue, "The Uncompleted Dossier,"*
> in The New York Review of Books, *Vol. XIV,*
> *No. 5, March 12, 1970, pp. 25-7, 30.*

V. S. Pritchett with Douglass A. Hughes   (interview date 1976)

[In the interview excerpted below, Pritchett comments on the strengths of the short story as a literary genre.]

[Hughes]: *For many years you've been a successful writer with the short story, novel, literary criticism, and travel books. In the Preface to* **The Sailor, Sense of Humor and Other Stories** *you've written that the short story is the only form of writing that has given you great pleasure. You say that despite difficulties of the form itself, you've found that the short story has stimulated you. I'd like you to talk briefly about the pleasures of writing the short story as opposed to other forms of literature.*

[Pritchett]: I think the short story has a certain amount of mixed excitement, that is to say, the excitement the poet feels when he has his image or his starting in his mind and watches it grow. It also has that almost sensational quality that the reporter feels when he sees something happen and then reports it exactly. The curious combination of the reporter and the poet in the short-story writer is a strange combination but I believe it exists. The other thing is that the short story is delightful because it is very much like looking at a picture. You can see the whole picture at once. A story is a thing which can be seen at once. You can't see *War and Peace, Middlemarch,* any long novel at once. Furthermore, the story has intensity in it. It's the intensity, I think, that attracts me.

You've suggested that the short story is a particularly apt form for our time "overwhelmed by enormous experience." You wrote in 1956 that we'd rather "glance at experience than look at it full in the face." Now, do you think that this remark still holds true for today, 1975?

I think it does. Nowadays the situation in which almost any of us lives in relation to society is becoming more and more complex and frightening. For instance, we may have to deal with terrorism and we certainly didn't before. We also have had to deal with human relationships in new ways. People may be ill and go to psychiatrists, to which people didn't go before. There are economic, interracial, and other difficulties that present themselves as frightful problems to the ordinary man. It requires an immense saturation in these subjects in order to be able to achieve some sort of detachment from them, which is necessary when you come to writing. You can't write, so to speak, from the middle of the storm, or not easily. So the short story, with its glancing view, can contain a great deal, can pay attention to aspects of these problems, which are very important, but it needn't state the whole of them. One of the advantages of the short story is that it allows us to isolate certain things in present day life.

How do you explain, or don't you think about, the critical neglect of the genre itself? Isn't it curious that the short story is not taken very seriously by critics?

Well, I think that is partially due to the general decline in the short story owing to the disappearance of periodicals. All the great short-story writers had periodicals which would publish them. The people loved reading stories. In a sense they had little else to do. They didn't have a television to look at, a motor car to drive, a swimming pool to swim in. They couldn't travel easily from one place to another. Therefore they read and one of their favorite forms of reading was the story. There were plenty of periodicals of very high quality. The evening newspaper had stories of very high quality, not just popular stuff.

I was just thinking that Maupassant's stories appeared in newspapers.

Maupassant's stories appeared in newspapers. So did Chekhov's and Poe's stories. That kind of thing has vanished. There followed then the magazines and little reviews. They have slowly ebbed away. The result has been that the public has lost this literary form that it used to enjoy. Secondly, I think short-story writers have always been rather few and far between. The number of first class short-story writers in any country has been very few compared with the number of novelists, shall we say. It is simply because the short story is a particularly difficult and special kind of art.

Let me interrupt for a second. There's one thing. If you take recent quality writers of the British short story: H. E. Bates, Sean O'Faolain, Frank O'Connor, Mary Lavin, and yourself. Let's take only those, all right? There's very little critical commentary on these writers considering their achievement. What I can't understand is why there should be 275 articles written next year on James Joyce and the works of these story writers should be almost totally ignored. That's what I'm getting at.

I know. It's very extraordinary, isn't it?

I think of the short story as the Neglected Genre.

In fact, there are very few books on the short story. Frank O'Connor wrote one. So did Sean O'Faolain.

H. E. Bates wrote one, though it is a historical survey.

Oh, yes, so he did. The short story is a subject that has been entirely neglected.

How do you explain that?

It may be that somehow the short story speaks for itself.

Do you really believe that? Isn't a short story much like a lyric poem?

Yes, yes, it is.

In many cases a story is very complicated and subtle and there are a lot of things that one can say about it.

Nobody does it, I must say. In fact, if you take the case of Turgenev, who wrote both short stories and novels—his stories differ very much from his novels. In any book on Turgenev the critic gives a brief chapter on his short stories, which contain some of his best work, and there are hundreds of pages about his novels.

All right, is it possible that we might conclude that critics or people generally really undervalue the story, and I particularly address this question to you because somewhere you've said that the short story is a minor art. Why would you depreciate it and consider it a minor art any more than a collection of lyric poems would be considered minor art?

When I said that I was being rather ironical because there was a period, which I think came to an end about ten years ago, when there was a very strong feeling that the short story was done for. The reason it was supposedly done for was that it's rather like the sonnet. It's a very complicated form of writing and it requires a certain skill. You can't compare a sonnet with *Paradise Lost* and you shouldn't do so. But on the other hand people do, in the back of their minds, say, oh it's short and therefore it must be much more important to write something long rather than a story. And that's what it amounts to.

That's exactly how I feel about it. It's so easy to depreciate the short story. I didn't realize you were being ironic in your remark.

I was being rather modest about it in order to make a dig. My statement was immediately denied by others when I wrote it. But people also did say that it was an inferior form of writing because it was essentially a craft. They were thinking, for example, of the immense amount of

craftsmanlike ingenuity which Kipling used, especially in his later stories, which were very elaborate. Or they were thinking of a Russian writer like Babel, who, to write a story of fifteen pages, would perhaps write a hundred and fifty pages and then reduce it, reduce it, reduce it. That's obviously a matter not of vision but of craftsmanship that has frequently been brought against short-story writers, that they are essentially craftsmen. I don't think it's true.

It may be true of some story writers. I think one could be only a craftsman and write readable stories, but it wouldn't be true of the best writers certainly.

It's not true, not at all. Another great thing about the short story is that the writer, the good one, always has a voice you can instantly recognize. You only have to read the first three lines and you can pretty well tell who wrote it. The actual pitch of his voice tells you straightaway. In a novelist this isn't necessarily so. It's very difficult to take test passages say from Dickens or George Eliot or Hardy. It's by no means certain that you'll recognize that distinct voice. The novelist is relying on the general public voice, no doubt of an educated kind, but nevertheless a general voice that everyone uses and understands. But the short-story writer is like someone who sings a song. The singer has his own voice. It isn't the voice of anyone else.

Did you ever consider writing a book of criticism on the short story?

No, never. I have written short critical articles about certain writers that I've admired. No, I think it's much better to write another story rather than write a book about short stories.

What do you think of Frank O'Connor as a critic of the short story?

I think he's extremely interesting about it because he had one particularly interesting theory, that the story was especially suited to anarchic societies. There were anarchic societies in Russia, America, and Ireland and there the short story flourished. In England, no, and therefore among English writers there was a long silence through the nineteenth century as far as the short story was concerned.

He also said that the short story deals with a submerged group, with the outsider. Do you think that this is true?

I suppose to some extent this is true. You don't feel, however, that Chekhov or Turgenev was an outsider. I think he may be right in saying that stories deal with a submerged part of the self, which is quite another matter. If you take the most conventional character you can think of, the most complete insider shall we say, and you write a story about him you are almost certain to choose that part of his person that is submerged or hidden. You're not likely to write about the surface, otherwise you'd become a photographer. I don't think the short-story writer is a photographer at all. Everyone feels himself to be exceptional and the writer tends to look at that part of the human being that is submerged, that separates the individual from others of his own kind.

In an introduction to the collected stories of Mary Lavin

you made an interesting observation. You said that the Russians, Italians, the Slavonic Jews, and the Irish excel at the short story. I'm curious why you left out the Americans. It seems to me that the Americans have succeeded marvelously with the short story.

Absolutely. I don't know why I left them out. I entirely agree with you.

In your autobiography you say that you object to the contention that you create characters in the Dickensian sense in your stories. Perhaps this is true, but to an American reader your fiction has an unmistakably British quality. You go on to say that far from being a traditional English writer there is a foreign element in your work. What do you mean by this foreign element?

Well, this theory about myself may be quite wrong but I felt myself not to be terribly interested in English life when I was young, before I went to live abroad. I spent six or seven years abroad between the ages of twenty and about twenty-seven. I had, as young men do, certain vanities in being rather foreign to my own environment. When I was in France I liked to feel myself a Frenchman and while in Spain to feel myself a Spaniard and hoped that some of this would rub off on me. This is partly the reason. And then as I got to know many writers that I admired, I realized that they had the same sort of feeling that they didn't quite belong to the community in which they lived. We were therefore people who had the feeling of living on a frontier between two possibilities. I think—I don't quite know how to put this—I think really it is the frontier spirit which I had very strongly felt and still do feel very much. About being Dickensian, many people say that about my writing and I certainly don't object to it because it's an enormous compliment. But on the other hand Dickens was a very great writer who was sort of centrally English in all of his comic characters. You've only to go out and down the street to meet them in two minutes. And they don't know they're being what they are. But Dickens saw and very deeply felt that what was happening to English people in his time was that they were working too hard, that the doctrine of work in the nineteenth century was just killing them. It was killing their souls, but they had this ability to construct a fantasy life which they gradually assumed to be real. He did everything he could to encourage the flourishing of this fantasy life. The best example I can think of is the alteration he made to an article that someone had written about the postal system for the paper he edited, *Household Words*. He had an article written on how the post office was organized and how you posted letters and what happened to them and so on. The writer had described the frantic scene at the post office at six o'clock in the evening when you had to get your mail posted in order to get it through at a cheap rate. At that hour you couldn't get into a post office because of the crowds pushing and shoving and even throwing their papers over the crowds to the counter. Dickens understood that the original writer was a rather dull fellow who described this scene. Dickens, in his alteration, began to exaggerate everything in the scene and finally described at the end how someone decided to throw the office boy clean across the crowd. Now this idea of throwing the office boy on to the

counter is a fantasy, but I'm sure many people in the crowd at that time thought: it's a pity we can't throw this boy across. This was a release. If he could see these exceptional fantasies that entered the imaginations of ordinary people, Dickens thought he could make them grow. He would be describing something that would be profoundly true of the English character. Well, I feel equally when I see someone who appears prosaic but who after I've got to know him suddenly reveals things about himself that are absolutely incredible. . . . I realize that the incredible is part of his real character. Well, in the sense that I focus on this incredible element sometimes I may be Dickensian but not in the sense of just going in for funny people. For most of the people I've written fantastic things about are not funny people at all.

You've said that every short story is a drama and for you the drama lies in the human personality. I think I understand what you mean by this, but I wonder why you emphasize character at the expense of events or situations. Wouldn't you agree that the situations, particularly unusual situations, play a very important part in most of your stories?

Yes they do, indeed. That's quite true. I think many writers, before they get down to the unusual situations, have one or two characters in mind. And sometimes these characters grow larger and larger of themselves and become, as it were, like stories. In others they are put in extraordinary situations and in fact their very characters attract unusual situations to them.

In revealing character you appear to be working throughout the story rather than in the Joycean manner of the epiphany. Would you agree?

Yes, I think on the whole I would, yes.

And the next question is: you've said that when Ulysses *was published you were living in Paris but you didn't read the novel until several years later. Did you read* Dubliners *early, when it first appeared?*

I read *Dubliners* very early.

Did those stories make an impression on you? Did they influence you?

I was very much influenced by Irish stories. In fact, I only began writing short stories when I went to Ireland [as a journalist] and found there were several interesting story writers there. I didn't know them, of course, but I knew their work. Joyce, of course, was one and Liam O'Flaherty was writing at that time. Sean O'Faolain may have written later. I suddenly recognized their curious poetic gift, if you understand poetic in the sense of a sensation, was very much an Irish gift and it did appeal to me enormously. The danger was that I should think of the Irish, as one often does, as just being funny because they say funny things. One had to grow out of that sort of thing and get at the real essence of what they were trying to say.

In commenting on the stories of Mary Lavin you've said that Irish storytellers tend to concentrate on the discrepancy between ordinary, everyday life and the self's hidden life.

Isn't this in fact your own approach to characterization, a disclosing of the duality of the individual?

It is very much so, yes. I never see people as being consistent with themselves at all.

Most of your characters live in a world of self-deception. Isn't that essentially what you're showing, that these characters are living in an illusion?

They're living partly in their imaginations. And after all, I think people . . . There's something I call self-imagination. We are what we are, but we often imagine ourselves as something else and it's that which I'm considering.

Then yours is a consistently ironic tone.

Yes, that is true.

Would it be fair to assume that your vision of life is that man lives in illusion?

Yes, certainly.

Would you accept the judgment that your work indicates that man's collective lot is one of failure and unhappiness?

Well, I think we live like tightrope walkers walking over a Niagara. Fortunately, we have enough—what should I say?—cussedness to survive the walk with some sort of balance.

It appears that your comic characters become grotesques— at least what might be considered grotesques—by dedicating themselves too unreservedly to their own personal view of reality, one which is cut off from conventional reality or truth. You talk about the essence of comedy as being "militancy." That's your word. Is militancy another word for fanaticism or the spirit of seriousness that Nietzsche speaks of?

No, I don't mean it in that sense. In comedy, I think, there's a general fight for survival that goes on. Almost every character feels himself entirely alone, and therefore he's engaged in a battle of wits with his purely imaginary enemies. I think this is very common in Jane Austen, a very militant writer in that sense.

Do you think that literature has a purpose, a function to serve? I ask this question knowing that in your whole literary career you've been very independent from ideological and philosophical positions, that you've been a very self-effacing writer. But do you see literature as having a function to serve in society?

It's a kind of secret means of communication between people. Literature enlarges our knowledge and possibilities of human nature to an extraordinary degree. It makes us aware of people, emotions, and ideas of which we are normally unaware or which we take for granted. It's really a secret communication.

Then you regard the writer more as an observer in the manner of Flaubert and Joyce than as a mover in the manner of Tolstoy and Dostoevsky?

I'm not a didactic writer. I really think that the writer is an observer, a recorder of human experience. But he himself may be observing in extreme difficulty; that is to say, he may be in the middle of something which he can't always clearly observe.

In your autobiography you mention the early influence on your writing: Stevenson, Chesterton, Anatole France. What about later influences? Was Hemingway an influence in his use of language?

Very much so, yes. When I wrote **"Sense of Humor"** it was very much under the influence of Hemingway, although it may not seem so to the reader. That was a story I had been trying to write for six or seven years. I had written various versions of it. I thought it wasn't any good and I set it aside. Then suddenly reading Hemingway I thought: my god, yes, I believe I can write it, and then I threw away my other versions and wrote it in a particular way.

Was "Many Are Disappointed" written at the same time?

Approximately the same time.

Because that story seems to me clearly to show Hemingway's influence in the language and tone.

Probably. He possibly had some influence, though I don't remember that quite so much. Yes, it must come under that. Certainly the thing people say I'm quite good at is writing dialogue, knowing how different kinds of people speak. Hemingway knew that and I, who never met any of those characters in the story **"Many Are Disappointed,"** suddenly realized how four men, going on a biking tour like that, would speak to each other. The background of the story is simply that I was once down in Cornwall and was bicycling or walking along and wanted a drink. I came to such a place as found in the story and there was the same kind of woman serving tea. I thought that it was very disappointing and went on. Afterward I thought how splendid it would be to have four men going along, each with his own particular fantasy or expectation, arriving at such a place. And that's how it grew.

Now that brings up another question. How your stories come about, how they're actually conceived and written. In reading about your life I get the feeling that a number of your stories have an autobiographical background.

That is so, yes.

But do you write some stories that are totally outside your experience, stories which are pure imagination?

I do. [Pause] I'm just trying to remember my stories.

There's one story I'm particularly fond of, "Blind Love."

That's totally outside my experience. The origin of that story was that I was told of a blind man who went to a faith healer.

It's a great story. Are you especially fond of it or is it just another story to you?

No. I think it's a good story, but it's not part of my experience.

Do you keep a notebook for your stories?

Yes, I do.

What I'm getting at here is how you actually go about writing stories. You have a notebook. Do you work every day on a story? Do you work when it moves you or when you get an idea? How do you work and how do the stories come about?

Well, I do, from time to time, make notes of things. All sorts of unusual things, like people speaking in the streets. Situations sometimes and sometimes I'll make a note of a particular feeling. And then sometimes from real life some incident occurs or some people I know will say something and I'll write it down. I think that if I make a list of these things they may stir some sort of story in me. But the story that results from such notes is *never* the story that is related to the people or events of real life. I get a lot of ideas for stories, but I find that I make false starts so I generally try to write three stories at the same time. If I write one I get stuck. Then I move on to the next one and I'll get stuck with that one. Then I move on to the next one and then I go back to the first one and continue.

In Midnight Oil *you say that the cost of literature is higher than most readers imagine and is getting higher. What did you mean by that?*

[Pause] I'm not really sure in what sense I meant that. But I must say I find the act of writing much more exacting now than I did when I was starting out, that is, after I had learned how to write. I believe writers continue to write well so long as they make difficulties for themselves. If you arrive at a certain point of success where you no longer have difficulties then your growth ceases. Your writing becomes easier and not so exacting and then you begin to go down hill. You become less interesting. So I think it is the concentration on difficulty which is important to writers. And actually the more experience you have the more exacting you become because you choose more obstacles.

Speaking of literary success, I recently came across a remark by W. H. Auden I'd like you to comment on. Auden wrote in the Introduction to Paul Valery's Analects: *"Aside from the money, literary success can give but small satisfaction to an author, even to his vanity. For what does literary success mean? To be condemned by persons who have not read his works and to be imitated by persons devoid of talent. There are only two kinds of literary glory that are worth winning but the writer who wins either will never know. One is to have been the writer, perhaps a quite minor one, in whose work some great master generations later finds an essential clue for solving some problem; the other is to become for someone else an example of the dedicated life, 'being secretly invoked, pictured, and placed by a stranger in an inner sanctum of his thoughts, so as to serve him as a witness, a judge, a father, and a hallowed mentor.'"*

I think that's rather a good statement. The great moment in a writer's life is having the excitement of his initial idea, the moment when a sudden vision comes: good heavens, I can do this. And then comes the appalling labor of trying to do it, when the writer may become increasingly disappointed and finally lose all self-confidence. And then the whole thing is over because he's finished it and it's left him with almost nothing. He's got to go on to the next thing. However, it is an enormous comfort to a writer and one of the great rewards of writing to find that what you've written has meant something to another writer or writers or to other people and that you're part of the continuity of literature. Of course, your quality as a writer is your own personal business, which you really want to perfect. You want to perfect yourself and that sort of self-perfection is its own reward. But I think that *every* writer is valuable insofar as he helps other writers. Last night, for example, I happened to pick up by accident Gibbon's *Decline and Fall of the Roman Empire* and read two or three pages. I'm not an historian and don't know anything about the Roman Empire; nevertheless, a few sentences there absolutely stuck in my mind. And I thought: thank god for Gibbon. You see, that started my mind working and so I'm grateful for Gibbon. (pp. 423-32)

V. S. Pritchett and Douglass A. Hughes, in an interview in Studies in Short Fiction, *Vol. XIII, No. 4, Fall, 1976, pp. 423-32.*

Eudora Welty (essay date 1978)

[*Welty is a well-known American novelist and short story writer whose work deals with life in the rural South. In the following review, she praises Pritchett's short stories.*]

This great and fascinating writer [V. S. Pritchett] is about the age of our century and has written short stories most of his way through it. With their abundance, they are of equally remarkable variety: Where would one look for the typical Pritchett story? But one always finds this—that any Pritchett story is all of it alight and busy at once, like a well-going fire. Wasteless and at the same time well fed, it shoots up in flame from its own spark like a poem or a magic trick, self-consuming, with nothing left over. He is one of the great pleasure-givers in our language.

Pritchett himself has said that the short story is his greatest love because he finds it challenging. The new collection makes it clear that neither the love nor the challenge has let him down.

As ever, the writing spouts with energy. Dialogue, in constant exchange, frisks like a school of dolphin. These are *social* stories: Life goes on in them without flagging. The characters that fill them—erratic, unsure, unsafe, devious, stubborn, restless and desirous, absurd and passionate, all peculiar unto themselves—hold a claim on us that is not to be denied. They demand and get our rapt attention, for in their revelation of their lives, the secrets of our own lives come into view. How much the eccentric has to tell us of what is central!

Once more, in [*Selected Stories*], the characters are everything. Through a character Pritchett can trace a frail thread of chivalry in the throatcutting trade of antique collecting. Through a character he finds a great deal of intrigue in old age. The whole burden of **"The Spree"** is grief and what his character is ever to do with it. Paradox comes naturally to Pritchett, and he has always preferred, and excelled in, the oblique approach; and I think all these varying stories in today's book are love stories.

One is called **"The Diver."** Panicking as his initiation into sex confronts him in the middle-aged Frenchwoman lying "naked and idle" on her bed—who mocks him with "You have never seen a woman before?"—the young English boy is surprised by his own brain beginning to act: He hears himself begin answering her with a preposterous lie. He is into another initiation—he is becoming a story writer as he stands there quaking. "It was her turn to be frightened." All being squared, the woman back in her earlier character of "a soft, ordinary, decent woman," that is when his heart begins to throb. "And everything was changed for me after this."

Of these 14 stories—chosen from four volumes published over the last nine years—**"The Diver"** is not the only one here to suggest that, in times of necessity or crisis, a conspiracy may form among the deep desires of our lives to substitute for one another, to masquerade sometimes as one another, to support, to save one another. These stories seem to find that human desire is really a *family* of emotions, a whole interconnection—not just the patriarch and matriarch, but all the children. All kin, and none of them born to give up. If anything happens to cut one off, they go on surviving in one another's skins. They become something new. In fact, they become storytellers.

In **"Blind Love,"** when Mr. Armitage employs Mrs. Johnson, two people have been brought together who have been afflicted beyond ordinary rescue. Mr. Armitage is blind; Mrs. Johnson has a very extensive and horrifying birthmark. Beneath her clothes, "She was stamped with an ineradicable bloody insult." When she was young and newly married, her husband had sent her packing for the horror of its surprise, for her having thus "deceived" him. Now, "as a punished and self-hating person, she was drawn to work with a punished man. It was a return to her girlhood: Injury had led her to injury." In the love affair that grows out of this doubleness, blindness and deceiving are played against each other, are linked together—as though each implied the other. How much does each really know? We watch to see what hurt does to vision—or *for* vision; what doubt does to faith, faith to doubt. These two magnetized people have selves hidden under selves; they have more than one visible or invisible skin. After they reach and survive a nearly fatal crisis of ambiguous revelation, the only possible kind, we see them contentedly traveling in tandem. "She has always had a secret. It still pleases Armitage to baffle people." But they are matched now in "blind love": They depend on each other altogether.

"The Marvelous Girl" is a double portrait. One side is blind love, love in the dark. The obverse side is a failed marriage in clear view. (It failed because "even unhappiness loses its tenderness and fascination.") A husband, from the back of a large audience, can see his wife seated on a stage in the glare of the light and the public eye, "a spectator of his marriage that had come to an end." She looks "smaller and more bizarre." When the lights suddenly go out in the auditorium, the darkness "extinguished everything. It stripped the eyes of sight. . . . One was suddenly naked in the dark from the boots upward. One could feel the hair on one's body growing and in the chatter one could hear men's voices grunting, women's

voices fast, breath going in and out, muscles changing, hearts beating. Many people stood up. Surrounded by animals like himself he too stood up, to hunt with the pack, to get out."

On the stairs he comes by accident up against his wife: "He heard one of the large buttons on his wife's coat click against a button on his coat. She was there for a few seconds: It seemed to him as long as their marriage."

Still in the dark, and like a dream, comes his discovery—it is his pursuit—of "the marvelous girl." And afterward, when the lights come on again, "they got up, scared, hot-faced, hating the light. 'Come on. We must get out,' he said. And they hurried from the lighted room to get into the darkness of the city."

We read these stories, comic or tragic, with an elation that stems from their intensity. In **"When My Girl Comes Home"** Pritchett establishes a mood of intensification that spreads far around and above it like a brooding cloud, far-reaching, not promising us to go away. We are with a family in England 10 years after the last World War as they face the return of a daughter, gone all this time, who is thought to be a prisoner of the enemy. Hilda, "rescued" at last from Japan, where she had not, after all, been tortured and raped but had done very well for herself, brings on a shock as excruciating as it is gradual when her shifting and cheapening tales begin to come out.

The youngest boy muses: "We must have all known in our different ways that we had been disturbed in a very long dream. We had been living on inner visions for years. It was an effect of the long war. England had been a prison. Even the sky was closed, and, like convicts, we had been driven to dwelling on fancies in our dreary minds. In the cinema," he says, and that cloud begins to reach overhead, "the camera sucks some person forward into an enormous closeup and holds a face there yards wide, filling the whole screen, all holes and pores, like some sucking octopus that might eat up an audience rows at a time . . . Hilda had been a close-up like this for us when she was lost and far away."

In the shock of reunion, the whole family—several generations and their connections—sees appearing, bit by bit, the evidence that all of them have been marred, too, have been driven, are still being driven and still being changed by the same war. Alone and collectively, they have become calloused as Hilda has been and, in some respect of their own, made monsters by their passage through an experience too big for them, as it was too big for Hilda—for anyone.

"Hilda had been our dream, but now she was home she changed as fast as dreams change," the boy tells us. "She was now, as we looked at her, far more remote to us than she had been all the years when she was away."

Finally, it is not Hilda's errant life in Japan but the "rescue," the return to the family circle, that wrecks her imperviousness. It wrecks the life at home, too. When the young narrator finds himself alone at the end with Hilda, "I wanted to say more. I wanted to touch her. But I couldn't. The ruin had made her untouchable."

None of the stories is livelier than these new stories of Pritchett's written of old age. Old bachelor clubman George is militant, astringent, biting, fearsomely grinning, in training with his cold baths, embattled behind his fossilized anecdotes, victoriously keeping alive ("he got up every day to win") on the adrenalin of outrage and of constituting himself a trial and a bore to everyone. But afraid. Afraid not of the North wind but of the East wind, afraid not that the Arch Enemy will get him but that the building will be sold out from under him.

> "O God," he groaned loudly, but in a manner so sepulchral and private that people moved respectfully away. It was a groan that seemed to come up from the earth, up from his feet, a groan of loneliness that was raging and frightening to the men around him. He had one of those moments when he felt dizzy, when he felt he was lost among unrecognizable faces, without names, alone, in the wrong club, at the wrong address even, with the tottering story of his life, a story which he was offering or, rather, throwing out as a lifeline for help.

What wins out over George is not the East wind or the Arch Enemy but the warm arms of a large, drinking, 40-year-old woman with a kind disposition and a giggle for his indignation, who "drops in" ("What manners!") out of his past that he had thought safely sealed behind anecdotes. She was the woman the old man had admired once "for being so complete an example of everything that made women impossible."

> It is thus that he faces the affronting fact that he had not after all succeeded in owning his own life and closing it to others; that he existed in other people's minds and that all people dissolved in this way, becoming fragments of one another, and nothing in themselves. . . . He knew, too, that he had once lived, or nearly lived.

Of all the stories of desiring, and of all the stories in this collection, **"The Camberwell Beauty"** is the most marvelous. It is a story of desiring and also of possessing—we are in a world of antique-shop keepers—and of possessing that survives beyond the death of desiring. It is a closed world, one that has its own hours, its own landscape inside nighttime warehouses, its edges the streets beneath the sodium lights. It has its own breed of people, its own language, its codes and spies and secrets and shames, jealousies, savageries, fantasies. And like some fairy tale itself, it has its own maiden, carried off and shut up and, you and I would think, wanting to accept rescue, but provided with a bugle to play if this should threaten.

"It broke my heart to think of that pretty girl living among such people and drifting into the shabbiness of the trade," says the young man—he is also of the trade—who discovers her and loses her when an old man named Pliny carries her off for himself and shuts her up in his shop. The boy cannot forget how she had written her name in the dust of a table top and left it unfinished: "I S A B—half a name, written by a living finger in the dust."

The young man is left "with a horror of the trade I had joined." He abhors "the stored up lust that seemed to pass between things and men like Pliny." It is not long before

"the fever of the trade had come alive in me: Pliny had got something I wanted." The end is unescapable—for all, that is, who are connected with the trade.

"The Camberwell Beauty" is an extraordinary piece of work. Densely complex and unnervingly beautiful in its evocation of those secret, packed rooms, it seems to shimmer with the gleam of its unreliable treasures. There is the strange device of the bugle—which, blown by Isabel, actually kills desire. All the while the story is filled with longing, it remains savage and seething and crass and gives off the unhidable smell of handled money.

Most extraordinarily of all, it expresses, not the confusion of one human desire with another, not sexuality confused with greed, but rather the culmination of these desires in their *fusion*.

"How unreal people looked in the sodium light," the defeated boy thinks as he walks in the street at the story's end. Or by the light of their obsessions.

Each story's truth is distilled by Pritchett through a pure concentration of human character. It is the essence of his art. And, of course, in plain fact, and just as in a story, it is inherent in the human being to create his own situation, his own plot. The paradoxes, the stratagems, the escapes, the entanglements, the humors and dreams, are all projections of the individual human being, all by himself alone. In its essence, Pritchett's work, so close to fantasy, is deeply true to life. (pp. 1, 39-40)

> *Eudora Welty, "A Family of Emotions," in* The New York Times Book Review, *June 25, 1978, pp. 1, 39-40.*

What extraordinary changes in society, manners, speech, ways of living, I have lived through. To live is to be out of date.

—V. S. Pritchett, in the preface to his Midnight Oil, *1971*.

Robert Towers (essay date 1980)

[*In the following excerpt, Towers reviews* On the Edge of the Cliff, and Other Stories.]

Pritchett is the least snobbish of English writers, a clear-eyed but amiable democrat who treats his characters with sublime fairness, playing no favorites, settling no scores. They are created substantially, with strong, sometimes eccentric outlines. Often their behavior is droll. But they are by no means "humors" characters in the manner of Dickens and his predecessors, for they have not been allowed to harden into crustacean-like rigidity; instead, they are presented as capable of sudden insights and moral qualms, of sudden reversals of course that suggest complexity and depth. Essentially Pritchett is a psychological realist who permits his characters to keep their options open while sparing them that diffusion or dissolution of ego so common in our psychologizing age. In this respect they seem more distinctively, more "archaically" English than American.

Pritchett's lovers are seldom beautiful, but they have a firmness of bone and contour that makes the (mostly) off-stage grappling of their bodies entirely credible without the whipped cream and cherries of pornographic detail. Bodies can be funny: "I liked watching her dress," writes the narrator of **"The Accompanist"**—"her legs and arms were thin, and as she put up her arms to fasten her bra and leaned forward to pull on her tights she seemed to be playing a game of turning herself into comic triangles." Bodies can be moving too, subject as they are to the grotesque tricks of time. In the remarkable title story, **"On the Edge of the Cliff,"** the seventyish writer called Harry violates one of the cardinal rules in the game of love that he plays with his mistress Rowena, who is twenty-five, by allowing her, for the first time, to see him naked. The violation occurs after Harry and Rowena have encountered a woman from his past, Daisy Pyke; filled with rage against time and Daisy, the old man impulsively decides to undress and plunge into Withy Hole, a frigid tidal pool on the Welsh coast where he and Daisy had swum decades before.

> He was standing there, his body furred with grey hair, his belly wrinkled, his thighs shrunk. Up went his bony arms.
>
> "You're not to! It will kill you! Your heart!" she shouted.
>
> He gave a wicked laugh, she saw his yellow teeth, and in he dived and was crawling and shouting in the water as he swam out farther, defying her, threshing the water, and then as she screamed at him, really frightened, he came crawling in like some ugly hairy sea animal, his skin reddened with cold, and stood dripping with his arms wide as if he was going to give a howl.

But Rowena, though frightened, is not repelled by what she has seen. That night, for the first time, she comes unbidden to his bed. " 'I've come to see the Ancient Mariner,' she said." This is only one of the many ironies upon which the story is hinged, all of them relevant to the dangers inherent in this particular game of love. Daisy, the fiftyish woman from Harry's past, a woman with "a hard little begging pushing mouth," turns out to have a lover young enough to be her son—a lover whom she is terrified of losing to Rowena if the couples continue to meet.

Like most of the stories in the collection, **"On the Edge of the Cliff "** is shrewdly constructed, though not at all, in the accepted sense, "well made." While full of twistings, the narrative line is sinewy; the surprises—and there are many in a good Pritchett story—never seem arbitrary. The play of language in the stories is also full of odd turnings, with a freshness of imagery that is sometimes startling and nearly always a source of delight. Seen from a great height, "the shallow sea [broke] idly, in changing lines of surf, like lips speaking lines that broke unfinished and could not be heard." In a small restaurant people "were talking loudly, so that bits of their lives seemed to

be flying around us. . . . " The cuckolded husband in **"The Fig Tree"** is "lazily well-made, a bufferish fellow in his late fifties, his drooping grey moustache is affable— 'honorable' is how I would describe the broad road of sun-burned baldness going over his head."

An abundance of such touches testifies to the flourishing condition of Pritchett's art. Containing only one story (**"The Spanish Bed"**) that I would consider a relative failure, *On the Edge of the Cliff* may well be his strongest collection to date. In both his vision and his craft, Pritchett has currently no equal as a short-story writer in England—and only a few elsewhere in the English-speaking world. (p. 26)

> *Robert Towers, "Fair Play," in* The New York Review of Books, *Vol. XXVII, No. 1, February 7, 1980, pp. 25-6.*

Walter Allen   (essay date 1981)

[*Allen is an English novelist, critic, and a distinguished popular historian. In the essay excerpted below, he discusses a selection of Pritchett's short fiction written between the 1930s and the 1970s.*]

Since the death of D. H. Lawrence, the outstanding English short-story writer has been V. S. Pritchett. Besides his short stories, he has written novels, literary criticism of great distinction, and two volumes of autobiography that are among the best of our time. In whatever genre he writes, he is always *sui generis,* marked by an unfailing curiosity about and a constant delight in the oddities and vagaries of human nature and by an exceedingly close observation of the human scene, all of which are expressed in a darting, idiosyncratic prose compounded of unexpected images and of brilliant, fresh generalization. It is a prose uncannily close to the speaking voice. The great influence on it is Dickens, though the Dickens that emerges in Pritchett's short stories is a Dickens who has absorbed the lessons of Dostoevsky and of Freud.

If there is one thing that Pritchett has made his own it is puritanism. He is, so to say, the connoisseur of puritanism in its characteristically English manifestations, which, in social terms, have generally been lower-middle class. Writing on puritanism in an essay on Gosse's *Father and Son,* he describes the territory of much of his own fiction:

> Extreme puritanism gives purpose, drama, and intensity to private life. . . . Outwardly, the extreme puritan appears narrow, crabbed, fanatical, gloomy, and dull; but from the inside—what a series of dramatic climaxes his life is, what a fascinating casuistry beguiles him, how he is bemused by the comedies of duplicity, sharpened by the ingenious puzzles of the conscience, and carried away by the eloquence of hypocrisy.

In that passage, Pritchett defines exactly the comedy of such short stories as **'It May Never Happen'**, **'The Saint'**, **'The Sailor'**, and **'Aunt Gertrude'**.

In these stories, which date from the late Thirties and the war years, an adolescent boy very much like the young Pritchett often appears as the centre of consciousness of the story. **'The Saint'** is the obvious way of entry into Pritchett's world.

At seventeen, the boy is introduced to and joins a sect which 'regarded it as "Error"—our name for Evil—to believe the evidence of our senses and if we had influenza or consumption, or had lost our money or were unemployed, we denied the reality of these things, saying that since God could not have made them they therefore did not exist.' His family is visited one Sunday for lunch by a man from the headquarters of the sect, Mr Hubert Timberlake.

> 'This is my son,' my father said introducing me. 'He thinks, he thinks, Mr Timberlake, but I tell him he only thinks he does ha, ha.' My father was a humorous man. 'He's always on the river,' my father continued. 'I tell him he's got water on the brain. I've been telling Mr Timberlake about you, my boy.'
>
> A hand as soft as the best quality chamois leather took mine. I saw a wide upright man in a double-breasted navy blue suit. He had a pink square head with very small ears and one of those torpid, enamelled smiles which are so common in our sex.
>
> 'Why, isn't that just fine?' said Mr Timberlake dryly. Owing to his contacts with Toronto he spoke with an American accent. 'What say we tell your father it's funny he thinks he's funny.'
>
> The eyes of Mr Timberlake were direct and colourless. He had the look of a retired merchant captain who had become decontaminated from the sea and had reformed and made money. His defence of me had made me his at once. My doubts vanished. Whatever Mr Timberlake believed must be true and as I listened to him at lunch I thought there could be no finer life than his.

After lunch, at Mr Timberlake's request, the boy takes him on the river.

> 'Now I want you to paddle us over to the far bank', he said, 'and then I'll show you how to punt.'
>
> Everything that Mr Timberlake said still seemed unreal to me. The fact that he was sitting in a punt of all commonplace material things was incredible, that he should propose to pole us up the river was terrifying. Suppose he fell into the river? At once I checked the thought. A leader of our church under the direct guidance of God could not possibly fall into the river.

But he does so all the same. He ignores the accident and its possible consequences, saying, 'If God made water it would be ridiculous to suggest He made it capable of harming his other creatures.' After a time they draw in and lie on the buttercups in the sun. At last, they rise to go.

> We both stood up and I let him pass in front of me. When I looked at him again I stopped dead. Mr Timberlake was no longer a man in a navy blue suit. He was blue no longer. He was transfigured. He was yellow. He was covered with buttercup pollen, a fine yellow paste of it made by the damp, from head to foot.
>
> 'Your suit,' I said.
>
> He looked at it. He raised his thin eyebrows a little, but he did not smile, or make any comment.
>
> The man is a saint, I thought. As saintly as any of those gold leaf figures in the churches of Sicily. Golden he sat in the punt, golden he sat for the next hour as I paddled him down the river. Golden and bored. Golden as we landed at the town and as we walked up the street back to my parent's house. There he refused to change his clothes or to sit by a fire. He kept his eye on the time for his train back to London. By no word did he acknowledge the disasters or the beauties of the world. If they were printed upon him it was as upon a husk.

The story ends sixteen years later when the narrator hears of Timberlake's death:

> I thought of our afternoon on the river. I thought of him hanging from the tree. I thought of him indifferent and golden, in the meadow. I understood why he had made for himself a protective, sedentary blandness, an automatic smile, a collection of phrases. He kept them on like the coat after his ducking. And I understood why—though I had feared it all the time we were on the river—I understood why he did not talk to me about the origin of evil. He was honest. The ape was with us. The ape that merely followed me was already inside Mr Timberlake eating at his heart.

Though relatively early, **'The Saint'** is probably the best-known of Pritchett's stories. It is indeed very fine and a complete success. But, for Pritchett, it is a comparatively simple work. It could be reduced in précis to an anecdote something like Johnson's comment on Berkeley, 'I refute him thus.' Richer in its amplitude and more searching into the crannies and recesses of the Puritan mind in its worldly manifestations, is **'It May Never Happen'**.

It is an exploration of the lower-middle class world of small business men in the home counties; one thinks inevitably of Dickens and Wells. It begins:

> I shall not forget the fingers that fastened me into the stiff collar. Or how I was clamped down under the bowler hat which spread my rather large ears outwards, and how, my nose full of the shop smell of a new suit, I went off for the first time to earn my living.
>
> 'You are beginning life,' they said.
>
> 'You have your foot on the first rung of the ladder,' they said.
>
> 'Excelsior!' my new Uncle Belton said. I was going to work in the office of one of my uncles, a new uncle, the second of my mother's sister, who had just married into the family.

So the theme is announced, a boy's initiation into what is called real life, and the way in which the announcement is made illustrates the high spirits with which Pritchett writes. The name of the firm the boy is entering is Belton and Phillimore. 'The push of Mr Belton, the designing of Mr Phillimore, his partner, made it irresistible.' Mr Belton, the new uncle, the first employer, is presented as follows:

> A new business, a new marriage, a new outlook on life—my brand new uncle looked as though he had come straight out of a shop window. He had been hardly more than a quarter of an hour in our house before we thought our paint looked shabby and the rooms small. The very curtains seemed to shrink like the poor as he talked largely of exports, imports, agencies, overheads, discounts, rebates, cut prices, and debentures. And when he had done with these, he was getting at what we paid for our meat, where we got our coal and how much at a time, telling us, too, where to buy carpets and clothes, gas fires, art pottery, and electric irons. He even gave us the name of a new furniture polish. It sounded like one of the books of the Old Testament. He walked around the house touching things, fingering picture-frames, turning chairs round, looking under tables, tapping his toes thoughtfully on the linoleum. Then he sat down and, lifting his foot restfully to his knees and exposing the striking pattern of his socks, he seemed to be working out how much we would get if we sold up house and home. The message, 'Sell up and begin again', flashed on and off in the smiles of his shining new face like morse.

The passage is typical of Pritchett and his way of building up a story, which is through the character-sketch, as in Dickens.

On his first morning of employment the boy Vincent travels to the office by train with his uncle. Again, the account of it is a masterly piece of comic writing.

> When he and I sat in the train that morning I thought Mr Belton looked larger.
>
> 'I don't want you to think I'm lecturing you, boy,' he said, 'but there are many boys who would give their right hand to walk straight into this business as you are doing.'
>
> 'Yes, uncle,' I said.
>
> 'A little thing—you must call me "Sir".'
>
> 'Yes, uncle,' I said. 'Sir.'
>
> 'And you must call Mr Phillimore "Sir".'
>
> I had forgotten all about Mr Belton's partner.
>
> 'But for Mr Phillimore you would not have had this chance,' Mr Belton said, detecting at once that I had forgotten. 'It's a very remarkable thing, it's really wonderful, some people would think more than wonderful, that Mr Phillimore agreed to it. He's a very busy man. A man with a great deal on his mind. There are people in the trade who would be glad to pay for the privilege of consulting Mr Phillimore. His word is law in the firm, and I want you to be most respectful to him. Don't forget to say "Good morning, sir" to him when you see him, and if he should offer

to shake hands you must, of course, shake hands with him. I think he may offer to shake hands, but he may not. If he rings his bell or asks you to do anything you must do it at once. Be quick and mind your manners. Open the door for him when he leaves the room. Mr Phillimore notices everything.'

> Naturally, Mr Belton had seemed all-powerful to me, and it awed me to hear that behind this god was yet another god to whom even he deferred. . . .
>
> 'I'll give you a little tip, boy,' he said, putting his hand on my knee, a touch that sent an uncomfortable thrill through my body and flushed me with all the shyness of my age. 'Do you mind if I give you a little piece of advice, something helpful?'
>
> 'No, uncle,' I murmured. 'Sir.'
>
> 'You needn't call me sir now,' he said, relaxing. 'If Mr Phillimore should ring for you,' he said, 'just remember the infant Samuel. You remember how when Our Lord called Samuel the boy said, "Speak Lord. Thy servant heareth." Well, just pause and say that, just quietly to yourself, before you go and see what Mr Phillimore wants. Don't hang around, of course. Sharp's the word. But say it.'
>
> My throat pinched, my mouth went dry. I should have said that Mr Belton was a religious man. His expression became dreamy.
>
> 'I think there'd be no harm in your saying it if I ring, too,' he said. Even he looked surprised after making this suggestion.

Mr Phillimore proves to be quite other than Vincent had expected. 'He was young, not more than thirty-five, and my first sight of Mr Phillimore suggested the frantic, yelping, disorganized expression of a copulating dog.' What we observe through Vincent's eyes is something very much like the break-up of a marriage between Belton and Phillimore, a break-up marked by jealousy, intrigue, flirtations and worse with business competitors, until the split is made final when Mr Phillimore actually joins one of the firm's rivals.

'It May Never Happen' is one of the most brilliant of Pritchett's early stories. In his stories of the Sixties and Seventies, behaviour that was once seen as special to puritanism is now presented as human nature *tout court*. Obsession, eccentricity, the passion to conform or dissent are now fundamental to all Pritchett's characters. And with this has gone a broadening of his canvas, so that now only part of his gallery of characters is recruited from the lower-middle class.

An excellent example of a late Pritchett story is **'The Camberwell Beauty'** which appeared in the collection of the same title published in 1974. It is a story about the antique trade as seen through the eyes of one who has been fascinated by it, dabbled in it, and failed in it. It is shown as a tight, self-contained world governed by fantasy:

> It is a trade that feeds illusions. If you go after

Georgian silver you catch the illusion, while you are bidding, that you are related to the rich families who owned it. You acquire imaginary ancestors. Or, like Pliny with a piece of Meissen he was said to keep hidden somewhere—you drift into German history and become a secret curator of the Victoria and Albert Museum—a place he often visited. August's lust for the 'ivories' gave to his horse-racing mind a private oriental side; he dreamed of rajahs, sultans, harems, and lavish gamblers which, in a man as vulgar as he was, came out, in sad reality, as a taste for country girls and the company of bookies. Illusions lead to furtiveness in everyday life and to sudden temptations; the trade is close to larceny, to situations where you don't ask where something has come from, especially for a man like August whose dreams had landed him in low company. He had started at the bottom and very early he 'received' and got twelve months for it.

The generalizations in that passage on the antique business and antique dealers are felt to be the fruits of fresh perception, shrewd and enlightening; we are presented with the psychology of a trade. And the character who makes the generalizations, the narrator, is noticeably quite different from the narrators of the stories of puritanism. There they are obviously personae for the young Pritchett himself, whereas in **'The Camberwell Beauty'** the narrator's analyses and descriptions of the trade are ways by which he is differentiated from his creator.

Pritchett has been publishing short stories for fifty years and during that time his art has continued to expand in scope and to deepen in penetration. One could instance **'Blind Love'** in the volume of that title published in 1969. It tells how a blind lawyer falls in love with his secretary-housekeeper, a woman whose emotional life has been ruined by a physical blemish. As a study of blindness and its effects on character one has to go back to Lawrence to find anything comparable. Witness this account of the secretary Mrs Johnson's first insights into her employer, Armitage:

> Mrs Johnson could not herself describe what keyed her up; perhaps, being on the watch? Her mind was stretched. She found herself translating the world to him and it took her time to realize that it did not matter that she was not 'educated up to it'. He obviously liked her version of the world, but it was a strain having versions. In the mornings she had to read his letters. This bothered her. She was very moral about privacy. She had to invent an impersonal, uninterested voice. His lack of privacy irked her; she liked gossip and news as much as any woman, but here it lacked the salt of the secret, the whispered, the found out. It was all information and statement. Armitage's life was an abstraction for him. He had to know what he could not see. What she liked best was reading legal documents to him. . . . When visitors came she noticed he stood in a fixed spot: he did not turn his head when people spoke to him and among all the head-turning and gesturing he was the still figure, the law-giver. But he was very cunning. If someone described a film they had seen, he was soon talking as if he had been there. Mrs John-

son, who had duties when he had visitors, would smile to herself at the surprise on the faces of people who had not noticed the quickness with which he collected every image or scene or character described.

'Blind Love' is a triumph of empathy and perception but as remarkable in an utterly different way is **'When My Girl Comes Home'**, which appeared in the collection of that name in 1961 and which I am tempted to think Pritchett's finest story. Certainly it is his finest and funniest evocation of working-class life. It is set in South London and describes, through the eyes of a young borough librarian, the dismay and bewilderment set up in her family when thirteen years after the war and imprisonment in a camp in Japan, Hilda, who had been married to an Indian named Singh, finally returns home.

It captures with great sympathy and without snobbishness English working-class manners, meaning by manners Lionel Trilling's 'a culture's hum and buzz of implication . . . the whole evanescent context in which its explicit statements are made . . . that part of a culture which is made up of half-uttered or unutterable expressions of value'. (pp. 268-75)

> *Walter Allen, "Chapter VI: Pritchett, Halward," in his* The Short Story in English, *Oxford at the Clarendon Press, 1981, pp. 268-80.*

Robert Kiely (essay date 1982)

[*In the following review of* Collected Stories, *Kiely characterizes Pritchett's short fiction as intellectually engaging.*]

In a long career filled with achievement, V. S. Pritchett, now in his ninth decade, has shown in his criticism, memoirs and short fiction the priceless virtue of not taking his readers by storm. Even as a young writer, he seemed to have the confidence not to strain for effect. He has always written with the assumption that intellectual concentration and emotional engagement are capable of being sustained, developed and deepened, that a writer need not always be feverishly "coming to the point." This attitude reflects something essential in his temperament, a narrative and expository talent, but also a patient respect for the reader's capacity for paying attention. He does not write as if he expects our minds to wander.

For a short-story writer, such a temperament and such talent might seem surprising. By definition, the form would appear to require something more abrupt, wit or irony in a phrase, a moment captured in a gesture or image. Two of the greatest and most influential short-story writers of the 20th century, James Joyce and Ernest Hemingway, demonstrated the extraordinary power of economy and radical condensation. In their stories, things typically come to a head in an instant of revelation.

But, like all inspired solutions to literary problems, the methods of these writers have been imitated to the point of rigor mortis. Who could wish to recount the tedious epiphanies, predictable disillusionments and vulgar catastrophes that have fallen like an avalanche of rubble on the innocent readers of the last four or five decades? It is hard to decide which is worse: the understated renditions of glimpsing the abyss or the more popular alternative of murder, suicide and rape galore. Either way, formula has too often been a substitute for imagination. And, even in the case of would-be stunners, when the writer nods, the reader yawns.

As an author of short stories, Pritchett has steadily pursued a course of quiet originality. He refuses to keep readers awake by trying to knock them dead. In his fiction, as in his other writing, we trust his art because we trust his judgment. And, in the long run, we find ourselves trusting both without having to sacrifice health and sanity. The selections in this new collection, which spans 50 years, have been chosen by the author from five volumes: *The Sailor, the Sense of Humor, and Other Stories, When My Girl Comes Home, Blind Love and Other Stories, The Camberwell Beauty and Other Stories,* and *On the Edge of the Cliff.*

Throughout his career, Pritchett has been a writer in the comic tradition who has taken life and his chosen genre very seriously. He is not a short-story writer who would have done better writing novels. Though his narratives are rich with detail and complex emotions, they are not overloaded with plots. They tend to focus on situations—a holiday, a visit, a meeting, a chore—with a unifying logic of their own. The situations, as he presents them, are neither isolated nor simple. They depend upon and imply events and often characters outside of the immediate frame of the story. Even lecture halls ("shabbied by hundreds, thousands, of meetings") and telephone booths ("unpleasantly warmed by the random emotions left behind in them") have their histories. Yet Pritchett's control is sufficiently strong to allow frequent intimations of "extrinsic" material without losing dramatic force.

Pritchett's opening lines are rarely arresting in the usual sense. He is capable of an eye-catching first sentence now and then. A story entitled **"The Saint"** begins: "When I was seventeen years old I lost my religious faith." But more typical are untidily long sentences with too many details and too many clauses: "She was kissing them all, hugging them, her arms bare in her summer dress, laughing and taking in a big draught of breath after every kiss, nearly knocking old Mrs. Draper off her feet, almost wrestling with Mrs. Fulmino, who was large and tall."

Or: " 'I'm beginning to be worried about Mr. "Wolverhampton" Smith,' said Mr. Armitage to Mrs. Johnson, who was sitting in his study with her notebook on her knee and glancing from time to time at the window."

To open a short story with such deliberately ungainly sentences is to take an interesting risk, but it is also to make a statement about the nature of the fiction to follow. The reader may be put off by too many names and seemingly unconnected parts, but he is also alerted to the idea that the world to which he is being introduced stretches beyond fastidious syntax. The beginning is not the Beginning. Whoever these characters are and whatever it is they are doing, we are forced to imagine an existence for them

that the narration casually, almost as if by accident, has tuned into in the midst of things.

One of the many English qualities of these very English stories is their way of making so little fuss over introductions. One listens in, as if to exchanges that seem to have been carried on, left off, and picked up again for years. How did it all begin? Well, never mind that. Who remembers, anyway? After a while you begin to get interested, and before you know it you are part of the dialogue. Like the best of English nonchalance, there is an art to it, and a gentle moral as well.

The human follies the stories expose are universal in their underlying causes, but they are all displayed in unmistakably British form. The lower-middle-class characters, seedy and slovenly among themselves, suddenly perk up when they think they are being judged. When a dowdy mum takes her little boy to the posh flat of her rich but disreputable sister, they are followed by the porter: " 'Take your cap off in the lift when you're with a lady,' she said to the boy, asserting to the porter that she was respectable."

How pathetic, how comical the type is! And how persistent! Thackeray would recognize it; so would Fielding; so, for that matter, would Chaucer. Perhaps it is the dogged durability and the fine patina of time-tested weaknesses that makes Pritchett so patient with them. He mimics and satirizes, but the sting is rarely sharp. He seems to forgive almost everything. His characters suffer enough from their imperfections without his having to take advantage of the privilege of authorial vengeance. Unlike some writers, he does not invent characters in order to punish them.

Even upper-class snobbery, as persistent a theme in British literature as respectability, is treated with relatively mild ridicule. When an aged bachelor named George goes to his club, he encounters "the Great Awful Thing," a new member of whom he disapproves:

> "Just the man I want to speak to," said Gaiterswell, picking up the menu in hands that George could only think of as thieving.
>
> "I didn't know you were a member," George choked out in words like lead shot.
>
> "Just elected."
>
> George gave a loud sniff.
>
> "Monstrous," said George, but holding on to manners said it under his breath.

Pritchett's most pervasive moral preoccupation—one that touches on and often embraces the others—is prejudice: the human tendency to protect the self through the belittlement of others, which, in its most general form, is a closing of the mind and heart to new information and experience. Pritchett's stories are filled with examples, large and small, of people making up their minds and then shutting them down: the old about the young; the young about the old; males and females; wives and husbands; parents and children; the beautiful and ugly; smart and stupid; rich and poor; respectable and disreputable.

The standard English disposition toward foreigners is on

display in a fine story, **"Handsome Is as Handsome Does,"** in which a middle-class couple spend a holiday in the south of France. Pierre, the proprietor of the pension where they stay, disturbs the husband because of his un-British mannerisms and courtliness.

> "He's a mean squirt," Coram said.
>
> "He's a liar," he said.
>
> "Look at him making those cigarettes."
>
> "We've known him a week and what's he do but cadge drinks and rides in the car. He's a fraud."

Pritchett allows this kind of talk to roll on until the reader feels the almost intolerable exasperation and frustration of Coram's wife. When it turns out that the old Frenchman is a better swimmer than his British detractor, Coram repudiates the sea along with the foreigners who bathe in it: " 'That water's dirty,' he said when he got back. The Mediterranean was a fraud: it was too warm, thick as syrup. He sat dripping on his wife's books."

Obviously, Pritchett has the satirist's gift, but he rarely stops there. It is as with catchy first lines and programmatic climaxes: He wishes to avoid what is too easy, both for the writer and the reader. It certainly is easy and fun to despise Coram and the dowdy mum and the snobbish octogenarian in his club. But it is Pritchett's way to unsettle the reader's own prejudices, to revive in us a lost hope for even his most "hopeless" cases. His stories are anything but sentimental. His characters are often middle-aged or old and living in moderate-to-desperate circumstances. He resists the temptation (possibly is not even tempted) to blast them off the face of the earth or transform them into heroes. But he shows us, and, furthermore, delights us by making us believe in, the human capacity to change and, particularly, to love.

Though few of his stories seem at first to be about love, many of the best—**"The Wheelbarrow," "The Key to My Heart," "Blind Love," "The Skeleton"** and **"The Lady from Guatemala,"** and even **"Handsome Is as Handsome Does"**—*become* love stories. Pritchett's material, like his openings, is unpromising. His characters often seem beyond caring, especially about themselves. A fastidious editor is pursued by an obsessive admirer; a scarred divorcée takes refuge with a blind man; an ancient celibate has his routine broken by a woman; a plain housewife hates her marriage. All are frozen into a life and an image of themselves; all are touched magically by thaw. The healing hand is deft and gentle. It does not leave us reeling but reflective. Pritchett's stories invite and merit rereading, and, what is more important, they encourage us to look again at those parts of life we like to think are settled. The most pernicious prejudices, his fiction shows, are the ones people have about themselves. He's a crafty one, as Coram would say, but there is wisdom and good humor in his craft. (pp. 5, 16)

> *Robert Kiely, "A Writer Who Trusts His Readers," in* The New York Times Book Review, *May 30, 1982, pp. 5, 16.*

> To put together a substantial if not complete collection of the stories from the seven volumes I have written in the last fifty years is a startling experience in old age. One comes across a procession of vanished selves. I see a crowd of old friends, too.
>
> **—V. S. Pritchett in the preface to his Collected Stories, *1982.***

William Peden   (essay date 1985)

[*In the following excerpt, Peden surveys Pritchett's stories published prior to 1960.*]

Pritchett's "literary" career began modestly enough, with a joke published in the *Paris Tribune.* It was followed by three essays in the *Christian Science Monitor,* and by extensive travel in Spain, in the United States, in Ireland (where he met William Butler Yeats, married, and began writing his first stories), back to Paris, and, eventually, England, where he dedicated himself to writing. I was "fanatical about writing," he stated; "the word and the sentence were my religion."

"Rain in the Sierra," Pritchett's first published story, came out in the *New Statesman.* **"Tragedy in a Greek Theatre,"** his second, had been immediately accepted by the *Cornhill.* He was paid well for the story; more important, it was anthologized in Edward J. O'Brien's prestigious annual collection, *Best British Short Stories* (1927), and in 1930 his first collection of short fiction, ***The Spanish Virgin and Other Stories,*** was in print.

Few of these early stories bear favorable comparison with the best of Pritchett's later work. The collection is interesting primarily for its range and variety, though it hardly suggests the directions his talent and dedication would take him and where they would continue to lead him until he had earned the reputation of being the "greatest living English short story writer."

"The Corsican Inn" is early Pritchett at his best. The story opens conventionally: "I had walked . . . twenty miles out of Ajaccio and climbed into the ranges of the interior." The narrator, with his guide, stops at an inn; on the wall is a portrait of a "glum young soldier with frightened sheepish eyes," signed by the president of the republic and inscribed "Mort pour la France." A loud-mouthed drunken youth staggers into the inn, knocks over a bottle of wine, and finally "with a snigger, and a gesture indicating . . . the photograph . . . and the pool of red wine . . . shouted in mock heroic tones: 'Mort pour la France!' and spat." The owner of the inn, the mother of the dead soldier, turns upon the blasphemer; her eyes, "like knives, cut through the awful silence, to the . . . bone."

And here the story ends, but the reader, like the narrator,

knows that all will be changed by the incident, and we share with him the truth of his final words concerning the blaspheming intruder: "There was no safe place for his gaze to hide in."

"Tragedy in a Greek Theatre" begins equally conventionally, almost a parody of the traditional story-within-a-story: "Those who used to go to Sicily for the winter will remember old William Bantock, the artist, who had such a delightful studio on the cliff at A—." Following the painter's death, the first-person narrator and the proprietor of the hotel who had been old Bantock's landlord open the "mystery room" that had been the artist's studio; the disclosure is predictable and less important than the characterization of Bantock, overwhelmed by his first experience in Etna and the grandeur of the Greeks. As was to be the case throughout his career, Pritchett's major preoccupation is with the revelation of character.

In marked contrast, **"The White Rabbit"** and **"The Cuckoo Clock"** are bizarre tours de force, the first centering upon an apparently "normal" and successful young executive, his two young children, a malignant governess, a pet rabbit and a "devilish" cat—a story with a chilling open-ended climax with reverberations as disturbing as those in James's *The Turn of the Screw;* the second, similarly impressive, is a mélange of fantasy, melodrama, illusion-versus-reality about a young boy who goes "alone . . . to spend the holidays" with aged relatives, a visit that glides brilliantly from realism to the macabre, a domain that Pritchett would seldom explore in his later stories.

"Fishy" and **"The Sack of Lights,"** on the other hand, are effective single-episode stories, a form in which Pritchett was to write with great effectiveness throughout his long career. The first concerns the return to Ireland of a man, penniless, after an absence of many years, and his reception in a local "fish dive"; the second, slight but equally memorable, is an expert characterization, completely devoid of plot per se, of an insane London charwoman.

Almost a decade was to elapse between *The Spanish Virgin* and *You Make Your Own Life* (1938; as had been the case with its predecessor, there was no United States edition). Pritchett's disastrous early marriage was behind him; he had recovered from "one nervous illness after another"; his family had "gone up in the world"; and most important of all he had remarried, a marriage that was to be as complete and meaningful as its predecessor had been a failure. He became, for the first time, whole, complete, assured, both as a man and a writer: "What cured me," he would write years later in the first volume of his autobiography, *Midnight Oil,* "was success in love, and in my work . . . . There is, I am sure, a direct connection between passionate love and the firing of the creative power. . . ."

The fourteen stories of *You Make Your Own Life* are highlighted by what was to become one of Pritchett's best-known and most frequently anthologized pieces, **"Sense of Humour."** The story had had its origins years before, in Ireland, its central character a lower-middle-class commercial traveler Pritchett had met when he was a reporter for the *Christian Science Monitor.* Characteristically, Prit-

chett worked and reworked the story before finally being satisfied with it: "that particular story presented many problems. . . . I had it on my hands for many years." Eventually revised and narrated in the first person largely through dialogue, it was rejected by many editors in England and the United States until, in 1937, John Lehmann accepted it for *New Writing.* It was a turning point in Pritchett's career, the first of his stories to "make a stir and give me what reputation I have as a writer of short stories. . . . [It] woke me up . . . and led me on to **'The Sailor,' 'The Saint,'** and **'Many Are Disappointed'** "; with it "I had become real at last."

Like most of Pritchett's best stories, **"Sense of Humour"** is a series of character revelations, relatively simple in narrative, decidedly complex in its implications. The real drama lies in the revelation of the reality beneath the exterior of three main characters, a lower-middle-class English commercial traveler, an attractive Irish girl with a "sense of humour" who clerks in the hotel where the salesman takes lodgings, and her "boy friend," a garage mechanic ("that half-wit at the garage," the traveler dubs him). Around this trio, one of whom dies a violent death, the author creates a mixture of revelations of sex-death-love-banality that leaves a stir of echoes likely to reverberate long in the reader's mind.

"Handsome Is As Handsome Does," the longest and perhaps the most ambitious story in the collection, presents an equally complex series of character revelations and reversals. Set in a French coastal pension, and built around an unattractive English couple in their forties, the story presents a tangled skein of human relations, climaxed by a near-drowning and a complicated love-revulsion relationship that ends with "two ugly people cut off from all others . . . helpless, halted, tangled people, outcasts in everything they did." Like so many of Pritchett's characters, the Corams are what the psychiatrist Edmund Bergler has termed "injustice collectors," neurotics who "suffer from a hidden need to feel that the world has wronged them."

Other notable stories range from the serious to the comic. Perhaps the most powerful—and certainly the most melodramatic—work in the entire collection is **"Miss Baker,"** somewhat heavy-handed, perhaps but unforgettable in its depiction of a young woman gone berserk in her search for the Lord. From its opening sentence—"When Easter came she knew that her time of fasting was drawing to a close"—to the acrid climax when she mistakes a drunken derelict for the Savior, Miss Baker is a grotesque in Sherwood Anderson's definition of the term, and her story is perhaps the angriest and harshest of Pritchett's satires against fundamentalist Christianity.

"Main Road," on the other hand, is a naturalistic study of the effect of poverty on the human spirit. As much sociological tract as conventional fiction, it presents a situation that would be quite at home in *The Grapes of Wrath* or any of the militantly Marxist stories of the American depression.

Pritchett is equally effective in some of his briefer pieces. **"You Make Your Own Life,"** for example, illustrates what he must have had in mind when he referred to the short story as a "flash that suddenly illumines, then passes." This account of a small-town barber, his wife, and a homicidal customer who seeks a most bizarre revenge is reminiscent of Hemingway in its economy and dialogue, together with an ending not unreminiscent of O. Henry—without in any way being derivative of either.

In marked contrast are pieces like **"The Aristocrat"** and **"Eleven O'Clock,"** the first an amusing characterization of an old man who enters a pub, does a conjuring trick or two, and trudges back into the snow—but only after having filched the watch of one of the spectators. **"Eleven O'Clock"** is a pure delight, about a milkman and a very good-natured—and concupiscent—Yorkshire-woman (a contemporary Wife of Bath whose "body seemed to be laughing at her fatness") who have their sport indoors while outside the milkman's mare is indulging *her* desires by nibbling almost to extinction the hedge coming into leaf outside the fat woman's house: " 'Been getting your greens, haven't you?' the milkman asks as he leaves the house. He stared at the mare and, bright under their blinkers, he saw the eyes of that cynical animal, secretive and glistening, gazing back at him."

"The Evils of Spain" is similarly unplotted, a series of conversations in a Madrid tavern, based on Pritchett's experience with the famous bullfighter Belmonte (whom he had met on a train to Spain, along with Arnold Bennett, Lord Beaverbrook, and Healy, the destroyer of Parnell and "the wickedest tongue in Ireland"). The now-familiar "Hemingway sound" permeates the story, and is particularly evident in the final paragraph: " 'No,' we said, 'Leave it [the soup]. We want it.' And then we said the soup was bad, and the wine was bad and everything he [the waiter] brought was bad, but the proprietor said the soup was good and the wine was good and we said in the end it was good. We told the proprietor the restaurant was good, but he said not very good, indeed bad."

"A Spring Morning" is a delight, a briskly narrated, warmhearted tale of a brief encounter between a working-class youth and two lively young shopgirls, a thoroughly pleasant single-episode piece that might very well have been written by H. E. Bates—and it is not presumptuous to assume that Bates would have liked it immensely.

It May Never Happen, Pritchett's third collection, was published in 1945; the American edition, the first volume of his short stories to be published in the United States, came out two years later. It is highlighted, perhaps, by **"The Sailor,"** which, like many of his stories, is based on fact or, more accurately, can be said *to grow out* of actual people and incidents, and had been conceived years before it was completed, when Pritchett, living alone in a cottage near Marlow, was aided by a "down and out sailor . . . who came down to look" after him. Like many of his stories, **"The Sailor"** was frequently revised before it was completed; it was to become his most-often anthologized story, though personally Pritchett "was not too keen on it."

The story begins simply enough: the narrator, in London for the day, meets a sailor with a penchant for getting lost, "hopelessly, blindly lost." Living alone in the country, the narrator takes the sailor home to be his manservant. "He lives in two worlds at once," the narrator tells the third major character, an alcoholic youngish woman known locally only as the "Colonel's daughter" who, like the sailor, lives a double life. To the world of the local inhabitants, she is loud-mouthed, coarse, obscene; in reality she is sensitive, not unintelligent, honest in her own way, and more than willing to have an affair with the narrator. He too is a split personality, living in two worlds, in one of which he is self-assured and slightly contemptuous; in the other withdrawn, uncertain, and unable to give or share sexually, emotionally, intellectually. In these terms, the drama is played out, partly comic, partly sick, a curious kind of life-death, attraction-repulsion drama not infrequent in Pritchett's works, and permeated with an odor of decay as palpable as the "sour smell at the edge of the wood, where, no doubt, a dead rabbit or pigeon was rotting."

"When I was seventeen years old I lost my religious faith. It had been unsteady for some time and then, very suddenly, it went as the result of an incident in a punt on the river outside the town where we lived." So begins **"The Saint,"** one of Pritchett's best and best-known stories—"a little masterpiece," H. E. Bates called it—at once serious and comic and without the sickly odor of decay that hovers over **"The Sailor."** The seventeen-year-old's uncle and aunt, not unlike Pritchett's unyielding Christian Science father, are members of a religious sect, the Purifiers; the narrative begins when the family is visited by a leader of the sect, Mr. Timberlake, "a man who had . . . performed many miracles—even, it was said . . . having twice raised the dead." The boy is taunted by his classmates and their Irish schoolmaster, and questions the validity of the Purifiers' belief that Error and Evil are illusory ("since God could not have made them," the Believers insist, "they therefore did not exist").

The boy's uncle talks to Mr. Timberlake about his nephew's doubts, and leader and boy go to the river to have a good talk while punting. In a scene at once hilarious and serious, the leader turns out to be inadequate both as punter and converter; almost decapitated by the overhanging branch of a willow tree, he desperately reaches for a stronger and higher branch. The result is disaster: "there he hung . . . above the water. . . . Too late with the paddle, ... I could not save him, . . . I did not believe what I saw; indeed, our religion taught us never to believe what we saw . . . only a miracle, I found myself saying, could save him."

Silently, Mr. Timberlake is suspended between tree and water. Was he, the boy thinks, "about to re-enact a well-known miracle? I hoped with all my will Mr. Timberlake would not walk upon the water. It was my prayer and not his that was answered."

Sixteen years pass. The narrator hears of Mr. Timberlake's death: he recalls that long-ago afternoon on the river, and "I understood why," he reflects, "though I had feared it all the time we were on the river—I understood why he did not talk to me about the origin of evil. He was honest. The ape was with us. The ape that merely followed me was already inside Mr. Timberlake eating out his heart."

"You Make Your Own Life," like **"The Saint,"** is apparently based on Pritchett's recollections of past experiences, in this case those of a youth working in the small-time upholstery business owned by his uncle and a Mr. Phillimore. Each partner is out to swindle the other, and the somewhat tedious story ends after the breakup of the firm and the narrator's last, and genuinely moving, sight of Mr. Phillimore:

> He was standing on London Bridge looking up at a high building where a man was cleaning windows.
>
> "I should die," I heard him say to someone in the crowd. Then he saw me. He bared his teeth as if he were going to spit, but changed his mind. His look suggested that I was the most ridiculous thing on earth. . . .

Much more amusing and lighthearted, **"The Chestnut Tree,"** is Pritchett's account of an apprentice of a London leather merchants' firm who is soon demoralized by a voluptuous but heavy-footed bookkeeper ("She was curving . . . with the swell of long breasts [and] . . . moved swan-like to her desk. But not like a swan in the water; like a swan on land. She waddled").

Then there is **"Pocock Passes,"** the remarkable story of a relationship between two very different kinds of men drawn together by fate and the fact that each is in his fifties, enormously fat, and a dedicated drinker. Utterly different, and one of Pritchett's favorites, **"Many Are Disappointed"** is a small gem, overwhelming in its simplicity, unerring in its selectivity: a story of isolation and simple goodness narrated in terms of the contrast between four young cyclists and the lonely owner of a rundown public house and her young daughter. Equally effective is a very good story of wartime England, **"The Voice,"** centering upon a Welsh clergyman buried beneath the debris of a bombed church. He is heard singing, and a member of the rescue party, a priest who regards the buried man as the "nearest thing to the devil himself," tumbles into the wreckage. "You were a fool to come down here after me. I wouldn't have done the same for you [the old man tells him]. . . . When you start feeling shaky . . . you'd better sing . . . the whiskey's gone. Sing, Lewis. Even if they don't hear, it does you good. Take the tenor, Lewis."

"The Ape" is atypical Pritchett, a blend of allegory and fantasy, with a cast including a talking pterodactyl and bands of apes interested in metaphysics, philosophy, and evolution. The fable ends with a revelation: one of the apes, who fought "like a god . . . with a science and ferocity such as we had never seen before," is finally subdued. The oldest ape examines the "panting creature" and finds the sight overwhelming: his backside is "bare and hairless—he had no tail. . . . 'It is man!' we cried. And our stomachs turned."

The remaining stories include **"The Lion's Den,"** another story of wartime England, centering upon a middle-aged father unworried by air raids. " 'He has faith,' his wife tells their son. 'He trusts in God. . . . he always did things in a big way' "; **"The Oedipus Complex,"** a good-natured burlesque of a most-amusing dentist; and several brief pieces of childhood, youth, and family relations (**"The Clerk's Tale," "Aunt Gertrude,"** and **"The Fly and the Ointment"**)—slight, perhaps, in comparison with stories like **"The Saint," "The Sailor,"** and **"Pocock Passes,"** but all characterized by admirable economy and balance, and Pritchett's quiet mastery of technique.

Pritchett's continuing preoccupation, from *The Spanish Virgin* through his most recent collection of short fiction, has been the revelation of character: individual human beings reacting with or against other individuals; with their own personal problems, dilemmas, and egos; with their environment; with things as they are. He has put the matter simply, succinctly, and effectively in his preface to *The Sailor, Sense of Humour, and Other Stories:* "It is difficult for a writer to define his own interest, but I think that I find the drama in human personality, in character rather than in events. . . . The drama has lain in the portrait, in the unconscious self-revelation of people. . . . It strikes me that the story lies in their double lives. . . . They dwell . . . in a solitude which they alone can populate. . . . for me the drama, the event, the plot, is the person; and the more fantastic, the more certain to be true."

Regardless of subject or setting, character or idea, Pritchett's best stories are *happenings:* they are trips, in a sense comparable to hallucinagenic trips. Something *happens,* revelations realized or unrealized, trivial or of vital importance to the individual even if, like the commercial traveler of **"Sense of Humour,"** he himself is unaware of their significance. Something happens, and having happened, the character has been changed, if ever so slightly. His process of moral vision, his essential identity, have been temporarily or permanently altered. This lifelong concern with individual human beings—occasionally unusual or odd or even at times bizarre although Pritchett emphatically denied that he was interested in eccentrics as such—is Pritchett's hallmark.

Equally important, perhaps, is that from his beginnings, despite his early acknowledged indebtedness to Hemingway and others, Pritchett was his own man, finding his own way, his own material, his own forms, and could say quite simply and honestly: "I do not write for the reader, for people, for society. I write for myself, for my own self-regarding pleasure, trying to excel and always failing on the excellence I desire." In these terms he has created a world authentically and convincingly his own, that of the English lower-middle to middle class, a world he knew "like the palm of [his] hand," a world of individuals whose small defeats, stalemates, or victories he depicts with calm but not disinterested detachment, a world viewed for the most part with a tempered skepticism and enlivened by his presentation of the strange, the bizarre, or the grotesque that exists in the ordinary, and the ordinary that is usually inherent in the unusual. It is not, for the most part, a happy world, though at times it is alive with gaiety and humor that can range from the very funny to the macabre. It is a world that has frequently been likened to that of Dickens—a concept Pritchett vigorously rejects—but which is more Thackerayan than Dickensian; Pritchett's Vanity Fair, like Thackeray's, is "not a moral place, certainly; nor a merry one, though very noisy" and one usually "more melancholy than mirthful."

Pritchett's people, like their counterparts in real life, are troubled by the awareness of their own failures and short-comings or elated at their small victories. They are disturbed by the recognition of their inadequacy or foolishness; more often than not they are lonely, sad, or disappointed. But they not only *endure,* as Faulkner's Negroes endured; they can be victors rather than victims, and their victories—small though they may be—are a tribute, perhaps, as a recent English critic has commented, to something inherent in the English character: "resilience, jauntiness, verve, inventiveness, courage, or downright cheek and the refusal to recognize or admit defeat." (pp. 143-51)

> William Peden, "V. S. Pritchett," in The English Short Story 1880-1945: A Critical History, *edited by Joseph M. Flora, Twayne Publishers, 1985, pp. 143-51.*

One carries around with one a huge collection of unoccupied characters who beg to become stories and to be justified. The sight of a woman catching a flea in a pub was the beginning of "Things as They Are."

—V. S. Pritchett in his "The Writer's Tale," Vogue, March 1981.

Walter Evans   (essay date 1985)

[*In the following excerpt, Evans considers two volumes of short stories published in the 1970s, highlighting Pritchett's ability to create believable characters.*]

Of all the writers actively engaged in the short story during the [1970s], V. S. Pritchett most truly deserves the title of old master. Of course, one expects wisdom, breadth of vision, and irony in stories brought down from a septuagenarian height, but that a man born in 1900 should produce such vigorous, witty, humor-tinged stories is a minor miracle. Of Pritchett's three volumes of short fiction published during the decade, the preferred one might well be his *Selected Stories,* which contains work from 1959 to 1978 from four different volumes; it seems appropriate, however, to concentrate on his two other collections, *The Camberwell Beauty* (1974) and *On the Edge of the Cliff* (1979). On the whole the earlier of the two seems slightly better, though most writers would be pleased to consider either the capstone of a career.

One feels uncomfortable labeling as formulaic some of Pritchett's favorite habits, but the stories of this decade often resolve themselves into love stories of a particular sort. The protagonist is usually a man, rather often a widower and sometimes distinctly old, a man at any rate of a certain degree of dignity, his self-conceit usually van-

quishing his irony in a close match (in **"The Rescue"** the role is played by a sixteen-year-old girl who "likes to see what a young man will do"—there are other variations), but that egotism loses in the final round to the special kind of madness represented by an eccentric female.

A more than minor miracle is the fact that the standard of his stories is so uniformly high, though individual stories do not often strain above that level into true greatness. The title story of *The Camberwell Beauty* does rise to such a level. It beautifully creates for us the tawdry, claustrophobic, insanely competitive, and jealous world of small-time antique dealers, managing a bare living largely through selling old furniture but each devoting his soul to a specialty: Georgian silver, Caughley ware, ivory. "At the heart of the trade is lust, but a lust that is a dream paralyzed by itself." Only well into the story does one learn that the "beauty" in question is not an antique but in fact a young woman who in adolescence was pirated from one dealer, August, by another, the ridiculous and ugly old Pliny; she is religiously coveted by a third, the narrator who has already failed in the trade. Apparently the first tried and failed to debauch Isabelle when she was his pubescent ward; the intentions of the last are unclear, though he seems to have a goal in the direction of physical consummation; but the second has lived with her for years as husband without being "horrible," as she puts it. Pliny never tries to get her in bed, though, she says, he "takes my clothes off before I go to bed. He likes to look at me. I am the most precious thing he has." The girl has already revealed an unsound mind (when alone she dresses in a cavalry helmet, bangs a drum, and occasionally blares on a horn to keep away potential kidnappers), but she remains, nevertheless, a "beauty." And the object of the desperate attentions of three different men.

The story works beautifully as an ironic peephole into the mentality of the collector but becomes a candidate for greatness when a reader notices the mirror in the peephole and realizes the extent to which the collector's insane lust for possession of a special example of Meissen or Dresden reflects a man's love for a particular woman. In what way, to what extent, does he desire to possess the object of his dreams? To what purpose? To what extent does lust of possession distort any "love"? The question rises from and transcends the story in a way characteristic of only the very finest fiction.

Throughout the two volumes Pritchett manages to compel our belief in a bewildering variety of individual characters: his protagonists range from young to very old men—all seemingly exactly right, whether a retired geologist, an active liberal journalist, a professional nurseryman, a small-time cloth merchant; Pritchett has a genius for creating lives into which a reader can enter. Especially surprising is his ability to create credible women who tend to exist outside the stereotypes normally assigned them by masculine writers. At one extreme would be the seventy-year-old protagonist and title character of **"Tea with Mrs. Bittell,"** but Pritchett manages to make bewitchingly appealing a gallery of women most male writers would automatically reject—women of a certain age, women given to anger and nagging, short stubby women who won't take no for an answer, women who are all bones and given to distraction, in **"Our Wife"** a woman who is truly "a noise and a nuisance." And though his stories tend to run to triangles involving two men and a woman, his characters seem virtually never to repeat themselves.

Technically Pritchett is fond of the throwaway ending, which tends to define the story as something like a slice of life (**"The Vice-Consul," "The Accompanist"**), albeit sometimes of extremely eccentric life (**"The Last Throw"**). His style is an unpretentious joy. At the shore "little families of whitecaps would appear" which "were like faces popping up or perhaps white hands shooting out and disappearing pointlessly. Yes, they were the pointless dead" (**"On the Edge of the Cliff"**). One character looks "around with that dishonest look a dog has when it is pretending not to hear its master's whistle" (**"The Spree"**). Another is a poet: "every so often he would go up to his room to sit on the sea wall, and as if he were some industrious hen, he would (as I once said) lay a poem" (**"Our Wife"**).

But Pritchett's final charm lies not in style or in character or in form or even in vision; his final charm comes from our sense that we are reading a genuinely classic writer in our own time. He is the real thing. (pp. 130-32)

> *Walter Evans, "The English Short Story in the Seventies," in* The English Short Story 1945-1980: A Critical History, *edited by Dennis Vannatta, Twayne Publishers, 1985, pp. 120-72.*

V. S. Pritchett with Ben Forkner and Philippe Séjourné (interview date 1986)

[*In the interview excerpted below, Pritchett discusses early influences on his work and describes what he believes are the characteristics of good short fiction.*]

A conversation with V. S. Pritchett:

One afternoon we chatted in the study of his Regents Park Terrace home. It is a pleasant room fronting a tree-shaded mews, comfortable and in its own way somewhat Dickensian, with plum-colored draperies, lime-green rug, books and pictures and a great glass case filled with brilliantly plumaged birds. Sitting on a lime-green sofa, Mr. Pritchett, a pipe-smoking, pink-and-white man wearing old-fashioned lime-green suspenders, was relaxing with a gin and water after an appearance on the BBC. We had been talking about the state of the short story in England and about his own stories in particular.

He disclaims any direct influence of Dickens, who in so many ways he seems to me to resemble. Nor did he think "there was anything Dickensian" about his characters.

"There are a lot of odd people in England," he said from the shadows of the lime-green sofa.

William Peden in the Saturday Review, *March 14, 1970.*

[Forkner]: *My first question is about your early life and the way it stimulated your interest in the short story. I know that you first began reading and writing short stories when you were in Ireland.*

[Pritchett]: That's true, yes. My beginning life was quite outside writing. I was a journalist and I was sent to Ireland during the Irish Civil War in the 20's after the Treaty when the two sides in the Rebellion fought each other, and I read a great deal of the Irish writers then such as Yeats, George Russell (A.E.), Liam O'Flaherty, Frank O'Connor, Sean O'Faolain, in fact all those remarkable writers. They had all read the Russians, and there was a tremendous interest in literature in Ireland. Dublin has got splendid bookshops . . .

You met Liam O'Flaherty?

I met him, I knew him fairly well. I admired his stories and from that it seemed to me that this is the form of writing I should try and do myself, because up till then I had written nothing else but sketches, descriptions of places, that kind of thing, but not a complete story. He was of course very interested in Chekhov and D. H. Lawrence, so there was a double entry into the short story via Ireland. In England, I don't think I had even read any Kipling in my twenties, though all my elders knew him by heart. In fact it was much later that I read English short stories. But Hemingway's dialogue attracted me.

And you've said it was a good period to begin writing short stories. There was an active interest, not only in Ireland, but . . .

Well, everywhere. There was in England—D. H. Lawrence, for example and Katherine Mansfield—and of course in France. In Ireland, there was a link with the Abbey Theatre where they produced a large number of one-act plays, and the one-act play was the thing which was becoming extremely popular in Europe outside Ireland. Really the idea had come to Ireland from Europe. Such plays are of course a step to the writing of short stories: it's adjacent to it. That was my beginning. However what I wrote then was very short, not much more than anecdotes, with a slight poetic tendency to them, but still anecdotes. Even the plainest short story is a poem.

Did you write them for publication?

Yes, I tried to get them published. Indeed I wrote one **"Rain in the Sierra"**, which was accepted in the paper called the *Irish Statesman* but never published. The paper went bust (laughter). Actually, I had travelled a good deal, you know, I had worked and lived in France, I then went to Dublin and to Spain. My first real published story of any scale: **"Tragedy in a Greek Theatre"** was published in the *Cornhill* and it was thought well of. I thought, well, I must be getting better because I can get a long story published. This story was set in Taormina.

One thing I noticed in going through your autobiographies is the importance of travelling and going across borders. You end A Cab at the Door *with these words: "I am pretty sure that although I am often described as a traditional English writer any originality in my writing is due to my having a foreign mind". You started writing when you started crossing frontiers? And looking back on your life in England?*

Yes, I think this is true. I left school when I was sixteen and I had a very modest education, but the one thing I was rather good at was languages and I was longing to get abroad and to see other countries. And especially the notion of crossing from one frontier to the other, as I felt that I had crossed frontiers in English life too. I had crossed the frontier out of rather modest lower middle class circumstances into the company of rather intellectual people. This transition from class to class and from country to country was very liberating to me.

And this is what you meant by being on the borderline when you write?

Yes, I do feel that. I feel it's a break with absolute realism; you're crossing from one portion of the mind to another portion, from reality to the imagination. It's the stimulus of doing that, I think, which has been important to me. It still is.

And at the same time you began talking about national character. You talk about the American South, somewhat, but mainly about the French character, the Spanish character, and the Irish character. In your stories too, people are often identified by their national character.

Yes, I think that is so, though theories of national character are very shaky. When I was young I was enormously opposed to the notion that other nations were alien, therefore they were "wrong", or that is to say, they had mistaken ideas and habits which, as a matter of fact, quite a large number of my very young contemporaries—especially schoolboys—firmly believed. The kind of Englishman I didn't much care for in those days was the kind who automatically went out to Europe, to India, to places abroad. They had such conventional and distorted views of the people they were living among. And I thought that the only thing that would interest me if I went to these places were the people themselves, and not the English colony. I tend to think all foreigners are right. Ireland was a great test because after all the Ireland of that period had been fighting the British up to then. Like many English people I loved being in Ireland, and the British and the Irish privately got on enormously well together, and that was quite a revelation to me.

Were they welcoming?

Oh, enormously, enormously.

You didn't know Yeats beforehand?

No I didn't know Yeats beforehand, I'd read him of course. I didn't know any Irish people.

James Stephens?

Yes and Frank O'Connor later on. I didn't know any of these people before. But Dublin is a small city, it had an intellectual society; if you were a journalist, as I was then, it was very easy to know them, and I was passionately interested in them, and I found even the most anti-British Irish (nominally anti-British Irish) in Ireland, just after the war, were far from hostile; we were on the friendliest

terms at once. I am capable of a little blarney myself—the Cockney kind!

And this was during a war.

It was actually during the Civil War, after the Treaty when Sinn Fein split.

[Séjourné]: *And in what year was that?*

That was in early 1922. The Rebellion was in 1916 and I had got to know some of the people in the Rebellion who were the most congenial company, especially the father of the present Prime Minister.

[Forkner]: *I can't remember exactly where in your autobiography you say that the Irish are especially gifted in the short story, and in that way they're similar to American Southerners.*

The two societies had certain resemblances.

Why do you think that's so?

That's a very hard question to answer. I think there's a similarity between a certain kind of person in the American South who is very much like the Anglo-Irish gentry, and in fact there was something like an Anglo-Irish situation in the South really. It is another version of a similar situation, of people who had large houses and estates, who ruled, or have been dominant, being suddenly dislodged, or gradually dislodged from their position. And especially Ireland and the South seem to me, from my reading too, as it were, colonies. They had known defeat. There had been large estates or plantations and their capital disappeared year after year. They say if you leave your capital still, it dies away in three to nine years.

Having no capital . . .

Nor I! (laughter), but I am fascinated by the theory. One of the best Anglo-Irish writers, Elizabeth Bowen, was herself the daughter of a colonial Irish family who became extremely poor in the south of Ireland, not so far from Limerick. It was a time when one met plenty of these people and their manners were delightful, they were very amusing, they were intelligent, but they were quite clearly crumbling as a social element.

How would that lend itself to the short story form?

Well, I would have thought that it lent itself because the novel depends enormously upon its sense of a stable social structure and the short story does not really depend on there being a social structure at all. Perhaps there is one of some sort, but it can direct itself to life outside the theoretical, or practical interest of the country. One of the problems I think that Chekhov had when he wanted to write a novel was that he did not quite have the breath for it: the society he lived in was despotic and anarchic. He had his opinions about it but that is another matter. He was detached from ideological politics.

I think you quoted Frank O'Connor somewhere about saying that some of the Irish, perhaps not so much the Anglo-Irish, but the Catholic Irish, are in a similar situation— though looking from down up, rather than from up down—, but they live in a rather anarchic society.

It is rather an anarchic society, yes. Or it was. I would have thought anyhow, there is a basic oral gift of story-telling in Ireland; in fact one might even go as far as to say it's their substitute for a morality, that's to say moral and ethical arguments soon turn into anecdotal and narrative ones. Telling a story as it were is partly a form of evasion, or it's a form of getting around serious difficulties by not propounding.

Yes.

I think the Irish particularly like their situations enlivened, whatever they are. In Britain there is on the whole, the general tendency to play down situations as much as possible. All countries have their hypocrisies.

That's a good distinction.

The thing we hate is situation. The Irish love situation (laughter).

Some of the American Southerners I know do much the same thing. They like to sort of over-emphasize a situation, even one of their own. By exaggerating, or dramatizing it, it becomes something else. It no longer needs to be addressed.

It becomes as it were a legend in the making. The other thing is there was at that time in Ireland, and I think there still is despite the pedantry, a very strong poetic gift. Sometimes just a mere ballad, at other times much more sophisticated, but it is there. The same gift exists in England but in an utterly different way; it comes out in quite a different form. But in Ireland it is very spontaneous, like Irish ballads. And as they sing it you feel that the ballad has come straight out of a lasting situation and the legend has grown around it.

I'd like to ask you about each of these Irish writers, but that would take us too long.

One thing that always struck me, if I may say so, about Liam O'Flaherty was a story of his in which—it's a summery day and it's by the sea and a butterfly's flying over the land, flying out to sea, and there it is going across the English Channel and you can see it for a long time and eventually it will disappear. Where does it disappear, does it cross the sea, does it fall down into the sea or what? The observer on the scene identifies himself as it were with the butterfly going across the sea. Of course it is a very slight idea but it's a very curious one, and a real one.

What's the title of that story?

I've forgotten. I think it appears in a book *The Tent*.

To shift to something a little bit different as far as your early interest in the short story: one thing I noticed in reading especially your first volume of autobiography, almost all through it you speak in terms of oppositions, between the north and south in England, or between your mother and father, or between your father's family and your mother's family. Not only many of your own short stories, but one characteristic of the short story form itself may be this sudden sharp opposition between two forces that you have to work for in a novel over a long time . . .

I think that sort of thing had a great influence on my story writing. It always has. There was a vast difference between my parents. My father came from Yorkshire and from village Yorkshire at that, and my mother—she was a Cockney—came from round the corner in London here; she came from Kentish Town, she worked in a shop; and the difference between the very talkative and the totally restless Cockney, with his rather superficial wit and his local stories and general mixture of merriment and sentiment is quite different from the stolid yet passionate Yorkshireman who is tough and blunt and doubts words and is moralistic. My father was a very religious man, my mother—she'd belong to any religion you offered to her to keep you quiet (laughter). I think in the first long story I wrote you get that conflict. I went to Sicily and in Taormina I saw a lot of painters, painting little pictures for tourists, and I got fascinated by one of them and he said it was so it could be put in a suitcase and this way it was an instant sale. And it became a kind of parable of the split between the artist and the businessman. That was the kind of thing which was really going on in my family because my father, although a businessman, and a religious man, had a certain degree of artist in him because he was a designer in the textile trade; he made all sorts of objects which were fashionable at that time but no longer are, and which showed a great deal of craftsman's skill, if not a pure artist's imagination. So in a way in that story it's reflected.

There are also figures in your family past. I was thinking especially of your Uncle Arthur who seemed such a sceptical and strong-minded man, and in your own stories you yourself are very much interested in showing the limitations of your characters' beliefs or ideas which is something your Uncle Arthur would have enjoyed.

I think, in the case of my Uncle Arthur, who is a very good example, he was just an ordinary working carpenter; he lived in York, and he was madly passionate about the famous cathedral. He knew every stone of it, measured the stones of it. He was a practical man but he had an extraordinary kind of semi-aesthetic gift, and similarly he loved everything in nature, but he did not stop at that. He would get on his bicycle and drive over to cliffs on the sea and dare himself to climb down the cliffs to collect birds' eggs. He had an absurd collection of bird's eggs—he would have filled this room—taken at the peril of his life and with a collector's care. He also collected insects, there were cases of every kind of known fly and irritant in English life at various stages. There they were in their cases, but he personally had obtained them. Well this is a kind of act of poetry, of folly and poetry in this otherwise practical carpenter, a poor man too. On the other hand, one other thing which has never ceased to surprise me, he had read that extraordinary psychological classic of the 17th century, Burton's *Anatomy of Melancholy,* which is the most extraordinary book of classical learning about neurosis and all that sort of thing, primitive psychology, early psychology. And he used to read this with absolute delight, with great pleasure—how much he understood I don't know.

He would quote from it?

He did quote from it, yes. And I think it was partly useful to him in his war with his brother-in-law, who was my grandfather, who was a Congregationalist minister, preacher, always referring to the Bible. Uncle Arthur used to say "Shut up! Burton, look it up in Burton" and he'd throw the Bible down. That sort of split in character is the thing that interests me, it still does.

That's another opposition between someone who has a strong religious belief and the other—your Uncle Arthur or your mother—. Your Uncle Arthur would fight against it and your mother would try to avoid it, perhaps, but there was still that opposition.

Absolutely so. There is still that opposition. It still fascinates me.

You said once that your first story was a lament. You said most of your stories had been laments. What did you mean by that?

The original thing which I wrote that about was a novel I started writing when I was ten; the germ of it was that I had read a long story by Washington Irving, a book for children about the Alhambra, and it was republished in a magazine with pictures. I read this and it gripped me completely and I decided I must write a novel about the recapture of Granada. I knew nothing about it at all except what I had read and very rapidly, like any schoolboy writer, I was longing to describe the battle. And I thought, "Oh, God, when all these men have been killed, what's going to happen?" I supposed I must get some of them wounded and call for ambulances, but there were no ambulances; and so the women would come and look for their dead husbands, and then they'd break into lamentations. The word "lamentations" impressed me very much and, in fact, I suppose, by transposition later on in life. I came to realize that people are always in a state of regret, or they are lamenting that such and such a thing did or did not happen. In small ways—I don't mean they are tearing their hair, but there is a split of sadness in life, a feeling of loss very often.

In most of your stories?

I am very conscious of that yes.

I'd like to ask a little more about the first short stories you read. You said that in Dublin you read D. H. Lawrence and Joyce's Dubliners.

Yes . . . yes, I read them, and I also read an English writer who is now rather forgotten but who was an extremely gifted writer of stories, in a very small compass, a man called A. E. Coppard. I admired his stories enormously. And in fact I used to know him, when I was living in the country. He was a nearby neighbour. And he was a very strange man; he was a warehouse-man's clerk or something like that who had decided to be a writer, so he had gone out and lived in a shed in the woods in Buckinghamshire, entirely on his own, with no sanitation and his drinking water from a well, in a shallow well in the earth. And he was a natural perfectly spontaneous man, not muddle-headed, he was absolutely clear-headed. I don't think he had any views about life in general, any kind of intellect, but he had a marvellous appreciation of the instant; he could describe a squirrel very well, he could describe a game-keeper, he could describe a couple of old farmers arguing about whether beef is better than veal to

eat, or what pork is like, and things like that. He had a great decorative sense of comedy. He was unfortunately, when I look back upon it, a rather folkish writer; he came at a period when the peasantry were dead really and they only existed in pockets in England, in little places, and their traditional customs by that time had almost gone. It was when suburbia spread out and the countryside died. That curious old England went out. Another writer who was very good, in the same way, in his early stories, who came later, was H. E. Bates. He wrote very well, very good English, had a good style, but was also brief.

[Séjourné]: *How old were you when you were reading these writers?*

Well, I suppose when I was in my twenties, I should think, when I came back from France. Because when I was in France I read simply nothing but French literature, French and Russian. I didn't read any Russian stories, but I did read a lot of French stories; I read Maupassant of course and many others. And when I came back to England—in fact I was rather too foreign when I came back—I was terribly soaked in French things and literature and language. It was very hard for me even to get French out of my head, and to be able to write English.

Do you think you may owe anything to Maupassant, for instance?

Well I think any short story writer does for one or two of his stories. I think he's bound to interest, especially the river stories, the boating stories of the river Seine. His style is very limpid; he was after all taught by Flaubert. And so he is, at that stage, a model. Any young writer is bound to turn to him for a period.

Now, may we turn to your success, your being hailed as one of the masters of the short story, and also you have been one of the most successful I would say from the public's point of view. What are the reasons for this success both with the critics and the public? Were they the same?

I think the public has come on rather more slowly. I think the critics were first, really. Many of my best early short stories I couldn't get published anywhere which seems to show there was not a public for them. A story like **"Sense of Humour"** which made me as it were tremendously admired by a small circle of people who knew. But up to then I'd never been able to find anyone to publish it. It was completely incomprehensible to them. I think the critics were the first. I suppose the critics really tended to be my contemporaries, probably the same age as myself.

I wondered whether the reason for your success was the great variety of subjects you were able to treat?

I think this is undoubtedly true. I've led a pretty restless life which is rather good for short story writers. And in that way one collects a good many subjects; and I think I've had a strange passage through society itself. I've been in almost any class of society. I mean I've found myself in it by accident for some reason or other, and I think I've had a journey through the English class system in a way, a more amusing one than most people, but still . . . I think also I have a rather ironical comic sense of life, and in fact that is an important point to me: I've always thought that the comic is really an aspect of the poetic. It is the sister of the poetic quality. And certainly my early writing—out of those Irish influences—was a strongly poetic, indeed sometimes over-poetic and the comic is the basic thing there. My fundamental view about the story is that it begins as a poetic insight, and that it is also a way of seeing through a situation, a "glimpse through" as someone has said in which you are in fact writing something perhaps like a short poem. I think the best examples of the short story in this sense are the sonnets of Shakespeare. Each sonnet is an intricate piece of poetry, but at the same time it is "a glimpse through" the life, a situation, the instance of feeling that he is evoking. It's more than an impression of surface. It cuts deeper than that.

Do you write easily, does it come easily to you?

No, not very easily. I make innumerable false starts. If I make a good start, then suddenly I get stumped. As Chekhov said: "the middle is the difficulty". I don't know how to go on. Or I don't know how to make the transition from this scene to the next scene. Things like those are things that are difficult for a short story writer, generally because he has too much piled up inside him, and doesn't know how to distribute it. Then I find I have to put it down and go back to look at it. And then I somehow see what I've got to do next. And when the story's done it's generally a failure towards the end of it. It's going downhill fast. And I must now try to control it. So I write most stories three or four times over. I don't think I've ever just dashed off a short story. It takes me quite a considerable time. I think very often the end of the story is something totally different. For example, I wrote a story called **"Neighbours"** about two years ago. I wanted to write a story about a woman's hairdresser who lived in London and went to work in a big shop in Piccadilly. I imagined this man, and I knew he was perpetually complaining about how people really traded on him in one way or another, how he was always called in to help in awkward situations and so on. I also noticed that he was a man who like myself didn't take a bus to the office. He walked all the way, from one end of Kensington right across the parks into Piccadilly. But he was also an ardent window-box gardener; knew a great deal about plants. All these pieces of information came into his character and I thought it would be a good subject. I began to see, of course he's gardening, he's gardening for women's hair. This sort of symbolism gripped me for a time, but I was over-loading it in the story. So I put the story aside, and then I suddenly realized—he had been talking about difficulties with his neighbour, a very boring woman who lived below him in her flat. That's another incident in the story—. I went away to Cornwall and I suddenly realized, my God! this is the place to put him. Let's take him away from his London place. And then I had the notion that he should meet this woman whom he dislikes, down there. He's staying at the same hotel. And then I had the sort of thing I wanted to write about. And so I had to scrap a lot of my verbiage, and come down to the main thing. And the main thing simply was—having had a very trying time with this lady—he hears from her that she's leaving her flat—she's married somebody down in the country—he'd been longing to avoid her and now he's terribly upset that she's now

gone and he's got nothing to complain about. This important aspect of life is gone. And it was only when I went down to Cornwall that I realised I must reimagine him. I'd heard too much about him. That I think is one of the important things about writing stories: if somebody begins to tell you a story, you have to say "Shut up, stop it". I don't want to know what *really* happened. I must reinvent.

So it's the poetic influx?

The poetic influx is absolutely at the heart of it, I'm sure.

Speaking about your method of working, I was struck by a sentence you use in one of your prefaces, you speak of "boiling down a hundred pages into twenty or thirty". Is that what you actually do? (laughter).

Well I think I actually do. Sometimes I've noticed that the story which perhaps runs from about fifteen to twenty pages, I look at the manuscript of it and I find I've got versions about *that* high. I've always been rather ashamed of that because I thought it shows how stupid I am. But I remember reading the memoirs of Babel, you know, the Russian. He wrote *The Red Cavalry,* a brilliant post-revolutionary. He was involved in the civil war after the Revolution and he's a marvellous laconic short story writer. Many of his stories are not more than three pages long. They're quite astonishing. Somebody was interviewing him and he came into the room and they found a pile of papers about a foot high; and Babel said, in a slightly nervous exhibitionist way: "that's my last short story of three pages". You do have to cut down, cut down, cut down. With your writing a narrative story of any kind it always seems to you first of all that every event has equal importance, that every bit of it ought to have three sentences to it; when sometimes three words is quite enough.

Well, I was wondering about that because sometimes I feel that some of your stories look like extracts from what might have been novels. Do you sometimes have this feeling that what you're writing might be developed into a novel or be part of a novel as well as be a short story?

I believe I don't think that really because when I wanted to write short stories and the publisher said he would not publish them unless I would write a novel, I was appalled because I had no idea how to construct a novel. So I read dozens of novels to see how you wrote a novel and I got more and more confused. I did manage to write one long slightly anecdotal story which was superficially, shall we say, the plan for a novel which I managed to turn into an apparent novel, but after that I was beginning to write novels in order to please this publisher, and ones which were certainly quite well written but they had no success. I found that really: short stories were much better. I'd much sooner write them. I have written, I suppose, two novels which are quite good. One has been republished lately: *Dead Man Leading.* And I also wrote *Mr. Beluncle* which is a transformed autobiography. These did succeed. I don't think my novels are very good. No one ever seems to mention them; I would not be surprised if some people thought them unreadable . . .

Going back to what Ben was saying a moment ago: I was

struck by the opening sentence of your Living Novel *when you complain of having read too many novels when you were young. Why is that? Why do you think it was wrong to read so many novels?*

Well I don't think I really did think that but I was always told so. I was brought up at the age when people tried to stop you reading novels. I was a voracious reader. I would not say I had read the whole of Walter Scott but I had read a good half of him by the time I was sixteen. And I had read the whole of Thackeray, most of Dickens and was on to Balzac and Tolstoy. I suppose it incited me to wish I could do that; but the labour in front of me seemed preposterous and enormous: how on earth shall I ever learn to be able to construct an edifice! I think for example in the Twenties (when I grew up) the people who distinguished themselves as novelists at that time had not read very much because they hated Victorian literature while I for instance was soaked in it. There was a revolt against the traditional English novel in general and its particular values and so on. My reading of French novels and Spanish novels liberated me from the enormous, rather crushing moral power of the Victorian novel. I don't think so now but that's what I thought at the time (laughter).

When you say that you have occasional difficulties in writing, does that mean that a number of your short stories were not completed or not proposed for publication?

Yes, some I scrapped or some I kept and read years later and thought "Good Heavens I know how to do this now". I know now how right Laurence Sterne was when he said that one cannot write until one "hears the tune in one's head". That's particularly true of short story-writers. You don't want an awful lot of facts, you don't want particularly an idea, but what you really want is to hear the tune of the first sentence and the note you wish to prolong. That's the thing to wait for.

There are certainly many young writers who get in touch with you and ask for your advice. What would you say are the main dangers for a young story writer, the main causes of failure?

I would have thought all sorts of wrong emphases in the writing. Poor slack English is a very common thing among . . . : when you're very young and write sentences which seem to hang like laundry on the line. It seems all right, but it is *not* all right (laughter). Also, much too much explicitness is a bad thing. There is no need to describe everything that goes on at the table where the family is sitting. There are certain things you should pick out. You should find ways of describing, say a street like this— just to get it in a sentence or two. You should also have a much better ear for ordinary speech than is common. That I do feel very strongly, because a lot of people, young writers, don't know how people speak. They give them written sentences to say instead of spoken sentences. Beware sentences that explain too much. A story must never explain, it must enact and suggest.

[Forkner]: *Did you practice taking down speech? I know you took notes when you were in the Appalachians.*

Yes, I did. I had a mania for taking a notebook with me and writing down every sentence that I could. I did it for years. I have stopped that now. Perhaps it is a bad thing; perhaps I should start again. But I have a trained memory for any kind of phrase, anything heard in a shop or in a train. A phrase was often more important to me than a sentence.

I think that question of speech is very important for young writers. Chiefly for the reason that people are not *writing* when they speak.

[Séjourné]: *Now speaking about your characters. In your novel* Dead Man Leading *you give the definition of what is the character of a bad novel, "the character who's got inextricably confused with the character of the author"* . . .

Yes, that's true.

Does that apply to the short story?

I would think it does. The author may have a character in his head, but I think he ought to be able to describe it without being too intricate about it. But, in general, I think the characters need to be liberated from their authors. That I think is important. There is a certain kind of first novel in which the hero is only too obviously a projection of the author in more favourable circumstances than in real life.

Still is not there a fair amount of autobiographical elements in your stories?

Oh, a great deal but transformed or filtered.

But that does not interfere?

That does not interfere at all, because to make things true they have to be made unlike yourself, they must appear not to be your view of them. You have to liberate your characters from yourself. You mustn't hang to them like the ghost at the feast. The ghost must be absent. They have to appear to be entirely on their own. I think it would be very difficult for me to write a portrait of myself. In fact I don't know where I would begin and indeed if I tried to put myself in a novel, or indeed in a story, I might put a tiny section of myself because it represented something in the story, but not otherwise.

Do you think that in your stories you have room to develop a true character, do you think the characters of a short story have the same vital energy as the characters in a novel? Have they got the same requirements as far as the writer is concerned?

They have a very different requirement. For instance, a full-length portrait in a novel by Tolstoy of Prince Andrew may only appear in a novel. It is intricately examined. It is examined morally, socially, with a good deal of detail, because such writers are generally describing not simply individuals but a state of society in which they live. And doing so, how they evolve from this society, or escape from it.

Now the short story writer only does that by indication and if he finds that a character is being, shall we say, ruined by society or by his social upbringing, he has to find a way of demonstrating this in one or two incidents, or in some reflection. He has to develop a certain sleight-of-hand. He's constantly reducing the size of the field he's got in front of him, but he's increasing the intensity. I think intensity is something very marked in the best short stories. They're not superficial in just hitting upon one or two things. They've chosen those things for a purpose which runs clean through the story. And which sharpens it . . .

In your view, is the character the center of the short story or is he only a medium through which something else is represented?

Well I think he's both that really. He is a character in the story, but also he represents things in the society around him. The ordinary human being has not got on his shoulders the burden of the novelist. He's got a greater burden, that of living (laughter). And so therefore he can be known for the aspects of this burden. For example, since it was something I wrote fairly recently, this question of the hairdresser. He's very comfortable in his flat. It's all rather decorative. He's a sort of homosexual. Anyway he is a man who's not much interested in women. He does his own cooking, and everything is absolutely just so. Being visited by a woman who is not like that, who is a widow and has got endless stories of her woes and difficulties and all the rest of it, whenever he meets her here or wherever she goes, he has an awful feeling "My God, let's keep away from ordinary life. Really she is a sample, she's human, she's awful". His feeling is that of somebody who cannot stand the boredom of any aspect of ordinary life. Yet, on the other hand, will go to enormous fuss, if anyone drops something on his sofa, some wine or something that spoils the velvet, he'll go all over London trying to find something that really cleans velvet (laughter).

I remember Arnold Bennet who was a writer I very much admired in many of his remarks about writing. He talks about one of his characters towards the end of a story as having to "bear the exquisite burden of life". Well I think that phrase is one I do rather feel. Only when I say "burden" I don't mean something that is really bowing me down but it is something I had to deal with. But I think the dealing with it should be exquisite, I mean to say it should be more delicate, perhaps more perceptive. I'm not very keen on a generalizing morality.

If characters are not completely developed in a short story, would you agree that they may be more like types than actually live characters. The French academic Alain Theil, whom you remember, said that he had found only ten types of female characters, such as the light woman, the unsatisfied woman, the deserted woman often divorced and so on . . . Would you agree with a definition like that or would you think it is unfair?

It's a generalization which may have a certain amount of truth but most of the novelists' or the short story writers' duty is to destroy generalization. Supposing I am faced with writing about one of his types, I should have to see that she is not a type. I should have to contradict the view. He might still say you're writing about a "light woman" but "you have never seen a light woman like this before" would be my answer. All human beings are different and I want to see the distinctions. There is something that takes them outside the generality.

One of the things that has always impressed me about Dickens—sometimes I have been compared, sometimes wrongly I think—people say his characters are done in caricature: I think that is totally untrue, almost totally untrue. Especially in the English characters. A large number of English people you see walking up and down the street are acting a part. They are concealing themselves from everyone by extraordinary acts of behaviour. Strange verbiage comes out of them, certain fantasies come flying out of them, which is part of their character. They see themselves curiously, I think, on some kind of private stage. And in England particularly where the sense of belonging to a society, where social pressures are strong, we tend to escape to our private stage. The sense of one's obligation to society, almost in any class under any circumstance, or one's role in society, is very strong indeed. But of course it's an unbearable burden. What you have, there's still yourself, this you are but up to a point. Now what do you live by? You live not by that, but possibly by some fantasy view of yourself or by some aspects of yourself which you hide from society, which you cherish, and large number of people are always seeing themselves—you see them in Camden-Town all day long—as being some one else. There used to be a newsagent here, a rather mocking character, and he would have a chat with you, and then he would suddenly put on a different voice and say: "Don't call us, we'll call you". He saw himself as a film producer sending an applicant away. All you were doing was buying a paper from him (laughter). I could see somehow or other he would assume that, instead of being behind a counter, he ought to be sitting in a cane chair in a studio in front of people asking for parts. He was exactly like that. I think many people are *adjacent* to life, not drowning in it.

Would you agree with the idea that because the short story is short it's easier for its authors to deal with characters whose personalities are fairly simple or who have strong characteristics to be easily . . .

That is perfectly true, yes. But even a simple character may have a moment of sudden drama in his daily life. H. E. Bates has one about a peasant who, as he ploughs a field, suddenly gets a message that his son had died. What the ploughman's "character" is, we don't know. We don't know what he is. We don't know what his character is. He is a ploughman. We can guess what a labouring ploughman's life is like. We can see he is a hard working man, that he is devoted to his job, and all the rest, but he can be made to seem a very powerful example of human being, of a humble human being with no characteristics except that he goes to work. Yet suddenly this blow occurs to him in the course of an ordinary day's work. In an ordinary day there is this devastating message which he will have to live through as the day passes. That day will be one of the dramas in the life of an ordinary man. The Russian writers have had the sense of the natural yet inexorable flux of the day passing through ourselves. That itself disposes of the need of plot or the elaboration of character. As that excellent critic John Bayley has said about Russian writing in general: for the Russians "the doors and windows of the human house are wide open; their minds are living in the open . . . ", in the passing hour. The story is, in essence, a poem.

Well you have introduced my next point speaking about the unnecessary plot, the limited importance of the plot. When reading your stories, I have some difficulty in deciding how important or unimportant the plot is for you. Is the plot of a story something that worries you?

No, not at all. I have to know what the beginning, middle and end is, if you mean that. But as far as an intrigue is concerned, or a complicated intrigue, no, I'm much more interested in the character, whose personality takes over. They certainly may get into trouble. I occasionally can think of plots which would turn them into anecdotes, I'm not very clever at that. In fact, I rather shy away when I see an anecdote coming up. They are too easy to invent, I try to avoid it. I don't say that I always do, I always feel that an anecdote part should be watched very carefully and, as much as possible, the end of the story should lie open, so that you feel, that your people have got to go on living when the story is over. However it is not necessarily so. Large numbers of good short stories have had rather tricky endings. Pushkin's "The Queen of Spades" is, in part, an elaborate, yet alarming conceit.

In fact there is a variety in your short stories?

Yes, Yes.

Some of them have a very clearly defined plot, for instance "The Necklace" or "Blind Love"... but if you take "The Two Brothers" it seems the story might have ended without a conclusion perhaps...

Yes, but it is an early story and happened to be "true".

...One of the two brothers leaves but he might have continued to live next door. Does that bother you?

No, it doesn't bother me. "The Necklace" I wrote as an exercise because I thought I had lost the ability to write a story. I was working on the *New Statesman* at the time and I was awfully busy. And I suddenly realized that I was running short of short stories, and I thought I'd better try and do something about it. And I remembered that Henry James had decided that he must really write a "necklace" story. The "necklace" story of Maupassant is the classic model and an astonishing number of writers have turned to that story and said "I must write a 'necklace' in a different way". And so I did it for that reason: it did release me.

But still you think for instance that a nice little twist at the end of the story may be a good trick: I am thinking for instance of "The Wheelbarrow"; suddenly we discover what the man's real interest is, but is it for you merely a technical trick or...

Not at all. It is a surprise, but it occurred to me in real life. I was giving up my house in the country, I decided that I couldn't be bothered to take the wheelbarrow with me, so I gave it to a local man who was the gardener. By this time I knew enough about country people to realize that whatever situation they got into, the "things" were the important thing to them. I knew the man coveted my wheelbarrow. It was natural for him to go for the useful object rather than for something else. Covetous self-interest is traditional of course. But I didn't think of it particularly as a trick but it certainly is an irony. That story was partic-

ularly interesting for me to write because it is about a Welsh miner. I do know the Welsh rather well. And when I read some of my stories I very often can remember from what particular real instant in life—or something like it—any sentence came from. And I've often thought—supposing I lost my memory—I could always go back to my stories and find the whole geography of my life, the travelling, friendships, goodness knows, in random detail, going back even into childhood. They don't belong to the period of the story necessarily. They sometimes go right back to childhood. I think childhood is an enormous source, the real well from which literature really comes. (pp. 12-33)

Is not there a danger, many people would say, of the short story becoming artificial with such components as the final twist, or the introduction of short bits of information at any point of the story that will serve to bring about the conclusion, or the necessary selection of components in which the role of the writer is too obvious? Do you think there is some truth in all that, that there is a danger for the short story?

Well there's the same sort of danger really that there is in the novel on a larger scale. I think if you try to write short stories well, you try and evade those things. I mean they stick out a mile when you read them through to you. And you think "No, that is really not so, not like the life I'm trying to put in". Nevertheless, there are a vast number of anecdotal stories which are like that. I think actually there is a public taste for the anecdote, that is much stronger than it is for the story which is not an anecdote. Maupassant, Maugham, even Chekhov sometimes, sinned in this way. One must of course distinguish between the "trick" ending and the "closed" ending in which the story has a fitting end. I think we've had far too many anecdotal stories. The twist can be avoided entirely by making it spring from the characters themselves. The finest stories have a natural, even intense musical power. I would have thought the number of people who like non-anecdotal short stories is the number of people who read poetry. One must distinguish between irony of life and mere wit. Experience often tells us that the comic and the dire are often opposite sides of each other, yet somehow united. We laugh and cry at the same time. Information is very bad in the short story. But I think there are the people who like it, they don't like stories to be over too quickly! People like to read novels as if they were getting into a nice hot bath you know. Lolling about in it. They like to "lose themselves". Whereas in the best stories you *find* yourself. I think that is undoubtedly true. The best stories wake you up. Even if they wake you up to preposterous things, they do wake you up.

If it does not wake you up, it is a bad short story?

It is a bad short story, that is it! I don't object to a certain amount of trickery, life is often bizarre and has its own wit. One of my "trick" stories, as you might recall, is the story I wrote about a dentist. This is straight from life. I didn't have any trouble at all in this. It was told to me by my dentist as he was struggling with my tooth. I knew him well and knew certain things about his life. He was a born non-penitent, but he needed to confess. He was a tremendous pursuer of young girls to whom he wrote poems. And in his surgery he had a file full of carefully type-written poems—written in the manner of one or two modern American poets—long poems. He would dish these out to girls and read them to persons like me to see "What do you think about this one". "She was a goddess but she had feet of clay" (laughter). Then he became more confessional, describing how he ran off with his father's mistress: frightful troubles and all the rest of it. He even interpreted it as a "touch of the Oedipus complex". It is unbelievable but there it is. And the fact that he should tell the story is perfect, it ends with his own polite, professional words. His *own* trick—not mine. Very English. The only thing that I had to do was to write it entirely in his abrupt dialogue, so that this is not the impersonal voice of the author speaking to you, but it's the dentist himself. He read it a year later when it was published and congratulated me and hoped I got well-paid for it!

Well, as you said, short stories should wake people up: is it for that reason that very often they tend to deal with rather unusual or extreme situations or characters?

That also happens, I suppose, but they don't always deal with such strange situations as my dentist. If you've got really extreme characters or strange situations, you must take care to be neutral. Strange situations are strange. It is one of the writer's duties to suggest the strangeness of ordinary life.

I was thinking of "The Satisfactory" for instance . . .

"The Satisfactory" yes.

This exchange of sex and food during the war, the lady providing extra food and the man giving sex in exchange.

That is a trick story, I think. Yet, I observed it in my daily visit to a restaurant where such a woman was feeding a man. There was a certain trade in food coupons during the war.

But is it not the extreme limit of something fairly usual . . . I mean it is usual to see a lady giving something nice to a man . . . but this is an extreme case, she hardly ate at all and he ate for two . . . (laughter).

It seemed comical and yet passionate to me—*a trouvail.* I don't claim it is a great story; it is a little farce. I don't see why one should not be able to write all kinds of stories. I've often thought when recalling people's criticism of the early Chekhov—you know he wrote some hilarious short stories—that a writer who can write short stories is able to write any kind of story, and if he can he'd better. Because if he's going to write a trick story and it obsesses him, then he'd better do it, to get it out of his system.

My last question for a conclusion would be: what future do you see for the short story? It seems that people are, maybe, less interested in short stories than they used to be fifty years ago? Is the short story dying out, do you think?

Well, the rise of the short story was due to the proliferation of magazines, monthly magazines, weekly magazines. People needed stories. Remember that novels, in the nineteenth century, were serialised month by month in magazines. Television is killing the magazines. It is very difficult to find any one to publish a short story. This won't stop stories being written. They do well in collections. But in Great Britain a writer is paid very little for individual stories—far less than in America where the rewards have been far larger. My two early stories **"A Sense of Humour"**, and **"The Sailor"**, I was paid £3 and £7 respectively, but they "made" my name. Had I been an American writer in my twenties I would have earned far more than that. I lived on literary journalism. So stories, the most important thing in my life, have had to take the back seat, in earning my living. But in the end, my collections of short stories have had enormous success in Germany, in the U.S., in Japan and in Great-Britain. I suppose it's the reward for having been paid very little at the start, but I don't know (laughter). Anyway that is how it is.

Television is the main enemy of all reading. People now are ceasing to read and certainly very few get the habit of reading in their childhood. In previous generations people read in their old age, because they had taken it up when they were children. Now children don't need to read a book.

You will say that television occasionally puts on a story for twenty minutes, isn't that a good idea? Well, they do that sometimes. But unfortunately the written short story is immediately distorted by television. It's rather like a novel being different when it's put on the stage. It's a different medium altogether. The radio is by far the best medium for stories: listeners are readers.

Have you had experiences with television?

"Blind Love" was done on television and some of it was rather well done. I watched it being made and they took a great deal of trouble. The only thing was that it was on a serious subject in which detail counts; on the screen it went at the speed of a horserace—a uniform speed. A short story does not go at uniform speed. It also changes direction. The television is very onespeed. If you went at the same pace you would be writing a novel.

Another of my television stories is **"The Wedding"**. I was afraid of that being done because it had to take place in the real country, among real country people, farmers and so on . . . And the television has had the habit of inventing a kind of standard English peasant type—people we always called "coming from Loamshire". I wouldn't have been able to bear this because I've known farmers very well indeed—in fact I've had them in my family and in my wife's family. Fortunately, the T.V. people took the story to a remote rural district in Yorkshire. Most of the actors were actual country men acting, and some came from that part of England. Their accents were true. There was not a touch of Broadcasting House in them. They spoke very naturally. They caught the note of frolic you need if you are going to describe a country wedding: the air of genial lust and general horseplay. The action of the story came to my mind from an actual wedding in which the young farmers had ropes tucked under their wedding clothes. The custom was to lasso some of the ladies like cattle which they manage very skilfully to do. The larking was rough but it was not detestable, it was human, even had an elegance. But they did it well, they didn't race it through, and they had a rather tricky subject because the rough farmer who was a rich widower (in my story) is determined to marry a country girl who was extremely well educated. In fact she teaches literature and is not a stuffy school Ma'am at all. She's a publishable literary critic. Improbable? Not at all. Read D. H. Lawrence. I know more than one instance. One has to make this possible. I think I know how to do that. I think they didn't quite, but they had a splendid girl for doing it, and I think they did it pretty well, but again it is the speed that seems to be wrong. I don't know, perhaps you could read that story in much less than half an hour—and the television was half an hour—perhaps you can read my story in a quarter of an hour, but that quarter of an hour would seem very long.

So you would not advise young short story writers to address themselves entirely to the T.V.? They should continue to write . . .

I think they must write . . . I think T.V. would mislead them . . . still, it depends . . . A good many people with talent are very open to experiment in new forms. Most of the good writers have been daring. They've taken risks, they constantly want to refresh their talents. Perhaps television will catch up with us. It is still in its adolescence. In the meantime we survive because there are still addicted readers who like to reflect as they read, and not merely to see instantly and to forget. (pp. 33-8)

> V. S. Pritchett, Ben Forkner, and Philippe Séjourné, in an interview in Journal of the Short Story in English, *No. 6, Spring, 1986, pp. 11-38.*

Geneviève Doze   (essay date 1986)

[*In the following essay, Doze offers two interpretations of "Many Are Disappointed."*]

V. S. Pritchett discovered literature by himself, as a child; he was first drawn to poetry, then found that prose was his natural medium, arguing that he had "never really enjoyed poetry for it was concerned with inner experience" and he "was very much an extrovert"; also that in prose "he found the common experience and the solid worlds where judgments were made and which one could firmly tread".

Nevertheless, both his critical writing and his fiction reveal the presence of the poet within, which may explain the attraction the short story, near kin to the poem, had for him. He introduces an element into "the common experience and the solid worlds" which is other than prosaic. From where he stands, "on the other side of a frontier", he listens and watches, fascinated by the mystery of the commonplace, tracing the singularity of everyday lives, opening doors to the imagination.

On leaving France, V. S. Pritchett explained that "with the possession of another language, he could become two persons". The variety of characters in his human comedy bear witness to his "passion . . . for identifying" himself "with people who were not" his "own and whose lives were alien to" his. The skill in finding the telling detail for characterization, the ear for the vernacular, the eye for description—he had wanted to be a painter, too, because "a

painting took one instantly through a door into another world, one like our own, but silent"—the fanciful, uninhibited imagery, the polysemic neologisms like "London . . . cabbaged with greenery" or "his . . . bull-necked way", explain the wealth of suggestion—a poet's—in his short stories. What is suggested is as cogent as what is explicitly said.

The thrift in Pritchett's language, which is whittled down to essentials, makes every detail significant, symbolic, emblematic; the narrative, within a delusively simple structure, tends naturally to the allegorical, although the open ending makes it impossible to attempt too precise an interpretation without being reductive.

Such is the case in **"Many Are Disappointed"**.

Like Gogol, V. S. Pritchett writes of "ordinary people, apparent nonentities, with an attentiveness capable of revealing deep currents of emotion beneath petty surfaces". No more ordinary people could be found than the characters in this story: a group of clerks on a cycling trip, a sickly woman who "does teas" in an isolated house, and her little girl. Nor could a narrative structure be simpler: it belongs to the primitive, picaresque type, with three phases—the arrival of the men, their irruption into the woman's life, their departure. The final phase resembles the first, without being identical.

The plot lies in the very absence of plot: the tale is about vacancy, loss, non-existence, going nowhere. The trappings of the classical tragedy are there, the unities strictly observed, but nothing happens, only a failed catharsis in a squalid kitchen.

The short story would seem to suit such a theme, with the freedom of narration which it affords, the use of multiple modes of expression, direct, indirect, free indirect speech, flowing into one another. In the first phase, short flashbacks, parentheses, descriptive passages, rhythmic prose stress the men's vitality; in the middle phase, centred round the woman, when dialogues play a greater part, the language is drab, the sentences short, the phrasing disjointed, revealing the tension and disturbance the men have brought. The final phase briefly returns to the characteristics of the first, with an ultimate echo of the middle one in the last sentence.

The shifting viewpoints, the discrepancy between the sensibility of the description and the inarticulateness of the characters in general, the coarseness of the men in particular, contribute to the sense of mystery the story creates, as though a subliminal consciousness were being brought to the surface, especially when the narrative focuses on the woman.

Graphically represented, the men draw a vector through the story, while a point which they cross stands for the woman. Significantly, her house is at a crossroads. The men are dynamic: "heads down to the wind", free to move, to change. They express themselves in space—the map, Harry's mania for Roman roads, which suggests connotations with Roman imperialism—they are off to "the land's end" on their "slim racing tyres". Their objective correlatives are circles: the steel wheels, Sid's gold ring, the golden sun of Ted's baldness, the coin given to the child, the cyclic pattern of the tale. In their end is their beginning. The men are whole, rounded. Their speech is determined imperative, expletive, reiterative, expressing achievement with *there's, here's, there it is,* possession and authority in the repeated use of *our*.

The men's course is barely deflected by the encounter with the woman. She belongs to another world, she is passive, static, submissive, with what V. S. Pritchett sees as "feminine traits" . . . "movements . . . as uncertain as the transparent jelly-fish as it washes back and forth in the current". She is immobile, confined within her house, waiting for things, people, to come to her. Living through vicarious experiences, counting the miles the men will ride to the next place. She is described as *timid, hesitating, anxious, afraid, fearful, amazed, wondering, placating, eager to please.*

The men give an impression of animal strength: "tall and large" "making the woman feel they will burst the walls", Harry "bullnecked", his "stubborn red neck"; "once they were outside, they stretched themselves in the open air". They are eager for a steak, beer, a girl "always waiting".

Ironically, the woman *is* waiting, but she is "not the woman 'Bert' had expected". She is tired, ludicrously and pathetically different from the stereotyped eroticism of Bert's dream: "there's a girl at the pub, a dark girl with bare arms and bare legs in a white frock . . . she just comes and puts her arms round you, and you can feel her skin through her frock and she brings you some beer. Same at the next place, same anywhere, different place different girl, or same girl—same girl always turning up, always waiting . . . waiting like all those songs". Instead, "she was a frail, drab woman . . . in a white blouse that drooped low over her chest . . . her hair was short, an impure yellow, and the pale skin of her face and her neck and her breast seemed to be moist as if she had just got out of bed".

She has nothing to please the men. The food she has to offer is spinsterish: bread and butter, tomatoes, tea; the tin in the sitting-room is symbolically empty. The ambiguity in the name of the pub the men had passed by, "The Queen's Arms", points out her inadequacies. She is married: the equation of being single and happiness is repeatedly mentioned; she sits drably in the kitchen, surrounded with "unwashed plates", the "remains of a meal", "unwashed clothes", while her husband's metonymic waistcoat implies as she holds it against her both loyalty and alienation.

The woman belongs to the vast and variegated host of unhappy females—especially married ones—who could be reminiscent of V. S. Pritchett's own mother, singing the sad rhyme: "Needles and pins / Needles and pins / When a man marries / His trouble begins". "Marriage", Pritchett says, "was a subject on which I had special knowledge". The comment: "Many are disappointed", is spoken like an aphorism by the woman; the use of the present tense gives it a universal bearing; it conveys a weight of experience, looking both into the past and the future.

The unanimist conviviality of the group of men, their jokes, the cohesion which is paradoxically stressed by the different and clearly defined roles of each member, the repeated use of *our* bring out the woman's loneliness: the little girl is merely a double exposure of her mother. The isolation is moral as well as material; the woman quotes her absent husband's rebuke, in its uncouth unpunctuated ungrammatical roughness: "you got your health what you want company for?", as though *she* were in the wrong.

Faced with the men, she summons up an absent community: "*they* call it the Tavern", "*many* are disappointed", I *always* do teas for *people*; "so as *people* can see". Her agitation, her inefficiency show how scarce customers are, how frequent her disappointments.

After the first shock in the confrontation of the two antithetic worlds, the narrative focuses alternately on the men in the sitting-room and on the woman and child in the kitchen, following the parallel revelations taking shape on either side.

The men are first "dumbfounded and angry at the ruddy sell", then the little girl's entry makes them smile and speak "more quietly because of the resemblance between the woman and her child". This, and the minute melancholy details in the description of the sitting-room suggest an insidious effect on their sensibilities, some realization of what the woman's life can be like:

> the cold room . . . they thought in the winter it must be damn cold. They thought of the ten drizzling miles to Handleyford . . . They listened to the cold clatter of the plates in the kitchen . . . There was the bare linoleum on the floor and the chill glass of the window. Outside was the road with blown sand at the edge and, beyond a wall, there were rows of cabbages, then a bit of field and the expressionless sky. There was no sound on the road. They—it occurred to them—had been the only sound on that road for hours.

All those dentals, all those soul-numbing words, drizzling, bare, chill, the rows of cabbages, the expressionless sky.

Then the final, ironical note, the "thick book called *The Marvels of Science*", trailing visions of self-improvement.

The long wait, punctuated by the coming and going of the woman, the monotonous *they's, there was, there were* convey what V. S. Pritchett has described as "the formidable pathos of human inertia, isolation and *ennui*". That something of this breaks through to the men is made manifest by the heightened interest expressed in: they *looked,* they *thought,* they *listened.*

Sid, the womanizer, is the only one to go any further, to cross the border-line between the two worlds, however briefly. While the others are perusing a map, moving on mentally, he ventures into the woman's territory. He alone had seen "her delicate stalk of neck . . . eyes like the pale wild scabious you see in ditches". He had been the intercessor she had looked at "as if he had performed a miracle"; now he is a dark angel. It is significant that the story should reach the peak of its intensity off-stage as it were, in the kitchen. The ascending process of emotion had started when "she spoke with delight as if a bell had sud-

denly tinkled inside her". Now, at its height, the realization that she has a right to feel lonely, her astonishment
"that someone should agree with her and not her husband" amount to an epiphany. There are elusive, subdued
erotic overtones in Sid's attitude—run-of-the-mill for
him—"he bent down so that his head nearly brushed the
woman's arm", recalling his leaning over the typists "to
tell them a story"—in the equivocal play with the gold
ring, as there are in the woman's excitement, the intimacy
of her observation: "she was fascinated because he took off
his glasses and she saw the deep serious shadows of his
eyes and the pale drooping of the naked lids. The eyes
looked tired and as if they had seen many things and she
was tired too". Yet there is something maternal as well in
this relationship, as there was when she looked at Bert:
"she glanced timidly and yet pityingly because he was the
youngest . . .".

The suggestion that she is ready to follow Sid: "taking the
child by the hand, she hurried over to him as if both of
them would cling to him. Excitedly, avidly, they followed
him to the other room", is brutally curtailed. The group
claim Sid once more, conscience-money is given to the
child, as in a sense, it had been given to the mother. "They
zipped up their jackets, stubbed their cigarettes, folded up
the map". Phonologically, semantically, the sentence is
final.

For the men, little seems to have changed: this time they
are riding *to* the sea, not *from the hidden sea, down*hill, not
up—a pilgrim's regress—*some* girl has replaced *same* girl,
perhaps qualifies their expectation. So much for experience. Only when they are all together, "heads down to the
wind", having recovered cohesion and drive, do they remember to look back. The collective "Good God", which
is all they have to say, can be taken to express relief, horror, pity, while the last vision of the woman and child,
"hands fluttering under the strong light of that high
place" and the conclusion: "It was a long time before they
went back into the house", in its stark simplicity tells the
weight of confinement, brief joy, resignation.

As V. S. Pritchett writes in **"The Cage Birds"**, "the place
was a fate". Thus may **"Many Are Disappointed"** be read
as a metaphor for the condition of woman, or the woman's
condition. An aura of mystery remains. Why "the
woman"? She has no name, and neither has her little girl.
Therein lies an opening into another dimension of this
story, a Romantic reading which will perforce be incomplete and hazardous.

The woman is the fulcrum supporting the tale, she, the
weakest element of all. *Her* solitude, *her* strangeness make
the encounter with the cyclists momentous. Her presence
behind the door, felt to be weird, retrospectively highlights
the eeriness that has been creeping into the narrative: a
slow crescendo of absence, loss, desolation has led to her:
"a deserted road", "a small red-brick house", "a single
chimney", "trailing out smoke", "cloud had covered the
sun like a grey hand", "the country had emptied and it
was astonishing to hear a bird", "there had been no villages, only long table-lands of common and bald wiry
grass for sheep and the isolated farm with no ivy on the
brick". The lexical and syntactic anthropomorphism of

sentences like "reeds were in the small meadows",
"hedges crawled uncut", "the whimper of the telegraph
wire on the hill", the insistency on the strange quality of
the "light from the hidden sea", the "strong white light
which seemed to be thrown up by great reflectors", give
a surrealist quality, "the sense of the mysterious within the
field of everyday reality" to the whole of the introductory
passage. Every object is etched with an uncanny precision
that makes it disturbing, however common it is—"the cart
tipped down, its shaft white with the winter's mud"—for
instance.

Out of time—the anachronic name "Tavern"—in the middle of nowhere, the four riders, four like the horsemen of
the Apocalypse, look like absurd knights with fur gaunt-
lets and bicycles for steeds, on a quest for beer and girls.
For all the absurdity, death is present, in nature, in the
connotations of crossroads where the Ancient Greeks
erected statues of Hecate, Christians erect crosses and
which are universally seen as propitious to intercessions
and revelations.

Here, the prophetess is a working-class Melisande; she
comes from elsewhere, "standing on the edge of another
country. The pale blue eyes seemed to be the pale sky of
a far away place where she had been living". Her immaturity, her child-like behaviour, the air of "continual wonder" on her face, in her voice, the epithets *dazed, amazed,
bewildered*, everything contributes to the impression of
mystery surrounding her. "I nearly died", she says; indeed, her pallor, "the high strong light . . . drank all colour from her", her smile "vacant like the smile fading on
an old photograph", her pale lips, her moist skin suggest
the shadow of death, like the shadow hanging over the
sun. She belongs with the heroines of eighteenth and nineteenth century literature, wasting away.

The house with the "emphatically closed door" is like a
tomb. Black is the predominant colour—on the sign, the
armchairs, the fern pattern. The plush is "damp and
sticky". The morbid atmosphere influences the men's
jokes: "Harry said they reckoned at home his grandad got
the cancer he died of from eating tomatoes day after day.
Bert, with his mouth full, said he'd read somewhere that
tea was the most dangerous drink of all".

The claustrophobic sitting-room is at the heart of this
reading of **"Many Are Disappointed"**. There is another
sitting-room in V. S. Pritchett's memory:

> when time went by so slowly and when we, too,
> were shut in a room with some grown-up who
> was occupied entirely by the enormous process
> of sitting. How they could sit! And sit alone!
> And how their figures grew larger and larger in
> our eyes, until their solitude and silence seemed
> to burst the room. It was, I think, one of the first
> intimations of mortality in childhood.

The sitting-room of the Tavern, seen as the antechamber
of death, may be part a burlesque allegory of the journey
of life.

There is no incompatibility between this reading and a
feminist one, inasmuch as they reflect V. S. Pritchett's

sense of the different levels on which life is lived, a sense which is the essence of his art. (pp. 59-66)

Geneviève Doze, "Two Tentative Readings of 'Many Are Disappointed' by V. S. Pritchett," in Journal of the Short Story in English, *No. 6, Spring, 1986, pp. 59-66.*

Claire Larriere   (essay date 1986)

[*In the following essay, Larriere discusses character interaction in Pritchett's short fiction.*]

The crisis which is at the heart of so many short stories is often brought about by the encounter of two characters. In V. S. Pritchett's stories, such encounters are all the more important as his characters are lonely individuals, who find it difficult to communicate with their fellow beings. The circumstances which bring about the encounters make up much of Pritchett's stories, but those circumstances are themselves determined by the character's temperaments and various idiosyncrasies: "For me the drama, the event, the plot, is the person; and the more fantastic, the more certain to be true".

Where, how, do the encounters between two Pritchettian characters take place? In very ordinary surroundings: the street, a pub, a hotel, a shop, at the dentist's or the barber's, in a house—generally, implicitly or explicitly, in England, with a few exotic exceptions, as in **"Rain in the Sierra"** or **"The Evils of Spain"**. The external conditions are rarely unusual. In this manner, the extraordinariness of certain encounters is enhanced by the ordinariness of the place. The first meeting between two characters is in some cases similar to a thunderbolt—thus the meeting in a pub between two obese men, Rogers and Pocock in **"Pocock Passes"** has the impact of a small explosion: "Atlas met Atlas, astonished to find each saddened by the burden of a world . . . Deep called unto deep: Rogers saw to his astonishment, not a stranger, but a brother. Not his blood brother, of course, but something closer—a brother in obesity". However, a short story by V. S. Pritchett can also deal with a moment in the course of regular relationships between one character and another (the hero and his interlocutor), and this moment is both revealing and fraught with consequences.

The relationship between the characters being determined by their temperaments, we can assert that each hero is bound to look for, and to find only certain types of interlocutors, as it is perhaps the case in real life. As a rule, Pritchett's characters take to three types of interlocutors.

The "soul mate" type has a magnetic impact on certain characters, who, though solitary, harbour gregarious tendencies. They brighten when they meet somebody as lonely and handicapped as themselves. It is the case of Rogers in **"Pocock Passes"**, of Mrs Johnson and Armitage in **"Blind Love"**, of Rachel and Gilbert (the former a divorcee, the latter a widower), in **"Did You Invite Me?"**. A few sufferers cling to individuals whose love and understanding they wrongly expect. Such is Charlie's case in **"The Two Brothers"** or Miss Tell's in **"The Satisfactory"**. An extreme instance of pathetic gullibility is Mrs Forster in

"Things As They Are"; she regularly gets drunk with a seemingly sympathetic woman to whom she confides her sentimental let-downs with the same regularity: as soon as Mrs Forster collapses, dead drunk, her companion grabs her bag and ransacks it, with the help of Frederick, the barman, "handsome, old and stupid".

The "receptacle" type is just a pair of ears, into which the hero pours his story. This type suits the character who wishes first and foremost to air his problems and for whom people's attention is more sought for than their compassion or their understanding. It is, to different degrees, the case of Sophia Barclay, the scandalmonger, in **"The Snag"** or of Miss Baker, in the story which bears her name, or of George Clark in **"The Skeleton"**. Like the dentist in **"The Oedipus Complex"**, whose martyred interlocutor will never be able to utter more than "Ah" and "Blah", these characters do not expect any remark from those they have chosen as confidents. If they cannot satisfy their need to talk to someone, they are liable to suffer intensely, like the old man in **"The Spree"**: "In these two years he seemed, because of his loneliness, to be dragging an increasing load of unsaid things behind him, things he had no one to tell . . . What he needed was not friends . . . he needed another stranger".

The most successful relationship between a hero and his "receptacle" is to be found in **"The Liars"**, where each of two characters is alternately a speaker and a "receptacle": their constant role-swapping prevents both Miss Randall and Harry from ever being passively receptive. Each knows not only the particulars of the other's story but the numerous embellishments he/she likes to adorn it with. The momentary "receptacle" is ever willing to hear his/her partner's story, not with the view to insuring the latter's attention when himself/herself becomes the narrator, but merely because the invention, the fantasizing of the story-teller acts as a stimulant on the listener. The following passage corresponds to one of the most inspired moments of the game:

> "The British bombed you, Harry?" "Not at all, it was one of father's bombs, home-made thing, it went off in the house." "Were you hurt, Harry?" "I was at my Auntie's. So I went to sea." "So you did, you told me, and the ship blew up too." "No ma'am it was the boiler. It was a Liverpool ship, the *Grantham*." "Two explosions, I don't believe you, Harry." "It's God's truth, ma'am. It was in New York harbour. But I'd left her in Buenos-Aires—there was always trouble on her." "And then you went to that hacienda—no, you got a job in a hotel first of all—isn't that it?" "Yes, in two or three hotels, ma'am, until this American lady took me up to her hacienda." "To look after the horses?" "That is correct." "This was the lady who rode her horse up the steps into the dining-room?" "No ma'am," said Harry, "she rode it right inside and up the marble staircase into her bedroom." "She couldn't, Harry. A mule, yes, but not a horse." "That part was easy for her, ma'am, it was getting the horse down that was the trouble. She called us, the Indian boy and myself, and we had to do that. Down twenty-five marble steps. She stood at the top shouting at us

'Mind the pictures'." "I suppose there was an explosion there, too, Harry?" "No ma'am, but there were butterflies as large as plates flying to the air, enough to knock you down" . . . "Harry", said the old lady one day, "you're as big a liar as my sister's husband used to be."

In his turn, Harry will humour the old lady's extravaganzas: the two partners are always perfectly receptive, without, however, becoming what we have called "soul mates".

The third type of interlocutor is very different from the preceding ones; this interlocutor presents no ambiguity and is easily spotted: he is the "beloved foe" type. But the relationships between the heroes and the so-called enemies who bewitch them are complex. Confronted with his "beloved foe", the hero is torn between what he feels to be a lucid and justified hatred and a sudden, irrepressible love. Thus the clergyman Lewis, in **"The Voice"**, who used to consider Morgan, the defrocked priest, as "the nearest human thing to the devil", suddenly decides, when he learns that Morgan is buried under the rubble at the bottom of a bomb hole, to risk his life to save him. However, until the end of his trying experience, Lewis keeps persuading himself that it is only Morgan's voice that is dear to him:

> "Morgan", they heard him call. "It's Lewis. We're coming. Can you hear?" He shouted for an axe and presently they heard him smashing with it. He was scratching like a dog or a rabbit. A voice like that to have stopped, to have gone! Lewis was thinking. How unbearable this silence was. A beautiful proud voice, the voice of a man, a voice like a tree, the soul of a man spreading in the air like the cedars of Lebanon.

That very voice, it is true, will at last reveal to Lewis the love which binds him to Morgan.

Some characters find several "beloved foes" in the course of their adventures, like Peacock, in **"The Fall"**, who plays the clown for their benefit. Others find several types of interlocutors, like the sailor, in the story which bears his name, who finds both a "receptacle"—his employer—and a "beloved foe"—a colonel's daughter, with whom he gets drunk, yielding to one of his innumerable and obsessive temptations.

Does their attraction for a "beloved foe" cure Pritchett's heroes of their loneliness? Do they find in this strange kind of brotherhood a reason for living and loving? Indeed, the "beloved foes" do not hate the heroes: they are foes only in the latter's eyes. The colonel's daughter has no intention of destroying the sailor, nor Morgan of dragging Lewis to hell, nor Peacock's acquaintances of deriding his family. But the conviction that one, or several individuals want to harm them give the heroes the feeling that they really exist. Thus they manifest a strange mixture of hate and gratefulness to their so-called enemies. The only exception to the rule is the young tramp in **"Main Road"**, whose hatred for his companion remains as unmitigated as it is compulsive: "First of all the younger man had begun hating him because he always got ahead. Then he hated his back and his figure and his ridiculous top-heavy

way of walking on his toes. He hated him because, in the intolerable space and emptiness of the country and of the sky, it was necessary to hate someone". The hero finds no security, no rewarding feature in his hatred; he is unable, and unwilling, to sublimate it, he will be dominated by it to the point of being tempted, after a first crime, to commit a much more serious one: "Food! He looked at the old man with contempt. What he wanted, his tortured hating soul cried out within him, was not food".

Everything would be simple—though, perhaps, less interesting—if the characters whom we have called the "interlocutors" of the heroes were not also tormented beings, in search themselves of a "soul mate", a "receptacle" or a "beloved foe". It is sometimes difficult to detect which of the interlocutors is the main character; is it Rogers or Pocock who is the hero in **"Pocock Passes"**, Mrs Johnson or Mr Armitage in **"Blind Love"**, Chatty or Magnolia in **"The Chain Smoker"**, Uncle Belton, or Phillimore in **"It May Never Happen"**, Harry or Miss Randall in **"The Liars"** etc.? The maintaining of an acute intensity of interest together with a great mobility of focalisation is a feat which Pritchett performs and the feat is all the more remarkable as his short stories are so often centred on inner adventures—adventures of a soul—rather than on spectacular eventful moments of life. As far as the possibility of there being several heroes is concerned, we can suggest that one of them generally proves more heroic than the others, for he is ready to undergo, or does undergo the ultimate consequence of his originality, that is the ultimate solitude—death.

It is precisely from the discrepancy between the hero's and his interlocutor's nature and search of a partner that the adventure originates in most of Pritchett's stories. The best example of this can again be found in **"Pocock Passes"**. In this story, two explosions occur. The first one, as we have seen, when Rogers comes across Pocock, whom he immediately considers as his "soul mate"; the second one, when Rogers discovers, together with the reader, that Pocock, when alive, was different from what he seemed to be and that he was not, like Rogers, in search of a "soul mate" but of a "receptacle". The adventure proper is the series of events which take place between the two explosions and particularly which provoke the second one, for between the impact of the two obese men's first meeting and the greater impact of the image of Pocock as it suddenly appears to Rogers, small shocks keep us breathless and increase the acuteness of the suspense. This "explosive" structure can be found in most of Pritchett's dramatic stories, like **"The Sailor"**, **"When My Girl Comes Home"**, **"The Two Brothers"**, **"The Scapegoat"**, **"It May Never Happen"** etc. The series of explosions lead either to a fatal misunderstanding, a final blow from life, or to a blissful self-liberation, a fulfilling sense of brotherhood. The structural variations lie in the importance of the main explosion(s) and mostly, when there are more than one, of the last one, which can provoke the death of a character, as in **"The Two Brothers"**, **"The Scapegoat"** or, on the contrary, bring about his happiness, as in **"The Voice"**.

It is not only human beings who strive for self-expression in Pritchett's stories: houses also have a compulsive individuality. They emit smells, like that of fresh paint or leather (the latter obviously a reminiscence of the author's personal experience). They wait for the slightest sign of recognition; the heroine of **"The Wheelbarrow"** comes, for the last time, to tidy up the house where she spent all her youth and which she believed, wrongly, soulless: "The house, so anonymous, so absurd, so meaningless and ghostless, had suddenly got her".

As the adventure, in Pritchett's stories, arises from a meeting which has a momentous impact on the characters, it is normal that the latter should try to look their best, or their most appealing at the moment of their encounter with the interlocutors who attract them; the duality between the real nature and the appearance of those characters is always underlined by Pritchett, mostly in his description of faces:

> The son noticed for the first time that like all big-faced men his father had two faces. There was the outer face like a soft warm and careless daub of innocent sealing wax and inside it, as if thumbed there by a seal, was a much smaller one, babyish, shrewd, scared and hard . . . Suddenly the father smiled and the little face was drowned in a warm flood of triumphant smiles from the bigger face.

The character's eyes can provoke a shock that was not always sought for nor expected: "There are glances that are collisions, scattering the air between like glass". But eyes also express a character's duality: "By nature Dr. Ray was a man of disguises and a new one with every sentence . . . If shrewdness was in one blue eye as sharp as a pellet, the other became watery with anxiety"—this image is scarcely believable if we take the description literally, but how expressive it becomes if we don't consider the message in each eye separately, but the look in the man's eyes as a whole . . .

It is perhaps the human voice, to which Pritchett is particularly sensitive, that best expresses the dual character of anyone:

> Effie has two voices and two kinds of laughter. Her usual voice is small and sweet—the matter-of-fact voice of a girl of five, and she uses it for things that are true. The laughter that goes with it is the high squeal that used to enchant us when she was little . . . her other voice is dry, abrupt, grown up, bold and mannish, and it drops to short, doggish barks of laughter. In this voice, Effie does not always tell the truth.

The way the characters walk is also significant:

> [Mrs Brackett] had a real liar's walk. It was her body that told the lies—I mean the way she walked, how her hips moved and her arms. Her tongue, I must say, usually told the truth. If it didn't, her head gave that shake to warn you she was going to try something on. That was why people who spread stories about her really liked her.

It happens nevertheless that the duality inherent in a character is not due to his desire to appear different from what he is, but is an innate feature, as innate as the terrible birth mark, the "great spreading ragged liver-coloured island of skin" on Mrs Johnson's breast in **"Blind Love"**; it sets her afire with lust, but her virtue is as ingrained as her birthmark is:

> It was a war with the inhabitant of the ragged island on her body. That creature craved for the furtive, for the hand that slipped under a skirt, for the scuffle in the back seat of a car, for a five-minute disappearance into a locked office. But the other Mrs Johnson, the cheerful one, was virtuous.

Strangely enough, the protean possibilities of Pritchett's characters make them not only true to life but true to themselves; whether in compliance with their nature or from the need to find an interlocutor (but are we not all naturally, from childhood or even from birth, in need of an interlocutor?) Pritchett's men and women are liars. But they are convincing, endearing liars. And is not the liar as a type a wonderful subject for a short story-writer? He offers him the occasion to tell, not one story, but many stories, with or without variants, within the framework of one. Indeed it is not only through their appearance but also through their speech that Pritchett's characters win over the interlocutors of their choice; this speech conforms to two requirements: the first is the economy inherent in the short story as a genre, the second is the economy imposed on the characters by their very search: they cannot afford to betray themselves, yet they must say enough to satisfy their craving and show they are worthy of interest. This makes their speech both pathetic and revealing; we shall quote once again Pocock and Rogers, these two true wonders:

> "Been having trouble with my foot", said Mr Pocock defiantly at Rogers. "It's the weight you carry", said Rogers.
>
> "I get it myself." Mr Pocock, as one heavy drinker to another, appreciated the tact of that lie.
>
> "I keep clear of doctors, old boy", said Mr Pocock. "Always have."
>
> "They cut you down", said Rogers, emptying his glass.
>
> "All wrong, old boy", said Mr Pocock. "Want to kill you."

Those two beings grope for each other, desire each other like lovers, with a mixture of daring and doubt. Their explosive meeting brings about the strongest but most delicate catharsis. (pp. 67-74)

> *Claire Larriere, "Explosions and Catharses," in* Journal of the Short Story in English, *No. 6, Spring, 1986, pp. 67-74.*

Cécile Oumhani   (essay date 1986)

[*In the essay below, Oumhani examines the recurring motif of water in Pritchett's short stories.*]

Speaking of his art, Pritchett says he is interested in those moments when the "inner life exposes itself unguardedly".

And indeed his short stories are mostly centered on a process of revelation through which a character appears under a new light. This preoccupation with revealing is to be felt in patterns of events and images that recur in a number of his short stories and highlight significant aspects of Pritchett's writing.

In several short stories, Pritchett's characters either fall or dive into the water and this experience marks a turning-point at which their inner nature becomes perceivable. Moreover this is generally followed by noticeable transformations in their relationship with other characters. Nakedness, as well as water, seems to play an important part in bringing to the fore a character's hidden life. It must also be said that the characters who are to encounter that plunge into the water all have in common a comparative degree of immaturity. Furthermore each sequence of events has a recognizable organisation.

The narrator of **"The Diver"** looks back on an early period of his life when he was considered innocent and foolish by his colleagues in the Paris office where he used to work. He recalls: "a sheet of glass seemed to come down between me and any female I saw". He not only suffered from a sexual block but also felt hindered from writing, which was what he wanted to do. His whole life was held back by those two obstacles which he could not overcome, until he accidentally fell into the river. He had been supervising the rescue of a cargo that had sunk into the water with a barge when the incident happened: "I crashed into cold darkness, water was running up my legs swallowing me". The fall into the water is associated with animals, through the appearance of the diver who had been hired to rescue the cargo and whom the narrator had been watching too closely when he fell. The diver is described as looking "like a swollen frog". The skins contained in the barge, which the diver was busy bringing up, are actually parts of animals, and the shape they take when hung to dry on poles, is said to evoke both animals and human beings: "It was like hanging up drowned animals—even, I thought, human beings". The diver, looking like an animal, and the skins associate human beings and animals. It is as if the narrator were recovering a part of himself that had remained repressed before, as if he were recognizing a more instinctive aspect of his nature, after his plunge into darker regions, symbolized by water.

His narrow escape immediately arouses admiration and concern among those who had mercilessly mocked him. Great stress is laid on the dangers he has faced and not quite staved off yet. Madame Chamson is worried: "You'll catch pneumonia", she said. And to Claudel: "You ought to have kept an eye on him. He might have drowned". Until that day, she had more or less ignored him but, on this occasion, she takes him to her shop to change clothes. He has to undress in front of her and stay naked while she fetches some dry clothes for him. After he finally manages to tell her a story he has invented, he is sexually initiated by her, thus doing away with his two problems: coming into contact with women and finding words to write. The fall into the water has been a liberation for the narrator and has allowed his personality to reveal itself in a dynamic way. Not only is it revealed to the reader but this also marks a shift in the narrator's position in the story. His relationships are altered and as the story finishes, the reader feels another perspective is opened up, where the narrator is placed in a leading position. Those who laughed at him or ignored him are awed and Madame Chamson confides: "I am afraid of that young Englishman. Have you seen his hands?"

The immersion into the water not only reveals the narrator but involves him in a process of initiation. The man in the bar where he is drinking rum after his rescue jokes about the four elements: "One moment he was on dry land, the next he was flying in the air, then plonk in the water. Three elements", said Claudel. "Only fire is missing", said the barman. This corresponds to the order in which the four elements are introduced when they symbolize the necessary stages towards initiation in Masonic rituals. The death connotation of the fall into the water constitutes another aspect in an initiation ritual. The death the narrator has escaped from is initiatory and has been instrumental in the disappearance of an old self and the emergence of a new one. The water itself appears as an element which is not altogether pure and reassuring, as strange animal-shapes come out of it. It seems rather to bring to light the darker regions of the self, where the character's instincts have been lurking, before the initiatory fall allows them to express themselves and alter the narrator's position in the story.

"The Rescue" deals with the same sort of transformation as **"The Diver"**. The narrator is a young girl whose mother is heavily involved in politics and various local activities. This has led her to bring home the persons she needs to help her. The latest recruit is Ellis, who spends his time admiring her: "he sat . . . gazing at Mother, worshipping her". He is caught up in a relation towards a mother-figure. Besides he is obviously hampered by sexual blocks and assumes a very puritanical attitude: "If I had my way, I would pass a law making adultery illegal. If a man or a woman committed it, they would be brought to the courts, fined two hundred pounds and imprisoned for two years". This hint of a recoil from sexual relations is reminiscent of the narrator of **"The Diver"**, who felt unable to speak to a woman. As if he refused to look inside himself and admit his potential nakedness, Ellis is persistently over-dressed: "In this hot weather he wore a thick suit, a waistcoat and woollen socks". Ellis is an immature character who, as a man, still has a passive and childish relation to his mother. Like the narrator of **"The Diver"**, he is laughed at because the uneven development of his personality makes him look awkward and ridiculous.

The narrator's mother has asked him to take part in the opening of a lido in a park. Crowds of people are in the water at the same time as Ellis, the narrator and her mother who is wearing an old-fashioned swimsuit. Soon after they have waded into the water, the narrator realizes her mother is drowning. Ellis who had already walked out, catches sight of her and steps in again just in time to save her. After she has come to, she is furious with the "horrible little man" with his arms around her and firmly denies that Ellis could be the person who rescued her. Death is strongly evoked, as the mother sinks, unconscious in the water. The ensuing commotion with people's comments on the "drowning woman" further accentuates this impression. She is described in words that suggest an animal-like creature: "She looked so slimy and wet and swollen in the face".

Stress has been laid on the mother's old-fashioned swimsuit and the feeling of shame it aroused in her daughter. The seminakedness of the mother is made to appear ugly through her swimsuit. Thus the fact that Ellis belongs to the narrator's generation and not to her mother's is indirectly pointed out. The overdressed Ellis is put in a situation in which he cannot but see his own partial nakedness as well as the mother's in her ugly swimsuit. Furthermore the circumstances have led her to a desperate need of help and Ellis has been drawn into taking action. Going into the water to save her finally makes him aware of a flaw in the object of his admiration. Interestingly enough the narrator in **"The Diver"** fell as he was *watching* the diver with his animal-like appearance. Ellis is made to *see* the mother as he goes into the water. Seeing is an important aspect of the experience of the water.

The episode brings about a decisive shift in Ellis's attitude towards the mother. Acting instead of worshipping has given him independence and shattered any possibility of pursuing a submissive relation. The mother-figure has symbolically drowned that evening in the lido, thus allowing Ellis to emerge as a full-grown man. He subsequently leaves the mother's house, soon followed by her daughter, who starts kissing him. Ellis is then compared to an animal: "We walked on and suddenly Ellis gave a peculiar jump, like a frog". They go to the park together and are then described by the narrator as if they were going under water: "The sky was like pink water above us and we were sinking, sinking, sinking". Once more water is linked to the sexual lives of the characters. Quite significantly the story ends on these words: "I taught him to swim that summer". The narrator suggests that she completed Ellis's sexual initiation, so that Ellis has gone through the same sort of experience as the narrator of **"The Diver"** who was initiated by Madame Chamson.

The story itself is structured on the same dynamic pattern: going into the water markedly alters the position of Ellis as a submissive, ridiculous character. The transformation places him, at the end of the story, in a totally different position and the ending opens up the perspective of a status of independence and maturity for Ellis. The motif of immersion ultimately appears as a rite of passage into adulthood, with initiation following Ellis's estrangement from the mother-figure.

At first sight **"Blind Love"** somewhat differs from **"The Diver"** and **"The Rescue"**, in so far as the characters who fall into water are much older than either the narrator of **"The Diver"** or Ellis. Armitage has been blind for twenty years and has to rely on the help of a housekeeper and secretary, Mrs Johnson. In spite of his handicap and owing to a highly elaborate organisation of his surroundings, he has kept up his legal business. In fact "law" is a word which does not only apply to his profession but to all the details of his everyday life: "They lived under fixed laws: no chair or table, even no ashtray must be moved. Every-

thing must be in its place". His blindness has led him to force a rigid framework onto the people and the objects around him. Armitage's infirmity not only implies a difficult and specific relation to the outside world but has also been the cause of the failure of his marriage, as his wife left him when he became blind. This inability to *see* brings to mind the narrator of **"The Diver"** changing because he *watched* the diver too closely.

Mrs Johnson is also plagued by a physical problem, which has brought about the end of a short-lived marriage. She has a terrible birthmark which stretches "from the neck over the left shoulder down to the breast and below". If Armitage's problem is not being able to see, hers lies in having to conceal and live with a secret. Both characters, although middle-aged, still have something in common with the narrator of **"The Diver"** and Ellis: they are incomplete, in the sense that they have been unable to achieve a fulfilled, balanced relationship in their first marriage. They both lack the experience of a mature, satisfactory love relationship.

In the third year of Mrs Johnson's presence in the house, Armitage takes a walk in the garden, when suddenly a rabbit and a dog rushing past him make him stumble and fall into the ice-covered swimming-pool. Mrs Johnson sees him fall "full length through the ice of the pool". The gardener helps him out and Mrs Johnson soon expresses her concern: "Towel", she cried. "Get it all off. You'll catch pneumonia". As in the other stories the idea of danger is underlined. Armitage resents Mrs Johnson's interference, her taking out clothes for him from the drawers and putting them on the bed have upset the "laws" and left him helpless. Only because everything was in its place could he find his way about the house. Her well-meaning gesture has only swept away his personal landmarks. His rage is compared to an animal's: "Half-naked to the waist, hairy on the chest and arms, he shocked because the rage seemed to be not in his mind but in his body like an animal's. The rage had the pathos of an animal's". That very evening he calls Mrs Johnson to his room, under the pretence that water has got into his watch, and sleeps with her. Once more the fall into the water is followed by a change in sexual attitudes.

The pattern of events and images is very similar to those described earlier. Ice is broken, physically and symbolically too. The rigidity Armitage had imposed on himself and others breaks at the same time as the ice that covered the swimming-pool. The image of the ice recalls the "sheet of glass" the narrator of **"The Diver"** felt between himself and women. It is also reminiscent of Ellis's wish to jail adulterers and thus separate them by walls. The ice, besides, suggests that, until it is broken, Armitage has repressed his sexual impulses. The fact that Mrs Johnson's helpfulness should upset him so much means that her presence as a woman has shattered the framework he had protected himself with until then. His fall into the water dramatically unmasks what he had doggedly tried to conceal and ignore. He is compelled to take off his clothes and is unwittingly prevented from finding others by Mrs Johnson. This first immersion motif has a strongly dynamic impact as it brings about an important shift in the two characters' relationship.

But this is only the first turning-point in the story, as tension gradually builds up for two reasons. Armitage is tormented by a mounting jealousy of the men who *saw* Helen Johnson. On her part she is obsessed by her birthmark and cannot bring herself to tell him about it and thus make him *see* it. Even though the ice has been broken, the process of revelation has not been completed yet and the crux of the problem is still seeing. Armitage starts going to a faith-healer, in the hope that he will recover his eyesight. Smith, the faith-healer, discovers Mrs Johnson's secret as he sees her in a swimsuit near the pool. Haunted by the idea that he may or may not have mentioned the birthmark to Armitage, she is eventually brought to the point of breaking down. After an outburst in which she tells Armitage about her secret, she walks out of the house and falls into the pool. As she is brought out of the water, an animal is mentioned: "A jeering bird flew up". The faith-healer is the indirect cause of this second immersion after which Armitage and Mrs Johnson are both healed. After telling Armitage about the birthmark, Mrs Johnson is cleansed of her obsessions in the water. Her problem was revealing, *letting* him *see;* Armitage's was *seeing*. After he is made to see the terrible mark, "which was like a ragged liver in a butcher's window", tension is at last released. Recognizing the partial ugliness of the object of his love is the condition of the fulfilment of their relation. His marriage had failed because of his blindness, his relationship with Helen Johnson becomes satisfactory after he has "seen". Only because she revealed her secret can she succeed in what she failed in at an earlier point of her life. The second fall has the same dynamic impact as the first, as it alters the relation of the two characters in a significant way. They finally reach a further stage in their maturity and the story ends with the opening up of a new perspective as they travel together in Italy.

"On the Edge of the Cliff " belongs to a different category of stories where the immersion motif neither alters the patterns of relationships nor indicates any maturing process. In this case the focus is more on the revelation of a character to the reader and the perspective in which the character is placed remains static. Harry, the central character in **"On the Edge of the Cliff "** is an elderly man living with a twenty-five year old girl. He has always been a womanizer and has spent his life collecting both flowers and women. The names of the women around him humorously underline the idea that he has always put them on the same plane as flowers: his wife was called Violet, the woman who played a mysterious part at some point of his life is Daisy, the girl is called Rowena, which is reminiscent of "rowan". When walking in the country, he keeps identifying birds and plants. He seems to entertain a passionate relation with nature: "He stopped impatiently to show her some small cushioned plant or stood on the cliff 's edge, like a prophet, pointing down to the falls of rock, the canyons . . . ". The word mania is even used to refer to his taste for the walk on the edge of the cliff: "He had a kind of mania about the Hole". His attitude towards nature is complex, as knowing about nature is for him a means of gaining a form of power. Rowena is afraid

of the Hole, but he overcomes any fear through his knowledge: "The place terrified Rowena and she held back, but he stumbled through the rough grasses to the edge, calling back bits of geology and navigation". The more he knows about the world around him, the better he can resist the anxiety passing time and approaching death inspire in him. In front of the Hole that fascinates him, he feels like saying to Rowena: "At my age one is always thinking about death".

The whole story revolves on the issues of telling the truth or pretending, seeing or not seeing. Harry's inability to come to terms with passing time reveals a degree of immaturity and makes him similar to the characters in the preceding stories. However it is the corollary self-deception which is brought to the foreground, rather than the question of Harry's maturity. His relation with a young girl imposes a particular code on both of them: "There are rules for old men who are in love with young girls, all the stricter when the young girls are in love with them. It has to be played as a game". In order to live up to the image he wants to give of himself, he cannot obey his impulses and tell Rowena what is on his mind. As far as the relation of the two characters is concerned, everything is ruled by the necessity of pretending. Once Harry's inner thoughts are envisaged it becomes obvious that their course is determined by self-deception. Significantly the story opens with these words:

> The sea-fog began to lift towards noon. It had been blowing in, thin and loose for two days, smudging the tops of the trees up the ravine where the house stood. "Like the cold breath of old men", Rowena wrote in an attempt at a poem, but changed the line, out of kindness to the "breath of ghosts", because Harry might take it personally.

The association of the sea-fog masking the scenery with the breath of old men hints at Harry's self-delusion.

Just before the dive into the sea, Harry takes Rowena to the fair, where she insists on having a go on the roundabout. His attention is drawn to a woman waving to "an idiotic young man riding backwards on a cow". She turns out to be Daisy, a fifty-year old woman, whom he thinks looks much younger. His inability to estimate her real age matches his own incapacity to see within himself. He feels very uncomfortable about meeting Daisy again, as her presence brings back unpleasant memories that will not be explained in great detail except by innuendo, even later on in the story. After the scene at the fair, Harry and Rowena start off for a walk on the cliff. Once they have come near the Hole, Rowena recalls that Harry used to bathe just round the corner with his wife and friends among whom was Daisy Pyke. She subsequently expresses the desire to swim too, but soon recoils from the ice-cold water. To her surprise Harry undresses and dives into the water, causing her some anxiety: "You're not to! It will kill you! Your heart!". When he comes out, he is compared to an animal: "he came crawling in like some ugly hairy sea-animal, his skin reddened with cold, and stood dripping with his arms wide as if he was going to give a howl". After his swim Harry is tormented: "he had broken one of his rules for old men. For the first time he had let her see him naked".

Rowena's attitude towards Harry changes after the episode: "He was astounded when she came into his room and got into his bed: she had not done this before. 'I've come to see the Ancient Mariner,' she said". As in the previous stories the immersion is accompanied by a modification of the sexual behaviour of the characters.

However, in the present case, the relationship is not essentially altered and the immersion motif is more significant as regards the process of revelation and the question of self-deception. This is clearly suggested by Rowena's address to Harry as the "Ancient Mariner". The immersion motif is soon followed by Daisy's call on Harry while Rowena is in town. To his surprise Harry hears that the "ridiculous young man" at the fair is not Daisy's son but her lover. This revelation casts a new light on the scene at the fair, which thus turns out to be the reflection in a mirror of Harry's own situation. He proves to be able to grasp its implications only when others than himself are concerned. Daisy's visit after the swim at Withy Hole appears as a further look in the heart of Harry and Rowena's relation. But it is an oblique look given through what Daisy says of her own relation with the young man and what she gathers about Harry and Rowena from her parallel experience. She pinpoints the self-delusion underlying their respective loves for much younger partners than themselves. She finally asks Harry not to meet again because their meeting would inevitably bring Rowena and Stephen together: "I know what would happen and so do you and I don't want to *see* it happen". She insists on the word *see* which is repeated later on: "I know it can't last", she said. "And you know it can't. But I don't want you to see it happen". At the beginning of the story, the fog masking the top of the trees is compared to the breath of old men, hinting at Harry's self-delusion. As the story unfolds the immersion motif definitely appears as inscribed in a process of revelation which is completed after Daisy's visit. The narrative technique provides the revelation through a reflection of Harry in another character who is more lucid at least in her speech. First the meeting at the fair with Rowena riding a giraffe and Stephen a cow introduces the ironical hint of children with a parent waiting for each of them at the side. Then after the swim at Withy Hole, Daisy's statements are revealingly reflected in Harry's mind as he thinks of the "little liar" whose favourite word used to be "honesty". Harry refuses to see things as they are and is forever engaged in a battle against time. The dive into the water will not alter him in any way and it is only part of a revealing process.

The ending of the story is quite different from the previous cases: nothing has changed in the game Rowena and Harry are playing. He mentions Daisy's visit as she returns and tells her that Stephen is not Daisy's son but her lover. Rowena replies: " 'You can't mean that', she said, putting on a very proper air. 'She's old enough—' but she stopped, and instead of giving him one of her light hugs, she rumpled his hair". The discrepancy already existing at the opening of the story between what they felt like saying but actually said continues at the end. The swim has had no dynamic impact on the existing patterns of relationship. The characters are shut in a static dimension and the end of the story is closed as the game that ruled their

relation at the beginning of the story is carried on as it ends. The dynamic element has been shifted to the relation between narration and reader. Harry's nakedness has not been revealed to himself or Rowena but to the reader who is shown a character "always thinking about death" who cannot come to terms with passing time.

"Handsome Is as Handsome Does" has a lot in common with **"On the Edge of the Cliff"** from the point of view of its structure. No new relationship pattern emerges among the characters after the immersion motif. On the other hand this motif allows the secret nature of a character to be unveiled to the reader. The Corams are on holiday in the South of France in a sea-side resort. They are presented as "an ugly pair". Coram rejects the people, the landscape around him, because they do not fit in with his limited experience of life. He keeps repeating that the proprietor of the hotel is a "fraud". Even "the Mediterranean was a fraud". From the start Coram refuses to see things as they are. Mrs Coram does not resist the changes that are subtly induced in her by her new surroundings and is gradually led to a crisis. She feels attracted to a young Jew they have just met. She has no children and Alex strikes her as being about the age of her son if she had had one: "Do you realize", she said, "we're nearly old enough to be his parents?". Being childless is a source of frustration to Mrs Coram and this gap in her experience recalls the incompleteness of the characters in the previous stories. Alex exerts a two-sided attraction on her, as he embodies the son she never had and is also a handsome young man as opposed to her ugly husband. The whole story is marked by the presence of water, as long parts of it are set on the beach. The partial nakedness of the characters beside the sea creates the necessary scene for a revelation which concerns deep-rooted aspects of the central character. It is on the beach that she becomes aware of Alex's handsome body, as he undresses to go into the water. The scene brings together Alex and Coram, at a short interval, in the same situation and Alex's handsomeness is negatively reflected and enhanced by Coram's own awkward and unattractive appearance. The technique, which recalls the reflections in **"On the Edge of the Cliff"**, obliquely foregrounds Mrs Coram's growing attraction to Alex. When he "came out of the water he seemed to be dry at once, as if some oil were in his skin", and this calls back the animal imagery accompanying immersion. Through this first and outwardly uneventful swim, Mrs Coram becomes conscious of a transformation within her. The first immersion in **"Handsome Is as Handsome Does"** triggers off a modification in the central character's sexual emotions. As Alex comes out of the water and asks her a question, Mrs Coram "was astonished by the pleasure it gave her".

Only with the second immersion does the story reach its climax. The Corams have gone to the beach with Monsieur Pierre, the proprietor of the hotel and Alex. Pierre's appearance is characterized by a mixture of masculine and feminine elements: "He had the hips of a woman". From the beginning Coram has been strongly prejudiced against him, as if there existed a secret rivalry between them. He maintains that Pierre cannot swim and only goes to the beach "to look at the women". Even when he is swimming, Coram claims he is not: " 'He's floating', said Tom. 'He's swimming', she said". Furthermore Monsieur Pierre makes statements which give women a supreme power, a right to be granted what they want: "Red wine or white? The wishes of women are the wishes of God". This remark is significantly made soon after Mrs Coram has had a distressing scene with her husband: "I want a child, Tom. What are we going to do? I must have a child". All this hints at the fact that Coram recognizes in Pierre a counterimage of himself he must therefore reject. Given the sexual connotations of swimming in the other stories, denying that Pierre can swim appears as a way of refusing his own incapacity to have a child.

Monsieur Pierre has gone into the water just before the story comes to its climax. Mrs Coram walks on the beach and her mood is attuned to the state of the sea, the description of the water enhancing her inner turmoil. A link is definitely established between her and the water, suggesting that what will happen next really concerns her: "the mounting chaos of the sea was like the confusion of her heart". Then she walks up with her husband to a promontory where they get a view which is very similar to Withy Hole in **"On the Edge of the Cliff"**: "the place was like a wide gulping mouth with jagged teeth". Both Mr and Mrs Coram "stood near together looking down at the hole with wonder and fear". Like Harry they face an image of water, evocative of passing time and death. Strikingly enough when water not only alludes to sexual attitudes, but also refers to human destiny, the scenes are no longer set near a river or a pool and a powerful sea-imagery comes into play. Didn't Mr Coram say to his wife that their childlessness "seemed to be the burden of their isolated lives"? Then as they stand, awed by the sea, Mrs Coram realizes Pierre is drifting towards a dangerous part of the coast. Coram refuses to dive in to save him. Only Alex goes to his rescue. The water is compared to an animal: "She saw a wave rise slowly like an animal just behind Pierre". Death is also present as the characters mention it several times. Pierre says: "That [. . .] is the second time I have looked death in the face". However the motif is enriched by the image of paternity lying behind Pierre's rescue by Alex. The two men are associated in Mrs Coram's mind, as if in a father-son relationship: "Two unconcerned men, making no fuss, one old and one young: Pierre and the Jew". Only a son can in a way rescue his father from the total annihilation of death. The Corams have no one to protect them from the threatening hole they are watching from the promontory.

Mrs Coram's crisis cannot be reduced to her physical attraction to Alex, as it is grounded in her deep-seated frustration at not having any children, a situation she indirectly blames her husband for: "Tom!" she said. "I shall have a child by someone else". The dive into the water reveals Mrs Coram in surroundings that have momentarily upset her usual attitudes. Soon after the rescue her sexual behaviour changes, and she walks into Alex's room, thus taking steps to put her inner fantasies into practice. She undresses in his presence and then has to face his astonishment and embarrassment. Worse the awareness that there is no desire inside her forces itself upon her with an ensuing feeling of shame. The crisis has not enabled Mrs

Coram to alter her position and relationships in any decisive way. In the end it only enhances her likeness to her husband. The same evening she tells English guests at the hotel how her husband rescued Pierre as he was drowning. The end of the story is closed and does not open up any perspective: "The Corams against the world". As in **"On the Edge of the Cliff"** the dive into the water is part of a revealing process through which the reader is shown the inner life of a character, without any prospect of change, as she and her husband remain enclosed in a static perspective.

"The Saint" is structured on a hybrid pattern and contains both static and dynamic elements, each corresponding to a particular character. The narrator recalls the incidents that brought about the loss of his religious faith. He was seventeen years old at the time and his family belonged to a sect which denied the existence of evil:

> We regarded it as "Error"—our name for Evil— to believe the evidence of our senses, and if we had influenza or consumption, or had lost our money or were unemployed, we denied the reality of these things, saying that since God could not have made them they therefore did not exist.

Gradually doubt creeps in and the narrator starts questioning his family's faith until Mr Timberlake, a very important figure in the sect, calls on them and takes him out for "a quiet talk". They go to the river and Timberlake insists on punting himself. Timberlake's outlook on life in its most day-to-day details is coloured by his belief that evil is only error. From the outset he appears to be one of those characters whose maturity is incomplete. However at that stage of the story, the narrator is also immature. The boy warns him against the branches of the weeping willows at the side. Humorously their existence as weeping willows is called in doubt by Timberlake: "Weeping willows—I'll give you a thought there. How Error likes to make us dwell on sorrow. Why not call them *laughing* willows?" Then he loses his balance and remains hanging to a branch above the water, after the boat has drifted on. Before the narrator can reach him, he sinks into the water with all his clothes on. The boy is immediately concerned about him: "Let me wring out your coat and waistcoat. You'll catch your death—". But he stops as he realizes that it is impossible for Timberlake to acknowledge the truth of the incident. Consistent with his belief, he refuses to take off his drenched clothes or admit anything has happened. He is not transformed by his fall in any way, and has only been revealed by it. On the other hand the episode marks a change in the boy. As Timberlake inevitably sinks, he is struck by the significance of the event: "It was at this moment I realized that the final revelation about man and society on earth had come to nobody and that Mr Timberlake knew nothing at all about the origin of evil". The boy is baptized into a new awareness through Timberlake's immersion. As the short story unfolds, he becomes more and more conscious of Timberlake's inadequacy and his estrangement from nature: "He was totally uninterested. By his questions—what is that church? Are there any fish in this river? Is that a wireless or a gramophone?—I understood that Mr Timberlake was formally acknowledging a world he did not live in". His faith in the sect hampers him from relating to the outside world. Symbolically his clothes become a hindrance to his movements: "Bunched in swollen clothes, he refused to take them off ". His obstinacy recalls Ellis's refusal to take off some of his clothes, in spite of the heat. Timberlake deliberately remains self-deluded. No prospect of change is opened to him and the story ends with the circumstances of his death, after a heart-attack, and the reflections it inspires in the narrator. Timberlake is shut in a static perspective, where he is revealed with no possibility of reaching a further stage in his maturity. If the end is closed for him, the narrator has been transformed by the fall which has a dynamic impact on him and allows him to move away from the sect and form his own ideas about life.

Pritchett's use of a motif of immersion in several short stories helps to understand some aspects of his writing. As has been shown, this motif consists of a recurrent pattern of imagery bringing together a series of elements: death, animal-like characteristics, nakedness and sex. It seems that by plunging his characters into water, Pritchett seeks to bring their primal dimension into sharp relief. He is concerned with their inner self and in his stories the perspective in depth is accentuated. Strikingly enough they are set in one place and the characters are not shown when travelling. The alterations that occur in them do not take place after they have covered a distance in time or in space. As it were the horizontal span of the story is not significant. On the other hand the changes correspond to a bringing into light or to the surface of the already existing features of a character. Pritchett's preoccupation is the underlying plane in his characters. It seems the surface of the water is a borderline separating the darker subconscious region from the diurnal one. His stories are set in one place because their movement aims at revealing the hidden face of an ever extant reality. It is not surprising that Pritchett should have been influenced by Freud, as has often been pointed out. The reversal of a two-sided reality that is brought into play either is a revelation to the reader or gives a character a new balance, altering his previous position in the story.

Pritchett considers his characters coherent entities that can be explored by lifting the layer of their outer self to reach their inner life. When compared with Modernist short story writers, his outlook appears very different. In Modernist short stories writers are in search of moments when the character becomes aware of being and can briefly overcome the impression that his self is forever fragmented. Pritchett's writing does not progress towards unity; rather he starts from a given apparent unity of characters and moves towards their inner divisions. Furthermore in Modernist short stories the reader is drawn into a position of symbiosis with the consciousness of a character, thus bringing about the merging of their respective angles of perception. Pritchett on the other hand places his reader in a position of observation where he is shown the unmasking of a character. He is interested in the different facets of a character, more than in an inner life in the Modernist sense of a consciousness.

In his writing Pritchett clearly delineates a triangular perspective, where point-of-view, character and reader are distinctly positioned, so as to allow the process of revelation to be brought into action. Much more could be said about his fascinating art of revealing as he resorts, in his other short stories, to various motifs, such as the clothes motif, in order to strip his characters of their social garb. (pp. 75-90)

Cécile Oumhani, "Water in V. S. Pritchett's Art of Revealing," in Journal of the Short Story in English, *No. 6, Spring, 1986, pp. 75-91.*

Michel Pouillard   (essay date 1986)

[*In the following essay, Pouillard demonstrates that Pritchett's "The Aristocrat" can be read as a one-act play.*]

The first recorded date of publication of **"The Aristocrat"** is 1938, in V. S. Pritchett's second volume of stories entitled *You Make Your Own Life.* Since then, this now well-known story has been selected and included in several collections offering representative samples of the modern English short story. The subject of **"The Aristocrat"** is easily summarized: a stranger claiming he is an old soldier walks into a public-house, wins the confidence and sympathy of those present by doing a few conjuring-tricks, and steals the gold watch of the richest customer, Mr. Murgatroyd. There is no real plot and hardly any climax but for the discovery of the theft in the last lines. However the story forms a self-contained whole which, as I propose to show, can be read as a one-act play, obviously a comedy if only because of the central theme, the deception of gullible people by an artful scoundrel.

The whole play takes place within the closed space of a public bar, The Prince of Denmark, on whose patrons the old man will play a rotten trick, and a French reader cannot but think of one of the three unities, viz. unity of place. The extremely simple scenery is more suggested than described as Pritchett merely mentions a few elements that could be found in any bar, the counter against which the publican and Murgatroyd are leaning, the bench on which four people are sitting, and the shelf under a mirror. The atmosphere in the bar is summed up in the very first paragraph: "The usual people were on the bench in the small bar, crowded, cheerful, and comfortable". The outside world is only hinted at and characterized by "the first flakes of March snow in the street". When the old man walks into the bar, he brings in "wet points of thawed snow on his long green shabby overcoat" and when he leaves, Mrs. Pierce, the publican, watches him go away through the window and remarks that "It's snowing hard now". As Theil suggests [in his *Les nouvelles de V. S. Pritchett,* 1982], the snow outside and on the stranger's coat provokes compassion for the poor old man, but it also symbolizes the intrusion of the hostile outside world into the comfortable, secure one of the public-house. So the bar both provides an atmosphere and serves as the stage on which all the characters are gathered and where the entire action takes place.

Setting the scenery and creating the atmosphere are one of the two major functions of the first page or so that constitutes the opening scene and reads as a prologue to the play itself. The feeling of security inside the bar is largely due to the ritual aspect of the scene which is indicated and underlined in the prologue that presents the spectator with a conventional social situation repeated every Saturday afternoon in the pub. As usual "it was at two o'clock and after a good lunch that Mr. Murgatroyd went into the Prince of Denmark", "the usual people were on the bench" including "the young Jewess who was always there on Saturday afternoon". It seems they have always known each other, and after a few remarks about the weather, they start the ceremony of the rounds the order of which is perfectly settled: "It was Mr. Sanders's round". The second function of the prologue is to introduce the protagonist, Mr. Murgatroyd, and the five members of the chorus, to whom I will return later on. As in a play then, the opening scene immediately plunges the reader-spectator into an already existing world with its code and rules, and acquaints him with some of the characters, among whom one of the two main ones. And if we remember Aristotle's assumption that comedy deals with ordinary people in everyday situations, surely this world and these people belong to the realm of comedy. In the concluding scene or epilogue, also a page or so, after the old man's exit, we see the same people in the same place and postures, resuming the same ritual interrupted by the intrusion of the stranger: "It was (Mr. Murgatroyd's) round". To that extent one might speak of a circular structure but the final disclosure of the truth brings in an important difference— Murgatroyd's watch, first mentioned at the very beginning of the story, has now disappeared and the cosy, secure feeling of the prologue is ruined: "Unable to do more because of the vast heaving and of his rage, Mr. Murgatroyd looked as though he would burst".

Between the practically static prologue and epilogue there takes place the long central scene containing the action proper and characterized by movement owing to the several tricks performed by the old man. His entrance upon the stage is theatrically presented and thrown into relief by the rhetorical repetition of "It was at this moment" and by the opposition between the long sentence summing up the activities of those already present and the short, sharp one introducing the new character:

> It was at this moment when they were busy with their glasses, all talking at once, when Mr. Murgatroyd unbuttoned his new coat and was easing out his disclaiming stomach and when the Jewess gave it a tap on the fourth button, with the words: "What you got in there, Mr. Murgatroyd?"—it was at this moment that a stranger came into the bar.

Albeit one can distinguish several stages corresponding to each of the tricks, the scene is more accurately described as forming a whole because of the central presence and role of the old man and of the development of his relations with the regulars of the pub. It is noticeable that during nearly the whole scene, in which there is as much acting as dialogue, the latter are shown as spectators watching the performance of the former, the impression we have of a play being enacted before them and before us being thus reinforced. The conjurer proves to be an extremely artful

and convincing actor as well as a skilful pick-pocket. Only on a second reading do we notice the moment when he steals the watch—"He even gave Mr. Murgatroyd a tap in the ribs and said he was sorry"—, which shows how difficult it is to detect cheating, stealing, and deception. It is the old man's art as a comedian that enables him to gull his audience and modify their feelings towards him. When he enters the scene they first feel curious and uneasy but he soon manages to win their sympathy—"There was a movement of sympathy"—, their confidence—"They were ashamed of their suspicions"—, their admiration—"his fingers captivated them"—, and eventually their compassion. When the old soldier leaves, they are both ashamed of having had such good dinners and sad that he should go but realize he is "a hungry old man" and understand he must now get some food with the coppers they have just given him. The overall movement from uneasiness and suspicion to confidence and sympathetic compassion underlines their gullibility but also contributes to the unity of the long central scene. The story thus progresses linearly and logically towards the final disclosure which reverses the feelings of Mr. Murgatroyd but is hardly a surprise for the reader.

The number of actors on the stage during the whole play is relatively limited. As already suggested, five of them can be regarded as choric characters while Mr. Murgatroyd and the old man are the traditional protagonist and antagonist. The five choric actors, four women and one man, are briefly characterized by a single predominant trait or attitude; Mrs. Pierce is "leaning with her fat forearms on the bar, musing like a cat"; Mrs. Sanders is "a woman pushed to the outskirts of everything and sitting on the extreme edge of the bench". Of Mr. Sanders, the man, compared to "a house-fly in the sun", we are given a more complete though brief portrait:

> He was a dogged little man with a waxed moustache and tobacco-stained fingers, one to nudge the ladies in the ribs with his sharp elbows, a jumping cracker at three-ten a week in the provision trade. And bald.

The anonymous Jewess is slightly different from the other members of the chorus, mainly because she is the only one who does not remain sitting and motionless. Almost as soon as Murgatroyd has come into the bar, she gets up and begins "walking up and down" and she is then described as "the dancing Jewess". Moving across the room from Murgatroyd to the old man she appears as a sort of link between them. Above all, because of her anonymity, because she physically touches Murgatroyd, looks him in the eyes, and is provocative to him, she is more akin to the stranger than to the other choric characters. The latter form a chorus insofar as they constitute a social, cultural group with a communal point of view and are little more than witnesses of an action in which they are not really involved. But they are devoid of the traditional chorus' wisdom and provide no norms by which the reader-spectator might judge the action and the behaviour of the protagonist and the antagonist.

Alain Theil has already pointed out the temporary ambiguity of the title. Because of his economic and social status, especially reflected in his clothes, Murgatroyd can for a while appear as the aristocrat, but Pritchett soon makes it clear whom the title applies to when he mentions "the aristocratic curve" of the stranger's moustache and later on plainly calls him "an aristocratic old man". The irony contained in the word will be revealed only at the end when the aristocrat turns out to be a common pick-pocket. Yet the ambiguous title already associates the two main characters. Besides, neither of them belongs to the group formed by the other customers: they are either richer or poorer, they never sit with them, but stand near the bar all the time. Yet Murgatroyd remains practically motionless, "entrenched against the counter", whereas the conjurer is "a restless old man" and never stops moving and fidgeting while performing his tricks.

For, as is often the case in comedy, the characterization of the two main personages largely rests on a number of contrasts. Mr. Murgatroyd is a well-fed, fat man of few words:

> He was a shy and important man. His eloquence was in the breadth of his shoulders, in the thick pink of his face after the first drink, in the full-moon expansion of his stomach under the smooth waistcoat and in the polish of his shoes.

The old man is tall and thin and when he opens his overcoat he is "seen to be even thinner than he had at first appeared to be"; even his lips are "two thin, stiff lines" and his nose is "lean and aquiline". He is obviously poor—"his long shabby green overcoat", "his clothes were worn", "his carefully darned jacket"—when Murgatroyd is well-off as evidenced by his gold watch, his new suit of clothes, his new Trilby hat, and his car outside the pub. In spite of his status and the respect shown to him in the restricted social circle where he enjoys his Saturday afternoons, Murgatroyd is essentially shy, embarrassed, passive, and defensive whereas the poor but dignified old man is self-confident, at ease, active, and aggressive. His aggressivity is reflected in his eyes and the glances he darts at people, a point repeatedly stressed by the narrator and underlined by the adjectives and images used: "giving each one of them a fine, quick calculating stab of his eyes", "those razor-cut glances". The opposition between protagonist and antagonist is thus strongly emphasized by the narrator even before the actual confrontation begins.

Though not perfectly omniscient—he has no access whatever to the old man's mind—the narrator is constantly present, faithfully reporting what is done and said on the stage. But he is not content to record and report; like all writers of comedies he is in no way neutral but obviously biased and largely responsible for the humorous coloration of the story. On a few occasions the dialogue in itself is comic as, for instance, in the evocation of military life at the end of the central scene, or Mrs. Pierce's and Mr. Sanders's would-be witty remarks about the weather:

> "Bit of an 'eat wave isn't it, Mr. Murgatroyd?", nodding to the first flakes of March snow in the street.

To this Mr. Sanders added his news:

> "Couple of cases of sunstroke in the Theobald's Road they tell me."

The presence of Mr. Murgatroyd brought out Mr. Sanders's wit.

However the narrator's brief comment on Mr. Sanders's wit exemplifies his constant tendency to underline the laughable foibles of his characters and his humorously ironic treatment of them. I have already quoted a few sentences and images characterizing Murgatroyd and some members of the chorus; this is the first mention of Mrs. Tagg feeling uneasy after the stranger's entrance: "Mrs. Tagg jostled her various selves together within her corsets and stared". Only the old man escapes Pritchett's irony but a few remarks here and there provide the reader with clues as to his true nature; the writer thus makes mention of his "quick crafty eyes", his "faintly triumphant smile", and, an even clearer pointer, "his thin, long, clever, hungry hands".

The main butt of the narrator's irony is Mr. Murgatroyd. His physique and clothes are humorously smiled at: "the full moon expansion of his stomach", "a pair of yellow gloves drooped in one hand like the most elegant of banana-skins". The main source of comedy, though, is his attitude in front of the old conjurer, for instance when the latter asks him for a sixpence in order to do one of his tricks. First Murgatroyd suspiciously hesitates, watched by the chorus:

> The old man looked round sharply.
>
> "Have you got a sixpence?" he jerked.
>
> Mr. Murgatroyd's smile died in his soul but remained fixed on his face. He coloured. He moved his lips. He concealed a swallow. He leaned farther back against the counter. Everyone was watching the crisis in Mr. Murgatroyd.

After the trick has been successfully performed he feels he cannot take the sixpence back:

> "Oh, I must give you your sixpence," he said to Mr. Murgatroyd. But Mr. Murgatroyd recoiled. He was shamed by the sight of his coin. He thickened with generosity, his skin gleamed with admiration and the flush of his second pint. He felt he was the leader of a delegation, the master of ceremonies, the mayor of a town; but too much of a man of the world to show it crudely.

As usual in comedy Mr. Murgatroyd is the main butt for ridicule and laughter because he is the main victim of the deceiver, the more so as he is the most suspicious and defensive of all the people present in the public-house as suggested in the very first lines of the story: "Mr. Murgatroyd went into the Prince of Denmark and took his stand four-square and defensive against the bar". But if he seems able to resist the young Jewess's advances, he is of course no match for the old man. The central theme of deception, related to that of appearances and reality, is introduced by and connected with the stranger's activity as a conjurer. Ironically enough the old man twice warns his audience and the reader against tricks and deception:

"It's all a swindle. The quickness of the hand deceiving the eye and human nature," he said.

"There's a trick in everything," said the old man.

But it is proof of his successful cleverness that he can afford to do so without arousing the suspicion of his victims who do not take the hint. So deception triumphs and when Murgatroyd discovers his watch has disappeared he has the same violent and laughable reaction as any stock comic character finding out he has been duped and robbed:

> His eyes popped wide and hard, his jaw dropped. He went very pale and then flushed to the colour of a beetroot.
>
> "Here," he blurted out, starting from the counter. "My watch. It was here. I know it was. It's gone. You saw it, Mrs. Pierce. You saw me take it out. It's gone. That artful old swine has pinched my watch!"
>
> He glared at them all.
>
> "Where is he?" he shouted. "Which way did he go? Look for him! Of all the thieves . . . ".

"The Aristocrat" illustrates Claire Larrière's assertions [in a doctorate thesis] that "chez Pritchett l'aventure naît d'une rencontre" and that "la vision du monde que Pritchett exprime dans ses nouvelles est perpétuellement teintée d'humour". However, its main interest lies not so much in the rather slight subject or the fairly commonplace theme, already dealt with in so many comedies, as in the presentation of the material and the handling of the theme. Owing to such elements and characteristics as I have tried to analyse—the restricted setting, the composition of the play, the nature and characterization of the actors, and the general humorous tone—it seems to me it is no distortion or exaggeration to suggest that **"The Aristocrat"** can be seen as a highly entertaining one-act comedy that could be acted on a stage. (pp. 93-100)

> *Michel Pouillard, "V. S. Pritchett's 'The Aristocrat' as a One-Act Comedy," in* Journal of the Short Story in English, *No. 6, Spring, 1986, pp. 93-100.*

Alain Theil (essay date 1986)

[*In the essay below, Theil suggests that Pritchett successfully utilizes traditional short story elements in unconventional ways.*]

V. S. Pritchett in his short stories paints the extraordinary. He is not alone of course in doing that. What the particular (inimitable?) Pritchettian brand of storytelling offers is the extraordinary, never the extraordinary for its own sake, but the extraordinary almost, so to speak, as a matter of course. Here again we may think of all those (K. Mansfield, T. F. Powys, E. Bowen, H. E. Bates among others) who have so deftly highlighted the outlandish, slightly dazing touch in the humdrum complexion of the yearly or weekly cycle. But again Pritchett brings to it the occasional extra touch of romping heartiness that gives the blend a character totally its own.

Why is a tale like **"The Landlord"** at once so pregnant, convincing and "of this time and place", and so obviously situated outside the range of the things to which we are ready to grant our belief? One of the highly improbable features of that story is the landlord's—the main character's—obliviousness of the legal deeds that have transferred the property of the semi-detached house to a buyer; while the latter at no moment finds a way or a will to tell him that his outrageous trespassing can no longer be borne! He who answers the above question will have come quite near to defining the nature of the Pritchettian lure upon the Pritchett enthusiast.

A distinct note of unfamiliarity and oddness is provided by elements, in many of Mr Pritchett's tales, bearing a relation to the heightened effects of the stage. For one thing, the characters often bear the stamp of the actor. Their language and conduct are, in many instances, those of the stage. Ranting and posturing are not unusual with them. They strut on and swagger off, bang doors, are prone to look at themselves in mirrors and strike attitudes. When deprived of the means to perform in the flesh (as the man and woman in **"The Liars"**), they do so by proxy, by pulling the strings of the private puppet show involving people and occasions they think they remember. A one-man audience is enough to set an Irish postman's imagination freewheeling in **"The Petrol Dump"**. In **"The Collection"**, the gentleman who takes the Sunday collection in the local chapel is so aware of the public's eye that his ego inflates to painful dimensions: bursting point is reached on his return home when his dream of universally-respected importance gets punctured. Another victim to a part devotedly played is Lippott (in **"Page and Monarch"**), who sees himself as the faithful hard-working trusted servant whose undescried endeavours permanently preserve the House of (multimillionaire) Schneider from collapse. Here and there the author's sleight of hand also turns a character into an impersonation of some famous figure. Miss Baker (in the eponymous story) is revealed to our bemused eyes as a twentieth-century Mary Magdalen first meeting her Saviour . . .

More than once, too, in these stories the material conditions for acting are created, as in **"The Speech"**, where a militant holds forth in a city-hall, or in **"The Aristocrat"**, where the patrons of a pub gape at the amateur illusionist (later exposed as a pickpocket), or in **"The Ladder"**, with Miss Richards indulging in a grotesque bout of sobbing, marooned on a platform above a drawing-room. On numerous other occasions through these tales an onlooker watches the main character's antics or petty ordeal, a situation recalling the basic actor/spectator relationship. What with this, what with the widespread use of direct speech, preferably delivered in short gushes by the protagonists, what with the character's names (Slooter, Phillimore, Alldraxen, Saxon, Brackett or Rougemont) and the exaggeration that often shows in the characters' gestures, fancies or general behaviour, not to speak of all that flavours of true farce, with many an instance in these tales of pure histrionics and a consistent drawing upon the resources of cinetics, the suggestion they convey of theatricality is very strong at times, resulting in a sense of a rather artificial world, one in which most of what happens does so on a kind of raised dais, somewhat above the daily scene. On a first appraisal, Pritchett's characters will therefore seem set apart from common humanity. At best they are felt to stand uncertainly on the line dividing the "real" person—with whom a reader can become identified and whose story he totally adheres to—from the rather incredible eccentric (of Dickensian descent, unless the kinship is rather on the side of Irish yarn-spinning) at a remove from our familiar experience. Sometimes, over and above the characters themselves, it is the situation in which they have more or less wittingly got trapped that looks extravagant, a case forcefully illustrated by the curious arrangement between the barber and his customer in **"You Make Your Own Life"**.

This alone, however, would not account for Mr Pritchett's enviable record as a story writer. He is much more than just an entertainer in the sense that we have outlined. Or again, such entertainment is on the surface, what bubbles over from the story's and its people's inner drama. To contend that the stories V. S. Pritchett writes are dead serious in their essence would not be going too far, in spite of the relative scarcity of interior monologues or renderings of the flux of moods and feelings one normally associates with serious narrative. On the one hand, there is the "mezzotint" stories group, tales that belong to various stages in his career and from which the "showy" features are almost altogether absent. They usually deal with the suppressed qualms that agitate ordinary self-effaced, unexpansive individuals. **"The Sniff"**, **"The Night-Worker"**, **"Many Are Disappointed"** are typical here. **"The Goldfish"** is steeped in a dreamlike atmosphere in which half delineated figures seem to mutter away over some ill-defined grievance.

On the other hand, we have those full-length portraits in a few pages of characters who, for all their amusing idiosyncrasies and superficial silly whims, move us by arousing in us the fellow-feeling for those who must cope with hardship or estrangement. The comedy, if any, is a veneer. What matters is the burden that drags the individual down. Besides, the key-characters (Sally in **"The Speech"**, George Clark in **"The Skeleton"**, Plymbell in **"The Satisfactory"**) enter the scene fully clad in a denseness of personal history and weighted with hidden sorrows or cumbered with inhibitions, complexes, grudges or lame scheming. What little of their past gradually filters down to us is enough to endow them with the thickness of life and make us genuinely concerned with regard to their predicament. We gather that the point of the story will not lie in, for example, some rhetorical reversal of circumstances, but that the final turn of events will have to do with the inward pressure that keeps this girl or that fellow quietly simmering day after day on the verge of a nasty crisis. Pritchett's are not cleverly put-together *anecdotic* stories. They tell us of failure and irritating failings, of mental illness and self-destroying cowardice, of the exhilaration of a glimpse into something ideal, of people made unsure (or on the contrary extroverts) by guilt, of people who derive a satisfaction from being sufferers. Further, the author

shows how one's personal liberty is put continually at risk (by unscrupulous exploiters of our foibles for instance) and can be thoroughly abdicated through the promptings of some minor or major folly; in which case one's sanity too becomes endangered. Tragedy lurks within the characters and within the folds of the tale.

At the junction of the flashy excess and comic gesturing—what we might call Pritchett's expressionism—and the tragic undertones, and partaking of both spheres, the extraordinary again, but of a kind that escapes immediate notice. For Pritchett's extraordinariness is often that of one of those minor cataclysms, that the casual observer's glance misses, come to perturb a colourless existence. The setting in fact is, as a rule, most ordinary (not like William Sansom's Slate Quarry pit or Vertical Ladder, not like the sun-scorched primitive places around the Mediterranean that have fascinated so many Anglo-Saxon storytellers). Homely, trivial circumstances are made to serve the author's purpose best and he works wonders with the restrictions imposed on the action by the recording of a conversation during a two hours' visit, or at a dance, or in a saloon bar. Whereas the drama in the common run of the stories we read finds its source in the irruption into the protagonist's life of an utter stranger from the exterior world, what trespassers here come to unsettle plans, disrupt peace of mind, shatter hard-earned hopes, are still of the protagonist's own world—which doesn't make less indeed the impact of the unforeseen. Exceptions are not easily found. Pocock (in **"Pocock Passes"**) is to a certain extent just another Rogers. As for the Guatemalan girl of **"The Editor Regrets . . . "**, we feel entitled to grant her no more independent existence (within the fiction) than an exotic shape arising out of Mr Drood's perturbed imagination and ailing conscience.

Indeed the extraordinary in many cases breeds from the invisible layers of the psyche, that innermost secret machinery capable to produce such erratic demeanour and fantastic results as those depicted in the story **"Citizen"**. Mythomania is one of V. S. Pritchett's favourite fields of investigation, as is phantasising of every description. Fleeting fantasies obscure the mind of many a Pritchettian hero, while more lasting ones, luxuriant and dangerous, provide the focus of analysis in several tales. In **"The Sack of Lights"** the extraordinary proceeds from the adoption of the deformed angle of vision of the slightly deranged ageing woman protagonist. The worst may come, for the character, of submitting to the great driving force of a fixed idea, but more than once the victim is a third person. The poetic *divertimento* **"A Serious Question"** revolves on the immature nonsense of a reticent childless wife who sets her husband's humblest claims at naught. Add all those who live their days in rampant bad faith, whose disingenuity, demurs and blurted-out answers concur after a while to blur every certainty: few characters remain whose peculiar mental cast doesn't hold the ferment of some complication. If with Pritchett the outside often catches the eye and gratifies one's sense of the preposterous or the openly ludicrous, the inside is more catching still and entrancingly uncommon, is in a word (one Pritchett the teller is addicted to), "astonishing". The very workings of the mind may become an object of wonder. See Mrs Prosser deliver as by rote a political harangue while her inward eye and awareness are busy reconstructing events (recent and remote) of her life and she herself grows bewildered by the discoveries she makes! (**"The Speech"**).

Once the importance of the interior scene has been realized, the significance of the outward display, by-play and at times horseplay appears. The latter are metaphoric expressions of the inner turmoil of emotions, trying thoughts or contradictory impulses harboured by the characters at bay. Exterior violence but connotes interior commotion, sometimes possibly in a symbolic manner as when the landlord's territorial encroachments are recorded presto, in speeded-up fashion, thus counterpointing Seugar's more and more inacceptable, less-than-human acceptance of the trespassing. The snarling fight of two dogs (in **"Did I Invite You?"**) is a sly, very oblique allusion to the uneasy relationship between a widower and a marriageable widow. A bachelor's brusque and ridiculous jiving at a dance betrays the dazed frustration and the anger that have been building up in him (**"Our Oldest Friend"**). The dizzy uninterrupted journeying of the lift in **"Slooter's Vengeance"** is a token of the operator's fury of indecision. **"The Fly in the Ointment"** has a father getting onto a table and making disorderly attempts at silencing a buzzing fly, while his thirty-year old son is left to watch the sorry chase and listen to the accompanying uncomplimentary remarks about his professional record and prospects. The harshness of the encounter of the absentee husband and the deserted wife (**"A Debt of Honour"**) is in direct proportion to the appeal this reprobate still exerts on the snubbed woman. To demonstrate the stagefall the protagonist of **"The Fall"** lets himself collapse bodily ten or fifteen times running onto a Reception Room's floor—an exhibition that masquerades as a symbol for the fundamentally disordered personality of the man, while (on the realistic plane) the falls afford him a kind of relief through unwitting self-punishment, and are, too, a desperate bid at public acknowledgement of his separate existence.

This is a typical example of V. S. Pritchett's use of the spectacular: its function is emblematic, it is used for revealing. He hardly ever resorts to it as an end in itself, not even in the case of the flustered teenager of **"A Spring Morning"** tilting her pail of suds from above upon her tactless suitor's head. And this in turn reminds us of Pritchett's rule of linking the spectacular with commonplace occurrences. The commonplace is transmuted and *becomes* spectacular and portentous, without any hint of or support from the fantastic playing a part in the process, as is the case with E. Bowen in similar circumstances, or with W. Sansom in his descriptions of people under stress whose mistaken senses conjure up about their heads an eerie, often frightening world. (Fantasy with Pritchett is of the intimate self, it quite dispenses with the tricks human perceptions are prone to.) A wife takes off all her clothes and dares her husband to paint her in the nude . . . A woman named Grace is trying on dresses when all of a sudden the "golden" dress reveals to her the golden woman she could be . . .

Grace Phillips's revelation about herself constitutes the climax of **"The Cage Birds"**. The crisis will come later, on

her return home where the intoxication engendered by her discovery predictably clashes with the scale of values set by her husband and regulating both their lives. His conspicuous lack of interest in what she would timidly impart to him of her afternoon experience douses the burning new light. Crisis is when the conflict born of a tangle of tensions comes to a head. As opposed to the tensions, which are the staple of human relations and as such figure the usual, crisis—the reader's secretly hoped-for reward—stands out as the exceptional, extraordinary moment in a story's pattern. One may well wish to assess the place held by it in Pritchett's stories, and how he handles it. The subject would indeed lend itself to a full-scale study, and we shall merely draw attention here to the most characteristic features, above all in connection with the theme we have set out to investigate.

Although crisis and violence seem to make a natural pair and go hand in hand, the identification must be resisted as far as Pritchett is concerned. Crisis with him seldom assumes the shape of physical violence: the mugging of a young peasant by a famished labourer (**"Main Road"**), the brief sexual scuffle of two adolescents (**"A Spring Morning"**), the horror of cutting one's throat as a final escape from psychopathic torment (**"The Two Brothers"**), the angry outburst of the landlady in **"The Corsican Inn"** and the rage the father in **"The Collection"** flies into at last (the outcome of the day-long strain of wearing a self-righteous mask) are indeed examples, but only to be picked from the lesser tales, that is, the shorter ones. In most other instances, outward violence, when present, only serves as a clue to the crisis that besets and shakes those concerned with often stunning force. It may have an obvious psychological relevance, as in the case of the rifle shot that brings down the jealously cared-for time-piece of **"The Cuckoo-Clock"**, or the sudden dismissal by frustrated Lippott of two loading-bay hands at Schneider House. It may provide a fitting counterpoint to the crisis that has two people striving at cross-purposes, as when the police in the early morning pounce down on the cheap hotel in **"The Honeymoon"** where the whimsical bride has flatly refused to go to bed with her mate . . .

Violence again, in its exterior garb, may be altogether absent from the story or from that part of it surrounding the crisis. This then will declare itself in a most subdued form and hardly claim our attention. Should such a practice extend to more of his stories than is actually the case, one might justly be tempted to label V. S. Pritchett an 'intimist' writer. The epithet would be at variance with that of expressionist we suggested before. Yet doesn't V. S. Pritchett's hall-mark (and originality) after all consist in the interplay of these opposites? The two modes are vying indeed for dominance in the scene (which is also one of the two turning-points in **"Handsome Is as Handsome Does"**) when disoriented, holiday-drugged Mrs Coram offers herself on the young man's bed and is refused. As well as in the superb slowmotion depicting of a minor disaster in **"The Saint"** (the missionary falls from the punt into the river), where determining crisis coincides with and involves a strong visual element, is outwardly catastrophic and spectacular, as it is on the inward plane of the character's consciousness: the boy's sharp recoil from the mendacious prophecy, "Accident does not happen", and the preacher's horror at encountering physical aggression, against which as we learn he was so studiously protecting himself all the time! The event comes to him as a challenge from a hostile world to his efforts at maintaining a frail balance between outward adverse agencies and a threatened self. We suppose he meekly admits to his defeat. But other Pritchettian characters, thus put to the test, will gallantly rise to the occasion and improvise according to their capacities. Thus, in **"The Diver"**, the young man who quickly spins a saving yarn in his time of need. Thus too in **"The Skeleton"**, where the protagonist must face up (as in five or six more stories) to the unexpected resurgence of a rather unsavoury past.

Challenge to be met at short notice is the first of the two main ways in which crisis is triggered off in these stories. The second one is conflict turning sour or gathering impetus and getting out of hand. Crisis here results either from a clash between two irreconcilables (one's fantasies or inadequacies and the inescapable claims of the real: see **"The Scapegoat"** among others) or from the interlocking of two antagonistic wills as someone attempts to crush, wreak revenge on or wrench some benefit from another person. The latter variety of human design is perhaps the most widely exemplified—we shall sample **"I Passed by your Window"**, **"The Sailor"**, **"The Necklace"** and, in the latest collection to date (*The Edge of the Cliff*), **"The Wedding"** and **"A Family Man"** (in which a man's mistress learns that she is being betrayed, and at the same time soothingly talks the wife, her visitor, into believing that husband William is nothing if unfaithful). In almost each of these, unsuccessful courting or mating supplies the central theme and the chief cause of the trouble.

Whether the crisis proceeds from the adding-up of incidents or other factors over a number of days, or on the contrary speedily builds up, breaks out then blows over in the course of a few hours, whether it is blatant or camouflaged, single or recurring, it gives the author an opportunity to assert his mastery in his chosen field, sometimes keeping even a practised reader in doubt as to the exact point in the tale when maximum focus is obtained and the genuine crisis (one may blindly read past it) or significant move take place, never in fact staking his all on one effect, however expertly prepared and brought off, but filling our mental space with ever more news, impressions, queries and narratory signals and messages, playing off against one another the serious and the jocular, the fool's pranks and the victimized man's musings, the flight of fancy and the difficulty of coping, strange inklings and bare down-to-earth fact.

Denseness, complexity and sheer vitality are qualities that more than any others set V. S. Pritchett's short stories (there are well-nigh a hundred of them) apart from those by competitors of his rank. The extraordinary here is that, instead of leaving the reader tired, confused and begging for less heady stuff, they are just the sort that we both remember best and are always willing to read over another time.

The clue to this is probably that his first and very sincere concern is man, and that he has something to say, too,

about how to live gregariously. Let moments of folly be pardoned. Let moments of hatred and anguish be got into perspective. It wasn't as bad as it seemed; and better lies in the offing. With the jabbering vexed protagonist of that short masterpiece (of the writer's very first batch), **"The Gnats"**, who arrived too late on the spot to shoot down the predatory heron, one will be grateful, after all, that the bird of beauty should escape and that ideal goals should still hover around to guide oneself by if need be. Mr Pritchett's stories end. Along with his great artistry, his sympathy and patience with his fellow-creatures remain. (pp. 101-10)

> Alain Theil, "V. S. Pritchett's Quiet Expressionism," in Journal of the Short Story in English, *No. 6, Spring, 1986, pp. 101-10.*

Because the short story has to be succinct, the art calls for a mingling of the skills of the rapid reporter or traveller with an eye for incident and ear for real speech, the instincts of the poet or the ballad-maker, and the sonnet writer's concealed discipline of form.

—V. S. Pritchett in his introduction to The Oxford Book of Short Stories, *1981*.

P. N. Furbank   (essay date 1989)

[*In the following review of* A Careless Widow, and Other Stories, *Furbank focuses on the title story.*]

To be a short-story writer, like being a lyric poet or a fireman, must entail a lot of waiting about. Novelists have something to be getting on with, whereas the short-story writer is dependent upon accidents, or upon the right kind of accident. This must have a fairly general effect on a short-story writer's life and outlook. It may for instance be wise for him or her not to have any very set theory about life or worked-out philosophy, or alternatively to have a philosophy of the accidental. Has V. S. Pritchett a philosophy? If so, he has kept it well hidden, and he is certainly not a generalizer.

Of course, there are two kinds of accident. There are the accidental conjunctions which life offers, opening up prospects of glory, pathos, absurdity and so on; and then there are the happy accidents of the pen. Which reminds one just how intertwined Pritchett's short-story writing is with his literary criticism. According to his own account, he agonizes and burns midnight oil over his stories but finds criticism comes with zest and ease; and half the charm of his famous *New Statesman* "middles" on classic authors was opportunism. At a certain point in these articles, after some preliminary skirmishing and scouting round, his pen would take off in a flurry of opportunistic and unpremeditated conceits. It was the moment of confidence, of having seized the secret of the book or author in hand, and the fact that week after week this moment came must have done a lot for his professional confidence. What came easily to him, and could be depended on to do so, was phrase-making; these "happy accidents" could be relied upon to happen. But it is important to realize that phrase-making, of a less showy and more chastened kind, is equally important to his stories. Quite often a whole story is inspired by a phrase; and in the opening story, **"A Careless Widow"**, in his new collection [*A Careless Widow, and Other Stories*] a mass of significance is effortlessly condensed in a single phrase: "She was ordinary life and ordinary life always went too far."

Still, to have lived this precarious waiting life for sixty years and to have done so without ever faking inspiration must have set Pritchett's mind running on professionalism and its requirements. But then, whether as cause or effect, his imagination has always been gripped by professions and trades. There is an impressive example of this in **"A Careless Widow"**. The protagonist is a hairdresser at a smart London establishment, a man who, "despite his doll's head of grey hair and the mesh of nervous lines on his long face", wants not at all to be typed as some stock notion of a hairdresser: limp-wristed, "gesticulating" and so on. His professional life is businesslike and impersonal; and his private life, with its well-chosen furniture and "perfect kitchen", is discriminating, beautifully organized and even more impersonal. He is a man of good will, very happy to be a support to his downstairs neighbour, a sloppy, floundering, rather lost widow, so long as the thing can be conducted according to proper rules. But ordinary life always goes too far; his neighbour goes too far when, as she is leaving his admirable flat, she coyly kisses him on the top of his head and then ruffles his hair to put it right. After this, what the rules prescribe is systematic evasion and putting-off.

But if at work he does not want to be anybody's "typical" hairdresser, on holiday—he likes strenuous, lonely, walking holidays—he does not want to be a hairdresser at all, he wants to slough off his London self altogether. What horror for him, then, on the first evening of his holiday, to hear a cry of "Lionel!" (his professional name) and find himself confronted by the widow. "What an unexpected pleasure", he manages; but she has spotted his horrified look, and his holiday, and hers too, will from now on be preoccupied with evasion.

This rich little imbroglio, which Henry James and Chekhov would have delighted in, is disentangled by Pritchett in finely moralistic and moving style. There is a fact hidden from Lionel: not so much that a professional self is not sloughed off at will as that it is his professional self, as opposed to some constructed "private" one, that knows how to feel. From a hint or two, amid the cross-purposes of their holiday, he gradually realizes that his neighbour may be remarrying and taking her nuisance-making self out of his life. The discovery slightly disturbs him, a fact which he puts down to mere dislike of change. He feels a little guilty at his own standoffishness and, noticing that she has had a change of hair-style, he compliments her. Instantly and unthinkingly, he drops into his professional pronoun "one" ("One can see the ears and the neck, the forehead is rounded"); he even gesticulates. But at this very moment he reads his own feelings better, has the sense of losing something unpredictably large, and begins to feel "the cold air of an empty flat".

There are two real winners in this collection, **"A Careless Widow"** and the succeeding story **"Cocky Olly"**; three, if you count the engaging final *jeu d'esprit* **"The Image Trade"**. It was a subtle stroke of Pritchett's to place those two opening stories side by side. For the implication of **"A Careless Widow"** and of a hundred other Pritchett stories is that if the middle-aged manage to hang together at all, it is by means of some professionalism or system or narrow set of rules, in other words by limits drawn and doors closed. By contrast the theme of **"Cocky Olly"**, told in the first person by a fourteen-year-old girl, is the sense of things opening out. Sarah's life begins to open out when she becomes involved with a neighbouring family with a larger-seeming, or anyway different, ethos. The dropped hints and obscure cultural references encountered there mortify but excite her, making the world seem deliciously large. At her new friends' home they play a game of Cocky Olly (Prisoner's Base), and the next few months of Sara's life, in their randomness and rushing around—there is an absurd, bickering odyssey with her new friends' neurotic and "artistic" son—are like an extended game of Cocky Olly. The whole loose, rambling shape of the story, the significances raised and then dropped and left behind, are cunningly designed to suggest a widening and opening of doors. The last words, ringing rather beautifully, are: "Then it was Cocky Olly again and all of us racing around."

In **"The Image Trade"** we are back, more wryly, with professionalism. A distinguished elderly author is visited by a famous photographer. As a writer he is deeply interested in all sorts of professions and trades. Or is he? Maybe only because it is a way, a quite false one, of "placing" people, and because people pay him to do it. The truth is, he is in "the image trade": in two seconds he has imagined, or pretended to imagine, that the photographer and his female companion are come to sell him second-hand false teeth, or that they are a pair of surgeons. To the end of his relationship with them, indeed, deeply interested or not, he is left totally baffled. What can be the meaning of all those bits and pieces, and of all the mad instructions, designed to make him look as he never remotely would in normal life? Will the photographer *never* stop giving his companion little punches and kicks? And is his photography any good? Is he an artist or just "a nosey collector of human instances, jellied in his darkroom"? If he is an artist, is he aiming to photograph his subjects, or merely his own soul? They are thoroughly rattling questions. They seem to require the author to reflect on his own profession and equipment, not to mention his face and body; and this, ruefully and very funnily, in Pritchett's best effervescent style, he proceeds to do.

P. N. Furbank, "The Professional Touch," in The Times Literary Supplement, *No. 4508, August 25-31, 1989, p. 917.*

John J. Stinson   (essay date 1992)

[*Stinson is an American educator whose specialty is modern British literature. In the following excerpt from his* V. S. Pritchett: A Study of the Short Fiction, *Stinson discusses Pritchett's stature as a short story writer and analyzes "Sense of Humour."*]

Pritchett's signature voice and approach are amply present [in **"Sense of Humor"**], whereas they were yet to be discovered in the earlier stories, which deserve only brief comment. But like other of his best work, often the title stories of collections—**"It May Never Happen," "When My Girl Comes Home,"** and **"The Camberwell Beauty"**—**"Sense of Humour"** causes doubt and uneasiness in the minds of critics. How else are we to explain not simply the absence of critical commentary but the exclusion from virtually every college anthology of this and all other Pritchett stories, whether highly successful or mediocre? The case is intriguing because, to a number of writers and reviewers—Margaret Drabble, Frank Kermode, Walter Allen, Paul Theroux, Robertson Davies, Eudora Welty, and William Trevor among them—Pritchett is *the* great English short-story writer of our time.

The answer to the question of Pritchett's neglect is obvious, remarkable only for its not being specifically remarked on after all these years. Simply put, it is that Pritchett provides fewer interpretive clues than most writers; consequently, neither critics nor general readers can arrive at tidily definitive interpretations of many of his stories. Pritchett's stories may be seen, in New Critical parlance, as inchoate or lacking in sufficient organic unity. Even if we allow for tensions and functional ambiguities, a few necessary clues (formal, symbolic, textural) will seem to be missing or to point in the wrong direction. Epiphanic moments are just as apt to bathe characters and readers in murky as in revealing light. While no critic focuses directly on these problems, Anatole Broyard seems to have something like it in mind as he querulously asks, "If one gave Mr. Pritchett the benefit of the doubt, if one assumed that his untidy stories cohered in some roundabout way, what then? Even if they worked, they would not be enough."

Readers will probably be more disconcerted by interpretive difficulties in Pritchett's stories because they are unsignaled: Pritchett is not thought to be anywhere near the cutting edge of experimentation, the place most readers identify with interpretive difficulty. They generally expect interpretive clear sailing in a Pritchett story when they note no fragmentariness, no twisted chronologies, no elaborately selfconscious plays with point of view, no formal obliquities of an obvious sort (**"When My Girl Comes Home"** being the single large exception). In a number of Pritchett's most important stories, they will meet what a leading theorist, Austin M. Wright, terms "mimetic resistance": some "unresolved contradiction at the level of character or action." Pritchett's various kinds of openness are, in one argument, not readily accepted or understood because short-story theory is not at a sufficiently sophisticated point of development to be able to describe or classify them. Nevertheless, Pritchett's methods are not all that surprising, in that suggestiveness, implicitness, and indi-

rection are the characteristic ingredients of the twentieth-century short story, and irony that of modern literature generally. In his own unfussy, unprogrammatic sort of way Pritchett carries these tendencies to the limit and in so doing demands much from both reader and critic.

Pritchett's is the art of severe selectivity. But his artful trick is to employ a rigorous selection while seeming to allow the story to unfold naturally, even casually. Pritchett, who acknowledges a general Hemingway influence, is, in a less obvious way than Hemingway, Stein, or Fitzgerald, his own kind of "leaver-outer." In the preface to his *Collected Stories* Pritchett writes of his typical procedure of "boiling down a hundred pages into twenty or thirty." This process of composition through excision gives rise to what we might call Pritchett's "haze effect," the sense that his characters, like figures in great Russian novels, or like people in real life who are not family members or intimate friends, seem surrounded by a haze that hides the edges of their personalities. The excisions affect the plot as well: unity becomes equivocal; how exactly the pieces of the plot hang together becomes problematic. Vagaries of plot, character, or structure seem designed, in Pritchett's best-known stories, to compel readers to engage in some ruminative reflection.

"Sense of Humour," Pritchett's first major story, the one he says signaled that he "had modestly arrived," both teases and entertains. Pritchett, whose remarks in interviews or autobiography are not guilefully calculated to self-advertise his stories' depths or dimensions, has simply labeled it "a piece of premature black comedy." It is that, but it is also a good deal more.

Readers of moderate sophistication will realize that the first-person narrator, who is also one of the story's two chief characters, can be trusted in the facts he reports but cannot be trusted in his judgments or ways of "seeing": his moral perceptions and ordinary human sensibilities have been severely dulled by a rigid, puritanical background that places its emphases on money, getting ahead, frugality, appearances, and respectability. Although Pritchett deals gently and compassionately with his characters and lacks the moral indignation of the satirist, his stories frequently carry a sting when they deal with people like this narrator, Arthur Humphrey, a commercial traveler whose type can be recognized in an American counterpart, the Willie Loman of his early and middle years. They form a series of hypocritical or morally obtuse members of the middle-class business community, people whose ordinary humanity has been twisted and severely diminished by adherence to such pervasive doctrines as that which views earthly prosperity as a harbinger of salvation.

As the story begins, Arthur informs the reader he is working a new sales territory for the first time. He does not wait for Monday morning, because he wants to attend two different churches on Sunday in the first town: "it pays in these small towns to turn up at church on Sundays, Presbyterians in the morning, Methodists in the evening," he says. From this alone readers might be led to view Arthur as a caricature out of the fiction of a Sinclair Lewis. But the story is not just a satiric cartoon or a black comic sketch; its sharply and cannily observed social details, rendered with all the right nuances, almost dare the reader to question why it should not be thought of as social realism. After all, the Arthur Humphreys of the real world are not only not obliterated by satire but hardly ever seem even to recognize themselves.

Readers can note the unerringly accurate ear for the speech of people of different social classes that Pritchett had developed by this time. In *Midnight Oil* Pritchett says, apropos **"Sense of Humour,"** "I think . . . that I gave the vernacular of that period a role it had not had up till then." The very first thing the reader of **Complete Collected Stories** encounters is the convincingly realistic sound of Arthur's voice:

> It started one Saturday. I was working new ground and I decided I'd stay at the hotel the weekend and put in an appearance at church.
>
> "All alone?" asked the girl in the cash desk.
>
> It had been raining since ten o'clock.
>
> "Mr. Good has gone," she said. "And Mr. Straker. He usually stays with us. But he's gone."
>
> "That's where they make their mistake," I said. "They think they know everything because they've been on the road all their lives."
>
> "You're a stranger here, aren't you?" she said.
>
> "I am," I said. "And so are you."
>
> "How do you know that?"
>
> "Obvious," I said. "Way you speak."
>
> "Let's have a light," she said.
>
> "So's I can see you," I said.
>
> That was how it started.

Using a smooth but aggressive conversational style common to his sort, Arthur soon makes up to the attractive desk clerk at the hotel, Muriel MacFarlane. They have some things in common: both have a macabre sense of humor (she attributes hers to being Irish), and both have made frugality a habit. Muriel's boyfriend, Colin Mitchell, a young fellow who works at a nearby garage, is tormented when Muriel goes out with Arthur. When Arthur takes Muriel out in his car, Colin almost always follows them on his motorbike. Arthur says Colin "seems to be a harum-scarum sort of half-wit to me," and Muriel replies, "And he spends every penny he makes." Arthur is blind to Colin's agony, regarding him, because of perceived class difference and Colin's inarticulateness, almost as a creature from another species. "I used to call him 'Marbles' because when he spoke he seemed to have a lot of marbles in his mouth," Arthur tells the reader. Arthur, in a demanding and superior way, confronts Colin about his always following Muriel and him: " 'She was my girl' was all he [Colin] said. He was pouring oil into my engine. He had some cotton wool in one hand and the can in the other. He wiped up the green oil that had overflowed, screwed on the cap, pulled down the bonnet, and whistled to himself." Readers will apprehend Colin's suffering far

more clearly than Arthur does; by this point in his career Pritchett was handling such dramatic ironies with great confidence and ease.

The relationship between Muriel and Arthur intensifies, and one bank holiday the two of them go for a visit to Arthur's parents' house. While there they receive a telephone call informing them that Colin has just been killed in an accident. He had been trying again to follow them on his motorbike but, passing other vehicles recklessly, had "gone clean off the saddle and under the Birmingham bus. The blood was everywhere. . . . What a mess!" Not surprisingly, one of Arthur's first thoughts is simply "Holiday ruined."

The combination of black comedy and the exposure of moral vacancy and hypocrisy continues to the end of the story. Colin's mother is assisted greatly in the funeral arrangements by virtue of the fact that Arthur's father is an undertaker and has a good eye for business. All quickly arrange to have Colin's body conveyed back to his own town in Arthur's father's hearse with, in order to save money, Arthur as the driver. Muriel decides she really ought to be with Colin on this occasion, but it is fairly clear she also wishes to be with Arthur: " 'No, no,' she said. 'I want to go with Colin. Poor Colin. He loved me and I didn't love him.' And she drew my hands down to her breasts." She rides in the front of the hearse with Arthur. Arthur thinks about the way Colin always followed behind them, and he is a bit uneasily aware that Colin is still behind them, no longer on his motorbike but now in his casket. Arthur and Muriel feel some awkwardness as they ride, but also a curious sense of satisfaction, almost elation. They like it that men lift their caps respectfully as they drive past in the hearse. The story ends with a broadly ironic remark from Muriel: "Look at that man there. Why doesn't he raise his hat? People ought to show respect for the dead."

The preceding summary is true both to the facts and to the basic tenor of the story. But it does not tell the whole truth about the story, or suggest its complexities. **"Sense of Humour"** is shaped and controlled, and it provides more of a sense of closure than many Pritchett stories. At its conclusion readers will have a sense of having moved closer to illumination. Still, they will also feel a sense of interpretive irresolution and elusiveness. A resonating core of mystery and complexity is in fact present in many of Pritchett's best stories, and it is this quality gives them their special character and memorability.

The lifelike complexity of the characters of both Arthur and Muriel accounts for our inability to pin down meaning absolutely, but this indefinite quality produces more satisfaction than frustration. Arthur and Muriel are a good deal more than walking exemplifications of moral vacancy. The remorseless modern business ethic, for example, has not completely suffocated Arthur's humanity. "I felt sorry for that fellow" and "I could have been friends with that fellow" (that is, were they not rivals in love) are Arthur's thoughts before Colin's death—at least as he reports them to the reader. As they ride back in the hearse, Muriel at one point begins to laugh, and Arthur chooses to shut her up: "Keep your sense of humour to yourself,' I said." This might well be only Arthur's middle-class respectability and hypocrisy at work, but it might also be some submerged sense of decency that is rising.

The story's largest mystery centers on an event that is in itself quite plausible: the first instance of sexual intercourse between Arthur and Muriel, on the very night of Colin's death. Space does not permit a discussion of the multiplicity of reasons for Muriel's giving herself to Arthur that night or for her repeatedly moaning "Colin, Colin, Colin" even as they made love. Muriel herself probably does not know fully; the pathways of the mind are dark and tangled. Arthur is troubled: "Did she love Colin all the time? Did she think I was Colin?" Readers can devise a scale of motivations for Muriel that range from the morally disgusting to the laudable. On the base end of the scale, she may have calculatedly seized on an opportunity for unprotected sexual intercourse as a means of levering Arthur into marriage. This motivation may seem unlikely, but Arthur is soon thinking that the unexpected sexual activity "had put my calculations out. I mean, supposing she had a baby. You see I had reckoned on waiting eighteen months or so." On the other end of the scale, readers might note that several times Muriel explains her behavior by saying, "I'm Irish. I've got a sense of humour." Such explanations might well mean, as Dean Baldwin suggests, that Muriel "can laugh at herself and the absurdities of human folly," that she is so fully in touch with the flow of the universe that she is able to accept life fully, and also death, which is but a part of life. Numerous possibilities, of course, exist in the middle of the scale. Commenting on the irreducibly mysterious motivations of Muriel, British reviewer Paul Binding has said that "we are changed—and devoured—by what we are unable to understand."

The interpretive ambiguities are more than a storyteller's tease: they are additional invitations for readers to reexamine the bases by which they define their own moral and psychological lives. (pp. 3-8)

> *John J. Stinson, in his* V. S. Pritchett: A Study of the Short Fiction, *Twayne Publishers, 1992, 149 p.*

Joseph Epstein   (essay date 1993)

[*In the following excerpt, Epstein discusses the enduring appeal of Pritchett's short fiction and critical essays and reviews* The Complete Collected Stories.]

V. S. Pritchett is a professional writer. At an earlier time, he would have been known as a man of letters, and John Gross, in the afterword to the new edition of his *Rise and Fall of the Man of Letters*, remarks that "no living man of letters had a better claim to be included" in his book than V. S. Pritchett. In fact, Pritchett was still very much in full sail when the first edition of Mr. Gross's book appeared in 1969. *A Cab at the Door*, the first of Pritchett's autobiographical volumes, had only just been announced—he would later write a second such volume, *Midnight Oil*—and much Pritchettian prose would flow under the bridge between then and now. The fluvial metaphor is perhaps allowable, since V. S. Pritchett has himself become something like the Ol' Man River of contempo-

rary English literature: now in his early nineties, he jus' keeps rollin', he keeps on rollin' along. In the recently published second volume of his autobiography, *You've Had Your Time*, Anthony Burgess mentions seeing "an ancient but thriving Victor Pritchett." To put Pritchett's age in perspective, it helps to know that he read Virginia Woolf's books when they were just out.

To commemorate his achievement, perhaps also to mark his endurance, Pritchett's publishers, both in England and in the United States, have recently issued two thick volumes of his work: the ***Complete Collected Stories*** and the *Complete Collected Essays;* the latter, more precisely, turns out to be the collected literary criticism. Taken together, these two books run to nearly 2,500 pages and weigh in, on our family French cooking scale, at just over seven pounds. These books, neither of which comes with an introduction or a prefatory word from their author or anyone else, are clearly meant as a tribute and one that provides the occasion to consider the now all-but-rounded-out career of a remarkable writer.

[V. S. Pritchett] is a throwback to a time when, in England, one could write about literature with the assumption that there was no need to teach or preach to your readers, but as if one were merely holding up one's end in an intelligent conversation. The assumption behind this seemed to be that your readers had of course read the same books you had; and that, if a new book was under discussion, they would soon read this book, too. Criticism in America has generally had more to do with teaching one's readers: introducing them to new subjects, straightening them out on old ones. An element of unspoken condescension often entered—and continues to enter—into the transaction. Criticism written by Americans has tended to be more thorough, that written by Englishmen—or at least   by   some   Englishmen—more   charming. V. S. Pritchett may be the last Englishman to have worked under the splendid assumption that his readers knew quite as much as he, were interested in pretty much the same things, and operated at the same level of sophistication. (pp. 19-20)

Not least among V. S. Pritchett's gifts is his ability to apprehend his own literary qualities. It is part of his talent for getting outside himself; a rare skill, it makes him in some ways his own best critic. In scattered comments in *Midnight Oil*, he limns his strengths and weaknesses, proclivities and antipathies with a nice detachment fitting to a writer who claims that "to strain after the essence of things has become a mania with me."

"I am no thinker or philosopher," Pritchett avers, truly enough. He knows that such truths as are available to him come through the impressions experience makes on him. He claims to have had a "vulgar instinct for survival." He also believes that "any originality in my writing is due to having something of a foreign mind," even though he is usually described as a traditionally English writer. "I have talent," he writes, "but no genius." That may well be true, but it has always seemed to me that the English language is deficient in not possessing a word that lies between the two; it would be a word that described how far talent, honed under the pressure of unrelenting hard work, can take one. This missing word would, I think, apply nicely to V. S. Pritchett. (pp. 21-2)

Although early in his career Pritchett produced a few novels, and he wrote more than one complete book on Spain, his reputation today rests on his work as a literary critic and as a short-story writer. Lucky is the writer who has found his forms, and these have been Pritchett's. "I have had to conclude," he writes in *Midnight Oil,* "that I am a writer who takes short breaths, and in consequence the story and the essay have been the best forms for me." (p. 22)

Pritchett has written vast quantities of both criticism and fiction, but his personality comes through much more clearly in his criticism. He is, as usual, quite aware of this fact, even though he reports that writing stories has given him greater pleasure than writing criticism. "In my criticism, perhaps even more than in my stories, I am self-portrayed. When I reread those essays written in such number over the last thirty years, I am surprised to see how much they are pitted with personal experience, and how much reaction to life itself, either nettled or expansive, has been packed into an epigram or an aside." One of the problems with other critics who have written fiction—Edmund Wilson and Lionel Trilling come to mind—is that they sound quite the same in their fiction as they do in their criticism, so that fiction becomes, like war and diplomacy for Clausewitz, chiefly criticism by other means.

Nothing of the kind is true of Pritchett. Only rarely is the storyteller in him likely to be mistaken for the critic, so differently do the two sound. While a V. S. Pritchett literary essay has its author's fingerprints all over it, I am not so sure that I could recognize a V. S. Pritchett short story without its author's name atop it. "The creative writer must know his own mind," Desmond MacCarthy once remarked, "the critic must also know the minds of other people." As a storyteller there is something ventriloquistic about Pritchett. *Voice,* the current cant word in university creative writing programs to describe the distinctive way a writer sounds, is not strong in Pritchett's fiction. He does many voices: he does the lower-middle and working classes in a hundred different voices. His own sometimes gets lost in the cacophony.

Is this a bad thing? Does it matter if there is nothing distinctively Pritchettian about a V. S. Pritchett short story? Isn't the main thing that a fair number simply are good stories—and the hell with their fitting a pattern or dovetailing into something sufficiently uniform to be called an *oeuvre?* Writers of great contemporary reputation—Eudora Welty, William Trevor, Robertson Davies—have weighed in with testimonials about the pleasure Pritchett's stories give and compare them with those of Joyce and Chekhov. One understands their having done so; one wants to admire Pritchett's stories.

Something about the quietly sedulous way Pritchett has written his fiction is immensely attractive. There is an admirably selfless quality to his storytelling. For one thing, he has, in his fiction, taken up a people forgotten by literature: the English lower-middle class of shopkeepers, sales-

men, dentists, minor manufacturers, publicans, clerks, antique dealers, and wives whose beauty and dreams have faded too quickly. What Pritchett once wrote about Gissing, may, in good part, also be said of him: "[His] discovery that in all character there sits a mind, and that the mind of the dullest is not dull because, at its very lowest, it will at least reflect the social dilemma into which it was born, is arresting." The point is connected with Pritchett's general view, set out in his criticism, that fiction ought not to disparage its characters or be written as if by foreigners living in their own country, which he believes a good deal of English and American fiction appears to have been.

Much of the program for Pritchett's own fiction seems to have been announced in his criticism. Apropos of Isaac Babel, Pritchett writes that "short story writers are poets," and that what the short story sets out to achieve is "an insight." Apropos of Borges, he notes that, "in the writer of short stories as in the poet, a distinctive voice, unlike all others, must arrest us," and he adds that the test of the artist is whether he can make his ideas walk, which is to say, come alive. Apropos of Kipling, he adds that the short story is "a form which depends on intensifying the subject, stamping a climate on it, getting at the essence of it."

Many of Pritchett's own stories exemplify these aesthetic axioms. Poetic though he may think the short-story form ultimately is or ought to be, his own vast output of stories includes almost every variety known to the form, and in my opinion his longer stories tend to be better than those in which he goes after more strictly poetic effects. "A short story," he writes in an essay on Flannery O'Connor, "ought to be faultless without being mechanical. The wrong word, a misplaced paragraph, an inadequate phrase or a convenient explanation, start fatal leaks in this kind of writing which is formally very close to poetry."

If Pritchett has a serious fault as a storyteller it is in his own impulse toward the poetic, which shows up in occasional small but disturbing touches. In one story a man sticks his hands in "his optimistic pockets"; in another a woman is wearing a "capable skirt"; another woman has "the disorder of a story"; a man is "as conceited as a gravestone"; another man has "an unreasonable chin and emotional knees"; yet another man stands "like a touchy exclamation mark"; and several clerks have "dejected buttocks," for which perhaps trousers with "optimistic pockets" ought to be recommended.

The stories are also sometimes studded with occasional aphoristic bits reminiscent of V. S. Pritchett's criticism. The narrator of **"The Sailor"** remarks: "Actually, I am in favour of snobbery, it is a sign of character. It's a bad thing to have, but it's a bad thing not to have had. You can't help having the diseases of your time." In the same story, the same character announces that "the secret of happiness is to find a congenial monotony." There are also numerous little touches straining after poetry and achieving it, such as a clergyman, in one story, comporting himself "like the actor walking in the sun of his own vanity"; or the man who, moving different parts of his body separately, "danced, as it were, in committee." Pritchett can be relied upon to have done his homework. If he writes about antique dealers, or window-washers, or bakers, he is always careful to get the niceties of these lines of work right. He often penetrates well beneath the surface of details to understand the drama playing there, a drama that is inseparable from a knowledge of such details. In **"The Camberwell Beauty,"** a story about the obsession of antique dealing, Pritchett writes:

> Mrs. Price—August's woman—was living with a man exactly like the others in the trade: he hated customers and hated parting with anything. By middle age these women have dead blank faces, they look with resentment and indifference at what is choking their shops; their eyes go smaller and smaller as the chances of getting rid of it become rarer and rarer and they are defeated. Kept out of the deals their husbands have among themselves, they see even their natural love of intrigue frustrated. This was the case of Mrs. Price, who must have been handsome in a big-boned way when she was young, but who had swollen into a drudge.

If a poet can hit the gong six or seven times, leaving behind that number of great poems, his claim to immortality, it has been said, is assured. The same ought perhaps to be true of storytellers, except that, as has been noted countless times, not least by V. S. Pritchett in his criticism, "how little a novelist's [or short-story writer's] choice of story and character widens or changes between his first book and his last." This seems to be true, too, of Pritchett's own stories, eighty-two of which are included in his *Complete Collected Stories,* with the added oddity that one of his best stories, **"Sense of Humour,"** is also among his earliest. Of these four-score and two stories, six or seven really are splendid. Among them I would include, along with **"Sense of Humour," "It May Never Happen," "The Saint," "The Camberwell Beauty," "The Sailor," "The Skeleton,"** and **"The Necklace."** For really splendid stories, that's a lot.

In his fiction, Pritchett is thought to be a comic writer. "Class is a funny thing," says a character, double-entendrically, in the story **"Noisy Flushes the Birds,"** and though Pritchett wrings much humor out of the sometimes extreme social limitations that are locked in by social class in England, his stories are more often striking in their darkness. Loneliness is the condition of so many of Pritchett's characters, who must make do with a life that has disappointed expectations, where expectations even existed in the first place. "There is a loneliness in fat," he remarks of the two fat men in one of his stories. An elderly homosexual, after tea and toast in the morning, "looked eagerly to see what was annoying in the papers—some new annoyance to add to a lifetime's accumulation of annoyances." **"The Two Brothers,"** another tale of loneliness, ends on the following sentences: "He took out a razor and became absorbed in the difficulty of cutting his throat. He was not quite dead when the Guards broke in and found him." Life, in Pritchett's stories, twists and breaks people apart.

The final story in the *Complete Collected Stories,* **"The Image Trade,"** which feels very autobiographical, is about an elderly writer named Pearson who is being photographed by a fashionable photographer named Zut. As the photographer is setting things up, the writer thinks:

> Dozens of photographs of me have been taken. I could show you my early slim-subaltern-on-the-Somme-waiting-to-go-over-the-top period. There was my Popular Front look in the Thirties and Forties, the jersey-wearing, all-the-world's-a-coal-mine period, with close-ups of the pores and scars of the skin and the gleam of sweat. There was the editorial look, when the tailor had to let out the waist of my trousers, followed by the successful smirk. In the Sixties the plunging neckline, no tie. Then back to collar and tie in my failed-bronze-Olympic period. Today I fascinate archaeologists—you know, the broken pillar of a lost civilisation. Come on, Zut. What do you want?

Later, when Pearson is presented with the finished photograph, he claims to see in its high-ceilinged, book-filled room not a room at all but "a dank cistern or aquarium of stale water. No sparkling anemone there but the bald head of a melancholy frog, its feet clinging to a log, floating in literature." Quite an arresting, not to say devastating, little image, that, suggesting that a career soaked in literature can turn a man at the end of a long life into a saddened frog. Must be something to it, viewed from within, or else Pritchett would not have thought of it.

And yet how different Pritchett's career looks from outside that room! Brick by brick, essay by essay, story by story, he has over the years built a modest yet quite sturdy literary edifice. Writing for a small and probably diminishing audience, he has never lowered his standard or sullied his integrity. In an essay on the novelist Ada Leverson, Pritchett claimed that her career proved that one could be both a minor novelist and yet a considerable artist. To bring this off, he felt, one required a freshness of view without borrowing the courage of anyone else's convictions; skill in construction and distinction in style; and a delight in one's own limits, so that even when one was dealing only with what seemed the surface of life one's seriousness and life-enhancing quality shone through. Pritchett might, of course, have been writing about himself—a doubtless minor writer, but a true artist who has written an uncommonly high number of essays and stories built to last. (pp. 25-7)

> *Joseph Epstein, "The Enduring V. S. Pritchett," in* The New Criterion, *Vol. XI, No. 7, March, 1993, pp. 19-27.*

FURTHER READING

Criticism

Baldwin, Dean R. *V. S. Pritchett.* Boston: Twayne Publishers, 1987, 135 p.

> Overview of Pritchett's fiction and nonfiction, with a bibliography of works by and about Pritchett.

Davies, Robertson. "V. S. Pritchett: Storyteller Supreme." *Book World—Washington Post* (25 April 1982): 1-2, 15.
Commentary on Pritchett's literary achievements as a short story writer, autobiographer, and essayist.

Journal of the Short Story in English (*Les Cahiers de la Nouvelle*), *Special Issue: V. S. Pritchett,* No. 6 (Spring 1986).
Collection of essays on various aspects of Pritchett's short stories. Some of these essays are included in the entry above.

Kermode, Frank. "A Modern Master." *The New York Review of Books* XXV, No. 13 (17 August 1978): 18-19.
Review of Pritchett's *Selected Stories* and critical commentary on Pritchett's contributions to modern literature.

Sheed, Wilfrid. "Racing the Clock with Greene and Pritchett." In his *The Morning After: Selected Essays and Reviews,* pp. 66-75. New York: Farrar, Straus & Giroux, 1971.
Compares two approaches to the portrayal of time and setting in the short fiction of Pritchett and Graham Greene.

Additional coverage of Pritchett's life and career is contained in the following sources published by Gale Research: *Contemporary Authors,* Vols. 61-64; *Contemporary Authors New Revision Series,* Vol. 31; *Contemporary Literary Criticism,* Vols. 5, 13, 15, 41; *Dictionary of Literary Biography,* Vol. 15; and *Major 20th-Century Writers.*

Thomas Pynchon

1937-

(Full name Thomas Ruggles Pynchon, Jr.) American novelist, short story writer, and nonfiction writer.

INTRODUCTION

Pynchon is widely regarded as one of the most eminent literary stylists in contemporary American fiction. Known primarily for such sprawling, labyrinthine novels as *V.* and *Gravity's Rainbow,* Pynchon also published several short stories early in his career, many of which prefigure issues that he later developed and expanded in his novels, such as fragmentation and alienation in a high-tech, information-saturated society and the human effort to find order in a universe seemingly governed by chaos.

Little is known of Pynchon's private life, due to his deliberate reclusion. Born in Glen Cove, New York, he graduated from Cornell University in 1958 with a degree in engineering. As a student at Cornell, Pynchon wrote at least four of his eight short stories, including his first published work, "Mortality and Mercy in Vienna," in which he used eucharistic imagery and allusions to Joseph Conrad's *Heart of Darkness* to detail a cocktail party massacre. In 1984, "The Small Rain," "Entropy," "Low-Lands," "Under the Rose," and "The Secret Integration" were collected and published as *Slow Learner: Early Stories,* with an uncharacteristic introduction by Pynchon. Because of the rare introspective and personal nature of the introduction, in which Pynchon disparagingly analyzes his stories and offers justification for their republication, it has at times received as much critical attention as have the stories themselves. Three of Pynchon's previously published stories were later revised and included in two of his novels. "Under the Rose" became chapter three of *V.,* and "The World (This One), the Flesh (Mrs. Oedipa Maas), and the Testament of Pierce Inverarity" and "The Shrink Flips" were both integrated into *The Crying of Lot 49.*

Critical response to Pynchon's short fiction has varied dramatically. While some commentators see the stories as important only in their relation to Pynchon's later, more highly regarded work, others believe they are developed enough as short pieces to stand on their own. Of the five included in *Slow Learner,* "Entropy" has received the most critical notice. Employing both Clausius's Second Law of Thermodynamics and Henry Adams's theory of entropic history—both of which hold that the transport of heat, or in Adams's case, multiplicity, within a closed system will cause the steady disintegration of that system—"Entropy" features the "lease-breaking" party of Meatball Mulligan and the efforts of Callisto and Aubade,

in the apartment above, to create an indoor environment not subject to the threat of entropy. Both systems collapse steadily into chaos over the course of the story. In "Low-Lands" Pynchon uses Dennis Flange's descent into the refuse of the Long Island sewer system as a metaphor for the human need for order and contentment, despite, Pynchon suggests, the impossibility of achieving either. "Under the Rose" explores both the historical incident at Fashoda (now Kodok) in 1898—in which British troops defeated an Arab army of 50,000, then challenged the French army, nearly provoking a European war—and its own self-referentiality as a fictionalized history. In "The Small Rain" Nathan "Lardass" Levine copes with an existential crisis while searching for corpses after a hurricane in Louisiana. "The Secret Integration" deals with several white children's reactions to their parents' racism when an African-American family moves into their neighborhood. Critics point out that themes of the usually fruitless search for a meaningful and undisturbed center in life link the stories to each other as well as to Pynchon's novels. Paul Gray has commented: "On the whole, Pynchon's early works are flawed but disciplined exercises by an apprentice who already senses the sorcerer he will become."

PRINCIPAL WORKS

SHORT FICTION

"Mortality and Mercy in Vienna" 1959 [published in journal *Epoch*]

*"The Small Rain" 1959 [published in journal *Cornell Writer*]

*"Entropy" 1960 [published in journal *Kenyon Review*]

*"Low-Lands" 1960 [published in journal *New World Writing*]

*"Under the Rose" 1961 [published in journal *Noble Savage*]

*"The Secret Integration" 1964 [published in magazine *Saturday Evening Post*]

"The World (This One), the Flesh (Mrs. Oedipa Maas), and the Testament of Pierce Inverarity" 1965 [published in magazine *Esquire*]

"The Shrink Flips" 1966 [published in journal *Cavalier*]

OTHER MAJOR WORKS

†*V.* (novel) 1963
‡*The Crying of Lot 49* (novel) 1966
Gravity's Rainbow (novel) 1973
Vineland (novel) 1990

*These works were collected and published as *Slow Learner: Early Stories* in 1984.

†This novel contains a chapter adapted from the earlier short story "Under the Rose."

‡This novel contains chapters adapted from the earlier short stories "The World (This One), the Flesh (Mrs. Oedipa Maas), and the Testament of Pierce Inverarity" and "The Shrink Flips."

CRITICISM

Joseph W. Slade (essay date 1974)

[*Slade is an American critic and educator whose works include* Thomas Pynchon, *from which the following excerpt is taken. Providing an overview of "Mortality and Mercy in Vienna," "Low-Lands," "Entropy," and "The Secret Integration," the essay explores major themes in the stories.*]

Although Pynchon's reputation [up to 1974] rests principally on his three novels, he has also published seven short stories in magazines. In chronological order they are **"Mortality and Mercy in Vienna,"** in *Epoch* (1959); **"Low-lands,"** *New World Writing* (1960); **"Entropy,"** *The Kenyon Review* (1960); **"Under the Rose,"** *The Noble Savage* (1961); **"The Secret Integration,"** *The Saturday Evening Post* (1964); **"The World (This One), The Flesh (Mrs. Oedipa Maas), and The Testament of Pierce Inverarity,"** *Esquire* (1965); and **"The Shrink Flips,"** *Cavalier* (1966).

In addition, he has written an essay entitled "A Journey into the Mind of Watts," *The New York Times Magazine* (1966). Of these shorter pieces three are slightly expanded versions of episodes in the novels: **"Under the Rose"** is taken from *V.,* while both **"The World (This One), The Flesh (Mrs. Oedipa Maas), and the Testament of Pierce Inverarity"** and **"The Shrink Flips"** are parts of *The Crying of Lot 49.* They will not be considered here. Those remaining are of interest because they are early examples of Pynchon's work, because they manifest themes—and characters—which appear later in his novels, or because they are significant in their own right. All three reasons justify a close look at Pynchon's first short story.

In **"Mortality and Mercy in Vienna,"** the thirty-year-old protagonist, Cleanth Siegel, thinks of his mind as a memory bank fed by computer cards from which he can recall information to make cocktail party conversation. The metaphor suggests one of Pynchon's most persistent concerns: technology and its relationship to human activity. More important in terms of this story is the recall of the author himself, for Pynchon uses *his* erudition not to make idle chatter but to create the rich stuff of his literature. For example, he borrows the title from *Measure for Measure,* one of Shakespeare's least pleasant comedies. In that play Duke Vincentio, aware that Vienna has become a lawless city, deputizes Angelo to clean it up, and gives him the authority to do so, including the power of life and death:

> In our remove be thou at full ourself;
> Mortality and mercy in Vienna
> Live in thy tongue and heart. . . .

In Pynchon's tale, Cleanth, who is supposed to find his girl friend at a party in Washington, D.C., inadvertently arrives early, meets his host, a Rumanian named David Lupescu, and discovers that they look very much alike. Lupescu too is startled by their Doppelgänger resemblance, and after installing Siegel as host, abandons the party to him, leaving behind a talismanic pig foetus (the first of several pigs in Pynchon's fiction) and these instructions: "As host you are a trinity: (a) receiver of guests"—ticking them off on his fingers—"(b) an enemy and (c) an outward manifestation, for *them,* of the divine body and blood." As an after-thought, as he flees "the jungle," Lupescu blurts, "Mistah Kurtz—he dead." The allusion is critical to an understanding of the story. Pynchon is invoking Conrad's *Heart of Darkness,* the literal and psychological jungle "where doubt itself is lost in an unexplored universe of incertitudes," to which Kurtz had hoped to bring civilization. Kurtz had been an agent of the International Society for the Suppression of Savage Customs. Siegel is a junior diplomat only recently returned from abroad to Washington, where he now serves on some unnamed commission. Washington, then, or more specifically, the area peopled by Lupescu's friends, would appear to be a "jungle," as in Conrad's tale, or a lawless place like Duke Vincentio's Vienna.

And it may be something else as well. "Mistah Kurtz—he dead" is also the epigraph of T. S. Eliot's "The Hollow Men." That Pynchon intends the double significance of the phrase is clear from additional references to Eliot in the story. Grossman, Siegel's roommate at Harvard, had read Eliot and Santayana as he degenerated from a healthy midwesterner into an effete Harvard type who now lives in Swampscott. Swampscott and Washington are part of an American waste land, Pynchon suggests, and the connection with Eliot's landscape is borne out by Siegel's thinking of himself as a prophet and a healer. By the time the party guests—"The Group"—arrive, singing a limerick about a man named Cheever and a beaver, Siegel in his Kurtz-role has developed "a light-headedness which he realized might be one of the first stages of hysteria but which he rather hoped was some vestige of the old nonchalance which had sustained him on the Continent for the past two years." In such a state he can even regard the limerick as profound.

Siegel is particularly susceptible to hysteria, it would appear, because of his background. He is the son of Catholic and Jewish parents, a genetic religious combination Pynchon will use later for Benny Profane in *V.* To Grossman, his roommate's Jesuitical side had prevented Siegel's being "kicked around or conscious of guilt or simply ineffective like so many of the other Jewish boys on campus." Yet, Grossman had said, "It is the seed of your destruction. . . . House divided against itself." Siegel's dual heritage has led to curious associations on his part. Instead of wanting to become a doctor, like the stereotypical Jewish son, Siegel equates healing with destruction; he remembers "sitting *shivah*" for a dead cousin while her husband cursed her doctor and the AMA.

In another allusion to Eliot, Lupescu designates Siegel a "Fisher of Souls." Siegel soon learns that he shares more than physical resemblance with the departed Rumanian. Something in their natures attracts the confidence of others; and in the past each has served as confidant and confessor for a "host of trodden-on and disaffected" people, the inhabitants of this modern waste land. Both the waste lands and the alienated characters will appear again and again in Pynchon's fiction, most notably in *The Crying of Lot 49,* and how the characters function in their sterile and sometimes hostile environment will become a major question. Siegel is not surprised when one by one the party guests tell him of his similarity to Lupescu and corner him in the Rumanian's "confessional," a bedroom decorated with crossed Browning Automatic Rifles hung on the wall. When Siegel prompts one penitent with a "Bless me father [for I have sinned]," she responds with "David said that too." This mock-priest hears confessions of decadent love affairs and emotional entanglements that increase his hysteria, "synopses and convolutions which should never have been exposed, revealing for Siegel the anatomy of a disease more serious than he had suspected. . . ." The waste land is blighted indeed.

Siegel finds one of the girls both enticing and repellent. A beautiful "sex machine," Debby Considine works for the State Department and has visited many countries, as she confesses to Siegel, there to pick up and later discard various males. Her latest prize and current escort is Irving Loon, an Ojibwa Indian she has acquired on a trip to Ontario. He stands now in a corner of the apartment like a "memento mori, withdrawn and melancholy." His melancholy triggers Siegel's memory banks. The resulting data

come from a Harvard anthropology course taught by a professor for whom "all cultures were equally mad; it was only the form that differed, never the content." According to the professor, the Ojibwa live so perpetually on the brink of starvation and extinction that the Indian brave succumbs to paranoia, convinced that the forces of nature are directed against him. Debby Considine has responded to what she, for lack of understanding, refers to as Irving Loon's ability to "come closer to something which city dwellers never find all their lives." Siegel can agree, but he knows what Debby does not: that the paranoia of the Ojibwas culminates in a peculiar psychosis, a personal identification with the Windigo, a destructive, cannibalistic spirit. Once he believes himself to be the Windigo, the starvation-prone Ojibwa comes to regard even his own relatives as "fat juicy beavers," a "host" to be killed and eaten.

Irving has already mentioned the Windigo to Debby, who mindlessly attributes the term to the Indian's "poetic, religious quality." Such language, uttered casually, pushes the "healer and prophet" deeper into hysteria. As soon as Debby introduces her confessor to her lover, Siegel tests his thesis by whispering "Windigo." Irving reacts with weird affection towards Debby, calling her "my beautiful little beaver." The innocently lewd limerick, now sinister, is an early example of Pynchon's skillful manipulation of motifs. Everything connects in his fiction, sometimes with so audible a click that critics accuse him of too great a passion for unity and artificial linkages.

Of all the members of the party, only Siegel knows what to make of the taciturn Indian, and if Irving behaves as anticipated then Siegel in his hysteria believes he has the power "to bring them a very tangible salvation. A miracle involving a host, true, but like no holy eucharist." At this point the allusions to Eliot and Conrad begin to swell. Eliot's waste land requires the imposition of a new mythology, a new religion, before it can be cleansed and healed of its sterility. Ironically, Siegel perceives in Irving Loon's primitive paranoia just the kind of healing the waste land needs. It will be a religion of retribution, of apocalypse. Conrad's Kurtz scrawls on his report to the International Society for the Suppression of Savage Customs the ominous words "Exterminate all the brutes." "The miracle *was* in his hands after all," Siegel's Jesuit side says to him: "It was just unfortunate that Irving Loon would be the only one partaking of any body and blood, divine or otherwise." Spurred by Siegel and seen only by him, the Ojibwa takes a rifle down from the wall of Lupescu's bedroom and searches happily for ammunition. Siegel leaves the party without saying anything to the guests sprawled under the pig foetus, and hears the first reports of Irving Loon's celebration of the host from the street outside. By loosing the berserk Indian, he has acted as prophet and healer to the waste land; he has healed its sickness by annihilation.

Pynchon possesses the enviable ability to blend fact and fantasy in such a way that the facts seem less credible than the fantasies. The Windigo psychosis is well documented by anthropologists but appears more preposterous than Lupescu's leaving his party to a stranger or hanging BAR's on his walls. As Pynchon becomes more adept at incorporating his wide knowledge into his stories, the line separating the real and the ridiculous will grow thinner. Of continuing relevance also are several of the motifs of **"Mortality and Mercy in Vienna."** The weightiest is paranoia, which for Pynchon, as for novelists like Joesph Heller, Ken Kesey, William Burroughs, and Norman Mailer, is a means of perception, a way of restructuring the world. While Irving Loon is probably the most extreme of Pynchon's paranoids, other paranoids in his fiction seem almost reasonable. After all, in an insane world—call it waste land or whatever—paranoia represents an attempt to establish sanity, to create order out of chaos. To believe however erroneously that the world is hostile is to establish a basis for action. A second motif involves an assumed moral superiority of "primitive" cultures over the decadent, "civilized" type. Superseding the Objiwas in later stories will be Maltese and Africans, cultures which have been laid waste by colonialism, but which still retain some spark of vitality. A third motif is a human penchant for annihilation as an alternative to a blighted world. The desire grows out of the "irresistibly fascinating" whisper like that which Kurtz hears in *Heart of Darkness*. As Conrad's Marlowe says of Kurtz's whisper, "it echoed loudly within him because he was hollow at the core. . . . " Cleanth Siegel suffers from a void within, and his whisper is amplified by the perception of a void without; Siegel and his successors in Pynchon's work can not tolerate such a vacuum.

While the mood of **"Mortality and Mercy in Vienna"** is somber, that of Pynchon's second story, **"Low-lands,"** is deliberately funny, marking the advent of what is usually called his black humor, a label which Bruce Jay Friedman defines—very appropriately, since Pynchon's story concerns a sailor—as sailing "into darker waters somewhere out beyond satire." The definition is doubly appropriate if one should regard T. S. Eliot's *The Waste Land* as satire, for **"Low-lands"** is almost a parody of that poem.

"Low-lands" differs from **"Mortality and Mercy"** in other respects also. Unlike Cleanth Siegel, Dennis Flange, the protagonist of **"Low-lands,"** retreats into passivity. His stasis is one of the things that makes the story less than successful, but from it Pynchon will learn to use multiple plots to carry his themes. In some ways Dennis Flange anticipates Benny Profane; he has the earmarks of the schlemihl. Actually he is more the prototype for the disaffected husband who appears as Roony Winsome in *V.* and as Mucho Maas in *The Crying of Lot 49*. A lawyer in the firm of Wasp and that (presumably) same Winsome, Flange has been married—childlessly—for seven years to a respectability-seeking wife, Cindy. Over the years they have drifted apart, an impasse for which Flange blames Cindy, although he is aware of the ironies of his having been a communications officer in the Navy. The whole problem, he believes, is somehow Freudian, an interpretation promoted by Flange's mad psychiatrist, Geronimo Diaz—another prototype, this time for Dr. Hilarius of *The Crying of Lot 49* and the insane scientists and healers of "The White Visitation" in *Gravity's Rainbow*—who claims that he is Paganini and that he has made a pact with the devil which has cost him his genius with the violin. Diaz's sessions with Flange consist chiefly of his serving his patient endless martinis and reading from "random-number tables from the Ebbinghaus nonsense syllable lists, ignoring everything that Flange would be trying to tell him." Such practices, taken together with Flange's former occupation in the Navy, are early indications of Pynchon's preoccupation with communication and information theory. Diaz's madness, however, is of "no known model or pattern," and Flange finds that his visits are a necessary corrective to a life too conventional and too rational.

Flange perceives that since his hitch in the Navy the routines of his life have eroded the romantic image he once held of himself as a stalwart Officer of the Deck, "fortune's elf-child and disinherited darling, young and randy and more a Jolly Jack Tar than anyone human could possibly be." Gradually he has regressed into passivity, becoming more and more fetal. His house, which he calls his "womb with a view," perches on a cliff overlooking Long Island Sound. It is a curious structure rising out of a tumulus of earth; beneath it are secret subterranean passages built by rum-runners during Prohibition. House and honeycombed tunnels form an "almost organic mound" to which Flange feels joined as if by umbilical cord, a place where he can practice "molemanship." Throughout Pynchon's work, undergrounds both literal and metaphorical are recurrent motifs. Tunnels and sewers appear in his early efforts as psychological and metaphysical arcs, as negative parabolas which will have a positive counterpart in the parabola of the V-2 rocket in *Gravity's Rainbow*. While Flange has tried to think of the house as a bower, and himself and Cindy as happy birds in it, it has not worked out that way. Cindy is too cold, too logical; she likes paintings by Mondrian, whose angled landscapes contrasts markedly with the surfaces Flange encounters later in the story. Theirs has been a sterile marriage.

A second motif in **"Low-lands"** evolves more slowly and eventually gives the story its title. It is a complex and ambiguous motif borrowed from Eliot. Flange, his memory pitched at the 30° list of a heaving vessel, dreams of the sea. There his Doppelgänger strides the rolling deck. The sea, Geronimo Diaz fatuously tells him, is mother to us all, since it generated life and still in a sense flows through human veins. So strong is Flange's affinity for the ocean that he cannot even tell a sea story when his buddies do, believing that

> if you are Dennis Flange and if the sea's tides are the same that not only wash along your veins but also billow through your fantasies then it is all right to listen to but not tell stories about that sea, because you and the truth of a true lie were thrown sometime way back into a curious contiguity and as long as you are passive you can remain aware of the truth's extent but the minute you become active you are somehow, if not violating a truth outright, at least screwing up the perspective of things, much as anyone observing subatomic particles changes the works, data and odds, by the act of observing.

This invoking of the Heisenberg principle of physics, this refusal or inability to become involved—which is one of the things he admires about his psychiatrist—is the key to Flange's personality, as it is to those of many other characters in Pynchon's stories. Flange's attitude is an assertion of passivity, a willingness to take events as they happen, to withdraw from participation. An obvious symbol for such passivity is the womb, but to it Pynchon here somewhat clumsily links another, the sea. In one respect, the sea suggests the amniotic fluid in which the fetus floats and the security the womb offers. At the same time the sea is dangerous: It can drown victims. Still a third aspect affects Flange, however. In his irrational moments he thinks of the sea as a "low-lands," a term he remembers from a sea-chanty. Viewed at certain times, the ocean seems "a waste land which stretches away to the horizon," a plain or desert which requires but one human figure "for completeness." Flange has come to think of his life as a flat surface, with "an assurance of perfect, passionless uniformity"; what he fears most is a convexity, a bulging of the planet's curvature that would leave him exposed. This vision of a flat surface, of course, is of a sea without water—in short, Eliot's waste land, arid and sterile. Flange imagines himself walking across this flat, solid sea from city to city. His psychiatrist considers this fantasy "a bizarre variation on the messiah complex," but Diaz, as might be expected, is only partly correct. Flange is the traveler of the waste land, similar to the protagonist of Eliot's poem, the man who draws the Tarot card of the Phoenician Sailor.

On the day of the story Flange has stayed home from work to drink wine and listen to Vivaldi with Rocco Squarcione, the local garbageman. Offended, Cindy stomps around upstairs, but at least leaves them alone; Flange wonders how anyone can stand a house without a second story. Cindy hits the ceiling, however, when another old buddy arrives. This is Pig Bodine, one of the best and most ubiquitous of Pynchon's minor characters, the all-round pervert and good natured if slightly sinister slob that his name implies. Cindy despises him, for good reason; on her wedding night Bodine had inveigled Dennis into having a few beers, and she had not heard from them until two weeks later, when her husband wired her from Cedar Rapids, Iowa. Now, fed up with his friends and his habits, she throws them all out and tells Flange not to come back. He goes docilely. "Maybe if they had had kids . . . ," he speculates only briefly.

In his garbage truck Rocco drives Bodine and Flange to the city dump, where the nightwatchman, a Negro named Bolingbroke, will put them up for the night. Pynchon borrows this name from Shakespeare to suggest mock royalty (Bolingbroke became Henry IV). Bolingbroke is a rootless former sailor of wide travel, having come into brief and comic contact with the absurdities of colonialism—another example of Pynchon's incipient interest in imperialism and injustice—before he retired to the dump. More to the point, Bolingbroke is king of the waste land; to Flange the dump is "an island or enclave in the dreary country around it, a discrete kingdom with Bolingbroke its uncontested ruler." Flange immediately perceives the predictable correspondence: The dump is a "low-lands." It is fifty feet below ground level but is inevitably rising as garbage fills it. This "fatedness" seizes and terrifies him, for it reminds him of his fear of convexity. He compares the gradual rise to a "maddeningly slow elevator . . . carrying you toward a known level to confer with some inevi-

table face on matters which had already been decided." By the time Pynchon writes *Gravity's Rainbow,* the accretion of debris or detritus will serve as his principal metaphor for the history of civilization. It is a frightening image: the waste land, in this case a literal one, sifting deeper and deeper in accumulated sterility.

Rocco leaves; Bolingbroke finds Pig and Dennis mattresses from a huge mountain of discarded household goods, the cast-off trash of a civilization, and then herds them into his ramshackle house with strange haste. Once inside, they begin the rather adolescent boozing which passes for camaraderie in so much of Pynchon's work. As they swap stories, Pynchon pulls out the stops in his eagerness to find amusing—if fuzzy—parallels for Eliot's *The Waste Land.* On his travels Bolingbroke has had an affair with a woman named Zenobia, a substitute for Eliot's Dido and Cleopatra. Allusions to Dante also echo Eliot's: Bolingbroke had once shipped on an Italian merchantman where he "shoveled coal as if into the fires of hell." For his part, in lieu of Eliot's Hanged Man, Dennis contributes a tale of a fraternity house escapade which ended with a stolen female cadaver hanging out of a window. When they have finished their muscatel, they turn in, but not before Bolingbroke warns the others not to pay attention to the gypsies who prowl the dump at night. His fear of them has caused him to put a strong lock on the door.

Some hours later Flange is awakened by a siren voice (Eliot: "voices singing out of empty cisterns and exhausted wells") calling to his Doppelgänger image of himself, as an "Anglo" with blond hair. Outside, before he can see who is calling, he trips one of Bolingbroke's booby-traps (laid for the gypsies), and disappears under a falling mountain of snow-tires. He is revived by a beautiful "angel," a girl only three and a half feet tall, who leads him to her home, a chamber deep underneath the dump reached by tunnels leading, ironically, from an abandoned GE refrigerator. The tunnel complex, complete with electricity stolen from the Long Island Lighting Company, she tells him, was built in the thirties by the Sons of the Red Apocalypse (the first of Pynchon's secret underground conspiracies) in preparation for revolution. When Federal agents arrested them all, the gypsies moved in.

The girl's name is Nerissa, which may also derive from Shakespeare (*The Merchant of Venice*), or Pynchon may be playing on "Nereids," the nymphs of the sea. Who she really is becomes apparent when she introduces Flange to her pet rat—the prototype of the rat Veronica in *V.* The rat's name is Hyacinth, and Nerissa is clearly the hyacinth girl of "The Burial of the Dead" section of *The Waste Land.* Nerissa wants Flange to be her husband; she had been told by a fortune teller named Violetta—Eliot's Madame Sosostris—that she would wed an Anglo like him. Flange considers. Noticing that Nerissa looks like a child, and the rat *her* child, he wonders again why he and Cindy never had children. He decides to stay:

> A child makes it all right. Let the world shrink
>   to a *boccie* ball.
> So of course he knew.

What he knows is not entirely clear. In Eliot's poem, the protagonist encounters the hyacinth girl in this passage:

"You gave me hyacinths first a year ago;
They called me the hyacinth girl."
—Yet when we came back, late, from the Hyacinth garden,
Your arms full, and your hair wet, I could not
Speak, and my eyes failed, I was neither
Living nor dead, and I knew nothing,
Looking into the heart of light, the silence.
Oed' und leer das meer [Waste and empty the sea].

Pynchon's story ends with Nerissa holding the rat Hyacinth in her arms and with Flange visualizing her in terms of sea images: "White caps danced across her eyes; sea creatures, he knew, would be cruising about in the submarine green of her heart." Of possible relevance also is the passage immediately following the one just quoted from *The Waste Land.* There Madame Sosostris tells the fortune of Eliot's protagonist. When he draws the Tarot card of the Phoenician Sailor, she predicts death by drowning, as a sacrifice for the redemption of the Waste Land.

Probably by intention on Pynchon's part, several interpretations are possible. Eliot's waste land suffers from failures of communication and love. Similar failures afflict Flange, and the dump, Pynchon's waste land, symbolizes his life. The dump is not a particularly good paradigm, however. As Eliot himself would say, it is not an "objective correlative" for Flange's condition, if only because we know too little about him, but it does represent an amusing and imaginative attempt to unite the motifs of water and waste made so famous by Eliot's poem. At the conclusion of **"Low-lands,"** Nerissa, who has much in common with the loving females Pynchon will develop later, offers Flange love, admiration for the image he has of himself, and the potentiality of fertility, although the rat, an indication of decay and disease in *The Waste Land,* is here at best a mocking promise. No real healing or redemption seems forthcoming, even if one assumes that Flange has symbolically died—drowned or buried by the falling snow tires—and risen; he is a miserable Messiah. Given his essential passivity, given his resemblance to other schlemihls in Pynchon's work, it is more likely that he has simply exchanged a "womb with a view" for a womb with no view at all, where, deep underneath the waste land, he is neither "living nor dead." He prefers withdrawal underground to the void, the emptiness above. Flange is inert—paralyzed by surfaces, surfaces Pynchon will convert into endless streets in his later fiction.

One of Pynchon's admirers, Richard Poirier, has observed [in *The Performing Self,* 1971] that "the signal 'self-destruct' might be said to flash whenever a reader of Pynchon presses too confidently at the point where he thinks he's located the 'meaning.' " Although usually the ambiguity adds to appreciation, in **"Low-lands"** it seems merely the confusion of the author, the product of inexperience infatuated with cleverness of the type which, as Burton Feldman says [in his essay "Anatomy of Black Humor," in *The American Novel since World War II,* 1969], renders Black Humor frequently too academic. Pynchon himself has Fausto Maijstral remark in *V.* that "Shakespeare and T. S. Eliot ruined us all." Although the story is pleasantly nutty, **"Low-lands"** is much less accom-plished than **"Mortality and Mercy in Vienna."** In the latter, Pynchon's literary allusions bear the weight of his ambiguity without effort. In **"Low-lands,"** because he too closely adapts Eliot's motifs, themselves very complex and ambiguous, the result is fuzziness. Moreover, the story is essentially static; at the end Flange returns full circle to a fetal state, and the plot does not advance. Nevertheless, elements of **"Low-lands"** presage motifs and incidents in Pynchon's later work: failures of communication, underground networks, oddballs who enjoy Vivaldi, loving females, images of history, midgets. Considered together, the first two stories exemplify the extremes of responses to the waste land of modern civilization: a desire for annihilation, for one's self or for others; and a desire for withdrawal, in order to protect one's self against the waste land's encroachment.

With **"Entropy,"** Henry Adams displaces T. S. Eliot as Pynchon's principal literary creditor, although references to de Sade, Faulkner, and Djuna Barnes crop up as well. If **"Low-lands"** demonstrates that the saturation of one's work with allusions to the work of others is tricky business, **"Entropy"** reestablishes the method as a valid artistic approach. In a philosophical sense, Pynchon would say, we are all influenced by cultural history, so that what others have thought and written affects us in many ways. Pynchon differs from most similarly oriented writers in one important respect, however: He is just as insistent on the cultural value of the sciences as of the humanities, and in **"Entropy"** he makes far-reaching allusions to both. Willard Gibbs and Ludwig Boltzmann are juxtaposed brilliantly with Henry Adams and Henry Miller. From Miller, Pynchon borrows a metaphor; **"Entropy"** begins with an epigraph from *Tropic of Cancer* in which Miller speaks of this age's depressing cultural and metaphysical climate as inclement weather:

> There will be more calamities, more death, more despair.
>
> Not the slightest indication of a change anywhere. . . . We must get into step, a lockstep toward the prison of death. There is no escape. The weather will not change.

With this metaphor Pynchon associates a second, from *The Education of Henry Adams:* the concept of entropy as historical process. Adams in turn had developed the concept from the work of the American physicist Willard Gibbs. By updating Gibbs with references to Boltzmann and Rudolf Clausius, who with Gibbs contributed to theories of chemical and physical equilibrium, Pynchon can make use of entropy as a term denoting the unavailability of energy in thermodynamic processes.

The classic formulations of these processes are the three Laws of Thermodynamics. The first states that heat can be converted into work (and work into heat), that the amount of work is always equal to the amount of heat, that heat can always be expressed in terms of energy, and that the amount of heat in a closed system is always constant. The first law is commonly known as the Principle of the Conservation of Energy: Energy cannot be created or destroyed. The third law states that every substance has a definite availability of energy to do work that approaches zero as the temperature approaches absolute zero. As energy becomes unavailable, the entropy will increase. For the purposes of Adams and Pynchon, the second law is the most important; it states that when a free exchange of heat takes place between two bodies as a self-sustaining and continuous process, the heat must always be transferred from the hotter to the colder body. In other words, the entropy is irreversible; it will always increase until the two bodies are uniformly cold, and without any remaining energy.

From his study of thermodynamics Rudolf Clausius perceived an analogy between heat-systems and the universe itself, as Sir William Dampier explains in *A History of Science:*

> Mechanical work can only be obtained from heat when heat passes from a hot body to a cold one. This process tends to diminish the difference of temperature, which is also diminished by conduction of heat, friction, and other irreversible processes. The availability of energy in an irreversible system is always becoming less, and its converse—the quantity called by Clausius the entropy—is always tending to a maximum. Thus the energy of an isolated system, and therefore (it was assumed) of the Universe, is slowly passing into heat, uniformly distributed and therefore unavailable as a source of useful work. Eventually, it was thought, by this dissipation of energy the Universe must become motionless and dead.

Clausius predicted that "heat-death" would occur when everything in the universe reached the same temperature, a prophecy Adams and Pynchon extend to human society, which is also a system. According to Adams, over history entropy increases; the world is running down. One manifestation of an increase in entropy is mounting chaos within the system as energy begins to disperse more and more randomly. Systems in good repair function in an orderly fashion, but as they succumb to entropy, order falls victim to chaos. Somewhat paradoxically, another manifestation of increasing energy, depending on the kind of system, is greater homogeneity among the system's parts. Healthy systems encompass diverse elements in relationship to one another, but as entropy increases, these elements lose their differentiation. Thus it is possible to speak of entropy as a measure of disorganization and unpredictability, and also as a measure of sameness and conformity.

But there are other kinds of systems and another kind of entropy. Complicating Pynchon's story is his introduction of communication theory. Within a communication system, many things can cause information to deteriorate; the effect of distortion and noise, say when two people are speaking on a telephone, can act like friction and conduction on energy within a thermodynamic system. In communication theory, entropy also represents the decay or loss of information, although the ramifications of the term grow complex. In *The Crying of Lot 49*, Pynchon explores the abstruse relationship between communication theory and thermodynamics; in **"Entropy,"** the term entropy in communications serves merely as counterpoint to the term as applied to the running down of the universe and society.

"Entropy" is skillfully constructed around the interlocking metaphors of weather and entropy in its double sense. Its structure can be visualized—by an analogy Pynchon would appreciate—as parallel vectors pointing in opposite directions. The two tracks provide compression and tension for the narrative. On one floor of a Washington, D. C., apartment house Meatball Mulligan's lease-breaking party, now in its second day, has been disintegrating into chaos steadily augmented by newly-arriving guests. In this respect, the party as a system is not exactly closed, since people do enter and leave, but Pynchon may be suggesting that social systems are not entirely isolated; that would seem to be the point, that Meatball does not try to wall himself off from the outside. By contrast, on the floor above a man named Callisto has perfected an ordered existence in a hermetically-sealed, ecologically stable flat at cost of isolation from the world. In fact, Callisto's apartment is a small-scale jungle, a "hothouse" in which he lives with a girl named Aubade, of French and Annamese ancestry—by which Pynchon may be hinting at exploitation by a technological colonialism. They do not go out, since Callisto fears the outside. He worries about the "heat-death" of the universe, a fixation abetted at the time of the story by the weather. For three days the mercury has registered 37 degrees outside; the weather will not change. Paranoiacally Callisto seizes on the phenomenon as an omen of the end.

The significance of the story's title is amplified in Callisto's ruminations, which are interspersed with the events of the party below. Callisto has awakened holding a sick bird; he has been nestling the creature against himself for three days, trying to revive it with heat from his own body and forestall the heat-death that comes to all things. The bird's illness is a microcosmic event in Callisto's world, for he has ordered his life and his environment into "a tiny enclave of regularity in the city's chaos, alien to the vagaries of the weather, of national politics, of any civil disorder." He is resisting entropy with a kind of love. It is the first such linkage of love and power in Pynchon's fiction:

> Henry Adams, three generations before his own, had stared aghast at Power; Callisto found himself now in much the same state over Thermodynamics, the inner life of that power, realizing like his predecessor that the Virgin and the dynamo stand as much for love as for power; that the two are indeed identical; and that love not only makes the world go 'round but also makes the boccie ball spin, the nebula precess.

It is the "sidereal" aspect of power that bothers Callisto; he knows that energy decays and that entropy is on the rise.

To Aubade Callisto dictates his memoirs, in third person, like Henry Adams. In doing so he recalls a mnemonic device from his undergraduate days for memorizing the Laws of Thermodynamics: "You can't win, things are going to get worse before they get better, who says they're going to get better," which ties the narrative to the weather-epigraph from Henry Miller. Now in middle-age, Callisto is forced to consider the thermodynamic equations of Gibbs, Boltzmann, and Clausius. Until now Callisto has been a disciple of Machiavelli, whose *The Prince* assumed that human agency (*virtú*) and chance (*fortuna*) governed the human condition in approximately equal proportions, "but the equations now introduced a random factor which pushed the odds to some unutterable and indeterminate ratio which he found himself afraid to calculate." Outside, the world appears to have gone chaotic: Madison Avenue rules America through a "consumerism" which has reduced people and things from healthy "differentiation to sameness, from ordered individuality to a kind of chaos." For Callisto entropy is a metaphor for decadence in society, and he predicts "a heat-death for his culture in which ideas, like heat-energy, would no longer be transferred, since each point in it would ultimately have the same quantity of energy; and intellectual motion would, accordingly, cease."

While Callisto treads his mental paces, below stairs Meatball Mulligan's party rollicks on. Meatball's guests range from the weird to the aimless, most of them pseudo-intellectuals, phony would-be expatriates, polyglots from the State Department, girls from the National Security Agency (whose prime function is code-breaking)—most of them employed in some way by the government and engaged in some form of communications. Dominating the rest are the Duke di Angelis quartet, a spaced-out group of musicians sporting sunglasses and smoking marijuana, thoroughly decadent. At one point the four decide to have a session—*sans* instruments. They tap their feet and swing their bodies to the inaudible strains of "Love For Sale," which is only moderately successful: "at least we ended together," says one. For their second number they try a variation on Gerry (not Meatball) Mulligan; they will *think* the root chords. Unfortunately, one soundlessly plays "I'll Remember April" while the other three launch into "These Foolish Things," a highly appropriate title. No one hears a note, of course, but this absurd exercise is directly related to Pynchon's theme. By playing without instruments, the quartet try to avoid noise and distortion, to overcome entropy, to communicate on a purely mental level. If the attempt is fruitless, it is no worse than Callisto's experiment in divorcing himself from the world.

Only Meatball provides a viable approach to the pervasive problem of entropy in both communications and thermodynamics. After waking with a hangover, and after fixing a tequila sour for "restoring order to his nervous system," he listens sympathetically to his friend Saul, who has just split from his wife Miriam; the fight was over communication theory. Saul works for the government on a top-secret project called MUFFET (Multi-Unit Factorial Field Electronic Calculator), and Miriam has been angered by Saul's speaking of "human behavior like a program fed into an IBM machine." Meatball claims not to know anything about communication theory. "Who does?" asks Saul. Perhaps, offers Mulligan, there is a "language barrier." Saul will not buy that:

> "If it is anything it's a kind of leakage. Tell a girl: 'I love you.' No trouble with two-thirds of that, it's a closed circuit. Just you and she, but that nasty four-letter word in the middle, *that's* the one you have to look out for. Ambiguity. Redundance. Irrelevance, even. Leakage. All this is

noise. Noise screws up your signal, makes for disorganization in the circuit."

Under Meatball's benign if inept influence, however, Saul finally admits that his friend's attitude is right. Nobody runs "at top efficiency," he concludes, and marriages are "sort of founded on compromises." By extrapolation, so is communication; one does the best one can to cope with entropy.

As the "system" of his party continues to decay, Mulligan does what he can to keep things functioning—not at top efficiency, but through compromise. Saul is dropping waterbags out the window, a girl is drowning in the bathtub, drunks are fighting, and horny sailors are gatecrashing in the belief they have found a whorehouse. Unlike Cleanth Siegel at a similar party, Meatball responds humanely. He has two choices: He can crawl in a closet and wait till everybody leaves, or he can "try to calm everybody down, one by one." The former option is tempting, and the latter involves hard work, but Pynchon is suggesting that hard work is the only legitimate means humans have to combat entropy in social systems and between ourselves. Hard as the job is, Meatball does "keep his lease-breaking party from deteriorating into total chaos"; he restores order among his different guests.

Contrapuntally, Aubade senses Callisto's rising terror with alarm. As one who comes from a colonialized country, Aubade is no stranger to compromise either. Moreover, she apprehends the world through sound, as "music which emerged at intervals from a howling darkness of discordancy." Aubade hears Callisto's words mingled with car horns on the street outside and the wild music from the speakers in Meatball's flat:

> The architectonic purity of her world was constantly threatened by such hints of anarchy: gaps and excrescences and skew lines, and a shifting or tilting of planes to which she had continually to readjust lest the whole structure shiver into a disarray of discrete and meaningless signals. Callisto had described the process once as a kind of "feedback": she crawled into dreams each night with a sense of exhaustion, and a desperate resolve never to relax that vigilance.

Words like "signals" and "feedback" belong to communication theory. Aubade expends her energy balancing the "signal-to-noise ratio." Exhausted himself, Callisto has rejected all post-World War I music as decadent, but Aubade speaks in accents of pure melody. He can not forget that war, and is still living in its aftermath.

When the bird he is cradling begins to die, Callisto, "helpless in the past," is paralyzed. Like Meatball, Aubade must make a choice, but unlike him she elects to allow disorder to penetrate an ordered system—because either way the system will decay. With bleeding hands she smashes the windows of the hothouse, and turns to wait

> until the moment of equilibrium was reached, when 37 degrees Fàhrenheit should prevail both outside and inside, and forever, and the hovering, curious dominant of their separate lives should resolve into a tonic of darkness and the final absence of all motion.

Death may be the consequence, but at least the hothouse has been opened to the life of the street. One must face the possibility of eventual annihilation, not try to arrest time. Aubade's act is an acknowledgment of the limited choices available. Callisto's love is not enough; love, like power, will decay. Mulligan shoulders responsibility for his life in time—and entropy is time's arrow. He merely retards the inevitable, but it is the only real choice he has. The choice, the polarity between hothouse and street, and the concept of entropy will structure Pynchon's novels.

"The Secret Integration," the first of Pynchon's stories to appear in a magazine of large circulation, is perhaps his least successful. Published after *V.*, it suffers from the very qualities that make the novel so engaging. *V.* is discursive and loose, but its diffusion is appropriate to its global setting. Equally loose, **"The Secret Integration"** is set in Mingeborough, Massachusetts, the Berkshire Mountain hometown of Tyrone Slothrop, protagonist of *Gravity's Rainbow*, and the small community cannot contain the multiple motifs of the plot. Actually the story seems to have been lifted from *Gravity's Rainbow*, where it left a small hole in the larger narrative. While we are criticizing it, we should note that perhaps because the story was written for *The Saturday Evening Post*, it has an air of cuteness about it, as if Pynchon, having become a recluse like J. D. Salinger, felt constrained to write like him too.

Nevertheless, **"The Secret Integration"** has its moments, and more importantly, has elements of considerable relevance to Pynchon's other work. As one might expect, paranoia, technical terminology, and communication and its failures are given prominence. One of the protagonists is a Salinger-type prodigy named Grover Snodd, a young mathematical genius. A couple of days a week he attends a nearby college, having been forced out of his school by what he believes is a cabal of parents and teachers incensed at his helping other kids with their homework. Among Grover's several hobbies is a radio receiver he has built, on which he and his friends listen to police calls and other hams, "disembodied voices, sometimes even as far away as the sea," which fill their dreams of the world beyond the mountains. Their TV sets only pick up one channel.

Grover's friends are a mixed group. They include Tim Santora, through whose eyes events are seen; Étienne Cherdlu (a play on Etaoin Shrdlu, the linotype operator's device), a boy who delights in practical jokes; Hogan Slothrop, brother to the Tyrone of *Gravity's Rainbow*, at nine the youngest member of Mingeborough's Alcoholics Anonymous, having renounced booze and gotten religion; Kim Dufay, a sixth-grader easily turned on by explosives, whose size 28A padded bra allows her to infiltrate PTA meetings; several minor characters like Nunzi Passarella, who has made his reputation by bringing a quarter-ton Poland China sow to school for Show-and-Tell; and Carl Barrington, a Negro boy new to the group. Actually, the story deals with how Carl came to be a member. Theirs is not so much a group as a conspiracy, a real one, led by Grover and directed against "the scaled-up world adults made, remade and lived in without" them, at "walls, at

anything else solid that happened to be around," at "inertia and stubbornness."

With the exception of Étienne Cherdlu's father, a junk man who believes people should worry about automation rather than skin color, the parents of Mingeborough's children are all bigots, hysterical at the thought of a black family moving into town and at the prospect of integration in general. "What's integration mean?" Tim Santora asks Grover. The only kind the math whiz ever heard of is

> "The opposite of differentiation," Grover said, drawing an x-axis, y-axis and curve on his green-board. "Call this function of x. Consider values of the curve any little increments of x"—drawing straight lines from the curve down to the x-axis, like the bars of a jail cell—"you can have as many of these as you want, see, as close together as you want."

> "Till it's all solid," Tim said.

> "No, it never gets solid. If this was a jail cell, and those lines were bars, and whoever was behind it could make himself any size he wanted to be, he could always make himself skinny enough to get free. No matter how close together the bars were."

Grover has sketched the possibilities of human freedom in a highly "integrated" social system. Wiser than most of Pynchon's characters, Grover knows that the lines are artificial, mathematical conveniences, and he also knows that a paradox is involved: without integration there can be no differentiation in a healthy society. In a viable system disparate elements function in concert. Despite his wisdom, however, Grover will be defeated by the cell bars of society's functions, for this is a story of childhood loss of innocence. Grover has been training the other kids in a subversive organization he has named Operation Spartacus after the Kirk Douglas movie. Financed by contributions from school milk money and by the sale of building materials stolen from a new housing project into which a black family proposes to move, the Spartacists make sodium bombs to disrupt the school and sabotage the local paper mill by stirring up machinery-stalling silt in the river from which the mill draws its water.

Most of their sorties are abortive, partly because most of Grover's followers are too young to understand Grover's plans of attack, his passion for "symmetry" in strategy, and partly because the kids can be stopped by the lines of force the adults have drawn. In one raid on their school, the children are enthusiastic until they reach the playing field lines chalked around the perimeter; they cannot pass. Grover theorizes that "the line figure in the grass might have reminded the little kids of chalk lines on a green-board." Grover tries to drill his troops by laying out lines on a practice field, but they lack adult authority, and Tim complains that the whole idea is unreal.

While the "Inner Junta" members of the group are not without sophistication, they are still fond of the trappings of adolescence. Their hideout is the mansion of "King Yrjö," an estate once owned, so legend has it, by a royal European pretender, and still inhabited by the ghost of the King's aide, a seven-foot-tall cavalry officer. It offers a suitable make-believe environment, and Grover and friends reach it in Huck Finn fashion, using an abandoned boat to cross the old canal system which surrounds the estate. Grover has almost given up on Operation Spartacus when Hogan Slothrop gets a call from the local Alcoholics Anonymous to go to the town's hotel to sit with a transient trying to kick the habit.

The transient turns out to be a Negro, the first the children have ever seen, an indigent jazz musician who has just played at the Lenox music festival. None of the adult A.A. members will have anything to do with a Negro, so they have sent Hogan in answer to the man's call, as a joke. Of course Hogan takes the assignment quite seriously, persuades Tim Santora to accompany him, and bravely sets off to calm the alky's jitters. At first offended by what he knows to be an insult on the part of Mingeborough's adults, Mr. McAfee, the black, warms to the ingenuousness of the boys and soon unburdens himself. His tales of isolation both racial and personal elicit their sympathy; they remind Tim of "all those cops and merchant captains and barge tenders over the radio, all those voices bouncing off the invisible dome in the sky and down to Grover's antenna and into Tim's dreams." In McAfee's voice Tim recognizes other drifters, relatives who disappeared during the Depression, riders on buses and freight trains. So lonely is McAfee that Tim tries to telephone long distance to a girl the man can hardly remember, but whose number he has been carrying in his wallet for years. As the telephone circuits open

> Tim's foot felt the edge of a certain abyss which he had been walking close to—for who knows how long?—without knowing. . . . It was night here . . . one single night over the entire land, making people, already so tiny in it, invisible too in the dark; and how hard it would be, how hopeless, to really find a person you needed suddenly, unless you lived all your life in a house like he did, with a mother and father.

Before pathos can overwhelm the scene, it is relieved by the arrival of Grover and Étienne Cherdlu, the latter decked in his skin diver's suit from attempting to sabotage the paper mill, both afraid the police are after them. Cherdlu's panic and McAfee's need for a drink soon do bring the cops, who arrest the Negro for vagrancy and run him out of town. The boys never see McAfee again, but his treatment by the adults has two consequences for the kids. The first is a retaliatory caper which momentarily rejuvenates Operation Spartacus; it is also an attempt "to resurrect a friend," McAfee. The kids rig up green flood lights along the railroad tracks, dress up in costumes and masks, and stage a night attack that terrifies a trainload of passengers. It is an affirmation of color, says Grover: "I feel different now and better for having been green, even sickly green, even for a minute."

The second consequence concerns Carl Barrington. The racism in Mingeborough reaches a head when the townspeople learn that blacks have actually moved into the new housing project. Tim and the other boys overhear their parents making hate-telephone calls to the newcomers, the Barringtons. The Inner Junta compensates by accepting Carl without reservation; it is a "secret integration." The point of the story, revealed at the end, is that the Barringtons have no children. Carl is imaginary, "put together out

---

An excerpt from "Entropy"

The last bass notes of *The Heroes' Gate* boomed up through the floor and woke Callisto from an uneasy sleep. The first thing he became aware of was a small bird he had been holding gently between his hands, against his body. He turned his head sidewise on the pillow to smile down at it, at its blue hunched-down head and sick, lidded eyes, wondering how many more nights he would have to give it warmth before it was well again. He had been holding the bird like that for three days: it was the only way he knew to restore its health. Next to him the girl stirred and whimpered, her arm thrown across her face. Mingled with the sounds of the rain came the first tentative, querulous morning voices of the other birds, hidden in philodendrons and small fan palms: patches of scarlet, yellow and blue laced through this Rousseau-like fantasy, this hothouse jungle it had taken him seven years to weave together. Hermetically sealed, it was a tiny enclave of regularity in the city's chaos, alien to the vagaries of the weather, of national politics, of any civil disorder. Through trial-and-error Callisto had perfected its ecological balance, with the help of the girl its artistic harmony, so that the swayings of its plant life, the stirrings of its birds and human inhabitants were all as integral as the rhythms of a perfectly-executed mobile. He and the girl could no longer, of course, be omitted from that sanctuary; they had become necessary to its unity. What they needed from outside was delivered. They did not go out.

"Is he all right," she whispered. She lay like a tawny question mark facing him, her eyes suddenly huge and dark and blinking slowly. Callisto ran a finger beneath the feathers at the base of the bird's neck; caressed it gently. "He's going to be well, I think. See: he hears his friends beginning to wake up." The girl had heard the rain and the birds even before she was fully awake. Her name was Aubade: she was part French and part Annamese, and she lived on her own curious and lonely planet, where the clouds and the odor of poincianas, the bitterness of wine and the accidental fingers at the small of her back or feathery against her breasts came to her reduced inevitably to the terms of sound: of music which emerged at intervals from a howling darkness of discordancy. "Aubade," he said, "go see." Obedient, she arose; padded to the window, pulled aside the drapes and after a moment said: "It is 37. Still 37." Callisto frowned. "Since Tuesday, then," he said. "No change." Henry Adams, three generations before his own, had stared aghast at Power; Callisto found himself now in much the same state over Thermodynamics, the inner life of that power, realizing like his predecessor that the Virgin and the dynamo stand as much for love as for power; that the two are indeed identical; and that love therefore not only makes the world go round but also makes the boccie ball spin, the nebula precess. It was this latter or sidereal element which disturbed him. The cosmologists had predicted an eventual heat-death for the universe (something like Limbo: form and motion abolished, heat-energy identical at every point in it); the meteorologists, day-to-day, staved it off by contradicting with a reassuring array of varied temperatures.

Thomas Pynchon, in his Slow Learner: Early Stories, *Little, Brown and Company, 1984.*

of phrases, images, possibilities that grownups had some-how turned away from, repudiated, left out at the edges of towns, as if they were auto parts in Étienne's father's junkyard." Carl will not survive an adult counterattack, however. From a day of planning strategy at King Yrjö's mansion the group of rebels returns to find the Barrington lawn completely covered with garbage. As the kids try to clear it away, they discover garbage from their own homes. It is too much. Carl decides he will go to live at King Yrjö's estate permanently: "he was entirely theirs, their friend and robot, to cherish, buy undrunk sodas for, or send into danger, or even, as now, to banish from their sight." Carl is being discarded, consigned to the junkheap of childish fantasies. And so is youthful rebellion. Each child leaves for "his own house, hot shower, dry towel, be-fore-bed television, good night kiss, and dreams that could never again be entirely safe."

Indeed, those dreams will never be safe. Tim Santora has already discovered that his dreams are full of "struggle down the long, inexhaustible network of some arithmetic problem where each step led to a dozen new ones." For Pynchon, networks are reality, and humans stumble through them. (pp. 19-45)

Joseph W. Slade, in his Thomas Pynchon, *Warner Paperback Library, 1974, 256 p.*

Robert Redfield and Peter L. Hays   (essay date 1977)

[*In the essay below, Redfield and Hays discuss the fugal structure of "Entropy."*]

Critical scholarship has identified and in some cases ana-lyzed a broad spectrum of Thomas Pynchon's source ma-terials, but less frequent have been explorations into the structural underpinnings of his literary creations. This ar-ticle will be devoted to just such an inquiry and will con-sider the fugue as a possible framework for the construc-tion of **"Entropy."**

Pynchon himself makes us abundantly aware of the notion of fugue by repeated mention of both the form and compo-sitional techniques used in it, such as counterpoint. In Pynchon's description of the season in which the story is set, he says, " . . . there are private meanderings, linked to the climate as if this spell were a stretto passage in the year's fugue." And toward its end, the story itself, as we shall presently see, seems to become a fugal stretto, a mu-sical device usually placed near the conclusion of the fugue, in which the themes are overlapped for the purpose of concentrated restatement. Aubade, her very name re-flecting a musical form, the troubadour's dawn song, con-verts her sense-impressions into music, stratifying them to eliminate the entropic noise element. She hears sound as note against note, *punctus contra punctum;* in other words, she hears constant counterpoint, the very essence of fugue. Thus, "Counterpointed against his words the girl heard the chatter of birds and fitful car honkings"; and while she caresses the branches of a mimosa in the hothouse enclave, we learn "That music rose in a tangled tracery: arabesques of order competing fugally with the improvised discords of the party downstairs." Similarly, as Callisto, seemingly

overheated by the exertion of his journeys into the past, begs for a cold compress, we read:

> The sound of his voice generated in the girl an answering scrap of melody. Her movement to-ward the kitchen, the towel, the cold water, and his eyes following her formed a weird and intri-cate canon; as she placed the compress on his forehead his sigh of gratitude seemed to signal a new subject, another series of modulations.

We first notice here an example of answering, the trading in music of a subject back and forth between voices, as in antiphony. The girl's motions and Callisto's eyes follow-ing her are then said to form a canon, a musical technique characterized by identical imitation of subject and answer, often a part of the fugal stretto.

This verbal implementation of musical structure, com-plete with appropriate vocabulary ("canon," "modula-tions"), is clear evidence of Pynchon's use of musical com-positional techniques and practices, especially fugue. Its dual meaning in Latin, depending on conjugation—*fugare,* "to chase, put to flight" and *fugere,* "to flee"—must have also been attractive to him, given both the rapid chasing from voice to voice of the various thematic frag-ments, as we shall see, and the escapism implicit in Callis-to's behavior. Let us now apply the basic attributes of the form to the story.

Counterpoint, the simultaneous sounding one against the other of the notes of melodies in separate voices, is the basic compositional technique of fugue. Pitch and charac-ter distinctions of the various voices help maintain a de-gree of melodic linearity, i.e., individual audibility, while each nonetheless contributes to a larger, more comprehen-sive musical whole. The very names designating the sing-ing voices imply the spatial arrangement which they as-sume both in actual pitch level and, in a very literal sense, on the written musical score itself: soprano, alto, tenor, bass.

If we scrutinize the construction of **"Entropy"** from a con-trapuntal point of view, some obvious parallels are re-vealed. Pynchon has chosen two contrasting households in which to convey to us two apparently distinct thematic threads. These living areas relate in a very real sense to musical voices: Callisto's apartment occupies the floor above Meatball's. Were we to do a lateral section of the apartment building, it would be very much as if we were looking at the upper two staves of a fourpart musical score. Further reference to the higher/lower implications of voicing can be drawn literally from the text itself. The first word of the story, "downstairs," places Meatball spa-tially beneath Callisto, who is rudely awakened by the "last bass notes of 'The Heroes' Gate' [which] boomed up through the floor."

Numerous, less-apparent distinctions between the two liv-ing groups serve to establish their individual characters and correspond to the textural identity of musical voices. Solipsist Callisto inhabits his hermetically sealed enclave and deals with intellectual attempts (science, books, phi-losophy) to preserve that which is delicate. His very name reflects elegance, meaning as it does "the most beautiful" in Greek. Meanwhile, Meatball Mulligan, "stew of odds and ends," moves about the overpopulated rooms of his exoteric domain—penetrated by the outside world from two directions and by no less than nine intruders—a domain in which is described the violent abuse of an intellectual text, the *Handbook of Chemistry and Physics,* and in which we are bombarded with vulgarities, linguistic and otherwise. Thus we perceive earthiness and lust underlying and in contrast to an upward striving toward the ideal.

Further specification of this voice character will be seen in the assignment of melodies, i.e., the thematic material to be presented by each level. Callisto's part, a sort of "cantus firmus," will express the conclusion he has drawn from an analysis of his own life and memories: that American culture and the world in general are rapidly approaching a heat-death, a moment when the irrevocable spread of entropic identity of energy levels will prevent energy exchange. This overall theme includes and yet is embellished by that emanating from Meatball's apartment, the breakdown of interpersonal communication as a result of the encroachment of entropic noise on informative signal. The essential identity of these two themes and their fusion toward the end of the story, however, allows us to conclude both that Meatball's fate will parallel Callisto's in spite of the former's apparent decisiveness and that we are dealing, not with a double fugue (the kind with two subjects simultaneously presented) as appearances might indicate, but with the progressive elaboration of a single subject.

The beginning of a fugue is normally the un-accompanied announcement of its subject. Pynchon achieves both this aspect of soloistic presentation and an awakening in us of an awareness of his topic's presence in other literary works by announcing it as an epigraph from a passage of Henry Miller's *Tropic of Cancer:* "We must get into step, a lock-step toward the prison of death. There is no escape. The weather will not change."

In the next several pages we discover the context in which the story will take place. With a virtual still-life view of Meatball as center, the descriptive eye moves outward in ever larger concentric circles, seeing first the party, then the city and nation, and finally the all-encompassing weather and its probable influence on the airy consistency of the human spirit. We realize that the mental attitudes of those present at the party must in some way be related to these unique atmospheric conditions. It is apparently a rainy Friday after several days of uncertain weather, gale-force winds, snow, bright sun, and the like. There reigns a feeling of climax, of a placing of the last straw, indeed of a stretto passage in fugue where the subject is announced in the next voice long before it has been concluded in the preceding one, and the resultant overlapping and thematic concentration produce a sense of anxiety and intense forward drive. There will be no time for the usual rest areas, the fugal episodes.

We now meet Callisto, who in clutching a dying bird to his breast hopes that the energy transfer will save its fragile life. (Recall Meatball's parallel embracing of an empty bottle in the initial description of the party. The theme of an embraced object has been introduced in one voice but does not seem to take on significance until it has been more adequately treated in the other.) An incipient suspense moves us to wonder if the life-giving heat will indeed transfer, as the theme echoed from the Miller epigraph receives a definitive exposition in one of Pynchon's voices, that of Callisto.

Callisto's trial-and-error invention, an enclave to protect his tiny world from the surrounding circles of invading energy chaos, is introduced to us, as is the theme of isolation and communications breakdown which will soon be extensively expanded on Meatball's lower pitch. Aubade keeps the two subjects before us by her frequent temperature readings, by her own system of information filtration, musical conversion, and by her desperate need to maintain the appropriate signal-to-noise relationship.

In Meatball's habitat the theme of enclave is immediately continued as Sandor Rojas announces the arrival of an apparent thief. Meatball allows a wet friend, Saul, to enter from the fire escape through a window, and the ensuing conversation centers on the problem of entropy in human communication, first seen above with Aubade. Saul's entrance has shown the third floor to be open to the outside world and has thus commented on the central theme. Almost immediately three coeds arrive through the front door, followed closely by five sailors. The aspect of enclosure versus exposure has here reached its limits.

Callisto, dictating his memoirs or final testament to Aubade, continues the sequential development of the heat-entropy theme. He searches back across the years for items of memory which corroborate his present fear and, shocked, encounters them in profusion. Remembered material from college courses and social phenomena he has experienced have a disturbing result: "He found himself, in short, restating Gibbs' prediction in social terms, and envisioned a heat-death for his culture in which ideas, like heat-energy, would no longer be transferred." The final outcome of the story is now evident.

Meatball and Saul again pick up the notion of the non-transference of ideas and develop it for us. Saul and his wife Miriam ("rebellion" in Aramaic) have lost touch with each other by arguing over computers acting like people versus people acting like computers—in short, over communication theory. Meatball's very manner of speaking reveals the loss factor in speech itself. Thereupon several outright errors in information transfer are presented to us by other characters, and another extreme is reached. The sailors have been wrongly told that Meatball's apartment is a "hoorhouse"; and Krinkles either misorders his description of Dave's accident to one of the coeds so that Dave wears protective gloves *after* a radiation overdose and thus, logically, can no longer play piano, or—more likely—lies to her. The girl's response indicates that she believes the misinformation. Total isolation of the individual sets in as Duke and the group initially attempt to play without those instruments which normally provide the vertical dimension, the chordal understructure, and then break totally free from organizing forces and just think, mentally perform, their music. Chaos is the obvious result, stated in Charles Ivesian tonal terms: "And they took off again, only it seemed Paco was playing in G sharp while the rest were in E flat, so they had to start all over."

All of these separate events combine to produce on Meatball's level a great crescendo of noise, the entropic element in communication. Eventually Meatball chooses to act rather than hide in a closet and is seen doling out wine, bedding down the drenched girl retrieved from the shower, and generally attempting a half-hearted restoration of order. But if entropy has conquered in the area of communication, we realize that its heat equalization cannot be far off.

As we cut back to Callisto, the catastrophe is upon us. In an appropriate contrast of musical terminology, Meatball's crescendo of noise anticipates the diminuendo of the tiny bird's life. The needed heat has indeed not transferred, and Callisto complains impotently against everything. The theme of entropy, worked to its conclusion on the third floor, is here carried forward to a dramatic suicide scene. Aubade, previously depicted with musical delicacy, bursts into a self-destructive fit, smashing out windows with her bare hands and rendering certain the entropic demise of the enclave.

Clearly the rapidly developing exchange of thematic motives between the two voices points toward a fugal stretto passage. While our minds' eyes have retained an idea suggested at Meatball's party, a related thought has been elaborated upon on Callisto's level. We have also seen examples in the reverse. The literary or filmic device used here, intercutting, parallels the antiphonal procedure of subject and answer exchange between voices. The subject itself, initially double in appearance, has been broken down into its motivic fragments, and each dealt with in one or more tiny separate scenes. A final, all-inclusive fusion has taken place. There is no need to examine each possible thematic fragment. It is the general exchange between the two voices of essentially similar material which points up the fugal nature of Pynchon's structural underpinnings.

The conclusion of the story highlights yet another musical construction much used in fugue. Meatball's plot has been worked out to the full as we see him take actions which will probably restore some measure of order to his chaotic celebration. This temporary turn for the better holds in our memory like a bass pedal point while Callisto's plot in the higher voice continues its forward development. And this tiny cadence delivers a neat conclusion to both threads of action. Regardless of Mulligan's piecemeal reactions, we realize that his entire group, if Callisto is right, will be overwhelmed by the same entropic cataclysm. Continuing the extensive use of musical terminology which has characterized the story, Pynchon avails himself of the magnetic dominant to tonic progression to bring his prophetic tale to a close:

> [Aubade] turned to face the man on the bed and wait with him until the moment of equilibrium was reached, when 37 degrees Fahrenheit should prevail both outside and inside, and forever, and the hovering, curious dominant of their separate lives should resolve into a tonic of darkness and the final absence of all motion.
>
> (pp. 50-4)

Robert Redfield and Peter L. Hays, "Fugue as a Structure in Pynchon's 'Entropy'," in Pacific

Coast Philology, *Vol. XII, October, 1977, pp. 50-5.*

Richard F. Patteson   (essay date 1979)

[*In the following essay, Patteson explores Pynchon's use of architecture and junk in his short stories to symbolize the deterioration and collapse of society.*]

Thomas Pynchon's fiction reveals a world continually in the process of falling apart. The source of nearly all major tension in his work can be traced to the conflict between the human need to create meaningful form and the unavoidable tendency toward formlessness in the universe. "Metaphor," as Fausto Maijstral writes in *V.,* "is a device, an artifice," and the creators of formal patterns "are alone with the task of living in a universe of things which simply are, and cloaking that innate mindlessness with comfortable and pious metaphor so that the 'practical' half of humanity may continue in the Great Lie. . . . " One of the most frequent and graphic ways in which Pynchon expresses these notions is through imagery of architecture and junk. Buildings and other shelters or enclosures are perhaps mankind's most obvious attempts to create forms that will protect him from whatever lies without, and junkyards are equally obvious reminders of the end to which all such structures finally come. Junk is, after all, only form out of control, form that has lost its significance, its use. Junk can no longer protect us from the knowledge of decay because it has itself decayed. Junk is (to use one of Pynchon's favorite words) refuse—that which is refused after it has ceased to work. It should not be surprising, therefore, to find in Pynchon characters who, unwilling to accept formlessness and disorder, attempt to construct orders—both physical (such as shelters) and purely conceptual (such as paranoid fantasies)—out of sundry types of waste. But all of these structures, whether houses built out of rubbish or "plots" like a history ordered by cause and effect, are in Fausto's words mere metaphors—necessary lies. (p. 39)

Form and junk, the house and the dump, figure as prominently in Pynchon's . . . short stories as they do in his novels. **"Entropy,"** Pynchon's best known of short work, consists of two interwoven narratives, one providing a kind of gloss on the other. On the ground floor of a Washington, D.C., apartment building a man named Meatball Mulligan hosts a raucous lease-breaking party, while the upstairs tenant, Callisto, attempts to save a freezing bird's life by sheltering it in his hand. Callisto, who fancies himself a latter-day Henry Adams, is an intellectual, and it is through him that Pynchon lays bare this theme. For several days the temperature outside has remained constant at thirty-seven degrees, and Callisto is convinced that the end of the world is near: "The cosmologists had predicted an eventual heat-death for the universe (something like Limbo: form and motion abolished, heat-energy identical at every point in it); the meteorologists, day-to-day, staved it off by contradicting with a reassuring array of varied temperatures." Callisto's own method of staving off disaster is to remake his apartment into an artificial, life-supporting environment: "Hermetically sealed, it was a tiny enclave of regularity in the city's chaos, alien to the vagaries of the weather, of national politics, of any civil disorder." Neither Callisto nor his girlfriend Aubade leaves the apartment for any reason. The significance of the architectural image here, a shelter against universal fallout, is unmistakable.

The use of entropy as a way of talking about the increasing disorganization of civilization is closely connected to the architecture/junk paradigm in Pynchon's fiction. Houses, apartments, shelters of all kinds, are islands of order in a chaotic world. Their usual function is to provide (or at least to suggest) stability and security. But many of Pynchon's houses and apartments, like the one in **"Entropy,"** are filled with parties that spin out of control. The house itself often turns into a dump, as refuse and unconscious bodies accumulate. This is what happens during Meatball Mulligan's lease-breaking party, and it is precisely this situation that Callisto wishes to deny.

Meatball himself tries to bring disorder under control, but in a different way. The party in Pynchon, as we have already noted, stands both for chaos and for the attempt to cast a form over chaos. Ordered disorder is Meatball Mulligan's goal—something poised between riot and ballet. Yet the very purpose of the party indicates the tendency toward disunity inherent in all of man's arrangements. The lease-breaking is one example of dissolution; there are many others. Forms break down in all sorts of ways. Like similar social gatherings in other Pynchon works, Meatball's party is characterized by random sex, destruction of property, and drunkenness to the point of oblivion. Personal relationships deteriorate rapidly. Meatball listens sympathetically to his friend Saul, whose wife Miriam has left him, but there is not much he can do. Saul and Miriam, it seems, had quarreled about communications theory, failing spectacularly to communicate with one another. On one occasion Miriam had even hurled at Saul "a *Handbook of Chemistry and Physics*"—virtually a Bible of cosmic order—missing her husband but breaking a window in the process. " 'Discipline must be maintained,' " Meatball remarks, while all around him discipline disintegrates.

Despite his failure as father-confessor to Saul, Meatball does not give up his efforts to bring the party under control. "The way he figured, there were only about two ways he could cope: (a) lock himself in the closet and maybe eventually they would all go away, or (b) try to calm everybody down, one by one." Opting for the second alternative (the first is really Callisto's shelter method), Meatball throws himself into the task of maintaining a semblance of order. His final sortie against chaos stands in sharp contrast to the response of Callisto and Aubade at the end of the story. As long as Callisto's artificial environment protects Aubade from the world outside, she is able to imagine "arabesques of order competing fugally with the improvised discords of the party downstairs." But when the bird dies, the fragile arabesques fall to pieces. Comfortable illusion is shattered. Surrendering to a disorder that she now sees as inescapable, Aubade smashes the window pane and waits, with Callisto, for the ordered individuality of their apartment to be engulfed by the chaos

without. On both floors disorder triumphs, and the house itself moves one step closer to junk.

The party is also the focal point of **"Mortality and Mercy in Vienna."** Once more, the location is Washington. The main character, Cleanth Siegel, has been invited to a party, but after he arrives, the host, David Lupescu, disappears and leaves Siegel in charge. During the course of the evening, Siegel, a career diplomat, finds himself, as the real host's surrogate, cast in the role of a priest. Intuitively following Lupescu's example, Siegel takes guests into the bedroom and hears their "confessions." But one of the guests is beyond help. An Ojibwa Indian named Irving Loon, in the grip of a type of paranoia peculiar to his tribe, feels "a concentration of obscure cosmic forces against him . . . which are bent on his destruction." Every Ojibwa boy "must experience a vision, after starving himself for several days. Often after seeing this vision he feels he has acquired a supernatural companion, and there is a tendency to identify." The supernatural figure usually evoked in the Windigo, "a mile-high skeleton made of ice . . . grabbing up humans by the handful and feeding on their flesh." When Siegel first guesses what might occur at the party, he pauses to consider the implications of his own position: "Because if this were true, Siegel had the power to bring them a very tangible salvation."

Instead of working the miracle, however, Siegel abandons his guests to anarchy and death. Just after he leaves the apartment, he hears screams, breaking glass, and a burst of rifle fire. [In his book *Thomas Pynchon* (1974)] Joseph Slade interprets Siegel's departure as the recognition of the need for "a new religion . . . of retribution, of apocalypse." By allowing Loon to run amok, Slade contends, Siegel "has acted as prophet and healer to the waste land; he has healed its sickness by annihilation." But much more likely, Siegel acquiesces in an annihilation that he cannot, in the end, prevent. In doing so, he allies himself with Callisto and Aubade rather than with Meatball Mulligan. The parallel between Siegel and Lupescu is at this point complete. Both are charged with maintaining order, if only momentarily, and both fail. Since there can be no lasting order, it is pointless to prolong the party's ineluctable self-destruction. Siegel realizes that all religion and ritual, including both Irving Loon's paranoia and Lupescu's party-giving, have a common source in the human impulse to create form out of chaos, even if the form be only an illusion. With Siegel's departure, party gives way to mindless violence, and Lupescu's wrecked apartment becomes the most gruesome dump of all.

Pynchon's other stories offer ways of responding to the breakdown of form, albeit not very satisfactory ones. **"The Secret Integration,"** on the surface a parable of race relations in the early sixties, is really about a peculiarly Pynchonesque initiation into adulthood. A band of disaffected but highly intelligent suburban children spend much of their time plotting ways to sabotage adult institutions, such as planting smoke bombs at PTA meetings. Pynchon makes it quite clear during the course of the story that the children are not really up to the task; each major offensive falls considerably short of success. In fact, the children, despite their anarchic impulses, are afraid to proceed too aggressively against the various shelters provided by the adult world. What they learn in the end is that there is no enduring shelter at all.

The source of nearly all major tension in Pynchon's work can be traced to the conflict between the human need to create meaningful form and the unavoidable tendency toward formlessness in the universe.

—*Richard F. Patteson*

A number of details in the story support this theme. The children's secret hideout is an old house in the process of turning to junk: "The outside was in fairly lousy shape: a lot of shingling was off, paint had peeled, room slates lay broken in piles where they'd slid and fallen. Windows had been mostly busted. . . . And everywhere the smell of old—eighty-year-old—wood." The place, moreover, is decorated with items such as "a multicolored model of a protein molecule . . . the Japanese TV and the sodium stockpile, a bunch of old transmission parts . . . concrete bust of Alf Landon . . . busted Mies van Rohe chair . . . assorted chandelier pieces, fragments of tapestries, teak newels, one fur overcoat they could hang around the neck of the bust and hide in sometimes, like a tent." The transmission parts are from the junkyard belonging to the father of one of the children. Étienne Cherdlu's father is the only sensitive adult in the story. When a black couple moves to town, the other parents make threatening telephone calls; Mr. Cherdlu warns that the real danger is not integration but automation. He fears a future of increasing dehumanization in which "the only jobs open will be in junkyards for busted machines." Even as Cherdlu hints darkly of a future increasingly given over to rubbish, the children use junk for shelter—the house, itself, most obviously, and the fur coat spread open "like a tent," but also all the other objects that add to the hideout's domesticity. Like Father Fairing in the New York sewers, like Fausto Maijstral beneath the rubble of Valetta, the children live within waste, at least for a time. They have created architectural form out of refuse. Their hideout is a fictional representation of what Norbert Wiener [in his book *The Human Use of Human Beings: Cybernetics and Society,* (1967)] calls "local enclaves whose direction seems opposed to that of the universe at large and in which there is a limited and temporary tendency for organization to increase." Wiener adds, "Life finds its home in some of these enclaves."

The children's most significant assemblage, however, is not a house, but a human being. When the black family, the Barringtons, move to town, the kids imagine that they have a son, Carl, who joins the gang. But at the end of the story, after the adults of the community have dumped a truckload of garbage in the Barrington's front yard, the children have to recognize their black friend for what he

is: "Carl has been put together out of phrases, images, possibilities that grownups had somehow turned away from, repudiated, left out at the edges of towns, as if they were auto parts in Étienne's father's junkyard." Like the hideout, Carl is a form made from junk, and the form falls into disuse at precisely the point at which garbage all but submerges the Barringtons' house. Not long before this, the children have begun to realize that their own plots, unlike those of the adults, must stop short of actual destruction. They fear most precisely what they learn from the Barrington incident: that there is no safe place, no form that does not end in junk. They are left at the end of the story, like Meatball Mulligan in **"Entropy,"** with no real solution. They will continue to dream of shelter, but those dreams will "never again be entirely safe," because now they know the truth.

The plot of **"Low-lands,"** like that of **"Entropy,"** hinges as much on the struggle for form as on the effects of dissolution. But in **"Low-lands"** the two elements are fused (rather than sandwiched) into a single dramatic piece. And also in **"Low-lands,"** the implications of the architecture/junk relationship can be seen more clearly than perhaps anywhere else in Pynchon's short fiction. The story opens with the disintegration of a family unit. New York attorney Dennis Flange annoys his wife Cindy one day by staying home from work to get drunk with the garbage man, Rocco Squarcione. Although disgusted at the company her husband keeps, Cindy manages to keep her anger under control until the arrival of Flange's old friend, Pig Bodine. At this point Cindy orders Flange out of the house and out of her life. Rocco takes Pig and Flange to the garbage dump, where they are given shelter by the dump's "uncontested ruler," a man called Bolingbroke. In the middle of the night Flange is awakened by Nerissa, a gypsy girl, who takes him to live with her in a baroque cavern under the dump. The disruptive forces that begin the story give way, for the time being, to the construction of a new order out of the very rubble of a fragmented civilization.

Pynchon takes care to stress that the breakdown of form in **"Low-lands"** is not limited to any one event. Pig Bodine, for instance, is AWOL from the Navy; the Episcopal priest who originally built the Flange house was a bootlegger; Flange's analyst is insane; Flange himself, although trained as a naval communications officer, cannot communicate with his own wife. The major disintegration in the story is in fact that of the Flange marriage. The process of deterioration culminates with Dennis and Cindy's separation, but it really begins seven years earlier, when Pig Bodine takes Flange out for "a few beers" on the night before the wedding: "This 'few beers' was sort of a rough estimate. Two weeks later Cindy received a telegram from Cedar Rapids, Iowa. It was from Flange and he was broke and horribly hung over." Cindy agrees to marry Flange "with the stipulation that she never set eyes on Pig again." For Flange, expulsion from home marks the beginning of a pilgrim's haphazard quest for the security and order that home represents. Joseph Slade claims that "unlike Cleanth Siegel . . . Flange retreats into passivity." It is Siegel, however, who retreats, even though his decision to do so may well be more deliberate (or less passive, in Slade's words) than Flange's drift toward the dump.

The junkyard at the end of Flange's brief journey is remarkably like the home he has left behind. Both are labyrinthine and womblike. Inside the Flange house, an "almost organic mound," are "priestholes and concealed passageways and oddly angled rooms." The gypsies' domain within the dump is "laced with a network of tunnels and rooms." And although Pynchon at first seems to distinguish between the respective topographies of home and dump, the differences, on closer inspection, can be seen as similarities. The Flange house is perched high on a cliff overlooking Long Island Sound, while the dump rises from within a huge pit. But both domiciles conceal depths beneath the appearance of heights. High and low are terms of differentiation which, in the long run, will cease to have any meaning as disorganization becomes more general. Pynchon's concrete symbol for that process is the gradual filling of the dump: "It was this peculiar quality of fatedness which struck Flange as he gazed off into the half-light while Rocco dumped the load: this thought that one day, perhaps fifty years from now, perhaps more, there would no longer be any hole: the bottom would be level with the streets." Like much else in **"Low-lands,"** the similarity between house and dump has a dual import. Flange finds another domestic order to replace the one he has lost, but all such orders are junk in the end.

Flange's preoccupation with the sea reinforces this double-edged theme. When his psychiatrist calls the sea "the true mother image for us all," Flange loses his temper, but only because the analyst strikes, almost literally, close to home—the sea's "ability to encompass," to be a "sustaining plasma." What the sea represents for Flange is the order, safety, and security of the home, and beyond that, of the womb. Yet it also represents the chaos that lies at the other end of the line. Flange associates the word "lowlands" in an old ballad with the sea during an eerie calm— "a minimum and dimensionless point . . . an assurance of perfect, passionless uniformity." The dump, likewise, contains a "dead center, the single point which implied an entire low country." This still point, unlike T. S. Eliot's, brings no glimpse of cosmic order, but rather a hint of cosmic disorder—the universe as a great junkyard.

Flange's acceptance of life with Nerissa embraces and replays these contradictions. She is "an angel"—his new spouse and mother, the hostess of a new party which must somehow be kept within bounds; but she is also the central figure in a bizarre parody of domesticity. The story ends on a note of paradox, as Flange gazes at Nerissa and agrees to stay: "Whitecaps danced across her eyes; sea creatures, he knew, would be cruising about in the submarine green of her heart." But which sea really dances across Nerissa's eyes—the sustaining plasma or the minimum, dimensionless point? For the moment, the illusion of form, sustenance, and protection obscures the reality of chaos. Unable to face disorder, Flange, like Callisto in **"Entropy,"** the children in **"The Secret Integration,"** and so many other Pynchon characters, constructs a fragile and certainly temporary shelter for himself: junk refash-

ioned into a home, fragments shored up against inevitable ruin. (pp. 41-7)

Richard F. Patteson, "Architecture and Junk in Pynchon's Short Fiction," in Illinois Quarterly, *Vol. 42, No. 2, Winter, 1979, pp. 38-47.*

Allon White   (essay date 1981)

[*White was an English educator and critic whose works include* The Uses of Obscurity *(1981) and* The Politics and Poetics of Transgression *(1986, coauthored with Peter Stallybrass). In the essay below on "Mortality and Mercy in Vienna," he argues that Pynchon equates rather than opposes antithetical notions to reveal ironic, and tragic, paradoxes in American culture.*]

'Mortality and Mercy in Vienna' by Thomas Pynchon, first published in 1959, is one of the finest short stories published since the war. It has the density, allusiveness and breadth of a full novel without losing the shock peripeteia of the classic short story. Indeed, the 'shocking' ending and its relation to the rest of the story are most revealing about Pynchon's writing as a whole and the contradictory tradition of American liberalism from which it issues. It coerces the central liberal values of humanist sympathy, compassion, care and concern ('Mercy') into a confrontation with violence, paranoia and an ironic acceptance of murder ('Mortality'). Written between the end of the Korean war and the beginning of the Vietnam war, Pynchon's story exposes the bitter 'paradox' of an American liberalism which finds, time and again, that the eventual form taken by its careful concern is brutality and violence.

Siegel, a young diplomat working for an unspecified Government commission arrives at a Washington party to discover that the host—a surprising *Doppelgänger* of himself—is just leaving and that he, Siegel, is now in charge. The party degenerates, people keep coming to Siegel to confess their problems and sins and he is embarrassed and annoyed by the frequency, the forced intimacy and above all by the content of these 'Confessionals'. But as the party accelerates to its chaotic climax, he notices that one of the guests, a displaced Ojibwa Indian called Irving Loon is about to suffer from a strange attack of the 'Windigo psychosis', an aberration of his own tribal culture which, any moment now, will turn him into a frenzied cannibal. Coolly, Siegel assesses what he should do. It takes him five seconds. He tells no one. As he walks out of the party he sees the Indian making towards an automatic rifle hung on the wall, and by the time he gets into the street he hears the first burst of fire and the first screams of the partygoers.

The question is: was Siegel's decision the result of a spiritual logic built up in hints and scraps throughout the story, or was it 'loony' (as the name Irving Loon suggests), a further bit of chaotic, anarchistic madness which simply pushed the break-down and degeneracy of the party to its own logical point of self-destruction?

The story itself proposes and balances both possibilities. **'Mortality and Mercy'** resembles in this Pynchon's earlier story **'Entropy'**, but also prefigures important aspects of

The Crying of Lot 49, V and *Gravity's Rainbow*. It plots a doubleness where the loonies look grimly sane, and the sane world looks like an asylum, or nightmare, or a chaotic party. Pynchon characters generally have some cosmic system which sometimes looks like a cybernetic theory, sometimes like the Book of Revelation—and yet the closer we get to the rationality of the cosmic system, the more it tends to dissolve into the grotesque, the paranoid, and in *this* story, the psychotic. Pynchon protagonists possess the unusual quality of being laconic obsessives. They move from the flip and the wry to metaphysical horror with elusive facility. Callisto, Irving Loon, Siegel, Oedipa Maas, Stencil, they all follow a trail which is like following a crazy paving to apocalypse. A trail which is either nuts and leading to paranoia and psychosis, or a trail which is the logical and sane revelation of some immense truth of an almost religious or mystical kind. The text is built upon this unknown, and the reader is held in a bizarre, fascinating narrative space, the singular quality of which is to make a radical identification of the forms of insanity and the forms of reason.

The title of the story is taken from *Measure for Measure,* and it is worth quoting the end of the Duke's speech in Act 1, Scene 1 where the phrase occurs:

> Spirits are not finely touch'd
> But to fine issues; nor nature never lends
> The smallest scruple of her excellence
> But, like a thrifty goddess, she determines
> Herself the glory of a creditor,
> Both thanks and use. But I do bend my speech
> To one that can my part in him advertise:
> Hold therefore, Angelo.
> In our remove, be thou at full ourself
> Mortality and Mercy in Vienna
> Live in thy tongue and heart.

Francis Douce in his *Illustrations of Shakespeare* (1807) gives us a gloss on the sentence, 'Mortality and Mercy in Vienna live in thy tongue and heart' which reads: 'I delegate to thy tongue the power of pronouncing sentence of death, and to thy heart the privilege of exercising mercy.' This is the charge which the old Duke puts upon Angelo, a sort of civic cleaning-up campaign to stamp out the corruption and vice to which he feels Vienna to have degenerated. We are familiar with the range of problems which arise in *Measure for Measure* when Angelo elides these two opposed powers granted him by the Duke: when Angelo *equates* 'the power of pronouncing sentence of death' with 'the privilege of exercising mercy'. The problematical disquiet of Shakespeare's play arises from the brutally forced identification of mortality with mercy, murder with forgiveness. In the sequence of actions in *Measure for Measure,* death is substituted for mercy and mercy for death so often that they appear to take on a sort of cold equivalence which calls everything into doubt. The profundity of this perverse equalling of mercy and murder is striking. If mercy equals murder, if the act of love and forgiveness is made somehow equivalent to the *crime* of murder, then all judgement is subverted. The ideas of law, value and judgement are radically perverted in a universe where mortality *is* mercy. Anything goes, and it's no longer possible to judge. It is this sinister world which Angelo

creates and which the end of the play, with the Duke's intervention, fails hopelessly to compensate for and correct: we are left with the pessimism of the primal identification.

Pynchon's story subverts its Shakespearean source whilst retaining a marvellous fidelity to the disturbing Jacobean equation at its heart. The obvious parallel to the Duke delegating responsibility to Angelo in *Measure for Measure* is Lupescu's delegation of the party to Siegel. And the parallel is emphasised by the name itself. 'Siegel' is the German word for 'seal' or 'impression' and this takes up the 'stamp/seal' image of *Measure for Measure,* and directly recalls the ducal stamp on the seal of commission which the Duke gives to Angelo at the beginning of the play. The power delegated by Lupescu to Siegel at the beginning of the party recalls the word-play of the Duke's first speech:

> I say, bid come before us Angelo.
> What figure of us, think you, he will bear?
> For you must know, we have with special soul
> Elected him our absence to supply;
> *Lent him our terror, drest him with our love . . .*

The oxymoron of that last line 'lent him our terror, drest him with our love', not only applies to the double qualities Lupescu bequeaths Siegel, but it begins to constitute *the* basic narrative structure of the story itself. **'Mortality and Mercy in Vienna'** is a narrative oxymoron where mutually exclusive opposites are forced into a close, ironic identification (like the very title of Pynchon's novel *Gravity's Rainbow*).

Thus the host of the party is called *David Lupescu.* 'David' is the Saviour, the shepherd, and the Christian symbolism of the pastor and his flock is invoked throughout. Siegel thinks: 'It was a slow process and dangerous because in the course of things it was very possible to destroy not only yourself but your flock as well. He took her hand. 'Come on', he said 'I'd like to meet Irving. Say for your penance ten Hail Marys and make a good Act of Contrition.' But although 'David' is the Shepherd, Lupescu is a Roumanian word meaning 'wolfish' (Lupescu is a Roumanian). David Lupescu is both shepherd and wolf, both guardian and destroyer of the flock. He is also (and also is not) the Host. When he runs out, he says to Siegel: ' "It's all yours, . . . You are now the host. As host you are a trinity. (*a*) receiver of guests"—ticking them off on his fingers—" (*b*) an enemy and (*c*) an outward manifestation for *them* of the divine body and blood." ' But by the end of the story, the guests have become the host, literally the body and the blood. As he leaves the impending mayhem, Siegel thinks that ' . . . this kind of penance was as good as any other; it was just unfortunate that Irving Loon, would be the only one partaking of any body and blood, divine or otherwise'.

It is as though the pastor had turned upon his flock and devoured it. Pynchon's eucharistic pun, which makes the host the guest, is paralleled by the ecumenical rapprochement of Jew and Jesuit in Siegel. Born of Jewish father and Catholic mother, these two warring factions within him (remember Grossmann's taunt at College that 'It is the seed of your destruction', he would murmur. 'House divided against itself?') the warring factions are by the end of the story resolved into a sort of paradoxical equivalence:

> He [Siegel] figured there were about sixty seconds to make a decision, and now the still small Jesuit voice, realising that the miracle *was* in his hands after all, for real, vaunted with the same sense of exhilaration Siegel had once felt seeing five hundred hysterical freshmen advancing on the women's dorms, knowing it was he who had set it all in motion. And the other, gentle part of him sang *kaddishes* for the dead and mourned over the Jesuit's happiness, realizing however that this kind of penance was as good as any other . . . It took no more than five seconds for the two sides to agree that there was really only one course to take.

Again, Pynchon has created a type of oxymoron whereby the active, manoeuvring Jesuit and the melancholy Jew become the same voice.

Terms which under ordinary circumstances are mutually exclusive are forced into a kind of identity where the one becomes a version of the other. The form is rather like a metaphor in which we cannot see which is the vehicle and which the tenor—there is no one referential set which controls the narrative: salvation *is* destruction; order *is* chaos; justice *is* psychosis; mercy *is* mortality. When Siegel sees what is going to happen, Pynchon writes: 'Siegel had the power to work for these parishioners a kind of miracle, to bring them a very tangible salvation. A miracle involving a host, true, but like no holy Eucharist.' This identification of the Christian mythic pattern of salvation and redemption with clinical psychosis is not a simple undermining of God by Freud. Siegel sees himself in the religious terminology of prophet and healer rather than the modern psychoanalytic counterpart of doctor and fortune-teller. Indeed Pynchon uses the terms of clinical psychiatry in his stories, but his analysts, like Geronimo Diaz in 'Lowlands' and Dr Hilarius in *The Crying of Lot 49* are usually raving mad. Once more, the oxymoron of terms is employed, and in both of those stories the patient becomes the analyst and vice versa, even though both also stay in their original roles. Thus the narrative operates to suspend interpretation and to fox judgement. The domestic suddenly gapes open and becomes the cosmic; a rather over-indulgent, slightly chaotic Washington party in the 1950s suddenly becomes the heart of darkness, a nightmare of evil. The mundane only has to flicker a little and it arches out into hysterical instability: a wry word in the bedroom is made to appear, in the next sentence, like a metaphysical indictment.

Debbie Considine's involved, messy story of the infidelity and bitching of the people at the party is at once an ironic parody of American divorce/partner-swapping culture and also the revelation of some universal moral infection. The story is given twice, once as situation comedy, the second time as a Joseph Conrad nightmare, and this forcing of the one through the other is a formal as well as material figure in the text—mystical overwriting and comic understatement are not simply juxtaposed but compressed by a switching mechanism which reveals them to be the positive and negative of the same pulse.

On the one hand Pynchon has a profoundly pessimistic reading of culture, and his use of entropic degeneration has been frequently noted. He is almost Spenglerian in his gloom about the decadence of modern social life. In **'Entropy,'** the short story written about two years before **'Mortality and Mercy,'** Callisto, the protagonist, is writing his autobiography:

> 'Nevertheless', continued Callisto, 'he found in entropy or the measure of disorganization for a closed system an adequate metaphor to apply to certain phenomena in his own world. He saw, for example, the younger generation responding to Madison Avenue with the same spleen he had once reserved for Wall Street, and in American "Consumerism" discovered a similar tendency from the least to the most probable, from differentiation to sameness, from ordered individuality to a kind of chaos. He found himself, in short, restating Gibbs' prediction in social terms, and envisioned a heat-death for his culture in which ideas, like heat-energy, would no longer be transferred, since each point in it would ultimately have the same quantity of energy.'

This indicates Pynchon's obsession with the entropic model of the world in which everything tends by a law of physics towards chaos and degeneration. It also gives us a gloss on the suddenly very grim, nihilistic thoughts which Seigel has at the end of the party, when once again he borrows from Conrad's *Heart of Darkness*:

> Lupescu . . . really had, like some Kurtz, been possessed by the heart of a darkness in which no ivory was ever sent out from the interior, but instead hoarded jealously by each of its gatherers to build painfully, fragment by fragment, temples to the glory of some imago or obsession, and decorated inside with the art work of dream and nightmare, and locked finally against a hostile forest, each 'agent' his own ivory tower, having no windows to look out of, turning further and further inward and cherishing a small flame behind the alter.

There is real bitterness in these lines. Solipsism, resulting from the extension of a hedonistic consumer culture, is for Pynchon a nightmare of decadence. Many of his characters are, in various ways, pigs. Pig Bodine recurs through his novels; Harvey Duckworth comes in carrying his girl piggy-back, there is Sam Fleischmann, Meatball Mulligan, Krinkles Porcino, and the symbol which hangs over the whole party, the pig's foetus which Lupescu hangs up at the beginning of the evening, when he says: 'Tonight. Of course. Why. Why not. Pig foetus. Symbol. God, what a symbol.'

The pig foetus suspended above the party has been put there by Lupescu in imitation of one used at a 'Dada exhibit in Paris on Christmas eve, 1919'. As such it infects the party with its own grotesque symbolism and foregrounds the surrealist dislocation of the story, what Seigel later calls 'this whole absurd surrealist atmosphere'. But the foetus is also an evident part of Pynchon's wider use of piggy animalism in this and other works. The stronger symbolic resonance of the pig characters and the pig foetus suspended above them, recalls the inherent iconic tradition which relates pigs to the inseparableness of sinful excess and sacrifice. In the Bestiaries (see F. C. Sillar and R. M. Meyler, *The Symbolic Pig*) the pig is said to signify 'Sinners and unclean persons or heretics; penitents who have become slack and have an eye for those sins which they have wept for, unclean and wanton men or spirits; foul thoughts and fleshly lusts from which proceed unproductive works, as though boiled away.'

This seems an accurate moralistic summary of Lupescu's friends at the party, and taken in conjunction with the series of confessions which constitute the ironic and degenerating religious lineaments of the plot, indexes the deeper connection between Pynchon's porcine preoccupations and the narrative itself—the murderous sacrifice of sinners which is also an act of mercy. This ironic equivalence is a central feature of the iconic tradition of the pig—particularly the Jacobean, which recurs endlessly in Pynchon's novels and relates back to the Shakespearean title of this story. In his fascinating book on literary metamorphosis, *The Gaping Pig* (1976), Irving Massey writes of the 'Elizabethan-Jacobean preoccupation with the pig caught in the open-mouthed squeal':

> The image produces the kind of uninterpretable paradox that is characteristic of metamorphosis. Is it a mockery of human laughter? Is it the agonized shriek of the animal? Laughter or desperation? A hideous expression of life, or the frozen face of death? In either case, it seems to belong to that metamorphic world that persistently ridicules our attempts at interpretation.

This seems to me perfectly apposite for Pynchon's use of the foetus and the ambiguous symbolic centre which it forms to his story. The filth, the chaos, the greed, the bloated, piggy self-centredness of the partygoers run as a leitmotif throughout, and lead, insistently, to that side of Pynchon which wants to 'exterminate all the brutes'. Like Angelo, who decreed death as a solution to the festering flesh-pots of corrupt Vienna, Siegel, Lupescu and Irving Loon are powerfully attracted by terrorism; Lupescu, like the Duke, 'lends Siegel his terror'. And there may be more than accident in the pun of Siegel's name, 'Sieg Heil'—and the reference to Vienna in the title may have as much to do with the birthplace of national socialism as with its Shakespearean source. Again one is caught: between a hinted parody of fascism and the gleaming desire for the final solution, the pure terror of Jacobean revenge. 'For the things that rule Irving Loon, the concentration of obscure cosmic forces . . . cynical terrorists, savage and amoral deities.'

Eliot's *Waste Land* and Conrad's *Heart of Darkness*, in addition to *Measure for Measure*, lie behind and in the story. T. S. Eliot's elegiac lament for the loss of spiritual vitality in modern city culture is caricatured in Debbie Considine's sentimental description of Irving Loon:

> He hasn't spoken a word for two days. I feel . . . that it's not only nostalgia for the wilderness, but almost as if somehow out there, in the hinterlands with nothing but snow and forests and a few beavers and moose, he has come close to something which city dwellers never find all their lives, may never even be aware exists, and

it's this that he misses, that the city kills or hides from him. I'll be damned thought Siegel. This broad is serious.

Irving is made the instrument of revenge on a spiritually desolate social group, and it is this as much as the vengeance of the exploited cultural minority—the Jew, the Ojibwa—which is in question. The story cannot be read simply as anti-imperialist, though the inset narrative about Grossmann is important. In Grossmann's gradual succumbing to East Coast cosmpolitanism we get a parallel to the sad story of Irving Loon, and a further index of Pynchon's preoccupation with the proliferating bourgeois culture which Siegel, at least, detests.

What interests me in the story though is not so much the relatively overt passages of critique as the political occlusion of the messianic and the domestic. The text does not simply 'hesitate' between opposed routes, salvation or psychosis, indeed, we're never really offered the choice. What it does is make us uncertain whether we're at a Washington party or on the eve of apocalypse.

We do not wait *eagerly to know,* for the mode of presentation is what we might call *ironic nihilist:* 'He shrugged. What the hell, stranger things had happened in Washington.' The horror of the black comedy is caught not in the extermination but in that shrug.

Any political critique of Pynchon should begin there: the shrugging off of murder. For when the solution or resolution is a spiralling identification of madness and religion, unable to prise apart mortality and mercy, the identification is not *neutral*—however full of 'modernist' suspensions it might seem to be. Like Francis Ford Coppola's *Apocalypse Now,* which ideologically it so closely resembles, Pynchon's story dissolves its revulsion and guilt about modern America into literary analogues and stylish paradox. It is an attempt to escape through the use of neutral formal equivalence, ironic equations of good and evil, and mythical and symbolic counterpoint. In fact, however, these devices only serve to make the helplessness of an ensnared liberalism all the more transparent. The poignancy of **'Mortality and Mercy in Vienna'** is revealed in that shrug, which is the real centre to the story. It indexes perfectly an inability and unwillingness to intervene in a world in which the traditional liberal humanist values have collapsed, a world in which mercy and mortality appear inseparable, and terrorism a kind of unfathomable justice. The shrug shows up the fine limits of Pynchon's story at the same time as revealing the moment (so often repeated in recent American history) when America's confused liberalism emerges as scandalously self-conscious indifference. (pp. 55-62)

> *Allon White, "Ironic Equivalence: A Reading of Thomas Pynchon's 'Mortality and Mercy in Vienna',"* in Critical Quarterly, *Vol. 23, No. 3, Autumn, 1981, pp. 55-62.*

Tony Tanner   (essay date 1982)

[*An English critic and educator, Tanner is the author of* The Reign of Wonder: Naivety and Reality in American Literature *(1965),* City of Words: American

Fiction, 1950-1970 *(1971), and* Problems and Roles of the American Artist as Portrayed by the American Novelist *(1971). In the following excerpt, Tanner surveys Pynchon's early short fiction.*]

Before considering Pynchon's early short fiction I want to make some general remarks concerning two phenomena—'rubbish' and 'codes'. Any reader of Pynchon will recognize that he has an extraordinary feeling for what society designates as 'rubbish'. No one can write so lyrically or elegiacally about, for example, a second-hand car lot, or an old mattress, than Pynchon; and what other writer, in the course of a long and moving passage about Advent during wartime, would consider embarking on a curiously poignant meditation triggered off by thinking about 'thousands of old used toothpaste tubes' (*Gravity's Rainbow*)? Many actual rubbish heaps or tips appear in his work—not as symbolic wastelands (though those are there too), but exactly as 'rubbish'. By extension, his work is populated by many of the categories (or non-categories) of people whom society regards as 'rubbish', socially useless junk: bums, hoboes, drifters, transients, itinerants, vagrants, the disinherited, the disaffected, derelicts, losers, victims. Pynchon is continually bringing such figures back from the relative invisibility to which society consigns them.

In this connection I want to introduce some statements made by Michael Thompson in his book, *Rubbish Theory.* Portions of the book can be faulted, but Thompson has a clear grasp of a point of central importance in Pynchon—namely, that what we regard as valuable and what we regard as rubbish are culturally determined.

> For the social order to be maintained there has to be some measure of agreement as to what is of value. People in different cultures may value different things, and they may value the same things differently, but all cultures insist upon some distinction between the valued and the valueless.

Thompson stresses that certain ways of discussing and categorizing things and people in society inevitably leave out some things (and people), literally overlooking them:

> serious adult thought in general, and sociology in particular, constitute a form of discourse that, of its very nature, is unable to make contact with certain regions of social life and, more important, . . . what goes in those regions is crucial for any understanding of society.

Pynchon would, I think, agree. He is the great writer of the overlooked, the left-out, and thus offers a challenge to our often unexamined assumptions about the valuable and the valueless, the estimable and the dismissible. And, as Thompson notes, society's value-categories are intimately connected with questions of power: 'the manner in which durability and transience are imposed upon the world of objects' is related to 'the control mechanism within the system'. At the simplest level, yesterday's kitsch may become today's valuable antiques. This need not be solely due to the manipulation of those who control the market, but those in positions of power in that particular market can have a lot of influence over which category an object

will be placed in. On a larger scale, society has a similar power over people. To use Thompson's words:

> only if one remains within severe cultural and temporal confines can one sustain the common-sense belief that rubbish is defined by intrinsic physical properties. Step outside these limits and one sees that the boundary between rubbish and non-rubbish moves in response to social pressures.

Among other things, Pynchon's work is constantly taking the reader outside the limits of his 'cultural and temporal confines'.

Values and valuations are not, of course, fixed. Society may withdraw as well as confer 'value': it is one of the ways in which societies change. Pynchon, like any great writer, makes us re-examine the dominant valuations of our age. His work is a counterforce to what Thompson designates as two kinds of blindness:

> there are those things or areas which we cannot see (though those with an entirely different 'game' may be able to see them), and there are those things or areas which we conspire not to see. When these latter intrude, and we cannot help but see them, we banish them from view (or, alternatively, neutralize their visibility) by assigning them to a unique cross-cultural category which may be labelled 'rubbish'.

Pynchon indeed plays a different 'game' and is constantly exposing the conspiracy of 'invisibility', that hidden social collusion—a kind of 'plot'—which decides and decrees what is valuable and what is 'rubbish'.

Having introduced the word 'plot', I can move on to make some general remarks about 'codes'. Pynchon's work is full of plots and codes—at every level, from political plots, spies, conspiracies and all kinds of private forms of communication, to larger, national, global, even metaphysical and religious questions concerning the possible presence or absence of plots, and more mystical kinds of illumination or 'messages' or communication (or 'communion', an important word for Pynchon) than the ciphers of espionage or the code of a secret society. Some precedent for this interest can be found in earlier American literature, most notably in the work of Poe. In his work there is not really any presence of 'nature' as one finds it in, say, Fenimore Cooper, but rather a series of cryptograms or clues which have to be decoded, interpreted, translated. The reader of Poe has to be a kind of detective (he, of course, effectively invented the detective story) and a cryptographer. This is true of Pynchon's readers—and many of his characters. In an essay entitled 'A Few Words on Secret Writing' Poe wrote:

> as we can scarcely imagine a time when there did not exist a necessity, or at least a desire, of transmitting information from one individual to another in such a manner as to elude general comprehension, so we may well suppose the practice of writing in cipher to be of great antiquity.

That 'necessity' or 'desire' is notably present in Pynchon's work. It is not, however, a simple matter of cracking a code. Nor is it in Poe. For example, in chapter 23 of *The*

Narrative of Arthur Gordon Pym the topography of a strange island is described. At one point the two men exploring the island find a series of 'indentures in the surface', but these are equivocal.

> With a very slight exertion of the imagination, the left, or more northerly of these indentures might have been taken for the intentional, though rude, representation of a human figure . . . the rest of them bore also some little resemblance to alphabetical characters, and Peters was willing, in all events, to adopt the idle opinion that they were really such.

Pym, on the other hand, is convinced that they are 'the work of nature'. Does nature have its own language of signs, or do we 'alphabetize' nature in looking at it?

The problem becomes a dominant one in Pynchon, where figures like Stencil in *V.* and Oedipa Maas in *Lot 49* have to try to work out whether they really are discovering clues, finding codes and seeing signs, or whether they are projecting or hallucinating in a plotless, clueless world. And, as we shall see, it is often in so-called 'rubbish' that they have to engage in their ambiguous quest for signs. The following quotation gives some sense of Pynchon's feeling for what we might call the esoteric message which may be concealed by the exoteric message, subtexts legible only to the initiated. Pynchon is referring to a secret society of those who have been struck by lightning (the enlightened?):

> Between congruent and identical there seems to be another class of look-alike that only finds the lightning-heads. Another world laid down on the previous one and to all appearances no different. Ha-*ha*! But the lightning-struck know, all right! . . . [they receive a] private monthly magazine *A Nickel Saved* (which looks perfectly innocent, old Ben Franklin after inflation, unless you know the other half of the proverb: ' . . . is a stockpile of nickel'. Making the *real* quote nickel-magnate Mark Hanna's 'You have been in politics long enough to know that no man in public office owes the public anything.' So the real title is *Long Enough,* which Those Who Know, know. The text of each issue of the magazine, when transformed this way, yields many interesting messages). To outsiders it's just a pleasant little club newsletter . . . (*Gravity's Rainbow*)

We can read Pynchon like 'outsiders', or like the lightning-struck. But Those Who Know, know.

Pynchon's first published story was **'The Small Rain'** (*The Cornell Writer*, 6 (March 1959)). There are already clearly discernible types, themes, even atmospheres, which he will develop in subsequent work. The main figure is Nathan Levine, who has deliberately enlisted in the army. He is stationed at some desolate piece of nowhere in Louisiana which he actually likes. He likes the inertia, the inaction, the repetition, the not having to think (he is a graduate from CCNY), and the not having to feel. This cherished immunity from feeling is to be a dominant and recurring phenomenon in Pynchon's work. He is also, paradoxically enough, a communications expert. However, his unit is suddenly ordered into action when a hurricane devastates the bayou country of southern Louisiana. Although Levine likes most of all to 'sleep' or drift off into pornographic novels—notably, one called *Swamp Wench*—the disaster stirs him into some kind of action and change. 'He was also starting to worry: to anticipate some radical change, perhaps, after three years of sand, concrete and sun.' This emergence into a degree of wakefulness and activity is provoked by two things: the disaster, and the hundreds of hideous corpses that have to be dragged from the water; and the college kids on the campus where they have been stationed. There is not only perpetual rain but the air is full of the smell of death. Levine begins to see the horror and the reality of it. He also sees how cut-off from it all the college kids are, 'each trying to look at it as something unusual and nothing they had ever been or would ever want ever to be part of.' Levine has a vision of a kind of life—or death-in-life—which is

> something like a closed circuit. Everybody on the same frequency. And after a while you forget about the rest of the spectrum and start believing that this is the only frequency that counts or is real. While outside, all up and down the land, there are these wonderful colors and x-rays and ultraviolets going on.

Too many people in Pynchon's world try to prolong life as 'a closed circuit' in some way or another, so that they can 'forget about the rest'. On impulse—it is not his official job—Levine joins the men on one of the tugs who are picking up the dead bodies. It is a wasteland indeed—'gray sun on gray swamp'—the rain not bringing fertility and new life, but death. The point is that Levine at least makes the gesture of doing something. 'Levine worked in silence like the others . . . realizing somehow that the situation did not require thought or rationalization. He was picking up stiffs. That was what he was doing.' It is as though the actual vision of—and contact with—death has brought him out of his anaesthetized and paralysed state. Not, of course, that he can do much about the situation, nor does he experience any miraculous transformation. But he acted, and it seems to indicate that he cannot go back into his old state. Instead, he sees himself living the life of a wanderer.

> He had a momentary, ludicrous vision of himself, Lardass Levine the Wandering Jew, debating on weekday evenings in strange and nameless towns with other Wandering Jews the essential problems of identity—not of the self so much as an identity of place and what right you really had to be anyplace.

We do not see his future, but just such displaced wanderers will roam through Pynchon's later fiction.

Near the end Levine picks up a coed who calls herself 'little Buttercup'. For a night in a cabin in a nearby swamp she is, indeed, his 'swamp wench'. Partly because his attitude towards women appears to be basically pornographic, and partly because of the girl's 'incapacity to give', there is no love, no human contact at all, in the coupling. Afterwards, Levine says 'In the midst of great death, the little death.' Doubtless he intends a pun (death as sexual

> Values and valuations are not, of course, fixed. Society may withdraw as well as confer 'value': it is one of the ways in which societies change. Pynchon, like any great writer, makes us re-examine the dominant valuations of our age.
>
> —Tony Tanner

climax), but it points to a larger truth: that what should be the act of love has been turned into an act of death. This deformation of sex into death—or the substitution of death for love—is one of the modern malaises to which Pynchon returns and which he analyses in his longer fiction. When Levine leaves the area, it is still raining, and he says to a friend, 'Jesus Christ I hate rain.' His friend answers, 'You and Hemingway. Funny, ain't it. T. S. Eliot likes rain.' This may be seen as a rejection of Eliot's values or poetic stance, though Levine is no Hemingway. Still, he has been shaken out of his nonchalance, that cultivated non-identity or emotional anonymity of the 'enlisted man'; he has lost some of his immunity from feeling. Although we last see him asleep (again), he cannot, we feel, ever go 'back' to the inert condition he was in at the start, living like a 'closed circuit', and forgetting all the rest.

Pynchon's next story was **'Mortality and Mercy in Vienna'** (published in *Epoch,* 9 (Spring 1959)). Summarized very reductively, it can be described as an account of a party in Washington (the first of many such parties in Pynchon's work which invariably degenerate into violence and chaos), at the end of which, we infer, a strange Indian from Ontario (Irving Loon) starts to massacre all the guests prior, again we infer, to eating them. Stated thus baldly, the idea of the story might seem to be just a piece of sick—very sick—humour. But into this remarkable story Pynchon has packed a number of very suggestive notions which are important in relation to his later work. We can start with the title, which comes from *Measure for Measure.* When the Duke, Vincentio, effectively 'abdicates' in the first scene, he hands over all his ducal power to Angelo:

> In our remove be thou at full ourself;
> Mortality and mercy in Vienna
> Live in thy tongue and heart.

The theme of self-removal and substitution of authority is central to Pynchon's story, in which Washington is depicted as being as degenerate and corrupt as the Vienna in Shakespeare's play, and in which a hugely disproportionate 'justice' is meted out to the errant and debauched guests, just as the death penalty imposed upon Claudio is quite incommensurable with his sin or crime of making Julietta ('fast my wife') pregnant. The problem, in both works, is how do you—can you, can anyone?—cure or heal a degenerate and, as it were, 'damned' society? In Shakespeare's play, Escalus offers a kind of pragmatic

doctoring, Angelo a would-be Messianic healing which is both hypocritical and inhuman, and the Duke a type of apocalyptic judgement which is truly just, therapeutic—and merciful.

Pynchon's story also starts with an abdication and a substitution. The main figure, Cleanth Siegel, a junior diplomat, arrives at a party only to find that his original host, Rachel, will not be there. Instead he finds a somewhat crazed man, David Lupescu, whom Siegel half recognizes as a *Doppelgänger* and who instantly seizes on Siegel as 'Mon semblable . . . mon frère' and also 'a sign, a deliverance'. He hands over responsibility for the party to Siegel with words that are loaded with religious resonance. 'It's all yours. You are now the host. As host you are a trinity: (a) receiver of guests . . . (b) an enemy and (c) an outward manifestation, for *them,* of the divine body and blood.' As he leaves, Siegel asks him where he is going, and Lupescu answers in words that deliberately invoke Conrad's *Heart of Darkness.* 'The outside . . . out of the jungle . . . Mistah Kurtz—he dead.' So by a use of literary reference or intertextuality, a device that Pynchon makes more use of than any other living writer—mixing writings, in Barthes's words—the Washington party is not only Shakespeare's Vienna but also Conrad's jungle (with a trace of Baudelaire's particular Paris). One question will be: how will Siegel act as the designated and chosen substitute 'host'? Like the Duke, or Angelo; like Marlow or Kurtz? Will he be a true host—or go crazy?

The question is quite central to Pynchon's work, so I shall go into it in a little more detail. Siegel is a mixed figure. His mother is a Catholic and he grows up religious, until he gives up his faith (at college he is known as Stephen—a nod at Joyce). But he retains inside him 'the still small Jesuit voice'. On the other hand there is a 'nimble little Machiavel' inside him who not only enjoys 'scheming and counterscheming' and 'manipulating campus opinion' but is also—as Machiavelli advised—capable of delegating cruel actions to others. (Machiavelli is an important figure in Pynchon's work.) He is, then, as one of his college friends murmurs, a 'House divided against itself ', the reference here, of course, being to Christ's words in Mark 3:24-6:

> How can Satan drive out Satan? If a kingdom is divided against itself, that kingdom cannot stand; if a household is divided against itself, that house will never stand: and if Satan is in rebellion against himself, he is divided and cannot stand: and that is the end of him.

As we discover, Siegel, finally, 'cannot stand'. When he was younger he had regarded himself as 'a kind of healer . . . a prophet actually, because if you cared about it at all you had to be both', though he was worried that one could easily become 'something less—a doctor, or a fortune-teller'. The possibility of any real healing and prophecy recurs throughout Pynchon. More generally, the problem becomes nothing less than how to be in the contemporary world, particularly if it is as infernal as the Washington party implies. One way is to cultivate disengagement, emotional immunity: keeping 'cool', to use a term deployed by Pynchon. But that, of course, can lead to paralysis and inhumanity. The other extreme is to want to be a great healer and prophet, but that can lead to a different kind of inhumanity—and madness (Kurtz). Pynchon's work is constantly seeking to discover something in between these two extremes.

In Siegel's case at the party he goes through different phases. He acts as a 'father confessor' to a number of 'the whole host of trodden-on and disaffected': he looks 'compassionate' and listens while people expose to him 'synapses and convolutions which should never have been exposed . . . the bad lands of the heart'. In his way he gives them 'absolution or penance, but no practical advice'. (Kurtz's eloquence contained no 'practical hints'; Marlow is more pragmatic.) But for a time he does attempt positive, practical, restorative work: 'This little Jesuit thing, this poltergeist, would start kicking around inside his head . . . and call him back to the real country where there were drinks to be mixed and *bon mots* to be tossed out carelessly and maybe a drunk or two to take care of.' This proto-religious instinct to 'take care' of people is supplemented by his 'true British staff-officer style to bite the jolly old bullet and make the best of a bad job'. But then he gets 'fed up' with the role he feels has been imposed upon him: 'It was a slow process and dangerous because in the course of things it was very possible to destroy not only yourself but your flock as well.' He starts to disengage himself.

The crisis is precipitated by the Indian, Loon (lunatic). Siegel remembers hearing about his tribe, the Ojibwa Indians, in an anthropology course. Because of their bleak and austere way of life, living always on the brink of starvation, this tribe is prone to 'psychopathy' and 'saturated with anxiety'. The Ojibwa hunter characteristically experiences a 'vision' after which

> he feels he has acquired a supernatural companion, and there is a tendency to identify . . . [for] the Ojibwa hunter, feeling as he does at bay, feeling a concentration of obscure cosmic forces against him and him alone, cynical terrorists, savage and amoral deities which are bent on his destruction, the identification may become complete.

This feeling or state of mind is one experienced by many subsequent figures in Pynchon's work. And, most importantly perhaps, these Indians have strong 'paranoid tendencies'—the first time the word 'paranoid' appears in Pynchon, but 'paranoia' is to become one of his central concerns. In the case of the Ojibwa their paranoia can lead to the 'Windigo psychosis', which, briefly, leads them to identify with a supernatural figure—the Windigo—who eats people, thus turning them into 'frenzied cannibals' who first 'gorge' themselves on their 'immediate family' and then start to devour people at random. From certain signs Siegel realizes that Irving Loon is very close to the 'Windigo psychosis' and is thus about to erupt into devastating violence and cannibalism. This does indeed bring the 'Moment of truth' for Siegel.

If he has read the signs correctly, 'Siegel has the power to work for these parishioners a kind of miracle, to bring them a very tangible salvation. A miracle involving a host,

true, but like no holy eucharist.' He has it in his power to 'save' the whole group; but he has lost his concern with them, thinking he 'should tell all these people to go to hell'. In effect he sends them there. He suddenly sees Irving Loon starting to load a rifle and realizes that the massacre is about to start. Siegel is 'paralyzed'. Then, realizing he has 'about sixty seconds to make a decision', the different parts of the house divided against itself—the Machiavel, the Jesuit, the gentle part, the 'John Buchan hero' part—agree that there is really only one course to take; 'it was just unfortunate that Irving Loon would be the only one partaking of any body and blood, divine or otherwise'. He issues no saving warnings but simply walks away, encased in a chilling indifference. As he hears the first screams and shots, 'He shrugged. What the hell, stranger things had happened in Washington.' Such insouciant callousness is a terrible sign of man's ability to dehumanize himself. Siegel has indeed allowed his 'flock' to be 'destroyed', and in the process he has destroyed himself—as a human being—as well. Satan cannot drive out Satan; and that is the end of him. Cleanth Siegel is not just an example of a failed healer, a false prophet. He is both a product and a representative of a society that has accepted—indeed, eagerly embraced—'mortality' on an ever-increasing scale, and has forgotten the 'mercy'.

'Low Lands' followed in 1960 (*New World Writing,* 16). In strict narrative terms it is about a lawyer named Dennis Flange who one day decides not to go to work so that he can drink with the garbage man, Rocco Squarcione. They are joined by an old navy friend of Flange, a gross figure named Pig Bodine (who recurs in later work). This is too much for Flange's wife Cindy and she orders them all out of the house. Rocco takes the others in his truck to a large garbage dump—vividly evoked by Pynchon, as we might expect—and introduces them to Bolingbroke, the watchman and 'king' of the dump. He puts them up for the night in his shack after they have told sea stories. Flange is awakened by a call from a girl who turns out to be a midget gypsy named Nerissa, who is convinced she will marry an 'Anglo'. She leads him by secret tunnels to her underground room. The story concludes with his agreeing to stay with her—at least for a while. The story takes place on three different levels: Flange's house above the sea; the dump at sea level; the subterranean complex of secret tunnels. Each has a different kind of residence: Flange's house was a minister's house from the 1920s; then there is the watchman's shack; finally Nerissa's room underground. There are connections: the house is full of secret tunnels associated with the smuggling that went on in the twenties, in which the minister was involved and to which he took a 'romantic attitude'; these are echoed by the network of underground tunnels beneath the dump, constructed in the thirties by a terrorist group called 'the Sons of the Red Apocalypse', and in the present time of the story occupied by gypsies.

As the story progresses, Flange moves further away from his wife, and further away from established society, first to the company of nonconformists and social derelicts, then yet further away to the gypsies—socially completely ostracized, 'rubbish' in social terms, and only able to 'live' by night. For 'further away' we could read 'deeper away', since for Flange the action is a continual descent. The house is up, the dump is down ('It seemed to Flange that they must be heading for the centre of the spiral, the low point') and the gypsy's room yet further down ('He had not realized that the junk pile ran to such a depth'). In every case, going from room to room Flange is going from womb to womb—as he knows—and perhaps prior to some regeneration and redemption (the ending leaves it deliberately equivocal; it might also be a descent into fantasy or even insanity). But a descent it is (Flange's 'Molemanship' is referred to), through varying strata of society's 'rubbish' (starting with the established society itself), and Flange is indeed burrowing. He is also drawn to the sea: 'he had read or heard somewhere in his pre-adolescence that the sea was a woman and the metaphor had enslaved him and largely determined what he became from that moment.' At times he also sees the sea as a 'waste land which stretches away to the horizon'. Nerissa the midget is a kind of mermaid of the dump. Flange's 'drowning' in the dump may make possible a sea change in his life, in his conception of the world. Just before he is summoned by Nerissa he falls asleep misquoting *The Tempest* and wondering whether he has perhaps 'suffered a sea change into something not so rare or strange'.

This leads us to another aspect of the whole story: among other things it is a tissue of references, allusions, quotations and misquotations, ironic echoes and parodies—mixed writings. Writers and works thus evoked in some way include T. S. Eliot (with a light travesty of the Waste Land myth), Shakespeare's *The Tempest, Henry IV* (Bolingbroke, of course), *The Merchant of Venice* (Nerissa is Portia's maid), *Alice's Adventures in Wonderland*, Keats's *Endymion*. More distinctly the story is a clear echo, and rewriting, of Washington Irving's story—so crucial for American literature—'Rip Van Winkle'. In all this mixing of writings and rewritings, Pynchon is not simply amusing himself or winking at learned readers. We should see this activity—which continues throughout his major works—more as a sifting (or 'burrowing' back) through not exactly the 'rubbish' and 'waste' of our literary past but through its accumulations to see what can be re-used (recycled, perhaps) for depicting his particular fictional world. We do not have to identify the other texts, but we do have to be alert for clues. Alert on all sides—noting, for example, that the 1920s are associated with the irresponsible 'romanticism' of the minister's house, while the 1930s saw the founding of 'the terrorist group called the Sons of the Red Apocalypse' when the whole social and political climate had changed. Pynchon is, among other things, a notable historical novelist, as *Gravity's Rainbow* was supremely to reveal. And again he can see that neither of the two suggested ways of being in—or against—society, worked or can work: the delusions of romanticism are matched by the delusions of apocalyptic revolutionary politics (they both used 'tunnels', but society still stood).

The story concludes with the beginning of the emergence of a new attitude in Flange, whether it is 'dream' or genuine transformation. Earlier we had read that he had a recurring dread of shrinkage—of himself, and of the world:

What he worried about was any eventual convexity, a shrinking, it might be, of the planet it-

self to some palpable curvature of whatever he would be standing on, so that he would be left sticking out like a projected radius, unsheltered and reeling across the empty lunes of his tiny sphere.

At the end, in Nerissa's room, he has a different attitude. And it is important to note that to Flange she looks like a child (just as her pet rat looks like her child): children are always a source of value in Pynchon and attitudes to them always indicative of something positive or negative in an adult. The story ends:

And then: I wonder why Cindy and I never had a child.

And: a child makes it all right. Let the world shrink to a *boccie* ball.

So of course he knew.

'Sure' he said. 'All right. I'll stay.' For a while, at least, he thought. She looked up gravely. Whitecaps danced across her eyes; sea creatures, he knew, would be cruising about in the submarine green of her heart.

So of course *we* do *not* know—except that something is happening to Flange, and that Pynchon has produced a text that is rare and strange, ranging through many moods and tones, dense with resonances and implications, and ending at an equivocal suspended moment which has a haunting beauty all its own.

'Entropy' was published in 1960 (*Kenyon Review*, 22). It is composed like a fugue, and relevant words like 'stretto', 'counterpoint' and 'fugue' occur in the text. The 'counterpoint' is mainly between two floors of a Washington apartment building. Downstairs one Meatball Mulligan is having a 'lease-breaking party' which seems to be degenerating into chaos. Upstairs a figure named Callisto and his girlfriend Aubade live in a curious fantasy room: a 'hothouse jungle it had taken him seven years to weave together. Hermetically sealed, it was a tiny enclave of regularity in the city's chaos, alien to the vagaries of the weather, of national politics, of any civil disorder.' 'They did not go out.' Outside there is rain and it is the season of the 'false spring'. Two notable conversations take place in the growing din of the party. One concerns communication theory.

Tell a girl: 'I love you'. No trouble with two-thirds of that, it's a closed circuit. Just you and she. But that nasty four-letter word in the middle *that's* the one you have to look out for. Ambiguity. Redundance. Irrelevance, even. Leakage. All this is noise. Noise screws up your signal, makes for disorganization in the circuit.

Upstairs Callisto and Aubade have indeed created a 'closed circuit', just he and she. But such hermetically maintained order is a form of death. Noise indeed 'screws up your signal', but this might have a potential value if you want to cause 'disorganization in the circuit'. This, I think, can apply to Pynchon's work, which does indeed make for 'disorganization' in the customary circuits. So we must be prepared for 'Ambiguity. Redundance. Irrelevance, even. Leakage.' They may be the condition for the emergence of new kinds of signal. On the other hand, as

Pynchon's story indicates, total noise—total chaos—would mean just no communication at all.

This problem is made clear in another form in the other conversation I wish to mention. There is a jazz quartet at the party and after pushing experimentation to the limit—there are distinct echoes of Gerry Mulligan and Ornette Coleman—they finally 'play' a completely silent piece, using no instruments. As the group's leader, the Duke, admits, the next logical extension 'is to think everything'. And thus to pass beyond music—and communication—altogether. The Duke says that they still have some problems, and Meatball says 'Back to the old drawing board.' ' "No, man," Duke said, "back to the airless void." ' Again this reflects on Pynchon's own position as a writer seeking some radically new form of fictional 'music'. He does not want to go back to 'the old drawing board'; but he knows that the 'airless void' is a place where no messages—no music—can take place at all.

An 'airless void' is something like what Callisto and Aubade have created in their 'hothouse' refuge. It is a deliberate retreat from the world. Drawing on Henry Adams and Gibbs, Callisto outlines his preoccupation with 'entropy' (an idea used not only in thermodynamics but in information theory); like Adams, Callisto speaks of himself in the third person:

> he found in entropy or the measure of disorgani-zation for a closed system an adequate metaphor to apply to certain phenomena in his own world . . . in American 'consumerism' discov-ered a similar tendency from the least to the most probable, from differentiation to sameness, from ordered individuality to a kind of chaos. He found himself, in short, restating Gibbs' pre-diction in social terms, and envisioned a heat-death for his culture in which ideas, like heat-energy, would no longer be transferred since each point in it would ultimately have the same quantity of energy; and intellectual motion would, accordingly, cease.

As he talks, he is trying to save the life of a young bird by warming it in his hands—transferring heat—but he finally fails, since he has indeed brought about an entropic state in his 'closed system'. What frightens him is that the tem-perature outside has remained at 37 degrees Fahrenheit for some days, and he takes this as an 'omen of apoca-lypse'. But while the idea of entropy is very important in Pynchon's work we should note that it is metaphor em-braced, not by the author, but by the self-isolated Callisto. (It is worth noting that at one point he is looking for 'cor-respondences' and he thinks of Sade, and what happens to Temple Drake in *Sanctuary,* and *Nightwood*—all works or authors alluding to acts of sexual perversion.)

While it might seem that there is a simple opposition be-tween the accelerating chaos downstairs and the calm up-stairs ('arabesques of order competing fugally with the im-provised discords of the party downstairs'), it is not, of course, so simple—as the conclusion intimates. Mulligan finds himself confronting a somewhat similar choice to that which confronted Siegel and confronts many other figures in Pynchon: give up, or try to do something?

The way he figured, there were only two ways he could cope: (a) lock himself in the closet and maybe eventually they would all go away, or (b) try to calm everybody down, one by one. (a) was certainly the more attractive alternative. But then he started thinking about that closet. It was dark and stuffy and he would be alone. . . . The other way was more a pain in the neck, but prob-ably better in the long run. So he decided to try and keep his lease-breaking party from deterio-rating into total chaos . . .

It might not be a radical solution, but it is a gesture against chaos, a neg-entropic act; while upstairs the girl Aubade finally breaks the window of their hothouse with her bare hands

> and turned to face the man on the bed and wait with him until the moment of equilibrium was reached, when 37 degrees Fahrenheit should prevail both outside and inside, and forever, and the hovering, curious dominant of their separate lives should resolve into a tonic of darkness and the final absence of all motion.

There is a kind of perfect music which acts like a 'closed system' and finally resolves all into a terminal sameness: there is a noise which might indeed lead to chaos (a termi-nal sameness of another kind) but which might also permit new signals and provoke some counterforce against chaos, against terminal sameness—against entropy. The attrac-tions of 'the closet' in the madness of the modern world are clear enough in Pynchon, but so is the need to resist those attractions in some way. The 'closed circuit', the sealed-off refuge, the hothouse world of fantasy, the dan-gerous seductiveness of metaphors of doom (like entropy): these can all lead to inhumanity and death. Pynchon, the writer, moves and manœuvres between the 'old drawing board' and the 'airless void'.

'Under the Rose' (*Noble Savage,* 3 (1961)) was later re-worked as chapter 3 in *V.,* but a few points should be noted about the story, since it revealed for the first time another dimension of Pynchon's imagination: his ability to recon-struct history for his own purposes (the astonishing range of this reconstructive gift was only to emerge fully in *Grav-ity's Rainbow*). It is set at the time of the Fashoda Crisis of 1898. This was the climax of a series of conflicts be-tween Great Britain and France, and although it resulted in the *entente* of 1904 it revealed the possible dangers of the international conflicts always latent in the period of late imperialism, and it could be seen, retrospectively, as an omen of the First World War. Fashoda was the strate-gic centre of the Egyptian Sudan, land of the Upper Nile, and both the British (under Kitchener) and the French (under Marchand) engaged in a race to capture it—forces converging on a single point (as they will on Malta in *V.*). National feelings ran so high that it did indeed bring the countries to the brink of war.

Pynchon's story is concerned with the spying that went on in the background—'spying's Free Masonry'—and the sense of the approach of some 'sure apocalypse'. One Ger-man spy longs for a big, final war, an Armageddon. The English spy, Porpentine, has 'conceived the private mis-sion of keeping off Armageddon'. But they are both 'comrade Machiavellians, still playing the games of the Renaissance'. All the spies operate 'in no conceivable Europe but rather in a zone forsaken by God, between the tropics of diplomacy, lines they were forbidden forever to cross'. A similar 'zone' is to reappear in *Gravity's Rainbow*. One spy looks forward to the possible great war as effecting a great 'cleaning': 'Armageddon would sweep the house of Europe so. Did that make Porpentine champion only of cobwebs, rubbish, offscourings?' And Pynchon, too? Porpentine is another of those Pynchon figures concerned with the problems of being a 'saviour'.

> Porpentine found it necessary to believe if one appointed oneself saviour of humanity that perhaps one must love that humanity only in the abstract. For any descent to the personal level can make a purpose less pure. Whereas a disgust at individual human perversity might as easily avalanche into a rage for apocalypse.

There are references to an increasing inclination to turn to the 'inanimate' (a girl 'daft for rocks', a man who has himself wired up so that he can operate like a machine), a dominant motif in *V*. Porpentine, old-fashioned, crosses a 'threshold' into 'humanity': it is fatal, and the story ends up with his death. The larger question posed—if there is a larger question than the problem of being 'human' in the modern world—is one that hangs over all Pynchon's subsequent work.

> It was no longer single combat. Had it ever been? . . . They were all in it; all had a stake, acted as a unit. Under orders. Whose orders? Anything human? He doubted . . . excused himself, silent, for wanting so to believe in a fight according to the duello, even in this period of history. But they—no, it—had not been playing those rules. Only statistical odds. When had he stopped facing an adversary and taken on a Force, a Quantity?

All the 'rules' of an earlier world have gone. There is now only a 'they'. Or, rather, an 'it'. We are entering the modern world.

Two more short pieces by Pynchon may conveniently be mentioned here, although they were written after the publication of *V*. **'The Secret Integration'** (*Saturday Evening Post*, 237 (19 December 1964)) concerns a group of boys led by Grover Snodd who indulge in various attempts at sabotaging the local paper mill or the school—an undertaking named Operation Spartacus (after the film). Most of them are childish adventure games, and as 'plots' they fail when it comes to the lines of authority laid down by the adult world, though there is some anarchic resentment against 'the sealed-up world adults made, remade and lived in without him'. The title refers to the events that follow the moving of a black family, the Barringtons, into the town of Mingeborough: the white adults are all bigots and behave hysterically at the presence of the black family in their community. Among other things, they cover the front lawn of the Barrington house with garbage. When the gang of boys discover this—and the gang includes the black boy Carl Barrington—they 'begin kicking through it looking for clues'. (Looking for clues in garbage is a recurrent activity in Pynchon!) The clues they find reveal

that a good deal of the garbage comes from their own homes. Through shame or feelings of helplessness they effectively abandon Carl, and he drifts away into the darkness, off to the old derelict mansion which is their secret hideout. Carl is in every sense a reject, and constructed out of rejections—indeed, we finally discover that he is an 'imaginary playmate'.

> Carl has been put together out of phrases, images, possibilities that grownups had somehow turned away from, repudiated, left out at the edges of the town, as if they were auto parts in Etienne's father's junkyard—things they could or did not want to live with but which the kids, on the other hand, could spend endless hours with, piecing together, rearranging, feeding, programming, refining. He was entirely theirs, their friend and robot, to cherish, buy undrunk sodas for, or send into danger or even, as now, at last, to banish from their sight.

So they leave their fantasy friend Carl and return 'each to his own house, hot shower, dry towel, before-bed television, good night kiss, and dreams that could never again be entirely safe'.

Another incident involves another black, a vagrant and a drifter named Mr McAfee. The children go to the hotel to try to help him (he is an alcoholic, and one of the children is already a member of Alcoholics Anonymous!). At one point the children try to telephone a girl the man once knew. This gives Tim an intimation of just what kind of terrifying loneliness is possible: 'Tim's foot felt at the edge of a certain abyss which he had been walking close to—for who knew how long—without knowing'; he sees 'how hard it would be, how hopeless, to really find a person you needed suddenly, unless you lived all your life in a house like he did, with a mother and father'. The white adults drive McAfee out of town next morning. Again, the children are really helpless. The town has certainly not accepted 'integration'. Tim asks his friend Grover, a maths prodigy, what the word 'integration' means:

> 'The opposite of differentiation,' Grover said, drawing an x-axis, y-axis and curve on his greenboard. 'Call this function of x. Consider values of the curve at any point little increments of x'—drawing straight vertical lines from the curve down to the x-axis, like the bars of a jail cell—'you can have as many of these as you want, see, as close together as you want.'

> 'Till it's all solid,' said Tim.

> 'No, it never gets solid. If this was a jail cell, and those lines were bars, and whoever was behind it could make himself any size he wanted to be, he could always make himself skinny enough to get free. No matter how close together the bars were.'

Grover knows that the lines are artificial, but in fact in the adult world they do operate as cell bars, and instead of integration plus differentiation this white society will try to maintain a rigid and exclusive sameness, as solid as it can make it. The ultimate emptiness and deadness of such a society is manifest in the new housing estate as perceived by the children:

But there was nothing about the little, low-rambling, more or less identical homes of North-umberland Estates to interest or to haunt . . . no small immunities, no possibilities for hidden life or otherworldly presence: no trees, secret routes, shortcuts, culverts, thickets that could be made hollow in the middle—everything in the place was out in the open, everything could be seen at a glance; and behind it, under it, around the corners of its houses and down the safe, gentle curves of its streets, you came back you kept coming back, to nothing: nothing but the cheerless earth.

The end of the story sees the end of fantasy, of rebellion and perhaps of innocence, for the children have encountered the nasty realities of adult prejudice inside their own comfortable homes. But this kind of man-made landscape of 'nothing' becomes an increasing source of dread in Pynchon's work. Elsewhere and in different ways the rebellion against the 'sealed-up world adults made' goes on—and must go on. (pp. 20-39)

> *Tony Tanner, in his* Thomas Pynchon, *Methuen, 1982, 95 p.*

Edward Mendelson   (essay date 1984)

[*An American educator and critic, Mendelson is the author of numerous books about W. H. Auden, as well as the editor of* Thomas Pynchon: A Collection of Critical Essays *(1978), and a contributor to* Mindful Pleasures: Essays on Thomas Pynchon *(1976). In the following review of* Slow Learner, *he calls the collection "an exhilarating spectacle of greatness discovering its powers."*]

The apprentice work of a major novelist makes better reading than the mature productions of a dozen minor ones. Thomas Pynchon wrote four of the five stories in [*Slow Learner*] around the age of 21, the fifth at 27. For all their energy and invention, they would now be forgotten had he written nothing else. But he went on to write *V.* (1963), *The Crying of Lot 49* (1966), and *Gravity's Rainbow* (1973), each in turn the most profound and accomplished American novel since the end of World War II. Readers who discovered Pynchon's stories in little magazines in the late 1950s would have seen in them an adroit young talent that might bear watching. Readers who discover them now will find an exhilarating spectacle of greatness discovering its powers.

To Pynchon himself the spectacle is embarrassing. Looking back from the vantage of his mid-40s, he sees only the slow learner of his title repeatedly committing faults he has still not fully outgrown. His introduction provides a relentlessly detailed catalogue of his youthful failings: "bad ear," "puerility," "adventitious lectures about tale-telling and geometry," "overwriting," "phony data," "stupid mistakes," "literary theft," "fancy footwork," "dumb theories," and more. The best he can say of his stories is that they might be useful as examples of bad writing, "illustrative of typical problems in entry-level fiction, and cautionary about some practices which younger writers might prefer to avoid." Pynchon's indictment of his younger self is accurate, but it is one-sided. It ignores the fact

that the faults of his stories proved to be virtues in embryo. He blundered; but he was exploring unknown territory. He stumbled; but he was learning virtuoso turns.

In his novels, however, he rarely made a false step. He achieved an inclusive vision of character and culture unparalleled in recent American writing. He integrated disparate realms of knowledge—social, psychological, linguistic, historical, scientific—without falsifying any one of them by making one the master-science that determines all the others. He understood that society and the psyche are intimately connected, but that the order of one could not be reduced to the order of the other. Neither Freud nor Marx gets the last word in Pynchon; neither, in fact, gets much to say at all. Pynchon's characters are shaped by the social world in the ways that everyone is shaped—by the patterns of the city, by the cycles of commerce, by the assumptions of the printed word—but which modern literature had largely forgotten until he began writing. Joyce and Mann look, by comparison, like innocents in a playground of poetic myths. To cite one example only, Pynchon takes seriously the ways in which his characters earn a living. Most characters in modern fiction hold down a job either as a sop to verisimilitude or as a source of glamour or pathos. Pynchon's characters think and act, like everyone, in terms derived partly from the work they spend much of their time performing. In *Gravity's Rainbow* the statistician Roger Mexico has mathematical probability ingrained in his thinking. It shapes his politics and his loves—yet he never collapses into an allegorical type signifying Mathematics.

Pynchon constructs his characters by giving equal weight to elements taken from public history (work, politics, ideas) and from personal history (sex, family, disease). His ability to make these elements cohere has burdened him, ironically enough, with a false reputation as a purveyor of grotesques. This says more about the unexamined assumptions held by critics than it does about Pynchon. A character like Brigadier Pudding, the coprophiliac fetishist of *Gravity's Rainbow,* will certainly seem grotesque to readers who assume personality is the product of interior processes that are essentially the same at all times and in all places. But the Brigadier is a logical product of his memories of the carnage at Ypres, his futile historical theories, and his combination of bureaucratic power and bureaucratic helplessness. There are no grotesques in Pynchon's novels for the simple reason that Pynchon acknowledges no standard (other than an ethical one) by which a character might be judged eccentric or extreme. He values the incorrigible uniqueness of his characters—and only directs his moral anger at them when they fail to do likewise.

He extends the same generosity to his fellow writers. In his introduction to *Slow Learner,* as much a cultural portrait of the late 1950s as an account of his own stories, he praises just about everyone who has written fiction in the past quarter-century. From Bellow and Kerouac to Barthelme and Le Carré, every writer he names is someone who either expanded possibilities for style, or enlarged the range of fictional subject matter, or took a trivial genre and made it serious. Apparently the only writer of the time who got everything wrong was the young Thomas

Pynchon. Only where Pynchon was especially entranced back then by some aspect of the period's culture does he find something to criticize now. There are surprises here for his readers. Having written novels that too often read like propaganda in a war between the virtuous young and the wicked old, he now keeps returning to what he calls "the puerility angle." He notes that the Beat movement and the hippie resurgence, which he honored, though ambiguously, in his novels, "placed too much emphasis on youth, including the eternal variety." Not that his essential loyalties have changed. He is quick to remember that the movement, "after all, was a sane and decent affirmation of what we all want to believe about American values." What bothers him now is the way the movement fed his own adolescent values and helped them play havoc with his writing.

Yet his stories resist adolescent values more often than they yield. The first, **"The Small Rain,"** takes one of Pynchon's favorite character types, a passive young man who lets an institution (here the peacetime army) do his thinking for him, and brings him to a voluntary confrontation with death. When the young man's unit is called in to provide communications for troops cleaning up after a hurricane, he slips into the crew of a tugboat gathering corpses left by the storm. Pynchon now sees this story as "defective" in the evasive way its narrator and characters deal with the subject of death ("When we speak of 'seriousness' in fiction ultimately we are talking about an attitude toward death"), but in judging it he has the moral exigencies of *The Crying of Lot 49* and *Gravity's Rainbow* for comparison. Pynchon also complains that he made someone's Southern accent crucial to the plot without taking the trouble to get the accent right. What he does not mention is that this botched effort led directly to the grand and exact polyphonies of *Gravity's Rainbow*.

Where Pynchon finds evasiveness in **"The Small Rain,"** he finds deliberate regression in **"Low-lands."** The main character of this story retreats from marriage into what may or may not be a fantasy relation with a three-and-a-half-foot-tall gypsy woman whose face and diction are like a child's. Earlier he had retreated from his honeymoon into a two-week drunk with his sailor buddies. Pynchon observes that this character is obviously a small boy inside, "although when I wrote this story I thought he was pretty cool." By focusing on the foreground defects of the story, Pynchon ignores some remarkable doings in back. The setting shifts from a house that hides a secret network of tunnels built by a smuggler during Prohibition to a junkyard laced by a network of tunnels built by forgotten terrorists during the Depression—and now populated by gypsies who may or may not be imaginary. The hidden networks of this story, and its passage from social dissent to private fantasy, served as preliminary sketches for all three of Pynchon's novels. There, hidden networks would come to signify social patterns as dense and complex as those in Balzac or Dickens, and the tempting passage from dissent to fantasy would end in fatal consequences.

Pynchon decries another aspect of this story with greater justice. He points to "an unacceptable level of racist, sexist and proto-Fascist talk," not only in the voice of one of the characters, but in his own narrative voice at the time. The time provided plenty of bad examples: "John Kennedy's role model James Bond was about to make his name by kicking Third World people around." Still, the narrative voice in **"Low-lands,"** he concludes, "remains that of a smart-assed jerk who didn't know any better, and I apologize for it."

When he turns to his next story Pynchon shows himself a better critic than his critics. "Disagreeable as I find **'Low-lands'** now, it's nothing compared to my bleakness of heart when I have to look at **'Entropy.'** " This is his most discussed and most anthologized story, largely because it includes straightforward expository versions of scientific issues later elaborated in his novels. While a lease-breaking party degenerates toward chaos in the apartment downstairs, middle-aged Callisto, in a closed bedroom one floor up, meditates on thermodynamics. Using the style Henry Adams used when meditating on power, Callisto does little more than meditate, on Pynchon's behalf. He speculates, for example, that cultures are subject to entropic decline just as thermodynamic systems are. Meanwhile, the temperature outside remains ominously constant, and the world settles into terminal stasis. Pynchon recalls in his introduction his "somber glee at any idea of mass destruction or decline"—a pose "fairly common, I hope, among pre-adults." The story is not without flashes of inspiration, or at least inspired silliness. In one of Pynchon's early forays into the realm of secret sympathies, he invents a jazz quartet that *thinks* the music, without instruments. After getting mixed up when one member thinks the wrong tune and another the wrong key, they start again as the leader comments, "Back to the airless void." The story, unfortunately, keeps returning to a schematic void of its own. As Pynchon observes in his introduction, "It is simply wrong to begin with a theme, symbol or other abstract unifying agent, and then try to force characters and events to conform to it."

Pynchon begins to redeem his early promise in the fourth story, **"Under the Rose."** This is a tale of international espionage set in Alexandria and Cairo in 1898. Pynchon broke through a six-month writer's block by looting everything but the plot from Baedeker's 1898 guide to Egypt. For the plot, John Buchan and his ilk provided material he could "steal, or let us say 'derive.' " Pynchon had made some self-mocking gestures toward writing historical fiction in **"Entropy,"** where, writing in 1958 or 1959, he offers picturesque details of Washington, D.C., "back then" in 1957. In **"Under the Rose"** he set himself the task of reconstructing a time and place he had never seen—and he also wrote the first of his stories whose characters seem to include no one remotely like himself. Also for the first time, he integrated his theoretical interests into the lives of his characters. A British spy, his sense of self based on a myth of personal heroism as the moving force in history, is forced to learn that history might be moved by larger, impersonal forces. Statistics may matter more than character. In effect, the revelation kills him. Pynchon records his debt to *The Prince* and *To the Finland Station* here, debts additional to those he owes Baedeker and Buchan. But what he now calls "literary theft" was his means of looking outside his own experience, of learning how to "shut up and listen"—something he says he began learning only later. In fact, he was able to build the vast historical panorama of *V.* around the kernel provided by **"Under the Rose"**; the story, much rewritten, became one of the novel's chapters. Pynchon was 22 when he wrote the story. Three years later—slow learner—he had finished *V.*

Two years afterward came **"The Secret Integration."** Although he works hard to list the defects of this story, even Pynchon finally has to admit it has virtues as well. Whether he is ready to accept responsibility for them is another matter: "Sometime in the last couple of decades, some company of elves must have snuck in and had a crack at it." The story follows a group of small-town children as they try to organize a Spartacist revolt of practical jokes against school and parents, partly in response to their parents' harassment of a black family that recently moved in. (Pynchon is responding, five years later, to his attitudes in **"Low-lands."**) One of the children in the group, the child of the black family, turns out in the end to have been an imaginary playmate, a fantasy abandoned when the group is forced to recognize both the ugliness of their parents' hatred and their own need for the safety their parents provide.

Pynchon achieved the moral and psychological complexity of this story through a means he now finds suspect—"the old Baedeker trick" of transferring his experience to a place he never knew, in this case a Berkshire town he read about in a W.P.A. guide. Discussing this "strategy of transfer," Pynchon seems almost ready to abandon the anonymity, the refusal of autobiography, that made possible the massive scale and sympathy of his novels, but which had also brought him notoriety as the invisible man of American letters. "Somewhere," he writes, "I had come up with the notion that one's personal life had nothing to do with fiction, when the truth, as everyone knows, is nearly the direct opposite." Yet the very next sentence shows that Pynchon is not throwing in his lot with writers who keep telling their own histories in ever more bloated forms. "The fiction," he continues, "that moved and pleased me then as now was precisely that which had been made luminous, undeniably authentic by having been found and taken up, always at a cost, from deeper, more shared levels of the life we all really live." It is the shared life that matters, not the life special to an author. This promises much for Pynchon's next novel, but it is also somewhat unfair to his previous ones. The complex particulars that he has always valued in his characters are signs of the uniqueness that—on a deep and shared level of the life we all really live—is everyone's birthright.

Pynchon does more to honor that birthright than any other living writer. By refusing to make himself the center of his fiction, he has earned without seeking it an authority beyond the reach of writers who follow the traditional American way of self-assertion. Pynchon's way was different from the start, and from the start he knew why it ought to be. When he wrote **"Low-lands"** he already knew enough to say this about an offstage character: "There are many ways of telling a sea-story, but perhaps because of the music and because the words had nothing to with per-

sonal legend, Delgado's way seemed tinged with truth of a special order." (pp. 36-9)

Edward Mendelson, "How Gravity Began," in The New Republic, *Vol. 191, Nos. 3 & 4, July 16 & 23, 1984, pp. 36-9.*

Richard F. Patteson   (essay date 1984)

[*In the following essay, Patteson provides a comparative analysis of chapter three of Pynchon's novel* V. *and his short story "Under the Rose," upon which that chapter is based, arguing that a narratological search for a "basic" story structure in either of the works serves to emphasize the indeterminacy of their structures.*]

One of the topics lately debated in the newly-christened field of narratology—whether a narrative has a "core" story underlying all possible manifestations of it—brings into sharper focus the persistent problem of indeterminacy in Thomas Pynchon's fiction. The issue has been joined most pointedly by Seymour Chatman and Barbara Herrnstein Smith. Chatman, along with a number of other theorists inspired by transformational linguistics, maintains that a narrative is composed of two parts, a "deep structure" (or "basic story") and its realizations (the story-as-told, or "discourse") [*Story and Discourse: Narrative Structure in Fiction and Film,* 1978]. Smith insists, in a carefully fashioned argument, that "for any particular narrative, there is no single *basically* basic story subsisting beneath it but, rather, an unlimited number of other narratives that can be *constructed in response* to it or *perceived as related* to it." Smith criticizes narratologists for relying too heavily on the dualistic (sign/signified) linguistic model as a "scaffolding" for their "two-leveled model of narrative." She offers an alternative conception of language (and of narrative) in which narratives are "regarded not only as *structures* but also as *acts,* the features of which are functions of the variable sets of conditions in response to which they are performed" ["Narrative Versions, Narrative Theories," *Critical Inquiry,* Autumn 1980]. Such a conception implies a sizable degree of indeterminacy within narrative. Indeed, while Chatman claims that a story can be manifested in different media and in different forms without losing the essential characteristics of its deep structure, Smith questions the very existence of such a structure. "For any given narrative," she contends, "there are always *multiple* basic stories that can be constructed in response to it because basic-ness is always arrived at by the exercise of some set of operations, in accord with some set of principles, that reflect some set of interests, all of which are, by nature, variable and multiple." In short, from Smith's point of view, any search for a "basic story" is bound to lead only to another version.

Pynchon, Khachig Tölöyan points out [in "Seven on Pynchon: The Novelist as Deconstructionist," *Novel,* Winter 1983], "underscores the struggle for the unequivocal determination and control of meaning-making." He enacts this struggle in various ways, including the creation of "competing stories seeking decisive closures, any one of which makes the reliability and closure of others impossible." Or, as Tony Tanner puts it [in his book *Thomas*

Pynchon, 1982], Pynchon's characters "move in a world of both too many and too few signs, too much data and too little information, too many texts but no reliable edition . . . ." Other fiction writers for a number of years have been exploring this very question—the existence or non-existence of a determinate truth underlying the corruptions and distortions of human perception. Many works of contemporary fiction are constructed in such a way as to imply that the notion of a "deep structure" apart from the individual text's articulation is at best improbable.

Contemporary writers frequently undermine the reader's faith in a "basic story" separate from the manifestation of a given text. In Robbe-Grillet's *Jealousy,* for instance, it is not possible to determine with certainty whether the centipede is killed before or after the trip to town. The automobile is said at one point (just after the trip) *never* to have given its owner any trouble; at another point (during the journey) the narrator suggests that the car is having trouble "again." These and many other apparent contradictions can of course be naturalized by the reader in terms of the narrator's obsession; sequential chronology is dissolved and reassembled within his mind. It is, nonetheless, impossible to reconstruct what "really" happens in Robbe-Grillet's novel. Equally problematic are narratives like [Samuel Beckett's] *Molloy,* which concludes with the assertions that it is midnight and raining, not midnight and not raining; and [Vladimir Nabokov's] *Pale Fire,* which literally mocks the hapless reader's search for the "underlying" story by incorporating within the text a multiplicity of versions from which to choose. The ultimate demolition of the "basic story" to date has been Marc Saporta's boxed novel, *Composition No. 1,* in which each shuffle of the unbound pages produces a different narrative. Obviously, a novel with an infinite number of versions (or shuffles) cannot have a single deep structure as Chatman means the term to be taken.

Pynchon's *V.,* although not so ostentatiously innovative in narrative method as these and other post-modernist works, is particularly useful to an examination of the problem of stories and their versions for two reasons. First, the novel's plot in large measure consists of Stencil's search for the "basic story" of *V.*—a truth about her beneath an indefinite number of manifestations or versions. Moreover, a section of Pynchon's book appears to exist in two textual manifestations, which are widely assumed by those who read them to be "versions" of the same basic narrative. I am referring here to Chapter Three of *V.* ("In which Stencil, a quick-change artist, does eight impersonations") and to the short story **"Under the Rose."** Both texts appear to be "about" the same "basic" events—espionage, a love affair involving one Victoria Wren, and a murder, all of which occur in Egypt at the time of the Fashoda crisis in 1898. But a closer look reveals important differences between the texts—differences that effectively thwart the reader's attempt to put together a "basic story" or a consistent, common narrative substructure.

Nearly all critics of *V.* have commented upon Stencil's quest as an exemplum of man's need to discover, or if necessary to create, a determinate structure of meaning beneath the flux and apparent randomness of the universe. Elaborating on this notion, Melvyn New argues [in "Profaned and Stenciled Texts: In Search of Pynchon's *V.,*" *Georgia Review,* Vol. 33, 1979] that the "human need to incorporate all fragments into an imagined whole" motivates not only Stencil's search but the critical act itself. *V.* can be seen as a meeting place for narratology and metaphysics. The universe is Stencil's discourse, in Chatman's terms. He seeks, he tries to conceive (in both senses of the word), a basic story—but in doing so only adds more variants: further fragments of discourse. The basic story remains elusive. And, as New suggests, Stencil's attempts to piece together the "real story" of V. parallel readers' attempts to piece together the "real story" *of V.*

There are innumerable hints throughout the novel that both Stencil's efforts and the readers' will prove futile. The street lamps described in the first chapter recede "in an asymmetric V to the east where it's dark and there are no more bars." This figure, the V whose constituent elements seem to have a common, basic point of origin (but in fact do not) stands as an emblem of Stencil's quest. Other details in the book contribute to a growing sense of something *not there,* of a gap where significance should be, of no-thing where something is anticipated. The vortex that takes Sidney Stencil's life is another V, but again, the figure is deceptive. Nothing, this time literally a vacuum, lies at the point of expected closure. Mondaugen's "sferics"—atmospheric radio disturbances—are a more interesting example because they constitute a sort of discourse for which Mondaugen is trying to find a "deep structure." But that structure does not exist. Even when the mad Lt. Weissmann "breaks" what he imagines to be Mondaugen's "code," the message is only that there is no message: " 'The world is all that the case is.' "

The two accounts of Victoria Wren's sojourn in Egypt—one within the novel, the other without—purport to relate the same "basic" events, yet they do so quite differently. In **"Under the Rose"** the tale is told by an omniscient narrator who spares no effort to fill in gaps, to provide necessary information, to tie up loose ends. The novel "version," on the other hand, is thoroughly "Stencilized." Herbert Stencil, dozing in a New York apartment, reconstructs the events of 1898 by imagining himself, through a series of "impersonations," as eight eyewitnesses. Very little in the chapter (we never know how much) is based upon fact. Moreover, the scenes that Stencil imagines are not so much seen and heard as overheard. The reader is given glimpses of characters, fragments of conversation, and above all, hypotheses (some of them contradicting others) about what is happening. The novel, then, contains its own subsidiary versions. Stencil's hypotheses, and the further hypotheses of the witnesses he impersonates, parallel what Smith maintains the reader does when he attempts to construct an underlying or "basic" story: he creates new versions.

"Under the Rose" is less complicated, and the occasional student who stumbles upon it might be forgiven if he erroneously concludes that he has found an important "key" to the novel. It is tempting even to see in **"Under the Rose"** a fully elaborated "basic story" of which the novel gives us only portions. But this inference is incorrect, for these two narratives differ in respects other than the amount of information imparted, and those differences determine whether, in this particular instance, a common "core story" can exist or even be plausibly hypothesized.

Because the number of discrete differences between the two texts is vast, I will confine my discussion to significant semantic variations. These fall into two broad categories, which I will, for lack of better terms, call quantitative and contradictive differences. Quantitative differences result from the addition or deletion of material which may plausibly fit into (or be stricken from) either text. Such material may also be fit into a composite version of the two texts without explicitly contradicting anything in either. These differences are not insignificant. They can greatly alter the reader's experience of the narrative. But they are not so radical as contradictive differences, which *cannot* logically be reconciled or brought into univocal focus.

Quantitative differences between the two Pynchon texts abound. David Cowart observes [in "Love and Death: Variations on a Theme in Pynchon's Early Fiction," *Journal of Narrative Technique,* Winter 1977] that many of the variations relate to the texts' difference in status. Because **"Under the Rose"** is an independently existing short story having to do primarily with espionage, material connected with Porpentine's murder is amplified and foregrounded. In Chapter Three of *V.,* Stencil's overall obsession with *V.* makes Victoria Wren the focal point. This is only partly true, however. The chapter is divided into eight segments. Porpentine (but not Victoria) appears prominently in four of them; both Porpentine and Victoria appear in four; in no section does Victoria appear without Porpentine. As for the short story, while it is certainly true that **"Under the Rose"** contains a far greater number of details about the political plot, it also contains a far greater number of details about Victoria Wren and her affair with Goodfellow. In fact, the wealth of background detail in the short story is a major quantitative difference between the two texts.

There is also material in Chapter Three that does not appear in **"Under the Rose."** Most of it concerns the private lives, and the inner lives, of Stencil's "impersonations." The first seven segments of Chapter Three are filtered through the perceptions of figures who appear as minor characters in the short story, while the last segment is related by a narrator who effaces himself utterly. Each of the seven narrators appearing in the text is given a distinctive personality and history—information absent from **"Under the Rose."** But this kind of material, like that having to do with Porpentine and the espionage plot, is ultimately assimilable into a narrative framework that could include information given in both accounts. Quantitative differences do not hinder the reader's construction or hypothesizing of a "basic story." Both texts, despite such differences, *can* share a narrative "core," although, clearly, that core must be imagined by the reader and is itself no more than a composite third "version."

Contradictive differences cannot be reconciled even in this way. One of the major contradictive differences between the two Pynchon texts concerns a cab ride in Cairo. In

"Under the Rose" Porpentine, upon arriving in Cairo, walks to the Hotel Victoria to visit a "friend" who produces coded instructions from the English Foreign Office. Afterward Porpentine catches a cab that takes him to a pharmacy near the Credit Lyonnais, where he picks up an envelope containing fifty pounds—payment for himself and Goodfellow. At Shepheard's Hotel, their Cairo headquarters, the two intelligence agents decode their instructions and make further plans. Later that night, Porpentine hires another cab and rides around the city until early morning. During this second cab ride, he visits an assortment of Cairenes: a girl who lives in the Quartier Rosetti, a jeweler in the Muski, a "minor Esthetic" with a connection at the British Consulate, and a pimp. He returns to his room at Shepheard's Hotel "at three in the morning."

In the novel the two cab rides are collapsed into one, and the driver (one of Stencil's impersonations) is the narrative focal point. Here, too, the excursion begins in front of the Hotel Victoria around mid-day, but the same ride, with the same driver, extends into the night. Furthermore, the order of Porpentine's errands is different. Gebrail the cab driver takes him *first* to the Quartier Rosetti, "then a few more stops along the Muski; then uphill to the Rond-Point, where Gebrail waited while the Englishman disappeared for half an hour into the Bazaars' pungent labyrinth." As evening approaches, Porpentine returns briefly to Shepheard's but climbs back into the *same* cab and orders Gebrail to take him to " 'a chemist's shop near the Credit Lyonnais.' " How Porpentine spends the next eight or nine hours is undisclosed. There are, of course, quantitative differences between the two accounts. The short story reveals more details about the reasons for Porpentine's various stops in Cairo, while the novel reveals more about the life and opinions of the cab driver. But these differences present no serious problem to the reader who is intent on constructing a hypothetical "basic story." The contradictive differences do present such a problem. Logic dictates that there must be either two cab rides or one. The visit to the pharmacy must occur either before most of the other stops, during early afternoon, or after them, at night. No "basic story" can reconcile these differences.

Much more important to both the short story and the novel are the circumstances surrounding Porpentine's murder. Once again, in **"Under the Rose"** there is greater elaboration on the actual events, but *the events themselves* are also different. In the short story, after a complicated altercation at the Ezbekiyeh Garden opera house, Porpentine pursues three enemy agents, Lepsius, Bongo-Shaftsbury, and Moldweorp, all the way to the pyramids. Joined by Goodfellow and Victoria Wren, Porpentine finally confronts his three adversaries and is shot dead by Bongo-Shaftsbury in the shadow of the sphinx. In the novel there is also a scuffle at the opera. Porpentine enters Lepsius' box and wrestles him to the floor (evidently to protect Lord Cromer, the British consul-general, or to draw his attention to potential danger from the enemy side). Bongo-Shaftsbury emerges from the shadows at this point and shoots Porpentine. In both texts the aim of Porpentine and Goodfellow is to avert a possible war between Britain and France by preventing the assassination of Cromer. **"Under the Rose"** renders all the intricacy of the political plotting and counter-plotting, while the novel's account, in the fashion of Robbe-Grillet, describes (with belabored "objectivity") only the bare events, omitting even the names of the principals. The really significant differences between the two accounts of this episode, however, are contradictive rather than quantitative. A single "basic story" may (perhaps) be told in different ways, with differing degrees of detail or explanatory information, but the "facts" of that story cannot contradict themselves. Porpentine cannot be murdered both at the opera and at the pyramids. The two sides of the V do not meet at the bottom; there can be no single, determinate sequence of events of which these two accounts are merely "versions."

Differences in narrative point of view, which I have touched on only lightly, can also be seen in quantitative and contradictive terms. As long as the omniscient narrator of **"Under the Rose"** imparts information absent from the novel, or conversely, as long as Stencil's "impersonations" in the novel impart information absent from the short story, textual differences resulting from differing points of view (and differing degrees of narrative authority) remain largely quantitative. For example, when Gebrail the cab driver reflects that " 'the city is only the desert in disguise,' " or when Waldetar the conductor thinks about his wife and three children (material that is not present in **"Under the Rose"**), nothing is added that would make construction of a "basic story" impossible.

But when the thoughts or words of a character/observer in the novel are attributed, by the omniscient narrator of the short story, to *another character,* the difference becomes contradictive. In the novel account, Yusef, the anarchist waiter who "kept abreast of current events," reflects that

> Sirdar Kitchener, England's newest colonial hero, recently victorious at Khartoum, was just now some 400 miles further down the White Nile, foraging about in the jungle; a General Marchand was also rumored in the vicinity. Britain wanted no part of France in the Nile Valley. M. Delcassé, Foreign Minister of a newly-formed French cabinet, would as soon go to war as not if there were any trouble when the two detachments met. As meet, everyone realized by now, they would.

In **"Under the Rose"** Porpentine is said to "ponder the Situation" in the following way:

> Sirdar Kitchener, England's newest colonial hero, recently victorious at Chartoum, was just now some four hundred miles further down the White Nile, foraging about in the jungle. A General Marchand was also rumored to be in the vicinity. Britain wanted no part of France in the Nile Valley. M. Delcassé Foreign Minister of a newly formed French cabinet, would as soon go to war as not if there were any trouble when the two detachments met. As meet, everyone realized by now, they would.

The linguistic differences between the two passages are negligible; the semantic difference is significant if these observations are Porpentine's instead of Yusef's. One might argue that a "basic story" can be constructed in which

both Yusef *and* Porpentine think about the Fashoda crisis, but it strains plausibility beyond the breaking point to imagine that such thoughts can be articulated in almost identical language.

When two accounts, however similar they might appear, contain contradictive differences such as those outlined above, it should be evident that there can be no "core story" of which the two accounts are, in Chatman's sense, textual manifestations. In other words, because of contradictive differences, *these particular narratives,* **"Under the Rose"** and Chapter Three of *V.,* cannot be thought of as two "versions" of the "same" story. That story cannot logically exist. But even if the differences between the two texts were only quantitative, any "basic story" would have to be fashioned by the reader to accommodate the differences, and the result would be, from Barbara Herrnstein Smith's point of view, another version. This is very close to Wolfgang Iser's notion that meanings are generated in part by the reader's "repair of indeterminacy." Meanings are provisional constructs, "the product of a rather difficult interaction between text and reader and not qualities hidden in the text." Seeking out a single, determinate meaning is not the same as looking for a "basic story," but the two pursuits do achieve similar results: the creation of another meaning, the creation of another version of "the" story. Smith of course goes still further, arguing that no narrative can *ever* have a single, determinate core or "basic story." The number of "basic stories" is always multiple and indefinite, and their construction depends upon a wide range of variable circumstances. Obviously this exercise in intertextuality does not prove either Chatman or Smith correct about the nature of narrative in general. What the comparison *does* do is suggest that conceptions of narrative and truth implicit in Pynchon's texts are closer to Smith's ideas than to Chatman's.

Rejecting the notion of a "basic story" existing somehow independent of or prior to a narrative's manifestation as text, Smith contends that "the best way to conceive of the sets of events that narratives seem to relate is not as specific, historically determinate, or otherwise stable and given phenomena but, rather, as the variable inferences and constructs that narratives characteristically elicit from their audiences or, indeed, as the various processes and activities of inferring, construing, projecting, hypothesizing, imagining, anticipating, and so forth, that constitute our characteristic *responses* to narrative." The events that Pynchon's narratives seem to relate stubbornly resist the reader's attempts to conceive them as determinate and stable. Those events finally have no existence apart from inference and hypothesis. At the beginning of Chapter Three of *V.* we are informed that Stencil's factual information about the Egyptian episode is scant: "He'd only veiled references to Porpentine in the journals. The rest was impersonation and dream." Stencil's entire quest, for that matter, is a series of "variable inferences and constructs." A character in *Gravity's Rainbow* explicitly wonders if "the Real Text" exists. The universe in which Stencil operates is one without a "basic story," and the reader's experience with the text parallels Stencil's experience with his world. The reader, like Stencil, must go on inferring, construing, projecting, hypothesizing, imagining, and anticipating.

The process never ends, for the indeterminacy of Pynchon's textual discourse cannot be separated from the indeterminacy of life itself. The "basic story" (or the "real, real story," as Mary McCarthy said in her unsuccessful effort to achieve a determinate reading of *Pale Fire* ["A Bolt from the Blue," *New Republic,* 4 June 1962] must always remain a gleam in the critic's eye.

The title of Pynchon's short story provides a small clue to the significance of these matters of "basic-ness" and difference. The phrase "under the rose," a translation of the Latin *sub rosa,* refers to the custom of hanging a rose over the council table to bind all those present to secrecy. Hence, anything done "under the rose" is done secretly. It is easy to see the relevance of this expression to Pynchon's espionage plot. The activities of Porpentine and Goodfellow, as well as those of their counterparts, are conducted *sub rosa.* One might even be tempted to see Stencil's—and the reader's—attempts to ferret out the "real story" of the novel's account as a raid on political, metaphysical, and narratological secrets.

But there is more. The custom of hanging a rose over the council table originated because the rose was associated with Harpokrates, who was once thought to be the Egyptian god of secrecy. Harpokrates was *not* the god of secrecy, however. He was the youthful manifestation of the god Horus, who had nothing to do with secrecy. The mistake dates from the Greco-Roman period of Egyptian history and apparently first arose because Harpokrates (literally, "the young Horus") is usually represented holding a finger to his lips—a conventional sign of youth, not secrecy, in Egyptian iconography. Latent in the expression, then, is a more powerful signal than the obvious one of secrecy. It is true that the phrase "under the rose" suggests hidden truth, or knowledge buried beneath the surface of things. But is also suggests, through its own etiology, the misinterpretation of truth, and perhaps even the relativity of knowledge. Error lies at the heart of the entire *sub rosa* tradition. The dual implication is appropriate. If anything is clear in Pynchon, it is that every interpretational foray—every raid on the secrets of deep structure and determinate meaning—leads inevitably to another version or, as the deconstructionists would have it, to a misinterpretation. Just as the absence of a common point of origin is the no-thing at the base of the street lamp V, the absence of a "basic story" is the no-thing underlying Pynchon's universe of discourse. Whatever may be generally said of narrative texts, in the case of Pynchon's texts, the text is all that is the case. (pp. 299-307)

> *Richard F. Patteson, "How True a Text? Chapter Three of* V. *and 'Under the Rose'," in* The Southern Humanities Review, *Vol. XVIII, No. 4, Fall, 1984, pp. 299-308.*

Joseph Tabbi   (essay date 1984)

[*In the essay below, Tabbi discusses the application in "Entropy" of the "Romantic metaphor," defined by literary critic M. H. Abrams as the use of breath and wind to demonstrate the relationship between "nature's outer motions and the interior life and emotions."*]

With his 1957 *Kenyon Review* essay on "The Correspondent Breeze: A Romantic Metaphor," M. H. Abrams helped to initiate a modern revaluation of Romantic literary practice. Having studied with Abrams at Cornell during the year this essay first appeared, Thomas Pynchon was among the first students Abrams influenced, and we retain the trace of this influence in the underlying structure and choice of words in Pynchon's early writing. For Abrams the recurrent motifs of breath and the wind in the greater Romantic lyric represent a predominant theme of continuity and interchange between nature's outer motions and the interior life and emotions:

> The wind is not only a property of the landscape, but also a vehicle for radical changes in the poet's mind. The rising wind . . . is correlated with a complex subjective process: the return to a sense of community after isolation, the renewal of life and emotional vigor after apathy and a deathlife torpor, and an outburst of creative power following a period of imaginative sterility.

Pynchon first responded to the Romantic metaphor in his early short story, **"Entropy,"** where we find a lyrical reconstruction of the season of "false spring" in Washington, D.C.:

> . . .as every good Romantic knows, the soul (*spiritus, ruach, pneuma*) is nothing, substantially, but air; it is only natural that warpings in the atmosphere should be recapitulated in those who breathe it. So that over and above the public components—holidays, tourist attractions— there are private meanderings, linked to the climate as if this spell were a *stretto* passage in the year's fugue: haphazard weather, aimless loves, unpredicted commitments: months one can easily spend *in* fugue, because oddly enough, later on, winds, rains, passions of February and March are never remembered in that city; it is as if they had never been.

A *stretto* is a tightened concluding passage of a fugue where component themes come rapidly together in periodic reinforcement. The music seems to generate from within a fleeting energy voiced in independence of its gathered elements. Through the figure from music, Pynchon implies a saving possibility that runs counter to his theme of entropic decline towards chaos and death: the threatening random motions of the city and its seasons shall be gathered and shaped into a regenerative combination with the casual passions of private experience. "As every good Romantic knows," this imaginative possibility resembles the imaginative linkage between inner passions and outer winds that the Romantic poets embraced in the metaphors of the wind harp and the correspondent breeze. Yet Pynchon treats the metaphor with irony: if such imaginative music is shaped in this false spring in Washington, it is yet unheard by those whose "private meanderings" make up a component strain. The irony no doubt involves the fact, first noticed and explored by Robert Redfield and Peter L. Hays [in "Fugue as Structure in Pynchon's 'Entropy,'" *Pacific Coast Philology,* (1977)], that Pynchon has written the story itself in the form of a fugue, setting the "improvised discords" of Meatball Mulligan's lease-breaking party downstairs in careful counterpoint to the isolated "arabesques of order" that the characters upstairs try (futilely) to sustain. Thus whereas Pynchon's narrative structure blends motions from inside and outside and implicitly connects the situations of diverse people, this all goes on unperceived by the characters in the story. Untouched by the sense of community and interaction his stylistic strategy implies, they move through Pynchon's fiction as through days lost in that state of temporary amnesia known to psychology as a "fugue." The events downstairs threaten endlessly to deteriorate into total confusion (though Meatball in the end does his best to restore order to his party), while upstairs the character Callisto interprets everything—the weather outside, personal remembrances, news from the world and occasional noise from below—to be nothing less than the onset of an entropic heat-death for his culture. "Fugue" in the second, psychological sense aptly describes Callisto's mental state because his overwhelming obsession with entropy causes him to lose touch with all that goes on around him. By artificially integrating the diverse "cities and seasons and casual passions of his days" into a reductive unity, Callisto essentially forgets whatever meaning these component memories can have held for him; their real distinctions blurred in his mind because of his obsession with entropy, "it is as if they had never been."

Pynchon thus restores his characters to a typically Romantic role, that of reconciling their internal passions to the natural world outside, but these characters fail to achieve emotional commerce with that world. This failure is reflected in the lack of physical interchange between inside and outside movements: although revellers ceaselessly enter Meatball's party from countless open doors and windows, nobody ever leaves. And Callisto and his companion Aubade occasionally take, but they never give anything back to their environment ("what they needed from outside was delivered. They did not go out."). Unlike the wind harp which merges winds and passions from inside and outside into the same gathering movement, or the correspondent breeze which generates new life and continuity in the poet and his natural surroundings, the pervasive metaphors of **"Entropy"** emphasize the unregenerative relations among people and their environment. Pynchon's characters at best perfect a false sense of continuity and a partial interchange with their perceived world; their private meanderings and casual passions find outward sympathy in a "false spring."

And yet despite Pynchon's ironic treatment of the Romantic metaphor, he nonetheless derives from "The Correspondent Breeze" an important organizing principle for the story's narrative. The *stretto*, like its Romantic analogues, generates new life and meaning from the limited thematic materials that comprise it. It is this second structural application that makes the Romantic ideal more than a standard by which to measure the extent of our modern malaise. Pynchon's narrative form implies a wholly communicative context in art from which "continuity" and "interchange" may reemerge with viable post-Romantic meanings. The fugal structure of **"Entropy"** unites the dual movements from inside and outside: Like the gathering correspondent breeze, but (unlike it) with-

out attributing the unifying subjective experience to a single observing presence. (pp. 61-3)

> *Joseph Tabbi, "Pynchon's Entropy," in* The Explicator, *Vol. 43, No. 1, Fall, 1984, pp. 61-3.*

Galen Strawson　(essay date 1985)

[*Strawson is an English educator and critic. In the following review, he provides a negative assessment of* Slow Learner, *criticizing what he considers its underdrawn characters, lifeless plots, and sluggish narration.*]

Re-reading the five short stories which he wrote and first published between 1958 and 1964, and has now collected in *Slow Learner,* Thomas Pynchon's initial reaction was "*Oh my God,* accompanied by physical symptoms we shouldn't dwell upon". What was he to do? At first he contemplated "some kind of a wall-to-wall rewrite". But time passed, and "middle-aged tranquility" gently supervened; 1958 was, after all, "another planet", as he remarked in his 1983 introduction to Richard Fariña's *Been Down So Long It Looks Like Up to Me.* And so he faced up to his former self, and republished his early stories untouched, "juvenile and delinquent" passages and all, "pretentious, goofy and ill-considered as they get now and then"— suitably preceded by an old-timer creative-writer introduction, semi-confessional, indulgently severe, serene with pedagogical distance. He republished them as *study-aids.*

> My best hope is that . . . these stories will still be of use with all their flaws intact, as illustrative of typical problems in entry-level fiction, and cautionary about some practices which younger writers might prefer to avoid.

Perhaps the first thing to say about *Slow Learner* is that the stories really are as bad as Pynchon says they are. With the exception of the last of them, **"The Secret Integration"** (1964), they are startlingly incompetent; falsely declamatory, painfully surreal, cripplingly self-conscious. Above all they are aimless, with an aimlessness rarely disturbed by any insight or striking image or linguistic *coup.* And yet the root ideas are sometimes quite good. And even the incompetence has a kind of charm: Pynchon's artfulness is so brilliantly unsuccessful that it keeps on flipping over into some sort of curious, second-order ingenuousness.

The first story is a good idea struggling to survive: in **"The Small Rain"** (1959), the intense tedium of army life at Fort Roach, Louisiana in July 1957 is suddenly interrupted; "Lardass" Levine, specialist 3/c, is forced to abandon his pursuit of perfect mental inanition in order to help out, in his capacity as a member of the 131st Signal Corps, with a hurricane disaster. This he does; he travels the flood waters in search of swollen corpses; he progresses through a series of situations; he is accidie in action. Events accumulate, piecemeal. Finally "some kind of sexual encounter appears to take place, though you'd never know it from the text", as Pynchon remarks: "The language suddenly gets too fancy to read." And then the story stops.

But it is in **"Low-lands"** and **"Entropy"** (both 1960) that Pynchon really hits bottom. These stories—in which the notorious Pig Bodine, later to feature in *V.* (1963) and *Gravity's Rainbow* (1973), makes his first appearance—record Pynchon's initial, confused, ravenously romantic and sexually frustrated surrender to the bizarre imperatives of late-Beat literary hip. **"Entropy"** examines two floors of a house in Washington DC: downstairs a laboriously excessive party moves timelessly into its third day; upstairs an ageing intellectual exquisite obsessed with the heat-death of the universe dictates his memoirs. Like parts of *V.*, it reads as if it had been coauthored by Daisy Ashford and William Burroughs, and it shares with them its fundamental impulse—Incurable Romanticism. It demands that ordinary life be epic, astoundingly so. With Kerouac, it craves city sorrow and sea sadness, sputtering and flaring with great gouts of portentous prose.

Pynchon's artfulness in *Slow Learner* is so brilliantly unsuccessful that it keeps on flipping over into some sort of curious, second-order ingenuousness.

—*Galen Strawson*

"Low-lands" is similar in its underlying motivation: a super-real drinking binge winds up in the town dump. . . . Dennis Flange, the much-shrunk but larger half of a bad marriage, decides to move in with a beautiful dwarf called Nerissa and her pet rat Hyacinth, deep beneath the garbage. . . . He is possessed by the sea, and language runs away:

> if the sea's tides are the same that not only wash along your veins but also billow through your fantasies then it is all right to listen to but not to tell stories about that sea, because you and the truth of a true lie were thrown sometime way back into a curious contiguity and as long as you are passive you can remain aware of the truth's extent but the minute you become active you are somehow, if not violating a convention outright, at least screwing up the perspective of things, much as anyone observing subatomic particles changes the works, data and odds, by the act of observing.

Certain parts of **"Under the Rose"** (1961) appeared, much altered, in Chapter three of *V.*, and the contrast between the two versions is striking. Clanking with unnecessary details, the story has none of the wasteful but genuine vigour of the novel; Pynchon clearly covered a great deal of ground in between the two. As it stands here, **"Under the Rose"** is a spatch-cocked tale of espionage in 1890s Egypt that is so extravagantly gauche and ignorant in its spasmodic archaisms, its fantasies of apocalypse, and its attempt at "jolly-ho, pip-pip" Englishness ("Porpentine recoiled, thinking: Lord love a duck. Bongo-Shaftesbury is insane"), that one is tempted by the hypothesis that the mismatch and muddle are intentional and secretly adroit. But they are not. Pynchon mentions Buchan, Machiavelli, Edmund Wilson's *To the Finland Station* and "many Vic-

torians" as influences behind the story. If he had read Conrad—*The Secret Agent, Under Western Eyes*—he would surely have been spared the authorship of **"Under the Rose"**.

In his introduction, middle-aged Pynchon suggests that young Pynchon was beginning to get somewhere with **"Under the Rose"**: "I think the characters are a little better, no longer just lying there on the slab but beginning at least to twitch some and blink their eyes open, although their dialogue still suffers from my perennial Bad Ear." This is very questionable, however. A lot happens in **"Under the Rose"**, but it lacks any genuine narrative motion, and none of the first four stories is a patch on **"The Secret Integration"** (1964), a comparatively assured and attractive story about three young white boys with racist parents who initiate a young black boy into their secret club—or so it seems at first.

Although he is "pretty content with how it holds up" as a story, Pynchon criticizes **"The Secret Integration"** for the "junkshop or randomly assembled quality" of many of its scenes. This criticism is perhaps just; but it applies with so much more force to the other four stories that **"The Secret Integration"** seems, by contrast, sweetly economical. For the first time in *Slow Learner,* Pynchon's characteristic factual accumulations seem to have a point, and to make a contribution to the story. For the first time, the characters start to move. For the first time, we have some evidence that the slow learner was actually learning something.

Galen Strawson, "Study-Aids from Another Planet," in The Times Literary Supplement, No. 4267, January 11, 1985, p. 41.

Malcolm Bradbury   (essay date 1985)

[*An English man of letters, Bradbury is best known as the author of such satiric novels as* Eating People Is Wrong *(1959) and* Stepping Westward *(1965). He has also written extensively on English and American literature, especially the works of E. M. Forster. In the review below, Bradbury praises the stories in* Slow Learner, *as well as the insight provided by Pynchon's introduction.*]

Pynchon is now recognised as one of the outstanding figures of post-war experimental fiction. He has become the post-modern Melville, the elusive learned author who, in *V.* (1963), *The Crying of Lot 49* (1966) and the difficult *Gravity's Rainbow* (1973) gave us a form of modern fiction that united complex technical experiment with post-atomic anxiety.

Pynchon has been viewed as a great novelist of our cybernetic age, and the great researcher-recorder of history as power. His work has also reinforced many influential ideas in contemporary criticism. His novels deconstruct on inspection. They are filled with literary references, or 'intertextuality', and insistently pursue signs, ciphers and codes. Plots become over-developed and absurd, comically named characters disappear as if they were outmoded concepts.

Pynchon's Traven-like obscurity as an unknown famous

author has helped this view of him. We could consider him a shrewd evader of the crass publicity machine who has gained more publicity by invisibility than by presence. However, he has become an example of the absentee author who has freely given us a multi-signifying, self-questioning text as obscure as the world itself—or the modern history that, in *V.* Herbert Stencil so futilely attempts to understand, while Benny Profane more wisely settles for pure randomness.

But now the veil has lifted a little. Pynchon-chasers have long known about a number of early short stories that circulated in elusive tiny editions or photocopies. *Slow Learner* contains five of these stories from 1958 to 1964 (a sixth, **'Mortality and Mercy in Vienna'** (1959), mysteriously escapes the net), mostly written when Pynchon was a Cornell undergraduate who also did a spell in the Navy.

The earliest stories—**'A Small Rain,' 'Low-lands,' 'Entropy'** and **'Under the Rose'**—show their academic origins. Several turn on the Stencil-Profane theme of the contrast between the world of the academy and the low-life world beyond. Their manner is also mixed, a learned prose contrasting with a very physical and comic reportage. Essential characters, names or themes will appear again. Indeed **'Under the Rose,'** a spy drama set around the Fashoda crisis, was massively reworked into *V.*

These stories also come with what the dust jacket rightly calls a 'disarming' introduction—a sly piece of self-irony where Pynchon remarks on the tiresomeness and adolescent sensibility of some of these pieces. Among those disarmed could be the critics who have pursued Pynchon with the weaponry described above. 'Do not underestimate the shallowness of my understanding,' Pynchon says about his use of the concept of entropy, on which so much critical effort has been exerted. A very present author prefers to speak not of intertextuality but of 'literary theft.' As for the famous swamping of characters by the universe of text, author does not confirm. Indeed he says, as a good writing teacher would, 'Get too conceptual, too cute and remote, and your characters die on the page.'

As for the contemporary crisis of fiction, Pynchon is sceptical. He locates his own starting-point at the end of the 1950s, when Modernism crossed over the Beat generation. He presents us with the plot of his own creative improvement, forward from apprentice pieces to the journeyman work of the impressive final story **'The Secret Integration.'** Pynchon's growth is towards a mixture of comedy and the recording of felt real experience. The fact is that he was, is, and always will be a great comic writer, a literary tease, and a playful language-maker who is governed by a strong moral sense and a desire to realise life in fiction.

Malcolm Bradbury, "The Invisible Man," in
The Observer, *January 13, 1985, p. 51.*

Richard Poirier (essay date 1985)

[*Poirier is an American critic and educator whose works include* A World Elsewhere: The Place of Style in American Literature *(1966),* The Renewal of Litera-

ture: Emersonian Reflections *(1987), and* Poetry and Pragmatism *(1992). He is also a founder and editor of* Raritan: A Quarterly Review. *In the following review, Poirier praises the stories in* Slow Learner, *but argues that Pynchon "misreads" his own stories in his introductory assessment.*]

With *V.* (1963), *The Crying of Lot 49* (1966) and *Gravity's Rainbow* (1973) to his credit so far, Thomas Pynchon, American of no known address, is possibly the most accomplished writer of prose in English since James Joyce. This is not to say that he is also the best novelist, whatever that would mean, but that sentence by sentence he can do more than any novelist of this century with the resources of the English-American language and with the various media by which it is made available to us, everything from coterie slangs to technological jargons, from film to economic history, from comic books to the poetry of T. S. Eliot, from the Baedeker to the Bible. The works of other novelists may prove, as the phrase would have it, more humanly satisfying than his, but Pynchon chooses to use his immense talents as a writer and encyclopedist to show why he cannot offer satisfactions of that kind. His jaunty complaints in the Introduction that the stories in *Slow Learner* fail to provide full, lifelike characters are for this reason alone so curious and irrelevant as to suggest either that he is kidding—and I am afraid he isn't—or that he is tired. I do not mean that in his fiction he is anti-humanist, but that what he finds of the human, when embodied or inscribed in language, is shown to be mostly grotesque, as names like Pig Bodine or Pierce Inverarity or Tantivy Mucker-Maffick or Scorpia Mossmoon will suggest, and that what he cherishes about human beings is scarcely discernible, except in those extraordinarily poignant catalogues of waste in which his writing abounds. In that respect he resembles Mucho Maas in *The Crying of Lot 49,* who stopped being a used-car salesman because 'he had believed in the cars. Maybe to excess.'

> how could he not, seeing people poorer than him come in, Negro, Mexican, cracker, a parade seven days a week, bringing the most godawful of trade-ins: motorised, metal extensions of themselves, of their families and what their whole lives must be like, out there so naked for anybody, a stranger like himself, to look at, frame cockeyed, rusty underneath, fender repainted in a shade just off enough to depress the value, if not Mucho himself, inside smelling hopelessly of children, supermarket booze, two, sometimes three generations of cigarette smokers, or only of dust—and when the cars were swept out you had to look at the actual residue of these lives, and there was no way of telling what things had been truly refused (when so little he supposed came by that out of fear most of it had to be taken and kept) and what had simply (perhaps tragically) been lost: clipped coupons promising savings of 5 or 10c, trading stamps, pink flyers advertising specials at the markets, butts, tooth-shy combs, help-wanted ads, Yellow Pages torn from the phone book, rags of old underwear or dresses that already were period costumes, for wiping your own breath off the inside of a windshield with so you could see whatever it was, a movie, a woman or car you covet-

ed, a cop who might pull you over just for drill, all the bits and pieces coated uniformly, like a salad of despair, in a gray dressing of ash, condensed exhaust, dust, body wastes—it made him sick to look, but he had to look . . . Even if enough exposure to the unvarying gray sickness had somehow managed to immunise him, he could still never accept the way each owner, each shadow, filed in only to exchange a dented, malfunctioning version of himself for another, just as futureless, automotive projection of somebody else's life.

Evidences of what in the Introduction he likes to call 'human reality' are, in his fiction, merely residual, scattered, and unavailable for any kind of consistent embodiment. He is therefore best thought of as a parodist of structure and of structuring, including his own. The most consistently reassuring evidence of the human in his writing is the writing itself, the energies of attachment and repulsion at work in his transitions from one subject or one idiom to another, the supple and unintimidated way in which he opens himself up to every aspect of contemporary existence. He revels in schemes, codes, systems that delight his interpreters; he is endlessly full of meaning. But it is meaning with a vengeance, while his sincerities reach out tentatively toward the unarticulated human life that, like the city dumps which hold so much of it, exists on the outskirts.

In his Introduction he is anxious not to make large claims for these early stories, dating from 1959, when he was 22, to 1964, and he indicates that, for him, *The Crying of Lot 49* is not a novel, though it was published as one, but a story 'in which I seem to have forgotten most of what I thought I'd learned up to then'. Why such essentially vain self-criticism? And if Pynchon really does feel so deprecatory, if the collection is therefore of mostly historical value, then by what critical scruple did he choose to omit the only other story he has published, **'Mortality and Mercy in Vienna'** (*Epoch,* Spring 1959), which is as good as all but two of the others, and why did he not include his one essay up to the publication of this book, 'A Journey into the Mind of Watts' (1966)? Had these been included, we would have had a far more useful collection of all his shorter pieces.

But Pynchon does not want anyone to think that his volume in any way sufficiently represents him. Instead he suggests again and again, even by means of the title, that he has since learned to do things in an importantly different way. Unquestionably he became far more ambitious, just as *The Waste Land* is more ambitious than, say, 'La Figlia che Piange'. And yet Eliot's earlier poem is an embryonic version of the later one, and these stories have a similar relation to *V.* or to *Gravity's Rainbow*. Pynchon wants to disguise this fact from himself and from us, as if to confirm that what he finds wanting in the stories, such as fullness of character and 'human reality', is supplied by the novels. In fact, they are not to be found in the novels either, and are not meant to be.

Pynchon is especially severe on a story called **'Entropy'**, one of the long-time favourites of those who like to suppose that his meanings can be pinned down if only readers

will bone up on such things as thermodynamics—a subject about which Pynchon, while majoring in English at Cornell, learned something in his courses on engineering physics. It is a story in which Meatball Mulligan is giving a frantic and exhausting three-day lease-breaking party on one level of an apartment, while upstairs Callisto and his girlfriend Aubade lie around, immobilised, thinking about the Laws of Thermodynamics, Henry Adams, heat death, and the imminent decline of all energy. It is a mostly charming, sometimes tiresome show-off piece, but the way it is laid out offers, as does the apartment itself, a neat diagram of how in the novels Pynchon apportions things on a more massive and complicated scale. It divides itself between torpor and pranks, between inertia and the wild projection of elaborate and possibly insane schemes, each feeding on the other but with all of it ultimately deadening. The story appeared in 1960 in *Kenyon Review,* where Robert Lowell would very likely have seen it, and where he would, I suspect, have found the penultimate line of his poem 'The Flaw', addressed to a woman lying beside him: 'Dear Figure curving like a question mark'. Callisto's girlfriend 'lay like a tawny question mark facing him'.

In any case, Pynchon now warns us not 'to underestimate the shallowness of my understanding of entropy', or of those scientists the story associates with it—Willard Gibbs, Rudolf Clausius and Norbert Weiner. But no one who *listens* to the way these matters are talked about by Callisto would ever have seriously cared how much Pynchon knew about them or didn't know. As offered up by Pynchon, the theory is evidence of a kind of pretentiousness on the part of pre-adult university graduates heavily sedated with classroom versions of literary Modernism and its by then fashionable excruciations. Pynchon chooses in the Introduction to confuse himself with his characters when he remarks: 'Given my undergraduate mood, Adams's sense of power out of control, coupled with Weiner's spectacle of universal heat-death and mathematical stillness, seemed just the ticket. But the distance and grandiosity of this led me to short change the humans in the story.' What 'humans' can he be talking about? Their absence, their 'short changing' of themselves, is precisely the point of the story. To complain about it is to miss the point.

He has a similar caveat about the first story he wrote, **'A Small Rain'**, published in 1959. There he introduces army specialist third class Nathan 'Lardass' Levine lying in his bunk in Fort Roach, Louisiana. Like Callisto in **'Entropy'**, Levine is 'drowsy', 'motionless', 'inert'. He is then moved as part of his unit to a college campus, the staging area for an operation in a nearby town all of whose inhabitants have been killed in a hurricane. The account of his surreptitious entry into the town is the best part of the story, filled with portents of apocalypse. Images of stasis and death are again juxtaposed with cut-up behaviour, especially on campus, and in the middle of it all is a scene of flaccid love-making between Levine and a co-ed: ' "In the midst of great death," Levine said, "the little death." And later "Ha. It sounds like a caption in *Life*. In the midst of *Life*. We are in death. Oh god." '

Pynchon once again misreads his own story, claiming that

'apparently I felt I had to put on a whole extra overlay of rain images and references to *The Waste Land* and *A Farewell to Arms.* I was operating on the motto "Make it literary," a piece of bad advice I made up all by myself and then took.' But even in the brief passage I've just quoted from the story it is obvious that it is not Pynchon but Levine who is 'literary'—he is said to have the highest IQ in the battalion—and that even he recognises how much he thereby loses of direct human feeling and experience. The story effectively satirises its own literariness. It makes no sense to suggest that 'I failed to recognise just for openers that the main character's problem was real and interesting enough to generate a story on its own,' since that is exactly what he does recognise.

It is equally wrong to say, as he does of another story, **'Low-lands'**, that its hero, a man named Flange, 'wants children—why it isn't clear—but not at the price of developing any real life shared with an adult woman. His solution to this is Nerissa, a woman with the size and demeanour of a child.' Pynchon seems compelled retrospectively to imagine alternatives which were never available to the characters in the first place and which are, besides, when compared with the dire cultural situations in which he originally put them, irrelevantly platitudinous. Flange nowhere expresses a desire to have children, and his taste for child-women is one shared by any number of Pynchon's males throughout his novels, which are heavily populated with barely pubescent bed partners. With the possible exception of Roger Mexico and Jessica Swanlake ('a young rosy girl in an ATS uniform') in the wartime London of *Gravity's Rainbow,* Pynchon does not find a place in his fiction for any such 'real-life' sharing or 'adulthood'.

If Pynchon is deciding that he ought to be more like E. M. Forster, to whom he makes a number of justly admiring allusions in *Gravity's Rainbow,* he will discover that he is probably only trying to avoid the rather bleaker implications of his much stronger affinity with Beckett, Borges and Burroughs. 'Only connect,' said Forster, who showed how difficult it was to do so. Everyone should want to 'connect': but though there are hints that Pynchon subscribes to the epigraph to section one of *Gravity's Rainbow,* which quotes Wernher von Braun to the effect that 'Nature does not know extinction; all it knows is transformation'—so that we'll all be connected some time anyway—Pynchon does seem to long for something closer to home, for what are popularly called fulfilling human relationships. And yet, in the world projected by his fiction, 'connections' are mostly disastrous, the results of an excess of paranoia to which there is no good alternative. 'There is something comforting—religious, if you want—about paranoia,' remarks Tyrone Slothrop, hero of *Gravity's Rainbow,* when he thinks he is losing his mind, and 'there is still also anti-paranoia, where nothing is connected to anything, a condition not many of us can bear for long.'

The distance Pynchon has travelled from the Modernism of Eliot, with its Classical and religiously orthodox tendencies, can be measured by comparing his paranoidal alternatives to the confident—and smug—distinction made by Eliot between the poet and the ordinary man, allowing for the possibility that someone may be both at once. 'The ordinary man,' he tells us, 'falls in love, or reads Spinoza, and these two experiences have nothing to do with each other, or with the noise of the typewriter or the smell of cooking; in the mind of the poet these experiences are always forming new wholes.' The point where Anglo-American Modernism breaks away from the Post-Modernism of someone like Pynchon is located exactly here: where amalgamations or the formation of 'new wholes' become in themselves the likely evidence either of chaos compounded or of systematic repression.

This is more or less the subject of the two most impressive stories in the collection, **'Under the Rose'** (1961) and **'The Secret Integration'**, which appeared in 1964, the year after the publication of *V.* **'Under the Rose'** is set in Egypt during the Fashoda Crisis of 1898 and has at its centre two British agents, Porpentine and Goodfellow, three German spies, Moldweorp, Lepsius and Bongo-Shaftsbury, and a girl named Victoria Wren, a prefiguration of the object of the quest of *V.,* where **'Under the Rose'** was to appear, in greatly revised form, as Chapter Three. Here, as in the other stories, Pynchon presupposes a condition of imminent crisis or blankness which excites in his characters all sorts of fun and games—'apocalypse', in Porpentine's phrase, 'as an excuse for a glorious beano'. But the rules of play are breached by Porpentine's gradual discovery that he cannot so surrender to the idea of the inevitable Final Clash as to stop feeling for the suffering of others. Even though he recognises that what he does can make no difference to the approaching Armageddon, he finds that his actions do matter to him. He begins to worry about the mistreatment by his competitors of a little girl on a train and of a whore whom he had seen Moldweorp slash with his cane one night in Rome. He is followed into the desert and shot by Moldweorp, and thinks, before he dies, that 'he'd crossed some threshold without knowing. Mongrel now, no longer pure . . . Mongrel, he supposed, is only another way of saying human.'

Pynchon is not satisfied with the story, though he likes it more than the others, and for reasons that by now, in the Introduction, have become nagging and tiresome. 'The problem here,' he writes, 'is like the problem with **"Entropy"**: beginning with something abstract—a thermodynamic coinage or the data in a guidebook—and only then going on to try to develop plot and character. This is simply, as we say in the profession, ass backwards. Without some grounding in human reality, you are apt to be left with another apprentice exercise, which is what this uncomfortably resembles.' Perhaps by 'profession' he means the oldest one in the world, because what is actually ass-backwards is his reading of his own story. Porpentine's whole career testifies to the insolubility, in such a world as his author allows, of the problem Pynchon wants in retrospect to have solved ahead of time. Before Porpentine's death, the one thing that 'made him, he believed, more human' was 'skylarking'—yet another form of Pynchon's pranksterism.

When Pynchon folded **'Under the Rose'** into the novel, he dropped some of the characters, including Moldweorp, and added a few others, but, more important, he substantially altered the mode of presentation. He wanted, it seems to me, to give the episode an enhanced political-human dimension. For one thing, he transformed what can be called his data bank for the story—Karl Baedeker's guide to Egypt for 1899—into an instrument of cultural imperialism, a kind of grid which preceeds the observer and determines what he will see and what he will not see. For another, instead of confining the point of view to Porpentine, the novel gives it to seven different figures. Three of these are Egyptian working-class people, the others are of various nationalities, but each is relatively anonymous and poor. None is given a place in the main plot, but all are allowed extensive musings on their daily lives, their loved ones, especially their children. Thus in the story Porpentine reports on climbing a tree so as to look into the hotel room where Victoria and Goodfellow are lying in bed: in the novel, however, this is changed so that Porpentine is himself the object of the half-amused, half-contemptuous scrutiny of a Syrian acrobatic burglar named Girgis who is crouching in the bushes outside Shepherd's Hotel. He thinks Porpentine is no more than 'another comic acrobat' trying unsuccessfully to break into the hotel, as he himself intends to do. Instead of a view *de haut en bas* we get, so to speak, a social and geographic view *de bas en haut*. By this process of distributing points of view to those outside 'Baedeker land' and its mentality, Pynchon is trying to find a conspicuous place in his writing for what he calls 'human reality', while leaving pretty much intact, because oblivious, the absurd behaviour of an imperialist European *haut monde*.

A similar juxtaposition of cultural forces is at work in 'Journey into the Mind of Watts', where, as against the 'basic realities', the 'bitter realities', of the black ghetto, Pynchon describes white Los Angeles as 'that creepy world full of pre-cardiac Mustang drivers who scream insults at one another only when the windows are up; of large corporations where Nice-guyship is the standing order regardless of whose executive back one may be endeavouring to stab; and of an enormous priest caste of shrinks who counsel moderation and compromise as the answer to all forms of hassle; among so much well-behaved unreality, it is next to impossible to understand how Watts may truly feel about violence.' The 'human reality' of Watts is under what he calls 'a siege of persuasion', of Baedeker mentality now projected by a vastly more powerful technology than existed at the turn of the century in Egypt—'the attempt to transmogrify the reality of Watts into the unreality of Los Angeles'.

He is inevitably drawn to such devastating cultural situations as these, and his notion that they allow for the representation of 'human reality' in any central or effective way is so obtuse as to sound like a concession to what in the Watts piece he mockingly calls 'the humanitarian establishment'. Baedeker world is now everywhere, and, as suggested by the title of the most affecting story in this collection, the only possible integration into the world of the people excluded from it is, perforce, **'The Secret Integration'**. The recalcitrant faction here is the Spartacus Gang, a bunch of middle-class pre-teen boys in New England's Berkshire County. Their pranks and practical jokes are di-

rected at 'hated institutions' like the school or the paper mill, and their 'patron saint' is one Crazy Sue Denham, 'that legendary and beautiful drifter who last century had roamed all this hilltop country exchanging babies and setting fires'. Essentially, the gang is opposed to the parental, grown-up world, as represented by the Parent Teacher's Association, but the boys all know that 'the reality would turn out to be considerably less than the plot' (as it customarily does in Pynchon), 'that something inert and invisible, something they could not be cruel to or betray (though who would have gone so far as to call it love?), would always be between them and any clear or irreversible step.' They know, that is, the security of warm beds and home.

It's Tom Sawyer time. But the story gradually turns into something closer to Huck Finn and his never resolved dilemma about Nigger Jim, with whom he could be loving and free only on the raft. One member of the gang is a black kid named Carl, child of the only black family in the neighbourhood. Some of the children have overheard their parents making anonymous and threatening phone calls to this family, but Pynchon very effectively does not register their reactions one way or another. The children take it in their stride, increasing the suspense over what the reader by now expects will be an inevitable conflict of loyalties. The crisis seems to occur near the end of the story, when the boys come upon heaps of garbage dumped on the black family's lawn. Among the orange peel and stubs of cigars—described in another of Pynchon's wonderful catalogues of the waste of ordinary lives—each child recognises 'the shadow-half of his family's life for all the week preceding'. In the face of such intimidating evidence and of the choices it demands, it is then revealed, however, that of course Carl does not exist at all except as a fantasy. 'He was what grown-ups, if *they'd* known, would have called, an "imaginary playmate" ': 'He was entirely theirs, their friend and robot, to cherish, buy undrunk sodas for, or send into danger, or even, as now, at last, to banish from their sight.' The white boys then 'rollicked off into the night's rain' by themselves, like Porpentine, who felt that 'a bit of skylarking . . . made him more human.' They go home to 'a good night kiss, and dreams that could never again be entirely safe'.

Whenever a character in Pynchon even so much as promises to embody or enact the excluded 'human' he is just as quickly made to dissolve. This is the representative destiny of Slothrop, who, in the last section of *Gravity's Rainbow*, is simply 'scattered'. 'It is doubtful he will ever be "found" again,' Pynchon reports, dropping into Army lingo, 'in the sense of "positively identified and detained".' This happens just after he is seen at a crossroads in the Zone—a version of occupied Germany—'crying, not a thing in his head, just feeling natural', as he looks upon a rainbow, 'driven down out of public clouds into Earth, green wet valleyed Earth'.

I suspect that Pynchon's own efforts as a person to remain outside any of the networks of American literary-cultural life is further evidence of his conviction that to let yourself be humanly 'known' or identified is just as quickly to be appropriated and dehumanised by the System, made part of some vast effort by which contemporary institutions and contemporary media sort and 'understand' people so as to destroy any fragments of resistant life and reality. In the face of accumulating renown he has gone to ever greater lengths to remain unknown and unknowable, unclassifiable as a person.

His whereabouts at any given time are revealed only to a very few associates; he has granted no interviews and revealed nothing about his personal life, though he hints in the Introduction that he has by now had some 'direct experience with marriage and parenting'. There's no way to confirm this, or even to know what he means by it. His dossier at Cornell, from which he graduated in 1959 'with distinction in all subjects', notably English literature and

---

An excerpt from Pynchon's introduction to *Slow Learner*

I enjoyed only a glancing acquaintance with the Beat movement. Like others, I spent a lot of time in jazz clubs, nursing the two-beer minimum. I put on hornrimmed sunglasses at night. I went to parties in lofts where girls wore strange attire. I was hugely tickled by all forms of marijuana humor, though the talk back then was in inverse relation to the availability of that useful substance. In 1956, in Norfolk, Virginia, I had wandered into a bookstore and discovered issue one of the *Evergreen Review,* then an early forum for Beat sensibility. It was an eye-opener. I was in the navy at the time, but I already knew people who would sit in circles on the deck and sing perfectly, in parts, all those early rock'n'roll songs, who played bongos and saxophones, who had felt honest grief when Bird and later Clifford Brown died. By the time I got back to college, I found academic people deeply alarmed over the *cover* of the *Evergreen Review* then current, not to mention what was inside. It looked as if the attitude of some literary folks toward the Beat generation was the same as that of certain officers on my ship toward Elvis Presley. They used to approach those among ship's company who seemed likely sources—combed their hair like Elvis, for example. "What's his message?" they'd interrogate anxiously. "What does he want?"

We were at a transition point, a strange post-Beat passage of cultural time, with our loyalties divided. As bop and rock'n'roll were to swing music and postwar pop, so was this new writing to the more established modernist tradition we were being exposed to then in college. Unfortunately there were no more primary choices for us to make. We were onlookers: the parade had gone by and we were already getting everything secondhand, consumers of what the media of the time were supplying us. This didn't prevent us from adopting Beat postures and props, and eventually as post-Beats coming to see deeper into what, after all, was a sane and decent affirmation of what we all want to believe about American values. When the hippie resurgence came along ten years later, there was, for a while anyway, a sense of nostalgia and vindication. Beat prophets were resurrected, people started playing alto sax riffs on electric guitars, the wisdom of the East came back in fashion. It was the same, only different.

Thomas Pynchon, in his introduction to Slow Learner, *Little, Brown and Company, 1984.*

---

physics, has mysteriously vanished; his Service records in the United States Navy during two years taken off from the university, 1955-1957, were destroyed in a fire. For several months after graduation he helped prepare technical documents for Boeing aircraft in Seattle, Washington, but fellow workers report that he often did his work in a cocoon he built round his desk with huge sheets of paper: he was a sort of aerospace Bartleby, as one commentator puts it. Where his photograph should appear in the Cornell Freshmen Register there is a blank square; and one of the two available photographs (the other is from the Navy) is in the Year Book of Oyster Bay High School on Long Island, whose principal has been asked by Pynchon not to discuss his time there. By contrast, the reclusive Salinger has given traces abundant enough to let Ian Hamilton plan a biography; and while Hawthorne, who had troubles with Pynchon's Calvinist ancestors for his characterisation in *The House of the Seven Gables* of Judge Pynchon, is famously credited with 12 years of deep isolation in his family home in Salem, he in fact saw a good number of people who reported on his activities, he took several recorded trips, and was missing from the public eye only because the public eye at that time had little reason to look for him. The unique degree of Pynchon's withdrawal from public scrutiny can be read as a refusal to surrender himself to forms of cultural power wherein knowledge of human life has become, in his view, inseparable from the effort to warp and control it, to reduce it to those compulsive plot-makings of which he is himself a master and a parodist. (pp. 18-20)

> *Richard Poirier, "Humans," in* London Review of Books, *Vol. 7, No. 1, January 24, 1985, pp. 18-20.*

John Dugdale   (essay date 1986)

[*In the review below, Dugdale praises* Slow Learner *for the comprehensive perspective it provides on Pynchon's development as a writer, but criticizes the introduction for its repeated instances of "unremitting and unhelpful self-deprecation."*]

> 'No apologia is any more than a romance—half a fiction—in which all the successive identities taken on and rejected by the writer as a function of linear time are treated as separate characters. The writing itself even constitutes another rejection, another "character" added to the past.'
> 'Confessions of Fausto Maijstral', *V.* Ch. 11.

Slow Learner, the only work by Pynchon to be published since *Gravity's Rainbow* (1973), consists of a new Introduction and five stories which originally appeared in several different outlets for fiction and are now collected for the first time. Four were written during 1958-59, in the author's final years at Cornell, and the remaining one, **'The Secret Integration'**, between his first and second novels, *V.* (1963) and *The Crying of Lot 49* (1966). Some or all of the stories will probably be familiar to the student of Pynchon's work, either because he has traced and photocopied the old periodical versions, or because he has come across them in anthologies or pirate pamphlet editions. They are, however, defamiliarised by being brought together in the new format, as paintings are by being hung in different rooms or exhibitions. It is strange to encounter them in chronological order, rather than according to the hazard of availability, and to read them as a collection, rather than separately. . . . **'Mortality and Mercy in Vienna'** is omitted without explanation, and **'Entropy'** is treated dismissively in the Introduction. The little-read **'Under the Rose'** and **'The Secret Integration'** occupy half the space of *Slow Learner* and are regarded more leniently. Oddest of all is to find the author's own voice mediating between the stories and the reader. As Pynchon continues to refuse all publicity, and has published scarcely any nonfiction, they were previously the creations of a name without a known biography, opinions, address, face or voice; a figure as inaccessible as his fictional Jacobean playwright, Richard Wharfinger.

The five stories are very diverse in setting and subject-matter: soldiers coping with a hurricane disaster in Louisiana (**'The Small Rain'**); a lawyer on a drinking binge which takes him to a waste tip on Long Island (**'Low-lands'**); two characters in the same apartment building in Washington D.C., one hosting a three-day-old party, the other seeking sanctuary from apocalypse by turning his room into a hothouse (**'Entropy'**); an English spy in Egypt at the time of the Fashoda crisis (**'Under the Rose'**); schoolkids in Massachusetts becoming aware of adult desolation and racism (**'The Secret Integration'**). Pynchon's body of work in short fiction deviates from the model of Joyce and Hemingway, where the stories are variations on a single subject, set in the same location and intended to form part of a structured collection. There is no consolidation of a characteristic form and subject-matter; indeed there seems to be a deliberate avoidance of self-repetition, with the only obvious continuity (two Washington party stories) eliminated in *Slow Learner* by the omission of **'Mortality and Mercy in Vienna'**. Even the placing of the stories with different periodicals suggests a conception of them as separate projects to be read discretely. The stories serve, like *Dubliners* and *In Our Time,* as preparation for the author's first novel, but they do so by being diverse rather than by the development of a consistent Pynchonesque manner, for the work in question is intermediate between a conventional novel and a heterogeneous collection of tales. As if to demonstrate their preparatory function, *V.* opens with three chapters which rework and permute elements from all the first five stories. Ch. 1 reintroduces Rachel from **'Mortality and Mercy in Vienna'** and Pig Bodine from **'Low-lands'**; its protagonist, the schlemiehl Benny Profane, is a merger of the former sailor Flange in **'Low-lands'** with the Jewish slob Levine in **'The Small Rain'**. Ch. 2 is a reprise of the sick Bohemian subculture of **'Entropy'**, with its chaotic party and avantgarde jazz performance. It also establishes the Herbert Stencil-Benny Profane double narrative, which is based on the Callisto-Mulligan fugue in the same story. Ch. 3 is **'Under the Rose'** transformed by the use of eight different narrative centres.

The original part of *Slow Learner,* the Introduction, skilfully interweaves comments on the stories—Pynchon's first discussion in print of his own work—with an engaging memoir which uses them as cues for anecdotes about Cornell, the Navy and the, 'strange post-Beat passage of cultural time' in the late 50s when they are mostly set. It is written in the colloquial and rather casual style he favours in blurbs for his friends' novels or in other recent non-fiction pieces:

> My first reaction, re-reading these stories, was 'oh my God', accompanied by physical symptoms we shouldn't dwell upon. My second thought was about some kind of wall-to-wall rewrite. These two impulses have given way to one of those episodes of middle-aged tranquillity, in which I now pretend to have reached a level of clarity about the young writer I was back then. I mean I can't just 86 this guy from my life.

As this indicates Pynchon finds little that pleases him in his early work. The only reason in the Introduction for republishing the stories is that they may serve as *negative* models for present-day young writers: 'my best hope is that, pretentious, goofy and ill-considered as they get now and then, these stories will still be of use with all their flaws intact, as illustrative of typical problems in entry-level fiction, and cautionary about some practices which younger writers might prefer to avoid'. It can be inferred that Pynchon felt a risk that the collection might be used in creative-writing classes in the U.S.A., and wished strongly to pre-empt the possibility of imitators by his adverse comments. These are among the pejorative terms he uses as he discusses the stories: pretentious, literary, fancy, cool, remote, hip, cute, theoretical, abstract, conceptual, overwritten. There are also criticisms of derivativeness and extraneous literary allusions, of immature attitudes to sex and death, a bad ear for dialogue and a 'smartassed' narrative voice. Above all the stories err, in their author's present view, in short-changing their characters. They fail in the primary task of the short story, which is apparently to create living characters who resolve or do not resolve problems in their lives which have general significance. (Pynchon does not make it clear whether his assertion of the central importance of plot and character applies just to 'entry-level' fiction or to all fiction). He writes of the stories suffering from the motto 'make it literary', and advocates instead a fiction which is unliterary, drawing on personal experience made luminous and accurate recording of American voices. The more artful a story (the more consciously it is a verbal textile, the more consciously a text among other texts) the more it is deplored. Significantly it is **'Entropy'**, where art is in the foreground and structure artificial, which he now finds particularly nauseating. Presumably the same considerations lead him to prefer the Twainian **'Secret Integration'** to *The Crying of Lot 49*, bizarrely described as a regression to 'my bad old ways'. The specific orientation and pre-emptive role of the Introduction to *Slow Learner* makes it quite different from other retrospective prefaces (e.g. James, Greene, Nabokov) and from a critical description of the stories. The texts are treated largely in terms of their nonachievments of conventional creative-writing class goals, and only a few aspects of each are considered. Occasionally, intriguing information is divulged, as in his remarks on adapting the techniques of surrealist art; or on the aim in the stories of 'sophisticating the Beat spirit'—

Against the undeniable power of tradition, we were attracted by such centrifugal lures as Norman Mailer's essay 'The White Negro', by the wide availability of recorded jazz, and a book I still believe is one of the great American novels, *On the Road,* by Jack Kerouac. . . . We were at a transition point, a strange post-Beat passage of cultural time, with our loyalties divided. As bop and rock'n'roll were to swing music and post-war pop, so was this new writing to the more established modernist tradition we were being exposed to then at college. Unfortunately there were no primary choices for us to make. We were onlookers: the parade had gone by and we were already getting everything secondhand, consumers of what the media of the time were supplying us.

In general, however, the Introduction consists of unremitting and unhelpful self-deprecation. Its value for the critic is more prospective than retrospective; it contributes more to the understanding of Pynchon's future fiction than to that of the stories it deals with, in so far as it sets out the terms of his rejection of the latter.

Concerned as it is with the use of the texts by young writers, the Introduction should not dictate the approach of other readers. I would want to argue, in common with earlier reviewers such as Richard Poirier [*London Review of Books,* 24 January 1985], that Pynchon is too harsh in his judgement of the stories; and to defend the tales against the teller, on two principal grounds. First, the management of perspective is more assured than Pynchon allows in the Introduction, and this partly extenuates some of the faults he remarks. One of the most interesting features of the short fiction is that almost from the outset it adopts a technique of narration which remains Pynchon's standard mode before *Gravity's Rainbow.* This is a third-person narration in a delicately shifting equilibrium between character-perspective and externality; it rests only briefly at either pole, with passages of a quasi-vocal interior monologue, and sentences when the protagonist is observed wholly from the outside. A narrative voice does not detach itself from the interior voice of the characters to position them for the reader or to clarify the fantastic and indeterminate moments in the texts. Having reached 'a level of clarity' about the characters and their era, Pynchon would now like to have had that clear view installed in the stories in the kind of overseer-narrator used in *Gravity's Rainbow.* But this is unnecessary, as the texts carefully register and re-register that they are in character-perspective; hence that the immature attitudes betrayed are those of the protagonist, and that the passages of 'overwriting' are not authorial lectures but attempts to render consciousnesses which are overfanciful and overloaded with information. Whatever Pynchon may say about his *biographical* identity with the characters ('almost but not quite me', 'I wish I could say that this is only Pig Bodine's voice') the words on the page preserve sufficient detachment. The re-published stories are studies of characters who have adolescent male attitudes about sex and death, who engage in, 'Racist, sexist and proto-Fascist talk', or who feel, 'somber glee at any idea of mass destruction or decline'. Only a foolish or careless reader of *Slow Learner* would confuse these sleepy slobs and fantasists with the implied author. In '**Mortality and Mercy in Vienna**', however, (a story ending with a massacre that the protagonist regards as miraculous) such a confusion is both more plausible and more dangerous, and it is quite probably on these grounds that it is excluded from the collection. The self-censorship is nonetheless regrettable, as the concern with sacrifice, violence and the sacred in the story indicates a direct continuity from the earliest Pynchon to *Gravity's Rainbow.*

Second, the Introduction presents the works as if they were attempts at uncomplicated conventional stories which fail, often because they are disrupted by abstract or book-learnt material. But they are unconventional stories which work, and can be read, on several levels. They are psychological studies of figures with a wide range of occupations, ages, fantasies and neuroses. They are ethical problem tales, dealing with the individual's response to meaningless mass death, a difficult marriage, a sick subculture, colour prejudice. They are miniature comedies, exploring ways of intruding seriousness amidst the jokes. They are experiments in blending realism and surrealism, with each of the last four stories incorporating an element of oneiric ambiguity: Nerissa in '**Low-lands**'; Callisto and Aubade in '**Entropy**'; the ending of '**Under the Rose**'; Carl in '**The Secret Integration**'. They are parts of Pynchon's appraisal of his literary inheritance, and comment through allusion on tradition. In the Introduction, for example, '**Under the Rose**' is compared unfavourably to Le Carré for, 'Complexity of plot and depth of character', but clearly Le Carré's spy fiction is much longer, and plot and character virtually exhaust his concerns. As Pynchon himself to some extent indicates, '**Under the Rose**' is multi-layered. It observes minutely the development of a paranoid's delusionary structure; it considers, with Henry Adams, whether history is personal or statistical; it junks together in surrealist fashion elements from a variety of Victorian and Modernist texts; it attempts playfully to recreate a place and period from Baedeker and other books; it relies on a 'strategy of transfer' whereby the Fashoda incident in 1898 acts as a parable about the Bomb, the looking-glass war of the C.I.A., and such events as the Quemoy and Matsu crisis; it floats a comparison, fundamental to *V.,* between the British Empire in its Kipling phase and Eisenhower's U.S.A.

The conception of a text which works on more than one level is implied by the titles of '**Under the Rose**' and '**The Secret Integration**', and by the punning image of a 'two-story' structure in both '**Low-lands**' and '**Entropy**'. In the three stories in the middle of *Slow Learner,* in particular, the anecdote of the protagonist is counterpointed against a set of ideas derived from, 'things I read for courses' (*V.,* Ch. 16). This body of material consists of themes introduced by the characters—psychoanalysis in '**Low-lands**', science in '**Entropy**', history in '**Under the Rose**'—and a cluster of literary allusions, insinuated by manipulation of detail. The story may be read simply on the manifest level, but there is thus also a latent dimension, which is not reducible to the extraneous overlay of 'theoretical stuff' and 'adventitious lectures' condemned in the Introduction. Understanding, at this latter level, is 'digging', in the 50s slang used in '**Entropy**'.

The early Joyce writes of, 'the hell of hells . . . the region, otherwise expressed, wherein everything is found to be obvious' (*Stephen Hero*). In early Pynchon too there is a need for something private or hidden, behind or under or inside. Where, 'everything . . . was out in the open, everything could be seen at a glance . . . you came back, you kept coming back, to nothing; nothing but the cheerless earth'. 'Life . . . without a second story', public surface without depth, text without subtext, is intolerable. Hence the dimension of the works which is kept secret, under the rose. Part of this shadow aspect involves the interaction of thematic concept and situation, but much (to the author's later regret) is an interrogation or arrangement of tradition. The second story of the texts therefore reflects the condition of being a second story, at second remove. The student Pynchon described in the Introduction is so well-read, and so given to experiencing at second-hand through books, that a 'first story', whether Shakespeare or Irving or Camus, has already been written whatever subject he chooses. He is so late in, and so saturated by, literary history, that there can be no pretence of providing the first treatment or instance of anything. (Even to report firsthand experience freshly and directly is to be Twainian). The abundant allusions are indicators of what he calls the degrees of literary theft: borrowing subject-matter, location, characters, mood; 'parodies on what someone else had already done' (*V.*, Ch. 10); writing aware of a predecessor but not influenced by him.

The, 'junkshop or randomly-assembled' allusions in the stories may seem merely capricious and opportunistic, at best surrealist as he uses the term, combining, 'inside the same frame elements not normally found together to produce illogical and startling effects'. However, *V.* suggests that the literary thefts and intertextual games are more carefully organised to establish his difference from particular traditions, and to elude them by alluding. The two interlaced narratives of the novel contrast Benny Profane, a rolling stone passing through various jobs and girlfriends in New York, 1956, and Herbert Stencil, who imagines past places like Egypt in 1898 in his hunt for a mysterious woman called V. The basic counterpoint is thus between American present and European past, but there is also a subordinate opposition between two artistic periods, both clustered around a world war, as Stencil's fictions tend to rework Modernist scenarios, and Benny prowls an absurdist city and falls in with a crowd of pseudo-Beat Bohemians. The same opposition is evident in **'Entropy'**, where Stravinsky is contrasted with the cool jazz of the 50s, and in less schematic form in most of the other stories. In **'The Small Rain'**, the first in the collection, a soldier is to be found reading, 'things like *Being and Nothingness* and *Form and Value in Modern Poetry*', Sartre and a survey of Modernism.

In the Introduction Pynchon refers to his 'divided loyalties' in the conflict of 'Beat vs. traditional fiction', yet, on the evidence of his work up to and including *V.,* he somewhat misrepresents the balance of forces. On the one hand, he says nothing positive about 'the undeniable power . . . of the more established modernist tradition', leaving this power to seem an undesirable enchantment. On the other, he is now nostalgic for a Beat movement which is never portrayed favourably in his fiction; the Whole Sick Crew are exhausted and decadent, and Benny's restless internal tourism is a parody of the Road myth. The more important influences after 1945 appear to be jazz (mentioned in three of the four contemporary stories) and French literature, not the subculture which took them up. The 'synthesis' *V.* strives for is not between Joyce and Kerouac, but between Modernism and a general postwar tendency manifested across the spectrum of art-forms from painting to the nouveau roman.

Pynchon's fiction up to and including *The Crying of Lot 49* has an often noted concern with attempting to transcend or reconcile binary oppositions, ethical, cultural, political, etc. (One of the senses of the title of *V.* is 'versus', i.e. both 'resistance' and 'intermediate between oppositions', e.g. God v. Caesar). These oppositions are never far from his literary conflict of loyalties. The binary 'ones and zeroes' at the end of *Crying* ('Behind the hieroglyphic streets there would either be a transcendent meaning, or only the earth') also represent the choice between an idealist and an anti-essentialist writing. The apparent moral motto of *V.*, 'Keep cool, but care', is spoken by a jazz musician and in context adumbrates a fusion between the tendencies of two different phases of twentieth century art. Even as a student Pynchon posits a third wave art after Modernism and post-Modernism (between 1938-60). First an art which is poetry or poetic, then one which is cool and anti-lyrical, then the synthesis which sorts out the valuable elements in both legacies, and is neither apocalyptic nor apathetic. But the jazz 'new conception' of **'Entropy'**, the notion of the third man or third person in **'Mortality and Mercy in Vienna'** and the various artists of *V.* are parodies of such a Messianic role. The blocked structures and endings of *V.* and *Crying* imply the impossibility of a third writing which transcends and succeeds the first two phases. Instead of a work which is genuinely *novel*, there can only be a quest for an 'excluded middle', a striving for a marriage ('compromises . . . a minimum basis for a workable thing) between what already exists. Nonetheless the project remains an ambitious one, and is already envisaged in the short stories. The reader of ***Slow Learner*** should not be persuaded by the new characters it adds to Pynchon's fiction (the 'slow learner' apprentice writer who somehow produced *V.* before he was 26, the amiable middle-aged recollector in tranquillity) to take them to be lesser works than they are. (pp. 156-64)

John Dugdale, " 'A Burglar, I Think: A Second-Story Man'," in The Cambridge Quarterly, *Vol. 15, No. 2, 1986, pp. 156-64.*

FURTHER READING

Criticism

Cooper, Peter L. *Signs and Symptoms: Thomas Pynchon and the Contemporary World.* Berkeley: University of California Press, 1983, 238 p.

Contains discussion of the short stories in an examination of Pynchon's place in contemporary American fiction and society.

Cowart, David. "Love and Death: Variations on a Theme in Pynchon's Early Fiction." *The Journal of Narrative Technique* 7, No. 3 (Winter 1977): 157-69.

Traces Pynchon's use of Puccini's opera *Manon Lescaut* to effect his characters' actions in "Under the Rose" and chapter three of *V.*

Dugdale, John. "Three Short Stories." In his *Thomas Pynchon: Allusive Parables of Power,* pp. 17-75. London: Macmillan, 1990.

Examines the allusive artistic and political subtexts of "Mortality and Mercy in Vienna," "Low-Lands," and "Entropy."

Fowler, Douglas. "Story into Chapter: Thomas Pynchon's Transformation of 'Under the Rose'." *The Journal of Narrative Technique* 14, No. 1 (Winter 1984): 33-43.

Comparative analysis of "Under the Rose" and the chapter in *V.* that Pynchon adapted from the story.

Madsen, Deborah L. "Postmodernist Allegory and the Postmodern Condition: *Slow Learner* and *Vineland.*" In her *The Postmodernist Allegories of Thomas Pynchon,* pp. 114-34. Leicester, England: Leicester University Press, 1991.

Argues that Pynchon uses in certain stories of *Slow Learner* and his novel *Vineland* a mimetic form of narrative distinct from allegory "to represent aspects of the

condition of postmodernity—especially . . . the issue of complicity."

Seed, David. "The Short Stories." In his *The Fictional Labyrinths of Thomas Pynchon,* pp. 13-70. Iowa City: University of Iowa Press, 1988.

Discusses the layers of symbolism and the unifying elements of contemporary American themes in the short stories.

Simons, John. "Third Story Man: Biblical Irony in Thomas Pynchon's 'Entropy'." *Studies in Short Fiction* 14, No. 1 (Winter 1977): 88-93.

Explores the biblical allusions contained in the Saul-Miriam sections of "Entropy" and their paradigmatic functioning in Pynchon's entropic theme.

Stark, John O. *Pynchon's Fictions: Thomas Pynchon and the Literature of Information.* Athens: Ohio University Press, 1980, 183 p.

Includes brief discussions of "Entropy," "Low-Lands," "Mortality and Mercy in Vienna," "The Secret Integration," and "Under the Rose" in an examination of how Pynchon's fiction attempts to integrate and organize the vast amounts of information available in contemporary society.

Wood, Michael. "The Apprenticeship of Thomas Pynchon." *The New York Times Book Review* (15 April 1984): 1, 28-9.

Positive appraisal of *Slow Learner.*

Additional coverage of Pynchon's life and career is contained in the following sources published by Gale Research: *Contemporary Authors,* **Vols. 17-20, rev. ed.;** *Contemporary Authors New Revision Series,* **Vol. 22;** *Contemporary Literary Criticism,* **Vols. 2, 3, 6, 9, 11, 18, 33, 62, 72;** *Dictionary of Literary Biography,* **Vol. 2;** *DISCovering Authors; Major 20th-Century Writers;* **and** *World Literature Criticism.*

Luisa Valenzuela

1938-

Argentinian short story writer, novelist, playwright, and journalist.

INTRODUCTION

Valenzuela is one of several prominent authors to have emerged in Argentina since the "boom," a period of innovation and excellence in Latin American literature during the 1960s. In her novels and short stories she juxtaposes surreal images and realistic settings—a technique known as magic realism—to explore themes of political and cultural repression. Valenzuela's fiction is frequently included in anthologies of Latin American and women writers and analyzed in comparative literature, women's studies, and Latin American studies courses.

Valenzuela was born in Buenos Aires. Her mother was a writer, and family friends included Argentinian literary notables Jorge Luis Borges and Ernesto Sábato. Valenzuela began working as a journalist at age seventeen and published her first short story at eighteen. An award-winning reporter, she worked for Buenos Aires newspapers *El Mundo* and *La Nación,* and edited *Crisis,* a magazine of literature, sociology, and politics. Valenzuela first gained attention as a fiction writer in 1966 with *Hay que sonreír,* a novel that depicts the submissive role of women in Argentinian society. Her first collection of short stories, *Los heréticos,* was published in 1967. In 1969 she received a Fulbright scholarship to participate in the University of Iowa's International Writers Program. During the 1970s and 1980s, Valenzuela lived and traveled extensively in the United States, Mexico, Argentina, and Spain, writing fiction and teaching creative writing. A writer-in-residence at Columbia University in 1978 and at New York University in 1985, she also served as a faculty member in the Creative Writing Division of New York University for several years. She resettled in Buenos Aires in 1990.

In her short stories Valenzuela blends diverse elements, including folklore, occult philosophy, and the tenets of psychoanalysis, to create surreal, experimental narratives in which she examines sociopolitical realities. In *Los heréticos,* for example, Valenzuela explores the ways in which the language of patriarchal religious institutions define feminine identity in Western Society. In *Aquí pasan cosas raras (Strange Things Happen Here)*, a collection of stories written during the height of political terrorism in Argentina in the 1970s, she uses wry wordplay and Argentinian slang to parody a world in which terrorism, censorship, and senseless killing are commonplace. Valenzuela's fic-

tion is characterized by its focus on themes of politics, language, and women, which are closely linked through images of violence, eroticism, death, and metamorphosis. Critics consider *Cambio de armas (Other Weapons)*, a collection of five tales featuring women willing to kill or die for their beliefs, representative of her work.

Valenzuela's use of magic realism emphasizes the surreal and bizarre more so than does the fiction of such pioneers of the technique as Gabriel García Márquez and Julio Cortázar. Accordingly, some critics find her stories less reflective of social or psychological reality than those of her contemporaries and claim that she is more interested in experimenting with literary form than in telling stories. Nonetheless, critics have also praised her inventive use of image, metaphor, and symbol, and numerous studies of her work have focused on her use of language to both convey meaning and create artistic form. Valenzuela's works have received significant acclaim in the United States, and she is well respected by other Hispanic writers. Cortázar has described Valenzuela as "Courageous—with neither self-censorship or prejudice—careful of her language—which is excessive when necessary but magnificently refined and modest as well, whenever reality is."

PRINCIPAL WORKS

SHORT FICTION

Los heréticos   1967
Aquí pasan cosas raras   1975
   [*Strange Things Happen Here,* 1979]
Clara: Thirteen Stories and a Novel   1976
Libro que no muerde   1980
Cambio de armas   1982
   [*Other Weapons,* 1985]
Donde viven las águilas   1983
   [*Up among the Eagles,* 1988]
Open Door   1989

OTHER MAJOR WORKS

Hay que sonreír   (novel)   1966
   [*Clara* published in *Clara: Thirteen Stories and a Novel,*
   1976]
El gato eficaz   (novel)   1972
Como en la guerra   (novel)   1977
   [*He Who Searches,* 1987]
Cola de lagartija   (novel)   1983
   [*The Lizard's Tail,* 1983]
Crimen del otra   (novel)   1989
Novela negra con argentinos   (novel)   1990
Realidad nacional desde la cama   (drama)   1990

CRITICISM

Luisa Valenzuela   (essay date 1986)

[*In the essay below, Valenzuela offers her reflections on the experience of being a writer.*]

The task of writing is at the same time heartrending and joyful. It is the discovery of one's own imagination, of the associations and the creative powers implicit in language, and a meticulous confrontation with something so denigrated and surprising as words can be.

The word is our tool and our enemy at the same time, it is the sword of Damocles sometimes suspended over our heads when we feel incapable of expressing it, of hitting on the key word, the Open Sesame that will allow us to enter into a new text. That is why I often say that literature, the production of literature, is a full-time curse. And not only because doubt springs up with each step or because the skepticism regarding the usefulness of writing is stated on each page, but also because it tears at the other side: the guilt, or the terror of not writing, of not writing each and every hour of life as is demanded by a certain dark desire so opposed to the other dark desire which pushes us out into the world and to that other thing we call life.

The distance isn't far between the chair where I have the idea and the desk where I will write it; it's insurmountable.

It's the same distance that lies between wanting to say it and not being able to say it. It's the resistance offered by words at being trapped as such. And we writers, with a butterfly net, always running after the blasted words, no longer with the intention of affixing them with a pin driven into the text, rigidly, but the intention of maintaining them alive, fluttering and changing, so that the text will have the necessary iridescence—perhaps called ambiguity—that will allow the reader to reinterpret it. As Barthes said: "The objective of literary work (of literature as work) consists of the reader no longer being the consumer but the creator of a text."

And in the literary puzzle, what I write isn't as interesting as how I write it (Felisberto Hernández and James Joyce insisted on the idea). In the articulation between the narrated anecdote and the style of narration is where the secret of the text resides and where we can witness the bewilderment of the word that can alternately assume the role of a faithful dog, a knife or dice.

An apparently innocent word acquires splendor and transforms itself thanks to the intention with which it is hurled from afar, thanks to that bed which has been prepared for it with piles of other words that precede it. And let's not speak about the silences, which are impossible to speak about anyway. What goes unsaid, that which is implied and omitted and censured and suggested, acquires the importance of a scream.

Inflexible semiologists talk about the "contamination" of the word when they speak of polysemy, meaning the disconcerting synonyms, the analogies, the varied connotations which disrupt the nature and functioning of every word.

As writers, we have our harvest with these so-called contaminations; we sharpen them, shine them, present them in the best way possible so that the light of the reading will bring out all its facets, even the most hidden ones, those most ignored by us and, as such, most delightful—the ones that elude our self-censorship, our internal repressions. (pp. 9-10)

> *Luisa Valenzuela, "Dangerous Words," in* The Review of Contemporary Fiction, *Vol. 6, No. 3, Fall, 1986, pp. 9-10.*

Marta Morello-Frosch   (essay date 1986)

[*In the following essay, Morello-Frosch discusses Valenzuela's depiction of Argentinian social and political oppression in "Other Weapons."*]

In several of her novels and short stories, Luisa Valenzuela has given ironic and often highly metaphorical accounts of the political and social events taking place in her native Argentina during the last two decades. In a collection of stories that appeared in the United States under the title **Other Weapons,** she includes some narratives that specifically refer to the reign of terror that ended in 1983 with the election of President Alfonsin.

These narratives have a distinctive feature in common: the space of resistance is located in the imaginary, in the seat of language, where being symbolically constructs reality, utters it, and thus validates the world. Accusations, polemics, encomium, and criticism are all collective acts of nomination. The speaking or uttering subject can thus construct and at times impose a vision of the world that can be opposed to the consensus or the dominant discourse. But the subject needs to establish differences between views, between perceptions, among beings and among periods, utterances and texts. In sum, the subject needs a collective and subjective memory that will furnish a context for his or her own practice. In the case of Luisa Valenzuela's stories, we encounter not only a discursive representation of violence, but a specific instance of this violence as a social practice.

In **"Other Weapons,"** Luisa Valenzuela conjures up the situation of a female oppositional force reduced to total passivity and isolation by her male captor-master. While the situation is socially and politically not uncommon, particularly in Latin America, what sets this narrative apart is the mode of entrapment and the structure of isolation it reveals, both of which transcend the usual capture-torture sequence. While the latter is a given, underlying the basic narrative as raw experience, it is the structuring, or the barriers imposed to the recall of such experience, the ones that bring the dramatic tension to the anecdote, which remains, otherwise, painfully common. The story narrates the life of a young woman with a military man. She is in a state of amnesia through mind-control that is drug induced, severed totally from her past, reduced to the condition of psychological tabula rasa, zero degree of consciousness, as she herself states. It is her total separateness from herself and others, both physically and psychologically, that brings about her peculiar mode of torture. It is particularly the latter one that can at times create anguish in an otherwise totally predictable sequence of days spent in comfortable isolation:

> Living like that, in the absolute present, in a world that's born every instant or at most was born a few days back (how many?) is like living in cotton wool: somewhat soft and warm, but with no taste at all. Not rough, either. There's little she can know about roughness in that completely soft, slightly rosy apartment, in the company of Martina, who talks ever so softly. But she senses roughness . . .

She feels bereft of a past, cut off from any familiar set of references that would make recognition with other subjects possible. As a result, she is unable to reconstitute herself as a subject, her relationship to the past severed, her relationship to the present restricted to one single mediator: he, who represents the only active presence near her, the maid Martina being merely an extension of his presence:

> Martina is also dark and hieratic and everything's in its place—one leaf to the right, one to the left, alternating. He did choose Martina. She was probably custom-made for him, because if it had been up to her she would probably have chosen someone full of life, one of those women who sing while they sweep the floor.

The maid, thus, does not provide any possibility of differ-

entiation, any otherness from him, any difference that may help Laura define herself. In fact, it is the repetition of her image in mirrors, the one added diabolical element, that contributes to her total disorientation. Self and self-as-other, distanced, mute, fixed, like multiplying pieces on a puzzle that becomes more and more difficult to solve, roadblocks to her recall of any past complete subjectivity.

The physical conditions of her confinement also add to her sense of loss. She is not even trapped like most prisoners in an ordinary cell, the limits to their world unequivocally set by harsh walls and the bars that allow a skimpy view of what is "out there," including the voices of the jail mates and guards outside reinforcing the perfect division of two separate worlds. Laura, on the contrary, lives in a small but comfortable apartment of soft pink walls, in the company of one person—he who comes and goes, and of the maid, who is an extension of his presence and of his will. The world outside is only glimpsed in the presence of two bodyguards—One and Two—who remain at the door whenever he is in residence. The door is locked. False keys carelessly displayed on the mantelpiece tantalize her with the notion that locks are to be opened, can and are meant to be opened, but, as she surmises, only by those who, like him, own the appropriate keys. This situation duplicates the condition of her mind, stirred by false keys in the course of the narrative, while she remains until the end unable to gain access to her memory. There are other sets of possible references that, like the mirror and the door, provide possible—and false—access to the past: a locked window that faces a sterile white wall—white, like the blank of her mind, uninscribed, or erased. The wall further indicates that Laura lives in a world of multiple signs similar to herself—mirror images—or blankness, without contrasts, or differences, hence without any possible means of comparison. In the apartment there is also a nuptial photograph, where she appears with him "wearing a veil and behind the veil, an absent expression," while he seems triumphant as any victor would. This again proves a mirror of their living situation; he knows, he acts, he commands, she obeys and does not know, she can only will a cup of tea or a plant. This last request of hers provides a carefully manicured specimen from a local florist, almost plastic in its perfection, like the rest of her surroundings, symmetric, without any reference to the world out there where plants grow limp, luxuriant, shrivelled, die. But if the *locus* provides no familiar set of references that may in any way aid her memory or suggest a link with the past, there is also the matter of language. Her language memory remains intact. She has stored all sorts of genetic signs, but she cannot individualize them, cannot insert them in a signifying chain that has continuity and spatial scope. She is unable to contextualize them for specific instances, since each one of these remains unique, isolated, part of no detectable process. Lacking a referential network, restricted to her own self, words, like consciousness, do not establish differential relationships for Laura. This is particularly obvious in her use of the name for him; he is Daniel, Pedro, Ariel, Alberto, Alfonso, Hector, any and none, lost in a set of nominal possibilities that cannot define, that make recognition impossible by a subject that cannot differentiate, he remains a nameless lover, only and surely a "he."

Names, like mirror images of self, do not assume their differentiating and relational function; they float, like her consciousness, unassigned, unreclaimed, unconstructed as concepts in a sea of indifferentiation. But in this cocoon of white walls, exchangeable names, and eternal present, there are two strong inscriptions: an ugly and recent scar that ascends her back, and a black hole of memory:

> An image that is undoubtedly charged with memories. (Where have all the memories gone? Where are they, going around knowing much more about her than she herself?) Something's hiding and sometimes she tries to reach a mental hand out to catch a memory on the wing, and that's impossible. It's impossible to have access to that corner of her brain where memory crouches, so she finds nothing: memory locked into itself as a defense.

This is evidence that she does retain language signs with which to shape her sense of estrangement, without knowing exactly from what she has been separated. She can only describe the unusual experience in her consciousness that remains like her gaze in the photograph, veiled, creating the image of the dark well to describe not only the emptiness of her state but also the disruption that this has brought to her life where everything is now unique, single, or interchangeable, which is the same, where names are given in series, or people named with numbers, like the bodyguards, like prisoners in cells. Because it is precisely in trying to describe her well that she begins to rebuild her past, not as experience but as a symbolic chain. For it is in the words that she uses—in the metaphors that in reversal to their usual function become a discourse for the real, not a construct of the imaginary—that she slowly reconstructs her past. Thus, metaphor becomes the discourse of experience, as language betrays that empty space, that fenced-in past, that begins to be filled with figures of speech, displaced locus for the real:

> Sometimes the sides of the well echo and it doesn't matter what they're trying to tell her although sometimes she does seem to receive a message—a whiplash—and she feels as though the soles of her feet were being burned and suddenly she crawls back up to her surface, the message is too much for her to bear, better to stay out of that black, vibrant well, better to move back into the candy-pink room which they tell her is hers.

The dark well may be telescoped into an imaginary gunsight at whose center he stands, while she, the docile helpless one, seems to be holding the rifle. The series of images tries to read this darkness as well as the sooty drippings of the only visible outside wall, as if these were Rorschach cards, articulating in this reading her artificially distanced and severed experience. Guided by the associative power of word signs, she resorts to the analogy of aggressive objects so that the picklock he carries in his pocket becomes "like a weapon to squeeze in her fist and hit with," the sight of a gaucho whip reminds her of a dynamite charge. The slowly evolving chain of verbal and non-verbal references becomes more complete to acquire full meaning in the end, when before fleeing after a coup, he hands to her the bag and gun with which she had threatened his life in

the past. At this point, a brutal return to history, to her being overpowered, tortured and reduced to a memoryless being, a woman without history, a living dead.

But if the story ends there, where her history and memory had been brutally cut off, the last paragraph precisely resumes the interrupted act of defense-aggression that she had initiated:

> She sees his back move away and feels like the fog is beginning to clear. She starts to understand a few things—what that black instrument is for, that thing he calls a gun. She lifts it and aims.

The narrative thus describes Laura's condition of internment as both a criminal and a patient, reduced by her male captor to the condition of total dependency and passivity, to be used by him in his regular appearances as his undisputed sex object, in joyless and often unsatisfying acts of possession. Such acts become near rituals to be witnessed by the two bodyguards—voyeurs who validate his power and his function. For if it is true, as the story suggests, that these eyes will be additional mirrors in which she can also see herself, it is also true that unlike the mirrors she will be an object for their gaze, for their possession through the peephole, and that she will not be able to recover her image. Like him, like Martina, like the mirrors, she will be looked at even in the most intimate and often involuntary acts, acted upon, a fetish to be traded in repeated acts of even visual possession. The male bonding of her captor with the observers, with the maid, with the visiting doctors, reinforces the total isolation that is levied upon her. Her being locked up, without any possible contact with the outside world, without any reference to the course of time, imprisoned in an absolute present, add to her intense estrangement. But it is the impossibility of memory, of mediating her personal history, the one that reduces her even more to the state of nonbeing, thus precluding any possibility of conscious relation with anyone, since her subjectivity has been amputated at the core. It is, however, from this sense of loss, from this consciousness of amputation, this almost visceral sense of incompleteness, that language comes to her rescue. It comes in unexpected forms of metaphorizing, an experience which is, indeed, unique, incomparable to any other that she can, at this moment, refer to. But words—signs—lie limply in her mind to be infused with new figurative vitality in her search for meaning. They come back for a second round of articulation, their materiality intact by the loss of memory, but their function undiminished. As in a photograph with a double superimposed exposure, words start referring to that empty well in terms of experience lived at the level of the skin. Thus, they reconstitute, as in ever more regular *lapsus,* a set of aggressive and brutal references that belie a past that has been kept, like Laura, locked up.

It may be profitable to point out that memory of pain and suffering seems to be in the history of abuse one of the more often cited deterrents to recurrence of aggression. Yet, it is precisely the absence of such memory, the one that seems to problematize Laura's otherwise protected life as a prisoner: the absence of desire—if one omits the sexual encounters—of initiative, of dialogue, of will. She is, in the broadest sense, the product of brain washing, capable of existing because there is in her no notion of any different time or situation. But it is these words, which had made her the object of tortures, that will, eventually, liberate her mind. Hers is a battle of the sign, not against the signs of others, but to recover the meanings she and her brethren infused in signs that seem no longer of use to her in her present condition. Luisa Valenzuela has managed to produce a narrative of extraordinary subtlety in which the problem of political and sexual oppression is reduced to that of restoration of meaning, of continuity, of communication with one's self and one's past, prerequisites to rebuilding subjectivity as social and historical beings, a project of national scope now being carried out in Argentina. What Laura manages to do is precisely that, and in her final act she allows for history to become unstuck, to follow its course while providing with her willful and daring action the end to a long period of dark wells and un-nominated silences. (pp. 82-6)

> *Marta Morello-Frosch, " 'Other Weapons': When Metaphors Become Real," in* The Review of Contemporary Fiction, *Vol. 6, No. 3, Fall, 1986, pp. 82-7.*

An excerpt from "Other Weapons"

There's only the sound of the clock, the syncopated tick-tock, and it's like a presence. So many almost presences, then, and no real presence, no voice calling her to pull her away from herself.

Not that his voice doesn't call her often. Not that his voice doesn't call out her name, Laura, sometimes from afar (from the other room) or just shout right into her ear when he's on top of her, calling just for the hell of it, imposing his presence, her obligation to be there and listen to him.

It's always like that with him, Juan, Mario, Alberto, Pedro, Ignacio, whatever he's called. No sense in changing his name, because his voice is always the same, and so are his demands: she should be with him, but not too much. He wants her to be erased, a malleable woman that he can put together as he pleases. She feels like clay, pliable under his touch, and she doesn't want to be, she refuses to be pliable, changing, and her inner voices howl in rage and hit against the walls of her body while he molds her at leisure.

Every so often she's overcome by these sudden rebellious bouts which are closely related to another feeling called fear. And then, nothing: then the tide recedes leaving nothing but a wet, wind-swept beach.

She wanders barefoot down the wet beach trying to pull herself back together after the horror she felt when the tide was high. So many waves washing over her, but not clearing her thoughts. The waves come in and then leave a sterile line of salty driftwood, which only allows for an indefinite, milder form of terror. She wanders aimlessly down the wet beach, and at the same time she is the beach, her own beach is her refuge; it isn't clay, it's wet sand he'd like to shape as he pleases. She's moist sand for him to build castles like a child. Castles in the air.

Sometimes he uses his voice for these purposes and names

---

her and names each part of her body in a doubtful attempt to reconstruct her.

That's the voice that sometimes calls her and can't break through her shell. Then there's the smile: his sort of strained smile. Only when he laughs—on those very rare occasions when he laughs—does something seem to awaken within her, and it isn't good. It's a deep pang, far removed from laughter.

So there isn't much of an incentive to call her to the surface and pull her out of her dark well. At any rate, nothing coming from outside the apartment, although suddenly something does, a doorbell ringing insistently snaps her back into the here and now. It's rare for that bell to ring like that; someone's desperately trying to be heard and he cautiously walks to the door to see who it is. She's on edge, a live wire, she hears the voices of others and doesn't try to understand them:

"I'm sorry. Colonel, there's an uprising. We had no other way to let you know. They rebelled. They're advancing towards your barracks with the tanks. Apparently the Third Regiment of Infantry is behind them. And the Navy. They're up in arms. Excuse me, Colonel, but we didn't know how to contact you."

He gets dressed in a hurry and leaves without saying goodbye, like so many other times. Only in more of a rush, and maybe forgetting to lock the door. But that's all. She's not concerned about any other details. Not even the voices she heard, which keep on resonating like an unexpected, hopeful sound which she doesn't try to interpret. Interpret? What for? Why should she try to understand something that's far beyond her meager capacity to understand?

> *Luisa Valenzuela in her* Other Weapons, *Ediciones del Norte, 1985.*

Dorothy S. Mull (essay date 1986)

[*In the essay below, Mull analyzes "Rituals of Rejection," characterizing the story as representative of Valenzuela's fiction in theme and style.*]

"Rituals of Rejection" ("Ceremonias de rechazo") is the third, and thus in a sense the centerpiece, of the five stories comprising Luisa Valenzuela's highly-acclaimed collection *Other Weapons* (*Cambio de armas,* 1982). Other stories in the volume—notably the first, **"Fourth Version,"** and the last, **"Other Weapons"**—have received well-deserved critical attention as complex, suggestive narratives offering a multiplicity of interpretations. In contrast, **"Rituals of Rejection"** would appear to require little in the way of critical analysis. The story describes a poignant but all too familiar scenario. A woman, here symbolically named Amanda, is enmeshed in a self-destructive relationship with an unworthy lover, and we witness her attempts, ultimately but perhaps not permanently successful, to free herself.

Yet the very simplicity of the plot—if it can be granted so elevated a name—allows us a clear view of some of Valenzuela's characteristic thematic concerns, motifs, and stylistic techniques. The issue of the locus of power in male-female relationships is obviously central, for example, and this is an issue fundamental to her work as a whole. Elsewhere, as in the story **"Other Weapons,"** it is often linked with the more general question of political struggle; even here, such a link is suggested by words like "torture" and "weapon." We also see in this story an emphasis on violence and mind-body conflict that is typical of Valenzuela's work. In addition, her characteristic preoccupation with cyclic processes and metamorphosis is very prominent; indeed, the situation is archetypal, involving a quest, a symbolic death, and a rebirth.

This concern with transformation is underscored both by the narrative point of view, shifting as it does between third- and first-person, and by dominant Valenzuelan motifs such as the mask, the dance, and the mirror. Further, the story is so enriched by echoes from literature (Dante), folklore, and ritual language of various kinds, some of it unfortunately lost in translation (incantations, prayers, social pleasantries, rhymes, formulaic speech from children's games), that it calls up responses much deeper than the simple plot would at first seem to warrant. Finally, the multifaceted surface of Valenzuela's prose sparkles with her signature wordplay, powerful rhythmic effects (achieved largely through incremental repetition), and extraordinary imaginative juxtapositions. Although her language is here much less ornate than it is in the more baroque passages of her novels, it provides ample evidence of her marked tendency to "think in metaphor."

The story is divided into four sections. In the first, Amanda waits in solitude for a telephone call from her lover, aptly nicknamed Coyote, who has once again abandoned her to take part in mysterious political activities that he will not explain. Although he insists, with characteristic evasiveness, that he is working for "the cause," Amanda's friends warn her that he could be an informer or even a policeman (the story is set in Buenos Aires). In spite of this possibility—or perhaps, as she says, partly because of it—she continues to make herself completely available to him. As the story opens, she is dancing around the telephone, conjuring it to ring with mock incantations, even resorting to black magic by drawing a chalk pentagram around it on the floor to attract Coyote's attention. When it remains obstinately silent, she finally gives up in disgust, "just barely containing her urge to give the phone a good kick and send it flying far away, where it belongs." The wry humor allows the protagonist to bear the pain of the situation, as often occurs in Valenzuela's work. However, the rest of the story describes Amanda's attempt to deliver just such a rejection to her lover, with whom the telephone is symbolically linked.

In the second section, Coyote has appeared at Amanda's house with no apology or explanation for his absence. They go to a Chinese restaurant, where he wields his fork ravenously while Amanda, equally hungry but for other pleasures, "takes him in delicately" with chopsticks "among bamboo shoots and black mushrooms, morsels of chicken, morsels of words and promises of love." But after the meal, just as she is happily boarding a bus in the belief that they are going home together (the sexual symbolism is obvious), Coyote suddenly tells her good-bye, saying

that he will call her the next day, "and Amanda, stepping back down from the bus, descends upon him and the sidewalk." Angrily, she insults him and marches off, but after turning right at the first corner and reaching the second, her fury dissipates and she turns right again so that she ends up going around the block and returning to the very spot where she left him. He embraces her in silence and presents her with a long-stemmed red rose. She accepts it, then tells him good-bye ("forever," Valenzuela adds in parentheses, the punctuation indicating both Amanda's unspoken resolve and Valenzuela's characteristic tendency toward afterthought and amplification).

But as the third and longest section of the story begins, we see that Amanda has by no means won the battle. She has had the telephone disconnected, but she recognizes that she needs to do more, since Coyote represents almost a part of herself, a part that must be ritualistically removed. So, after preparing a bath with perfumed bath salts, she puts on white face cream as the symbolic mask she needs for "exiting from the stage" and stepping into a new and better life. As she waits for this mask to work its magic, overtones of self-denial, masochism, violence, and even death are very prominent: "I'm a fire burning its own flames, the white face says, facing the insane mirror, barely moving its mouth." Rinsing the cream off, Amanda observes that her artificial pallor—the "whitewash" of her "facade"—vanishes down the drain. What returns to her, however, is not only her original skin coloring but also her original suffering. (In the Spanish text, the rhyme "colores"/"dolores" reinforces the parallel.) Not completely satisfied, wanting to do something more drastic to reach her essential self and rid herself of Coyote's influence, she applies another facial mask, a transparent coating that smooths her features until they appear angelic, then violently peels it off and scrubs her face with an abrasive bath mitt.

With her skin now smarting and burning, Amanda decides that she had better proceed "with less fanaticism and more tenderness. One shouldn't erase one's face quite so literally." She paints a mask around her eyes with orange face cream, smears white cream on her forehead and chin, and draws ritualistic patterns on her face with lipstick and eyeliner. Thus "tattooed," she prepares to enter her bath, which has cooled and needs to be refilled, but before doing so, she notices that her legs are unshaven. With kaleidoscopic rapidity, her thoughts shift from a mock invocation ("Protect us, oh Aura, . . . from hairy legs that in moments of true bliss may hinder the hand that caresses") to a reminiscence of childhood to a very real, very anguished sexually charged lament for her lover. As she tries to decide whether her break with Coyote has been an act of bravery or of cowardice, a rejection "so as not to be rejected," Amanda plucks at her legs "with fury and tweezers, a contradictory combination." Finally, in a violent scene bringing to mind witches' cauldrons, she strips the hair off with steaming hot black wax.

Thus "purified"—returned, in a sense, to a hairless prepubescent state—Amanda at last prepares to enter the bath. But it has again cooled off and must again be emptied. Filling it for the third time, she adds pine-scented salts, and the fragrance reminds her of the forests where she spent her summers as a child. As memories flood her mind, she remembers how the tiny toads in the forest used to deposit a few drops of urine in her hand when she attempted to catch them. At first she dismisses this as a "useless defense" but then decides that it may be worth trying. In the end (the passage is an artistic tour de force), she releases her own urine into the bathwater, and Valenzuela describes her as "sumptuously" submerged in a sea permeated by her own fluids, "surrounded by her own self. Ecstatic. Her private inner heat now surrounding her in the pine forest with sunbeams filtering through the branches and giving her a halo of sorts. A golden aura amid the white foam." And the "halo," the "golden aura," now belongs not to some haloed deity that she must invoke, but to herself, now no longer in Coyote's embrace (and grasp), but triumphantly surrounded by a part of her own body.

One thing remains: to dispose of the rose, now withered and dead. The next morning, in the fourth and final section of the story, Amanda picks it up and carries it toward the turbid waters of the River Plate. After walking three blocks—an echo of her earlier three-block walk away from and back toward Coyote, except that she now proceeds "knowing her destination"—she glimpses or envisions a person dressed in white "as in Dante's sonnet" (possibly herself, although the identification is not made explicit in the Spanish text). Amanda observes that this figure looks more like a nurse than like "long-lost Beatrice," and concludes that this is appropriate, since what she wants is to cure herself of her unrequited passion, not to die because of it as the nineteenth-century romantic tradition would dictate.

Nevertheless, she feels that she is committing a subversive act by walking toward the river to throw away the dead rose. In her mind, the rose that Coyote held is not only like a broken mirror that brings bad luck but also a kind of weapon that "makes her run a thousand risks. [Hers would be] an ironic fate: imprisoned for carrying a rose." (And what she is doing *is* subversive, for she is freeing herself, at least for a time, from the dependence of women on men that underpins many social structures.) The rose, of course, has multiple meanings. It was given by Coyote as an "offering" in a gesture that, for Amanda, was an "offense," but at a deeper level it represents a dangerous weapon, sexual passion, and throwing it away is an act of severance. As she herself comments, *"Sic transit,"* the unspoken *"gloria"* being not the *"gloria mundi"* (for that is what she is trying to recapture) but the past glory of Coyote that she hopes to efface from her memory.

As suggested above, the physical paths traced by Amanda in the story reflect her growing independence. In the first scene, her obsessive dance around the telephone is focused on an object identified with Coyote, circumscribed by the walls of the room, circular and thus theoretically neverending, and ultimately fruitless. In the second scene, her journey around the block begins promisingly but is also ultimately unsuccessful. In this final scene, however, she knows her goal, and the river—unlike her mute telephone and silent lover—receives her with a "lapping of tame, soft waves, a welcoming sigh." Described in a beau-

tiful, memorable metaphor as a vast vicuña poncho "rippled by a secret breath," the river of vicuña, soft and precious, stands in marked contrast to Coyote, an animal of rough coat and rougher ways—a predator, a thief, a devourer of flesh, including carrion. (We recall his greedy attack on the food in the Chinese restaurant, in contrast to Amanda's slow, delicate approach with chopsticks.)

The vicuña has also been on the endangered species list for years, and this leads us—through a metaphorical byway—to an important aspect of the story: although Amanda ends in triumph, she understands that other Coyotes may eventually enter her life. She says that she will try to be "solid within, to stop the game from repeating itself," but the possibility is there, for her name is, after all, Amanda. Although "the Coyotean cycle" may have closed, the phrase itself implies eternal recurrence. Amanda herself identifies Coyote with her unfulfilled desire, and those familiar with Valenzuela's other work may remember Luis Cernuda's observation—reproduced on the cover of the Spanish edition of her 1977 novel *Como en la guerra (He Who Searches)*—that "el deseo es una pregunta cuya respuesta no existe" ("desire is a question that has no answer"). Desire is the human condition, and therefore one must assume, however reluctantly, that Amanda's freedom is tenuous and may be transitory.

Nevertheless, it *is* freedom, symbolized by her appropriation of roles formerly held by Coyote. During her walk home from the river, for example, she digs up a plant and brings it back to her garden as he used to do. In the final scene, she is neither entangled in the "jungle" associated with Coyote nor immersed in the comforting but unreal "pine forest" of the bath. Rather, she is surrounded by her own garden, a garden that she herself cultivates and waters. As she dances there, showering herself and the plants with a hose that Coyote has bought and installed, both the phallic symbolism and the regeneration theme are obvious. Whereas before with the telephone she had danced without song and without success and whereas before during the bath scene her mirror had revealed only a death-white face, at the end of the story she is singing and the mirror reflects her whole body—nude, wet, and engaged in that most self-sufficient of activities, calisthenics—and "confirms her song."

The song may also be intended to suggest a renewed ability to write. The metaphor is ancient, writing is a recurrent theme in Valenzuela's work, and Amanda has told us that, once free of Coyote, she will be able to indulge in "more gratifying—albeit solitary—activities: writing, for example, answering all those letters." (Previously, her "writing" has been limited to the chalk pentagram and the bizarre designs that she draws on her own face; and she ultimately destroys them both, stepping on the pentagram and allowing the designs to dissolve in the heat of the bathwater.)

The possibility of a metaphorical equation between singing and renewed creativity is strengthened by the fact that, in the final pages of the story, Valenzuela openly relates the exterior to the interior, the visible to the invisible world. We may have deduced that the beautiful maroon-leaved woodland plant represents the protagonist herself (a similar symbol is used in **"Other Weapons"**), but it is Valenzuela who tells us that the plant is "proof of how Amanda no longer needs the Coyote to tend her outer garden. And the inner one? It may be the same one, inside and out, merging."

This linkage between external acts and internal change is central to the story. What we see is the ritual transformation of a cowed, obsessed woman to a free, self-sufficient one—a symbolic death and rebirth, complete with aspects of purification (entering the bath), renunciation (discarding the rose), and vegetation rites (transplanting the maroon-leaved plant, which, unlike the rose, is rooted in earth and will not wither). Through her own initiative, Amanda has carried out a series of acts that transform her from the meek person whom Coyote addresses as "mamacita" to a goddesslike state approaching that of the archetypal Mother Earth.

What is more, she is a self-sufficient Mother Earth who supplies her own life-giving water so that vegetation can grow. We recall that Coyote, in contrast, has been described as a vampire who sucks out her vital fluids. Water in its many forms—the bath, urine, a golden cup of tea that "tastes like sunlight," the river, and so on—is an organizing metaphor in the story. The message is clear: by acting rather than languidly waiting to be acted upon, Amanda has granted herself new life.

The opposition between waiting and acting—and, implicitly, between death and life—is set up in the quasi-syllogistic opening sentence ("To wait, seated in a chair, is the deadest form of dead anticipation, and waiting [is] the most uninspired form of death, so Amanda finally manages to . . . set her anxiety in motion") and informs the narrative throughout. While circling the telephone, for example, Amanda muses that "the dance helps you forget the rigor mortis of absence and waiting. You shake your hair out, you shake up your thoughts." Later, after she discards the rose, her new, freer motion is linked with a more authentic renovation (a hair image is again glanced at): "Amanda takes off, wandering through the park of Palermo, and the sweet scent of eucalyptus starts combing through her soul, reconstructing it for her and giving her back all she had lost while following the Coyote's tracks."

A related theme is the play between the infernal and the celestial—the violent extremes of experience so prominent in Valenzuela's work as a whole. At the outset, for example, Coyote is described as a "mediator between heaven and hell." Although this phrase may reflect certain Indian legends in which the coyote has positive, even Promethean aspects, at the simplest level it obviously refers to Amanda's ecstasy when she is sexually united with her lover and her despondency when she is not. "When I'm with him, the unconfessable in me runs wild—my darkest desires grow wings, and I can feel angelic, even though it's just the opposite." Coyote controls and guides Amanda's life, but it is a perverse sort of "guidance" that leaves her no room for growth. Later on, we find a passing reference to another powerful guide, Beatrice, Dante's companion in the *Paradiso* and his major source of inspiration. Although, as noted above, Beatrice is here pointedly trans-

formed into a nurselike figure, the allusion stands, and it is important for several reasons.

First, it suggests the possibility that the structure of Valenzuela's narrative reiterates the tripartite structure of the *Divine Comedy,* i.e., that Amanda makes an allegorical journey from a personal Hell (with Coyote either absent from her life, as in the first section of the story, or present but perennially elusive, as in the second), through Purgatory (the cleansing rituals of the third section; the hot wax may even reflect the purifying fire of *Purgatorio* XXVII) to Paradise (the joyous garden scene of the fourth and final section). (We note that the main action of the story takes place on three consecutive days, and that the events of those days correspond to the Hell-Purgatory-Paradise sequence described above.) The reiteration would be partly ironic, of course, in that the culmination of Dante's journey is reunion with Beatrice and a vision of the Celestial Rose in the *Paradiso,* while at the end of **Rituals of Rejection"** Amanda is alone and triumphantly *free* of the rose, though surrounded by vegetation.

The fact that a female protagonist is implicitly compared with a male, Dante, is also significant, for it suggests Valenzuela's characteristic openness—her resistance to boundaries and categories. (In interviews, she has repeatedly said that she is fascinated by transsexuality, and many of her works touch on this theme.) Still another important facet of the allusion to Dante is the specific mention of his sonnet on Beatrice, especially if, as seems possible, Valenzuela is remembering not only the famous "Tanto gentile" (*Vita Nuova* XXVI) but also "A ciascun' alma presa, e gentil core," which immediately follows Dante's description of Beatrice as dressed in purest white (III). The focus of the latter poem is not on the well-known revitalizing, beneficent powers of love but on its cruelty. Beatrice is envisioned sitting on the lap of the God of Love, who has a terrifying aspect and who forces her to eat Dante's burning heart, which he holds in his hand. Although the image of the eaten heart was a medieval commonplace, today it shocks. It reminds us of the destructive nature of Amanda's obsession with Coyote before she breaks free through ritual transformation.

The phrase "ritual transformation" is here used advisedly. It has been chosen because its convenient grammatical ambiguity—is the word "ritual" an adjective or a noun?—conveys a fundamental dualism in the story as a whole. Not only do we have the "transformation" of the protagonist, we also have the transformation of ritual itself. For the ceremonies devised by Amanda are not the conventional tribal rites familiar to us all—characteristically public, carried out in groups, and male-dominated. On the contrary, Amanda's are idiosyncratic ("of her own invention,") and performed in solitude. Perhaps most important, they represent an ironic inversion of beautification rites that are associated with the enticement rather than the rejection of males in our culture.

Amanda's rituals—applying "practical" cosmetic masks, putting on makeup, removing body hair, taking a scented bath—could all, under different circumstances, have been acts aimed at seduction. Here, however, they are transformed. The cosmetic masks and hair removal are not intended to enhance her skin but to strip away the "old" Amanda, the one addicted to Coyote. The garish, primitive makeup, which is itself a kind of mask, is not designed to compliment her features but to obscure them—or, to put it another way, to allow a previously hidden part of her personality to emerge. (The mask is an extremely important motif in Valenzuela's writing; and she has commented—with her characteristic spirit of contradiction—that what interests her is the *un*masking made possible by the use of the mask.) Finally, Amanda's bath, discussed in detail above, does initially scent her body with the aroma of pine, but this "cosmetic" effect is far overshadowed by the most un-cosmetic addition of urine to the bathwater. The bath is a defense and an assertion of self, not a beautification ritual designed to please someone else.

The ironic inversion (or subversion) of traditional values and associations is, as several critics have pointed out, a fundamental feature of Valenzuela's work. It is related to her radical questioning of constructs often thought of as dominated by males, by logic, and by conventional categorization. One aspect of this questioning is Valenzuela's insistence on breaking apart, altering, and/or combining traditional words in untraditional ways. Her coinage of the appellation *bolastristes* for Coyote in the present story (Spanish text) is a typical example. (Literally "sadballs," and vaguely lyrical as well as sexual, it appears in the English as "little bastard.") As Magnarelli has put it, "Valenzuela seems determined to prove that she is not at the mercy of language, that she does have power and control over that medium."

In **"Rituals of Rejection,"** Valenzuela goes far beyond mere questioning of tradition, whether tradition takes the form of a word, a relationship between unequals, or a beautification rite. Carefully structured, economically but poetically written, the story is not merely a rejection but an affirmation. It is a celebration of the independent self—a self that no longer needs to seek validation in a man's embrace, a self that can rejoice in seeing itself reflected not in a man's eyes, but in a mirror, free and whole and strong. As such, the story is in many ways more positive than any of the rest in *Other Weapons.* Here there is violence, but it is transcended; here there is death, but it is overcome. The protagonist's "weapon" is not merely the written word, or the spoken one, or fantasy, or amnesia, or a revolver. It is her body itself, and what she does with that body. (pp. 88-95)

> *Dorothy S. Mull, "Ritual Transformation in Luisa Valenzuela's 'Rituals of Rejection',"* in The Review of Contemporary Fiction, *Vol. 6, No. 3, Fall, 1986, pp. 88-96.*

Zulma Nelly Martinez   (essay date 1986)

[*In the following excerpt, Martinez discusses the philosophical issues she perceives underlying "Where the Eagles Dwell."*]

Luisa Valenzuela's deceptively simple **"Where the Eagles Dwell"** is undoubtedly one of her most compelling short stories to date. At first glance the tale simply describes the protagonist's demise among the outlandish people inhabiting the mountaintop—the enticing region "where the eagles dwell." Further reading, however, discloses a metatext that raises a variety of philosophical issues. Among others, the story addresses the implications of the gradual shift, presently underway in the West, from a mechanical to a holistic view of the world.

Valenzuela's narration challenges traditional mechanicism, which she sees as largely responsible for the Western proclivity to reduce human existence to mechanical motion and to turn beings into lifeless automatons. This state, aptly categorized as a state of "robotitude" by the well-known feminist Mary Daly [in her *Gyn/Ecology*], is magnificently allegorized in Valenzuela's tale. Inasmuch as it also contains a suggestion of "roboticide" (to quote from Daly once again), the story subtly suggests the transition from the mechanical worldview, which interprets reality as essentially fragmented and devoid of life, to the holistic model, which sees the world as being essentially interrelated and infused with life.

The holistic interpretation is primarily developing under the impact of the New Physics and of consciousness research. Work in both fields of endeavor is making it increasingly evident that the release of long repressed energies in our world is reawakening the life force itself, a force that tends to weave together what Western culture has so mercilessly torn asunder and to *heal* the world by rendering it *whole.*

"Where the Eagles Dwell" is structured on the basis of the strict separation between the upper and the lower realms. This underlines the fact that fragmentation leads to a hierarchical polarization which consecrates some portions of reality and denigrates others. Although Valenzuela's narration deals primarily with the dualisms mind/matter, conscious/unconscious, rational/non-rational, and life/death, it likewise alludes to the rigid division between male and female, self and other. Let us remember, however, that at the basis of Western dichotomization lies the stringent separation of mind and matter institutionalized by the Cartesian cogito. Ultimately, it is the absolute supremacy of the rational mind in the Western world that the story questions.

Narrated in the first person by its protagonist, **"Where the Eagles Dwell"** tells of a woman who leaves the lowlands she inhabits to ascend the mountaintop. The fear of confronting the precipices down below prevents her eventual descent and return home, and thus she finds herself captive in a strange world that threatens to overpower her. The story essentially deals with the woman's struggle for survival and final deliverance from the inhospitable land, a land she rightly sees as the land of the "living" dead.

In effect, by centering their existence exclusively on the mind, the residents of the mountain have drastically fragmented reality and cut themselves off from life. Oblivious to the contingencies of everyday existence, the villagers spend their time constructing fantastic mental worlds which they are incapable of materializing, however, because in this realm materialization implies degradation—a "fall" into the physical world and hence into an inexorable progress toward death.

By mechanically reiterating their futile mental activity, the mountain dwellers have succeeded in arresting the flow of time, and hence in this world everything relentlessly endures. Although they have reached adulthood, they do not age; although they copulate, they do not reproduce; although they die, their bodies do not decay. As the cycle of life is suspended, they are caught "on a wheel that turns but does not move": an endless turning which dooms them to remain in a death-conferring, ever-reiterated now.

Valenzuela suggests that people who live by arresting life are in effect already dead: "Life entails a progression towards death. To remain stagnant is to be *already* dead" (author's italics). Thus the parallel village erected on the opposite side of the mountain to house the dead constitutes an appropriate symbol of a life spent in dispossessing the world of life.

Clearly Valenzuela goes further than the machine and the robot metaphor, for, in her fictional world, life is not only seen as reduced to eternally identical motion but also as already nullified or as "petrified." The image of "the stone" and the awareness of its perils, which haunt the protagonist, expresses her fear of the ultimate nullification presumably involved in death. (This nihilistic notion is further dramatized, it will be recalled, by the fact that the villagers no longer reproduce.)

That the dead town mirrors the village of the "living" is ironic since the former provides the only "reflection" in an otherwise reflectionless universe. Valenzuela presents this world as devoid of mirrors and of reflecting waters of any kind, a universe where nothing reflects anything and where entities are self-contained. In this essentially solipsistic world even language is expendable, for the language they speak no longer serves the purpose of allowing people to communicate through a set of shared meanings. It is a lifeless language whose meaning has long been forgotten and which permits them to relate only by interpreting intonations and pauses, facial expressions and sighs.

Valenzuela's point is well made. To live exclusively within the boundaries of the mind, however formidable its power, is tantamount to dealing life a lethal blow. In the villagers Valenzuela has symbolized the flight into the realm of mind that turns out to be a flight into the realm of death. In her protagonist, conversely, she has allegorized a passionate love of life—a yearning to redeem the world from death, a yearning which can only be fulfilled when she has redeemed herself.

Although the story focuses primarily on a single night, the course the woman follows is gradual. At first she merely struggles to turn away from the mind and celebrate the material universe by searching to rediscover both her body and the natural world. Thus she often runs barefoot, seeking to become one with nature and her myriad objects, and takes occasional pictures of herself, attempting to identify with her body and its gradual decay. (It will be recalled that there are no mirrors in the place.)

As she heals the split between the mind and matter, the unnamed narrator readies herself for a decisive confrontation with her unconscious. It is clear that the terrifying abysses which have prevented her return home symbolize the frightening depths of the unconscious mind which she must face to be redeemed from death.

The momentous confrontation occurs on a clear night filled with the rattle of cans placed on the houses of the dead. As the protagonist prepares to shoot the last picture of herself (she has one frame left), a startling luminosity, produced by the moonlight shining on the cans, causes her to release the shutter. Rather than capturing her image, the camera photographs a "veiled stone wall," an incident the woman hardly notices, however, for she is now transfigured by the unexpected effulgence. Suddenly, seized by an uncontrollable urge, the narrator clutches all the pictures and rushes downhill: "They are calling me from down below, the call coming from the left, and I respond and at first I run down the precarious road and when there is no longer a road I struggle on nonetheless, I stumble and climb and stumble again and hurt myself . . . at times I lose my footing and slip and slide . . . with my body I attempt to stop myself. The thorns tear my flesh but they also prevent me from sliding further. . . . In despair I struggle on for I must continue."

In this splendid scene Valenzuela depicts her protagonist as a woman transformed by passion—the passion, undoubtedly, that attends all formidable insights. By heeding a call that seems to emanate from the entrancing radiance (but which, in reality, arises from within), the woman accedes to a descent into the depths of mind which is underscored by her perilous descent downhill toward the city of the dead: her shed blood and torn flesh, by which her inner death is reflected in the external realm, consecrate the world. In other words, the protagonist dies to her deadly fragmentation and is reborn to a life-bestowing wholeness—a wholeness that bonds her to the others and ultimately unites her with the life force: the sacred source of life.

Calmly and assuredly now, all sense of urgency gone, she marches on to the secret city to redeem the dead: "I will reach the city of the dead and I will give them the successive expressions of my face and at last I will be able to set out on my journey back to the lowlands, no longer fearing the stone because I will carry the last picture with me and I am in the picture and I am the stone." By attaching to the faces of the dead the photos of the successive expressions of her own face, the protagonist symbolically restores the dead to life. Thus she may affirm at the close of the story that she "is in the picture" and that she is "the stone"—the former assertion alluding to her mutating self and hence to life, the latter to the stone and hence to death. Within herself, as within the entire universe, life and death coexist—a life that perpetually unfolds and enfolds, manifests and returns to the unmanifest.

The fact that the protagonist-narrator of Valenzuela's story is a woman is not coincidental. The author is evidently hinting at the view, presently held by many, that the emergence of women will be *the* decisive force in healing the Western world of its death orientation.

Throughout its history, Western culture has been fundamentally masculine, the male of the species consistently regarded as the repository of the power of the mind, the privileged being rising above the carnal, the material and the nonrational—the domains traditionally linked to woman. "Male and female," writes a well-known feminist, "have been related to each other as mind and body. The male owns and subordinates the female just as the mind controls and manipulates the body," or just as the ego subjugates the unconscious drives.

Exiled from the culture-making processes, woman has in fact remained more closely aligned with and attuned to the elements of reality that man has obsessively struggled to subdue. Not surprisingly, the image of the carnal, lustful and demonic female, incarnated in the witch, has haunted the Western mind throughout history. Clearly the witch embodies the everpresent danger of uncontrollable forces lurking in the shadows, a danger finally materialized in our world with the advent of feminism.

Modern witchcraft underlies a contemporary brand of feminism regarded as "spiritual" by some of its adherents—the notion of "spirit" in this instance pointing to that of the life-giving world soul. This discloses the subtle relation between the release of long-repressed energies in the field of science and the emergence of the long-repressed female in the social sphere, for, in fact, woman embodies the life force—the creative, transformative principle.

Intrinsically linked to the cycles of birth and rebirth both in the human and the natural worlds (let us recall that the earth has been consistently perceived as female), woman possesses a more profound awareness of reality's inherent tendency to endlessly transform itself. Thus the moon in its three phases—waxing, full, and waning—has become the main metaphor for modern witchcraft and hence of spiritual feminism. Valenzuela's heroine, let it be remembered, is impelled by the moon-generated radiance to set out on the sacred task of transforming herself and the world she inhabits. In this respect, she incarnates the witch.

Inasmuch as they honor the essential oneness of the world, spiritual feminists regard their commitment to social change as necessarily grounded on a commitment to their inner selves: only a mind that has transcended fragmentation is empowered to reach out and heal others and ultimately to link with the life force itself.

It is evident, then, that holism involves the mind in a special way, for it is human awareness of the world's interrelatedness that sets the interrelatedness in motion—as if the universe itself sought recreation by rediscovering the long-repressed bond with the human mind.

By moving from the isolated ego-consciousness to the awareness of wholeness, Valenzuela's protagonist effectively retraces the steps that mark the Western mind's progressive estrangement from the vital source, and hence the implication of a return home at the close of **"Where the Eagles Dwell."**

In a world like ours, haunted by the specter of annihilation, the holistic stance is obviously essential. Therein lies the ultimate significance of Luisa Valenzuela's tale. (pp. 109-13)

Zulma Nelly Martinez, "Luisa Valenzuela's 'Where the Eagles Dwell': From Fragmentation to Holism," in The Review of Contemporary Fiction, *Vol. 6, No. 3, Fall, 1986, pp. 109-15.*

What society accepts or rejects ought not concern the female writer. What cannot be said even by her because it remains censured in her dark subconscious—that is serious. They are the only truths worth being written.

—*Luisa Valenzuela, in* Women's Voices from Latin America, *1985*.

Barbara Pauler Fulks   (essay date 1988)

[*In the following essay, Fulks presents a close analysis of "La palabra asesino."*]

Luisa Valenzuela, an Argentinian who has lived and worked in France and the United States, was connected with the *Tel Quel* literary movement in Paris in the 1960s. Other members of this group included Julia Kristeva, Roland Barthes, and Tzvetan Todorov. Jacques Lacan was delivering his lectures on psychoanalysis during the same period. Valenzuela acknowledges the influence Lacan has had on her writing. His structuring of the unconscious, the idea of multiple significations for a signifier and the image of the dismembered body are Lacanian constructs present in her prose. The 1960s constellation of a new theory of language, a psychoanalysis based on this theory, and a revolutionary feminism would seem to demand a new and different fictional voice. Valenzuela's prose addresses the problematics of language, gender and self.

How does the feminine voice penetrate the monolithic structure of masculine discourse? **"La palabra asesino"** is an exploration of this problem. "Ella," the first word of the story, foregrounds gender. The text will be narrated from a feminine point of view, a transgression of traditional Latin American configuration of assumed or explicit masculine narration with the feminine order serving as a catalyst for action and thought. The use of the pronoun serves various functions. First, as a linguistic term, *ella* is a deictic pointer. As a third-person pronoun, it situates the narrator and reader at a distance from the character. The reader is not invited to enter the more intimate I/you relationship of first-person narration, rather, she and the narrator will be observers of this character. Second, "ella" is a generic (or gyneric) pronoun. "She" lacks a proper name which would establish her individuality and specificity. The textual proper name is also an echo of a social order in which women, bearing the names of fathers and/or husbands, are exchanged as property. Thus, in the first textual word, the reader apprehends a space (as observer), an order (the feminine), and an absence (proper social identity).

The opening sentence provides a paradigm for the narration to follow and sets up a hermeneutic puzzle for the reader. "Ella merodea por la vida en busca de una respuesta." Because the verb is in the present tense and the pronoun as yet lacks corporeality, the sentence could be read as an observation on the feminine condition or plight: the quest for an answer. What is striking here and what shifts the observation from cliché to renovation is the opening of space for the feminine. The quest motif in masculine literature is common; the realm of the feminine character is traditionally confined to the interior space of home and hearth. The verb "merodea" situates this character at large in the world and attributes to her the capacity to assume the various connotations of the verb: plunder, pillage, rob. What she robs and what answer she is looking for are the questions to be unraveled in the text.

The second sentence negates the validity of the quest: "Las respuestas no existen." Presented in the form of a dictum, an authoritative pronouncement, the reader may question the genesis of the statement. Is the narrator intruding in the text or is the statement a discovery of the character, "ella"? The question is important because if it is the narrator's voice, the reader is instructed along with "ella" not to look for answers. If it represents the character's voice, the reader is still free to separate herself from the character's plight. What is the character's plight? I am going to interpret it as the quest for self-knowledge or identity situated in language in a gendered subject.

Post-Freudian psychoanalytic theory provides a basis for an understanding of the notion of self. According to Lacan, identity is constituted through language. The gendered subject enters the Symbolic Order or the world of language through a metaphoric rupture from the mother and entry into the Word or Law of the Father. This entry into the Symbolic Order is problematical for the female. Language is a preconstituted monolithic representation of a social order when the subject enters. The feminine in this symbolic order is construed as an absence, a lack. If possession of the Phallus (the Word) provides the male subject access to discourse, where is the phallusless feminine order located? "Woman is excluded by the nature of words, meaning that the phallic definition poses her as exclusion."

In *Speculum of the Other Woman,* Luce Irigaray demonstrates the result of woman's non-status in language. The phallocentric discourse of patriarchy interprets reality in what Irigaray calls "The Law of the Self-same." The logic of this law advances sets of binary oppositions such as the following: light/dark, order/chaos, rationality/irrationality, male/female. In each set, the left-hand term is a presence, the right-hand an absence. Thus, instead of representing oppositions, the terms are the positive and negative poles of the same quality. Femininity is cast as the absence of masculinity. In the privileged discourses of traditional philosophy, literature, and psychoanalysis, the feminine is held up as a metaphorical mirror in which male interprets himself.

Valenzuela's prose seeks a new epistemology, a new way of apprehending or making "reality." **"La palabra asesino"** is divided into nine sections, each of which develops a motif of the nature of self-knowledge. The first section introduces the theme of knowledge with the verbs *saber* and *conocer*. The repetition of *conocer* implies a process of knowing which leads to an end: "para saber hay que . . . conocer y conocer." The quest is presented as dangerous, "quizá no se vuelva," and painful, "en carne viva," and it leads to desire.

Desire is a key concept of post-Freudian psychoanalytic discourse bearing both sexual and linguistic dimensions. In Lacan's theory, desire originates when the child experiences its self or body as separated from that of the mother. Before this separation, the child is part of what Lacan labels the Imaginary Order. As Toril Moi interprets Lacan:

> The Imaginary corresponds to the pre-Oedipal period when the child believes itself to be a part of the mother, and perceives no separation between itself and the world. In the Imaginary there is no difference and no absence, only identity and presence. The Oedipal crisis represents the entry into the Symbolic Order. This entry is also linked to the acquisition of language. In the Oedipal crisis the father splits up the dyadic unity between mother and child and forbids the child further access to the mother and the mother's body. The phallus, representing the Law of the Father (or the threat of castration), thus comes to signify separation and loss to the child [Toril Moi, *Sexual/Textual Politics*].

This desire for the mother is repressed and the child develops a sense of self and other. The self, however, is constituted upon a lack. The pronoun, I, is constantly shifting and unity is never achieved. Language also is symbolic of loss. The act of naming represents a lack of the object named. There is no single, unified relationship between the signified and the signifier. Words are constantly slipping into other connotations. The desire for a unity of meaning, like the desire for union with the mother, is continually displaced.

Social institutions are reflective of this desire for unity, according to Julia Kristeva. Theorizing desire as the origin of monotheism, she writes:

> There is one unity: an increasingly purified community discipline, that is isolated as a transcendent principle and which thereby ensures the survival of the group. This unity which is represented by the God of monotheism is sustained by a desire that pervades the community, a desire which is at once stirring and threatening. Remove this threatening desire, the dangerous support of cohesion, from man; place it beside him and create a supplement for what is lacking in this man who speaks to his God; and you have woman, who has no access to the word, but who appears as the pure desire to seize it, or as that which ensures the permanence of the divine paternal function for all humans: that is, the desire to continue the species [*The Kristeva Reader*].

Kristeva is describing one institution, religion, but the theory applies to all social institutions which are inscribed in language as unities of meaning. As Valenzuela puts it: "El deseo cabe en todas partes."

Desire also has a sexual dimension, but if woman has no access to the word in the Symbolic Order, then her desire cannot be expressed in the language of patriarchy, which defines her desire in terms of masculine desire. There seems to be an impasse here, an insurmountable blockage for the feminine order. Kristeva has, however, in very abstract theoretical discourse, postulated the unconscious as providing the means to break through the monolithic system of language. The unconscious functions not *in* language but as an inner pressure or pulsion *under* language. This pressure can be found in the silent spaces or gaps in the language system, in what cannot be written or spoken, and is more likely to be found in the discourse of marginalized groups in the social system. Returning to Valenzuela's story, we find desire described as "una pulsión interna, un latido de ansiedad incontenible."

In the second segment of Valenzuela's text the masculine enters as a speaking, dialogic self. He is not given a proper name, but he attains corporeality through the social and historical details of his life. He has a past and a future. He is a subject in space and in time. These concrete details of age, relationship to social institutions and a project for the future contrast with the indefinite position of *ella* in the previous segment. His space has been one of confinement in institutions. He is signalled as a marginal member of society, like the feminine order. He and she meet during "una amable fiesta." Mikhail Bakhtin describes the incursion of subversive discourse or parody in the Middle Ages as occurring in an atmosphere of holidays and festivals. Authoritative discourse breaks down in a festive mode, perhaps in the nature of Kristeva's internal pressures bearing on the Symbolic Order. Valenzuela describes the party as "lejos de toda barrera."

The motif of the second segment, the contrast between the senses of touch and sight, develops the theme of self-knowledge in the introductory section. The eye, a sign of vision and illumination, is the privileged sense organ in the patriarchal discourse of authority. According to Irigaray, "the predominance of the visual, and of the discrimination and individualization of form, is particularly foreign to female eroticism. Woman takes pleasure more from touching than from looking." [Luce Irigaray, *This Sex Which Is Not One*]. In Valenzuela's text there is a cluster of vision-related words surrounding *él:* "no oculta," "revela," "mirar," "ojo a ojo," "aclaración." "She" takes all the clarifications as only pieces of him; her knowledge of him comes from the touch of his skin.

The following segment moves from texture to text. In the first paragraph there is further development of light-relational comparisons. He is literally ("piel") and figuratively ("pasado") dark, but transparent. She, on the other hand, is opaque. In Lacan's metaphorical mirror of self, the masculine becomes a subject as a result of his reflected mirror image. Sight and light are privileged here because without light (enlightenment) nothing would be seen. This subject, *él,* is dark—subversive in the social order—but transparent; his subjectivity or self can be imagined. Feminine subjectivity or self is empty space where no light enters.

In order to have a sense of form, a self, an ego, she wears his skin and colors herself with his color. She wears a mask of his self to understand him better. With this texture the textuality begins. The narration calls attention to itself as writing: "tantos hilos que parecen ir atándose hasta simular la trama. Como si configuraran un entendimiento." And so, distanced from realism by several layers—it is only a simulacrum of a simulacrum—the reader enters a plot.

The plot begins with a tactile body, his body, and the metaphorical associations it evokes in the narrator: "animal de la noche," "piel de boa constrictor," "la selva." Touch words abound in the first paragraph: "la mano," "acaricia," "tocado," "tacto," "la yema de los dedos." Beginning in a context of sexual presence, both temporal (present tense) and corporeal (*su cuerpo*), the narration shifts to incorporate past and future references. With the repetition of "a lo largo de" and the substitution of "años" for "su cuerpo" the narrator anticipates future time ("recuperará"), and ties it to a distant past time—"algo tan antiguo y sabio como una porcelana S'ung o las tapas de un volumen encuadernado en cuero de Rusia." The male body

Dust jacket for Argentine edition of Other Weapons.

here is being abstracted and made archetypal, an inversion of the uses made of the female body in literature. This narrated male body is a shell, a speaking skin whose self-narration reads as superficial as his covering. The inner consciousness in this text belongs to *ella*.

In the second paragraph of this section the reader is advised at the outset not to naturalize "his" narration into some sort of realistic account. Two kinds of narration are contrasted. Hers, "ensoñaciones literarias," are related to the unconscious dream world. His are related to the mimesis of drawing, describing through speech. In her rendition of his history the discourse becomes a rapid concatenation of preterite verbs: "vivió," "peleó," "robó," "se nutrió," "pegó." The explosive alliteration of hard *c* sounds of "un corte drástico a la droga," "la cura cold turkey" contrasts with the fluid, sibilant feminine discourse of the previous paragraph: "acaricia," "tersura," "sedosa," "lujurioso," "selva." His text traces his need for nurture from mother to lover. She, as mother, will feed him—"gota a gota" suggests mother's milk. As goddess she will renounce self, "como un acto de amor religioso." As lover she will also feed him: "el placer que él le brinda a ella lo alimenta." Mother, goddess and lover are traditional feminine images in masculine literature. They are images of lack from a feminist perspective, male imaging female in his own image. As this section closes, the Edenic garden, "sin tiempo y sin espacio," is confronted with "la noción de muerte," and the narration focuses on a specific time, "esta noche."

Valenzuela has said, "without life there is no death; without death there is no life. By denying death we automatically deny life." This statement may be applied to the longest section of **"la palabra asesino."** Death is explored from various angles, embracing both the metaphorical and the empirical. The first sentence signals the metaphorical realm of death and poses the narrator as victim: "ella admite no saber qué le va a matar antes, si las ensoñaciones literarias o la calentura." "Las ensoñaciones literarias" is a repetition which was previously used to describe the narrator's writing as a search for self-identity rather than a mimetic description of reality. The quest here is a process of investigating the feminine self in relation with and opposed to the masculine self. According to both psychoanalysis and modern theories of language, identity is always an opposition. As Jacqueline Rose posits woman's psychic dilemma:

> what could be a place without identity, other than a falling into the realm of the unnameable body without language, a realm to which women have often and so oppressively been confined? . . . The act of differentiation-recognition of the other leads—if not to violence—then, at least, and of necessity, to psychic pain.

The literary act is thus a threatening one.

"La calentura," a sexual metaphor, is also posed as threatening. According to Garfield:

> Valenzuela adheres to many of Georges Bataille's ideas which link orgasm and death to religious experience, taboo and transgression, desire

and terror, and anguish. Eroticism embodies the violence and violation of death, a temporary negation of individuality on the part of two mortals who aspire to a fleeting union with eternity, the 'little death' of an orgasm that erases for a moment their isolated existences.

Bataille's pornographic novels also equate the face with the genitals [Susan Rubin Suleiman, "Pornography, Transgression, and the Avant-Garde: Bataille's *Story of the Eye.*" *The Poetics of Gender.* Ed. Nancy K. Miller.] and in this section of Valenzuela's text there is a constant shifting from the narrator's detailed, erotic descriptions of "his" face to an investigation and judgment of his empirical actions so that a relationship between body and action is established. His face is described in terms of size and shape which are also applicable to his sexual organ: "afilada," "altos," "recta," (repeated three times), "larguísimos," "punta," "rosada," "de no huesos." His justification for his crimes is that his victims did not like his face: "No les gustó mi cara." "She" verbally explores his face, equating it to his penis and then rejects his explanation and shifts her attention to his shotgun, a shift which moves the text from the metaphorical order characterizing the feminine narration to the empirical order of specific actions in time and space.

The narrator's quest for self-knowledge requires her to interpret and judge his actions, not only in the realm of her desire, but also in the realm of a real social order. She finds his justifications of murder wanting and her judgment of him takes the shape of a still unspoken word: "ha enunciado interiormente la palabra asesino." Her reflections on death then take her from judging his actions in the anti-social world of crime to a consideration of violence and death perpetrated on a national level. His violence is associated with that of young male Somocistas trained in torture who, when asked to draw a human figure, can only draw mutilated bodies.

The narrator is forced to contaminate herself in this "orden subvertido por la muerte." Continuing the juxtaposition of sex and violence on a metaphorical level, she posits water and fire as the two possibilities of disaster. She has described not to avoid the connections her quest have suggested. She assumes the image of a bird and the verbal associations multiply. "Imitar al pato" connects the bird image to masochism, playing a victim. "Las infames posiciones sin gracia, los despatarramientos" connects the feminine open-leg sexual position to the notion of death. Her sex is described as emitting an "olor marítimo." Water seems to suggest a primal, womblike state, the status of the Lacanian subject previous to the entry into the Symbolic Order. The subject in the Imaginary (Lacanian) or Semiotic (Kristevan) Order has no sense of body image, no sense of self, and so is not even actually a subject. The feminine order, with no access to language of the Symbolic Order is awash in this area of no-meaning, non-self.

Fire, the other symbolic possibility of disaster, is also connected to sexual desire and self-destruction. The metaphors of heat, fire, firearms, destruction, and death are associated with his and other males' propensity to violence.

The water imagery continues with the reflexive verb

"sondearse," referring to his quest for self. His specular image, focused on the sense of vision, is characterized by her as a false one, inverted and distant. The male quest is narcissistic, a search for self which negates Other. He can only use her as a mirror to see himself reflected, reinforcing his subjectivity while denying her as radical Other.

At the end of this section, the narrator describes herself as on the verge of madness brought on by the contradictions of loving an assassin and perhaps loving him because he is an assassin. The pattern of sadism and masochism as embodied in the male and female orders can only be broken by her entry into his order, the order of cruelty: "Qué más le queda a ella? Ella misma salir a matar, salir a subvertir el orden."

In the following section the narrator's shift into the masculine order brings her face to face with the possibility of violence: "Este hombre me va a golpear." Since she is now in his order she feels the immanence of a confrontation. She shifts again from the empirical to the textual order to leave him "estampado en el papel, sacándoselo cold turkey." The vaguely referential bird imagery that she had used to suggest herself, "plumas cerosas," has been displaced by the violent connotations of cold turkey. Thus she imagines that she, as torturer, has inflicted lash marks on his back.

Changing places again, she fantasizes herself as victim in the next section. This fantasy lends itself to a much more realistic reading than the female sadist fantasy of the previous section because of its juxtaposition to the narration of his history. Just as he had murdered in the past, so had he tied up his wife. His cruelty is always textually tied to empirical reality and then associated with larger acts of social violence such as the war in Viet Nam and the Nicaraguan dictatorship.

She finally reaches a state of crisis in which she figuratively shatters into pieces. The mirror image is replaced by a fluidity untranslatable by language: "no hay palabras que traduzcan el vórtice del torbellino." She is in a space beyond the specular image of the Symbolic Order, a space of self-disintegration which leads to "la tentación del salto" or a breakthrough into self-knowledge. When she shouts "asesino," she is born into the Symbolic Order, the Law of the Fathers. Whether the word is an accusation of him or a calling to him from her desire, it is an epithet of judgment enunciated from the feminine space of subjectivity.

The segmented form of this text echoes the fragmented feminine morphology. There is no unity, only pieces of the self. Moreover, the feminine self can only be conceptualized in its position of opposition to the masculine self which in turn denies the existence of the feminine except as a reflection of its self. There can be no confrontation of Self and Other in a relationship in which the masculine sees only one self. **"La palabra asesino"** investigates an attempt to break through this impasse, to find a feminine voice. Each segment explores a piece of self viewed through the masculine and feminine orders. Relationship to knowledge, sensory perceptions, self-narration, language, socialization, violence, sex and death are elaborat-

ed from opposing perspectives. The narrator's breakthrough from the Imaginary Order to the Symbolic Order of language has been achieved at tremendous psychic cost. Her first act of naming signals her birth as a subject, but what position this subject will assume in relationship to the Other is the open end of this text. (pp. 179-88)

Barbara Pauler Fulks, "A Reading of Luisa Valenzuela's Short Story, 'La palabra asesino'," in Monographic Review/Revista Monográfica, *Vol. IV, 1988, pp. 179-88.*

Valenzuela on the situation of the woman writer:

We artists, in general, tend to believe ourselves to be a special race, but this is only one more aspect of our illusions. For that very reason, a woman writer's situation is different from a man's, since it is a matter of one more reflexion of woman's place with respect to man. And I don't want to begin with complaints, that are not always so, about problems concerning publishing or being translated. No. I prefer to circumscribe my comments to a simple fact, which Tillie Olsen points out so well: a woman, who manages a house and raises children, lacks the free time so necessary for writing. And, above all, she lacks a wife to support her in everything and, if necessary, to act as her secretary. I believe that those are the basic problems, besides an undeniable lack of recognition on the part of the publishing house machinery in Hispanic America that separates us most from the Nobel Prize.

Luisa Valenzuela, in Women's Voices from Latin America, *by Evelyn Picon Garfield, 1985.*

Denise M. Marshall   (essay date 1989)

[In the excerpt below, Marshall offers a favorable review of The Open Door.*]*

Valenzuela's tapestries are captured for us in **Open Door** in these thirty-two stories, fourteen of them published in English for the first time. One of the chief pleasures of reading Valenzuela is her improbable images, fantastic colors, and ineffable design. The title of the collection, **Open Door,** is apt, for it swings wide a portal on the fictional worlds of a writer from whom English readers have been shut away. While Valenzuela's other stories have been published in English, they are now quite difficult to find. **Open Door** includes selections from them all—it serves as overview, introduction, and perhaps an impetus for reissuing her other collections. In the magnificent variety of these short stories, Valenzuela has put together a kaleidoscopic vision where each facet opens a new vista onto the strange, the odd, the familiar, and the human.

Valenzuela's narratives swirl around fantastic realities where color and shape hold sway over the mind; language forms that landscape's tints and habitations, whether of human structure or natural coruscations. Language forms the mindscapes of her characters, as their words take shape from and give form to their environments. In the mindscape, thought, action and word fuse reality and imagination into what happens. And that transcends other reality or imagination. The territory melds familiar with strange, emotional with detached, imagination with reason, lyrical with grotesque. "The step from watching over the bread [money] to watching over the flower isn't that great if you're liberal with your puns" muses the security guard for a financial corporation. Fond of the building plants, he fantasizes caring for them, and this small desire triggers a transformation "as if someone had given him the famous kiss on his sleeping forehead, as if he had awakened, illuminated."

A liberality with puns leads easily into the plastic quality these stories invest in language. One of Valenzuela's greatest talents is her remarkable ability to sculpt words and sentences. Puns here are both play with words and words playing inside the field of language. "The senses and gods intersect in this part of the world, assuming these parts are of the world and not strung over the Andes, just beyond arm's reach." This playfulness of language creates a humor intrinsic to the point of view and expressed fluidly throughout. "They survive, growing wise, and for that very reason, nobody wants to listen to them." But the double-edged humor often points to hard-earned wisdom, little appreciated truths, and unexpected disaster. "The things now floating downriver, unsettling everyone, are subtle, anchored to the huge water lilies, almost like words. That is, they are messages; they are disasters." The language as it yields up this play and this humor is sinuous and surprising. In the kaleidoscope of Valenzuela, surprise is the flash in the facets.

Surprise informs the narrative technique as well. The delighted reader cannot predict the outcome of language, plot, or character. Perhaps the only predictability is the sureness of the author's touch, and in that we are content. Surprise occurs in the familiar wandering through these pages under strange new names. Celery munchers are possibly doing it "as a sign of nonconformity . . . or perhaps they're doing it out of a sense of superiority . . . " Walls are built to keep out nature but a thistle foils the plan. Another part of the surprise of these stories is the transformations with which Valenzuela is fascinated, from transformations of thought to fantastical transformation of one being into another. She pursues these transformations to their sources and imagines the process as emblematic. Thus, the faceted spaces inside her kaleidoscope are interrelated in such a way that the sense of a network of connection is an inescapable part of reading any of these stories. What we don't know is which facet is going to flash next, and that is the joy of discovery and recognition that is the *Open Door.*

> Denise M. Marshall, "Among Eagles and Lizards," in Belles Lettres: A Review of Books by Women, *Vol. 4, No. 2, Winter, 1989, p. 3.*

Patricia Rubio   (essay date 1989)

[*In the following essay, Rubio examines the relationship between the narrative structure of Valenzuela's works and her vision of life.*]

Luisa Valenzuela's writing belongs to that class of con-temporary works Umberto Eco has called "open works." In them the harmonious representation of reality, supported by logic and syllogism, is replaced by a more ample and complex vision in which the laws of causality cease to operate in a linear fashion. The ordered *Weltanschauung* of the standard realist narrative—the tradition to which *Clara,* Valenzuela's first novel, and **The Heretics,** her first collection of short stories, belong—disintegrates in the face of desire, cruelty, the instinctual, the magical, the fantastic, the sickly. The rules governing ordinary discourse are trampled on. The causality governing the typical realist plot is replaced by association and disjunction. The objective of Valenzuela's writing is not the mimetic representation of reality, but rather the creation of fictive worlds bearing witness to their own process of mutation. Valenzuela's writing, at least in the works I will be referring to, neither affirms nor defines; instead, it questions constantly, interrogating the world and, in the process, also interrogating itself.

One of the central structural units of many of these open texts is the fragment. Because, in Octavio Paz's words, the fragment is an "errant particle," it implies the destruction of linearity, both in the discourse and in the story, and leads to opening or dispersion in multiple directions. The order governing both the enunciation and the enunciated of realist narrative reveals the prevalence of a rational vision of the world; the fragment is by contrast an expression of the irrational and surprising.

The fragment is most especially an essential element in Valenzuela's most ambitious works, including *Cat-O-Nine-Deaths, He Who Searches,* **Book That Doesn't Bite,** and a great number of the short stories collected in **Strange Things Happen Here.** "We are fragmented," says Valenzuela; "nothing is univocal; there is no unity; God is unity; we are pieces." Such a view is already present in the first novel, *Clara.* [In a footnote, the critic adds: "In *Clara,* the protagonist's body is first fragmented in illusory terms, by means of a circus trick—the Aztec flower—which produces in the spectator the illusion that the victim's head is being separated from the body. The novel, however, closes when the executor of the trick, Clara's husband, is truly ready to cut her throat."] In it, as in some of Valenzuela's later texts, fragmentation does not affect the structure of the text, but is present, as a thematic concern. The characters in these stories may be victims of physical dismemberment, as in the case of the main character in *Clara* and **"My daily horse,"** or they may be fragmented by a dualist and mechanistic understanding of the world, as in the case of the protagonist of **"Up Among the Eagles."** In most of the tales in **Strange Things Happen Here** and **Up Among the Eagles,** as in several stories of **Other Weapons,** we find that the fragmentation goes beyond individual experience and is a characteristic of the society at large, a pervasive consequence of political persecution, torture, and fear. The country as a whole may be said to be fragmented, with division between those who live in the city and those who live in the hinterland; between the oppressors who live comfortably, and the others who are underground. These others perceive the "strange things" that reveal the country's fragmentation and understand that the tranquility of the official order is mere appearance.

But the fragmentation in Valenzuela is extraordinarily various. The narrative of *Cat-O-Nine-Deaths* is composed of a series of microstories none of which turns upon ordered causality. Almost none of these texts, furthermore, develops a narrative line from beginning to end. The fragments are pieces of experiences, sensations, bits of dreams, imaginings, sudden occurrences, organized by association or by way of strategic juxtaposition. Between one story and the next, and within the stories themselves, there are spaces that remain unfilled. The following passage characteristically reveals Valenzuela's procedures:

> He told her tomorrow we'll see each other and she, naively, believed him. How could a cat woman fail to see the cat? And how was it that he, who was so much the rat, didn't know how to escape her? This cat had eyes of brass and in the village it was snowing. Beneath the snow a poster declared that God was alive and well in Argentina.

Between the various fragments one finds recurring elements: there are the cats of death and the dogs of life, or the narrator's crippled friend who makes several intermittent appearances. Certain thematic units also recur, such as the relationship between eros and thanatos, or between language and eroticism; other topics include the absurdity of the idea of progress, and an incisive denunciation of Argentinian fascism. These concerns, sometimes mentioned in passing, other times dealt with in–depth, give the text a certain unity, while simultaneously dispersing it in several directions at once. There is no specific focus, no center; only fragments which are constantly being further fragmented. No wonder the narrator of *Cat-O-Nine-Deaths,* acknowledging the atomization of the story, says "nothing has happened here and nothing will happen."

In *He Who Searches,* Valenzuela develops a story propelled by the traditional motif of the search. This, however, does not insure the novel's unity; rather, it ironizes it. Although the story progresses, it appears and dissolves like rings of smoke, questioning and undoing itself at every turn. Almost at the center of the novel the university professor, a protagonist in search of the woman with whom he has had many encounters, says: "There has never been anybody here, this room has been deserted for more than a thousand years and if she passed through here a few days ago then my theory is proven: she is nobody." **"Fourth Version,"** in *Other Weapons,* offers a similar, although less radical structure. The text one reads is made up of pre-existent fragments (or pre-texts), and the so-called "fourth version" corresponds to the ordering that the narrative voice has given to these fragments:

> There are so many pages written . . . I read and reread and at times order and reorder them randomly. I stumble across complex components and bump into multiple beginnings. I study, discard and recover them and try to place them appropriately in a furious attempt to revitalize the puzzle.

The writing, then, does not entail developing a story but

creating a text which itself becomes the search for new ways of exploring meaning, connectedness, order, disorder.

The fragmentation of the story obviously affects every dimension of the narrative: the categories of time and space are made to inform a new vision of the world in which indeterminacy and discontinuity replace definiteness and certainty, and simultaneity replaces succession. Wandering takes precedence over directedness. "If I am in Buenos Aires how I love to wander at daybreak through the Village," says the narrative voice of *Cat-O-Nine-Deaths,* and in *He Who Searches* we read, "Here I am: traveling the Moebius strip through America because the space where she is to be found is not Euclidian space nor is her time the same time of which we're dimly aware when we see our skin aging." In Luisa Valenzuela's worlds, Euclidian space is but one of several spacial dimensions. The others can only be formulated by non-Euclidian geometry. The fragmented text puts the reader, sometimes dimly, sometimes sharply, in touch with those other, literary geometries, prompting us to seek unexplored pieces of reality and to participate in the destruction of the usual modes of apprehending the world.

Characters also partake in this process of fragmentation which proceeds from the progressive dissolution of their names (Beatriz, Bea, Be, B or AZ, in *He Who Searches,* or Bella, Bella, B in **"Fourth Version"**), to their physical obliteration: "I am afraid of falling apart, . . . I am afraid of exploding and spattering all four walls, afraid that a part of me, only a part, may reach her in her image" (*He Who Searches*). In **"Neither the Most Terrifying Nor the Most Memorable,"** a short story in *Strange Things Happen Here,* we find the most radical fragmentation of the character unit. In this story parts of the protagonist's body become city spaces, producing in the end a cubistic image involving the human body and the city: "His mouth is the block between Corrientes and Lavalle, at Anchorena (the produce market) with a little intersecting street that is the Calle Gardel, where sometimes he sings a nostalgic song and sometimes whistles to call the dog." In general, one can say that Valenzuela's characters are mutants, partly human, partly paper figures, who don't, at least in the works we have cited, achieve a definite human configuration. Take for example the following scene from *Cat-O-Nine-Deaths:*

> He has two lively little partridge eyes, the pointy ears of a cub and the teeth of a wild boar—all nicely kept in their little containers in the fridge.

The most radical dissolution occurs in the narrative discourse itself. Logically and normatively ordered discourse yields to one which denies its own capacity to represent. The discourse becomes opaque and diffuse, and in its expansion it seeks to establish itself as the sole "reality." We find in Valenzuela's work an interest in stretching language to its maximum, in affirming its reality as an object of inquiry. Most of her texts possess logomimetic characteristics in the sense that the words on the page establish themselves as signifiers with no evident value or meaning. The intention to destroy the meaning associated with a specific signifier is unmistakable. Valenzuela achieves this either by negating or by affirming—but always to the breaking point—the ambiguity of the linguistic sign. In her narrative, for example, the word "dog" *does* bite, as some of the texts and the title of *Book that Doesn't Bite* ironically reveal. The destruction of univocal meaning, on the other hand, is achieved, for example, by accumulating various meanings for one signifier: "Corriendo el albur, corriendo la liebre, corriendo el Amok . . . acabó claro está, estirando la pata" ("Running the risk, running scared, running amok, he ended up croaking"). In this example the meaning of the word "correr" (to run) slides in each expression into another meaning, and in the Spanish, it ends up in "estirando la pata," which literally means "stretching the leg," a colloquial expression akin to "kicking the bucket." Neologisms, the coupling or rupturing of words in order to create new ones, along with the use of "nonsense", also contribute to the dissolution of meaning. This is what Valenzuela is getting at in *Cat-O-Nine-Deaths* when she writes: "that's how my ludicrousidity unfolds to reveal what makes me feel good and well-disposed, it's what's attractive in me, what's fun." ("Mi ludicidad aflora así a revuelo para biendisponerme, es lo pático en mí, lo divertente.") The "exploration of the word, the kind of prostituted word we use daily," as Valenzuela has expressed it, is central to her assault on established systems of meaning and to the unfolding of her writerly temperament.

Other varieties of fragmentation include the abandonment of the paragraph, the destruction of syntax, the fragmented sentence and a punctuation system which introduces disorder rather than order into the sentence. Valenzuela also frequently incorporates literal translations of sayings—usually from English—which in the Spanish version do not evoke their original meaning and thus become nonsensical. The text thus finds itself in continuous metamorphosis and, as Nelly Martínez has indicated, "proclaims the defeat of logos and announces the closure of western episteme" ["*El gato eficaz* de Luisa Valenzuela," *Revista canadiense de estudios hispánicos* (1979)].

The fragmentation of the discourse also determines the handling of the narrative voice. Contrary to the narrator in realist fiction, who is easy to characterize, who often possesses total control over the narrated world, and whose word is reliable and of paramount importance for the understanding of the text, Valenzuela's narrator is in constant mutation: s/he is a transvestite, bisexual or hermaphrodite; s/he/it is an animal or an object, both singular and plural, sometimes combining both modes in one instance. In *He Who Searches* the narrator is typically slippery: "He (I shall henceforth call him I) knows (I know) that they will do us no harm; I know(s) many more things . . . " The comments offered by the narrator contribute to the reader's confusion, and rarely orient the reading process. Their function is clearly to underscore the ambiguity, even the mendacity, of the text: "The paper is a trap and nothing coming from it can be remembered. The paper is a trap, I am a trap made out of paper and printed characters." So we read in *Cat-O-Nine-Deaths*. The kaleidoscopic vision of the narrative voice suggests the possibility of multiple readings and interpretations. The reader, lacking elementary guidance, has to penetrate the verbal jungle in

order to find possible ways of ordering a puzzle in constant mutation.

> To die . . . to make room for someone else to assume my obligation and attempt to complete puzzles or break the heads s/he loves the most. But always very carefully, apologizing, following my mysteries step by step, making, for example, an apologia for the escape of truth, the escaped-truth.

The image of the text as a puzzle is important, not only because it refers back both to the fragmentary structure of the text and to the fact that it is only a point of departure requiring the reader's complicity for its completion, but also because it contributes to the conception of the text as a space and an object of play. In her texts Valenzuela refers principally to two games: chess, in which a set of rules regulates the moves available to the players; and puzzles, which are not regulated and the execution of which depends exclusively on the individual trying to complete them. There is another opposition between these two games that further emphasizes what I have been saying thus far: in chess, there is a hierarchy determining the value of the pieces, and hence the relative importance of the moves. In a puzzle, all the pieces or fragments are of equal value, and binary oppositions, such as white/black, do not exist. Valenzuela's definition of her narrative as a puzzle affirms its fragmentariness, and also alludes to its iconoclastic intentions.

There is, however, another element of game playing that seems worth mentioning, and that has to do with the very meaning of the term *play*. We are all familiar with the conventional idea of *play* associated with the word "ludens," but to "have play" (in Spanish, "tener juego") also means that two or more pieces are loosely linked together, that there is a space between the pieces which permits flexibility and thus gives the object freedom. This understanding of the word *play* is, I believe, important for the deciphering of the texts I have been considering. In Valenzuela's texts one does not reorder what exists, but rather searches for what is there as well as for what is not, for what needs a space for expression even though it is nowhere represented. Between one fragment and another there is such a space wherein the fragments may be said to "have play." And it is through this play, within the interstices between fragments, that Valenzuela's texts find their authentic meaning. (pp. 287-96)

> *Patricia Rubio, "Fragmentation in Luisa Valenzuela's Narrative," in* Salmagundi, *Nos. 82 & 83, Spring & Summer, 1989, pp. 287-96.*

Luisa Valenzuela with Marie-Lise Gazarian Gautier (interview date 1989)

[The following is an excerpt from three interviews Gautier conducted with Valenzuela in 1980, 1983, and 1988.]

[Gautier]: *[Jorge Luis] Borges said that he worked with a few themes which he carried over from work to work. Do you find that each novel or short story that you write is a total break from the previous work, or is each new book a modified version of the same theme?*

[Valenzuela]: I think it is both. The style, I feel, usually changes. I am always looking for different things to say and new ways of saying them. But there are small, or perhaps big obsessions, that come back again and again in a writer's work. One of my obsessions is with heresies, that very subtle point where any religion falls into heresy. Practically all living religions are heresies of the original dogma, and I find them marvelous because a human being should not be dogmatic at all. And there is also the theme of a search that comes back again and again in many of my works. I am still waiting to know what I am searching for.

Many of your characters are searching for identity. Will you explain why?

The Argentines are searching for an identity. We have a very undefined identity, which is also part of our charm, in a way. Because we are half European and did not have a great Indian culture from our past to support us, we do not believe in the past so much. But I do not know whether we even believe in the present, that is the trouble. At the same time, we are very literary people.

Do you think of yourself as a novelist or a short-story writer?

I think of myself as a writer. I don't like to put labels on things. I would just say that writing is a hard way of life. I don't like it too much. I do not think I like it too much.

Then why do you write?

It is a necessity and it is a great joy when writing is going on very well. When you are really doing fine, writing is fabulous, but there is all this inner struggle, and the inner fight of knowing you are not writing enough, and you are not doing it well enough. So, sometimes short stories come to me and sometimes a novel grows on its own.

When you start writing do you know whether it will be a short story or a novel?

Yes, although my first novel started out as a short story and turned into a novel, which surprised me very much. But now I know perfectly well what it is going to be at the outset, because the rhythm of a story is far different from that of a novel.

Could you describe your style, or is that difficult for you?

My style changes, it is a search for my own voice. The trouble is that the search never ends because one's voice is always changing. Voice is everything, language is everything, so I think the only way we can express ourselves is through this voice. It can be exterior or interior, but what is really important for me is language. I usually play with it a lot and mostly let it play with me.

You have said that your novels are "an active dialogue with the reader." Do you think of the reader when you write?

When writing, I think of myself as a reader. I enjoy it and surprise myself. I cannot write when I am not surprised, so I hope to do the same to the reader. I am always trying to present different possibilities and sufficient ambiguity in

writing, so that the reader can add his own level of reading to the work.

Are your characters figments of your imagination or are they derived from your personal experiences?

It is a cross between both. The experience might trigger an imaginative character. I seldom use myself as a character, although now I am trying to. But it is very hard because stories derived from my real life have no element of surprise for me. I am trying to be very much in touch with what we call reality, so I can allow it to grow on its own and not limit it to what I know for sure.

You have given seminars on the art of writing in many universities and also in Hispanic communities. Have you learned from your students?

You always learn a lot. Borges used to say that parents learn from their children, and as he never had children he learned from Bioy Casares. I learn a lot from my students. I do not think you can teach anybody to be a good writer. That is not only a natural gift but also a great struggle in which you have to look and fight all the time. But you can teach people this act of freedom, which writing is all about. And you receive that freedom at the same time as you give it. More than anything else, I would tell young people to say everything, to be very courageous about it and not to censor themselves.

Could you discuss the importance of disguise, mask, and change of identity in your works?

They are especially important in *Strange Things Happen Here.* I think that we are always using masks, we are never ourselves. You were laughing at me when I was trying to fix my hair before we started the interview, but that is my mask and I was trying to show a good face. The knowledge of our masks and the possibility of interrelating with others through these masks and disguises is very important. We are wearing them because we never have real access to our unconscious desire. The minute we become conscious of it, we lose it. So, the only way to reach certain strings of that desire is by wearing a mask.

Did you start writing because of your mother, Luisa Mercedes Levinson, who was an author in her own right?

I started writing in spite of my mother's career. There were many writers who came to our home, so I wanted to be a painter or a mathematician or something completely different. One day, I decided it would be very easy to write a short story which could be as good as any written by my mother's friends. I then wrote my first story and everything started growing on its own.

Are you a feminist writer?

I am against labels. I am a feminist in the sense that I am fighting for women to have all opportunities and freedom. What we women writers are looking for is a woman's language. We were never allowed to express ourselves in a very free way. So when women started writing they used an everyday pattern of speech which had been imposed on them by men. And I know there is a woman's language, which is very visceral and very strong, and not at all this nice, rhythmic sort of thing which men tried to make us believe is women's speech.

So you think women write differently from men?

The difference is very subtle. It is not a different way of writing, it is a different approach to language. Language is sex, an idea which we never want to recognize.

What is women's place in Latin American literature today?

Women's place is unfortunately the place society will allow us to have, for the time being. There are very fine women writers such as Clarice Lispector, who was an extraordinary writer and should have been part of the Boom. She belonged to the same generation as Cabrera Infante, so why was she not included in the Boom? Because she was a woman.

Can you explain how rebellion and freedom are vital parts of your works?

I hope they are. Freedom is a search. We do not usually have it, but we are looking for it. We try to express it by showing our own inner freedom whenever we can. And the rebellion must be there constantly. If we forget to be rebels we are no longer writing, we are not being artists. If we repeat what has already been done or said, it is worthless.

Has censorship affected your writing?

When I wrote **Strange Things Happen Here,** it was a moment of great violence in Argentina, and I was fighting to be able to say what was going on without being censored. That was a rather unconscious challenge, but it was there. So I managed to do something very positive for my style of writing, because that book became a metaphor for everything that was going on at the time. I was really playing my game then. (pp. 296-300)

Who are the writers who have influenced you the most?

I think everyone has influenced me. Every writer influences all the others. Even the most horrible things I have read have influenced me. It would be a cliché to list the writers I care for most. However, I will mention Borges, Cortázar, and Bioy Casares. But I greatly enjoy other writers. I loved Carlos Fuentes's *Terra Nostra.* I started using it as a puzzle of time and space. We are all discoverers. That is why I also love the last of Carpentier's books, *El arpa y la sombra* (*The Harp and the Shadow*), which is the story of Christopher Columbus. He really did not discover a new world because he already knew there was a world there. Writers are like that. We feel as if we were discovering new lands, but we have in fact already heard of them from other writers. We are just making our humble explorations. Nevertheless, the trip can be full of risks, and we have to create our lies and our deceptions well so as to make the story worthwhile.

. . . . .

Luisa, you are cosmopolitan and at the same time very Latin American. How do you reconcile living outside Argentina and yet manage to hold on to your indigenous roots?

I think roots come from many parts. A good sense of perspective is the most important thing for me, because I think that when one is involved in a situation, one can't always see it very clearly. My first revelation in this respect came when I was in Iowa in 1979. It was then that I discovered that Argentina really was a Latin American culture, steeped in Latin American tradition. We Argentines have always believed we were so European, which is absolutely not true.

Speaking of you, Carlos Fuentes once said, "Luisa Valenzuela is the heiress of Latin American literature. She wears an ornate baroque crown, and yet she walks barefoot." Do you feel a responsibility as the heir to your continent?

I think it is far too generous of Carlos to say something like that. I don't believe one assumes responsibilities in that sense—we are always heirs to our continent. It is not a question of living up to that legacy, but rather a matter of looking it squarely in the face. I think there is some degree of courage required in facing things as they are, because many ugly truths must be faced as well. I write as an attempt to learn what is beneath the surface. In this sense, my continent is a little confusing, but all the more interesting because of it.

You began writing as a journalist who managed to infiltrate places where women had never been allowed. Now that you are a novelist, do you carry your experiences as a journalist into your work?

I think one is inseparable from the other. The journalist I once was, and still am, continues to influence the way I look at my surroundings—it has taught me many things. Thanks to journalism, I have learned how to synthesize, how to narrate a story as concisely as possible. This is something which I have carried over into my books, to the occasional dismay of my readers, who say they have to read every page twice because there is too much information on it. Journalism has also taken me to vastly different worlds from the ones I was used to. I was a *redactora estrella* (star reporter) for a popular magazine, so I was sent to boxing matches, world soccer championships, and the like. This gave free expression to a very vital part of my character. Ironically, I have chosen a very quiet and sedate profession, writing fiction, which contradicts this need to run free.

Can you say something about the interplay of fantasy and reality, the third dimension you have created in your work?

I have a feeling that reality is much wider than what we see. I think everything is real; what happens is that we label as real only the most evident things. We have limited the boundaries of reality too formally. In the final analysis, everything that goes through our minds is real, including dreams, poetry, and a whole gamut of elements which we do not usually associate with reality. We are like horses with blinders, and the only thing I try to do is to take the blinders off and see all sides of reality, the known as well as the dark aspects of reality, which people call fantasy. Cortázar was very aware of this, and he used to refer to the pataphysical idea of worlds complementary to this one. I think he was very correct, obviously. We are immersed in a reality which there is no need to limit. When we do so, it is out of ignorance, pure and simple.

Do you think the woman as a writer has a responsibility to other women?

I don't agree with that use of the term "responsibility." If a woman writer felt she had a direct responsibility, the result would probably be a messy confusion in her writing and her actions. Responsibility must be intrinsic; it must come together with a profound and basic ideology. If this is the case, then when a person acts those inner tenets will express themselves either directly or indirectly. Obviously, since we are women, we speak to other women, but we direct ourselves to anyone who may be willing to listen.

You have said, "I strive so that my stories may be ambiguous, so that they say more than what is apparent." Why do you like to carry that ambiguity to art?

Because I don't think a written work ends with the last word. There is never a last word. When someone reaches that point, the dialogue with the author is only beginning. Then suddenly the reader is acting and creating a new reading. Every reading represents a new awareness of the work. I am very concerned that there be different possibilities and an array of mythical, political or other foundations.

In an interview you held in Buenos Aires in April of 1983, you said, "I think my literature is vibrant and my life is literary." Could you explain this a little?

As far as saying that my literature is vibrant, that is a wish—I would like it to be so. There is not the slightest doubt, however, that my life is literary. It is very difficult for me to separate life and literature. I live through certain situations which I know I am propelling; it is like someone who pushes against the wall to reach another reality. I try to force certain situations to their extreme to see what lies behind them. One always tries to break the toy to see what is inside. In the same way, I want to take life apart to see what is inside. My experiences as a writer are all my life. I don't ever stop writing, even when I am walking or riding the subway. Writing is a sort of screen separating me from the rest of the world, even to the extent of making me miss some part of real life. Then again, real life is writing too, so I don't know.

Your mother, Luisa Mercedes Levinson, was a writer. Do you see some likeness between your work and hers?

I don't see any likeness; we speak with very different voices. During the last years of her life, however, we were beginning to approach similar themes. We viewed them from different angles with our own very personal perspectives, but we did share some obsessions, and I think this is fascinating. (pp. 301-05)

Why are you so drawn to magic?

Because I think it is a part of life. It comprises all the activities of the right hemisphere of our brain, to put it as scientifically as possible. There is a facet of the mind that we call magic for lack of a better word, which I think is fascinating in all its expressions and insightful about things we don't know how to explain.

Why do you like to play with symbols and metaphors so much?

Because they help us understand. Because we need to grasp the full scope of language. I think this is a great contribution of the latest wave of Latin American literature—a reappraisal of language, of the sort the French are so fond of engaging, an analysis of the metaphorical and metonymical structure of language. It is thanks to this freedom one gives to words that imagination grows, and that the spectrum of ideas becomes so much broader, because it is the very words which are guiding you to take the next step.

Do you conceive of literature as a game or a weapon?

As a weapon *and* as a game, but not in the derogatory sense of that word. I think games are among the most important components of life. This is the *homo ludens*—it is this meaning which we are rescuing now, through that game of imagination and invention which is going on in physics with the work of microphysicists. A nebulous poetical area remains wherein one can invent and be wrong and continue inventing . . . because nothing is as real as it seems.

What are some of the recurrent themes in your work?

That is very difficult for me to say. It is for the critics to discover and resolve them. I think masks have been there since the beginning, like cats and critters of that nature, although I believe this is all a bit limiting. I think my work is constantly changing, but the obsessions remain.

What do you feel upon seeing your name in the North American press mentioned in the same breath as the writers of the Boom, like Fuentes, Vargas Llosa and Cortázar?

I am happy I guess, although we should all be there, not just me. Because there are a number of writers of my generation who should be on that list as well, there is a long way to go yet.

You have said, "New York is the most surrealist place on this earth." Why are the ideas for your books born here, and why do you have to isolate yourself from New York to be able to write?

I said that about New York to counter that "surrealist" label North Americans apply to Latin American literature. I don't believe in those tags, I don't think Latin American literature is surrealistic. Surrealism is something very precise and limited, it is the exaltation of madness. Our literature is very rational in certain respects. New York is a completely crazy city, full of contradictions and superimposed elements—people don't see that here because they don't focus on that reality, but we Latin Americans do see it. This is greatly stimulating, but I must isolate myself before the city swallows me up. I need to return to Spanish, to surround myself with it, and that's why I often travel to Mexico. The language spoken around me is very important.

So you consider Mexico a second home?

In the same way that New York is a second home. I have a lot of second homes.

Are you a poet?

We are all poets. We all have a little bit of the poet, the doctor, and the madman in us. I am a poet and a doctor and a madwoman. But I write very little poetry, although I did recently. It is the facet of my craft in which I indulge the least, although there is a certain poetry to my prose.

How did you meet Julio Cortázar?

I met him by accident in Mexico and then I saw him again at a convention in Frankfurt. It was there that we became close friends. He was an extraordinary human being.

What about Jorge Luis Borges?

I have known Borges since childhood, as he was a close friend of my mother's. They even wrote a story together called "La hermana de Eloísa" ("Heloise's Sister"). They laughed a lot when they wrote it; it was truly fantastic, and it was a sort of apprenticeship in the joys of writing for me.

Along with María Teresa León, Rafael Alberti's wife, and their daughter Aitana, you were part of the magazine Quince Abriles *in Buenos Aires.*

I began writing in that magazine by doing an interview with Mirtha Legrand, the well-known Argentine actress. I was a pretty awful writer then, but by the time I was seventeen I was much better.

What makes up the creative process which takes you from the idea for a novel to the finished product?

It consists in the happiness of continual discovery. It is a question of surmounting obstacles, because the conception one has of a novel can be very limited and imprecise. When I conceive a novel in very narrow and specific terms, it is very difficult for me to write, and it doesn't take off. What is important, therefore, is to have certain steady elements, and then give the characters a free rein, so that the novel begins to write itself.

What kind of relationship do you have with your characters? Do you lead them or do they lead you?

I try never to have power struggles with anybody, not even with my characters. They lead me because I want them to be as alive as possible. They start growing on their own and they even go against my feelings on occasion. That's when I feel I am writing well, when I can express my unconscious thoughts without needing a mask. Either the characters have become the mask or there is a part of my unexpressed self which is able to say, "That's true," without it necessarily being my personal truth. (pp. 307-10)

You work with the themes of censorship, exile, and human rights. What does freedom mean to you?

Everything. Creating is impossible without freedom. I find it sinister to say that censorship is good for literature because it stimulates the imagination of writers. Censorship castrates, and in the long run the castration is total. (pp. 311-12)

Can you speak about your book **Other Weapons** *a little?*

It is a story about a woman who has been tortured to such an extent that she has a complete loss of memory. The story, which is more of a novel really, develops as she recovers snippets of her memory. The title indicates a change from weapons of torture to sexual weapons. I had to reread the story many times, because it is a very precise tale requiring a lot of polish, and each time was more painful than the last. Finally, when they sent me the proofs to the book, I could read it no longer. In fact, I haven't read the translation either for the same reason. Had I realized how difficult it would be to face the novel's elements of eroticism, horror, and death, I would have censored the tale completely.

Do you feel more comfortable as a novelist or as a storyteller?

That's very difficult to answer. Speaking in a literary sense, I like the short story more than the novel. It is very hard to put together a collection of stories. With each story one has to start anew, whereas a novel, if it is already on track, flows of its own volition. It is a great pleasure when this happens, and situations become more complex and unpredictable—and then, all of a sudden, everything is set straight again. (p. 312)

. . . . .

You have mentioned to me in a previous interview that some of the themes in your work are heresies and a quest, and you have even said, "I am still waiting to know what I am searching for." Did you find out the answer to your quest?

Fortunately, I haven't, because I suppose that the day I find the answer to that, I will stop writing, or worse still, I will be dead. I think that life is a search for the reason of the quest, or what you are after. So the interesting thing is simply to keep on going. I don't think I'll ever find an answer. I don't think there is an answer.

What is Argentina to you now that it has recovered its freedom?

That is a very difficult question because Argentina is my homeland, of course, and in a sense it is my home. But it's a home far away from home and I don't know if I'll ever really want to go back to stay. I would like to go and spend time there, however. Even if Argentina has found its freedom, I don't find my freedom in Argentina, because I am trapped by my own past. If you leave your homeland and then you go back to it, it's never the same as what you left. You haven't gone through that period of change, so you are not altogether a part of it. It's just a place of nostalgia then, but since I am not a nostalgic person, it's a non-place in a sense, although it's also a place of comfort and reassurance.

Does it mean that the need for freedom will no longer be an essential part of your writing?

The need for freedom is an essential part of my life; in a sense it is a part of everything. It's not a question of freedom or no freedom—I don't think freedom is that superficial. Argentina has found democracy, and it's going through a very good time, if you don't think of the economy. But there is no internal freedom; there is too much pain, the wounds are too deep. People are too subjected to rules, more than rules, regulations, of course regulations of fashions and fads. So the search for freedom is an important part of my personality and I hope of everybody else's. (pp. 314-15)

Can you explain the importance of humor and irony in your work?

It is essential. I think humor is more important. Irony, however, is a necessary by-product, although we shouldn't be too proud of it. I don't think I would relate to anybody without a sense of humor, and I don't think I could keep on moving in life without it. When I am down, I remind myself of that and I perk up. Even when humor is not in my work, I have a feeling there is irony or cynicism or some biased way of saying things which could be more or less funny. Humor allowed me to break the barriers of censorship in more than one way, because not only was I evading the censors, wherever they were, I was forcing the reader to read me. Otherwise, he would have put the book down. The main reason for having a sense of humor in writing is to allow oneself to say things that otherwise one wouldn't dare even acknowledge. But they suddenly come out through jokes.

Now that you can express that truth freely, does it mean that humor is going to be left out of your work?

The truth that cannot be uttered is not the truth that the censors, or the people or the government will punish you for expressing. The deep unspeakable thing is what you don't dare say, because it is your own dark side relating to other dark sides. So that is always there crouching somewhere inside you, trying to avoid being brought out in the open, and wanting to come out nevertheless. Humor, therefore, is always necessary and is unrelated to external freedom.

What is the force that propels your writing?

I wish I knew, because then I would switch it on when I need to. I don't know.

When I talk with you I always find that there is a special magic around you. Do you think that the world of the occult is watching over us?

I think that we are the world of the occult; it's not that it's watching over us, it is there all the time. So it is only that we refuse to see part of the reality that surrounds us.

Why is it so important to you?

Because it is another vision. The South American Indians said that you have to learn to look twice, simultaneously. You have to learn the straightforward vision that encompasses everything that is out there and recognize it, and also the lateral vision that shows you the world of shadows. There is another world, there is a magical thinking which has lost all its charm. Scientists now speak of the lateralization of the brain. There is the right side of the brain too, and you have to think about it. It is as simple as that.

But for you it is another dimension?

No, it is the same dimension that is absolutely embedded in the other; they are interlinked, you can't separate them, that is why I said it is not watching over us—we are part

of that too. But we don't want to acknowledge it. That's why Americans think the Latin American novel is surrealistic when it is totally realistic!

Are masks as important to you now as they once were? I see we are still surrounded by them.

Much less; most of them are in crates. They have been internalized. I have a friend who was speaking to me about the naked masks, and the naked masks in African art are invisible. So sometimes the dancer comes in and his face is showing, but you know he is wearing a mask because he is performing a certain ceremony, and that is a naked mask, an invisible mask. And now I am exploring these masks, which are much more abstract. But it is never a form of unmasking, because I don't believe in the possibility of being unmasked. I think we are like onions, there is always another layer behind it.

Do you wear a mask?

We all do. Unfortunately, I don't think there is a way to avoid wearing a mask. I always recall Oscar Wilde saying, "Give me a mask, and I'll tell you the truth." So perhaps sometimes we want to don that other mask, the one that will allow us to really be ourselves and see our inner truth.

And yet, when I talk to you, I feel that I know you and that there is nothing standing between us.

Because it is not a mask to disguise my feelings; I think it is not a dishonest mask, it is an honest mask.

Is style more important to you than characters?

I wouldn't phrase it like that. In Joyce's words: "I am more interested in how you say it than what you say." Words and language are more important to me than anecdotes or situations. I am more interested in what is being said in spite of ourselves.

Do you mean going beyond words?

No, words go so far that you can never reach them. I am more interested in going beyond the psychological possibilities of the character I am building. And suddenly the language this character is using really depicts a picture that is much more true to itself than what I was trying to do.

Words in spite of ourselves.

Yes, language speaks through us, as they say nowadays. It says much more than we realize we are saying or want to say.

Do you feel closer to the Spanish language being in New York, Buenos Aires, or Mexico?

I feel very close to language in Argentina, of course. You are touching an important point there, because perhaps I feel too close to language in Buenos Aires, and that is why I am always running away from it. Because if you are really immersed in the stew, you don't see the ingredients.

Where do you write best?

In Mexico, which is midway between Buenos Aires and the United States, but now I manage to write well in my own country.

Do you feel that there has been an evolution in your style?

I feel that there has been a real change in my style. It has evolved, because I think I have sharpened the instrument and I now use words as weapons more and more. But one cannot presume to dominate language, because that would really be a fascist pretension. I am allowing language to become more fluent. I have a feeling that every time I write, and write well, I see more clearly than before. Language is to me like a house, the home in which I feel most comfortable. Each brick is a particular word and has to be laid in an exact position to maintain the whole structure.

Do you feel close to all your books?

Yes, I feel close to certain situations in them. I feel close to them when I write them. But I am also indifferent because I don't open them after they have been published.

How do you feel during the actual process of writing?

When it is going well, I usually feel elated and I think it is a great thing to do. Sometimes when I am tackling a very difficult subject matter, however, I feel I have to tear the book out of my system. Then I don't feel elated at all, except for the fact that I am working in a world with language, and that gives me great drive, great energy, even if I am telling horrible stories with horrible situations. (pp. 315-19)

Why is your work so powerful?

Because I have a sense of what should be said in spite of myself. It is also a trap because there are some very tender, sweet things that I love. This is when you start fighting the barriers of censorship again. The other day Susan Sontag asked me if I had a fascination with sadomasochism and I replied, "No, I don't," to which she said, "Well, it comes out in your books." After this conversation, I realized that it is not that I am fascinated by the dark part of our nature, but merely that I acknowledge it. Coming from a beautiful country which suddenly became the cradle of torturers, I cannot avoid acknowledging the existence of evil things and their power over people. I look for the horrible and put it out in the open, so that it will not come out of hiding at a moment when I don't want it to.

Do you write for a purpose then?

I always think there should be a purpose, although I could also say, "No, I write for no purpose whatsoever." But then I start wondering, "What the heck do I write for anyway?" I write to shake people up. I used to think that I wrote to pull the rug from under the readers' feet and I would say, "This is the reality you see but there are also all these other possibilities and things going on at the same time." Even in the most banal and innocent statement, there are dark and somber aspects of human nature hidden. (pp. 319-20)

> *Luisa Valenzuela and Marie-Lise Gazarian Gautier, in an interview in* Interviews with Latin American Writers *by Marie-Lise Gazarian Gautier, Dalkey Archive Press, 1989, pp. 293-322.*

FURTHER READING

Criticism

Gold, Janet. "Feminine Space and the Discourse of Silence: Yolanda Oreamuno, Elena Poniatowska, and Luisa Valenzuela." In *In the Feminine Mode: Essays on Hispanic Women Writers,* edited by Noël Valis and Carol Maier, pp. 195-203. Canbury, N.J.: Associated University Presses, 1990.

> Comparative analysis of theme and symbolism in selected short stories written by three Hispanic women.

Magnarelli, Sharon. *Reflections/Refractions: Reading Luisa Valenzuela.* New York: Peter Lang Publishing, 1988, 243 p.

> Collection of essays and an interview focusing on the themes of language, politics, and religion in Valenzuela's writings.

Interview

Garfield, Evelyn Picon. "Luisa Valenzuela." In her *Women's Voices from Latin America,* pp. 141-65. Detroit: Wayne State University Press, 1985.

> Interview with Valenzuela focusing on her pre-1980 works; includes an introduction to the content, themes, and style of Valenzuela's fiction.

Additional coverage of Valenzuela's life and work is contained in the following sources published by Gale Research: *Contemporary Authors,* Vol. 101; *Contemporary Authors New Revision Series,* Vol. 32; *Contemporary Literary Criticism,* Vol. 31; *Dictionary of Literary Biography,* Vol. 113; and *Hispanic Writers.*

Villiers de l'Isle-Adam

1838-1889

(Full name Jean-Marie Mathias Philippe-Auguste, Comte de Villiers de l'Isle-Adam) French playwright, short story writer, novelist, and poet.

INTRODUCTION

Villiers's works, which ranged from satirical humor to occult horror, were an important influence on a generation of French writers that included Joris-Karl Huysmans and Stéphane Mallarmé. However, his uncompromising idealism and criticisms of bourgeois ethics were out of step with popular tastes, and the reading public ignored much of his work. Although Villiers had hoped to achieve fame as a dramatist, his most successful literary efforts were in the short story genre, and critics generally consider the ironic, fantastic, and disturbing stories collected in *Contes cruels* (*Cruel Tales*) to be his most sophisticated work.

Born in Brittany, Villiers was the only child of a family beset by financial instability. He took great pride in his noble lineage, however, and some biographers claim that his quest for literary greatness stemmed from his desire to redeem the grandeur and prestige accorded his family name in the era before the French Revolution. In the late 1850s he moved to Paris with his family. There he frequented the city's cafés and salons and established a reputation as a gifted conversationalist and raconteur. Although his early efforts at prose and drama attracted praise in literary circles, he remained virtually unknown to the public. In the early 1860s he established a friendship with the French poet Charles Baudelaire, who introduced Villiers to the works of Edgar Allan Poe. Villiers's subsequent short fiction, particularly his interest in the macabre and the grotesque, is often attributed to his admiration for Poe's fiction. During the 1860s and 1870s Villiers wrote several plays and numerous short stories. Popular and financial success, however, continued to elude him until 1883 when he published *Cruel Tales,* his first collection of short stories. Over the next six years, Villiers published four more collections of short fiction as well as a novel. He died of cancer in 1889.

In his short fiction Villiers proclaimed his belief in the efficacy of otherworldly forces and expressed a disdain for materialism and scientism. In "Les demoiselles de Bienfilâtre" ("The Bienfilâtre Sisters") he satirized what he considered bourgeois society's preoccupation with material gain by suggesting that prostitution can be a respectable profession in a society in which respectability is based on financial profit. His condemnations of science often centered on the insensitivity of doctors and scientists who sacrifice humans and animals in their quest for knowledge. The doctor in "L'héroisme du docteur Hallindonhill," for instance, murders a patient he has cured in order to dis-

cover how the cure worked, while the scientist in "Le tueur de cygnes" kills several swans to prove that they sing as they die. In such works as "L'intersigne" ("The Sign") and *Claire Lenoir,* Villiers expressed his fascination with occult phenomena and the intervention of supernatural forces in everyday life. The protagonist of "The Sign" receives numerous cryptic and otherworldly communications which are revealed at the end of the story to have been premonitions of his friend's death, while Doctor Tribulat Bonhomet, the main character of *Claire Lenoir,* discovers through a scientific investigation that a woman's husband returned from the dead and beheaded her former lover.

In assessing Villiers's short fiction, critics have concentrated on the ambiguous and disturbing qualities of his works. "Véra," for example, is often cited by critics as a tale whose meaning is unclear since Villiers did not reveal whether or not the title character has actually returned to her husband after her death. Other commentators have noted that Villiers often attempted to disorient his audience by leading his readers to question their reactions to his characters. In "Sombre récit, conteur plus sombre" ("Sombre Tale, Sombre Teller"), Villiers embedded several narratives by different narrators into a single story, throughout which the protagonist criticizes one of the narrators, D—, for amusing a group of people at a dinner party with the story of someone's death and for manipulating the elements of the narrative for theatrical effect. At the conclusion of the story, the protagonist relates his account of the dinner party to a friend and realizes that in highlighting certain aspects of D—'s narration, he too is guilty of manipulating events for emotional effect. Critics contend that this "cruel twist" at the end forces readers to reevaluate the protagonist, their relationship to the story as an audience, and their gullibility. As A. W. Raitt has stated: "One is nearly always obliged to think twice before one can be sure one has penetrated to the hidden meaning of Villiers's stories; they do not immediately offer up all their secrets as do most tales, but contain shifting and unsuspected depths of irony and meditation."

PRINCIPAL WORKS

SHORT FICTION

*Claire Lenoir 1867; published in journal *Revue des lettres et des arts*
  [*Claire Lenoir,* 1925]
Contes cruels 1883
  [*Sardonic Tales,* 1927; also published as *Cruel Tales,* 1963]
Akëdysséril 1886
L'amour suprême 1886
Tribulat Bonhomet 1887
Histoires insolites 1888
Nouveaux contes cruels 1888
Nouveaux contes cruels et Propos d'au delà 1893

OTHER MAJOR WORKS

Deux essais de poésie (poetry) 1858
Premières poésies (poetry) 1859
Isis (unfinished novel) 1862
Elën (drama) [first publication] 1865
Morgane (drama) [first publication] 1866; also published as *Le prétendant* [revised edition], 1965
La révolte (drama) 1870
  [*The Revolt* published in *The Revolt and The Escape,* 1901]
Le nouveau monde (drama) 1883
L'Eve future (novel) 1886
  [*Eve of the Future Eden,* 1981; also published as *Tomorrow's Eve,* 1982]
Axël (drama) [first publication] 1890
  [*Axël,* 1925]
Chez les passants (essays and satire) 1890
L'evasion (drama) [first publication] 1891
  [*The Escape* published in *The Revolt and The Escape,* 1901]
Correspondance générale. 2 vols. (letters) 1962

Œuvres complètes. 2 vols. (dramas, essays, novels, poetry, and short stories) 1986

*This work was included in the volume *Tribulat Bonhomet.*

CRITICISM

Joris-Karl Huysmans (essay date 1884)

[*Huysmans was a French novelist, critic, essayist, and short story writer. His most influential work, the novel* A rebours *(1884;* Against the Grain, *1922), became a manifesto of the Decadent movement in European literature.* Against the Grain *portrays the inward struggle and spiritual crisis of Huysmans's protagonist, Des Esseintes, who became the prototype of the decadent connoisseur who celebrates the superiority of imagination over reality. In the following excerpt from* Against the Grain, *Huysmans compares Villiers's work to that of Edgar Allan Poe.*]

[The] cerebral clinic where, vivisecting in a stifling atmosphere, this spiritual surgeon [Poe] became, as soon as his attention wandered, the prey of his imagination, which sprayed about him, like delicious miasmas, angelic, dream-like apparitions, was for Des Esseintes a source of indefatigable conjectures; but now that his neurosis had grown worse, there were days when reading these works exhausted him. . . .

He therefore had to hold himself in check and only rarely indulge in these formidable elixirs, just as he could no longer visit with impunity his red entrance-hall and feast his eyes on the horrors of Odilon Redon and the tortures of Jan Luyken.

And yet, when he was in this frame of mind, almost anything he read seemed insipid after these terrible philtres imported from America. He would therefore turn to Villiers de l'Isle-Adam, in whose scattered writings he discovered observations just as unorthodox, vibrations just as spasmodic, but which, except perhaps in *Claire Lenoir,* did not convey such an overwhelming sense of horror. (p. 192)

Claire Lenoir was the first of a series of stories linked together by the generic title of *Histoires moroses.* Against a background of abstruse speculations borrowed from old Hegel, there moved two deranged individuals, a Doctor Tribulat Bonhomet who was pompous and puerile, and a Claire Lenoir who was droll and sinister, with blue spectacles as big and round as five-franc pieces covering her almost lifeless eyes.

This story concerned a commonplace case of adultery, but ended on a note of indescribable terror when Bonhomet, uncovering the pupils of Claire's eyes as she lay on her deathbed, and probing them with monstrous instruments, saw clearly reflected on the retina a picture of the husband brandishing at arm's length the severed head of the lover and, like a Kanaka, howling a triumphant war-chant.

Based on the more or less valid observation that, until decomposition sets in, the eyes of certain animals, oxen for instance, preserve like photographic plates the image of the people and things lying at the moment of death within the range of their last look, the tale obviously owed a great deal to those of Edgar Allan Poe, from which it derived its wealth of punctilious detail and its horrific atmosphere.

The same was true of **"L'Intersigne,"** which had later been incorporated in the *Contes cruels,* a collection of stories of indisputable talent which also included **"Véra,"** a tale Des Esseintes regarded as a little masterpiece.

Here the hallucination was endowed with an exquisite tenderness; there was nothing here of the American author's gloomy mirages, but a well-nigh heavenly vision of sweetness and warmth, which in an identical style formed the antithesis of Poe's Beatrices and Ligeias, those pale, unhappy phantoms engendered by the inexorable nightmare of black opium.

This story too brought into play the operations of the will, but it no longer showed it undermined and brought low by fear; on the contrary, it studied its intoxication under the influence of a conviction which had become an obsession, and it also demonstrated its power, which was so great that it could saturate the atmosphere and impose its beliefs on surrounding objects.

Another book of Villiers', *Isis,* he considered remarkable for different reasons. The philosophical lumber that littered *Claire Lenoir* also cluttered up this book, which contained an incredible hotch-potch of vague, verbose observations on the one hand and reminiscences of hoary melodramas on the other—oubliettes, daggers, rope-ladders, in fact all the romantic bric-à-brac that would reappear, looking just as old-fashioned, in Villiers' *Elën* and *Morgane. . . .* (pp. 193-94)

The heroine of this book, a Marquise Tullia Fabriana, who was supposed to have assimilated the Chaldean learning of Poe's women and the diplomatic sagacity of Stendhal's Sanseverina-Taxis, not content with all this, had also assumed the enigmatic expression of a Bradamante crossed with an antique Circe. These incompatible mixtures gave rise to a smoky vapour in which philosophical and literary influences jostled each other around, without managing to sort themselves out in the author's mind by the time he began writing the prolegomena to this work, which was intended to fill no less than seven volumes.

But there was another side to Villiers' personality, altogether clearer and sharper, marked by grim humour and ferocious banter; when this side was uppermost, the result was not one of Poe's paradoxical mystifications, but a lugubriously comic jeering similar to Swift's bitter raillery. A whole series of tales, **"Les Demoiselles de Bienfilâtre," "L'Affichage céleste," "La Machine à gloire"** and **"Le plus beau dîner du monde"** revealed a singularly inventive and satirical sense of humour. All the filthiness of contemporary utilitarian ideas, all the money-grubbing ignominy

of the age were glorified in stories whose pungent irony sent Des Esseintes into raptures of delight.

In this realm of biting, poker-faced satire, no other book existed in France. (p. 194)

> *Joris-Karl Huysmans, in a chapter in his* Against Nature, *translated by Robert Baldick, Penguin Books Ltd., 1959, pp. 178-200.*

Arthur Symons　(essay date 1925)

[*Symons was a critic, poet, and short story writer who first gained notoriety in the 1890s as an English decadent. He later became one of the most important critics of the modern era, and his* The Symbolist Movement in Literature *(1899) established an appropriate vocabulary with which to define the new aesthetic—one that communicated a concern with dreamlike states, imagination, and a reality that exists beyond the boundaries of the senses. In the following excerpt, which was published as an introduction to his translation of* Claire Lenoir, *Symons asserts that the disparate themes and tones of Villiers's works are different manifestations of his cynicism.*]

In the literature of the fantastic there are few higher names than that of the Comte de Villiers de l'Isle Adam—a writer whose singular personality and work render him perhaps the most extraordinary figure in the contemporary world of letters. The descendant of a Breton house of fabulous antiquity, his life has been, like his works, a paradox, and an enigma. He has lived, as he says, somewhere, "par politesse," ceaselessly experimenting upon life, perhaps a little too consciously, with too studied an extravagance of attitude, but at least brilliantly, and with dramatic contrast. An immense consciousness of his own genius, a pride of race, a contempt, artistic and aristocratic, of the common herd, and, more especially, of the *bourgeois* multitude of letters and of life:—it is to moods of mind like these, permanent with him, that we must look for the source of that violent and *voulu* eccentricity which mars so much of his work, and gives to all of it so disdainful an air. It is unfortunate, I think, when an artist condescends so far as to take notice of the Philistine element in which an impartial Providence has placed him. These good people we have always with us, and I question if any spiritual arms are of avail against them. They are impervious, impalpable; they do not know when they are hit. But to Villiers "les gens de sens commun" are an incessant preoccupation. He is aware of his failure of temper, and writes at the head of a polemical preface, "Genus irritabile vatum." But he does not take the hint, and the common-sense people whom he despises have the satisfaction of viewing the contortions into which they provoke him.

In considering the work of Villiers we are brought face to face with a writer who seems to be made up of contradictions. Any theory, if it be at all precise, must proceed by making exceptions. Here is a writer who is at once a transcendentalist and a man of the world, a cynic and a believer in the things of the spirit. He is now [Jonathan] Swift, now [Jacques-Henri] Bernadin de St. Pierre, now [Charles] Baudelaire or [Heinrich] Heine. In reading him you pass from exaltation to buffoonery with the turn of a page, and are never quite sure whether he is speaking seriously or in jest. Above all, everywhere, there is irony; and the irony is of so fine a point, and glances in so many directions, that your judgment is distracted, interrupted, contradicted and confused in a whirlwind of conflicting impressions. And I cannot but be conscious that some things might have to be said differently if it were possible to unearth and take into consideration those *œuvres de jeunesse* of which the author himself has not a copy.

Villiers has written much; but practically it is little exaggeration to say that he is a man of one book. The volume of *Contes Cruels* (published in 1880) includes, I believe, work of many periods; it contains specimens of every style its author has attempted, and in every kind the best work that he has done. The book as a whole is a masterpiece, and almost every separate tale is a masterpiece. I can think of no other collection of tales in any language on which so various and finely gifted a nature has lavished itself; none with so wide a gamut of feeling, none which is so Protean a manifestation of genius. The *Tales* of Edgar Poe alone surpass it in sheer effect, the *Twice-Told Tales* of Hawthorne alone approach it in variety of delicate sensation; both, compared with its shifting and iridescent play of colours, are but studies in monochrome. Around this supreme work we may group the other volumes—all more or less imperfect, and at their best but as so many pages the more towards the single masterpiece. *La Révolte,* a drama in one act in prose, represented at the Vaudeville May 6, 1870, has something of the touch of certain *Contes Cruels,* it is at least not unworthy of a place near them. *L'Eve Future* (1886), that most immense and ferocious of pleasantries, is simply one of the scientific burlesques of the *Contes* swollen out into a huge volume, where it is likely to die of plethora. The volume of the same year, called after its first tale *L'Amour Suprême,* attempts to be a second set of *Contes Cruels;* it has nothing of their distinction, except in *Akëdysséril,* and though striking and clever, is little more than clever and striking. *Tribulat Bonhomet,* which appeared in 1887—"une bouffonnerie enorme et sombre, couleur du siècle," as the author has called it—is largely made up of an "Etude physiologique" published in 1867; like *L'Eve Future,* it lacks all sense of proportion—any touch of the restraining hand. In the two later volumes, *Historie Insolites* (1888), and *Nouveaux Contes Cruels* (1889), there are occasional glimpses of the early mastery, as in the fascinating horror of **"La Torture par l'Esperance,"** and the delicate cynicism of **"Les Amies de Pension"**; on the whole, however, they must be classed with the miscellaneous volume of 1886. . . . I shall speak chiefly of the *Contes Cruels,* for I believe it is by these that Villiers will live; and I shall try to classify them after a fashion, in order to approach one after another the various sides of this multiform and many-sided genius.

First and before all, Villiers is a humorist, and he is a humorist who has no limitations, who has command of every style, who has essayed every branch of the literature of the fantastic. Frankly, I say this is a pity; but with such a nature this prodigality—a prodigality which is partly pure unconsciousness, partly sheer bravo—was no doubt inevitable. The consequence has been that we have to lament the comparatively small yield from what is unquestionably, to my way of thinking, the richest vein of ore. There are some half-dozen of tales—all contained in the *Contes Cruels*—which, for certain of the rarest qualities of writing—subtleties, delicate perversities, exquisite complexities of irony essentially modern—can be compared, so far as I know, with nothing outside the *Petits Poèmes en Prose* of Baudelaire. **"Les Demoiselles de Bienfilâtre," "Maryelle," "Sentimentalisme," "Le Convive des Dernières Fêtes," "La Reine Ysabeau"**—one might add the solitary poem inserted, jewel amid jewels, amongst the prose—these pieces, with which one or two others have affinities of style though not of temper, constitute a distinct division of M. Villiers' work. They are all, more or less, studies in modern love, supersubtle and yet perfectly finished little studies, so light in touch, manipulated with so delicate a finesse, so exquisite and unerring a tact, that the most monstrous paradoxes, the most incredible assumptions of cynicism, become possible, become acceptable. Of them all I think the masterpiece is **"Les Demoiselles de Bienfilâtre"**; and it is one of the most perfect little works of art in the world. The mockery of the thing is elemental; cynicism touches its zenith. It becomes tender, it becomes sublime. A perversion simply monstrous appears, in the infantine simplicity of its presentment, touching, credible, heroic. The edge of laughter is skirted by the finest of inches; and, as a last charm, one perceives, through the irony itself—the celestial, the elementary irony—a faint and sweet perfume as of a perverted odour of sanctity. The style has the delicacy of the etcher's needle. From beginning to end every word has been calculated, and every word is an inspiration. No other tale quite equals this supreme achievement; but in **"Maryelle,"** in **"Sentimentalisme,"** and the others, there is the same note, and a perfection often only less absolute. **"Maryelle"** and **"Sentimentalisme"** are both studies in a special type of woman, speculations round a certain strange point of fascination; and they render that particular type with the finest precision, and, if I may say so, sympathy. The one may be called a comedy, the other a tragedy. The experiences they record are comic (in the broad sense), certainly, and tragic to the men who undergo them; and in both, under the delicate lightness of the style—the gentle, well-bred, *disengaged* tone of a *raconteur* without reserve or afterthought, or with all that scrupulously hid—there is a sort of double irony, a crisscross and intertexture of meanings and suggestions, a cynicism which turns, in spite of itself, to poetry, or a poetry which is really the other side of cynicism. **"La Reine Ysabeau"** and **"Le Convive des Dernières Fêtes"** sound a new note, the note of horror. The former stands almost by itself in the calm cruelty of its style, the singular precision of the manner in which its atrocious complication of love, vengeance, and fatality is unrolled before our eyes—the something enigmatical in the march of the horrible narrative told almost with tenderness. Its serenity is the last refinement of the irony with which this incredible episode arraigns the justice of things. From the parenthesis of the first sentence to the "Priez pour eux," every touch tells, and every touch is a surprise. Very different, and yet in certain points akin to it, is the strange tale of **"Le Convive des Dernières Fêtes,"** perhaps after the more epic chronicle of **"La Reine Ysabeau,"** the finest of Villiers' tales of enigmatical horror. Quietly as the tale is told, full as it is of complications, and developed through varying episodes, it holds us as the Ancient Mariner held the wedding guest. It is with a positive physical sensation that we read it, an instinctive shiver of fascinated and terrified suspense. There is something of the same *frisson* in the latter part of **Tribulat Bonhomet,** and in the marvellous little study in the supernatural, **"L'Intersigne,"** one of the most impressive of Villiers' works. But here the sensation is not due to effects really out of nature; and the element of horror—distinct and peculiar as is the impression it leaves upon the mind—is but one among the many elements of the piece. In these thirty pages we have a whole romance, definitely outlined characters, all touched with the same *bizarrerie*—the execution-mad Baron, Clio la Cendree, Antoine Chantilly, and Susannah Jackson; the teller of the tale, the vague C . . . , and the fantastic Doctor. Narrow as is the space, it is surcharged with emotion; a word, a look, a smile, a personal taste, is like the touching of an electric button; and, indeed, it is under the electric light that one fancies these scenes to enact themselves—scenes which have as little in common with mere daylight as their personages with average humanity. It is a world in which the virtues have changed with their names, and coquette with the vices; and in masque and domino one is puzzled to distinguish the one from the other. It is a world of exquisite, delicately depraved beings trembling with sensibility. Irony is their breath of life, paradox their common speech. And the wizard who has raised these ghosts seems to stand aside and regard them with a sarcastic smile.

What is Villiers' view of life? it may occur to us to ask; is he on the side of the angels? That is a question it is premature to answer; we have to look next on another and a widely different aspect of the fantastic edifice of his work.

The group of tales we have been considering reveals the humourist in his capacity of ironical observer: their wit is a purely impersonal mockery, they deal with life from the point of view of the artist, and they are pre-eminently artistic, free from any direct purpose of pre-occupation. In the pseudoscientific burlesques, and the kindred satires on ignorant and blatant mediocrity, the smile of the Comic Muse has given place to "Laughter holding both his sides"; absurdity caps absurdity, order and measure seem to be flung to the winds, and in this new Masque of Anarchy sharp blows are given, the jests are barbed, and they fly not quite at random. "L'Esprit du siècle," says Villiers, "ne l'oublions pas, est aux machines." And it is in the mechanical miracles of modern science that he has found a new and unworked and inexhaustible field of satire. Jules Verne has used these new discoveries with admirable skill in his tales of extravagant wonder; Villiers seizes them as a weapon, and in his hands it becomes deadly, and turns back upon the very age which forged it; as a means of comedy and the comedy becomes soberly Rabelaisian, boisterous and bitter at once, sparing nothing, so that he can develop the deliberate plan of "an apparatus for the chemical analysis of the last sigh," make a sober proposal for the utilization of the sky as a means of advertisement (**"Affichage Celeste"),** and describe in all its detail and through all its branches the excellent invention of Bathybius Bottom, **"La Machine à Gloire,"** a mechanical contrivance for obtaining dramatic success with the expense and inconvenience of that important institution, the Claque. In these wild and whirling satires, which are at bottom as cold and biting as Swift, we have a quite new variety of style, a style of patchwork and grimaces, a style under which the French language—the language of [Jacques-Bénigne] Bossuet and [Jean de] La Bruyère—almost collapses. Familiar words take new meanings, and flash through all the transformations of the pantomime before our eyes; strange words start up from forgotten corners; words and thoughts, never brought together since Babel, clash and stumble into a protesting combination; and in the very aspect of the page there is something startling. The absurdity of these things is so extreme, an absurdity so supremely serious, that we are carried almost beyond laughter, and on what is by virtue of its length the most important of the scientific burlesques, *L'Eve Future,* it is almost impossible to tell whether the author is really in sober earnest or whether the whole thing is a colossal joke. (pp. xiii-xxviii)

So far we have had the humourist, a humourist who appears to be cynic to the backbone, cynic equally in the Parisian perversities of **"Les Demoiselles de Bienfilâtre"** and the scientific hilarity of **"La Machine à Gloire."** But we have now to take account of one of those "exceptions" of which I spoke—work which has nothing of the humourist in it, work in which there is not a trace of cynicism, work full of spirituality and all the virtues. **"Virginie et Paul"** is an idyl of young love comparable only with that yet lovelier idyl, the magical chapter in *Richard Feverel.* This Romeo and Juliet are both fifteen, and their little moment of lovers' chat, full of the poetry of the most homely and natural things, is brought before us in a manner so exquisitely true, so perfectly felt, that it is not even sentimental. Every word is a note of music, a song of nightingales among the roses—*per amica silentia lunæ*—and there is not a false note in it, no exaggeration, nothing but absolute truth and beauty. The strange and charming little romance of **"L'Inconnue"** is another of these tales of ingenuous love, full of poetry fresh from lovers' hearts, and with a delicate rhythmical effect in its carefully modulated style. **"L'Amour Suprême,"** a less perfect work of art, exhales the same aroma of tender and etherealized affection—an adoring and almost mystic love of the ideal incarnated in woman. In the bizarre narrative of **"Véra,"** which recalls the supernatural romances of Poe, there is again this strange spirituality of tone; and in the dazzling prose poem of *Akëdyssëril*—transfigured prose glowing with Eastern colour; a tale of old-world passion full of barbaric splendour, and touched, for all its remoteness, with the human note—in this epic fragment, considered in France, I believe, to be, in style, at least, Villiers' masterpiece, it is humanity transfigured in the light of the ideal that we contemplate. Humanity transfigured in the light of the ideal!—think for a moment of **"Les Demoiselles de Bienfilâtre,"** of "[L'Appareil pour] L'Analyse chimique du Dernier Soupir"! What, then, are we to believe? Has Villiers two natures, and can he reconcile irreconcilable opposites? Or if one is the real man, which one? And what of the other? What, in a word, is the true Villiers? "For, as he thinketh in his heart, so is he."

The question is not a difficult one to answer; it depends upon an elementary knowledge of the nature of that perfectly intelligible being, the cynic. The typical cynic is essentially a tender-hearted, sensitive idealist; his cynicism is in the first instance a recoil, then, very often, a disguise. Most of us come into the world without any very great expectations, not looking for especial loftiness in our neighbours, not very much shocked if every one's devotion to the ideal is not on a level with, perhaps, ours. We go on our way, if not exactly "rejoicing," at least without positive discomfort. Here and there, however, a soul nurtured on dreams and nourished in the scorn of compromise finds its way among men and demands of them perfection. There is no response to the demand. Entranced by an inaccessible ideal, the poor soul finds that its devotion poisons for it all the wells of earth. And this is the birth of what we call a cynic. The cynic's progress is various, and seldom in a straight line. It is significant to find that in the Ibsen-like drama, *La Révolte,* one of Villiers' comparatively early works, the irony has a perfectly serious point, and aims directly at social abuses. The tableau is a scene, an episode, taken straight from life, a piece of the closest actuality; there is no display, no exaggeration, all is simple and straightforward as truth. The laughter in it is the broken-hearted laughter, sadder than tears, of the poet, the dreamer, before the spectacle of the world. It is obviously the work of one who is a mocker through his very passion for right and good, his sense of the infinite disproportion of things. Less obviously, but indeed quite really,

is the enormous and almost aimless mockery of some of these tales of his the reverse of a love of men and a devotion to the good and the beautiful. Cynicism is a quality that develops, and when we find it planted in the brain of a humourist there is simply no accounting for the transformations through which it may run. Thus the gulf which seems to separate **"Les Demoiselles de Bienfilâtre"** from **"L'Inconnue"** is after all nothing but a series of steps. Nor is it possible for one who judges art as art to regret this series of steps; for it is precisely his cynicism that has become the "note," the rarest quality, of this otherwise unballasted genius; it is as a cynic that he will live—a cynic who can be pitiless and tender, Rabelaisian and Heinesque, but imaginative, but fantastically poetical, always. (pp. xxix-xxxiv)

> *Arthur Symons, in an introduction to* Claire Lenoir *by Villiers de l'Isle-Adam, translated by Arthur Symons, Albert & Charles Boni, 1925, pp. xiii-xxxiv.*

A. W. Raitt   (essay date 1963)

[*An English educator and critic, Raitt specializes in nineteenth-century French literature and has written two book-length studies of Villiers:* Villiers de l'Isle-Adam et le mouvement symboliste *(1965) and* The Life of Villiers de l'Isle-Adam *(1981). In the following essay, he comments on the themes, style, and philosophical intent of the stories in* Cruel Tales.]

The **Cruel Tales,** which had been appearing piecemeal since 1867, were first published in book form in 1883. Their author, Jean-Marie-Mathias-Philippe-Auguste, Comte de Villiers de l'Isle-Adam, by then a man of forty-four, was a writer of fitfully blazing genius, the object of fanatical admiration by contemporaries as distinguished as Mallarmé and Verlaine and the butt of scornful derision by the public at large. Convinced that he was born to add new lustre by his art to the long line of famous ancestors to which he optimistically laid claim, he had always refused to demean himself to mundane occupations, for which in any case his mercurial temperament totally unfitted him, and with obstinate pride had continued for twenty years to produce plays, novels, short stories, and poems so foreign to the taste of his times that publishers sneered at them and they found little audience save among his literary friends. The result was that he had long since been reduced to the most abject penury, the small resources of the family of already impoverished Breton aristocracy to which he belonged having been gleefully dissipated by his eccentric father. The **Cruel Tales** themselves were often written on dirty, crumpled scraps of paper stained with the coffee and wine of the café tables at which Villiers, generally more or less homeless, spent much of his time. When the volume appeared it did much to establish his reputation, especially among the younger generation, who saw in him one of the masters of the growing Symbolist movement. But even though this belated recognition was reinforced by the publication of other major works—several more volumes of short stories, a remarkable novel entitled *The Future Eve,* which is a passionate philosophical inquiry as well as a Verne-like piece of scientific antici-

---

Vincent O'Sullivan on Villiers and Edgar Allan Poe: Many are given to talk loosely about Poe and Villiers being in the same category. Villiers admired Poe, partly no doubt because Baudelaire and Mallarmé admired him; I think he may have desired to write like Poe if he could. But he could not; his personality was too marked. No two men more unlike than Poe and Villiers both as men and as artists ever existed. As artist Villiers never deals in physical horror; his effects are cerebral. Fear, which dominates in some of Poe's best stories, is totally absent from those of Villiers. Arrogance, often present in stories by Villiers, is totally absent from Poe's. How Poe affected Villiers, it seems to me, was in leading him to exhibitions of scientific and mechanical erudition which most readers have not the power to control. . . . The fact is that neither Poe nor Villiers had any education in science worth speaking of during their youth, and their after lives were not such as give an opportunity for exact study of abstruse subjects. About the only other resemblance between Poe and Villiers is that although they both bring women fairly often into their tales they leave them mere shadows, "out of space, out of time,"—Poe always, and Villiers too always, except when the woman is there as a target for his scorn and irony. *Vincent O'Sullivan, in his "The Tales and Stories of Villiers de l'Isle-Adam," in* The Dublin Magazine, *April-June 1940.*

pation, and his great and sombre tragedy *Axël*—it had come too late to save him. Worn out by years of privation and debt, overcome by the responsibility of having to provide for an illiterate mistress and her two sons, sceptical of the welcome the public now gave him, he died in 1889, at the height of his fame but sadly aware that, at least in his own eyes, his mission on earth was still unfulfilled.

At first sight, the *Cruel Tales* betray little of this fantastic and tormented existence. The sumptuousness of their style, the richness of their settings, the apparent remoteness from any confessional element, even the resoundingly aristocratic name of their author, could easily give the impression that they were the pastime of some elegant and moneyed amateur—and that is no doubt how Villiers would have liked them to be read. But their coruscating surface only partly hides the drama of Villiers's life. Permanently at odds with the spirit of the age in which he lived, Villiers delights in denouncing its idols, but his bitter irony does not stay on a level of abstract expostulation; many of his tales are the fruit of his own most humiliating experiences. The unfortunate young genius in 'Two Augurs', for instance, has had a career exactly parallel to Villiers's own, and the publisher who refuses his works is identifiable as Émile de Girardin, one of the pundits of the Second Empire press. Similarly, most of the characters of 'Sombre Tale, Sombre Teller' can be unmasked as dramatists and actors whose facile successes had, in Villiers's view, made the public impervious to the philosophical drama which he had striven in vain to create on the Parisian stage. In a different register, the eloquent and moving indictment of the fickleness of the mob in 'The Impatient Mob' (which Remy de Gourmont called 'the most grandly written story in the French language') is plainly inspired by his failure to convince his contemporaries of the validity of his message as the herald of a new form of idealist art.

Villiers the individual is equally present in the more romantic and emotive tales. The fascination with gold which he had inherited from his father is memorably evoked in the rhythmic prose of 'Occult Memories':

> Among the splendour of the dew, I walk alone beneath the arches of the dark alleyways, as my Ancestor walked beneath the crypts of the sparkling tombs. I, too, instinctively avoid, I know not why, the baneful rays of the moon and the harmful company of human beings. Yes, I avoid them when I walk like this, alone with my dreams. For then I feel that I carry in my soul the light of the barren riches of countless forgotten kings.

In 'The Sign', despite the reminiscences of Poe's 'Fall of the House of Usher', one is conscious that Villiers is thinking of his uncle, a country priest in Brittany with whom he had frequently stayed in his youth. It can be deduced from Villiers's correspondence that the heroine of 'Maryelle', with her startling ideas on fidelity preserved in inconstancy, was in fact one of his mistresses. 'The Eleventh-Hour Guest' is none other than Villiers in disguise; he may never have gone so far as to play the hangman himself, but it is well attested that he had a morbid obsession with public executions. The furious misogyny of 'The

Unknown Woman' reflects the innumerable disappointments of his search for an impossible ideal in love. One may even detect in 'Sentimentality' and 'Sombre Tale, Sombre Teller' another private worry which appears to have disturbed him at intervals throughout his career: the fear that the constant practice of literary mimetism would eventually destroy his capacity for feeling spontaneous personal emotion. It is certain too that he saw himself as the melancholy hero of 'Véra', as the mysteriously doomed 'Duke of Portland' (a highly romanticized interpretation of the oddities by which the Fifth Duke had made himself notorious in Villiers's time), even as the aspirant Magus in 'The Messenger'.

Were it not for these constant reminders of a vibrant human personality beneath the often impassive presentation, the philosophic intentions of the *Cruel Tales* might risk turning them into abstract allegories. For Villiers was deeply committed in the struggle of ideas which dominated French intellectual life in the latter part of the nineteenth century, and almost all his stories have some ulterior purpose in the conflict between scientism and positivism on the one hand and idealism, whether Christian or not, on the other. An unorthodox but impassioned Catholic, a dabbler in the occult sciences, a fanatical believer in metaphysical idealism, Villiers rarely set pen to paper without wishing to demonstrate one or other of the ideas which were dear to him. In 'Véra', for instance, Villiers originally set out to convince his readers that it was possible to call up the spirits of the dead by occult means; he then revised the story and added a further episode to show that the reappearance of the dead Véra is only the creation of D'Athol's imagination—since only our own thoughts are real to us, we are free to create our own reality if we believe in it with sufficient urgency. Divine prescience forms the subject of 'The Messenger', the relativity of moral concepts that of 'The Bienfilâtre Sisters', the nature and use of language that of 'The Unknown Woman', the possibility of premonitory visions that of 'The Sign'. Villiers was fascinated by the intervention in human affairs of mysterious, otherworldly forces, the existence of which in his work is a constant challenge to the assumptions of materialism—the materialism which excites him to those angry and derisive onslaughts which form the basis of so many of his stories. The objects of these attacks include attachment to money in 'Celestial Publicity' and 'Virginia and Paul', faith in political panaceas in 'Vox Populi', the commercialization of art in 'Two Augurs', the supposed virtues of the bourgeoisie in 'The Brigands', and the arrogance of science in 'Doctor Tristan's Treatment'. This combination of vision and satire in the *Cruel Tales* is one of the hallmarks of Villiers's work.

Villiers's individuality stands out more clearly if one compares him with some other famous French short-story writers. He has none of the cosy picturesqueness of Daudet; apart from a brief but evocative sketch of the Breton countryside in 'The Sign' and one or two striking townscapes, such as the one which opens 'The Desire to be a Man' or the one which he ingeniously satirizes in 'The Very Image', he takes little interest in description. Nor has he Maupassant's gift for the realistic delineation of character—on the rare occasions where his primary aim is psychological dissection, as in **'Antonie'**, **'The Eleventh-Hour Guest'**, or **'Maryelle',** he proceeds much more in the manner of Poe's case-histories of lurid abnormalities. Indeed, he sometimes even eschews the sharp narrative outlines associated with the French short story as practised by Mérimée and Maupassant: **'Vox Populi'** and **'Occult Memories'** are as much prose poems as they are tales. That he has an astonishing talent for suspenseful anecdote is undeniable—he was an outstanding *raconteur* in conversation, and stories such as **'Véra'** and **'The Sign'** are as masterful in the gradual unfolding of their plot as anything any of his rivals wrote. But it is rare for him to tell a story simply for its own sake—**'Queen Ysabeau'** is perhaps the only example in this collection, and it is not one of the best.

One is thus less struck by the impression of manual dexterity conveyed by so many short-story writers from Mérimée onwards than by the essential strangeness of Villiers's tales. He deliberately and invariably tries to disturb his readers, either by transporting them to the distant realms of his own prolific imagination, as in **'The Messenger'**, or by making them see their world through the distorting prism of his unorthodox view of it, as in those fantasies like **'Celestial Publicity'** where he insidiously extols some fictitious but plausible invention in order to reveal the ridicule inherent in modern habits of mind. That is why one is nearly always obliged to think twice before one can be sure one has penetrated to the hidden meaning of Villiers's stories; they do not immediately offer up all their secrets as do most tales, but contain shifting and unsuspected depths of irony and meditation. For the same reason, they do not pall on rereading, since their attraction lies in a background of subtle intentions and not in the meretricious thrill of a surprise ending (even though they often supply that too). Villiers's belief that his generation was in danger of spiritual atrophy through too exclusive concentration on the material side of life has as its corollary that only shock tactics could jolt his fellow-men out of their complacency; who would dare say that such a message is irrelevant today? He once wrote a tale called **'The Disturber'**—that is a title which he himself richly deserved.

The style as much as the subject-matter is made to contribute to this disorientation of the reader. Villiers detested prosaic realism and continually sought to make his writing as unusual, as individual, as surprising as he could, whether in the mock-heroics of **'Doctor Tristan's Treatment'**, with its sudden glimpses of unwonted perspectives through the fog of verbiage, or in the sustained and elevated harmonies of **'The Sign'**. Rare words, curious inversions, unlikely juxtapositions, complex and involuted clauses, cunningly calculated poetic rhythms, a multiplicity of typographical devices, abrupt changes of tone—all is designed to make one feel that here is something new, something unique, something which, as he said of *The Future Eve,* has 'neither a precedent, nor anything congeneric with it, nor anything analogous to it'. Sometimes, it is true, this striving for solemn effect can degenerate into self-conscious posturing, in which the style and the subject-matter seem to have lost contact with each other, as happens in **'The Messenger'**, where Villiers sacrifices to a frigid Parnassian splendour. Sometimes, too, he over-

works the trick of parodying the exaggerations of his opponents, and the pseudo-scientific pieces are liable to become wearisome with their relentless exploitation of a single joke. But at its best Villiers's style has extraordinary power and beauty—a beauty which has drawn tribute from authors as diverse as Mallarmé, Valéry, Barrès, and Yeats.

These qualities yield a volume of short stories quite unlike any other, whether it be by Poe, Mérimée, Maupassant, Chekhov, Katherine Mansfield, or Somerset Maugham. Villiers's understanding of character may be less convincing than theirs, his evocation of atmosphere less absorbing, his technical skill less perfect. But he has something which is uniquely his and which no other short-story writer can match: his genius for imparting simultaneously emotional excitement and intellectual stimulation. A French critic, urged to read the works of some new author who was said to have exceptional talents for description, plot, psychology, and style, asked simply: 'Yes, but has he a *voice?*' In Villiers's case, there can be no doubt about the answer. He has a voice which is unmistakably his own and which rings out as powerfully today as it did when he first raised it in protest against the abuses and errors of his time. (pp. v-xi)

> *A. W. Raitt, in an introduction to* Cruel Tales
> *by Villiers de l'Isle-Adam, translated by Robert Baldick, Oxford University Press, London, 1963, pp. v-xi.*

Ivor A. Arnold   (essay date 1972)

[In the following excerpt, Arnold analyzes the traits and thematic import of Villiers's style through a detailed examination of the imagery in his short fiction.]

With the exception of [M.] Deenen in her *Le Merveilleux dans l'oeuvre de Villiers de l'Isle-Adam,* no one has approached Villiers directly through his images, and this is the task we set ourselves in this study. It should be noted here that the technique used is one based on Riffaterrian contextual *i.e.* qualitative analysis, and that no statement is exclusively "statistical", although quantitative statements are made with a view to generating qualitative statements of value. It should also be clear from what follows that we define "image" in the broadest sense as literary expression oriented to the response of the imagination to a variety of literary stimuli, including the more specific categories of imaginative (image-provoking) figures of speech.

Villiers' fiction employs traditional mechanisms of narrative and descriptive exposition with particular mannerisms, the discussion of which would be beyond the scope of this study. It should at least be noted, however, that within the framework of this more or less "normal" affabulation there is a very high frequency of expository techniques intended expressly to convey the basic structural dichotomy—the conflict of the Real and the Ideal; these appear as vehicles of theoretical abstraction presented in a noticeably discursive manner at odds with the dramatic intent. The moral or didactic mode in fact obtrudes onto the fictional message-chain to a greater degree than metaphorical expressivity. Despite the proportionate restraint of the latter's role, however, analysis of the imagery is more intricately revealing, and, as is so often the case, offers more precise indications to the nature of the style.

In approximately 200,000 words of figurative language, we found that only 10,000 (or 5 per cent) appear in "imaginative" writing, which in fact leans heavily on non-figurative kinds of semantic and syntatic avocation. The figures that do appear do not correlate with any specific manner of thematic groups: they are evenly distributed among all tale types, although they account for a smaller proportion of the figurative language in the more polemic, "excoriating" *contes* such as **"La Machine à Gloire,"** **"L'Affichage céleste,"** and make up an above average proportion of the exotic-descriptive tales such as **"L'Annonciateur"** and *Akëdysséril:* as a formal category, metaphor is not a stylistic indicator.

If we classify imaginative figures into types, we find that, of close to 600 instances, including modes not normally classed as "metaphorical" (allusive comparison, paradox, oxymoron, periphrasis—about 70 in all), a mere 130 are simple metaphors, whereas only 106 are simple comparisons (of the latter, 35 are integral components of larger figures and hence not in stylistic relief). Futhermore, of the combined total of 236, at least 60 are unconscious clichés of the type: *blanc comme la neige, le feu des étoiles, i.e.,* rhetorically apt, even expressive, but in no way striking to the imagination, nor acting in any way to vary the tonal level in which they occur. Thus the most common figures of classical and romantic style account for less than one-third of Villiers' figurative "atmosphere", in terms of mode, far less in terms of bulk.

In contrast, the mass of figurative language is represented by what we call "visions"—imaginative shifts of viewpoint provoking a dualistic perception of a setting in terms of "reality" and "appearance"—which vary in length from a few of no more than 10 words to many that occupy one-half of a page of text; and "conceits"—dynamic, multi-term, sustained metaphors that are "visionary", too, in character, springing as they do from the interplay of tensions between "reality" and the ideal imagination, elaborately intellectualised and integrated into physical correlatives of metaphysial "truth", or erotic fantasy. Statistically, there are some 130 of the former and almost 120 of the latter.

The more striking similes are, for the most part, highly conventional creations, almost stereotyped echoes of "unearthly" atmospheres of medieval or modern romance, and their subjects are drawn from both formal and natural beauty, in clichés of artistic composition:

> Elle se détachait comme un lys sur les ténèbres étoilés . . .

> . . . oiseaus-mouches pareils à de petites pierres précieuses incrustés d'ailes . . .

> . . . sa chevelure, que le vent n'ose effleurer, couvre ses épaules surnaturelles comme le feuillage des saules sur les eaux d'argent . . .

> . . . Telle la poussière d'une route que rougit,

avant l'ombre définitive, quelque dernier rayon de l'Occident.

occasionally distorting a familiar sight or experience:

> La Seine charriait ses bateaux marchands pareils à des hannetons démesurés;

> Et il me sembla brusquement, que les cristaux, les figures, les draperies (. . .) s'éclairaient d'une mauvaise lueur, d'une rouge lueur . . . pareille à certains effets de théâtre.

On occasion they betray an earthy, wry humour, as in the description of the spectators to Le Mahoin's execution:

> . . . pressés comme de véritables harengs,

but by far the most common employ the colour of the melodrama which, although it too presents little variety of pattern, bestows on the tenor of a comparison a ready-made aura of familiar touches of chill and horror that prompt predictable responses of affectivity.

Of all the similes noted, not more than 20 per cent are thrown into any real relief in context, either by their form or by their content; in the case of metaphor, the proportion is only a little higher: 25 per cent, but some, as in the following illustrative selection, are of more interest, as reflecting certain Villieresque affinities.

Stormy evocations of Breton landscapes and seascapes, for example, abound in many a vehicle: *triomphale tempête, grondement éloigné des batteries; tonnante acclamation; des tonnerres de tambour; les éclairs de leurs javelots; l'océan de ces joies languides; mille éclairs de sensations; faire valoir ces landes immenses; ce nébuleux sentiment; mes idées étaient pâles et brumeuses; ses yeux aux lueurs de violettes après un orage* as do clichés of "passion": *genre de beauté en fièvre; votre amant doit être quelque enfant sauvage enchaîné par vos malices . . .* and other images of violence and animal energy: *ils avaient assassiné leur corps* (fig. sense); *doué d'une vigueur de tigre; dents de panthère: l'encolure d'un taureau; un rugissement de délivrance et de joie* and the predilection for violence may be expressed in kinds of pyrotechnic images; at least these furnish some of the more striking of his metaphors, for example:

> . . . il avait donc fallu cette fusée d'inconséquences pour entraîner ce bouquet final . . .

Villiers also scores particularly with floral incongruity, especially when reinforced with accumulation and concrete-abstract coupling:

> [. . . Souvente fois, le préfet de la ville y jetait négligemment, en manière de carte de visite,] une touffe choisie, un bouquet inopiné de sergents de ville . . . (**"Les Demoiselles de Bienfilâtre"**)

and:

> [. . . Sur la terrasse, entre la rangée de fiacres et le vitrage,] une pelouse de femmes, une floraison de chignons, échappés du crayon de Guys . . . (*ibid.*)

Of greater import is a major pattern of related images—

the conceit and the "vision"—for in these the pervasive Idealism, both metaphysical and erotic, that invests Villiers' work is fundamental. In both extent and content they bear outstanding witness to the psychical preoccupations that dominate the imaginative modes.

Conceits were noted in 32 out of 70 stories and anecdotes, their use being associated with three representative topics or themes: Woman and earthly love (8); the artist and the Philistine (12); the Absolute, the occult, Death, Nobility, and God (12). The first group, however, contain a greater proportionate concentration: in these eight (accounting for approximately 40 per cent of the linguistic material containing the devices) there are 54 conceits, in comparison with no more than 56 in the remaining 24 tales, and the individual instances in the first group tend to be more sustained (esp. in *Akëdysséril*) than in the others. There is also a clear division represented here between this group (**"Véra," "Virginie et Paul," "Sentimentalisme," "Maryelle," "L'Amour suprême,"** *Akëdysséril,* **"La Maison du bonheur," "L'Etonnant couple Moutonnet"**) with its predominantly sensual figures, and the remainder, which, despite a greater diversity of themes and plots, tend to be highlighted by conceits of metaphysical association.

Visions have a slightly broader distribution (38 out of 70), occurring largely in the same contexts as conceits (the additional tales nearly all appear in *Histoires insolites,* and fall into the same thematic groups); but the sensual emphasis is much less marked (the proportion of visions appearing in the "amatory" group noted above to the remainder is closer to 1:2); and there is no sharp separation between sensual and metaphysical, both categories appearing in all groups. The greatest concentration of this device occurs in the metaphysical tales: **"Duke of Port-land"** (7); **"Le Convive des dernières fêtes"** (9); **"Le Désir d'être un homme"** (7); and **"L'Annonciateur"** (6); and in the sensual-metaphysical **"Véra"** (7), and *Akëdysséril* (17).

Not all Villiers' conceits are characterised by elaborateness and length; a small number consist of a few words only, being distinguished from simple metaphor entirely by the unexpectedness of the images they contain, and by the startling dissimilarity of vehicle and tenor, or by the insistently "metaphysical" character of the secondary subject:

> . . . un sourire tout emparadisé de voluptés. . . . il avait brisé le magnétique fil de sa trame radieuse avec une seule parole . . . (*ibid.*)

but they are usually of three or more terms, unamplified but densely arranged, with the crucial mixtures of earthly and heavenly; passionate and Platonic; natural and supernatural; permanent and ephemeral underlying the metaphorical tension:

> . . . leur sensibilité crédule, tout imbue d'angéliques larmes . . .

> . . . les syllabes pâlies par la brume des années . . .

Such conceits only become syntactically intricate when one or more of the terms is hypotactically extended in all its relevant detail. The figure gains in its open-ended power of suggestion, but the textual mass tends to overshadow the context it is meant to illuminate: the logical symbolism is pursued to the bitter end and the writer's reluctant reversion to macro-context comes so late as to almost obscure the basic meaning-train:

> Comme ces larmes de verre, agrégées illogiquement, et cependant si solides qu'un coup de maillet sur leur partie épaisse ne les briserait pas, mais qui tombent en une subite et impalpable poussière si l'on en casse l'extrémité plus fine que la pointe d'une aiguille, tout s'était évanoui . . . (**"Véra"**);

Such intricate images are common in Villiers' imaginative prose. Comparable in complexity, but of a different order, are those cases, usually of a metaphysical nature, where it is the metaphor, not the syntax, that is multidimensional. Here disparate elements or planes are interlocked in a single metaphoric base from which only a significance beyond nature and reason can arise.

A sensual mysticity lies at the heart of most of these literal illogicalities; they seem to betray a deep need to wrench apart the normal physical order and reconstruct, at least in symbol, a world that would reconcile the most abject and most exalted in man's nature, and dissolve the immediate in the Absolute. Nowhere is this more plain than in *Akëdysséril,* where Villiers embodies in the passionate but frigid queen at once his yearning for the physical Ideal—beauty, power, glory, noble detachment—and his insurmountable sense of disenchantment:

> [Alors le Serviteur de Sivà, tournant vers elle sa blême face de granit, lui répondit . . .]

Drawing of Villiers de l'Isle-Adam at age twenty by Lemercier de Neuville.

. . . C'est que, jeune femme, ta nuit nuptiale ne fut qu'étoilée. Son étincelante pâleur fut toute pareille à celle de mille bleus crépuscules, réunis au firmament, et se voilant à peine les uns les autres. L'éclair de Kâmadéva, le Seigneur de l'amour, ne les traversa que d'une pâleur un peu plus lumineuse, mais fugitive! Et ce n'est pas en ces douces nuits que les coeurs humains peuvent subir le choc de sa puissante foudre . . .

It is clear from these few and assorted examples of Villiers' conceptual exuberance that there is no calculated proportioning of form to concept: the tense exigencies of the contextual moment may limit length and shape to a brief appositional intrusion; or the linguistic enthusiasm stimulated by a particularly fanciful flight of imagination may lead him to linger, thence to elaborate, and frequently abandon himself to the free associative process to the point where the macro-context is, for a time, lost from view. It is the intensity of involvement, not aesthetic considerations of "fit", that govern the greater or lesser elaboration of a conceit. It is a highly "self-conscious" device, in which, by its very nature, form and content are almost inseparable considerations. Yet it is true to say that their relationship is a very loose one: as we have seen, an especially startling association may be very tersely expressed, but there is as much impact in the sheer mass and open-ended suggestibility of a conceit that has simply evolved from an initially trite cliché.

We have already noted how Villiers' conceits are distributed among three major topic-types: woman and earthly love; philistinism and art; the absolute and the occult. These themes, of course, embrace opposites. Erotic passion conflicts with neo-platonic exaltation. Artistic unworldliness fights crass literary commercialism. The finite masks of appearances belie the transcendentalism of Cosmic reality, be it of Faith or Magic. These oppositions are closely—but not precisely—reflected in the principal themes, or fields, of the vehicles used to convey them.

Here, again, there are three groups: the traditional "amorous"; the metaphysical-sensual; ritualistic transfiguration—each extending their particular associative aura into, and beyond, a network of micro-contextual frames.

As the phrase implies, the amorous conceits exploit to the full the commonplaces of a venerable convention: pathetic fallacy, exaggeration, personification. Objects—necklaces, precious gems—closely associated with the loved ones are animated with a lover's pangs; twin souls in amorous mourning renounce a fruitless sacrifice on the altar of love; a lover pleads for liberation from his soul's prison; a beloved's eyes are veils of mourning, lowered over their "beauteous night"; the threshold of Paradise threatens to become an abyss of despair.

In all cases, there is a re-creation of the expressive-didactic tone that pervades much neo-Petrarchan poetry, for example, and there is a certain automatism in its use. But, at times, one feels the full force of a cosmic opposition, a yoking of the ethereal to the earthy, in a conceit of love that contrives to skirt preciosity without restraint of invention:

. . . Et c'est aussi pourquoi bien des amants—

oh! les prédestinés!—ont su, dès ici-bas, au dédain de leurs sens mortels, sacrifier les baisers, renoncer aux étreintes et, les yeux perdus en une lointaine extase nuptiale, projeter, ensemble, la dualité même de leur être dans les mystiques flammes du Ciel. A ces coeurs élus, tout trempés de foi, la Mort n'inspire que des battements d'espérance; *en eux, une sorte d'Amour-phénix a consumé la poussière de ses ailes pour ne renaître qu'immortel;* ils n'ont accepté de la terre que l'effort seul qu'elle nécessite pour s'en détacher . . . (**"L'Amour suprême"**);

or, more soberly (in spite of its presence in one of Villiers' most ironic contexts):

. . . Un premier amour jette dans le coeur de profondes racines qui étouffent jusqu'aux germes des sentiments antérieurs . . . (**"Les Demoiselles de Bienfilâtre"**)

and comes close to assimilating these figures to the group that follows.

In the metaphysical-sensual group, the relative dosage of each component depends to a great extent on the thematic weight of each in the major context. **"L'Annonciateur"** is a novella whose theme and atmosphere stress the mortality of earthly things, even at the moment of invoking the Absolute. The conceits and visions are wholly "metaphysical", with correlatives of Heaven and Earth mingling in quite a different way.

For illustration we need only compare the use of "germe" in the previous example to its function in the following:

. . . L'âme de Salomon, germe divin, est mêlée aux reflets de ce signe victorieux où s'épure, doucement, la lueur des étoiles . . .

or the symbols of finitude in the description of Helcias, the aged High Priest, "l'interprète des symboles, le ministre des pouvoirs occultes", who, despite a life-long pursuit of "sublime purity", is consigned by an inscrutable Deity to a remote point in Chaos and denied his deliverance from the Universe:

. . . Il est pareil à une pierre volcanique qui, animée d'une impulsion terrible, serait retenue au bord du cratère par la vertu d'une loi miraculeuse, et qui se consumerait de sa vitesse intérieure . . .

The dosage is different, on the other hand, in **"L'Amour suprême"**, where it is indeed universal and ideal Love that is paramount, yet where the voluptuous quality is not diminished but maintained and transcended by its imagery of sublimation, purification, and exaltation:

Ainsi, l'humanité subissant, à travers les âges, l'enchantement du mystérieux Amour, palpite à son seul nom sacré.

Toujours elle en divinisa l'immuable essence, transparue sous le voile de la vie,—car les espoirs inapaisés ou déçus que laissent au coeur humain les fugitives illusions de l'amour terrestre lui font toujours pressentir que nul ne peut posséder son réel idèal, sinon dans la lumière créatrice d'où il émane . . .

In both of these contexts one notes the recurring "captive" motif (Helcias is "... *retenue* (...) *par la vertu d'une loi* ... "; is "... *rivé* (...) *haletant comme une victime* ..."; so, too, "*humanité*" lies bound by "*l'enchantement du mystérieux Amour*"; *fugitives illusions*" is a figure turned on its head: the "literal" meaning of the "figurative" sense "*fugitive*" ['fleeting'] invokes the 'ideal' image of the human heart, a self-deluding 'figitive' from the 'real'.)

But one is impressed, in context, less by its presence than by its *place* in the conceit. The 'captive' is syntactically 'enveloped' by the transcendent or sublime to form a stylistic correlative of the motif, *i.e.*

> ... animée d'une impulsion terrible (...) retenue (...) par la vertu d'une loi miraculeuse ...
>
> ... surpris et rivé par le regard d'un Etre ...
>
> ...l'humanité [, subissant, à travers les âges,] l'enchantement du mystérieux Amour, ...

and there are other instances of this 'symbolism' of syntax mirroring motif-within-conceit (of which most are sensual in nature).

The Occult partakes of the metaphysical, the unattainable 'beyond' and the usually meaningless 'here-and-now' can draw together and even momentarily fuse in occult phenomena, where the infinite circumscribes and illuminates a transfigured finite. The 'faith' of the spiritualist moves in the supernatural, where the worlds of the Ideal and the Occult may intermingle without contradiction.

Thus, as the above examples already suggest, the metaphysical element may enter the metaphysical-sensual conceit indirectly, through the evocation of occult 'correspondences' that are presumed to communicate with the cosmic 'beyond'. Their metaphoric force lies in the esoteric symbolism that unites various vehicles into a recognizable pattern of cabalism, regardless of theme or macro-context.

Of this the clearest cases occur in 'amorous' contexts, where we find a marked insistence on ritual acts of emblematic objects such as those used in the practice of occult rites: gold, silver, crystal, roses, wax, parchment, essences, phials, and the infliction of pain—the device occurs so frequently that a complete list would be tedious.

Appraising the poetry of Léon Dierx, in *Une soirée chez Nina de Villard,* Villiers wrote:

> ... Sans l'inquiétude mystique dont elle est saturée, elle serait d'un sensualisme idéal ...
>
> C'est qu'en cette poésie vibrent des accents d'un charme triste, auquel il faut être initié de naissance pour les comprendre et pour les aimer (...)
>
> Et le fait est que la sensation d'*adieux,* qu'éveille sa poésie, oppresse par sa mystérieuse intensité; le sombre de ses *Ruines* et de ses *Arbres,* et de ses *Femmes* aussi, et de ces *Cieux,* surtout! donnent l'impression d'un deuil d'âme occulte et glaçant. Ses vers, pareils à des diamants pâles, respirent un tel détachement de vivre qu'en vérité ... ce

> serait à craindre quelque fatal renoncement, chez ce poète (...)

A degree of self-portraiture here is clearly evident; he might well have been speaking of his own art, for the dominant theme of his conceits is, above all, that of a yearning to escape through the 'veil' separating this world from that of authentic 'reality'. Thus, the 'veil', that only the ideal or the occult can penetrate, is a metaphysical cliché for Villiers:

> Un voile de bonheur et d'amour semblait les envelopper tous les deux, aux lueurs silencieuses du firmament ... (**"Le Secret de la belle Ardiane"**);

one which he is very inclined to use, therefore, in a mood of disenchantment:

> Alors que les seize ans vous enveloppaient de leur ciel d'illusions, avez-vous aimé une toute jeune fille? ... (**"Virginie et Paul"**);

or with outright irony:

> ... Olympe, en effet, venait de voir, vaguement, les pièces de métal sacré reluire entre les doigts transfigurés de Maxime (...) Un voile se déchira. C'était le miracle! ... (**"Les Demoiselles de Bienfilâtre"**);

But there is no irony in the following, where the veil becomes a sort of diaphanous envelope, a mysterious 'threshold' of the spirit, materialised into quasi-real substance:

> ... Vieillard, il te fallut que chacun d'eux se sentit solitaire! ... Isolés, pouvaientils, ces enfants, échanger ce seul regard qui eût traversé les nébuleuses fumées de tes vengeances comme un rayon de soleil? ... (*Akëdysséril*):

or, with a less filmy 'threshold' to Heaven:

> ... Mais, entre les accalmies de toute cette triomphale tempête, une voix perdue s'élevait du côté de la grille mystique. Le vieux homme, la nuque renversée contre le pilori de ses barreaux, roulant ses prunelles mortes vers le ciel ... psalmodiait, augural intercesseur, sa phrase maintenant mystérieuse ... (**"Vox populi"**).

Another occult bridge to the 'beyond' is furnished by the notion of the 'magic mirror', which may only reflect reality, but under certain circumstances reveals supernatural images. In this it enjoys the same occult power as the human eye which, again at certain special moments, may at will reflect or project the spiritual world into an ordinary environment.

> ... Les deux religieux (...) possédaient aussi des fronts extraordinaires et des prunelles pénétrées d'un rayonnement intérieur tel que je n'en ai jamais rencontré l'équivalent. Leur regard attestait la permanence du coeur et de l'esprit en l'unique pensée de Dieu ... (**"Entrevue à Solesmes"**).

In **"L'Annonciateur"** the twin notions converge in a summary conceit of a complex and bizarre teleology:

. . . Cependant, de même qu'en un miroir d'airain, posé à terre, se reproduisent, en leur illusion, les profondes solitudes de la nuit et ses mondes d'étoiles, ainsi les Anges, à travers les voiles translucides de la vision, peuvent impressioner les prunelles des prédestinés, des saints, des mages! C'est la terre seule, brouillard oublié, que ne distinguent plus ces prunelles élues; elles ne repercutent que l'infinie-Clarté . . .

If the ineffable may be seen in both darkness and light, it may be heard in the wind, but it is a sound for the 'elect' only: the priest:

. . . Puis, tout se perd dans l'obscurité. Et le souffle sacré des prophètes passe, dans le vent, à travers les ruines des murs chananéens . . . (**"L'Annonciateur"**);

or the poet:

. . . le seul poète est celui qui ne peut qu'aboyer magnifiquement sa pensée . . . la rugir parfois, la tonner souvent . . . Mais on ne l'entend jamais que dans les rafales . . . Tant pis pour ceux qui n'entendent pas la langue du pays d'où souffle en mes vers le vent de l'éternité . . . (**"Les Filles de Milton"**)

and such language may work apparent evil, not in incantation, but through 'strange consonances' that impart bizarre emblematic powers to the impalpable. So believes Akëdyssëril, accusing the High Priest of Sivà of defying her wishes for a humane death for the royal lovers whose throne she has usurped (it transpires that the evil is transcended: the High Priest's subtle tortures have immeasurably enhanced the Ideality of their death-in-love):

. . . Le verbe de tes lèvres revêt, alors, les reflets bleus et froids des glaives, de l'écaille des dragons, des pierreries. Il enlace, fascine, déchire, éblouit, envenime, étouffe . . . et il a des ailes! Ses occultes morsures font saigner l'amour à n'en plus guérir . . .

. . . . .

Et selon tes vouloirs, la mortelle malice qui anime ta sifflante pensée, jamais ne louange que pour dissimuler les obliques flèches de tes réserves, qui seules, importent . . .

The cabalistic, the occult, and the transcendent inspire most of Villiers' characteristic conceits; but we would be in error if we failed to note certain isolated but significant deviations from this pattern. It is a striking fact that nearly all these devices are visionary, and, for the most part, they are visual, too. Villiers' special love of music,—and particularly the music of Wagner—is poorly represented, as is his passion for the theatre.

Of the former, we can offer only a few metaphysical clichés:

. . . Au milieu du grand silence, un rossignol, âme de la nuit, fait scintiller une pluie de notes magiques . . . (**"Virginie et Paul"**);

. . . Et des mesures de valses s'envolaient, du brillant des violons, lans la nuit . . . (**"L'Amour suprême"**);

which share with the following, equally undistinguished, the traditional bird-flight motif:

. . . A ces mots (. . .) Eulalie, Bertrande et Cécile Rousselin,——dont les rires s'étaient envolés plus loin que les oiseaux du ciel . . . (**"Le Jeu des Grâces"**);

. . .——On eût dit éternels enfants, destinés à mourir comme les oiseaux s'envolent . . . (**"La Maison du bonheur"**);

of the latter, two instances, the contextually effective cliché of **"Le Desir d'être un homme"** (in which the old 'Thespian' bids a melodramatic adieu to his profession):

. . . Il fallait descendre en toute hâte du chariot de Thespis et le regarder s'éloigner, emportant les camarades! Puis, voir les oripeaux et les banderoles qui, le matin, flottaient au soleil jusque sur les roues, jouets du vent joyeux de l'Espérance, les voir disparaître au coude lointain de la route, dans le crépuscule . . .

and the Molieresque evocation of "L'Amour sublime", in which the 'ethereal' lovers take conversational leave of the earthbound, jealous husband:

. . . par d'insensibles fissures, la conversation glissait entre les mains (cependant bien serrées) du conservateur, et s'enfuyait en rêves mystiques . . .

The supernatural element in Villiers' imaginative writing is still more patent in what we have chosen to term his 'visions'.

There are pictorial evocations that correspond to mental images either of unnatural phenomena or of unnatural arrangements of phenomena that project distorted views or interpretations of real settings into a stream of narrative. Clearly, many of the conceits we have discussed have a 'vision' integral to the secondary element: the point of comparison or contrast is with the unreal, the transcedent, or the occult, and the reader must re-imagine the vision in order to bridge the metaphorical gap.

Visions, in themselves, are non-metaphoric. Rather they stem from the dualistic viewpoint of the writer himself, who sees objects and acts both as the 'are', and as correspondences of 'other' worlds. Futhermore, unlike conceits, they are not dynamic syntheses, but static—or at least 'arrested'—compositions of objects or acts that momentarily place the reader in the equally ephemeral surreal world of the writer. Conceits stimulate the imagination to grasp strange analogies between different phenomenological planes, and tend therefore to the didactic, *i.e.,* they resemble a kind of puzzle whose solution enlightens and instructs: visions simply evoke, for while a metaphor may be the means of preparing and implementing the visionary shift of viewpoint, the vision itself is only intended to cast a different, fleeting light over the scene, without implied commentary.

A straightforward example from **"Vera"** may serve to illustrate.

Count Athol has buried his young wife in the family vault,

and, at noon, returns to meditate behind the closed doors of the mausoleum:

> . . . De l'encens brûlait sur un trépied, devant le cercueil: une couronne lumineuse de lampes, au chevet de la jeune défunte, l'étoilait . . .

The details of the scene are presented factually; the physical focus: *lampes* is real; 'couronne' and 'étoilait' are, separately, all but fossilized metaphors. But their conjunction and arrangement suggest more: the disposition of the lamps is like a halo or corona, and the head of the coffin, faintly luminous in a 'starry' light, becomes a focal point of a 'transcendental' light-effect whose source seems, through semantic intensification, to be the Heavens. It is as though the walls of the mausoleum now retreat before the Infinite, admitted through the free-floating, unstopped sentence-end. The verbal components thus achieve a totality of sensory and ultra-sensory impression in which the metaphors are not 'mixed' but complementary in an overall oneness of effect, transcending the metaphors and reflecting a particular 'vision of association' in the author's imagination.

In the more than 100 visions that we noted, this transcendentalism represents a constant, if non-ordered reflection of the author's basic disposition, a verbal projection of psychic moods sparked from the fundamental conviction as to the duality of experience at certain moments, when the dichotomy between the stuff of physical reality and its inner coherence is exposed to view.

This sense of verbal 'otherworldliness' springs in part from the associative groupings of certain types of recurring suggestion; it is also the result of an 'atmosphere' arising from an almost incantational accumulation of a number of stock properties of supernatural apparatus which take on a momentary force independent of the events of the context, with the effect of raising what is already a generally considerable expressive tension to further, almost impossible heights: the feeling of the unnatural is doubly intensified.

It may be found in the vocabulary of gothic melodrama, overlaid with menace: *brouillards, fumée, pins sauvages, règne de Henri IV, richesses féodales, archers, chevaliers de pierre, croisades, héroisme, fantômes, armes,* or in allusions to patterns of medieval or pagan terrorism—explicit:

> . . . Comment accorder mes souvenirs habituels avec ces intenses idées lointaines de meurtre, de silence profond, de brume, de faces effarées, de flambeaux et de sang, qui surgissaient dans ma conscience . . . (**"Le Convive des dernières fêtes"**);

or by accretion:

> . . . Au-devant d'eux marchait un enfant, aussi en livrée de deuil, et ce page agitait, une fois par minute, le court battement d'une cloche pour avertir au loin que l'on s'écartât sur le passage du promeneur. Et l'aspect de cette petite troupe laissait une impression aussi glaçante que le cortège d'un condamné . . . (**"Duke of Portland"**)

—or by indirect allusion, as in the following theatrical reminder of Villiers' admiration for Shakespeare's *Hamlet*:

> . . . Devant cet homme s'ouvrait la grille du rivage; l'escorte le laissait seul et il s'avançait alors au bord les flots. Là, comme perdu en un pensif désespoir et s'enivrant de la désolation de l'espace, il demeurait taciturne, pareil aux spectres de pierre de la plateforme, sous les vents, la pluie et les éclairs, devant le mugissement de l'Océan. Après une heure de cette songerie, le morne personnage, toujours accompagné des lumières et précédé du glas de la cloche, reprenait vers le donjon, le sentier d'où il était descendu . . . (**"Duke of Portland"**);

In the following, a macabre symbolism adds another, bizarre, dimension to the Parisian scene, transmogrified by featureless, Breughel-like figures and 'ominously' looming porticos:

> . . . [un bâtiment carré] s'était dressé dans la brume comme une apparition de pierre, et, malgré la rigidité de son architecture, malgré la buée morne et fantastique dont il s'était enveloppé, je lui reconnus, tout de suite, un certain air d'hospitalité cordiale qui me rasséréna l'esprit.
>
> . . . . .
>
> Plusieurs individus, les jambes allongés, la tête élevée, les yeux fixes, l'air positif, paraissaient méditer . . . (**"A s'y méprendre"**)

while in other examples visions of stylised horror and monstrousness evoke the '*monstrum horrendum informe ingens*' of mythology:

> . . . Le vent se plaignait sur les rocheuses ravines, entre les sapins qui se ployaient et craquaient, confondant leurs branches nues, pareilles aux cheveux d'une tête renversée avec horreur. La Gorgone courait dans les nuées, dont les voiles semblaient mouler sa face . . . (**"Impatience de la foule"**);
>
> . . . Et, surplombant dans les cieux mêmes, ces confins de l'horizon, de démesurées figures d'êtres divins (. . .) siégeaient, évasant leurs genoux dans l'immensité . . . (*Akëdysséril*).

Such passages testify to Villiers' deep awareness of the grotesque and ominous in natural phenomena, his innate sense of awe for the unknowable and the superhuman. The visions are 'larger than life', sophisticated refinements of the deep-seated primitive fascination for the repellant and the awe-inspiring.

Similar in effect, but stemming from a more painterly orientation, are the distorted and 'bloated' visions that occur from time to time. Although there is a certain kinship with both images of monstrousness and of decay in that the abnormal and thus 'frightful' is accentuated, unlike the foregoing examples, usually interspersed with narrative or description, these visions tend to be associated with, and subordinate to, a clear intention to create mood. They often give the impression of being gratuitous, perhaps of mere tricks of the subconscious, especially when they appear at variance with the context.

Thus they may take the form of independent 'still life' compositions within a mood of Romantic 'spleen':

> Les camélias, dont les touffes se gonflaient au bout de leurs tiges d'archal, débordaient les cristaux sur la table. (**"Le Convive des dernières fêtes"**)

or occur as mere shadowed distortions:

> . . . Une bruine froide mouillait l'atmosphère. Des passants noirs, obombrés de parapluies difformes, s'entrecroisaient . . .

Occasionally, there is a brief but significant cracking of the smooth surface of appearances, rather than a distortion. A visionary shift lets in a shaft of light from another level of reality in an occult glimpse of supernatural or elemental powers:

> . . . Le silence qui accueillit les paroles de C*** fut solennel comme si la Mort eût laissé voir, brusquement, sa tête chauve entre les candélabres . . . (**"Le Convive des dernières fêtes"**)

and the resumption of the "normal" macro-context, in spite of the authority of its mass, does not completely erase the effect from the reader's consciousness. For all its brief duration, the associative forces of 'otherworldly' suggestion supply a counter-contextual energy of a higher order than that of an ordinary shift between semantic levels; their mood-intensifying value lingers on appreciably longer by reason of its inherent affective awesomeness.

In the youthful **"Souvenirs occultes,"** these effects are converged in a complex vision of latent horror, derived from the association of the contorted, the 'bloated', the decomposed and decomposing. A natural description thrown into violent relief against an already intensely exotic context, projects a multi-sensorial vision of dense semantic and formal intricacy, heightened by occult and emblematic overtones in an integrated, if self-conscious composition of menace:

> . . . Ni souffles, ni ramages, ni fontaines, en la calme horreur de ces régions. Les bengalis, eux-mêmes, s'éloignent, ici, des vieux ébéniers, ailleurs leurs arbres. Entre les décombres, accumulés dans les éclaircies, d'immenses et monstrueuses éruptions de très longues fleurs, calices funestes où brûlent, subtils, les esprits du Soleil, s'élancent, striées d'azur, nuancées de feu, veinées de cinabre, pareilles aux radieuses dépouilles d'une myriade de paons disparus. Un air chaud de mortels aromes pèse sur les muets débris: et c'est comme une vapeur de cassolettes funéraires, une bleu, enivrante et torturante sueur de parfums . . .

This early passage is a key one, for the strangely apt coupling of 'radieuses dépouilles' reflects in microcosm an essential structural 'yoking of opposites' in Villiers' cosmology, *i.e.*, an association of decay and light, in which the latter may take many forms, and where the contrast may be projected at sundry levels of context.

Villiers' intense—and perhaps wistful—fascination for the 'hard, bright things of earth' is constantly metamorphosed into a brilliantly 'illuminated' reality, crumbling into momentarily glowing ashes or erupting into conflagration, *i.e.*, into the light of the fire that consumes in violence—literally:

> . . . Deux heures après, les flamboiements d'un sinistre immense, jaillissant de grande magasins de pétrole, d'huiles et d'allumettes, se répercutaient sur toutes les vitres du faubourg du Temple . . .
>
> . . . . .
>
> Les voitures, prisonnières, ne circulaient plus. Tout le monde vociférait. On distinguait des cris lointains parmi le crépitement terrible du feu. Les victimes hurlaient, saisies par cet enfer, et les toits des maisons s'écroulaient sur elles . . . (**"Le Désir d'être un homme"**);

or figuratively:

> . . . Cependant le crépuscule s'azurait, les flammes dorées s'éteignaient, et dans la pâleur du ciel, déjà—des étoiles (. . .) (**Akëdysséril**).

Visions of infinite space combined with bright, heraldic colours and recurrent shafts of heavenly light inevitably prompt comparison with the 'visions' of William Blake, both as painter and poet, although it is beyond the intent and scope of this study to establish particular similarities. However, many of Villiers' literary visions reveal a like preoccupation with concrete expressions of the power of Spirit over Creatures and the divine significance of Matter. In Villiers, they take the form of modes of moral significance (conventional or understood), emblematic compositions which may be static or dynamic, although in the latter case there is emphasis on pure configuration.

Thus the use of the guillotine in **"Le Secret de l'échafaud"** to carry the earthbound thoughts into the infinite:

> . . . Seule, emplissant l'espace et bornant le ciel, la guillotine semblait prolonger sur l'horizon l'ombre de ses deux bras levés, entre lesquels, bien loin, là-haut, dans le bleuissement de l'aube, on voyait scintiller la dernière étoile . . .

where 'semblait' points, not a comparison, but an illusion of perspective, and it is the association of the referend: *'deux bras levés'* with the visual component that create the emblem.

Such composite visions, so invested with mysticity, resemble details from some grandiose tableau of primitive art. But, as with such details, they display a deceptive unity; the open form of composition, the depth, the multiplicity of focus and the consequent appearance of 'ordered chaos' that often characterize the whole, are not apparent in the part. In the novelle that are themselves gigantic metaphysical-sensual visions of the Ideal imagination—*Akëdysséril* and **"L'Annonciateur"**—the broad, movement-filled canvas is a particularly effective means of animating a kind of Jacob's ladder of perpetual interplay between multiple planes of action, *i.e.*, between the mass and the élite, between the élite and the divine. It entails an accumulation of lesser image-pictures woven through a compatible narrative-pattern. It envelops the reader in a profound sensation of exotic and 'spine-chilling' tone-colour while its heaped-up massiveness and intricacy at a relatively simple level of trope enhance the feeling of the totality of the experience adumbrated by the plot and symbol-characters. Relying heavily on a variety of metaphorical figures and the occasional 'vision' rather than on dense or startling relief, it attains to a high level of visionary intensity adequate to suspend disbelief without distracting from the didactic element.

Thus most of Villiers' 'visions' spring from and vitalize an inherent metaphysical-physical dualism which is a cardinal feature, not only of the novelle **"L'Annonciateur"** and *Akëdysséril,* but of the longer 'contes' of otherwordly or supernatural association: **"Le Convive des dernières fêtes," "Le Désir d'être un homme," "La Maison du bonheur," "L'Amour suprême," "Conte de fin d'été"** and the briefer but no less intense **"Véra," "L'Affichage céleste," "Duke of Portland," "Virginie et Paul," "Les Amants de Tolède," "L'Elu des Rêves," "Les Filles de Milton,"** and **"La Céleste aventure."** And though it may be said that their primary function is to provide instantaneous evocation of the 'unreal', it is also true that they provide, besides, remarkable 'windows' through which to view the totality of their creator's worldview.

The intent of the fiction of Villiers de l'Isle-Adam is preeminently moral and the prose is couched in a didactic mode highly charged with the tension of Idealism and disenchantment in perpetual conflict. Villiers' typical expressivity is a dense, polysyllabic, "traditional" rhetoric, frequently modified and tautened,—and at times rendered violent—by disjunctive forms and highly convoluted syntax. His style ranges from peroration to irony (often grounded in banality, cliché, and deliberate ambiguity) to passionate near-incoherence. Although meaning is often enhanced with conventional symbolism, the texture of the rhetoric is generally excessively ratiocinative, tending to obscure meaning with complex syntactic figures and intricate hypotaxis, and moreover prone to high affective tension and multiple and unexpected shifts of register and style-type.

Within this general texture there is a highly significant occurrence of image-patterns, dominated by conceits and "visions" and heavy with ornaments of the occult: the horrendous, the transfigured, the ritualistic. The "visions" often take "painterly" form, dynamically composed into fluid, "arrested", emblematic, or "open-formed" tableaux, with a predilection for mixtures of the sensual and apocalyptic in the major "canvases."

Of the two major image-types, the conceit is the more conventional. This is usually densely arranged with mixtures of opposites or of logical illogicalities, the latter form functioning psychologically in place of the more direct paradox, noticeably rare in Villiers. There is a loose relationship of form and concept: fanciful flights of the imagination often lead to excessive elaboration and an obscuring of the original motivation. Conceits that pertain to love tend to be more conventional and stress the mortality of earthly experience; mystical conceits stress sensuality and reflect Villiers' obsession with occult "correspondences", expressed in esoteric symbolism, cabalistic paraphernalia, blazoning and, occasionally, enigma.

Visions are projected in alternating, interpenetrating

and/or multi-focal planes which, especially in the more massive instances, eschew synthesis. The effect is very frequently combined with stock "gothic" properties to create melodramic tension: luminous distortions, macabre symbolism, images of decay and decomposition, and a feeling of the play of supernatural forces. The total effect of massiveness and intricacy stems from the desire for completeness of impression and richness of affective impact, without regard for the norms of *mesure,* coherence and balance of a classical tradition.

Villiers' expressive-figurative language by its very nature resists compact formalisation. The *strings* of characteristics—thematic and formal—that emerge from this study are clearly to be assimilated in their totality to similar, although not identical, patterns that have been shown to be present in the literature of the late and post-Renaissance. Careful typological distinctions have been made by students of this literature between the styles of that period in different countries of Europe and the epoch-style has even been separated into substyles such as Baroque, High Baroque, Metaphysical, Mannerist, *précieux.* Such niceties are irrelevant out of the context of their epoch, although there is much to be said for finding in Villiers' Weltanschauung a historical correlative with the spirit and deeds of the Counter-Reformation.

Villiers de l'Isle-Adam has been characterized in Lansonian terms as a *"romantique attarde".* But in the Villieresque strings of style characteristics there is a textual convergence with baroque style-sets too pronounced to be obscured by a ready allusion to the broad concept of Romanticism. And to assert simply that the Romantics had their own peculiar forms of violence and excessiveness, together with temperaments akin both to Villiers and to many baroque writers, is to underestimate the conclusive stylistic evidence of Villiers' image-technique as a basic indicator to his style. (pp. 123-44)

> *Ivor A. Arnold, "Villiers de l'Isle-Adam: Image-Technique in the Shorter Fiction," in* Orbis Litterarum, *Vol. 27, No. 2, 1972, pp. 122-44.*

The cruelty emphasized in the title *Contes cruels,* experienced by many of the characters, is perhaps most subtly exerted upon the reader, whose convictions about reality are constantly tested and challenged.

—John Blaise Anzalone, in his "Jean-Marie Mathias Philippe-Auguste, Comte de Villiers de l'Isle-Adam," in Dictionary of Literary Biography, *Vol. 123, 1992.*

Horst S. Daemmrich   (essay date 1972)

[Daemmrich is a German-born American educator and

critic. In the following excerpt, he uses two stories by Villiers, "Duke of Portland" and "A s'y méprendre," as examples of how modern literary works may be seen as "infernal" versions of fairy tales.]

The efflorescence of the fairy tale as genre and the interest in folk and fairy tale motifs during the time of German Romanticism has been documented exhaustively. With the advent of Romanticism in Europe, basic fairy tale motifs have also recurred in literature. Frequently they are not recognized, because the fairy tale's familiar setting, timeless characters, temporal unity, and the concurrence of reality and supra-reality are absent. The fairy tale exhibits a distinct pattern: it proceeds from a situation of challenge, disorder, or conflict, to one of resolution or restoration of order. And though the hero is threatened by the possibility of failure he invariably succeeds in his quest and journey. He is rewarded with happiness in life by either remaining innocent, gaining worldly riches, or attaining truth. After being tested he actually experiences the spiritual rebirth promised to the tragic hero in literature in the form of increased self-knowledge. Consequently, the reader who perceives the archetypal form hidden in a fairy tale motif may fail to identify it in a literary work which portrays man's existential situation, his passion and action in a specific historic and cultural setting. Furthermore, fairy tale motifs in fiction or plays are often transformed or completely inverted.

Such inversions can be the result of a deliberate and playful manipulation which sets up a sharp contrast between the universal, ageless archetype and a singular human fate. Inversions can also spring from the conscious or unconscious rejection of the archetype. This pattern, consistent with a tragic or absurd view of the world, is characterized by a demonic modulation which questions the validity of the archetype and transforms the joyous acclamation of life into a somber appraisal of man's destiny. Inverted motifs constitute basic structural units in narratives and plays. Their identification should lead to the recognition of an important structural pattern in literature and consequently enhance critical appraisals. In the light of traditional motifs such inversions should be called infernal fairy tales.

In some tales the demonic imagery seems to express the author's "ironic mode." Frequently, however, it forms the basis for a profoundly pessimistic design of caged man. In the perspective of intellectual history, infernal fairy tales balance the optimistic view of the world expressed in traditional fairy tales; one might even argue that infernal tales express man's existential situation more faithfully than fairy tales, which appear almost as inversions of life. (pp. 85-6)

The motif of the Quest for Life and its variations are found in many fairy tales, among them, "The Brave Tailor," "Cinderella," "The Three Ravens," and "The Devil with Three Golden Hairs." Its characteristic elements can be perceived most clearly in the tales of "The Princess on the Glass Mountain," "The Raven," and "Prince Swan." The tale of the "Princess on the Glass Mountain" relates how a young man retains his pure heart, successfully overcomes all obstacles, and finally rides up the mountain of glass to win the fair princess. In "The Raven" a man encounters in a dark forest the enchanted princess who implores him to free her. All he has to do is to resist the lure of an old woman and refuse her food and drink in order to stay awake for the princess. Despite her admonition he is enticed to drink on three successive days by the old woman and fails his test. After leaving bread, meat, and wine which will always replenish themselves, that is, symbols of eternal life and rejuvenation, the princess disappears to the mountain of glass. Hopelessly, the man searches for her in a dark forest which symbolizes the existential uncertainty of life. Finally he overcomes three giants, wins a magic horse, rides to the top of the mountain and liberates the princess.

The pattern of the tales reveals a struggle between man's idealistic vision and his earthly, confining instincts which is hidden in the conflict between the fair princess and the evil woman, the virgin and the temptress. . . . The hero yearns for pure light but falls prey to temptations in his quest for self-realization. The ultimate success of the quest does not depend on heroic qualities nor does it spring from a rebellious assertion against nature. Indeed, the hero frequently needs the help of nature which he receives from friendly animals and insects; just as often he relies on shrewdness or even resorts to trickery. But while he initially fails to surmount the obstacles which he encounters during his trials, he is eventually redeemed because he remains faithful to his ideal during the long, arduous journey in the forests of darkness. By retaining a pure heart and remaining true to his quest he can ultimately scale the shimmering mountain of glass that reaches far into the sky and thus realize his vision. (p. 89)

Allusions to, demonic modulations and inversions of, the motif of the Quest for Life seem to increase toward the end of the nineteenth and the beginning of the twentieth century. They are apparent in the fiction of Jean Marie de Villiers de l'Isle-Adam, Hugo von Hofmannsthal, and Isak Dinesen (Karen Blixen), to name three authors from different countries. A prevalent pattern in these narratives is the transformation of vistas of life and potential self-realization in the world to visions of alienation, death, destruction, and existential failure. The pattern is frequently enforced by imagery of distortion, oppressive squalor, and the cage. Two tales from Villiers de l'Isle-Adam's collection **Contes cruels** (1883) provide good examples. In **"Duke of Portland,"** the young, wealthy, and popular Duke journeys to the Middle East. Suddenly, without understanding the reasons for his urge, he decides to visit the last victim of the ancient incurable form of leprosy, an outcast banned in horror from society. It seems as if a mysterious demonic fate guides his action: "no one escapes his destiny." Descending into the cave of the leper, the Duke, "bold to the point of madness," insists upon shaking the man's hand and immediately contracts the disease. Thereupon he buries himself in his manor and dies imprisoned in his own cage.

In the narrative **"A s'y méprendre!"** the basic theme of active self-realization in the world is inverted to a confrontation with death. On a cold, drizzly November day the narrator calls a carriage in order to attend a previously arranged business meeting. While waiting on the threshold of a building resembling all and any buildings in his life, he follows a sudden impulse to step in and greet the hostess. Upon entering, he finds himself confronted by dead businessmen, who are entertained by Death. They had already ended their journey, for they failed to perceive the true significance of life, by confusing activity with existential commitment: "Certainly, in order to escape their harassed existence, most of the people in the room had assassinated their bodies, thus hoping for some more well-being."

Horrified, the narrator tries to escape by leaping into a coach, which has disgorged more dead businessmen. During the ensuing trip through the streets of Paris, he observes that the passing scenery has assumed the appearance of death. Still determined to follow his destiny, he alights at the café designated as the site of the planned meeting, only to find once again a room filled with dead associates. At this point he begins to understand that "in order to escape the burden of their intolerable, nagging conscience, most of the people in the room had long ago assassinated their 'souls,' thus hoping for some more well-being." And yet the narrator-protagonist fails to understand the real significance of his visionary experience. He leaves silently, returns to his home, and renounces his profession and life. (pp. 91-2)

The inversion of archetypal fairy tale motifs shows several common features. Instead of anticipating a happy ending, the motifs arouse a feeling of impending disaster. Joy in life is marred by the finality of isolation or death. The possibility of a successful self-realization in the world is questioned or negated and the theme of enslavement replaces that of freedom. Finally the motifs focus attention on man's existential anguish and the suffering of all those who face a wretched, absurd world. (p. 95)

> Horst S. Daemmrich, "The Infernal Fairy Tale: Inversion of Archetypal Motifs in Modern European Literature," in Mosaic: A Journal for the Comparative Study of Literature and Ideas, *Vol. III, No. 14, Spring, 1972, pp. 85-95.*

Ivor Arnold (essay date 1974)

[*In the following essay, Arnold analyzes Villiers's descriptive style.*]

Villiers de L'Isle Adam's descriptive style is not the product of a deliberately refined painterly aesthetic as, for example, that of the Goncourt brothers. It is rather adapted to the literary moment, an instrument for establishing appropriate setting and atmosphere at the behest of narrative circumstance and subordinated to more engrossing moral ends.

The general literary aesthetic of the 1860's–1880's in France for descriptive writing was "art for art's sake," a loose blend of the descriptive and rhetorical forms of Flaubert (realism, verbal beauty, "fit"), with those of the Goncourts (phenomenalism and the nominal phrase), availing itself too to some extent of the *phrase décadente* of Ver-

laine and the incantations and wrenched disjunctions of Mallarmé, but maintaining a stubborn loyalty to the older traditional rhetoric of expressive prose. Villiers' personal descriptive style is highly representative of this general aesthetic particularly in its uneasy combination of the "old" and the "new" rhetoric, but its salient features are a special emphasis on the more widely accepted features of *écriture artiste,* an unusually wide use of descriptive rhetoric of the Romantic era, and large doses of Parnassian exoticism. These create an overall heterogeneity which in large measure is to be explained by the overriding conformity to the principle of "fit," a principle that made correspondence of style to subject almost a national "law" of stylistics.

The most conspicuous and the most interesting influence on Villiers' descriptive style is, without doubt, that of *écriture artiste,* the prose technique introduced by Jules and Edmond de Goncourt in the 1860's. The more extreme stylistic features of their aesthetic were practised by few others, but, in more modified form, gained widespread acceptance. M. G. Loesch, in his *Die impressionistische Syntax der Goncourt* (diss., 1919) made a careful stylistic analysis of the style and its aesthetic, and his findings are invaluable for the establishment of a basis of comparison.

As Loesch indicates, the basis of the technique is the application of contemporary art-forms to literary prose, to effect a systematic transition of the Impressionist theories of form and light to descriptive writing. Not only did it seek to achieve comparable pictorial effects, it also claimed that the phenomenological approach of direct representation could, in literature, be applied to the rendition of emotion as well, i.e., direct impressions of the "colour" and "form" both of environment and sentiment were deemed possible through a syntax deliberately calculated to eliminate the classic interpretative role of the artist.

This, briefly, is not to be achieved by abandoning completely the classic mode, with its careful attention to balance, harmony and coherence as ends in themselves. Rather the classic virtues are to be relegated to a minor rôle, in favour of a "dynamic phenomenalism," emphasizing objectivity, impersonality and the neglect of causality, stressing evocation instead of delineation, and tending to substitute the chronological for the more "normal" logical order of sentence so as to achieve a kind of impressionistic control over the information transmitted to the reader's imagination.

So, at the syntactic level, we find that the chief device is the nominal expression with its highly affective impact of image—static or dynamic—thrust upon the reader's "mind's eye" instantaneously, undiluted as far as possible by commentary or mere rhetorical flow, closely articulated by disjunctive contraction into single, dense, and complete images, and elaborated by means of "radiations" of complex, heterogeneous accumulations of subordinate phrases and clauses with a minimum of grammatical connectives. For evocation, we find, too, an intricate system of affectively or "impressionistically" placed epithets and widespread nominalisation of adjectives in order to achieve a similar order of perception (e.g., "les ivresses de bonheur"). So, too, the "impressionistic" noun-pluralisation, the long series of pictorial phrases, the use of asyndetic strings, with repetition of demonstratives, or repetition of nouns with change of, or omission of article, all designed to simulate the intensity, overlap, and "high-frequency emissions" of the visual and psychic information "quanta" that constitute sense-data.

Of these features, only a certain number occur with frequency in Villiers' modified form of "écriture artiste."

Nominalism in Villiers is confined to the heaping of substantival images with the occasional substantivisation of epithet; the zero degree use of *c'est, c'était,* etc., and the more affective *voici que;* the occasional example of singular abstract noun replacing concrete verb; and the gratuitous pluralisation of the noun where the singular form suffices:

> . . . C'était son premier soir de jeunesse! Il avait vingt ans. C'était son entrée dans un monde de flamme, d'oubli, *de banalités,* d'or et de plaisirs . . . (**"L'Inconnue"**)

These devices may be combined with impressionistic order, and, to this end, inversion:

> . . . Sur un siège de cèdre, aux pieds des chroubïm lumineux de Trône et entouré de ses rudes guibborim, est assis, voûté, pâle et sans boire, et le glaive sur les genoux, le Sar-des-gardes Ben Jëhu. C'est l'antique exécuteur du rebelle Adônia . . .

Verb-noun plural forms on occasion stand alone:

> . . . Au dehors, il faisait une pluie terne et fine, semée de neige; une nuit glaciale;—*des bruits de voitures, des cris de masques,* la sortie de l'Opéra. C'était les hallucinations de Gavarni, de Deveria, de Gustave Doré . . . (**"Le Convive des dernières fêtes"**);

but often blend significantly with appropriate evocations of light in the Impressionist manner:

> . . . J'oubliai donc toute préoccupation. Ce furent bientôt, des scintillements de concetti, des aveux légers, de ces baisers vagues (pareils au bruit de ces feuilles de fleurs que les belles distraites font claquer sur le dessus de leurs mains), ce furent des feux de sourires et de diamants . . .;

although the presence of the twin "conceits," one typically in parenthesis, produces a particularly Villieresque convergence.

The Goncourt mannerism of ordering a descriptive sentence phenomenologically or chronologically is widespread at this period, and in Villiers examples are legion. As already illustrated in one of the above examples, it very frequently entails inversion of subject and verb, together with deliberate effects of suspense obtained by disjointing the sentence with accumulated detail, or adverbial qualification:

> Il y a quelques annés, florissait, orgueil de nos boulevards, certain vaste et lumineux café, situé presque en face d'un de nos théâtres de genre, dont le fronton rappelle celui d'un temple païen . . . (**"Les Demoiselles de Bienfilâtre,"**);

> . . . Sur la terrasse, entre la rangée de fiacres et le vitrage, une pelouse de femmes, une floraison de chignons échappés du crayon de Guys, attifées de toilettes invraisemblables, se prélassaient sur les chaises, auprès des guéridons de fer battu peints en vert espérance. Sur ces guéridons étaient délivrés des breuvages . . .

It may produce a wholly "picturesque" scenic pattern:

> . . . Une sorte de sentier, en pente vers la mer, une sinueuse allée, creusée entre des étendues de roches et bordée, tout au long, de pins sauvages, ouvre, en bas, ses lourdes grilles dorées sur le sable même de la plage, immergé aux heures de reflux . . . (**"Duke of Portland"**);

or trace a set of purely psychological impressions:

> Sa disparition de Mabille, ses allures nouvelles, la discrète élégance de ses toilettes sombres, ses airs, enfin, de *noli me tangere,* joints à de certaines *réticences* qu'employaient désormais ses favorisés en parlant d'elle, tout cela m'intriguait un peu les esprits au sujet de cette séduisante fille, célèbre, jadis, dans ces soupers où son fin et joli babil galvanisait jusqu'aux princes les plus moroses de la Gomme—et que je désire appeler Maryelle . . . (**"Maryelle"**)

In either case, the writer tends to satisfy grammatical requirements with a bare verb of minimal expressivity, so far separated from its real subject that the logical linkage is destroyed, leaving it a mere appendage to the phenomenological mass (here: *"sentier"* . . . *"ouvre";* *"disparition,"* . . . *cela m'intriguait* "), to the point where even the central figure succumbs to effacement, resulting in the very common *"phrase à éventail"*:

> . . . Une chaise dépaillée, une ombre de table, une écuelle, sous un jour de souffrance, dit à tabatière, creusé dans la toiture;—et, dans un enfoncement, au plus sombre du bouge, un grabat sur lequel *un très vieux homme,* en loques de mendiant, à la face hébétée et blanche—en laquelle transparaissait déjà la Tête de mort,—semblait râler, les yeux fixes—étreignant en sa main droite pendante un crochet de chiffonnier . . . (**"L'Elu des rêves"**)

Attributive anteposition, while a consistently calculated effect for the Goncourts, is largely an automatic device in Villiers, i.e., in passages of "modified" *écriture artiste* he normally anteposes epithets traditionally placed after the noun, so that there is, in these contexts, a diminution of the affective or phenomenological effect. Stylistic effectiveness is restored in some contexts, where anteposition is compounded (especially in a triad: " . . . *une bleue, enivrante et torturante sueur de parfums"* (**"Souvenirs occultes"**), and Villiers has a particular tendency to antepose participles, both present and past, in which case the verbal element benefits phenomenologically from its unusual location before its subject (cf. the effect of anticipation of, e.g., *"une environnante conviction," "ce stupéfiant discours," "une négligée élégance," "cette inattendue perfidie"*).

In a style where accumulation is a normal device, only extreme or special features will result in notable *mise-en-*

relief. The *écriture artiste* technique of reiterating or heaping up images by subtle variations of parallel form is not frequent in Villiers; it is generally confined to an occasional example of pluralised verb-abstractions:

> . . . Autour de lui, sous les puissantes vibrations tombées du beffroi,—dehors, là-bas, au delà du mur de ses yeux—,des piétinements de cavalerie, et, par éclats, des sonneries aux champs, des acclamations mêlées aux salves des Invalides, aux cris fiers des commandements, des bruissements d'acier, des tonnerres de tambours scandant des défilés interminables d'infanterie, toute une rumeur de gloire lui arrivait! Son ouïe suraiguë percevait jusqu'à des flottements d'étendards aux lourdes franges frôlant des cuirasses . . . (**"Vox populi"**);

heaped adjective-phrases in near-parallel:

> . . . Annah, ou plutôt Susannah Jackson, la Circé écossaise, *aux cheveux plus noirs que la nuit, aux regards de sarisses, aux petites phrases acidulées,* étincelait, indolemment, dans le velours rouge . . . (**"Le Convive des dernières fêtes"**);

or massed, complex adverb-phrases, most often temporal in nature (i.e., exploiting a form in keeping with an "impressionistic" perception of "points" in time) in a binary-ternary pattern (2 × 3):

> —En 1876, au solstice de l'automne, vers ce temps où le nombre, toujours croissant, des inhumations accomplies à la légère,—beaucoup trop précipitées enfin,—commen çait à révolter la Bourgeoisie parisienne et à la plonger dans les alarmes un certain soir, sur les huit heures, à l'issue d'une séance de spiritisme des plus curieuses, je me sentis, en rentrant chez moi, sous l'influence de ce spleen héréditaire . . . (**"L'Intersigne"**);

and even (though rarely) a massed conglomeration of disparate sentence-members in a *"phrase à éventail "*:

> . . . En l'une de ces chambres,—dont le riche ameublement, les tentures cordouanes, les arbustes, les vitraux ensoleillés, les tableaux, tranchaient sur la nudité des autres séjours,—se tenait debout, cette aurore-là, les pieds nus sur des sandales, au centre de la rosace d'un tapis byzantin, les mains jointes, les vastes yeux fixes, un maigre vieillard, de taille géante, vêtu de la simarre blanche à croix rouge, le long manteau noir aux épaules, la barrette noire sur le crâne, le chapelet de fer à la ceinture. Blafard, brisé de macérations, saignant, sans doute, sous le calice invisible qu'il ne quittait jamais, il considérait une alcôve où se trouvait, drapé et festonné de guirlandes, un lit opulent et moelleux. Cet homme avait nom Tomas de Torquemada . . . (**"Les Amants de Tolède"**)

Just as frequently, however, Villiers will couch a descriptive passage in the routine expressivity of new rhetoric, with its sonorities, its eloquent balance, its even progression. Such passages may well exhibit some of the features illustrated in our examples of *écriture artiste,* but—perhaps influenced by a stylistic identification with the "goût suranné" which enshrouds the following passage—their effect is lost as logic and elegance take precedence. This passage from **"The Duke of Portland"** (which exhibits some of the purest examples of phenomenological nominalism) is a prime example. One notes how the unobtrusive impressionistic inversion and preposed adverbs alternate delicately with the regular movement of subject-verb order and a minimum of anteposed epithets to achieve what is an "old-fashioned" *reportage,* rather than an impression. The writer's prime aesthetic objective, in this case, at least, is a "well-turned" style, not painterly impressionism, and rhetoric triumphs:

> . . . Souvent, en effet, vers cette heure-là même, dans les détours de l'allée qui descendait vers l'Océan, un gentleman, enveloppé d'un manteau, le visage recouvert d'un masque d'étoffe noire auquel était adaptée une capuce circulaire qui cachait toute la tête, s'acheminait, la lueur d'un cigare à la main longuement gantée, vers la plage. Comme par une fantasmagorie d'un goût suranné, deux serviteurs aux cheveux blancs le précédaient; deux autres le suivaient, à quelques pas, élevant de fumeuses torches rouges.
>
> Au-devant d'eux marchait un enfant, aussi, en livrée de deuil, et ce page agitait, une fois par minute, le court battement d'une cloche pour avertir au loin que l'on s'écartât sur le passage du promeneur. Et l'aspect de cette troupe laissait une impression aussi glaçante que le cortège d'un condamné . . .

Possibly for similar reasons of "fit," or, more simply, perhaps prompted by an unconscious feeling for tonal associations, Villiers sometimes plainly reverts to Romantic "passion," drawing upon the time-honoured devices of lyric evocation (alliteration, imitative harmony, "picturesque" nature, and sentimental reverie):

> . . . Le vent se plaignait sur les rocheuses ravines, entre les sapins qui se ployaient et craquaient, confondant leurs branches nues . . . (**"Impatience de la foule"**);

and:

> . . . Voici l'heure de l'isolement: les bruits du travail se sont tus dans le faubourg; mes pas m'ont conduit jusqu'ici, au hasard. Cette bâtisse fut, autrefois, une vieille abbaye. Un rayon de lune fait voir l'escalier de pierre, derrière la grille, et illumine à demi les vieux saints sculptés (etc.) . . . (**"Virginie et Paul"**);

but such pure reversion is not typical; more often his nonimpressionist descriptive rhetoric betrays the early formation of Parnassianism. Then we have a different aesthetic, one of a passion for borrowed terms and "precise" orthography, cadenced movement, careful, restrained diction, the concentration on syntactic congruence to architectural form, and a subordination of verbal euphony.

Romantic lyricism, Parnassianism, *écriture artiste* all play a part in Villiers' descriptive style. Indeed we are repeatedly confronted in his descriptive writing by *mixtures,* in which it is the complex design of *dosages,* varying from instance to instance according to the particular psycholinguistic purpose, that is its definition. In a word, Villiers' style is usually derivative in unconscious manner, for the most part drawing like so many others on a common fund of epoch-styles past and present, and it would be false to single out any one as a specific stylistic model. But Villiers was an artist as much as he was a moralist, and it is clearly in the more commonly practised forms of *écriture artiste* that his style is at its most "art-conscious" and deliberate. (pp. 874-81)

> Ivor Arnold, "Villiers de l'Isle-Adam and 'écriture artiste'," in The French Review, *Vol. XLVII, No. 5, April, 1974, pp. 874-81.*

Arthur Symons on Villiers's attitude toward science:

Villiers' revolt against Science, so far as Science is materialistic, and his passionate curiosity in that chimera's flight towards the invisible, are one and the same impulse of a mind to which only mind is interesting. *Toute cette vieille Extériorité, maligne, compliquée, inflexible,* that illusion which Science accepts for the one reality: it must be the whole effort of one's consciousness to escape from its entanglements, to dominate it, or to ignore it, and one's art must be the building of an ideal world beyond its access, from which one may indeed sally out, now and again, in a desperate enough attack upon the illusions in the midst of which men live.

Arthur Symons, in his The Symbolist Movement in Literature, *1899.*

William T. Conroy, Jr. (essay date 1978)

[In the following excerpt, Conroy surveys Villiers's short stories.]

Villiers' tales had been appearing piecemeal since 1867, but it was only in 1883 that they were published collectively as *Contes cruels.* Of the twenty-eight tales in the volume, nineteen had been published between 1867 and 1879. Most of these had gone through several publications and revisions, and Villiers again submitted them to correction before including them in the volume. If the changes in many only affected details, those in **"L'Intersigne,"** **"L'Annonciateur"** (**"Azraël"**), and **"Le Secret de l'ancienne musique"** (**"Le Chapeau chinois"**) were more substantial. The remaining nine stories were conceived after 1880, and three in fact had no publication prior to the appearance of the collection.

Of the works written after 1880, three satirize the bourgeoisie and the materialism of the age. **"Deux Augures,"** for instance, is a conversation between a supposed aspiring journalist and a newspaper director. The latter rejects the young man's article as too good in the democratic era when "Above all, [have] no genius!" and "Be mediocre" are the rules of the game. While based on reality—the journalist embodying characteristics of Villiers, the director those of publishing magnate Emile de Girardin—the story assumes the proportions of caricature, and the direc-

tor becomes a symbol of the "lucrative cynicism of the powerful press." In **"Fleurs de ténèbres"** (1880), Villiers satirizes the practicality and emotional insensitivity of his contemporaries, who even resell flowers used at funerals, so they do not "wither *uselessly* on the fresh tombs." The satire of **"Les Brigands"** (1882) is particularly truculent. The landowners of Nayrac join forces to go collect their rents, although they know the rumors of highway robbers are false. On their way home, they meet landlords of neighboring Pibrac, who have also banded together. Imagining the tenants' stories to be true, each group mistakes the other for bandits. A battle to save "their lives and their money" results in a general massacre. The tale ends with "the real brigands (that is, the half-dozen poor devils guilty, at most, of having taken a few crusts . . .)" collecting the money from the dead bodies and fleeing across the border. In ridiculing the bourgeoisie's fear of the popular classes and its desire to defend its possessions at any cost, Villiers uses three interesting satiric devices. First, the characters are drawn in caricatural terms. Then, he describes the landlords' departure in language that parodies chivalric epics. "Our heroes," he writes, were singing a "heroic song," while "the ladies," their wives, "were looking in admiration at these modern paladins and stuffing their pockets with cough drops." Finally, it is with sheer irony that the landowners, knowing the falsity of the rumors, fall victim to the tenants' stories and mistake their counterparts for robbers.

"Duke of Portland" is a tale of mystery and suspense, partially based on the historic William Bentinck, fifth duke of Portland (1800-1879). After returning to England from the East, Lord Richard abruptly retires to a solitary existence in the family manor. Queen Victoria, who has sent inquiries to the recluse, shudders when she reads a letter from him, while Héléna, the queen's reader, who is betrothed to Portland, falls into a faint. A year later, while the elite of English aristocracy gather at Portland for one of the seasonal balls given but not attended by the duke, this mysterious character, masked, wrapped in a cloak, and preceded by a page ringing a bell, makes his way to the beach. There, he meets Héléna, bids her farewell until next they meet, and dies. Three days later, true to his memory and hopeful of reunion in eternity, Héléna takes the veil. Only at the end, as the narrative returns to the moment of the tale's beginning, does Villiers clarify the mystery. In the East, the noble Richard contracted leprosy by charitably visiting one of its victims and shaking his hand.

"Vox populi" (1880, 1881) is a poetic tale consisting of three scenes and a conclusion. In the first scene, set in 1868 during the Second Empire, the people have gathered to see the "grand review on the Champs-Elysées that day" of Napoleon's anniversary. Amid the cheers is heard the melodic plea of a beggar: "Have pity on a poor blind man, if you please!" The second scene, set in 1870 during the Third Republic, also depicts a "grand review on the Champs-Elysées that day," the crowd's applause, and the beggar's prayer. Another "grand review on the Champs-Elysées that day" is presented in scene three, set in 1871 during and after the Commune. The same action occurs. The masses cheer a leader; the beggar, eyes raised toward heaven, whimpers: "Have pity on a poor blind man, if you please!" The repetition of the same action at different historical periods, the use of identical words to open and close the three scenes, and the tale's conclusion underline the repetitive nature of history and its immutable truths. The people, eager to give their allegiance, are forever intellectually blind. By contrast, the seer, symbolized by a blind beggar who . . . is privy to eternal truths, understands their real desires. Unfortunately, advice given by the "Speaker of the people's secret thoughts" constantly goes unheeded. The story's title, referring to the Latin slogan "Vox populi, vox Dei" ("The voice of the people is the voice of God"), is meant ironically.

The three remaining works, less easily classified, present pictures of cruel individuals. **"Le Désir d'être un homme"** (1882), for instance, is a bizarre psychological study of an aging actor, Esprit Chaudval, who, after impersonating other people for so long, desires to experience an emotion of his own and "be a man." In hopes of feeling remorse, he sets a fire that claims nearly a hundred victims. But he is disappointed, for, a victim of his acting profession, he can feel no emotion of his own, "no menacing phantom." **"La Reine Ysabeau"** (1880), a pseudohistorical narrative set in the early fifteenth century, draws a portrait of the wife of France's King Charles VI (1368-1422). Having learned that her favorite, Vidame de Maulle, has wagered that he can seduce Bérénice Escabala, Queen Ysabeau cunningly has him accused of arson and condemned to death. On the eve of the execution, Maulle's heroic lawyer changes places with the condemned man, who escapes in the former's dress. The exchange makes no difference to Ysabeau. To erase Maulle's name "from the list of the living, she order[s] the sentence to be carried out *anyway*." **"Maryelle,"** a tale within a tale, satirically depicts a courtesan who sees no contradiction between her need to accept gentlemen's favors and her fidelity, "in thought as in sensations," to her young lover Raoul.

We can now make several concluding remarks about this collection. The tales as a whole bear the heavy imprint of the author. The noble Portland and the young writer of **"Deux Augures"** are projections of himself; Maryelle is surely based on one of the society women he had met. **"Vox populi"** contains memories of parades on the Champs-Elyés. Yet these experiences are transformed, through symbols and poetic imagination, to another level of meaning. Behind almost all the stories is the idea of the nobility of idealism (**"Véra," "Duke of Portland," "L'Intersigne"**), the inhumanity of positivism and bourgeois values (**"Les Demoiselles de Bienfilâtre," "Deux Augures," "L'Affichage céleste," "Les Brigands"**), or the unceasing conflict between the two (**"Vox populi," "Virginie et Paul," "Sentimentalisme"**). The choice of the collection's title is a happy one, for cruelty, either in the situation described or in the mordant satiric style employed, is a feature common to virtually all the stories. Now some tales, like **"L'Appareil pour l'analyse chimique du dernier soupir"** or **"La Machine à gloire,"** may disappoint us because they lack subtlety; others, like **"Fleurs de ténèbres,"** because they are undeveloped. And the inclusion of seven poems from his earlier works seems an outright mistake: Although arranged to present a series of emotions and col-

lectively called "Conte d'amour" (1880), the poems hardly constitute a tale. Nevertheless, one still has to agree with Mallarmé that the collection contains "a sum of extraordinary Beauty." No wonder the **Contes cruels** established Villiers as a leader of the literary avant-garde in the eyes of the younger generation. No wonder, too, that the volume still haunts us today. (pp. 106-09)

After the brilliance of the **Contes cruels,** Villiers' later collections—*L'Amour suprême* (1886), *Histoires insolites* (1888), *Nouveaux Contes cruels* (1888)—are somewhat disappointing. Many works in the first two volumes, like **"Les Expériences du Dr. Crookes,"** about supposed scientific experiments confirming the occult, are long and rambling. Others suffer from lack of action; **"La Maison du bonheur"** is really a description of two elect souls who flee a vulgar world. Narratives like **"Le Droit du passé," "Le Tzar et les grands-ducs,"** and **"Une Entrevue à Solesmes"** are personal and historical anecdotes rather than imagined tales. Furthermore, of the eight **Nouveaux Contes cruels,** most are derivative. Four are based on borrowed material, while three repeat, with little variation, themes and techniques of earlier tales. **"Les Amies de pension,"** for instance, recalls **"Les Demoiselles de Bienfilâtre,"** as **"Le Chant du coq"** recalls **"L'Annonciateur."** And if **"L'Amour du naturel"** is about the effects of materialism on life, not just love, it calls to mind the earlier **"Virginie et Paul"** by its idyllic setting, dialogue, and characters whose names are borrowed from other literary works.

Nevertheless, the three collections contain some notable exceptions, and in these Villiers attains the high artistic level of the **Contes cruels. "L'Amour suprême,"** after which the collection of 1886 is named, is a story of supreme love fulfilled in death. After claiming that people have been willing to "sacrifice kisses [and] forego embraces" to avoid "the unfulfilled hopes" and "illusions of worldly love," the narrator illustrates the idea with his own experience. During a ball at the Ministry of Foreign Affairs, he unexpectedly met Lysiane d'Aubelleyne, whom he had known and loved years ago in Brittany. About to flee the "tangible world where we ourselves are only appearances," she came that night only to affront, according to Carmelite custom, "the world's temptations before professing her vows." She consented to see the narrator once again the following morning in the chapel of Notre-Dame-des-Champs. When he arrived, a priest was reciting the mass of the dead. The white-draped bier, candles, and nuns indicated that an induction ceremony was to take place. He now realized Mlle d'Aubelleyne had invited him to witness the profession of her vows, her dying to the world. Toward the ceremony's end, her eyes met his. Their love, like that of Portland and Héléna, will be fulfilled in death, for in her eyes he read the promise of an "eternal rendezvous."

Although the narrator is surprised by this outcome, Villiers' imagery has in fact prepared the reader. Mlle d'Aubelleyne's purity and death to the world is reflected the moment we see her in her pale complexion, her eyes "of white lilies," and the black dress decorated with lilies. Her comparison to Beatrice, whose love from afar raised Dante's own to a spiritual dimension, suggests the role she will play at the end, where, incidentally, the image is repeated and developed. The tolling of midnight, foreshadowing the death bell of the religious ceremony, suggest a future death as Villiers compares it to a "formless bird of wind, sonorous echoes and darkness," Finally, the meeting of Mlle d'Aubelleyne and the narrator on a balcony, detached from the clamor of the worldly gathering, facing the eternal stars, foreshadows their eventual meeting beyond the sense world, in eternity.

True love and its incompatibility with the world are also the theme of "Les Amants de Tolède" (*Histoires insolites*). To preserve an innocent couple's love from the onslaught of disillusioning reality, Tomas de Torquemada, the grand inquisitor of Spain, submits them to what he calls the "trial by Happiness." Binding them naked, setting them upon the marriage bed, he leaves them alone "to their immense joy." Their purity permits them to experience absolute love. After they are unbound, however, they have no desire to repeat the incident. Henceforth, they live almost separately in their own apartments, dying without posterity, for they realize that they have experienced a sublime and unique moment and that any attempt to relive it can only be a disappointment.

Four satiric tales from the collections are worth noting. The first, "Le Secret de l'échafaud" (*L'Amour suprême*), is based on contemporary executions, experimentation with the dead, and two historical characters, Dr. Edmond-Désiré Couty de La Pommerais and Dr. Armand Velpeau. La Pommerais, who is awaiting execution for murder, receives a visit from Velpeau. After indicating that a much-debated point is whether conscious life persists in the brain after decapitation, the latter proposes to the former an experiment that will resolve the question. After the blade falls, La Pommerais is to wink his right eye three times if he is aware of life. La Pommerais agrees, and moments after the execution, Velpeau anxiously leans over the severed head to observe the results. The right eye, however, winks only once. The inscrutable sign and the inconclusive result of the experiment make the point of the satire clear. Life and death are enigmas. In vain, cruel experimenters like Velpeau poke, prod, and profane the dead; science is incapable of answering the fundamental questions of life.

"L'Héroïsme du docteur Hallidonhill" (*Histoires insolites*) is about a London physician who offhandedly prescribes a dubious cure—a stay in Nice and a diet of watercress—to a skeleton of a patient, for whom he has already given up all hope. When after six months the skeleton returns a giant, Hallidonhill does not hesitate to sacrifice to science the life he has saved. Grabbing a revolver, he shoots the patient in order to examine the body and explain "the arch-miraculous action of watercress." The point of the satire is clear: Modern-day science, treating men like guinea pigs, is indifferent to human values. But, despite the serious topic, the work is never heavy or morose. Through exaggeration and irony (as in the title itself), the satire not only instructs, it also amuses.

"La Légende de l'éléphant blanc" (*L'Amour suprême*) at first strikes one as being nothing more than an amusing narrative. Out of national pride, Lord W*** hires tamers to capture a legendary white elephant from Burma and transport it back to the London Zoo. Having captured the sacred beast, the tamers dye it black to get it out of the country. They are done in by their own ruse. They cannot remove the dye, and Lord W*** is unwilling to pay for a white elephant that is black. Behind this literal level, however, lies a symbolic meaning. By its rarity, color, and sacredness, the elephant, like the swans in "Le Tueur de cygnes," represents the artist, that rare person who lives apart from the materialistic world and contemplates the divine. Villiers uses the symbol to satirize the unwillingness of practical men to respect that sacredness and society's desire to exploit the artist, even removing from him his very identity.

"Les Plagiaires de la foudre" (*Histoires insolites*), a kind of fable, also has a satiric intent. On a Pacific island, a breed of parrots imitate the sound of thunder. By their "talent," they scare the other inahbitants away. Their know-how is nevertheless limited. Try as they may, the "feathered sycophants" cannot imitate the cry of the eagle or the roar of the lion. Clearly, Villiers is ridiculing those writers, who gain some success by imitating mediocre talents but who are at a loss when it comes to a true genius.

Another tale involving the guillotine, "Les Phantasmes de M. Redoux" (*Histoires insolites*), is worth noting especially for the way it combines satire with terror. At first we are amused by the satirical portrait of Antoine Redoux, esteemed citizen of Paris, typical bourgeois, whose controlled existence prevents him from ever realizing his fantasies. When the slightly inebriated protagonist, in London on business, yields to the fantasy of playing King Louis XVI and gets caught under a guillotine late one night in Madame Tussaud's Wax Museum, our feelings begin to change. Momentarily, out of hatred for everything Redoux represents, we rejoice that his head may at any instant fall under the blade from above. Then, as Villiers suggests the captive's horror by describing external manifestations—chattering of teeth, whitening of hair and beard—desire for revenge leaves us. We identify with the terrified human being, and we imagine ourselves under the unstable blade, waiting for the inevitable.

Finally, there are in these collections two tales of suspense and terror that are superb. The first is "Catalina" (*L'Amour suprême*). To rest his mind from the study of German philosophy, the narrator of the tale journeys to Spain. In Santander, he meets an old friend, Lieutenant Gérard de Villebreuse, who has just arrived from Guiana and is bringing to the Zoological Museum of Madrid a collection of hummingbirds, orchid bulbs, and a treasure. Discussion of the treasure is interrupted by the appearance of Catalina, a "flower girl of the wharf." Suddenly, Gérard remembers that it is the anniversary of his mother's death and that he must return to his ship. He invites his friend to spend the night with Catalina in his hotel room. In the middle of the night, the narrator is awakened by "old wood splitting." From a distant church, midnight sounds. The pendulum, however, seems to be in the room, "successively striking now the masonry of the wall, now the partition of a neighboring room." The wind seems to produce a "hissing of damp wood." The narrator hears people fleeing the hotel and notices Catalina, now awake, shivering and unable to speak. To his cries for explanations, the fleeing occupants retort that he is crazy "to sleep with the Devil in the room!" Igniting a rolled-up newspaper, the narrator spies a gigantic python that has loosened itself from its ropes. He now understands: This is Gérard's treasure, its swinging body has produced the sound of the pendulum, and its tongue the hissing sound. Panic-stricken, the narrator grabs Catalina and flees. Taking a steamer, he returns home immediately, happy to leave "the contingencies of the world of phenomena" for the abstract world of philosophy.

What is ingenious in this tale is the build up of suspense and the intensity of terror. When the narrator first awakes in the hotel room, it is unclear whether the splitting, thumping, and hissing sounds are real or the product of imagination. It is possible that the narrator, like so many characters in Poe, is just an excitable, nervous individual. When people start fleeing, the reader realizes that there is something objective to fear. But what? Although Catalina's teeth are chattering, one wonders whether she is the source of danger, perhaps a person carrying a curse. She is from exotic Havana, and the tale is, after all, named for her. Moreover, the people fleeing the hotel decry the narrator's "sleeping with the Devil in the room," and no one else is ostensibly present. Our fear abates slightly when the narrator lights the newspaper and the unknown danger becomes known. But not for long. Villiers' detailed description of the snake's coils, its swaying body inching closer and closer (reminiscent of the pendulum in Poe's immortal tale), and its darting tongue revivify our terror.

The second tale of terror, **"La Torture par l'espérance"** (*Nouveaux Contes cruels*), is also marked by echoes of Poe. Villiers himself seems to acknowledge a debt to the American, for the story bears an epigraph—"Oh! for a voice to speak"—taken from "The Pit and the Pendulum." There is, however, a significant difference between the two tales: If much of the terror in Poe's work derives from the description of the pendulum, the slow ienxorable approach of a physical danger, here the terror is provoked more subtly through psychological means. A fear of recapture obsesses the protagonist, and the reader shares the agony.

This tale, in truth, is a masterpiece. Not only is it concise, a little over seventeen hundred words, but the plot is of extreme simplicity. In a first part, the Spanish grand inquisitor announces to heretic Rabbi Aser Abarbanel that tomorrow he will submit to an *auto da fé*. Then, finding his cell unlocked, the rabbi makes his way down a deserted corridor toward freedom. In a third part, met by the inquisitor, he realizes that "all the stages of this fatal evening were only an arranged torture, that of Hope." The tale is a masterpiece, lastly and above all, because it sustains a single impression of terror throughout the entire narrative, right from mention of the inquisitor at the beginning to his reappearance at the end.

These nine tales show that Villiers remained as before a vibrant short story writer. (pp. 120-25)

William T. Conroy, Jr., in his Villiers de l'Isle-Adam, *Twayne Publishers, 1978, 167 p.*

Esther Rashkin   (essay date 1981)

[*In the following excerpt, Rashkin focuses on the fantastic elements in "Véra."*]

> (. . .) the way of paradoxes is the way of truth.
> Oscar Wilde,
> *The Picture of Dorian Gray*

The attempt to define the "fantastic" in literature has preoccupied literary critics for some time. Tzvetan Todorov, in his *Introduction à la littérature fantastique,* has written perhaps the most comprehensive description of the genre. Not concerned with the interpretation of individual texts, Todorov's aim is to establish a science or "poetics" of the fantastic by describing the verbal, syntactic, and semantic structures manifest in fantastic literature: "Nous considérons l'oeuvre littéraire comme une structure qui peut recevoir un nombre indéfini d'interprétations (. . .). Notre tâche (. . .) est la description de cette structure creuse (. . .). (. . .) il s'agit (. . .) pour nous de *décrire une configuration plutôt que de nommer un sens.*"

In arriving at his definition of the fantastic, Todorov reiterates this emphasis on structure as opposed to content. He contends that the fantastic occurs when the implicit reader of the text (that is, the character in the text who functions as a reader and with whom the real reader identifies) hesitates between two possible explanations of the story's events. If this reader can explain the tale by the laws of reality or natural coincidence, the work belongs to the genre called "l'étrange." If, on the contrary, the events of the story can only be accounted for by a supernatural occurrence, the text is said to be "merveilleux." Only when the hesitation of the implicit reader is sustained by the text to the very end, thereby making it impossible to choose between a natural or supernatural explanation, is the text considered "purely fantastic."

Based on these genre distinctions, Todorov concludes that Villiers de l'Isle-Adam's short story **"Véra"** is not purely fantastic but "fantastique merveilleux." While noting that the text continually hesitates between the natural and the supernatural, he claims that all ambiguity is ultimately resolved by the tale's conclusion when a supernatural explanation is provided for the events that occur.

Now while Todorov's descriptions of the fantastic are insightful, provocative, and worthy of extensive study, for the purpose of this essay, it is the legitimacy of his classification of Villiers' tale that interests us. Does Todorov's categorization of **"Véra"** as "fantastique-merveilleux," when judged on the basis of his own model of the fantastic, in fact prove to be an accurate one? Is the perpetual ambiguity and hesitation produced by the text actually resolved by its conclusion? In order to find out, let us take a second look at **"Véra"**—a look aimed less at describing the fantastic through the structural elements of the text than at analyzing how the text itself restructures our perception of the fantastic.

First a brief summary of the tale. After locking the mausoleum where his wife of just six months lay entombed, the Count d'Athol returns to Véra's now-empty bedroom, horrified by the idea of living without her. As his thoughts take him back to their brief but passionate existence together, the count suddenly senses that Véra, in some mysterious way, is present with him in the room. Convinced of the reality of this presence, he begins to live with Véra as if she were in fact alive. This bizarre existence continues for a year until, on the evening of the anniversary of her death, Véra appears before the count, no longer an invisible phantom but a perceivable and tangible reality. In the original version of the story, published in 1874, the text ends at this point: a moment of supreme ecstasy, as the count and Véra merge forever into one immortal being.

Apparently dissatisfied with this ending, Villiers published the story two years later with a second conclusion. In it the count suddenly awakens from his ecstatic union with Véra only to discover that in reality she is dead. At this moment Véra disappears from sight, literally vanishing into the air. Her departure, however, is not without a trace. The count's desperate plea for a sign, for an indication of the path that will lead him back to Véra, is answered by the perplexing appearance of the key to her tomb. It is this key that the count himself had tossed back into the mausoleum swearing never to return, and that now drops mysteriously from the bed onto the floor of the room.

It is apparent even from this brief summary that the second ending of the story represents, on some level, a negation, an inversion, or a reversal of the original conclusion. This reversibility, in itself extremely problematic, raises several immediate questions. What is the significance of such a reversal? How is the meaning of the text affected by the reversal of its conclusion? In what ways is the inversion of the two endings emblematic of the structure of the entire text? How can the enigmatic relationship of these two conclusions be seen as an indication of how to read the text?

Taking a cue from this last question, I will begin by establishing a reading of the text up to and including its original ending, analyzing those elements that are thematized by the narration to this point. I will then evaluate the implications of the text's own transgression of this limit; that is, the meaning of the text's apparent dissatisfaction with itself.

The text begins with two quotations. The epigraph (an apparent citation from Hegel) states that "La forme du corps lui est plus *essentielle* que sa substance," while the first sentence of the narrative asserts that "L'Amour est plus fort que la Mort." Both sentences have dialectical structures; both embody oppositions in which one pole exerts a force over and thereby masters the other. The former defines form as more essential or more important than substance; the latter names love as the conqueror of death. The presence of these two assertions at the head of the narration seems to indicate that they are in some way emblematic of the meaning of the entire text. It is by questioning the validity of this hypothesis that our reading will progress; that is, by determining whether the remainder of the text sustains these dialectical claims of mastery, or functions instead to subvert them; by investigating whether the truth implied by both quotations is irreversible, or serves instead to problematize on a textual level the concept of absolute and unambiguous truth.

The first event narrated by the text, the death of Véra, immediately appears to contradict the idea that love is stronger than death. In a moment of extreme passion between Véra and d'Athol, death conquers love; Véra dies at the moment of orgasm: "La Mort, subite, avait foudroyé. La nuit dernière, sa bien-aimée s'était évanouie en des joies si profondes, s'était perdue en de si exquises étreintes, *que son coeur, brisé de délices, avait défailli* (. . .)."

Yet, if the initial event of the text appears to contradict the idea of the supremacy of love over death, the count's reaction to Véra's absence may be seen as an attempt to eliminate this contradiction by denying or rejecting death as conqueror of love. In locking her sepulcher, d'Athol gently tosses the key through the iron gate onto the steps leading to her tomb. "—Pourquoi ceci? . . . *A coup sûr* d'après quelque résolution mystérieuse *de ne plus revenir.*" D'Athol refuses to return to the tomb; he refuses to remember, to consciously accept Véra's death. By burying the key, the count metaphorically buries the memory of his loss.

This gesture of negating death coincides in the text with an attempt to negate the temporal mode in which death exists as a reality for d'Athol. It coincides with an attempt to negate the present: "(. . .) il revoyait la chambre veuve. La croisée (. . .) était ouverte (. . .).—Et là, là, dans l'ombre, *la pendule, dont il avait brisé le ressort pour qu'elle ne sonnât plus d'autres heures.*"

By breaking the clock in Véra's room, the count kills time. But if this murder of time signals the brutal halting of a temporal progression into the future, it also marks the eternal suspension of the past, of the time in which Véra lived. Indeed d'Athol's rather startling behavior appears motivated by some strange attraction to the past. The origin of this attraction is revealed in the description of his life prior to Véra's tragic end:

> (. . .) toutes les difficultés [du] monde (. . .) s'étaient évanouis devant *la tranquille certitude qu'ils eurent* (. . .) *l'un de l'autre.* (. . .) certaines idées, celles de *l'âme,* par exemple, de *l'Infini de Dieu même,* * *étaient comme voilées à leur entendement.* (. . .)
>
> Ils devinrent le battement de l'être l'un de l'autre. En eux, l'esprit pénétrait si bien le corps, que leurs formes leur semblaient intellectuelles, et que les baisers, mailles brûlantes, les enchaînaient dans *une fusion idéale* (*Villiers' italics).

D'Athol's life with Véra in the past is portrayed as an ideal fusion of two beings, as an existence based on the immediacy of sensation, devoid of the ambiguity and uncertainty associated with such concepts as "the soul, infinity, or God." The death of Véra, therefore, represents for d'Athol not only the loss of an object of desire but the loss of the certainty of his own existence. His negation of Véra's death marks a negation of the loss of his own life in the past as an absolute and perfect totality. Thus when, after Véra's death, d'Athol wonders to himself, "Ainsi elle était partie! . . . *Où donc! . . . Vivre maintenant?* Pour quoi faire? . . . C'était impossible, absurde" (Villiers' italics), it is not the possibility of living that he rejects but the possibility of living in the present, in the here and now, that he declares impossible. While denying the present, the count affirms the possibility of living in another time, in another temporal mode in which it would be possible to recover the certainty and totality of his past experience—another temporal mode in which Véra, the source of his certitude, would exist, despite her death, as "present for d'Athol."

The enigmatic nature of Véra's location—of the time and place in which d'Athol may recover her as present—is underscored by the narrative itself when the count, returning alone from her tomb, observes her empty bedroom: "Ainsi elle etait partie! . . . *Où* donc! . . . " (Villiers' italics). Although Véra's death is recounted in detail by the text just one page earlier, she is described here not as dead but as having gone elsewhere, as merely being absent. At the same time, the notion of absence itself is made ambiguous by the impersonal pronoun "elle" which refers to Véra following her death: "Le comte regarda, autour de lui (. . .) les bijoux, le collier de perles, (. . .) les lourds flacons de parfums qu'*Elle* ne respirerait plus" (Villiers' italics). By definition a substitute, the pronoun "Elle" is used as a proper name in the text by virtue of the capital letter "E." Thus, whereas on the one hand Véra is referred to by a linguistic substitute as absent and anonymous ("elle"), the personalization of the pronoun ("*Elle*") grammatically subverts this description by specifically naming Véra as absence and anonymity itself. Véra is identified not merely in spite of but in terms of her anonymity. Although named as absent, she is paradoxically designated at the same moment as identifiable, recoverable, as somehow present in her absence.

The ambiguous character of Véra's presence, of the specific place where she may be possessed, is at least partially resolved by the motto embroidered on her slippers: "*Qui verra Véra l'aimera*" (Villiers' italics). Véra is defined as lovable, while love itself is described as contingent upon perception. However, the certainty of perception, its infallibility as a determinant of presence, is put into question syntactically by the phonetic play of the signifiers "verra" and "Véra." The aural exchangeability of these words reflects the ambiguity of Véra's own status in the text. Véra is either an image or illusion that exists solely because it is perceived ("verra"), or she is a real person who truly exists, independent of visual deception ("Véra"; derived from the Latin "versus, vera, verum" meaning "truth or reality").

The motto, then, does not reveal where Véra is recoverable; it poses instead another question. If love, presence, and truth are defined as contingent upon perception, while perception is itself portrayed as susceptible to error and delusion, how can one recognize the truth? Where is the real? An initial response is given in the text immediately following the count's denial of Véra's death: "Les heures passèrent. Il regardait, par la croisée, la nuit qui s'avançait dans les cieux: et la Nuit lui apparaissait *personnelle* (. . .)" (Villiers' italics).

"La Nuit," a metaphor of time, is described as "personnelle," as familiar or recognizable. When the count looks at

Caricature of Villiers de l'Isle-Adam by Coll-Toc for Les Hommes d'Aujourd'hui *(1886).*

the night sky, it is not the forward progression of time that he perceives ("la nuit qui s'avançait dans les cieux") but a particular moment in time already known to him. D'Athol sees a moment of his own past; and it is at the precise instant of this perception that he senses for the first time that Véra is present with him in the room.

Véra is thus a function not of the reality of the present but of the memory of the past. She exists for d'Athol as an effect of repetition, as an effect of his perception of the past in the present. If the count's attempts to negate death and deny the present represent his desire to recuperate Véra and be reunited with her as a totality, then it is only by radically transgressing all temporal limits, by totally obliterating the distinctions between the present and the past, that such a recuperation becomes possible. Véra exists in the present only to the extent that d'Athol forgets the present. She is perceived as alive only because d'Athol forgets the reality of her death: "D'Athol, en effet, *vivait absolument dans l'inconscience de la mort de sa bien-aimée! Il ne pouvait que la trouver toujours présente* (. . .)."

The real for d'Athol becomes a function of the forgetting of reality. More precisely, it becomes a function of the forgetting of the distinction between reality and fiction. Véra herself is named in terms of this forgetting. She is referred to by an expression which itself represents the dissolution of difference and the attendant reversibility of reality and fiction—"l'Illusion": "Tantôt, sur un banc du jardin, les jours de soleil, il lisait, à haute voix, les poésies qu'elle aimait; tantôt, le soir, auprès du feu, les deux tasses de thé sur un guéridon, il causait avec l'*Illusion* souriante, assise, à ses yeux, sur l'autre fauteuil" (Villiers' italics).

The capital "I" of "Illusion" transforms the word grammatically from a common noun to a proper noun. Véra is not merely described as an illusion but is named as such. However, the act of naming in itself gives Véra a measure of reality; it gives her a specific referential identity in language. Therefore, by naming Véra "the Illusion," the literal meaning of the word "illusion," as it pertains to Véra, is forgotten. While named in language as an illusion, Véra is referred to by language as real and present. Within the discourse of the text itself, illusion becomes a metaphor or substitute for reality; truth ("Véra") becomes synonymous with "Illusion"; and the real becomes virtually indistinguishable from the imaginary:

> Les jours, les nuits, les semaines s'envolèrent. (. . .) Et des phénomènes singuliers se passaient maintenant, *où il devenait difficile de distinguer le point où l'imaginaire et le réel étaient identiques.* Une présence flottait dans l'air: une forme s'efforçait de transparaître, de se tramer sur *l'espace devenue indéfinissable.*

If the distinction between the real and the imaginary is put into question by d'Athol's desire to negate Véra's death, the exact nature of this desire is itself rendered problematic by the peculiar way in which the count lives his life with Véra:

> D'Athol vivait double, en illuminé. Un visage doux et pâle, entrevu comme l'éclair, entre deux clins d'yeux; un faible accord frappé au piano, tout à coup; un baiser qui lui fermait la bouche au moment où il allait parler, des affinités de pensées *féminines** qui s'éveillaient en lui en réponse à ce qu'il disait, un dédoublement de lui-même tel qu'il sentait, comme en un brouillard fluide, le parfum vertigineusement doux de sa bien-aimée auprès de lui, et, la nuit, entre la veille et la sommeil, des paroles entendues très bas; tout l'avertissait. *C'était une négation de la Mort* élevée, enfin, à une puissance inconnue! (*Villiers' italics).

D'Athol imagines himself as both man and woman, as the union of Véra and himself. However, by playing Véra's role as well as his own, his identity is not merely doubled or duplicated ("D'Athol vivait *double*"), but is at the same time divided or split (un *dédoublement* de lui-même"). The moment d'Athol imagines himself as the embodiment of both Véra and himself, he becomes alienated or separated from his identity as a man. He becomes, if only in part, a woman ("des affinités de pensées *féminines* (. . .) s'éveillaient en lui"), and his integrity as a complete being dissolves in a moment of symbolic emasculation or death.

D'Athol's double life, then, while appearing to represent the ultimate synthesis with Véra he desires, more accurately signals the loss of his own identity as a totality. By attempting to master death and recover Véra as alive,

d'Athol ironically ends up recreating death. His double life becomes a living death, not so much a "négation de la Mort," as the text seems to claim, but an affirmation or repetition of death.

Indeed each negation by d'Athol of Véra's loss masks his true desire to reaffirm that loss. Each gesture which seems to deny death merely disguises his desire to repeat death. This becomes evident when, at the moment the count appears to acknowledge the loss of Véra by placing on her pillow "une immortelle," a flower traditionally symbolic of mourning, he simultaneously negates his own gesture. He excuses it as a mere joke, as a means of humoring Véra in her own self-deception: "Le jour de *sa** fête, il plaça, par *plaisanterie, une immortelle* dans le bouquet qu'il jeta sur l'oreiller de Véra.—*Puisqu'elle se croit morte,* dit-il" (*Villiers' italics).

What then is the reason for d'Athol's unacknowledged desire to repeat death? What does such a repetition accomplish?

Death is by definition an unrepeatable and unique event. It marks with absolute finality the end of time and thus represents an irrevocable subversion of temporal continuity. By repeating death, d'Athol erases its uniqueness and its specificity as a temporal end point. Its identity as a radically discontinuous event is forgotten, replaced instead by the continuity of repetition itself. Death is no longer perceived by d'Athol as death but as the temporal equivalent of life.

Thus, when the count is finally reunited with Véra on the anniversary of her death (an event which is itself a figure of repetition), this union is not the effect of a negation of death but of the subversion of the opposition between life and death. If their union is described in the text as "oblivious" (oublieuse) and "immortal," it is because it is made possible by the killing of memory and by the murder of death itself:

> Un frais éclat de rire musical éclaira de sa joue le lit nuptial; le comte se retourna. Et là, devant ses yeux, faite de volonté et de souvenir, accoudée, fluide, sur l'oreiller de dentelles, sa main soutenant ses lourds cheveux noirs, sa bouche délicieusement entr'ouverte en un sourire tout emparadisé de voluptés, belle à en mourir, enfin! la comtesse Véra le regardait un peu endormie encore.
>
> —Roger! . . . dit-elle d'une voix lointaine.
>
> Il vint auprès d'elle. Leurs lèvres s'unirent dans une joie divine,—*oublieuse,—immortelle!*
>
> Et ils s'aperçurent, *alors,* qu'ils n'étaient, réellement, qu'*un seul être* (Villiers' italics).

An interpretation of the meaning of the text up to its original ending now appears possible. If the "murder of death" is the ultimate result of d'Athol's fiercely passionate desire to recuperate Véra, it seems reasonable to assume, as the first sentence of the text asserts, that "love is stronger than death." Correspondingly, if the "killing of memory" permits d'Athol to regain the certitude and totality of his past existence with Véra and to be united with her in one complete and transcendent spirit or essence ("*un seul être*"), then we may conclude that spirit is indeed superior to matter or, as the text's epigraph declares, that "form is more essential than substance."

However, if the two principal questions posed by the text appear to be resolved, a third one emerges at this point to take their place—the identity of the "pale conqueror" alluded to in the motto inscribed beneath d'Athol's coat of arms:

> [La voiture] s'arrêta devant le portail d'un vaste hôtel seigneurial (. . .) le cintre était surmonté de l'écusson de pierre, aux armes de l'antique famille des comtes d'Athol, savoir: *d'azur, à l'étoile abîmée d'argent*, avec la devise 'PALLIDA VICTRIX,' sous la couronne retroussée d'hermine au bonnet princier (Villiers' italics).

Upon first glance, d'Athol himself appears to fit the description, since he succeeds in both conquering death and recuperating Véra. Moreover, he is described on several occasions as appearing physically "pale." But d'Athol is not alone in conforming to the inscription. As we noted earlier, the count first senses Véra's presence at the moment the night appears "personal" to him. At this same moment, he sees the planet Venus emerging from the night sky, a planet whose description corresponds in several ways to the inscription "Pallida Victrix";

> (. . .) la Nuit lui apparaissait *personnelle*; elle lui semblait une reine marchant, avec mélancolie, dans l'exil, et l'agrafe de diamant de sa tunique de deuil, Vénus, seule, brillait, au-dessus des arbres, perdue au fond de l'azur.
>
> —C'est Véra, pensa-t-il (Villiers' italics).

Venus, the "goddess" of love, corresponds in gender to the feminine adjective "Pallida," and thus to the grammatically female identity of the pale conqueror. Venus is also the symbol of love par excellence, the symbol of that which, according to the text, conquers death.

Yet an even greater link between Venus and the pale conqueror may be found by comparing their physical descriptions. The words "Pallida Victrix" are *mise en abîme*, inscribed on an azur background with a star "abîmée" in silver that gives the illusion of infinite depth at its center. Venus, known alternately as the morning or evening "star," is similarly described as a (pale) diamond emerging from out of an abyss, as literally "lost in the azur depths of the sky."

Thus, with both d'Athol and Venus appearing to fit the description of the pale conqueror, the exact identity of the character referred to by the motto remains ambiguous. This ambiguity is increased when, just moments after the count and Véra are apparently joined in their transcendant union, d'Athol's memory suddenly returns:

> Tout à coup, le comte d'Athol tressaillit, comme frappé d'*une réminiscence fatale*.
>
> —Ah! maintenant, *je me rappelle*! . . . dit-il. Qu'ai-je donc? *Mais tu es morte*!
>
> A l'instant même, (. . .) l'ardente et blanche vision rentra dans l'air et s'y perdit.

D'Athol's memory is "fatal" in every sense of the word. By remembering that he has killed memory and murdered the reality of Véra's death, the count, ironically, kills forgetting and murders the fiction of Véra's life. Just as the initial event of the text—Véra's ecstatic death in the arms of the count—it is death that conquers love and the physical reality of substance that proves more essential than form. The polarities of life and death, reality and fiction, the past and the present, and male and female (whose reversal in the text permitted the transcendent union of Véra and d'Athol in the first ending of the story) are once again reversed. Death itself replaces d'Athol and Venus as the pale conqueror, while the count returns to the alienating uncertainty of an existence without his beloved.

If this reversal of the meaning of the original conclusion brings d'Athol back to a state of disunion and loss, it also evokes within the reader a sense of confusion and ambiguity. How can the reader determine the "true meaning" of the text with any degree of certainty if what appears to be its meaning at one moment is abruptly reversed by the text in the next moment; if the superiority of love over death and form over substance is asserted by the narrative at one point only to be subverted by it at another? Can such a "true meaning" in fact exist or be understood? Is not the very possibility of understanding itself ultimately put into question by this structure of reversal?

The last event of the text, the appearance of the key to Véra's tomb, may be seen as a response to these questions:

> L'atmosphère était, maintenant, celle des défunts.
>
> (. . .)—Oh! murmura-t-il, c'est donc fini!—Perdue! . . . Toute seule!—Quelle est la route, maintenant, pour parvenir jusqu'à toi? Indique-moi le chemin qui peut me conduire vers toi! . . .
>
> Soudain, comme une réponse, un objet brillant tomba du lit nuptial, sur la noire fourrure, avec un bruit métallique: un rayon de l'affreux jour terrestre l'éclaira! . . . L'abandonné se baissa, le saisit, et un sourire sublime illumina son visage en reconnaissant cet objet: *c'était la clef du tombeau.*

What is the exact status of this key which, according to the narrative, suddenly drops from out of nowhere onto the floor of Véra's room? Does the key really exist, or is it merely an illusion fabricated by d'Athol's imagination? Is it incontrovertible proof that Véra was in fact present in the room in some supernatural form, thereby reiterating the text's initial conclusion that love is stronger than death and form more essential than substance? Or is the key merely an hallucination, a visual effect of the count's passionate desire to recuperate Véra and thus, conversely, a confirmation of the assertions of the second ending of the narrative that death conquers love and substance is superior to form? Furthermore, if the key does exist, if the reader assumes that it is somehow sent by Véra in response to d'Athol's pleas, what then is its function? Does it represent the mechanical means by which d'Athol may reenter the tomb and repossess Véra as dead? Or does it function metaphorically by implying that only through his own death can d'Athol hope to be reunited with Véra in some extra-physical realm?

Paradoxical as it may seem, the key appears capable of either affirming or denying the conclusions of both the first and the second endings of the narrative. The information contained within the text does not permit the reader to decide with any certainty which of the contradictory explanations evoked by the key is in fact signified by it.

Yet, if the meaning of the key is in itself thoroughly ambiguous, its function in the text is less so. It is precisely by failing to indicate whether the truth of the narrative is established by the first ending or by the second which reverses it that the key implies these conclusions are infinitely reversible and that the "true meaning" of the text is impossible to determine. And if the key fails to identify the first or second ending as symbolic of the text's true meaning, it is because the key itself has no meaning. It does not "contain" a signification that can be uncovered by the reader. Described as "silver and shining," the key recalls the star "abîmée d'argent" in the background of d'Athol's family crest. It is thus described as part of a "structure en abîme"—a structure whose meaning or reality is constantly displaced by an infinite series of mirror-like reflections.

The key then inscribes meaning in the text by virtue of the ambiguity that its presence generates. It conveys meaning not because of its transparency but in spite of its opaqueness; not by explaining what it means but by resisting explanation. This pure signifier has significance only in terms of and in reference to other signifiers: to the two conflicting conclusions of the story. It functions not by establishing the meaning of the text but by perpetually displacing, dislocating, or de-centering it.

The entire text is in fact constituted by this constant displacement, by the infinite reversibility of its meaning. As a result, the text itself is unable to master its meaning. Although capable of insisting upon the reversals and resulting ambiguity of its signification, it remains unable to resolve that ambiguity. Thus, while the title **"Véra"** signifies on some level "truth," the text is by no means the proprietor of that truth. The reader, in turn, unable to isolate a meaning or truth the text itself does not know, becomes mystified by the very object he or she tries to demystify. The reading which results can only be a reflection of the text's own distorted view of itself.

It is this distinction, this persistent de-centering, up to and including the appearance of the key, that Todorov has overlooked in his reading of **"Véra"**:

> (. . .) tout au long de la nouvelle, on peut hésiter entre: croire à la vie après la mort; ou penser que le comte qui y croit est fou. Mais à la fin, le comte découvre dans sa chambre la clé du tombeau de Véra; or cette clé, il l'avait jetée luimême à l'intérieur du tombeau; *il faut donc que ce soit Véra, la morte, qui l'ait apportée.* [critic's italics]

By assuming that the key has been sent by Véra and that through some supernatural force she has returned from the dead, Todorov short-circuits the inherent undecidability of the narrative. He attributes to the story a signifi-

cation that it itself never claims. The text, as we have seen, never ceases to hesitate between the natural and the supernatural, between the conflicting ideas that (1) Véra's presence is an effect of d'Athol's madness and that (2) it is a result of some transcendent, extra-physical force. Thus, while Todorov's description of the narrative places him in the position of assuming a certain mastery over its signification, the narrative itself is concerned with preventing the reader from attaining that position, from locating him or herself in a place from which to objectively perceive the story's truth or utter any neutral discourse about its meaning. **"Véra,"** in other words, is not explainable by the supernatural; it is not an example of what Todorov calls the "fantastique-merveilleux." **"Véra,"** contrary to Todorov's description of the tale, but (ironically) according to his own definition of the fantastic, is a purely fantastic text. (pp. 460-71)

Esther Rashkin, "Truth's Turn: Rereading the Fantastic in Villiers' 'Véra'," in The Romanic Review, *Vol. LXXII, No. 4, November, 1981, pp. 460-71.*

Irony is present almost everywhere in *Contes cruels,* and the unwary reader can easily find himself trapped in a maze of apparent contradictions, until he realizes that he has involuntarily exposed the fallibility of his own mental processes.

—*A. W. Raitt, in his* The Life of Villiers de l'Isle-Adam, *1981.*

Esther Rashkin   (essay date 1982)

[*In the following essay, Rashkin argues that the protagonist of "L'intersigne" is uncertain of his father's identity and that the question facing the reader is whether the text can reveal the truth about the protagonist's paternity. (An expanded version of this essay appears in Rashkin's* Family Secrets and the Psychoanalysis of Narrative, *Princeton University Press, 1992.)*]

> Le récit révèle, mais en le révèlant, cache un secret: plus exactement, il le porte.
>
>   Maurice Blanchot

First published in 1867, **"L'Intersigne"** is the earliest of Villiers de l'Isle-Adam's *Contes cruels.* Hailed by Castex [in *Le Conte fantastique en France*] as "l'un des chefs d'oeuvres de la littérature fantastique française," the story is concerned with the baron Xavier de la V***, a young man prone to frequent attacks of spleen, who decides to leave Paris, where he lives with his father, and seek peace of mind during a visit with his longtime friend Maucombe, the priest of Saint-Maur. Upon arriving at the vicarage, however, his sense of well-being is erased by two bizarre hallucinations—visions in which both the house and the priest appear before him as hauntingly decrepit images, devoid of life. Xavier's anxiety increases when, in the middle of the night, he perceives the image of a priest standing in the doorway to his room, solemnly holding out a black cloak. When Xavier is unexpectedly called back to Paris the next day, Maucombe offers to accompany him part of the way. As a penetrating rain begins to fall, Xavier persuades his friend to return home lest he fall ill. Agreeing to do so, Maucombe holds out his black cloak, in a gesture identical to that of the priest in Xavier's vision, and insists that the baron wear it for protection. Horrified by this inexplicable coincidence, Xavier flees Saint-Maur, leaving the cloak at a nearby hostel to be returned to Maucombe. Not until he arrives back in Paris does the baron learn that the priest had caught a chill on the open road and had died, three days after his departure, wrapped in the cloak he had given Xavier—the cloak he had brought back from the holy land and that had touched "THE TOMB."

The pattern of readings engendered by this series of events is remarkable for its consistency. Whether it is Gourevitch suggesting [in *Villiers de l'Isle-Adam*] that in "**L'Intersigne**," " . . . c'est la limite entre l'univers et celui des correspondances mystérieuses que Villiers nous invite à franchir," or Castex himself concluding [in his edition of *Contes cruels: Nouveaux contes cruels*] that "Villiers a prétendu montrer . . . que nous recevons, dans notre sommeil, des révélations d'un autre monde . . . ," the story has repeatedly sent its readers to the folklore and superstition of Brittany in search of the meaning of its title. "Les intersignes," writes Castex, quoting from Anatole Le Braz's *La Légende de la mort,* a work detailing Breton legends, "Les intersignes annoncent la mort. Mais la personne à qui se manifeste l'intersigne est rarement celle que la mort menace . . . Les intersignes sont comme l'ombre, projetée en avant, de ce qui doit arriver."

It is this definition that has led critics to interpret the hallucinations and bizarre coincidences recounted in the story as a series of *intersignes* or premonitions warning of the priest's death. The critics' reliance on this meaning to the exclusion of all others, however, has caused them to ignore the specificity of Villiers's tale. By taking the text's title to be the key to the text's truth, they have disregarded the highly individual descriptions of Xavier's visions, the cloak, and the tomb which not only constitute the story but distinguish it from all other tales of premonition. In reading "**L'Intersigne**," it is my intent to analyze these descriptions in terms of the entire story, to look beyond the text's title to the function and meaning of the narrative itself.

We first meet Xavier emerging from a spiritualist séance—an experience he describes as "curieuse," as apparently more mystifying than enlightening. Immediately following this session, aimed at altering one's consciousness and communicating with the dead, he suffers an attack of spleen. The sequential relationship between these two events is the first indication that the onset of Xavier's anxiety is related to his unsuccessful séance, to his failure to receive some communication from the beyond. Indeed, although never explicitly stated, it gradually becomes evident that his trip to Saint-Maur is designed not merely to escape his spleen but to uncover its cause. This is implicit

in Xavier's desire to go "hunting" in Saint-Maur, and in his description of his trip as a "holy pilgrimage"—as a search for some mystical and salutary wisdom beyond common awareness.

This unspoken motive is also evident in Xavier's description of Maucombe. Not only is the priest a "savant . . . et docte recteur" who can "set things right" (rectus) by giving strength and guidance to those with whom he speaks ("conversation fortifiante"); he is also an intermediary, a liaison between Xavier and some higher truth ("ce parfait confesseur d[e] Dieu"). Gifted with an "intelligence mystique," Maucombe represents a link with what lies beyond reason and logic, a means of access by which Xavier may reach and ultimately possess a mystical knowledge that eludes him. The priest functions in Xavier's eyes as a medium, as a person identical to the one in a spiritualist séance, through whom contact is made with the other world. And it is ultimately with Maucombe that Xavier will try to recreate just such a séance, that he will attempt to repeat the scene through which the unknown may be known. Xavier himself alludes to this by calling the evenings he and Maucombe will spend together "viellées," connoting "vigils for the dead."

Xavier's description of Saint-Maur as a site where altered states of awareness can be achieved also conveys this unspoken desire to repeat the séance: "Ici l'on peut s'asseoir sur la pierre de la mélancolie!—Ici les rêves morts ressuscitent, devançant les moments de la tombe! . . . ici la vue du ciel exalte jusqu'à l'oublie. Like the séance in Paris, Saint-Maur is a place where something dead ("pierre"—tombstone) or hidden, as in a dream long dead ("rêves morts"), can become very close ("s'asseoir") while simultaneously remaining obscure and undefinable ("mélancolie"—humeur *noire*). It is a place where a trancelike state of consciousness ("exalte jusqu'à l'oublie") is associated with recalling something dead ("les rêves morts ressuscitent") and perceiving a beyond ("la vue du ciel").

Yet, if Xavier's choice of Saint-Maur as a refuge is motivated by a secret wish to communicate with the beyond and learn some mysterious truth, the series of hallucinations he experiences reveals a totally contradictory desire. His haunting vision of Maucombe's house embodies this paradox:

> Etait-ce bien la maison que j'avais vue tout à l'heure? Quelle ancienneté me dénonçaient, *maintenant,* [Villiers's italics] les longues lézardes, entre les feuilles pâles?—Cette bâtisse avait un air étranger; . . . le portail hospitalier m'invitait avec ses trois marches; mais, en concentrant mon attention sur ces dalles grises, je vis qu'elles venaient d'être polies, *que des traces de lettres creusées y restaient encore,* et je vis bien qu'elles provenaient du cimetière voisin,—dont les croix noires m'apparaissaient, à présent, de côté, à une centaine de pas . . . et les échos du lugubre coup du marteau, que je laissai retomber, . . . retentirent *comme les vibrations d'un glas.*

The passage functions on two levels simultaneously. The pale, dying leaves, the front steps made from tombstones, the neighboring cemetery with its black crosses, and the ringing of a death knell all connote the presence or close proximity of the dead. Yet, those buried in the cemetery exist only as anonymous crosses; the person for whom the death knell tolls is unknown; and the tombstones, which serve normally to identify the dead, are illegible, their markings almost totally effaced by the passage of time. While the figures constituting Xavier's vision point to the presence of the dead, they carefully preserve the secret of their identity. Although they bring Xavier into closer contact with some truth from the beyond, they simultaneously separate him from that truth by revealing it as distant ("Quelle *ancienneté* me dénonçaient") and strange ("— Cette bâtisse avait *un air étranger*").

The rhetoric of Xavier's hallucinations reveals the double structure in which he is caught—a structure in which something is both hidden and revealed, strange and familiar, far and close; a structure that reflects the inherent contradiction of his real desire. For while Xavier wishes to know something, he also wishes to remain ignorant of it. It is this conflict that explains why, at the moment he abandons his self-control (he speaks of being "le jouet d'une hallucination") and lapses into the altered state of consciousness he believes crucial to uncover the truth, a censoring mechanism seems to take over, obscuring the meaning of what is revealed. It is almost as if, on some level, Xavier fears the content of the knowledge he wants to obtain; as if, unwittingly, he realizes that its revelation would actually threaten him in some way. The rhetoric of Xavier's vision thus functions as a mask of the truth beyond his awareness, as a screen that simultaneously protects him from and blinds him to its frightening content.

We see this same structure of conflict in Xavier's second hallucination, his vision of Maucombe:

> La figure qui était devant moi n'était pas, ne pouvait pas être celle du souper! ou, du moins, si je la reconnaissais vaguement, il me semblait que je ne l'avais vue, en réalité qu'en ce moment-ci. Une seule réflexion me fera comprendre: l'abbé me donnait, humainement, la *seconde* [Villiers's italics] sensation que, *par une obscure correspondance,* sa maison m'avait fait éprouver.
>
> La tête que je contemplais était grave, très pâle, d'une pâleur de mort, et les paupières étaient baissées . . . je fermai les yeux. Quand je les rouvris . . . le bon abbé était toujours là,—mais je le reconnaissais maintenant!—A la bonne heure! Son sourire amical dissipait en moi toute inquiétude. L'impression n'avait pas duré le temps d'adresser une question. C'avait été un saisissement,—une sorte d'hallucination.

Described moments earlier as being in excellent health, Maucombe's inexplicably death-like and unearthly appearance "corresponds" in some obscure way to Xavier's first hallucination. Yet, the correspondence between the two visions is not based merely on their mutual resistance to meaning but on the identity of their modes of resistance. The hallucinations correspond because their very obscurity is generated by the same paradoxical system of desire: a system in which the familiar suddenly appears strange ("La tête que je contemplais était . . . *d'une pâleur de mort* ") and the near eerily distant ("La figure . . . devant

moi . . . ne pouvait pas être celle du souper!"); a system that protects at the very moment it imperils.

What then is the content of the forbidding truth whose absence evokes within Xavier this bizarre conflict between the wish to know and not know, between the desire for visual insight and intellectual blindness? Xavier's third hallucination provides some clues:

> . . . je fus au milieu de la chambre . . . Comme je m'approchais de la porte, une tache de braise, partie du trou de la serrure, vint errer sur ma main et sur ma manche . . .
>
> Une chose me paraissait surprenante: la *nature* [Villiers's italics] de la tache qui courait sur ma main. C'était une lueur glacée, sanglante, n'éclairant pas . . .—Mais, *en vérité,* ce qui sortait ainsi du trou de la serrure me causait l'impression *du regard phosphorique d'un hibou*!
>
> . . . la porte s'ouvrit . . . En face de moi, dans le corridor, se tenait, debout, une forme haute et noire,—un prêtre, le tricorne sur la tête. La lune l'éclairait tout entier, à l'exception de la figure . . .
>
> Le souffle *de l'autre monde* enveloppait ce visiteur . . .
>
> Tout à coup, le prêtre éleva le bras, avec lenteur, vers moi. Il me présentait une chose lourde et vague. C'était un manteau. Un grand manteau noir, un manteau de voyage. Il me le tendait, comme pour me l'offrir! . . .

Projected into an altered and almost trance-like state of consciousness resembling the séance in Paris, Xavier once again perceives what appears to be a message from the beyond, a hint as to the content of the information he desires to attain. His description of the light wandering on his sleeve as "une tache . . . sanglante" suggests that the knowledge eluding him, although preserved in a frozen ("glacée") and intact state resistant to understanding ("n'éclairant pas"), is nevertheless connected with a familial or "blood" affair capable of shaming or "tainting" those touched by it. Yet, no sooner is this fragment of information revealed than Xavier's censoring mechanism, reacting to a threat posed by his increased proximity to the truth (the stain which wanders on his sleeve is literally "within his grasp"), denies the accuracy of his first impression and substitutes for the stain an image devoid of all connotations of familial shame: "—Mais, *en vérité,* ce qui sortait ainsi du trou de la serrure me causait l'impression *du regard phosphorique d'un hibou*!"

This substitution is by no means insignificant, however. While Xavier may prevent or at least defer the unveiling of some possibly odious truth in replacing the stain by the owl, his description of the bird (a mythological symbol of wisdom and knowledge) as a "glowing luminescence" emerging from the dark marks it as a symbol of the mode by which truth or meaning can be revealed. In portraying a "bird of wisdom" as a bright gleam in the midst of darkness, Xavier exchanges a figure threatening to reveal the truth for a figure revealing the form by which truth is manifest in the dream: as light within shadow, as illumination within obscurity. While Xavier's metonymic displacement prevents the truth from emerging, it simultaneously preserves the structure by which that emergence takes place. While his fear of knowing causes him to deny the content of what is revealed, his desire to know leads him to retain the form of that revelation.

The rhetorical exchange of the mode of revelation for revelation itself is again evident in Xavier's description of the priest's gesture. If the priest's sacrifice of the cloak signifies the unmasking and transmission of some message from the beyond ("Le souffle *de l'autre monde* enveloppait ce visiteur"), the cloak, whose meaning at this point in the text is totally mysterious ("une chose *lourde et vague*"), conceals the content of that message. An object which covers and uncovers, the cloak functions metaphorically by veiling the very meaning it itself conveys. It both reveals and hides, protects Xavier from the fearful truth it contains while symbolizing the mode by which that truth is exposed.

What, then, should we make of Xavier's experience on the open road when Maucombe offers him his cloak for protection on his journey back to Paris? What is different about this scene which seems to be essentially identical to the scene of Xavier's third vision, but which evokes within him the strongest sense of fear and horror he has yet experienced? Quite simply, the difference is Maucombe himself. The identity of the priest in Xavier's nocturnal vision is unknown, his face hidden in shadow. Only on the road to Paris is Maucombe revealed to be at the center of this drama, to be the person who actually offers the cloak and literally uncovers himself before Xavier.

The uncovering, then, not of an unknown priest but of Maucombe himself terrifies Xavier and somehow brings him closer than any of his other hallucinatory experiences to the horrifying truth he seeks. It is this fact that marks a crucial shift in the text. Until this point, Xavier's visions could be read as messages from the beyond, as signs of some otherworldly knowledge he both desires and fears. The dramatic uncloaking of Maucombe on the open road, however (foreshadowed by the substitution of the priest for the house in Xavier's second hallucination), reveals that the tormenting hallucinations Xavier suffers are somehow representative of something that is not (or cannot be?) said between the two men; that these visions in some way link Maucombe with Xavier; that what Xavier desires to know is not an otherworldly truth but a mystery (a secret?) associated with Maucombe. Is Maucombe withholding something from Xavier concerning their relationship? Does Xavier suspect that the truth he seeks is related to the priest? The text, thus far, provides no conclusive answers to these enigmas. The last event of the story, however, offers an important clue. When Xavier arrives back home, his father gives him a letter, sent by Maucombe's servant Nanon, announcing that the priest died from a chill caught on the open road three days after Xavier's departure. His last words, as transcribed by Nanon, revealed that he died "heureux *d'être enveloppé* à son dernier soupir *et enseveli dans le manteau* qu'il avait rapporté de son pèlerinage en terre sainte, *et qui avait touché* [Villiers's italics] LE TOMBEAU.

The cloak "touched the tomb." But what is concealed within the tomb, and whose tomb is it? Most readers have assumed it to be Christ's tomb. The assigning of this particular referent to a term whose meaning suggests a link with other elements in the text is, I think, too hasty. For Nanon's letter states an immediate connection between the tomb and the cloak, the latter itself being associated with Xavier's two preceding visions in his room and on the road. The cloak, in turn, wraps Maucombe at the moment of his death. A chain is thus established linking the hallucinations, the cloak, Maucombe, and the tomb. Nanon's message, in other words, not only discloses that the cloak covered something buried within a tomb; it identifies the tomb as a symbol of some buried *secret* tormenting Xavier. The tomb becomes a figure (like the hallucinations, the cloak, and Maucombe) that both reveals and hides, both holds and withholds its mysterious contents.

The problem now remains of determining the secret hidden within this symbolic tomb. The attempt to do so leads back to the beginning of the tale, to the sentence of the narrative that marks its point of origin: "Un soir d'hiver . . . nous prenions le thé autour d'un bon feu, chez l'un de nos amis, *le baron Xavier de la V**** . . . Xavier is introduced in terms of a lack: the lack of his "nom de famille," of his father's name—a lack symbolized by three asterisks (***). Ironically, it is these signs, whose apparent emptiness begins the text, that permit us to fill in the meaning that has thus far been so elusive. For despite its monumental opacity, the text suggests by this first sentence that it is the absence of a name that is covered over by the enigmatic chain of visions that constitute the narrative. Through the traces of its own elliptical beginning, the text implies that the secret Xavier both seeks and fears, the secret which in some mysterious way concerns both him and Maucombe, is the fact that he does not know the identity of his father, that the father with whom he lives is not who Xavier thinks he is. Xavier, the text ultimately (and silently) reveals, is a bastard. And his father is the priest, Maucombe.

This conclusion is supported in several substantial ways by the text. While in Paris, Xavier refers to his spleen as "héréditaire," as something caused by or originating with his parent(s). When we recall that this spleen intensifies immediately following his participation in a séance, it becomes clear that his interest in spiritualism is not aimed at gaining some knowledge from beyond this world, but at learning some secret from *beyond his awareness*. His hallucinations can now be seen as revealing the content of this secret. While the first vision points to something abnormal concerning the house of Maucombe ("house" also connotes "lineage"), the second hallucination directly implicates the priest in this abnormality. Xavier's third vision, in turn, describes the nature of Maucombe's involvement—his association with some blood or familial shame ("tache sanglante"). (Although the priest in the dream is anonymous, the connection with Maucombe is self-evident since Xavier is in his home.) With Maucombe's offer of the cloak on the open road, the priest is conclusively identified as the subject of Xavier's hallucinations; he is literally exposed as both the bearer and the object of the familial secret tormenting the baron. Indeed, the name

Maucombe itself identifies the priest in this way: as a man "weighed down by" or implicated (combe — incombe: weighs down upon) in some "evil" (mau — mal) or morally shameful deed. The very words the priest speaks also reinforce this idea. For it is Maucombe, responding to Xavier's expression of friendship toward him, who speaks of the *parenté divine* that ties them together.

But if the hallucinations and the priest's name sustain the contention that Xavier is a bastard, fathered by Maucombe, it is perhaps the epigraph of the text that most succinctly and conclusively confirms the relationship between the two men. For the narrative is preceded by the words of Saint-Bernard—an abbot like Maucombe—who, in his *Meditations* on the *Preparation for the Last Judgment,* describes man as an "imperfect" and "inferior" being who was born of "fetid sperm" and *who does not remember his origin*:

> Attende, homo, quid fuisti ante ortum et quod eris usque ad occasum. *Profecto fuit quod non eras.* Postea, *de vili materia factus,* in utero matris de sanguine menstruali nutritus, tunica tua fuit *pellis secundina.* Deinde, in vilissimo panno involutus, progressus es ad nos,—sic indutus et ornatus! *Et non memor es quae sit origo tua. Nihil est aliud homo quam sperma foetidum . . .*

> Listen, man, to what you were before being born, and to what you will be in the end. *Perfect was what you were not.* Afterward, *you were made from lowly material,* nourished in your mother's womb from menstrual blood, your tunic was from *inferior hide.* Next, covered in the most vile rag, you advanced toward us,—in this way clothed and adorned! *And you do not remember what your origin was. Man is nothing else than fetid sperm . . .*

Indeed, Xavier neither "remembers" his origins nor resolves the enigma of his experiences at Saint-Maur. When he recounts his tale to a group of friends gathered at his home, he does so "without commentary," without making any attempt to explain the meaning of the events he relates: "—Voici une histoire . . . *que je n'accompagnerai d'aucun commentaire. Elle est véridique. Peut-être la trouverez-vous impressionnante.*" The significance of this lack of interpretation becomes apparent when we recall the events surrounding Xavier's departure from Maucombe's house.

Upon leaving Saint-Maur, Xavier claims to have finally escaped from death ("Je sortais de la Mort"). In fact, the moment of his departure signals the precise opposite: the moment of his embrace *by* death. For in fleeing Saint-Maur, Xavier is literally wrapped (*ceint*) in the cloak which enshrouds the *sein-mort,* which covers at death (*mort*) the father to whose "breast" he was once held. It is in the absence of this cloak (which he leaves behind) and the hallucinations, which he experiences in Maucombe's presence and which linked him with the priest, that Xavier is compelled to transform the mysterious events he experiences into a story. By narrating his story, Xavier retains contact with the secret beyond his awareness; he remains in touch with his father Maucombe. Not at all the disinterested reporter of events he appears to be, Xavier is a man "living with the dead," with the ghostly presence of his real father encrypted within the very words of his tale. Xavier's narrative becomes the tomb of Maucombe's secret—a tomb that Xavier, unwittingly, carries with him always.

"L'Intersigne" is a text that illustrates the formation of such an entombed secret. While Maucombe is alive, the possibility always exists, despite the shame associated with his crime, that he will reveal the truth to Xavier, his bastard son. In fact, the priest's reaction to Xavier's premature departure from Saint-Maur seems to cloak his intention to do just this: "La grande affaire, *c'est le salut: j'esperais être pour quelque chose dans le vôtre . . .* " With the death of Maucombe, the possibility of such a revelation disappears. The priest does not leave his son without a legacy, however. Xavier becomes the unwitting caretaker of his father's secret. By narrating his tale, he keeps alive the truth buried with Maucombe while at the same time barring its disclosure. He preserves intact the secret silently transmitted to him by his father while ignoring not only its content but the very fact that it exists. Indeed, if Xavier is unable to comment on the tale he narrates, it is because he has no idea of what it contains, no notion of the phantom that has been transmitted to him. Xavier's narration is thus literally a *ghost story*: a story about how a secret, kept by the father, concerning his child, becomes a ghost within that child—a ghost that haunts but is never perceived; a ghost born from the grave of the father that survives within a crypt (the narrative) created by the son.

But if Xavier's narrative is a "crypt," so too are the key words it contains: *manteau, tombeau, Maucombe, Saint-Maur.* Each of these terms hides encrypted within it a reference to the others. In order to interpret the meaning of the cloak, for example, the reader must uncover within it its link (indicated earlier) to the tomb, Maucombe, and Saint-Maur. To understand the significance of the tomb, the reader must decipher its connection with the cloak, Saint-Maur, and Maucombe. It is this pattern of encrypting, this structure in which words are buried within other words, that finally permits us to understand the title of Villiers's text. For *intersignes* are not, in this tale at least, premonitions of death, as the critics have asserted. They are words "within words," symbols or rhymes that reveal the text's meaning only when the reader goes beneath the surface of the narrative; only when he or she looks beyond the signs within the text to see the signs "within the signs"—to see, literally, a chain of *inter-signes.*

Thus, while certain critics have let themselves be convinced of the revelatory nature of the text's title, a more careful reader examining the entire text will be inevitably persuaded of its bogus authenticity. For what evokes feelings of anxiety, doubt, and fear in reading **"L'Intersigne"** is not merely the fact that a character in the text is haunted by mysterious visions (or ghosts) that may or may not be real and that may (or may not) forewarn of impending death. It is the fact that these visions or ghosts are themselves haunted by the secrets they hide—secrets that only the language of the "ghosts," i.e., the language of the story, can reveal. The dilemma faced by the reader is thus not to decide whether or not the ghosts perceived by Xavier are harbingers of death, but to know whether the text itself can ever unveil what it encrypts. **"L'Intersigne"** is a tale that never ceases to engage the reader in this dilemma. For the trap set by Villiers's text is a special one. It is a trap that catches its prey, not because it is so cleverly concealed, but because it is so uncannily revealed. (pp. 65-76)

> *Esther Rashkin, "Secret Crimes, Haunted Signs: Villiers's L'Intersigne',"* in Stanford French Review, *Vol. 6, No. 1, Spring, 1982, pp. 65-76.*

Villiers is contemptuous of the Spiritualist's feats which are irrelevant to the Christian. He condemns their doctrines as a diabolical temptation, forbidden to the Christian and unprofitable to him, since they contribute nothing to his vision of God.

—*Margaret Groves, in her "Villiers de l'Isle-Adam and Sir William Crookes," in* French Studies, *April 1975.*

Nancy C. Mellerski   (essay date 1986)

[*In the following essay, which was originally presented at the seventh International Conference on the Fantastic in the Arts in March 1986, Mellerski discusses foreshadowing, déjà vu, and duplication in Villiers's "L'intersigne" and interprets how the "intersigne" functions to subvert the reader's understanding of meaning in the text.*]

Villiers de l'Isle-Adam's short story, **"L'Intersigne,"** is as much an investigation of the nature of the fantastic in and through language as it is a portrayal of a fantastic event. Like Villiers's **"Véra,"** where the problem of truth is already posed in the title, the signifier *intersigne* suggests a problem to be explored: What is the nature of the interval between life and death? Is there a gap into which the fantastic may insert itself, or in which the fantastic will operate? **"Véra"** plays upon the double function of a key (open/close) to establish a permanent bipolarity in the story of le comte d'Athol and his beloved wife. As Esther Rashkin has noted [in "Truth's Turn: Rereading the Fantastic in Villiers' 'Véra'," *Romanic Review* (1981)], the presence of the key does not resolve the contradictions that characterize the plot of this particular story; rather, it suggests that the conclusions in the two published versions of the narrative "are infinitely irreversible and that the 'true meaning' of the text is impossible to determine." The fantastic in **"Véra,"** therefore, arises from the nature of the count's double life, which poses an ambiguity (truth/lie) that ultimately resists explanation.

In **"L'Intersigne,"** the persistence of doubling again serves

to maintain an ambivalence, here between life and death. Through a text supersaturated with déjà vu, mirror images, foreshadowings, and repeated events, Villiers creates a linguistic interval between signifier and signified, a place (Saint-Maur) and a character (*le saint mort*), into which the fantastic will penetrate, expand, and elaborate at one and the same time a meaning and a lack of meaning. As its name implies, the *intersigne* serves to dissolve the boundaries of two separating categories, thereby creating a new space of transformation that will operate according to what Bakhtin has termed a dialogical way of seeing/reading. That is, the unitary and reductive narrative that defines nineteenth-century realism will be exchanged for a discourse which constantly questions the nature of the real. The result, in Villiers's tale, will be the polysemic text that Rosemary Jackson identifies [in her *Fantasy: The Literature of Subversion*] as characteristic of the fantastic genre: a narrative that forces us to shift our vision from fixed units and objects to the spaces between them. Like **"Véra,"** **"L'Intersigne"** will resist the formulation of a final truth.

The *intersigne,* according to Anatole Le Braz [in his *La légende de la mort*], is a child of Breton folklore. It announces the coming of death, but rarely to the person who is directly threatened. When someone is to die, another near and dear to him will be forewarned, for "les intersignes sont comme l'ombre, projetée en avant, de ce qui doit arriver" (*intersignes* are like the foreshadowing of what must happen). The prefiguration of death in the title of Villiers's short story takes the narrative form of an aborted exchange. The narrator, Xavier de la V***, while visiting his old friend the Abbé Maucombe in Brittany, is surprised and terrified by a nocturnal visitor outside his door. The visitor, seemingly a priest, silently offers Xavier a large black cloak. Xavier refuses it, slams the door, and takes refuge in his bed, thinking himself the victim of a hideous nightmare. Another day passes, and Xavier departs for the village from which he will return to Paris, accompanied partway through the forest by the Abbé Maucombe. A cold rain begins to fall, and the abbot offers Xavier his black cloak, for the narrator has forgotten his own. Xavier accepts the cloak with misgivings, and when he reaches the village, leaves directions for it to be returned to his friend. Upon arriving in Paris, Xavier learns that the abbot has since died of a chill that he caught in the forest, and has been buried in the same black cloak. The aborted nocturnal exchange has thus been replayed in the forest, with fatal results.

The *intersigne* is therefore the locus of fantastic discourse in this story, functioning as a structure of exchange: information about a forthcoming death is revealed, unbeknownst to the narrator. The real meaning of the gesture is not learned until much later, when it is too late to prevent the event from happening as it was foretold. It is precisely this exchange function that structures the entire story, for, as we shall see, the text is articulated through a series of *intersignes,* or lexical exchanges that inscribe the presence of the fantastic through a complex web of foreshadowings and narrative mirrors.

The first of these occurs even before Xavier has left Paris

for Brittany. Alone in his room, suffering from spleen, he contemplates his face in the mirror and notes that it is "mortellement pâle" (deathly pale). Discontent, he attempts to shake his moroseness, "enseveli" (buried) in a large old armchair. The choice of adverb and verb here is by no means accidental; Xavier has just been present at a seance which seems to have been provoked by a quantity of hasty burials in the city. His preoccupation with death is interrupted by the thought of a voyage he might make to see the Abbé Maucombe. The text therefore establishes at the very beginning a link between Xavier's morbid thoughts and the fate of his distant friend. The reader, it might be said, is already in the presence of an *intersigne*, though one does not yet know it. We are, in fact, in exactly the same situation as Xavier will be during the first night he spends at the abbot's house.

Xavier's arrival at the Abbé Maucombe's presbytery near Saint-Maur provides another occasion for a type of foreshadowing; here, it is an experience of a curious form of déjà vu. His first impression is that of a charming country home covered in climbing vines and flowers, its windows brightly illuminated by the rays of the setting sun. The beauty of the site is such that Xavier hesitates to knock on the door, preferring to enjoy for one moment longer the calm of the *campagne déserte* (lonely countryside). This delay is enough, however, to allow the text to veer toward melancholy and death: "Ici les rêves morts ressuscitent, devançant les moments de la tombe! Si tu veux avoir le véritable désir de mourir, approche: ici la vue du ciel exalte jusqu'à l'oubli" (Here dead dreams are brought back to life, in advance of the moments of the grave. If you wish to have the true desire to die, come near: here the view of heaven excites one to forgetfulness). Xavier turns back toward the house, and is stunned to see that it has exchanged its identity for another: it is now ancient and crumbling; its windows are lit by "les rayons d'agonie du soir" (the dying rays of evening); the steps appear to be made of tombstones from a local cemetery, and the doorknocker resounds "comme les vibrations d'un glas" (like the echoes of a death knell). [In a footnote, Mellerski states: "The reference to Poe's "House of Usher" is obvious here, the same *lézardes* (cracks) that fissure the Abbé Maucombe's cottage walls echo those that widen and tear apart Roderick and Madeleine's ancestral home. This instance of intertextual exchange might also be said to function as an *intersigne;* the adept reader will interpret it as a prefiguration of mortal events in Villiers's story.'] Significantly, the tombstone steps still bear "traces de lettres creusées" (traces of engraved letters) whose content Xavier does not reveal (cannot read?). These "signs" of death early in the narrative reinforce not only the idea of foreshadowing (as in the verb *devancer*), but also the ambiguity that will result from Xavier's "misreading" of later events.

By itself, the transformation of the house forms a simple *intersigne;* when combined with a future duplication, it assumes the proportions of a structure of exchange. The subject of this later episode is a description of the Abbé Maucombe himself. After dinner on the night of his arrival, Xavier offers the reader a portrait of the priest, a man still young and strong, whose eyes burn with mystical intelligence. Indeed, he says, "il me paraissait enfin d'une santé

vigoureuse: les années l'avaient fort peu atteint" (he seemed to me to be in vigorous health; the years had hardly touched him). After a discussion of God and mortality, the two take leave of one another in the corridor outside Xavier's room, but the latter is horrified to catch a glimpse of a different Abbé Maucombe in the light of a burning candle. He appears now to be "agonisant," his face pale, "d'une pâleur de mort . . . " (dying . . . with the pallor of death). Like the transformation of the Abbot's house, which occurred as Xavier observed the rays of the sun setting on the horizon and reflecting in the waters of a pond, so the "vivace reflect" (bright reflection) of the candle introduces a textual double. Xavier himself notes that "l'abbé me donnait, humainement, la *seconde* sensation que, par une obscure correspondance, sa maison m'avait fait éprouver" (the abbot gave me, in human form, the second sensation that his house, by some odd correspondence, had made me feel). It is even clearer now that this second experience of déjà vu is meant to warn of death to come. When the abbot wishes Xavier goodnight a *second* time, the text underlines that fact that the experience Xavier has undergone twice is one that has occurred between the lines. In the space of time it has taken for the Abbé Maucombe to speak the same words twice, a foreshadowing of death has entered the text. Further, by creating an identification between the house and its owner, Villiers has effected a linguistic exchange, exemplifying the "odd correspondence" that Xavier mentions. The place, Saint-Mauer, indeed reflects its inhabitant, the future *saint mort* (dead saint).

The central episode of the story occurs within the next three pages, and once again Villiers takes care to introduce it with a textual *intersigne:* Xavier cannot sleep; he is disturbed by odd sounds in the night, and particularly by those of wood-eating insects, the "horloges-de-mort" (deathwatch beetles) that inhabit the walls of the abbot's house. [In a footnote, Mellerski states: "Death-watch beetles, as their name suggests, are also linked with folkloric beliefs in portents of death. Their presence here, just before the appearance of the *intersigne,* creates another instance of a doubled foreshadowing similar to that of the engraved steps."] The description of the nocturnal visit by the ghostly priest is in itself a clichéd fantastic situation: the moon illuminates the room with its pale flame, and the clock strikes midnight. A mysterious light burns through the keyhole of the door, staining Xavier's sleeve with an icy, bloody glow. Transfixed by the "tache" (stain), Xavier remarks that the light passing through the keyhole "me causait l'impression du regard phosphorique d'un hibou!" (gave me the impression of an owl's phosphoric gaze). As the priest offers the cloak, "un oiseau de nuit, avec un cri hideux" (a nightbird, with a hideous cry) flies between the two protagonists. Xavier is terrified, but ascribes the event to a dream or to somnambulism.

On the following day (the next chapter), however, the text of **"L'Intersigne"** goes beyond cliché, and introduces a form of the fantastic peculiar to this story. Xavier attempts, at breakfast, to recount his nocturnal experience to the Abbé Maucombe, but at the moment of describing the gesture made by the *intersigne,* he is interrupted by the arrival of a letter from his father. His story is quickly for-

gotten by the narrator, but the event has merely been de-
ferred, not obliterated. By itself, this minor duplication
functions as another *intersigne,* since Xavier's unfinished
tale of exchange mirrors the same interrupted gesture of
the previous night.

The foreshadowed offering of the cloak is ultimately realized in a forest setting, but lexically and syntactically the
text merely reproduces the scene that has taken place the
night before in Xavier's room. Significantly, it is introduced by a reference to the same cemetery that is the
source of the tombstone steps leading to the Abbé Maucombe's house, and whose inscriptions Xavier was unable
to decipher. The moon is again a pale flame, and the light
of the keyhole, previously the subject of a metaphor, now
really does issue from an owl with phosphorescent eyes.
The stain on Xavier's sleeve has been transformed into a
glow "qui tremblait sur le grand bras d'une yeuse" (that
trembled on the large branch of a live oak). The abbot
himself duplicates the manner and gestures of the *intersigne* in the earlier chapter. More significantly, he *repeats*
his words as he offers Xavier the cloak: "Ainsi prenez,—
prenez ce manteau!—J'y tiens beaucoup! . . . (Therefore
take—take this cloak. I absolutely insist on it—very
much!). At the very moment of exchange, the text reproduces itself exactly:

> En face de moi, dans le corridor, se tenait, deb-
> out, une forme haute et noire,—un prêtre, le tri-
> corne sur la tête. La lune l'éclairait tout entier,
> à l'exception de la figure: je ne voyais que le feu
> de ses deux prunelles qui me considéraient avec
> une solennelle fixité.
>
> [Facing me in the hallway stood a tall black
> form: a priest, his three-cornered hat on his
> head. The moon illuminated him entirely, except
> for his face. I could see only the fire of his two
> pupils which held me in a solemn stare.]
>
> L'abbé, en prononçant ces paroles, me tendait
> son manteau noir. Je ne voyais pas sa figure, à
> cause de l'ombre que projetait son large tricorne:
> mais je distinguai ses yeux *qui me considéraient
> avec une solennelle fixité.*
>
> [The abbot, on saying these words, held out his
> black cloak to me. I did not see his face, because
> of the shadow projected by his wide three-
> cornered hat. But I noticed his eyes, which held
> me in a solemn stare.]

The scene closes with Xavier in flight, but not before a
final echo of the *intersigne* makes itself heard. Just as Xavier had previously felt the nightbird, uttering a horrible
cry, brush by his face, he now experiences a vastly multiplied version of the same event: "Et voici que, venue du
fond de l'horizon, du fond de ces bois décriés, une volée
d'orfraies, à grand bruit d'ailes, passa, en criant
d'horribles syllabes inconnues, au dessus de ma tête"
(And then, rising from far away on the horizon, from deep
within these lonely woods, a flock of rooks passed over my
head, loudly beating their wings, crying horrible unknown
syllables). The "unknown syllables" of the birds (like the
unread[able] inscriptions on the tombstone steps) remind
us that where the *intersigne* accomplished its foreshadowing in silence, the real exchange must be inscribed verbally

in order for the text to realize literally what has only been
figural.

Dorothy Kelly, in a recent study of the role of effacement
in the fantastic text ["The Ghost of Meaning: Language
in the Fantastic," *Sub-stance* (1982)], notes that the uncanny arises when a text puts its own preestablished limits
into question. Using Charles Nodier's "Ines de Las Sier-
ras" as an example, she points out that while the heroine's
first appearance suggests a ghostly phenomenon, the reader is finally unable to reinterpret it as either canny or uncanny. The second version of Ines's appearance, which is
meant to explain her presence in the castle, forces us to use
the same illogic in our supposedly correct reading that we
had used to evaluate events during her first appearance.
Kelly notes that "certain parts [of the first version] resist
reappropriation into the realistic explanation provided by
the second part. . . . As ineradicable elements of the supernatural, insufficiently erased, they represent the endurance or the return of the supernatural *in* the realistic." She
concludes that the "repetition of the events in two *different* contexts of supposed fiction and supposed reality constitutes the uncanny and supernatural aspect" of the story.
This useful definition of fantastic language as the locus of
an aporia, a suspension between the categories of the figural and the literal, fiction and reality, supernatural and real
may be applied and extended in an evaluation of Villiers's
manipulation of the fantastic in **"L'Intersigne."**

If the first sign of the fantastic is a form of repetition, or
a foreshadowing of the literal through the figural, Villiers's story is a masterly exercise in all the possibilities
that such repetition might provide. Indeed, though the
text proceeds chronologically, covering one full week of
time, its structure is in fact nonlinear in a more important
sense. We have seen how the central episodes, the *intersigne* and its realization, are foreshadowed by two other
descriptions that operate in the same duplicatory manner.
The entire text, however, is structured and framed by such
displacement and reproduction.

In an article on the structure of **"L'Intersigne,"** ["Logique
et chronologique dans 'L'Intersigne' de Villiers de l'Isle-
Adam," *Annales de la faculté des lettres et sciences humaines de Nice* (1977)] André Labarrère indicates that
Villiers's short story frequently employs a device in which
a seemingly anecdotal detail (such as Xavier's forgotten
cloak, or the fact that he leaves his address with Nanon)
later becomes a crucial structural element. Labarrère
compares this device to a cinematic insert whose real importance will be understood much later in the sequence of
the plot. In Villiers's text, however, chronology and logic
overlap for the act is at the same time being reported on
as it is happening. This is, I think, tantamount to characterizing the moment of exchange through the *intersigne* as
a moment when the figural meaning of the fantastic text
must be construed literally. The text actually suppresses
any distinction between real and unreal, and suspends itself in a intermediary zone between signifier and signified.

It might be argued that in the second published version of
his story, Villiers came perilously close to veering toward
a resolution of the fantastic into the *merveilleux chrétien.*
Additional details concerning the cloak's association with

the tomb of Christ suggest a false transcendance through religious myth and seem to attempt to domesticate the fantastic ambiguity of the experience of the *intersigne*. Similarly, a change of epigraph directs the reader's attention toward sacred matters and away from the displacement and reproduction that we have seen as central to fantastic discourse in this tale. The original epigraph is from Sir Graft's *Inquiry into Dark Science;* it reads "Oh! Oh! que signifie ce télescope, Harris? je vois doubler le Ciel et la Terre" (What does this telescope mean, Harris? I see that Heaven and Earth are *increased twofold*). The second published version of the story replaces this epigraph with one from Saint Bernard's *Meditations* on the *Preparation for the Last Judgment,* and reminds man of his original, imperfect nature. It would seem, therefore, that Villiers was somehow "uncomfortable" with the original, highly ambiguous ending to the tale. But as we have seen, the sacred origin of the cloak maintains a properly *textural* relationship with the beginning of the narrative, and can therefore be inserted into the network established previously: death-spleen-mirror is now "cloaked" at both ends of the story by references to resurrection.

Given the narrative complexity of Villiers's text, we can agree with Rashkin [in "Secret Crimes, Haunted Signs: Villiers' 'L'Intersigne.'" *Stanford French Review* (1982)] when she rejects the notion that reading the *intersigne* as simply a premonition of death (as other critics have done) will exhaust the meaning of this tale. On the other hand, to read "*intersignes* [as] words 'within words,' symbols or rhymes that reveal the text's meaning only when the reader goes beneath the surface of the narrative" is unfortunately to fall into the very "trap" that this particular fantastic text sets for the reader. A narrative that so carefully displaces and duplicates its signs is precisely one that resists recuperation of hidden meanings, and denies the signifying activity that realist narrative claims for its own. For this reason, we must read **"L'Intersigne"** as exemplary of the discourse of nonsignification, as Jackson terms the fantastic—or even, perhaps, as that of oversignification, wherein everything and nothing can be meaningful.

Villiers's interrogation of the ways in which we interpret the world, and the world of the text, is therefore developed on both linguistic and epistemological levels. In much the same fashion that the ghostly *intersigne* represents, in Gillian Beer's terms [in "Ghosts," *Essays in Criticism* (1978)], an "insurrection" rather than the resurrection of the dead, so, too, Villiers's use of duplication, déjà vu, and foreshadowing creates a structure in which each textual mirror reflects a narrative "revolt" against the surface logic of the whole. As a result, the function of the *intersigne* must be understood not only as the means by which our vision is shifted to the intervals between things, but also, and perhaps more importantly, as properly subversive of our desire to read *for* meaning, and to read *in* meanings. (pp. 135-41)

> *Nancy C. Mellerski, "Structures of Exchange in Villiers de l'Isle-Adam's 'L'Intersigne',"* in The Shape of the Fantastic: Selected Essays from the Seventh International Conference on the Fantastic in the Arts, *edited by Olena H.*

> *Saciuk, Greenwood Press, Inc., 1990, pp. 135-42.*

Anthony Zielonka   (essay date 1987)

[*In the essay below, Zielonka examines irony and satire in "Les demoiselles de Bienfilâtre."*]

Villiers de l'Isle-Adam is recognized as one of the masters of satire in nineteenth-century French literature. In his **Contes cruels** (1883), in addition to tales of mystery, humor, fantasy and exoticism, we find several satirical stories which take as their target a variety of inventions of modern science, of new developments in advertizing, as well as more universal themes such as man's selfishness, greed, hypocrisy and materialism. The aim of this note is to examine the ways in which irony and satire are used by Villiers in the first story of this collection: **"Les Demoiselles de Bienfilâtre"**. Although this was not the first of the short stories to be written or published, it seems fitting that it was with this fine satirical tale that Villiers chose to open the collection.

One of the essential features of satire is that it has an object, which can be a situation, an attitude, a form of behavior or a set of values. The satirist singles out an object for his criticism and pokes fun at it or makes it appear ridiculous. The writer can utilize various forms of irony, of humor, of parody, exaggeration, bathos, and even of burlesque, in his treatment of this object. As Northrop Frye writes in the *Anatomy of Criticism:* "Two things, then, are essential to satire; one is wit or humor founded on fantasy or a sense of the grotesque or absurd, the other is an object of attack."

What is being satirized in this story is the social and moral climate in France in the early years of the Third Republic. Villiers illustrates and passes judgment on this society's preoccupation with money and with materialistic values. In this parody of the Romantic theme of the fallen woman who is redeemed when she falls in love, traditional Christian values have become distorted and inverted, and nobody, not even the clergy, the traditional guardians of Christian morality, is able to change or reverse this situation. Villiers chooses irony as the main weapon or vehicle of his satire. In his hands, it becomes a complicated and ambiguous instrument which makes his stories such engaging and entertaining reading.

Villiers opens the story by stating what appears to be a general truth or moral:

> Pascal nous dit qu'au point de vue des faits, le
> Bien et le Mal sont une question de "latitude".
> En effet, tel acte humain s'appelle crime, ici,
> bonne action, là-bas, et réciproquement.

He goes on to give examples of the diversity of moral standards and of norms of behavior around the world, concentrating on different peoples' attitudes to old people and to sexual morality. He is thus making a serious point about the relativity of moral principles. Yet, even here, at the beginning of what is ostensibly a fable, he treats the conventions of this genre ironically. The tale is a parody of a fable because, in it, conventional moral values are not overturned in some distant and exotic land but in the very heart of Paris. In fact, irony, which dominates the whole story, appears even before the narrative itself begins. [In his introduction to *Contes cruels, Nouveaux contes* (1968)] P.-G. Castex has commented upon the ironic dimensions of the title and on the fact that, in the manuscript, Villiers had entitled this story "L'Innocente".

In the course of this story, considerable irony is derived from the juxtaposition of different characters' viewpoints, from mutual misunderstandings and from the exaggeration of the situation in which they find themselves. The readers are thus given a superior vantage-point from which they can observe and laugh at the incongruity of the situation. The characters, each of whom has a limited view of events, reveal themselves to be naïve, gullible and, ultimately, ludicrous. Frye has shown that this privileged perspective, enjoyed by the reader, is characteristic of the *ironic* mode (*Anatomy*).

However, the narrator also plays an important role in disclosing the ironic dimensions of the story. He does this by making interjections and comments on the actions and speeches of the characters as well as by foregrounding elements of vocabulary and style which draw attention to the unusual aspects of the situation. When describing the ladies who wait for clients on the café-terrace he uses an odd and unflattering combination of bird imagery and makes a strikingly understated observation:

> Les yeux tenaient de l'émerillon et de la volaille. Les unes conservaient sur leurs genoux un gros bouquet, les autres un petit chien, les autres rien. Vous eussiez dit qu'elles attendaient quelqu'un.

This is one example of the way in which a writer can give his readers clues to enable them to detect his irony. As D. C. Muecke points out [in *Irony* (1970)]: ". . . the half-concealment is part of the ironist's artistic purpose and the detection and appreciation of the camouflage is a large part of the reader's pleasure."

One of the principal sources of irony (and of humor) in this text is the unexpected association of positive attributes, such as diligence, conscientiousness and piety with what is normally regarded as an immoral profession. Here, the euphemisms with which Villiers refers to Olympe and Henriette's profession connote virtue and respectability. Prostitution is never referred to directly. Villiers calls the two sisters "Soeurs de joie" and "ces ouvrières 'qui vont en journée la nuit' ", and writes of "leur commerce" and "les affaires". They are dedicated, hardworking girls who have based a traditional Christian morality on a decidedly unorthodox acceptance of prostitution as a profession. This inversion of Christian morality is the major source of irony and satire in the story. Villiers clearly exaggerates a phenomenon which he sees in contemporary society and criticizes it by making it appear comic. In a morality based entirely on financial gain, with a consequently cynical attitude to love, their dedication to their work suffices to make what they do respectable.

It is only when Olympe betrays this materialistic morality, by falling in love with a poor student, that she is castigated as a sinner: "Un jour, la plus jeune, Olympe, tourna

mal . . . Bref, elle fit une faute: elle aima." The narrator playfully exaggerates and dramatizes her "offence" and gives the impression that he shares the dominant view of morality. He expresses sympathy for Henriette, who is shunned by everybody as a result of her sister's "fall". He describes her shocked reaction to Olympe's loss of interest in her work and in keeping up appearances. We are also shown the full extent of the shame and dishonor that Olympe has brought upon her family. The narrator adopts a mock-serious tone throughout; he systematically misuses the noble and Classical examples to which he refers, as here, in the account of Henriette's final attempt to "save" her sister, in the café:

> Pareille à la Mallonia déshonorée par Tibère et se présentant devant le Sénat romain pour accuser son violateur, avant de se poignarder en son désespoir, Henriette entra dans la salle des austères . . . il se fit un religieux silence: il s'agissait de juger.

Olympe's sense of shame becomes so intense that it literally causes her death. She recognizes the mortal sin that she has committed by daring to love a man without thinking of financial gain.

The conclusion of the story consists of an almost farcical succession of misunderstandings. Since only the reader is able to see the full truth of the situation, he alone is able to appreciate the full irony of what is happening. The priest who comes to administer the last rites to Olympe and to give her absolution misunderstands what she says to him and approves of her expression of regret at having abandoned her previously irreproachable way of life. His credulity and naïvety prevent him from seeing the ambiguity of her remorse.

Olympe, too, misunderstands what is happening when Maxime rushes into her room with the money that his parents have sent him to enable him to pay his examination fees. She shrinks back from him because his very presence reminds her of her "sin", and does not notice the money he has brought, which Villiers mockingly calls "cette significative circonstance atténuante". The priest misinterprets her rejection of Maxime, which he regards as a rejection of her former immoral association with the student. He also misunderstands her final joy on seeing that Maxime has brought her some money after all:

> . . . le prêtre pensa qu'elle se sentait sauvée et que d'obscures visions séraphiques transparaissaient pour elle sur les mortelles ténèbres de la dernière heure.

Olympe's viewpoint is juxtaposed with that of the priest, producing a sharp contrast. She sees the golden coins as a "métal sacré", as the proof of a miracle which has redeemed her, whilst the reader realizes that she has merely succeeded in corrupting the student. In his use of the verb "racheter", here, Villiers makes an almost sacrilegious pun, since Maxime's money is the means of Olympe's redemption but is also, literally, a payment for her services.

The supreme irony comes at the end of the text. Villiers portrays Olympe's last moments as a mystical vision. A moment of total confusion and misunderstanding is presented as a moment of divine enlightenment. Her dying utterance, "Il a éclairé!", ironically echoes Goethe's supposed last words, which form the epigraph to the story: "De la lumière!" (pp. 157-61)

> *Anthony Zielonka, "Irony and Satire in 'Les Demoiselles de Bienfilâtre' by Villiers de l'Isle-Adam," in* French Literature Series, *Vol. XIV, 1987, pp. 157-61.*

Villiers de l'Isle-Adam, like the legendary Janus, has two faces. There is one that sees the world through tired eyes, filled with bitterness and regret, as an evil to be fled. But there is a second, the face of a visionary, seeking a world where human spirituality can flourish.

—John Blaise Anzalone, in his "Jean-Marie Mathias Philippe-Auguste, Comte de Villiers de l'Isle-Adam," in Dictionary of Literary Biography, *Vol. 123, 1992.*

Ross Chambers (essay date 1988)

[*In the excerpt below, Chambers explores the symbolic meanings of the cloaks in "L'intersigne."*]

Attempts at a limiting definition of the fantastic are bound to fail because the fantastic is *at once* a specific genre (a part of literature) and something that is specific to literature (and so coextensive with it). A recent paper by Catherine Lowe proposes persuasively that the fantastic is the manifestation in literature of that which eludes theory, and consequently of that ungraspable uncanniness that defines the literary itself. I will follow her lead in not worrying too much about the fantastic as a specific genre (or even—to use Rosemary Jackson's word—mode) but I will take the fantastic to be paradigmatic of the general category of the fictional, for my interest is in learning from it what it can teach about the intriguing problem of the authority of fictional narrative.

Fictional authority poses many questions: some major ones are the following. How is it that a text presented as, and recognized as, a "fiction"—as non-factual, untrue, a fabrication—can acquire *authority,* in the sense that it is accorded attention by empirical readers? What *kind* of authority can this be (what kind of attention does such a text draw)? And—even more curiously—how is it that such texts acquire authority by figuring their own acquisition of authority? To these questions I propose first to supply rather sketchy "answers" that correspond to the hypotheses I am currently working with, and then to test their explanatory value by undertaking a brief reading of **"L'Intersigne."**

A fictional text simulates the transmission of information from a "narrator" to a "narratee." Thus, in **"L'Intersigne,"** a general narrator reports to a general narratee an event which, as it happens, is another act of storytelling. To a group of friends ("gens de pensée") gathered around a fireside and taking tea on a winter's evening (propitious circumstances for an effective tale), a pale young man contributed a story because it concerned a topic of interest ("la *nature* de ces coïncidences qui . . . ") that had arisen in conversation:

> —Voici une histoire, nous dit-il, que je n'accompagnerai d'aucun commentaire. Elle est véridique. Peut-être la trouverez-vous impressionnante.
>
> Nous allumâmes nos cigarettes et nous écoutames . . . .

Because of the absence of commentary, both the audience of baron Xavier's story and the general narratee are left to draw their own conclusions concerning the relevance of the story to the "nature" of certain coincidences; but that is not really the point. The point is for the tale to work its effect, to be "impressionnant."

And so the rest of the text (a fiction) records its (fictive) storyteller's (fictive) story as (fictively) told to the (fictive) narratees. Contrary to the baron's assertion, there is absolutely nothing "véridique" here. Nor is the frame-story necessarily any more truthful—and even if it were, it would be entirely pointless if the framed narrative did not itself carry the force of authority. The narratees (the group of friends listening to the baron's tale, but also the general narratee), are clearly produced as receiving the stories as acts of veridiction. But any *reader*—as distinct from the narratees produced in the text—who might seek truthful knowledge here (that is, the transmission of information that could be accepted and acted upon as, in some sense, factual or real) would be a naïve reader, that is, not a "reader" at all. Yet, the fact that empirical readers of fiction nevertheless *simulate* a belief in narrative information of a fictive kind is a matter of common experience and observation; and it leads to the question: *why?* What, for a reader, is to be gained by *reading in the narratee position,* that is, by simulating an appropriate response to the rhetorical devices of "faire croire" (here, the bald statement: "Elle est véridique," for instance) deployed by a fictive narrator anxious to produce interest in his, or sometimes her, story? (That baron Xavier's story does not fall flat and succeeds in "impressing" at least part of his audience is indicated, of course, by the fact that one member of the group has become the general narrator of **"L'Intersigne"**: this personage clearly deems the story "impressionnante" enough to be worth repeating, even though he does not, and cannot, on his own account endorse the affirmation of its truthfulness.)

Any narrative, fictional or otherwise (let us assume that the distinction fictional/true has at least a pragmatic validity), that depends for its authority on the transmission of information (knowledge, experience, etc.) is subject to a law of diminishing returns. As the information is delivered there is an expenditure of authority such that, by the time the final pieces of information have been revealed, it is approaching (or has reached) zero. In this light, one understands the tendency observable in many narratives, to save the more vital pieces of information until the end: it is a device for maintaining narrative authority, as manifested in the narratee's "interest," for the duration of the narrative. But one notices also, in many endings, a significant deployment of textual "work" whose function appears to be to prolong the addressee's reflection on the story—and hence the narrative's authority—*beyond* its formal end. This new form of attention and interest, however, cannot depend on the reception of information (the role attributed to the narratee), which has come to an end with the end of the story; indeed, it is often stimulated by a certain withholding of information (as unavailable, unsayable, etc.). For the question now is not: what is the information being conveyed? but: what does this information (and the manner of its being conveyed) *mean*?

In short, a narrative that has not already raised, or begun to raise, the question of its significance has in its ending a *last chance* to appeal to an addressee who now is of a different sort, being the subject, not so much of a *libido sciendi* as of a *libido interpretandi*. Such an addressee is no longer, even by simulation, a narratee whose attitudes to the narrative are *controlled* by the narrator as subject of the discourse; for one of *this* addressee's objects of interest will be, precisely, the narrator-narratee relation itself and the mode of the story's telling. Such an addressee will have become, in short, a *reader* to whom the narrative discourse has the type of interest characteristic of a "text," a type of interest that can be described, in a word, as interpretability.

My hypothesis, then, is that fictional narratives can be understood as discursive apparatuses that "convert" their narratee into a reader; and that the reason, therefore, why empirical readers are so willing to simulate the forms of belief and interest attributed to the narratee, as the presumed subject of a desire to *know,* is that it is only in this way that they may have something to *interpret* and may thus enjoy the *real* (not simulated) pleasures of the *libido interpretandi,* that is, of collaborating with the text in the production of meaning. It is consequently on the seduction of the reader's *libido interpretandi* through the simulated *libido sciendi* of the narratee that fictional narratives depend for the long-term authority of their discourse, it being understood that interpretability is limitless and subject to a law, not of decreasing, but of increasing returns. The more one interprets, the more there is to understand . . .

One can put this another way by saying that narrative devices of *expenditure* of authority (the "knowledge" that is transmitted and the corresponding work of "faire croire") are supplemented by textual devices of restraint, or better still of *reserve,* since it is the "unsaid" in any text that becomes the object of its interpretation—but this unsaid constitutes a *reservoir* of signification that seems inexhaustible. The trick of narrative authority, in fiction, is consequently *so to expend* narrative information (in what I call the "narrative function" of discourse) that a significant *reserve of textual authority*—of interpretability—becomes available (in what I call the "textual function"). That, I believe, in broad outline, is the operation we refer

Villiers de l'Isle-Adam in his later years.

to when we discuss the "interest" we take in a fictional text.

Figuration (the opposite of literality—again I assume the pragmatic validity of the distinction) is one of the names we give to interpretability. A figure is a piece of discursive information that is treated as the object of an act of reading, the agency of a signifying practice and hence a reserve of meaning, in which signification is at once withheld (not given as information) and made available (as in a reservoir). *Self*-figuration—also called self-referentiality or reflexivity—is consequently of the essence in fictional narrative because it is the means whereby narratives are able to produce themselves as *interpretable discourse* and to tap the reserve of authority associated with interpretability. Although our culture has many institutions devoted to the tasks of determining which pieces of discourse will qualify as interpretable fictions and of teaching some of the ways in which they can be interpreted, a text produces itself as "readable" in the first instance by figuring itself as a specific kind of communicative act (and hence, ultimately, always as "text"). In so doing, it produces a "space" between itself as figuring-text and itself as figured-text, a tiny difference of the text from itself, which is the "space" of reading, the "difference" that both invites and permits interpretation. There is, of course, a conundrum here, since it takes an act of reading to perceive in the text the self-figuration that produces it as an object of reading (and so produces the reader as its textual addressee). But that conundrum is coextensive with the conundrum of fiction itself, which "becomes" fiction through being recognized (i.e., read) as such—whereupon the signs of its fictionality (and notably its self-referentiality) become readable.

These, then, are the hypotheses I am currently working with in answer to the questions about the authority of fiction I raised at the outset. In **"L'Intersigne,"** to get back now to Villiers, a change of overcoats takes place. Xavier, in his role as protagonist, forgets his warm *houppelande* at the inn and is loaned, instead, the thin and worn, but strangely "doubled" *manteau* the abbé Maucombe has brought back to Brittany from the Holy Land. With the abbé's *over*coat on his shoulders Xavier is *over*come (or *over*whelmed) by an eery sense of the world as "intersigne," as open—that is—onto a limitless transcendence. It would be easy, too easy, to understand this change of overcoats as a figure of the distinction between the "real" and the "fantastic" on which many theories of the fantastic as a *genre* seem to rely. Taking the fantastic, however, as a paradigm of the fictional, I will discuss the change of coats rather as a figure of the conversion of narratee into reader on which the authority of fiction depends.

I will take it, that is, as an example of textual self-figuration, and more specifically as a figure of the text's reliance for its authority—for that which prevents the dismissive shrug of the shoulders that all narratives fear—on different modes of rhetorical *enveloppement* (the *enveloppement* that is a "faire croire" and the *enveloppement* that is a "donner à lire"), and in particular on the integration of one mode with the other. The mode of the *houppelande,* warm and comforting like a cosy Parisian tea-party on a wintry evening, is replaced by—but is not discontinuous with—the mode of the *manteau,* thin and worn and open to the icy wind and penetrating damp of the supernatural, but nevertheless "redoublé avec une espèce de tendresse bizarre," and able to exert the "poids secret" that prevents Xavier from shrugging his shoulders. It has powers of another order, those of a discourse haunted by the inexhaustible otherness that can be called death, the uncanny or, quite simply, the interpretable, and which the text itself produces as a form of charity, the Christian (or "Christian"?) charity personified by the abbé. It warms, then, in another way.

But Xavier does not keep the abbé's *manteau:* he returns to his *houppelande* and to Paris, sending the *manteau* back to the Breton abbé, whose shroud it then becomes. The text thus asserts, I think, the value and the necessity of its own doubleness, as the agency of a "narrative" (*houppelande*) function and a "textual" (*manteau*) function that, by definition, work together and cannot be separated from each other. The condition of the "textual function" (of interpretability) is that there be a "narrative function" (the transmission of information); but the "narrative function" is in a precise sense meaningless unless it is *doubled* by a discourse whose very thinness, like that of the abbé's coat,

makes it "double" in its turn, eery and haunted because open onto a transcendance of interpretability.

There are, then, two forms of doubleness—a double doubling—to be taken account of in reading **"L'Intersigne."** Between the modern universe of Paris, where spleen is treated with iron and senna-tea, and the region of Basse-Bretagne, with the village of Saint-Maur (note the homology with "mort") where lives the abbé Maucombe and to which Xavier repairs in hopes of curing his melancholy through hunting (an unconscious "chasse spirituelle"), a certain dichotomy is carefully maintained. To one the screech of owls, to the other that of the train. It is the Parisians, says the abbé, who are fanatical in their modern beliefs; it is more "reasonable" to choose "pour foi, la plus utile, puisque nous sommes libres et que nous devenons notre croyance"; his preference goes, then, not to "le siècle des lumières" but to "la Lumière des siècles"—the very light that, on a number of occasions in Brittany, Xavier will see streaming from various pairs of numinous eyes. In Paris, we realize, doors are carefully—indeed "sournoisement"—locked, and have a secret mechanism which is their "pride"; but in Saint-Maur, pride is denounced, in a quotation from Joseph de Maistre, as that which stands between humanity and God; and doors are opened simply by lifting the latch when they do not swing open "largement, lentement, silencieusement" of their own accord, to reveal a terrifying dream-figure (yet it is not a dream), offering a cloak as a message, it seems, from and of the other world.

In this carefully developed double paradigm, Xavier's *houppelande*—which he takes, along with hat, gloves and hunting-rifle, on his train-journey but "forgets" at the inn—figures, then, the Parisian mode of *enveloppement,* a method of *keeping out* the truth of the spiritual world—of God, of death—as one locks a door "à triple tour" to protect one's property, the property Xavier will return to Paris to defend in his lawsuit:

> —Eh! c'est qu'il s'agit de presque toute ma fortune! murmurai-je.
>
> —La fortune, c'est Dieu! dit simplement Maucombe.

The abbé's *manteau,* like Brittany, is characterized on the other hand by an openness that gives it a doubleness of its own. For Saint-Maur is a place of second sight and "*seconde* sensation," where a presbytery in a serene landscape can become, in the blink of an eye, a glimpse of death, with its cracked walls, its windows luminous (with the "Lumière des siècles" . . .) in the "agonie du soir," its steps now *legible* ("je vis . . . que des lettres creusées y restaient encore") as tombstones—or where, again, the abbé himself, from being a man in his prime, can suddenly reveal himself as "un agonisant qui se tenait debout, là, près de ce lit." The *manteau* brought back from a pilgrimage and which is said in a "singular" but *repeated* phrase to have "*touché* LE TOMBEAU ," clearly figures the closeness of Breton reality to its otherworldly double; and the abbé, at his death, is "heureux . . . d'être enveloppé . . . et enseveli" in the precious cloak.

These terms ("enveloppé," "enseveli") and especially their

implied equivalence are significant. But the doubleness of Brittany is figured too by the *redoublement* of the cloak's threadbare cloth, which it owes to the work of patching and darning it has undergone ("il était très vieux et même rapiécé, recousu, redoublé. . . ," so that it is not so much lined with, as *thickened by* the "charité profonde" that Xavier reads into its construction: it has been "redoublé avec une espèce de tendresse bizarre." The image is of a threadbare openness that achieves its density through the work of sewing, patching and darning that clearly—indeed conventionally—figures writing as the production of text(ure) but simultaneously signifies here the good works of charity. And it is this thickness that gives the worn old coat the heaviness ("un poids secret") that will prevent Xavier from shrugging off the terrifying intimations he is vouchsafed.

But the selfsame thickness makes the *manteau* simultaneously an equivalent, as well as the opposite, of the *houppelande;* and it points to the fact that Paris and Brittany are themselves not so much opposed as they are in a mirror-relationship. They form a chiasmus, of which the dialogic play of "siècle des lumières" and "Lumière des siècles" is one of the major emblems; and it is this chiasmic relation that permits communication—notably but not exclusively in the form of travel—between the two. Thus, if the reality of Saint-Maur opens onto the other world, so too, in its own way, does the enclosed world of Paris, a place where "des inhumations accomplies à la légère—beaucoup trop précipitées enfin" are of concern and a seance can plunge Xavier into the "noire obsession" of his "spleen héréditaire"—the very spleen that will send him to Brittany in search of its cure. For this reason, Paris and Brittany can be seen, in terms suggested by the construction of the *manteau,* as being in a relation, not of difference and distance so much as of *redoublement* of each other: the continuity between them, symbolized by Xavier's voyage to Brittany to meet the abbé who has returned from a more distant voyage, is more important than their, no less real, differences. Brittany is to Paris as the thickness of charity (and of the other world) is to the thin stuff of the abbé's *manteau:* not a separate *lining,* but of a piece with it.

Consequently, it is important to note that there is a continuity of overcoats also, since Xavier forgets his *houppelande* only to replace it by the *manteau* which he will send back to Saint-Maur when, on his return to Paris, he gets back his *houppelande,* or, as he says, "reconquers" it at the inn. If the overcoats are taken to be figures of narrative discourse, then their doubleness and continuity, their interchangeability, can be immediately related to the textual thickness that Villiers's narrative constructs and enacts for itself, notably through its framing devices. The framing story begins in Paris, among a group of "gens de pensée" discussing "un sujet des plus sombres"; the framed story in turn begins in a Paris of spleen and alarm occasioned by various manifestations (*spiritisme,* premature burial) of the permeable interface between the world of the living and that of the dead; and it then moves into the transcendental thickness of the world of Brittany before returning once more to Paris. With more space, I would want to show also that the title, the dedication, the epi-

graph, as well as this double *entrée en matière,* mark the writing of the whole opening page—as the strategic place where the discursive character of the text is determined—as a place of particularly intense *travail de couture,* "rapiécé, recousu, redoublé" like the *manteau* itself. But it is more important to point out that what is figured by the relation of the overcoats and enacted by the "layering" of the textual discourse is, in each case, something like the continuity and mutual dependency that characterize the relation of "narrative" and "textual" functions on which the authority of fiction depends.

For not only does the *houppelande* lead to the *manteau* and back again, but the *manteau* itself, not content with being "redoublé" in the transcendent sense we have seen, has a kind of double existence that relates it also to a diurnal, non-transcendental world, and hence ultimately to Paris and the discursive mode that corresponds to it. The *manteau* appears first in the "dream"-visitation when the dark, priestly figure, his eyes streaming with light, proffers it wordlessly, and Xavier sees "un grand manteau noir, un manteau de voyage." But the real terror occurs the following day, since this time it is the world of "reality" that doubles the "dream"-world (rather than the other way around, as has previously been the case) and the abbé repeats the gesture performed by his nocturnal *alter ego,* but now fastening the cloak around the young man's unresisting shoulders. "Il me jeta le manteau sur les épaules, me l'agrafa . . . pendant que, sans forces, je fermais les paupières." This is clearly the moment when Xavier's submission to the terrifying authority of the world of Brittany is at its peak.

This moment, it is true, is that of the declining day and the onset of a wintry night. But the nocturnal visitation has a much less alarming diurnal double, as well, in the *morning* scene of the next day, when over a sunny and very everyday breakfast (the abbé is reading a newspaper), Xavier narrates the story of his disturbed night. At the crucial moment of the proffering of the *manteau,* he is interrupted by a message from . . . Paris—a letter from his father concerning worldly affairs (the threatened fortune), but brought by the maid Nanon, whose *second* identity as an angel ("sa vaste coiffe avait des battements d'ailes,"—unless of course she is an owl?—has already been established: " . . . la porte de la salle à manger s'ouvrit, Nanon . . . entra, dans le rayon du soleil, au beau milieu de la conversation, et, m'interrompant, me tendit un papier . . . ." Where the *manteau,* in one sense, is doubled by the "other world," there is, then, another doubling here (the door, the apparition in a ray of light, the message) between the nocturnal *manteau* episode and the world of sunlight, newspapers and business letters from Paris, the world to which the *houppelande* belongs. And, in case the discursive relevance of this scene to the text as a whole should escape us, let us recall that Xavier is here doubling his nocturnal experience by relating it over the breakfast table (just as, in Paris, he will again relate it, but over the teacups of afternoon).

Brittany, then, has "news" of Paris as well as of the other world—but Paris, too, with its spiritist obsessions and its melancholics, has some sort of (fore-)knowledge of Brittany, and of what it represents. Xavier, before his departure, sees his mortal pallor in the glass (as he will see death in Brittany), and sinks into his armchair: "je m'ensevelis dans un *ample* fauteuil, *vieux* meuble . . . , etc." (my emphases): the chair clearly foreshadows the cloak that has touched the tomb, in which Xavier will be wrapped and the abbé, in due course, "enseveli." And, after his visit, the letter *from* Xavier's father, received in the Breton dining-room, has as its counterpart the letter *to* Xavier's father, penned by Nanon, and received in the Parisian *salon,* bringing to it the terrifying news of the abbé's death. So the important fact is not simply that the overcoats are continuous with one another but that they are, like the news of Paris in Brittany and the news of Brittany in Paris, *interchangeable in both directions.* After the *houppelande* has been forgotten and replaced by the *manteau,* the *manteau* will be exchanged again for the *houppelande,* in which Xavier returns to Paris.

And it is only then—after this double exchange of coats—that Xavier finally gets the good night's sleep he has longed for all this time, through Parisian sleeplessness and Breton *éveil.* With his feet comfortably warm in the train, "enveloppé dans ma houppelande reconquise," he achieves the "bonne nuit" that he had been, precisely, "désireux de conquérir." The metaphor of conquest (both the baron and the abbé have had military experience) conflates the voyage-pilgrimage theme with that of the crusade; but, in so doing, it simultaneously underscores the circularity of the voyages undertaken, whether that of the abbé to Palestine (and back to Brittany) or that of Xavier to Brittany (and back to Paris). The "bonne nuit" the young man finally enjoys in his *houppelande* is consequently not a sign of complacency and comfort so much as it represents a conquest, something gained: the integration into his Parisian experience of what he has learned (or learned to *see*) in Brittany—and hence the cure of his melancholy. But Xavier's return to the *houppelande* figures also his conquest of discursive power, through the integration of the two types of narrative authority, a "faire croire" relating to narrative knowledge and a "donner à lire" implying interpretability. And it is this power that he will mobilize in telling his story (a veridiction that he hopes will prove "impressionnante") to his Parisian friends, in an act of storytelling that can be taken, in turn, to represent, *en abyme,* the discursive situation the text itself seeks to produce.

The association of both the *houppelande* and the *manteau* with specific types of discourse is difficult to ignore. Like the worn cloak strengthened with charity, the "conversation fortifiante" of the abbé has the power to overwhelm and envelop its addressee, who becomes entirely passive. Compare: "J'étais fatigué: j'écoutais, sans répondre" and "Il me jeta le manteau sur les épaules . . . pendant que, sans forces, je fermais les paupières." But this authoritarian manner of the abbé's nevertheless requires interpretation on the receiver's or hearer's part; the abbé's gnomic utterances, like the *manteau,* have their own *redoublement,* which is the underlying "charity" that inspires them. "Une charité profonde, sans doute, portait l'abbé Maucombe à donner en aumônes le prix d'un manteau neuf: du moins, je m'expliquai la chose de cette façon"—

here, precisely, as he examines the coat's construction, one sees Xavier in the act of furnishing the interpretation it requires. But the "charité profonde" to be read in the abbé's discourse has less to do with almsgiving and more to do with a project of salvation on Xavier's behalf ("La grande affaire, c'est le salut: j'espérais être pour quelque chose dans le vôtre,"; and it is *this* charity—for so we as readers are led to interpret the situation—that underlies the insistence of the abbé's discourse at the moment of proffering the cloak: "ainsi *prenez,—prenez ce manteau!* J'y tiens beaucoup! . . . beaucoup!—ajouta-t-il avec un ton inoubliable." For the italics instruct us, as readers, to look for *more* here, in the abbé's action, than self-abnegating courtesy: the words betray something like secret knowledge on his part of the extraordinary and supernatural powers we are supposed to attribute to the *manteau.* And it is this secret, unsaid dimension of supernatural "knowledge"—as opposed to the strict information conveyed by its "véridique" discourse—that we are invited, as readers, to attribute in turn to Xavier's story, and to Villier's text. Therein lies its eery, "impressionnant" quality.

The *houppelande,* too, is enveloping; and it can be associated with another form of "authoritarian" discourse, another sort of insistence: that of baron Xavier baldly affirming the truth of his story. There is no mention of its having a lining or *redoublement* (a *houppelande* is thick by definition, "souvent ouaté et fourré," as the *Petit Robert* says)—but the thickness of the *houppelande* is significantly associated with a theme of forgetting. The sentence that tells us of Xavier's forgetting of the coat at the inn itself comes as an afterthought (the information has been forgotten at its right place in the narrative), and as a parenthesis in the discourse: ("J'avais oublié ma houppelande dans ma chambre, au Soleil d'Or."). Once "reconquered," it is the occasion of another forgetting, this time of the *manteau:* "Là-dessus je m'endormis, enfin, d'un bon sommeil, oubliant complètement ce que je devais traiter désormais de coïncidence insignifiante." But this phrasing (which is close to being logically contradictory) shows that what is at work in Xavier's forgetfulness is the phenomenon of repression: he has not consigned the *manteau* (and the whole episode of Saint-Maur) to oblivion, but it can elude his psychic censorship—the locked door of his Parisian mind—only by passing as a "coïncidence insignifiante." It will take the letter from Nanon announcing the abbé's death to restore its terrifying force.

If, then, the *houppelande* seems to be the sign of a density in the discourse of "Paris" that results from the duplicity (doubleness) of repression, it is important to notice other instances, in Xavier's speech, that indicate the repression of "Saint-Maur" and its return. During the sunny breakfast scene, there is a parapraxis:

> —Avez-vous passé une bonne nuit, mon cher Xavier? me demanda-t-il.
>
> —Excellente! répondis-je distraitement (par habitude et sans accorder attention le moins du monde à ce que je disais).

Xavier has passed a terrifying night—the night of the visitation. But there is, of course, a sense (in the perspective of "salut") in which the night *has* been excellent, not be-

cause he has achieved the sleep he was counting on but because of the message, whether dreamed or not, that has
kept him *awake.* His unconscious knows this and speaks
in his discourse. But, then, it had already manifested its
knowledge of the beneficence of Brittany at the moment
of his initial decision to quit Paris, counteracting another
of Xavier's forgettings:

> A peine cette pensée me fut-elle venue, à
> l'instant même où je me décidai pour cette ligne
> de conduite, le nom d'un vieil ami, oublié depuis
> des années, l'abbé Maucombe, me passa dans
> l'esprit.
>
> —L'abbé Maucombe! . . . dis-je à voix basse.

It is not necessary to rehearse here the evidence of widespread "knowledge" of what we now call the unconscious
process in the literature, "fantastic" or otherwise, of the
nineteenth century. We can safely conclude, however, that
if the narrator's "Parisian" discourse is associated with his
houppelande, it is because it is structured by repression,
and that what it represses—and what consequently returns in that discourse—is the doubleness, or interpretability, the openness onto the beyond that is characteristic
of the *manteau,* and of the simple but profound speech of
the Breton abbé. Xavier, telling his tale to his Parisian
friends, quite naturally uses the Parisian style of discourse,
as indicated by the "faire croire" rhetoric of his "Elle est
véridique." But as a returnee from Brittany *he himself embodies the return of the repressed,* and he makes of his Parisian discourse the site of a massive manifestation of that
repressed, not only in the form of the *matière de Bretagne*
he recounts (his experience at Saint-Maur) but also in the
form of the discursive interpretability that goes with it.
And so, not only does his story have the characteristics of
the *houppelande* ("Elle est véridique") but also it has those
of the *manteau* (and of the abbé's own weighty discourse):
"Peut-être la trouverez-vous impressionnante."

To map these conclusions briefly onto the theory set forth
at the beginning of this article, we can say that the information expended by Xavier's story as it unfolds is the
knowledge of what happened to him in Brittany; but we
are warned to read this discourse of information in terms
of what it "forgets" or represses (and consequently incorporates): the *reserve* of signification revealed by discourse
in its interpretability. Like the *manteau* and the *houppelande,* the discourse of the text is interchangeably a discourse of knowledge and a discourse that is interpretable
(a discourse of death, of the unknown . . .). But the
knowledge that the text expends (what happened in Saint-
Maur) proves to be precisely the knowledge (of interpretability) that the text *needs its reader to have* in order for
it to enjoy the reserve of authority that "returns" in it and
cannot be exhausted. It is all a matter of getting us to
change overcoats. (pp. 63-75)

> *Ross Chambers, "Changing Overcoats: Vil-
> liers' 'L'Intersigne' and the Authority of Fic-
> tion," in* L'Esprit Createur, *Vol. XXVIII, No.
> 3, Fall, 1988, pp. 63-77.*

FURTHER READING

Biography

du Pontavice de Heussey, Robert. *Villiers de l'Isle-Adam: His
Life and Works.* Translated by Lady Mary Loyd. London:
William Heinemann, 1894, 286 p.

Biography by Villiers's nephew.

Raitt, Alan W. "The Last Days of Villiers de l'Isle-Adam."
French Studies 8, No. 3 (July 1954): 233-49.

Presents an account of Villiers's marriage on his deathbed.

———. "Villiers de l'Isle-Adam in 1870." *French Studies*
XIII, No. 4 (October 1959): 332-48.

Detailed account of Villiers's activities and whereabouts
at the outset of the Franco-Prussian War.

———. "The Poet and the Prime Minister: Villiers de l'Isle-
Adam and the Marquess of Salisbury." *French Studies*
XXXIV, No. 4 (October 1980): 401-16.

Documents the relationship between Villiers and the
British Prime Minister Marquess of Salisbury, to whom
Villiers dedicated two stories.

———. *The Life of Villiers de l'Isle-Adam.* Oxford: Oxford
University Press, 1981, 452 p.

Extensive biography in which Raitt attempts to distinguish between the reality and legend of Villiers's life in
order to present a "detailed and reliable account of how
Villiers de l'Isle-Adam actually spent his time."

Criticism

Anzalone, John. "Villiers de l'Isle-Adam and the Gnostic
Tradition." *The French Review* 57, No. 1 (October 1983):
20-7.

Asserts that Villiers's work reflects a "gnostic 'sensitivity' " which Anzalone defines as "a call to the pursuit of
individual spiritual fulfillment against the backdrop of
a tragic, universal fall."

Cogman, P. W. M. "Subversion of the Reader in Villiers's
'Sombre récit, conteur plus sombre'." *Modern Language Review* 83, No. 1 (January 1988): 30-9.

Identifies the narrative techniques Villiers employed in
"Sombre récit, conteur plus sombre" to disorient the
reader.

Conroy, William T., Jr. *Villiers de l'Isle-Adam.* Boston:
Twayne Publishers, 1978, 167 p.

Critical and biographical survey.

Rose, Marilyn Gaddis. "Entropy and Redundancy in Decadent Style: Translating Villiers de l'Isle-Adam." *Sub-Stance,*
No. 16 (1977): 144-48.

Claims that Villiers is "*a,* if not *the,* quintessential Decadent," and contends that the use of redundancy in Decadent writing is a device to create a feeling of entropy.

———. "Decadence in Villiers de l'Isle-Adam and His Followers." *Orbis Litterarum* 36, No. 2 (1981): 141-54.

Surveys Villiers's influence on other writers and contends that "Conte d'Amour," a poem sequence from
Contes cruels, is typical of Decadent literary style in its
excess, redundancy, and crypticism.

Additional coverage of Villiers's life and career is contained in the following sources published by Gale Research: *Dictionary of Literary Biography,* Vol. 123 and *Nineteenth-Century Literature Criticism,* Vol. 3.

Appendix:

Select Bibliography of General Sources on Short Fiction

BOOKS OF CRITICISM

Allen, Walter. *The Short Story in English.* New York: Oxford University Press, 1981, 413 p.

Aycock, Wendell M., ed. *The Teller and the Tale: Aspects of the Short Story* (Proceedings of the Comparative Literature Symposium, Texas Tech University, Volume XIII). Lubbock: Texas Tech Press, 1982, 156 p.

Averill, Deborah. *The Irish Short Story from George Moore to Frank O'Connor.* Washington, D.C.: University Press of America, 1982, 329 p.

Bates, H. E. *The Modern Short Story: A Critical Survey.* Boston: Writer, 1941, 231 p.

Bayley, John. *The Short Story: Henry James to Elizabeth Bowen.* Great Britain: The Harvester Press Limited, 1988, 197 p.

Bennett, E. K. *A History of the German Novelle: From Goethe to Thomas Mann.* Cambridge: At the University Press, 1934, 296 p.

Bone, Robert. *Down Home: A History of Afro-American Short Fiction from Its Beginning to the End of the Harlem Renaissance.* Rev. ed. New York: Columbia University Press, 1988, 350 p.

Bruck, Peter. *The Black American Short Story in the Twentieth Century: A Collection of Critical Essays.* Amsterdam: B. R. Grüner Publishing Co., 1977, 209 p.

Burnett, Whit, and Burnett, Hallie. *The Modern Short Story in the Making.* New York: Hawthorn Books, 1964, 405 p.

Canby, Henry Seidel. *The Short Story in English.* New York: Henry Holt and Co., 1909, 386 p.

Current-García, Eugene. *The American Short Story before 1850: A Critical History.* Twayne's Critical History of the Short Story, edited by William Peden. Boston: Twayne Publishers, 1985, 168 p.

Flora, Joseph M., ed. *The English Short Story, 1880-1945: A Critical History.* Twayne's Critical History of the Short Story, edited by William Peden. Boston: Twayne Publishers, 1985, 215 p.

Foster, David William. *Studies in the Contemporary Spanish-American Short Story.* Columbia, Mo.: University of Missouri Press, 1979, 126 p.

George, Albert J. *Short Fiction in France, 1800-1850.* Syracuse, N.Y.: Syracuse University Press, 1964, 245 p.

Gerlach, John. *Toward an End: Closure and Structure in the American Short Story.* University, Ala.: The University of Alabama Press, 1985, 193 p.

Hankin, Cherry, ed. *Critical Essays on the New Zealand Short Story.* Auckland: Heinemann Publishers, 1982, 186 p.

Hanson, Clare, ed. *Re-Reading the Short Story.* London: MacMillan Press, 1989, 137 p.

Harris, Wendell V. *British Short Fiction in the Nineteenth Century.* Detroit: Wayne State University Press, 1979, 209 p.

Huntington, John. *Rationalizing Genius: Idealogical Strategies in the Classic American Science Fiction Short Story.* New Brunswick: Rutgers University Press, 1989, 216 p.

Kilroy, James F., ed. *The Irish Short Story: A Critical History.* Twayne's Critical History of the Short Story, edited by William Peden. Boston: Twayne Publishers, 1984, 251 p.

Lee, A. Robert. *The Nineteenth-Century American Short Story.* Totowa, N. J.: Vision / Barnes & Noble, 1986, 196 p.

Leibowitz, Judith. *Narrative Purpose in the Novella.* The Hague: Mouton, 1974, 137 p.

Lohafer, Susan. *Coming to Terms with the Short Story.* Baton Rouge: Louisiana State University Press, 1983, 171 p.

Lohafer, Susan, and Clarey, Jo Ellyn. *Short Story Theory at a Crossroads.* Baton Rouge: Louisiana State University Press, 1989, 352 p.

Mann, Susan Garland. *The Short Story Cycle: A Genre Companion and Reference Guide.* New York: Greenwood Press, 1989, 228 p.

Matthews, Brander. *The Philosophy of the Short Story.* New York: Longmans, Green and Co., 1901, 83 p.

May, Charles E., ed. *Short Story Theories.* Athens, Oh.: Ohio University Press, 1976, 251 p.

McClave, Heather, ed. *Women Writers of the Short Story: A Collection of Critical Essays.* Englewood Cliffs, N. J.: Prentice-Hall, 1980, 171 p.

Moser, Charles, ed. *The Russian Short Story: A Critical History.* Twayne's Critical History of the Short Story, edited by William Peden. Boston: Twayne Publishers, 1986, 232 p.

New, W. H. *Dreams of Speech and Violence: The Art of the Short Story in Canada and New Zealand.* Toronto: The University of Toronto Press, 1987, 302 p.

Newman, Frances. *The Short Story's Mutations: From Petronius to Paul Morand.* New York: B. W. Huebsch, 1925, 332 p.

O'Connor, Frank. *The Lonely Voice: A Study of the Short Story.* Cleveland: World Publishing Co., 1963, 220 p.

O'Faolain, Sean. *The Short Story.* New York: Devin-Adair Co., 1951, 370 p.

Orel, Harold. *The Victorian Short Story: Development and Triumph of a Literary Genre.* Cambridge: Cambridge University Press, 1986, 213 p.

O'Toole, L. Michael. *Structure, Style and Interpretation in the Russian Short Story.* New Haven: Yale University Press, 1982, 272 p.

Pattee, Fred Lewis. *The Development of the American Short Story: An Historical Survey.* New York: Harper and Brothers Publishers, 1923, 388 p.

Peden, Margaret Sayers, ed. *The Latin American Short Story: A Critical History.* Twayne's Critical History of the Short Story, edited by William Peden. Boston: Twayne Publishers, 1983, 160 p.

Peden, William. *The American Short Story: Continuity and Change, 1940-1975.* Rev. ed. Boston: Houghton Mifflin Co., 1975, 215 p.

Reid, Ian. *The Short Story.* The Critical Idiom, edited by John D. Jump. London: Methuen and Co., 1977, 76 p.

Rhode, Robert D. *Setting in the American Short Story of Local Color, 1865-1900.* The Hague: Mouton, 1975, 189 p.

Rohrberger, Mary. *Hawthorne and the Modern Short Story: A Study in Genre.* The Hague: Mouton and Co., 1966, 148 p.

Shaw, Valerie, *The Short Story: A Critical Introduction.* London: Longman, 1983, 294 p.

Stephens, Michael. *The Dramaturgy of Style: Voice in Short Fiction.* Carbondale, Ill.: Southern Illinois University Press, 1986, 281 p.

Stevick, Philip, ed. *The American Short Story, 1900-1945: A Critical History.* Twayne's Critical History of the Short Story, edited by William Peden, Boston: Twayne Publishers, 1984, 209 p.

Summers, Hollis, ed. *Discussion of the Short Story.* Boston: D. C. Heath and Co., 1963, 118 p.

Vannatta, Dennis, ed. *The English Short Story, 1945-1980: A Critical History.* Twayne's Critical History of the Short Story, edited by William Peden. Boston: Twayne Publishers, 1985, 206 p.

Voss, Arthur. *The American Short Story: A Critical Survey.* Norman, Okla.: University of Oklahoma Press, 1973, 399 p.

Walker, Warren S. *Twentieth-Century Short Story Explication: New Series, Vol. 1: 1989-1990.* Hamden, Conn.: Shoe String, 1993, 366 p.

Ward, Alfred C. *Aspects of the Modern Short Story: English and American.* London: University of London Press, 1924, 307 p.

Weaver, Gordon, ed. *The American Short Story, 1945-1980: A Critical History.* Twayne's Critical History of the Short Story, edited by William Peden. Boston: Twayne Publishers, 1983, 150 p.

West, Ray B., Jr. *The Short Story in America, 1900-1950.* Chicago: Henry Regnery Co., 1952, 147 p.

Williams, Blanche Colton. *Our Short Story Writers.* New York: Moffat, Yard and Co., 1920, 357 p.

Wright, Austin McGiffert. *The American Short Story in the Twenties.* Chicago: University of Chicago Press, 1961, 425 p.

CRITICAL ANTHOLOGIES

Atkinson, W. Patterson, ed. *The Short-Story.* Boston: Allyn and Bacon, 1923, 317 p.

Baldwin, Charles Sears, ed. *American Short Stories.* New York: Longmans, Green and Co., 1904, 333 p.

Charters, Ann, ed. *The Story and Its Writer: An Introduction to Short Fiction.* New York: St. Martin's Press, 1983, 1239 p.

Current-García, Eugene, and Patrick, Walton R., eds. *American Short Stories: 1820 to the Present.* Key Editions, edited by John C. Gerber. Chicago: Scott, Foresman and Co., 1952, 633 p.

Fagin, N. Bryllion, ed. *America through the Short Story.* Boston: Little, Brown, and Co., 1936, 508 p.

Frakes, James R., and Traschen, Isadore, eds. *Short Fiction: A Critical Collection.* Prentice-Hall English Literature Series, edited by Maynard Mack. Englewood Cliffs, N.J.: Prentice-Hall, 1959, 459 p.

Gifford, Douglas, ed. *Scottish Short Stories, 1800-1900.* The Scottish Library, edited by Alexander Scott. London: Calder and Boyars, 1971, 350 p.

Gordon, Caroline, and Tate, Allen, eds. *The House of Fiction: An Anthology of the Short Story with Commentary.* Rev. ed. New York: Charles Scribner's Sons, 1960, 469 p.

Greet, T. Y., et. al. *The Worlds of Fiction: Stories in Context.* Boston: Houghton Mifflin Co., 1964, 429 p.

Gullason, Thomas A., and Caspar, Leonard, eds. *The World of Short Fiction: An International Collection.* New York: Harper and Row, 1962, 548 p.

Havighurst, Walter, ed. *Masters of the Modern Short Story.* New York: Harcourt, Brace and Co., 1945, 538 p.

Litz, A. Walton, ed. *Major American Short Stories.* New York: Oxford University Press, 1975, 823 p.

Matthews, Brander, ed. *The Short-Story: Specimens Illustrating Its Development.* New York: American Book Co., 1907, 399 p.

Menton, Seymour, ed. *The Spanish American Short Story: A Critical Anthology.* Berkeley and Los Angeles: University of California Press, 1980, 496 p.

Mzamane, Mbulelo Vizikhungo, ed. *Hungry Flames, and Other Black South African Short Stories.* Longman African Classics. Essex: Longman, 1986, 162 p.

Schorer, Mark, ed. *The Short Story: A Critical Anthology.* Rev. ed. Prentice-Hall English Literature Series, edited by Maynard Mack. Englewood Cliffs, N. J.: Prentice-Hall, 1967, 459 p.

Simpson, Claude M., ed. *The Local Colorists: American Short Stories, 1857-1900.* New York: Harper and Brothers Publishers, 1960, 340 p.

Stanton, Robert, ed. *The Short Story and the Reader.* New York: Henry Holt and Co., 1960, 557 p.

West, Ray B., Jr., ed. *American Short Stories.* New York: Thomas Y. Crowell Co., 1959, 267 p.

Short Story Criticism Indexes

Literary Criticism Series
Cumulative Author Index

SSC Cumulative Nationality Index
SSC Cumulative Title Index

How to Use This Index

The main references

Calvino, Italo
 1923-1985.....CLC **5, 8, 11, 22, 33, 39,**
          73; SSC 3

---

list all author entries in the following Gale Literary Criticism series:

CLC = *Contemporary Literary Criticism*
CLR = *Children's Literature Review*
CMLC = *Classical and Medieval Literature Criticism*
DC = *Drama Criticism*
LC = *Literature Criticism from 1400 to 1800*
NCLC = *Nineteenth-Century Literature Criticism*
PC = *Poetry Criticism*
SSC = *Short Story Criticism*
TCLC = *Twentieth-Century Literary Criticism*

The cross-references

See also CANR 23; CA 85-88;
 obituary CA 116

---

list all author entries in the following Gale biographical and literary sources:

AAYA = *Authors & Artists for Young Adults*
AITN = *Authors in the News*
BLC = *Black Literature Criticism*
BW = *Black Writers*
CA = *Contemporary Authors*
CAAS = *Contemporary Authors Autobiography Series*
CABS = *Contemporary Authors Bibliographical Series*
CANR = *Contemporary Authors New Revision Series*
CAP = *Contemporary Authors Permanent Series*
CDALB = *Concise Dictionary of American Literary Biography*
CDBLB = *Concise Dictionary of British Literary Biography*
DA = *DISCovering Authors*
DLB = *Dictionary of Literary Biography*
DLBD = *Dictionary of Literary Biography Documentary Series*
DLBY = *Dictionary of Literary Biography Yearbook*
HLC = *Hispanic Literature Criticism*
HW = *Hispanic Writers*
JRDA = *Junior DISCovering Authors*
MAICYA = *Major Authors and Illustrators for Children and Young Adults*
MTCW = *Major 20th-Century Writers*
SAAS = *Something about the Author Autobiography Series*
SATA = *Something about the Author*
WLC = *World Literature Criticism, 1500 to the Present*
YABC = *Yesterday's Authors of Books for Children*

Literary Criticism Series
Cumulative Author Index

Antoine, Marc
See Proust, (Valentin-Louis-George-Eugene-) Marcel

Antoninus, Brother
See Everson, William (Oliver)

Antonioni, Michelangelo 1912- ..... **CLC 20**
See also CA 73-76

Antschel, Paul 1920-1970...... **CLC 10, 19**
See also Celan, Paul
See also CA 85-88; CANR 33; MTCW

Anwar, Chairil 1922-1949 .... **TCLC 22**
See also CA 121

Apollinaire, Guillaume .. **TCLC 3, 8, 51; PC 7**
See also Kostrowitzki, Wilhelm Apollinaris de

Appelfeld, Aharon 1932- .... **CLC 23, 47**
See also CA 112; 133

Apple, Max (Isaac) 1941-........ **CLC 9, 33**
See also CA 81-84; CANR 19; DLB 130

Appleman, Philip (Dean) 1926- ..... **CLC 51**
See also CA 13-16R; CAAS 18; CANR 6, 29

Appleton, Lawrence
See Lovecraft, H(oward) P(hillips)

Apteryx
See Eliot, T(homas) S(tearns)

Apuleius, (Lucius Madaurensis)
125(?)-175(?)................ **CMLC 1**

Aquin, Hubert 1929-1977......... **CLC 15**
See also CA 105; DLB 53

Aragon, Louis 1897-1982....... **CLC 3, 22**
See also CA 69-72; 108; CANR 28; DLB 72; MTCW

Arany, Janos 1817-1882........ **NCLC 34**

Arbuthnot, John 1667-1735.......... **LC 1**
See also DLB 101

Archer, Herbert Winslow
See Mencken, H(enry) L(ouis)

Archer, Jeffrey (Howard) 1940- .... **CLC 28**
See also BEST 89:3; CA 77-80; CANR 22

Archer, Jules 1915- .... **CLC 12**
See also CA 9-12R; CANR 6; SAAS 5; SATA 4

Archer, Lee
See Ellison, Harlan

Arden, John 1930- .... **CLC 6, 13, 15**
See also CA 13-16R; CAAS 4; CANR 31; DLB 13; MTCW

Arenas, Reinaldo 1943-1990 .... **CLC 41**
See also CA 124; 128; 133; HW

Arendt, Hannah 1906-1975 .... **CLC 66**
See also CA 17-20R; 61-64; CANR 26; MTCW

Aretino, Pietro 1492-1556 .... **LC 12**

Arghezi, Tudor 1880-1967 .... **CLC 80**
See also Theodorescu, Ion N.

Arguedas, Jose Maria
1911-1969 .... **CLC 10, 18**
See also CA 89-92; DLB 113; HW

Argueta, Manlio 1936-............ **CLC 31**
See also CA 131; HW

Ariosto, Ludovico 1474-1533........ **LC 6**

Aristides
See Epstein, Joseph

Aristophanes
450B.C.-385B.C.... **CMLC 4; DA; DC 2**

Arlt, Roberto (Godofredo Christophersen)
1900-1942 .... **TCLC 29**
See also CA 123; 131; HW

Armah, Ayi Kwei 1939-.. **CLC 5, 33; BLC 1**
See also BW; CA 61-64; CANR 21; DLB 117; MTCW

Armatrading, Joan 1950- .... **CLC 17**
See also CA 114

Arnette, Robert
See Silverberg, Robert

Arnim, Achim von (Ludwig Joachim von Arnim) 1781-1831 .... **NCLC 5**
See also DLB 90

Arnim, Bettina von 1785-1859.... **NCLC 38**
See also DLB 90

Arnold, Matthew
1822-1888 ..... **NCLC 6, 29; DA; PC 5; WLC**
See also CDBLB 1832-1890; DLB 32, 57

Arnold, Thomas 1795-1842 ...... **NCLC 18**
See also DLB 55

Arnow, Harriette (Louisa) Simpson
1908-1986 .... **CLC 2, 7, 18**
See also CA 9-12R; 118; CANR 14; DLB 6; MTCW; SATA 42, 47

Arp, Hans
See Arp, Jean

Arp, Jean 1887-1966.............. **CLC 5**
See also CA 81-84; 25-28R; CANR 42

Arrabal
See Arrabal, Fernando

Arrabal, Fernando 1932- ... **CLC 2, 9, 18, 58**
See also CA 9-12R; CANR 15

Arrick, Fran.................... **CLC 30**

Artaud, Antonin 1896-1948 ..... **TCLC 3, 36**
See also CA 104

Arthur, Ruth M(abel) 1905-1979.... **CLC 12**
See also CA 9-12R; 85-88; CANR 4; SATA 7, 26

Artsybashev, Mikhail (Petrovich)
1878-1927 .... **TCLC 31**

Arundel, Honor (Morfydd)
1919-1973 .... **CLC 17**
See also CA 21-22; 41-44R; CAP 2; SATA 4, 24

Asch, Sholem 1880-1957 .... **TCLC 3**
See also CA 105

Ash, Shalom
See Asch, Sholem

Ashbery, John (Lawrence)
1927- ...... **CLC 2, 3, 4, 6, 9, 13, 15, 25, 41, 77**
See also CA 5-8R; CANR 9, 37; DLB 5; DLBY 81; MTCW

Ashdown, Clifford
See Freeman, R(ichard) Austin

Ashe, Gordon
See Creasey, John

Ashton-Warner, Sylvia (Constance)
1908-1984 .... **CLC 19**
See also CA 69-72; 112; CANR 29; MTCW

Asimov, Isaac
1920-1992 ...... **CLC 1, 3, 9, 19, 26, 76**
See also BEST 90:2; CA 1-4R; 137; CANR 2, 19, 36; CLR 12; DLB 8; DLBY 92; JRDA; MAICYA; MTCW; SATA 1, 26, 74

Astley, Thea (Beatrice May)
1925- .... **CLC 41**
See also CA 65-68; CANR 11, 43

Aston, James
See White, T(erence) H(anbury)

Asturias, Miguel Angel
1899-1974 .... **CLC 3, 8, 13**
See also CA 25-28; 49-52; CANR 32; CAP 2; DLB 113; HW; MTCW

Atares, Carlos Saura
See Saura (Atares), Carlos

Atheling, William
See Pound, Ezra (Weston Loomis)

Atheling, William, Jr.
See Blish, James (Benjamin)

Atherton, Gertrude (Franklin Horn)
1857-1948 .... **TCLC 2**
See also CA 104; DLB 9, 78

Atherton, Lucius
See Masters, Edgar Lee

Atkins, Jack
See Harris, Mark

Atticus
See Fleming, Ian (Lancaster)

Atwood, Margaret (Eleanor)
1939- ..... **CLC 2, 3, 4, 8, 13, 15, 25, 44; DA; PC 8; SSC 2; WLC**
See also BEST 89:2; CA 49-52; CANR 3, 24, 33; DLB 53; MTCW; SATA 50

Aubigny, Pierre d'
See Mencken, H(enry) L(ouis)

Aubin, Penelope 1685-1731(?)........ **LC 9**
See also DLB 39

Auchincloss, Louis (Stanton)
1917- .... **CLC 4, 6, 9, 18, 45**
See also CA 1-4R; CANR 6, 29; DLB 2; DLBY 80; MTCW

Auden, W(ystan) H(ugh)
1907-1973 ...... **CLC 1, 2, 3, 4, 6, 9, 11, 14, 43; DA; PC 1; WLC**
See also CA 9-12R; 45-48; CANR 5; CDBLB 1914-1945; DLB 10, 20; MTCW

Audiberti, Jacques 1900-1965 ...... **CLC 38**
See also CA 25-28R

Auel, Jean M(arie) 1936-.......... **CLC 31**
See also AAYA 7; BEST 90:4; CA 103; CANR 21

Auerbach, Erich 1892-1957 .... **TCLC 43**
See also CA 118

Augier, Emile 1820-1889 .... **NCLC 31**

August, John
See De Voto, Bernard (Augustine)

Augustine, St. 354-430.......... **CMLC 6**

Aurelius
See Bourne, Randolph S(illiman)

Baroja (y Nessi), Pio 1872-1956 .... **TCLC 8**
See also CA 104

Baron, David
See Pinter, Harold

Baron Corvo
See Rolfe, Frederick (William Serafino
Austin Lewis Mary)

Barondess, Sue K(aufman)
1926-1977 .... **CLC 8**
See also Kaufman, Sue
See also CA 1-4R; 69-72; CANR 1

Baron de Teive
See Pessoa, Fernando (Antonio Nogueira)

Barres, Maurice 1862-1923 .... **TCLC 47**
See also DLB 123

Barreto, Afonso Henrique de Lima
See Lima Barreto, Afonso Henrique de

Barrett, (Roger) Syd 1946- .... **CLC 35**
See also Pink Floyd

Barrett, William (Christopher)
1913-1992 .... **CLC 27**
See also CA 13-16R; 139; CANR 11

Barrie, J(ames) M(atthew)
1860-1937 .... **TCLC 2**
See also CA 104; 136; CDBLB 1890-1914;
CLR 16; DLB 10; MAICYA; YABC 1

Barrington, Michael
See Moorcock, Michael (John)

Barrol, Grady
See Bograd, Larry

Barry, Mike
See Malzberg, Barry N(athaniel)

Barry, Philip 1896-1949 .... **TCLC 11**
See also CA 109; DLB 7

Bart, Andre Schwarz
See Schwarz-Bart, Andre

Barth, John (Simmons)
1930- ...... **CLC 1, 2, 3, 5, 7, 9, 10, 14,
27, 51; SSC 10**
See also AITN 1, 2; CA 1-4R; CABS 1;
CANR 5, 23; DLB 2; MTCW

Barthelme, Donald
1931-1989 ...... **CLC 1, 2, 3, 5, 6, 8, 13,
23, 46, 59; SSC 2**
See also CA 21-24R; 129; CANR 20;
DLB 2; DLBY 80, 89; MTCW; SATA 7,
62

Barthelme, Frederick 1943-........ **CLC 36**
See also CA 114; 122; DLBY 85

Barthes, Roland (Gerard)
1915-1980 .... **CLC 24**
See also CA 130; 97-100; MTCW

Barzun, Jacques (Martin) 1907- .... **CLC 51**
See also CA 61-64; CANR 22

Bashevis, Isaac
See Singer, Isaac Bashevis

Bashkirtseff, Marie 1859-1884 ... **NCLC 27**

Basho
See Matsuo Basho

Bass, Kingsley B., Jr.
See Bullins, Ed

Bass, Rick 1958-................ **CLC 79**
See also CA 126

Bassani, Giorgio 1916-............. **CLC 9**
See also CA 65-68; CANR 33; DLB 128;
MTCW

Bastos, Augusto (Antonio) Roa
See Roa Bastos, Augusto (Antonio)

Bataille, Georges 1897-1962 .... **CLC 29**
See also CA 101; 89-92

Bates, H(erbert) E(rnest)
1905-1974 .... **CLC 46; SSC 10**
See also CA 93-96; 45-48; CANR 34;
MTCW

Bauchart
See Camus, Albert

Baudelaire, Charles
1821-1867 ..... **NCLC 6, 29; DA; PC 1;
WLC**

Baudrillard, Jean 1929- .... **CLC 60**

Baum, L(yman) Frank 1856-1919 ... **TCLC 7**
See also CA 108; 133; CLR 15; DLB 22;
JRDA; MAICYA; MTCW; SATA 18

Baum, Louis F.
See Baum, L(yman) Frank

Baumbach, Jonathan 1933- ...... **CLC 6, 23**
See also CA 13-16R; CAAS 5; CANR 12;
DLBY 80; MTCW

Bausch, Richard (Carl) 1945- ...... **CLC 51**
See also CA 101; CAAS 14; CANR 43;
DLB 130

Baxter, Charles 1947-......... **CLC 45, 78**
See also CA 57-60; CANR 40; DLB 130

Baxter, George Owen
See Faust, Frederick (Schiller)

Baxter, James K(eir) 1926-1972 .... **CLC 14**
See also CA 77-80

Baxter, John
See Hunt, E(verette) Howard, Jr.

Bayer, Sylvia
See Glassco, John

Beagle, Peter S(oyer) 1939-......... **CLC 7**
See also CA 9-12R; CANR 4; DLBY 80;
SATA 60

Bean, Normal
See Burroughs, Edgar Rice

Beard, Charles A(ustin)
1874-1948 .... **TCLC 15**
See also CA 115; DLB 17; SATA 18

Beardsley, Aubrey 1872-1898 ..... **NCLC 6**

Beattie, Ann
1947- .... **CLC 8, 13, 18, 40, 63; SSC 11**
See also BEST 90:2; CA 81-84; DLBY 82;
MTCW

Beattie, James 1735-1803 .... **NCLC 25**
See also DLB 109

Beauchamp, Kathleen Mansfield 1888-1923
See Mansfield, Katherine
See also CA 104; 134; DA

Beaumarchais, Pierre-Augustin Caron de
1732-1799 .... **DC 4**

**Beauvoir, Simone (Lucie Ernestine Marie
Bertrand) de**
1908-1986 .... **CLC 1, 2, 4, 8, 14, 31, 44,
50, 71; DA; WLC**
See also CA 9-12R; 118; CANR 28;
DLB 72; DLBY 86; MTCW

Becker, Jurek 1937-............ **CLC 7, 19**
See also CA 85-88; DLB 75

Becker, Walter 1950-............. **CLC 26**

Beckett, Samuel (Barclay)
1906-1989 ...... **CLC 1, 2, 3, 4, 6, 9, 10,
11, 14, 18, 29, 57, 59; DA; WLC**
See also CA 5-8R; 130; CANR 33;
CDBLB 1945-1960; DLB 13, 15;
DLBY 90; MTCW

Beckford, William 1760-1844 .... **NCLC 16**
See also DLB 39

Beckman, Gunnel 1910-............ **CLC 26**
See also CA 33-36R; CANR 15; CLR 25;
MAICYA; SAAS 9; SATA 6

Becque, Henri 1837-1899........ **NCLC 3**

Beddoes, Thomas Lovell
1803-1849 .... **NCLC 3**
See also DLB 96

Bedford, Donald F.
See Fearing, Kenneth (Flexner)

Beecher, Catharine Esther
1800-1878 .... **NCLC 30**
See also DLB 1

Beecher, John 1904-1980.......... **CLC 6**
See also AITN 1; CA 5-8R; 105; CANR 8

Beer, Johann 1655-1700............. **LC 5**

Beer, Patricia 1924-.............. **CLC 58**
See also CA 61-64; CANR 13; DLB 40

Beerbohm, Henry Maximilian
1872-1956 .... **TCLC 1, 24**
See also CA 104; DLB 34, 100

Begiebing, Robert J(ohn) 1946-..... **CLC 70**
See also CA 122; CANR 40

Behan, Brendan
1923-1964 .... **CLC 1, 8, 11, 15, 79**
See also CA 73-76; CANR 33;
CDBLB 1945-1960; DLB 13; MTCW

Behn, Aphra
1640(?)-1689 .... **LC 1; DA; DC 4; WLC**
See also DLB 39, 80, 131

Behrman, S(amuel) N(athaniel)
1893-1973 .... **CLC 40**
See also CA 13-16; 45-48; CAP 1; DLB 7,
44

Belasco, David 1853-1931 .... **TCLC 3**
See also CA 104; DLB 7

Belcheva, Elisaveta 1893- .... **CLC 10**

Beldone, Phil "Cheech"
See Ellison, Harlan

Beleno
See Azuela, Mariano

Belinski, Vissarion Grigoryevich
1811-1848 .... **NCLC 5**

Belitt, Ben 1911-................. **CLC 22**
See also CA 13-16R; CAAS 4; CANR 7;
DLB 5

Bell, James Madison
1826-1902 .... **TCLC 43; BLC 1**
See also BW; CA 122; 124; DLB 50

Bell, Madison (Smartt) 1957- ...... **CLC 41**
See also CA 111; CANR 28

Bell, Marvin (Hartley) 1937-..... **CLC 8, 31**
See also CA 21-24R; CAAS 14; DLB 5;
MTCW

Bell, W. L. D.
  See Mencken, H(enry) L(ouis)

Bellamy, Atwood C.
  See Mencken, H(enry) L(ouis)

Bellamy, Edward 1850-1898 ...... **NCLC 4**
  See also DLB 12

Bellin, Edward J.
  See Kuttner, Henry

Belloc, (Joseph) Hilaire (Pierre)
  1870-1953 .... **TCLC 7, 18**
  See also CA 106; DLB 19, 100; YABC 1

Belloc, Joseph Peter Rene Hilaire
  See Belloc, (Joseph) Hilaire (Pierre)

Belloc, Joseph Pierre Hilaire
  See Belloc, (Joseph) Hilaire (Pierre)

Belloc, M. A.
  See Lowndes, Marie Adelaide (Belloc)

Bellow, Saul
  1915- ...... **CLC 1, 2, 3, 6, 8, 10, 13, 15,**
      25, 33, 34, 63, 79; DA; SSC 14; WLC
  See also AITN 2; BEST 89:3; CA 5-8R;
      CABS 1; CANR 29; CDALB 1941-1968;
      DLB 2, 28; DLBD 3; DLBY 82; MTCW

Belser, Reimond Karel Maria de
  1929- .... **CLC 14**

Bely, Andrey .... **TCLC 7**
  See also Bugayev, Boris Nikolayevich

Benary, Margot
  See Benary-Isbert, Margot

Benary-Isbert, Margot 1889-1979 ... **CLC 12**
  See also CA 5-8R; 89-92; CANR 4;
      CLR 12; MAICYA; SATA 2, 21

Benavente (y Martinez), Jacinto
  1866-1954 .... **TCLC 3**
  See also CA 106; 131; HW; MTCW

Benchley, Peter (Bradford)
  1940- .... **CLC 4, 8**
  See also AITN 2; CA 17-20R; CANR 12,
      35; MTCW; SATA 3

Benchley, Robert (Charles)
  1889-1945 .... **TCLC 1**
  See also CA 105; DLB 11

Benedikt, Michael 1935- .... **CLC 4, 14**
  See also CA 13-16R; CANR 7; DLB 5

Benet, Juan 1927-................ **CLC 28**

Benet, Stephen Vincent
  1898-1943 .... **TCLC 7; SSC 10**
  See also CA 104; DLB 4, 48, 102; YABC 1

Benet, William Rose 1886-1950 ... **TCLC 28**
  See also CA 118; DLB 45

Benford, Gregory (Albert) 1941-.... **CLC 52**
  See also CA 69-72; CANR 12, 24;
      DLBY 82

Bengtsson, Frans (Gunnar)
  1894-1954 .... **TCLC 48**

Benjamin, David
  See Slavitt, David R(ytman)

Benjamin, Lois
  See Gould, Lois

Benjamin, Walter 1892-1940 ...... **TCLC 39**

Benn, Gottfried 1886-1956........ **TCLC 3**
  See also CA 106; DLB 56

Bennett, Alan 1934- .... **CLC 45, 77**
  See also CA 103; CANR 35; MTCW

Bennett, (Enoch) Arnold
  1867-1931 .... **TCLC 5, 20**
  See also CA 106; CDBLB 1890-1914;
      DLB 10, 34, 98

Bennett, Elizabeth
  See Mitchell, Margaret (Munnerlyn)

Bennett, George Harold 1930-
  See Bennett, Hal
  See also BW; CA 97-100

Bennett, Hal .... **CLC 5**
  See also Bennett, George Harold
  See also DLB 33

Bennett, Jay 1912- .... **CLC 35**
  See also AAYA 10; CA 69-72; CANR 11,
      42; JRDA; SAAS 4; SATA 27, 41

Bennett, Louise (Simone)
  1919- .... **CLC 28; BLC 1**
  See also DLB 117

Benson, E(dward) F(rederic)
  1867-1940 .... **TCLC 27**
  See also CA 114; DLB 135

Benson, Jackson J. 1930-......... **CLC 34**
  See also CA 25-28R; DLB 111

Benson, Sally 1900-1972 .... **CLC 17**
  See also CA 19-20; 37-40R; CAP 1;
      SATA 1, 27, 35

Benson, Stella 1892-1933........ **TCLC 17**
  See also CA 117; DLB 36

Bentham, Jeremy 1748-1832 ..... **NCLC 38**
  See also DLB 107

Bentley, E(dmund) C(lerihew)
  1875-1956 .... **TCLC 12**
  See also CA 108; DLB 70

Bentley, Eric (Russell) 1916-....... **CLC 24**
  See also CA 5-8R; CANR 6

Beranger, Pierre Jean de
  1780-1857 .... **NCLC 34**

Berger, Colonel
  See Malraux, (Georges-)Andre

Berger, John (Peter) 1926- ...... **CLC 2, 19**
  See also CA 81-84; DLB 14

Berger, Melvin H. 1927-.......... **CLC 12**
  See also CA 5-8R; CANR 4; CLR 32;
      SAAS 2; SATA 5

Berger, Thomas (Louis)
  1924-.......... **CLC 3, 5, 8, 11, 18, 38**
  See also CA 1-4R; CANR 5, 28; DLB 2;
      DLBY 80; MTCW

Bergman, (Ernst) Ingmar
  1918- .... **CLC 16, 72**
  See also CA 81-84; CANR 33

Bergson, Henri 1859-1941........ **TCLC 32**

Bergstein, Eleanor 1938-........... **CLC 4**
  See also CA 53-56; CANR 5

Berkoff, Steven 1937-............. **CLC 56**
  See also CA 104

Bermant, Chaim (Icyk) 1929- ...... **CLC 40**
  See also CA 57-60; CANR 6, 31

Bern, Victoria
  See Fisher, M(ary) F(rances) K(ennedy)

Bernanos, (Paul Louis) Georges
  1888-1948 .... **TCLC 3**
  See also CA 104; 130; DLB 72

Bernard, April 1956- .... **CLC 59**
  See also CA 131

Bernhard, Thomas
  1931-1989 .... **CLC 3, 32, 61**
  See also CA 85-88; 127; CANR 32;
      DLB 85, 124; MTCW

Berrigan, Daniel 1921-............. **CLC 4**
  See also CA 33-36R; CAAS 1; CANR 11,
      43; DLB 5

Berrigan, Edmund Joseph Michael, Jr.
  1934-1983
  See Berrigan, Ted
  See also CA 61-64; 110; CANR 14

Berrigan, Ted.................... **CLC 37**
  See also Berrigan, Edmund Joseph Michael,
      Jr.
  See also DLB 5

Berry, Charles Edward Anderson 1931-
  See Berry, Chuck
  See also CA 115

Berry, Chuck..................... **CLC 17**
  See also Berry, Charles Edward Anderson

Berry, Jonas
  See Ashbery, John (Lawrence)

Berry, Wendell (Erdman)
  1934- .... **CLC 4, 6, 8, 27, 46**
  See also AITN 1; CA 73-76; DLB 5, 6

Berryman, John
  1914-1972 ...... **CLC 1, 2, 3, 4, 6, 8, 10,**
                          13, 25, 62
  See also CA 13-16; 33-36R; CABS 2;
      CANR 35; CAP 1; CDALB 1941-1968;
      DLB 48; MTCW

Bertolucci, Bernardo 1940-........ **CLC 16**
  See also CA 106

Bertrand, Aloysius 1807-1841 .... **NCLC 31**

Bertran de Born c. 1140-1215 ..... **CMLC 5**

Besant, Annie (Wood) 1847-1933 ... **TCLC 9**
  See also CA 105

Bessie, Alvah 1904-1985.......... **CLC 23**
  See also CA 5-8R; 116; CANR 2; DLB 26

Bethlen, T. D.
  See Silverberg, Robert

Beti, Mongo.............. **CLC 27; BLC 1**
  See also Biyidi, Alexandre

Betjeman, John
  1906-1984 .... **CLC 2, 6, 10, 34, 43**
  See also CA 9-12R; 112; CANR 33;
      CDBLB 1945-1960; DLB 20; DLBY 84;
      MTCW

Bettelheim, Bruno 1903-1990 ...... **CLC 79**
  See also CA 81-84; 131; CANR 23; MTCW

Betti, Ugo 1892-1953.............. **TCLC 5**
  See also CA 104

Betts, Doris (Waugh) 1932-.... **CLC 3, 6, 28**
  See also CA 13-16R; CANR 9; DLBY 82

Bevan, Alistair
  See Roberts, Keith (John Kingston)

Beynon, John
  See Harris, John (Wyndham Parkes Lucas)
      Beynon

Bialik, Chaim Nachman
  1873-1934 .... **TCLC 25**

Bickerstaff, Isaac
See Swift, Jonathan

Bidart, Frank 1939- .... **CLC 33**
See also CA 140

Bienek, Horst 1930-........... **CLC 7, 11**
See also CA 73-76; DLB 75

Bierce, Ambrose (Gwinett)
1842-1914(?) ...... **TCLC 1, 7, 44; DA;
SSC 9; WLC**
See also CA 104; 139; CDALB 1865-1917;
DLB 11, 12, 23, 71, 74

Billings, Josh
See Shaw, Henry Wheeler

Billington, Rachel 1942-.......... **CLC 43**
See also AITN 2; CA 33-36R

Binyon, T(imothy) J(ohn) 1936- .... **CLC 34**
See also CA 111; CANR 28

Bioy Casares, Adolfo 1914-.... **CLC 4, 8, 13**
See also CA 29-32R; CANR 19, 43;
DLB 113; HW; MTCW

Bird, C.
See Ellison, Harlan

Bird, Cordwainer
See Ellison, Harlan

Bird, Robert Montgomery
1806-1854 .... **NCLC 1**

Birney, (Alfred) Earle
1904- .... **CLC 1, 4, 6, 11**
See also CA 1-4R; CANR 5, 20; DLB 88;
MTCW

Bishop, Elizabeth
1911-1979 ...... **CLC 1, 4, 9, 13, 15, 32;
DA; PC 3**
See also CA 5-8R; 89-92; CABS 2;
CANR 26; CDALB 1968-1988; DLB 5;
MTCW; SATA 24

Bishop, John 1935-.............. **CLC 10**
See also CA 105

Bissett, Bill 1939-................ **CLC 18**
See also CA 69-72; CANR 15; DLB 53;
MTCW

Bitov, Andrei (Georgievich) 1937-... **CLC 57**
See also CA 142

Biyidi, Alexandre 1932-
See Beti, Mongo
See also BW; CA 114; 124; MTCW

Bjarme, Brynjolf
See Ibsen, Henrik (Johan)

Bjornson, Bjornstjerne (Martinius)
1832-1910 .... **TCLC 7, 37**
See also CA 104

Black, Robert
See Holdstock, Robert P.

Blackburn, Paul 1926-1971 ...... **CLC 9, 43**
See also CA 81-84; 33-36R; CANR 34;
DLB 16; DLBY 81

Black Elk 1863-1950 .... **TCLC 33**

Black Hobart
See Sanders, (James) Ed(ward)

Blacklin, Malcolm
See Chambers, Aidan

Blackmore, R(ichard) D(oddridge)
1825-1900 .... **TCLC 27**
See also CA 120; DLB 18

Blackmur, R(ichard) P(almer)
1904-1965 .... **CLC 2, 24**
See also CA 11-12; 25-28R; CAP 1; DLB 63

Black Tarantula, The
See Acker, Kathy

Blackwood, Algernon (Henry)
1869-1951 .... **TCLC 5**
See also CA 105

Blackwood, Caroline 1931- .... **CLC 6, 9**
See also CA 85-88; CANR 32; DLB 14;
MTCW

Blade, Alexander
See Hamilton, Edmond; Silverberg, Robert

Blaga, Lucian 1895-1961 .... **CLC 75**

Blair, Eric (Arthur) 1903-1950
See Orwell, George
See also CA 104; 132; DA; MTCW;
SATA 29

Blais, Marie-Claire
1939- .... **CLC 2, 4, 6, 13, 22**
See also CA 21-24R; CAAS 4; CANR 38;
DLB 53; MTCW

Blaise, Clark 1940-............... **CLC 29**
See also AITN 2; CA 53-56; CAAS 3;
CANR 5; DLB 53

Blake, Nicholas
See Day Lewis, C(ecil)
See also DLB 77

Blake, William
1757-1827 ..... **NCLC 13, 37; DA; WLC**
See also CDBLB 1789-1832; DLB 93;
MAICYA; SATA 30

Blasco Ibanez, Vicente
1867-1928 .... **TCLC 12**
See also CA 110; 131; HW; MTCW

Blatty, William Peter 1928-......... **CLC 2**
See also CA 5-8R; CANR 9

Bleeck, Oliver
See Thomas, Ross (Elmore)

Blessing, Lee 1949-.............. **CLC 54**

Blish, James (Benjamin)
1921-1975 .... **CLC 14**
See also CA 1-4R; 57-60; CANR 3; DLB 8;
MTCW; SATA 66

Bliss, Reginald
See Wells, H(erbert) G(eorge)

Blixen, Karen (Christentze Dinesen)
1885-1962
See Dinesen, Isak
See also CA 25-28; CANR 22; CAP 2;
MTCW; SATA 44

Bloch, Robert (Albert) 1917-....... **CLC 33**
See also CA 5-8R; CANR 5; DLB 44;
SATA 12

Blok, Alexander (Alexandrovich)
1880-1921 .... **TCLC 5**
See also CA 104

Blom, Jan
See Breytenbach, Breyten

Bloom, Harold 1930- .... **CLC 24**
See also CA 13-16R; CANR 39; DLB 67

Bloomfield, Aurelius
See Bourne, Randolph S(illiman)

Blount, Roy (Alton), Jr. 1941- ..... **CLC 38**
See also CA 53-56; CANR 10, 28; MTCW

Bloy, Leon 1846-1917........... **TCLC 22**
See also CA 121; DLB 123

Blume, Judy (Sussman) 1938-... **CLC 12, 30**
See also AAYA 3; CA 29-32R; CANR 13,
37; CLR 2, 15; DLB 52; JRDA;
MAICYA; MTCW; SATA 2, 31

Blunden, Edmund (Charles)
1896-1974 .... **CLC 2, 56**
See also CA 17-18; 45-48; CAP 2; DLB 20,
100; MTCW

Bly, Robert (Elwood)
1926- .... **CLC 1, 2, 5, 10, 15, 38**
See also CA 5-8R; CANR 41; DLB 5;
MTCW

Bobette
See Simenon, Georges (Jacques Christian)

Boccaccio, Giovanni 1313-1375
See also SSC 10

Bochco, Steven 1943-............. **CLC 35**
See also CA 124; 138

Bodenheim, Maxwell 1892-1954 ... **TCLC 44**
See also CA 110; DLB 9, 45

Bodker, Cecil 1927-.............. **CLC 21**
See also CA 73-76; CANR 13; CLR 23;
MAICYA; SATA 14

Boell, Heinrich (Theodor) 1917-1985
See Boll, Heinrich (Theodor)
See also CA 21-24R; 116; CANR 24; DA;
DLB 69; DLBY 85; MTCW

Boerne, Alfred
See Doeblin, Alfred

Bogan, Louise 1897-1970..... **CLC 4, 39, 46**
See also CA 73-76; 25-28R; CANR 33;
DLB 45; MTCW

Bogarde, Dirk .... **CLC 19**
See also Van Den Bogarde, Derek Jules
Gaspard Ulric Niven
See also DLB 14

Bogosian, Eric 1953- .... **CLC 45**
See also CA 138

Bograd, Larry 1953-.............. **CLC 35**
See also CA 93-96; SATA 33

Boiardo, Matteo Maria 1441-1494 .... **LC 6**

Boileau-Despreaux, Nicolas
1636-1711 .... **LC 3**

Boland, Eavan 1944-........... **CLC 40, 67**
See also DLB 40

Boll, Heinrich (Theodor)
1917-1985 .... **CLC 2, 3, 6, 9, 11, 15, 27,
39, 72; WLC**
See also Boell, Heinrich (Theodor)
See also DLB 69; DLBY 85

Bolt, Lee
See Faust, Frederick (Schiller)

Bolt, Robert (Oxton) 1924-........ **CLC 14**
See also CA 17-20R; CANR 35; DLB 13;
MTCW

Bomkauf
See Kaufman, Bob (Garnell)

Bonaventura.................... **NCLC 35**
See also DLB 90

Bond, Edward 1934-....... **CLC 4, 6, 13, 23**
See also CA 25-28R; CANR 38; DLB 13;
MTCW

Cameron, Peter 1959-............ **CLC 44**
See also CA 125

Campana, Dino 1885-1932........ **TCLC 20**
See also CA 117; DLB 114

Campbell, John W(ood, Jr.)
1910-1971 .... **CLC 32**
See also CA 21-22; 29-32R; CANR 34;
CAP 2; DLB 8; MTCW

Campbell, Joseph 1904-1987 .... **CLC 69**
See also AAYA 3; BEST 89:2; CA 1-4R;
124; CANR 3, 28; MTCW

Campbell, (John) Ramsey 1946- .... **CLC 42**
See also CA 57-60; CANR 7

Campbell, (Ignatius) Roy (Dunnachie)
1901-1957 .... **TCLC 5**
See also CA 104; DLB 20

Campbell, Thomas 1777-1844 .... **NCLC 19**
See also DLB 93

Campbell, Wilfred................. **TCLC 9**
See also Campbell, William

Campbell, William 1858(?)-1918
See Campbell, Wilfred
See also CA 106; DLB 92

Campos, Alvaro de
See Pessoa, Fernando (Antonio Nogueira)

Camus, Albert
1913-1960 .... **CLC 1, 2, 4, 9, 11, 14, 32,**
63, 69; DA; DC 2; SSC 9; WLC
See also CA 89-92; DLB 72; MTCW

Canby, Vincent 1924-............ **CLC 13**
See also CA 81-84

Cancale
See Desnos, Robert

Canetti, Elias 1905- ...... **CLC 3, 14, 25, 75**
See also CA 21-24R; CANR 23; DLB 85,
124; MTCW

Canin, Ethan 1960-............... **CLC 55**
See also CA 131; 135

Cannon, Curt
See Hunter, Evan

Cape, Judith
See Page, P(atricia) K(athleen)

Capek, Karel
1890-1938 ..... **TCLC 6, 37; DA; DC 1;**
WLC

See also CA 104; 140

Capote, Truman
1924-1984 ...... **CLC 1, 3, 8, 13, 19, 34,**
38, 58; DA; SSC 2; WLC
See also CA 5-8R; 113; CANR 18;
CDALB 1941-1968; DLB 2; DLBY 80,
84; MTCW

Capra, Frank 1897-1991........... **CLC 16**
See also CA 61-64; 135

Caputo, Philip 1941-.............. **CLC 32**
See also CA 73-76; CANR 40

Card, Orson Scott 1951- .... **CLC 44, 47, 50**
See also CA 102; CANR 27; MTCW

Cardenal (Martinez), Ernesto
1925- .... **CLC 31**
See also CA 49-52; CANR 2, 32; HW;
MTCW

Carducci, Giosue 1835-1907....... **TCLC 32**

Carew, Thomas 1595(?)-1640........ **LC 13**
See also DLB 126

Carey, Ernestine Gilbreth 1908-.... **CLC 17**
See also CA 5-8R; SATA 2

Carey, Peter 1943-............ **CLC 40, 55**
See also CA 123; 127; MTCW

Carleton, William 1794-1869...... **NCLC 3**

Carlisle, Henry (Coffin) 1926-...... **CLC 33**
See also CA 13-16R; CANR 15

Carlsen, Chris
See Holdstock, Robert P.

Carlson, Ron(ald F.) 1947-........ **CLC 54**
See also CA 105; CANR 27

Carlyle, Thomas 1795-1881 .. **NCLC 22; DA**
See also CDBLB 1789-1832; DLB 55

Carman, (William) Bliss
1861-1929 .... **TCLC 7**
See also CA 104; DLB 92

Carossa, Hans 1878-1956........ **TCLC 48**
See also DLB 66

Carpenter, Don(ald Richard)
1931- .... **CLC 41**
See also CA 45-48; CANR 1

Carpentier (y Valmont), Alejo
1904-1980 .... **CLC 8, 11, 38**
See also CA 65-68; 97-100; CANR 11;
DLB 113; HW

Carr, Emily 1871-1945........... **TCLC 32**
See also DLB 68

Carr, John Dickson 1906-1977 ...... **CLC 3**
See also CA 49-52; 69-72; CANR 3, 33;
MTCW

Carr, Philippa
See Hibbert, Eleanor Alice Burford

Carr, Virginia Spencer 1929-....... **CLC 34**
See also CA 61-64; DLB 111

Carrier, Roch 1937-........... **CLC 13, 78**
See also CA 130; DLB 53

Carroll, James P. 1943(?)-......... **CLC 38**
See also CA 81-84

Carroll, Jim 1951- .... **CLC 35**
See also CA 45-48; CANR 42

Carroll, Lewis .... **NCLC 2; WLC**
See also Dodgson, Charles Lutwidge
See also CDBLB 1832-1890; CLR 2, 18;
DLB 18; JRDA

Carroll, Paul Vincent 1900-1968.... **CLC 10**
See also CA 9-12R; 25-28R; DLB 10

Carruth, Hayden 1921- .... **CLC 4, 7, 10, 18**
See also CA 9-12R; CANR 4, 38; DLB 5;
MTCW; SATA 47

Carson, Rachel Louise 1907-1964... **CLC 71**
See also CA 77-80; CANR 35; MTCW;
SATA 23

Carter, Angela (Olive)
1940-1992 ...... **CLC 5, 41, 76; SSC 13**
See also CA 53-56; 136; CANR 12, 36;
DLB 14; MTCW; SATA 66;
SATA-Obit 70

Carter, Nick
See Smith, Martin Cruz

Carver, Raymond
1938-1988 ... **CLC 22, 36, 53, 55; SSC 8**
See also CA 33-36R; 126; CANR 17, 34;
DLB 130; DLBY 84, 88; MTCW

Cary, (Arthur) Joyce (Lunel)
1888-1957.............**TCLC 1, 29**
See also CA 104; CDBLB 1914-1945;
DLB 15, 100

Casanova de Seingalt, Giovanni Jacopo
1725-1798 .... **LC 13**

Casares, Adolfo Bioy
See Bioy Casares, Adolfo

Casely-Hayford, J(oseph) E(phraim)
1866-1930 .... **TCLC 24; BLC 1**
See also CA 123

Casey, John (Dudley) 1939-........ **CLC 59**
See also BEST 90:2; CA 69-72; CANR 23

Casey, Michael 1947-.............. **CLC 2**
See also CA 65-68; DLB 5

Casey, Patrick
See Thurman, Wallace (Henry)

Casey, Warren (Peter) 1935-1988... **CLC 12**
See also CA 101; 127

Casona, Alejandro................. **CLC 49**
See also Alvarez, Alejandro Rodriguez

Cassavetes, John 1929-1989........ **CLC 20**
See also CA 85-88; 127

Cassill, R(onald) V(erlin) 1919-... **CLC 4, 23**
See also CA 9-12R; CAAS 1; CANR 7;
DLB 6

Cassity, (Allen) Turner 1929- .... **CLC 6, 42**
See also CA 17-20R; CAAS 8; CANR 11;
DLB 105

Castaneda, Carlos 1931(?)-......... **CLC 12**
See also CA 25-28R; CANR 32; HW;
MTCW

Castedo, Elena 1937- .... **CLC 65**
See also CA 132

Castedo-Ellerman, Elena
See Castedo, Elena

Castellanos, Rosario 1925-1974..... **CLC 66**
See also CA 131; 53-56; DLB 113; HW

Castelvetro, Lodovico 1505-1571..... **LC 12**

Castiglione, Baldassare 1478-1529 ... **LC 12**

Castle, Robert
See Hamilton, Edmond

Castro, Guillen de 1569-1631........ **LC 19**

Castro, Rosalia de 1837-1885 ..... **NCLC 3**

Cather, Willa
See Cather, Willa Sibert

Cather, Willa Sibert
1873-1947 .... **TCLC 1, 11, 31; DA;**
SSC 2; WLC
See also CA 104; 128; CDALB 1865-1917;
DLB 9, 54, 78; DLBD 1; MTCW;
SATA 30

Catton, (Charles) Bruce
1899-1978 .... **CLC 35**
See also AITN 1; CA 5-8R; 81-84;
CANR 7; DLB 17; SATA 2, 24

Cauldwell, Frank
See King, Francis (Henry)

Caunitz, William J. 1933- .... **CLC 34**
See also BEST 89:3; CA 125; 130

Causley, Charles (Stanley) 1917-..... **CLC 7**
See also CA 9-12R; CANR 5, 35; CLR 30;
DLB 27; MTCW; SATA 3, 66

Caute, David 1936-............... **CLC 29**
See also CA 1-4R; CAAS 4; CANR 1, 33;
DLB 14

Cavafy, C(onstantine) P(eter)...... **TCLC 2, 7**
See also Kavafis, Konstantinos Petrou

Cavallo, Evelyn
See Spark, Muriel (Sarah)

Cavanna, Betty .... **CLC 12**
See also Harrison, Elizabeth Cavanna
See also JRDA; MAICYA; SAAS 4;
SATA 1, 30

Caxton, William 1421(?)-1491(?)..... **LC 17**

Cayrol, Jean 1911-............... **CLC 11**
See also CA 89-92; DLB 83

Cela, Camilo Jose 1916-..... **CLC 4, 13, 59**
See also BEST 90:2; CA 21-24R; CAAS 10;
CANR 21, 32; DLBY 89; HW; MTCW

Celan, Paul .... **CLC 53**
See also Antschel, Paul
See also DLB 69

Celine, Louis-Ferdinand
.... **CLC 1, 3, 4, 7, 9, 15, 47**
See also Destouches, Louis-Ferdinand
See also DLB 72

Cellini, Benvenuto 1500-1571 .... **LC 7**

Cendrars, Blaise
See Sauser-Hall, Frederic

Cernuda (y Bidon), Luis
1902-1963 .... **CLC 54**
See also CA 131; 89-92; DLB 134; HW

Cervantes (Saavedra), Miguel de
1547-1616 ..... **LC 6, 23; DA; SSC 12;**
WLC

Cesaire, Aime (Fernand)
1913-............. **CLC 19, 32; BLC 1**
See also BW; CA 65-68; CANR 24, 43;
MTCW

Chabon, Michael 1965(?)-......... **CLC 55**
See also CA 139

Chabrol, Claude 1930-............ **CLC 16**
See also CA 110

Challans, Mary 1905-1983
See Renault, Mary
See also CA 81-84; 111; SATA 23, 36

Challis, George
See Faust, Frederick (Schiller)

Chambers, Aidan 1934-........... **CLC 35**
See also CA 25-28R; CANR 12, 31; JRDA;
MAICYA; SAAS 12; SATA 1, 69

Chambers, James 1948-
See Cliff, Jimmy
See also CA 124

Chambers, Jessie
See Lawrence, D(avid) H(erbert Richards)

Chambers, Robert W. 1865-1933... **TCLC 41**

Chandler, Raymond (Thornton)
1888-1959 .... **TCLC 1, 7**
See also CA 104; 129; CDALB 1929-1941;
DLBD 6; MTCW

Chang, Jung 1952-............... **CLC 71**
See also CA 142

Channing, William Ellery
1780-1842 .... **NCLC 17**
See also DLB 1, 59

Chaplin, Charles Spencer
1889-1977 .... **CLC 16**
See also Chaplin, Charlie
See also CA 81-84; 73-76

Chaplin, Charlie
See Chaplin, Charles Spencer
See also DLB 44

Chapman, George 1559(?)-1634...... **LC 22**
See also DLB 62, 121

Chapman, Graham 1941-1989 ..... **CLC 21**
See also Monty Python
See also CA 116; 129; CANR 35

Chapman, John Jay 1862-1933..... **TCLC 7**
See also CA 104

Chapman, Walker
See Silverberg, Robert

Chappell, Fred (Davis) 1936-.... **CLC 40, 78**
See also CA 5-8R; CAAS 4; CANR 8, 33;
DLB 6, 105

Char, Rene(-Emile)
1907-1988 .... **CLC 9, 11, 14, 55**
See also CA 13-16R; 124; CANR 32;
MTCW

Charby, Jay
See Ellison, Harlan

Chardin, Pierre Teilhard de
See Teilhard de Chardin, (Marie Joseph)
Pierre

Charles I 1600-1649.............. **LC 13**

Charyn, Jerome 1937-........ **CLC 5, 8, 18**
See also CA 5-8R; CAAS 1; CANR 7;
DLBY 83; MTCW

Chase, Mary (Coyle) 1907-1981 ...... **DC 1**
See also CA 77-80; 105; SATA 17, 29

Chase, Mary Ellen 1887-1973....... **CLC 2**
See also CA 13-16; 41-44R; CAP 1;
SATA 10

Chase, Nicholas
See Hyde, Anthony

Chateaubriand, Francois Rene de
1768-1848 .... **NCLC 3**
See also DLB 119

Chatterje, Sarat Chandra 1876-1936(?)
See Chatterji, Saratchandra
See also CA 109

Chatterji, Bankim Chandra
1838-1894 .... **NCLC 19**

Chatterji, Saratchandra .... **TCLC 13**
See also Chatterje, Sarat Chandra

Chatterton, Thomas 1752-1770 .... **LC 3**
See also DLB 109

Chatwin, (Charles) Bruce
1940-1989 .... **CLC 28, 57, 59**
See also AAYA 4; BEST 90:1; CA 85-88;
127

Chaucer, Daniel
See Ford, Ford Madox

Chaucer, Geoffrey
1340(?)-1400 .... **LC 17; DA**
See also CDBLB Before 1660

Chaviaras, Strates 1935-
See Haviaras, Stratis
See also CA 105

Chayefsky, Paddy .... **CLC 23**
See also Chayefsky, Sidney
See also DLB 7, 44; DLBY 81

Chayefsky, Sidney 1923-1981
See Chayefsky, Paddy
See also CA 9-12R; 104; CANR 18

Chedid, Andree 1920-............ **CLC 47**

Cheever, John
1912-1982 ...... **CLC 3, 7, 8, 11, 15, 25,**
64; DA; SSC 1; WLC
See also CA 5-8R; 106; CABS 1; CANR 5,
27; CDALB 1941-1968; DLB 2, 102;
DLBY 80, 82; MTCW

Cheever, Susan 1943-......... **CLC 18, 48**
See also CA 103; CANR 27; DLBY 82

Chekhonte, Antosha
See Chekhov, Anton (Pavlovich)

Chekhov, Anton (Pavlovich)
1860-1904 .... **TCLC 3, 10, 31; DA;**
SSC 2; WLC
See also CA 104; 124

Chernyshevsky, Nikolay Gavrilovich
1828-1889 .... **NCLC 1**

Cherry, Carolyn Janice 1942-
See Cherryh, C. J.
See also CA 65-68; CANR 10

Cherryh, C. J. .... **CLC 35**
See also Cherry, Carolyn Janice
See also DLBY 80

Chesnutt, Charles W(addell)
1858-1932 .. **TCLC 5, 39; BLC 1; SSC 7**
See also BW; CA 106; 125; DLB 12, 50, 78;
MTCW

Chester, Alfred 1929(?)-1971....... **CLC 49**
See also CA 33-36R; DLB 130

Chesterton, G(ilbert) K(eith)
1874-1936 .... **TCLC 1, 6; SSC 1**
See also CA 104; 132; CDBLB 1914-1945;
DLB 10, 19, 34, 70, 98; MTCW;
SATA 27

Chiang Pin-chin 1904-1986
See Ding Ling
See also CA 118

Ch'ien Chung-shu 1910-........... **CLC 22**
See also CA 130; MTCW

Child, L. Maria
See Child, Lydia Maria

Child, Lydia Maria 1802-1880 .... **NCLC 6**
See also DLB 1, 74; SATA 67

Child, Mrs.
See Child, Lydia Maria

Child, Philip 1898-1978........ **CLC 19, 68**
See also CA 13-14; CAP 1; SATA 47

Childress, Alice
1920-........ **CLC 12, 15; BLC 1; DC 4**
See also AAYA 8; BW; CA 45-48;
CANR 3, 27; CLR 14; DLB 7, 38; JRDA;
MAICYA; MTCW; SATA 7, 48

Chislett, (Margaret) Anne 1943-.... **CLC 34**

Chitty, Thomas Willes 1926-....... **CLC 11**
See also Hinde, Thomas
See also CA 5-8R

Chomette, Rene Lucien 1898-1981 . . **CLC 20**
See also Clair, Rene
See also CA 103

Chopin, Kate . . . . **TCLC 5, 14; DA; SSC 8**
See also Chopin, Katherine
See also CDALB 1865-1917; DLB 12, 78

Chopin, Katherine 1851-1904
See Chopin, Kate
See also CA 104; 122

Chretien de Troyes
c. 12th cent. - . . . . **CMLC 10**

Christie
See Ichikawa, Kon

Christie, Agatha (Mary Clarissa)
1890-1976 . . . . . . **CLC 1, 6, 8, 12, 39, 48**
See also AAYA 9; AITN 1, 2; CA 17-20R;
61-64; CANR 10, 37; CDBLB 1914-1945;
DLB 13, 77; MTCW; SATA 36

Christie, (Ann) Philippa
See Pearce, Philippa
See also CA 5-8R; CANR 4

Christine de Pizan 1365(?)-1431(?) . . . . **LC 9**

Chubb, Elmer
See Masters, Edgar Lee

Chulkov, Mikhail Dmitrievich
1743-1792 . . . . **LC 2**

Churchill, Caryl 1938- . . . . **CLC 31, 55**
See also CA 102; CANR 22; DLB 13;
MTCW

Churchill, Charles 1731-1764 . . . . **LC 3**
See also DLB 109

Chute, Carolyn 1947- . . . . **CLC 39**
See also CA 123

Ciardi, John (Anthony)
1916-1986 . . . . **CLC 10, 40, 44**
See also CA 5-8R; 118; CAAS 2; CANR 5,
33; CLR 19; DLB 5; DLBY 86;
MAICYA; MTCW; SATA 1, 46, 65

Cicero, Marcus Tullius
106B.C.-43B.C. . . . . **CMLC 3**

Cimino, Michael 1943- . . . . **CLC 16**
See also CA 105

Cioran, E(mil) M. 1911- . . . . **CLC 64**
See also CA 25-28R

Cisneros, Sandra 1954- . . . . **CLC 69**
See also AAYA 9; CA 131; DLB 122; HW

Clair, Rene . . . . **CLC 20**
See also Chomette, Rene Lucien

Clampitt, Amy 1920- . . . . **CLC 32**
See also CA 110; CANR 29; DLB 105

Clancy, Thomas L., Jr. 1947-
See Clancy, Tom
See also CA 125; 131; MTCW

Clancy, Tom . . . . **CLC 45**
See also Clancy, Thomas L., Jr.
See also AAYA 9; BEST 89:1, 90:1

Clare, John 1793-1864 . . . . **NCLC 9**
See also DLB 55, 96

Clarin
See Alas (y Urena), Leopoldo (Enrique
Garcia)

Clark, Al C.
See Goines, Donald

Clark, (Robert) Brian 1932- . . . . **CLC 29**
See also CA 41-44R

Clark, Eleanor 1913- . . . . **CLC 5, 19**
See also CA 9-12R; CANR 41; DLB 6

Clark, J. P.
See Clark, John Pepper
See also DLB 117

Clark, John Pepper 1935- . . **CLC 38; BLC 1**
See also Clark, J. P.
See also BW; CA 65-68; CANR 16

Clark, M. R.
See Clark, Mavis Thorpe

Clark, Mavis Thorpe 1909- . . . . **CLC 12**
See also CA 57-60; CANR 8, 37; CLR 30;
MAICYA; SAAS 5; SATA 8, 74

Clark, Walter Van Tilburg
1909-1971 . . . . **CLC 28**
See also CA 9-12R; 33-36R; DLB 9;
SATA 8

Clarke, Arthur C(harles)
1917- . . . . . . **CLC 1, 4, 13, 18, 35; SSC 3**
See also AAYA 4; CA 1-4R; CANR 2, 28;
JRDA; MAICYA; MTCW; SATA 13, 70

Clarke, Austin 1896-1974 . . . . **CLC 6, 9**
See also CA 29-32; 49-52; CAP 2; DLB 10,
20

Clarke, Austin C(hesterfield)
1934- . . . . **CLC 8, 53; BLC 1**
See also BW; CA 25-28R; CAAS 16;
CANR 14, 32; DLB 53, 125

Clarke, Gillian 1937- . . . . **CLC 61**
See also CA 106; DLB 40

Clarke, Marcus (Andrew Hislop)
1846-1881 . . . . **NCLC 19**

Clarke, Shirley 1925- . . . . **CLC 16**

Clash, The . . . . **CLC 30**
See also Headon, (Nicky) Topper; Jones,
Mick; Simonon, Paul; Strummer, Joe

Claudel, Paul (Louis Charles Marie)
1868-1955 . . . . **TCLC 2, 10**
See also CA 104

Clavell, James (duMaresq)
1925- . . . . **CLC 6, 25**
See also CA 25-28R; CANR 26; MTCW

Cleaver, (Leroy) Eldridge
1935- . . . . **CLC 30; BLC 1**
See also BW; CA 21-24R; CANR 16

Cleese, John (Marwood) 1939- . . . . . **CLC 21**
See also Monty Python
See also CA 112; 116; CANR 35; MTCW

Cleishbotham, Jebediah
See Scott, Walter

Cleland, John 1710-1789 . . . . **LC 2**
See also DLB 39

Clemens, Samuel Langhorne 1835-1910
See Twain, Mark
See also CA 104; 135; CDALB 1865-1917;
DA; DLB 11, 12, 23, 64, 74; JRDA;
MAICYA; YABC 2

Cleophil
See Congreve, William

Clerihew, E.
See Bentley, E(dmund) C(lerihew)

Clerk, N. W.
See Lewis, C(live) S(taples)

Cliff, Jimmy . . . . **CLC 21**
See also Chambers, James

Clifton, (Thelma) Lucille
1936- . . . . **CLC 19, 66; BLC 1**
See also BW; CA 49-52; CANR 2, 24, 42;
CLR 5; DLB 5, 41; MAICYA; MTCW;
SATA 20, 69

Clinton, Dirk
See Silverberg, Robert

Clough, Arthur Hugh 1819-1861 . . **NCLC 27**
See also DLB 32

Clutha, Janet Paterson Frame 1924-
See Frame, Janet
See also CA 1-4R; CANR 2, 36; MTCW

Clyne, Terence
See Blatty, William Peter

Cobalt, Martin
See Mayne, William (James Carter)

Coburn, D(onald) L(ee) 1938- . . . . . . **CLC 10**
See also CA 89-92

Cocteau, Jean (Maurice Eugene Clement)
1889-1963 . . . . **CLC 1, 8, 15, 16, 43; DA;
WLC**
See also CA 25-28; CANR 40; CAP 2;
DLB 65; MTCW

Codrescu, Andrei 1946- . . . . **CLC 46**
See also CA 33-36R; CANR 13, 34

Coe, Max
See Bourne, Randolph S(illiman)

Coe, Tucker
See Westlake, Donald E(dwin)

Coetzee, J(ohn) M(ichael)
1940- . . . . **CLC 23, 33, 66**
See also CA 77-80; CANR 41; MTCW

Coffey, Brian
See Koontz, Dean R(ay)

Cohen, Arthur A(llen)
1928-1986 . . . . **CLC 7, 31**
See also CA 1-4R; 120; CANR 1, 17, 42;
DLB 28

Cohen, Leonard (Norman)
1934- . . . . **CLC 3, 38**
See also CA 21-24R; CANR 14; DLB 53;
MTCW

Cohen, Matt 1942- . . . . **CLC 19**
See also CA 61-64; CAAS 18; CANR 40;
DLB 53

Cohen-Solal, Annie 19(?)- . . . . **CLC 50**

Colegate, Isabel 1931- . . . . **CLC 36**
See also CA 17-20R; CANR 8, 22; DLB 14;
MTCW

Coleman, Emmett
See Reed, Ishmael

Coleridge, Samuel Taylor
1772-1834 . . . . **NCLC 9; DA; WLC**
See also CDBLB 1789-1832; DLB 93, 107

Coleridge, Sara 1802-1852 . . . . **NCLC 31**

Coles, Don 1928- . . . . **CLC 46**
See also CA 115; CANR 38

Colette, (Sidonie-Gabrielle)
1873-1954 . . . . . . **TCLC 1, 5, 16; SSC 10**
See also CA 104; 131; DLB 65; MTCW

Collett, (Jacobine) Camilla (Wergeland)
1813-1895 . . . . **NCLC 22**

Cowley, Malcolm 1898-1989 . . . . . . CLC 39
   See also CA 5-8R; 128; CANR 3; DLB 4,
   48; DLBY 81, 89; MTCW

Cowper, William 1731-1800 . . . . . . NCLC 8
   See also DLB 104, 109

Cox, William Trevor 1928- . . . CLC 9, 14, 71
   See also Trevor, William
   See also CA 9-12R; CANR 4, 37; DLB 14;
   MTCW

Cozzens, James Gould
   1903-1978 . . . . CLC 1, 4, 11
   See also CA 9-12R; 81-84; CANR 19;
   CDALB 1941-1968; DLB 9; DLBD 2;
   DLBY 84; MTCW

Crabbe, George 1754-1832 . . . . . . NCLC 26
   See also DLB 93

Craig, A. A.
   See Anderson, Poul (William)

Craik, Dinah Maria (Mulock)
   1826-1887 . . . . NCLC 38
   See also DLB 35; MAICYA; SATA 34

Cram, Ralph Adams 1863-1942 . . . . TCLC 45

Crane, (Harold) Hart
   1899-1932 . . . . TCLC 2, 5; DA; PC 3;
                                           WLC
   See also CA 104; 127; CDALB 1917-1929;
   DLB 4, 48; MTCW

Crane, R(onald) S(almon)
   1886-1967 . . . . CLC 27
   See also CA 85-88; DLB 63

Crane, Stephen (Townley)
   1871-1900 . . . . TCLC 11, 17, 32; DA;
                                       SSC 7; WLC
   See also CA 109; 140; CDALB 1865-1917;
   DLB 12, 54, 78; YABC 2

Crase, Douglas 1944- . . . . CLC 58
   See also CA 106

Crashaw, Richard 1612(?)-1649 . . . . . . LC 24
   See also DLB 126

Craven, Margaret 1901-1980 . . . . . . CLC 17
   See also CA 103

Crawford, F(rancis) Marion
   1854-1909 . . . . TCLC 10
   See also CA 107; DLB 71

Crawford, Isabella Valancy
   1850-1887 . . . . NCLC 12
   See also DLB 92

Crayon, Geoffrey
   See Irving, Washington

Creasey, John 1908-1973 . . . . CLC 11
   See also CA 5-8R; 41-44R; CANR 8;
   DLB 77; MTCW

Crebillon, Claude Prosper Jolyot de (fils)
   1707-1777 . . . . LC 1

Credo
   See Creasey, John

Creeley, Robert (White)
   1926- . . . . . CLC 1, 2, 4, 8, 11, 15, 36, 78
   See also CA 1-4R; CAAS 10; CANR 23, 43;
   DLB 5, 16; MTCW

Crews, Harry (Eugene)
   1935- . . . . CLC 6, 23, 49
   See also AITN 1; CA 25-28R; CANR 20;
   DLB 6; MTCW

Crichton, (John) Michael
   1942- . . . . CLC 2, 6, 54
   See also AAYA 10; AITN 2; CA 25-28R;
   CANR 13, 40; DLBY 81; JRDA;
   MTCW; SATA 9

Crispin, Edmund . . . . CLC 22
   See also Montgomery, (Robert) Bruce
   See also DLB 87

Cristofer, Michael 1945(?)- . . . . CLC 28
   See also CA 110; DLB 7

Croce, Benedetto 1866-1952 . . . . . . TCLC 37
   See also CA 120

Crockett, David 1786-1836 . . . . NCLC 8
   See also DLB 3, 11

Crockett, Davy
   See Crockett, David

Croker, John Wilson 1780-1857 . . NCLC 10
   See also DLB 110

Crommelynck, Fernand 1885-1970 . . CLC 75
   See also CA 89-92

Cronin, A(rchibald) J(oseph)
   1896-1981 . . . . CLC 32
   See also CA 1-4R; 102; CANR 5; SATA 25,
   47

Cross, Amanda
   See Heilbrun, Carolyn G(old)

Crothers, Rachel 1878(?)-1958 . . . . . TCLC 19
   See also CA 113; DLB 7

Croves, Hal
   See Traven, B.

Crowfield, Christopher
   See Stowe, Harriet (Elizabeth) Beecher

Crowley, Aleister . . . . TCLC 7
   See also Crowley, Edward Alexander

Crowley, Edward Alexander 1875-1947
   See Crowley, Aleister
   See also CA 104

Crowley, John 1942- . . . . CLC 57
   See also CA 61-64; CANR 43; DLBY 82;
   SATA 65

Crud
   See Crumb, R(obert)

Crumarums
   See Crumb, R(obert)

Crumb, R(obert) 1943- . . . . CLC 17
   See also CA 106

Crumbum
   See Crumb, R(obert)

Crumski
   See Crumb, R(obert)

Crum the Bum
   See Crumb, R(obert)

Crunk
   See Crumb, R(obert)

Crustt
   See Crumb, R(obert)

Cryer, Gretchen (Kiger) 1935- . . . . . CLC 21
   See also CA 114; 123

Csath, Geza 1887-1919 . . . . TCLC 13
   See also CA 111

Cudlip, David 1933- . . . . CLC 34

Cullen, Countee
   1903-1946 . . . . . TCLC 4, 37; BLC 1; DA
   See also BW; CA 108; 124;
   CDALB 1917-1929; DLB 4, 48, 51;
   MTCW; SATA 18

Cum, R.
   See Crumb, R(obert)

Cummings, Bruce F(rederick) 1889-1919
   See Barbellion, W. N. P.
   See also CA 123

Cummings, E(dward) E(stlin)
   1894-1962 . . . . . . CLC 1, 3, 8, 12, 15, 68;
                                        DA; PC 5; WLC 2
   See also CA 73-76; CANR 31;
   CDALB 1929-1941; DLB 4, 48; MTCW

Cunha, Euclides (Rodrigues Pimenta) da
   1866-1909 . . . . TCLC 24
   See also CA 123

Cunningham, E. V.
   See Fast, Howard (Melvin)

Cunningham, J(ames) V(incent)
   1911-1985 . . . . CLC 3, 31
   See also CA 1-4R; 115; CANR 1; DLB 5

Cunningham, Julia (Woolfolk)
   1916- . . . . CLC 12
   See also CA 9-12R; CANR 4, 19, 36;
   JRDA; MAICYA; SAAS 2; SATA 1, 26

Cunningham, Michael 1952- . . . . CLC 34
   See also CA 136

Cunninghame Graham, R(obert) B(ontine)
   1852-1936 . . . . TCLC 19
   See also Graham, R(obert) B(ontine)
   Cunninghame
   See also CA 119; DLB 98

Currie, Ellen 19(?)- . . . . CLC 44

Curtin, Philip
   See Lowndes, Marie Adelaide (Belloc)

Curtis, Price
   See Ellison, Harlan

Cutrate, Joe
   See Spiegelman, Art

Czaczkes, Shmuel Yosef
   See Agnon, S(hmuel) Y(osef Halevi)

D. P.
   See Wells, H(erbert) G(eorge)

Dabrowska, Maria (Szumska)
   1889-1965 . . . . CLC 15
   See also CA 106

Dabydeen, David 1955- . . . . CLC 34
   See also BW; CA 125

Dacey, Philip 1939- . . . . CLC 51
   See also CA 37-40R; CAAS 17; CANR 14,
   32; DLB 105

Dagerman, Stig (Halvard)
   1923-1954 . . . . TCLC 17
   See also CA 117

Dahl, Roald 1916-1990 . . . . . CLC 1, 6, 18, 79
   See also CA 1-4R; 133; CANR 6, 32, 37;
   CLR 1, 7; JRDA; MAICYA; MTCW;
   SATA 1, 26, 73; SATA-Obit 65

Dahlberg, Edward 1900-1977 . . . CLC 1, 7, 14
   See also CA 9-12R; 69-72; CANR 31;
   DLB 48; MTCW

Dale, Colin . . . . TCLC 18
   See also Lawrence, T(homas) E(dward)

DeLillo, Don
1936- ..... **CLC 8, 10, 13, 27, 39, 54, 76**
See also BEST 89:1; CA 81-84; CANR 21;
DLB 6; MTCW

de Lisser, H. G.
See De Lisser, Herbert George
See also DLB 117

De Lisser, Herbert George
1878-1944 .... **TCLC 12**
See also de Lisser, H. G.
See also CA 109

Deloria, Vine (Victor), Jr. 1933- .... **CLC 21**
See also CA 53-56; CANR 5, 20; MTCW;
SATA 21

Del Vecchio, John M(ichael)
1947- .... **CLC 29**
See also CA 110; DLBD 9

de Man, Paul (Adolph Michel)
1919-1983 .... **CLC 55**
See also CA 128; 111; DLB 67; MTCW

De Marinis, Rick 1934- .... **CLC 54**
See also CA 57-60; CANR 9, 25

Demby, William 1922- ..... **CLC 53; BLC 1**
See also BW; CA 81-84; DLB 33

Demijohn, Thom
See Disch, Thomas M(ichael)

de Montherlant, Henry (Milon)
See Montherlant, Henry (Milon) de

de Natale, Francine
See Malzberg, Barry N(athaniel)

Denby, Edwin (Orr) 1903-1983 ..... **CLC 48**
See also CA 138; 110

Denis, Julio
See Cortazar, Julio

Denmark, Harrison
See Zelazny, Roger (Joseph)

Dennis, John 1658-1734 .... **LC 11**
See also DLB 101

Dennis, Nigel (Forbes) 1912-1989 .... **CLC 8**
See also CA 25-28R; 129; DLB 13, 15;
MTCW

De Palma, Brian (Russell) 1940- .... **CLC 20**
See also CA 109

De Quincey, Thomas 1785-1859 ... **NCLC 4**
See also CDBLB 1789-1832; DLB 110

Deren, Eleanora 1908(?)-1961
See Deren, Maya
See also CA 111

Deren, Maya .... **CLC 16**
See also Deren, Eleanora

Derleth, August (William)
1909-1971 .... **CLC 31**
See also CA 1-4R; 29-32R; CANR 4;
DLB 9; SATA 5

de Routisie, Albert
See Aragon, Louis

Derrida, Jacques 1930- .... **CLC 24**
See also CA 124; 127

Derry Down Derry
See Lear, Edward

Dersonnes, Jacques
See Simenon, Georges (Jacques Christian)

Desai, Anita 1937- .... **CLC 19, 37**
See also CA 81-84; CANR 33; MTCW;
SATA 63

de Saint-Luc, Jean
See Glassco, John

de Saint Roman, Arnaud
See Aragon, Louis

Descartes, Rene 1596-1650 .... **LC 20**

De Sica, Vittorio 1901(?)-1974 ..... **CLC 20**
See also CA 117

Desnos, Robert 1900-1945 .... **TCLC 22**
See also CA 121

Destouches, Louis-Ferdinand
1894-1961 .... **CLC 9, 15**
See also Celine, Louis-Ferdinand
See also CA 85-88; CANR 28; MTCW

Deutsch, Babette 1895-1982 .... **CLC 18**
See also CA 1-4R; 108; CANR 4; DLB 45;
SATA 1, 33

Devenant, William 1606-1649 ...... **LC 13**

Devkota, Laxmiprasad
1909-1959 .... **TCLC 23**
See also CA 123

De Voto, Bernard (Augustine)
1897-1955 .... **TCLC 29**
See also CA 113; DLB 9

De Vries, Peter
1910-1993 .... **CLC 1, 2, 3, 7, 10, 28, 46**
See also CA 17-20R; 142; CANR 41;
DLB 6; DLBY 82; MTCW

Dexter, Martin
See Faust, Frederick (Schiller)

Dexter, Pete 1943- .... **CLC 34, 55**
See also BEST 89:2; CA 127; 131; MTCW

Diamano, Silmang
See Senghor, Leopold Sedar

Diamond, Neil 1941- .... **CLC 30**
See also CA 108

di Bassetto, Corno
See Shaw, George Bernard

Dick, Philip K(indred)
1928-1982 .... **CLC 10, 30, 72**
See also CA 49-52; 106; CANR 2, 16;
DLB 8; MTCW

Dickens, Charles (John Huffam)
1812-1870 ...... **NCLC 3, 8, 18, 26; DA**
See also CDBLB 1832-1890; DLB 21, 55,
70; JRDA; MAICYA; SATA 15

Dickey, James (Lafayette)
1923- .... **CLC 1, 2, 4, 7, 10, 15, 47**
See also AITN 1, 2; CA 9-12R; CABS 2;
CANR 10; CDALB 1968-1988; DLB 5;
DLBD 7; DLBY 82; MTCW

Dickey, William 1928- .... **CLC 3, 28**
See also CA 9-12R; CANR 24; DLB 5

Dickinson, Charles 1951- .... **CLC 49**
See also CA 128

Dickinson, Emily (Elizabeth)
1830-1886 .. **NCLC 21; DA; PC 1; WLC**
See also CDALB 1865-1917; DLB 1;
SATA 29

Dickinson, Peter (Malcolm)
1927- .... **CLC 12, 35**
See also AAYA 9; CA 41-44R; CANR 31;
CLR 29; DLB 87; JRDA; MAICYA;
SATA 5, 62

Dickson, Carr
See Carr, John Dickson

Dickson, Carter
See Carr, John Dickson

Didion, Joan 1934- ..... **CLC 1, 3, 8, 14, 32**
See also AITN 1; CA 5-8R; CANR 14;
CDALB 1968-1988; DLB 2; DLBY 81,
86; MTCW

Dietrich, Robert
See Hunt, E(verette) Howard, Jr.

Dillard, Annie 1945- .... **CLC 9, 60**
See also AAYA 6; CA 49-52; CANR 3, 43;
DLBY 80; MTCW; SATA 10

Dillard, R(ichard) H(enry) W(ilde)
1937- .... **CLC 5**
See also CA 21-24R; CAAS 7; CANR 10;
DLB 5

Dillon, Eilis 1920- .... **CLC 17**
See also CA 9-12R; CAAS 3; CANR 4, 38;
CLR 26; MAICYA; SATA 2, 74

Dimont, Penelope
See Mortimer, Penelope (Ruth)

Dinesen, Isak .... **CLC 10, 29; SSC 7**
See also Blixen, Karen (Christentze
Dinesen)

Ding Ling .... **CLC 68**
See also Chiang Pin-chin

Disch, Thomas M(ichael) 1940- ... **CLC 7, 36**
See also CA 21-24R; CAAS 4; CANR 17,
36; CLR 18; DLB 8; MAICYA; MTCW;
SAAS 15; SATA 54

Disch, Tom
See Disch, Thomas M(ichael)

d'Isly, Georges
See Simenon, Georges (Jacques Christian)

Disraeli, Benjamin 1804-1881 .. **NCLC 2, 39**
See also DLB 21, 55

Ditcum, Steve
See Crumb, R(obert)

Dixon, Paige
See Corcoran, Barbara

Dixon, Stephen 1936- .... **CLC 52**
See also CA 89-92; CANR 17, 40; DLB 130

Doblin, Alfred .... **TCLC 13**
See also Doeblin, Alfred

Dobrolyubov, Nikolai Alexandrovich
1836-1861 .... **NCLC 5**

Dobyns, Stephen 1941- .... **CLC 37**
See also CA 45-48; CANR 2, 18

Doctorow, E(dgar) L(aurence)
1931- .... **CLC 6, 11, 15, 18, 37, 44, 65**
See also AITN 2; BEST 89:3; CA 45-48;
CANR 2, 33; CDALB 1968-1988; DLB 2,
28; DLBY 80; MTCW

Dodgson, Charles Lutwidge 1832-1898
See Carroll, Lewis
See also CLR 2; DA; MAICYA; YABC 2

Dodson, Owen (Vincent)
1914-1983 . . . . **CLC 79; BLC 1**
See also BW; CA 65-68; 110; CANR 24;
DLB 76

Doeblin, Alfred 1878-1957. . . . . . . **TCLC 13**
See also Doblin, Alfred
See also CA 110; 141; DLB 66

Doerr, Harriet 1910- . . . . **CLC 34**
See also CA 117; 122

Domecq, H(onorio) Bustos
See Bioy Casares, Adolfo; Borges, Jorge
Luis

Domini, Rey
See Lorde, Audre (Geraldine)

Dominique
See Proust, (Valentin-Louis-George-Eugene-)
Marcel

Don, A
See Stephen, Leslie

Donaldson, Stephen R. 1947-. . . . . . . **CLC 46**
See also CA 89-92; CANR 13

Donleavy, J(ames) P(atrick)
1926- . . . . **CLC 1, 4, 6, 10, 45**
See also AITN 2; CA 9-12R; CANR 24;
DLB 6; MTCW

Donne, John
1572-1631 . . . . **LC 10, 24; DA; PC 1**
See also CDBLB Before 1660; DLB 121

Donnell, David 1939(?)-. . . . . **CLC 34**

Donoso (Yanez), Jose
1924- . . . . **CLC 4, 8, 11, 32**
See also CA 81-84; CANR 32; DLB 113;
HW; MTCW

Donovan, John 1928-1992 . . . . **CLC 35**
See also CA 97-100; 137; CLR 3;
MAICYA; SATA 29

Don Roberto
See Cunninghame Graham, R(obert)
B(ontine)

Doolittle, Hilda
1886-1961 . . . . . **CLC 3, 8, 14, 31, 34, 73;
DA; PC 5; WLC**
See also H. D.
See also CA 97-100; CANR 35; DLB 4, 45;
MTCW

Dorfman, Ariel 1942-. . . . . **CLC 48, 77**
See also CA 124; 130; HW

Dorn, Edward (Merton) 1929-. . . **CLC 10, 18**
See also CA 93-96; CANR 42; DLB 5

Dorsan, Luc
See Simenon, Georges (Jacques Christian)

Dorsange, Jean
See Simenon, Georges (Jacques Christian)

Dos Passos, John (Roderigo)
1896-1970 . . . . . . **CLC 1, 4, 8, 11, 15, 25,
34; DA; WLC**
See also CA 1-4R; 29-32R; CANR 3;
CDALB 1929-1941; DLB 4, 9; DLBD 1;
MTCW

Dossage, Jean
See Simenon, Georges (Jacques Christian)

Dostoevsky, Fedor Mikhailovich
1821-1881 . . . . . **NCLC 2, 7, 21, 33; DA;
SSC 2; WLC**

Doughty, Charles M(ontagu)
1843-1926 . . . . **TCLC 27**
See also CA 115; DLB 19, 57

Douglas, Ellen
See Haxton, Josephine Ayres

Douglas, Gavin 1475(?)-1522. . . . . . . **LC 20**

Douglas, Keith 1920-1944 . . . . **TCLC 40**
See also DLB 27

Douglas, Leonard
See Bradbury, Ray (Douglas)

Douglas, Michael
See Crichton, (John) Michael

Douglass, Frederick
1817(?)-1895 . . . . . **NCLC 7; BLC 1; DA;
WLC**
See also CDALB 1640-1865; DLB 1, 43, 50,
79; SATA 29

Dourado, (Waldomiro Freitas) Autran
1926- . . . . **CLC 23, 60**
See also CA 25-28R; CANR 34

Dourado, Waldomiro Autran
See Dourado, (Waldomiro Freitas) Autran

Dove, Rita (Frances) 1952-. . . **CLC 50; PC 6**
See also BW; CA 109; CANR 27, 42;
DLB 120

Dowell, Coleman 1925-1985. . . . . . . **CLC 60**
See also CA 25-28R; 117; CANR 10;
DLB 130

Dowson, Ernest Christopher
1867-1900 . . . . **TCLC 4**
See also CA 105; DLB 19, 135

Doyle, A. Conan
See Doyle, Arthur Conan

Doyle, Arthur Conan
1859-1930 . . . . . . **TCLC 7; DA; SSC 12;
WLC**
See also CA 104; 122; CDBLB 1890-1914;
DLB 18, 70; MTCW; SATA 24

Doyle, Conan 1859-1930
See Doyle, Arthur Conan

Doyle, John
See Graves, Robert (von Ranke)

Doyle, Sir A. Conan
See Doyle, Arthur Conan

Doyle, Sir Arthur Conan
See Doyle, Arthur Conan

Dr. A
See Asimov, Isaac; Silverstein, Alvin

Drabble, Margaret
1939- . . . . **CLC 2, 3, 5, 8, 10, 22, 53**
See also CA 13-16R; CANR 18, 35;
CDBLB 1960 to Present; DLB 14;
MTCW; SATA 48

Drapier, M. B.
See Swift, Jonathan

Drayham, James
See Mencken, H(enry) L(ouis)

Drayton, Michael 1563-1631. . . . . **LC 8**

Dreadstone, Carl
See Campbell, (John) Ramsey

Dreiser, Theodore (Herman Albert)
1871-1945 . . . . . . **TCLC 10, 18, 35; DA;
WLC**
See also CA 106; 132; CDALB 1865-1917;
DLB 9, 12, 102; DLBD 1; MTCW

Drexler, Rosalyn 1926- . . . . **CLC 2, 6**
See also CA 81-84

Dreyer, Carl Theodor 1889-1968. . . . **CLC 16**
See also CA 116

Drieu la Rochelle, Pierre(-Eugene)
1893-1945 . . . . **TCLC 21**
See also CA 117; DLB 72

Drop Shot
See Cable, George Washington

Droste-Hulshoff, Annette Freiin von
1797-1848 . . . . **NCLC 3**
See also DLB 133

Drummond, Walter
See Silverberg, Robert

Drummond, William Henry
1854-1907 . . . . **TCLC 25**
See also DLB 92

Drummond de Andrade, Carlos
1902-1987 . . . . **CLC 18**
See also Andrade, Carlos Drummond de
See also CA 132; 123

Drury, Allen (Stuart) 1918-. . . . . **CLC 37**
See also CA 57-60; CANR 18

Dryden, John
1631-1700 . . . **LC 3, 21; DA; DC 3; WLC**
See also CDBLB 1660-1789; DLB 80, 101,
131

Duberman, Martin 1930-. . . . . **CLC 8**
See also CA 1-4R; CANR 2

Dubie, Norman (Evans) 1945-. . . . . . **CLC 36**
See also CA 69-72; CANR 12; DLB 120

Du Bois, W(illiam) E(dward) B(urghardt)
1868-1963 . . . . **CLC 1, 2, 13, 64; BLC 1;
DA; WLC**
See also BW; CA 85-88; CANR 34;
CDALB 1865-1917; DLB 47, 50, 91;
MTCW; SATA 42

Dubus, Andre 1936-. . . . . **CLC 13, 36**
See also CA 21-24R; CANR 17; DLB 130

Duca Minimo
See D'Annunzio, Gabriele

Ducharme, Rejean 1941-. . . . . **CLC 74**
See also DLB 60

Duclos, Charles Pinot 1704-1772 . . . . . **LC 1**

Dudek, Louis 1918- . . . . **CLC 11, 19**
See also CA 45-48; CAAS 14; CANR 1;
DLB 88

Duerrenmatt, Friedrich
1921-1990 . . . . . . **CLC 1, 4, 8, 11, 15, 43**
See also Durrenmatt, Friedrich
See also CA 17-20R; CANR 33; DLB 69,
124; MTCW

Duffy, Bruce (?)-. . . . . **CLC 50**

Duffy, Maureen 1933- . . . . **CLC 37**
See also CA 25-28R; CANR 33; DLB 14;
MTCW

Dugan, Alan 1923- . . . . **CLC 2, 6**
See also CA 81-84; DLB 5

du Gard, Roger Martin
See Martin du Gard, Roger

Duhamel, Georges 1884-1966 .... **CLC 8**
See also CA 81-84; 25-28R; CANR 35;
DLB 65; MTCW

Dujardin, Edouard (Emile Louis)
1861-1949 .... **TCLC 13**
See also CA 109; DLB 123

Dumas, Alexandre (Davy de la Pailleterie)
1802-1870 .... **NCLC 11; DA; WLC**
See also DLB 119; SATA 18

Dumas, Alexandre
1824-1895 .... **NCLC 9; DC 1**

Dumas, Claudine
See Malzberg, Barry N(athaniel)

Dumas, Henry L. 1934-1968 ..... **CLC 6, 62**
See also BW; CA 85-88; DLB 41

du Maurier, Daphne
1907-1989 .... **CLC 6, 11, 59**
See also CA 5-8R; 128; CANR 6; MTCW;
SATA 27, 60

Dunbar, Paul Laurence
1872-1906 .... **TCLC 2, 12; BLC 1; DA;**
PC 5; SSC 8; WLC
See also BW; CA 104; 124;
CDALB 1865-1917; DLB 50, 54, 78;
SATA 34

Dunbar, William 1460(?)-1530(?) .... **LC 20**

Duncan, Lois 1934-............... **CLC 26**
See also AAYA 4; CA 1-4R; CANR 2, 23,
36; CLR 29; JRDA; MAICYA; SAAS 2;
SATA 1, 36, 75

Duncan, Robert (Edward)
1919-1988 .... **CLC 1, 2, 4, 7, 15, 41, 55;**
PC 2
See also CA 9-12R; 124; CANR 28; DLB 5,
16; MTCW

Dunlap, William 1766-1839 .... **NCLC 2**
See also DLB 30, 37, 59

Dunn, Douglas (Eaglesham)
1942-...................... **CLC 6, 40**
See also CA 45-48; CANR 2, 33; DLB 40;
MTCW

Dunn, Katherine (Karen) 1945-..... **CLC 71**
See also CA 33-36R

Dunn, Stephen 1939-................ **CLC 36**
See also CA 33-36R; CANR 12; DLB 105

Dunne, Finley Peter 1867-1936.... **TCLC 28**
See also CA 108; DLB 11, 23

Dunne, John Gregory 1932-........ **CLC 28**
See also CA 25-28R; CANR 14; DLBY 80

Dunsany, Edward John Moreton Drax
Plunkett 1878-1957
See Dunsany, Lord; Lord Dunsany
See also CA 104; DLB 10

Dunsany, Lord.................... **TCLC 2**
See also Dunsany, Edward John Moreton
Drax Plunkett
See also DLB 77

du Perry, Jean
See Simenon, Georges (Jacques Christian)

Durang, Christopher (Ferdinand)
1949-.................... **CLC 27, 38**
See also CA 105

Duras, Marguerite
1914-...... **CLC 3, 6, 11, 20, 34, 40, 68**
See also CA 25-28R; DLB 83; MTCW

Durban, (Rosa) Pam 1947-........ **CLC 39**
See also CA 123

Durcan, Paul 1944-........... **CLC 43, 70**
See also CA 134

Durrell, Lawrence (George)
1912-1990 .... **CLC 1, 4, 6, 8, 13, 27, 41**
See also CA 9-12R; 132; CANR 40;
CDBLB 1945-1960; DLB 15, 27;
DLBY 90; MTCW

Durrenmatt, Friedrich
.... **CLC 1, 4, 8, 11, 15, 43**
See also Duerrenmatt, Friedrich
See also DLB 69, 124

Dutt, Toru 1856-1877.......... **NCLC 29**

Dwight, Timothy 1752-1817...... **NCLC 13**
See also DLB 37

Dworkin, Andrea 1946-.......... **CLC 43**
See also CA 77-80; CANR 16, 39; MTCW

Dwyer, Deanna
See Koontz, Dean R(ay)

Dwyer, K. R.
See Koontz, Dean R(ay)

Dylan, Bob 1941-...... **CLC 3, 4, 6, 12, 77**
See also CA 41-44R; DLB 16

Eagleton, Terence (Francis) 1943-
See Eagleton, Terry
See also CA 57-60; CANR 7, 23; MTCW

Eagleton, Terry .... **CLC 63**
See also Eagleton, Terence (Francis)

Early, Jack
See Scoppettone, Sandra

East, Michael
See West, Morris L(anglo)

Eastaway, Edward
See Thomas, (Philip) Edward

Eastlake, William (Derry) 1917-..... **CLC 8**
See also CA 5-8R; CAAS 1; CANR 5;
DLB 6

Eberhart, Richard (Ghormley)
1904-............... **CLC 3, 11, 19, 56**
See also CA 1-4R; CANR 2;
CDALB 1941-1968; DLB 48; MTCW

Eberstadt, Fernanda 1960-........ **CLC 39**
See also CA 136

Echegaray (y Eizaguirre), Jose (Maria Waldo)
1832-1916 .... **TCLC 4**
See also CA 104; CANR 32; HW; MTCW

Echeverria, (Jose) Esteban (Antonino)
1805-1851 .... **NCLC 18**

Echo
See Proust, (Valentin-Louis-George-Eugene-)
Marcel

Eckert, Allan W. 1931-.......... **CLC 17**
See also CA 13-16R; CANR 14; SATA 27,
29

Eckhart, Meister 1260(?)-1328(?) .. **CMLC 9**
See also DLB 115

Eckmar, F. R.
See de Hartog, Jan

Eco, Umberto 1932-........... **CLC 28, 60**
See also BEST 90:1; CA 77-80; CANR 12,
33; MTCW

Eddison, E(ric) R(ucker)
1882-1945 ....**TCLC 15**
See also CA 109

Edel, (Joseph) Leon 1907-...... **CLC 29, 34**
See also CA 1-4R; CANR 1, 22; DLB 103

Eden, Emily 1797-1869 .... **NCLC 10**

Edgar, David 1948-.............. **CLC 42**
See also CA 57-60; CANR 12; DLB 13;
MTCW

Edgerton, Clyde (Carlyle) 1944- .... **CLC 39**
See also CA 118; 134

Edgeworth, Maria 1767-1849...... **NCLC 1**
See also DLB 116; SATA 21

Edmonds, Paul
See Kuttner, Henry

Edmonds, Walter D(umaux) 1903-.. **CLC 35**
See also CA 5-8R; CANR 2; DLB 9;
MAICYA; SAAS 4; SATA 1, 27

Edmondson, Wallace
See Ellison, Harlan

Edson, Russell .... **CLC 13**
See also CA 33-36R

Edwards, G(erald) B(asil)
1899-1976 .... **CLC 25**
See also CA 110

Edwards, Gus 1939-.............. **CLC 43**
See also CA 108

Edwards, Jonathan 1703-1758.... **LC 7; DA**
See also DLB 24

Efron, Marina Ivanovna Tsvetaeva
See Tsvetaeva (Efron), Marina (Ivanovna)

Ehle, John (Marsden, Jr.) 1925-.... **CLC 27**
See also CA 9-12R

Ehrenbourg, Ilya (Grigoryevich)
See Ehrenburg, Ilya (Grigoryevich)

Ehrenburg, Ilya (Grigoryevich)
1891-1967 .... **CLC 18, 34, 62**
See also CA 102; 25-28R

Ehrenburg, Ilyo (Grigoryevich)
See Ehrenburg, Ilya (Grigoryevich)

Eich, Guenter 1907-1972 .... **CLC 15**
See also CA 111; 93-96; DLB 69, 124

Eichendorff, Joseph Freiherr von
1788-1857 .... **NCLC 8**
See also DLB 90

Eigner, Larry.................... **CLC 9**
See also Eigner, Laurence (Joel)
See also DLB 5

Eigner, Laurence (Joel) 1927-
See Eigner, Larry
See also CA 9-12R; CANR 6

Eiseley, Loren Corey 1907-1977..... **CLC 7**
See also AAYA 5; CA 1-4R; 73-76;
CANR 6

Eisenstadt, Jill 1963- .... **CLC 50**
See also CA 140

Eisner, Simon
See Kornbluth, C(yril) M.

Ekeloef, (Bengt) Gunnar
1907-1968 .... **CLC 27**
See also Ekelof, (Bengt) Gunnar
See also CA 123; 25-28R

Ekelof, (Bengt) Gunnar............. **CLC 27**
See also Ekeloef, (Bengt) Gunnar

Evtushenko, Evgenii Aleksandrovich
    See Yevtushenko, Yevgeny (Alexandrovich)

Ewart, Gavin (Buchanan)
    1916- . . . . **CLC 13, 46**
    See also CA 89-92; CANR 17; DLB 40;
    MTCW

Ewers, Hanns Heinz   1871-1943 . . . **TCLC 12**
    See also CA 109

Ewing, Frederick R.
    See Sturgeon, Theodore (Hamilton)

Exley, Frederick (Earl)
    1929-1992 . . . . **CLC 6, 11**
    See also AITN 2; CA 81-84; 138; DLBY 81

Eynhardt, Guillermo
    See Quiroga, Horacio (Sylvestre)

Ezekiel, Nissim   1924- . . . . **CLC 61**
    See also CA 61-64

Ezekiel, Tish O'Dowd   1943- . . . . **CLC 34**
    See also CA 129

Fagen, Donald   1948- . . . . **CLC 26**

Fainzilberg, Ilya Arnoldovich   1897-1937
    See Ilf, Ilya
    See also CA 120

Fair, Ronald L.   1932- . . . . **CLC 18**
    See also BW; CA 69-72; CANR 25; DLB 33

Fairbairns, Zoe (Ann)   1948- . . . . **CLC 32**
    See also CA 103; CANR 21

Falco, Gian
    See Papini, Giovanni

Falconer, James
    See Kirkup, James

Falconer, Kenneth
    See Kornbluth, C(yril) M.

Falkland, Samuel
    See Heijermans, Herman

Fallaci, Oriana   1930- . . . . **CLC 11**
    See also CA 77-80; CANR 15; MTCW

Faludy, George   1913- . . . . **CLC 42**
    See also CA 21-24R

Faludy, Gyoergy
    See Faludy, George

Fanon, Frantz   1925-1961 . . . **CLC 74; BLC 2**
    See also BW; CA 116; 89-92

Fanshawe, Ann   . . . . **LC 11**

Fante, John (Thomas)   1911-1983 . . . **CLC 60**
    See also CA 69-72; 109; CANR 23;
    DLB 130; DLBY 83

Farah, Nuruddin   1945- . . . . . **CLC 53; BLC 2**
    See also CA 106; DLB 125

Fargue, Leon-Paul   1876(?)-1947 . . . **TCLC 11**
    See also CA 109

Farigoule, Louis
    See Romains, Jules

Farina, Richard   1936(?)-1966 . . . . . . **CLC 9**
    See also CA 81-84; 25-28R

Farley, Walter (Lorimer)
    1915-1989 . . . . **CLC 17**
    See also CA 17-20R; CANR 8, 29; DLB 22;
    JRDA; MAICYA; SATA 2, 43

Farmer, Philip Jose   1918- . . . . **CLC 1, 19**
    See also CA 1-4R; CANR 4, 35; DLB 8;
    MTCW

Farquhar, George   1677-1707 . . . . **LC 21**
    See also DLB 84

Farrell, J(ames) G(ordon)
    1935-1979 . . . . **CLC 6**
    See also CA 73-76; 89-92; CANR 36;
    DLB 14; MTCW

Farrell, James T(homas)
    1904-1979 . . . . **CLC 1, 4, 8, 11, 66**
    See also CA 5-8R; 89-92; CANR 9; DLB 4,
    9, 86; DLBD 2; MTCW

Farren, Richard J.
    See Betjeman, John

Farren, Richard M.
    See Betjeman, John

Fassbinder, Rainer Werner
    1946-1982 . . . . **CLC 20**
    See also CA 93-96; 106; CANR 31

Fast, Howard (Melvin)   1914- . . . . . . **CLC 23**
    See also CA 1-4R; CAAS 18; CANR 1, 33;
    DLB 9; SATA 7

Faulcon, Robert
    See Holdstock, Robert P.

Faulkner, William (Cuthbert)
    1897-1962 . . . . . **CLC 1, 3, 6, 8, 9, 11, 14,
        18, 28, 52, 68; DA; SSC 1; WLC**
    See also AAYA 7; CA 81-84; CANR 33;
    CDALB 1929-1941; DLB 9, 11, 44, 102;
    DLBD 2; DLBY 86; MTCW

Fauset, Jessie Redmon
    1884(?)-1961 . . . . **CLC 19, 54; BLC 2**
    See also BW; CA 109; DLB 51

Faust, Frederick (Schiller)
    1892-1944(?) . . . . **TCLC 49**
    See also CA 108

Faust, Irvin   1924- . . . . **CLC 8**
    See also CA 33-36R; CANR 28; DLB 2, 28;
    DLBY 80

Fawkes, Guy
    See Benchley, Robert (Charles)

Fearing, Kenneth (Flexner)
    1902-1961 . . . . **CLC 51**
    See also CA 93-96; DLB 9

Fecamps, Elise
    See Creasey, John

Federman, Raymond   1928- . . . . . . **CLC 6, 47**
    See also CA 17-20R; CAAS 8; CANR 10,
    43; DLBY 80

Federspiel, J(uerg) F.   1931- . . . . **CLC 42**

Feiffer, Jules (Ralph)   1929- . . . . **CLC 2, 8, 64**
    See also AAYA 3; CA 17-20R; CANR 30;
    DLB 7, 44; MTCW; SATA 8, 61

Feige, Hermann Albert Otto Maximilian
    See Traven, B.

Fei-Kan, Li
    See Li Fei-kan

Feinberg, David B.   1956- . . . . **CLC 59**
    See also CA 135

Feinstein, Elaine   1930- . . . . **CLC 36**
    See also CA 69-72; CAAS 1; CANR 31;
    DLB 14, 40; MTCW

Feldman, Irving (Mordecai)   1928- . . . . **CLC 7**
    See also CA 1-4R; CANR 1

Fellini, Federico   1920- . . . . **CLC 16**
    See also CA 65-68; CANR 33

Felsen, Henry Gregor   1916- . . . . **CLC 17**
    See also CA 1-4R; CANR 1; SAAS 2;
    SATA 1

Fenton, James Martin   1949- . . . . **CLC 32**
    See also CA 102; DLB 40

Ferber, Edna   1887-1968 . . . . **CLC 18**
    See also AITN 1; CA 5-8R; 25-28R; DLB 9,
    28, 86; MTCW; SATA 7

Ferguson, Helen
    See Kavan, Anna

Ferguson, Samuel   1810-1886 . . . . . **NCLC 33**
    See also DLB 32

Ferling, Lawrence
    See Ferlinghetti, Lawrence (Monsanto)

Ferlinghetti, Lawrence (Monsanto)
    1919(?)- . . . . **CLC 2, 6, 10, 27; PC 1**
    See also CA 5-8R; CANR 3, 41;
    CDALB 1941-1968; DLB 5, 16; MTCW

Fernandez, Vicente Garcia Huidobro
    See Huidobro Fernandez, Vicente Garcia

Ferrer, Gabriel (Francisco Victor) Miro
    See Miro (Ferrer), Gabriel (Francisco
    Victor)

Ferrier, Susan (Edmonstone)
    1782-1854 . . . . **NCLC 8**
    See also DLB 116

Ferrigno, Robert   1948(?)- . . . . **CLC 65**
    See also CA 140

Feuchtwanger, Lion   1884-1958 . . . . . **TCLC 3**
    See also CA 104; DLB 66

Feydeau, Georges (Leon Jules Marie)
    1862-1921 . . . . **TCLC 22**
    See also CA 113

Ficino, Marsilio   1433-1499 . . . . **LC 12**

Fiedeler, Hans
    See Doeblin, Alfred

Fiedler, Leslie A(aron)
    1917- . . . . **CLC 4, 13, 24**
    See also CA 9-12R; CANR 7; DLB 28, 67;
    MTCW

Field, Andrew   1938- . . . . **CLC 44**
    See also CA 97-100; CANR 25

Field, Eugene   1850-1895 . . . . **NCLC 3**
    See also DLB 23, 42; MAICYA; SATA 16

Field, Gans T.
    See Wellman, Manly Wade

Field, Michael . . . . **TCLC 43**

Field, Peter
    See Hobson, Laura Z(ametkin)

Fielding, Henry
    1707-1754 . . . . **LC 1; DA; WLC**
    See also CDBLB 1660-1789; DLB 39, 84,
    101

Fielding, Sarah   1710-1768 . . . . **LC 1**
    See also DLB 39

Fierstein, Harvey (Forbes)   1954- . . . **CLC 33**
    See also CA 123; 129

Figes, Eva   1932- . . . . **CLC 31**
    See also CA 53-56; CANR 4; DLB 14

Finch, Robert (Duer Claydon)
    1900- . . . . **CLC 18**
    See also CA 57-60; CANR 9, 24; DLB 88

Franklin, (Stella Maraia Sarah) Miles
1879-1954 .... **TCLC 7**
See also CA 104

Fraser, Antonia (Pakenham)
1932- .... **CLC 32**
See also CA 85-88; MTCW; SATA 32

Fraser, George MacDonald 1925-.... **CLC 7**
See also CA 45-48; CANR 2

Fraser, Sylvia 1935- .... **CLC 64**
See also CA 45-48; CANR 1, 16

Frayn, Michael 1933-...... **CLC 3, 7, 31, 47**
See also CA 5-8R; CANR 30; DLB 13, 14;
MTCW

Fraze, Candida (Merrill) 1945- ..... **CLC 50**
See also CA 126

Frazer, J(ames) G(eorge)
1854-1941 .... **TCLC 32**
See also CA 118

Frazer, Robert Caine
See Creasey, John

Frazer, Sir James George
See Frazer, J(ames) G(eorge)

Frazier, Ian 1951-................ **CLC 46**
See also CA 130

Frederic, Harold 1856-1898...... **NCLC 10**
See also DLB 12, 23

Frederick, John
See Faust, Frederick (Schiller)

Frederick the Great 1712-1786 ...... **LC 14**

Fredro, Aleksander 1793-1876..... **NCLC 8**

Freeling, Nicolas 1927- .... **CLC 38**
See also CA 49-52; CAAS 12; CANR 1, 17;
DLB 87

Freeman, Douglas Southall
1886-1953 .... **TCLC 11**
See also CA 109; DLB 17

Freeman, Judith 1946-........... **CLC 55**

Freeman, Mary Eleanor Wilkins
1852-1930 .... **TCLC 9; SSC 1**
See also CA 106; DLB 12, 78

Freeman, R(ichard) Austin
1862-1943 .... **TCLC 21**
See also CA 113; DLB 70

French, Marilyn 1929-...... **CLC 10, 18, 60**
See also CA 69-72; CANR 3, 31; MTCW

French, Paul
See Asimov, Isaac

Freneau, Philip Morin 1752-1832.. **NCLC 1**
See also DLB 37, 43

Freud, Sigmund 1856-1939 .... **TCLC 52**
See also CA 115; 133; MTCW

Friedan, Betty (Naomi) 1921-...... **CLC 74**
See also CA 65-68; CANR 18; MTCW

Friedman, B(ernard) H(arper)
1926- .... **CLC 7**
See also CA 1-4R; CANR 3

Friedman, Bruce Jay 1930-.... **CLC 3, 5, 56**
See also CA 9-12R; CANR 25; DLB 2, 28

Friel, Brian 1929-.......... **CLC 5, 42, 59**
See also CA 21-24R; CANR 33; DLB 13;
MTCW

Friis-Baastad, Babbis Ellinor
1921-1970 .... **CLC 12**
See also CA 17-20R; 134; SATA 7

Frisch, Max (Rudolf)
1911-1991 ..... **CLC 3, 9, 14, 18, 32, 44**
See also CA 85-88; 134; CANR 32;
DLB 69, 124; MTCW

Fromentin, Eugene (Samuel Auguste)
1820-1876 .... **NCLC 10**
See also DLB 123

Frost, Frederick
See Faust, Frederick (Schiller)

Frost, Robert (Lee)
1874-1963 .... **CLC 1, 3, 4, 9, 10, 13, 15,
26, 34, 44; DA; PC 1; WLC**
See also CA 89-92; CANR 33;
CDALB 1917-1929; DLB 54; DLBD 7;
MTCW; SATA 14

Froy, Herald
See Waterhouse, Keith (Spencer)

Fry, Christopher 1907-....... **CLC 2, 10, 14**
See also CA 17-20R; CANR 9, 30; DLB 13;
MTCW; SATA 66

Frye, (Herman) Northrop
1912-1991 .... **CLC 24, 70**
See also CA 5-8R; 133; CANR 8, 37;
DLB 67, 68; MTCW

Fuchs, Daniel 1909-1993 .... **CLC 8, 22**
See also CA 81-84; 142; CAAS 5;
CANR 40; DLB 9, 26, 28

Fuchs, Daniel 1934- .... **CLC 34**
See also CA 37-40R; CANR 14

Fuentes, Carlos
1928- ...... **CLC 3, 8, 10, 13, 22, 41, 60;
DA; WLC**
See also AAYA 4; AITN 2; CA 69-72;
CANR 10, 32; DLB 113; HW; MTCW

Fuentes, Gregorio Lopez y
See Lopez y Fuentes, Gregorio

Fugard, (Harold) Athol
1932- .... **CLC 5, 9, 14, 25, 40, 80; DC 3**
See also CA 85-88; CANR 32; MTCW

Fugard, Sheila 1932- .... **CLC 48**
See also CA 125

Fuller, Charles (H., Jr.)
1939- .... **CLC 25; BLC 2; DC 1**
See also BW; CA 108; 112; DLB 38;
MTCW

Fuller, John (Leopold) 1937-....... **CLC 62**
See also CA 21-24R; CANR 9; DLB 40

Fuller, Margaret .... **NCLC 5**
See also Ossoli, Sarah Margaret (Fuller
marchesa d')

Fuller, Roy (Broadbent)
1912-1991 .... **CLC 4, 28**
See also CA 5-8R; 135; CAAS 10; DLB 15,
20

Fulton, Alice 1952-............... **CLC 52**
See also CA 116

Furphy, Joseph 1843-1912....... **TCLC 25**

Fussell, Paul 1924-............... **CLC 74**
See also BEST 90:1; CA 17-20R; CANR 8,
21, 35; MTCW

Futabatei, Shimei 1864-1909 ...... **TCLC 44**

Futrelle, Jacques 1875-1912 ...... **TCLC 19**
See also CA 113

G. B. S.
See Shaw, George Bernard

Gaboriau, Emile 1835-1873...... **NCLC 14**

Gadda, Carlo Emilio 1893-1973 .... **CLC 11**
See also CA 89-92

Gaddis, William
1922-....... **CLC 1, 3, 6, 8, 10, 19, 43**
See also CA 17-20R; CANR 21; DLB 2;
MTCW

Gaines, Ernest J(ames)
1933- .... **CLC 3, 11, 18; BLC 2**
See also AITN 1; BW; CA 9-12R; CANR 6,
24, 42; CDALB 1968-1988; DLB 2, 33;
DLBY 80; MTCW

Gaitskill, Mary 1954-............. **CLC 69**
See also CA 128

Galdos, Benito Perez
See Perez Galdos, Benito

Gale, Zona 1874-1938 .... **TCLC 7**
See also CA 105; DLB 9, 78

Galeano, Eduardo (Hughes) 1940-... **CLC 72**
See also CA 29-32R; CANR 13, 32; HW

Galiano, Juan Valera y Alcala
See Valera y Alcala-Galiano, Juan

Gallagher, Tess 1943-.......... **CLC 18, 63**
See also CA 106; DLB 120

Gallant, Mavis
1922- .... **CLC 7, 18, 38; SSC 5**
See also CA 69-72; CANR 29; DLB 53;
MTCW

Gallant, Roy A(rthur) 1924- .... **CLC 17**
See also CA 5-8R; CANR 4, 29; CLR 30;
MAICYA; SATA 4, 68

Gallico, Paul (William) 1897-1976 ... **CLC 2**
See also AITN 1; CA 5-8R; 69-72;
CANR 23; DLB 9; MAICYA; SATA 13

Gallup, Ralph
See Whitemore, Hugh (John)

Galsworthy, John
1867-1933 .... **TCLC 1, 45; DA; WLC 2**
See also CA 104; 141; CDBLB 1890-1914;
DLB 10, 34, 98

Galt, John 1779-1839........... **NCLC 1**
See also DLB 99, 116

Galvin, James 1951-.............. **CLC 38**
See also CA 108; CANR 26

Gamboa, Federico 1864-1939...... **TCLC 36**

Gann, Ernest Kellogg 1910-1991.... **CLC 23**
See also AITN 1; CA 1-4R; 136; CANR 1

Garcia, Cristina 1958-........... **CLC 76**
See also CA 141

Garcia Lorca, Federico
1898-1936 .... **TCLC 1, 7, 49; DA;
DC 2; PC 3; WLC**
See also CA 104; 131; DLB 108; HW;
MTCW

Garcia Marquez, Gabriel (Jose)
1928- .... **CLC 2, 3, 8, 10, 15, 27, 47, 55;
DA; SSC 8; WLC**
See also Marquez, Gabriel (Jose) Garcia
See also AAYA 3; BEST 89:1, 90:4;
CA 33-36R; CANR 10, 28; DLB 113;
HW; MTCW

Gard, Janice
See Latham, Jean Lee

Gard, Roger Martin du
See Martin du Gard, Roger

Gardam, Jane 1928-............ **CLC 43**
See also CA 49-52; CANR 2, 18, 33;
CLR 12; DLB 14; MAICYA; MTCW;
SAAS 9; SATA 28, 39

Gardner, Herb.................. **CLC 44**

Gardner, John (Champlin), Jr.
1933-1982 ..... **CLC 2, 3, 5, 7, 8, 10, 18,**
28, 34; SSC 7
See also AITN 1; CA 65-68; 107;
CANR 33; DLB 2; DLBY 82; MTCW;
SATA 31, 40

Gardner, John (Edmund) 1926-..... **CLC 30**
See also CA 103; CANR 15; MTCW

Gardner, Noel
See Kuttner, Henry

Gardons, S. S.
See Snodgrass, W(illiam) D(e Witt)

Garfield, Leon 1921-............. **CLC 12**
See also AAYA 8; CA 17-20R; CANR 38,
41; CLR 21; JRDA; MAICYA; SATA 1,
32

Garland, (Hannibal) Hamlin
1860-1940 .... **TCLC 3**
See also CA 104; DLB 12, 71, 78

Garneau, (Hector de) Saint-Denys
1912-1943 .... **TCLC 13**
See also CA 111; DLB 88

Garner, Alan 1934-............... **CLC 17**
See also CA 73-76; CANR 15; CLR 20;
MAICYA; MTCW; SATA 18, 69

Garner, Hugh 1913-1979 .... **CLC 13**
See also CA 69-72; CANR 31; DLB 68

Garnett, David 1892-1981 .... **CLC 3**
See also CA 5-8R; 103; CANR 17; DLB 34

Garos, Stephanie
See Katz, Steve

Garrett, George (Palmer)
1929-................. **CLC 3, 11, 51**
See also CA 1-4R; CAAS 5; CANR 1, 42;
DLB 2, 5, 130; DLBY 83

Garrick, David 1717-1779 .... **LC 15**
See also DLB 84

Garrigue, Jean 1914-1972 .... **CLC 2, 8**
See also CA 5-8R; 37-40R; CANR 20

Garrison, Frederick
See Sinclair, Upton (Beall)

Garth, Will
See Hamilton, Edmond; Kuttner, Henry

Garvey, Marcus (Moziah, Jr.)
1887-1940 .... **TCLC 41; BLC 2**
See also BW; CA 120; 124

Gary, Romain .... **CLC 25**
See also Kacew, Romain
See also DLB 83

Gascar, Pierre .... **CLC 11**
See also Fournier, Pierre

Gascoyne, David (Emery) 1916-.... **CLC 45**
See also CA 65-68; CANR 10, 28; DLB 20;
MTCW

Gaskell, Elizabeth Cleghorn
1810-1865 .... **NCLC 5**
See also CDBLB 1832-1890; DLB 21

Gass, William H(oward)
1924-... **CLC 1, 2, 8, 11, 15, 39; SSC 12**
See also CA 17-20R; CANR 30; DLB 2;
MTCW

Gasset, Jose Ortega y
See Ortega y Gasset, Jose

Gautier, Theophile 1811-1872 ..... **NCLC 1**
See also DLB 119

Gawsworth, John
See Bates, H(erbert) E(rnest)

Gaye, Marvin (Penze) 1939-1984 ... **CLC 26**
See also CA 112

Gebler, Carlo (Ernest) 1954-....... **CLC 39**
See also CA 119; 133

Gee, Maggie (Mary) 1948-......... **CLC 57**
See also CA 130

Gee, Maurice (Gough) 1931-....... **CLC 29**
See also CA 97-100; SATA 46

Gelbart, Larry (Simon) 1923-... **CLC 21, 61**
See also CA 73-76

Gelber, Jack 1932-........ **CLC 1, 6, 14, 79**
See also CA 1-4R; CANR 2; DLB 7

Gellhorn, Martha Ellis 1908- ... **CLC 14, 60**
See also CA 77-80; DLBY 82

Genet, Jean
1910-1986 ... **CLC 1, 2, 5, 10, 14, 44, 46**
See also CA 13-16R; CANR 18; DLB 72;
DLBY 86; MTCW

Gent, Peter 1942-................. **CLC 29**
See also AITN 1; CA 89-92; DLBY 82

Gentlewoman in New England, A
See Bradstreet, Anne

Gentlewoman in Those Parts, A
See Bradstreet, Anne

George, Jean Craighead 1919-...... **CLC 35**
See also AAYA 8; CA 5-8R; CANR 25;
CLR 1; DLB 52; JRDA; MAICYA;
SATA 2, 68

George, Stefan (Anton)
1868-1933 .... **TCLC 2, 14**
See also CA 104

Georges, Georges Martin
See Simenon, Georges (Jacques Christian)

Gerhardi, William Alexander
See Gerhardie, William Alexander

Gerhardie, William Alexander
1895-1977 .... **CLC 5**
See also CA 25-28R; 73-76; CANR 18;
DLB 36

Gerstler, Amy 1956-.............. **CLC 70**

Gertler, T. .... **CLC 34**
See also CA 116; 121

Ghalib 1797-1869 .... **NCLC 39**

Ghelderode, Michel de
1898-1962 .... **CLC 6, 11**
See also CA 85-88; CANR 40

Ghiselin, Brewster 1903-.......... **CLC 23**
See also CA 13-16R; CAAS 10; CANR 13

Ghose, Zulfikar 1935-............. **CLC 42**
See also CA 65-68

Ghosh, Amitav 1956-............. **CLC 44**

Giacosa, Giuseppe 1847-1906 ...... **TCLC 7**
See also CA 104

Gibb, Lee
See Waterhouse, Keith (Spencer)

Gibbon, Lewis Grassic .... **TCLC 4**
See also Mitchell, James Leslie

Gibbons, Kaye 1960-............. **CLC 50**

Gibran, Kahlil 1883-1931........ **TCLC 1, 9**
See also CA 104

Gibson, William 1914-........ **CLC 23; DA**
See also CA 9-12R; CANR 9, 42; DLB 7;
SATA 66

Gibson, William (Ford) 1948- ... **CLC 39, 63**
See also CA 126; 133

Gide, Andre (Paul Guillaume)
1869-1951 .... **TCLC 5, 12, 36; DA;**
SSC 13; WLC
See also CA 104; 124; DLB 65; MTCW

Gifford, Barry (Colby) 1946-....... **CLC 34**
See also CA 65-68; CANR 9, 30, 40

Gilbert, W(illiam) S(chwenck)
1836-1911 .... **TCLC 3**
See also CA 104; SATA 36

Gilbreth, Frank B., Jr. 1911-....... **CLC 17**
See also CA 9-12R; SATA 2

Gilchrist, Ellen 1935-.. **CLC 34, 48; SSC 14**
See also CA 113; 116; CANR 41; DLB 130;
MTCW

Giles, Molly 1942-............... **CLC 39**
See also CA 126

Gill, Patrick
See Creasey, John

Gilliam, Terry (Vance) 1940-....... **CLC 21**
See also Monty Python
See also CA 108; 113; CANR 35

Gillian, Jerry
See Gilliam, Terry (Vance)

Gilliatt, Penelope (Ann Douglass)
1932-1993 .... **CLC 2, 10, 13, 53**
See also AITN 2; CA 13-16R; 141; DLB 14

Gilman, Charlotte (Anna) Perkins (Stetson)
1860-1935 .... **TCLC 9, 37; SSC 13**
See also CA 106

Gilmour, David 1949-............. **CLC 35**
See also Pink Floyd
See also CA 138

Gilpin, William 1724-1804....... **NCLC 30**

Gilray, J. D.
See Mencken, H(enry) L(ouis)

Gilroy, Frank D(aniel) 1925-........ **CLC 2**
See also CA 81-84; CANR 32; DLB 7

Ginsberg, Allen
1926- ...... **CLC 1, 2, 3, 4, 6, 13, 36, 69;**
DA; PC 4; WLC 3
See also AITN 1; CA 1-4R; CANR 2, 41;
CDALB 1941-1968; DLB 5, 16; MTCW

Ginzburg, Natalia
1916-1991 .... **CLC 5, 11, 54, 70**
See also CA 85-88; 135; CANR 33; MTCW

Giono, Jean 1895-1970.......... **CLC 4, 11**
See also CA 45-48; 29-32R; CANR 2, 35;
DLB 72; MTCW

Author Index

Grumbach, Doris (Isaac)
1918- . . . . **CLC 13, 22, 64**
See also CA 5-8R; CAAS 2; CANR 9, 42

Grundtvig, Nicolai Frederik Severin
1783-1872 . . . . **NCLC 1**

Grunge
See Crumb, R(obert)

Grunwald, Lisa 1959- . . . . **CLC 44**
See also CA 120

Guare, John 1938- . . . . **CLC 8, 14, 29, 67**
See also CA 73-76; CANR 21; DLB 7;
MTCW

Gudjonsson, Halldor Kiljan 1902-
See Laxness, Halldor
See also CA 103

Guenter, Erich
See Eich, Guenter

Guest, Barbara 1920- . . . . **CLC 34**
See also CA 25-28R; CANR 11; DLB 5

Guest, Judith (Ann) 1936- . . . . **CLC 8, 30**
See also AAYA 7; CA 77-80; CANR 15;
MTCW

Guild, Nicholas M. 1944- . . . . **CLC 33**
See also CA 93-96

Guillemin, Jacques
See Sartre, Jean-Paul

Guillen, Jorge 1893-1984 . . . . **CLC 11**
See also CA 89-92; 112; DLB 108; HW

Guillen (y Batista), Nicolas (Cristobal)
1902-1989 . . . . **CLC 48, 79; BLC 2**
See also BW; CA 116; 125; 129; HW

Guillevic, (Eugene) 1907- . . . . **CLC 33**
See also CA 93-96

Guillois
See Desnos, Robert

Guiney, Louise Imogen
1861-1920 . . . . **TCLC 41**
See also DLB 54

Guiraldes, Ricardo (Guillermo)
1886-1927 . . . . **TCLC 39**
See also CA 131; HW; MTCW

Gunn, Bill . . . . **CLC 5**
See also Gunn, William Harrison
See also DLB 38

Gunn, Thom(son William)
1929- . . . . **CLC 3, 6, 18, 32**
See also CA 17-20R; CANR 9, 33;
CDBLB 1960 to Present; DLB 27;
MTCW

Gunn, William Harrison 1934(?)-1989
See Gunn, Bill
See also AITN 1; BW; CA 13-16R; 128;
CANR 12, 25

Gunnars, Kristjana 1948- . . . . **CLC 69**
See also CA 113; DLB 60

Gurganus, Allan 1947- . . . . **CLC 70**
See also BEST 90:1; CA 135

Gurney, A(lbert) R(amsdell), Jr.
1930- . . . . **CLC 32, 50, 54**
See also CA 77-80; CANR 32

Gurney, Ivor (Bertie) 1890-1937 . . . **TCLC 33**

Gurney, Peter
See Gurney, A(lbert) R(amsdell), Jr.

Gustafson, Ralph (Barker) 1909- . . . . **CLC 36**
See also CA 21-24R; CANR 8; DLB 88

Gut, Gom
See Simenon, Georges (Jacques Christian)

Guthrie, A(lfred) B(ertram), Jr.
1901-1991 . . . . **CLC 23**
See also CA 57-60; 134; CANR 24; DLB 6;
SATA 62; SATA-Obit 67

Guthrie, Isobel
See Grieve, C(hristopher) M(urray)

Guthrie, Woodrow Wilson 1912-1967
See Guthrie, Woody
See also CA 113; 93-96

Guthrie, Woody . . . . **CLC 35**
See also Guthrie, Woodrow Wilson

Guy, Rosa (Cuthbert) 1928- . . . . **CLC 26**
See also AAYA 4; BW; CA 17-20R;
CANR 14, 34; CLR 13; DLB 33; JRDA;
MAICYA; SATA 14, 62

Gwendolyn
See Bennett, (Enoch) Arnold

H. D. . . . . **CLC 3, 8, 14, 31, 34, 73; PC 5**
See also Doolittle, Hilda

Haavikko, Paavo Juhani
1931- . . . . **CLC 18, 34**
See also CA 106

Habbema, Koos
See Heijermans, Herman

Hacker, Marilyn 1942- . . . . **CLC 5, 9, 23, 72**
See also CA 77-80; DLB 120

Haggard, H(enry) Rider
1856-1925 . . . . **TCLC 11**
See also CA 108; DLB 70; SATA 16

Haig, Fenil
See Ford, Ford Madox

Haig-Brown, Roderick (Langmere)
1908-1976 . . . . **CLC 21**
See also CA 5-8R; 69-72; CANR 4, 38;
CLR 31; DLB 88; MAICYA; SATA 12

Hailey, Arthur 1920- . . . . **CLC 5**
See also AITN 2; BEST 90:3; CA 1-4R;
CANR 2, 36; DLB 88; DLBY 82; MTCW

Hailey, Elizabeth Forsythe 1938- . . . **CLC 40**
See also CA 93-96; CAAS 1; CANR 15

Haines, John (Meade) 1924- . . . . **CLC 58**
See also CA 17-20R; CANR 13, 34; DLB 5

Haldeman, Joe (William) 1943- . . . . . **CLC 61**
See also CA 53-56; CANR 6; DLB 8

Haley, Alex(ander Murray Palmer)
1921-1992 . . . **CLC 8, 12, 76; BLC 2; DA**
See also BW; CA 77-80; 136; DLB 38;
MTCW

Haliburton, Thomas Chandler
1796-1865 . . . . **NCLC 15**
See also DLB 11, 99

Hall, Donald (Andrew, Jr.)
1928- . . . . **CLC 1, 13, 37, 59**
See also CA 5-8R; CAAS 7; CANR 2;
DLB 5; SATA 23

Hall, Frederic Sauser
See Sauser-Hall, Frederic

Hall, James
See Kuttner, Henry

Hall, James Norman 1887-1951 . . . **TCLC 23**
See also CA 123; SATA 21

Hall, (Marguerite) Radclyffe
1886(?)-1943 . . . . **TCLC 12**
See also CA 110

Hall, Rodney 1935- . . . . **CLC 51**
See also CA 109

Halliday, Michael
See Creasey, John

Halpern, Daniel 1945- . . . . **CLC 14**
See also CA 33-36R

Hamburger, Michael (Peter Leopold)
1924- . . . . **CLC 5, 14**
See also CA 5-8R; CAAS 4; CANR 2;
DLB 27

Hamill, Pete 1935- . . . . **CLC 10**
See also CA 25-28R; CANR 18

Hamilton, Clive
See Lewis, C(live) S(taples)

Hamilton, Edmond 1904-1977 . . . . **CLC 1**
See also CA 1-4R; CANR 3; DLB 8

Hamilton, Eugene (Jacob) Lee
See Lee-Hamilton, Eugene (Jacob)

Hamilton, Franklin
See Silverberg, Robert

Hamilton, Gail
See Corcoran, Barbara

Hamilton, Mollie
See Kaye, M(ary) M(argaret)

Hamilton, (Anthony Walter) Patrick
1904-1962 . . . . **CLC 51**
See also CA 113; DLB 10

Hamilton, Virginia 1936- . . . . **CLC 26**
See also AAYA 2; BW; CA 25-28R;
CANR 20, 37; CLR 1, 11; DLB 33, 52;
JRDA; MAICYA; MTCW; SATA 4, 56

Hammett, (Samuel) Dashiell
1894-1961 . . . . **CLC 3, 5, 10, 19, 47**
See also AITN 1; CA 81-84; CANR 42;
CDALB 1929-1941; DLBD 6; MTCW

Hammon, Jupiter
1711(?)-1800(?) . . . . **NCLC 5; BLC 2**
See also DLB 31, 50

Hammond, Keith
See Kuttner, Henry

Hamner, Earl (Henry), Jr. 1923- . . . **CLC 12**
See also AITN 2; CA 73-76; DLB 6

Hampton, Christopher (James)
1946- . . . . **CLC 4**
See also CA 25-28R; DLB 13; MTCW

Hamsun, Knut . . . . **TCLC 2, 14, 49**
See also Pedersen, Knut

Handke, Peter 1942- . . **CLC 5, 8, 10, 15, 38**
See also CA 77-80; CANR 33; DLB 85,
124; MTCW

Hanley, James 1901-1985 . . . **CLC 3, 5, 8, 13**
See also CA 73-76; 117; CANR 36; MTCW

Hannah, Barry 1942- . . . . **CLC 23, 38**
See also CA 108; 110; CANR 43; DLB 6;
MTCW

Hannon, Ezra
See Hunter, Evan

Hansberry, Lorraine (Vivian)
1930-1965 .... **CLC 17, 62; BLC 2; DA;
DC 2**
See also BW; CA 109; 25-28R; CABS 3;
CDALB 1941-1968; DLB 7, 38; MTCW

Hansen, Joseph 1923- .... **CLC 38**
See also CA 29-32R; CAAS 17; CANR 16

Hansen, Martin A. 1909-1955..... **TCLC 32**

Hanson, Kenneth O(stlin) 1922- .... **CLC 13**
See also CA 53-56; CANR 7

Hardwick, Elizabeth 1916- .... **CLC 13**
See also CA 5-8R; CANR 3, 32; DLB 6;
MTCW

Hardy, Thomas
1840-1928 ...... **TCLC 4, 10, 18, 32, 48;
DA; PC 8; SSC 2; WLC**
See also CA 104; 123; CDBLB 1890-1914;
DLB 18, 19, 135; MTCW

Hare, David 1947- .... **CLC 29, 58**
See also CA 97-100; CANR 39; DLB 13;
MTCW

Harford, Henry
See Hudson, W(illiam) H(enry)

Hargrave, Leonie
See Disch, Thomas M(ichael)

Harlan, Louis R(udolph) 1922- ..... **CLC 34**
See also CA 21-24R; CANR 25

Harling, Robert 1951(?)- .... **CLC 53**

Harmon, William (Ruth) 1938-..... **CLC 38**
See also CA 33-36R; CANR 14, 32, 35;
SATA 65

Harper, F. E. W.
See Harper, Frances Ellen Watkins

Harper, Frances E. W.
See Harper, Frances Ellen Watkins

Harper, Frances E. Watkins
See Harper, Frances Ellen Watkins

Harper, Frances Ellen
See Harper, Frances Ellen Watkins

Harper, Frances Ellen Watkins
1825-1911 .... **TCLC 14; BLC 2**
See also BW; CA 111; 125; DLB 50

Harper, Michael S(teven) 1938- .. **CLC 7, 22**
See also BW; CA 33-36R; CANR 24;
DLB 41

Harper, Mrs. F. E. W.
See Harper, Frances Ellen Watkins

Harris, Christie (Lucy) Irwin
1907- .... **CLC 12**
See also CA 5-8R; CANR 6; DLB 88;
JRDA; MAICYA; SAAS 10; SATA 6, 74

Harris, Frank 1856(?)-1931....... **TCLC 24**
See also CA 109

Harris, George Washington
1814-1869 .... **NCLC 23**
See also DLB 3, 11

Harris, Joel Chandler 1848-1908 ... **TCLC 2**
See also CA 104; 137; DLB 11, 23, 42, 78,
91; MAICYA; YABC 1

Harris, John (Wyndham Parkes Lucas)
Beynon 1903-1969 .... **CLC 19**
See also CA 102; 89-92

Harris, MacDonald
See Heiney, Donald (William)

Harris, Mark 1922- .... **CLC 19**
See also CA 5-8R; CAAS 3; CANR 2;
DLB 2; DLBY 80

Harris, (Theodore) Wilson 1921-.... **CLC 25**
See also BW; CA 65-68; CAAS 16;
CANR 11, 27; DLB 117; MTCW

Harrison, Elizabeth Cavanna 1909-
See Cavanna, Betty
See also CA 9-12R; CANR 6, 27

Harrison, Harry (Max) 1925-...... **CLC 42**
See also CA 1-4R; CANR 5, 21; DLB 8;
SATA 4

Harrison, James (Thomas)
1937-............... **CLC 6, 14, 33, 66**
See also CA 13-16R; CANR 8; DLBY 82

Harrison, Kathryn 1961-.......... **CLC 70**

Harrison, Tony 1937-............. **CLC 43**
See also CA 65-68; DLB 40; MTCW

Harriss, Will(ard Irvin) 1922-...... **CLC 34**
See also CA 111

Harson, Sley
See Ellison, Harlan

Hart, Ellis
See Ellison, Harlan

Hart, Josephine 1942(?)- .... **CLC 70**
See also CA 138

Hart, Moss 1904-1961 .... **CLC 66**
See also CA 109; 89-92; DLB 7

Harte, (Francis) Bret(t)
1836(?)-1902 .... **TCLC 1, 25; DA;
SSC 8; WLC**
See also CA 104; 140; CDALB 1865-1917;
DLB 12, 64, 74, 79; SATA 26

Hartley, L(eslie) P(oles)
1895-1972 .... **CLC 2, 22**
See also CA 45-48; 37-40R; CANR 33;
DLB 15; MTCW

Hartman, Geoffrey H. 1929-....... **CLC 27**
See also CA 117; 125; DLB 67

Haruf, Kent 19(?)- .... **CLC 34**

Harwood, Ronald 1934-........... **CLC 32**
See also CA 1-4R; CANR 4; DLB 13

Hasek, Jaroslav (Matej Frantisek)
1883-1923 .... **TCLC 4**
See also CA 104; 129; MTCW

Hass, Robert 1941-............. **CLC 18, 39**
See also CA 111; CANR 30; DLB 105

Hastings, Hudson
See Kuttner, Henry

Hastings, Selina................... **CLC 44**

Hatteras, Amelia
See Mencken, H(enry) L(ouis)

Hatteras, Owen................... **TCLC 18**
See also Mencken, H(enry) L(ouis); Nathan,
George Jean

Hauptmann, Gerhart (Johann Robert)
1862-1946 .... **TCLC 4**
See also CA 104; DLB 66, 118

Havel, Vaclav 1936-........ **CLC 25, 58, 65**
See also CA 104; CANR 36; MTCW

Haviaras, Stratis .... **CLC 33**
See also Chaviaras, Strates

Hawes, Stephen 1475(?)-1523(?) ..... **LC 17**

Hawkes, John (Clendennin Burne, Jr.)
1925- ...... **CLC 1, 2, 3, 4, 7, 9, 14, 15,
27, 49**
See also CA 1-4R; CANR 2; DLB 2, 7;
DLBY 80; MTCW

Hawking, S. W.
See Hawking, Stephen W(illiam)

Hawking, Stephen W(illiam)
1942- .... **CLC 63**
See also BEST 89:1; CA 126; 129

Hawthorne, Julian 1846-1934 ..... **TCLC 25**

Hawthorne, Nathaniel
1804-1864 ...... **NCLC 39; DA; SSC 3;
WLC**
See also CDALB 1640-1865; DLB 1, 74;
YABC 2

Haxton, Josephine Ayres 1921- .... **CLC 73**
See also CA 115; CANR 41

Hayaseca y Eizaguirre, Jorge
See Echegaray (y Eizaguirre), Jose (Maria
Waldo)

Hayashi Fumiko 1904-1951...... **TCLC 27**

Haycraft, Anna
See Ellis, Alice Thomas
See also CA 122

Hayden, Robert E(arl)
1913-1980 .... **CLC 5, 9, 14, 37; BLC 2;
DA; PC 6**
See also BW; CA 69-72; 97-100; CABS 2;
CANR 24; CDALB 1941-1968; DLB 5,
76; MTCW; SATA 19, 26

Hayford, J(oseph) E(phraim) Casely
See Casely-Hayford, J(oseph) E(phraim)

Hayman, Ronald 1932-............ **CLC 44**
See also CA 25-28R; CANR 18

Haywood, Eliza (Fowler)
1693(?)-1756 .... **LC 1**

Hazlitt, William 1778-1830...... **NCLC 29**
See also DLB 110

Hazzard, Shirley 1931- .... **CLC 18**
See also CA 9-12R; CANR 4; DLBY 82;
MTCW

Head, Bessie
1937-1986 .... **CLC 25, 67; BLC 2**
See also BW; CA 29-32R; 119; CANR 25;
DLB 117; MTCW

Headon, (Nicky) Topper 1956(?)- ... **CLC 30**
See also Clash, The

Heaney, Seamus (Justin)
1939- .... **CLC 5, 7, 14, 25, 37, 74**
See also CA 85-88; CANR 25;
CDBLB 1960 to Present; DLB 40;
MTCW

Hearn, (Patricio) Lafcadio (Tessima Carlos)
1850-1904 .... **TCLC 9**
See also CA 105; DLB 12, 78

Hearne, Vicki 1946-.............. **CLC 56**
See also CA 139

Hearon, Shelby 1931-............. **CLC 63**
See also AITN 2; CA 25-28R; CANR 18

Heat-Moon, William Least......... **CLC 29**
See also Trogdon, William (Lewis)
See also AAYA 9

Hebert, Anne 1916- .... **CLC 4, 13, 29**
See also CA 85-88; DLB 68; MTCW

Hecht, Anthony (Evan)
1923- .... **CLC 8, 13, 19**
See also CA 9-12R; CANR 6; DLB 5

Hecht, Ben 1894-1964 .... **CLC 8**
See also CA 85-88; DLB 7, 9, 25, 26, 28, 86

Hedayat, Sadeq 1903-1951........ **TCLC 21**
See also CA 120

Heidegger, Martin 1889-1976 ...... **CLC 24**
See also CA 81-84; 65-68; CANR 34;
MTCW

Heidenstam, (Carl Gustaf) Verner von
1859-1940 .... **TCLC 5**
See also CA 104

Heifner, Jack 1946- .... **CLC 11**
See also CA 105

Heijermans, Herman 1864-1924 ... **TCLC 24**
See also CA 123

Heilbrun, Carolyn G(old) 1926-.... **CLC 25**
See also CA 45-48; CANR 1, 28

Heine, Heinrich 1797-1856 .... **NCLC 4**
See also DLB 90

Heinemann, Larry (Curtiss) 1944- .. **CLC 50**
See also CA 110; CANR 31; DLBD 9

Heiney, Donald (William)
1921-1993 .... **CLC 9**
See also CA 1-4R; 142; CANR 3

Heinlein, Robert A(nson)
1907-1988 ...... **CLC 1, 3, 8, 14, 26, 55**
See also CA 1-4R; 125; CANR 1, 20;
DLB 8; JRDA; MAICYA; MTCW;
SATA 9, 56, 69

Helforth, John
See Doolittle, Hilda

Hellenhofferu, Vojtech Kapristian z
See Hasek, Jaroslav (Matej Frantisek)

Heller, Joseph
1923- .... **CLC 1, 3, 5, 8, 11, 36, 63; DA;**
WLC
See also AITN 1; CA 5-8R; CABS 1;
CANR 8, 42; DLB 2, 28; DLBY 80;
MTCW

Hellman, Lillian (Florence)
1906-1984 ...... **CLC 2, 4, 8, 14, 18, 34,**
44, 52; DC 1
See also AITN 1, 2; CA 13-16R; 112;
CANR 33; DLB 7; DLBY 84; MTCW

Helprin, Mark 1947- ..... **CLC 7, 10, 22, 32**
See also CA 81-84; DLBY 85; MTCW

Helyar, Jane Penelope Josephine 1933-
See Poole, Josephine
See also CA 21-24R; CANR 10, 26

Hemans, Felicia 1793-1835 ...... **NCLC 29**
See also DLB 96

Hemingway, Ernest (Miller)
1899-1961 .... **CLC 1, 3, 6, 8, 10, 13, 19,**
30, 34, 39, 41, 44, 50, 61, 80; DA; SSC 1;
WLC
See also CA 77-80; CANR 34;
CDALB 1917-1929; DLB 4, 9, 102;
DLBD 1; DLBY 81, 87; MTCW

Hempel, Amy 1951- .... **CLC 39**
See also CA 118; 137

Henderson, F. C.
See Mencken, H(enry) L(ouis)

Henderson, Sylvia
See Ashton-Warner, Sylvia (Constance)

Henley, Beth .... **CLC 23**
See also Henley, Elizabeth Becker
See also CABS 3; DLBY 86

Henley, Elizabeth Becker 1952-
See Henley, Beth
See also CA 107; CANR 32; MTCW

Henley, William Ernest
1849-1903 .... **TCLC 8**
See also CA 105; DLB 19

Hennissart, Martha
See Lathen, Emma
See also CA 85-88

Henry, O......... **TCLC 1, 19; SSC 5; WLC**
See also Porter, William Sydney

Henryson, Robert 1430(?)-1506(?).... **LC 20**

Henry VIII 1491-1547............. **LC 10**

Henschke, Alfred
See Klabund

Hentoff, Nat(han Irving) 1925- ..... **CLC 26**
See also AAYA 4; CA 1-4R; CAAS 6;
CANR 5, 25; CLR 1; JRDA; MAICYA;
SATA 27, 42, 69

Heppenstall, (John) Rayner
1911-1981 .... **CLC 10**
See also CA 1-4R; 103; CANR 29

Herbert, Frank (Patrick)
1920-1986 .... **CLC 12, 23, 35, 44**
See also CA 53-56; 118; CANR 5, 43;
DLB 8; MTCW; SATA 9, 37, 47

Herbert, George 1593-1633 .... **LC 24; PC 4**
See also CDBLB Before 1660; DLB 126

Herbert, Zbigniew 1924- .... **CLC 9, 43**
See also CA 89-92; CANR 36; MTCW

Herbst, Josephine (Frey)
1897-1969 .... **CLC 34**
See also CA 5-8R; 25-28R; DLB 9

Hergesheimer, Joseph
1880-1954 .... **TCLC 11**
See also CA 109; DLB 102, 9

Herlihy, James Leo 1927- .... **CLC 6**
See also CA 1-4R; CANR 2

Hermogenes fl. c. 175- .... **CMLC 6**

Hernandez, Jose 1834-1886...... **NCLC 17**

Herrick, Robert 1591-1674 ..... **LC 13; DA**
See also DLB 126

Herring, Guilles
See Somerville, Edith

Herriot, James 1916- .... **CLC 12**
See also Wight, James Alfred
See also AAYA 1; CANR 40

Herrmann, Dorothy 1941- .... **CLC 44**
See also CA 107

Herrmann, Taffy
See Herrmann, Dorothy

Hersey, John (Richard)
1914-1993 .... **CLC 1, 2, 7, 9, 40**
See also CA 17-20R; 140; CANR 33;
DLB 6; MTCW; SATA 25

Herzen, Aleksandr Ivanovich
1812-1870 .... **NCLC 10**

Herzl, Theodor 1860-1904........ **TCLC 36**

Herzog, Werner 1942- .... **CLC 16**
See also CA 89-92

Hesiod c. 8th cent. B.C.- .... **CMLC 5**

Hesse, Hermann
1877-1962 .... **CLC 1, 2, 3, 6, 11, 17, 25,**
69; DA; SSC 9; WLC
See also CA 17-18; CAP 2; DLB 66;
MTCW; SATA 50

Hewes, Cady
See De Voto, Bernard (Augustine)

Heyen, William 1940- .... **CLC 13, 18**
See also CA 33-36R; CAAS 9; DLB 5

Heyerdahl, Thor 1914-........... **CLC 26**
See also CA 5-8R; CANR 5, 22; MTCW;
SATA 2, 52

Heym, Georg (Theodor Franz Arthur)
1887-1912 .... **TCLC 9**
See also CA 106

Heym, Stefan 1913- .... **CLC 41**
See also CA 9-12R; CANR 4; DLB 69

Heyse, Paul (Johann Ludwig von)
1830-1914 .... **TCLC 8**
See also CA 104; DLB 129

Hibbert, Eleanor Alice Burford
1906-1993 .... **CLC 7**
See also BEST 90:4; CA 17-20R; 140;
CANR 9, 28; SATA 2; SATA-Obit 74

Higgins, George V(incent)
1939- .... **CLC 4, 7, 10, 18**
See also CA 77-80; CAAS 5; CANR 17;
DLB 2; DLBY 81; MTCW

Higginson, Thomas Wentworth
1823-1911 .... **TCLC 36**
See also DLB 1, 64

Highet, Helen
See MacInnes, Helen (Clark)

Highsmith, (Mary) Patricia
1921- .... **CLC 2, 4, 14, 42**
See also CA 1-4R; CANR 1, 20; MTCW

Highwater, Jamake (Mamake)
1942(?)- .... **CLC 12**
See also AAYA 7; CA 65-68; CAAS 7;
CANR 10, 34; CLR 17; DLB 52;
DLBY 85; JRDA; MAICYA; SATA 30,
32, 69

Hijuelos, Oscar 1951- .... **CLC 65**
See also BEST 90:1; CA 123; HW

Hikmet, Nazim 1902(?)-1963....... **CLC 40**
See also CA 141; 93-96

Hildesheimer, Wolfgang
1916-1991 .... **CLC 49**
See also CA 101; 135; DLB 69, 124

Hill, Geoffrey (William)
1932- ....**CLC 5, 8, 18, 45**
See also CA 81-84; CANR 21;
CDBLB 1960 to Present; DLB 40;
MTCW

Hill, George Roy 1921- .... **CLC 26**
See also CA 110; 122

Hill, John
See Koontz, Dean R(ay)

Hill, Susan (Elizabeth) 1942- .... **CLC 4**
See also CA 33-36R; CANR 29; DLB 14;
MTCW

Hillerman, Tony 1925-........... **CLC 62**
See also AAYA 6; BEST 89:1; CA 29-32R;
CANR 21, 42; SATA 6

Hillesum, Etty 1914-1943 .... **TCLC 49**
See also CA 137

Hilliard, Noel (Harvey) 1929-...... **CLC 15**
See also CA 9-12R; CANR 7

Hillis, Rick 1956-................ **CLC 66**
See also CA 134

Hilton, James 1900-1954........ **TCLC 21**
See also CA 108; DLB 34, 77; SATA 34

Himes, Chester (Bomar)
1909-1984 ... **CLC 2, 4, 7, 18, 58; BLC 2**
See also BW; CA 25-28R; 114; CANR 22;
DLB 2, 76; MTCW

Hinde, Thomas .... **CLC 6, 11**
See also Chitty, Thomas Willes

Hindin, Nathan
See Bloch, Robert (Albert)

Hine, (William) Daryl 1936-....... **CLC 15**
See also CA 1-4R; CAAS 15; CANR 1, 20;
DLB 60

Hinkson, Katharine Tynan
See Tynan, Katharine

Hinton, S(usan) E(loise)
1950-................. **CLC 30; DA**
See also AAYA 2; CA 81-84; CANR 32;
CLR 3, 23; JRDA; MAICYA; MTCW;
SATA 19, 58

Hippius, Zinaida .... **TCLC 9**
See also Gippius, Zinaida (Nikolayevna)

Hiraoka, Kimitake 1925-1970
See Mishima, Yukio
See also CA 97-100; 29-32R; MTCW

Hirsch, E(ric) D(onald), Jr. 1928-... **CLC 79**
See also CA 25-28R; CANR 27; DLB 67;
MTCW

Hirsch, Edward 1950- .... **CLC 31, 50**
See also CA 104; CANR 20, 42; DLB 120

Hitchcock, Alfred (Joseph)
1899-1980 .... **CLC 16**
See also CA 97-100; SATA 24, 27

Hoagland, Edward 1932-......... **CLC 28**
See also CA 1-4R; CANR 2, 31; DLB 6;
SATA 51

Hoban, Russell (Conwell) 1925- .. **CLC 7, 25**
See also CA 5-8R; CANR 23, 37; CLR 3;
DLB 52; MAICYA; MTCW; SATA 1, 40

Hobbs, Perry
See Blackmur, R(ichard) P(almer)

Hobson, Laura Z(ametkin)
1900-1986 .... **CLC 7, 25**
See also CA 17-20R; 118; DLB 28;
SATA 52

Hochhuth, Rolf 1931-........ **CLC 4, 11, 18**
See also CA 5-8R; CANR 33; DLB 124;
MTCW

Hochman, Sandra 1936-......... **CLC 3, 8**
See also CA 5-8R; DLB 5

Hochwaelder, Fritz 1911-1986...... **CLC 36**
See also Hochwalder, Fritz
See also CA 29-32R; 120; CANR 42;
MTCW

Hochwalder, Fritz................ **CLC 36**
See also Hochwaelder, Fritz

Hocking, Mary (Eunice) 1921-..... **CLC 13**
See also CA 101; CANR 18, 40

Hodgins, Jack 1938-.............. **CLC 23**
See also CA 93-96; DLB 60

Hodgson, William Hope
1877(?)-1918 .... **TCLC 13**
See also CA 111; DLB 70

Hoffman, Alice 1952-............. **CLC 51**
See also CA 77-80; CANR 34; MTCW

Hoffman, Daniel (Gerard)
1923-................. **CLC 6, 13, 23**
See also CA 1-4R; CANR 4; DLB 5

Hoffman, Stanley 1944-........... **CLC 5**
See also CA 77-80

Hoffman, William M(oses) 1939-... **CLC 40**
See also CA 57-60; CANR 11

Hoffmann, E(rnst) T(heodor) A(madeus)
1776-1822 .... **NCLC 2; SSC 13**
See also DLB 90; SATA 27

Hofmann, Gert 1931-............. **CLC 54**
See also CA 128

Hofmannsthal, Hugo von
1874-1929 .... **TCLC 11; DC 4**
See also CA 106; DLB 81, 118

Hogan, Linda 1947-.............. **CLC 73**
See also CA 120

Hogarth, Charles
See Creasey, John

Hogg, James 1770-1835.......... **NCLC 4**
See also DLB 93, 116

Holbach, Paul Henri Thiry Baron
1723-1789 .... **LC 14**

Holberg, Ludvig 1684-1754 .... **LC 6**

Holden, Ursula 1921-............. **CLC 18**
See also CA 101; CAAS 8; CANR 22

Holderlin, (Johann Christian) Friedrich
1770-1843 .... **NCLC 16; PC 4**

Holdstock, Robert
See Holdstock, Robert P.

Holdstock, Robert P. 1948-........ **CLC 39**
See also CA 131

Holland, Isabelle 1920- .... **CLC 21**
See also CA 21-24R; CANR 10, 25; JRDA;
MAICYA; SATA 8, 70

Holland, Marcus
See Caldwell, (Janet Miriam) Taylor
(Holland)

Hollander, John 1929-...... **CLC 2, 5, 8, 14**
See also CA 1-4R; CANR 1; DLB 5;
SATA 13

Hollander, Paul
See Silverberg, Robert

Holleran, Andrew 1943(?)-......... **CLC 38**

Hollinghurst, Alan 1954-.......... **CLC 55**
See also CA 114

Hollis, Jim
See Summers, Hollis (Spurgeon, Jr.)

Holmes, John
See Souster, (Holmes) Raymond

Holmes, John Clellon 1926-1988.... **CLC 56**
See also CA 9-12R; 125; CANR 4; DLB 16

Holmes, Oliver Wendell
1809-1894 .... **NCLC 14**
See also CDALB 1640-1865; DLB 1;
SATA 34

Holmes, Raymond
See Souster, (Holmes) Raymond

Holt, Victoria
See Hibbert, Eleanor Alice Burford

Holub, Miroslav 1923-............. **CLC 4**
See also CA 21-24R; CANR 10

Homer c. 8th cent. B.C.- ..... **CMLC 1; DA**

Honig, Edwin 1919- .... **CLC 33**
See also CA 5-8R; CAAS 8; CANR 4;
DLB 5

Hood, Hugh (John Blagdon)
1928- .... **CLC 15, 28**
See also CA 49-52; CAAS 17; CANR 1, 33;
DLB 53

Hood, Thomas 1799-1845........ **NCLC 16**
See also DLB 96

Hooker, (Peter) Jeremy 1941-...... **CLC 43**
See also CA 77-80; CANR 22; DLB 40

Hope, A(lec) D(erwent) 1907-.... **CLC 3, 51**
See also CA 21-24R; CANR 33; MTCW

Hope, Brian
See Creasey, John

Hope, Christopher (David Tully)
1944- .... **CLC 52**
See also CA 106; SATA 62

Hopkins, Gerard Manley
1844-1889 .... **NCLC 17; DA; WLC**
See also CDBLB 1890-1914; DLB 35, 57

Hopkins, John (Richard) 1931-...... **CLC 4**
See also CA 85-88

Hopkins, Pauline Elizabeth
1859-1930 .... **TCLC 28; BLC 2**
See also CA 141; DLB 50

Hopley-Woolrich, Cornell George 1903-1968
See Woolrich, Cornell
See also CA 13-14; CAP 1

Horatio
See Proust, (Valentin-Louis-George-Eugene-)
Marcel

Horgan, Paul 1903- .... **CLC 9, 53**
See also CA 13-16R; CANR 9, 35;
DLB 102; DLBY 85; MTCW; SATA 13

Horn, Peter
See Kuttner, Henry

Hornem, Horace Esq.
See Byron, George Gordon (Noel)

Horovitz, Israel 1939-............ **CLC 56**
See also CA 33-36R; DLB 7

Horvath, Odon von
See Horvath, Oedoen von
See also DLB 85, 124

Horvath, Oedoen von 1901-1938... **TCLC 45**
See also Horvath, Odon von
See also CA 118

Horwitz, Julius 1920-1986........ **CLC 14**
See also CA 9-12R; 119; CANR 12

Hospital, Janette Turner 1942-..... **CLC 42**
See also CA 108

Hostos, E. M. de
See Hostos (y Bonilla), Eugenio Maria de

Hostos, Eugenio M. de
See Hostos (y Bonilla), Eugenio Maria de

Hostos, Eugenio Maria
See Hostos (y Bonilla), Eugenio Maria de

Hostos (y Bonilla), Eugenio Maria de
1839-1903 .... TCLC **24**
See also CA 123; 131; HW

Houdini
See Lovecraft, H(oward) P(hillips)

Hougan, Carolyn 1943- .... CLC **34**
See also CA 139

Household, Geoffrey (Edward West)
1900-1988 .... CLC **11**
See also CA 77-80; 126; DLB 87; SATA 14, 59

Housman, A(lfred) E(dward)
1859-1936 ...... TCLC **1, 10; DA; PC 2**
See also CA 104; 125; DLB 19; MTCW

Housman, Laurence 1865-1959 ..... TCLC **7**
See also CA 106; DLB 10; SATA 25

Howard, Elizabeth Jane 1923- ... CLC **7, 29**
See also CA 5-8R; CANR 8

Howard, Maureen 1930- ..... CLC **5, 14, 46**
See also CA 53-56; CANR 31; DLBY 83; MTCW

Howard, Richard 1929- ...... CLC **7, 10, 47**
See also AITN 1; CA 85-88; CANR 25; DLB 5

Howard, Robert Ervin 1906-1936 ... TCLC **8**
See also CA 105

Howard, Warren F.
See Pohl, Frederik

Howe, Fanny 1940- .... CLC **47**
See also CA 117; SATA 52

Howe, Julia Ward 1819-1910 ..... TCLC **21**
See also CA 117; DLB 1

Howe, Susan 1937- .... CLC **72**
See also DLB 120

Howe, Tina 1937- .... CLC **48**
See also CA 109

Howell, James 1594(?)-1666 .... LC **13**

Howells, W. D.
See Howells, William Dean

Howells, William D.
See Howells, William Dean

Howells, William Dean
1837-1920 ...... TCLC **41, 7, 17**
See also CA 104; 134; CDALB 1865-1917; DLB 12, 64, 74, 79

Howes, Barbara 1914- .... CLC **15**
See also CA 9-12R; CAAS 3; SATA 5

Hrabal, Bohumil 1914- .... CLC **13, 67**
See also CA 106; CAAS 12

Hsun, Lu .... TCLC **3**
See also Shu-Jen, Chou

Hubbard, L(afayette) Ron(ald)
1911-1986 .... CLC **43**
See also CA 77-80; 118; CANR 22

Huch, Ricarda (Octavia)
1864-1947 .... TCLC **13**
See also CA 111; DLB 66

Huddle, David 1942- .... CLC **49**
See also CA 57-60; DLB 130

Hudson, Jeffrey
See Crichton, (John) Michael

Hudson, W(illiam) H(enry)
1841-1922 .... TCLC **29**
See also CA 115; DLB 98; SATA 35

Hueffer, Ford Madox
See Ford, Ford Madox

Hughart, Barry 1934- .... CLC **39**
See also CA 137

Hughes, Colin
See Creasey, John

Hughes, David (John) 1930- .... CLC **48**
See also CA 116; 129; DLB 14

Hughes, (James) Langston
1902-1967 ..... CLC **1, 5, 10, 15, 35, 44; BLC 2; DA; DC 3; PC 1; SSC 6; WLC**
See also BW; CA 1-4R; 25-28R; CANR 1, 34; CDALB 1929-1941; CLR 17; DLB 4, 7, 48, 51, 86; JRDA; MAICYA; MTCW; SATA 4, 33

Hughes, Richard (Arthur Warren)
1900-1976 .... CLC **1, 11**
See also CA 5-8R; 65-68; CANR 4; DLB 15; MTCW; SATA 8, 25

Hughes, Ted
1930- .... CLC **2, 4, 9, 14, 37; PC 7**
See also CA 1-4R; CANR 1, 33; CLR 3; DLB 40; MAICYA; MTCW; SATA 27, 49

Hugo, Richard F(ranklin)
1923-1982 .... CLC **6, 18, 32**
See also CA 49-52; 108; CANR 3; DLB 5

Hugo, Victor (Marie)
1802-1885 .. NCLC **3, 10, 21; DA; WLC**
See also DLB 119; SATA 47

Huidobro, Vicente
See Huidobro Fernandez, Vicente Garcia

Huidobro Fernandez, Vicente Garcia
1893-1948 .... TCLC **31**
See also CA 131; HW

Hulme, Keri 1947- .... CLC **39**
See also CA 125

Hulme, T(homas) E(rnest)
1883-1917 .... TCLC **21**
See also CA 117; DLB 19

Hume, David 1711-1776 .... LC **7**
See also DLB 104

Humphrey, William 1924- .... CLC **45**
See also CA 77-80; DLB 6

Humphreys, Emyr Owen 1919- ..... CLC **47**
See also CA 5-8R; CANR 3, 24; DLB 15

Humphreys, Josephine 1945- .... CLC **34, 57**
See also CA 121; 127

Hungerford, Pixie
See Brinsmead, H(esba) F(ay)

Hunt, E(verette) Howard, Jr.
1918- .... CLC **3**
See also AITN 1; CA 45-48; CANR 2

Hunt, Kyle
See Creasey, John

Hunt, (James Henry) Leigh
1784-1859 .... NCLC **1**

Hunt, Marsha 1946- .... CLC **70**

Hunter, E. Waldo
See Sturgeon, Theodore (Hamilton)

Hunter, Evan 1926- .... CLC **11, 31**
See also CA 5-8R; CANR 5, 38; DLBY 82; MTCW; SATA 25

Hunter, Kristin (Eggleston) 1931-... CLC **35**
See also AITN 1; BW; CA 13-16R; CANR 13; CLR 3; DLB 33; MAICYA; SAAS 10; SATA 12

Hunter, Mollie 1922- .... CLC **21**
See also McIlwraith, Maureen Mollie Hunter
See also CANR 37; CLR 25; JRDA; MAICYA; SAAS 7; SATA 54

Hunter, Robert (?)-1734 .... LC **7**

Hurston, Zora Neale
1903-1960 ...... CLC **7, 30, 61; BLC 2; DA; SSC 4**
See also BW; CA 85-88; DLB 51, 86; MTCW

Huston, John (Marcellus)
1906-1987 .... CLC **20**
See also CA 73-76; 123; CANR 34; DLB 26

Hustvedt, Siri 1955- .... CLC **76**
See also CA 137

Hutten, Ulrich von 1488-1523 .... LC **16**

Huxley, Aldous (Leonard)
1894-1963 ..... CLC **1, 3, 4, 5, 8, 11, 18, 35, 79; DA; WLC**
See also CA 85-88; CDBLB 1914-1945; DLB 36, 100; MTCW; SATA 63

Huysmans, Charles Marie Georges
1848-1907
See Huysmans, Joris-Karl
See also CA 104

Huysmans, Joris-Karl .... TCLC **7**
See also Huysmans, Charles Marie Georges
See also DLB 123

Hwang, David Henry
1957- .... CLC **55; DC 4**
See also CA 127; 132

Hyde, Anthony 1946- .... CLC **42**
See also CA 136

Hyde, Margaret O(ldroyd) 1917- ... CLC **21**
See also CA 1-4R; CANR 1, 36; CLR 23; JRDA; MAICYA; SAAS 8; SATA 1, 42

Hynes, James 1956(?)- .... CLC **65**

Ian, Janis 1951- .... CLC **21**
See also CA 105

Ibanez, Vicente Blasco
See Blasco Ibanez, Vicente

Ibarguengoitia, Jorge 1928-1983 .... CLC **37**
See also CA 124; 113; HW

Ibsen, Henrik (Johan)
1828-1906 .... TCLC **2, 8, 16, 37, 52; DA; DC 2; WLC**
See also CA 104; 141

Ibuse Masuji 1898-1993 .... CLC **22**
See also CA 127; 141

Ichikawa, Kon 1915- .... CLC **20**
See also CA 121

Idle, Eric 1943- .... CLC **21**
See also Monty Python
See also CA 116; CANR 35

Jewett, (Theodora) Sarah Orne
1849-1909 . . . . TCLC 1, 22; SSC 6
See also CA 108; 127; DLB 12, 74;
SATA 15

Jewsbury, Geraldine (Endsor)
1812-1880 . . . . NCLC 22
See also DLB 21

Jhabvala, Ruth Prawer
1927- . . . . CLC 4, 8, 29
See also CA 1-4R; CANR 2, 29; MTCW

Jiles, Paulette 1943- . . . . CLC 13, 58
See also CA 101

Jimenez (Mantecon), Juan Ramon
1881-1958 . . . . TCLC 4; PC 7
See also CA 104; 131; DLB 134; HW;
MTCW

Jimenez, Ramon
See Jimenez (Mantecon), Juan Ramon

Jimenez Mantecon, Juan
See Jimenez (Mantecon), Juan Ramon

Joel, Billy . . . . CLC 26
See also Joel, William Martin

Joel, William Martin 1949-
See Joel, Billy
See also CA 108

John of the Cross, St. 1542-1591 . . . . LC 18

Johnson, B(ryan) S(tanley William)
1933-1973 . . . . CLC 6, 9
See also CA 9-12R; 53-56; CANR 9;
DLB 14, 40

Johnson, Benj. F. of Boo
See Riley, James Whitcomb

Johnson, Benjamin F. of Boo
See Riley, James Whitcomb

Johnson, Charles (Richard)
1948- . . . . CLC 7, 51, 65; BLC 2
See also BW; CA 116; CAAS 18;
CANR 42; DLB 33

Johnson, Denis 1949- . . . . CLC 52
See also CA 117; 121; DLB 120

Johnson, Diane 1934- . . . . CLC 5, 13, 48
See also CA 41-44R; CANR 17, 40;
DLBY 80; MTCW

Johnson, Eyvind (Olof Verner)
1900-1976 . . . . CLC 14
See also CA 73-76; 69-72; CANR 34

Johnson, J. R.
See James, C(yril) L(ionel) R(obert)

Johnson, James Weldon
1871-1938 . . . . TCLC 3, 19; BLC 2
See also BW; CA 104; 125;
CDALB 1917-1929; CLR 32; DLB 51;
MTCW; SATA 31

Johnson, Joyce 1935- . . . . CLC 58
See also CA 125; 129

Johnson, Lionel (Pigot)
1867-1902 . . . . TCLC 19
See also CA 117; DLB 19

Johnson, Mel
See Malzberg, Barry N(athaniel)

Johnson, Pamela Hansford
1912-1981 . . . . CLC 1, 7, 27
See also CA 1-4R; 104; CANR 2, 28;
DLB 15; MTCW

Johnson, Samuel
1709-1784 . . . . LC 15; DA; WLC
See also CDBLB 1660-1789; DLB 39, 95,
104

Johnson, Uwe
1934-1984 . . . . CLC 5, 10, 15, 40
See also CA 1-4R; 112; CANR 1, 39;
DLB 75; MTCW

Johnston, George (Benson) 1913- . . . CLC 51
See also CA 1-4R; CANR 5, 20; DLB 88

Johnston, Jennifer 1930- . . . . CLC 7
See also CA 85-88; DLB 14

Jolley, (Monica) Elizabeth 1923- . . . CLC 46
See also CA 127; CAAS 13

Jones, Arthur Llewellyn 1863-1947
See Machen, Arthur
See also CA 104

Jones, D(ouglas) G(ordon) 1929- . . . . CLC 10
See also CA 29-32R; CANR 13; DLB 53

Jones, David (Michael)
1895-1974 . . . . CLC 2, 4, 7, 13, 42
See also CA 9-12R; 53-56; CANR 28;
CDBLB 1945-1960; DLB 20, 100; MTCW

Jones, David Robert 1947-
See Bowie, David
See also CA 103

Jones, Diana Wynne 1934- . . . . CLC 26
See also CA 49-52; CANR 4, 26; CLR 23;
JRDA; MAICYA; SAAS 7; SATA 9, 70

Jones, Edward P. 1950- . . . . CLC 76
See also CA 142

Jones, Gayl 1949- . . . . CLC 6, 9; BLC 2
See also BW; CA 77-80; CANR 27;
DLB 33; MTCW

Jones, James 1921-1977 . . . . CLC 1, 3, 10, 39
See also AITN 1, 2; CA 1-4R; 69-72;
CANR 6; DLB 2; MTCW

Jones, John J.
See Lovecraft, H(oward) P(hillips)

Jones, LeRoi . . . . CLC 1, 2, 3, 5, 10, 14
See also Baraka, Amiri

Jones, Louis B. . . . . CLC 65
See also CA 141

Jones, Madison (Percy, Jr.) 1925- . . . CLC 4
See also CA 13-16R; CAAS 11; CANR 7

Jones, Mervyn 1922- . . . . CLC 10, 52
See also CA 45-48; CAAS 5; CANR 1;
MTCW

Jones, Mick 1956(?)- . . . . CLC 30
See also Clash, The

Jones, Nettie (Pearl) 1941- . . . . CLC 34
See also CA 137

Jones, Preston 1936-1979 . . . . CLC 10
See also CA 73-76; 89-92; DLB 7

Jones, Robert F(rancis) 1934- . . . . . . CLC 7
See also CA 49-52; CANR 2

Jones, Rod 1953- . . . . CLC 50
See also CA 128

Jones, Terence Graham Parry
1942- . . . . CLC 21
See also Jones, Terry; Monty Python
See also CA 112; 116; CANR 35; SATA 51

Jones, Terry
See Jones, Terence Graham Parry
See also SATA 67

Jong, Erica 1942- . . . . CLC 4, 6, 8, 18
See also AITN 1; BEST 90:2; CA 73-76;
CANR 26; DLB 2, 5, 28; MTCW

Jonson, Ben(jamin)
1572(?)-1637 . . . . LC 6; DA; DC 4; WLC
See also CDBLB Before 1660; DLB 62, 121

Jordan, June 1936- . . . . CLC 5, 11, 23
See also AAYA 2; BW; CA 33-36R;
CANR 25; CLR 10; DLB 38; MAICYA;
MTCW; SATA 4

Jordan, Pat(rick M.) 1941- . . . . CLC 37
See also CA 33-36R

Jorgensen, Ivar
See Ellison, Harlan

Jorgenson, Ivar
See Silverberg, Robert

Josipovici, Gabriel 1940- . . . . CLC 6, 43
See also CA 37-40R; CAAS 8; DLB 14

Joubert, Joseph 1754-1824 . . . . NCLC 9

Jouve, Pierre Jean 1887-1976 . . . . . . CLC 47
See also CA 65-68

Joyce, James (Augustine Aloysius)
1882-1941 . . . . . . TCLC 3, 8, 16, 35; DA;
SSC 3; WLC
See also CA 104; 126; CDBLB 1914-1945;
DLB 10, 19, 36; MTCW

Jozsef, Attila 1905-1937 . . . . TCLC 22
See also CA 116

Juana Ines de la Cruz 1651(?)-1695 . . . LC 5

Judd, Cyril
See Kornbluth, C(yril) M.; Pohl, Frederik

Julian of Norwich 1342(?)-1416(?) . . . . LC 6

Just, Ward (Swift) 1935- . . . . CLC 4, 27
See also CA 25-28R; CANR 32

Justice, Donald (Rodney) 1925- . . CLC 6, 19
See also CA 5-8R; CANR 26; DLBY 83

Juvenal c. 55-c. 127 . . . . CMLC 8

Juvenis
See Bourne, Randolph S(illiman)

Kacew, Romain 1914-1980
See Gary, Romain
See also CA 108; 102

Kadare, Ismail 1936- . . . . CLC 52

Kadohata, Cynthia . . . . CLC 59
See also CA 140

Kafka, Franz
1883-1924 . . . . TCLC 2, 6, 13, 29, 47;
DA; SSC 5; WLC
See also CA 105; 126; DLB 81; MTCW

Kahn, Roger 1927- . . . . CLC 30
See also CA 25-28R; SATA 37

Kain, Saul
See Sassoon, Siegfried (Lorraine)

Kaiser, Georg 1878-1945 . . . . TCLC 9
See also CA 106; DLB 124

Kaletski, Alexander 1946- . . . . CLC 39
See also CA 118

Kalidasa fl. c. 400- . . . . CMLC 9

Kallman, Chester (Simon)
1921-1975 . . . . **CLC 2**
See also CA 45-48; 53-56; CANR 3

Kaminsky, Melvin 1926-
See Brooks, Mel
See also CA 65-68; CANR 16

Kaminsky, Stuart M(elvin) 1934- . . . **CLC 59**
See also CA 73-76; CANR 29

Kane, Paul
See Simon, Paul

Kane, Wilson
See Bloch, Robert (Albert)

Kanin, Garson 1912- . . . . **CLC 22**
See also AITN 1; CA 5-8R; CANR 7;
DLB 7

Kaniuk, Yoram 1930- . . . . **CLC 19**
See also CA 134

Kant, Immanuel 1724-1804 . . . . . . **NCLC 27**
See also DLB 94

Kantor, MacKinlay 1904-1977 . . . . . . **CLC 7**
See also CA 61-64; 73-76; DLB 9, 102

Kaplan, David Michael 1946- . . . . . . **CLC 50**

Kaplan, James 1951- . . . . **CLC 59**
See also CA 135

Karageorge, Michael
See Anderson, Poul (William)

Karamzin, Nikolai Mikhailovich
1766-1826 . . . . **NCLC 3**

Karapanou, Margarita 1946- . . . . **CLC 13**
See also CA 101

Karinthy, Frigyes 1887-1938 . . . . . . **TCLC 47**

Karl, Frederick R(obert) 1927- . . . . . **CLC 34**
See also CA 5-8R; CANR 3

Kastel, Warren
See Silverberg, Robert

Kataev, Evgeny Petrovich 1903-1942
See Petrov, Evgeny
See also CA 120

Kataphusin
See Ruskin, John

Katz, Steve 1935- . . . . **CLC 47**
See also CA 25-28R; CAAS 14; CANR 12;
DLBY 83

Kauffman, Janet 1945- . . . . **CLC 42**
See also CA 117; CANR 43; DLBY 86

Kaufman, Bob (Garnell)
1925-1986 . . . . **CLC 49**
See also BW; CA 41-44R; 118; CANR 22;
DLB 16, 41

Kaufman, George S. 1889-1961 . . . . . **CLC 38**
See also CA 108; 93-96; DLB 7

Kaufman, Sue . . . . **CLC 3, 8**
See also Barondess, Sue K(aufman)

Kavafis, Konstantinos Petrou 1863-1933
See Cavafy, C(onstantine) P(eter)
See also CA 104

Kavan, Anna 1901-1968 . . . . **CLC 5, 13**
See also CA 5-8R; CANR 6; MTCW

Kavanagh, Dan
See Barnes, Julian

Kavanagh, Patrick (Joseph)
1904-1967 . . . . **CLC 22**
See also CA 123; 25-28R; DLB 15, 20;
MTCW

Kawabata, Yasunari
1899-1972 . . . . **CLC 2, 5, 9, 18**
See also CA 93-96; 33-36R

Kaye, M(ary) M(argaret) 1909- . . . . **CLC 28**
See also CA 89-92; CANR 24; MTCW;
SATA 62

Kaye, Mollie
See Kaye, M(ary) M(argaret)

Kaye-Smith, Sheila 1887-1956 . . . . . **TCLC 20**
See also CA 118; DLB 36

Kaymor, Patrice Maguilene
See Senghor, Leopold Sedar

Kazan, Elia 1909- . . . . **CLC 6, 16, 63**
See also CA 21-24R; CANR 32

Kazantzakis, Nikos
1883(?)-1957 . . . . **TCLC 2, 5, 33**
See also CA 105; 132; MTCW

Kazin, Alfred 1915- . . . . **CLC 34, 38**
See also CA 1-4R; CAAS 7; CANR 1;
DLB 67

Keane, Mary Nesta (Skrine) 1904-
See Keane, Molly
See also CA 108; 114

Keane, Molly . . . . **CLC 31**
See also Keane, Mary Nesta (Skrine)

Keates, Jonathan 19(?)- . . . . **CLC 34**

Keaton, Buster 1895-1966 . . . . **CLC 20**

Keats, John
1795-1821 . . . **NCLC 8; DA; PC 1; WLC**
See also CDBLB 1789-1832; DLB 96, 110

Keene, Donald 1922- . . . . **CLC 34**
See also CA 1-4R; CANR 5

Keillor, Garrison . . . . **CLC 40**
See also Keillor, Gary (Edward)
See also AAYA 2; BEST 89:3; DLBY 87;
SATA 58

Keillor, Gary (Edward) 1942-
See Keillor, Garrison
See also CA 111; 117; CANR 36; MTCW

Keith, Michael
See Hubbard, L(afayette) Ron(ald)

Kell, Joseph
See Wilson, John (Anthony) Burgess

Keller, Gottfried 1819-1890 . . . . **NCLC 2**
See also DLB 129

Kellerman, Jonathan 1949- . . . . **CLC 44**
See also BEST 90:1; CA 106; CANR 29

Kelley, William Melvin 1937- . . . . . . **CLC 22**
See also BW; CA 77-80; CANR 27; DLB 33

Kellogg, Marjorie 1922- . . . . **CLC 2**
See also CA 81-84

Kellow, Kathleen
See Hibbert, Eleanor Alice Burford

Kelly, M(ilton) T(erry) 1947- . . . . . . **CLC 55**
See also CA 97-100; CANR 19, 43

Kelman, James 1946- . . . . **CLC 58**

Kemal, Yashar 1923- . . . . **CLC 14, 29**
See also CA 89-92

Kemble, Fanny 1809-1893 . . . . . . **NCLC 18**
See also DLB 32

Kemelman, Harry 1908- . . . . **CLC 2**
See also AITN 1; CA 9-12R; CANR 6;
DLB 28

Kempe, Margery 1373(?)-1440(?) . . . . . **LC 6**

Kempis, Thomas a 1380-1471 . . . . **LC 11**

Kendall, Henry 1839-1882 . . . . . . **NCLC 12**

Keneally, Thomas (Michael)
1935- . . . . . . **CLC 5, 8, 10, 14, 19, 27, 43**
See also CA 85-88; CANR 10; MTCW

Kennedy, Adrienne (Lita)
1931- . . . . **CLC 66; BLC 2**
See also BW; CA 103; CABS 3; CANR 26;
DLB 38

Kennedy, John Pendleton
1795-1870 . . . . **NCLC 2**
See also DLB 3

Kennedy, Joseph Charles 1929- . . . . . . **CLC 8**
See also Kennedy, X. J.
See also CA 1-4R; CANR 4, 30, 40;
SATA 14

Kennedy, William 1928- . . . **CLC 6, 28, 34, 53**
See also AAYA 1; CA 85-88; CANR 14,
31; DLBY 85; MTCW; SATA 57

Kennedy, X. J. . . . . **CLC 42**
See also Kennedy, Joseph Charles
See also CAAS 9; CLR 27; DLB 5

Kent, Kelvin
See Kuttner, Henry

Kenton, Maxwell
See Southern, Terry

Kenyon, Robert O.
See Kuttner, Henry

Kerouac, Jack . . . . . **CLC 1, 2, 3, 5, 14, 29, 61**
See also Kerouac, Jean-Louis Lebris de
See also CDALB 1941-1968; DLB 2, 16;
DLBD 3

Kerouac, Jean-Louis Lebris de 1922-1969
See Kerouac, Jack
See also AITN 1; CA 5-8R; 25-28R;
CANR 26; DA; MTCW; WLC

Kerr, Jean 1923- . . . . **CLC 22**
See also CA 5-8R; CANR 7

Kerr, M. E. . . . . **CLC 12, 35**
See also Meaker, Marijane (Agnes)
See also AAYA 2; CLR 29; SAAS 1

Kerr, Robert . . . . **CLC 55**

Kerrigan, (Thomas) Anthony
1918- . . . . **CLC 4, 6**
See also CA 49-52; CAAS 11; CANR 4

Kerry, Lois
See Duncan, Lois

Kesey, Ken (Elton)
1935- . . . . . . **CLC 1, 3, 6, 11, 46, 64; DA;
WLC**
See also CA 1-4R; CANR 22, 38;
CDALB 1968-1988; DLB 2, 16; MTCW;
SATA 66

Kesselring, Joseph (Otto)
1902-1967 . . . . **CLC 45**

Kessler, Jascha (Frederick) 1929- . . . . **CLC 4**
See also CA 17-20R; CANR 8

Kettelkamp, Larry (Dale) 1933- . . . . **CLC 12**
See also CA 29-32R; CANR 16; SAAS 3;
SATA 2

Keyber, Conny
See Fielding, Henry

Keyes, Daniel 1927- . . . . **CLC 80; DA**
See also CA 17-20R; CANR 10, 26;
SATA 37

Khayyam, Omar
1048-1131 . . . . **CMLC 11; PC 8**

Kherdian, David 1931- . . . . **CLC 6, 9**
See also CA 21-24R; CAAS 2; CANR 39;
CLR 24; JRDA; MAICYA; SATA 16, 74

Khlebnikov, Velimir . . . . **TCLC 20**
See also Khlebnikov, Viktor Vladimirovich

Khlebnikov, Viktor Vladimirovich 1885-1922
See Khlebnikov, Velimir
See also CA 117

Khodasevich, Vladislav (Felitsianovich)
1886-1939 . . . . **TCLC 15**
See also CA 115

Kielland, Alexander Lange
1849-1906 . . . . **TCLC 5**
See also CA 104

Kiely, Benedict 1919- . . . . **CLC 23, 43**
See also CA 1-4R; CANR 2; DLB 15

Kienzle, William X(avier) 1928- . . . . **CLC 25**
See also CA 93-96; CAAS 1; CANR 9, 31;
MTCW

Kierkegaard, Soren 1813-1855. . . . **NCLC 34**

Killens, John Oliver 1916-1987. . . . . **CLC 10**
See also BW; CA 77-80; 123; CAAS 2;
CANR 26; DLB 33

Killigrew, Anne 1660-1685. . . . . **LC 4**
See also DLB 131

Kim
See Simenon, Georges (Jacques Christian)

Kincaid, Jamaica
1949- . . . . **CLC 43, 68; BLC 2**
See also BW; CA 125

King, Francis (Henry) 1923- . . . . . **CLC 8, 53**
See also CA 1-4R; CANR 1, 33; DLB 15;
MTCW

King, Stephen (Edwin)
1947- . . . . **CLC 12, 26, 37, 61**
See also AAYA 1; BEST 90:1; CA 61-64;
CANR 1, 30; DLBY 80; JRDA; MTCW;
SATA 9, 55

King, Steve
See King, Stephen (Edwin)

Kingman, Lee. . . . . **CLC 17**
See also Natti, (Mary) Lee
See also SAAS 3; SATA 1, 67

Kingsley, Charles 1819-1875 . . . . . **NCLC 35**
See also DLB 21, 32; YABC 2

Kingsley, Sidney 1906- . . . . **CLC 44**
See also CA 85-88; DLB 7

Kingsolver, Barbara 1955- . . . . **CLC 55**
See also CA 129; 134

Kingston, Maxine (Ting Ting) Hong
1940- . . . . **CLC 12, 19, 58**
See also AAYA 8; CA 69-72; CANR 13,
38; DLBY 80; MTCW; SATA 53

Kinnell, Galway
1927- . . . . **CLC 1, 2, 3, 5, 13, 29**
See also CA 9-12R; CANR 10, 34; DLB 5;
DLBY 87; MTCW

Kinsella, Thomas 1928- . . . . **CLC 4, 19**
See also CA 17-20R; CANR 15; DLB 27;
MTCW

Kinsella, W(illiam) P(atrick)
1935- . . . . **CLC 27, 43**
See also AAYA 7; CA 97-100; CAAS 7;
CANR 21, 35; MTCW

Kipling, (Joseph) Rudyard
1865-1936 . . . . . . **TCLC 8, 17; DA; PC 3;
SSC 5; WLC**
See also CA 105; 120; CANR 33;
CDBLB 1890-1914; DLB 19, 34;
MAICYA; MTCW; YABC 2

Kirkup, James 1918- . . . . **CLC 1**
See also CA 1-4R; CAAS 4; CANR 2;
DLB 27; SATA 12

Kirkwood, James 1930(?)-1989 . . . . . . **CLC 9**
See also AITN 2; CA 1-4R; 128; CANR 6,
40

Kis, Danilo 1935-1989 . . . . **CLC 57**
See also CA 109; 118; 129; MTCW

Kivi, Aleksis 1834-1872 . . . . **NCLC 30**

Kizer, Carolyn (Ashley)
1925- . . . . **CLC 15, 39, 80**
See also CA 65-68; CAAS 5; CANR 24;
DLB 5

Klabund 1890-1928. . . . . **TCLC 44**
See also DLB 66

Klappert, Peter 1942- . . . . **CLC 57**
See also CA 33-36R; DLB 5

Klein, A(braham) M(oses)
1909-1972 . . . . **CLC 19**
See also CA 101; 37-40R; DLB 68

Klein, Norma 1938-1989 . . . . **CLC 30**
See also AAYA 2; CA 41-44R; 128;
CANR 15, 37; CLR 2, 19; JRDA;
MAICYA; SAAS 1; SATA 7, 57

Klein, T(heodore) E(ibon) D(onald)
1947- . . . . **CLC 34**
See also CA 119

Kleist, Heinrich von 1777-1811. . . . **NCLC 2**
See also DLB 90

Klima, Ivan 1931- . . . . **CLC 56**
See also CA 25-28R; CANR 17

Klimentov, Andrei Platonovich 1899-1951
See Platonov, Andrei
See also CA 108

Klinger, Friedrich Maximilian von
1752-1831 . . . . **NCLC 1**
See also DLB 94

Klopstock, Friedrich Gottlieb
1724-1803 . . . . **NCLC 11**
See also DLB 97

Knebel, Fletcher 1911-1993. . . . . **CLC 14**
See also AITN 1; CA 1-4R; 140; CAAS 3;
CANR 1, 36; SATA 36; SATA-Obit 75

Knickerbocker, Diedrich
See Irving, Washington

Knight, Etheridge
1931-1991 . . . . **CLC 40; BLC 2**
See also BW; CA 21-24R; 133; CANR 23;
DLB 41

Knight, Sarah Kemble 1666-1727 . . . . . **LC 7**
See also DLB 24

Knowles, John
1926- . . . . **CLC 1, 4, 10, 26; DA**
See also AAYA 10; CA 17-20R; CANR 40;
CDALB 1968-1988; DLB 6; MTCW;
SATA 8

Knox, Calvin M.
See Silverberg, Robert

Knye, Cassandra
See Disch, Thomas M(ichael)

Koch, C(hristopher) J(ohn) 1932- . . . **CLC 42**
See also CA 127

Koch, Christopher
See Koch, C(hristopher) J(ohn)

Koch, Kenneth 1925- . . . . **CLC 5, 8, 44**
See also CA 1-4R; CANR 6, 36; DLB 5;
SATA 65

Kochanowski, Jan 1530-1584. . . . . . . **LC 10**

Kock, Charles Paul de
1794-1871 . . . . **NCLC 16**

Koda Shigeyuki 1867-1947
See Rohan, Koda
See also CA 121

Koestler, Arthur
1905-1983 . . . . **CLC 1, 3, 6, 8, 15, 33**
See also CA 1-4R; 109; CANR 1, 33;
CDBLB 1945-1960; DLBY 83; MTCW

Kogawa, Joy Nozomi 1935- . . . . **CLC 78**
See also CA 101; CANR 19

Kohout, Pavel 1928- . . . . **CLC 13**
See also CA 45-48; CANR 3

Koizumi, Yakumo
See Hearn, (Patricio) Lafcadio (Tessima
Carlos)

Kolmar, Gertrud 1894-1943 . . . . **TCLC 40**

Konrad, George
See Konrad, Gyoergy

Konrad, Gyoergy 1933- . . . . . . **CLC 4, 10, 73**
See also CA 85-88

Konwicki, Tadeusz 1926- . . . . . **CLC 8, 28, 54**
See also CA 101; CAAS 9; CANR 39;
MTCW

Koontz, Dean R(ay) 1945- . . . . **CLC 78**
See also AAYA 9; BEST 89:3, 90:2;
CA 108; CANR 19, 36; MTCW

Kopit, Arthur (Lee) 1937- . . . . **CLC 1, 18, 33**
See also AITN 1; CA 81-84; CABS 3;
DLB 7; MTCW

Kops, Bernard 1926- . . . . **CLC 4**
See also CA 5-8R; DLB 13

Kornbluth, C(yril) M. 1923-1958. . . . **TCLC 8**
See also CA 105; DLB 8

Korolenko, V. G.
See Korolenko, Vladimir Galaktionovich

Korolenko, Vladimir
See Korolenko, Vladimir Galaktionovich

Korolenko, Vladimir G.
See Korolenko, Vladimir Galaktionovich

Korolenko, Vladimir Galaktionovich
1853-1921 . . . . TCLC 22
See also CA 121

Kosinski, Jerzy (Nikodem)
1933-1991 . . . . CLC 1, 2, 3, 6, 10, 15, 53,
70
See also CA 17-20R; 134; CANR 9; DLB 2;
DLBY 82; MTCW

Kostelanetz, Richard (Cory) 1940- . . CLC 28
See also CA 13-16R; CAAS 8; CANR 38

Kostrowitzki, Wilhelm Apollinaris de
1880-1918
See Apollinaire, Guillaume
See also CA 104

Kotlowitz, Robert 1924- . . . . CLC 4
See also CA 33-36R; CANR 36

Kotzebue, August (Friedrich Ferdinand) von
1761-1819 . . . . NCLC 25
See also DLB 94

Kotzwinkle, William 1938- . . . CLC 5, 14, 35
See also CA 45-48; CANR 3; CLR 6;
MAICYA; SATA 24, 70

Kozol, Jonathan 1936- . . . . CLC 17
See also CA 61-64; CANR 16

Kozoll, Michael 1940(?)- . . . . CLC 35

Kramer, Kathryn 19(?)- . . . . CLC 34

Kramer, Larry 1935- . . . . CLC 42
See also CA 124; 126

Krasicki, Ignacy 1735-1801 . . . . NCLC 8

Krasinski, Zygmunt 1812-1859 . . . . NCLC 4

Kraus, Karl 1874-1936 . . . . TCLC 5
See also CA 104; DLB 118

Kreve (Mickevicius), Vincas
1882-1954 . . . . TCLC 27

Kristeva, Julia 1941- . . . . CLC 77

Kristofferson, Kris 1936- . . . . CLC 26
See also CA 104

Krizanc, John 1956- . . . . CLC 57

Krleza, Miroslav 1893-1981 . . . . CLC 8
See also CA 97-100; 105

Kroetsch, Robert 1927- . . . . . . CLC 5, 23, 57
See also CA 17-20R; CANR 8, 38; DLB 53;
MTCW

Kroetz, Franz
See Kroetz, Franz Xaver

Kroetz, Franz Xaver 1946- . . . . CLC 41
See also CA 130

Kroker, Arthur 1945- . . . . CLC 77

Kropotkin, Peter (Aleksieevich)
1842-1921 . . . . TCLC 36
See also CA 119

Krotkov, Yuri 1917- . . . . CLC 19
See also CA 102

Krumb
See Crumb, R(obert)

Krumgold, Joseph (Quincy)
1908-1980 . . . . CLC 12
See also CA 9-12R; 101; CANR 7;
MAICYA; SATA 1, 23, 48

Krumwitz
See Crumb, R(obert)

Krutch, Joseph Wood 1893-1970. . . . CLC 24
See also CA 1-4R; 25-28R; CANR 4;
DLB 63

Krutzch, Gus
See Eliot, T(homas) S(tearns)

Krylov, Ivan Andreevich
1768(?)-1844 . . . . NCLC 1

Kubin, Alfred 1877-1959 . . . . TCLC 23
See also CA 112; DLB 81

Kubrick, Stanley 1928- . . . . CLC 16
See also CA 81-84; CANR 33; DLB 26

Kumin, Maxine (Winokur)
1925- . . . . CLC 5, 13, 28
See also AITN 2; CA 1-4R; CAAS 8;
CANR 1, 21; DLB 5; MTCW; SATA 12

Kundera, Milan
1929- . . . . CLC 4, 9, 19, 32, 68
See also AAYA 2; CA 85-88; CANR 19;
MTCW

Kunitz, Stanley (Jasspon)
1905- . . . . CLC 6, 11, 14
See also CA 41-44R; CANR 26; DLB 48;
MTCW

Kunze, Reiner 1933- . . . . CLC 10
See also CA 93-96; DLB 75

Kuprin, Aleksandr Ivanovich
1870-1938 . . . . TCLC 5
See also CA 104

Kureishi, Hanif 1954(?)- . . . . CLC 64
See also CA 139

Kurosawa, Akira 1910- . . . . CLC 16
See also CA 101

Kuttner, Henry 1915-1958 . . . . TCLC 10
See also CA 107; DLB 8

Kuzma, Greg 1944- . . . . CLC 7
See also CA 33-36R

Kuzmin, Mikhail 1872(?)-1936 . . . . TCLC 40

Kyd, Thomas 1558-1594 . . . . . . LC 22; DC 3
See also DLB 62

Kyprianos, Iossif
See Samarakis, Antonis

La Bruyere, Jean de 1645-1696 . . . . . . LC 17

Lacan, Jacques (Marie Emile)
1901-1981 . . . . CLC 75
See also CA 121; 104

Laclos, Pierre Ambroise Francois Choderlos
de 1741-1803 . . . . NCLC 4

La Colere, Francois
See Aragon, Louis

Lacolere, Francois
See Aragon, Louis

La Deshabilleuse
See Simenon, Georges (Jacques Christian)

Lady Gregory
See Gregory, Isabella Augusta (Persse)

Lady of Quality, A
See Bagnold, Enid

La Fayette, Marie (Madelaine Pioche de la
Vergne Comtes 1634-1693 . . . . . . LC 2

Lafayette, Rene
See Hubbard, L(afayette) Ron(ald)

Laforgue, Jules 1860-1887 . . . . NCLC 5

Lagerkvist, Paer (Fabian)
1891-1974 . . . . CLC 7, 10, 13, 54
See also Lagerkvist, Par
See also CA 85-88; 49-52; MTCW

Lagerkvist, Par
See Lagerkvist, Paer (Fabian)
See also SSC 12

Lagerloef, Selma (Ottiliana Lovisa)
1858-1940 . . . . TCLC 4, 36
See also Lagerlof, Selma (Ottiliana Lovisa)
See also CA 108; CLR 7; SATA 15

Lagerlof, Selma (Ottiliana Lovisa)
See Lagerloef, Selma (Ottiliana Lovisa)
See also CLR 7; SATA 15

La Guma, (Justin) Alex(ander)
1925-1985 . . . . CLC 19
See also BW; CA 49-52; 118; CANR 25;
DLB 117; MTCW

Laidlaw, A. K.
See Grieve, C(hristopher) M(urray)

Lainez, Manuel Mujica
See Mujica Lainez, Manuel
See also HW

Lamartine, Alphonse (Marie Louis Prat) de
1790-1869 . . . . NCLC 11

Lamb, Charles
1775-1834 . . . . NCLC 10; DA; WLC
See also CDBLB 1789-1832; DLB 93, 107;
SATA 17

Lamb, Lady Caroline 1785-1828 . . NCLC 38
See also DLB 116

Lamming, George (William)
1927- . . . . CLC 2, 4, 66; BLC 2
See also BW; CA 85-88; CANR 26;
DLB 125; MTCW

L'Amour, Louis (Dearborn)
1908-1988 . . . . CLC 25, 55
See also AITN 2; BEST 89:2; CA 1-4R;
125; CANR 3, 25, 40; DLBY 80; MTCW

Lampedusa, Giuseppe (Tomasi) di . . . TCLC 13
See also Tomasi di Lampedusa, Giuseppe

Lampman, Archibald 1861-1899 . . NCLC 25
See also DLB 92

Lancaster, Bruce 1896-1963 . . . . CLC 36
See also CA 9-10; CAP 1; SATA 9

Landau, Mark Alexandrovich
See Aldanov, Mark (Alexandrovich)

Landau-Aldanov, Mark Alexandrovich
See Aldanov, Mark (Alexandrovich)

Landis, John 1950- . . . . CLC 26
See also CA 112; 122

Landolfi, Tommaso 1908-1979 . . . CLC 11, 49
See also CA 127; 117

Landon, Letitia Elizabeth
1802-1838 . . . . NCLC 15
See also DLB 96

Landor, Walter Savage
1775-1864 . . . . NCLC 14
See also DLB 93, 107

Landwirth, Heinz 1927-
See Lind, Jakov
See also CA 9-12R; CANR 7

Lane, Patrick 1939- . . . . CLC 25
See also CA 97-100; DLB 53

Loy, Mina .... **CLC 28**
See also Lowry, Mina Gertrude
See also DLB 4, 54

Loyson-Bridet
See Schwob, (Mayer Andre) Marcel

Lucas, Craig 1951- .... **CLC 64**
See also CA 137

Lucas, George 1944- .... **CLC 16**
See also AAYA 1; CA 77-80; CANR 30;
SATA 56

Lucas, Hans
See Godard, Jean-Luc

Lucas, Victoria
See Plath, Sylvia

Ludlam, Charles 1943-1987 ..... **CLC 46, 50**
See also CA 85-88; 122

Ludlum, Robert 1927- .... **CLC 22, 43**
See also AAYA 10; BEST 89:1, 90:3;
CA 33-36R; CANR 25, 41; DLBY 82;
MTCW

Ludwig, Ken. .... **CLC 60**

Ludwig, Otto 1813-1865. .... **NCLC 4**
See also DLB 129

Lugones, Leopoldo 1874-1938 ..... **TCLC 15**
See also CA 116; 131; HW

Lu Hsun 1881-1936 .... **TCLC 3**

Lukacs, George .... **CLC 24**
See also Lukacs, Gyorgy (Szegeny von)

Lukacs, Gyorgy (Szegeny von) 1885-1971
See Lukacs, George
See also CA 101; 29-32R

Luke, Peter (Ambrose Cyprian)
1919- .... **CLC 38**
See also CA 81-84; DLB 13

Lunar, Dennis
See Mungo, Raymond

Lurie, Alison 1926- .... **CLC 4, 5, 18, 39**
See also CA 1-4R; CANR 2, 17; DLB 2;
MTCW; SATA 46

Lustig, Arnost 1926- .... **CLC 56**
See also AAYA 3; CA 69-72; SATA 56

Luther, Martin 1483-1546 .... **LC 9**

Luzi, Mario 1914- .... **CLC 13**
See also CA 61-64; CANR 9; DLB 128

Lynch, B. Suarez
See Bioy Casares, Adolfo; Borges, Jorge
Luis

Lynch, David (K.) 1946- .... **CLC 66**
See also CA 124; 129

Lynch, James
See Andreyev, Leonid (Nikolaevich)

Lynch Davis, B.
See Bioy Casares, Adolfo; Borges, Jorge
Luis

Lyndsay, SirDavid 1490-1555 .... **LC 20**

Lynn, Kenneth S(chuyler) 1923- .... **CLC 50**
See also CA 1-4R; CANR 3, 27

Lynx
See West, Rebecca

Lyons, Marcus
See Blish, James (Benjamin)

Lyre, Pinchbeck
See Sassoon, Siegfried (Lorraine)

Lytle, Andrew (Nelson) 1902- ...... **CLC 22**
See also CA 9-12R; DLB 6

Lyttelton, George 1709-1773 .... **LC 10**

Maas, Peter 1929- .... **CLC 29**
See also CA 93-96

Macaulay, Rose 1881-1958 ..... **TCLC 7, 44**
See also CA 104; DLB 36

Macaulay, Thomas Babington
1800-1859 .... **NCLC 42**
See also CDBLB 1832-1890; DLB 32, 55

MacBeth, George (Mann)
1932-1992 .... **CLC 2, 5, 9**
See also CA 25-28R; 136; DLB 40; MTCW;
SATA 4; SATA-Obit 70

MacCaig, Norman (Alexander)
1910- .... **CLC 36**
See also CA 9-12R; CANR 3, 34; DLB 27

MacCarthy, (Sir Charles Otto) Desmond
1877-1952 .... **TCLC 36**

MacDiarmid, Hugh..... **CLC 2, 4, 11, 19, 63**
See also Grieve, C(hristopher) M(urray)
See also CDBLB 1945-1960; DLB 20

MacDonald, Anson
See Heinlein, Robert A(nson)

Macdonald, Cynthia 1928- ...... **CLC 13, 19**
See also CA 49-52; CANR 4; DLB 105

MacDonald, George 1824-1905 ..... **TCLC 9**
See also CA 106; 137; DLB 18; MAICYA;
SATA 33

Macdonald, John
See Millar, Kenneth

MacDonald, John D(ann)
1916-1986 .... **CLC 3, 27, 44**
See also CA 1-4R; 121; CANR 1, 19;
DLB 8; DLBY 86; MTCW

Macdonald, John Ross
See Millar, Kenneth

Macdonald, Ross..... **CLC 1, 2, 3, 14, 34, 41**
See also Millar, Kenneth
See also DLBD 6

MacDougal, John
See Blish, James (Benjamin)

MacEwen, Gwendolyn (Margaret)
1941-1987 .... **CLC 13, 55**
See also CA 9-12R; 124; CANR 7, 22;
DLB 53; SATA 50, 55

Machado (y Ruiz), Antonio
1875-1939 .... **TCLC 3**
See also CA 104; DLB 108

Machado de Assis, Joaquim Maria
1839-1908 .... **TCLC 10; BLC 2**
See also CA 107

Machen, Arthur................... **TCLC 4**
See also Jones, Arthur Llewellyn
See also DLB 36

Machiavelli, Niccolo 1469-1527 .. **LC 8; DA**

MacInnes, Colin 1914-1976 ...... **CLC 4, 23**
See also CA 69-72; 65-68; CANR 21;
DLB 14; MTCW

MacInnes, Helen (Clark)
1907-1985 .... **CLC 27, 39**
See also CA 1-4R; 117; CANR 1, 28;
DLB 87; MTCW; SATA 22, 44

Mackay, Mary 1855-1924
See Corelli, Marie
See also CA 118

Mackenzie, Compton (Edward Montague)
1883-1972 .... **CLC 18**
See also CA 21-22; 37-40R; CAP 2;
DLB 34, 100

Mackenzie, Henry 1745-1831 .... **NCLC 41**
See also DLB 39

Mackintosh, Elizabeth 1896(?)-1952
See Tey, Josephine
See also CA 110

MacLaren, James
See Grieve, C(hristopher) M(urray)

Mac Laverty, Bernard 1942- .... **CLC 31**
See also CA 116; 118; CANR 43

MacLean, Alistair (Stuart)
1922-1987 .... **CLC 3, 13, 50, 63**
See also CA 57-60; 121; CANR 28; MTCW;
SATA 23, 50

Maclean, Norman (Fitzroy) 1902-1990
See also CA 102; 132; SSC 13

MacLeish, Archibald
1892-1982 .... **CLC 3, 8, 14, 68**
See also CA 9-12R; 106; CANR 33; DLB 4,
7, 45; DLBY 82; MTCW

MacLennan, (John) Hugh
1907-1990 .... **CLC 2, 14**
See also CA 5-8R; 142; CANR 33; DLB 68;
MTCW

MacLeod, Alistair 1936- .... **CLC 56**
See also CA 123; DLB 60

MacNeice, (Frederick) Louis
1907-1963 .... **CLC 1, 4, 10, 53**
See also CA 85-88; DLB 10, 20; MTCW

MacNeill, Dand
See Fraser, George MacDonald

Macpherson, (Jean) Jay 1931- ...... **CLC 14**
See also CA 5-8R; DLB 53

MacShane, Frank 1927- .... **CLC 39**
See also CA 9-12R; CANR 3, 33; DLB 111

Macumber, Mari
See Sandoz, Mari(e Susette)

Madach, Imre 1823-1864 .... **NCLC 19**

Madden, (Jerry) David 1933- .... **CLC 5, 15**
See also CA 1-4R; CAAS 3; CANR 4;
DLB 6; MTCW

Maddern, Al(an)
See Ellison, Harlan

Madhubuti, Haki R.
1942- .... **CLC 6, 73; BLC 2; PC 5**
See also Lee, Don L.
See also BW; CA 73-76; CANR 24; DLB 5,
41; DLBD 8

Madow, Pauline (Reichberg) .... **CLC 1**
See also CA 9-12R

Maepenn, Hugh
See Kuttner, Henry

Maepenn, K. H.
See Kuttner, Henry

Maeterlinck, Maurice 1862-1949 ... **TCLC 3**
See also CA 104; 136; SATA 66

Maginn, William 1794-1842 .... **NCLC 8**
See also DLB 110

Mahapatra, Jayanta 1928- .... **CLC 33**
See also CA 73-76; CAAS 9; CANR 15, 33

Mahfouz, Naguib (Abdel Aziz Al-Sabilgi)
1911(?)-
See Mahfuz, Najib
See also BEST 89:2; CA 128; MTCW

Mahfuz, Najib .... **CLC 52, 55**
See also Mahfouz, Naguib (Abdel Aziz
Al-Sabilgi)
See also DLBY 88

Mahon, Derek 1941- .... **CLC 27**
See also CA 113; 128; DLB 40

Mailer, Norman
1923- ...... **CLC 1, 2, 3, 4, 5, 8, 11, 14,
28, 39, 74; DA**
See also AITN 2; CA 9-12R; CABS 1;
CANR 28; CDALB 1968-1988; DLB 2,
16, 28; DLBD 3; DLBY 80, 83; MTCW

Maillet, Antonine 1929- .... **CLC 54**
See also CA 115; 120; DLB 60

Mais, Roger 1905-1955 .... **TCLC 8**
See also BW; CA 105; 124; DLB 125;
MTCW

Maitland, Sara (Louise) 1950- ..... **CLC 49**
See also CA 69-72; CANR 13

Major, Clarence
1936- .... **CLC 3, 19, 48; BLC 2**
See also BW; CA 21-24R; CAAS 6;
CANR 13, 25; DLB 33

Major, Kevin (Gerald) 1949- .... **CLC 26**
See also CA 97-100; CANR 21, 38;
CLR 11; DLB 60; JRDA; MAICYA;
SATA 32

Maki, James
See Ozu, Yasujiro

Malabaila, Damiano
See Levi, Primo

Malamud, Bernard
1914-1986 ..... **CLC 1, 2; 3, 5, 8, 9, 11,
18, 27, 44, 78; DA; WLC**
See also CA 5-8R; 118; CABS 1; CANR 28;
CDALB 1941-1968; DLB 2, 28;
DLBY 80, 86; MTCW

Malaparte, Curzio 1898-1957 ..... **TCLC 52**

Malcolm, Dan
See Silverberg, Robert

Malherbe, Francois de 1555-1628 ..... **LC 5**

Mallarme, Stephane
1842-1898 .... **NCLC 4, 41; PC 4**

Mallet-Joris, Francoise 1930- ...... **CLC 11**
See also CA 65-68; CANR 17; DLB 83

Malley, Ern
See McAuley, James Phillip

Mallowan, Agatha Christie
See Christie, Agatha (Mary Clarissa)

Maloff, Saul 1922- .... **CLC 5**
See also CA 33-36R

Malone, Louis
See MacNeice, (Frederick) Louis

Malone, Michael (Christopher)
1942- .... **CLC 43**
See also CA 77-80; CANR 14, 32

Malory, (Sir) Thomas
1410(?)-1471(?) .... **LC 11; DA**
See also CDBLB Before 1660; SATA 33, 59

Malouf, (George Joseph) David
1934- .... **CLC 28**
See also CA 124

Malraux, (Georges-)Andre
1901-1976 ...... **CLC 1, 4, 9, 13, 15, 57**
See also CA 21-22; 69-72; CANR 34;
CAP 2; DLB 72; MTCW

Malzberg, Barry N(athaniel) 1939- ... **CLC 7**
See also CA 61-64; CAAS 4; CANR 16;
DLB 8

Mamet, David (Alan)
1947- .... **CLC 9, 15, 34, 46; DC 4**
See also AAYA 3; CA 81-84; CABS 3;
CANR 15, 41; DLB 7; MTCW

Mamoulian, Rouben (Zachary)
1897-1987 .... **CLC 16**
See also CA 25-28R; 124

Mandelstam, Osip (Emilievich)
1891(?)-1938(?) .... **TCLC 2, 6**
See also CA 104

Mander, (Mary) Jane 1877-1949... **TCLC 31**

Mandiargues, Andre Pieyre de ...... **CLC 41**
See also Pieyre de Mandiargues, Andre
See also DLB 83

Mandrake, Ethel Belle
See Thurman, Wallace (Henry)

Mangan, James Clarence
1803-1849 .... **NCLC 27**

Maniere, J.-E.
See Giraudoux, (Hippolyte) Jean

Manley, (Mary) Delariviere
1672(?)-1724 .... **LC 1**
See also DLB 39, 80

Mann, Abel
See Creasey, John

Mann, (Luiz) Heinrich 1871-1950... **TCLC 9**
See also CA 106; DLB 66

Mann, (Paul) Thomas
1875-1955 .... **TCLC 2, 8, 14, 21, 35, 44;
DA; SSC 5; WLC**
See also CA 104; 128; DLB 66; MTCW

Manning, David
See Faust, Frederick (Schiller)

Manning, Frederic 1887(?)-1935 ... **TCLC 25**
See also CA 124

Manning, Olivia 1915-1980 ...... **CLC 5, 19**
See also CA 5-8R; 101; CANR 29; MTCW

Mano, D. Keith 1942- .... **CLC 2, 10**
See also CA 25-28R; CAAS 6; CANR 26;
DLB 6

Mansfield, Katherine
.... **TCLC 2, 8, 39; SSC 9; WLC**
See also Beauchamp, Kathleen Mansfield

Manso, Peter 1940- .... **CLC 39**
See also CA 29-32R

Mantecon, Juan Jimenez
See Jimenez (Mantecon), Juan Ramon

Manton, Peter
See Creasey, John

Man Without a Spleen, A
See Chekhov, Anton (Pavlovich)

Manzoni, Alessandro 1785-1873 .. **NCLC 29**

Mapu, Abraham (ben Jekutiel)
1808-1867 .... **NCLC 18**

Mara, Sally
See Queneau, Raymond

Marat, Jean Paul 1743-1793 .... **LC 10**

Marcel, Gabriel Honore
1889-1973 .... **CLC 15**
See also CA 102; 45-48; MTCW

Marchbanks, Samuel
See Davies, (William) Robertson

Marchi, Giacomo
See Bassani, Giorgio

Margulies, Donald .... **CLC 76**

Marie de France c. 12th cent. -.... **CMLC 8**

Marie de l'Incarnation 1599-1672.... **LC 10**

Mariner, Scott
See Pohl, Frederik

Marinetti, Filippo Tommaso
1876-1944 .... **TCLC 10**
See also CA 107; DLB 114

Marivaux, Pierre Carlet de Chamblain de
1688-1763 .... **LC 4**

Markandaya, Kamala .... **CLC 8, 38**
See also Taylor, Kamala (Purnaiya)

Markfield, Wallace 1926- .... **CLC 8**
See also CA 69-72; CAAS 3; DLB 2, 28

Markham, Edwin 1852-1940 ..... **TCLC 47**
See also DLB 54

Markham, Robert
See Amis, Kingsley (William)

Marks, J
See Highwater, Jamake (Mamake)

Marks-Highwater, J
See Highwater, Jamake (Mamake)

Markson, David M(errill) 1927- .... **CLC 67**
See also CA 49-52; CANR 1

Marley, Bob .... **CLC 17**
See also Marley, Robert Nesta

Marley, Robert Nesta 1945-1981
See Marley, Bob
See also CA 107; 103

Marlowe, Christopher
1564-1593 ..... **LC 22; DA; DC 1; WLC**
See also CDBLB Before 1660; DLB 62

Marmontel, Jean-Francois
1723-1799 .... **LC 2**

Marquand, John P(hillips)
1893-1960 .... **CLC 2, 10**
See also CA 85-88; DLB 9, 102

Marquez, Gabriel (Jose) Garcia...... **CLC 68**
See also Garcia Marquez, Gabriel (Jose)

Marquis, Don(ald Robert Perry)
1878-1937 .... **TCLC 7**
See also CA 104; DLB 11, 25

Marric, J. J.
See Creasey, John

Marrow, Bernard
See Moore, Brian

Marryat, Frederick 1792-1848 .... **NCLC 3**
See also DLB 21

Marsden, James
See Creasey, John

McCarthy, Mary (Therese)
1912-1989 ... **CLC 1, 3, 5, 14, 24, 39, 59**
See also CA 5-8R; 129; CANR 16; DLB 2;
DLBY 81; MTCW

McCartney, (James) Paul
1942- .... **CLC 12, 35**

McCauley, Stephen (D.) 1955- ..... **CLC 50**
See also CA 141

McClure, Michael (Thomas)
1932- .... **CLC 6, 10**
See also CA 21-24R; CANR 17; DLB 16

McCorkle, Jill (Collins) 1958-...... **CLC 51**
See also CA 121; DLBY 87

McCourt, James 1941-............. **CLC 5**
See also CA 57-60

McCoy, Horace (Stanley)
1897-1955 .... **TCLC 28**
See also CA 108; DLB 9

McCrae, John 1872-1918......... **TCLC 12**
See also CA 109; DLB 92

McCreigh, James
See Pohl, Frederik

McCullers, (Lula) Carson (Smith)
1917-1967 .... **CLC 1, 4, 10, 12, 48; DA;
SSC 9; WLC**
See also CA 5-8R; 25-28R; CABS 1, 3;
CANR 18; CDALB 1941-1968; DLB 2, 7;
MTCW; SATA 27

McCulloch, John Tyler
See Burroughs, Edgar Rice

McCullough, Colleen 1938(?)-...... **CLC 27**
See also CA 81-84; CANR 17; MTCW

McElroy, Joseph 1930- .... **CLC 5, 47**
See also CA 17-20R

McEwan, Ian (Russell) 1948- ... **CLC 13, 66**
See also BEST 90:4; CA 61-64; CANR 14,
41; DLB 14; MTCW

McFadden, David 1940-........... **CLC 48**
See also CA 104; DLB 60

McFarland, Dennis 1950- .... **CLC 65**

McGahern, John 1934-........ **CLC 5, 9, 48**
See also CA 17-20R; CANR 29; DLB 14;
MTCW

McGinley, Patrick (Anthony)
1937- .... **CLC 41**
See also CA 120; 127

McGinley, Phyllis 1905-1978 ...... **CLC 14**
See also CA 9-12R; 77-80; CANR 19;
DLB 11, 48; SATA 2, 24, 44

McGinniss, Joe 1942-............. **CLC 32**
See also AITN 2; BEST 89:2; CA 25-28R;
CANR 26

McGivern, Maureen Daly
See Daly, Maureen

McGrath, Patrick 1950-........... **CLC 55**
See also CA 136

McGrath, Thomas (Matthew)
1916-1990 .... **CLC 28, 59**
See also CA 9-12R; 132; CANR 6, 33;
MTCW; SATA 41; SATA-Obit 66

McGuane, Thomas (Francis III)
1939- .... **CLC 3, 7, 18, 45**
See also AITN 2; CA 49-52; CANR 5, 24;
DLB 2; DLBY 80; MTCW

McGuckian, Medbh 1950-........ **CLC 48**
See also DLB 40

McHale, Tom 1942(?)-1982...... **CLC 3, 5**
See also AITN 1; CA 77-80; 106

McIlvanney, William 1936-........ **CLC 42**
See also CA 25-28R; DLB 14

McIlwraith, Maureen Mollie Hunter
See Hunter, Mollie
See also SATA 2

McInerney, Jay 1955-............ **CLC 34**
See also CA 116; 123

McIntyre, Vonda N(eel) 1948- ..... **CLC 18**
See also CA 81-84; CANR 17, 34; MTCW

McKay, Claude ... **TCLC 7, 41; BLC 3; PC 2**
See also McKay, Festus Claudius
See also DLB 4, 45, 51, 117

McKay, Festus Claudius 1889-1948
See McKay, Claude
See also BW; CA 104; 124; DA; MTCW;
WLC

McKuen, Rod 1933-............. **CLC 1, 3**
See also AITN 1; CA 41-44R; CANR 40

McLoughlin, R. B.
See Mencken, H(enry) L(ouis)

McLuhan, (Herbert) Marshall
1911-1980 .... **CLC 37**
See also CA 9-12R; 102; CANR 12, 34;
DLB 88; MTCW

McMillan, Terry (L.) 1951-..... **CLC 50, 61**
See also CA 140

McMurtry, Larry (Jeff)
1936- .... **CLC 2, 3, 7, 11, 27, 44**
See also AITN 2; BEST 89:2; CA 5-8R;
CANR 19, 43; CDALB 1968-1988;
DLB 2; DLBY 80, 87; MTCW

McNally, Terrence 1939-...... **CLC 4, 7, 41**
See also CA 45-48; CANR 2; DLB 7

McNamer, Deirdre 1950-.......... **CLC 70**

McNeile, Herman Cyril 1888-1937
See Sapper
See also DLB 77

McPhee, John (Angus) 1931- ...... **CLC 36**
See also BEST 90:1; CA 65-68; CANR 20;
MTCW

McPherson, James Alan
1943- .... **CLC 19, 77**
See also BW; CA 25-28R; CAAS 17;
CANR 24; DLB 38; MTCW

McPherson, William (Alexander)
1933- .... **CLC 34**
See also CA 69-72; CANR 28

McSweeney, Kerry .... **CLC 34**

Mead, Margaret 1901-1978........ **CLC 37**
See also AITN 1; CA 1-4R; 81-84;
CANR 4; MTCW; SATA 20

Meaker, Marijane (Agnes) 1927-
See Kerr, M. E.
See also CA 107; CANR 37; JRDA;
MAICYA; MTCW; SATA 20, 61

Medoff, Mark (Howard) 1940- ... **CLC 6, 23**
See also AITN 1; CA 53-56; CANR 5;
DLB 7

Meged, Aharon
See Megged, Aharon

Meged, Aron
See Megged, Aharon

Megged, Aharon 1920-............. **CLC 9**
See also CA 49-52; CAAS 13; CANR 1

Mehta, Ved (Parkash) 1934-....... **CLC 37**
See also CA 1-4R; CANR 2, 23; MTCW

Melanter
See Blackmore, R(ichard) D(oddridge)

Melikow, Loris
See Hofmannsthal, Hugo von

Melmoth, Sebastian
See Wilde, Oscar (Fingal O'Flahertie Wills)

Meltzer, Milton 1915-............. **CLC 26**
See also AAYA 8; CA 13-16R; CANR 38;
CLR 13; DLB 61; JRDA; MAICYA;
SAAS 1; SATA 1, 50

Melville, Herman
1819-1891 .... **NCLC 3, 12, 29; DA;
SSC 1; WLC**
See also CDALB 1640-1865; DLB 3, 74;
SATA 59

Menander
c. 342B.C.-c. 292B.C.... **CMLC 9; DC 3**

Mencken, H(enry) L(ouis)
1880-1956 .... **TCLC 13**
See also CA 105; 125; CDALB 1917-1929;
DLB 11, 29, 63; MTCW

Mercer, David 1928-1980.......... **CLC 5**
See also CA 9-12R; 102; CANR 23;
DLB 13; MTCW

Merchant, Paul
See Ellison, Harlan

Meredith, George 1828-1909... **TCLC 17, 43**
See also CA 117; CDBLB 1832-1890;
DLB 18, 35, 57

Meredith, William (Morris)
1919- .... **CLC 4, 13, 22, 55**
See also CA 9-12R; CAAS 14; CANR 6, 40;
DLB 5

Merezhkovsky, Dmitry Sergeyevich
1865-1941 .... **TCLC 29**

Merimee, Prosper
1803-1870 .... **NCLC 6; SSC 7**
See also DLB 119

Merkin, Daphne 1954-............ **CLC 44**
See also CA 123

Merlin, Arthur
See Blish, James (Benjamin)

Merrill, James (Ingram)
1926- ...... **CLC 2, 3, 6, 8, 13, 18, 34**
See also CA 13-16R; CANR 10; DLB 5;
DLBY 85; MTCW

Merriman, Alex
See Silverberg, Robert

Merritt, E. B.
See Waddington, Miriam

Merton, Thomas
1915-1968 .... **CLC 1, 3, 11, 34**
See also CA 5-8R; 25-28R; CANR 22;
DLB 48; DLBY 81; MTCW

Merwin, W(illiam) S(tanley)
1927-...... **CLC 1, 2, 3, 5, 8, 13, 18, 45**
See also CA 13-16R; CANR 15; DLB 5;
MTCW

Montale, Eugenio 1896-1981... **CLC 7, 9, 18**
See also CA 17-20R; 104; CANR 30;
DLB 114; MTCW

Montesquieu, Charles-Louis de Secondat
1689-1755 .... **LC 7**

Montgomery, (Robert) Bruce 1921-1978
See Crispin, Edmund
See also CA 104

Montgomery, L(ucy) M(aud)
1874-1942 .... **TCLC 51**
See also CA 108; 137; CLR 8; DLB 92;
JRDA; MAICYA; YABC 1

Montgomery, Marion H., Jr. 1925-.. **CLC 7**
See also AITN 1; CA 1-4R; CANR 3;
DLB 6

Montgomery, Max
See Davenport, Guy (Mattison, Jr.)

Montherlant, Henry (Milon) de
1896-1972 .... **CLC 8, 19**
See also CA 85-88; 37-40R; DLB 72;
MTCW

Monty Python .... **CLC 21**
See also Chapman, Graham; Cleese, John
(Marwood); Gilliam, Terry (Vance); Idle,
Eric; Jones, Terence Graham Parry; Palin,
Michael (Edward)
See also AAYA 7

Moodie, Susanna (Strickland)
1803-1885 .... **NCLC 14**
See also DLB 99

Mooney, Edward 1951- .... **CLC 25**
See also CA 130

Mooney, Ted
See Mooney, Edward

Moorcock, Michael (John)
1939- .... **CLC 5, 27, 58**
See also CA 45-48; CAAS 5; CANR 2, 17,
38; DLB 14; MTCW

Moore, Brian
1921- .... **CLC 1, 3, 5, 7, 8, 19, 32**
See also CA 1-4R; CANR 1, 25, 42; MTCW

Moore, Edward
See Muir, Edwin

Moore, George Augustus
1852-1933 .... **TCLC 7**
See also CA 104; DLB 10, 18, 57, 135

Moore, Lorrie .... **CLC 39, 45, 68**
See also Moore, Marie Lorena

Moore, Marianne (Craig)
1887-1972 .... **CLC 1, 2, 4, 8, 10, 13, 19,
47; DA; PC 4**
See also CA 1-4R; 33-36R; CANR 3;
CDALB 1929-1941; DLB 45; DLBD 7;
MTCW; SATA 20

Moore, Marie Lorena 1957-
See Moore, Lorrie
See also CA 116; CANR 39

Moore, Thomas 1779-1852........ **NCLC 6**
See also DLB 96

Morand, Paul 1888-1976 .... **CLC 41**
See also CA 69-72; DLB 65

Morante, Elsa 1918-1985....... **CLC 8, 47**
See also CA 85-88; 117; CANR 35; MTCW

Moravia, Alberto...... **CLC 2, 7, 11, 27, 46**
See also Pincherle, Alberto

More, Hannah 1745-1833 .... **NCLC 27**
See also DLB 107, 109, 116

More, Henry 1614-1687............ **LC 9**
See also DLB 126

More, Sir Thomas 1478-1535 ...... **LC 10**

Moreas, Jean.................... **TCLC 18**
See also Papadiamantopoulos, Johannes

Morgan, Berry 1919-.............. **CLC 6**
See also CA 49-52; DLB 6

Morgan, Claire
See Highsmith, (Mary) Patricia

Morgan, Edwin (George) 1920-..... **CLC 31**
See also CA 5-8R; CANR 3, 43; DLB 27

Morgan, (George) Frederick
1922- .... **CLC 23**
See also CA 17-20R; CANR 21

Morgan, Harriet
See Mencken, H(enry) L(ouis)

Morgan, Jane
See Cooper, James Fenimore

Morgan, Janet 1945- .... **CLC 39**
See also CA 65-68

Morgan, Lady 1776(?)-1859...... **NCLC 29**
See also DLB 116

Morgan, Robin 1941-............. **CLC 2**
See also CA 69-72; CANR 29; MTCW

Morgan, Scott
See Kuttner, Henry

Morgan, Seth 1949(?)-1990 .... **CLC 65**
See also CA 132

Morgenstern, Christian
1871-1914 .... **TCLC 8**
See also CA 105

Morgenstern, S.
See Goldman, William (W.)

Moricz, Zsigmond 1879-1942 ..... **TCLC 33**

Morike, Eduard (Friedrich)
1804-1875 .... **NCLC 10**
See also DLB 133

Mori Ogai .... **TCLC 14**
See also Mori Rintaro

Mori Rintaro 1862-1922
See Mori Ogai
See also CA 110

Moritz, Karl Philipp 1756-1793 ...... **LC 2**
See also DLB 94

Morland, Peter Henry
See Faust, Frederick (Schiller)

Morren, Theophil
See Hofmannsthal, Hugo von

Morris, Bill 1952-............... **CLC 76**

Morris, Julian
See West, Morris L(anglo)

Morris, Steveland Judkins 1950(?)-
See Wonder, Stevie
See also CA 111

Morris, William 1834-1896 .... **NCLC 4**
See also CDBLB 1832-1890; DLB 18, 35, 57

Morris, Wright 1910-... **CLC 1, 3, 7, 18, 37**
See also CA 9-12R; CANR 21; DLB 2;
DLBY 81; MTCW

Morrison, Chloe Anthony Wofford
See Morrison, Toni

Morrison, James Douglas 1943-1971
See Morrison, Jim
See also CA 73-76; CANR 40

Morrison, Jim .... **CLC 17**
See also Morrison, James Douglas

Morrison, Toni
1931- .... **CLC 4, 10, 22, 55; BLC 3; DA**
See also AAYA 1; BW; CA 29-32R;
CANR 27, 42; CDALB 1968-1988;
DLB 6, 33; DLBY 81; MTCW; SATA 57

Morrison, Van 1945- .... **CLC 21**
See also CA 116

Mortimer, John (Clifford)
1923- .... **CLC 28, 43**
See also CA 13-16R; CANR 21;
CDBLB 1960 to Present; DLB 13;
MTCW

Mortimer, Penelope (Ruth) 1918-.... **CLC 5**
See also CA 57-60

Morton, Anthony
See Creasey, John

Mosher, Howard Frank 1943-...... **CLC 62**
See also CA 139

Mosley, Nicholas 1923-........ **CLC 43, 70**
See also CA 69-72; CANR 41; DLB 14

Moss, Howard
1922-1987 .... **CLC 7, 14, 45, 50**
See also CA 1-4R; 123; CANR 1; DLB 5

Mossgiel, Rab
See Burns, Robert

Motion, Andrew 1952- .... **CLC 47**
See also DLB 40

Motley, Willard (Francis)
1912-1965 .... **CLC 18**
See also BW; CA 117; 106; DLB 76

Mott, Michael (Charles Alston)
1930- .... **CLC 15, 34**
See also CA 5-8R; CAAS 7; CANR 7, 29

Mowat, Farley (McGill) 1921- ..... **CLC 26**
See also AAYA 1; CA 1-4R; CANR 4, 24,
42; CLR 20; DLB 68; JRDA; MAICYA;
MTCW; SATA 3, 55

Moyers, Bill 1934-............... **CLC 74**
See also AITN 2; CA 61-64; CANR 31

Mphahlele, Es'kia
See Mphahlele, Ezekiel
See also DLB 125

Mphahlele, Ezekiel 1919-... **CLC 25; BLC 3**
See also Mphahlele, Es'kia
See also BW; CA 81-84; CANR 26

Mqhayi, S(amuel) E(dward) K(rune Loliwe)
1875-1945 .... **TCLC 25; BLC 3**

Mr. Martin
See Burroughs, William S(eward)

Mrozek, Slawomir 1930-........ **CLC 3, 13**
See also CA 13-16R; CAAS 10; CANR 29;
MTCW

Mrs. Belloc-Lowndes
See Lowndes, Marie Adelaide (Belloc)

Mtwa, Percy (?)-................ **CLC 47**

Mueller, Lisel 1924-........... **CLC 13, 51**
See also CA 93-96; DLB 105

Muir, Edwin 1887-1959 .... **TCLC 2**
See also CA 104; DLB 20, 100

Muir, John 1838-1914 . . . . TCLC 28

Mujica Lainez, Manuel
    1910-1984 . . . . CLC 31
    See also Lainez, Manuel Mujica
    See also CA 81-84; 112; CANR 32; HW

Mukherjee, Bharati 1940- . . . . CLC 53
    See also BEST 89:2; CA 107; DLB 60;
    MTCW

Muldoon, Paul 1951- . . . . CLC 32, 72
    See also CA 113; 129; DLB 40

Mulisch, Harry 1927-. . . . . CLC 42
    See also CA 9-12R; CANR 6, 26

Mull, Martin 1943-. . . . . CLC 17
    See also CA 105

Mulock, Dinah Maria
    See Craik, Dinah Maria (Mulock)

Munford, Robert 1737(?)-1783 . . . . LC 5
    See also DLB 31

Mungo, Raymond 1946-. . . . . CLC 72
    See also CA 49-52; CANR 2

Munro, Alice
    1931- . . . . CLC 6, 10, 19, 50; SSC 3
    See also AITN 2; CA 33-36R; CANR 33;
    DLB 53; MTCW; SATA 29

Munro, H(ector) H(ugh) 1870-1916
    See Saki
    See also CA 104; 130; CDBLB 1890-1914;
    DA; DLB 34; MTCW; WLC

Murasaki, Lady . . . . CMLC 1

Murdoch, (Jean) Iris
    1919- . . . . . . CLC 1, 2, 3, 4, 6, 8, 11, 15,
                                    22, 31, 51
    See also CA 13-16R; CANR 8, 43;
    CDBLB 1960 to Present; DLB 14;
    MTCW

Murphy, Richard 1927- . . . . CLC 41
    See also CA 29-32R; DLB 40

Murphy, Sylvia 1937-. . . . . CLC 34
    See also CA 121

Murphy, Thomas (Bernard) 1935-. . . CLC 51
    See also CA 101

Murray, Albert L. 1916- . . . . CLC 73
    See also BW; CA 49-52; CANR 26; DLB 38

Murray, Les(lie) A(llan) 1938- . . . . . CLC 40
    See also CA 21-24R; CANR 11, 27

Murry, J. Middleton
    See Murry, John Middleton

Murry, John Middleton
    1889-1957 . . . . TCLC 16
    See also CA 118

Musgrave, Susan 1951- . . . . CLC 13, 54
    See also CA 69-72

Musil, Robert (Edler von)
    1880-1942 . . . . TCLC 12
    See also CA 109; DLB 81, 124

Musset, (Louis Charles) Alfred de
    1810-1857 . . . . NCLC 7

My Brother's Brother
    See Chekhov, Anton (Pavlovich)

Myers, Walter Dean
    1937- . . . . CLC 35; BLC 3
    See also AAYA 4; BW; CA 33-36R;
    CANR 20, 42; CLR 4, 16; DLB 33;
    JRDA; MAICYA; SAAS 2; SATA 27, 41,
    71

Myers, Walter M.
    See Myers, Walter Dean

Myles, Symon
    See Follett, Ken(neth Martin)

Nabokov, Vladimir (Vladimirovich)
    1899-1977 . . . . . CLC 1, 2, 3, 6, 8, 11, 15,
                    23, 44, 46, 64; DA; SSC 11; WLC
    See also CA 5-8R; 69-72; CANR 20;
    CDALB 1941-1968; DLB 2; DLBD 3;
    DLBY 80, 91; MTCW

Nagai Kafu . . . . TCLC 51
    See also Nagai Sokichi

Nagai Sokichi 1879-1959
    See Nagai Kafu
    See also CA 117

Nagy, Laszlo 1925-1978. . . . . CLC 7
    See also CA 129; 112

Naipaul, Shiva(dhar Srinivasa)
    1945-1985 . . . . CLC 32, 39
    See also CA 110; 112; 116; CANR 33;
    DLBY 85; MTCW

Naipaul, V(idiadhar) S(urajprasad)
    1932-. . . . . CLC 4, 7, 9, 13, 18, 37
    See also CA 1-4R; CANR 1, 33;
    CDBLB 1960 to Present; DLB 125;
    DLBY 85; MTCW

Nakos, Lilika 1899(?)- . . . . CLC 29

Narayan, R(asipuram) K(rishnaswami)
    1906- . . . . CLC 7, 28, 47
    See also CA 81-84; CANR 33; MTCW;
    SATA 62

Nash, (Frediric) Ogden 1902-1971 . . CLC 23
    See also CA 13-14; 29-32R; CANR 34;
    CAP 1; DLB 11; MAICYA; MTCW;
    SATA 2, 46

Nathan, Daniel
    See Dannay, Frederic

Nathan, George Jean 1882-1958 . . . TCLC 18
    See also Hatteras, Owen
    See also CA 114

Natsume, Kinnosuke 1867-1916
    See Natsume, Soseki
    See also CA 104

Natsume, Soseki . . . . TCLC 2, 10
    See also Natsume, Kinnosuke

Natti, (Mary) Lee 1919-
    See Kingman, Lee
    See also CA 5-8R; CANR 2

Naylor, Gloria
    1950- . . . . CLC 28, 52; BLC 3; DA
    See also AAYA 6; BW; CA 107; CANR 27;
    MTCW

Neihardt, John Gneisenau
    1881-1973 . . . . CLC 32
    See also CA 13-14; CAP 1; DLB 9, 54

Nekrasov, Nikolai Alekseevich
    1821-1878 . . . . NCLC 11

Nelligan, Emile 1879-1941. . . . . . . TCLC 14
    See also CA 114; DLB 92

Nelson, Willie 1933-. . . . . CLC 17
    See also CA 107

Nemerov, Howard (Stanley)
    1920-1991 . . . . CLC 2, 6, 9, 36
    See also CA 1-4R; 134; CABS 2; CANR 1,
    27; DLB 6; DLBY 83; MTCW

Neruda, Pablo
    1904-1973 . . . . . CLC 1, 2, 5, 7, 9, 28, 62;
                                    DA; PC 4; WLC
    See also CA 19-20; 45-48; CAP 2; HW;
    MTCW

Nerval, Gerard de 1808-1855. . . . . . NCLC 1

Nervo, (Jose) Amado (Ruiz de)
    1870-1919 . . . . TCLC 11
    See also CA 109; 131; HW

Nessi, Pio Baroja y
    See Baroja (y Nessi), Pio

Nestroy, Johann 1801-1862. . . . . . . NCLC 42
    See also DLB 133

Neufeld, John (Arthur) 1938- . . . . . . CLC 17
    See also CA 25-28R; CANR 11, 37;
    MAICYA; SAAS 3; SATA 6

Neville, Emily Cheney 1919-. . . . . . . CLC 12
    See also CA 5-8R; CANR 3, 37; JRDA;
    MAICYA; SAAS 2; SATA 1

Newbound, Bernard Slade 1930-
    See Slade, Bernard
    See also CA 81-84

Newby, P(ercy) H(oward)
    1918- . . . . CLC 2, 13
    See also CA 5-8R; CANR 32; DLB 15;
    MTCW

Newlove, Donald 1928- . . . . CLC 6
    See also CA 29-32R; CANR 25

Newlove, John (Herbert) 1938-. . . . . CLC 14
    See also CA 21-24R; CANR 9, 25

Newman, Charles 1938-. . . . . CLC 2, 8
    See also CA 21-24R

Newman, Edwin (Harold) 1919- . . . . CLC 14
    See also AITN 1; CA 69-72; CANR 5

Newman, John Henry
    1801-1890 . . . . NCLC 38
    See also DLB 18, 32, 55

Newton, Suzanne 1936- . . . . CLC 35
    See also CA 41-44R; CANR 14; JRDA;
    SATA 5

Nexo, Martin Andersen
    1869-1954 . . . . TCLC 43

Nezval, Vitezslav 1900-1958 . . . . . . TCLC 44
    See also CA 123

Ngema, Mbongeni 1955- . . . . CLC 57

Ngugi, James T(hiong'o) . . . . CLC 3, 7, 13
    See also Ngugi wa Thiong'o

Ngugi wa Thiong'o 1938-. . . CLC 36; BLC 3
    See also Ngugi, James T(hiong'o)
    See also BW; CA 81-84; CANR 27;
    DLB 125; MTCW

Nichol, B(arrie) P(hillip)
    1944-1988 . . . . CLC 18
    See also CA 53-56; DLB 53; SATA 66

Nichols, John (Treadwell) 1940-. . . . CLC 38
    See also CA 9-12R; CAAS 2; CANR 6;
    DLBY 82

Nichols, Leigh
See Koontz, Dean R(ay)

Nichols, Peter (Richard)
1927- . . . . **CLC 5, 36, 65**
See also CA 104; CANR 33; DLB 13;
MTCW

Nicolas, F. R. E.
See Freeling, Nicolas

Niedecker, Lorine 1903-1970. . . . **CLC 10, 42**
See also CA 25-28; CAP 2; DLB 48

Nietzsche, Friedrich (Wilhelm)
1844-1900 . . . . **TCLC 10, 18**
See also CA 107; 121; DLB 129

Nievo, Ippolito 1831-1861 . . . . **NCLC 22**

Nightingale, Anne Redmon 1943-
See Redmon, Anne
See also CA 103

Nik.T.O.
See Annensky, Innokenty Fyodorovich

Nin, Anais
1903-1977 . . . . . . **CLC 1, 4, 8, 11, 14, 60;**
SSC 10
See also AITN 2; CA 13-16R; 69-72;
CANR 22; DLB 2, 4; MTCW

Nissenson, Hugh 1933- . . . . **CLC 4, 9**
See also CA 17-20R; CANR 27; DLB 28

Niven, Larry . . . . **CLC 8**
See also Niven, Laurence Van Cott
See also DLB 8

Niven, Laurence Van Cott 1938-
See Niven, Larry
See also CA 21-24R; CAAS 12; CANR 14;
MTCW

Nixon, Agnes Eckhardt 1927- . . . . . **CLC 21**
See also CA 110

Nizan, Paul 1905-1940. . . . . **TCLC 40**
See also DLB 72

Nkosi, Lewis 1936- . . . . **CLC 45; BLC 3**
See also BW; CA 65-68; CANR 27

Nodier, (Jean) Charles (Emmanuel)
1780-1844 . . . . **NCLC 19**
See also DLB 119

Nolan, Christopher 1965- . . . . **CLC 58**
See also CA 111

Norden, Charles
See Durrell, Lawrence (George)

Nordhoff, Charles (Bernard)
1887-1947 . . . . **TCLC 23**
See also CA 108; DLB 9; SATA 23

Norfolk, Lawrence 1963- . . . . **CLC 76**

Norman, Marsha 1947- . . . . **CLC 28**
See also CA 105; CABS 3; CANR 41;
DLBY 84

Norris, Benjamin Franklin, Jr.
1870-1902 . . . . **TCLC 24**
See also Norris, Frank
See also CA 110

Norris, Frank
See Norris, Benjamin Franklin, Jr.
See also CDALB 1865-1917; DLB 12, 71

Norris, Leslie 1921- . . . . **CLC 14**
See also CA 11-12; CANR 14; CAP 1;
DLB 27

North, Andrew
See Norton, Andre

North, Anthony
See Koontz, Dean R(ay)

North, Captain George
See Stevenson, Robert Louis (Balfour)

North, Milou
See Erdrich, Louise

Northrup, B. A.
See Hubbard, L(afayette) Ron(ald)

North Staffs
See Hulme, T(homas) E(rnest)

Norton, Alice Mary
See Norton, Andre
See also MAICYA; SATA 1, 43

Norton, Andre 1912- . . . . **CLC 12**
See Norton, Alice Mary
See also CA 1-4R; CANR 2, 31; DLB 8, 52;
JRDA; MTCW

Norway, Nevil Shute 1899-1960
See Shute, Nevil
See also CA 102; 93-96

Norwid, Cyprian Kamil
1821-1883 . . . . **NCLC 17**

Nosille, Nabrah
See Ellison, Harlan

Nossack, Hans Erich 1901-1978 . . . . . **CLC 6**
See also CA 93-96; 85-88; DLB 69

Nosu, Chuji
See Ozu, Yasujiro

Nova, Craig 1945- . . . . **CLC 7, 31**
See also CA 45-48; CANR 2

Novak, Joseph
See Kosinski, Jerzy (Nikodem)

Novalis 1772-1801 . . . . **NCLC 13**
See also DLB 90

Nowlan, Alden (Albert) 1933-1983 . . **CLC 15**
See also CA 9-12R; CANR 5; DLB 53

Noyes, Alfred 1880-1958 . . . . **TCLC 7**
See also CA 104; DLB 20

Nunn, Kem 19(?)- . . . . **CLC 34**

Nye, Robert 1939- . . . . **CLC 13, 42**
See also CA 33-36R; CANR 29; DLB 14;
MTCW; SATA 6

Nyro, Laura 1947- . . . . **CLC 17**

Oates, Joyce Carol
1938- . . . . . . **CLC 1, 2, 3, 6, 9, 11, 15, 19,**
33, 52; DA; SSC 6; WLC
See also AITN 1; BEST 89:2; CA 5-8R;
CANR 25; CDALB 1968-1988; DLB 2, 5,
130; DLBY 81; MTCW

O'Brien, E. G.
See Clarke, Arthur C(harles)

O'Brien, Edna
1936- . . . **CLC 3, 5, 8, 13, 36, 65; SSC 10**
See also CA 1-4R; CANR 6, 41;
CDBLB 1960 to Present; DLB 14;
MTCW

O'Brien, Fitz-James 1828-1862. . . **NCLC 21**
See also DLB 74

O'Brien, Flann . . . . **CLC 1, 4, 5, 7, 10, 47**
See also O Nuallain, Brian

O'Brien, Richard 1942- . . . . **CLC 17**
See also CA 124

O'Brien, Tim 1946- . . . . **CLC 7, 19, 40**
See also CA 85-88; CANR 40; DLBD 9;
DLBY 80

Obstfelder, Sigbjoern 1866-1900 . . . **TCLC 23**
See also CA 123

O'Casey, Sean
1880-1964 . . . . **CLC 1, 5, 9, 11, 15**
See also CA 89-92; CDBLB 1914-1945;
DLB 10; MTCW

O'Cathasaigh, Sean
See O'Casey, Sean

Ochs, Phil 1940-1976 . . . . **CLC 17**
See also CA 65-68

O'Connor, Edwin (Greene)
1918-1968 . . . . **CLC 14**
See also CA 93-96; 25-28R

O'Connor, (Mary) Flannery
1925-1964 . . . . **CLC 1, 2, 3, 6, 10, 13, 15,**
21, 66; DA; SSC 1; WLC
See also AAYA 7; CA 1-4R; CANR 3, 41;
CDALB 1941-1968; DLB 2; DLBY 80;
MTCW

O'Connor, Frank . . . . **CLC 23; SSC 5**
See also O'Donovan, Michael John

O'Dell, Scott 1898-1989 . . . . **CLC 30**
See also AAYA 3; CA 61-64; 129;
CANR 12, 30; CLR 1, 16; DLB 52;
JRDA; MAICYA; SATA 12, 60

Odets, Clifford 1906-1963 . . . . **CLC 2, 28**
See also CA 85-88; DLB 7, 26; MTCW

O'Doherty, Brian 1934- . . . . **CLC 76**
See also CA 105

O'Donnell, K. M.
See Malzberg, Barry N(athaniel)

O'Donnell, Lawrence
See Kuttner, Henry

O'Donovan, Michael John
1903-1966 . . . . **CLC 14**
See also O'Connor, Frank
See also CA 93-96

Oe, Kenzaburo 1935- . . . . **CLC 10, 36**
See also CA 97-100; CANR 36; MTCW

O'Faolain, Julia 1932- . . . . **CLC 6, 19, 47**
See also CA 81-84; CAAS 2; CANR 12;
DLB 14; MTCW

O'Faolain, Sean
1900-1991 . . . . **CLC 1, 7, 14, 32, 70;**
SSC 13
See also CA 61-64; 134; CANR 12;
DLB 15; MTCW

O'Flaherty, Liam
1896-1984 . . . . **CLC 5, 34; SSC 6**
See also CA 101; 113; CANR 35; DLB 36;
DLBY 84; MTCW

Ogilvy, Gavin
See Barrie, J(ames) M(atthew)

O'Grady, Standish James
1846-1928 . . . . **TCLC 5**
See also CA 104

O'Grady, Timothy 1951- . . . . **CLC 59**
See also CA 138

O'Hara, Frank
1926-1966 . . . . **CLC 2, 5, 13, 78**
See also CA 9-12R; 25-28R; CANR 33;
DLB 5, 16; MTCW

O'Hara, John (Henry)
    1905-1970 ...... **CLC 1, 2, 3, 6, 11, 42**
    See also CA 5-8R; 25-28R; CANR 31;
    CDALB 1929-1941; DLB 9, 86; DLBD 2;
    MTCW

O Hehir, Diana 1922- .... **CLC 41**
    See also CA 93-96

Okigbo, Christopher (Ifenayichukwu)
    1932-1967 ...... **CLC 25; BLC 3; PC 7**
    See also BW; CA 77-80; DLB 125; MTCW

Olds, Sharon 1942-............ **CLC 32, 39**
    See also CA 101; CANR 18, 41; DLB 120

Oldstyle, Jonathan
    See Irving, Washington

Olesha, Yuri (Karlovich)
    1899-1960 .... **CLC 8**
    See also CA 85-88

Oliphant, Margaret (Oliphant Wilson)
    1828-1897 .... **NCLC 11**
    See also DLB 18

Oliver, Mary 1935-............ **CLC 19, 34**
    See also CA 21-24R; CANR 9; DLB 5

Olivier, Laurence (Kerr)
    1907-1989 .... **CLC 20**
    See also CA 111; 129

Olsen, Tillie
    1913- .... **CLC 4, 13; DA; SSC 11**
    See also CA 1-4R; CANR 1, 43; DLB 28;
    DLBY 80; MTCW

Olson, Charles (John)
    1910-1970 ..... **CLC 1, 2, 5, 6, 9, 11, 29**
    See also CA 13-16; 25-28R; CABS 2;
    CANR 35; CAP 1; DLB 5, 16; MTCW

Olson, Toby 1937- .... **CLC 28**
    See also CA 65-68; CANR 9, 31

Olyesha, Yuri
    See Olesha, Yuri (Karlovich)

Ondaatje, (Philip) Michael
    1943-................**CLC 14, 29, 51, 76**
    See also CA 77-80; CANR 42; DLB 60

Oneal, Elizabeth 1934-
    See Oneal, Zibby
    See also CA 106; CANR 28; MAICYA;
    SATA 30

Oneal, Zibby .... **CLC 30**
    See also Oneal, Elizabeth
    See also AAYA 5; CLR 13; JRDA

O'Neill, Eugene (Gladstone)
    1888-1953 ...... **TCLC 1, 6, 27, 49; DA;
                                        WLC**
    See also AITN 1; CA 110; 132;
    CDALB 1929-1941; DLB 7; MTCW

Onetti, Juan Carlos 1909- .... **CLC 7, 10**
    See also CA 85-88; CANR 32; DLB 113;
    HW; MTCW

O Nuallain, Brian 1911-1966
    See O'Brien, Flann
    See also CA 21-22; 25-28R; CAP 2

Oppen, George 1908-1984 .... **CLC 7, 13, 34**
    See also CA 13-16R; 113; CANR 8; DLB 5

Oppenheim, E(dward) Phillips
    1866-1946 .... **TCLC 45**
    See also CA 111; DLB 70

Orlovitz, Gil 1918-1973 .... **CLC 22**
    See also CA 77-80; 45-48; DLB 2, 5

Orris
    See Ingelow, Jean

Ortega y Gasset, Jose 1883-1955 ... **TCLC 9**
    See also CA 106; 130; HW; MTCW

Ortiz, Simon J(oseph) 1941- .... **CLC 45**
    See also CA 134; DLB 120

Orton, Joe .... **CLC 4, 13, 43; DC 3**
    See also Orton, John Kingsley
    See also CDBLB 1960 to Present; DLB 13

Orton, John Kingsley 1933-1967
    See Orton, Joe
    See also CA 85-88; CANR 35; MTCW

Orwell, George
    .... **TCLC 2, 6, 15, 31, 51; WLC**
    See also Blair, Eric (Arthur)
    See also CDBLB 1945-1960; DLB 15, 98

Osborne, David
    See Silverberg, Robert

Osborne, George
    See Silverberg, Robert

Osborne, John (James)
    1929- .... **CLC 1, 2, 5, 11, 45; DA; WLC**
    See also CA 13-16R; CANR 21;
    CDBLB 1945-1960; DLB 13; MTCW

Osborne, Lawrence 1958- .... **CLC 50**

Oshima, Nagisa 1932- .... **CLC 20**
    See also CA 116; 121

Oskison, John M(ilton)
    1874-1947 .... **TCLC 35**

Ossoli, Sarah Margaret (Fuller marchesa d')
    1810-1850
    See Fuller, Margaret
    See also SATA 25

Ostrovsky, Alexander
    1823-1886 .... **NCLC 30**

Otero, Blas de 1916-1979......... **CLC 11**
    See also CA 89-92; DLB 134

Otto, Whitney 1955-............. **CLC 70**
    See also CA 140

Ouida .... **TCLC 43**
    See also De La Ramee, (Marie) Louise
    See also DLB 18

Ousmane, Sembene 1923- .. **CLC 66; BLC 3**
    See also BW; CA 117; 125; MTCW

Ovid 43B.C.-18th cent. (?)... **CMLC 7; PC 2**

Owen, Hugh
    See Faust, Frederick (Schiller)

Owen, Wilfred (Edward Salter)
    1893-1918 ...... **TCLC 5, 27; DA; WLC**
    See also CA 104; 141; CDBLB 1914-1945;
    DLB 20

Owens, Rochelle 1936-............. **CLC 8**
    See also CA 17-20R; CAAS 2; CANR 39

Oz, Amos 1939- ... **CLC 5, 8, 11, 27, 33, 54**
    See also CA 53-56; CANR 27; MTCW

Ozick, Cynthia 1928-...... **CLC 3, 7, 28, 62**
    See also BEST 90:1; CA 17-20R; CANR 23;
    DLB 28; DLBY 82; MTCW

Ozu, Yasujiro 1903-1963 .... **CLC 16**
    See also CA 112

Pacheco, C.
    See Pessoa, Fernando (Antonio Nogueira)

Pa Chin
    See Li Fei-kan

Pack, Robert 1929-............... **CLC 13**
    See also CA 1-4R; CANR 3; DLB 5

Padgett, Lewis
    See Kuttner, Henry

Padilla (Lorenzo), Heberto 1932-... **CLC 38**
    See also AITN 1; CA 123; 131; HW

Page, Jimmy 1944-............... **CLC 12**

Page, Louise 1955-............... **CLC 40**
    See also CA 140

Page, P(atricia) K(athleen)
    1916- .... **CLC 7, 18**
    See also CA 53-56; CANR 4, 22; DLB 68;
    MTCW

Paget, Violet 1856-1935
    See Lee, Vernon
    See also CA 104

Paget-Lowe, Henry
    See Lovecraft, H(oward) P(hillips)

Paglia, Camille (Anna) 1947-....... **CLC 68**
    See also CA 140

Paige, Richard
    See Koontz, Dean R(ay)

Pakenham, Antonia
    See Fraser, Antonia (Pakenham)

Palamas, Kostes 1859-1943 .... **TCLC 5**
    See also CA 105

Palazzeschi, Aldo 1885-1974 .... **CLC 11**
    See also CA 89-92; 53-56; DLB 114

Paley, Grace 1922-.... **CLC 4, 6, 37; SSC 8**
    See also CA 25-28R; CANR 13; DLB 28;
    MTCW

Palin, Michael (Edward) 1943- ..... **CLC 21**
    See also Monty Python
    See also CA 107; CANR 35; SATA 67

Palliser, Charles 1947-........... **CLC 65**
    See also CA 136

Palma, Ricardo 1833-1919........ **TCLC 29**

Pancake, Breece Dexter 1952-1979
    See Pancake, Breece D'J
    See also CA 123; 109

Pancake, Breece D'J.............. **CLC 29**
    See also Pancake, Breece Dexter
    See also DLB 130

Panko, Rudy
    See Gogol, Nikolai (Vasilyevich)

Papadiamantis, Alexandros
    1851-1911 .... **TCLC 29**

Papadiamantopoulos, Johannes 1856-1910
    See Moreas, Jean
    See also CA 117

Papini, Giovanni 1881-1956....... **TCLC 22**
    See also CA 121

Paracelsus 1493-1541............. **LC 14**

Parasol, Peter
    See Stevens, Wallace

Parfenie, Maria
    See Codrescu, Andrei

Parini, Jay (Lee) 1948- .... **CLC 54**
    See also CA 97-100; CAAS 16; CANR 32

Park, Jordan
    See Kornbluth, C(yril) M.; Pohl, Frederik

Parker, Bert
    See Ellison, Harlan

Parker, Dorothy (Rothschild)
    1893-1967 . . . . **CLC 15, 68; SSC 2**
    See also CA 19-20; 25-28R; CAP 2;
    DLB 11, 45, 86; MTCW

Parker, Robert B(rown) 1932- . . . . . . **CLC 27**
    See also BEST 89:4; CA 49-52; CANR 1,
    26; MTCW

Parkes, Lucas
    See Harris, John (Wyndham Parkes Lucas)
    Beynon

Parkin, Frank 1940- . . . . **CLC 43**

Parkman, Francis, Jr.
    1823-1893 . . . . **NCLC 12**
    See also DLB 1, 30

Parks, Gordon (Alexander Buchanan)
    1912- . . . . **CLC 1, 16; BLC 3**
    See also AITN 2; BW; CA 41-44R;
    CANR 26; DLB 33; SATA 8

Parnell, Thomas 1679-1718 . . . . **LC 3**
    See also DLB 94

Parra, Nicanor 1914- . . . . **CLC 2**
    See also CA 85-88; CANR 32; HW; MTCW

Parrish, Mary Frances
    See Fisher, M(ary) F(rances) K(ennedy)

Parson
    See Coleridge, Samuel Taylor

Parson Lot
    See Kingsley, Charles

Partridge, Anthony
    See Oppenheim, E(dward) Phillips

Pascoli, Giovanni 1855-1912 . . . . . . **TCLC 45**

Pasolini, Pier Paolo
    1922-1975 . . . . **CLC 20, 37**
    See also CA 93-96; 61-64; DLB 128;
    MTCW

Pasquini
    See Silone, Ignazio

Pastan, Linda (Olenik) 1932- . . . . . . **CLC 27**
    See also CA 61-64; CANR 18, 40; DLB 5

Pasternak, Boris (Leonidovich)
    1890-1960 . . . . . . **CLC 7, 10, 18, 63; DA;
                                    PC 6; WLC**
    See also CA 127; 116; MTCW

Patchen, Kenneth 1911-1972 . . . **CLC 1, 2, 18**
    See also CA 1-4R; 33-36R; CANR 3, 35;
    DLB 16, 48; MTCW

Pater, Walter (Horatio)
    1839-1894 . . . . **NCLC 7**
    See also CDBLB 1832-1890; DLB 57

Paterson, A(ndrew) B(arton)
    1864-1941 . . . . **TCLC 32**

Paterson, Katherine (Womeldorf)
    1932- . . . . **CLC 12, 30**
    See also AAYA 1; CA 21-24R; CANR 28;
    CLR 7; DLB 52; JRDA; MAICYA;
    MTCW; SATA 13, 53

Patmore, Coventry Kersey Dighton
    1823-1896 . . . . **NCLC 9**
    See also DLB 35, 98

Paton, Alan (Stewart)
    1903-1988 . . . . . . **CLC 4, 10, 25, 55; DA;
                                    WLC**
    See also CA 13-16; 125; CANR 22; CAP 1;
    MTCW; SATA 11, 56

Paton Walsh, Gillian 1937-
    See Walsh, Jill Paton
    See also CANR 38; JRDA; MAICYA;
    SAAS 3; SATA 4, 72

Paulding, James Kirke 1778-1860 . . **NCLC 2**
    See also DLB 3, 59, 74

Paulin, Thomas Neilson 1949-
    See Paulin, Tom
    See also CA 123; 128

Paulin, Tom . . . . **CLC 37**
    See also Paulin, Thomas Neilson
    See also DLB 40

Paustovsky, Konstantin (Georgievich)
    1892-1968 . . . . **CLC 40**
    See also CA 93-96; 25-28R

Pavese, Cesare 1908-1950 . . . . **TCLC 3**
    See also CA 104; DLB 128

Pavic, Milorad 1929- . . . . **CLC 60**
    See also CA 136

Payne, Alan
    See Jakes, John (William)

Paz, Gil
    See Lugones, Leopoldo

Paz, Octavio
    1914- . . . . **CLC 3, 4, 6, 10, 19, 51, 65;
                                    DA; PC 1; WLC**
    See also CA 73-76; CANR 32; DLBY 90;
    HW; MTCW

Peacock, Molly 1947- . . . . **CLC 60**
    See also CA 103; DLB 120

Peacock, Thomas Love
    1785-1866 . . . . **NCLC 22**
    See also DLB 96, 116

Peake, Mervyn 1911-1968 . . . . . . **CLC 7, 54**
    See also CA 5-8R; 25-28R; CANR 3;
    DLB 15; MTCW; SATA 23

Pearce, Philippa . . . . **CLC 21**
    See also Christie, (Ann) Philippa
    See also CLR 9; MAICYA; SATA 1, 67

Pearl, Eric
    See Elman, Richard

Pearson, T(homas) R(eid) 1956- . . . . **CLC 39**
    See also CA 120; 130

Peck, John 1941- . . . . **CLC 3**
    See also CA 49-52; CANR 3

Peck, Richard (Wayne) 1934- . . . . . . **CLC 21**
    See also AAYA 1; CA 85-88; CANR 19,
    38; JRDA; MAICYA; SAAS 2; SATA 18,
    55

Peck, Robert Newton 1928- . . . . **CLC 17; DA**
    See also AAYA 3; CA 81-84; CANR 31;
    JRDA; MAICYA; SAAS 1; SATA 21, 62

Peckinpah, (David) Sam(uel)
    1925-1984 . . . . **CLC 20**
    See also CA 109; 114

Pedersen, Knut 1859-1952
    See Hamsun, Knut
    See also CA 104; 119; MTCW

Peeslake, Gaffer
    See Durrell, Lawrence (George)

Peguy, Charles Pierre
    1873-1914 . . . . **TCLC 10**
    See also CA 107

Pena, Ramon del Valle y
    See Valle-Inclan, Ramon (Maria) del

Pendennis, Arthur Esquir
    See Thackeray, William Makepeace

Pepys, Samuel
    1633-1703 . . . . **LC 11; DA; WLC**
    See also CDBLB 1660-1789; DLB 101

Percy, Walker
    1916-1990 . . . . **CLC 2, 3, 6, 8, 14, 18, 47,
                                    65**
    See also CA 1-4R; 131; CANR 1, 23;
    DLB 2; DLBY 80, 90; MTCW

Perec, Georges 1936-1982 . . . . **CLC 56**
    See also CA 141; DLB 83

Pereda (y Sanchez de Porrua), Jose Maria de
    1833-1906 . . . . **TCLC 16**
    See also CA 117

Pereda y Porrua, Jose Maria de
    See Pereda (y Sanchez de Porrua), Jose
    Maria de

Peregoy, George Weems
    See Mencken, H(enry) L(ouis)

Perelman, S(idney) J(oseph)
    1904-1979 . . . **CLC 3, 5, 9, 15, 23, 44, 49**
    See also AITN 1, 2; CA 73-76; 89-92;
    CANR 18; DLB 11, 44; MTCW

Peret, Benjamin 1899-1959 . . . . **TCLC 20**
    See also CA 117

Peretz, Isaac Loeb 1851(?)-1915 . . . **TCLC 16**
    See also CA 109

Peretz, Yitzkhok Leibush
    See Peretz, Isaac Loeb

Perez Galdos, Benito 1843-1920 . . . **TCLC 27**
    See also CA 125; HW

Perrault, Charles 1628-1703 . . . . **LC 2**
    See also MAICYA; SATA 25

Perry, Brighton
    See Sherwood, Robert E(mmet)

Perse, St.-John . . . . **CLC 4, 11, 46**
    See also Leger, (Marie-Rene Auguste) Alexis
    Saint-Leger

Peseenz, Tulio F.
    See Lopez y Fuentes, Gregorio

Pesetsky, Bette 1932- . . . . **CLC 28**
    See also CA 133; DLB 130

Peshkov, Alexei Maximovich 1868-1936
    See Gorky, Maxim
    See also CA 105; 141; DA

Pessoa, Fernando (Antonio Nogueira)
    1888-1935 . . . . **TCLC 27**
    See also CA 125

Peterkin, Julia Mood 1880-1961 . . . . **CLC 31**
    See also CA 102; DLB 9

Peters, Joan K. 1945- . . . . **CLC 39**

Peters, Robert L(ouis) 1924- . . . . **CLC 7**
    See also CA 13-16R; CAAS 8; DLB 105

Petofi, Sandor 1823-1849 . . . . **NCLC 21**

Petrakis, Harry Mark 1923- . . . . **CLC 3**
    See also CA 9-12R; CANR 4, 30

Petrarch 1304-1374 . . . . **PC 8**

Petrov, Evgeny . . . . **TCLC 21**
    See also Kataev, Evgeny Petrovich

Petry, Ann (Lane) 1908- . . . . . **CLC 1, 7, 18**
    See also BW; CA 5-8R; CAAS 6; CANR 4;
    CLR 12; DLB 76; JRDA; MAICYA;
    MTCW; SATA 5

Petursson, Halligrimur 1614-1674 .... **LC 8**

Philipson, Morris H. 1926- .... **CLC 53**
See also CA 1-4R; CANR 4

Phillips, David Graham
1867-1911 .... **TCLC 44**
See also CA 108; DLB 9, 12

Phillips, Jack
See Sandburg, Carl (August)

Phillips, Jayne Anne 1952- ..... **CLC 15, 33**
See also CA 101; CANR 24; DLBY 80;
MTCW

Phillips, Richard
See Dick, Philip K(indred)

Phillips, Robert (Schaeffer) 1938-... **CLC 28**
See also CA 17-20R; CAAS 13; CANR 8;
DLB 105

Phillips, Ward
See Lovecraft, H(oward) P(hillips)

Piccolo, Lucio 1901-1969 .... **CLC 13**
See also CA 97-100; DLB 114

Pickthall, Marjorie L(owry) C(hristie)
1883-1922 .... **TCLC 21**
See also CA 107; DLB 92

Pico della Mirandola, Giovanni
1463-1494 .... **LC 15**

Piercy, Marge
1936- .... **CLC 3, 6, 14, 18, 27, 62**
See also CA 21-24R; CAAS 1; CANR 13,
43; DLB 120; MTCW

Piers, Robert
See Anthony, Piers

Pieyre de Mandiargues, Andre 1909-1991
See Mandiargues, Andre Pieyre de
See also CA 103; 136; CANR 22

Pilnyak, Boris .... **TCLC 23**
See also Vogau, Boris Andreyevich

Pincherle, Alberto 1907-1990 ... **CLC 11, 18**
See also Moravia, Alberto
See also CA 25-28R; 132; CANR 33;
MTCW

Pinckney, Darryl 1953- .... **CLC 76**

Pindar 518B.C.-446B.C. .... **CMLC 12**

Pineda, Cecile 1942-.............. **CLC 39**
See also CA 118

Pinero, Arthur Wing 1855-1934 ... **TCLC 32**
See also CA 110; DLB 10

Pinero, Miguel (Antonio Gomez)
1946-1988 .... **CLC 4, 55**
See also CA 61-64; 125; CANR 29; HW

Pinget, Robert 1919- .... **CLC 7, 13, 37**
See also CA 85-88; DLB 83

Pink Floyd .... **CLC 35**
See also Barrett, (Roger) Syd; Gilmour,
David; Mason, Nick; Waters, Roger;
Wright, Rick

Pinkney, Edward 1802-1828 ..... **NCLC 31**

Pinkwater, Daniel Manus 1941-.... **CLC 35**
See also Pinkwater, Manus
See also AAYA 1; CA 29-32R; CANR 12,
38; CLR 4; JRDA; MAICYA; SAAS 3;
SATA 46

Pinkwater, Manus
See Pinkwater, Daniel Manus
See also SATA 8

Pinsky, Robert 1940-........ **CLC 9, 19, 38**
See also CA 29-32R; CAAS 4; DLBY 82

Pinta, Harold
See Pinter, Harold

Pinter, Harold
1930- ..... **CLC 1, 3, 6, 9, 11, 15, 27, 58,
73; DA; WLC**
See also CA 5-8R; CANR 33; CDBLB 1960
to Present; DLB 13; MTCW

Pirandello, Luigi
1867-1936 .... **TCLC 4, 29; DA; WLC**
See also CA 104

Pirsig, Robert M(aynard)
1928- .... **CLC 4, 6, 73**
See also CA 53-56; CANR 42; MTCW;
SATA 39

Pisarev, Dmitry Ivanovich
1840-1868 .... **NCLC 25**

Pix, Mary (Griffith) 1666-1709 .... **LC 8**
See also DLB 80

Pixerecourt, Guilbert de
1773-1844 .... **NCLC 39**

Plaidy, Jean
See Hibbert, Eleanor Alice Burford

Planche, James Robinson
1796-1880 .... **NCLC 42**

Plant, Robert 1948- .... **CLC 12**

Plante, David (Robert)
1940- .... **CLC 7, 23, 38**
See also CA 37-40R; CANR 12, 36;
DLBY 83; MTCW

Plath, Sylvia
1932-1963 ..... **CLC 1, 2, 3, 5, 9, 11, 14,
17, 50, 51, 62; DA; PC 1; WLC**
See also CA 19-20; CANR 34; CAP 2;
CDALB 1941-1968; DLB 5, 6; MTCW

Plato 428(?)B.C.-348(?)B.C.... **CMLC 8; DA**

Platonov, Andrei .... **TCLC 14**
See also Klimentov, Andrei Platonovich

Platt, Kin 1911- .... **CLC 26**
See also CA 17-20R; CANR 11; JRDA;
SAAS 17; SATA 21

Plick et Plock
See Simenon, Georges (Jacques Christian)

Plimpton, George (Ames) 1927-..... **CLC 36**
See also AITN 1; CA 21-24R; CANR 32;
MTCW; SATA 10

Plomer, William Charles Franklin
1903-1973 .... **CLC 4, 8**
See also CA 21-22; CANR 34; CAP 2;
DLB 20; MTCW; SATA 24

Plowman, Piers
See Kavanagh, Patrick (Joseph)

Plum, J.
See Wodehouse, P(elham) G(renville)

Plumly, Stanley (Ross) 1939- ...... **CLC 33**
See also CA 108; 110; DLB 5

Poe, Edgar Allan
1809-1849 ..... **NCLC 1, 16; DA; PC 1;
SSC 1; WLC**
See also CDALB 1640-1865; DLB 3, 59, 73,
74; SATA 23

Poet of Titchfield Street, The
See Pound, Ezra (Weston Loomis)

Pohl, Frederik 1919- .... **CLC 18**
See also CA 61-64; CAAS 1; CANR 11, 37;
DLB 8; MTCW; SATA 24

Poirier, Louis 1910-
See Gracq, Julien
See also CA 122; 126

Poitier, Sidney 1927-............. **CLC 26**
See also BW; CA 117

Polanski, Roman 1933- .... **CLC 16**
See also CA 77-80

Poliakoff, Stephen 1952- .... **CLC 38**
See also CA 106; DLB 13

Police, The...................... **CLC 26**
See also Copeland, Stewart (Armstrong);
Summers, Andrew James; Sumner,
Gordon Matthew

Pollitt, Katha 1949- .... **CLC 28**
See also CA 120; 122; MTCW

Pollock, (Mary) Sharon 1936-...... **CLC 50**
See also CA 141; DLB 60

Pomerance, Bernard 1940-........ **CLC 13**
See also CA 101

Ponge, Francis (Jean Gaston Alfred)
1899-1988 .... **CLC 6, 18**
See also CA 85-88; 126; CANR 40

Pontoppidan, Henrik 1857-1943 ... **TCLC 29**

Poole, Josephine .... **CLC 17**
See also Helyar, Jane Penelope Josephine
See also SAAS 2; SATA 5

Popa, Vasko 1922- .... **CLC 19**
See also CA 112

Pope, Alexander
1688-1744 .... **LC 3; DA; WLC**
See also CDBLB 1660-1789; DLB 95, 101

Porter, Connie (Rose) 1959(?)- ..... **CLC 70**
See also CA 142

Porter, Gene(va Grace) Stratton
1863(?)-1924 .... **TCLC 21**
See also CA 112

Porter, Katherine Anne
1890-1980 ...... **CLC 1, 3, 7, 10, 13, 15,
27; DA; SSC 4**
See also AITN 2; CA 1-4R; 101; CANR 1;
DLB 4, 9, 102; DLBY 80; MTCW;
SATA 23, 39

Porter, Peter (Neville Frederick)
1929- .... **CLC 5, 13, 33**
See also CA 85-88; DLB 40

Porter, William Sydney 1862-1910
See Henry, O.
See also CA 104; 131; CDALB 1865-1917;
DA; DLB 12, 78, 79; MTCW; YABC 2

Portillo (y Pacheco), Jose Lopez
See Lopez Portillo (y Pacheco), Jose

Post, Melville Davisson
1869-1930 .... **TCLC 39**
See also CA 110

Potok, Chaim 1929- .... **CLC 2, 7, 14, 26**
See also AITN 1, 2; CA 17-20R; CANR 19,
35; DLB 28; MTCW; SATA 33

Potter, Beatrice
See Webb, (Martha) Beatrice (Potter)
See also MAICYA

Potter, Dennis (Christopher George)
   1935- .... CLC **58**
   See also CA 107; CANR 33; MTCW

Pound, Ezra (Weston Loomis)
   1885-1972 ...... CLC **1, 2, 3, 4, 5, 7, 10,**
               13, 18, 34, 48, 50; DA; PC 4; WLC
   See also CA 5-8R; 37-40R; CANR 40;
   CDALB 1917-1929; DLB 4, 45, 63;
   MTCW

Povod, Reinaldo 1959- .... CLC **44**
   See also CA 136

Powell, Anthony (Dymoke)
   1905- .... CLC **1, 3, 7, 9, 10, 31**
   See also CA 1-4R; CANR 1, 32;
   CDBLB 1945-1960; DLB 15; MTCW

Powell, Dawn 1897-1965 .... CLC **66**
   See also CA 5-8R

Powell, Padgett 1952- .... CLC **34**
   See also CA 126

Powers, J(ames) F(arl)
   1917- .... CLC **1, 4, 8, 57; SSC 4**
   See also CA 1-4R; CANR 2; DLB 130;
   MTCW

Powers, John J(ames) 1945-
   See Powers, John R.
   See also CA 69-72

Powers, John R. .... CLC **66**
   See also Powers, John J(ames)

Pownall, David 1938- .... CLC **10**
   See also CA 89-92; CAAS 18; DLB 14

Powys, John Cowper
   1872-1963 .... CLC **7, 9, 15, 46**
   See also CA 85-88; DLB 15; MTCW

Powys, T(heodore) F(rancis)
   1875-1953 .... TCLC **9**
   See also CA 106; DLB 36

Prager, Emily 1952- .... CLC **56**

Pratt, E(dwin) J(ohn)
   1883(?)-1964 .... CLC **19**
   See also CA 141; 93-96; DLB 92

Premchand .... TCLC **21**
   See also Srivastava, Dhanpat Rai

Preussler, Otfried 1923- .... CLC **17**
   See also CA 77-80; SATA 24

Prevert, Jacques (Henri Marie)
   1900-1977 .... CLC **15**
   See also CA 77-80; 69-72; CANR 29;
   MTCW; SATA 30

Prevost, Abbe (Antoine Francois)
   1697-1763 .... LC **1**

Price, (Edward) Reynolds
   1933- .... CLC **3, 6, 13, 43, 50, 63**
   See also CA 1-4R; CANR 1, 37; DLB 2

Price, Richard 1949- .... CLC **6, 12**
   See also CA 49-52; CANR 3; DLBY 81

Prichard, Katharine Susannah
   1883-1969 .... CLC **46**
   See also CA 11-12; CANR 33; CAP 1;
   MTCW; SATA 66

Priestley, J(ohn) B(oynton)
   1894-1984 .... CLC **2, 5, 9, 34**
   See also CA 9-12R; 113; CANR 33;
   CDBLB 1914-1945; DLB 10, 34, 77, 100;
   DLBY 84; MTCW

Prince 1958(?)- .... CLC **35**

Prince, F(rank) T(empleton) 1912- .. CLC **22**
   See also CA 101; CANR 43; DLB 20

Prince Kropotkin
   See Kropotkin, Peter (Aleksieevich)

Prior, Matthew 1664-1721 .... LC **4**
   See also DLB 95

Pritchard, William H(arrison)
   1932- .... CLC **34**
   See also CA 65-68; CANR 23; DLB 111

Pritchett, V(ictor) S(awdon)
   1900- ...... CLC **5, 13, 15, 41; SSC 14**
   See also CA 61-64; CANR 31; DLB 15;
   MTCW

Private 19022
   See Manning, Frederic

Probst, Mark 1925- .... CLC **59**
   See also CA 130

Prokosch, Frederic 1908-1989.... CLC **4, 48**
   See also CA 73-76; 128; DLB 48

Prophet, The
   See Dreiser, Theodore (Herman Albert)

Prose, Francine 1947- .... CLC **45**
   See also CA 109; 112

Proudhon
   See Cunha, Euclides (Rodrigues Pimenta) da

Proust, (Valentin-Louis-George-Eugene-)
   Marcel
   1871-1922 ... TCLC **7, 13, 33; DA; WLC**
   See also CA 104; 120; DLB 65; MTCW

Prowler, Harley
   See Masters, Edgar Lee

Prus, Boleslaw .... TCLC **48**
   See also Glowacki, Aleksander

Pryor, Richard (Franklin Lenox Thomas)
   1940- .... CLC **26**
   See also CA 122

Przybyszewski, Stanislaw
   1868-1927 .... TCLC **36**
   See also DLB 66

Pteleon
   See Grieve, C(hristopher) M(urray)

Puckett, Lute
   See Masters, Edgar Lee

Puig, Manuel
   1932-1990 .... CLC **3, 5, 10, 28, 65**
   See also CA 45-48; CANR 2, 32; DLB 113;
   HW; MTCW

Purdy, A(lfred Wellington)
   1918- .... CLC **3, 6, 14, 50**
   See also CA 81-84; CANR 42

Purdy, Al
   See Purdy, A(lfred Wellington)
   See also CAAS 17; DLB 88

Purdy, James (Amos)
   1923- .... CLC **2, 4, 10, 28, 52**
   See also CA 33-36R; CAAS 1; CANR 19;
   DLB 2; MTCW

Pure, Simon
   See Swinnerton, Frank Arthur

Pushkin, Alexander (Sergeyevich)
   1799-1837 ...... NCLC **3, 27; DA; WLC**
   See also SATA 61

P'u Sung-ling 1640-1715 .... LC **3**

Putnam, Arthur Lee
   See Alger, Horatio, Jr.

Puzo, Mario 1920- .... CLC **1, 2, 6, 36**
   See also CA 65-68; CANR 4, 42; DLB 6;
   MTCW

Pym, Barbara (Mary Crampton)
   1913-1980 .... CLC **13, 19, 37**
   See also CA 13-14; 97-100; CANR 13, 34;
   CAP 1; DLB 14; DLBY 87; MTCW

Pynchon, Thomas (Ruggles, Jr.)
   1937- ..... CLC **2, 3, 6, 9, 11, 18, 33, 62,**
                        72; DA; SSC 14; WLC
   See also BEST 90:2; CA 17-20R; CANR 22;
   DLB 2; MTCW

Qian Zhongshu
   See Ch'ien Chung-shu

Qroll
   See Dagerman, Stig (Halvard)

Quarrington, Paul (Lewis) 1953-.... CLC **65**
   See also CA 129

Quasimodo, Salvatore 1901-1968 ... CLC **10**
   See also CA 13-16; 25-28R; CAP 1;
   DLB 114; MTCW

Queen, Ellery .... CLC **3, 11**
   See also Dannay, Frederic; Davidson,
   Avram; Lee, Manfred B(ennington);
   Sturgeon, Theodore (Hamilton); Vance,
   John Holbrook

Queen, Ellery, Jr.
   See Dannay, Frederic; Lee, Manfred
   B(ennington)

Queneau, Raymond
   1903-1976 .... CLC **2, 5, 10, 42**
   See also CA 77-80; 69-72; CANR 32;
   DLB 72; MTCW

Quevedo, Francisco de 1580-1645.... LC **23**

Quin, Ann (Marie) 1936-1973 .... CLC **6**
   See also CA 9-12R; 45-48; DLB 14

Quinn, Martin
   See Smith, Martin Cruz

Quinn, Simon
   See Smith, Martin Cruz

Quiroga, Horacio (Sylvestre)
   1878-1937 .... TCLC **20**
   See also CA 117; 131; HW; MTCW

Quoirez, Francoise 1935- .... CLC **9**
   See also Sagan, Francoise
   See also CA 49-52; CANR 6, 39; MTCW

Raabe, Wilhelm 1831-1910 .... TCLC **45**
   See also DLB 129

Rabe, David (William) 1940-... CLC **4, 8, 33**
   See also CA 85-88; CABS 3; DLB 7

Rabelais, Francois
   1483-1553 .... LC **5; DA; WLC**

Rabinovitch, Sholem 1859-1916
   See Aleichem, Sholom
   See also CA 104

Radcliffe, Ann (Ward) 1764-1823 .. NCLC **6**
   See also DLB 39

Radiguet, Raymond 1903-1923 .... TCLC **29**
   See also DLB 65

Radnoti, Miklos 1909-1944 .... TCLC **16**
   See also CA 118

Ribeiro, Darcy 1922- . . . . **CLC 34**
    See also CA 33-36R

Ribeiro, Joao Ubaldo (Osorio Pimentel)
    1941- . . . . **CLC 10, 67**
    See also CA 81-84

Ribman, Ronald (Burt) 1932- . . . . **CLC 7**
    See also CA 21-24R

Ricci, Nino 1959- . . . . **CLC 70**
    See also CA 137

Rice, Anne 1941- . . . . **CLC 41**
    See also AAYA 9; BEST 89:2; CA 65-68;
    CANR 12, 36

Rice, Elmer (Leopold)
    1892-1967 . . . . **CLC 7, 49**
    See also CA 21-22; 25-28R; CAP 2; DLB 4,
    7; MTCW

Rice, Tim 1944- . . . . **CLC 21**
    See also CA 103

Rich, Adrienne (Cecile)
    1929- . . . . **CLC 3, 6, 7, 11, 18, 36, 73, 76;**
                                            PC 5
    See also CA 9-12R; CANR 20; DLB 5, 67;
    MTCW

Rich, Barbara
    See Graves, Robert (von Ranke)

Rich, Robert
    See Trumbo, Dalton

Richards, David Adams 1950- . . . . . . **CLC 59**
    See also CA 93-96; DLB 53

Richards, I(vor) A(rmstrong)
    1893-1979 . . . . **CLC 14, 24**
    See also CA 41-44R; 89-92; CANR 34;
    DLB 27

Richardson, Anne
    See Roiphe, Anne Richardson

Richardson, Dorothy Miller
    1873-1957 . . . . **TCLC 3**
    See also CA 104; DLB 36

Richardson, Ethel Florence (Lindesay)
    1870-1946
    See Richardson, Henry Handel
    See also CA 105

Richardson, Henry Handel. . . . . **TCLC 4**
    See also Richardson, Ethel Florence
    (Lindesay)

Richardson, Samuel
    1689-1761 . . . . **LC 1; DA; WLC**
    See also CDBLB 1660-1789; DLB 39

Richler, Mordecai
    1931- . . . . **CLC 3, 5, 9, 13, 18, 46, 70**
    See also AITN 1; CA 65-68; CANR 31;
    CLR 17; DLB 53; MAICYA; MTCW;
    SATA 27, 44

Richter, Conrad (Michael)
    1890-1968 . . . . **CLC 30**
    See also CA 5-8R; 25-28R; CANR 23;
    DLB 9; MTCW; SATA 3

Riddell, J. H. 1832-1906 . . . . **TCLC 40**

Riding, Laura. . . . . **CLC 3, 7**
    See also Jackson, Laura (Riding)

Riefenstahl, Berta Helene Amalia 1902-
    See Riefenstahl, Leni
    See also CA 108

Riefenstahl, Leni. . . . . **CLC 16**
    See also Riefenstahl, Berta Helene Amalia

Riffe, Ernest
    See Bergman, (Ernst) Ingmar

Riley, James Whitcomb
    1849-1916 . . . . **TCLC 51**
    See also CA 118; 137; MAICYA; SATA 17

Riley, Tex
    See Creasey, John

Rilke, Rainer Maria
    1875-1926 . . . . **TCLC 1, 6, 19; PC 2**
    See also CA 104; 132; DLB 81; MTCW

Rimbaud, (Jean Nicolas) Arthur
    1854-1891 . . . . . **NCLC 4, 35; DA; PC 3;**
                                            WLC

Rinehart, Mary Roberts
    1876-1958 . . . . **TCLC 52**
    See also CA 108

Ringmaster, The
    See Mencken, H(enry) L(ouis)

Ringwood, Gwen(dolyn Margaret) Pharis
    1910-1984 . . . . **CLC 48**
    See also CA 112; DLB 88

Rio, Michel 19(?)-. . . . . **CLC 43**

Ritsos, Giannes
    See Ritsos, Yannis

Ritsos, Yannis 1909-1990. . . . . **CLC 6, 13, 31**
    See also CA 77-80; 133; CANR 39; MTCW

Ritter, Erika 1948(?)-. . . . . **CLC 52**

Rivera, Jose Eustasio 1889-1928. . . **TCLC 35**
    See also HW

Rivers, Conrad Kent 1933-1968. . . . . . **CLC 1**
    See also BW; CA 85-88; DLB 41

Rivers, Elfrida
    See Bradley, Marion Zimmer

Riverside, John
    See Heinlein, Robert A(nson)

Rizal, Jose 1861-1896. . . . . **NCLC 27**

Roa Bastos, Augusto (Antonio)
    1917- . . . . **CLC 45**
    See also CA 131; DLB 113; HW

Robbe-Grillet, Alain
    1922- . . . . . . **CLC 1, 2, 4, 6, 8, 10, 14, 43**
    See also CA 9-12R; CANR 33; DLB 83;
    MTCW

Robbins, Harold 1916-. . . . . **CLC 5**
    See also CA 73-76; CANR 26; MTCW

Robbins, Thomas Eugene 1936-
    See Robbins, Tom
    See also CA 81-84; CANR 29; MTCW

Robbins, Tom. . . . . **CLC 9, 32, 64**
    See also Robbins, Thomas Eugene
    See also BEST 90:3; DLBY 80

Robbins, Trina 1938- . . . . **CLC 21**
    See also CA 128

Roberts, Charles G(eorge) D(ouglas)
    1860-1943 . . . . **TCLC 8**
    See also CA 105; DLB 92; SATA 29

Roberts, Kate 1891-1985 . . . . **CLC 15**
    See also CA 107; 116

Roberts, Keith (John Kingston)
    1935- . . . . **CLC 14**
    See also CA 25-28R

Roberts, Kenneth (Lewis)
    1885-1957 . . . . **TCLC 23**
    See also CA 109; DLB 9

Roberts, Michele (B.) 1949-. . . . . . . **CLC 48**
    See also CA 115

Robertson, Ellis
    See Ellison, Harlan; Silverberg, Robert

Robertson, Thomas William
    1829-1871 . . . . **NCLC 35**

Robinson, Edwin Arlington
    1869-1935 . . . . **TCLC 5; DA; PC 1**
    See also CA 104; 133; CDALB 1865-1917;
    DLB 54; MTCW

Robinson, Henry Crabb
    1775-1867 . . . . **NCLC 15**
    See also DLB 107

Robinson, Jill 1936- . . . . **CLC 10**
    See also CA 102

Robinson, Kim Stanley 1952- . . . . . . **CLC 34**
    See also CA 126

Robinson, Lloyd
    See Silverberg, Robert

Robinson, Marilynne 1944- . . . . **CLC 25**
    See also CA 116

Robinson, Smokey. . . . . **CLC 21**
    See also Robinson, William, Jr.

Robinson, William, Jr. 1940-
    See Robinson, Smokey
    See also CA 116

Robison, Mary 1949-. . . . . **CLC 42**
    See also CA 113; 116; DLB 130

Rod, Edouard 1857-1910 . . . . **TCLC 52**

Roddenberry, Eugene Wesley 1921-1991
    See Roddenberry, Gene
    See also CA 110; 135; CANR 37; SATA 45

Roddenberry, Gene . . . . **CLC 17**
    See also Roddenberry, Eugene Wesley
    See also AAYA 5; SATA-Obit 69

Rodgers, Mary 1931-. . . . . **CLC 12**
    See also CA 49-52; CANR 8; CLR 20;
    JRDA; MAICYA; SATA 8

Rodgers, W(illiam) R(obert)
    1909-1969 . . . . **CLC 7**
    See also CA 85-88; DLB 20

Rodman, Eric
    See Silverberg, Robert

Rodman, Howard 1920(?)-1985. . . . . **CLC 65**
    See also CA 118

Rodman, Maia
    See Wojciechowska, Maia (Teresa)

Rodriguez, Claudio 1934-. . . . . **CLC 10**
    See also DLB 134

Roelvaag, O(le) E(dvart)
    1876-1931 . . . . **TCLC 17**
    See also CA 117; DLB 9

Roethke, Theodore (Huebner)
    1908-1963 . . . . . . **CLC 1, 3, 8, 11, 19, 46**
    See also CA 81-84; CABS 2;
    CDALB 1941-1968; DLB 5; MTCW

Rogers, Thomas Hunton 1927- . . . . . **CLC 57**
    See also CA 89-92

Rogers, Will(iam Penn Adair)
    1879-1935 . . . . **TCLC 8**
    See also CA 105; DLB 11

Rogin, Gilbert 1929-. . . . . **CLC 18**
    See also CA 65-68; CANR 15

Rohan, Koda .... TCLC 22
See also Koda Shigeyuki

Rohmer, Eric.................... CLC 16
See also Scherer, Jean-Marie Maurice

Rohmer, Sax .... TCLC 28
See also Ward, Arthur Henry Sarsfield
See also DLB 70

Roiphe, Anne Richardson 1935- ... CLC 3, 9
See also CA 89-92; DLBY 80

Rojas, Fernando de 1465-1541 ...... LC 23

Rolfe, Frederick (William Serafino Austin
Lewis Mary) 1860-1913...... TCLC 12
See also CA 107; DLB 34

Rolland, Romain 1866-1944...... TCLC 23
See also CA 118; DLB 65

Rolvaag, O(le) E(dvart)
See Roelvaag, O(le) E(dvart)

Romain Arnaud, Saint
See Aragon, Louis

Romains, Jules 1885-1972 .... CLC 7
See also CA 85-88; CANR 34; DLB 65;
MTCW

Romero, Jose Ruben 1890-1952 ... TCLC 14
See also CA 114; 131; HW

Ronsard, Pierre de 1524-1585....... LC 6

Rooke, Leon 1934- .... CLC 25, 34
See also CA 25-28R; CANR 23

Roper, William 1498-1578......... LC 10

Roquelaure, A. N.
See Rice, Anne

Rosa, Joao Guimaraes 1908-1967 ... CLC 23
See also CA 89-92; DLB 113

Rosen, Richard (Dean) 1949-...... CLC 39
See also CA 77-80

Rosenberg, Isaac 1890-1918...... TCLC 12
See also CA 107; DLB 20

Rosenblatt, Joe .... CLC 15
See also Rosenblatt, Joseph

Rosenblatt, Joseph 1933-
See Rosenblatt, Joe
See also CA 89-92

Rosenfeld, Samuel 1896-1963
See Tzara, Tristan
See also CA 89-92

Rosenthal, M(acha) L(ouis) 1917-... CLC 28
See also CA 1-4R; CAAS 6; CANR 4;
DLB 5; SATA 59

Ross, Barnaby
See Dannay, Frederic

Ross, Bernard L.
See Follett, Ken(neth Martin)

Ross, J. H.
See Lawrence, T(homas) E(dward)

Ross, Martin
See Martin, Violet Florence
See also DLB 135

Ross, (James) Sinclair 1908- ...... CLC 13
See also CA 73-76; DLB 88

Rossetti, Christina (Georgina)
1830-1894 ... NCLC 2; DA; PC 7; WLC
See also DLB 35; MAICYA; SATA 20

Rossetti, Dante Gabriel
1828-1882 .... NCLC 4; DA; WLC
See also CDBLB 1832-1890; DLB 35

Rossner, Judith (Perelman)
1935- .... CLC 6, 9, 29
See also AITN 2; BEST 90:3; CA 17-20R;
CANR 18; DLB 6; MTCW

Rostand, Edmond (Eugene Alexis)
1868-1918 .... TCLC 6, 37; DA
See also CA 104; 126; MTCW

Roth, Henry 1906- .... CLC 2, 6, 11
See also CA 11-12; CANR 38; CAP 1;
DLB 28; MTCW

Roth, Joseph 1894-1939......... TCLC 33
See also DLB 85

Roth, Philip (Milton)
1933- ...... CLC 1, 2, 3, 4, 6, 9, 15, 22,
31, 47, 66; DA; WLC
See also BEST 90:3; CA 1-4R; CANR 1, 22,
36; CDALB 1968-1988; DLB 2, 28;
DLBY 82; MTCW

Rothenberg, Jerome 1931-....... CLC 6, 57
See also CA 45-48; CANR 1; DLB 5

Roumain, Jacques (Jean Baptiste)
1907-1944 .... TCLC 19; BLC 3
See also BW; CA 117; 125

Rourke, Constance (Mayfield)
1885-1941 .... TCLC 12
See also CA 107; YABC 1

Rousseau, Jean-Baptiste 1671-1741 ... LC 9

Rousseau, Jean-Jacques
1712-1778 .... LC 14; DA; WLC

Roussel, Raymond 1877-1933 ..... TCLC 20
See also CA 117

Rovit, Earl (Herbert) 1927-........ CLC 7
See also CA 5-8R; CANR 12

Rowe, Nicholas 1674-1718........... LC 8
See also DLB 84

Rowley, Ames Dorrance
See Lovecraft, H(oward) P(hillips)

Rowson, Susanna Haswell
1762(?)-1824 .... NCLC 5
See also DLB 37

Roy, Gabrielle 1909-1983....... CLC 10, 14
See also CA 53-56; 110; CANR 5; DLB 68;
MTCW

Rozewicz, Tadeusz 1921-........ CLC 9, 23
See also CA 108; CANR 36; MTCW

Ruark, Gibbons 1941- .... CLC 3
See also CA 33-36R; CANR 14, 31;
DLB 120

Rubens, Bernice (Ruth) 1923-... CLC 19, 31
See also CA 25-28R; CANR 33; DLB 14;
MTCW

Rudkin, (James) David 1936- ...... CLC 14
See also CA 89-92; DLB 13

Rudnik, Raphael 1933-............. CLC 7
See also CA 29-32R

Ruffian, M.
See Hasek, Jaroslav (Matej Frantisek)

Ruiz, Jose Martinez .... CLC 11
See also Martinez Ruiz, Jose

Rukeyser, Muriel
1913-1980 .... CLC 6, 10, 15, 27
See also CA 5-8R; 93-96; CANR 26;
DLB 48; MTCW; SATA 22

Rule, Jane (Vance) 1931-........... CLC 27
See also CA 25-28R; CAAS 18; CANR 12;
DLB 60

Rulfo, Juan 1918-1986......... CLC 8, 80
See also CA 85-88; 118; CANR 26;
DLB 113; HW; MTCW

Runeberg, Johan 1804-1877...... NCLC 41

Runyon, (Alfred) Damon
1884(?)-1946 .... TCLC 10
See also CA 107; DLB 11, 86

Rush, Norman 1933-............. CLC 44
See also CA 121; 126

Rushdie, (Ahmed) Salman
1947- .... CLC 23, 31, 55
See also BEST 89:3; CA 108; 111;
CANR 33; MTCW

Rushforth, Peter (Scott) 1945- ..... CLC 19
See also CA 101

Ruskin, John 1819-1900......... TCLC 20
See also CA 114; 129; CDBLB 1832-1890;
DLB 55; SATA 24

Russ, Joanna 1937-.............. CLC 15
See also CA 25-28R; CANR 11, 31; DLB 8;
MTCW

Russell, George William 1867-1935
See A. E.
See also CA 104; CDBLB 1890-1914

Russell, (Henry) Ken(neth Alfred)
1927- .... CLC 16
See also CA 105

Russell, Willy 1947-.............. CLC 60

Rutherford, Mark .... TCLC 25
See also White, William Hale
See also DLB 18

Ruyslinck, Ward
See Belser, Reimond Karel Maria de

Ryan, Cornelius (John) 1920-1974 ... CLC 7
See also CA 69-72; 53-56; CANR 38

Ryan, Michael 1946- .... CLC 65
See also CA 49-52; DLBY 82

Rybakov, Anatoli (Naumovich)
1911- .... CLC 23, 53
See also CA 126; 135

Ryder, Jonathan
See Ludlum, Robert

Ryga, George 1932-1987 .... CLC 14
See also CA 101; 124; CANR 43; DLB 60

S. S.
See Sassoon, Siegfried (Lorraine)

Saba, Umberto 1883-1957 .... TCLC 33
See also DLB 114

Sabatini, Rafael 1875-1950 .... TCLC 47

Sabato, Ernesto (R.) 1911-...... CLC 10, 23
See also CA 97-100; CANR 32; HW;
MTCW

Sacastru, Martin
See Bioy Casares, Adolfo

Sacher-Masoch, Leopold von
1836(?)-1895 .... NCLC 31

Sayles, John (Thomas)
    1950- .... **CLC 7, 10, 14**
    See also CA 57-60; CANR 41; DLB 44

Scammell, Michael .... **CLC 34**

Scannell, Vernon 1922- .... **CLC 49**
    See also CA 5-8R; CANR 8, 24; DLB 27;
    SATA 59

Scarlett, Susan
    See Streatfeild, (Mary) Noel

Schaeffer, Susan Fromberg
    1941- .... **CLC 6, 11, 22**
    See also CA 49-52; CANR 18; DLB 28;
    MTCW; SATA 22

Schary, Jill
    See Robinson, Jill

Schell, Jonathan 1943- .... **CLC 35**
    See also CA 73-76; CANR 12

Schelling, Friedrich Wilhelm Joseph von
    1775-1854 .... **NCLC 30**
    See also DLB 90

Scherer, Jean-Marie Maurice 1920-
    See Rohmer, Eric
    See also CA 110

Schevill, James (Erwin) 1920- .... **CLC 7**
    See also CA 5-8R; CAAS 12

Schiller, Friedrich 1759-1805 .... **NCLC 39**
    See also DLB 94

Schisgal, Murray (Joseph) 1926- ..... **CLC 6**
    See also CA 21-24R

Schlee, Ann 1934- .... **CLC 35**
    See also CA 101; CANR 29; SATA 36, 44

Schlegel, August Wilhelm von
    1767-1845 .... **NCLC 15**
    See also DLB 94

Schlegel, Johann Elias (von)
    1719(?)-1749 .... **LC 5**

Schmidt, Arno (Otto) 1914-1979.... **CLC 56**
    See also CA 128; 109; DLB 69

Schmitz, Aron Hector 1861-1928
    See Svevo, Italo
    See also CA 104; 122; MTCW

Schnackenberg, Gjertrud 1953- ..... **CLC 40**
    See also CA 116; DLB 120

Schneider, Leonard Alfred 1925-1966
    See Bruce, Lenny
    See also CA 89-92

Schnitzler, Arthur 1862-1931 ...... **TCLC 4**
    See also CA 104; DLB 81, 118

Schor, Sandra (M.) 1932(?)-1990 ... **CLC 65**
    See also CA 132

Schorer, Mark 1908-1977 .... **CLC 9**
    See also CA 5-8R; 73-76; CANR 7;
    DLB 103

Schrader, Paul (Joseph) 1946- ...... **CLC 26**
    See also CA 37-40R; CANR 41; DLB 44

Schreiner, Olive (Emilie Albertina)
    1855-1920 .... **TCLC 9**
    See also CA 105; DLB 18

Schulberg, Budd (Wilson)
    1914- .... **CLC 7, 48**
    See also CA 25-28R; CANR 19; DLB 6, 26,
    28; DLBY 81

Schulz, Bruno
    1892-1942 .... **TCLC 5, 51; SSC 13**
    See also CA 115; 123

Schulz, Charles M(onroe) 1922- .... **CLC 12**
    See also CA 9-12R; CANR 6; SATA 10

Schumacher, Ernst Friedrich
    1911-1977 .... **CLC 80**
    See also CA 81-84; 73-76; CANR 34

Schuyler, James Marcus
    1923-1991 .... **CLC 5, 23**
    See also CA 101; 134; DLB 5

Schwartz, Delmore (David)
    1913-1966 ...... **CLC 2, 4, 10, 45; PC 8**
    See also CA 17-18; 25-28R; CANR 35;
    CAP 2; DLB 28, 48; MTCW

Schwartz, Ernst
    See Ozu, Yasujiro

Schwartz, John Burnham 1965- .... **CLC 59**
    See also CA 132

Schwartz, Lynne Sharon 1939- ..... **CLC 31**
    See also CA 103

Schwartz, Muriel A.
    See Eliot, T(homas) S(tearns)

Schwarz-Bart, Andre 1928- .... **CLC 2, 4**
    See also CA 89-92

Schwarz-Bart, Simone 1938- .... **CLC 7**
    See also CA 97-100

Schwob, (Mayer Andre) Marcel
    1867-1905 .... **TCLC 20**
    See also CA 117; DLB 123

Sciascia, Leonardo
    1921-1989 .... **CLC 8, 9, 41**
    See also CA 85-88; 130; CANR 35; MTCW

Scoppettone, Sandra 1936- .... **CLC 26**
    See also CA 5-8R; CANR 41; SATA 9

Scorsese, Martin 1942- .... **CLC 20**
    See also CA 110; 114

Scotland, Jay
    See Jakes, John (William)

Scott, Duncan Campbell
    1862-1947 .... **TCLC 6**
    See also CA 104; DLB 92

Scott, Evelyn 1893-1963........... **CLC 43**
    See also CA 104; 112; DLB 9, 48

Scott, F(rancis) R(eginald)
    1899-1985 .... **CLC 22**
    See also CA 101; 114; DLB 88

Scott, Frank
    See Scott, F(rancis) R(eginald)

Scott, Joanna 1960- .... **CLC 50**
    See also CA 126

Scott, Paul (Mark) 1920-1978.... **CLC 9, 60**
    See also CA 81-84; 77-80; CANR 33;
    DLB 14; MTCW

Scott, Walter
    1771-1832 .... **NCLC 15; DA; WLC**
    See also CDBLB 1789-1832; DLB 93, 107,
    116; YABC 2

Scribe, (Augustin) Eugene
    1791-1861 .... **NCLC 16**

Scrum, R.
    See Crumb, R(obert)

Scudery, Madeleine de 1607-1701..... **LC 2**

Scum
    See Crumb, R(obert)

Scumbag, Little Bobby
    See Crumb, R(obert)

Seabrook, John
    See Hubbard, L(afayette) Ron(ald)

Sealy, I. Allan 1951- .... **CLC 55**

Search, Alexander
    See Pessoa, Fernando (Antonio Nogueira)

Sebastian, Lee
    See Silverberg, Robert

Sebastian Owl
    See Thompson, Hunter S(tockton)

Sebestyen, Ouida 1924- .... **CLC 30**
    See also AAYA 8; CA 107; CANR 40;
    CLR 17; JRDA; MAICYA; SAAS 10;
    SATA 39

Secundus, H. Scriblerus
    See Fielding, Henry

Sedges, John
    See Buck, Pearl S(ydenstricker)

Sedgwick, Catharine Maria
    1789-1867 .... **NCLC 19**
    See also DLB 1, 74

Seelye, John 1931- .... **CLC 7**

Seferiades, Giorgos Stylianou 1900-1971
    See Seferis, George
    See also CA 5-8R; 33-36R; CANR 5, 36;
    MTCW

Seferis, George .... **CLC 5, 11**
    See also Seferiades, Giorgos Stylianou

Segal, Erich (Wolf) 1937- .... **CLC 3, 10**
    See also BEST 89:1; CA 25-28R; CANR 20,
    36; DLBY 86; MTCW

Seger, Bob 1945-................. **CLC 35**

Seghers, Anna .... **CLC 7**
    See also Radvanyi, Netty
    See also DLB 69

Seidel, Frederick (Lewis) 1936-..... **CLC 18**
    See also CA 13-16R; CANR 8; DLBY 84

Seifert, Jaroslav 1901-1986..... **CLC 34, 44**
    See also CA 127; MTCW

Sei Shonagon c. 966-1017(?) ...... **CMLC 6**

Selby, Hubert, Jr. 1928- ..... **CLC 1, 2, 4, 8**
    See also CA 13-16R; CANR 33; DLB 2

Selzer, Richard 1928-............. **CLC 74**
    See also CA 65-68; CANR 14

Sembene, Ousmane
    See Ousmane, Sembene

Senancour, Etienne Pivert de
    1770-1846 .... **NCLC 16**
    See also DLB 119

Sender, Ramon (Jose) 1902-1982 .... **CLC 8**
    See also CA 5-8R; 105; CANR 8; HW;
    MTCW

Seneca, Lucius Annaeus
    4B.C.-65................... **CMLC 6**

Senghor, Leopold Sedar
    1906- .... **CLC 54; BLC 3**
    See also BW; CA 116; 125; MTCW

Serling, (Edward) Rod(man)
    1924-1975 .... **CLC 30**
    See also AITN 1; CA 65-68; 57-60; DLB 26

Serna, Ramon Gomez de la
See Gomez de la Serna, Ramon

Serpieres
See Guillevic, (Eugene)

Service, Robert
See Service, Robert W(illiam)
See also DLB 92

Service, Robert W(illiam)
1874(?)-1958 ...... TCLC 15; DA; WLC
See also Service, Robert
See also CA 115; 140; SATA 20

Seth, Vikram 1952-............... CLC 43
See also CA 121; 127; DLB 120

Seton, Cynthia Propper
1926-1982 .... CLC 27
See also CA 5-8R; 108; CANR 7

Seton, Ernest (Evan) Thompson
1860-1946 .... TCLC 31
See also CA 109; DLB 92; JRDA; SATA 18

Seton-Thompson, Ernest
See Seton, Ernest (Evan) Thompson

Settle, Mary Lee 1918- .... CLC 19, 61
See also CA 89-92; CAAS 1; DLB 6

Seuphor, Michel
See Arp, Jean

Sevigne, Marie (de Rabutin-Chantal) Marquise
de 1626-1696 .... LC 11

Sexton, Anne (Harvey)
1928-1974 .... CLC 2, 4, 6, 8, 10, 15, 53;
DA; PC 2; WLC
See also CA 1-4R; 53-56; CABS 2;
CANR 3, 36; CDALB 1941-1968; DLB 5;
MTCW; SATA 10

Shaara, Michael (Joseph Jr.)
1929-1988 .... CLC 15
See also AITN 1; CA 102; DLBY 83

Shackleton, C. C.
See Aldiss, Brian W(ilson)

Shacochis, Bob .... CLC 39
See also Shacochis, Robert G.

Shacochis, Robert G. 1951-
See Shacochis, Bob
See also CA 119; 124

Shaffer, Anthony (Joshua) 1926-.... CLC 19
See also CA 110; 116; DLB 13

Shaffer, Peter (Levin)
1926- .... CLC 5, 14, 18, 37, 60
See also CA 25-28R; CANR 25;
CDBLB 1960 to Present; DLB 13;
MTCW

Shakey, Bernard
See Young, Neil

Shalamov, Varlam (Tikhonovich)
1907(?)-1982 .... CLC 18
See also CA 129; 105

Shamlu, Ahmad 1925- .... CLC 10

Shammas, Anton 1951-............ CLC 55

Shange, Ntozake
1948- .. CLC 8, 25, 38, 74; BLC 3; DC 3
See also AAYA 9; BW; CA 85-88; CABS 3;
CANR 27; DLB 38; MTCW

Shanley, John Patrick 1950-....... CLC 75
See also CA 128; 133

Shapcott, Thomas William 1935- ... CLC 38
See also CA 69-72

Shapiro, Jane.................... CLC 76

Shapiro, Karl (Jay) 1913- .. CLC 4, 8, 15, 53
See also CA 1-4R; CAAS 6; CANR 1, 36;
DLB 48; MTCW

Sharp, William 1855-1905 .... TCLC 39

Sharpe, Thomas Ridley 1928-
See Sharpe, Tom
See also CA 114; 122

Sharpe, Tom..................... CLC 36
See also Sharpe, Thomas Ridley
See also DLB 14

Shaw, Bernard................... TCLC 45
See also Shaw, George Bernard

Shaw, G. Bernard
See Shaw, George Bernard

Shaw, George Bernard
1856-1950 .... TCLC 3, 9, 21; DA; WLC
See also Shaw, Bernard
See also CA 104; 128; CDBLB 1914-1945;
DLB 10, 57; MTCW

Shaw, Henry Wheeler
1818-1885 .... NCLC 15
See also DLB 11

Shaw, Irwin 1913-1984....... CLC 7, 23, 34
See also AITN 1; CA 13-16R; 112;
CANR 21; CDALB 1941-1968; DLB 6,
102; DLBY 84; MTCW

Shaw, Robert 1927-1978 .... CLC 5
See also AITN 1; CA 1-4R; 81-84;
CANR 4; DLB 13, 14

Shaw, T. E.
See Lawrence, T(homas) E(dward)

Shawn, Wallace 1943- .... CLC 41
See also CA 112

Sheed, Wilfrid (John Joseph)
1930- .... CLC 2, 4, 10, 53
See also CA 65-68; CANR 30; DLB 6;
MTCW

Sheldon, Alice Hastings Bradley
1915(?)-1987
See Tiptree, James, Jr.
See also CA 108; 122; CANR 34; MTCW

Sheldon, John
See Bloch, Robert (Albert)

Shelley, Mary Wollstonecraft (Godwin)
1797-1851 .... NCLC 14; DA; WLC
See also CDBLB 1789-1832; DLB 110, 116;
SATA 29

Shelley, Percy Bysshe
1792-1822 .... NCLC 18; DA; WLC
See also CDBLB 1789-1832; DLB 96, 110

Shepard, Jim 1956-............... CLC 36
See also CA 137

Shepard, Lucius 1947-............ CLC 34
See also CA 128; 141

Shepard, Sam
1943- .... CLC 4, 6, 17, 34, 41, 44
See also AAYA 1; CA 69-72; CABS 3;
CANR 22; DLB 7; MTCW

Shepherd, Michael
See Ludlum, Robert

Sherburne, Zoa (Morin) 1912-...... CLC 30
See also CA 1-4R; CANR 3, 37; MAICYA;
SATA 3

Sheridan, Frances 1724-1766........ LC 7
See also DLB 39, 84

Sheridan, Richard Brinsley
1751-1816 ... NCLC 5; DA; DC 1; WLC
See also CDBLB 1660-1789; DLB 89

Sherman, Jonathan Marc.......... CLC 55

Sherman, Martin 1941(?)-......... CLC 19
See also CA 116; 123

Sherwin, Judith Johnson 1936-... CLC 7, 15
See also CA 25-28R; CANR 34

Sherwood, Robert E(mmet)
1896-1955 .... TCLC 3
See also CA 104; DLB 7, 26

Shiel, M(atthew) P(hipps)
1865-1947 .... TCLC 8
See also CA 106

Shiga, Naoya 1883-1971.......... CLC 33
See also CA 101; 33-36R

Shimazaki Haruki 1872-1943
See Shimazaki Toson
See also CA 105; 134

Shimazaki Toson.................. TCLC 5
See also Shimazaki Haruki

Sholokhov, Mikhail (Aleksandrovich)
1905-1984 .... CLC 7, 15
See also CA 101; 112; MTCW; SATA 36

Shone, Patric
See Hanley, James

Shreve, Susan Richards 1939-...... CLC 23
See also CA 49-52; CAAS 5; CANR 5, 38;
MAICYA; SATA 41, 46

Shue, Larry 1946-1985............ CLC 52
See also CA 117

Shu-Jen, Chou 1881-1936
See Hsun, Lu
See also CA 104

Shulman, Alix Kates 1932- ...... CLC 2, 10
See also CA 29-32R; CANR 43; SATA 7

Shuster, Joe 1914- .... CLC 21

Shute, Nevil..................... CLC 30
See also Norway, Nevil Shute

Shuttle, Penelope (Diane) 1947- ..... CLC 7
See also CA 93-96; CANR 39; DLB 14, 40

Sidney, Mary 1561-1621 .... LC 19

Sidney, Sir Philip 1554-1586.... LC 19; DA
See also CDBLB Before 1660

Siegel, Jerome 1914- .... CLC 21
See also CA 116

Siegel, Jerry
See Siegel, Jerome

Sienkiewicz, Henryk (Adam Alexander Pius)
1846-1916 .... TCLC 3
See also CA 104; 134

Sierra, Gregorio Martinez
See Martinez Sierra, Gregorio

Sierra, Maria (de la O'LeJarraga) Martinez
See Martinez Sierra, Maria (de la
O'LeJarraga)

Sigal, Clancy 1926-................ CLC 7
See also CA 1-4R

Smith, Iain Crichton 1928- .... **CLC 64**
See also CA 21-24R; DLB 40

Smith, John 1580(?)-1631 .... **LC 9**

Smith, Johnston
See Crane, Stephen (Townley)

Smith, Lee 1944-............. **CLC 25, 73**
See also CA 114; 119; DLBY 83

Smith, Martin
See Smith, Martin Cruz

Smith, Martin Cruz 1942-........ **CLC 25**
See also BEST 89:4; CA 85-88; CANR 6,
23, 43

Smith, Mary-Ann Tirone 1944-..... **CLC 39**
See also CA 118; 136

Smith, Patti 1946- .... **CLC 12**
See also CA 93-96

Smith, Pauline (Urmson)
1882-1959 .... **TCLC 25**

Smith, Rosamond
See Oates, Joyce Carol

Smith, Sheila Kaye
See Kaye-Smith, Sheila

Smith, Stevie .... **CLC 3, 8, 25, 44**
See also Smith, Florence Margaret
See also DLB 20

Smith, Wilbur A(ddison) 1933-..... **CLC 33**
See also CA 13-16R; CANR 7; MTCW

Smith, William Jay 1918- .... **CLC 6**
See also CA 5-8R; DLB 5; MAICYA;
SATA 2, 68

Smith, Woodrow Wilson
See Kuttner, Henry

Smolenskin, Peretz 1842-1885.... **NCLC 30**

Smollett, Tobias (George) 1721-1771 .. **LC 2**
See also CDBLB 1660-1789; DLB 39, 104

Snodgrass, W(illiam) D(e Witt)
1926- .... **CLC 2, 6, 10, 18, 68**
See also CA 1-4R; CANR 6, 36; DLB 5;
MTCW

Snow, C(harles) P(ercy)
1905-1980 ...... **CLC 1, 4, 6, 9, 13, 19**
See also CA 5-8R; 101; CANR 28;
CDBLB 1945-1960; DLB 15, 77; MTCW

Snow, Frances Compton
See Adams, Henry (Brooks)

Snyder, Gary (Sherman)
1930- .... **CLC 1, 2, 5, 9, 32**
See also CA 17-20R; CANR 30; DLB 5, 16

Snyder, Zilpha Keatley 1927-...... **CLC 17**
See also CA 9-12R; CANR 38; CLR 31;
JRDA; MAICYA; SAAS 2; SATA 1, 28,
75

Soares, Bernardo
See Pessoa, Fernando (Antonio Nogueira)

Sobh, A.
See Shamlu, Ahmad

Sobol, Joshua .... **CLC 60**

Soderberg, Hjalmar 1869-1941 .... **TCLC 39**

Sodergran, Edith (Irene)
See Soedergran, Edith (Irene)

Soedergran, Edith (Irene)
1892-1923 .... **TCLC 31**

Softly, Edgar
See Lovecraft, H(oward) P(hillips)

Softly, Edward
See Lovecraft, H(oward) P(hillips)

Sokolov, Raymond 1941-.......... **CLC 7**
See also CA 85-88

Solo, Jay
See Ellison, Harlan

Sologub, Fyodor .... **TCLC 9**
See also Teternikov, Fyodor Kuzmich

Solomons, Ikey Esquir
See Thackeray, William Makepeace

Solomos, Dionysios 1798-1857 ... **NCLC 15**

Solwoska, Mara
See French, Marilyn

Solzhenitsyn, Aleksandr I(sayevich)
1918- ...... **CLC 1, 2, 4, 7, 9, 10, 18, 26,
34, 78; DA; WLC**
See also AITN 1; CA 69-72; CANR 40;
MTCW

Somers, Jane
See Lessing, Doris (May)

Somerville, Edith 1858-1949 ..... **TCLC 51**
See also DLB 135

Somerville & Ross
See Martin, Violet Florence; Somerville,
Edith

Sommer, Scott 1951- .... **CLC 25**
See also CA 106

Sondheim, Stephen (Joshua)
1930- .... **CLC 30, 39**
See also CA 103

Sontag, Susan 1933-... **CLC 1, 2, 10, 13, 31**
See also CA 17-20R; CANR 25; DLB 2, 67;
MTCW

Sophocles
496(?)B.C.-406(?)B.C..... **CMLC 2; DA;
DC 1**

Sorel, Julia
See Drexler, Rosalyn

Sorrentino, Gilbert
1929- .... **CLC 3, 7, 14, 22, 40**
See also CA 77-80; CANR 14, 33; DLB 5;
DLBY 80

Soto, Gary 1952-.............. **CLC 32, 80**
See also AAYA 10; CA 119; 125; DLB 82;
HW; JRDA

Soupault, Philippe 1897-1990 ...... **CLC 68**
See also CA 116; 131

Souster, (Holmes) Raymond
1921- .... **CLC 5, 14**
See also CA 13-16R; CAAS 14; CANR 13,
29; DLB 88; SATA 63

Southern, Terry 1926- .... **CLC 7**
See also CA 1-4R; CANR 1; DLB 2

Southey, Robert 1774-1843 .... **NCLC 8**
See also DLB 93, 107; SATA 54

Southworth, Emma Dorothy Eliza Nevitte
1819-1899 .... **NCLC 26**

Souza, Ernest
See Scott, Evelyn

Soyinka, Wole
1934- ..... **CLC 3, 5, 14, 36, 44; BLC 3;
DA; DC 2; WLC**
See also BW; CA 13-16R; CANR 27, 39;
DLB 125; MTCW

Spackman, W(illiam) M(ode)
1905-1990 .... **CLC 46**
See also CA 81-84; 132

Spacks, Barry 1931-............. **CLC 14**
See also CA 29-32R; CANR 33; DLB 105

Spanidou, Irini 1946- .... **CLC 44**

Spark, Muriel (Sarah)
1918- .... **CLC 2, 3, 5, 8, 13, 18, 40;
SSC 10**
See also CA 5-8R; CANR 12, 36;
CDBLB 1945-1960; DLB 15; MTCW

Spaulding, Douglas
See Bradbury, Ray (Douglas)

Spaulding, Leonard
See Bradbury, Ray (Douglas)

Spence, J. A. D.
See Eliot, T(homas) S(tearns)

Spencer, Elizabeth 1921-.......... **CLC 22**
See also CA 13-16R; CANR 32; DLB 6;
MTCW; SATA 14

Spencer, Leonard G.
See Silverberg, Robert

Spencer, Scott 1945-............. **CLC 30**
See also CA 113; DLBY 86

Spender, Stephen (Harold)
1909- .... **CLC 1, 2, 5, 10, 41**
See also CA 9-12R; CANR 31;
CDBLB 1945-1960; DLB 20; MTCW

Spengler, Oswald (Arnold Gottfried)
1880-1936 .... **TCLC 25**
See also CA 118

Spenser, Edmund
1552(?)-1599 .... **LC 5; DA; PC 8; WLC**
See also CDBLB Before 1660

Spicer, Jack 1925-1965 ...... **CLC 8, 18, 72**
See also CA 85-88; DLB 5, 16

Spiegelman, Art 1948-............ **CLC 76**
See also AAYA 10; CA 125; CANR 41

Spielberg, Peter 1929-............. **CLC 6**
See also CA 5-8R; CANR 4; DLBY 81

Spielberg, Steven 1947- .... **CLC 20**
See also AAYA 8; CA 77-80; CANR 32;
SATA 32

Spillane, Frank Morrison 1918-
See Spillane, Mickey
See also CA 25-28R; CANR 28; MTCW;
SATA 66

Spillane, Mickey .... **CLC 3, 13**
See also Spillane, Frank Morrison

Spinoza, Benedictus de 1632-1677 .... **LC 9**

Spinrad, Norman (Richard) 1940-... **CLC 46**
See also CA 37-40R; CANR 20; DLB 8

Spitteler, Carl (Friedrich Georg)
1845-1924 .... **TCLC 12**
See also CA 109; DLB 129

Spivack, Kathleen (Romola Drucker)
1938- .... **CLC 6**
See also CA 49-52

Spoto, Donald 1941-.............. **CLC 39**
See also CA 65-68; CANR 11

Springsteen, Bruce (F.) 1949- ...... **CLC 17**
See also CA 111

Spurling, Hilary 1940-............ **CLC 34**
See also CA 104; CANR 25

Squires, (James) Radcliffe
1917-1993 .... **CLC 51**
See also CA 1-4R; 140; CANR 6, 21

Srivastava, Dhanpat Rai 1880(?)-1936
See Premchand
See also CA 118

Stacy, Donald
See Pohl, Frederik

Stael, Germaine de
See Stael-Holstein, Anne Louise Germaine
Necker Baronn
See also DLB 119

Stael-Holstein, Anne Louise Germaine Necker
Baronn 1766-1817 .... **NCLC 3**
See also Stael, Germaine de

Stafford, Jean 1915-1979... **CLC 4, 7, 19, 68**
See also CA 1-4R; 85-88; CANR 3; DLB 2;
MTCW; SATA 22

Stafford, William (Edgar)
1914-1993 .... **CLC 4, 7, 29**
See also CA 5-8R; 142; CAAS 3; CANR 5,
22; DLB 5

Staines, Trevor
See Brunner, John (Kilian Houston)

Stairs, Gordon
See Austin, Mary (Hunter)

Stannard, Martin 1947- .... **CLC 44**
See also CA 142

Stanton, Maura 1946- .... **CLC 9**
See also CA 89-92; CANR 15; DLB 120

Stanton, Schuyler
See Baum, L(yman) Frank

Stapledon, (William) Olaf
1886-1950 .... **TCLC 22**
See also CA 111; DLB 15

Starbuck, George (Edwin) 1931-.... **CLC 53**
See also CA 21-24R; CANR 23

Stark, Richard
See Westlake, Donald E(dwin)

Staunton, Schuyler
See Baum, L(yman) Frank

Stead, Christina (Ellen)
1902-1983 .... **CLC 2, 5, 8, 32, 80**
See also CA 13-16R; 109; CANR 33, 40;
MTCW

Stead, William Thomas
1849-1912 .... **TCLC 48**

Steele, Richard 1672-1729 .... **LC 18**
See also CDBLB 1660-1789; DLB 84, 101

Steele, Timothy (Reid) 1948-....... **CLC 45**
See also CA 93-96; CANR 16; DLB 120

Steffens, (Joseph) Lincoln
1866-1936 .... **TCLC 20**
See also CA 117

Stegner, Wallace (Earle)
1909-1993 .... **CLC 9, 49**
See also AITN 1; BEST 90:3; CA 1-4R;
141; CAAS 9; CANR 1, 21; DLB 9;
MTCW

Stein, Gertrude
1874-1946 ...... **TCLC 1, 6, 28, 48; DA;**
WLC
See also CA 104; 132; CDALB 1917-1929;
DLB 4, 54, 86; MTCW

Steinbeck, John (Ernst)
1902-1968 ...... **CLC 1, 5, 9, 13, 21, 34,**
45, 75; DA; SSC 11; WLC
See also CA 1-4R; 25-28R; CANR 1, 35;
CDALB 1929-1941; DLB 7, 9; DLBD 2;
MTCW; SATA 9

Steinem, Gloria 1934-............ **CLC 63**
See also CA 53-56; CANR 28; MTCW

Steiner, George 1929-............ **CLC 24**
See also CA 73-76; CANR 31; DLB 67;
MTCW; SATA 62

Steiner, K. Leslie
See Delany, Samuel R(ay, Jr.)

Steiner, Rudolf 1861-1925 .... **TCLC 13**
See also CA 107

Stendhal 1783-1842.... **NCLC 23; DA; WLC**
See also DLB 119

Stephen, Leslie 1832-1904 .... **TCLC 23**
See also CA 123; DLB 57

Stephen, Sir Leslie
See Stephen, Leslie

Stephen, Virginia
See Woolf, (Adeline) Virginia

Stephens, James 1882(?)-1950...... **TCLC 4**
See also CA 104; DLB 19

Stephens, Reed
See Donaldson, Stephen R.

Steptoe, Lydia
See Barnes, Djuna

Sterchi, Beat 1949-.............. **CLC 65**

Sterling, Brett
See Bradbury, Ray (Douglas); Hamilton,
Edmond

Sterling, Bruce 1954-............. **CLC 72**
See also CA 119

Sterling, George 1869-1926 ...... **TCLC 20**
See also CA 117; DLB 54

Stern, Gerald 1925- .... **CLC 40**
See also CA 81-84; CANR 28; DLB 105

Stern, Richard (Gustave) 1928-... **CLC 4, 39**
See also CA 1-4R; CANR 1, 25; DLBY 87

Sternberg, Josef von 1894-1969..... **CLC 20**
See also CA 81-84

Sterne, Laurence
1713-1768 .... **LC 2; DA; WLC**
See also CDBLB 1660-1789; DLB 39

Sternheim, (William Adolf) Carl
1878-1942 .... **TCLC 8**
See also CA 105; DLB 56, 118

Stevens, Mark 1951- .... **CLC 34**
See also CA 122

Stevens, Wallace
1879-1955 .... **TCLC 3, 12, 45; DA;**
PC 6; WLC
See also CA 104; 124; CDALB 1929-1941;
DLB 54; MTCW

Stevenson, Anne (Katharine)
1933- .... **CLC 7, 33**
See also CA 17-20R; CAAS 9; CANR 9, 33;
DLB 40; MTCW

Stevenson, Robert Louis (Balfour)
1850-1894 .... **NCLC 5, 14; DA;**
SSC 11; WLC
See also CDBLB 1890-1914; CLR 10, 11;
DLB 18, 57; JRDA; MAICYA; YABC 2

Stewart, J(ohn) I(nnes) M(ackintosh)
1906- .... **CLC 7, 14, 32**
See also CA 85-88; CAAS 3; MTCW

Stewart, Mary (Florence Elinor)
1916- .... **CLC 7, 35**
See also CA 1-4R; CANR 1; SATA 12

Stewart, Mary Rainbow
See Stewart, Mary (Florence Elinor)

Stifter, Adalbert 1805-1868...... **NCLC 41**
See also DLB 133

Still, James 1906-................ **CLC 49**
See also CA 65-68; CAAS 17; CANR 10,
26; DLB 9; SATA 29

Sting
See Sumner, Gordon Matthew

Stirling, Arthur
See Sinclair, Upton (Beall)

Stitt, Milan 1941-................ **CLC 29**
See also CA 69-72

Stockton, Francis Richard 1834-1902
See Stockton, Frank R.
See also CA 108; 137; MAICYA; SATA 44

Stockton, Frank R. .... **TCLC 47**
See also Stockton, Francis Richard
See also DLB 42, 74; SATA 32

Stoddard, Charles
See Kuttner, Henry

Stoker, Abraham 1847-1912
See Stoker, Bram
See also CA 105; DA; SATA 29

Stoker, Bram .... **TCLC 8; WLC**
See also Stoker, Abraham
See also CDBLB 1890-1914; DLB 36, 70

Stolz, Mary (Slattery) 1920-....... **CLC 12**
See also AAYA 8; AITN 1; CA 5-8R;
CANR 13, 41; JRDA; MAICYA;
SAAS 3; SATA 10, 71

Stone, Irving 1903-1989........... **CLC 7**
See also AITN 1; CA 1-4R; 129; CAAS 3;
CANR 1, 23; MTCW; SATA 3;
SATA-Obit 64

Stone, Oliver 1946-.............. **CLC 73**
See also CA 110

Stone, Robert (Anthony)
1937- .... **CLC 5, 23, 42**
See also CA 85-88; CANR 23; MTCW

Stone, Zachary
See Follett, Ken(neth Martin)

Stoppard, Tom
1937- ...... **CLC 1, 3, 4, 5, 8, 15, 29, 34, 63; DA; WLC**
See also CA 81-84; CANR 39; CDBLB 1960 to Present; DLB 13; DLBY 85; MTCW

Storey, David (Malcolm)
1933- .... **CLC 2, 4, 5, 8**
See also CA 81-84; CANR 36; DLB 13, 14; MTCW

Storm, Hyemeyohsts 1935- .... **CLC 3**
See also CA 81-84

Storm, (Hans) Theodor (Woldsen)
1817-1888 .... **NCLC 1**

Storni, Alfonsina 1892-1938 .... **TCLC 5**
See also CA 104; 131; HW

Stout, Rex (Todhunter) 1886-1975 ... **CLC 3**
See also AITN 2; CA 61-64

Stow, (Julian) Randolph 1935- .. **CLC 23, 48**
See also CA 13-16R; CANR 33; MTCW

Stowe, Harriet (Elizabeth) Beecher
1811-1896 .... **NCLC 3; DA; WLC**
See also CDALB 1865-1917; DLB 1, 12, 42, 74; JRDA; MAICYA; YABC 1

Strachey, (Giles) Lytton
1880-1932 .... **TCLC 12**
See also CA 110; DLBD 10

Strand, Mark 1934- ...... **CLC 6, 18, 41, 71**
See also CA 21-24R; CANR 40; DLB 5; SATA 41

Straub, Peter (Francis) 1943- ...... **CLC 28**
See also BEST 89:1; CA 85-88; CANR 28; DLBY 84; MTCW

Strauss, Botho 1944- .... **CLC 22**
See also DLB 124

Streatfeild, (Mary) Noel
1895(?)-1986 .... **CLC 21**
See also CA 81-84; 120; CANR 31; CLR 17; MAICYA; SATA 20, 48

Stribling, T(homas) S(igismund)
1881-1965 .... **CLC 23**
See also CA 107; DLB 9

Strindberg, (Johan) August
1849-1912 ...... **TCLC 1, 8, 21, 47; DA; WLC**
See also CA 104; 135

Stringer, Arthur 1874-1950 .... **TCLC 37**
See also DLB 92

Stringer, David
See Roberts, Keith (John Kingston)

Strugatskii, Arkadii (Natanovich)
1925-1991 .... **CLC 27**
See also CA 106; 135

Strugatskii, Boris (Natanovich)
1933- .... **CLC 27**
See also CA 106

Strummer, Joe 1953(?)- .... **CLC 30**
See also Clash, The

Stuart, Don A.
See Campbell, John W(ood, Jr.)

Stuart, Ian
See MacLean, Alistair (Stuart)

Stuart, Jesse (Hilton)
1906-1984 .... **CLC 1, 8, 11, 14, 34**
See also CA 5-8R; 112; CANR 31; DLB 9, 48, 102; DLBY 84; SATA 2, 36

Sturgeon, Theodore (Hamilton)
1918-1985 .... **CLC 22, 39**
See also Queen, Ellery
See also CA 81-84; 116; CANR 32; DLB 8; DLBY 85; MTCW

Sturges, Preston 1898-1959 .... **TCLC 48**
See also CA 114; DLB 26

Styron, William
1925- .... **CLC 1, 3, 5, 11, 15, 60**
See also BEST 90:4; CA 5-8R; CANR 6, 33; CDALB 1968-1988; DLB 2; DLBY 80; MTCW

Suarez Lynch, B.
See Bioy Casares, Adolfo; Borges, Jorge Luis

Suarez Lynch, B.
See Borges, Jorge Luis

Su Chien 1884-1918
See Su Man-shu
See also CA 123

Sudermann, Hermann 1857-1928 .. **TCLC 15**
See also CA 107; DLB 118

Sue, Eugene 1804-1857 .... **NCLC 1**
See also DLB 119

Sueskind, Patrick 1949- .... **CLC 44**

Sukenick, Ronald 1932- ..... **CLC 3, 4, 6, 48**
See also CA 25-28R; CAAS 8; CANR 32; DLBY 81

Suknaski, Andrew 1942- .... **CLC 19**
See also CA 101; DLB 53

Sullivan, Vernon
See Vian, Boris

Sully Prudhomme 1839-1907 ...... **TCLC 31**

Su Man-shu .... **TCLC 24**
See also Su Chien

Summerforest, Ivy B.
See Kirkup, James

Summers, Andrew James 1942- ..... **CLC 26**
See also Police, The

Summers, Andy
See Summers, Andrew James

Summers, Hollis (Spurgeon, Jr.)
1916- .... **CLC 10**
See also CA 5-8R; CANR 3; DLB 6

Summers, (Alphonsus Joseph-Mary Augustus) Montague 1880-1948 .... **TCLC 16**
See also CA 118

Sumner, Gordon Matthew 1951- .... **CLC 26**
See also Police, The

Surtees, Robert Smith
1803-1864 .... **NCLC 14**
See also DLB 21

Susann, Jacqueline 1921-1974....... **CLC 3**
See also AITN 1; CA 65-68; 53-56; MTCW

Suskind, Patrick
See Sueskind, Patrick

Sutcliff, Rosemary 1920-1992 ...... **CLC 26**
See also AAYA 10; CA 5-8R; 139; CANR 37; CLR 1; JRDA; MAICYA; SATA 6, 44; SATA-Obit 73

Sutro, Alfred 1863-1933.......... **TCLC 6**
See also CA 105; DLB 10

Sutton, Henry
See Slavitt, David R(ytman)

Svevo, Italo .... **TCLC 2, 35**
See also Schmitz, Aron Hector

Swados, Elizabeth 1951- .... **CLC 12**
See also CA 97-100

Swados, Harvey 1920-1972 .... **CLC 5**
See also CA 5-8R; 37-40R; CANR 6; DLB 2

Swan, Gladys 1934- .... **CLC 69**
See also CA 101; CANR 17, 39

Swarthout, Glendon (Fred)
1918-1992 .... **CLC 35**
See also CA 1-4R; 139; CANR 1; SATA 26

Sweet, Sarah C.
See Jewett, (Theodora) Sarah Orne

Swenson, May
1919-1989 .... **CLC 4, 14, 61; DA**
See also CA 5-8R; 130; CANR 36; DLB 5; MTCW; SATA 15

Swift, Augustus
See Lovecraft, H(oward) P(hillips)

Swift, Graham 1949- .... **CLC 41**
See also CA 117; 122

Swift, Jonathan
1667-1745 .... **LC 1; DA; WLC**
See also CDBLB 1660-1789; DLB 39, 95, 101; SATA 19

Swinburne, Algernon Charles
1837-1909 ...... **TCLC 8, 36; DA; WLC**
See also CA 105; 140; CDBLB 1832-1890; DLB 35, 57

Swinfen, Ann .... **CLC 34**

Swinnerton, Frank Arthur
1884-1982 .... **CLC 31**
See also CA 108; DLB 34

Swithen, John
See King, Stephen (Edwin)

Sylvia
See Ashton-Warner, Sylvia (Constance)

Symmes, Robert Edward
See Duncan, Robert (Edward)

Symonds, John Addington
1840-1893 .... **NCLC 34**
See also DLB 57

Symons, Arthur 1865-1945 .... **TCLC 11**
See also CA 107; DLB 19, 57

Symons, Julian (Gustave)
1912- .... **CLC 2, 14, 32**
See also CA 49-52; CAAS 3; CANR 3, 33; DLB 87; DLBY 92; MTCW

Synge, (Edmund) J(ohn) M(illington)
1871-1909 .... **TCLC 6, 37; DC 2**
See also CA 104; 141; CDBLB 1890-1914; DLB 10, 19

Syruc, J.
See Milosz, Czeslaw

Szirtes, George 1948- .... **CLC 46**
See also CA 109; CANR 27

Tabori, George 1914- .... **CLC 19**
See also CA 49-52; CANR 4

Tagore, Rabindranath
1861-1941 . . . . **TCLC 3; PC 8**
See also CA 104; 120; MTCW

Taine, Hippolyte Adolphe
1828-1893 . . . . **NCLC 15**

Talese, Gay 1932- . . . . **CLC 37**
See also AITN 1; CA 1-4R; CANR 9;
MTCW

Tallent, Elizabeth (Ann) 1954- . . . . . **CLC 45**
See also CA 117; DLB 130

Tally, Ted 1952- . . . . **CLC 42**
See also CA 120; 124

Tamayo y Baus, Manuel
1829-1898 . . . . **NCLC 1**

Tammsaare, A(nton) H(ansen)
1878-1940 . . . . **TCLC 27**

Tan, Amy 1952- . . . . **CLC 59**
See also AAYA 9; BEST 89:3; CA 136;
SATA 75

Tandem, Felix
See Spitteler, Carl (Friedrich Georg)

Tanizaki, Jun'ichiro
1886-1965 . . . . **CLC 8, 14, 28**
See also CA 93-96; 25-28R

Tanner, William
See Amis, Kingsley (William)

Tao Lao
See Storni, Alfonsina

Tarassoff, Lev
See Troyat, Henri

Tarbell, Ida M(inerva)
1857-1944 . . . . **TCLC 40**
See also CA 122; DLB 47

Tarkington, (Newton) Booth
1869-1946 . . . . **TCLC 9**
See also CA 110; DLB 9, 102; SATA 17

Tarkovsky, Andrei (Arsenyevich)
1932-1986 . . . . **CLC 75**
See also CA 127

Tartt, Donna 1964(?)- . . . . **CLC 76**
See also CA 142

Tasso, Torquato 1544-1595 . . . . **LC 5**

Tate, (John Orley) Allen
1899-1979 . . . . **CLC 2, 4, 6, 9, 11, 14, 24**
See also CA 5-8R; 85-88; CANR 32;
DLB 4, 45, 63; MTCW

Tate, Ellalice
See Hibbert, Eleanor Alice Burford

Tate, James (Vincent) 1943- . . . **CLC 2, 6, 25**
See also CA 21-24R; CANR 29; DLB 5

Tavel, Ronald 1940- . . . . **CLC 6**
See also CA 21-24R; CANR 33

Taylor, Cecil Philip 1929-1981 . . . . . **CLC 27**
See also CA 25-28R; 105

Taylor, Edward 1642(?)-1729 . . . . **LC 11; DA**
See also DLB 24

Taylor, Eleanor Ross 1920- . . . . **CLC 5**
See also CA 81-84

Taylor, Elizabeth 1912-1975 . . . **CLC 2, 4, 29**
See also CA 13-16R; CANR 9; MTCW;
SATA 13

Taylor, Henry (Splawn) 1942- . . . . . . **CLC 44**
See also CA 33-36R; CAAS 7; CANR 31;
DLB 5

Taylor, Kamala (Purnaiya) 1924-
See Markandaya, Kamala
See also CA 77-80

Taylor, Mildred D. . . . . **CLC 21**
See also AAYA 10; BW; CA 85-88;
CANR 25; CLR 9; DLB 52; JRDA;
MAICYA; SAAS 5; SATA 15, 70

Taylor, Peter (Hillsman)
1917- . . . . . . **CLC 1, 4, 18, 37, 44, 50, 71;**
SSC 10
See also CA 13-16R; CANR 9; DLBY 81;
MTCW

Taylor, Robert Lewis 1912- . . . . **CLC 14**
See also CA 1-4R; CANR 3; SATA 10

Tchekhov, Anton
See Chekhov, Anton (Pavlovich)

Tcherniak, Nathalie 1900-
See Saurraute, Nathalie

Teasdale, Sara 1884-1933 . . . . **TCLC 4**
See also CA 104; DLB 45; SATA 32

Tegner, Esaias 1782-1846 . . . . **NCLC 2**

Teilhard de Chardin, (Marie Joseph) Pierre
1881-1955 . . . . **TCLC 9**
See also CA 105

Temple, Ann
See Mortimer, Penelope (Ruth)

Tennant, Emma (Christina)
1937- . . . . **CLC 13, 52**
See also CA 65-68; CAAS 9; CANR 10, 38;
DLB 14

Tenneshaw, S. M.
See Silverberg, Robert

Tennyson, Alfred
1809-1892 . . **NCLC 30; DA; PC 6; WLC**
See also CDBLB 1832-1890; DLB 32

Teran, Lisa St. Aubin de . . . . **CLC 36**
See also St. Aubin de Teran, Lisa

Teresa de Jesus, St. 1515-1582 . . . . . . **LC 18**

Terkel, Louis 1912-
See Terkel, Studs
See also CA 57-60; CANR 18; MTCW

Terkel, Studs . . . . **CLC 38**
See also Terkel, Louis
See also AITN 1

Terry, C. V.
See Slaughter, Frank G(ill)

Terry, Megan 1932- . . . . **CLC 19**
See also CA 77-80; CABS 3; CANR 43;
DLB 7

Tertz, Abram
See Sinyavsky, Andrei (Donatevich)

Tesich, Steve 1943(?)- . . . . **CLC 40, 69**
See also CA 105; DLBY 83

Teternikov, Fyodor Kuzmich 1863-1927
See Sologub, Fyodor
See also CA 104

Tevis, Walter 1928-1984 . . . . **CLC 42**
See also CA 113

Tey, Josephine . . . . **TCLC 14**
See also Mackintosh, Elizabeth
See also DLB 77

Thackeray, William Makepeace
1811-1863 . . **NCLC 5, 14, 22; DA; WLC**
See also CDBLB 1832-1890; DLB 21, 55;
SATA 23

Thakura, Ravindranatha
See Tagore, Rabindranath

Tharoor, Shashi 1956- . . . . **CLC 70**
See also CA 141

Thelwell, Michael Miles 1939- . . . . . **CLC 22**
See also CA 101

Theobald, Lewis, Jr.
See Lovecraft, H(oward) P(hillips)

Theodorescu, Ion N. 1880-1967
See Arghezi, Tudor
See also CA 116

The Prophet
See Dreiser, Theodore (Herman Albert)

Theriault, Yves 1915-1983 . . . . **CLC 79**
See also CA 102; DLB 88

Theroux, Alexander (Louis)
1939- . . . . **CLC 2, 25**
See also CA 85-88; CANR 20

Theroux, Paul (Edward)
1941- . . . . **CLC 5, 8, 11, 15, 28, 46**
See also BEST 89:4; CA 33-36R; CANR 20;
DLB 2; MTCW; SATA 44

Thesen, Sharon 1946- . . . . **CLC 56**

Thevenin, Denis
See Duhamel, Georges

Thibault, Jacques Anatole Francois
1844-1924
See France, Anatole
See also CA 106; 127; MTCW

Thiele, Colin (Milton) 1920- . . . . **CLC 17**
See also CA 29-32R; CANR 12, 28;
CLR 27; MAICYA; SAAS 2; SATA 14,
72

Thomas, Audrey (Callahan)
1935- . . . . **CLC 7, 13, 37**
See also AITN 2; CA 21-24R; CANR 36;
DLB 60; MTCW

Thomas, D(onald) M(ichael)
1935- . . . . **CLC 13, 22, 31**
See also CA 61-64; CAAS 11; CANR 17;
CDBLB 1960 to Present; DLB 40;
MTCW

Thomas, Dylan (Marlais)
1914-1953 . . . **TCLC 1, 8, 45; DA; PC 2;**
SSC 3; WLC
See also CA 104; 120; CDBLB 1945-1960;
DLB 13, 20; MTCW; SATA 60

Thomas, (Philip) Edward
1878-1917 . . . . **TCLC 10**
See also CA 106; DLB 19

Thomas, Joyce Carol 1938- . . . . **CLC 35**
See also BW; CA 113; 116; CLR 19;
DLB 33; JRDA; MAICYA; MTCW;
SAAS 7; SATA 40

Thomas, Lewis 1913- . . . . **CLC 35**
See also CA 85-88; CANR 38; MTCW

Thomas, Paul
See Mann, (Paul) Thomas

Thomas, Piri 1928- . . . . **CLC 17**
See also CA 73-76; HW

Thomas, R(onald) S(tuart)
1913- . . . . CLC 6, 13, 48
See also CA 89-92; CAAS 4; CANR 30;
CDBLB 1960 to Present; DLB 27;
MTCW

Thomas, Ross (Elmore) 1926- . . . . . . CLC 39
See also CA 33-36R; CANR 22

Thompson, Francis Clegg
See Mencken, H(enry) L(ouis)

Thompson, Francis Joseph
1859-1907 . . . . TCLC 4
See also CA 104; CDBLB 1890-1914;
DLB 19

Thompson, Hunter S(tockton)
1939- . . . . CLC 9, 17, 40
See also BEST 89:1; CA 17-20R; CANR 23;
MTCW

Thompson, Jim 1906-1977(?) . . . . . . CLC 69

Thompson, Judith . . . . CLC 39

Thomson, James 1700-1748 . . . . LC 16

Thomson, James 1834-1882 . . . . . NCLC 18

Thoreau, Henry David
1817-1862 . . . . . . NCLC 7, 21; DA; WLC
See also CDALB 1640-1865; DLB 1

Thornton, Hall
See Silverberg, Robert

Thurber, James (Grover)
1894-1961 . . . CLC 5, 11, 25; DA; SSC 1
See also CA 73-76; CANR 17, 39;
CDALB 1929-1941; DLB 4, 11, 22, 102;
MAICYA; MTCW; SATA 13

Thurman, Wallace (Henry)
1902-1934 . . . . TCLC 6; BLC 3
See also BW; CA 104; 124; DLB 51

Ticheburn, Cheviot
See Ainsworth, William Harrison

Tieck, (Johann) Ludwig
1773-1853 . . . . NCLC 5
See also DLB 90

Tiger, Derry
See Ellison, Harlan

Tilghman, Christopher 1948(?)- . . . . . CLC 65

Tillinghast, Richard (Williford)
1940- . . . . CLC 29
See also CA 29-32R; CANR 26

Timrod, Henry 1828-1867 . . . . NCLC 25
See also DLB 3

Tindall, Gillian 1938- . . . . CLC 7
See also CA 21-24R; CANR 11

Tiptree, James, Jr. . . . . CLC 48, 50
See also Sheldon, Alice Hastings Bradley
See also DLB 8

Titmarsh, Michael Angelo
See Thackeray, William Makepeace

**Tocqueville, Alexis (Charles Henri Maurice
Clerel Comte)** 1805-1859 . . . . . NCLC 7

Tolkien, J(ohn) R(onald) R(euel)
1892-1973 . . . . CLC 1, 2, 3, 8, 12, 38;
DA; WLC
See also AAYA 10; AITN 1; CA 17-18;
45-48; CANR 36; CAP 2;
CDBLB 1914-1945; DLB 15; JRDA;
MAICYA; MTCW; SATA 2, 24, 32

Toller, Ernst 1893-1939 . . . . TCLC 10
See also CA 107; DLB 124

Tolson, M. B.
See Tolson, Melvin B(eaunorus)

Tolson, Melvin B(eaunorus)
1898(?)-1966 . . . . CLC 36; BLC 3
See also BW; CA 124; 89-92; DLB 48, 76

Tolstoi, Aleksei Nikolaevich
See Tolstoy, Alexey Nikolaevich

Tolstoy, Alexey Nikolaevich
1882-1945 . . . . TCLC 18
See also CA 107

Tolstoy, Count Leo
See Tolstoy, Leo (Nikolaevich)

Tolstoy, Leo (Nikolaevich)
1828-1910 . . . . . TCLC 4, 11, 17, 28, 44;
DA; SSC 9; WLC
See also CA 104; 123; SATA 26

Tomasi di Lampedusa, Giuseppe 1896-1957
See Lampedusa, Giuseppe (Tomasi) di
See also CA 111

Tomlin, Lily . . . . CLC 17
See also Tomlin, Mary Jean

Tomlin, Mary Jean 1939(?)-
See Tomlin, Lily
See also CA 117

Tomlinson, (Alfred) Charles
1927- . . . . CLC 2, 4, 6, 13, 45
See also CA 5-8R; CANR 33; DLB 40

Tonson, Jacob
See Bennett, (Enoch) Arnold

Toole, John Kennedy
1937-1969 . . . . CLC 19, 64
See also CA 104; DLBY 81

Toomer, Jean
1894-1967 . . . . CLC 1, 4, 13, 22; BLC 3;
PC 7; SSC 1
See also BW; CA 85-88;
CDALB 1917-1929; DLB 45, 51; MTCW

Torley, Luke
See Blish, James (Benjamin)

Tornimparte, Alessandra
See Ginzburg, Natalia

Torre, Raoul della
See Mencken, H(enry) L(ouis)

Torrey, E(dwin) Fuller 1937- . . . . CLC 34
See also CA 119

Torsvan, Ben Traven
See Traven, B.

Torsvan, Benno Traven
See Traven, B.

Torsvan, Berick Traven
See Traven, B.

Torsvan, Berwick Traven
See Traven, B.

Torsvan, Bruno Traven
See Traven, B.

Torsvan, Traven
See Traven, B.

Tournier, Michel (Edouard)
1924- . . . . CLC 6, 23, 36
See also CA 49-52; CANR 3, 36; DLB 83;
MTCW; SATA 23

Tournimparte, Alessandra
See Ginzburg, Natalia

Towers, Ivar
See Kornbluth, C(yril) M.

Townsend, Sue 1946- . . . . CLC 61
See also CA 119; 127; MTCW; SATA 48,
55

Townshend, Peter (Dennis Blandford)
1945- . . . . CLC 17, 42
See also CA 107

Tozzi, Federigo 1883-1920 . . . . TCLC 31

Traill, Catharine Parr
1802-1899 . . . . NCLC 31
See also DLB 99

Trakl, Georg 1887-1914 . . . . TCLC 5
See also CA 104

Transtroemer, Tomas (Goesta)
1931- . . . . CLC 52, 65
See also CA 117; 129; CAAS 17

Transtromer, Tomas Gosta
See Transtroemer, Tomas (Goesta)

Traven, B. (?)-1969 . . . . CLC 8, 11
See also CA 19-20; 25-28R; CAP 2; DLB 9,
56; MTCW

Treitel, Jonathan 1959- . . . . CLC 70

Tremain, Rose 1943- . . . . CLC 42
See also CA 97-100; DLB 14

Tremblay, Michel 1942- . . . . CLC 29
See also CA 116; 128; DLB 60; MTCW

Trevanian (a pseudonym) 1930(?)- . . . CLC 29
See also CA 108

Trevor, Glen
See Hilton, James

Trevor, William
1928- . . . . CLC 7, 9, 14, 25, 71
See also Cox, William Trevor
See also DLB 14

Trifonov, Yuri (Valentinovich)
1925-1981 . . . . CLC 45
See also CA 126; 103; MTCW

Trilling, Lionel 1905-1975 . . . . CLC 9, 11, 24
See also CA 9-12R; 61-64; CANR 10;
DLB 28, 63; MTCW

Trimball, W. H.
See Mencken, H(enry) L(ouis)

Tristan
See Gomez de la Serna, Ramon

Tristram
See Housman, A(lfred) E(dward)

Trogdon, William (Lewis) 1939-
See Heat-Moon, William Least
See also CA 115; 119

Trollope, Anthony
1815-1882 . . . . . . NCLC 6, 33; DA; WLC
See also CDBLB 1832-1890; DLB 21, 57;
SATA 22

Trollope, Frances 1779-1863 . . . . . NCLC 30
See also DLB 21

Trotsky, Leon 1879-1940 . . . . TCLC 22
See also CA 118

Trotter (Cockburn), Catharine
1679-1749 . . . . LC 8
See also DLB 84

Trout, Kilgore
See Farmer, Philip Jose

Trow, George W. S. 1943-......... **CLC 52**
See also CA 126

Troyat, Henri 1911-.............. **CLC 23**
See also CA 45-48; CANR 2, 33; MTCW

Trudeau, G(arretson) B(eekman) 1948-
See Trudeau, Garry B.
See also CA 81-84; CANR 31; SATA 35

Trudeau, Garry B.................. **CLC 12**
See also Trudeau, G(arretson) B(eekman)
See also AAYA 10; AITN 2

Truffaut, Francois 1932-1984....... **CLC 20**
See also CA 81-84; 113; CANR 34

Trumbo, Dalton 1905-1976 .... **CLC 19**
See also CA 21-24R; 69-72; CANR 10;
DLB 26

Trumbull, John 1750-1831....... **NCLC 30**
See also DLB 31

Trundlett, Helen B.
See Eliot, T(homas) S(tearns)

Tryon, Thomas 1926-1991 .... **CLC 3, 11**
See also AITN 1; CA 29-32R; 135;
CANR 32; MTCW

Tryon, Tom
See Tryon, Thomas

Ts'ao Hsueh-ch'in 1715(?)-1763....... **LC 1**

Tsushima, Shuji 1909-1948
See Dazai, Osamu
See also CA 107

Tsvetaeva (Efron), Marina (Ivanovna)
1892-1941 .... **TCLC 7, 35**
See also CA 104; 128; MTCW

Tuck, Lily 1938-................. **CLC 70**
See also CA 139

Tunis, John R(oberts) 1889-1975 ... **CLC 12**
See also CA 61-64; DLB 22; JRDA;
MAICYA; SATA 30, 37

Tuohy, Frank.................... **CLC 37**
See also Tuohy, John Francis
See also DLB 14

Tuohy, John Francis 1925-
See Tuohy, Frank
See also CA 5-8R; CANR 3

Turco, Lewis (Putnam) 1934- ... **CLC 11, 63**
See also CA 13-16R; CANR 24; DLBY 84

Turgenev, Ivan
1818-1883 ...... **NCLC 21; DA; SSC 7;**
WLC

Turner, Frederick 1943-........... **CLC 48**
See also CA 73-76; CAAS 10; CANR 12,
30; DLB 40

Tusan, Stan 1936-................ **CLC 22**
See also CA 105

Tutu, Desmond M(pilo)
1931- .... **CLC 80; BLC 3**
See also BW; CA 125

Tutuola, Amos
1920- .... **CLC 5, 14, 29; BLC 3**
See also BW; CA 9-12R; CANR 27;
DLB 125; MTCW

Twain, Mark
... **TCLC 6, 12, 19, 36, 48; SSC 6; WLC**
See also Clemens, Samuel Langhorne
See also DLB 11, 12, 23, 64, 74

Tyler, Anne
1941- .... **CLC 7, 11, 18, 28, 44, 59**
See also BEST 89:1; CA 9-12R; CANR 11,
33; DLB 6; DLBY 82; MTCW; SATA 7

Tyler, Royall 1757-1826.......... **NCLC 3**
See also DLB 37

Tynan, Katharine 1861-1931 ...... **TCLC 3**
See also CA 104

Tytell, John 1939-............... **CLC 50**
See also CA 29-32R

Tyutchev, Fyodor 1803-1873..... **NCLC 34**

Tzara, Tristan .... **CLC 47**
See also Rosenfeld, Samuel

Uhry, Alfred 1936-............... **CLC 55**
See also CA 127; 133

Ulf, Haerved
See Strindberg, (Johan) August

Ulf, Harved
See Strindberg, (Johan) August

Unamuno (y Jugo), Miguel de
1864-1936 .... **TCLC 2, 9; SSC 11**
See also CA 104; 131; DLB 108; HW;
MTCW

Undercliffe, Errol
See Campbell, (John) Ramsey

Underwood, Miles
See Glassco, John

Undset, Sigrid
1882-1949 .... **TCLC 3; DA; WLC**
See also CA 104; 129; MTCW

Ungaretti, Giuseppe
1888-1970 .... **CLC 7, 11, 15**
See also CA 19-20; 25-28R; CAP 2;
DLB 114

Unger, Douglas 1952-............ **CLC 34**
See also CA 130

Unsworth, Barry (Forster) 1930-.... **CLC 76**
See also CA 25-28R; CANR 30

Updike, John (Hoyer)
1932- ...... **CLC 1, 2, 3, 5, 7, 9, 13, 15,**
23, 34, 43, 70; DA; SSC 13; WLC
See also CA 1-4R; CABS 1; CANR 4, 33;
CDALB 1968-1988; DLB 2, 5; DLBD 3;
DLBY 80, 82; MTCW

Upshaw, Margaret Mitchell
See Mitchell, Margaret (Munnerlyn)

Upton, Mark
See Sanders, Lawrence

Urdang, Constance (Henriette)
1922- .... **CLC 47**
See also CA 21-24R; CANR 9, 24

Uriel, Henry
See Faust, Frederick (Schiller)

Uris, Leon (Marcus) 1924-....... **CLC 7, 32**
See also AITN 1, 2; BEST 89:2; CA 1-4R;
CANR 1, 40; MTCW; SATA 49

Urmuz
See Codrescu, Andrei

Ustinov, Peter (Alexander) 1921- .... **CLC 1**
See also AITN 1; CA 13-16R; CANR 25;
DLB 13

V
See Chekhov, Anton (Pavlovich)

Vaculik, Ludvik 1926- .... **CLC 7**
See also CA 53-56

Valenzuela, Luisa 1938-... **CLC 31; SSC 14**
See also CA 101; CANR 32; DLB 113; HW

Valera y Alcala-Galiano, Juan
1824-1905 .... **TCLC 10**
See also CA 106

Valery, (Ambroise) Paul (Toussaint Jules)
1871-1945 .... **TCLC 4, 15**
See also CA 104; 122; MTCW

Valle-Inclan, Ramon (Maria) del
1866-1936 .... **TCLC 5**
See also CA 106; DLB 134

Vallejo, Antonio Buero
See Buero Vallejo, Antonio

Vallejo, Cesar (Abraham)
1892-1938 .... **TCLC 3**
See also CA 105; HW

Valle Y Pena, Ramon del
See Valle-Inclan, Ramon (Maria) del

Van Ash, Cay 1918-.............. **CLC 34**

Vanbrugh, Sir John 1664-1726 ...... **LC 21**
See also DLB 80

Van Campen, Karl
See Campbell, John W(ood, Jr.)

Vance, Gerald
See Silverberg, Robert

Vance, Jack..................... **CLC 35**
See also Vance, John Holbrook
See also DLB 8

Vance, John Holbrook 1916-
See Queen, Ellery; Vance, Jack
See also CA 29-32R; CANR 17; MTCW

Van Den Bogarde, Derek Jules Gaspard Ulric
Niven 1921-
See Bogarde, Dirk
See also CA 77-80

Vandenburgh, Jane .... **CLC 59**

Vanderhaeghe, Guy 1951- .... **CLC 41**
See also CA 113

van der Post, Laurens (Jan) 1906- ... **CLC 5**
See also CA 5-8R; CANR 35

van de Wetering, Janwillem 1931- .. **CLC 47**
See also CA 49-52; CANR 4

Van Dine, S. S. .... **TCLC 23**
See also Wright, Willard Huntington

Van Doren, Carl (Clinton)
1885-1950 .... **TCLC 18**
See also CA 111

Van Doren, Mark 1894-1972..... **CLC 6, 10**
See also CA 1-4R; 37-40R; CANR 3;
DLB 45; MTCW

Van Druten, John (William)
1901-1957 .... **TCLC 2**
See also CA 104; DLB 10

Van Duyn, Mona (Jane)
1921- .... **CLC 3, 7, 63**
See also CA 9-12R; CANR 7, 38; DLB 5

Van Dyne, Edith
  See Baum, L(yman) Frank

van Itallie, Jean-Claude 1936-........ **CLC 3**
  See also CA 45-48; CAAS 2; CANR 1;
    DLB 7

van Ostaijen, Paul 1896-1928 ..... **TCLC 33**

Van Peebles, Melvin 1932- ...... **CLC 2, 20**
  See also BW; CA 85-88; CANR 27

Vansittart, Peter 1920-............ **CLC 42**
  See also CA 1-4R; CANR 3

Van Vechten, Carl 1880-1964 ...... **CLC 33**
  See also CA 89-92; DLB 4, 9, 51

Van Vogt, A(lfred) E(lton) 1912-..... **CLC 1**
  See also CA 21-24R; CANR 28; DLB 8;
    SATA 14

Vara, Madeleine
  See Jackson, Laura (Riding)

Varda, Agnes 1928- .... **CLC 16**
  See also CA 116; 122

Vargas Llosa, (Jorge) Mario (Pedro)
  1936- ... **CLC 3, 6, 9, 10, 15, 31, 42; DA**
  See also CA 73-76; CANR 18, 32, 42; HW;
    MTCW

Vasiliu, Gheorghe 1881-1957
  See Bacovia, George
  See also CA 123

Vassa, Gustavus
  See Equiano, Olaudah

Vassilikos, Vassilis 1933-......... **CLC 4, 8**
  See also CA 81-84

Vaughn, Stephanie................ **CLC 62**

Vazov, Ivan (Minchov)
  1850-1921 .... **TCLC 25**
  See also CA 121

Veblen, Thorstein (Bunde)
  1857-1929 .... **TCLC 31**
  See also CA 115

Vega, Lope de 1562-1635........... **LC 23**

Venison, Alfred
  See Pound, Ezra (Weston Loomis)

Verdi, Marie de
  See Mencken, H(enry) L(ouis)

Verdu, Matilde
  See Cela, Camilo Jose

Verga, Giovanni (Carmelo)
  1840-1922 .... **TCLC 3**
  See also CA 104; 123

Vergil 70B.C.-19B.C. .... **CMLC 9; DA**

Verhaeren, Emile (Adolphe Gustave)
  1855-1916 .... **TCLC 12**
  See also CA 109

Verlaine, Paul (Marie)
  1844-1896 .... **NCLC 2; PC 2**

Verne, Jules (Gabriel)
  1828-1905 .... **TCLC 6, 52**
  See also CA 110; 131; DLB 123; JRDA;
    MAICYA; SATA 21

Very, Jones 1813-1880........... **NCLC 9**
  See also DLB 1

Vesaas, Tarjei 1897-1970......... **CLC 48**
  See also CA 29-32R

Vialis, Gaston
  See Simenon, Georges (Jacques Christian)

Vian, Boris 1920-1959 .... **TCLC 9**
  See also CA 106; DLB 72

Viaud, (Louis Marie) Julien 1850-1923
  See Loti, Pierre
  See also CA 107

Vicar, Henry
  See Felsen, Henry Gregor

Vicker, Angus
  See Felsen, Henry Gregor

Vidal, Gore
  1925- ..... **CLC 2, 4, 6, 8, 10, 22, 33, 72**
  See also AITN 1; BEST 90:2; CA 5-8R;
    CANR 13; DLB 6; MTCW

Viereck, Peter (Robert Edwin)
  1916-......................... **CLC 4**
  See also CA 1-4R; CANR 1; DLB 5

Vigny, Alfred (Victor) de
  1797-1863 .... **NCLC 7**
  See also DLB 119

Vilakazi, Benedict Wallet
  1906-1947 .... **TCLC 37**

Villiers de l'Isle Adam, Jean Marie Mathias
    Philippe Auguste Comte
  1838-1889 .... **NCLC 3; SSC 14**
  See also DLB 123

Vincent, Gabrielle a pseudonym...... **CLC 13**
  See also CA 126; CLR 13; MAICYA;
    SATA 61

Vinci, Leonardo da 1452-1519...... **LC 12**

Vine, Barbara .... **CLC 50**
  See also Rendell, Ruth (Barbara)
  See also BEST 90:4

Vinge, Joan D(ennison) 1948-...... **CLC 30**
  See also CA 93-96; SATA 36

Violis, G.
  See Simenon, Georges (Jacques Christian)

Visconti, Luchino 1906-1976....... **CLC 16**
  See also CA 81-84; 65-68; CANR 39

Vittorini, Elio 1908-1966...... **CLC 6, 9, 14**
  See also CA 133; 25-28R

Vizinczey, Stephen 1933-.......... **CLC 40**
  See also CA 128

Vliet, R(ussell) G(ordon)
  1929-1984 .... **CLC 22**
  See also CA 37-40R; 112; CANR 18

Vogau, Boris Andreyevich 1894-1937(?)
  See Pilnyak, Boris
  See also CA 123

Vogel, Paula A(nne) 1951-......... **CLC 76**
  See also CA 108

Voight, Ellen Bryant 1943- .... **CLC 54**
  See also CA 69-72; CANR 11, 29; DLB 120

Voigt, Cynthia 1942- .... **CLC 30**
  See also AAYA 3; CA 106; CANR 18, 37,
    40; CLR 13; JRDA; MAICYA;
    SATA 33, 48

Voinovich, Vladimir (Nikolaevich)
  1932- .... **CLC 10, 49**
  See also CA 81-84; CAAS 12; CANR 33;
    MTCW

Voltaire
  1694-1778 ... **LC 14; DA; SSC 12; WLC**

von Daeniken, Erich 1935- .... **CLC 30**
  See also von Daniken, Erich
  See also AITN 1; CA 37-40R; CANR 17

von Daniken, Erich............... **CLC 30**
  See also von Daeniken, Erich

von Heidenstam, (Carl Gustaf) Verner
  See Heidenstam, (Carl Gustaf) Verner von

von Heyse, Paul (Johann Ludwig)
  See Heyse, Paul (Johann Ludwig von)

von Hofmannsthal, Hugo
  See Hofmannsthal, Hugo von

von Horvath, Odon
  See Horvath, Oedoen von

von Horvath, Oedoen
  See Horvath, Oedoen von

von Liliencron, (Friedrich Adolf Axel) Detlev
  See Liliencron, (Friedrich Adolf Axel)
    Detlev von

Vonnegut, Kurt, Jr.
  1922-...... **CLC 1, 2, 3, 4, 5, 8, 12, 22,**
    40, 60; DA; SSC 8; WLC
  See also AAYA 6; AITN 1; BEST 90:4;
    CA 1-4R; CANR 1, 25;
    CDALB 1968-1988; DLB 2, 8; DLBD 3;
    DLBY 80; MTCW

Von Rachen, Kurt
  See Hubbard, L(afayette) Ron(ald)

von Rezzori (d'Arezzo), Gregor
  See Rezzori (d'Arezzo), Gregor von

von Sternberg, Josef
  See Sternberg, Josef von

Vorster, Gordon 1924-............ **CLC 34**
  See also CA 133

Vosce, Trudie
  See Ozick, Cynthia

Voznesensky, Andrei (Andreievich)
  1933-.................... **CLC 1, 15, 57**
  See also CA 89-92; CANR 37; MTCW

Waddington, Miriam 1917-........ **CLC 28**
  See also CA 21-24R; CANR 12, 30;
    DLB 68

Wagman, Fredrica 1937-.......... **CLC 7**
  See also CA 97-100

Wagner, Richard 1813-1883....... **NCLC 9**
  See also DLB 129

Wagner-Martin, Linda 1936-...... **CLC 50**

Wagoner, David (Russell)
  1926-................... **CLC 3, 5, 15**
  See also CA 1-4R; CAAS 3; CANR 2;
    DLB 5; SATA 14

Wah, Fred(erick James) 1939-...... **CLC 44**
  See also CA 107; 141; DLB 60

Wahloo, Per 1926-1975 .... **CLC 7**
  See also CA 61-64

Wahloo, Peter
  See Wahloo, Per

Wain, John (Barrington)
  1925-............. **CLC 2, 11, 15, 46**
  See also CA 5-8R; CAAS 4; CANR 23;
    CDBLB 1960 to Present; DLB 15, 27;
    MTCW

Wajda, Andrzej 1926-............ **CLC 16**
  See also CA 102

Wakefield, Dan 1932-............. **CLC 7**
See also CA 21-24R; CAAS 7

Wakoski, Diane
1937-........... **CLC 2, 4, 7, 9, 11, 40**
See also CA 13-16R; CAAS 1; CANR 9;
DLB 5

Wakoski-Sherbell, Diane
See Wakoski, Diane

Walcott, Derek (Alton)
1930- .... **CLC 2, 4, 9, 14, 25, 42, 67, 76;**
BLC 3
See also BW; CA 89-92; CANR 26;
DLB 117; DLBY 81; MTCW

Waldman, Anne 1945- .... **CLC 7**
See also CA 37-40R; CAAS 17; CANR 34;
DLB 16

Waldo, E. Hunter
See Sturgeon, Theodore (Hamilton)

Waldo, Edward Hamilton
See Sturgeon, Theodore (Hamilton)

Walker, Alice (Malsenior)
1944- ...... **CLC 5, 6, 9, 19, 27, 46, 58;**
BLC 3; DA; SSC 5
See also AAYA 3; BEST 89:4; BW;
CA 37-40R; CANR 9, 27;
CDALB 1968-1988; DLB 6, 33; MTCW;
SATA 31

Walker, David Harry 1911-1992.... **CLC 14**
See also CA 1-4R; 137; CANR 1; SATA 8;
SATA-Obit 71

Walker, Edward Joseph 1934-
See Walker, Ted
See also CA 21-24R; CANR 12, 28

Walker, George F. 1947- .... **CLC 44, 61**
See also CA 103; CANR 21, 43; DLB 60

Walker, Joseph A. 1935- .... **CLC 19**
See also BW; CA 89-92; CANR 26; DLB 38

Walker, Margaret (Abigail)
1915- .... **CLC 1, 6; BLC 3**
See also BW; CA 73-76; CANR 26;
DLB 76; MTCW

Walker, Ted.................... **CLC 13**
See also Walker, Edward Joseph
See also DLB 40

Wallace, David Foster 1962- .... **CLC 50**
See also CA 132

Wallace, Dexter
See Masters, Edgar Lee

Wallace, Irving 1916-1990....... **CLC 7, 13**
See also AITN 1; CA 1-4R; 132; CAAS 1;
CANR 1, 27; MTCW

Wallant, Edward Lewis
1926-1962 .... **CLC 5, 10**
See also CA 1-4R; CANR 22; DLB 2, 28;
MTCW

Walpole, Horace 1717-1797......... **LC 2**
See also DLB 39, 104

Walpole, Hugh (Seymour)
1884-1941 .... **TCLC 5**
See also CA 104; DLB 34

Walser, Martin 1927-............. **CLC 27**
See also CA 57-60; CANR 8; DLB 75, 124

Walser, Robert 1878-1956....... **TCLC 18**
See also CA 118; DLB 66

Walsh, Jill Paton.................. **CLC 35**
See also Paton Walsh, Gillian
See also CLR 2; SAAS 3

Walter, Villiam Christian
See Andersen, Hans Christian

Wambaugh, Joseph (Aloysius, Jr.)
1937-..................... **CLC 3, 18**
See also AITN 1; BEST 89:3; CA 33-36R;
CANR 42; DLB 6; DLBY 83; MTCW

Ward, Arthur Henry Sarsfield 1883-1959
See Rohmer, Sax
See also CA 108

Ward, Douglas Turner 1930-....... **CLC 19**
See also BW; CA 81-84; CANR 27; DLB 7,
38

Ward, Peter
See Faust, Frederick (Schiller)

Warhol, Andy 1928(?)-1987........ **CLC 20**
See also BEST 89:4; CA 89-92; 121;
CANR 34

Warner, Francis (Robert le Plastrier)
1937-...................... **CLC 14**
See also CA 53-56; CANR 11

Warner, Marina 1946-............ **CLC 59**
See also CA 65-68; CANR 21

Warner, Rex (Ernest) 1905-1986.... **CLC 45**
See also CA 89-92; 119; DLB 15

Warner, Susan (Bogert)
1819-1885 .... **NCLC 31**
See also DLB 3, 42

Warner, Sylvia (Constance) Ashton
See Ashton-Warner, Sylvia (Constance)

Warner, Sylvia Townsend
1893-1978 .... **CLC 7, 19**
See also CA 61-64; 77-80; CANR 16;
DLB 34; MTCW

Warren, Mercy Otis 1728-1814... **NCLC 13**
See also DLB 31

Warren, Robert Penn
1905-1989 .... **CLC 1, 4, 6, 8, 10, 13, 18,**
39, 53, 59; DA; SSC 4; WLC
See also AITN 1; CA 13-16R; 129;
CANR 10; CDALB 1968-1988; DLB 2,
48; DLBY 80, 89; MTCW; SATA 46, 63

Warshofsky, Isaac
See Singer, Isaac Bashevis

Warton, Thomas 1728-1790........ **LC 15**
See also DLB 104, 109

Waruk, Kona
See Harris, (Theodore) Wilson

Warung, Price 1855-1911........ **TCLC 45**

Warwick, Jarvis
See Garner, Hugh

Washington, Alex
See Harris, Mark

Washington, Booker T(aliaferro)
1856-1915 .... **TCLC 10; BLC 3**
See also BW; CA 114; 125; SATA 28

Wassermann, (Karl) Jakob
1873-1934 .... **TCLC 6**
See also CA 104; DLB 66

Wasserstein, Wendy
1950- .... **CLC 32, 59; DC 4**
See also CA 121; 129; CABS 3

Waterhouse, Keith (Spencer)
1929- .... **CLC 47**
See also CA 5-8R; CANR 38; DLB 13, 15;
MTCW

Waters, Roger 1944-............. **CLC 35**
See also Pink Floyd

Watkins, Frances Ellen
See Harper, Frances Ellen Watkins

Watkins, Gerrold
See Malzberg, Barry N(athaniel)

Watkins, Paul 1964-............. **CLC 55**
See also CA 132

Watkins, Vernon Phillips
1906-1967 .... **CLC 43**
See also CA 9-10; 25-28R; CAP 1; DLB 20

Watson, Irving S.
See Mencken, H(enry) L(ouis)

Watson, John H.
See Farmer, Philip Jose

Watson, Richard F.
See Silverberg, Robert

Waugh, Auberon (Alexander) 1939-.. **CLC 7**
See also CA 45-48; CANR 6, 22; DLB 14

Waugh, Evelyn (Arthur St. John)
1903-1966 ...... **CLC 1, 3, 8, 13, 19, 27,**
44; DA; WLC
See also CA 85-88; 25-28R; CANR 22;
CDBLB 1914-1945; DLB 15; MTCW

Waugh, Harriet 1944- .... **CLC 6**
See also CA 85-88; CANR 22

Ways, C. R.
See Blount, Roy (Alton), Jr.

Waystaff, Simon
See Swift, Jonathan

Webb, (Martha) Beatrice (Potter)
1858-1943 .... **TCLC 22**
See also Potter, Beatrice
See also CA 117

Webb, Charles (Richard) 1939-...... **CLC 7**
See also CA 25-28R

Webb, James H(enry), Jr. 1946-.... **CLC 22**
See also CA 81-84

Webb, Mary (Gladys Meredith)
1881-1927 .... **TCLC 24**
See also CA 123; DLB 34

Webb, Mrs. Sidney
See Webb, (Martha) Beatrice (Potter)

Webb, Phyllis 1927-............. **CLC 18**
See also CA 104; CANR 23; DLB 53

Webb, Sidney (James)
1859-1947 .... **TCLC 22**
See also CA 117

Webber, Andrew Lloyd............. **CLC 21**
See also Lloyd Webber, Andrew

Weber, Lenora Mattingly
1895-1971 .... **CLC 12**
See also CA 19-20; 29-32R; CAP 1;
SATA 2, 26

Webster, John 1579(?)-1634(?) .... **DC 2**
See also CDBLB Before 1660; DA; DLB 58;
WLC

Webster, Noah 1758-1843 .... **NCLC 30**

Wedekind, (Benjamin) Frank(lin)
1864-1918 . . . . **TCLC 7**
See also CA 104; DLB 118

Weidman, Jerome 1913- . . . . **CLC 7**
See also AITN 2; CA 1-4R; CANR 1;
DLB 28

Weil, Simone (Adolphine)
1909-1943 . . . . **TCLC 23**
See also CA 117

Weinstein, Nathan
See West, Nathanael

Weinstein, Nathan von Wallenstein
See West, Nathanael

Weir, Peter (Lindsay) 1944- . . . . **CLC 20**
See also CA 113; 123

Weiss, Peter (Ulrich)
1916-1982 . . . . **CLC 3, 15, 51**
See also CA 45-48; 106; CANR 3; DLB 69,
124

Weiss, Theodore (Russell)
1916- . . . . **CLC 3, 8, 14**
See also CA 9-12R; CAAS 2; DLB 5

Welch, (Maurice) Denton
1915-1948 . . . . **TCLC 22**
See also CA 121

Welch, James 1940- . . . . **CLC 6, 14, 52**
See also CA 85-88; CANR 42

Weldon, Fay
1933(?)- . . . . **CLC 6, 9, 11, 19, 36, 59**
See also CA 21-24R; CANR 16;
CDBLB 1960 to Present; DLB 14;
MTCW

Wellek, Rene 1903- . . . . **CLC 28**
See also CA 5-8R; CAAS 7; CANR 8;
DLB 63

Weller, Michael 1942- . . . . **CLC 10, 53**
See also CA 85-88

Weller, Paul 1958- . . . . **CLC 26**

Wellershoff, Dieter 1925- . . . . **CLC 46**
See also CA 89-92; CANR 16, 37

Welles, (George) Orson
1915-1985 . . . . **CLC 20, 80**
See also CA 93-96; 117

Wellman, Mac 1945- . . . . **CLC 65**

Wellman, Manly Wade 1903-1986 . . **CLC 49**
See also CA 1-4R; 118; CANR 6, 16;
SATA 6, 47

Wells, Carolyn 1869(?)-1942 . . . . . . **TCLC 35**
See also CA 113; DLB 11

Wells, H(erbert) G(eorge)
1866-1946 . . . . **TCLC 6, 12, 19; DA;**
SSC 6; WLC
See also CA 110; 121; CDBLB 1914-1945;
DLB 34, 70; MTCW; SATA 20

Wells, Rosemary 1943- . . . . **CLC 12**
See also CA 85-88; CLR 16; MAICYA;
SAAS 1; SATA 18, 69

Welty, Eudora
1909- . . . . . . **CLC 1, 2, 5, 14, 22, 33; DA;**
SSC 1; WLC
See also CA 9-12R; CABS 1; CANR 32;
CDALB 1941-1968; DLB 2, 102;
DLBY 87; MTCW

Wen I-to 1899-1946 . . . . **TCLC 28**

Wentworth, Robert
See Hamilton, Edmond

Werfel, Franz (V.) 1890-1945 . . . . . . **TCLC 8**
See also CA 104; DLB 81, 124

Wergeland, Henrik Arnold
1808-1845 . . . . **NCLC 5**

Wersba, Barbara 1932- . . . . **CLC 30**
See also AAYA 2; CA 29-32R; CANR 16,
38; CLR 3; DLB 52; JRDA; MAICYA;
SAAS 2; SATA 1, 58

Wertmueller, Lina 1928- . . . . **CLC 16**
See also CA 97-100; CANR 39

Wescott, Glenway 1901-1987 . . . . . . **CLC 13**
See also CA 13-16R; 121; CANR 23;
DLB 4, 9, 102

Wesker, Arnold 1932- . . . . **CLC 3, 5, 42**
See also CA 1-4R; CAAS 7; CANR 1, 33;
CDBLB 1960 to Present; DLB 13;
MTCW

Wesley, Richard (Errol) 1945- . . . . . . **CLC 7**
See also BW; CA 57-60; CANR 27; DLB 38

Wessel, Johan Herman 1742-1785 . . . . **LC 7**

West, Anthony (Panther)
1914-1987 . . . . **CLC 50**
See also CA 45-48; 124; CANR 3, 19;
DLB 15

West, C. P.
See Wodehouse, P(elham) G(renville)

West, (Mary) Jessamyn
1902-1984 . . . . **CLC 7, 17**
See also CA 9-12R; 112; CANR 27; DLB 6;
DLBY 84; MTCW; SATA 37

West, Morris L(anglo) 1916- . . . . . **CLC 6, 33**
See also CA 5-8R; CANR 24; MTCW

West, Nathanael
1903-1940 . . . . **TCLC 1, 14, 44**
See also CA 104; 125; CDALB 1929-1941;
DLB 4, 9, 28; MTCW

West, Owen
See Koontz, Dean R(ay)

West, Paul 1930- . . . . **CLC 7, 14**
See also CA 13-16R; CAAS 7; CANR 22;
DLB 14

West, Rebecca 1892-1983 . . **CLC 7, 9, 31, 50**
See also CA 5-8R; 109; CANR 19; DLB 36;
DLBY 83; MTCW

Westall, Robert (Atkinson)
1929-1993 . . . . **CLC 17**
See also CA 69-72; 141; CANR 18;
CLR 13; JRDA; MAICYA; SAAS 2;
SATA 23, 69; SATA-Obit 75

Westlake, Donald E(dwin)
1933- . . . . **CLC 7, 33**
See also CA 17-20R; CAAS 13; CANR 16

Westmacott, Mary
See Christie, Agatha (Mary Clarissa)

Weston, Allen
See Norton, Andre

Wetcheek, J. L.
See Feuchtwanger, Lion

Wetering, Janwillem van de
See van de Wetering, Janwillem

Wetherell, Elizabeth
See Warner, Susan (Bogert)

Whalen, Philip 1923- . . . . **CLC 6, 29**
See also CA 9-12R; CANR 5, 39; DLB 16

Wharton, Edith (Newbold Jones)
1862-1937 . . . . **TCLC 3, 9, 27; DA;**
SSC 6; WLC
See also CA 104; 132; CDALB 1865-1917;
DLB 4, 9, 12, 78; MTCW

Wharton, James
See Mencken, H(enry) L(ouis)

Wharton, William (a pseudonym)
. . . . **CLC 18, 37**
See also CA 93-96; DLBY 80

Wheatley (Peters), Phillis
1754(?)-1784 . . . . **LC 3; BLC 3; DA;**
PC 3; WLC
See also CDALB 1640-1865; DLB 31, 50

Wheelock, John Hall 1886-1978 . . . . **CLC 14**
See also CA 13-16R; 77-80; CANR 14;
DLB 45

White, E(lwyn) B(rooks)
1899-1985 . . . . **CLC 10, 34, 39**
See also AITN 2; CA 13-16R; 116;
CANR 16, 37; CLR 1, 21; DLB 11, 22;
MAICYA; MTCW; SATA 2, 29, 44

White, Edmund (Valentine III)
1940- . . . . **CLC 27**
See also AAYA 7; CA 45-48; CANR 3, 19,
36; MTCW

White, Patrick (Victor Martindale)
1912-1990 . . **CLC 3, 4, 5, 7, 9, 18, 65, 69**
See also CA 81-84; 132; CANR 43; MTCW

White, Phyllis Dorothy James 1920-
See James, P. D.
See also CA 21-24R; CANR 17, 43; MTCW

White, T(erence) H(anbury)
1906-1964 . . . . **CLC 30**
See also CA 73-76; CANR 37; JRDA;
MAICYA; SATA 12

White, Terence de Vere 1912- . . . . . . **CLC 49**
See also CA 49-52; CANR 3

White, Walter F(rancis)
1893-1955 . . . . **TCLC 15**
See White, Walter
See also CA 115; 124; DLB 51

White, William Hale 1831-1913
See Rutherford, Mark
See also CA 121

Whitehead, E(dward) A(nthony)
1933- . . . . **CLC 5**
See also CA 65-68

Whitemore, Hugh (John) 1936- . . . . . **CLC 37**
See also CA 132

Whitman, Sarah Helen (Power)
1803-1878 . . . . **NCLC 19**
See also DLB 1

Whitman, Walt(er)
1819-1892 . . . . . **NCLC 4, 31; DA; PC 3;**
WLC
See also CDALB 1640-1865; DLB 3, 64;
SATA 20

Whitney, Phyllis A(yame) 1903- . . . . **CLC 42**
See also AITN 2; BEST 90:3; CA 1-4R;
CANR 3, 25, 38; JRDA; MAICYA;
SATA 1, 30

Whittemore, (Edward) Reed (Jr.)
1919- . . . . **CLC 4**
See also CA 9-12R; CAAS 8; CANR 4;
DLB 5

Whittier, John Greenleaf
1807-1892 . . . . **NCLC 8**
See also CDALB 1640-1865; DLB 1

Whittlebot, Hernia
See Coward, Noel (Peirce)

Wicker, Thomas Grey 1926-
See Wicker, Tom
See also CA 65-68; CANR 21

Wicker, Tom . . . . **CLC 7**
See also Wicker, Thomas Grey

Wideman, John Edgar
1941- . . . . **CLC 5, 34, 36, 67; BLC 3**
See also BW; CA 85-88; CANR 14, 42;
DLB 33

Wiebe, Rudy (Henry) 1934-... **CLC 6, 11, 14**
See also CA 37-40R; CANR 42; DLB 60

Wieland, Christoph Martin
1733-1813 . . . . **NCLC 17**
See also DLB 97

Wieners, John 1934- . . . . **CLC 7**
See also CA 13-16R; DLB 16

Wiesel, Elie(zer)
1928- . . . . **CLC 3, 5, 11, 37; DA**
See also AAYA 7; AITN 1; CA 5-8R;
CAAS 4; CANR 8, 40; DLB 83;
DLBY 87; MTCW; SATA 56

Wiggins, Marianne 1947- . . . . **CLC 57**
See also BEST 89:3; CA 130

Wight, James Alfred 1916-
See Herriot, James
See also CA 77-80; SATA 44, 55

Wilbur, Richard (Purdy)
1921- . . . . **CLC 3, 6, 9, 14, 53; DA**
See also CA 1-4R; CABS 2; CANR 2, 29;
DLB 5; MTCW; SATA 9

Wild, Peter 1940- . . . . **CLC 14**
See also CA 37-40R; DLB 5

Wilde, Oscar (Fingal O'Flahertie Wills)
1854(?)-1900 . . . . **TCLC 1, 8, 23, 41; DA;
SSC 11; WLC**
See also CA 104; 119; CDBLB 1890-1914;
DLB 10, 19, 34, 57; SATA 24

Wilder, Billy . . . . **CLC 20**
See also Wilder, Samuel
See also DLB 26

Wilder, Samuel 1906-
See Wilder, Billy
See also CA 89-92

Wilder, Thornton (Niven)
1897-1975 . . . . . . **CLC 1, 5, 6, 10, 15, 35;
DA; DC 1; WLC**
See also AITN 2; CA 13-16R; 61-64;
CANR 40; DLB 4, 7, 9; MTCW

Wilding, Michael 1942- . . . . **CLC 73**
See also CA 104; CANR 24

Wiley, Richard 1944- . . . . **CLC 44**
See also CA 121; 129

Wilhelm, Kate . . . . **CLC 7**
See also Wilhelm, Katie Gertrude
See also CAAS 5; DLB 8

Wilhelm, Katie Gertrude 1928-
See Wilhelm, Kate
See also CA 37-40R; CANR 17, 36; MTCW

Wilkins, Mary
See Freeman, Mary Eleanor Wilkins

Willard, Nancy 1936- . . . . **CLC 7, 37**
See also CA 89-92; CANR 10, 39; CLR 5;
DLB 5, 52; MAICYA; MTCW;
SATA 30, 37, 71

Williams, C(harles) K(enneth)
1936- . . . . **CLC 33, 56**
See also CA 37-40R; DLB 5

Williams, Charles
See Collier, James L(incoln)

Williams, Charles (Walter Stansby)
1886-1945 . . . . **TCLC 1, 11**
See also CA 104; DLB 100

Williams, (George) Emlyn
1905-1987 . . . . **CLC 15**
See also CA 104; 123; CANR 36; DLB 10,
77; MTCW

Williams, Hugo 1942- . . . . **CLC 42**
See also CA 17-20R; DLB 40

Williams, J. Walker
See Wodehouse, P(elham) G(renville)

Williams, John A(lfred)
1925- . . . . **CLC 5, 13; BLC 3**
See also BW; CA 53-56; CAAS 3; CANR 6,
26; DLB 2, 33

Williams, Jonathan (Chamberlain)
1929- . . . . **CLC 13**
See also CA 9-12R; CAAS 12; CANR 8;
DLB 5

Williams, Joy 1944- . . . . **CLC 31**
See also CA 41-44R; CANR 22

Williams, Norman 1952- . . . . **CLC 39**
See also CA 118

Williams, Tennessee
1911-1983 . . . . . **CLC 1, 2, 5, 7, 8, 11, 15,
19, 30, 39, 45, 71; DA; DC 4; WLC**
See also AITN 1, 2; CA 5-8R; 108;
CABS 3; CANR 31; CDALB 1941-1968;
DLB 7; DLBD 4; DLBY 83; MTCW

Williams, Thomas (Alonzo)
1926-1990 . . . . **CLC 14**
See also CA 1-4R; 132; CANR 2

Williams, William C.
See Williams, William Carlos

Williams, William Carlos
1883-1963 . . . . **CLC 1, 2, 5, 9, 13, 22, 42,
67; DA; PC 7**
See also CA 89-92; CANR 34;
CDALB 1917-1929; DLB 4, 16, 54, 86;
MTCW

Williamson, David (Keith) 1942-... **CLC 56**
See also CA 103; CANR 41

Williamson, Jack . . . . **CLC 29**
See also Williamson, John Stewart
See also CAAS 8; DLB 8

Williamson, John Stewart 1908-
See Williamson, Jack
See also CA 17-20R; CANR 23

Willie, Frederick
See Lovecraft, H(oward) P(hillips)

Willingham, Calder (Baynard, Jr.)
1922- . . . . **CLC 5, 51**
See also CA 5-8R; CANR 3; DLB 2, 44;
MTCW

Willis, Charles
See Clarke, Arthur C(harles)

Willy
See Colette, (Sidonie-Gabrielle)

Willy, Colette
See Colette, (Sidonie-Gabrielle)

Wilson, A(ndrew) N(orman) 1950- . . **CLC 33**
See also CA 112; 122; DLB 14

Wilson, Angus (Frank Johnstone)
1913-1991 . . . . **CLC 2, 3, 5, 25, 34**
See also CA 5-8R; 134; CANR 21; DLB 15;
MTCW

Wilson, August
1945- . . . . . **CLC 39, 50, 63; BLC 3; DA;
DC 2**
See also BW; CA 115; 122; CANR 42;
MTCW

Wilson, Brian 1942- . . . . **CLC 12**

Wilson, Colin 1931- . . . . **CLC 3, 14**
See also CA 1-4R; CAAS 5; CANR 1, 22,
33; DLB 14; MTCW

Wilson, Dirk
See Pohl, Frederik

Wilson, Edmund
1895-1972 . . . . **CLC 1, 2, 3, 8, 24**
See also CA 1-4R; 37-40R; CANR 1;
DLB 63; MTCW

Wilson, Ethel Davis (Bryant)
1888(?)-1980 . . . . **CLC 13**
See also CA 102; DLB 68; MTCW

Wilson, John 1785-1854 . . . . **NCLC 5**

Wilson, John (Anthony) Burgess
1917- . . . . **CLC 8, 10, 13**
See also Burgess, Anthony
See also CA 1-4R; CANR 2; MTCW

Wilson, Lanford 1937- . . . . **CLC 7, 14, 36**
See also CA 17-20R; CABS 3; DLB 7

Wilson, Robert M. 1944- . . . . **CLC 7, 9**
See also CA 49-52; CANR 2, 41; MTCW

Wilson, Robert McLiam 1964- . . . . . **CLC 59**
See also CA 132

Wilson, Sloan 1920- . . . . **CLC 32**
See also CA 1-4R; CANR 1

Wilson, Snoo 1948- . . . . **CLC 33**
See also CA 69-72

Wilson, William S(mith) 1932- . . . . . **CLC 49**
See also CA 81-84

Winchilsea, Anne (Kingsmill) Finch Counte
1661-1720 . . . . **LC 3**

Windham, Basil
See Wodehouse, P(elham) G(renville)

Wingrove, David (John) 1954-. . . . . . **CLC 68**
See also CA 133

Winters, Janet Lewis . . . . **CLC 41**
See also Lewis, Janet
See also DLBY 87

Winters, (Arthur) Yvor
1900-1968 . . . . **CLC 4, 8, 32**
See also CA 11-12; 25-28R; CAP 1;
DLB 48; MTCW

Winterson, Jeanette 1959-......... **CLC 64**
See also CA 136

Wiseman, Frederick 1930-......... **CLC 20**

Wister, Owen 1860-1938 .... **TCLC 21**
See also CA 108; DLB 9, 78; SATA 62

Witkacy
See Witkiewicz, Stanislaw Ignacy

Witkiewicz, Stanislaw Ignacy
1885-1939 .... **TCLC 8**
See also CA 105

Wittig, Monique 1935(?)-......... **CLC 22**
See also CA 116; 135; DLB 83

Wittlin, Jozef 1896-1976 .... **CLC 25**
See also CA 49-52; 65-68; CANR 3

Wodehouse, P(elham) G(renville)
1881-1975 ... **CLC 1, 2, 5, 10, 22; SSC 2**
See also AITN 2; CA 45-48; 57-60;
CANR 3, 33; CDBLB 1914-1945;
DLB 34; MTCW; SATA 22

Woiwode, L.
See Woiwode, Larry (Alfred)

Woiwode, Larry (Alfred) 1941-... **CLC 6, 10**
See also CA 73-76; CANR 16; DLB 6

Wojciechowska, Maia (Teresa)
1927-...................... **CLC 26**
See also AAYA 8; CA 9-12R; CANR 4, 41;
CLR 1; JRDA; MAICYA; SAAS 1;
SATA 1, 28

Wolf, Christa 1929-....... **CLC 14, 29, 58**
See also CA 85-88; DLB 75; MTCW

Wolfe, Gene (Rodman) 1931-....... **CLC 25**
See also CA 57-60; CAAS 9; CANR 6, 32;
DLB 8

Wolfe, George C. 1954-.......... **CLC 49**

Wolfe, Thomas (Clayton)
1900-1938 ... **TCLC 4, 13, 29; DA; WLC**
See also CA 104; 132; CDALB 1929-1941;
DLB 9, 102; DLBD 2; DLBY 85; MTCW

Wolfe, Thomas Kennerly, Jr. 1931-
See Wolfe, Tom
See also CA 13-16R; CANR 9, 33; MTCW

Wolfe, Tom .... **CLC 1, 2, 9, 15, 35, 51**
See also Wolfe, Thomas Kennerly, Jr.
See also AAYA 8; AITN 2; BEST 89:1

Wolff, Geoffrey (Ansell) 1937- ..... **CLC 41**
See also CA 29-32R; CANR 29, 43

Wolff, Sonia
See Levitin, Sonia (Wolff)

Wolff, Tobias (Jonathan Ansell)
1945-................... **CLC 39, 64**
See also BEST 90:2; CA 114; 117; DLB 130

Wolfram von Eschenbach
c. 1170-c. 1220 .... **CMLC 5**

Wolitzer, Hilma 1930-........... **CLC 17**
See also CA 65-68; CANR 18, 40; SATA 31

Wollstonecraft, Mary 1759-1797...... **LC 5**
See also CDBLB 1789-1832; DLB 39, 104

Wonder, Stevie .... **CLC 12**
See also Morris, Steveland Judkins

Wong, Jade Snow 1922-.......... **CLC 17**
See also CA 109

Woodcott, Keith
See Brunner, John (Kilian Houston)

Woodruff, Robert W.
See Mencken, H(enry) L(ouis)

Woolf, (Adeline) Virginia
1882-1941 ..... **TCLC 1, 5, 20, 43; DA;
SSC 7; WLC**
See also CA 104; 130; CDBLB 1914-1945;
DLB 36, 100; DLBD 10; MTCW

Woollcott, Alexander (Humphreys)
1887-1943 .... **TCLC 5**
See also CA 105; DLB 29

Woolrich, Cornell 1903-1968...... **CLC 77**
See also Hopley-Woolrich, Cornell George

Wordsworth, Dorothy
1771-1855 .... **NCLC 25**
See also DLB 107

Wordsworth, William
1770-1850 .... **NCLC 12, 38; DA; PC 4;
WLC**
See also CDBLB 1789-1832; DLB 93, 107

Wouk, Herman 1915-......... **CLC 1, 9, 38**
See also CA 5-8R; CANR 6, 33; DLBY 82;
MTCW

Wright, Charles (Penzel, Jr.)
1935-................... **CLC 6, 13, 28**
See also CA 29-32R; CAAS 7; CANR 23,
36; DLBY 82; MTCW

Wright, Charles Stevenson
1932-................ **CLC 49; BLC 3**
See also BW; CA 9-12R; CANR 26;
DLB 33

Wright, Jack R.
See Harris, Mark

Wright, James (Arlington)
1927-1980........... **CLC 3, 5, 10, 28**
See also AITN 2; CA 49-52; 97-100;
CANR 4, 34; DLB 5; MTCW

Wright, Judith (Arandell)
1915-.................... **CLC 11, 53**
See also CA 13-16R; CANR 31; MTCW;
SATA 14

Wright, L(aurali) R. 1939-........ **CLC 44**
See also CA 138

Wright, Richard (Nathaniel)
1908-1960 .... **CLC 1, 3, 4, 9, 14, 21, 48,
74; BLC 3; DA; SSC 2; WLC**
See also AAYA 5; BW; CA 108;
CDALB 1929-1941; DLB 76, 102;
DLBD 2; MTCW

Wright, Richard B(ruce) 1937- ...... **CLC 6**
See also CA 85-88; DLB 53

Wright, Rick 1945-............... **CLC 35**
See also Pink Floyd

Wright, Rowland
See Wells, Carolyn

Wright, Stephen 1946-............ **CLC 33**

Wright, Willard Huntington 1888-1939
See Van Dine, S. S.
See also CA 115

Wright, William 1930-............ **CLC 44**
See also CA 53-56; CANR 7, 23

Wu Ch'eng-en 1500(?)-1582(?)........ **LC 7**

Wu Ching-tzu 1701-1754 .... **LC 2**

Wurlitzer, Rudolph 1938(?)- ... **CLC 2, 4, 15**
See also CA 85-88

Wycherley, William 1641-1715.... **LC 8, 21**
See also CDBLB 1660-1789; DLB 80

Wylie, Elinor (Morton Hoyt)
1885-1928 .... **TCLC 8**
See also CA 105; DLB 9, 45

Wylie, Philip (Gordon) 1902-1971... **CLC 43**
See also CA 21-22; 33-36R; CAP 2; DLB 9

Wyndham, John
See Harris, John (Wyndham Parkes Lucas)
Beynon

Wyss, Johann David Von
1743-1818 .... **NCLC 10**
See also JRDA; MAICYA; SATA 27, 29

Yakumo Koizumi
See Hearn, (Patricio) Lafcadio (Tessima
Carlos)

Yanez, Jose Donoso
See Donoso (Yanez), Jose

Yanovsky, Basile S.
See Yanovsky, V(assily) S(emenovich)

Yanovsky, V(assily) S(emenovich)
1906-1989 .... **CLC 2, 18**
See also CA 97-100; 129

Yates, Richard 1926-1992 ..... **CLC 7, 8, 23**
See also CA 5-8R; 139; CANR 10, 43;
DLB 2; DLBY 81, 92

Yeats, W. B.
See Yeats, William Butler

Yeats, William Butler
1865-1939 ..... **TCLC 1, 11, 18, 31; DA;
WLC**
See also CA 104; 127; CDBLB 1890-1914;
DLB 10, 19, 98; MTCW

Yehoshua, A(braham) B.
1936-.................... **CLC 13, 31**
See also CA 33-36R; CANR 43

Yep, Laurence Michael 1948-...... **CLC 35**
See also AAYA 5; CA 49-52; CANR 1;
CLR 3, 17; DLB 52; JRDA; MAICYA;
SATA 7, 69

Yerby, Frank G(arvin)
1916-1991 .... **CLC 1, 7, 22; BLC 3**
See also BW; CA 9-12R; 136; CANR 16;
DLB 76; MTCW

Yesenin, Sergei Alexandrovich
See Esenin, Sergei (Alexandrovich)

Yevtushenko, Yevgeny (Alexandrovich)
1933-............. **CLC 1, 3, 13, 26, 51**
See also CA 81-84; CANR 33; MTCW

Yezierska, Anzia 1885(?)-1970 ..... **CLC 46**
See also CA 126; 89-92; DLB 28; MTCW

Yglesias, Helen 1915-.......... **CLC 7, 22**
See also CA 37-40R; CANR 15; MTCW

Yokomitsu Riichi 1898-1947 ..... **TCLC 47**

Yonge, Charlotte (Mary)
1823-1901 .... **TCLC 48**
See also CA 109; DLB 18; SATA 17

York, Jeremy
See Creasey, John

York, Simon
See Heinlein, Robert A(nson)

Yorke, Henry Vincent 1905-1974 ... **CLC 13**
See also Green, Henry
See also CA 85-88; 49-52

SSC Cumulative Nationality Index

SSC Cumulative Title Index

Title Index

"The Cone" (Wells)　6:361, 383

"Coney Island" (Beattie)　11:25-6, 29

"The Conference" (Singer)　3:385, 388

"A Conference of the Powers" (Kipling)　5:259

"The Confessional" (O'Faolain)　13:293

"The Confession of Brother Grimes" (Warren)　4:390, 394, 396

"A Conflict Ended" (Freeman)　1:196-97, 199

"Confused" (Singer)　3:384

"The Conger Eel" (O'Flaherty)　6:269, 274

El congreso ("The Assembly"; *The Congress*) (Borges)　4:27-8

The Congress (Borges)
See *El congreso*

"The Conjurer's Revenge" (Chesnutt)　7:6-7, 10, 18, 42

The Conjure Woman (Chesnutt)　7:2-5, 7-12, 14, 26, 30, 33, 38-40, 43

"The Conjuring Contest" (Dunbar)　8:122, 149

"Con legítimo orgullo" ("With Justifiable Pride") (Cortazar)　7:94

"The Connoisseur" (de la Mare)　14:70, 82

The Connoisseur, and Other Stories (de la Mare)　14:70

"The Connor Girls" (O'Brien)　10:334, 341

"A Conquest of Humility" (Freeman)　1:198

"The Conscript" (Balzac)　5:12-13

"Consequences" (Cather)　2:110-11, 115

"Conservatory" (Barthelme)　2:51

"A Consolatory Tale" (Dinesen)　7:164, 186, 193, 200

"The Constant Tin Soldier" (Andersen)
See "The Steadfast Tin Soldier"

"A Constellation of Events" (Updike)　13:402

"Conte de fin d'été" (Villiers de l'Isle Adam)　14:390

Contes cruels (*Sardonic Tales*) (Villiers de l'Isle Adam)　14:377-78, 380-81, 391, 395-96, 403, 411

Contes cruels: Nouveaux contes cruels (Villiers de l'Isle Adam)　14:404, 412

Contes de la bécasse (Maupassant)　1:257

Contes drolatiques (*Droll Stories*) (Balzac)　5:19-21

Contes philosophiques (Balzac)
See *Romans et contes philosophiques*

"The Contessina" (Bowen)　3:40

"The Contest" (Paley)　8:388, 394, 398

"The Contest of the Minstrels" (Hoffmann)
See "Der Kampf der Sänger"

"Continuity of Parks" (Cortazar)　7:54, 70, 83

"The Contract" (Anderson)　1:52

"The Convalescence of Jack Hamlin" (Harte)　8:247, 249

"The Conventional Wisdom" (Elkin)　12:99

"A Conversation" (Aiken)　9:14

"A Conversation" (Turgenev)　7:335

"Conversation at Night" (Bunin)
See "A Night Conversation"

"The Conversation of Eiros and Charmion" ("Eiros and Charmion") (Poe)　1:402

"Conversation Piece, 1945" ("Double Talk") (Nabokov)　11:109-10, 112-13, 127

"Conversations at Night" (Le Guin)　12:211, 213, 216

"Conversations with Goethe" (Barthelme)　2:51

"A Conversation with My Father" (Paley)　8:390, 392, 395, 399-402, 405, 407, 415-16, 418

"Converse at Night" (Dinesen)　7:168, 171, 186

"The Conversion of Aurelian McGoggin" (Kipling)　5:261, 274

"The Conversion of Sum Loo" (Cather)　2:102

"The Convert" (Lavin)　4:165-68

"A Convert of the Mission" (Harte)　8:216, 254

"Cookie" (Taylor)　10:382, 390

"Cool Air" (Lovecraft)　3:258, 262, 274

"The Cop and the Anthem" (Henry)　5:173, 187

"Copenhagen Season" (Dinesen)　7:166, 169-71, 186, 190-91

"Un coq chanta" (Maupassant)　1:272

"Cora Unashamed" (Hughes)　6:109-10, 118-19, 121-23, 129

"The Cornet Yelagin Affair" (Bunin)
See "The Elaghin Affair"

"The Corn Planting" (Anderson)　1:37

"Correspondence" (McCullers)　9:332-34, 343, 345, 358

A Correspondence (Turgenev)　7:317-18, 320, 324-26, 328, 361

"The Corsican Inn" (Pritchett)　14:268, 298

"Cortísimo metraje" ("Short Feature") (Cortazar)　7:95

"Cosmic Casanova" (Clarke)　3:133

Le cosmicomiche (*Cosmicomics*) (Calvino)　3:92-6, 98-100, 103-04, 106-07, 110, 112, 116-17

Cosmicomics (Calvino)
See *Le cosmicomiche*

Cosmopolitans (Maugham)　8:366, 380

"The Cost of Living" (Gallant)　5:130, 140-41, 149

Costumes by Eros (Aiken)　9:4, 28

"The Cottagette" (Gilman)　13:126, 145

"Councillor Krespel" (Hoffmann)
See "Rat Krespel"

"A Council of State" (Dunbar)　8:122, 124-25, 128, 136, 141, 144, 150

"A Council of War" (Gilman)　13:143

"Counsel for Oedipus" (O'Connor)　5:370

"Counterparts" (Joyce)　3:200-01, 205, 209, 226, 231, 234, 246, 249

"Countess" (Le Fanu)
See "A Passage in the Secret History of an Irish Countess"

"The Counting-House" (Turgenev)　7:313

"The Count of Crow's Nest" (Cather)　2:100, 102

"The Count of Monte Cristo" (Calvino)　3:93, 95-6

"The Country Church" (Irving)　2:244

"The Country Doctor" (Kafka)
See "Ein landarzt"

"The Country Husband" (Cheever)　1:90, 100-02

"The Country Inn" (Turgenev)
See "The Inn"

"The Country of the Blind" (Wells)　6:361-62, 368-73, 376-79, 383-84, 391-92, 399-400, 405

The Country of the Blind, and Other Stories (Wells)　6:359-61, 366, 380, 391-92

The Country of the Pointed Firs (Jewett)　6:152, 154-55, 157, 162-66, 168-69, 174-82

"Country Society" (Bates)　10:118

"A Country Tale" (Dinesen)　7:168-69

"The Count's Courtship" (de la Mare)　14:66, 81, 86

"The Coup de Grâce" (Bierce)　9:55-6, 75-7

"Le coup de pistolet" (Merimee)　7:277

"A Couple of Fools" (Bates)　10:131

"A Couple of Hamburgers" (Thurber)　1:418-19

"The Courting of Dinah Shadd" (Kipling)　5:260, 263-64, 274

"The Courting of Sister Wisby" (Jewett)　6:152, 160, 162, 178

"Court in the West Eighties" (McCullers)　9:342, 345, 356

"A Courtship" (Faulkner)　1:151, 178

"Courtship" (O'Brien)　10:334, 341

"The Courtship of Mr. Lyon" ("Mr. Lyon") (Carter)　13:6, 9, 25, 30-31

"Cousin Larry" (Parker)　2:280, 283

"Cousin Poor Lesley and the Lousy People" (Elkin)　12:117

"Cousins" (Bellow)　14:43, 46, 58

"Cousin Teresa" (Saki)　12:295, 302, 312

Covering End (James)　8:296

"The Coward" (Barnes)　3:18-22

"A Coward" (Wharton)　6:414

"The Cow's Death" (O'Flaherty)　6:274

"The Cowslip Field" (Bates)　10:120, 131-32, 139

"The Coxon Fund" (James)　8:317, 348

Crab Apple Jelly (O'Connor)　5:362, 364, 371, 377-78, 380, 383

"The Cracked Looking-Glass" (Porter)　4:327, 329-30, 339-40, 342, 360

"Cracker Prayer" (Hughes)　6:138

The Crapshooter (Steinbeck)　11:248

"Crazy, Crazy, Now Showing Everywhere" (Gilchrist)　14:154

"The Crazy Hunter" (Boyle)　5:58-9, 61-3, 65-6, 68-9

The Crazy Hunter: Three Short Novels (Boyle)　5:66

"Crazy Sunday" (Fitzgerald)　6:47, 52, 60-1, 77-9

"Created He Them" (London)　4:253

"The Creative Impulse" (Maugham)　8:369, 378-79

"The Creative Instinct" (Maugham)　8:358

"The Creature" (O'Brien)　10:332-33

"The Creatures" (de la Mare)　14:65, 80, 83, 85

Creatures of Circumstance (Maugham)　8:380

Credos and Curios (Thurber)　1:424

"Cremona Violin" (Hoffmann)　13:225

"Cressy" (Harte)　8:221

"Crevasse" (Faulkner)　1:147

"Crewe" (de la Mare)　14:73, 80, 84, 88-9, 90-1

"Criers and Kibitzers, Kibitzers and Criers" (Elkin)　12:94-5, 116-18

"The Crime at Pickett's Mill" (Bierce)　9:98

"Le crime au père Boniface" (Maupassant)　1:274

"The Crime of Gabriel Gale" (Chesterton)　1:124

"The Crime of Professor Sandwich" (Benet)　10:149

"The Crime Wave at Blandings" (Wodehouse)　2:344, 346, 349

"The Cripple" (Andersen)　6:13

"Critical Mass" (Clarke)　3:134

"Critique de la vie quotidienne" (Barthelme)　2:39-40, 42, 55

"Croatoan" (Ellison)　14:115-17, 128

Title Index

Title Index

Title Index

Title Index

Title Index

Title Index

Title Index

ISBN 0-8103-8470-1

90000

9 780810 384705